D0082969

Oversize
HF
5823
.W455
2012

Advertising & IMC

Principles & Practice

Ninth Edition

Sandra Moriarty
University of Colorado

Nancy Mitchell
University of Nebraska–Lincoln

William Wells
University of Minnesota

Nyack College
Wilson Library

Prentice Hall
Boston   Columbus   Indianapolis   New York   San Francisco   Upper Saddle River
Amsterdam   Cape Town   Dubai   London   Madrid   Milan   Munich   Paris   Montreal   Toronto
Delhi   Mexico City   Sao Paulo   Sydney   Hong Kong   Seoul   Singapore   Taipei   Tokyo

OCLC#
6401 32969

Editorial Director: Sally Yagan
Editor in Chief: Eric Svendsen
Acquisitions Editor: Melissa Sabella
Editorial Project Manager: Meeta Pendharkar
Editorial Assistant: Elisabeth Scarpa
Director of Marketing: Patrice Lumumba Jones
Senior Marketing Manager: Anne Fahlgren
Marketing Assistant: Melinda Jensen
Senior Managing Editor: Judy Leale
Project Manager: Becca Richter Groves
Senior Operations Supervisor: Arnold Vila
Operations Specialist: Cathleen Petersen
Senior Art Director: Janet Slowik

Art Director: Steve Frim
Interior Designer: DePinho Design and Yellow Dog Designs
Cover Designer: DePinho Design
Cover Art: Precision Graphics and DePinho Design
Manager, Rights and Permissions: Hessa Albader
Media Editor: Denise Vaughn
Media Project Manager, Production: Lisa Rinaldi
Full-Service Project Management: S4Carlisle Publishing Services
Composition: S4Carlisle Publishing Services
Printer/Binder: Quebecor World Color/Versailles
Cover Printer: Lehigh-Phoenix Color/Hagerstown
Text Font: 10/12 Times

Credits and acknowledgments borrowed from other sources and reproduced, with permission, in this textbook appear on appropriate page within text (or on page 628).

Microsoft® and Windows® are registered trademarks of the Microsoft Corporation in the U.S.A. and other countries. Screen shots and icons reprinted with permission from the Microsoft Corporation. This book is not sponsored or endorsed by or affiliated with the Microsoft Corporation.

Copyright © 2012, 2009, 2006, 2003, 2000 Pearson Education, Inc., publishing as Prentice Hall, One Lake Street, Upper Saddle River, New Jersey 07458. All rights reserved. Manufactured in the United States of America. This publication is protected by Copyright, and permission should be obtained from the publisher prior to any prohibited reproduction, storage in a retrieval system, or transmission in any form or by any means, electronic, mechanical, photocopying, recording, or likewise. To obtain permission(s) to use material from this work, please submit a written request to Pearson Education, Inc., Permissions Department, One Lake Street, Upper Saddle River, New Jersey 07458.

Many of the designations by manufacturers and seller to distinguish their products are claimed as trademarks. Where those designations appear in this book, and the publisher was aware of a trademark claim, the designations have been printed in initial caps or all caps.

Library of Congress Cataloging-in-Publication Data
Moriarty, Sandra E. (Sandra Ernst)
   Advertising & IMC: principles & practice / Sandra Moriarty, Nancy Mitchell, William Wells.
-- 9th ed.
     p. cm.
   Includes bibliographical references and index.
   ISBN 978-0-13-216364-4 (alk. paper)
1. Advertising. I. Mitchell, Nancy, 1950- II. Wells, William, 1926- III. Title.
   HF5823.W455 2012
   659.1--dc22   2010023721

10 9 8 7 6 5 4 3 2 1

Prentice Hall
is an imprint of

www.pearsonhighered.com

ISBN 10:   0-13-216364-0
ISBN 13: 978-0-13-216364-4

This Ninth Edition is dedicated to all the students who have inspired us with their questions and ideas and all the colleagues who have challenged us with new thoughts and new findings. Most of all we dedicate this book to all of our many contributors—the students, graduates, professors, and professionals who have contributed their thoughts, creative work, and professional experiences to this edition.

BRIEF CONTENTS

CONTENTS

Preface xix

PART 2 PRINCIPLE: BE TRUE TO THY BRAND

PART 3 PRACTICE: WHERE IS CREATIVE HEADED?

PART 4 PRACTICE: WHERE ARE MEDIA HEADED?

PART 5 PRINCIPLES: IMC AND TOTAL COMMUNICATION

ABOUT THE AUTHORS

Sandra Moriarty, Ph.D., *Professor Emerita, University of Colorado at Boulder*

Sandra Moriarty is cofounder of the Integrated Marketing Communication graduate program at the University of Colorado. Now retired, she has also taught at Michigan State University, University of Kansas, and Kansas State University, where she earned her Ph.D. in education. She specialized in teaching the campaign course and courses on the creative side—both writing and design. She has worked in government public relations, owned an advertising and public relations agency, directed a university publications program, and edited a university alumni magazine. She has been a consultant on integrated marketing communication with agencies such as BBDO and Dentsu, the largest advertising agency in the world, and with their clients in the United States, Europe, and Asia. Professor Moriarty has published widely in scholarly journals on marketing communication and visual communication topics and has authored 12 books on advertising, branding, integrated marketing communication, marketing, visual communication, and typography. A classic book on integrated marketing, *Driving Brand Value,* was written with coauthor Tom Duncan. Most recently she has authored the *Science and Art of Branding* with Giep Franzen, University of Amsterdam. International versions of her books include Spanish, Chinese, Taiwanese, Korean, and Japanese editions and also an English-language version for India. She has spoken to groups and presented seminars in most European countries, as well as Mexico, Japan, Korea, India, New Zealand, and Turkey.

Nancy Mitchell, Ph.D., *Professor, University of Nebraska–Lincoln*

Nancy Mitchell is professor of advertising in the College of Journalism and Mass Communications at the University of Nebraska–Lincoln (UNL), where she has taught since 1990. She served as chair of the advertising department for 11 years before heading the graduate program in her college. In addition to her teaching responsibilities, she is now Director of General Education at UNL. Prior to her tenure at the University of Nebraska, she taught at West Texas A&M University. She has taught a variety of courses, including advertising principles, design, copywriting, research and strategy, and campaigns and media ethics. She worked as an advertising professional for 15 years before entering academe. She gained experience as a copywriter, designer, editor, fund-raiser, and magazine editor in an array of businesses, including a large department store, a publishing company, an advertising agency, a newspaper, and a Public Broadcasting System affiliate. Her research focuses on creating effective advertising messages to underrepresented groups, ethical issues, and assessment of student learning. Nationally, she served as Advertising Division head for the Association for Education in Journalism and Mass Communications. She serves on the editorial boards for the *Journal of Advertising Education* and *Journalism and Mass Communication Educator*.

William Wells, Ph.D., *Professor Emeritus, University of Minnesota, and former Executive Vice President, DDB, Chicago*

One of the industry's leading market and research authorities, Bill Wells is a retired professor of advertising at the University of Minnesota's School of Journalism and Mass Communication. Formerly Executive Vice President and Director of Marketing Services at DDB Chicago, he is the only representative of the advertising business elected to the Attitude Research Hall of Fame. He earned a Ph.D. from Stanford University and was formerly professor of psychology and marketing at the University of Chicago. He joined Needham, Harper–Chicago as Director of Corporate Research. Author of the Needham Harper Lifestyle study as well as author of more than 60 books and articles, Dr. Wells also published *Planning for ROI: Effective Advertising Strategy*. He was recognized by the American Academy of Advertising in 2010 for his dedication and commitment to advertising and previously received the AAA's "Distinguished Service Award."

PREFACE

Advertising can cause you to stop and watch, or even stop and think. It can make you laugh, or squirm in your seat, or bring tears to your eyes. It can inspire you to read about a new product or remember a favorite brand when you're walking down the aisle in a supermarket. Advertising can also leave you free to change the channel or turn a page without being aware of having seen the brand message at all. So the question for you as a student of marketing communication is: Did it work?

But you're not the only one facing that question. It's clear from the headlines in industry publications that marketers want to know if their ads and other marketing communication efforts work. Marketing communication, particularly advertising, costs money—a lot of money in many cases—and marketers want proof that their advertising and marketing communication is efficient and effective.

That's why this textbook, *Advertising & IMC: Principles & Practice,* is dedicated not only to explaining advertising and other areas of brand communication—such as public relations, direct marketing, and sales promotion—but also to investigating what makes marketing communication effective.

The challenge for this Ninth Edition is to pin down the basic principles and best practices in an industry that is undergoing radical change—old media are shape-shifting and in some cases disappearing; new media are emerging and merging with old media as well as developing entirely new functions. The practice of advertising, in particular, faces new challenges in an interactive age where consumers are more in charge—actively selecting and designing their own media world and engaging with their friends in new forms of social media. This Ninth Edition reflects these changes as it challenges its readers to assume control not only of their media choices, but of their bigger role as consumers of products, ideas, and media.

WHAT'S NEW IN *PRINCIPLES & PRACTICE,* NINTH EDITION

1. New emphasis on enduring principles in a changing industry

Keeping up with the dynamic world of advertising and marketing communication is a challenge for any textbook. Recent developments facing the industry including the evolving world of digital media and the varied consumer responses to the Great Recession remind us to think about principles that anchor our profession. Although we recognize that the marketing communication environment is in an increasing state of upheaval, we also believe that the basic principles of advertising and marketing communication are enduring and will help the industry adjust to the changing marketplace. We call attention to these enduring principles throughout *Principles & Practice* as we describe how the practices are affected by these new situations.

2. Increased IMC focus

To reflect a wider view of advertising among consumers and within the industry, we have refocused the positioning of *Principles & Practice* to add a more obvious discussion of integrated marketing communication (IMC). The word *advertising*, in other words, has come to refer to a variety of marketing communication tools and functions. From the very first edition, *Principles & Practice* has contained discussions about IMC, but in this edition we have made that orientation clear. This broader focus includes all the various forms of marketing communication—multiplatform, as well as multimedia—and the discussion is embedded seamlessly throughout the book.

3. Increased brand focus

We have introduced brand communication in previous editions, but with the more extensive use of IMC concepts in the Ninth Edition, we also have adjusted the language in *Principles & Practice* to focus on the point of the communication, which we see as a brand. In other words, instead of talking about an advertisement as if it were an end in itself, we now talk about brand communication. This recognizes that the ad, or any other marketing communication message, has to be about something. And that something—the focus of all these communication efforts—is the brand.

4. New set of IMC principles

For most of this book's life, we have made an effort to identify key principles and draw attention to them as call-outs in the margins. With the increased emphasis on IMC in the Ninth Edition, we have also made an effort to develop a set of 10 key IMC-based principles for brand communication. They evolve within the chapters as various IMC concepts are introduced and explained and come together as a set in a much revised Chapter 18, "The IMC Umbrella." This IMC wrap-up chapter explains IMC campaigns and distinguishes campaigns from the management of a Total Communication program.

5. Language adjustment

To reflect this broader focus on brands and IMC, we also needed to adjust the language throughout *Principles & Practice*. In the Ninth Edition students will read about brand communication, not just ads and advertisements. We still refer to ads, but only when we are talking specifically about that function. When we talk about the wider world of "advertising," we refer to marketing or brand communication.

6. Creative chapters moved ahead of media chapters

Creative thinking is a basic requirement in all areas of marketing communication. To emphasize that and to respond to adopters and reviewers who prefer to teach creative before media, Part 3 now focuses on the creative side and message strategy; Part 4 focuses on the media side.

7. Rewritten and reorganized media chapters reflecting changes in industry

In our first point on this list, we mentioned the changes in the media industry; which include the growth of social media and the assault on traditional media. In recognition of this new media environment, we have totally rewritten and reorganized the media chapters in *Principles & Practice*. The first media chapter, which is now Chapter 11, is completely new. It provides an overview of this new media world with a special emphasis on the exciting new opportunities to engage with consumers. It also introduces the basic concepts necessary to evaluate and compare media options. The second chapter is also completely rewritten and now combines all the traditional media in one discussion. The third chapter is more tightly focused on digital media; and the fourth chapter puts it all together in a discussion on media planning and buying including, of course, the new media.

8. New interactive and social media discussions

We note the special role that social media play in marketing communication strategies. What has happened is a huge change in the way advertising, both in its traditional and wider meanings, operate. It's a paradigm shift with the entire industry moving from one-way targeted media to two-way interactive media. The idea that the audience is in control not only of what media they choose, but also what content they see (including messages generated by other consumers), means companies have to engage, rather than target prospective customers. And engagement means companies have to listen, as well as deliver messages. And listening is much more complicated because it's not just one customer calling a customer service line, but rather sharing information online among family and thousands of "friends" on social media, such as Facebook. Throughout *Principles & Practice*, the Ninth Edition recognizes the impact and implications of this shift from company-controlled to consumer-controlled media.

9. New Principled Practice boxes

We've added a new feature called *Principled Practice*. In previous editions we included ethics discussions in our *Matter of Principle* and *Matter of Practice* boxes. In the Ninth Edition we have designated a separate feature for these ethics boxes and titled it *Principled Practice* to help students think critically about current issues in the industry.

10. New pedagogical tools

- A new award-winning American Advertising Federation National Student Advertising Competition (AAF NSAC) case for the Century Council appears in the Appendix, and questions referring to the case were added at the end of each chapter.
- BrandRevive is a new assignment at the end of each chapter that guides the student through the activities involved in developing a brand campaign plan, in this case for some older, perhaps forgotten brand that needs a new lease for space in the minds of consumers. If students engage in this assignment continuously throughout the course, they will develop a campaign plan for their portfolio.
- A new MyLab website for *Principles & Practice* has been created. Content from the text has been moved to this site to provide more integration between the printed text and the online support materials and activities.

WHY MARKETING COMMUNICATION?

We are using the phrase *marketing communication* or *brand communication* because what used to be known as *advertising* has expanded beyond the familiar ads in print media and commercials on radio and television.

Electronic and social media have opened up new ways to communicate online with consumers about a brand. Alternative and nontraditional forms, such as *guerilla marketing* that reaches people in surprising ways in unexpected places, have opened up new opportunities to engage people with brand messages through memorable experiences.

Creating buzz and dialogue have replaced the old practice of targeting messages at consumers. A new goal is to enlist word-of-mouth conversations to reinforce and extend the power of the more traditional marketing communication forms.

This wider view of *advertising* includes an array of communication tools. We mentioned public relations, direct marketing, and sales promotion, but those are just a few of the tools in the brand communication toolkit. We will describe the use of these various forms of brand communication as *integrated marketing communication* (IMC), which refers to the strategic use of multiple forms of communication to engage different types of consumers who have an interest in or connection to a brand.

So the two most central themes for this introductory brand communication textbook are effectiveness and integration and they will be discussed throughout the chapters that follow.

WHAT IS EFFECTIVENESS?

During a recent Super Bowl, an ad for Anheuser-Busch called "Applause" showed people in an airport spontaneously applauding a group of American troops

The Facets Model of Effects

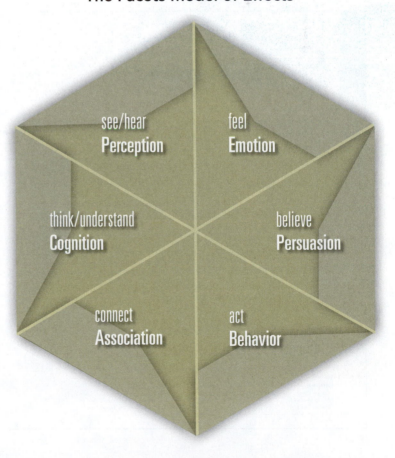

see/hear
Perception

feel
Emotion

think/understand
Cognition

believe
Persuasion

connect
Association

act
Behavior

returning home. Even the audience watching from their living rooms was inclined to join in with applause as part of this graceful display of respect and appreciation. It was touching. Memorable. Beautifully photographed. And the people seemed real, not rehearsed. But was it an effective ad? What was it trying to accomplish? Did the viewers remember it as an Anheuser-Busch ad and, if so, did it affect their opinions of that company and its brands?

What is effective advertising? Is it marketing communication that gets talked about? Is it a message like the Anheuser-Busch commercial that touches your emotions and inspires you to applaud? What, exactly, does it mean to say that an advertisement "works"?

Our answer is that brand communication is effective if it creates a desired response in the audience. A brand message *that works* is advertising that affects people; it gets results that can be measured. To better understand how this impact is created by a message, this textbook will highlight the principles and best practices of the industry.

Principles & Practice uses the *Facets Model of Advertising Effects* to better explain brand communication strategies, consumer responses, and effectiveness. The facets model is like a diamond or a crystal whose surfaces represent the different types of responses generated by a brand message. This model and the ideas it represents are used throughout the book to help explain such things as how objectives are decided on, what strategies deliver what kind of effects, and how an advertisement and other forms of marketing communication are evaluated based on their objectives.

Principles & Practices

Marketing communication messages are part inspiration and part hard work, but they are also a product of clear and logical thinking. Ultimately marketing communication is evaluated on its ability to generate a desired consumer response that meets a set of carefully crafted objectives.

In most cases, consumers have little idea what the objectives are because that information generally isn't made public—and you sometimes can't tell from the ad itself. But think about the "Applause" ad. From what we've told you, what do you think the ad's ob-

CHAPTER 8

The Creative Side

CHAPTER KEY POINTS

1. How do we explain the science and art of creative strategy, as well as the important parts of a creative brief?
2. What are some key message strategy approaches?
3. Can creative thinking be defined, and how does it lead to a Big Idea?
4. What characteristics do creative people have in common, and what is their typical creative process?
5. What issues affect the management of creative strategy and its implementation?

Frontier: A Whole Different Animal

When low-cost carrier Frontier Airlines started up in 1994, it took off with animals emblazoned on the tails of its planes. Frontier's distinctive aircraft tails, all of which depict a variety of different wildlife, have made Frontier's brand name synonymous with the airline's Western heritage. Years of award-winning advertising have firmly established the airline with its talking animals on the planes' tails as a favorite of consumers in the Denver market and beyond.

The economic downturn of 2008 and 2009, however, grounded much of Frontier's advertising as the airline was forced into bankruptcy because of a cash-flow problem. Luckily, it emerged from the downturn with a new owner who recognized the value of the brand and its award-winning advertising.

Frontier's agency, Grey Worldwide, realized that Denverites were elated that their hometown airline and its beloved animals would live to see another day. A narrow window to celebrate this great news emerged. And once again, Creative Directors Shawn Couzens and Gary Ennis turned to Larry, Jack, Flip, and the rest of the gang for the perfect solution. The campaign had to be written and produced quickly and affordably—so it could air while the news was still fresh. And so, in just a few short weeks, the "Still the One" campaign was born.

This is just one example of how nimble the Frontier campaign is. No matter what the message, or how quick the turnaround, the animals can always deliver it in a way that's engaging and relevant. In fact, the animals have proven so popular, they may end up being the airline's single most important asset when it comes to the brand's ultimate survival.

So how did it all start? In 2003, Grey Worldwide brought the tail animals to life by creating a likable cast of characters—each different and unique in its own way. The humorous ad campaign broke away from the buttoned-up approach used by most airlines by creating an "episodic sitcom" much like *Seinfeld* or *Cheers*. As a result, consumers built an emotional attachment to the brand and its spokes-animals. And with each new commercial, that connection grew stronger as Frontier continued to evolve the campaign.

Aaron Knauer
DIA Correspondent

BREAKING NEWS

It's a Winner

Campaigns:	Company:	Agency:	Awards:
"Still the One," "Flip to Mexico," "Leather Seats"	Frontier Airlines	Grey Worldwide	Gold Effie (for sustained success), Silver Clio, Silver Effie, Gold Mobius ("Best of Show" Nomination) for "Flip to Mexico"

jectives are? To sell beer? To get viewers to run out and buy the brand? Actually, the ad seems to be a bit removed from a straight sales pitch.

An educated guess—and that's what you will be better able to make after reading this book—is that perhaps its objective is simply to make people feel good, to see the goodness in a simple patriotic gesture—and, ultimately, to associate that feeling of goodness and warmth with the brand. Does it work? How did you feel when you read over the description of the ad? Even without seeing the commercial, you may have found that the idea touched your emotions and increased your respect or liking for the brand. To write objectives, however, you must have some understanding of how these messages work.

This book presents both principles and practices of effective brand communication. You will find principles in the margins of the text in every chapter. In addition, boxes and other features elaborate on both the principles and practices related to the topic of each chapter.

In this Ninth Edition, we take you behind the scenes of many award-winning campaigns, such as the "Aflac," "Altoids," and "Wii" campaigns, to uncover the hard work and explain the objectives, the inspiration, and the creative ideas behind some great campaigns. You will see how the ideas come together; you will live through the decision making; and you will understand the risks the message creators faced.

We also have contributions from highly experienced professionals, as well as our Ad Stars, graduates from advertising and marketing communication programs around the country who were nominated by their professors to be featured in this book. We showcase their work throughout the book. They also have written *Inside Stories* that explain strategies and what they have learned on the job, as well as *A Day in the Life* features that provide insight into various career opportunities in marketing communication.

The Proof

Advertisers and marketers want proof that their marketing communication is effective and efficient. Likewise, you should want proof about the value of your textbooks. You will learn in this book that all advertising claims need to be supported. That's why we make the claim—and, yes, this is an advertisement—that *Advertising & IMC: Principles & Practice* is the book to read to learn about effective brand communication. We are making a bold claim, but here is how we back it up.

Advertising & IMC: Principles & Practice is time tested. That's why it has continued as one of the market leaders for more than 20 years. It continues to be in touch with the most current practices in the industry, but it also presents the fundamental principles in ways that will give you a competitive edge. That's why students keep this textbook on their shelves as an important reference book as they move through their major. One thing we hear from our young professional Ad Stars is that they continue to rely on this book as they make their transition to professional life, and you can find it on many of their office shelves, as well. The principles in this book are enduring and your understanding of the practices of the field can jump-start your career.

ᴾᴱᴬᴿˢᴼᴺ mymarketinglab

mymarketinglab (www.mypearsonmarketinglab.com) gives you the opportunity to test yourself on key concepts and skills, track your own progress through the course, and use the personalized study plan activities—all to help you achieve success in the classroom.

The MyLab that accompanies *Advertising & IMC: Principles & Practice* includes:

- Part Ending Cases: Each part incorporates a case study that features award-winning campaigns recognized by the NY American Marketing Association as outstanding examples of effectiveness.
- Ad Exercises: View a variety of advertisements and test your understanding of how they apply IMC concepts.

Plus:

- Personalized study plans—Pre- and post-tests with remediation activities directed to help you understand and apply the concepts where you need the most help.
- Interactive elements—A wealth of hands-on activities and exercises let you experience and learn firsthand, whether it is with the online e-book where you can search for specific keywords or page numbers, highlight specific sections, enter notes right on the e-book page, and print reading assignments with notes for later review or with other materials.
- Mini-simulations—These simulations help you move beyond the basics with interactive simulations that place you in a realistic marketing situation that requires you to make decisions based on marketing concepts.

Find out more at www.mypearsonmarketinglab.com.

CONTRIBUTORS

Advisory Board VIPs

Shawn M. Couzens
Vice President and Creative Director, Grey Worldwide, New York

Susan Mendelsohn
Ph.D., President, Susan Mendelsohn Consultants, Chicago, Illinois

William H. Weintraub
Chief Marketing Officer (Retired), Coors Inc., Boulder, Colorado

Constance Cannon Frazier
Chief Operating Officer, AAF, Washington, D.C.

John Paluszek
Senior Counsel, Ketchum, New York

Karl Weiss
President/CEO, Market Perceptions, Inc., Denver, Colorado

Larry Kelley
Partner, Media Director, and Chief Planning Officer, FKM, and Professor, University of Houston, Texas

Ivan L. Preston
Journalism and Mass Communications Professor Emeritus, University of Wisconsin, Madison

Robert Witeck
CEO, Witeck-Combs Communications, Washington, D.C.

Regina Lewis
Ph.D., Vice President of Consumer Insights, Intercontinental Hotels Group, Atlanta, Georgia

David Rittenhouse
Senior Partner, Media Director, Neo@Ogilvy, New York

Charles E. Young
Ph.D., Founder and CEO, Ameritest, Albuquerque, New Mexico

Contributors: Ad Stars

Masura Ariga
Group Account Director, Dentsu Inc., Tokyo, Japan

Ed Chambliss
Vice President, Team Leader, The Phelps Group, Santa Monica, California

Andy Dao
Copywriter, Leo Burnett, Chicago, Illinois

Heather Beck
Senior Media Planner, Melamed Riley Advertising, Cleveland, Ohio

Diego Contreras
Art Director, Crispin Porter + Bogusky, Boulder, Colorado

Michael Dattalico
Owner, Musion Creative, LLC, Gainesville, Florida

Jeremy Boland
Art Director and Photographer, Borders Perrin Norrander, Portland, Oregon

Amanda Correa
Brand Manager, The Richards Group, Dallas, Texas

Elisa Guerrero
Freelancer, Fort Worth, Texas

John Brewer
President & CEO, Billings Chamber of Commerce/CVB, Billings, Montana

Jennifer L. Cunningham
Account Manager, Yello, Orlando, Florida

Amy Hume
Communications Consultant, University of Colorado–Denver

Chris Hutchinson
Art Director, Wieden + Kenney, Portland, Oregon

Karl Schroeder
Senior Writer, Coates Kokes, Portland, Oregon

Steven Tran
Marketing Graduate, University of Illinois at Chicago

Ingvi Logason
Principal, H:N Marketing Communications, Reykjavik, Iceland

Heather M. Schulz
Ph.D. Candidate in Advertising, University of Texas at Austin

Trent Walters
Brand Management Team Leader, The Richards Group, Dallas, Texas

Lara Mann
Senior Copywriter, DraftFCB, Chicago, Illinois

Peter Stasiowski
Marketing & Communications Manager, Interprint, Inc. Pittsfield, Massachusetts

Jennifer Wolfe-Kimbell
Senior Marketing Manager, Vail Resorts, Broomfield, Colorado

Matt Miller
Art Director, Leo Burnett, Chicago, Illinois

Kate Stein
Senior Finance and Mass Communications Graduate, University of Florida

Lisa Yansura
Outreach Coordinator, Quantum House, West Palm Beach, Florida

Amy Niswonger
Design Instructor, School of Advertising Art, Dayton, Ohio

Aaron Stern
Freelance Copywriter, New York, NY

Wendy Zomnir
Creative Director & Founding Partner, Urban Decay, Costa Mesa, California

Holly Duncan Rockwood
Director of Corporate Communications, Electronic Arts, San Francisco, California

Mark Thomson
President, Thomson Productions, Des Moines, Iowa

Sonia Montes Scappaticci
Business Development Director, Branded Entertainment, Catmandu Entertainment, Detroit, Michigan

Contributors: Pros & Profs

Edd Applegate
Professor, Middle Tennessee State University, Murfreesboro

Bruce Bendinger
Owner, The Copy Workshop, Chicago, Illinois

Clarke Caywood
Professor and Director, Graduate Program in Public Relations, Medill School of Journalism, Northwestern University, Evanston, Illinois

Bill Barre
Lecturer, University of Wisconsin, Eau Claire

Daryl Bennewith
Strategic Director, TBWA Group, Durban, South Africa

Jason Chambers
Associate Professor and Assistant Dean, College of Media, University of Illinois, Urbana

Ann Barry
Associate Professor, Boston College, Massachusetts

Edoardo Teodoro Brioschi
Professor and Chair of Economica and Techniques of Business Communication, Università Cattolica del Sacro Cuore, Milan, Italy

Jason Cormier
Cofounder and Managing Partner, Room214.com, Boulder, Colorado

Fred Beard
Professor, Gaylord College of Journalism and Mass Communication, University of Oklahoma, Norman

Sheri Broyles
Interim Chair, Department of Strategic Communications, Mayborn School of Journalism, University of North Texas, Denton

Linda Correll
Assistant Professor, Southern Illinois University, Carbondale

Joel Davis
Professor, School of Journalism & Media Studies, San Diego State University

Marieke de Mooij
Consultant, Cross Cultural Communication, The Netherlands

Bonnie Drewniany
Associate Professor, University of South Carolina, Columbia

Tom Duncan
IMC Founder and Director Emeritus, University of Colorado, and Daniels School of Business, University of Denver

Steve Edwards
Professor, Termerlin Advertising Institute, Southern Methodist University, Dallas, Texas

Gary Ennis
Vice President and Creative Director, Grey Worldwide, New York

Pat Fallon
Cofounder and Chair, Fallon Worldwide, Minneapolis, Minnesota

Tom Fauls
Associate Professor, Director of Advertising Program, College of Communication, Boston University, Massachusetts

Giep Franzen
Founder, FHB/BBDO, and Founder, SWOCC, a foundation at the University of Amsterdam for scientific research in brand communication, Amsterdam, The Netherlands

Jami Fullerton
Professor, Oklahoma State University, Stillwater

Arlene Gerwin
Marketing Consultant and President, Bolder Insights, Boulder, Colorado

Thomas Groth
Professor, Department of Communication Arts, University of West Florida, Pensacola

Jean M. Grow
Associate Professor, Diederich College of Communication, Marquette University, Milwaukee, Wisconsin

Scott R. Hamula
Associate Professor and Program Director, Integrated Marketing Communications, Roy H. Park School of Communications, Ithaca College, New York

Thomas Harris
Public Relations Consultant and Author, Cofounder of Golin/Harris Communications, Highland Park, Illinois

Donald Jugenheimer
Principal and Partner, In-Telligence Inc., Las Cruces, New Mexico

Alice Kendrick
Professor, Southern Methodist University, Dallas, Texas

Peggy Kreshel
Associate Professor, Department of Advertising, University of Georgia, Athens

Dean Krugman
Professor, Department of Advertising and Public Relations, Grady College of Journalism and Mass Communication, University of Georgia, Athens

Hairong Li
Associate Professor, Department of Advertising, Public Relations, and Retailing, Michigan State University, East Lansing

Linda Maddox
Professor of Marketing and Advertising, George Washington University, Washington, D.C.

Karen Mallia
Assistant Professor, University of South Carolina, Columbia

James Maskulka
Associate Professor of Marketing, Lehigh University, Bethlehem, Pennsylvania

Michael McNiven
Assistant Professor, Rowan University, Glassboro, New Jersey

George Milne
Associate Professor, University of Massachusetts–Amherst

Keith Murray
Associate Dean, College of Business, Bryant University, Smithfield, Rhode Island

Connie Pechmann
Professor, Paul Merage School of Business, University of California–Irvine

Jimmy Peltier
Professor, University of Wisconsin–Whitewater

Joseph E. Phelps
Department Chair, Department of Advertising and Public Relations, University of Alabama, Tuscaloosa

Marilyn Roberts
Dean, College of Communication and Media Sciences, Zayed University, United Arab Emirates

Herbert Rotfeld
Professor of Marketing, Auburn University, Alabama

Mike Rothschild
Professor Emeritus, School of Business, University of Wisconsin, and Consultant/Researcher, Madison, Wisconsin

Edward Russell
Professor, Advertising, S. I. Newhouse School of Public Communications, Syracuse University, New York

Sheila Sasser
Professor of Advertising Creativity, IMC, and Marketing, College of Business, Eastern Michigan, University College of Business, Ypsilanti

Fred Senn
Founding Partner, Fallon Worldwide, Minneapolis, Minnesota

Brian Sheehan
Associate Professor, S. I. Newhouse School of Public Communications, Syracuse University, New York

Mark Stuhlfaut
Assistant Professor, University of Kentucky, Lexington

John Sweeney
Professor, Head of Advertising and Director of Sports Communication Program, University of North Carolina–Chapel Hill

Ronald E. Taylor
Professor, Director of School of Advertising and Public Relations, University of Tennessee–Knoxville

Wan-Hsiu Sunny Tsai
Assistant Professor, School of Communication, University of Miami, Florida

Bruce G. Vanden Bergh
Professor, Department of Advertising, Public Relations, and Retailing, Michigan State University, East Lansing

Joyce M. Wolburg
Professor and Associate Dean, Diederich College of Communication, Marquette University, Milwaukee, Wisconsin

Reviewers

Alex Ortiz *Texas Tech University*
Amy Wojciechowski *West Shore Community College*
Carol Johanek *Washington University*
David Basch *SUNY at New Paltz*
Deborah Niemer *Oakland Community College–Royal Oak*
Dennis Morgan *Orange Coast College*
Denver D'Rozario *Howard University*
Donnalyn Pompper *Temple University*
Douglas Russell *University of Denver*
Dr. Alan Wiman *Rider University*
Jane Bekta *Fashion Institute of Technology*
Jeffrey Green *New York University*
Jennifer Theakston *School Craft College*
Karen Stewart *Stockton College*
Maggie Lears *Towson University*
Marilyn Easter *San Jose State University*
Mary Vermillion *DePaul University*
Michael Scherb *Ramapo College of New Jersey*
Michelle Lantz *Lansing Community College*
Mike Goldberg *Berkeley College & University of Phoenix*
Parimal Bhagat *Indiana University of Pennsylvania*
Patricia Thompson *Virginia Commonwealth University*
Ralph Giacobbe *Southern Illinois University–Edwardsville*
Robert Spademan *Cleveland State University*
Robin Tanner *University of Wisconsin–Madison*
Sonya Grier *American University*
Steven LeShay *Wilmington University*
Susan Ascher *Baruch College of CUNY*
Walter Sweedo *Lehigh Carbon Community College*

Advertising & IMC

Principles & Practice

ENDURING PRINCIPLES IN TIMES OF TURMOIL

This is one of the most exciting times to take an advertising course because of all the changes in the industry—new technology, new media, new types of consumers and media users, new ways of looking at marketing communication, and new economic challenges. It's also a great time to be studying the basics of advertising because this is the era of back to basics.

From 2008 through 2010, the depressing economic scene, which was complicated by scary shifts in media, played out like a really bad reality show. Analysts and experts worried about traditional business practices and called for new business models that would create turnarounds and breakthroughs.

Unchanging Truths in Times of Change

Rather than redefine the field to deal with the effects of the recession, Bill Weintraub, one of this book's Advisory Board members and a marketing expert who led marketing teams at Procter & Gamble, Tropicana, Kellogg's, and Coors, insists that the basic truths in marketing communication are immutable:

> I don't believe the underlying principles of marketing and communication should ever change. Regardless of the economy, new media, changes in culture, etc. I don't accept that these superficial changes in the marketing environment are relevant in terms of how intelligent business practices should be conducted.

So what are the immutable principles that guide the practice of marketing communication? Advisory Board member Regina Lewis, who has been in charge of consumer insights for InterContinental Hotel Group and Dunkin' Brands, says:

> I believe firmly that even—especially!—in a downturn, the basics of branding by connecting with consumer values lie at the heart of success. During tough economic times, uniquely positioning your brand (a strategy based on knowing how consumers think and feel about your brand versus competitive brands) is essential. And communicating about your brand in a way that is highly meaningful to consumers becomes more important. This is my philosophy.

Viewpoints of Bill Weintraub, retired Coors chief marketing officer, and Regina Lewis, vice president of Global Consumer Insights for the InterContinental Hotel Group

We agree with Weintraub and Lewis that branding, positioning, and communication are the foundations of brand success. We've elaborated on their thoughts to compile seven principles that we believe express marketing and marketing communication basics—even in economic downturns. These principles are central themes in this textbook:

1. *Brand* Build and maintain distinctive brands that your customers love.
2. *Position* Identify your competitive advantage in the minds of consumers.
3. *Consume* Focus on consumers and match your brand's strengths to consumer needs and wants.
4. *Message* Identify your best prospects and engage them in a brand conversation.
5. *Media* Know how to best reach and connect with your target audience.
6. *Integrate* Know how to connect the dots and make everything in the marketing communication toolkit work together.
7. *Evaluate* Track everything you do so you know what works.

As you will see in this book, effective advertising and marketing communication are founded on basic, enduring principles. The principles and practices described in this book provide direction even when the economy crashes. That doesn't mean that brand communication is unchanging. In fact, the practices are dynamic and continually adapting to changing marketplace conditions. But the basic principles are unchanging even in times of change.

In the chapters that follow, these principles and practices will be explained, as will the key practices of advertising and marketing communication. In Part 1, the first two chapters focus on defining advertising and marketing and explaining where marketing communication fits. Chapter 3 analyzes the ethics and social responsibility of marketing and communication.

1

The New World of Marketing Communication

WHOPPERFREAKOUT.COM

Campaign:	Company:	Agency:	Award:
"Whopper Freakout"	Burger King	Crispin Porter + Bogusky	Grand Effie and Gold Effie in Restaurants category

CHAPTER KEY POINTS

1. What is advertising, how has it evolved, and what does it do in modern times?
2. How have the key concepts of marketing communication developed over time?
3. How is the industry organized—key players, types of agencies, and jobs within agencies?
4. How is the practice of advertising changing?

Ingredients for a Burger Freakout

Imagine the reaction store managers would receive if they announced to their customers, "Today this Burger King is a Whopper-free zone." No more Whoppers. That's precisely what happened in a Las Vegas Burger King. The announcement was part of a social experiment designed to see how consumers would react if they couldn't get their beloved burgers. In the process it showed the power of advertising to be relevant and effective in confirming that the Whopper is "America's favorite burger," and it increased sales. Here's the inside scoop.

Ad agency Crispin Porter + Bogusky (CPB) faced this challenge: the Crispin team had to "take a product that has been around for 50 years and sells more than a billion units annually and make it interesting enough that the campaign would increase sales during a highly competitive period." And they had to do it using no marketing tools other than advertising. Adding to the challenge, CPB had to accomplish this in a competitive environment: McDonald's consistently outspends Burger King three to one.

The solution: CPB knew that America loves the Whopper. The agency figured it wasn't enough to just announce that BK's burger is the best. Who would care? Instead of telling facts about the product, the agency figured it had to demonstrate that it was the best burger in a compelling manner. *Here's your first advertising lesson:* To convince consumers, show them the truth about the product—don't just tell them about it—and do it memorably.

Just who eats Whoppers? Burger King knows its core demographic (its biggest group of consumers) is 18- to 24-year-old males, and it sure knows how to connect with those dudes. Past promotional efforts included sponsorships with the National Football League and NASCAR and tie-ins with *The Simpsons Movie*. Its chicken sandwich was launched with the "Subservient Chicken" website. Who could forget the creepy King mascot who shows up in weird places? The Whopper commands a loyal and passionate following from those who love the weird—and who aren't counting calories.

To grab the attention of Whopper lovers, CPB came up with a big idea, a prank. It devised an experiment that deprived consumers of their beloved Whopper—something that hadn't been done before in the burger war. To enact the deprivation

5

strategy, the agency took over a Burger King in Las Vegas for a single day and video-taped with hidden cameras the reactions of consumers who were either told that Whoppers had been permanently removed from the BK menu or given a competitor's burger such as a Big Mac or Wendy burger instead of a Whopper.

Actors were used as Burger King employees, but real consumers —not actors— reacted to the bad burger news. TV commercials created from these scenes drove viewers to *www.whopperfreakout.com,* where they could watch an 8-minute documentary about the experiment. The agency hoped that this would catch on with consumers who would then pass the word and generate more web traffic. Ad Lesson #2: The best advertising is word-of-mouth endorsements from friends.

Did it work? Customers freaked out. Turn to the end of the chapter to find out how wildly successful this campaign has been. And if you want to see more of this campaign, check out *www.bk.com/en/us/campaigns/whopper-freakout.html.*

Sources: Effie brief provided by New York American Marketing Association; Eleftheria Parpis, "BK's 'Whopper Freakout' Wins Grand Effie," June 3, 2009, www.adweek.com; Li Evans, "Whopper Freakout Shows Burger King Is King of Viral Marketing," January 13, 2008, www.searchmarketinggurus.com; Suzanne Vranica, "Hey, No Whopper on the Menu?! Hoax by Burger King Captures Outrage," *The Wall Street Journal,* February 8, 2008, www.wsj.com; Andrew Martin, "Gulp! Burger King Is on the Rebound," *The New York Times,* February 10, 2008, www.nytimes.com; www.whopperfreakout.com.

The Burger King "Whopper Freakout" campaign is an example of an award-winning effort that proved how much America loves the Whopper. But what made it successful? In the Part 1 opener we made the point that, in spite of economic downturns, the basic principles remain important. The Burger King story demonstrates the importance of a dramatic idea, as well as the power of word of mouth. In this chapter we'll define advertising and its role in marketing communication, explain how its basic concepts and practices evolved, and describe the agency world. We'll conclude by analyzing the changes facing marketing communication.

WHAT IS ADVERTISING?

You've seen thousands, maybe millions of commercial messages, so how would you define advertising, which is the most visible of all the forms of marketing communication that we will be discussing in this book? It may sound silly to ask such an obvious question. But where would you start if your instructor asked you for a definition of advertising?

At its most basic, the purpose of advertising has always been to sell a *product,* which can be *goods, services,* or *ideas.* Although there have been major changes in recent years from dying print media to merging and converging digital forms, the basics of advertising, as we said in the Part 1 opener, are even more important in turbulent times. To better understand advertising's development as a commercial form of communication, it helps to understand how advertising's definition and its basic roles have evolved over the years.

* *Identification* Advertising *identifies a product and/or the store where it's sold.* In its earliest years, and this goes back as far as ancient times, advertising focused on identifying a product and where it was sold. Some of the earliest ads were simply signs with the name or graphic image of the type of store—cobbler, grocer, or blacksmith.
* *Information* Advertising *provides information about a product.* Advances in printing technology at the beginning of the Renaissance spurred literacy and brought an explosion of printed materials in the form of posters, handbills, and newspapers. Literacy was no longer the badge of the elite and it was possible to reach a general audience with more detailed information about products. The word **advertisement** first appeared around 1655, and by 1660 publishers were using the word as a heading in newspapers for commercial information. These messages announced land for sale, runaways (slaves and servants), transportation (ships arriving, stagecoach schedules), and goods for sale from local merchants.

Because of the importance of commercial information, these ads were considered news and in many cases occupied more space in early newspapers than the news stories.

- **Persuasion** *Advertising persuades people to buy things.* The Industrial Revolution accelerated social change, as well as mass production. It brought the efficiency of machinery not only to the production of goods, but also to their distribution. Efficient production plus wider distribution meant that manufacturers could offer more products than their local markets could consume. With the development of trains and national roads, manufacturers could move their products around the country. For widespread marketing of products, it became important to have a recognizable brand name, such as Ivory or, more recently, Burger King. Also large groups of people needed to know about these goods, so along with industrial mechanization and the opening of the frontier came even more use of new communication media, such as magazines, catalogs, and billboards that reached more people with more enticing forms of persuasion. P. T. Barnum and patent medicine makers were among the advertising pioneers who moved promotion from identification and information to a flamboyant version of persuasion called *hype*—graphics and language characterized by exaggeration, or hyperbole.

Over the years, identification, information, and persuasion have been the basic elements of marketing communication and the focus of advertising. So how do we define it now realizing that advertising is dynamic and constantly changing to meet the demands of society and the marketplace? We can summarize a modern view of advertising with the following definition:

> **Advertising** is a paid form of persuasive communication that uses mass and interactive media to reach broad audiences in order to connect an identified sponsor with buyers (a target audience), provide information about products (goods, services, and ideas), and interpret the product features in terms of the customer's needs and wants.

This definition has a number of elements and as we review them, we will also point out where the definition is changing because of new technology, media shifts, and cultural changes. (Another source for definitions in the advertising and marketing area is the American Marketing Association Dictionary, which you can find at *www.marketingpower.com/_layouts/Dictionary.aspx*.)

Advertising is usually *paid* for by the advertiser (Burger King, for example) who has a product to *sell* (the Whopper), although some forms of advertising, such as public service announcements (PSAs), use donated space and time. Not only is the message paid for, but the sponsor is identified. Advertising began as *one-way* communication—from an advertiser to a targeted audience. Digital media, however, have opened the door to interesting new forms of *two-way* and *multiple-way* brand-related communication such as word-of-mouth conversations among friends or consumer-generated messages sent to a company. The viral video of Whopper customers' disbelieving responses became a hit on YouTube when shared among friends.

Advertising generally reaches a *broad audience* of *potential customers,* either as a *mass audience* or in smaller *targeted* groups. However *direct-response* advertising, particularly those practices that involve digital communication, has the ability to address individual members of the audience. So some advertising can deliver *one-to-one* communication but with a large group of people.

In traditional advertising, the message is conveyed through different kinds of *mass media,* which are largely *nonpersonal* messages. This nonpersonal

CLASSIC

P. T. Barnum was a pioneer in advertising and promotion. His flamboyant circus posters were more than just hype. What are the other roles they performed?

characteristic, however, is changing with the introduction of more *interactive* types of media, as the Whopper case demonstrates. Richard Edelman, CEO of the Edelman agency, emphasizes the emerging importance of *word of mouth,* which is personal communication through new media forms rather than what he describes as "scripted messages in a paid format."[1]

Most advertising has a defined strategy and seeks to *inform* consumers and/or make them *aware* of a brand, company, or organization. In many cases, it also tries to *persuade* or influence consumers to do something, such as buy a product or check out a brand's website. Persuasion may involve *emotional* messages as well as information. In an unusual use of messages tied to feelings, the Burger King "deprivation strategy" was designed to elicit negative responses to competitors' burgers that were substituted for the Whopper.

Keep in mind that, as we have said, a *product* can be a *good, service,* or *idea.* Some nonprofits, for example, use ads to "sell" memberships, get volunteers and donations, or advocate controversial positions.

Is Advertising the Only Tool in the Promotional Toolkit?

It's not the only tool, although it may be the biggest. In the United States, advertising is a $30 billion industry.[2] Advertising often is seen as the driving force in marketing communication because it commands the largest budget, as well as the largest number of agencies and professionals.

To get an idea of the scope of the advertising industry, consider Tables 1.1 and 1.2, which give some indication of the size of the advertising industry by breaking out the top 10 advertising categories and advertisers. In Table 1.1 look at how spending changed in the course of a year from 2008 to 2009 based on Third Quarter (January to September) figures. Which categories and advertisers were on the increase and which decreased and what do you think accounts for those changes?

As we said, advertising's original purpose was to sell something, but over the years, other promotional tools, with different sets of strengths, have developed to help meet that objective. For example, providing information, particularly about some new feature or a new product, is sometimes better handled through *publicity* or public relations. *Direct-response* advertising, such as catalogs and flyers sent to the home or office, can also provide more information in more depth than traditional ads that are limited in space and time. *Specialties* that carry brand logos as reminders or incentives to buy are handled by *sales promotion* companies. Communication with employees and shareholders about brands and campaigns is usually handled by *public relations*.

In other words, a variety of promotional tools can be used to identify, inform, and persuade. Professionals see differences in all of these areas, but many people just see them all as

Table 1.1   Top Ten Advertising Categories by Ad Expenditure

Category	2009 Advertising Spending ($m)	% Change Since 2008
1. Automotive	$7,492	−30.8
2. Telecom	6,190	.4
3. Financial services	5,673	−23.7
4. Local services & amusements	5,610	−15.0
5. Direct response	4,916	−12.0
6. Miscellaneous retail	4,751	−17.4
7. Food and candy	4,550	−2.2
8. Restaurants	4,204	2.4
9. Personal care products	4,082	−9.2
10. Pharmaceuticals	3,484	−.6

Source: TNS Media Intelligence Reports U.S. Advertising Expenditures Declined 14.7 Percent in First Nine Months of 2009, TNS Media Intelligence, December 8, 2009, *www.tns-mi.com/news/2009-Ad-Spending-Q3.htm.*

Table 1.2   Top Ten U.S. Advertisers

Company	2009 Advertising Spending ($m)	% Change Since 2008
1. Procter & Gamble	$1,941	−15.9
2. Verizon	1,892	−5.8
3. General Motors	1,353	−15.5
4. AT&T	1,339	−6.1
5. Johnson & Johnson	1,037	−1.3
6. News Corp	947.8	−9.4
7. Sprint Nextel	913	51.1
8. Pfizer Inc	897	11.9
9. Time Warner	875	−10.7
10. General Electric	764	−12.9

Source: "TNS Media Intelligence Reports U.S. Advertising Expenditures Declined 14.7 Percent in First Nine Months of 2009, TNS Media Intelligence, December 8, 2009, *www.tns-mi.com/news/2009-Ad-Spending-Q3.htm.*

promotion, or lump them together and call them *advertising.* The proper name for this bundle of tools, however, is **marketing communication (marcom),** an umbrella term that refers to all forms of communication about a brand that appear in a variety of media. Although we are focusing on advertising in this initial chapter, the book will focus on this expanded concept of marketing communication. Chapter 2 will provide more information about this wider world of brand communication.

Why Advertising?

Advertising obviously plays a role in both communication and marketing as we've been discussing. In addition to marketing communication, advertising also has a role in the functioning of the economy and society. Consider the launch of the Apple Macintosh in 1984, which was successful because of the impact of one advertisement, a television commercial generally considered to be the greatest ever made. As you read about this "1984" commercial in the *A Matter of Practice,* note how this commercial demonstrated all four functions—marketing, communication, social, and economic.

Marketing and Communication Roles   In its marketing communication role, advertising transforms a product into a distinctive brand by creating an **image** and personality that goes beyond straightforward product features. The "1984" commercial demonstrated how a personality could be created for a computer (innovative), one that showcased it as a creative tool that breaks through the rigid systems of other computer brands (IBM?). As advertising showcases brands, it also creates consumer demand (lines of customers the following day at stores where the Macintosh was sold) and makes statements that reflect social issues and trends (opening up the new category of personal computers for non-experts). So in addition to marketing and communication, advertising has economic and social roles.

Economic and Societal Roles   Advertising flourishes in societies that enjoy economic abundance, in which supply exceeds demand. In these societies, advertising extends beyond a primarily informational role to create a demand for a particular brand. In the case of the "Whopper Freakout" campaign, the decision was to make the product disappear in order to generate **buzz,** as well as reinforce a high level of demand for the brand by loyal customers.

Most economists presume that, because it reaches large groups of potential consumers, advertising brings cost efficiencies to marketing and, thus, lower prices to consumers. The more people know about a product, the higher the sales—and the higher the level of sales, the cheaper the product. Think about the high price of new products, such as a computer, HDTVs, and cell phones or other new technology. As demand grows, as well as competition, prices begin to drop.

Principle
Advertising *creates* cost efficiencies by increasing demand among large groups of people resulting in higher levels of sales and, ultimately, lower prices.

A MATTER OF PRACTICE

The Greatest Commercial Ever Made

The advertiser was Apple, the product was its new Macintosh, and the client—the person handling the advertising responsibility and making decisions—was Steve Jobs, Apple's CEO, who wanted a "thunderclap" ad. The agency was California-based Chiat/Day (now TBWA\Chiat\Day). The medium was the Super Bowl. The "supplier" was legendary British film director Ridley Scott of *Alien* and *Blade Runner* fame. The audience was the 96 million people watching Super Bowl XVIII that winter day in January 1984, and the target audience was all those in the audience who were trying to decide whether to buy a personal computer.

It's a basic principle in advertising: The combination of the right product at the right time in the right place with all the right people involved can create something magical—in this case, Jobs' thunderclap. It also required a cast of 200 and a budget of $900,000 for production and $800,000 for the 60-second time slot. By any measure, it was a big effort.

The storyline was a takeoff on George Orwell's science fiction novel about the sterile mind-controlled world of *1984*. An audience of mindless, gray-skinned drones (who were actually skinheads from the streets of London) watches a massive screen image of "Big Brother" spouting an ideological diatribe. Then an athletic young woman in bright red shorts runs in, chased by helmeted storm troopers, and throws a sledgehammer at the screen. The destruction of the image is followed by a burst of fresh air blowing over the open-mouthed drones as they "see the light." In the last shot the announcer reads the only words in the commercial as they appear on screen:

On January 24th, Apple Computer will introduce Macintosh. And you'll see why 1984 won't be like "1984."

Was it an easy idea to sell to the client?

First of all, some Apple executives who first saw the commercial were terrified that it wouldn't work because it didn't look like any commercial they had ever seen. After viewing it, several board members put their heads down in their hands. Another said, "Who would like to move on firing Chiat/Day immediately?" Legend has it that Apple's other founder, Steve Wozniak, took out his checkbook and told Jobs, "I'll pay for half if you pay for the other half." The decision to air the commercial finally came down to Jobs, whose confidence in the Chiat/Day creative team gave him the courage to run the ad.

Was it effective?

On January 24, long lines formed outside computer stores carrying the Macintosh, and the entire inventory sold out in one day. The initial sales goal of 50,000 units was easily surpassed by the 72,000 units sold in the first 100 days. More would have been sold if production had been able to keep up with demand.

The "1984" commercial is one of the most talked-about and remembered commercials ever made. Every time someone draws up a list of best commercials, it sits at the top, and it continues to receive accolades more than two decades later. If you haven't seen it, check it out at *www.apple-history.com* or *http://s153506479 .onlinehome.us/1984.html* and decide for yourself.

Remember, the commercial only ran once—an expensive spot on the year's most-watched television program. The commercial turned the Super Bowl from just another football game into the advertising event of the year. What added to its impact was the hype before and after it ran. People knew about the spot because of press coverage prior to the game, and they were watching for it. Coverage after the game was as likely to talk about the "1984" spot as the football score. Advertising became news and watching Super Bowl commercials became an event. That's why *Advertising Age's* critic Bob Garfield calls it "the greatest TV commercial ever made."

The debate continues about whether the "Big Brother" character was designed to represent IBM. What do you think?

Watch "1984" on:" *www.youtube.com/watch?v=OYecfV3ubP8* or *http://video.google.com/videoplay?docid=-715862862672743260*
About TBWA\Chiat\Day: *https://www.tbwachiat.com/*
An interview with Ridley Scott about making "1984": *www.youtube.com/watch?v=BjiRErZBC8I*

Sources: Kevin Maney, "Apple's '1984' Super Bowl Commercial Still Stands as Watershed Event," *USA Today,* January 28, 2004: 3B; Liane Hansen (Host), "Steve Hayden Discusses a 1984 Apple Ad Which Aired During the Super Bowl," National Public Radio Weekend Edition, February 1, 2004; Bradley Johnson, "10 Years after '1984': The Commercial and the Product That Changed Advertising," *Advertising Age,* June 1994: 1, 12–14; Curt's Media, "The 1984 Apple Commercial: The Making of a Legend," *www.isd.net/cmcalone/cine/1984.html.*

Two contrasting points of view explain how advertising creates economic impact. In the first, the rational view, advertising is seen as a vehicle for helping consumers assess value through price cues and other information, such as quality, location, and reputation. Advocates of this viewpoint see the role of advertising as a means to objectively provide price/value information, thereby creating more *rational economic decisions*. By focusing on images and emotional responses, the second approach appeals to consumers making a decision on *nonprice, emotional appeals*. This emotional view explains how images and psychological appeals influence consumer decisions. This type of advertising is believed to be so persuasive that it decreases the likelihood a consumer will switch to an alternative product, regardless of the price charged.

In addition to informing us about new and improved products, advertising also mirrors fashion and design trends and adds to our aesthetic sense. Advertising has an educational role in that it teaches about new products and their use. It may also expose social issues—some say the "1984" commercial symbolically proclaimed the value of computer literacy "for the rest of us," those who weren't slaves to the hard-to-operate PC systems of the time. It helps us shape an image of ourselves by setting up role models with which we can identify (a woman athlete liberating the gray masses), and it gives us a way to express ourselves in terms of our personalities (smash the screen image of Big Brother) and sense of style (red shorts—the only color in the drab environment) through the things we wear and use. It also presents images capturing the diversity of the world in which we live. These social roles have both negative and positive dimensions, which we will discuss in Chapter 3.

What Are the Most Common Types of Advertising?

There isn't just one kind of advertising. In fact, advertising is a large and varied industry. Different types of advertising have different roles. Considering all the different advertising situations, we can identify seven major types of advertising:

1. *Brand advertising,* the most visible type of advertising, is referred to as *national* or *consumer* advertising. Brand advertising, such as that for the Apple Macintosh in the classic "1984" commercial, focuses on the development of a long-term brand identity and image.

2. *Retail* or *local advertising* focuses on retailers, distributors, or dealers who sell their merchandise in a certain geographical area; retail advertising has information about products that are available in local stores. The objectives focus on stimulating store traffic and creating a distinctive image for the retailer. Local advertising can refer to a retailer, such as T. J. Maxx, or a manufacturer or distributor who offers products in a fairly restricted geographic area.

3. *Direct-response advertising* tries to stimulate an immediate response by the customer to the seller. It can use any advertising medium, particularly direct mail and the Internet. The consumer can respond by telephone, mail, or over the Internet, and the product is delivered directly to the consumer by mail or some other carrier.

4. *Business-to-business (B2B) advertising,* also called *trade advertising,* is sent from one business to another. It includes messages directed at companies distributing products as well as industrial purchasers and professionals such as lawyers and physicians. Advertisers place most business advertising in professional publications.

5. *Institutional advertising,* also called **corporate advertising,** focuses on establishing a corporate identity or winning the public over to the organization's point of view. Tobacco companies, for example, run ads that focus on the positive things they are doing. The ads for a pharmaceutical company showcasing leukemia treatment also adopt that focus.

6. *Nonprofit advertising* is used by not-for-profit organizations, such as charities, foundations, associations, hospitals, orchestras, museums, and religious institutions, to reach customers (hospitals, for example), members (the Sierra Club), and volunteers (Red Cross). It is also used to solicit donations and other forms of program participation. The *"Truth"*® campaign for the American Legacy Foundation, which tries to reach teenagers with antismoking messages, is an example of nonprofit advertising.

7. *Public service advertising* provides messages on behalf of a good cause, such as stopping drunk driving (as in ads from Mothers Against Drunk Driving) or preventing child abuse. Also called **public service announcements (PSAs),** advertising and public relations professionals usually create them **pro bono** (free of charge) and the media donate the space and time.

Cool leather.
Soft suede.
Hot savings. Hurry.

Fashion never waits. That's why now's the time to shop T.J.Maxx for the latest leather and suede at simply incredible prices. Think jackets, shirts, and skirts in all the coolest colors, plus classic browns and blacks. Fashion forward to T.J.Maxx.

Starts Sunday, August 8

T·J·maxx you should go®

Leather and suede are always tough to resist. At these prices, you won't have to.

Arrives Sunday, August 8... hurry in for best selection.

T·J·maxx

Retailers sometimes advertise nationally, but much of their advertising is targeted to a specific market, such as this direct-mail piece for T. J. Maxx.

This institutional ad for a pharmaceutical trade association uses a heart-tugging visual and copy to show consumers the value of the organization's activities—producing pharmaceutical drugs that help save lives.

Most people get their Aflac policies through payroll deduction at their workplace. This B2B ad explains to businesspeople how Aflac insurance can be part of an employee benefit package at no direct cost to the company.

Although these categories identify characteristics of various types of advertising, there are many commonalities. In practice, all types of advertising demand creative, original messages that are strategically sound and well executed, and all of them are delivered through some form of media. Furthermore, advertisements can be developed as single ads largely unrelated to other ads by the same advertiser or as a **campaign,** a term that refers to a set of related ads that are variations on a theme. They are used in different media at different times for different segments of the audience and to keep attracting the **attention** of the target audience. Let's now consider the development of key advertising concepts and practices.

HOW DID CURRENT PRACTICES AND CONCEPTS DEVELOP?

As illustrated in the timeline in Figure 1.1 the advertising industry is dynamic and is affected by changes in technology, media, and the economic and social environment. But this history is far more than names and dates. The timeline reflects how the principles and practices of a multibillion-dollar industry have evolved.[3]

Eras and Ages

The timeline divides the evolution of advertising into five stages, which reflect historical eras and the changes that lead to different philosophies and styles of advertising. As you read through this, note how changing environments, in particular media advancements, have changed the way advertising functions. (For more historical information check out the extensive timeline at *http://adage.com/century/ timeline/index.html* or Duke's John W. Hartman for Sales, Advertising & Marketing History at *http://library.duke. edu/digitalcollections/eaa*. Another source for classic ads is *www.vintageadbrowser.com*.)

This ad promotes a brand, Crest White Strips, and provides information about the product, as well as reasons to buy it.

The Early Age of Print   Industrialization and mechanized printing spurred literacy, which encouraged businesses to advertise beyond just their local place of business. Ads of the early years look like what we call **classified advertising** today. Their objective was to *identify products* and *deliver information* about them including where they were being sold. The primary medium of this age was *print,* particularly newspapers, although handbills and posters were also important, as well as hand-painted signs. The first newspaper ad appeared in 1704 for Long Island real estate, and Benjamin Franklin's *Pennsylvania Gazette* ran the first advertising section in 1729. The first *magazine* ads appeared in 1742 in Franklin's *General Magazine.*

The Early Age of Agencies   The 19th century brought the beginning of what we now recognize as the advertising industry. Volney Palmer opens the *first ad agency* in 1848 in Philadelphia. The J. Walter Thompson agency is formed in 1864, the oldest advertising agency still in existence. P.T. Barnum brings a Swedish singer to the United States and uses a blitz of newspaper ads, handbills, and posters, one of the first *campaigns.* In 1868 the N.W. Ayer agency begins the *commission system* for placing ads—advertising professionals initially were agents or brokers who bought space and time on behalf of the client for which they received a commission, a percentage of the media bill. The J. Walter Thompson agency invents *the account executive* position, a person who acts as a liaison between the client and the agency.

As advertisers and marketers became more concerned about creating ads that worked, professionalism in advertising began to take shape. Here, also, is when it became important to have a definition or a theory of advertising. In the 1880s, advertising was referred to by advertising legend Albert Lasker as *"salesmanship in print* driven by a *reason why."* Those two phrases became the model for stating an ad *claim* and explaining the *support* behind it.

On the retail side, department store owner John Wanamaker hired John E. Powers in 1880 as the store's full-time *copywriter* and Powers crafted an advertising strategy of *"ads as news."* The McCann agency, which began in 1902, also developed an agency philosophy stated as *"truth well told"* that emphasized the agency's role in crafting the ad message. *Printer's Ink,* the advertising industry's first trade publication, appeared in 1888. In the early 1900s, the J. Walter Thompson

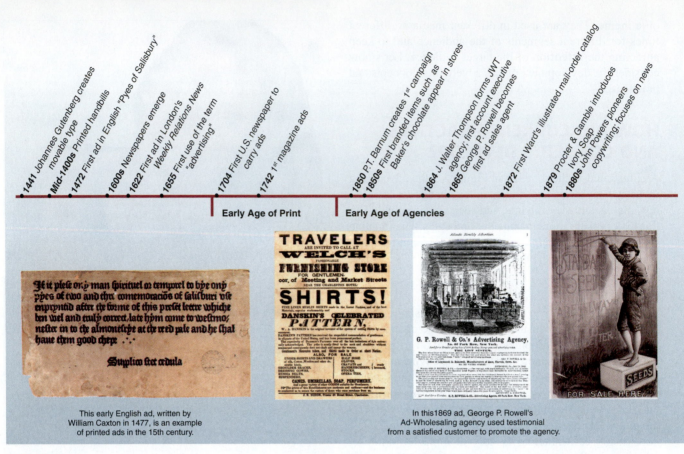

FIGURE 1.1
Advertising Timeline

agency begins publishing its "Blue Books," which explained how advertising works and compiled media data as an industry reference.

By the end of the 19th century advertisers began to give their goods brand names, such as Baker's Chocolate and Ivory Soap. The purpose of advertising during this period was to create demand, as well as a visual identity, for these new brands. Inexpensive brand-named products, known as *packed goods,* began to fill the shelves of grocers and drug stores. The questionable ethics of hype and *puffery,* which is exaggerated promises, came to a head in 1892 when *Ladies Home Journal* banned patent medicine advertising. But another aspect of hype was the use of powerful graphics that dramatized the sales message.

In Europe, the visual quality of advertising improved dramatically as artists who were also *illustrators,* such as Toulouse-Lautrec, Aubrey Beardsley, and Alphonse Mucha, brought their craftsmanship to posters and print ads, as well as magazine illustrations. Because of the artistry, this period is known as the *Golden Age.* The artist role moved beyond illustration to become the **art director** in 20th-century advertising.

The Scientific Era   In the early 1900s professionalism in advertising was reflected in the beginnings of a professional organization of large agencies, which was officially named the American Association of Advertising Agencies (known also as 4As) in 1917 (*www.aaa.org*). In addition to getting the industry organized, this period also brought a refining of professional practices. As 19th-century department store owner John Wanamaker commented, "Half the money I spend on advertising is wasted and the trouble is I don't know which half." That statement partly reflected a need to know more about how advertising works, but it also recognized the need to better target the message.

In the early 20th-century, modern professional advertising adopted scientific *research* techniques. Advertising experts believed they could improve advertising by blending science and art. Two leaders were Claude Hopkins and John Caples. At the height of Hopkins' career, he was Lord & Thomas's best-known copywriter. Highly analytical, he conducted *tests of his copy* to refine his advertising methods, an approach explained in his 1923 book, *Scientific Advertising.* John Caples, vice president of Batten, Barton, Durstine and Osborn (BBDO), published *Tested Advertising Methods* in 1932. His theories about the *pulling power of headlines* also were based on extensive tests. Caples was known for changing the style of advertising writing, which had been

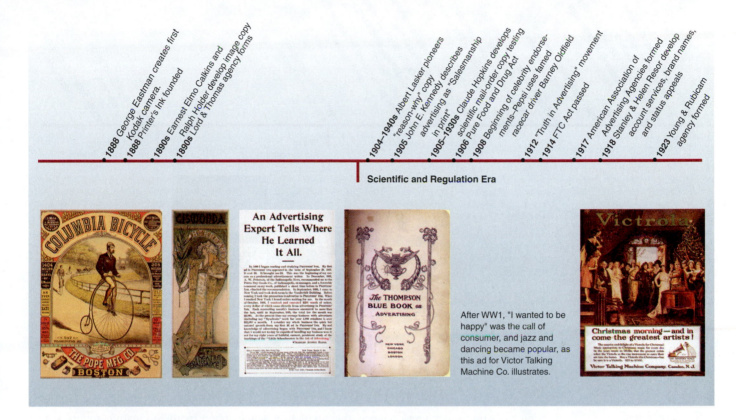

1888 George Eastman creates first Kodak camera.

1888 Printer's Ink founded

1890s Earnest Elmo Calkins and Ralph Holder develop image copy

1890s Lord & Thomas agency forms

1904–1940s Albert Lasker pioneers "reason-why" copy

1905 John E. Kennedy describes advertising as "Salesmanship in print"

1905–1930s Claude Hopkins develops scientific mail-order copy testing

1906 Pure Food and Drug Act

1908 Beginning of celebrity endorsements—Pepsi uses famed racecar driver Barney Oldfield

1912 "Truth in Advertising" movement

1914 FTC Act passed

1917 American Association of Advertising Agencies formed

1918 Stanley & Helen Resor develop account services, brand names, and status appeals

1923 Young & Rubicam agency formed

Scientific and Regulation Era

After WW1, "I wanted to be happy" was the call of consumer, and jazz and dancing became popular, as this ad for Victor Talking Machine Co. illustrates.

wordy and full of exaggerations. During the 1930s and 1940s, Daniel Starch, A. C. Nielsen, and George Gallup founded research organizations that are still part of today's advertising industry.

During and after the Great Depression, Raymond Rubicam emerged as an advertising power and launched his own agency with John Orr Young, a Lord & Thomas copywriter under the name of Young and Rubicam. Their work was known for intriguing headlines and fresh, original approaches to advertising ideas.

Targeting, the idea that messages should be directed at particular groups of prospective buyers, evolved as media became more complex. Advertisers realized that they could spend their budgets more efficiently by identifying those most likely to purchase a product, as well as the best ways to reach them. The scientific era helped media better identify their audiences. In 1914 the Audit Bureau of Circulation (ABC) was formed to standardize the definition of paid circulation for magazines and newspapers. Media changes saw print being challenged by *radio advertising* in 1922. Radio surpassed print in ad revenue in 1938.

The world of advertising agencies and management of advertising developed rapidly in the years after World War II. The J. Walter Thompson (JWT) agency, which still exists today, led the boom in advertising during this period. The agency's success was due largely to its *creative copy* and the *management* style of the husband-and-wife team of Stanley and Helen Resor. Stanley developed the concept of *account services* and expanded the account executive role into strategy development; Helen developed innovative copywriting techniques. The Resors also coined the **brand name** concept as a strategy to associate a *unique identity* with a particular product as well as the concept of *status appeal* to persuade nonwealthy people to imitate the habits of rich people (*www.jwt.com*).

Television commercials came on the scene in the early 1950s and brought a huge new revenue stream to the advertising industry. In 1952 the Nielsen rating system for TV advertising became the primary way to measure the reach of *TV commercials*.

This period also saw marketing practices, such as *product differentiation* and *market segmentation* incorporated into advertising strategy. The idea of *positioning,* carving out a unique spot in people's minds for the brand, was developed by Al Ries and Jack Trout in 1969.

The Creative Revolution The creative power of agencies exploded in the 1960s and 1970s, a period marked by the resurgence of art, inspiration, and intuition. Largely in reaction to the

1930s Radio advertising surpasses magazines as leading advertising medium
1932 John Caples applies scientific methods to mail-order copy and headlines
1940 Clyde Bedell develops "selling stratagems"
1950s TV becomes important advertising medium
1950s Rosser Reeves develops "Unique Selling Proposition"
1960s Leo Burnett creates brand icons and "inherent drama"
1960s David Ogilvy develops research-based image advertising and storytelling
1960s Bill Bernbach focuses on the art of persuasion
1969 Internet beginning
1970s E-mail begins
1989 Web is born
2001 New focus on social concerns
2008–2009 Economy crashes worldwide

Creative Revolution

Era of Accountability

Era of Change: Integration, International, and Internet

Who can forget Pepsi's use of celebrity endorsements in the 1980s?

Due to the 9/11 attacks, advertising takes on a new social responsiblilty focus.

FIGURE
1.1   (continued)

emphasis on research and science, this revolution was inspired by three creative geniuses: Leo Burnett, David Ogilvy, and William Bernbach.

Leo Burnett was the leader of what came to be known as the *Chicago school of advertising.* He believed in finding the *"inherent drama"* in every product. He also believed in using *cultural archetypes* to create mythical characters who represented American values, such as the Jolly Green Giant, Tony the Tiger, the Pillsbury Doughboy, and his most famous campaign character, the Marlboro Man (*www.leoburnett.com*).

Ogilvy, founder of the Ogilvy & Mather agency, is in some ways a paradox because he married both the *image school* of Rubicam and the *claim school* of Lasker and Hopkins. He created enduring brands with *symbols,* such as the Hathaway Man and his mysterious eye patch for the Hathaway shirt maker, and handled such quality products as Rolls-Royce, Pepperidge Farm, and Guinness with product-specific and information-rich claims (*www.ogilvy.com*).

The Doyle, Dane, and Bernbach (DDB) agency opened in 1949. From the beginning, William Bernbach—with his acute sense of words, design, and creative concepts—was considered to be the most innovative advertising creative person of his time. His advertising touched people—and persuaded them—by focusing on *feelings and emotions.* He explained, "There are a lot of great technicians in advertising. However, they forget that advertising is persuasion, and persuasion is not a science, but an art. Advertising is the art of persuasion."[4] Bernbach is known for the understated Volkswagen campaign that ran at a time when car ads were full of glamour and bombast. The campaign used headlines such as "Think Small" with accompanying picture of a small VW bug (*www.ddb.com*).

The Era of Accountability and Integration   Starting in the 1970s, the industry-wide focus was on *effectiveness.* Clients wanted ads that produced sales, so the emphasis was on research, testing, and measurement. To be accountable, advertising and other marketing communication agencies recognized that their work had to prove its value. After the dot.com boom and economic downturn in the 1980s and 1990s, this emphasis on accountability became even more important, and advertisers demanded proof that their advertising was truly **effective** in accomplishing its *objectives* as stated in the strategy.

Social responsibility is another aspect of accountability. Although advertising regulation has been in place since the early 1900s with the passage of the Pure Food and Drug Act in 1906 and

SHOWCASE

The pro bono Handgun Control campaign was designed as a wake-up call following the Columbine High School shootings. Chris Hutchinson, art director at Weiden + Kennedy, explained that "Children killing children with guns is a very real issue and we wanted to communicate the horror of this. The visuals are meant to shock juxtaposing toys with gun violence."

Chris Hutchinson graduated from the advertising program at the University of Oregon. He was nominated to have his work showcased in this text by Professor Charles Frazer.

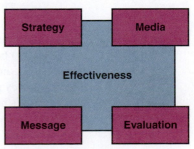

the creation of the **Federal Trade Commission** in 1914, it wasn't until 1971 that the National Advertising Review Board was created to monitor questions of *taste and social responsibility.* Charges of using sweatshops in low-wage countries and an apparent disregard for the environment concerned critics such as Naomi Klein, who wrote the best-selling book *No Logo* and Marc Gobe who wrote *Citizen Brands.* One highly visible campaign that demonstrates this commitment is the "Truth" campaign developed by Crispin Porter + Bogusky along with Arnold Worldwide to provide informative documentary-style print ads and television commercials that inform youth about the dangers of smoking without preaching to them.

As the *digital era* brought nearly instantaneous means of communication, spreading *word of mouth* among a social network of consumers, companies became even more concerned about their practices and **reputation.** The recession that began in December 2007 and subsequent headlines about bad business practices, such as the Bernard Madoff "Ponzi" scheme, made consumers even more concerned about *business ethics.*

We also characterize this as the era when integrated marketing communication became important. **Integrated marketing communication (IMC)** is another technique that managers began to adopt in the 1980s as a way to better coordinate their brand communication. Integration and consistency makes marketing communication more efficient and thus more financially accountable.

So What Are the Key Components of Advertising?

In this brief review of how advertising developed over some 300 years, a number of key concepts were introduced all of which will be discussed in more detail in the chapters that follow. But let's summarize these concepts in terms of a simple set of key components that describe the practice of advertising: strategy, message, media, and evaluation (see Figure 1.2):

- *Strategy* The logic behind an advertisement is stated in objectives that focus on areas such as sales, news, psychological appeals, emotion, branding and brand

Strategy		Media
	Effectiveness	
Message		Evaluation

FIGURE 1.2
Four Components of Advertising

reputation, as well as the position and differentiation of the product from the competition, and segmenting and targeting the best prospects.

- *Message* The concept behind a message and how that message is expressed is based on research and consumer insights with an emphasis on creativity and artistry.
- *Media* Various media have been used by advertisers over the centuries including print (hand-bills, newspapers, magazines), outdoor (signs and posters), broadcast (radio and television), and now digital media. Targeting ads to prospective buyers is done by matching their profiles to media audiences. Advertising agency compensation was originally based on the cost of buying time or space in the media.
- *Evaluation* Effectiveness means meeting objectives and in order to determine if that has happened, there must be testing. Standards also are set by professional organizations and companies that rate the size and makeup of media audiences, as well as advertising's social responsibility.

This section briefly identified how various jobs and professional concepts emerged over time. Let's now put the agency world under a microscope and look deeper at the structure of the industry.

THE AGENCY WORLD

In the discussion of definitions and the evolution of advertising practices, we briefly introduced agencies, but as a student of advertising and marketing communication you need to know more about how agencies are organized and how they operate.

Who Are the Key Players?

As we discuss the organization of the industry, consider that all the key players also represent job opportunities you might want to consider if you are interested in working in advertising or some area of marketing communication. The players include the advertiser (referred to by the agency as the *client*) who sponsors the message, the agency, the media, and the **suppliers** who provide expertise. The *A Matter of Practice* box about the greatest television commercial ever made introduced a number of these key players and illustrated how they all make different contributions to the final advertising.

The Advertiser Advertising begins with the **advertiser,** which is the company that sponsors the advertising about its business. In the "1984" story, Apple Computer was the advertiser, and Steve Jobs, the company's CEO, made the final decision to run the then-controversial commercial. The advertiser is the number one key player. Management of this function usually lies with the marketing department but in smaller companies, such as Urban Decay Cosmetics, the advertising decisions may lie with the owner, founder, or partners in the business. Wende Zomnir is not only a founding partner of Urban Decay Cosmetics, she is also an advertising graduate and a marketing communication professional.

Most advertisers have a marketing team that initiates the advertising effort by identifying a marketing problem advertising can solve. For example, Apple executives knew that the Macintosh easy-to-use computer platform needed to be explained and that information about the launch of the new computer would need to reach a large population of potential computer buyers. Advertising was essential to the success of this new product.

The marketing executive (with input from the corporate officers and others on the marketing team) also hires the advertising agency—for Burger King this was Crispin Porter + Bogusky—and other marketing communication agencies as needed. In professional jargon, the advertiser (Burger King) becomes the agency's *client*. As the client, the advertiser is responsible for monitoring the work and paying the agency for its work on the account. That use of the word *account* is the reason agency people refer to the advertiser as *the account* and the agency person in charge of that advertiser's business as the *account manager.*

The marketing team makes the final decisions about strategy including the target audience and the size of the advertising budget. This team approves the advertising or marketing communication plan, which contains details outlining the message and media strategies. In Chapter 2 we'll explain more about how this marketing team functions.

THE INSIDE STORY

A Passion for the Business

Wende Zomnir, *Creative Director and Founding Partner, Urban Decay Cosmetics*

Being the creative force behind a brand like Urban Decay makes me responsible for cranking out great ideas. And in the 13 years I've been doing this, I've figured out a few things about how to generate creative ideas with which people connect. It begins with a passion for the business. Here are my seven principles about how to run a business creatively:

1. *Feel a passion for your brand.* Everyone in product development, design, PR, merchandising, sales, and marketing at Urban Decay loves our makeup and deeply connects to our position as the counterculture icon in the realm of luxury makeup.

2. *Spot emerging trends.* Our best ideas don't start from analysts telling us what the trends are. My creative team and I talk about what kinds of colors, visual icons, textures, and patterns we are craving and start from there. Our job at Urban Decay is to lead graphically with our product design and formulation. Recently we launched a volumizing mascara called Big Fatty and played off the connotations in the name, infusing the formula with hemp oil and wrapping the mascara vial in an Age of Aquarius–inspired print. Shortly after the product's release, a supplier to the cosmetics industry came in to show us a version of our own mascara, giving us a presentation on the coming trends. It's annoying, but when this happens, we know we're doing our job.

3. *Cultivate your inner voice.* You also need to develop a gut instinct for what will work. I felt that skulls were going to be huge because everyone in the office was craving them on T-shirts, shoes, key rings, and so forth. We decided to put them on our seasonal holiday compacts in 2005. And the same season that Marc Jacobs launched them, so did we. We had distributors begging us to sell them a version without the skull, but we stood firm and wouldn't change it because we knew it was right. And you know what? The same distributors who balked placed the biggest reorders and complained that we couldn't stock them fast enough.

4. *Check your ego.* Listening to that inner voice IS something you can cultivate, but you've got to check your ego at the door in order to do it. That can be hard, because being a creative leader means you've probably generated a lot of great ideas that work. So, you've got confidence in your concepts and your ability to deliver, but you have to be able to admit others have great ideas, too.

5. *Cherry-pick the best ideas.* Gut instinct is important, BUT—and this is big—even more crucial is being able to listen to all the ideas and sort out the junk. After you sort through everything, then pick the very best concept, even if it's NOT your idea.

6. *Little ideas are important, too.* You've got to rally everyone behind your Big Idea, but realize that all those little ideas that prop up the big one are great, too. That's what makes so many of our products work in the marketplace: a big idea supported by little ideas—and the people who develop them.

7. *Be flexible.* My final important creative principle is flexibility. Knowing when to be flexible has resulted in some of the best work we've created here. While working on a body powder for summer that was to be impregnated with water for a cooling sensation on the skin, we ran into production problems. We wanted a powder, but I decided to add flavor instead. That edible body powder became a huge subbrand for us, spawning multiple flavors and generating huge amounts of press and revenue. The cooling powder would have been late, had quality control issues, and probably would have lasted a season.

Wende Zomnir (aka Ms. Decay) graduated from the University of North Texas where she was a student of Professor Sheri Broyles.

Check out Urban Decay at *www.urbandecay.com/; www.myspace.com/urbandecaycosmetics;* and *http://twitter.com/UrbanDecay411.*

The distinctive personality of Urban Decay Cosmetics is seen in its packaging, as well as its products' names, such as the Ammo Group, and colors: "Smog," "Mildew," and "Oil Slick."

Big companies may have hundreds of agencies working for them, although they normally have an **agency-of-record (AOR)** that does most of their business and may even manage or coordinate the work of other agencies.

The Agency   The second player is the **advertising agency** (or other types of marketing communication agencies) that creates, produces, and distributes the messages. The working arrangement between advertiser and agency is known as the *agency–client partnership.* Both the "1984" story and the BK deprivation scheme demonstrated how important it is to cultivate a strong sense of trust between the agency and its clients because these were both risky ideas.

An advertiser uses an outside agency because it believes the agency will be more efficient in creating advertising messages than the advertiser would be on its own. Successful agencies such as Crispin Porter + Bogusky typically have strategic and creative expertise, media knowledge, workforce talent, and the ability to negotiate good deals for clients. The advertising professionals working for the agency are experts in their areas of specialization and passionate about their work.

Not all advertising professionals work in agencies. Large advertisers, either companies or organizations, manage the advertising process either by setting up an **advertising department** (sometimes called **marketing services**) that oversees the work of agencies or by setting up their own in-house agency, as we see in Figure 1.3. Tasks performed by the company's marketing services department include the following: select the agencies; coordinate activities with vendors, such as media, production, and photography; make sure the work gets done as scheduled; and determine whether the work has achieved prescribed objectives.

The Media   The third player in the advertising world is the media. The emergence of mass media has been a central factor in the development of advertising because mass media offers a way to reach a widespread audience. In traditional advertising, the term **media** refers to all of the channels of communication that carry the message from the advertiser to the audience and from consumers back to companies. We refer to these media as **channels** because they deliver messages, but they are also companies, such as your local newspaper or radio station.

Some of these media conglomerates are huge, such as Time Warner and Viacom. Time Warner, for example, is a $40 billion company with some 38,000 employees. It owns HBO, Time Inc., Turner Broadcasting, and Warner Brothers, among other media companies. You can learn more about this media conglomerate at *www.timewarner.com.* **Media vehicles** are the specific programs, such as *60 Minutes* or *The Simpsons,* or magazines—*The New York Times, Advertising Age, Woman's Day.*

Note that **media** is plural when it refers to various channels, but singular—**medium**—when it refers to only one form, such as newspapers.

Each medium (newspaper, radio or TV station, billboard company, etc.) has a department that is responsible for selling ad space or time. These departments specialize in assisting advertisers in

FIGURE 1.3

Two Advertising Organization Structures

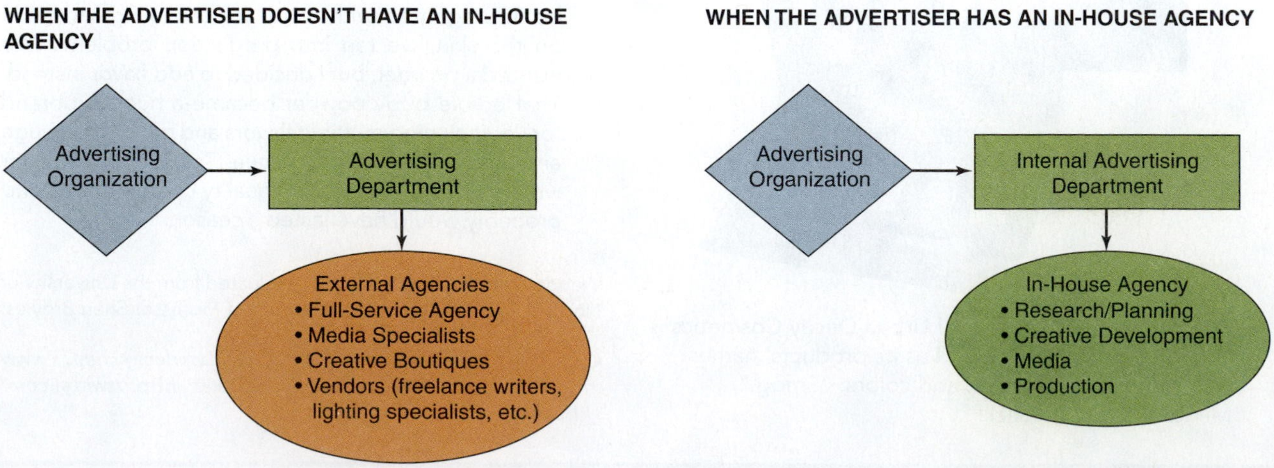

WHEN THE ADVERTISER DOESN'T HAVE AN IN-HOUSE AGENCY

Advertising Organization → Advertising Department → External Agencies
• Full-Service Agency
• Media Specialists
• Creative Boutiques
• Vendors (freelance writers, lighting specialists, etc.)

WHEN THE ADVERTISER HAS AN IN-HOUSE AGENCY

Advertising Organization → Internal Advertising Department → In-House Agency
• Research/Planning
• Creative Development
• Media
• Production

comparing the effectiveness of various media as they try to select the best mix of media to use. Many media organizations will assist advertisers in the design and production of advertisements. That's particularly true for local advertisers using local media, such as a retailer preparing an advertisement for the local newspaper.

The primary advantage of advertising's use of **mass media** is that the costs to buy time in broadcast media, space in print media, and time and space in digital media are spread over the tremendous number of people that these media reach. For example, $3 million may sound like a lot of money for one Super Bowl ad, but when you consider that the advertisers are reaching more than 100 million people, the cost is not so extreme. One of the big advantages of mass-media advertising is that it can reach a lot of people with a single message in a very cost-efficient form.

Principle
Advertising is cost efficient when it uses mass media to reach large numbers of prospective consumers.

Professional Suppliers and Consultants   The fourth player in the world of advertising include artists, writers, photographers, directors, producers, printers, and self-employed freelancers and consultants. In the "1984" story, the movie director Ridley Scott was a supplier in that Chiat/Day contracted with him to produce the commercial. This array of suppliers mirrors the variety of tasks required to put together an ad. Other examples include freelance copywriters and graphic artists, songwriters, printers, market researchers, direct-mail production houses, telemarketers, and public relations consultants. Why would the other advertising players hire an outside supplier? There are many reasons. The advertiser or the agency may not have expertise in a specialized area, their people may be overloaded with work, or they may want a fresh perspective. They also may not want to incur the overhead of full-time employees.

Types of Agencies

We are primarily concerned with advertising agencies in this chapter, but other areas such as public relations, direct marketing, sales promotion, and the Internet have agencies that provide specialized promotional help, as well.

The A-List awards by *Advertising Age* recognize cutting-edge agencies that rank high in three areas: First they are creative—*Ad Age* calls them "widely imaginative"—in developing brand strategies and executions. Second, they are fast growing and winners of some of the biggest new business pitches. Finally, they are recognized for their effectiveness. In other words, their work leads to measurable results. Note that the agencies in the following list represent big and small agencies, as well as full-service and specialized agencies. At the top of the list is the agency of the year, Crispin Porter + Bogusky, the agency behind the Burger King "Whopper Freakout" campaign.

A-List of Advertising Agencies

1. *Crispin Porter + Bogusky* This agency used to be a medium-size, independent Miami hotshop, but now it's a big national creative power from Miami and Boulder, Colorado, known for its provocative work for Burger King, Old Navy, and Coke Zero, among other powerhouse clients (*www.cpbgroup.com*).
2. *TBWA/Chiat/Day* This L.A.-based agency creates what it calls its "disruptive ideas" for global clients such as Visa and Adidas. This is the agency behind the legendary "1984" ad for Apple's Macintosh (*www.tbwa.com*).

Advertising relies on the expertise of many different people, such as television producers, graphic designers, photographers, printers, and musicians.

3. *Goodby, Silverstein & Partners* The previous year's Agency of the Year, San Francisco–based Goodby continues to be recognized not only for its creative efforts, but also for building big brands, such as Doritos and General Electric, as well as the classic "Got Milk" campaign (*www.goodbysilverstein.com*).

4. *R/GA* Originally a specialized digital agency, R/GA now operates more like a full-service agency that prides itself on forging deep, lasting connections with consumers for its clients, which include Nike and Apple's iTunes (*www.rga.com*).

5. *Tribal DDB* Primarily a digital agency, New York–based Tribal is also creative, collaborative, and brand savvy. Its work includes an award-winning TV commercial for Deutsche Telekom, as well as other new media and viral projects for Philips, Wrigley, and McDonald's (*www.tribalddb.com*).

6. *Mindshare* Mindshare is a global media network that offers media and communication planning, interactive marketing, branded entertainment, sports marketing, and marketing effectiveness analyses to such clients as IBM, Unilever, and American Express (*www.mindshareworld.com*).

7. *The Martin Agency* More than a regional shop from Richmond, Virginia, this agency continues to be recognized for great creative spots, such as those for Geico (*www.martinagency.com*).

8. *Vidal Partnership* The largest independent Hispanic agency in the United States, Vidal operates as an integrated full-service marketing communication agency and handles campaigns for Wendy's, Home Depot, JCPenney, and Johnson & Johnson (*www.vidal-partnership.com*).

9. *Rapp* A giant in direct marketing, Rapp is redefining relationship marketing for its customers, such as Macy's, Audi, ExxonMobile, and General Electric (*www.rapp.com*).

10. *Deutsch* The New York–based Deutsch full-service agency believes in connecting with and motivating an audience on behalf of clients such as Evian, GM, and PlayStation (*www.deutschinc.com*).

Source: Adapted from Parekh Rupal, "Agency of the Year: Crispin Porter + Bogusky," *Advertising Age,* January 19, 2009, *http://adage.com/agencya-list08/article?article_id=133815.*

In addition to agencies that specialize in advertising and other areas of marketing communication, there are also consulting firms in marketing research and branding that offer specialized services to other agencies, as well as advertisers. Since these various types of marketing communication areas are all part of an integrated marketing communication approach, we cover many of these functions in separate chapters later in the book.

Full-Service Agencies   In advertising, a **full-service agency** includes the four major staff functions of account management, creative services, media planning, and account planning, which includes research. A full-service advertising agency also has its own finance and accounting department, a **traffic department** to handle internal tracking on completion of projects, a department for broadcast and **print production** (sometimes organized within the creative department), and a human resources department.

Let's take a minute to look inside one full-service agency, Crispin Porter + Bogusky, which was named Agency of the Year by *Adweek* and *Advertising Age,* as well as *Ad Age*'s sister publication *Creativity.* CPB celebrates some $140 million in revenue and employs nearly 900 in its two offices in Miami and Boulder, Colorado. The agency is known for its edgy, pop-culture approach to strategy. You probably know Burger King's weird "king" character, and you read about its "Whopper Freakout" campaign at the beginning of this chapter. Maybe you have been introduced to some of Old Navy's "SuperModelquins," the talking mannequins in the opening story you'll read later in Chapter 5. That's the kind of provocative work that *Ad Age* calls "culturally primal."[5] It infiltrates the social scene and creates buzz. Although known for its creative work, CPB also has an innovative product design think tank that has come up with such ideas as a public bike rental program, a portable pen version of WED-40, and BK's popular Burger Shots sliders.

In-House Agencies   Like a regular advertising agency, an **in-house agency** produces ads and places them in the media, but the agency is a part of the advertiser's organization, rather than an outside company. Companies that need closer control over their advertising have their own internal in-house agencies. An in-house agency performs most, and sometimes all, of the functions of an outside advertising agency and produce materials, such as point-of-sale displays, sales team literature, localized ads and promotions, and coupon books, that larger agencies have a hard time producing cost effectively. Retailers, for example, find that doing their own advertising and media placement provides cost savings, as well as the ability to meet fast-breaking deadlines. Some fashion companies, such as Ralph Lauren, also create their own advertising in house to maintain complete control over the brand image and the fashion statement it makes. Check out this in-house agency at *http://about.ralphlauren.com/campaigns/default.asp.*

Specialized Agencies   Many agencies do not follow the traditional full-service agency approach. They either specialize in certain functions (writing copy, producing art, or media buying), audiences (minority, youth), industries (health care, computers, agriculture, business-to-business communication), or markets (minority groups such as Asian, African American, or Hispanic). In addition, some agencies specialize in other marketing communication areas, such as branding, direct marketing, sales promotion, public relations, events and sports marketing, packaging, and point-of-sale promotions. Sometimes one-client agencies are created to handle the work of one large client. Let's take a look at two special types of agencies:

- **Creative boutiques** are ad agencies, usually small (two or three people to a dozen or more), that concentrate entirely on preparing the creative execution of the idea, or the creative product. A creative boutique has one or more writers or artists on staff, but generally no staff for media, research, or strategic planning. Typically, these agencies can prepare advertising to run in print and broadcast media, as well as in out-of-home (such as outdoor and transit advertising), Internet, and alternative media. Creative boutiques usually serve companies directly, but are sometimes retained by full-service agencies that are overloaded with work.
- **Media-buying services** specialize in the purchase of media for clients. They are in high demand for many reasons, but three reasons stand out. First, media has become more complex as the number of choices has grown—think of the proliferation of new cable channels, magazines, and radio stations. Second, the cost of maintaining a competent media department has escalated. Third, media-buying services often buy media at a low cost because they can group several clients' purchases together to get discounts from the media because of the volume of their media buys.

Agency Networks and Holding Companies   Finally let's talk about **agency networks,** which are large conglomerations of agencies under a central ownership. Agency networks are all of the offices that operate under one agency name, such as DDB Worldwide (200 offices in 90 countries) or BBDO Worldwide (287 offices in 79 countries). You can read more about these agencies and their networks at *www.ddb.com* and *www.bbdoworldwide.com.*

   Holding companies include one or more advertising agency networks, as well as other types of marketing communication agencies and marketing services consulting firms. The four largest are WPP Group, Interpublic, Omnicom, and Publicis. WPP, for example, includes the J. Walter Thompson Group, Ogilvy & Mather Worldwide, Young & Rubicam, Grey Global Group, and Bates advertising networks, as well as the Berlin Cameron creative agency, public relations agencies Hill and Knowlton, Ogilvy Public Relations, and Burson-Marsteller; direct-response company Wunderman; research firms Millward Brown and Research International; media firms Mindshare and Mediaedge:cia; and branding and corporate identity firms Landor and Lambie-Naim, to name a few. Most of those firms are also networks with multiple offices. For an inside look at a big holding company, check out WPP at *www.wpp.com.*

How Are Agency Jobs Organized?

In addition to the chief executive officer, if the agency is large enough, it usually has one or more vice presidents, as well as department heads for the different functional areas. We will concentrate on five of those areas: account management; account planning and research; creative development and production; media research, planning, and buying; and internal services.

Account Management   The **account management** (sometimes called **account services**) function acts as a liaison between the client and the agency. It ensures that the agency focuses its resources on the client's needs. The account team summarizes the client's communication needs and develops the basic "charge to the agency," which the account manager presents to the agency's team. The **account executive** (called the *content manager* at the Crispin Porter + Bogusky agency) is responsible for interpreting the client's marketing research and strategy for the rest of the agency. The *Day in the Life* story focuses on the work of an account executive at CPB.

Once the client and agency together establish the general guidelines for a campaign, the account management team supervises the day-to-day development. Account management in a major agency typically has three levels: the *management supervisor,* who provides leadership on strategic issues and looks for new business opportunities; the *account supervisor,* who is the key executive working on a client's business and the primary liaison between the client and the

A DAY IN THE LIFE

Tweets from the Front Line

Jennifer Cunningham, *Content Manager, Crispin Porter + Bogusky*

As a content manager (account executive) at Crispin Porter + Bogusky's Boulder office, I never know what's in store for me on any given day. What I DO know is that the days will never be boring. From presenting creative to clients, to going on late-night caffeine runs for teams pulling all-nighters . . . anything goes.

Though tasks vary from day to day, part of my job is to constantly stay up to date on the latest and greatest technologies and trends. Now, I'm no tech expert but if a client asks for my opinion on brand integration on Twitter, for example, I better know what they're talking about.

And since Twitter is all the rage right now, here's a day in my shoes at CP+B via real-time tweets:

- Parking. Better hustle, have a 9:30 meeting and need some coffee first! (Had a late night last night sending a print ad to the printer—when ads are due, I stay in the office and help make sure everyone has approved it before it goes out.) *9:08*
- Reading all my morning e-mails—my clients are on East Coast time so their workday started 2+ hours ago. *9:19*
- Content team status—this is an informal weekly meeting to ensure everyone knows what's up on the account. *9:32*
- Confirming teams are ready for an 11 A.M. client presentation. Creatives here don't let ANY work out the door unless it's perfect. But sometimes perfection doesn't sync with the client call times. . . . *9:55*
- Writing setup slides for the presentation—this includes recapping our assignment, thoughts on the work, and background info. *10:08*
- Don't have the creative yet—checking in with teams, starting to get a little nervous. *10:30*
- Talked with my creative director—they're making the last few tweaks on the presentation, but they're running 10 to 15 minutes behind. *10:41*
- Calling my client. She's running behind too—starting late will be "just fine." Whew. *10:49*
- Call from another client—the publisher is saying they didn't receive our print ad last night. Asking if we can look into it . . . oh boy. *10:53*

- E-mailing my print producer to check in with the publisher. *10:55*
- E-mailing my media planner to ensure we won't miss our insertion deadline. *10:56*
- Got the presentation! Looks awesome—have a feeling the clients will love these ideas. *11:10*
- On the call—reinforcing the strategy and schedules as the creatives present ideas. *11:22*
- Recapping the presentation call to make sure the creative teams have clear feedback for revisions and to ensure our clients had the same take-aways from the call. *12:01*
- Hopping on a media call—gathering info for Production, so we can start work once ideas from the presentation are approved. *1:11*
- Reviewing invoices over lunch—have to make sure our billing is accurate and that we stay on budget for projects. *2:03*
- Call with Business Affairs—just finalized legal approvals on scripts and the contracts for celebrity talent for our next TV spot. Pretty exciting! *3:15*
- Whew—lost track of time. Rereleased the print ad for the publication. Confirmed teams are working on feedback. Put together a post-campaign analysis to see how we met our goals number-wise on our last project. Participated in a brainstorming session for another account—gotta help where you can. *6:08*
- Wrapping up—need to walk my dog at home. *6:31*
- Hopping back on my computer for a couple more e-mails and prep for tomorrow. All in all a pretty good day. *8:15*
- Finishing up this day-in-the-life—hope you enjoyed reading it. Good luck should you pursue a career in advertising! There's never a dull moment. *9:01*

To learn more about Crispin Porter + Bogusky, check out *www.cpbgroup .com.*
Jennifer Cunningham is a graduate of the advertising program at the University of Colorado. She was a student of Professor Kendra Gale.

agency; and the *account executive* (as well as *assistant account executives*), who is responsible for day-to-day activities and operates like a project manager. A smaller agency will combine some of these levels. Of course, individual agencies also have their own titles for these positions, such as the "content manager" title used at CPB.

Account Planning and Research   Full-service agencies usually have a separate department specifically devoted to planning and sometimes to research as well. Today the emphasis in agency research is on developing an advertising message concept that focuses on the consumer's perspective and relationship with the brand. The **account planning** group gathers all available intelligence on the market and consumers and acts as the voice of the consumer. Account planners are strategic specialists who prepare comprehensive information about consumers' wants, needs, and relationship to the client's brand and recommendations on how the advertising should work to satisfy those elements based on insights they derive from consumer research.

Creative Development and Production   A creative group includes people who write (*copywriters*), people who design ideas for print ads or television commercials (*art directors*), and people who convert these ideas into television or radio commercials (*producers*). Many agencies build a support group around a team of an art director and copywriter who work well together. In addition to these positions, the broadcast production department and art studio are two other areas where creative personnel can apply their skills.

Media Research, Planning, and Buying   Agencies that don't rely on outside media specialists have a media department that recommends to the client the most efficient means of delivering the message to the target audience. That department has three functions: research, planning, and buying. Because the media world is so complex, it is not unusual for some individuals to become experts in certain markets or types of media.

Internal Operations   The departments that serve the operations within the agency include the traffic department and print production, as well as the more general financial services and human resources (personnel) departments. The traffic department is the lifeblood of the agency, and its personnel keep track of everything that happens.

How Are Agencies Paid?

Advertising agencies are a big business. Procter & Gamble, for example, spends nearly $5 billion annually on global advertising. With that kind of money on the table, you can imagine that the agency–client relationship is under pressure from both sides. Agencies want to get more work and get paid more; clients want to cut costs and make their advertising as cost effective as possible.

Agencies derive their revenues and profits from three main sources: commissions, **fees,** and retainers. For years, a 15 percent **commission** on media billings was the traditional form of compensation. That's actually how agencies got started back in the 19th century. For those few accounts still using a commission approach, the rate is rarely 15 percent; it is more likely lower and subject to negotiation between agency and client.

Many advertisers now use a fee system either as the primary compensation tool or in combination with a commission system. The **fee system** is comparable to the system by which advertisers pay their lawyers and accountants. The client and agency agree on an hourly fee or rate or may negotiate a charge for a specific project. This fee can vary by department, or it may be a flat hourly fee for all work regardless of the salary level of the person doing the work. Charges are also included for out-of-pocket expenses, travel, and other standard items.

An agency also may be put on a monthly or yearly **retainer.** The amount billed per month is based on the projected amount of work and the hourly rate charged. This system is most commonly used by public relations agencies.

A more recent trend in agency compensation is for advertisers to pay agencies on the basis of their performance. One consultant recommends that this arrangement be based on paying the agency either a percentage of the client's sales or a percentage of the client's marketing budget. Procter & Gamble is a pioneer in trying to apply this system. Another version of this idea is that agencies share in the profits of their client when they create a successful campaign, but that also means they have a greater financial risk in the relationship should the advertising not create the intended impact.

Another innovation in agency compensation is called **value billing,** which means that the agency is paid for its creative and strategic ideas, rather than for executions and media placements.

Sarah Armstrong, Coke's director of worldwide media and communication, has urged the industry to shift to "value-based" forms of compensation that reward agencies based on effectiveness—whether they make the objectives they set for their advertising.[6]

HOW IS THE PRACTICE OF ADVERTISING CHANGING?

We would like to end this review of advertising basics by talking about the future of advertising. Because of the recent Great Recession, Mike Carlton, an industry commentator, says, "[C]learly we are at a point in time when things will never be quite the same again for our industry." But there are still some exciting changes that open up opportunities for new professionals entering the field.

Consumer in Charge

As Jim Stengel, Procter & Gamble's former global marketing officer, has said, "[I]t's not just about doing great TV commercials: The days of pounding people with images, and shoving them down their eyeballs are over. The consumer is much more in control now."[7] This change is causing some shifts in the way the advertising business operates.

In 2009 CareerBuilder dismissed one of the most creative agencies—Portland-based Wieden + Kennedy, who had created five great Super Bowl ads for the job-posting website—and took its advertising in house. The reason is that the company wants ordinary consumers to create 25-second commercials for the brand. That will not only bring publicity, but also save bucks. CareerBuilder, through its in-house agency, will still pay for production of the winning ad and buy the ad time. Not only will this move bring more opportunities for *consumer-generated advertising* (at the expense of advertising agencies), the company estimates it will save around 15 to 20 percent of its annual marketing costs.[8]

Other brands that have used consumer-generated ads include Frito-Lay, Converse, Master-Card, and L'Oreal. Frito-Lay received thousands of media mentions for its Super Bowl ad contest on such programs as *The Tonight Show, The View,* and *Good Morning America.* You can check out Doritos' collection of consumer-generated Super Bowl ads in the "Crash the Super Bowl" contest at *www.crashthesuperbowl.com/#/winners.*

Consumer involvement in advertising is a bigger issue than just ad agencies losing their clients. In fact, consumers have been taking control of media and marketing for a number of years through Wikipedia, Twitter, and other newly democratized information sources. YouTube, MySpace, and Facebook have invited everyone into the ad distribution game. The Internet is a new world of interaction and consumer-initiated contacts that are creating entirely new ways of communicating with potential customers. That's why in 2006, *Time* magazine spotted the trend and named "You the Consumer" as its Person of the Year and then in 2007 *Advertising Age* named the consumer its "Agency of the Year."

Blurring Lines and Converging Media

One of the biggest changes impacting the advertising industry is the changing media environment. Television used to be the big gun, and it still eats up the biggest part of the budget, but the old networks (CBS, NBC, ABC, FOX) are only half as important as they used to be as the number of cable channels has exploded.

The big bomb that has fragmented the media world is digital media, which appear in so many different forms that it's impossible to keep up with them. The newspaper industry has been particularly hurt as it has realized that much, if not most, of its content can be accessed more easily and quickly in a digital format. So are newspapers dead?

Traditional media are trying to adjust by transforming themselves into new digital formats, as well. So what do you call online versions of newspapers and magazines? Are they still print when they appear on a screen? And new personal media—iPhones, iPods, iPads, BlackBerries, Kindles—are real shape-changers. They can be phones, music players, calendars, and sources of local and national information, as well as cameras, video viewers, book readers, Web surfers, and video game players. Changes such as these need to be considered when putting together media plans, a challenge that will be discussed in Part 3.

Advertising agencies make most of their money from television spots and print media. However, as we've mentioned, both of those revenue streams are threatened by economics and the changing media landscape. As Mike Carlton explains, "TV spots and other traditional work as the economic backbone of the agency business will just not work much longer."[9] However, Carlton also calls for agencies to take a stronger leadership role in the development of brand strategy, particularly for the more complex forms of marketing communication with their blurred, merged, and converged media.

Accountability and Effectiveness

Given the recent recession, you can guess that efficiency is an advantage in this new advertising world, which has been emphasizing accountability for a couple of decades. The other critical client concern is effectiveness, which is another way to look at accountability in marketing communication.

We mentioned that CareerBuilder had taken its advertising in house partly to drive a consumer-generated advertising program, but also to save costs, which is critical in an economic downturn. The need for efficiency is complicated by crack-ups in the agency–client relationships. Agencies that are creative in finding new ways to deliver cost efficiencies have a real advantage in their client dealings.

Effectiveness   Along with the ongoing need for efficiencies, there's always a concern about effectiveness, or accountability as it's sometimes called, but this has become even more important in difficult times. The recent recession forced the advertising industry to become even more serious about creating advertising that delivers results and then proving the effectiveness of the advertising work once it's completed. Effectiveness is a theme that you will see discussed throughout this book.

So what is **effectiveness?** Effective ads are ads that work. That is, they deliver the message the advertiser intended and consumers respond as the advertiser hoped they would. Ultimately, advertisers such as Burger King want consumers to buy and keep buying their goods and services. To get to that point, ads must first effectively communicate a message that motivates consumers to respond.

The most important characteristic of advertising is that it is purposeful: Ads are created to have some effect, some impact on the people who read or see their message. We refer to this as advertising's **effects,** the idea being that effective advertising messages will achieve the advertiser's desired impact and the target audience will respond as the advertiser intended. This desired impact is formally stated as a set of **objectives,** which are statements of the measurable goals or results that the advertising is intended to achieve. In other words, advertising works if it achieves its objectives.

Principle
Advertising is effective if it achieves its objectives.

Award Shows   This chapter opened with the Burger King campaign, which was identified as award-winning advertising. The Effie award, named for a shortened form of the word *effective,* is given by the New York Chapter of the American Marketing Association (AMA) to advertising and other forms of marketing communication that have been proven to be not only creative, but more importantly, effective. That means the campaigns were guided by measurable objectives, and evaluation after the campaign determined that the effort did, in fact, meet or exceed the objectives. (Check out the Effies at *www.effie.org*.) Other award shows that focus on effectiveness are the Advertising and Marketing Effectiveness (AME) awards by the New York Festivals company, Canada's Cassie Awards, and the London-based Institute of Practitioners (IPA) Award. Check out these award programs at *www.ameawards.com, www.cassies.ca,* and *www.ipa.co.uk*.

Other award shows judge factors such as creative ideas, for example, the Clios by a private award-show company, a New York–based advertising association's One Show, and the Cannes Lions Awards by a French award-show company. Awards are also given for media plans (*Adweek*'s Media Plan of the Year) and art direction (New York–based Art Directors Club award show). These awards can be found at *www.clioawards.com, www.canneslions.com, www.adweek .com,* and *www.adcglobal.org/awards/annual*.

Other professional areas also have award shows that reward such things as clever promotional ideas. For example, the Reggies are given by the Promotion Marketing Association, and outstanding public relations efforts are recognized by the Public Relations Society of America's Silver Anvil Award.

Integrated Marketing Communication (IMC)

We mentioned that effectiveness is a central theme for this book, but another concept that we will discuss throughout is *integration.* As we mentioned earlier in our timeline, the search for effective communication has led many companies to focus on the consistency of their brand communication in order to more efficiently establish a coherent brand perception. We call that practice *integrated marketing communication* or *IMC.* In other words, everything that sends a brand message is a point of concern for those managing brand communication. To be effective, these messages need to complement one another and present the same basic brand strategy.

*First Principle
of IMC*
Everything
communicates.

The point is that brand communication involves more than just advertising. We refer to the **First Principle of IMC** as *everything communicates.* And that means all marketing communication *media* (print, broadcast, out-of-home, and digital), as well as all marketing communication *platforms* (advertising, public relations, events and sponsorships, and direct response) and other new forms, such as guerilla marketing and online social media. All communication efforts are planned for maximum synergy.

Looking Ahead

This chapter has provided an introduction to many of the basic concepts of advertising, as well as IMC. We'll continue that introduction of principles and practices in Chapter 2 as we explain the bigger picture of advertising and its role in marketing communication and marketing. Marketing communication agencies play an important role in puzzling out new ways to interact with customers and cement brand relationships.

IT'S A WRAP

WHOPPER*FREAKOUT*.COM

Best Burger, Best Campaign, Best Practices

The focus on effectiveness and results is the theme of this textbook, and throughout the book we will introduce you to practices that generate effectiveness. We'll end each chapter with the results of the campaign that introduced the chapter—in this case, the Grand Effie–winning "Whopper Freakout" campaign for Burger King. The freakout campaign for Whopper's 50th anniversary demonstrates the power of having a brand identity so strong that customers not only remember it, but demand it.

So here's the rest of the Whopper story. It's a story of consumer shock and outrage: "If Burger King doesn't have the Whopper, they might as well change their name to Burger Queen," and "What are you going to put on the logo now—home of the 'whatever we got'?" griped outraged customers. When one stunned would-be Whopper eater was given a Big Mac instead, he said, "I hate McDonald's."

These comments were all captured on tape and played and replayed on the special website by intrigued viewers 5 million times. Fourteen million more watched it and the TV spots on YouTube. The agency figures this all led to a 300+ percent increase in Web chatter about Burger King, which it estimates was about a fifth of the paid media. That means it received about 20 percent of the media for free as consumers spread the word. Burger King successfully captured its audience with a viral hit. *Ad lesson #3:* Smart thinking can help you compete with competitors with bigger budgets.

Was the campaign effective? Did the captivated audience buy the burgers? The answer: the quarterly sales increased by double digits. At the beginning of this case, you read about two goals for the campaign. One was to reaffirm that the Whopper is America's most-loved burger, and the other was to increase the sales of the burger. This campaign achieved both of these measurable objectives.

What a way to celebrate the 50th anniversary of the Whopper. To make the golden anniversary more golden, the campaign was awarded a Gold Effie in the Restaurants category and the coveted Grand Effie, the top award given to acknowledge effectiveness for the campaign's "boldness and creativity across multiple media platforms, delivering real cultural relevance and above all, outstanding business results." *Ad lesson #4:* Awards mean nothing if they don't achieve the business goals.

Key Points Summary

1. **What is advertising, how has it evolved, and what does it do in modern times?** The definition of advertising has evolved over time from identification to information and persuasion, as well as selling. In modern times, advertising is persuasive communication that uses mass and interactive media to reach broad audiences in order to connect an iden-

tified sponsor with buyers and provide information about products. It performs communication, marketing, economic, and societal roles. Seven types of advertising define the industry: brand, retail or local, direct response, B2B, institutional, nonprofit, and public service.

2. **How have the key concepts of marketing communication developed over time?** A review of the evolution of advertising practice identifies the source of many of the key concepts currently used in advertising. These concepts can be grouped into the four key components of advertising: strategy (objectives, appeals, branding, positioning and differentiation, and segmenting and targeting), message (creative concept based on research and consumer insight, creativity and artistry), media (the evolution of print, broadcast, outdoor, and digital, as well as the practice of matching targets to media audiences and compensation based on the media buy), and evaluation (effectiveness in terms of meeting objectives, testing, standards).

3. **How is the industry organized—key players, types of agencies, and jobs within agencies?** The key players begin with the advertiser, the organization or brand behind the advertising effort. Other players include the agency that prepares the advertising, the media that run it, and the professional suppliers and consultants who contribute expertise. The three types of agencies are full-service, in-house, and specialized agencies. There are also networks of agencies with many offices, as well as holding companies that own many different kinds of agencies. Agency jobs are varied in expertise and provide a number of career opportunities for all kinds of skill sets: account management, planning and research, creative (writing, art direction, production), and media (research, planning, buying). Agencies are paid in different ways, including by commission based on a percent of media costs, with a fee system based on estimated project costs or hourly billing, or with a monthly retainer. Value billing is based on creative and strategic ideas rather than media costs.

4. **How is the practice of advertising changing?** A number of changes are creating new forms of advertising, such as consumer-initiated ideas and advertising executions, blurring lines between marcom areas and tools, media that are changing shape and merging with other media forms, new forms of client–agency relationships, and value-marketing practices that emerged from the recession.

Words of Wisdom: Recommended Reading

Jaffe, Joseph, *Life after the 30-Second Spot: Energize Your Brand with a Bold Mix of Alternatives to Traditional Advertising,* Hoboken, NJ: John Wiley, 2005.

Ogilvy, David, *Ogilvy on Advertising,* New York: Vintage Books, 1985.

Othmer, James, *Adland: Searching for the Meaning of Life on a Branded Planet,* New York: Doubleday, 2009.

Steel, Jon, *Perfect Pitch: The Art of Selling Ideas and Winning New Business,* Hoboken, NJ: John Wiley, 2007.

History

Applegate, Edd, *Personalities and Products: A Historical Perspective on Advertising in America,* Westport, CT: Greenwood Press, 1998.

Fox, Stephen, *The Mirror Makers: A History of American Advertising and its Creators,* Champaign, IL: University of Illinois Press, 1997.

Twitchell, James, *Twenty Ads That Shook the World: The Century's Most Groundbreaking Advertising and How It Changed Us All,* New York: Three Rivers Press, 2000.

Tungate, Mark, *Adland: A Global History of Advertising,* Philadelphia: Kogan Page, 2007.

Key Terms

account executive, p. 24
account management, p. 23
account planning, p. 25
account services, p. 23
advertisement, p. 6
advertiser, p. 18
advertising, p. 7
advertising agency, p. 20
advertising department, p. 20
agency networks, p. 23
agency-of-record (AOR), p. 20
art director, p. 14

attention, p. 13
brand advertising, p. 11
brand name, p. 15
business-to-business (B2B) advertising, p. 11
buzz, p. 9
campaign, p. 12
channels (media), p. 20
classified advertising, p. 13
commission, p. 25
corporate advertising, p. 11
creative boutique, p. 23

direct-response advertising, p. 11
effective, p. 16
effectiveness, p. 27
effects, p. 27
Federal Trade Commission (FTC), p. 17
fee, p. 25
fee system, p. 25
full-service agency, p. 22
holding companies, p. 23
image, p. 9

in-house agency, p. 22
institutional advertising p. 11
integrated marketing communication (IMC), p. 17
local advertising, p. 11
marketing communication (marcom), p. 9
marketing services, p. 20
mass media, p. 21
media, p. 20
media-buying services, p. 23
media vehicles, p. 20

Review Questions

1. Analyze the Burger King campaign discussed in this chapter and compare it to key aspects of the modern definition of advertising.

2. Advertising plays four general roles in society. Define and explain each one in the context of the "1984" commercial featured in this chapter.

3. What are the four components of advertising and what key concepts and practices do they represent?

4. Trace the evolution of advertising and the current developments that shape the practice of advertising. What are the most important periods in the development of advertising and what changes did they bring?

5. Who are the four key players in the world of advertising, and what are the responsibilities of each?

6. We discussed five categories of agency jobs. Explain each one and identify where your own personal skills might fit.

7. What challenges are affecting the current practice of advertising? In particular, why is effectiveness important to advertisers?

Discussion Questions

1. Look through the ads in this textbook and find examples that focus on each of the three definitional orientations—identification, information, and persuasion. Explain how each ad works and why you think it demonstrates that focus. Which do you think is most effective and why do you feel that way?

2. Many industry experts feel that Apple's "1984" commercial is the best television commercial ever made. Watch it online at *www.youtube.com/watch?v=OYecfV3ubP8* and analyze how it works. How many of the basic advertising practices and concepts that we introduced in the historical timeline of Figure 1.1 does it demonstrate? Why do you think the experts are so impressed with this ad?

3. You belong to an organization that wants to advertise a special event it is sponsoring. You are really concerned that the group not waste its limited budget on advertising that doesn't work. Outline a presentation you would make to the group's board of directors that explains advertising strengths and why advertising is important for this group. Then explain the concept of advertising effectiveness. In this situation, what would be effective and what wouldn't be? How would you determine whether an ad works or not?

4. *Three-Minute Debate:* In class, Mark tells the instructor that all this "history of advertising" stuff is irrelevant. The instructor asks the class to consider why it is important to understand the historical review of advertising definitions and practices. What would you say either in support of Mark's view or to change his mind? Organize into small teams with pairs of teams taking one side or the other. Develop a three-minute presentation for the class that explains the position your team has taken on this issue.

Take-Home Projects

1. *Portfolio Project:* Leo Burnett, a giant of the advertising industry, always kept a file he called "Ads Worth Saving," ads that struck him as effective for some reason. This was his portfolio of ideas. He explained that he would go through that file, not looking for ideas to copy, but because these great ads would trigger thoughts about how to solve some problem. So throughout this book, we will invite you to start your own portfolio. In some cases the assignments will ask you to find good (or bad) work and explain why you evaluate them as you do. In other cases, we'll ask you to actually do something—write, design, propose—or create something that you could take to an interview that demonstrates your understanding of the principles we talk about in this book.

   A Facebook Profile: For this first assignment, choose one of the people from the historical discussions in this chapter, someone you believe influenced the development of modern marketing communication. Research this person on the Internet and build a personal profile including samples of work if you can find some. Present your report as if it were a Facebook page. Make sure your presentation explains why you believe this person was important.

2. *Mini-Case Analysis:* Every chapter in this textbook opens with an award-winning case. For this assignment you will be asked to analyze why it was effective and, in many cases, come up with ideas for how that campaign could be extended to another year or another market.

Burger King Freakout: Reread the Burger King "Whopper Freakout" campaign that was introduced at the beginning of this chapter and wrapped up at the end of the chapter. Go online and see if you can find any other information about this campaign. What are the strong points of this campaign? Why has it won awards and why was it deemed effective? If you were on the BK team, would you recommend that this campaign be continued or is it just a one-time idea? In other words, what happens next? Is there a spin-off? Develop a one-page analysis and proposal for the next year.

Team Project: The BrandRevive Campaign

There are a number of brands that have been somewhat forgotten by consumers, or maybe never had much of a brand presence in consumer minds because of a lack of marketing communication effort. These are brands that need revitalization, rebranding, or repositioning. Some of those brands, listed below, are consumer goods but there are also services, a business-to-business marketer, a couple of nonprofit organizations, and an event. All of these could use some help building or rebuilding their brands. In other words, there are a variety of brands and types of categories from which you can choose:

- *Post's Grape Nuts* cereal, at over 110 years old, has been a mainstay on grocery shelves for more than a century and has a small band of dedicated and loyal fans. Unfortunately, the brand has been in decline for many years.
- *Ramen* noodles are based on a popular Japanese product. In the United States the packaged noodles are a low-budget dish on which college students are known to subsist.
- *Goody Beauty Products* are big in discount and drugstores, but the company has never run a national brand campaign and the brand name is largely unknown.
- *Bag Balm,* a hand lotion in a distinctive green tin, is good for farmers and others with dry, beat-up skin. You can find this product on the bottom shelf in many drugstores.
- *Ovaltine,* like Grape Nuts, is another very old brand that may have a small group of loyal customers, but has been largely forgotten by most consumers.
- *Laura Ashley,* a brand of apparel and a retailer, has been struggling since the 1990s and has lost a lot of its popularity.
- *Avaya* is a large B2B company that has a small presence in the mind of general consumers and, like Geico demonstrated, could benefit by becoming better known to a more general audience.
- Other services that could all use brand rejuvenation include *A&W Restaurants, Zale Jewelers, Discover Card, Ask.com, Amtrak,* and *TraveLodge.*
- The *Anti-Defamation League* is a nonprofit that promotes respect for cultural differences.
- *Goodwill* collects and sells used clothing and household goods.
- The *Mardi Gras* in New Orleans needs a new position and marketing strategy that will reach a broader audience and bring people back to New Orleans.

So here's your chance to work as a member of a BrandRevive team and develop a full-blown campaign to reinvigorate one of these brands. We'll be using this brand revitalization project throughout this book as an end-of-chapter exercise. By the time you have finished the book, you will have developed a complete marketing communication campaign to revitalize one of these old, fading, or largely unknown brands.

So where do you begin? For this first chapter assignment, your objective is to get organized and do some background research to determine which brand your team would like to revitalize.

How to Get Started

- After forming your team (we recommend three or four people), choose three brands from the previous list to consider for this BrandRevive assignment:
- To help you narrow your three choices down to the one your team wants to focus on, split your team up and explore the history of the three brands and their companies. Go online and visit your library for historical, as well as current, background information.
- In a paragraph, develop a short profile for each brand and identify its key problems.
- After reviewing this preliminary background information, as a team choose the brand your group wants to spend the semester working on.
- For your chosen brand, do more research and build a brand history, as well as a corporate history.
- Write up your findings in a review that is no longer than one double-spaced page. Convert your key findings into a PowerPoint presentation that is no longer than three slides. Prepare and practice to give this presentation to your class.

Hands-On Case

The Century Council

Read the Century Council case in the Appendix before coming to class.

1. In class, discuss the following:
   a. In what ways does the Century Council case reflect the expanded definition of what advertising is?
   b. How does the case illustrate the various roles that advertising campaigns can perform?
2. Write a one-page explanation of the campaign.

2

Integrated Brand Communication

It's a Winner

Campaign:	Company:	Agency:	Award:
"Wii Would Like to Play"	Nintendo of America	Leo Burnett USA, Golin Harris, Starcom Worldwide	Grand Effie and Gold Effie for New Product or Service Category

CHAPTER KEY POINTS

1. How is marketing defined, what is the marketing process, and what are marketing's key concepts?
2. How does marketing communication contribute to the development of a brand?
3. What is integrated marketing communication and what are its key concepts?
4. How is brand communication evolving during a time of change?

Wii Wages Campaign in Video Game War

Imagine that you just landed your dream job with agency Leo Burnett, and you are in charge of marketing Wii, a new video game for Nintendo. Here's the situation you're facing. Once the category leader, Nintendo's sales have plummeted so much that one industry consultant advised your company to abandon the fight to compete in the video game war. You think about the formidable rivalry from the Microsoft's popular Xbox 360 and Sony's PlayStation 3. What do you do? Where do you start?

What makes Nintendo's Wii campaign *Ad Lesson #1* is the insightful thinking about those people whom the advertising aims to convince to become Wii consumers. Think about PlayStation 3 and Xbox 360 users. They're usually male and avid gamers—guys who like difficult and often violent games. Nintendo could have chased those hardcore users. But it didn't. Instead, Nintendo chose to appeal to an audience who'd been turned off by video games—moms, families, even residents in nursing homes. Nintendo zigged when the competition zagged.

Such a bold strategy was not without risk. Some in the industry scoffed at the daunting task of trying to persuade nonusers to become Wii enthusiasts. Nintendo's research showed that nonplayers voiced similar complaints about games for other systems: they were too hard or complicated to learn. The nonplayers said they enjoyed challenging games such as crossword puzzles and Sudoku, participating in sports leagues, and connecting with other people socially. They weren't game averse, but they held negative perceptions about video games.

Nintendo responded to the research findings with a Big Idea. Why not invite the nonplayers to participate? Rather than talking about the power of the processor or pixel count as its competitors did, the "Wii Would Like to Play" campaign focused on features that made its product different: motion-sensitive controllers and prices lower than the competition's. It lured people off their couches and intrigued them by showing a wide age range of people—family and friends—who actively and interactively played simple games together.

Proving that Wii isn't just for kids, Nintendo crafted a different kind of marketing effort for a different kind of video game. Its multimillion-dollar campaign let potential consumers touch, see, and experience the new game—*Ad Lesson #2*.

Nintendo's ambassador program featured parties for multigenerational families, hard-core gamers, and modern moms. Others experienced Wii at malls, retail midnight madness events, music/video tours, and online social networking communities. Before Wii was even launched, it was featured in *South Park*, showed up on the front page of *The Wall Street Journal*, and other popular media including *People* magazine, NPR, and *BusinessWeek*.

Other efforts to spread the word included a MySpace page, which attracted a million page views, brand partnerships with 7-Eleven, Pringles Snack Stacks, and Comedy Central. Wii also showed up on the Discovery Channel, Animal Planet, and Discovery Kids Network.

Given the need to teach people how to play the game on their home TV screens, an important venue was in-person demonstrations either in stores or at events, such as trade shows and video game expositions. The opening photo of this chapter shows the president of Nintendo and the general manager of the entertainment division playing a game of tennis on a large video screen during the Electronic Entertainment Expo in Hollywood.

How well did the marketing communication strategy work in launching this new brand? Turn to the end of the chapter to see the amazing results for this new brand introduction. And if you want to see more of the campaign, check out *http://us.wii.com/viewer_tvcm_usa.jsp?vid=5*.

Sources: "Wii Would Like to Play," Effie Awards Brief of Effectiveness and Press Release, www.nyama.org; "Leo Burnett Wins Grand Effie for Nintendo," June 4, 2008, www.adweek.com; "Study Says Nintendo Tops in Game Ads," February 24, 2009, www.mediapost.com; Chris Kohler, "Nintendo's Wii Marketing Blitz Detailed," November 13, 2006, www.wired.com; David Eaves, "WiiNomics . . . Nintendo's Scarcity Strategy Keeps Paying Dividends," December 11, 2008, www.eaves.ca.

This chapter will give you a foundation for thinking about solving problems for clients. The Nintendo story demonstrates how marketing communication can help accomplish marketing objectives. It illustrates some fundamentals that will help you think through challenges you're likely to face in your career. This chapter starts with an explanation of the basic principles of marketing. We then explore the important concept of branding and why it is so heavily dependent on marketing communication. Finally we explain the concept of integrated marketing communication.

WHAT IS MARKETING?

A company like Nintendo needs effective marketing communication in order for its products to succeed in the marketplace. However, to succeed, a product must also offer customers value, and much of a product's value is created by marketing decisions that determine the product's design and ease of use, distribution, and pricing, as well as its marketing communication.

Marketing is designed to build brand and customer relationships that generate sales and profits or, in the case of nonprofits, memberships, volunteers, and donations. In turbulent times like the marketing communication industry has been through with the Great Recession, it is useful to remember the point we made in the Part I opener—that most of the basic marketing practices and principles are not only still viable, but may provide the only way through the chaos. So let's start by defining basic marketing concepts and see how they relate to marketing communication.

Why Marketing 101?

Some of you reading this textbook are marketing majors but others have not had and may never take a marketing course. For that reason, we will present here a quick crash course in those aspects of marketing that are most relevant to marketing communication.

A process and a discipline, **marketing** is the way a product is designed, tested, produced, branded, packaged, priced, distributed, and promoted. The American Marketing Association

(AMA) updated its definition of the term in 2007 as "Marketing is the activity, set of institutions, and processes for creating, communicating, delivering, and exchanging offerings that have value for customers, clients, partners, and society at large."[1] It is a function within an organization that focuses on managing customer relationships to benefit all of a brand's **stakeholders**—by stakeholders we mean all the individuals and groups who have a stake in the success of the brand. Positive relationships create value for a brand.

Traditionally, the objective of most marketing programs has been to sell products, which we define as *goods, services,* or *ideas.* This is accomplished by matching a product's availability—and the company's production capabilities—to the consumer's need, desire, or demand for the product. As you may remember from Wende Zomnir's *The Inside Story* in Chapter 1, her role as a founder and creative director for Urban Decay Cosmetics is to lead the market with edgy product designs and formulations that appeal to fashion-conscious young women.

Goods and services are identified in terms of their **product category.** By category, we mean the classification to which the product is assigned. For example, Harley-Davidson is in the motorcycle category, Apple Macintosh is in the computer category, and Burger King is in the fast-food category. Marketing managers manipulate the **marketing mix,** also called the **four Ps,** which refers to the *product* (design, performance), its *price,* the *place* where it is made available (distribution), and its *promotion* (marketing communication).

SHOWCASE

The Urban Decay product line of cosmetics projects a street-smart attitude embodied in its packaging and product names.

A graduate of the University of North Texas, Wende Zomnir was nominated by Professor Sheri Broyles to be featured in this book.

The Concept of Exchange   Marketing helps to create demand for a product leading to an **exchange**—that is, the act of trading something of value (money) for a desired product, either goods or service. The company makes a product and offers it for sale at a certain price; the customer gives money to the company to buy that product. Money is exchanged for goods or services. Demand, however, drives the exchange. With the Wii launch, for example, bloggers noted that Nintendo strategically controlled how many games were produced, and the scarcity seemed to create even more demand and, in turn, publicity for the new Wii system.

In addition to economic exchange, marketing also facilitates *communication exchange.* Marketing communication provides both information (facts, ideas, brand image cues) and the opportunity for customer–company interaction. In other words, people have to know about it before they can buy it or sign up for it or donate to it. That is why the Wii launch involved a large array of marketing communication tools, including new types of **contact points** with customers. Beyond awareness, the new social media, such as Facebook, MySpace, Twitter, and YouTube, also make it possible to have truly interactive communication with consumers. The Wii campaign illustrates how MySpace can be used to generate a conversation about a new product.

Who Are the Key Players?   The marketing industry is a complex network of professionals, all of whom are involved in creating, producing, delivering, and selling something to customers. The four categories of key players include (1) marketers, (2) suppliers and vendors, (3) distributors and retailers, and 4) marketing partners, such as agencies. Consider also that these positions represent jobs, so you can use this information as a career guide should you be interested in working in marketing.

The **marketer,** also referred to (from the agency's point of view) as the *client,* is any company or organization behind the brand—that is, the organization, company, or manufacturer producing the product or service and offering it for sale. The *Day in The Life* story describes the job of a marketing and communication manager, Peter Stasiowski, who works on the "client side." Stasiowski first started his career as an art director at Gargan Communications

A DAY IN THE LIFE

A View from the Marketing Communication Front Line

Peter Stasiowski, *Marketing and Communication Manager, Interprint, Inc.*

There's a big difference between working for an ad agency, where the focus is on promoting many clients, and becoming an individual company's lone marketing professional, where the focus is on promoting the company that signs your paycheck.

The most obvious changes, such as fine-tuning one marketing plan instead of juggling several, give way to more subtle and important differences. When I traded my agency title of art director and creative director for my current position as marketing and communications manager for an industrial printing company, I went from working with a group of people dedicated to practicing good marketing communications to working with a group dedicated to printing good décor paper for its customers in the laminate industry.

In my case, the opportunities to expand my marketing skills beyond commercial art into areas like copywriting and financial planning came with the responsibility to make good marketing decisions without the security of an ad agency's team behind me.

At its core, a day in my life as the marketing and communications manager for Interprint is spent communicating clear messages to the right markets as efficiently as possible. For example, to the broad laminate market, I write 90 percent of the articles for Interprint's promotional magazine about everything from our latest printing technologies to our environmental stewardship programs.

I'm also responsible for speaking with newspaper reporters, either to answer their questions or to promote a press release. Then there's coordinating the construction of trade show exhibits, planning press conferences, and, yes, designing print advertising. It's all meant to get the good word out to the right eyes and ears.

At the end of the day, my reward is knowing that as I dive deeper into the fabric of one company and learn what messages and media resonate with its customers, I gain both a broader skill set and the unfiltered feedback that ensures increasingly successful marketing efforts into the future.

For more about Interprint, check out the company's fact sheet at *http://usa .interprint.com/media.*

Peter Stasiowski is a graduate of the advertising program at the University of West Florida. He and his work were nominated by Professor Tom Groth to be featured in this book.

in Massachusetts. In addition to his story, he has provided two business-to-business ads that he designed for his company.

The materials and ingredients used in producing a product are obtained from other companies, referred to as *suppliers* or *vendors*. The phrase **supply chain** is used to refer to this complex network of suppliers who produce components and ingredients that are then sold to the manufacturer. The **distribution chain** or **channel of distribution** refers to the various companies involved in moving a product from its manufacturer to its buyers. Suppliers and distributors are also partners

36

in the communication process and their marketing communication often supports the brand. Marketing relationships also involve cooperative programs and alliances between two companies that work together as *marketing partners* to create products and promotions. For example, Leo Burnett created brand partnerships for Wii with 7-Eleven, Pringles, and Comedy Central.

What Are the Most Common Types of Markets? The word **market** originally meant the place where the exchange between seller and buyer took place. Today we speak of a market not only as a place (the New England market), but also as a particular type of buyer—for example, the youth market or the motorcycle market. The phrase **share of market** refers to the percentage of the total sales in a product category a particular brand has.

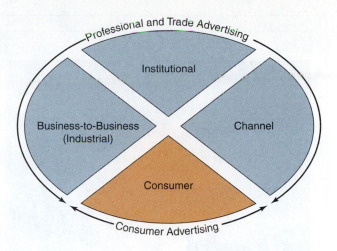

FIGURE 2.1

Four Types of Markets The consumer market, which is the target of consumer advertising is important but it is only one of four types of markets. The other three are reached through professional and trade advertising.

As Figure 2.1 shows, the four main market types are (1) consumer, (2) business-to-business (industrial), (3) institutional, and (4) channel markets. We can further divide each of these markets by size or geography (local, regional, national, or international).

- **Consumer markets** consist of people who buy goods and services for personal or household use. As a student, you are considered a member of the consumer market for companies that sell jeans, athletic shoes, sweatshirts, pizza, music, textbooks, backpacks, computers, education, checking accounts, bicycles, and a multitude of other products that you buy at drugstores and grocery stores, which the marketing industry refers to as **package goods** (In Europe these are called **fast-moving consumer goods or fmcg.**)
- **Business-to-business (B2B) markets** consist of companies that buy products or services to use in their own businesses or in making other products. General Electric, for example, buys computers to use in billing and inventory control, steel and wiring to use in the manufacture of its products, and cleaning supplies to use in maintaining its buildings. Advertising in this category tends to be heavy on factual content and information but it can also be beautifully designed as Peter Stasiowski's ads for Interprint demonstrate (see the previous *Day in the Life* feature).
- **Institutional markets** include a wide variety of nonprofit organizations, such as hospitals, government agencies, and schools that provide services for the benefit of society. Universities, for example, are in the market for furniture, cleaning supplies, computers, office supplies, groceries, audiovisual material, paper towels, and toilet paper, to name a few. Such ads are similar to B2B ads in that they are generally heavy on facts and light on emotional appeals.
- **Channel markets,** as discussed earlier, include members of the distribution chain, which is made up of businesses we call **resellers,** or **intermediaries. Channel marketing,** the process of targeting a specific campaign to members of the distribution channel, is more important now that manufacturers consider their distributors to be partners in their marketing programs. As giant retailers such as Walmart become more powerful, they can even dictate to manufacturers what products their customers want to buy and how much they are willing to pay for them.

Most advertising dollars are spent on consumer markets, although B2B advertising is becoming almost as important. Firms usually reach consumer markets through mass media and other marketing communication tools. They typically reach the other three markets—industrial, institutional, and channel or reseller—through trade and professional advertising in specialized media, such as trade journals, professional magazines, and direct mail, but even more so through personal sales and trade shows and promotions.

Why Is Services Marketing Important? When some people think about "products," they only think about goods. This is unfortunate because services are the dominant part of the economy in most developed countries. Health care, for example, is one of the largest industries in the United States and it is a service industry.

Marketing a service-based business, however, is different in a number of ways from marketing goods. For one thing, the product—insurance, banking, travel planning—is often intangible, although some services that "touch things" have a more tangible dimension, such as lawn

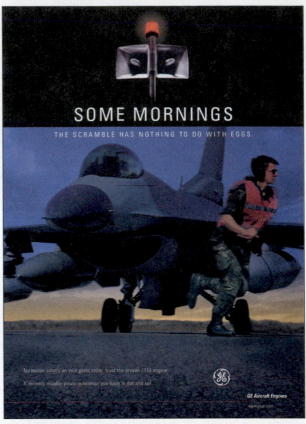

This group of ads demonstrates advertising directed at the three types of markets: consumer (Keds), institutional (GE aircraft engines), and channel ("Ka-ching"). What are the similarities and differences in these three types of advertisements?

Principle

In many economies, services marketing, which is intangible and creates a more personal relationship with the customer, dominates goods marketing.

care, car rentals, restaurants, and dental work. But even those services are not as tangible as buying a car or a video game.

Note that many goods manufacturers also offer a service—technical advice and setup, parts and repair, financing, and so forth. Most companies have a **customer service** operation that provides follow-up services for many goods and also answers questions and deals with complaints about products. But it's more than just customer service. The global media VP at Kraft Foods, for example, refers to Kraft's iPhone application as providing important "connectivity between consumers, brands, and content that they love."[2]

Another difference between a good and a service is the relationship between the provider of the service and the customer. In services marketing, the relationship is often closer and more personal than the relationship between a manufacturer and the buyer of its goods. Another difference is that a service usually involves a delivery process that may present many opportunities for messages to be delivered. Think about your last airline flight—how many contact points did you encounter in the experience—making a reservation, checking in, the flight itself, and getting your baggage. How many messages did you receive during that process and were they all positive?

How Does the Marketing Process Work?

The primary goal of the marketing process is to create and execute a **marketing plan,** which is a document that sets up objectives and proposes strategies for using marketing elements to achieve the objectives. The process of creating a marketing plan—and managing its execution—begins with marketing research. The research process helps marketers make a set of key strategic and tactical decisions that guide deployment of the marketing mix. The marketing planning process is outlined below. In later chapters on research and planning, we'll explore these topics in more detail.

Steps in the Marketing Planning Process

Step 1. *Research* the consumer market and the competitive marketplace and develop a **situation analysis** or a **SWOT analysis** (strengths, weaknesses, opportunities, threats).

Step 2. Set *objectives* for the marketing effort.

Step 3. Assess consumer needs and wants relative to the product; *segment* the market into groups that are likely to respond; *target* specific markets.

Step 4. *Differentiate* and *position* the product relative to the competition.

Step 5. Develop the *marketing mix strategy:* develop strategies for product design and performance criteria, pricing, distribution, and marketing communication.

Step 6. *Execute* the strategies.

Step 7. *Evaluate* the effectiveness of the strategy.

CLASSIC

Ads for Lydia Pinkham's Vegetable Compound appeared in newspapers in the 1870s with claims that the product "goes to the very root of all female complaints." How do products and advertising like this compare with modern-day pharmaceutical advertising?

What Key Concepts Drive Marketing Practices?

Historically marketers developed a product and then found a market for it. This is referred to as a **product-driven philosophy.** The great inventive period surrounding the Industrial Revolution saw patent medicines and over-hyped advertising flourish. Lydia Pinkham's Vegetable Compound, for example, made outrageous claims for a tonic with a base of 18 percent alcohol.[3] It was certainly good for what ails you.

The marketing concept, which turned marketers' attention toward consumer needs and wants, has nudged marketing closer to a customer-focused philosophy rather than one based on production.

Focus on Consumers   The **marketing concept** says marketing should focus first on identifying the needs and wants of the customer, rather than just the company's production capabilities. The marketing concept involves two steps: (1) determine through research what the customer needs and wants and (2) develop, manufacture, market, and service goods that fill those needs and wants—that is, create solutions for customers' problems.

Principle
Customer-focused marketing is designed to address consumer needs and wants.

A STAR ALLIANCE MEMBER ✪

©2004 United Air Lines, Inc. All Rights Reserved.

After eight years of being voted best frequent flyer program, where else is there to go? Up, of course.

Mileage Plus is proud to have been voted the best frequent flyer program for the past eight years by the readers of *Business Traveler* magazine. And we know the best way to thank you is to make the program even better. To join or to find out more, visit united.com/joinmp today.

UNITED
Mileage Plus®

This United Airlines ad demonstrates a corporate orientation. Do you believe it is effective? Why?

Ideally, marketers are able to match consumer needs and wants to their products, either those in the current line or prospective products in *research and development (R&D)*. In business-to-business marketing, the customer may even be involved as a partner in designing a new product or service.

Marketing communication can be designed to acquire consumer feedback that leads to insights into consumer decision making. This information then feeds back into marketing plans, where it can stimulate new **product developments** that are better designed to more efficiently and effectively meet customer needs. The consumer-generated content mentioned in Chapter 1 has a parallel in marketing. For example, Threadless.com, an online T-shirt retailer, invited consumers to create a T-shirt design and upload it to the site where other consumers get to vote for winners that will be offered for sale on the site.[4]

In advertising, the difference between a product and a consumer focus lies in the orientation of the ad. Is it addressing a consumer's benefit or a product's feature? Ideally it will do both by interpreting product features in terms of consumer benefits. United Airlines uses a consumer-focused approach for its Escapes vacation planning service and a product focus for its Mileage Plus frequent flyer program, which is shown here.

A note about terminology: We often use the words *consumer* and *customer* interchangeably, but there are some differences in meaning. **Consumer** is a general term for people who buy and use products and services, which is almost all of us. It's similar to the phrase *general public*. (However, we also make a distinction between consumer and trade products and promotions, which recognizes that businesses and organizations also buy and use products and services, as well as individual consumers.) The word **customer,** however, refers to someone who has purchased a specific brand or visited a specific retailer. Customers have a closer link to a brand or a store because they have taken action by buying or visiting. By virtue of that action, these people can be said to have a relationship with a brand or store.

Differentiation, Competitive Advantage, and Positioning   Although customer-centric marketing is important, marketing experts also point to the importance of **differentiation** as a selling strategy. They recommend strategies that are informed by consumers, but led by fundamental marketing decisions that make the brand stand out as different from its competition, a process known as **positioning.**[5]

How a brand is different and superior in some way is called **competitive advantage.** This concept is referred to in marketing strategy as **product differentiation.** The point of difference is seen in the way the product is positioned relative to its competitors. We'll talk about positioning more in the branding discussion later in this chapter and in Chapter 7. A product can be differentiated and therefore positioned in a variety of ways: by price, design, performance, distribution, and brand image. In a market-driven economy, product features and claims, such as quality and cheaper price, help marketers establish an advantage over the competition.

A classic example of differentiation is Maytag washers, which are sold based on their quality of design and construction and, hence, reliability. This perception of reliability has been instilled by marketing communication and the use of the famous "lonely repairman" brand character. The brand's slogan, "The Dependability People," also personalizes the product and adds a note of employee responsibility to the image. This differentiation strategy is based on the

The Wii video game has the advantage of a large video screen. It was important with the Nintendo Wii introduction to provide hands-on demonstrations in places like malls and stores so prospects could feel how the Wii works. Experiencing how the product performs by getting potential customers to try it was a key to the success of the new product introduction.

quality of the product, as well as on creating a brand position in the minds of consumers.

Added Value   Another reason marketing communication activities are useful, both to consumers and to marketers, is that they add value to a product. **Added value** refers to a marketing communication activity that makes the product more valuable, useful, or appealing to the consumer. With no added value, why pay more for one brand over the competition? A motorcycle is a motorcycle, but a Harley-Davidson is a highly coveted bike because of the brand image created by its advertising. Advertising and other marketing communication not only showcase the product's value but also may add value by making the product appear more desirable. Providing news and useful information of interest to consumers is another way that advertising adds value, as the United ad demonstrates. An example comes from a commercial for Idaho Potatoes, which provides information about peeling potatoes as a strategy to reinforce its dominance of its category.

Dawn Wells, who played Mary Ann on *Gilligan's Island*, demonstrates a trick about peeling potatoes in this commercial for Idaho Potatoes, the only potato that has successfully been branded.

Other aspects of marketing strategy can add value. For example, the more convenient the product is to buy, the more valuable it is to the customer. Likewise, the lower the price, the more useful features a product has, or the higher its quality, the more a customer may value it. Ensuring the product's utility and convenience is one of the tasks of customer-oriented marketing and the point of many advertisements. These other aspects that add value are found in the marketing mix strategy.

What Is the Marketing Mix?

As mentioned earlier and as shown in Figure 2.2, the traditional marketing mix includes four primary elements, sometimes referred to as the "four Ps": the product, its price and place of distribution, and its promotion (marketing communication).* To a marketing manager, marketing communication is just one part of the marketing mix. The importance of marketing communication relative to the other three Ps differs by product category and sometimes even by brand. The following list explains the components of the marketing mix:

The Product   The focus of the Four Ps is the product (goods, service, or ideas). Design, performance, and quality are key elements of a product's success. Some products, such as Puma's athletic shoes and apparel, are known for their design, which becomes a major **point of differentiation** from competitors. Performance is important for technical products, such as Nintendo's Wii, particularly when they are introduced to the market. A product launch for a new brand such as Sprint's Android or Apple's iPad depends on announcements in the media usually involving both publicity and advertising. The goals of the communication are to build awareness of the new

Product
- Design and development
- Performance
- Branding
- Packaging

Price
- Psychological pricing
- Sales
- Price/value

Place (Distribution)
- Channels
- Market coverage
- Push–pull
- Co-op advertising

Promotion (Marketing Communication)
- Personal selling
- Advertising
- Sales promotion
- Point of purchase
- Customer service
- Public relations
- Direct marketing
- Merchandising
- Packaging
- Events, sponsorships

FIGURE 2.2

The Four Elements of the Marketing Mix
The four marketing mix elements and their related tools and marketing communication techniques are the basic components of marketing. Marketing communication is shown in the middle and overlapping because the other three—product, price, and place—all have communication effects.

*The term *marketing mix* was introduced by Harvard advertising management professor Neil Border in 1953; the four Ps were popularized by Michigan State marketing professor E. Jerome McCarthy in 1960.

This sign for McDonald's highlights its $1 items. The $1 menu has become a competitive battleground for the fast-food category.

brand and to explain how this new product works and how it differs from competitors.

Product performance—how it handles or is used—sends the loudest messages about a product or brand and determines whether or not the product is purchased again or the buyer recommends it to others. Computer buyers, for example, will assess performance by asking: Is it easy to use? Does it crash? How big is its memory? Quality is another product feature that is often linked to upscale brands, such as Mercedes and Rolex. The idea is that if the product is well engineered and its manufacturer maintains a high standard of quality, then the brand will last and perform at a high level.

Pricing   The **price** a seller sets for a product is based not only on the cost of making and marketing the product, but also on the seller's expected margin of profit. Ultimately, the price of a product is based on what the market will bear, the competition, the economic well-being of the consumer, the relative value of the product, and the consumer's ability to gauge that value, which is referred to as the *price/value proposition*. An example is the familiar Redbox kiosks offering videos for rent at $1 a night. These started in McDonald's and now are found in many other locations.[6]

With the exception of price information delivered at the point of sale, advertising is often the primary vehicle for telling the consumer about price, as the McDonald's breakfast promotion flyer demonstrates. The term **price copy,** which is the focus of much retail advertising, refers to advertising copy devoted primarily to this type of information. A number of other pricing strategies, however, can affect how the price is communicated or signaled in advertising. During the Great Recession, fast-food chains, as well as Walmart and, of course, discount and dollar stores, depended on a *value pricing* strategy using the $1 price to signal money-saving offers.[7] Some prices are relatively standard, such as those at movie theaters. In contrast, *promotional pricing* is used to communicate a dramatic or temporary price reduction through terms such as *sale, special,* and *today only.*

The price sends a message. **Psychological pricing** strategies use marketing communication to manipulate the customer's judgment of value. For example, ads showing *prestige pricing*—in which a high price is set to make the product seem worthy or valuable—may be illustrated by photographs of the "exceptional product" in luxury settings or by copy explaining the reasons for a high price. Consider a watch that costs $500—what does that price say? On one hand, it may say that it's a prestige or quality product; on the other hand, it might suggest that the watch is expensive, maybe too expensive. In fact, the meaning of the price is dependent on the context provided by the marketing communication, which puts the price in perspective.

Place (Distribution)   It does little good to offer a good or service that will meet customers' needs unless you have a mechanism for making the product available and handling the exchange of payment for the product. What marketers call **distribution** includes the channels used to make the product easily accessible to customers.

Puma, for example, is growing the market for its shoes and athletic apparel because of its unusual approach to distribution. Its *channel marketing* strategy delivers Puma products to exclusive and mass-market audiences, selling its edgy designs to trendy retailers and then placing its more mainstream products in mall stores. Foot Locker might sell the GV special, a style based on a retro Puma tennis shoe from its glory days 30 years ago; at the same time an independent fashion store might carry a basketball shoe in fabrics like snakeskin or lizard. In recent years, Puma has expanded its distribution program to include its own stores, which greet customers with a unique shopping environment reflecting the personality of the Puma brand.

The choice of a distribution channel also sends messages. The image of an athletic shoe, like Puma, can be quite different if it's sold in Kmart, as opposed to Nordstrom. Marketing managers consider a variety of channels when choosing distribution strategies.

The Internet has brought another distribution question. "Clicks or bricks" is a phrase used to describe whether a product is sold online (clicks) or in a traditional store (bricks). Another distribution strategy involves the use of intermediaries, such as retailers. **Direct marketing** companies, such as Lands' End and Dell, distribute their products directly without the use of a reseller.

The sale is totally dependent on the effectiveness of the direct-response advertising. The more familiar strategy of distributing the product through one or more distributors and retailers is what we described earlier as *channel marketing.*

Another distribution-related strategy involves the distinction between push and pull strategies. A **push strategy** directs marketing efforts at resellers, and success depends on the ability of these intermediaries to market the product, which they often do with their own advertising. In contrast, a **pull strategy** directs marketing efforts at the consumer and attempts to pull the product through the channel by intensifying consumer demand. The decision to use a push or pull strategy determines, to some extent, the audience to be targeted and the nature of the demand to be addressed by the message.

Marketing Communication   The last of the Four Ps is *promotion,* or what we call **marketing communication** (marcom, for short), which includes such tools as advertising, public relations, sales promotion, direct response, events and sponsorships, point of sale, digital media, and the communication aspects of packaging, as well as personal sales, and a number of new forms of online and place-based communication that have emerged recently. The rest of the book is focused on this element—our goal is to help you understand how marketing communication works to support a marketing plan.

In Figure 2.2, note how we positioned marketing communication in the center of the Four Ps. The point is, as you may remember from our **First Principle of IMC** in Chapter 1 that *everything communicates.* In practice, we can rephrase that to say *everything in the marketing mix can send a message.* How the product is designed and how it performs, where the brand is sold, and at what price—all of these marketing decisions send messages about the brand's position, quality, and image.

In fact, we can rephrase that first principle again as *"Everything a brand does, and sometimes what it doesn't do, can send a message."* Unintentional messages come from brand experiences; for example, a long wait on a customer service help line or the inability of a company representative to answer a product safety question sends the message that the company doesn't value a customer's time or safety. Those messages can be more powerful—in a negative way—than anything said in the advertising. That's why it's necessary to monitor all marketing elements from a communication perspective.

> **Principle**
> Every part of the marketing mix, not just marketing communication—sends a message.

The same creative spirit that drives Puma's product design also drives its marketing communication, which typically uses nontraditional ways to connect with customers, such as word of mouth and other marcom programs that promote the brand on the street and on the feet of its devotees, as well as on the Internet. Retailers praise Puma for its eye-catching, in-store merchandising displays. Other clever ideas include promotions at sushi restaurants during the World Cup held in Japan and South Korea. Puma got a well-known sushi chef to create a special Puma sushi roll that was served in select Japanese restaurants in cities around the world. These restaurants also discretely announced the sponsorship through Puma-branded chopsticks, sake cups, and napkins. At the same time, Puma partnered with the U.K.-based Terence Conran design shop to sell an exclusive version of its World Cup soccer boot and held weekend sushi-making events at the Conran home furnishings store.

One type of communication that we don't discuss in depth in this book is personal sales because in most companies it is managed separately from marketing communication. Because that area is particularly important to marketing programs, however, we'll briefly introduce it here. **Personal sales** relies on face-to-face contact between the marketer and a prospective customer, rather than contact through media. In contrast to most advertising, whose effects are often delayed, marketers use **personal selling** to create immediate sales to people who are shopping for a product. In Nintendo's case, it was important to have trained salespeople demonstrate how to play the Wii video game.

The different types of personal selling include sales calls at the place of business by a field representative (field sales), assistance at an outlet by a sales clerk (retail selling), and calls by a representative who goes to consumers' homes (door-to-door selling). Marketing communication works as a partner with sales programs to develop **leads,** the identification of potential customers, or **prospects. Lead generation**

Founded in Germany in 1948, Puma was famous initially as a producer of innovative athletic-training shoes. A global brand that now includes fashion-statement apparel and accessories, as well as footwear, it has left its paw prints in more than 80 countries. Go to *www.puma.com* to see Puma's newest designs. How important is design to this manufacturer and how can you assess that and other marketing mix decisions from this website?

is a common objective for trade promotion and advertising. Personal sales are even more important in business-to-business marketing for reaching key decision makers within a company who can authorize a purchase.

The management challenge, then, is to manage all of the messages delivered by all aspects of the marketing mix, including marketing communication, so they work together to present the brand in a coherent and consistent way.[8]

WHAT IS MARCOM'S ROLE IN BRANDING?

A management function that creates the tangible and intangible elements of a brand is called **branding.** Through effective marketing communication that establishes a unique identity, the brand engages the hearts and minds of consumers in a process that differentiates similar products from each other.

Given your experience, how would you define a brand? You have pieces of a definition from our previous questions: past positive experience, familiarity, a promise, a position, an image. Here's how we would define a **brand:** *A perception, often imbued with emotion, which results from experiences with and information about a company or a line of products.* Other definitions point to a mixture of tangible and intangible attributes, as well as the symbolic importance of the trademark, which stands for the brand, and the value the brand offers to both the consumer and the company. We'll explain these factors in the following discussion.

Principle

A brand is more than a product. Companies make products but sell brands.

A brand is more than a product. Hamburgers are products—but the Big Mac and Whopper are brands. Toothpaste is a product (also the product category)—Colgate and Crest are brands of toothpaste. Branding applies to services as well as goods—State Farm and the U.S. Postal Service (USPS) are also brands—and to nonprofits, such as United Way and Habitat for Humanity

In fact, all organizations with a name can be considered brands. The *A Matter of Practice* feature explains how organization brands are distinct from product brands. In particular, as international branding expert Giep Franzen explains: "Organizations should be aware that simply by existing and interacting with others, an organization is branding itself. So branding the organization is inevitable. It is going to happen whether the process is managed or not."

Sometimes the difference between brands in the same product category lies in product features—how the hamburger is made and the chemistry of the toothpaste—but often we choose one brand over another because of a difference in the brand impressions we carry. Companies make products but they sell brands. A brand differentiates a product from its competitors and makes a promise to its customers.

Second Principle of IMC

A brand is a unified vision (the art) and a complex system (the science).

Branding involves a complex set of philosophies and activities. A successful brand is the product of both science—in the management of a complex system of activities—and art—a vision of the essence of the brand in which all the pieces and parts fit together perfectly in a coherent brand perception.[9] This is the **Second Principle of IMC:** *A brand is a unified vision (the art) and a complex system (the science).* In other words, marketing communicators are managing a multiplicity of brand activities and programs that are interrelated and only work well to the extent that they work together. When they work together with a single vision of the brand essence, like a great orchestra, the pieces and parts fit together perfectly generating meaning and creating something value. That's the art of **brand management.**

How Does a Brand Acquire Meaning?

A brand is, in fact, a perception—an identification that we assign to the products we know and use. What do we mean by that?

Think about this: why does one brand sell twice the number of products as another when there is no basic difference in product attributes or performance and both brands sell for the same price? The answer is—a difference in the brand meaning. Meaning-making ideas and images are what marketing communication delivers to brands. This perception, this **brand meaning,** is the one thing a brand has that can't be copied. Competitors can make a similar product, but it's difficult for them to make the same brand because brand meaning is built on personal impressions.

A Brand Is a Perception   A brand, then, is basically a perception loaded with emotions and feelings (intangible elements), not just a trademark or package design (tangible elements). Tangible features are things you can observe or touch, such as a product's design, ingredients, components,

The Complex World of Organization Branding

Giep Franzen, *Founder of FHB/BBDO, a leading advertising agency in the Netherlands, and also founder of SWOCC, a foundation at the University of Amsterdam for scientific research in brand communication*

Until about the 1990s brands were mainly attached to products and services. Companies, retailers, and media operating under a corporate name were aware of the fact that their entity had a "corporate image," but they usually did not look upon their name as a brand unless it was used to identify their offerings to the consumers.

Banks were banks, shops were shops, magazines were just magazines. That has changed dramatically. Bank names, retail names, and magazine titles almost overnight became brands. And now, at the end of the first decade of the 21st century, almost anything with a name is regarded as a brand—persons, communities, locations, countries, orchestras, baseball teams, and what have you. *Branding* no longer is the exclusive realm of package goods, durables, and services—it is an all-encompassing phenomenon that relates to all organizations and entities in society.

The word *corporate* is less appropriate to represent this new kind of branding because its connotations are so much dominated by "business." But *corporate* also implies "organizations"—both profit and nonprofit—and therefore we prefer to refer to "organization branding," which also better distinguishes this class of brands from product brands.

Before accepting the concept of *organization branding*, we need to understand what organizations are. This is where the concept of "identity" comes in. Identity is the set of interdependent, central, unique, and salient characteristics that define an entity. It is the essence of an organization. Identity refers to a relative consistency of appearances, values, beliefs, attitudes, and behaviors— agreement in the defining and meaningful attributes of an organization.

Organizational branding is a harmonization of the organization's identity and its image. The values inside the organization should be compatible with the brand values that are being communicated, recognized, and valued by customers and other consumers.

The brand is the linchpin between an organization and stakeholders. It expresses the organization, lives in the minds of consumers, and should be relevant for their interests.

The model below illustrates the three building blocks that our team of scholars at the SWOCC Foundation believe are important in managing an organization brand. The categories are Organization Identity, Consumer/Customer Characteristics, and a category we call "Brand Framework," which includes all the components attached to the brand by the organization, and related to it by the consumers and other stakeholders. Here is a brief summary of the elements included in these categories and in this model:

- **Organization Identity** Identifiers, business category, physical identity, history, organization culture, behaviors, outlook, ideology, performance, and reputation.
- **Consumer/Customer Characteristics** Sociodemographics, needs and goals, values and lifestyles situations, category experiences and attitudes, and brand relationships.
- **Brand Framework** Brand signs, brand architecture, brand domains and products, brand presence, brand experiences, brand meanings, brand essence, brand function, brand positioning, brand evaluation, brand relationships, market brand equity.

The model below illustrates the nature of the relationship between the three building blocks. They are mostly self-evident. "Brand Orientation" is an approach in which the management of an organization revolves around the creation, development, and protection of its brand.

Obviously the influence of the elements varies over different types of organizations. This means that there cannot be a "one-size-fits-all" model for organization branding. For each type of organization, the most relevant elements have to be identified and assembled in a situation-specific model.

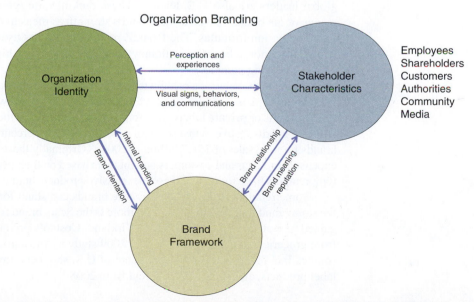

Organization Branding

Organization Identity — Perception and experiences / Visual signs, behaviors, and communications — Stakeholder Characteristics

Employees
Shareholders
Customers
Authorities
Community
Media

Brand orientation / Internal branding

Brand relationship / Brand meaning reputation

Brand Framework

size, shape, and performance. Intangibles include the product's perceived value, its brand image, positive and negative impressions and feelings, and past experiences customers have had with the brand or company. Intangibles are just as important as the tangible features because they create the emotional bonds people have with their favorite brands and because they are impossible for the competition to copy.

But even intangibles can lend monetary value and legal protection to a brand's unique identity. Read Tales of Twitterjacking at *www.pearsonhighered.com/moriarty* and consider the importance of a brand presence in a situation faced by Twitter: the hacking and hijacking of its accounts.

All the impressions created by a brand's tangible and intangible features come together as a brand concept—the brand and what it means—that exists in people's hearts and minds. It results not only from experiences with the product, but also from messages acquired from marketing communication. Such impressions are particularly important in what we call **parity products** such as soap, gasoline, and other products with few distinguishing features. For these products, feelings about the brand can become the critical point of difference.

The meaning of a brand is an aggregation of everything a customer (or other stakeholder) sees, hears, reads, or experiences about a company or a specific brand. This meaning, however, cannot be totally controlled by management. A company can *own* a brand name and brand symbol and *influence* to some degree what people think about the brand, but it can't dictate the brand impression because that exists in people's minds and is derived, as we've said, from their personal experiences.

Principle

A brand transforms products into something more meaningful than the product itself.

Brand Transformation   A basic principle of branding is that a brand transforms a product—goods as well as services—into something more meaningful than the product itself. A Tiffany watch is more than a timepiece—it is also different from a Swatch even if they both have the same basic components, and both are different from a generic Kmart watch with an unknown brand name. **Brand transformation** creates this difference by enriching the brand meaning. Brand meanings are more complex than impressions because of what they symbolize. The Tiffany brand symbolizes quality, sophistication, and luxury; a Swatch brand is fun and fashionable; a generic watch is inexpensive and utilitarian.

The development of the Ivory Soap brand by Procter & Gamble in 1879 represented a major advance in branding because of the way its makers built a meaningful brand concept to transform a parity product—soap—into a powerful brand—Ivory. Just as the Macintosh "1984" commercial in Chapter 1 represents one of the all-time great ads, Ivory represents one of the all-time great marketing stories.

For some products and categories, the brand is a huge factor in consumer decision making. We say a brand creates value for consumers in the sense that it makes it easier to find and repurchase a familiar product. Table 2.1 lists the top 20 brands in the world based on estimates of their brand value. Google is the first $100 billion brand and has been in the number one spot for the previous three years. Analyze this list and see if you can determine how many of the global leaders are also U.S. leaders. These rankings are typically based on financial performance of the brand, as well as the brand's strength as measured by various types of proprietary brand valuation formulas. The BrandZ methodology was used to create this list by Millward Brown Optimor, a brand consultancy company, in partnership with the WPP global communication holding company.

Compare the value of a recognized brand to a generic brand and a store brand. **Generic brands** were originally sold in a black-and-white no-frills package at low prices. **Store brands,** also called **house brands** or **private labels**, are products manufactured to the store's requirements and labeled with a brand distinctive to that store. In supermarkets, 15 percent of the sales, on average, are store brands for total sales of $54.7 billion in 2009.[10] Originally these store brands were assigned to inexpensive products and customers bought them based on their price. In periods of economic downturn, retailers have found that these inexpensive products hold more value for frugal customers.

Some retailers realize that their store brands can stand for quality and value. Craftsman is the store brand for Sears tools and Kenmore is the Sears brand for appliances—both of these have gained acceptance as quality brands. Kirkland, Costco's private label, shows up on everything from groceries to men's dress shirts. A 2009 study by the market research firm Information Resources Inc. found that nearly 80 percent of U.S. shoppers now think positively about private-label products, an increase of 7 percent from 2008.[11]

A MATTER OF PRINCIPLE

It's Pure and It Floats

A basic principle of branding is that a brand takes on meaning when it makes a product distinctive within its product category. Procter & Gamble accomplished that by creating identity elements for its soap brand Ivory before anyone had thought of making a bar of soap a distinctive product. The Ivory brand identity system also called attention to innovative features of the product. Here's the background story about how Ivory came to be one of the first and most successful brands of all time.

Before the Civil War, homemakers made their own soap from lye, fats (cooking grease), and fireplace ashes. It was a soft, jelly-like, yellowish soap that would clean things adequately, but if it fell to the bottom of a pail, it dissolved into mush. In Victorian times, the benchmark for quality soap was the highly expensive castile bar—a pure white soap imported from the Mediterranean and made from the finest olive oil.

William Procter and James Gamble, who were partners in a candle-making operation, discovered a formula that produced a uniform, predictable bar soap, which they provided in wooden boxes to both armies during the Civil War. This introduced the concept of mass production and opened up a huge market when the soldiers returned to their homes with a demand for the bars of soap. But back at home the bars of soap were still yellow and sunk to the bottom.

Procter & Gamble hired a chemist to create a white bar equivalent to the legendary castile bar. The chemist's work represented the first time scientific-based research and development (R&D) was used to design a product. In 1878 P&G white soap was invented. It was a modest success until the company began getting requests for the "soap that floats." One legend is that a worker in 1879 accidentally left the soap-mixing machine operating during lunch, resulting in an unusually frothy mixture. Recent research, however, has found that James Gamble may have always intended for Ivory to float. Whether accident or intention, it led to one of the world's greatest statements of a product benefit: "It floats."

Other decisions also helped make it a branding breakthrough. In 1879 one of the P&G family was in

church listening to a scripture about ivory palaces and proposed that the white bar be renamed Ivory Soap. Now the great product had a great name as well as a great product benefit. Rather than asking for soap—soap was soap—and taking a bar from the barrel, customers could now ask for a specific product they liked by name.

But that wasn't the end of P&G's branding innovations. A grandson who was determined to match the quality of the legendary castile soap again turned to chemists and independent laboratories to determine the purity of both castile and Ivory. In 1882 the research found that the total impurities in Ivory added up to only 0.56 percent, which was actually lower than that of the castile bars. By turning that into a positive, Harley Procter wrote the legendary slogan that Ivory is "99 and 44/100 percent pure." Thus was born a pledge of quality that became one of the most famous brand slogans in marketing history.

Note: To read more about the history of this famous brand, check out *www.ivory.com/purefun_history.htm.*

Sources: Charles Goodrum and Helen Dalrymple, *Advertising in America,* New York: Harry N. Abrams, 1990; Laurie Freeman, "The House That Ivory Built: 150 Years of Procter & Gamble," *Advertising Age,* August 20, 1987: 4–18, 164–220; "P&G History: History of Ivory," June 2004, *www.pg.com.*

Table 2.1   Top 20 Brands Based on Brand Value

Global Brand Top 20	2009 Brand Value ($m)	% Change from 2008
1. Google	$100,039	16
2. Microsoft	76,249	8
3. Coca-Cola	67,625	16
4. IBM	66,622	20
5. McDonald's	66,575	34
6. Apple	63,113	14
7. China Mobile	61,283	7
8. General Electric	59,793	−16
9. Vodafone	53,727	45
10. Marlboro	49,460	33
11. Walmart	41,083	19
12. ICBC (Industrial and Commercial Bank of China)	38,056	36
13. Nokia	35,163	−20
14. Toyota	29,907	−15
15. UPS	27,842	−9
16. BlackBerry	27,478	100
17. Hewlett-Packard	26,745	−9
18. BMW	23,945	−15
19. SAP	23,615	9
20. Disney	23,110	−3

Sources: "BrandZ™ Top 100 Most Valuable Global Brands 2009," Millward Brown Optimor Report, *www.millwardbrown.com/Sites/ Optimor/Media/Pdfs/en/BrandZ/BrandZ-2009-Report.pdf;* "BRANDZ™ Top 100 Most Valuable Global Brands Now Worth $2 Trillion," Millward Brown Optimor Press Release, April 29, 2009.

What Are the Key Components of a Brand?

Although Franzen and the SWOCC team investigating the nature of organization branding (see the earlier *A Matter of Practice* feature) identified many elements in branding, for our discussion here we will only consider three key strategic decisions—identity, position and promise, and image and personality—that guide the development and management of a brand.

Principle

If branding is successful, then you refer to a specific brand by name, rather than its general category label.

Brand Identity   A critical function of branding is to create a separate **brand identity** for a product within a product category. Analyze the language you use in talking about your own things. Do you buy chips or Doritos? Do you drink a soft drink or a Pepsi? Do you wear tennis shoes or Nikes?

Logos help identify a product or idea. Which of these logos do you think are the most effective?

If branding works, then you refer to a specific brand by name, rather than a generic category when discussing a product. Brand identity cues are generally the brand name and the symbol used as a logo—think of the "swish" graphic that symbolizes Nike and the leaping cat for Puma.

The choice of a brand name for new products is tested for memorability and relevance. The idea is that the easier it is to recognize the identity cues, the easier it will be to create awareness of the brand. That also makes it easy to find and repurchase a brand, which is an important factor in customer repurchase decisions. Successful brand names have several characteristics:

- **Distinctive** A common name that is unrelated to a product category, such as Apple for a computer, ensures there will be no similar names creating confusion. It can also be provocative, as in the Virgin line.
- **Association** Subaru, for example, chose Outback as the name for its rugged SUV hoping the name would evoke the adventure of the Australian wilderness.
- **Benefit** Some brand names relate to the brand promise, such as Slim-Fast for weight loss and Head & Shoulders for dandruff control shampoo.
- **Heritage** Some brand names reflect the maker, such as H&R Block, Kellogg's, and Dr. Scholl's. The idea is that there is credibility in a product when makers are proud to put their names on it, particularly in some international markets, such as Japan, where the company behind the brand is an important part of the brand image.
- **Simplicity** To make a brand name easier to recognize and remember, brand names are often short and easy to pronounce, such as Tide, Bic, and Nike. Because of the increase in multinational marketing, it is also important that names properly translate into other languages.

When Coke moved into the Chinese market in the late 1970s, it faced the immediate problem of translating its well-known brand name into Chinese. Of course, there are no equivalent Chinese words for *Coca* or *Cola,* and phonetic-based translations were meaningless. The ingenious solution was to use a group of four characters 可口可乐 the first half means "tasty" or "delicious," the next two characters together mean "really happy." Although it has come to stand as a generic phrase for cola, the name for Coke in Chinese is roughly "tasty happy" cola. So Coke owns the category. The effectiveness of the Chinese trademark has been an important factor in making Coca-Cola the leading soft drink in China.[12]

Brand names are important but recognition is often based on a distinctive graphic. In fact, the word *brand* comes from branding of cattle, a practice that used a distinctive design element to represent the name of the ranch to which the cattle belonged. A number of elements contribute to the visual identity—logos, trademarks, characters and other visual cues, such as color and distinctive typefaces.

Although the distinctive logo is known around the world, Coca-Cola's brand name needed to be represented in Chinese characters that had meaning for the Chinese market.

A **logo** is similar to a cattle brand in that it stands for the product's source. A **trademark** is a legal sign that indicates ownership. Originally these were simple symbols or initials that silversmiths etched into their products, the "mark of the trade." In modern times, trademarks may include logos, other graphic symbols, or even unusual renderings of the brand name, such as the distinctive Coca-Cola script. A trademark is registered with the government and the company has exclusive use of its trademark as long as it is used consistently for that product alone.

Problems can arise when a brand name dominates a product category, such as Kleenex and Xerox. In such situations, the brand name becomes a substitute label for the category label. Refrigerator, laundromat, zipper, and aspirin lost the legal right to their names when they became generic category names. Band-Aid and Q-tips, although legally registered as indicated by their use of the registration symbol®,

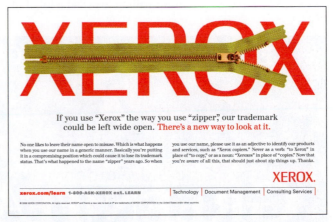

Xerox has a long-running campaign that seeks to protect its name as a brand. Ads such as this warn against using *Xerox* as a general term for a copy machine or as a verb for making a copy.

Principle

Brand communication sets expectations for what will happen when the product is used through the virtual contract of a brand promise.

have also crept into common usage as generic names—"It's a band-aid for the budget"—so they, too, are in danger of having their brand names become generic category labels.

Brand Position and Promise   Beyond the basic identification elements, another strategic decision in brand development involves deciding the correct **brand position.** We mentioned earlier that positioning is a way to identify the location a product or brand occupies in consumers' minds relative to its competitors—higher, lower, bigger, more expensive. Related to position is the **brand promise.** From a consumer viewpoint, the value of a brand lies in the promise it makes. "It floats" and "99 and 44/100 percent pure" are both promises that identify key selling points for Ivory Soap. In other words, the brand through its communication sets expectations for what a customer believes will happen when the product is used. Because of past experience and advertising messages, you know what to expect—that's what a brand promise means.

Consistency is the backbone of a promise. The promise needs to be delivered not just by the advertising but at all points of contact with a brand. Furthermore, the brand has to deliver on the promise. Many weak brands suffer from overpromising. Using hype and exaggeration, they promise more than they can deliver and consumers end up disappointed. If a cough drop promises relief from throat irritation, then it better deliver that relief. If it also promises good taste, then it better not disappoint with a bitter medicinal flavor. Successfully identifying and then delivering the promise are part of the platform for building a long-term brand relationship with customers.

Brand Image and Personality   Another aspect of brand meaning is brand image, which refers to something more complex than a brand impression. More specifically a **brand image** is a mental picture or idea about a brand that contains associations—luxury, durable, cheap—as well as emotions. These associations and feelings result primarily from the content of advertising and other marketing communication. For example, what do you think of when you think of the Marines, Ben & Jerry's ice cream, the Chicago Cubs, or Celestial Seasonings teas?

A **brand personality** symbolizes the personal qualities of people you know—bold, fun, exciting, studious, geeky, daring, boring, whatever. Probably the greatest brand personality ever created was for Harley-Davidson. How do you describe the Harley brand personality? Partly it's the people who you associate with the brand, people you may think of as black-leather, devil-may-care individuals who are a little on the outlaw side. It doesn't matter that in their real lives, Harley owners may be doctors, lawyers, or professors. When they put on that black jacket and climb on the bike, they are renegades of the road. The Harley brand personality reflects the people who ride it, and the people who ride it reflect the Harley brand personality.

Principle

Brands speak to us through their distinctive images and personalities.

Each brand sends a different message because of the image or personality it projects through its marketing communication. If you give your mother a Tiffany watch, she knows you care and were willing to spend a lot of money to demonstrate your caring. If you give a friend a Swatch, you may be saying you think she's a *fashionista* and someone who likes to make a fashion statement. If you give your little brother a generic watch from Walmart, you might be saying that he needs a timepiece that works even though he may lose it or break it. Brands speak to us through their images and personalities.

A brand takes on a distinctive meaning as the branding elements—identity, position, promise, image, and personality—come together to create a coherent and unified perception.[13]

How Is Brand Equity Developed?

Branding not only differentiates products, but also increases their value. A brand and what it symbolizes can affect how much people are willing to pay for it—and that's true for computers, as well as cars and cornflakes. Brand studies consistently

Celestial Seasonings uses its distinctive packages to send messages to consumers about its brand image. In what way do packages like this reinforce the brand personality?

find that in blind taste tests, people perceive the recognizable brand as tasting better than an unknown brand, even when the sample is identical. It's only a perception in their minds, not an actual taste. And when identical products carry different labels, people will pay more for the recognizable brand. Why do you suppose that's so?

Brand Value   Branding not only differentiates products, but also increases their value to consumers. The value of branding lies in the power of familiarity and trust to win and maintain consumer acceptance. If a well-known brand name has been tested over time, it's familiar and dependable, plus it carries the associations created through the marketing communication. All of these qualities add value to the brand and make it possible to give a familiar brand a premium price compared to unknown brands. The ACW Ironworks branding campaign is an example of how a brand identity is designed and conveyed through various types of marketing communication.

Brand value comes in two forms—the value to a consumer and the value to the corporation. The first is a result of the experiences a customer has had with a brand; the second is a financial measure, which we call brand equity.

On the customer side, some brands have loyal users who purchase the brand repeatedly. Powerful brands are those that retain their customers who will repeatedly buy the product or service. **Brand relationship** programs that lead to *loyalty* are important brand strategies. Brand relationship communication, therefore, aims to deliver reminders about familiar brands and build trust. **Brand loyalty** programs offer rewards for repeat business. The frequent flyer and frequent buy programs, for example, provide incentives to loyal customers.

Brands also have a financial value that can be plotted on corporate balance sheets. This **brand equity** is the intangible value of the brand based on the relationships with its

Third Principle of IMC
Brand relationships drive brand value.

SHOWCASE
This branding campaign by the AdLab student agency at Boston University for ACW Ironworks featured a logo design, a business card, and print advertising.

Intel Inside is an example of ingredient branding, in which a computer manufacturer advertises that it is using Intel chips as a testimony to the product's quality. On what brands have you seen this Intel Inside logo exhibited? Do you think ingredient branding like this works?

stakeholders, as well as intellectual property, such as product formulations. These are intangible assets beyond the tangible ones of plants, equipment, and land. When a company is sold, a figure is calculated for the value of its brands—that's the intangible side of corporate valuation.

Our **Third Principle of IMC,** then, is that *brand relationships drive brand value.* That's because brand relationships are built on a foundation of positive brand experiences and truthful brand communication. The part of brand equity that is based on relationships is also referred to as **goodwill.** It lies in the accumulation of positive brand relationships, which can be measured as a level of personal attachment to the brand that has revenue-producing potential.

Leveraging Brand Equity   Brand managers will sometimes leverage brand equity through a **brand extension,** which is the use of an established brand name with a related line of products. In effect, they launch new products but use the established name because it is already recognized and respected. Because the brand is known, it carries with it associations and feelings, as well as a certain level of trust. The disadvantage is that the extension may dilute the meaning of the brand or may even boomerang negatively. Usually the extension practice is used for related products, although Virgin, which started out as a brand name for an airline, has had some success adapting its brand name to various unrelated categories from bottled beverages to mobile phone services, and music stores.

Another practice is **co-branding,** which is a strategy that uses two brand names owned by two separate companies to create a partnership offering. Co-branding is a common practice for credit cards, such as the Visa and United Airlines Mileage Plus card. The new brand name is Mileage Plus but the card carries both the Visa and United Airlines identity information. The idea is that the partnership provides customers with value from both brands.

A strong brand may be attractive to other business partners, as well, through a practice called **brand licensing.** In effect, a partner company rents the brand name and transfers some of its brand equity to another product. The most common example comes from sport teams whose names and logos are licensed to makers of all kinds of goods—shirts, caps, mugs, and other memorabilia. You may also be aware of the practice of brand licensing for your own school. Universities and colleges generate lots of money by licensing their names, logos, and mascots to apparel makers, among many others.

Another way to leverage a brand is through **ingredient branding,** which refers to the use of a brand name for a component used in manufacturing in advertising and other promotion. The most well-known example is the "Intel Inside" phrase and logo used by other computer makers to call attention to the quality of the chips it uses in manufacturing its products. Other examples of bragging about the quality of components are found in advertising for outdoor wear that announces the use of Gore-Tex, a lightweight, warm, water-resistant fabric, and in food advertising that promotes the use of NutraSweet or Hershey's chocolate. For ingredient branding to be successful, the ingredient must have a high level of awareness and be known as a premium product.

The point of this review of branding practices is that the way a product is made or how it performs its services is no longer the primary differentiating point. Marketing strategy isn't as much about promoting product features as it is about creating brand meanings. It isn't about gaining new customers, but rather about building strong brand relationships.

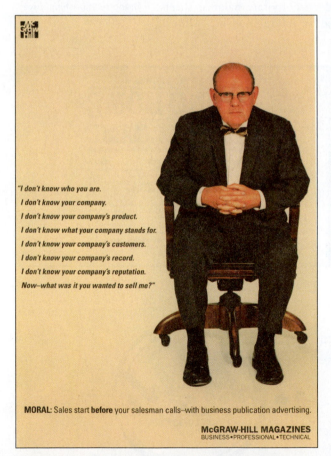

"I don't know who you are.
I don't know your company.
I don't know your company's product.
I don't know what your company stands for.
I don't know your company's customers.
I don't know your company's record.
I don't know your company's reputation.
Now—what was it you wanted to sell me?"

MORAL: Sales start **before** your salesman calls—with business publication advertising.

McGRAW-HILL MAGAZINES
BUSINESS•PROFESSIONAL•TECHNICAL

CLASSIC
This ad ran in 1958 but it continues to show up in marketing and communication books as an example of how important it is to understand the client's business and branding situation. Furthermore, it helps to have brand awareness and a positive brand identity before you try to make a sale.

Ultimately, the stronger a brand is, the more value it has to all its stakeholders. Understanding how brands are built and managed requires an understanding of relationship-building communication as the classic McGraw-Hill "client" ad illustrates.

Most of the added value that comes from an effective brand strategy is driven by marketing communication. Since positive brand relationships generate profits and accumulate as brand equity, the success of branding depends on communication. In other words, advertising and other marketing communication tools are the drivers of strong brands and create marketing success stories.

WHY INTEGRATED MARKETING COMMUNICATION?

We mentioned earlier that advertising is only one type of marketing communication. The important thing to remember is that **integrated marketing communication (IMC)** is the practice of unifying all marketing communication messages and tools as well as the messages from the marketing mix decisions, so that they send a consistent message promoting the brand's strategy.[14]

Lingwall's study of IMC education observed that "IMC has gained significant ground among practitioners in public relations, advertising, and marketing over the past 15 years."[15] In fact, IMC is still a new concept and both professionals and professors are engaged in defining the field and explaining how it works.

Total Brand Communication

Several things make the practice of IMC different from advertising. One is its focus on branding and brand communication. Duncan and Mulhern, the authors of a symposium report, explain that, "IMC is, among other things, a process for doing advertising and promotion better and more effectively in the process of building brands."[16]

Tom Duncan, one of the architects of this new professional area, explains that IMC originally started out as focused on creating "one voice, one look" marketing communication, but companies broadened that focus as they realized the need for greater consistency for all aspects of brand communication and customer relationships.[17] So the meaning of IMC has expanded beyond traditional marketing communication and encompasses what we are calling in this book "total brand communication."

It might be helpful to consider how all of the communication we've been discussing fits together. Here's the scheme: advertising and other marcom areas comprise the tools of marketing communication in an IMC program. On a broader level, traditional marcom tools work with other marketing mix communication messages to deliver brand communication. Those relationships are depicted in Figure 2.3.

Organizing for IMC

One area of particular concern to managers is the coordination of all of the agencies involved in creating the various brand messages. Maurice Levy, CEO of the Paris-based Publicis Groupe holding company, has criticized the way his agencies coordinate their work on behalf of a brand. He contends that the giant company has suffered from a "silo mentality" that hurts clients. He asks, "How do we stop confusing clients with contradictory points of view coming from teams each defending their little piece of turf—to the detriment of the client's interests?"[18] Check out the Publicis website, *www.publicisgroupe.com,* to see how complex this problem can be for a large international agency.

An IMC program is even more complex than a traditional **advertising plan** because it uses more marcom tools and addresses more audiences. So another principle, the **Fourth Principle of IMC,** states that *you can't be integrated externally if you are not integrated internally.* This principle identifies the critical

Principle
Most of the added value that comes from an effective brand strategy and accumulates as brand equity is driven by marketing communication.

Fourth Principle of IMC
You can't be integrated externally if you are not integrated internally.

FIGURE 2.3

The Hierarchy of Brand Communication

Brand Strategy

Marcom Plan

Specific MC Areas (Adv, PR, etc.)

THE INSIDE STORY

Who's the Integrator Here, Anyway?

Ed Chambliss, *Vice President and Team Leader, The Phelps Group*

I love smaller clients. I'm talking about clients who have little-to-no marketing department. Those clients who recognize the importance of integrated marketing communication (IMC), but don't know how to actually make it happen. They come to us and say, "Here—you be the integrator." That's because most smaller clients are smart enough to know they don't know everything and that's why you hire a specialist. In this case, a specialist in IMC.

Over time, however, smaller clients become larger clients. And larger clients need in-house marketing departments, and marketing departments need marketing directors, and marketing directors need to be the integrators because, well, that's their job.

Which leaves a lot of marketing directors wondering, "If I'm the integrator, why should I hire an IMC agency? Why don't I just hire a bunch of agencies that are each 'best in breed' and then I'll integrate all of them myself?" It's a fair question. And one that should be answered with other questions. To start, does the marketing director really know how to be an integrator? That is, do they have the formal training in how to create an organization and processes that can orchestrate all of the brand **touch points**, both outbound and inbound, across multiple suppliers? Or do they merely believe that integration sounds like a great idea and think they can make it happen?

Chances are, the marketing director isn't one of the handful of trained IMC specialists out there. More likely, they're a specialist in one particular area of marketing communication who has been promoted into the "integrator" position. For these clients, hiring an IMC agency is a shortcut to integration. An IMC agency can advise the marketing director about how to best integrate their internal organization while doing all of the external heavy lifting that true integration requires.

If the marketing director is trained in IMC, then they'll already be asking these questions: "Are the 'best of breed' agencies I want to hire used to working in an integrated fashion? Or am I going to spend all of my time trying to get them to understand that the overall puzzle is more important than just their one piece?"

This is where an IMC agency shines again. Whether a client hires us to do everything or just one particular type of work, they know that we understand the bigger picture. As one of my IMC-trained clients (who, by the way, hires us only for online work) says, "You guys get it. You understand the big picture. With other agencies, it's like explaining color to a blind man."

In the end, integration needs to happen, so a smart marketing director will assemble the team that has the best possible chance of making it a reality. If it works, the marketing director can take all of the credit. But if integration doesn't happen, there's no credit to take. Only blame.

For more about the Phelps agency, check out *www .thephelpsgroup.com.*

Chambliss graduated from the University of Colorado–Boulder with a master's degree in integrated marketing communication. He was nominated to be featured in this book by Professor Tom Duncan.

---

management implications of IMC. In terms of practice, managing and monitoring all of these messages is an organizational problem best solved through **cross-functional organization,** which means a team is created involving members from all of the relevant parts of a company that interact with customers, other stakeholders, and with outside agencies. Its members represent all of the areas and tools that control contact points and interact with brand customers and other key stakeholders. This cross-functional team operates with a singular brand vision as it plans marketing communication, monitors its impact, and tracks consumer response. Who is in charge of planning all of these brand-building opportunities? On one hand the marketing and communication manager on the client side, such as Peter Stasiowski who was featured earlier in this chapter in the *Day in the Life* box, is in charge. But marketing communication managers work in partnership with agency managers who also provide guidance about such things as IMC strategies. Ed Chambliss, in his *The Inside Story,* discusses the qualifications needed to be an IMC manager, whether on the client side or the agency side. You can also check the website at the end of the *The Inside Story* feature for more information on The Phelps Group, a true IMC-focused agency.

IMC Principles and Practices

In Chapter 1 and in this chapter we have introduced several IMC principles, as well as practices that guide the use of integrated marketing communication. We'll continue to introduce these principles in the chapters that follow, but just to help you summarize what we've discussed so far, here are the first four.

First Principle of IMC: Everything communicates.
  Practice 1.1: Everything in the marketing mix can send a message.
  Practice 1.2: Everything a brand does, and sometimes what it doesn't do, can send a message.

Second Principle of IMC: A brand is a unified vision (the art) and a complex system (the science).

Third Principle of IMC: Brand relationships drive brand value.

Fourth Principle of IMC: You can't be integrated externally if you are not integrated internally.

Integrated marketing communication is an important philosophy, as well as practice. It is a major theme in this book and we will continue to discuss it in the chapters that follow.

BRAND COMMUNICATION IN A TIME OF CHANGE

In Chapter 1, we concluded that advertising is a dynamic industry and subject to challenges and change. The same is true of marketing and all areas of marketing communication. The recession of the late 2000s challenged many marketing practices but some companies came through it more easily than others. General Mills, for example, supported its big-name brands by increasing its marketing budgets. The company focused, however, on what it calls "high ROI (return on investment) areas," such as multicultural consumers, **digital marketing,** and its international markets and global brands.[19] So let's consider ways in which the practice of marketing is changing, particularly in this post-recession period.

Accountability

Similar to the concern for effectiveness in advertising, accountability is a hot issue in marketing. Marketing managers are being challenged by senior management to prove that their decisions lead to the most effective marketing strategies. In other words, was this the best way to launch a new brand or expand into a new territory?

Jim Stengel, retired global marketing officer for P&G and now a UCLA business professor, mentioned several of these areas in an analysis of changing practices in marketing and the need they created for better measurement of effectiveness. He called attention to two major areas of concern—accountability and global marketing.[20] Accountability is what Stengel called for in his quest for better measurement.

Marketing managers are under pressure to deliver business results measured in terms of sales increases, the percentage share of the market the brand holds, and corporate **return on investment (ROI).** The calculation of ROI determines how much money the brand made compared to its expenses. In other words, what did the marketing program cost, and what did it deliver in sales?

Advertising and other marketing communication agencies are creating tools and techniques to help marketers evaluate the efficiency and effectiveness of their marketing communication expenditures. The Interpublic Group, for example, a large marketing communication holding company, has created the Marketing Accountability Partnership to determine what marketers' dollars accomplish or how they can be better used.[21] The issue of accountability is made more complicated by the growing use of global marketing.

Global Marketing

Marketers have moved into global markets, in some cases as a deliberate strategy and in other cases because international competitors have moved into their own markets. General Mills

Here are a few brands that represent different types of geographical marketing strategies. Sainsbury's, an example of regional marketing, is the largest grocery retailer in the United Kingdom with stores in Great Britain, Wales, Scotland, and Northern Ireland. IKEA furniture stores are found in various countries but the company keeps its base and image firmly anchored in Sweden and represents Scandinavian functional design and craftsmanship. Coca-Cola, of course, is one of the best known brands in the world and its logo is recognized everywhere.

survived the Great Recession by emphasizing its international markets and global brands, as well as multicultural consumers in all the markets, including in the United States.[22]

The growth in global marketing activities is increasing dramatically, so it's helpful to understand some of what makes global marketing different from national marketing. In most countries markets are composed of local, regional, international, and global brands. A **local brand** is one marketed in a single country. A **regional brand** is one marketed throughout a region (for example, North America, Europe, China, India). An **international brand** is available in a number of different countries in various parts of the world. A **global brand** is available virtually everywhere in the world, such as Coca-Cola.

Marketing programs that manage and promote the same brand in several countries or globally are practicing **international marketing.** International marketing communication did not appear in any organized manner until the 20th century.

International marketing and marketing communication are not the exclusive province of large companies. Bu Jin, an innovative small Colorado company, creates and markets martial arts products worldwide. With only eight full-time employees, its products serve a high-end international market. Most of Bu Jin's business is driven by its catalog. (Check it out at *www.bujindesign.com*.) Service providers also market internationally. Airlines and transportation companies that serve foreign markets, such as United and UPS, are, in effect, exporting a service.

Regardless of the company's form or style of management, the shift from national to international management requires new tools for marketers, including one language (often English), one control mechanism (the budget), and one strategic plan (the brand strategy).

The choice of an agency or agencies for international marketing depends, in part, on whether the brand's messages are *standardized* across all markets or *localized* to accommodate cultural differences. If the company wants to take a highly standardized approach in international markets, it is likely to favor international agencies that can handle marketing communication for the product in both the domestic and international markets. A localized effort, in contrast, favors use of local agencies for planning and implementation in all of the countries where the product is distributed. The issue of standardized versus global advertising is discussed in more detail in Chapter 18.

Looking Ahead

In this changing marketplace, how responsible the brand is seen to be in terms of its impact on society and the environment can be important to the brand's strategy. Social responsibility is the focus of the next chapter and presents issues related to the social impact of marketing communication, as well as marcom ethics and regulation.

IT'S A WRAP

Winning Video Game War with Wii

Leo Burnett's Wii campaign for Nintendo beat the competition at their own game. The results of the campaign were nothing short of a blowout. For its short-term goal, Nintendo wanted to sell 600,000 units from its launch in November through the end of the year. It nearly doubled that goal, outselling its Sony rival by more than 50 percent during that period. A midterm objective aimed to make Nintendo a rival with Sony and Microsoft by gaining at least a third of the market by the end of 2007. It beat the year-end goal in less than six months. Amazingly in July sales topped the combined sales for both Xbox 360 and PlayStation 3. The long-term goal of fundamentally changing how people experience video games paid off too. Wii parties became the rage. The key purchasers, moms, decided that the Wii was okay for their families. All sorts of people from young families to retirees caught the Wii bug, got off the couch, and started to play.

Nintendo was honored for its effective efforts with a Grand Effie. "Leo Burnett's marketing strategy for the Wii will forever change the gaming industry and its dialogue with consumers," said Deborah Meyer, who chaired the Grand Effie jury. This phenomenal marketing effort continues to pay dividends, as Nintendo recently was judged tops in game ads for effectiveness and impact in print, television, and digital media.

Key Points Summary

1. **How is marketing defined, what is the marketing process, and what are marketing's key concepts?** Marketing is the way a product is designed, branded, distributed, and promoted, as well as a set of processes for creating customer relationships that benefit the organization and its stakeholders. Key concepts that affect the planning of marketing communication include the *marketing concept,* which refers to a focus on customers; the *exchange,* which refers to communication and interaction, as well as money traded for goods or services; *competitive advantage,* which means that the product is differentiated and superior in some way to its competitors, and *added value,* which refers to the way that a product takes on features that are valued by consumers at each step of the marketing process.

   The *key players* are the marketer, the suppliers and vendors, the channels of distribution, and marketing partners such as agencies. In addition to services marketing, the four *types of markets* are consumer, business-to-business, institutional, and channels. The *marketing process* leads to the development and execution of a marketing plan and the steps moved from research, to setting objectives, assessing consumer needs and wants, segmenting and targeting the market, differentiating and positioning the product, developing the marketing mix, and evaluating the effectiveness of the plan. The *marketing mix* includes the product, its pricing and distribution, and the marketing communication.

2. **How does marketing communication contribute to the development of a brand?** A brand is a perception created from information as well as experiences with the company and its line of products. It's intangible but it generates value in the form of brand equity. A brand perception takes on meaning by *transforming* the product into something

unique and distinctive and by making a *promise* that sets customers' expectations. The *branding process* includes establishing a brand *identity* through both name and symbols, defining the *brand image* and *personality,* and developing *brand relationships* with loyal customers that contribute to the financial value of the brand, called *brand equity.* Marketing communication is the primary driver of brand meanings and brand relationships.

3. **What is integrated marketing communication and what are its key concepts?** IMC can be described as total communication, which means that everything that sends a message is monitored for its impact on the brand image. Central to IMC is the practice of unifying all marketing communication messages and tools to send a consistent brand message. Not only does this maximize consistency, it also creates *synergy,* such that a group of coordinated messages has more impact than marketing communications that are independent of each other. IMC recognizes a variety of *stakeholders* who contribute to the brand conversation, as well as a multitude of *touch points* where messages are delivered including marketing mix messages, as well as more formal planned marketing communication.

4. **How is brand communication evolving during a time of change?** Accountability and global marketing are two key emergent themes. Tough economic times have led to increased calls for accountability. Investments in marketing communication must show that they are money well spent. This focus highlights the need for developing tools to measure the effectiveness of the investments. Growth in global marketing demonstrates a strategic opportunity to build business internationally. With this dramatic growth comes a need for marketing communicators to fully understand those audiences with whom they are trying to build relationships.

Words of Wisdom: Recommended Reading

Andersen, Kurt, *Reset: How This Crisis Can Restore Our Values and Renew America,* New York: Random House, 2009.

Dru, Jean-Marie, *Beyond Disruption: Changing the Rules in the Marketplace,* New York: John Wiley, 2002.

Fanzen, Giep, and Sandra Moriarty, *The Science and Art of Branding,* Armonk, NY: M.E. Sharpe, 2009.

Gilbreath, Bob, *The Next Evolution of Marketing: Connect with Your Customers by Marketing with Meaning,* New York: McGraw-Hill and Bridge Worldwide, 2010.

Jaffe, Joseph, *Life after the 30-Second Spot: Energize Your Brand with a Bold Mix of Alternatives to Traditional Advertising,* Hoboken, NJ: John Wiley, 2005.

Levine, Rick, Christopher Locke, Doc Searls, and David Weinberger, *The Cluetrain Manifesto,* 10th Anniversary ed., New York: Basic Books, 2009.

Schmetterer, Bob, *Leap! A Revolution in Creative Business Strategy,* Hoboken, NJ: John Wiley, 2003.

Wipperfurth, Alex, *Brand Hijack: Marketing without Marketing,* New York: Penguin, 2005.

Key Terms

added value, p. 41
advertising plan, p. 53
brand, p. 44
brand equity, p. 51
brand extension, p. 52
brand identity, p. 48
brand image, p. 50
brand licensing, p. 52
brand loyalty, p. 51
brand management, p. 44
brand meaning, p. 44
brand personality, p. 50
brand position, p. 50
brand promise, p. 50
brand relationship, p. 51
brand transformation, p. 46
brand value, p. 51
branding, p. 44
business-to-business (B2B) market, p. 37
channel market, p. 37
channel marketing, p. 37
channel of distribution, p. 36
co-branding, p. 52
competitive advantage, p. 40

consumer, p. 40
consumer markets, p. 37
contact points, p. 35
cross-functional organization, p. 54
customer, p. 40
customer service p. 38
differentiation, p. 40
digital marketing, p. 55
direct marketing, p. 42
distribution, p. 42
distribution chain, p. 36
exchange, p. 35
fast-moving consumer goods (fmcg), p. 37
four Ps, p. 35
generic brands, p. 46
global brand, p. 56
goodwill, p. 52
house brands, p. 46
ingredient branding, p. 52
institutional markets, p. 37
integrated marketing communication (IMC), p. 53

intermediaries, p. 37
international brand, p. 56
international marketing, p. 56
lead generation, p. 43
leads, p. 43
local brand, p. 56
logo, p. 49
market, p. 37
marketer, p. 35
marketing, p. 34
marketing communication, p. 43
marketing concept, p. 39
marketing mix, p. 35
marketing plan, p. 39
package goods, p. 37
parity products, p. 46
personal sales, p. 43
personal selling, p. 43
point of differentiation, p. 41
positioning, p. 40
price, p. 42
price copy, p. 42

private labels, p. 46
product category, p. 35
product development, p. 40
product differentiation, p. 40
product-driven philosophy, p. 39
prospects, p. 43
psychological pricing, p. 42
pull strategy, p. 43
push strategy, p. 43
regional brand, p. 56
resellers, p. 37
return on investment (ROI), p. 55
share of market, p. 37
situation analysis, p. 39
stakeholders, p. 35
store brands, p. 46
supply chain, p. 36
SWOT analysis, p. 39
touch points, p. 54
trademark, p. 49

Review Questions

1. What is the definition of marketing, and where does marketing communication fit within the operation of a marketing program?

2. In general, outline the structure of the marketing industry and identify the key players.

3. Explain how marketing communication relates to the four key marketing concepts and to the marketing mix.

4. Explain how brand meaning and brand value are created.

5. Define integrated marketing communication and explain its approach to audience, media, and message.

Discussion Questions

1. When identical products carry different labels, people will pay more for the recognized brand. Explain why that is so.

2. Coca-Cola is the most recognizable brand in the world. How did the company achieve this distinction? What has the company done in its marketing mix in terms of product, price, distribution, and marketing communications that has created such tremendous brand equity and loyalty? How has advertising and other forms of marketing communication aided in building the brand?

3. List your favorite brands and from that list do the following analyses:

   a. Think about the categories where it is important to you to buy your favorite brand. For which categories does the brand not make a difference? Why is that so?

   b. In those categories where you have a favorite brand, what does that brand represent to you? Is it something that you've used and liked? Is it comfortable

familiarity—you know it will be the same every time? Is it a promise—if you use this, something good will happen? Is it something you have always dreamed about owning? Why are you loyal to this brand?

4. *Three-Minute Debate* This chapter stressed integration of advertising with other components of the marketing mix. A classmate argues that advertising is a small part of the marketing process and relatively unimportant; another says advertising is the most important communication activity and needs to get the bulk of the budget. If you were in marketing management for Kellogg cereals, how would you see advertising supporting the marketing mix? Does advertising add value to each of these functions for Kellogg? Do you think it is a major responsibility for the marketing manager? What would you say either in support of or in opposition to your classmates' views? Working with a small team of your classmates, present your point of view to your class.

Take-Home Projects

1. *Portfolio Project* Look through the ads in this textbook or in other publications and find an example of an advertisement that you think demonstrates the marketing concept, i.e., a focus on consumer needs and wants, and another ad that you think does not represent an effective application of the marketing concept. Compare the two and explain why you evaluated them as you did. Copy both ads and mount them and your analysis in your portfolio.

2. *Mini-Case Analysis* In the Wii case, Nintendo believed that the market for video games—primarily males and kids—

could be broadened to include women, as well as an older family market. Summarize how Nintendo arrived at that insight. Pretend you have been assigned to the Wii account for the next year after this launch. What would you want to know to determine if this strategy has been successful? In terms of marketing and communication, what might Wii do in the next stage of this campaign to maintain its marketing edge? Write up your ideas in a one-page position paper to turn in to your instructor.

Team Project: The BrandRevive Campaign

In Chapter 1, we introduced the need for old, forgotten, and minimally known brands to be revitalized and you were asked to choose from among a list of brands that need revitalization, rebranding, or repositioning. As we explained, this is an assignment that will continue throughout the book leading to a complete campaign for the brand you chose. For Chapter 1, you did an initial review of the brand and company history for that assignment.

For this chapter, the next step in your BrandRevive project is to do more in-depth background research on the brand and category. Split your team with some going online and others visiting your school's library to find all of the relevant articles and other marketing information that you can about the category and your brand's place in it. If you chose a consumer good or service with a physical location, visit a store and analyze what you see there in terms of its presentation and competitive situation. Also visit the brand's home page and collect what information you can find there about the brand and its marketing strategy.

- Based on your background research, rough out what you believe to be the branding strategy.
- Then summarize what you believe to be the brand's marketing mix strategy.
- Find out what you can about advertising and marketing communication spending both for your brand, your competitors' brands, and the category. This will provide a benchmark for your budget.
- Write up your findings in a brand review that is no longer than four double-spaced pages. Convert your key findings into a PowerPoint presentation that is no longer than four slides. Prepare and practice to give this presentation to your class.

Hands-On Case

The Century Council

Read the Century Council case in the Appendix before coming to class.

1. How might the marketing mix of major beer and liquor companies be relevant to a campaign to curb binge drinking on college campuses?
2. How might "teaching responsible drinking" curb binge drinking on campus?
3. Why do you think liquor companies would want to fund "The Stupid Drink" campaign to curb binge drinking on campus?
4. Prepare a one-page statement explaining how "The Stupid Drink" campaign will actually help beer and alcohol marketers.

3

Brand Communication and Society

plant this page.
save a bee.

Nature needs honey bees. We all do. After all, they're responsible for
pollinating one third of all the foods we eat. But they're disappearing at an alarming rate.
Help us bring them back. Plant this page filled with bee-friendly wildflower seeds under a thin layer

It's a Winner

Campaign:	Company:	Agency:	Awards:
"Häagen-Dazs Loves Honey Bees"	Häagen-Dazs	Goodby, Silverstein & Partners; Ketchum	2009 Gold Effie Winner; 2009 Festival of Media, Media Responsibility Award; Cannes Lions 2009 PR Lion

LOVE IS ETERNAL

LET ALL YOU DO COME FROM LOVE

©JOANNE FINK • WWW.ZENSPIRATIONS.COM

1. What is the social impact of brand communication?
2. What ethical and social responsibilities do communicators bear?
3. Why and how is advertising regulated?

Häagen-Dazs Creates a Buzz about Bees

Did you know that honeybee colonies are disappearing at an alarming rate? In the last three years a third of their colonies in the United States have died, which puts much of our natural food supply at risk. Honeybees help pollinate about a third of every bite that Americans eat—from fruits to nuts. The cause of the crisis is not entirely known, but some of this loss is attributed to colony collapse disorder or "CCD." When this condition happens, bees mysteriously abandon their hives.

How does this crisis relate to Häagen-Dazs? This premium ice cream uses only all-natural ingredients, and bee pollination is essential for ingredients in nearly half of its flavors. It's in the best interest of the company, as well as the bees, to resolve the problem. This is the story about how a company practices social responsibility, or shows concern for the welfare of others, and profits from the experience.

Faced with a need to ramp up sales and inject zip into the Häagen-Dazs brand (whose main competitor is funkier, socially conscious Ben & Jerry's), the client asked its ad agency, Goodby, Silverstein & Partners, and the PR firm Ketchum to accomplish these objectives with no increase in budget. In such a situation, it made sense to generate a buzz that could extend the impact of its message beyond the limited media budget for advertising. What Häagen-Dazs discovered was a problem more important than the brand.

Summarizing the situation, three factors led to the big idea for the campaign: a brand known for its all-natural ingredients, consumers who are increasingly concerned about sustainability and environmental issues, and a critical issue. The idea centered on a simple equation: 1/2 of Häagen-Dazs ice cream flavors + 1/3 of what we eat − honeybees = a bigger-than-ice-cream problem.

To help find a solution, Häagen-Dazs's ad agency, Goodby, Silverstein & Partners, and public relations firm, Ketchum, created the "Häagen-Dazs Loves Honey Bees" program. Häagen-Dazs kicked off its multifaceted efforts to help solve the honeybee mystery by giving substantial research grants to Penn State and UC

Jef I. Richards, University of Texas, and Joseph E. Phelps, University of Alabama, contributed to the review of this chapter.

Davis scientists. An expert advisory "Bee Board," comprised of scientists and bee-keepers, served as sources for news media. Häagen-Dazs created *advertorials*, advertising that looks like editorial matter in newspapers or magazines, about the bee problem, which ran in key magazines, such as *National Geographic* and *Gourmet*. Häagen-Dazs even created a new flavor, Vanilla Honey Bee, and earmarked the profits for CCD research.

Other components of the program spread the message to its audience. The *www.helpthehoneybees.com* site educated consumers about the crisis and invited their involvement. The online presence allowed consumers to purchase T-shirts and even send "bee-mail" to friends. Häagen-Dazs funded a six-minute documentary about CCD that is available on the Serious Eats website (*www.seriouseats.com*). A "Bee Dance" video was launched on YouTube. Häagen-Dazs encouraged consumer involvement by distributing more than a million free bee-friendly seeds in HD loves HB packets.

Häagen-Dazs counted on the people who heard its message to spread the word. For example, a reader who happened to be an employee of Whole Foods read the *National Geographic* piece and inspired Northern California Whole Foods stores to create honeybee displays featuring Häagen-Dazs and CCD.

Although the bee problem was the center of the communication, selling a brand was still important. Häagen-Dazs hopes that when you crave premium ice cream, you'll choose its Vanilla Honey Bee or Dulce de Leche over Ben & Jerry's Cherry Garcia or Phish Food flavors, partly because it's a brand that cares.

Was this effort to be socially responsible successful? In what ways? Turn to the end of the chapter to see how Häagen-Dazs measured the effectiveness of these efforts.

Sources: "Häagen-Dazs Loves Honey Bees," Effie Awards Brief of Effectiveness, *www.nyama.org*; *www.helpthehoneybees .com*; Michael Bush, "Häagen-Dazs Saves the Honeybees," May 8, 2009, *http://adage.com*; Gavin O'Malley, "Viewers Swarm to Häagen-Dazs Bee-Friendly Viral Video," August 21, 2008, *www.mediapost.com*; Juliana Barbassa, "Food Companies Target Honey Bee Health Problems," December 1, 2008, *www.nytimes.com*; "Häagen-Dazs Brand Boosts Image and Sales with 'Häagen-Dazs Loves Honey Bees' Campaign," *www.ketchum.com*; "Häagen-Dazs: Honey, Let's Lick the Problem," June 2009, *www.advertolog.com*.

Caring for the environment and promoting a product can be mutually beneficial, as the "Häagen-Dazs Loves Honey Bees" case demonstrates. By raising public awareness about the plight of the honeybees, Häagen-Dazs also benefited its ice cream business. This chapter reminds us that as communicators we make choices. We have the power to use our talents to leave the world a bit better than we found it. This chapter helps you explore the impact of brand communication on society. We present ongoing debates about the power of advertising, look at issues related to social responsibility, and contemplate emerging issues related to digital media. You will examine your personal and professional ethics related to brand communication. Finally, you will read about the legal aspects of advertising and regulatory processes that are in place to make sure harmful communication is minimized.

WHAT IS THE SOCIAL IMPACT OF BRAND COMMUNICATION?

Häagen-Dazs's campaign to align itself with a good cause demonstrates that marketing communication might help make the world a little better. The Häagen-Dazs case shows that marketers can think beyond the campaign's immediate benefits to consider how their actions might affect a larger sphere—society and the natural environment. Donating a fortune to help the unfortunate, as Bill and Melinda Gates of Microsoft fame have done, is another way for companies to prove their worth. Think about all of the companies such as Nestlé, Coca-Cola, AT&T, Target, and Walmart who pitched in to help victims of the Haiti earthquake.

"Avon Commits $1 Million to Support Relief Efforts" in earthquake-ravaged Haiti. "Coca-Cola Commits to Climate Friendly Refrigeration." "Kraft Foods Employees Honor Dr. Martin Luther King Jr.'s Legacy Across the Country." These headlines[1] demonstrate that professional brand communicators have the potential to do good, although too many examples show that communicators sometimes fail to act responsibly.

Advertising and other forms of marketing communication are used effectively for social marketing, as well as for selling stuff, which also can be a good thing. Advertising can be used to counter bad behaviors and promote good behavior. Read *The Inside Story* at *www.pearsonhighered.com/moriarty* about a University of Florida campaign against drinking and driving developed by Adwerks, Florida's student-run advertising agency.

Do you think advertising itself is inherently good or bad for society? Most of the time people use advertising for neutral or good purposes, meaning they value a brand's **social responsibility.** To emphasize the importance of this topic, sprinkled throughout this book are *A Principled Practices* boxes that discuss issues of social and ethical responsibility.

Advertising sometimes draws criticism for its social impact and much of the discussion that follows is focused on advertising because it is so highly visible. Check out *www.AdBusters.org* for a look inside the world of advertising criticism. We start this chapter with three important debates concerning the role of advertising and marketing communication as institutions in society that will help you understand different aspects of social responsibility.

CLASSIC

A J. Walter Thompson ad written by legendary ad man James Young was so startling that readers begged the *Ladies Home Journal* to stop running the ad. It was considered disgusting then, but how do you see it now?

What Are the Debates about Marcom's Social Role?

In this section we review some of the issues related to advertising's role in society. Our intention is to review the criticisms, but understand that we believe that advertising is a good force in society and in our economy even though it may sometimes be used in ways that generate concern. Three topics generate debate about advertising and marketing communication's role in society. They focus on demand creation, shaping versus mirroring of social trends, and the overcommercialization of society.

Demand Creation   Some critics charge that advertising causes **demand creation,** which results when an external message drives people to feel a need or want—sometimes unnecessarily. A 2009 Harris Poll indicated that two-thirds of Americans believed ad agencies were at least partially to blame for the recent economic crisis because they caused people to buy things they couldn't afford.[2] Others reject this notion. Does advertising create demand for products people don't need? Has advertising convinced you to buy products you don't need?

Let's start the discussion by considering deodorants. Did you know that no one used deodorants much until about 1919? People didn't worry about having body odor. An ad for a new product, Odorono (great name, and it's still being used, by the way), targeted women because everyone assumed that men were supposed to emit bad odors and women would be the more likely users of the product. The launch ad in *Ladies' Home Journal* so offended readers that about 200 people canceled their subscription. The ads were effective, however. Sales for the deodorant rose 112 percent.[3] Did advertising make women buy something they didn't even know they needed? Was that a bad thing?

If you think it doesn't happen today, think about Unilever's Axe product. Axe pioneered the new category of body spray for men in 2002. Did guys know before 2002 that they needed scented body spray? Is it a good thing advertising convinces people to buy products like deodorants and body sprays? Can such advertising improve consumers' lives?

Companies often conduct significant research to find out what consumers want before they launch new products. If people do not want the products being marketed, they do not buy them. Advertising may convince people to buy a product—even a bad one—once. If they try the product and don't like it, they won't buy it again. So to some extent advertising creates demand. At the same time, it is important to remember that audiences may refuse to purchase the product if they don't feel a need for it.

Principle
If people do not want the products being marketed, they do not buy them.

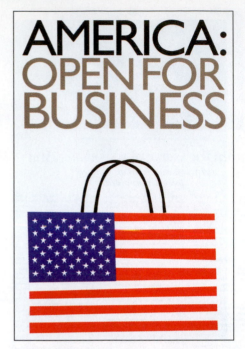

The poster "America: Open for Business" is an example of a message aimed at stimulating business after 9/11. The RED campaign demonstrates a collaborative effort by a number of corporations, including Gap, to fight AIDS in Africa. Do you think messages like these can impact social trends?

Shaping versus Mirroring   Another important debate about advertising's role in society questions the limits of its influence. At what point does advertising cross the line between reflecting social values and creating them? Professionals believe they are reflecting the values of their society. Critics argue that advertising has repeatedly crossed this line, influencing vulnerable groups, such as children and young teenagers, too strongly.

A case in point: Do ultra-thin models in advertising cause young women to have eating disorders, as some have claimed? While it is probable that the images women and girls see influence them in some ways, it's difficult to say that these images directly and solely cause the problem, because many factors in a person's environment potentially influence eating choices. Some research, however, supports the view that advertising is partly to blame; advertising may contribute to the problem. What do you think?

Can advertising manipulate people's choices? Critics of advertising argue that advertising can create social trends and has the power to dictate how people think and act. They believe that even if an individual ad cannot control behavior, the cumulative effects of nonstop television, radio, print, Internet, and outdoor ads can be overwhelming. Others contend that effective brand communication spots trends and then develops messages that connect target audiences with the trends. In other words, if people are interested in achieving healthy lifestyles, you will see ads that use health appeals as an advertising strategy. In this way, advertising mirrors values rather than sets them. Do you agree with that argument?

One example of using advertising to try to change society and improve the world while still selling products is the RED campaign, instigated by U2 singer Bono in conjunction with major companies like Apple, Gap, and Hallmark. The purpose of the campaign is to sell RED-branded products to help fight AIDS and HIV in Africa. Does Product RED advertising mirror a societal concern for Africans' welfare or does it shape how we think about the problem, or both? Another example of attempting to influence society is the award-winning "Open for Business" poster that appeared after the 9/11 tragedy.

This shaping-versus-mirroring debate is the most central issue we address in considering advertising's role in society. What drives consumers to behave or believe as they do? Is it advertising, or is it other forces? Why do women buy cosmetics, for example? Are they satisfying a deep cultural need for beauty, or were they manipulated by advertising to believe in the hope that cosmetics offer? Women can even purchase a product by the cosmetics company Philosophy called Hope in a Jar. Or have their families and friends socialized them to believe they look better with cosmetics than without? Advertising and society's values are probably interactive, so the answer to the debate may simply be that advertising both mirrors and shapes values.

Overcommercialization   Does advertising lead people to be too materialistic? The second half of the 20th century is notable for the rise of a materialistic consumer culture in the Western world. Did advertising create this culture, or does it simply reflect a natural striving for the good life?

Some argue that advertising heightens expectations and primes the audience to believe that the answer is always a product. If you have a headache, what do you do? You take a pill. What is left unsaid by an advertisement is that you might get rid of the headache just as easily by taking a nap, drinking less alcohol or more water, or taking a walk to relieve stress. Nobody pays for ads to tell you about alternatives. Consumers, however, are not always passively doing what advertisers tell them. As we have said, they have the power to refuse to buy what is being sold.

Another facet of this debate relates to a problem that emerges if the walls blur between advertising and news and entertainment. If advertising becomes intertwined with news, how will audiences know whether news stories are free from editorial pressure from sponsors who want to control what is said about their brands? As product placement becomes increasingly prevalent, how does that affect entertainment? Does the influence of advertising, for example, change how we watch football games and other sporting events? Does it bother you that Coke has more than 2,000 product placements in *American Idol,* especially when a lot of viewers are under 16?[4]

Other Social Responsibility Issues

To help you understand issues that advertisers face when they can have a direct impact and make a difference to society, we'll discuss six key topics: (1) taste and offensive advertising, (2) sex appeals, (3) diversity issues, (4) message-related issues, (5) product-related issues, and (6) emerging issues with digital media. If you're interested in these and other related topics, visit the Advertising Educational Foundation website at *www.aef.com* for more information.

Poor Taste and Offensive Advertising   Although certain ads might be in bad taste in any circumstance, viewer reactions are affected by such factors as sensitivity to the product category, timing (if the message is received in the middle of dinner, for example), and other circumstances, such as whether the person is alone or with others when viewing the message. Some television ads, for example, might not bother adults watching alone but would make them uncomfortable if children were watching.

Also, questionable ads become offensive in the wrong context. Advertisers and media outlets must try to be sensitive to such objections. Recently, outraged advertisers including Applebee's, General Mills, and Kraft pulled ads from Fox News Channel's *Glenn Beck* program after the host called President Obama a "racist" with a "deep-seated hatred for white people."[5]

We all have our own ideas about what constitutes good taste. Unfortunately, these ideas vary so much that creating general guidelines for good taste in advertising is difficult. Different things offend different people at different times. In addition, taste changes over time. What was offensive yesterday may not be considered offensive today. The Odorono ad offended people in 1919, but would it today? By today's standards that advertisement seems pretty tame. Today's questions of taste center on the use of sexual innuendo, nudity, vulgarity, and violence. What about the Axe ads for male body sprays? Do you find them offensive or in good taste?

An ad can be offensive to the general public even if the targeted audience accepts it. Brand communicators would be wise to conduct research to gauge the standards of taste for the general population as well as the specific target audience. If they fail to do so, advertisers risk alienating potential consumers. Such was the case with Abercrombie and Fitch's sexually explicit ads aimed at young teens that spawned a grassroots campaign to stop the company's marketing tactics. Some might argue that any publicity is good publicity, and offensive advertising calls attention to your product in a memorable way.

The *A Principled Practice* box by Herbert Rotfeld discusses this topic in more detail.

Principle
Good taste is a difficult standard to apply because different things offend different people at different times.

Sex Appeals and Body Image   Advertising that portrays women (or men) as sex objects is considered demeaning and sexist, particularly if sex is not relevant to the product. Sometimes ads use sex appeals that are relevant to the product, such as those used by Victoria's Secret. The ethical question then is how sexy is too sexy. Transit authorities in two Canadian cities decided Virgin Mobile's ads were too racy for the public and asked the company to pull risqué ads from bus shelters that showed embracing couples and invited viewers to "Hook up fearlessly."[6] Explicitly using sex appeals to sell may not always be appropriate as Professor Rotfeld argued in the *A Principled Practice* feature.

Playing on consumers' insecurities about their appearance presents advertisers with a classic ethical dilemma because self-image advertising can be seen as contributing to self-improvement, but sometimes, such advertising is questionable because it leads to dangerous practices. Some critics charge that women place their health at risk in order to cultivate an unrealistic or even unhealthy physical appearance. Supermodels don't always project healthy portrayals of women. Critic and author Jean Kilbourne claimed, "ads are aimed at the very heart of girls' insecurities' because of the ideal image of beauty that they portray: 'an absolutely perfect-looking young woman who's incredibly thin'."[7]

Do you think advertising sends this message? Messages that only feature thin models normalize the thin ideal of beauty. Young women and even men can become obsessed with their weight to the point that they believe they are attractive only if they are unnaturally thin. The "Dove Campaign for Real Beauty" that you'll read about in Chapter 5 defies the notion that women need to be thin to be beautiful.

A PRINCIPLED PRACTICE

Pizza, Tacos, and Truck Parts: Sex in Advertising

Herbert Jack Rotfeld, *Professor of Marketing, Auburn University*

An advertisement for a pizza place near a college campus ran an advertisement in the school paper that read, "Put a hot piece between your lips. We're hot and easy, fast and cheesy." In another city, a Mexican restaurant showed a Lycra-clad woman posed with her hands on her hips over the headline, "Tickle my taco."

In each case, the advertiser probably thought it was good advertising, not realizing that the irrelevant use of sex distracts and hinders any communication or persuasion to the target. It should be intuitively obvious that a product is sexually relevant for marketing communication only if people would make a purchase for a sexual reason. While breath mints, clothes, or exercise equipment may be purchased by some people to enhance their self-image of sex appeal, it is doubtful that anyone buys pizza or tacos for anticipation of an orgasmic experience.

A truck supply company owner thought he had client-grabbing pictures on his business calendars with the monthly display of exposed female anatomy, but when many of his customers forgot his company name or "lost" his phone number, he finally realized that the secretaries and office managers who gave the truckers the necessary purchase order forms would never allow such lewd displays on their office walls.

The misplaced marketing problem is more than just simple misdirection and distraction. The people who wrote or produced these ads lost track of what they are trying to say to the target audience. After years of talking to advertisers and watching them produce these less-than-optimal efforts, one realizes that some of the advertising creators believe that publicity garnered by offending people is always beneficial. Instead of communication, attention of any kind—to anything, at any cost—is their goal.

However, advertising is a very limited and limiting form of communication; it is costly to undertake and difficult to carry out successfully. The marketing question of how best to communicate is a conservative one, but it is also an effort to maximize the likelihood of a favorable consumer response. In the end, there is a communication job to be done.

Too often, advertising writers seem focused on titillating each other with the overuse of lewd imagery, exposed breasts, and other distractions. In the end, sex does not sell.

The same problem of physical appearance exists for men, particularly young men, although the muscular ideal body may not lead to the same health-threatening reactions that young women face, unless men resort to steroids to attain this image. The standard of attractiveness is a sociocultural phenomenon that both mirrors and shapes our ideals. Responsible advertisers, therefore, have begun using models of more normal size and weight as a way to reduce the pressure on young people.

Diversity and Stereotypes   Athletic blacks, feeble seniors, sexy Italians, smart Asians. You're probably familiar with these and other examples of stereotypes. A **stereotype** is a representation of a cultural group that emphasizes a trait or group of traits that may or may not communicate an accurate representation of the group. Sometimes the stereotype is useful (athletes are fit) and aids communication by using easily understood symbolic meanings, but sometimes the stereotype relies on a characteristic that is negative or exaggerated and, in so doing, reduces the group to a caricature. This is the problem with portraying older adults as all being absentminded or feeble, for instance.

The issue of stereotyping also raises the shaping-versus-mirroring question. For example, stereotyping women as sex objects is a practice that is deeply embedded in our culture, however negatively some might see that value. Using such strategies also makes advertising a participant in shaping and reinforcing that cultural value.

Intentionally or not communicators choose how they portray people in their ads. Whether you believe advertising has the ability to shape our values and our view of the world or whether it mirrors society, communicators have a responsibility to ensure that what is portrayed is accurate and representative. Diversity has become an issue as advertisers struggle to target, as well as portray, people outside the white, straight mainstream market.

Next we discuss some of the most common problems found in the way advertising portrays people.

Gender Stereotypes   Stereotyped gender images abound in the media—dumb blondes, the rugged western Marlboro man, and the clueless buffoon who appears in ads, comics, and programs as a bungling dad are all examples. One of the most important lessons media teach is how people fit into culturally shared gender and racial roles. The way men and women are cast as characters in advertisements and programs can create or reinforce cultural stereotypes.[8]

Historically, advertising has portrayed gender in distinct and predictable stereotypes. Men are usually shown as strong, independent, and achievement oriented; women are shown as nurturing and empathetic, but softer and more dependent, and they are told that the products being advertised will make their lives less stressful and more manageable. Men are often negatively stereotyped as well. The organization *FathersAndHusbands.org* formed to promote positive images of men in the media.

A study of gender representation in 1,300 prime-time commercials found that although women make most purchases of goods and services, they are underrepresented as primary characters during most prime-time commercials, except for health and beauty products. Women are cast as younger, supportive counterparts to men, and older women remain the most underrepresented group.[9] However, many marketers are recognizing the diversity of women's roles. In the 1990s, advertisers did a better job of depicting women—and men—in roles that were more than one dimensional.[10] They functioned in multiple roles, not just as career women or supermoms, and men even appeared as house-husbands and nurturing fathers.

THE BLIND ARE ALSO COLOR BLIND

CLASSIC
"Color Blind"
This was an ad created by the Carson/Roberts agency in 1964 during debate over the Civil Rights Voting Guarantee Bill. It is included in the AIGA Design Archives. AIGA is the leading graphic design association.

A few adventurous companies have even begun to show images of gays in advertising to general audiences. Such images have appeared fairly extensively in mainstream fashion advertising for brands such as Calvin Klein, Benetton, and Banana Republic. The coming-out episode of ABC's *Ellen* was groundbreaking in more ways than just programming—it was the first time advertisers used prime-time network TV to reach gay and lesbian viewers. Now it's not unusual to see gays and lesbians portrayed as multidimensional characters on shows such as *Glee, Modern Family,* and *Grey's Anatomy.* Viacom's LOGO, a 24-hour gay channel, is supported by a host of national advertisers trying to reach this audience.

Racial and Ethnic Stereotypes   Think about sports teams like the Washington Redskins, Kansas City Chiefs, or Cleveland Indians that reduce Native Americans to a caricature, and you'll know why some critics claim that racial and ethnic groups are stereotyped in advertising. Do you believe these team names and logos represent negative stereotypes and, if so, what should be done about them when millions of dollars have been invested in them as brands? The portrayal of Italian Americans as ignorant Mafioso types in a Verizon Wireless commercial prompted one blogger to complain, "It is so common to see Italian Americans negatively portrayed by Hollywood and Madison Avenue that our society doesn't think twice when we see garbage such as this. . . ."

Should we permit the media to profit from all the unflattering and nasty stereotypes about blacks, Jews, Asians, Muslims, Irish, and Latinos?"[11]

Cultural Differences in Global Advertising   In the global economy advertisers seek worldwide audiences for their products. As they do so, advertisers sometimes make mistakes of overlaying their worldview on that of another culture without thinking about the impact of their advertising. Many oppose the move to a global perspective because of concerns about the homogenization of cultural differences. **Marketing imperialism** or **cultural imperialism** is a term used to describe what happens when Western culture is imposed on others, particularly the Middle East, Asian, and African cultures. Some Asian and Middle Eastern countries are critical of what they see as America's materialism and disrespectful behavior toward women and elders. They worry that **international advertising** and media will encourage their young people to adopt these viewpoints.

Cultural differences are very real, and we will talk more about them throughout the book. Consider that respect for culture and local customs is so important that insensitivity to local customs can make an ad completely ineffective. Customs can be even stronger than laws. When advertising to children age 12 or older was approved in Germany, for example, local customs were so strong that companies risked customer revolt by advertising. In many countries, naming a competitor in comparative advertising is considered bad form.

Age-Related Stereotypes   Another group that critics say is often subject to stereotyping is senior citizens, a growing segment of the population with increasing amounts of disposable income. In a focus group of women in their 50s, participants had trouble keeping their comments polite when viewing a series of health care ads that showed older women in primarily sedentary activities. One explained that even though she has arthritis, she still wants to see ads that show arthritis sufferers working out in a gym, rather than "silver-haired couples walking along the beach with a golden retriever."[12]

Barbara Champion, president of a research firm specializing in the maturing market, observed:

> The needs of maturing consumers, depending on mental and physical acuity as well as life-stage factors, are often different from one another. Whether a consumer is an empty-nester whose children have grown up and left home, a grandparent, a retiree, a widow, or in need of assisted living, for example, will greatly affect how, when, and why goods and services are purchased."[13]

Many of the ads for Viagra speak to a specific segment of the population and do so in a tasteful, tactful way.

Advertising to Children   Marketing to youth is one of the most controversial topics in the industry. One reason why advertising to children attracts so much attention is that children are seen as vulnerable. Children do not always know what is good for them and what is not. Concerned adults want to make sure that they protect impressionable minds from exploitation marketers. They want to help children learn to make good choices.

A current issue that's being addressed relates to selling soft drinks, candy, and food with high fat and sugar content to children. Recognizing that obesity among youth is a major health problem, the Council of Better Business Bureaus launched the Children's Food and Beverage Advertising Initiative to help 10 major corporations set guidelines to cut down on junk food advertising. The companies, which are responsible for producing almost two-thirds of the food and drink advertising for children under 12, include General Mills, McDonald's, Coca-Cola, PepsiCo, Hershey, and Kellogg.

Marketing alcohol to black teens is another important issue because of the use of rappers like Ice-T to promote malt liquors and the dozens of pages of alcohol ads that appear in black youth–culture magazines such as *Vibe*. A Georgetown University study contends that the alcohol beverage industry is marketing far more heavily to African American young people than to others in that age group.

You'll read more about the important issue of advertising to children in the regulation section of this chapter.

Message-Related Issues   Even though most advertisers try to create messages that communicate fairly and accurately, marketers need to understand what is not considered acceptable so they can avoid unethical and even illegal behavior. Advertising claims are considered to be unethical if they are false, misleading, or deceptive. In the drive to find something to say about a product that will catch attention and motivate the audience to respond, advertisers sometimes stretch the truth. **False advertising,** which is a type of misleading advertising, is simply a message that is untrue. Misleading claims, puffery, comparative advertising, endorsements, and product demonstrations are explained next.

Misleading Claims and Puffery   The target of the heaviest criticism for being misleading is weight-loss advertising, as well as other back-of-the-magazine, self-improvement advertisements for health and fitness products. In a study of 300 weight-loss ads, the Federal Trade Commission (FTC), a regulatory body, found that ads for weight-loss products sometimes make "grossly exaggerated" claims and that dieters need to beware of ads for dietary supplements, meal replacements, patches, creams, wraps, and other products. (The FTC is described more completely in the regulation section.) The study found that 40 percent of the ads made at least one representation that was almost certainly false, and 55 percent made a claim that was very likely false or at least lacked adequate substantiation.[14]

Misleading claims are not just a problem in the United States. The London-based Barclays credit card was forced by the U.K. government to withdraw an advertising campaign that promised "0 percent forever." The ad was deemed deceptive because borrowers would enjoy the no-interest offer for only as long as it took for the balance to be cleared. In other words, all new spending on the card would be charged the standard interest rate.[15]

Not all exaggerated claims are considered misleading. **Puffery** is defined as "advertising or other sales representations, which praise the item to be sold with subjective opinions, superlatives, or exaggerations, vaguely and generally, stating no specific facts."[16] Campbell Soup, for example, has used the slogan "M'm!, M'm!, Good!" which is vague and can't really be proven or disproven. It's a classic example of puffery, generally deemed to be of little concern to regulators looking for false or misleading claims because it is so innocuous.

Because obviously exaggerated "puffing" claims are legal, the question of puffery is mainly an ethical one. According to the courts, consumers expect exaggerations and inflated claims in advertising, so reasonable people wouldn't believe that these statements ("puffs") are literal facts. However, empirical evidence on the effectiveness of puffery is mixed. Some research suggests that the public might expect advertisers to be able to prove the truth of superlative claims, and other research indicates that reasonable people do not believe such claims. This is particularly important when advertising to children who might not know the difference between fact and opinion. Noted advertising scholar Ivan Preston does not think all puffs deserve to be protected legally as he explains in the *A Matter of Principle* feature that follows.

Comparative Advertising   We're used to seeing advertisers take on their competition in an ad—Mac vs. PC, Dunkin' Donuts vs. Starbucks, Campbell's Soup vs. Progresso. Although it is perfectly legitimate to compare a marketer's product favorably against a competitor, regulations govern the use of **comparative advertising** if it can be challenged as misleading.

Advertisers face the common threat that competitors will misrepresent their products. Although no one expects a competitor to be totally objective, advertisers have legal recourse to object to unfair comparisons. U.S. law permits awards of damages from an advertiser who "misrepresents the nature, characteristics, qualities, or geographic origin in comparative advertising." Recently, a New York court granted Weight Watchers International a temporary restraining order against Jenny Craig, claiming that Jenny Craig's advertising made deceptive claims about its success rate.[17]

Advertisers who engage in comparative advertising know that research in support of their competitive claims must be impeccable. The Dunkin' Donuts ad compares its coffee to Starbucks and backs up its claim with a national taste test.

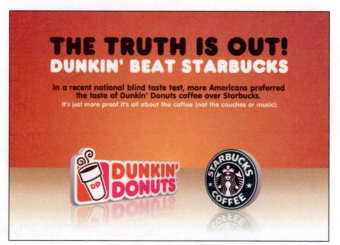

Dunkin' Donuts hopes to convince coffee drinkers to switch from Starbucks based on results from a national taste test.

Principle
Advertising claims are unethical if they are false, misleading, or deceptive.

Principle
Puffery may be legal, but if it turns off the target audience nothing is gained by using such a strategy.

Preston on Puffery

Ivan L. Preston, *Professor Emeritus, University of Wisconsin*

I believe some forms of puffery ought to be prohibited. Let me explain by first defining what it is. Puffs are statements that evaluate and present values about a thing rather than facts that state what it is or does. Puffs are offered as the opinions of the source presenting them. In the regulatory context they are almost always called *puffery* or *puffs*, but evaluations or opinions is what they are. Here's a list of six varieties of puffs, listed by strength:

1. *The Strongest Is Best* That means no competitor equals you. In the United States, Nestlé's says it makes the very best chocolate, and Gillette is the best a man can get, and Goodyear has the best tires in the world. Other ways of saying *best* include terms such as *most comfortable, longest lasting, tastiest*—anything that says you're alone at the top of the list.
2. *Best Possible* As in "Nothing cleans stains better than Clorox." This type is also a claim to be at the top, except to claim that nobody is better allows for others to be just as good. It's a clever claim, because research shows that many consumers think it means better than all others.
3. *Better* You are better than another, or better than many, or just better. The pain reliever Advil says: Advil works better. If it explicitly says better than all others, it goes in category 1, so this number 3 is for claims that don't claim explicitly to be better than all others. It's often used when competing mainly against just one other brand.

4. *Good and Specially Good* The next two categories are both Good, but Specially Good involves strong statements such as *great*. Weber says its barbecue grill is "great" outdoors. Coty calls its perfume "extraordinary." Many products claim to be wonderful or fantastic; Bayer aspirin works wonders. But these claims do not say best or better explicitly.
5. *Good Is Just Plain Good* An insurance company says "You're in good hands with Allstate." Campbell's Soup is "M'm!, M'm!, Good!" Those are weaker claims, lower on the scale.
6. *Subjective Claims* These statements use words that are not explicitly evaluative, but people are likely to take them as valuations. A sports network refers to itself as "Sports Heaven." A candy maker says, "There's a smile in every Hershey bar."

I hypothesize that evidence from consumers would show that the strongest puffs, especially the first category, are most likely to lead to consumer perceptions that are false and can produce deception. Those at the bottom, especially number 6, are least likely to produce such problems. Examples such as the smile in the candy bar, I think are more likely to be seen as fanciful or joking rather than serious.

Puffery in the United States can be factually false and legal. The only puffery I'm talking about prohibiting legally is the false kind. Puffery is an issue only when deception is an issue, and deception is an issue only when there's a claim. Not all ad content is a claim. A lot of it is intended only to get attention so that consumers will stay with the ad and see the part where there is a claim. Other ad content shows sheer enthusiasm, such as appeals to action like "Take a look at this." So remember, no claim, no problem.

Under the law, companies/plaintiffs are required to prove five elements to win a false-advertising lawsuit about an ad making a comparative claim:

1. False statements have been made about either product.
2. The ads actually deceived or had the tendency to deceive a substantial segment of the audience.
3. The deception was "material" or meaningful. In other words, the plaintiff must show that the false ad claim is likely to influence purchasing decisions.
4. Falsely advertised goods are sold in interstate commerce.
5. The suing company has been or likely will be injured as a result of the false statements, either by loss of sales or loss of goodwill.

In addition to the federal laws, consumers also may rely on state laws governing unfair competition and false ad claims if the consumer is the victim of a false comparative claim.

Endorsements and Demonstrations A popular advertising strategy is the use of a spokesperson who endorses a brand. That's a perfectly legal strategy, unless the endorser doesn't actually use the product. An **endorsement** or **testimonial** is any advertising message that consumers believe reflects the opinions, beliefs, or experiences of an individual, group, or institution. However, if consumers can reasonably ascertain that a message does not reflect the announcer's opinion, the message isn't an endorsement and may even be misleading.

Consider the billboard of President Obama wearing a Weatherproof-brand jacket during his visit to the Great Wall of China. The company put the image on its website for a time and promoted "the Obama jacket" until the White House asked that they take down the billboard. It claimed the ad was misleading because the company never received approval or an endorsement from the president.[18]

Weatherproof, an apparel company stirred up controversy with its Time Square billboard showing President Obama wearing what looked to be one of its jackets. Do you think this was a misleading use of a public image?

The increasing prominence of digital media raises another ethical dilemma. Is it acceptable for company representatives to pose as consumers or pay bloggers to post endorsements as customer reviews online? The Word of Mouth Marketing Association says no. Its ethics code[19] explicitly prohibits consumers from taking cash from manufacturers, suppliers, or their representatives for making recommendations, reviews, or endorsements, unless full disclosure is provided. Do you think it was ethical that Ford loaned 100 bloggers its new Fiesta[20] to drive and presumably chat about on the Internet? Under what conditions? We'll probably see lots more examples of **blogola**, also referred to as flogging (sponsored conversations), in the future.[21]

Federal regulations require that endorsers must be qualified by experience or training to make judgments, and they must actually use the product. If endorsers are comparing competing brands, they must have tried those brands as well. Those who endorse a product improperly may be liable if the government determines there is deception.

Product demonstrations in television advertising also must not mislead consumers. This mandate is especially difficult for advertisements of food products because such factors as hot studio lights and the length of time needed to shoot the commercial can make the product look unappetizing. Think about the problems of shooting ice cream under hot lights. Because milk looks gray on television, advertisers often substitute a mixture of glue and water. The question is whether the demonstration falsely upgrades the consumers' perception of the advertised brand. The FTC evaluates this kind of deception on a case-by-case basis.

One technique some advertisers use to sidestep restrictions on demonstrations is to insert disclaimers or "supers," verbal or written words in the ad that indicate exceptions to the advertising claim made. You've probably seen car commercials that start with beauty shots of the product. Suddenly, the message is less clear; for several seconds five different, often lengthy, disclaimers flash on the screen in tiny, eye-straining type, including "See dealers for details and guaranteed claim form" and "Deductibles and restrictions apply."

Product-Related Issues   Marketers need to consider carefully what they choose to produce and advertise. Some key areas of concern include controversial products, unhealthy or dangerous products such as alcohol and tobacco, and prescription drugs. The decision to produce the product lies with the marketing department and the company's business objectives, but advertising is frequently in the spotlight because of its visibility.

Before an agency can create an ad for a client, it must consider the nature of the client company and its mission, marketing objectives, reputation, available resources, competition, and, most importantly, product line. Can the agency and its staff honestly promote the products being advertised? What would you do if you were a copywriter for an agency that has a political client you don't support? Several agencies have resigned from profitable tobacco advertising accounts because of the medical evidence about the harm cigarettes cause. In cases where the agency works on a controversial account, there are still ethical ways to approach the business.

Controversial Products   Marketing communication reflects the marketing and business ethics of its clients and, because of its visibility, sometimes gets the blame for selling controversial, unsafe,

Principle

The ethics of selling a controversial or unsafe product lies with the marketing department; however, marketing communication may be criticized because it is the visible face of marketing.

or dangerous products. For example, products that were once considered not suitable to advertise, such as firearms, gambling, hemorrhoid preparations, feminine hygiene products, pantyhose and bras, laxatives, condoms, and remedies for male erectile dysfunctions have become acceptable, although advertising for them may still be offensive to some people.

Some products are controversial for political reasons or because of environmental issues. Oil companies, for example, have been criticized for their practices and are constantly trying to prove their role as good corporate citizens. The Shell ad, which comes from Iceland, is an example of a company that is changing its practices to deliver on its social responsibility mission.

Unhealthy or Dangerous Products   One way to make ethical decisions is to choose the route that minimizes potential harm. Because there has been so much negative publicity about the health effects of eating a steady diet of heavily processed food, food companies, particularly fast-food producers such as McDonald's and KFC, have reacted to charges of culpability in the nation's obesity problem. McDonald's slimmed down Ronald McDonald, added healthier choices to its menu, and moved away from using cholesterol-causing saturated fats when making French fries. Disney launched efforts to serve healthier food in its theme parks as an effort to improve the diets of children. Wendy's reduced the amount of trans fats it uses for cooking.[22]

One of the most heated advertising issues in recent years has been about tobacco advertising. Although Congress passed a law that banned cigarette advertising on television and radio starting in 1971, that did not resolve the issue. Proponents of the ban on cigarette advertising argue that since cigarettes have been shown to cause cancer as well as other illnesses, encouraging tobacco use promotes sickness, injury, or death for the smoker and those inhaling secondhand smoke. They argue that further restricting advertising on those products would result in fewer sales and fewer health problems for America as a whole.

Opponents of advertising bans counter with the argument that prohibiting truthful, nondeceptive advertising for a legal product is unconstitutional and a violation of their free speech rights. They feel that censorship is more of a problem than advertising a legal product, even if it is unhealthy.

In recognition of the growing public concerns about cigarette marketing, tobacco companies have voluntarily curbed their advertising and pulled ads from magazines with high levels of youth readership and from most outdoor billboards. Most major tobacco companies also run anti-smoking ads aimed at teenagers. Philip Morris has virtually stopped advertising and shifted

SHOWCASE

To solve a local crisis in Iceland with its image, Shell used a campaign based on the slogan "Shell—with you all the way." The campaign demonstrated how Shell is involved and "travels" with customers from youth to adulthood, from work to home, from the present to the future—shaping the society that people want to build.

This ad was contributed by Ingvi Logason, principal in HÉR&NÚ, Reykjavik, Iceland. A graduate of Western Florida University, his work was nominated for inclusion in this book by Professor Tom Groth.

its budget to events and other promotions that reach its customers, rather than trying to use advertising to reach new customers.

In 1996 a governmental agency established a set of restrictions applicable to tobacco advertisers. Among these were a ban on outdoor ads within 1,000 feet of a school or playground and a rule that limited ads to black-and-white, text only, in magazines with 55 percent readership under the age of 18. The restrictions also stipulated that $150 million be provided to fund anti-smoking ads targeting children. Following the 1996 action, most states have received initial payments from the $206 billion master settlement agreement to be supplied by tobacco companies over a 25-year period. Approximately half the money goes to fund TV and print ads warning children about the dangers of smoking; the other half pays for promotions such as loyalty cards, all-expenses-paid teen summits, and various events. The anti-smoking *truth®* campaign aimed at teens was supported through these efforts.

Banning tobacco advertising is not unique to the United States. Many other countries have even stronger restrictions against such advertising. A near-total advertising ban in the United Kingdom took effect in early 2003, and similar restrictions were launched in the European Union two years later. Canada and New Zealand have banned tobacco advertising, and Australia and Malaysia have prohibited nearly all forms of it.

The ethics of advertising liquor is another concern. The biggest issue for the spirits industry is charges of advertising to underage drinkers. In 2003 the FTC became so concerned that it asked several major liquor producers to detail their marketing practices and target audiences and to explain how they had implemented the promises made in a 1999 report to Congress. About the same time a lawsuit filed in the District of Columbia charged that alcohol marketers were actively engaged in trying to establish brand loyalty among underage consumers.

Liquor executives contend that they follow voluntary advertising guidelines to avoid images and time slots that appeal to kids. That stance has been hard to keep, however, because every major brand is trying to win over young consumers.

The Distilled Spirits Council, a trade organization representing producers and marketers of distilled spirits sold in the United States, offers a model for industry self-regulation. Its Code of Responsible Practices for Beverage Alcohol Advertising and Marketing encourages members to follow the guidelines set forth in the code when promoting their products.

For many years companies themselves and the four biggest networks—ABC, NBC, CBS, and Fox—imposed a voluntary restriction on television advertising for liquor. However, in November 1996 the voluntary ban was dropped by the Distilled Spirits Council of the United States, after Seagram's ran a commercial on an ABC affiliate. Commercials for distilled spirits are increasingly visible on television.[23]

The beer industry has been the target of strong criticism for several years. Although it is unlikely that beer advertising will be banned, some companies sensitive to public opinion have initiated proactive programs that educate and discourage underage drinkers.

Prescription drugs are another problem area. In 1997, the government loosened its controls on pharmaceutical advertising. As a result, the amount of prescription drug advertising has skyrocketed. While these print and TV ads have proven very successful in terms of increased sales, various consumer groups, government agencies, and insurance companies have been quite critical of them. In one study, for example, the National Institute of Health Care Management found that direct-to-consumer prescription advertising has led to an increase in requests for costlier drugs, when the less expensive generic drug would be just as effective.[24]

Also, some doctors claim that they are being pressured to write inappropriate prescriptions because their patients are influenced by the drug ad claims. Other doctors say they appreciate that the advertising has caused consumers to become more active in managing their own health and more informed about their drug options.

In recent health care reform efforts, some lawmakers targeted the $4.3 billion ad sector for elimination because they believe these ads contribute to the high cost of health care.[25] Whether this will ever materialize is up in the air. In the meantime, this advertising is legal. For guidelines pertaining to advertising prescription drugs, see the U.S. Food and Drug Administration's website: *www.fda.gov/Drugs/ResourcesForYou/Consumers/PrescriptionDrugAdvertising/default.htm.*

Emerging Issues   One study surveyed industry leaders to see if they thought ethical issues changed over time.[26] Their answer: Traditional ethical issues, such as the importance of being honest and respectful in communication, are essentially the same, but different ones are emerging as a result of the changing digital media landscape. Industry leaders explained the risk of not telling the truth was low in traditional media because so many checks and balances exist in the forms of laws, guidelines, and other policing mechanisms. The checks and balances related to the Internet and blogosphere, however, aren't as well established, and a consensus about what constitutes ethical behavior hasn't fully developed for the Web.

Also marketers' loss of control over their messages, transparency, and privacy on the Internet are key factors relating to ethical practices. The leaders noted the difficulty and complexity related to developing regulation and controls for digital media practices like blogola and paid viral marketing. Photographers complain when their images are taken from sites like Flickr and used in ads without their permission. It's particularly a problem with user-generated ads.

Social Responsibility, Branding, and Integrity   There is even an IMC dimension to social responsibility. **Cause marketing,** which is marketing that supports a good cause such as Habitat for Humanity, is a common practice for many companies. Companies can send employee teams to work on food banks or homeless shelters, or the company can donate money or sponsor fund-raisers—but those efforts are often short term.

On a higher level of social responsibility is the use of **mission marketing,** which refers to marketing that aligns the basic business practices and position of a brand with some cause such as the environment or sustainability. This practice adds value to a brand and leads to a positive brand perception, as well as brand loyalty and stakeholder commitment. Ben & Jerry's, Tom's of Maine, and the Body Shop are all supporters of good environmental practices in sourcing their ingredients. Starbucks has become a supporter of ethically grown and traded coffee beans through its "Shared Planet" program. In other words, it's more than a short-term support of a cause—these commitments are deeply embedded in the essence and operations of the brand and they lead to a more passionate brand loyalty from all their stakeholders.

Mission marketing demonstrates our **Fourth Principle of IMC:** *Integration equals integrity.* You may not know this, but the Latin for both *integration* and *integrity* come from the same root words, *integrare,* "to make whole," and *integritas,* "wholeness." In IMC, when brand communication is managed as a whole (i.e., when all of the pieces and parts work together), then it achieves integrity. A brand with integrity is driven by a singular vision and that can, and should, include good citizenship.

Green marketing, for example, is more than just an advertising theme that resonates as consumers become concerned about questions of global warming. It can also drive business decisions and impact product design and packaging for everything from diapers to cars to plastic water bottles. Companies concerned with this issue calculate the pollution created by their products—in manufacturing, use, and disposal. Walmart, for example, announced in 2009 that it would provide environmental impact information for all of its products.[27]

Fourth Principle of IMC

Integration equals integrity.

WHAT ARE COMMUNICATORS' ETHICAL RESPONSIBILITIES?

By now you are familiar with many of the ethical and social issues facing marketing communication. How does this involve you? This section will give you a better understanding about what we mean by ethics and provide some decision-making tools as you encounter ethical dilemmas. Let's start by considering a Benetton campaign that challenged personal and professional ethics.

Ethics are the "shoulds" and "oughts" of behavior. Ethics are the "right thing to do." Defining what is right can be challenging. What one person says is right isn't always what others define to be appropriate. Ethics and morals are closely related, but they are not synonymous. **Morals** are frameworks for right actions and are more the domain of religion and philosophy. Examples of moral systems are the Ten Commandments from the Judeo-Christian religious tradition or the Buddhists' Eightfold Path. These moral systems provide a framework for behavior.

Although ethics reflect what is right and wrong, the difficulty lies in making choices from equally compelling or competing options, as in the Benetton example—how should you behave when the answer is unclear? We know that doing the right thing is ethical, but it's sometimes hard to know what the right thing is. Sometimes there's no one right answer. Consider, for example, this situation: You are a graphic designer. You want to use a picture you found on the Internet, and

PRACTICAL TIPS

Brilliant or Offensive Advertising?

Fred Beard, Professor of Advertising, *University of Oklahoma*

A photo of a priest kissing a nun. An emaciated AIDS victim at the moment of death, attended by his distraught family. An African guerrilla holding an AK-47 and a human leg bone. A dead soldier's bloody uniform.

So began Italian clothing maker Benetton's selfless, noble, and global advertising effort to encourage brotherhood and condemn indifference to human suffering. Or, depending on whom else you ask, so began a cynical and self-serving effort to take advantage of the world's pain and suffering with a purpose no more noble than selling T-shirts and sweaters, with shock and calculated offense being the primary tactics.

When the "United Colors of Benetton" campaign started in 1990, creative director Oliviero Toscani was given free rein. What followed was a steady stream of symbolic, shocking, and often upsetting ads that were only identifiable as Benetton's by a small, green logo. Toscani's 18-year tenure with Benetton ended in 2000, following a firestorm of controversy over the "We, On Death Row" campaign, which was designed to draw attention to the "plight" of 26 convicted murderers in the United States.

Why would an advertiser purposely want to offend people? Benetton certainly isn't alone. The use of "shockvertising" has grown as advertisers have learned that controversy encourages attention and often creates a media buzz far surpassing the reach and frequency of the original media buys. Ethically speaking, though, should advertisers care if they offend people?

The fact is, few people either inside or outside advertising would argue that the presentation of a potentially offensive message is always morally wrong. What questions should we ask to be able to decide for ourselves whether or not an advertising campaign like the "United Colors of Benetton" crosses the line? Here's a start:

- Is it inherently wrong to present words and images that will undoubtedly offend most people if the goal is to draw attention to humanitarian issues and problems?
- Does it make a difference if the goal of widely offensive advertising is solely to sell products?
- Do people have a right not to see ads that offend them? Because some media, such as TV and outdoor advertising, are more intrusive than others, does the medium make a difference?
- What do advertising codes of ethics say about audience offense? Are advertisers professionally and morally obligated to follow them?
- To whom do advertisers owe the most responsibility—their own organizations and stakeholders, society, consumers, other advertising professionals?

Considering these questions, where do you come down on the Benetton ads? Should the company have censored them—or let them run? What would you have done if you were the Benetton marketing manager?

you don't want to copy it unethically. How much do you have to change the digital picture before it becomes your own?

Determining what constitutes ethical behavior happens on many levels. Individually, advertisers call on their own moral upbringing. The various marcom industries provide codes of ethics and standards of self-regulation. The government helps regulate marcom practices through legal means.

Personal and Professional Ethics

Ethical decisions are usually complex and involve navigating a moral maze of conflicting forces: strategy versus ethics, costs versus ethics, effectiveness versus ethics, etc. They demand the ability to do what ethicists call "moral reasoning."[28] In the end, if you are a responsible professional making a decision about a strategy or an execution tactic to be used in an advertisement, you must be aware of industry standards as well as ethical questions that underlie the core issues we have discussed in this chapter.

More importantly, personal judgment and moral reasoning rest on an intuitive sense of right and wrong, a moral compass that tells you when an idea is misleading, insensitive, too over the top, or too manipulative. And then you need the courage to speak up and tell your colleagues. Do you think that the Benetton advertising passes your personal standards for good advertising?

Professionals in advertising by and large see themselves as ethical people. However, polls indicate that the public tends to see them differently. In a recent Honesty and Ethics Poll conducted by the Gallup organization, advertising practitioners ranked near the bottom, with nurses, doctors and pharmacists at the top.[29] Advertising practitioners ranked ahead of HMO managers and car salesmen. (Interestingly, members of Congress and Senators ranked lower than advertisers.) That poll suggests the public is not persuaded that advertising professionals are guided by

A MATTER OF PRACTICE

Advertising Gets No Respect!

Steve Edwards, Associate Professor of Advertising, *Southern Methodist University*

Why is the profession of advertising ranked just above being a used-car salesman on surveys of ethical practices? Why should you care? Advertising has tremendous power to shape our attitudes about our world and ourselves, inform people of important ideas, and change behavior. Yet, advertising students will graduate and get jobs paying less than students in finance, accounting, marketing, or engineering. Why?

Advertising surrounds us and is accessible everywhere and, as with anything that is plentiful, is undervalued. If you have water flowing from the tap, let it flow. But if you were in a desert with a single bottle of water that same resource becomes precious.

People tend to underestimate the effects of advertising on themselves, while overestimating its effects on others. And, while consumers enjoy the information or entertainment advertising provides, they underestimate the knowledge and skills needed to advertise effectively and thus devalue the profession.

Professions are strong to the degree that (1) they are identified and differentiated by their specialized knowledge, (2) they educate new members, and (3) they make the value of their knowledge/work clear to the wider society. Think about why doctors are well respected.

Strengthening the profession of advertising starts with you. Become an advocate for the field. Start by (1) developing an understanding of how advertising affects society both positively and negatively, (2) be able to define the specialized knowledge of advertising that others have not studied, and (3) educate others about the power of the industry.

Specifically, pay attention to the economic versus social effects of advertising. Criticisms of advertising often focus on specific ads that encourage socially undesirable behaviors (overconsumption in general or underage drinking), target impressionable children, or stereotype certain societal groups. Anti-consumerist organizations such as Adbusters.org promote "buy nothing day" and offer social criticism of advertising using spoof ads. However, people rarely think of the importance of communication messages focused on hygiene, poverty, AIDS, obesity, recycling, alcoholism, literacy, etc., but it is through advertising that we learn about such things.

It is also through advertising that consumers learn that BMW is *The Ultimate Driving Machine*, or that the Toyota Prius "helps save gas and helps the environment." The choices we make as consumers are based on the fundamental values we deem important. And yes, advertising, along with other large societal institutions (e.g., religion or government), helps set or reinforce an agenda for what we as a society value. But it is due in part to advertising that consumers are educated about products in the marketplace and, by making purchase decisions, can force companies to improve products or lower prices to compete.

Advertising is a powerful force and should be respected, but advocates are needed.

Where are you in this debate about the value of advertising? Do you see yourself as an advocate or a critic? If you were at a party, could you defend yourself as a student of advertising—perhaps even an advertising professional?

AAAA's Creative Code

We, the members of the American Association of Advertising Agencies, in addition to supporting and obeying the laws and legal regulations pertaining to advertising, undertake to extend and broaden the application of high ethical standards. Specifically, we will not knowingly create advertising that contains:

- False or misleading statements or exaggerations, visual or verbal
- Testimonials that do not reflect the real opinion of the individual(s) involved
- Price claims that are misleading
- Claims insufficiently supported or that distort the true meaning or practicable application of statements made by professional or scientific authority
- Statements, suggestions, or pictures offensive to public decency or minority segments of the population.

We recognize that there are areas that are subject to honestly different interpretations and judgment. Nevertheless, we agree not to recommend to an advertiser, and to discourage the use of, advertising that is in poor or questionable taste or that is deliberately irritating through aural or visual content or presentation.

Comparative advertising shall be governed by the same standards of truthfulness, claim substantiation, tastefulness, etc. as apply to other types of advertising.

FIGURE 3.1
The AAAA's Creative Code

Source: Courtesy of the American Association of Advertising Agencies. Reprinted with permission.

ethical standards. Read the *A Matter of Practice* feature and begin to think about how you might improve society with your life's work.

Industry standards can provide help with a decision about what is or is not ethically correct. Many professions write a **code of ethics** to help guide practitioners toward ethical behavior. Advertising is no different. Professional ethics are often expressed in a code of standards that identifies how professionals in the industry should respond when faced with ethical questions. The American Association of Advertising Agencies (AAAA) begins its "Standards of Practice" with the line: "We hold that a responsibility of advertising agencies is to be a constructive force in business." The core of the statement, the Creative Code, is reproduced in Figure 3.1.

In the wake of highly public business scandals such as the collapse of Enron in 2001, many firms are responding with their own codes of ethics. If this subject interests you, you can look up these codes in a collection compiled by the Center for the Study of Ethics in the Professions at the Illinois Institute of Technology (*http://ethics.iit.edu/codes/*).

International Standards and Codes

Standards of professional behavior are not found only in the United States or other Western countries. Singapore, for example, has an ad code specifically designed to prevent Western-influenced advertising from impairing Asian family values. Malaysia's requirement that all ads be produced in the country not only keeps that country's advertising aligned with its own standards and cultural values, it also cuts back dramatically on the number of foreign ads seen by its public. Advertisers who violate the ethical code of conduct in Brazil can be fined up to $500,000 or imprisoned for up to five years. This punishment would certainly prompt an advertiser to be careful.

In the Netherlands, industry members have encouraged the formation of an "ethical office" to oversee all agencies, advertisers, and media. That office is responsible for reviewing advertisements to ensure that they comply with the Dutch Advertising Code and general ethical principles. In Swedish advertising agencies, an executive known as the "responsible editor" is trained and experienced in marketing law; that editor reviews all advertisements and promotional materials to ensure that they are legally and ethically acceptable.

Ethical Decision-Making Tools

Codes of ethics can be helpful to guide your actions. However, they are broad statements and do not explain what you should do in every circumstance you encounter. Developing a strong personal and professional sense of right and wrong is a prerequisite to being able to exercise responsible judgment when you're confronted with an ethical dilemma. We include some tools that you might find helpful. The *Practical Tips* box lists some questions that might prompt clearer thinking about murky ethical problems.

PRACTICAL TIPS

An Ethics Checklist for Marketing Communicators

1. In terms of its social impact, does this advertisement . . .
   - violate public standards of good taste?
   - reinforce negative stereotypes?
   - damage people's self-image and create insecurities?
   - promote materialism?
   - create false wants and false hope?
   - contribute to cultural pollution?
   - market dangerous products?
2. In terms of its strategic decisions, does this advertisement . . .
   - target vulnerable groups?
   - harm children?
   - appeal to base motivations such as envy and greed?
   - drive demand for unnecessary purchases?
   - prey on people's fears unnecessarily?
   - undercut people's self-image and self-concept?
   - make unsubstantiated claims?
3. In terms of its tactics, does this advertisement . . .
   - use ideas, words, or images that are offensive or insensitive?
   - use inappropriate stereotypes?
   - manipulate people's emotions unnecessarily?
   - make false, deceptive, or misleading claims?
   - use unfair comparisons?
   - create endorsements or demonstrations that exaggerate or lie?
   - use unnecessary scare or shock tactics?
   - use puffery?

One model that might guide you is the TARES Test of Ethical Advertising.[30] The five-part test defines action-guiding principles directed toward making ethical decisions in the realm of professional persuasion. The communication passes the test if it is **t**ruthful, **a**uthentic, **r**espectful, **e**quitable and **s**ocially (TARES) responsible. These specific questions can guide your thinking:

1. Are the ad claims in the message *Truthful*? Are visual and verbal claims truthful? Are omissions deceptive?
2. Is the claim an *Authentic* one? Is there a sincere need for the product? Are the reasons given for purchasing the product genuinely appealing?
3. Does the ad treat the receiver with *Respect*? Does it include inaccurate stereotypes or degrading language?
4. Is there *Equity* between the sender and the receiver? Would the receiver of the ad need to be unusually well informed or brilliant to understand the ad? Is some hidden prejudice masked within the ad?
5. Is the ad *Socially* responsible?

There are other models. Alternatively, you could use the Potter Box (see Figure 3.2), which asks communication decision makers to consider four aspects of the dilemma. They need to (1) identify and understand the *facts,* (2) outline the *values* inherent in the decision, (3) apply relevant philosophical *principles,* and (4) articulate the competing *loyalties.* Using this model assumes you have some understanding of philosophical principles. None of these tools will give you a single, right answer. They will, however, help you examine the problem from a number of angles and think systematically about the problem.

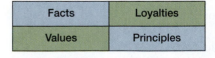

Facts	Loyalties
Values	Principles

FIGURE 3.2

The Potter Box
The Potter Box is a tool that allows you to analyze an ethical situation and puzzle out the relationships between and among facts, values, principles, and loyalties.

Source: Ralph B. Potter, "The Logic of Moral Argument," in Toward a Discipline of Social Ethics, ed. Paul Deats (Boston: Boston University Press, 1972).

WHY AND HOW IS ADVERTISING REGULATED?

While it would be ideal if individuals and companies always made socially responsible choices and everyone could agree that those choices resulted in proper actions, sometimes that does not occur and there is a need for regulatory or legal action. The company may decide it is acceptable to advertise certain products, and the government may decide otherwise.

Various systems are in place to monitor the social responsibility of advertising and other brand communication, including laws, government regulatory bodies, professional oversight groups, and industry self-regulation. Figure 3.3 identifies the organizations with oversight responsibility for advertising and groups them in terms of five specific categories: government, media, industry, public or community groups, and the competition. Let's examine each of those systems.

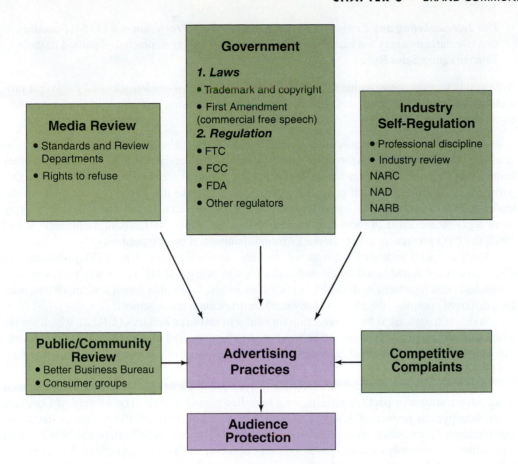

FIGURE 3.3
Advertising Review
and Regulation

Marketing Communication's Legal Environment

Making and enforcing laws are the domain of government. Congress makes laws, while courts interpret those laws in specific situations to create case law. Regulatory agencies in the executive branch of the federal government also play a role by enforcing laws related to advertising. The following list summarizes important advertising legislation, most of which shows the growing authority of regulatory bodies, such as the Federal Trade Commission (FTC) to regulate advertising:

Key Advertising Legislation

- *Pure Food and Drug Act (1906)* Forbids the manufacture, sale, or transport of adulterated or fraudulently labeled foods and drugs in interstate commerce. Supplanted by the Food, Drug and Cosmetic Act of 1938; amended by Food Additives Amendment in 1958 and Kefauver-Harris Amendment in 1962.
- *Federal Trade Commission Act (1914)* Establishes the commission, a body of specialists with broad powers to investigate and to issue cease-and-desist orders to enforce Section 5, which declares that "unfair methods of competition in commerce are unlawful."
- *Wheeler-Lea Amendment (1938)* Prohibits unfair and deceptive acts and practices regardless of whether competition is injured; places advertising of foods and drugs under FTC jurisdiction.
- *Lanham Act (1947)* Provides protection for trademarks (slogans and brand names) from competitors and also encompasses false advertising.
- *Magnuson-Moss Warranty/FTC Improvement Act (1975)* Authorizes the FTC to determine rules concerning consumer warranties and provides for consumer access to means of redress, such as the "class action" suit. Also expands FTC regulatory powers over unfair or deceptive acts or practices and allows it to require restitution for deceptively written warranties costing the consumer more than $5.
- *FTC Improvement Act (1980)* Provides the House of Representatives and Senate jointly with veto power over FTC regulation rules. Enacted to limit the FTC's powers to regulate "unfairness" issues in designing trade regulation rules on advertising.

- *The Telemarketing and Consumer Fraud Act and Abuse Protection Act (1994)* Specifies that telemarketers may not call anyone who requests not to be contacted. Resulted in the Telemarketing Sales Rules.

In this section, we examine two pivotal areas of case law—trademarks and copyright protection and the First Amendment—as they pertain to advertising and other areas of marketing communication.

Trademark and Copyright Protection   A **trademark** is a brand, corporate or store name, or distinctive symbol that identifies the seller's brand and thus differentiates it from the brands of other sellers. A trademark can be registered through the Patent and Trademark Office (PTO) of the Department of Commerce, which gives the organization exclusive use of the mark, as long as the trademark is maintained as an identification of a specific product. Registered trademarks enjoy more legal protection than those that are not registered. Under the Lanham Trademark Act of 1947, the PTO protects unique trademarks from infringement by competitors.

Even an audio trademark is protected, as a case in the European Union (EU) illustrates. A distinctive audio sound based on the noise of a cock crowing and the way it was represented in Dutch had been registered with the EU's trademark office. When this sound trademark was used by a different company, the first company sued for trademark infringement.

A recent trademark issue is protection for **uniform resource locators (URLs),** which are Internet domain names. URLs need to be registered to be protected just like any other trademark. They are issued on a first-come, first-served basis for any domain name not identical to an existing brand name.

A **copyright** gives an organization the exclusive right to use or reproduce original work, such as an advertisement or package design, for a specified period of time. The Library of Congress controls copyright protection. Copyrighting of coined words, phrases, illustrations, characters, and photographs can offer some protection from other advertisers who borrow too heavily from competitors. Commonly used designs or symbols, however, cannot be copyrighted. Nor can ideas be copyrighted. For a copyright to be obtained, a work must be fixed in a tangible medium. Copyright infringement can occur when a product is used in an ad without proper permission. A sweet example: The maker of Peeps, those marshmallow chicks and bunnies, sued American Greetings for using pictures of Peeps without authorization.[31]

Marketing Communication and the First Amendment   The most basic federal law that governs advertising and other forms of marketing communication is the First Amendment to the U.S. Constitution. The First Amendment states that Congress shall make no law "abridging the freedom of speech, or of the press." How have courts applied the First Amendment to advertising? First Amendment protection extends to **commercial speech,** which is speech that promotes commercial activity. However, that protection is not absolute; it is often restricted. The Supreme Court generally applies a different standard to commercial speech than it does to other forms of speech, such as that enjoyed by the press and filmmakers, because the conditions are different for different forms of speech.

Protection of advertising as commercial speech has varied over the years. In 1980, in conjunction with its ruling on *Central Hudson Gas and Electric v. Public Service Commission of New York,* the Supreme Court established a test that determines to what extent the government can restrict advertising. This decision also stipulated the degree to which advertising is considered commercial speech, although a recent 2010 Supreme Court decision enhanced the free speech rights of corporations, particularly for political speech.

A number of cases have attempted to change the common view of advertising as commercial speech. Most notably, the Supreme Court struck down a Massachusetts law that restricted tobacco advertising. Free speech advocates applauded the decision while critics of tobacco companies lamented. Although no one expects advertising to have the same constitutional protection of free speech that is given to individuals, courts throughout the country are narrowing the gap.

The Supreme Court permits some restrictions on commercial speech. For example, the court has held that false or misleading commercial speech can be banned. Even truthful commercial speech can be restricted if the government can prove the public good demands such restrictions.[32] The courts have also ruled that such acts as the federal ban on junk faxes is valid and that businesses' right to commercial speech does not include printing their advertisements on other people's fax machines.

Essentially, the Supreme Court has ruled that only truthful commercial speech is protected, not misleading or deceptive statements. Because the nation's courts continue to reinterpret how the First Amendment applies in different cases, advertisers need to keep close track of legal developments. The following list summarizes First Amendment decisions by the U.S. Supreme Court that affect advertising:

First Amendment Rulings on Commercial Speech

- *Valentine v. Chrestensen (1942)* The Constitution protects free expression but not purely commercial advertising. The Court seemed to be saying that advertising isn't "speech" under the First Amendment, and it's questionable whether the Court actually intended the "purely commercial" wording to have any real meaning.
- *Virginia State Board of Pharmacy v. Virginia Citizens Consumer Council (1976)* States cannot prohibit pharmacists from advertising prices of prescription drugs because the free flow of information is indispensable.
- *Central Hudson Gas & Electric Corporation v. Public Service Commission of New York (1980)* Public Service Commission's prohibition of promotional advertising by utilities is found to be unconstitutional, placing limitations on government regulation of unlawful, non-deceptive advertising.
- *Posadas de Puerto Rico Associates v. Tourism Company of Puerto Rico (1986)* Puerto Rican law banned advertising of gambling casinos to residents of Puerto Rico. A significant point in this case was Associate Justice of the Supreme Court Rehnquist's comment that the greater power of a legislature to ban gambling altogether most certainly included the lesser power to ban only the advertising of gambling.
- *Cincinnati v. Discovery Network (1993)* The Court ruled that the Cincinnati City Council violated the First Amendment's protection of commercial speech when it banned news racks of advertising brochures from city streets for aesthetic and safety reasons, while permitting newspaper vending machines.
- *Edenfield v. Fane (1993)* The Court ruled that Florida's prohibition of telephone solicitation by accountants was unconstitutional.
- *U.S. v. Edge Broadcasting (1993)* Broadcasting gambling is a vice, so the legislature has the greater power to ban it along with the lesser power to ban advertising of it.
- *44 Liquormart, Inc. v. Rhode Island (1996)* The Court ruled that two Rhode Island statutes that banned advertising for alcohol prices were unconstitutional.
- *Glickman v. Wileman Bros. & Elliott, Inc. (1997)* The Court ruled that a mandatory generic advertising program, issued in accord with marketing orders of the Agricultural Marketing Act, did not infringe on the free speech rights of fruit growers.
- *New York Times Co. v. Sullivan (1964)* The Court ruled that the First Amendment protects criticism of the government that appeared in advertising even though it included some minor factual errors.
- *Rubin v. Coors Brewing (1995)* The Court reaffirmed the regulation of commercial speech when it ruled that Coors could publish the alcohol content on its label despite the Federal Alcohol Administration Act prohibition of doing so.
- *Greater New Orleans Broadcasters Assn. v. U.S. (1999)* The Court ruled that federal law prohibits some, but not all broadcast advertising of lotteries and casino gambling.
- *Citizens United v. Federal Election Commission (2010)* The Court ruled that government may not ban political spending by corporations in candidate elections.

International Laws and Regulations   As advertisers, agencies, and media become more global, it will be imperative for the players to understand local laws in the countries in which they operate. Marketing practices, such as pricing and price advertising, vary in their legal and regulatory restrictions.

Some product categories, such as over-the-counter (OTC) drugs, are particularly difficult to work with because regulations about their marketing and advertising are different in every country. Advertising for certain types of products is banned. Thailand prohibits tobacco ads, as does Hungary. In Hong Kong, outdoor display advertising of tobacco products is banned. Malaysia has banned most forms of tobacco advertising, including print, TV, radio, and billboards. However, these restrictions are fairly ineffective as a result of **indirect advertising** that features a product other than the primary (controversial) product. Examples of these techniques in Malaysia are quite plentiful. Billboards with the Salem, Benson & Hedges, and Winston names dot the landscape, but they're not advertising cigarettes. They're advertising the companies' travel, clothing, and restaurant businesses.

There also are differences in the legal use of various marketing communication tools. A contest or promotion might be successful in one country and illegal in another. Different laws and self-regulatory codes about direct marketing exist in different European Union countries. For example, France requires an opt-in clause to a mailing or questionnaire asking permission to add the customer's name to a mailing list.[33] Germany prohibits companies from making unsolicited telephone calls and faxes to consumers. Because of the difficulty in complying with widely varying laws, international advertisers often work with either local agencies or with international agencies that have local affiliates and experts who know the local laws and can identify potential legal problems.

Marketing Regulatory Environment

In addition to specific legislation that affects the practice of marketing communication, there are also government bodies that oversee the application of these laws and establish standards and regulations that marketers must meet. The Federal Trade Commission (FTC) is the primary body that oversees marketing communication, but a number of other agencies are also involved in regulating the messages sent to consumers, as summarized in the following list:

Specialized Government Agencies That Affect Advertising

Agency	*Effect on Advertising*
Federal Trade Commission (*www.ftc.gov*)	Regulates credit, labeling, packaging, warranties, and advertising.
Food and Drug Administration (*www.fda.gov*)	Regulates packaging, labeling, and manufacturing of food and drug products.
Federal Communications Commission (*www.fcc.gov*)	Regulates radio and television stations and networks.
U.S. Postal Service (*www.usps.gov*)	Controls advertising by monitoring materials sent through the mail.
Bureau of Alcohol, Tobacco, and Firearms (*www.atf.treas.gov*)	Division of the U.S. Treasury Department that regulates advertising for alcoholic beverages.
U.S. Patent and Trademark Office (*www.uspto.gov*)	Oversees trademark registration to protect against patent infringement.
Library of Congress (*www.loc.gov*)	Provides controls for copyright protection.

In addition to the FTC, the Food and Drug Administration (FDA) and the **Federal Communications Commission (FCC)** are dynamic components of the regulatory environment. Let's look in more depth at their missions and the type of practices they regulate.

Federal Trade Commission (FTC) Established by Congress in 1914 to oversee business, the FTC is the primary agency governing the advertising industry. Its main focus with respect to advertising is to identify and eliminate ads that deceive or mislead the consumer. Some FTC responsibilities include the following:

- *Unfairness* Initiate investigations against companies that engage in unfair competition or deceptive practices.
- *Deception* Regulate acts and practices that deceive businesses or consumers and issue cease-and-desist orders where such practices exist. Cease-and-desist orders require that the practice be stopped within 30 days; an order given to one firm is applicable to all firms in the industry.
- *Violations* When the FTC finds a violation of the law, such as a deceptive or unfair practice, it mandates (1) a cease-and-desist order, (2) an affirmative disclosure, or (3) corrective advertising.

Specifically, the FTC oversees false advertising and in recent years that oversight has focused on health and weight-loss business practices, 900 telephone numbers, telemarketing, and advertising that targets children and the elderly. The FTC hosts the National Do Not Call Registry to help citizens keep from receiving unwanted telemarketing calls. The FTC monitors the ratings system and the advertising practices of the film, music, and electronic games industries. Periodically, it issues progress reports to Congress on youth-oriented entertainment advertising to make sure that ads for products with potentially objectionable content—primarily violent or sexual content—are not seen on media targeted to youth. The FTC's reports to Congress cover advertising on television and websites as well as print media.

The existence of a regulatory agency such as the FTC influences advertisers' behavior. Although most cases never reach the FTC, advertisers prefer not to risk long legal battles with the agency. Advertisers are also aware that competitors may complain to the FTC about a questionable advertisement. Such a move can cost the offending organization millions of dollars.

The FTC revised its guidelines governing testimonial advertisements, bloggers, and celebrity endorsements in October 2009 for the first time since 1980. These guidelines toughen rules for endorsements and testimonials by requiring that the results touted by endorsers are likely to be typical. The revisions also now cover bloggers who must disclose any free products or other compensation they get in exchange for their endorsements.[34]

Food and Drug Administration (FDA)   The FDA is the regulatory division of the U.S. Department of Health and Human Services that oversees package labeling, ingredient listings, and advertising for food and drugs. It also determines the safety and purity of foods and cosmetics. In particular, the FDA is a watchdog for drug advertising, specifically in the controversial area of direct-to-consumer ads for prescription drugs. Its job is first to determine whether drugs are safe and then to see that these drugs are marketed in a responsible way. Marketing includes promotional materials aimed at doctors as well as consumers.

For pharmaceutical companies, advertising is a commercial free speech issue, and the industry has brought pressure on the FDA to make direct-to-consumer advertising rules for prescription drugs more understandable, simpler, and clearer.

Federal Communications Commission (FCC)   The FCC, formed in 1934 to protect the public interest in broadcast communication, can issue and revoke licenses to radio and television stations. The FCC also has the power to ban messages, including ads, that are deceptive or in poor taste. The agency monitors only advertisements that have been the subject of complaints and works closely with the FTC to eliminate false and deceptive advertising. The FCC takes actions against the media, whereas the FTC is concerned with advertisers and agencies.

Other Regulatory Bodies   In addition to the FTC, the FDA, and the FCC, several other federal agencies regulate advertising. Most other federal agencies that regulate advertising are limited to a certain type of advertising, product, or medium. We have already discussed the Patent Office and the Library of Congress and their roles in protecting copyrights and trademarks. Let's now look at other key regulatory agencies:

- *Bureau of Alcohol, Tobacco, and Firearms* The Bureau of Alcohol, Tobacco, and Firearms (BATF) within the Treasury Department regulates deception in advertising and establishes labeling requirements for the liquor industry. This agency's power comes from its authority to issue and revoke annual operating permits for distillers, wine merchants, and brewers. Because there is a danger that public pressure could result in banning all advertisements for alcoholic beverages, the liquor industry strives to maintain tight controls on its advertising.
- *The U.S. Postal Service (USPS)* The USPS regulates direct-mail and magazine advertising and has control over the areas of obscenity, lotteries, and fraud. To give you an idea of the magnitude of the U.S. Postal Service's responsibility, the Direct Marketing Association estimated spending on direct mail at $54 billion in 2008, even in a period of declining spending on the medium.[35] Consumers who receive advertisements in the mail that they consider sexually offensive can request that no more mail be delivered from that sender. The postmaster general also has the power to withhold mail that promotes lotteries. Fraud can include a number of questionable activities, such as implausible, get-rich-quick schemes.
- *The States' Attorneys General* The National Association of Attorneys General seeks to regulate advertising at the state level. Members of this organization have successfully brought suits in their respective states against such advertising giants as Coca-Cola, Kraft, and Campbell Soup. More recently, numerous attorneys general have led the way against the tobacco industry and have supported the advertising restrictions discussed earlier.

The Impact of Regulation

In our discussion of issues we mentioned several that have spurred governmental regulation, such as children's advertising, deception, and claim substantiation. In this section we discuss these regulations in terms of the government agencies taking responsibility for them.

The FTC and Children's Advertising   Developing responsible advertising aimed at audiences of children is a critical issue. The FTC and other governmental agencies have gotten involved with the regulation of marketing to children.

After a 1978 study found that the average child viewed more than 20,000 TV commercials per year, a heated debate ensued. One side favored regulation because of children's inability to evaluate advertising messages and make purchasing decisions. The other side opposed regulation, arguing that many self-regulatory mechanisms already existed and the proper place for restricting advertising to children was in the home.

In response, the FTC initiated proceedings to study possible regulations of children's television. Despite the FTC's recommendations, the proceedings did not result in new federal regulations until 1990. In the interim, self-regulation in the advertising industry tried to fill this void.

The National Advertising Division (NAD) of the Council of Better Business Bureaus, Inc., set up a group charged with helping advertisers deal with children's advertising in a manner sensitive to children's special needs. The Children's Advertising Review Unit (CARU), established in 1974, evaluates advertising directed at children under the age of 12.

In 1990 Congress passed the Children's Television Advertising Practice Act, which placed 10.5-minute-per-hour ceilings for commercials in children's weekend television programming and 12-minute-per-hour limits for weekday programs. The act also set rules requiring that commercial breaks be clearly distinguished from programming, barring the use of program characters to promote products.

Advocates for children's television continue to argue that many stations made little effort to comply with the 1990 act and petitioned the Federal Communications Commission to increase the required number of educational programs to be shown daily. In 1996, broadcasters, children's advocates, and the federal government reached an agreement requiring all TV stations to air three hours of children's educational shows a week.

Regulating Deception   Ultimately, advertisers want their customers to trust their products and advertising, so many take precautions to ensure that their messages are not deceptive, misleading, or unreasonable. **Deceptive advertising** is intended to mislead consumers by making claims that are false or by failure to make full disclosure of important facts, or both. The current FTC policy on deception contains three basic elements:

1. *Misleading* Where there is representation, omission, or practice, there must be a probability that it will mislead the consumer.
2. *Reasonableness* The perspective of the "reasonable consumer" is used to judge deception. The FTC tests reasonableness by looking at whether the consumer's interpretation or reaction to an advertisement is reasonable.
3. *Injurious* The deception must hold the probability of material injury. Here, "material" is defined as "affecting consumers' choice or behavior regarding the product or service." In other words, the deception is likely to influence consumers' decision making about products and services.

This policy makes deception difficult to prove because the criteria are rather vague and hard to measure. It also creates uncertainty for advertisers who must wait for congressional hearings and court cases to discover what the FTC will permit.

Regulating Substantiation   An area of particular concern to the FTC in determining whether or not an advertisement is misleading is **claim substantiation.** The advertiser should have a reasonable basis for making a claim about product performance or run the risk of an FTC investigation. Food claims, such as those focused on calories or carbohydrates, must be supported by research about nutrition. Even claims in auto advertising, as the Chevy Equinox ad demonstrates, need proof. Consequently, an advertiser should always have data on file to substantiate any claims it makes in its advertisements. Also, ideally, this research should be conducted by an independent research firm.

The FTC determines the reasonableness of claims on a case-by-case basis. In general, the FTC considers these factors:

- **Type and Specificity of Claim** For example, Computer Tutor claims you can learn the basics of using a computer by simply going through its three-CD set.
- **Type of Product** FedEx promises a certain delivery time, regardless of weather, mechanical breakdown, and so forth. This product has a great many uncontrollable variables compared to Heinz ketchup, which the company promises will be "thick."
- **Possible Consequences** A website that claims it is secure can cause serious damage to its customers if, in fact, it is not.
- **Degree of Reliance** Business-to-business customers depend on the many claims made by their vendors. Therefore, if XPEDX (yes, that's how it's spelled), a manufacturer of boxes and other packages, claims in its ad that it can securely deliver any size product, it had better deliver.
- **Type and Accessibility of Evidence** The type of evidence could range from testimonials from satisfied customers to complex product testing in multiple laboratories. It could be made available through an 800-number request or online.
- **What Substantiation is Reasonable** What do experts in this area believe is reasonable proof of a claim?

This ad claims the Chevy Equinox is the most fuel efficient car in its category. Note the four footnotes that explain how the claim is supported.

Remedies for Deception and Unfair Advertising Common sources of complaints concerning deceptive or unfair advertising practices are competitors, the public, and the FTC's own monitors. After the FTC determines that an ad is deceptive, the first step in the regulation process is to issue a **consent decree.** The FTC simply notifies the advertiser of its finding and asks the advertiser to sign a consent decree agreeing to stop the deceptive practice. Most advertisers do sign the decree to avoid the bad publicity.

Duracell was forced to modify one of its ads after Energizer complained that the ad inferred that Duracell CopperTop batteries would last three times longer than other heavy-duty and super-heavy-duty batteries. The ad didn't mention Energizer by name, but Energizer charged the ad was "false and misleading" because consumers would think the comparison was with other alkaline batteries, such as Energizer. In fact, the CopperTop does not last longer than other alkaline batteries. The ad was modified with a disclaimer.[36]

It is important for students of advertising to understand the legal ramifications of deceptive and unfair advertising. Under some circumstances the FTC holds advertisers and their agencies accountable. Essentially, an agency is liable for deceptive advertising along with the advertiser when the agency is an active participant in the preparation of the ad and knows or has reason to know that it is false or deceptive.

If a complaint seems justified, the commission can follow several courses of action:

- **Cease-and-Desist Orders** When an advertiser refuses to sign a consent decree and the FTC determines that the deception is substantial, it issues a **cease-and-desist order.** The process leading to the issuance of a cease-and-desist order is similar to a court trial. An administrative law judge presides. FTC staff attorneys represent the commission, and the accused parties are entitled to representation by their lawyers. If the administrative judge decides in favor of the FTC, the judge issues an order requiring the respondents to cease their unlawful practices. The advertiser can appeal the order to the full five-member commission.
- **Corrective Advertising** The FTC may require **corrective advertising** when consumer research determines that an advertising campaign has perpetuated lasting false beliefs. Under this remedy, the FTC orders the offending person or organization to produce messages for consumers that correct the false impressions the ad made. The purpose of corrective advertising is not to punish an advertiser but to prevent it from continuing to deceive consumers. The FTC may require a firm to run corrective advertising even if the campaign in question has been discontinued.

A landmark corrective advertising case is *Warner-Lambert v. FTC*. According to the FTC, Warner-Lambert's campaign for Listerine mouthwash, which ran for 50 years, had been deceiving customers, leading them to think that Listerine could prevent or reduce the severity of sore throats and colds. The company was ordered to run a corrective advertising campaign, mostly on television, for 16 months at a cost of $10 million.

Interestingly, after the Warner-Lambert corrective campaign ran its course, 42 percent of Listerine users continued to believe that the mouthwash was being advertised as a remedy for sore throats and colds, and 57 percent of users rated cold and sore throat effectiveness as a key reason for purchasing the brand.[37] These results raised doubts about the effectiveness of corrective advertising to change impressions and have affected recent court decisions.

• **Consumer Redress** The Magnuson-Moss Warranty-FTC Improvement Act of 1975 empowers the FTC to obtain consumer redress when a person or a firm engages in deceptive practices. A judge can order any of the following: cancellation or reformation of contracts, refund of money or return of property, payment of damages, and public notification.

Media Review of Advertising

The media attempts to regulate advertising by screening and rejecting ads that violate their standards of truth and good taste. Most networks have a Standards and Practices Department that screens every ad and gives approval before the ad can run. Each individual medium has the discretion to accept or reject a particular ad. For example, *Reader's Digest* does not accept tobacco and liquor ads, and many magazines and television stations do not show condom ads. The major television networks craft their own standards and guidelines.

The First Amendment gives any publisher the right to refuse to publish anything the company does not want to publish, and this sometimes creates battles between media companies and advertisers. For example, some billboard companies in Utah refused to run billboards for a Wasatch Beer company brand named Polygamy Porter. The brand's slogan "Why have just one!" and headlines such as "Take Some Home for the Wives" were deemed offensive to the state's Mormon population. A similar brouhaha arose when the state's Brighton Ski Resort promoted its four-person lifts with a billboard during the Salt Lake City Olympics that read "Wife. Wife. Wife. Husband." The billboard company that banned the beer ads received letters both for and against its stand, which indicates the difficulty of such decisions.

Self-Regulation

Rather than wait for laws and regulatory actions, responsible advertisers take the initiative and establish individual ethical standards that anticipate and even go beyond possible complaints. Such a proactive stance helps the creative process and avoids the kinds of disasters that result from violating the law or offending members of society.

Advertisers practice three types of self-regulation: self-discipline, industry self-regulation, and self-regulation by public and community groups.

Self-Discipline An organization such as an advertising agency exercises self-discipline when it develops, uses, and enforces norms within its own practices. Self-discipline starts with the individuals in the agency or organization. It is each person's responsibility to recognize ethical issues and be intentional about their behavior. We hope that this chapter will help you think about making choices that you deem the right thing to do in your career.

Virtually all major advertisers and advertising agencies have in-house ad review procedures, including reviews by agency and client attorneys. These employees help ensure that work is legal. Typically the attorneys are concerned with how claims are phrased and substantiated. Are the claims verifiable? Is there research and data to prove the truth of the claims? Is there anything in the wording that could be misinterpreted or misleading? Is there anything deceptive in the visual images?

Several U.S. companies (Colgate-Palmolive, General Foods, AT&T) have their own codes of behavior and criteria that determine whether advertisements are acceptable. Companies without such codes tend to have informal criteria that they apply on an ad-by-ad basis. At a minimum, advertisers and agencies should have every element of a proposed ad evaluated by an in-house committee, lawyers, or both.

Industry Self-Regulation When the development, use, and enforcement of norms comes from the industry, the term used is *industry self-regulation*. In the case of both advertisers and advertising agen-

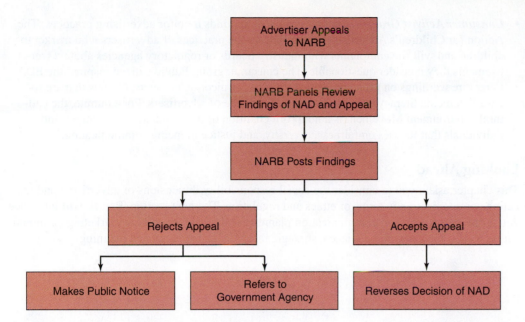

FIGURE 3.4

The NARB Appeal Process Consumers or groups submitting a complaint to NAD and NARB go through this process. The ultimate power of NAD and NARB is the threat of passing the claim to the FTC. Usually, cases are settled before that point.

cies, the most effective attempts at pure self-regulation have come through industry groups, such as the Advertising Review Council (ARC) and the Better Business Bureau. In 1971 several professional advertising associations in conjunction with the Council of Better Business Bureaus established the National Advertising Review Council, which negotiates voluntary withdrawal of national advertising that professionals consider deceptive. The National Advertising Division (NAD) of the Council of Better Business Bureaus and the National Advertising Review Board (NARB) are the two operating arms of the National Advertising Review Council. None of these are government agencies.

NAD is made up of people from the field of advertising. It evaluates complaints submitted by consumers, consumer groups, industrial organizations, and advertising firms. NAD also does its own industry monitoring. After NAD receives a complaint, it may ask the advertiser in question to substantiate claims made in the advertisement. If that substantiation is deemed inadequate, NAD representatives ask the advertiser to change or withdraw the offending ad. When a satisfactory resolution cannot be found, NAD refers the case to NARB.

NARB is a 50-member regulatory group that represents national advertisers, advertising agencies, and other professional fields. When the advertiser appeals a case to NARB, it faces a review panel of five people: three advertisers, one agency person, and one public representative. This NARB panel reviews the complaint and the NAD staff findings and holds hearings to let the advertiser present its case. If the case remains unresolved after the process, NARB can (1) publicly identify the advertiser and the facts about the case and (2) refer the complaint to the appropriate government agency, usually the FTC. Although neither NAD nor NARB has any real power other than threatening to invite government intervention, these groups have been effective in controlling cases of deception and misleading advertising. Figure 3.4 summarizes the NARB appeal process.

Self-Regulation by Public and Community Groups The advertising industry voluntarily involves nonindustry representatives, such as the Better Business Bureau or the media, in the development, application, and enforcement of norms. Local and consumer activist groups represent two ways in which self-regulation occurs in this manner:

- *Local Group* At the local level, self-regulation has been supported by the Better Business Bureau (BBB). The BBB (*www.bbb.org*) functions much like the national regulatory agencies and also provides local businesses with advice concerning the legal aspects of advertising. Approximately 250 local and national bureaus made up of advertisers, agencies, and media, have screened hundreds of thousands of advertisements for possible violations of truth and accuracy. Although the BBB has no legal power, it receives and investigates complaints and maintains files on violators. It also assists local law enforcement officials in prosecuting violators. The ease with which the BBB can be accessed on the Internet has prompted businesses to be more careful about complying with its standards.

- *Consumer Activist Group* Consumer groups of all kinds monitor advertising practices. The Action for Children's Advertising group follows the practices of advertisers who market to children and will file complaints with industry boards or regulatory agencies about advertisements they consider questionable. The consumer group Public Citizen inspired the FDA to require warnings on print ads for certain types of nicotine products. Groups that are focused on media literacy also review the performance of advertisers. For example, the Cultural Environment Movement is a nonprofit coalition of independent organizations and individuals that focuses on fairness, diversity, and justice in media communication.[38]

Looking Ahead

This chapter asked you to consider the social responsibility dimensions of advertising and marketing communication in terms of ethics and regulation. The next section, Part II, will introduce you to the basics of brand communication planning with chapters on how marketing communication works, the consumer audience, strategic research, and strategy and planning.

Häagen-Dazs loves Honey Bees™

IT'S A WRAP

It's a Winner, Just Bee-Cause

As noted at the beginning of this chapter, the crisis of the honeybees is bigger than ice cream—it affects a significant part of the food chain. The work Häagen-Dazs has done to illuminate the problem and work toward a solution demonstrates that profits are only one measure of a brand's success. Acting socially responsible is part of the formula for good business.

Christine Chen, deputy director of communication strategy at Goodby, Silverstein & Partners, said the campaign was successful in part because the honeybee issue was a natural fit with Häagen-Dazs. She said,

> That [connection] made it more than just some cause we say we care about. It was something that probably came as a surprise to consumers because it was a way they never really thought about the brand before. The idea was to get people to think about the problem first and foremost and then to understand Häagen-Dazs's connection to it and become motivated to do something about it.

Although the bee crisis continues, more resources are focused on solving the mystery. Häagen-Dazs along with other bee-involved brands such as Burt's Bees were invited to testify before the House Agricultural Subcommittee, and they successfully convinced congressional members to allocate funding for the CCD issue.

The investment in the problem paid good dividends for the brand as well. The honeybee buzz had a positive impact on sales. Unaided brand awareness of Häagen-Dazs rose from 29 to 36 percent. It generated lots of publicity. It made 125 million impressions, which is the number of people who may have seen something in the media about the crisis. This number of impressions had been set as the yearlong goal and was achieved in quick order—during the campaign's first week. The viral "Bee Dance" video on YouTube received more than a million hits in the first month, proving once again, the power of the Internet.

"Häagen-Dazs Loves Honey Bees" won a swarm of awards for this campaign, including a Gold Effie; 2009 Festival of Media, Media Responsibility Award; Cannes Lions 2009 PR Lion; 2009 PRWeek Award for Cause-Related Campaign of the Year; and the 2009 Silver SABRE (Superior Achievement in Branding and Reputation) Award.

Ad lesson learned: Acting socially responsibility is good business.

Key Points Summary

1. **What is the social impact of brand communication?** To some extent advertising does create demand for products; however, the power of advertising to do this is hard to measure. The shape-versus-mirror debate is a central issue in considering advertising's role in society. Critics of advertising tend to believe that it has the power to shape social trends and the way people think and act; advertising professionals tend to believe that it mirrors values rather than sets them. In fact, advertising and society's values are probably interactive so the answer may simply be that advertising both mirrors and shapes values. Whether or not advertising causes society to become overcommercialized relates to the criticism that buying products appears to be the solution to every problem. Counterarguments emerge from the position that consumers can make intelligent choices about what they need.

2. **What ethical and social responsibilities do communicators bear?** Advertisers have a social responsibility to make good ethical choices. At the root of ethical behavior is the individual decision maker's set of moral values. When faced with a dilemma of equally compelling choices, advertisers can consult their personal values, professional codes of ethics, and international standards of ethical behavior to guide their moral decision making.

3. **Why and how is advertising regulated?** In a complex society there is usually not one answer to what constitutes "right" behavior. Regulatory agencies help enforce advertising standards. Several governmental bodies help regulate advertising:

   - The FTC is the agency primarily concerned with identifying and eliminating deceptive advertising.
   - The FDA oversees advertising related to food and drugs.
   - The FCC monitors advertising broadcast by radio and television stations.
   - Other regulatory bodies with some advertising oversight include the Bureau of Alcohol, Tobacco, and Firearms, the U.S. Postal Service, the Patent and Trademark Office, the Library of Congress, and the states' attorneys general offices.

   In addition to governmental oversight, advertising is also self-regulated. Individuals working in the field need to act responsibly to make ethical and legal choices. Advertising agencies have in-house ad review procedures and legal staff that monitor the creation of advertising. The industry has a number of bodies that review advertising, such as the National Advertising Review Council, the National Advertising Division of the Better Business Bureau, and the National Advertising Review Board. Other bodies include the various media review boards, competitors who are concerned about unfair advertising that might harm their brands, and public and community groups that represent either local or special-interest groups.

Words of Wisdom: Recommended Reading

Christians, Clifford G., Mark Fackler, Kathy Brittain McKee, Peggy J. Kreshel, and Robert H. Woods, *Media Ethics: Cases and Moral Reasoning*, 8th ed., Boston: Allyn & Bacon, 2008.

Hovland, Roxanne, Joyce Wolburg, Eric Haley, and Ron Taylor, *Readings in Advertising, Society and Consumer Culture,* Armonk, NY: M.E. Sharpe, 2007.

Klein, Naomi, *No Logo,* 10th Anniversary ed., New York: Picador Press/St. Martin's Press, 2009.

Pardun, Carol J. (Ed.), *Advertising and Society: Controversies and Consequences*, Chichester, UK: Wiley-Blackwell, 2009.

Reichert, Tom (Ed.), *Issues in American Advertising: Media, Society and a Changing World,* Chicago: The Copy Workshop, 2008.

Key Terms

blogola, p. 73
cause marketing, p. 76
cease-and-desist order, p. 87
claim substantiation, p. 86
code of ethics, p. 79
commercial speech, p. 82
comparative advertising, p. 71
consent decree, p. 87

copyright, p. 82
corrective advertising, p. 87
cultural imperialism, p. 70
deceptive advertising, p. 86
demand creation, p. 65
endorsement, p. 72
ethics, p. 76
false advertising, p. 71

Federal Communications Commission (FCC), p. 84
green marketing, p. 76
indirect advertising, p. 83
international advertising, p. 70
marketing imperialism, p. 70
mission marketing, p. 76
morals, p. 76

puffery, p. 71
social responsibility, p. 65
stereotype, p. 68
testimonial, p. 72
trademark, p. 82
uniform resource locators (URLs), p. 82

Review Questions

1. Explain the debate over whether advertising shapes or mirrors society. If you were to take a side in this debate, which side would you choose?

2. What do you consider the most pressing ethical issues facing advertisers? Explain.

3. Explain how trademarks and copyrights are legally protected, and why the First Amendment is important to advertisers.

4. In addition to the FTC, what other governmental bodies are involved in regulating advertising practices?

5. Define ethics. How do you determine what is ethical? If you are called on to make a decision about the promotion of an event for one of your clients, where does the ultimate consideration lie? What questions would you ask?

Discussion Questions

1. The Dimento Game Company has a new basketball video game. To promote it, "Slammer" Aston, an NBA star, is signed to do the commercial. Aston is shown in the commercial with the game controls as he speaks these lines: "This is the most challenging court game you've ever tried. It's all here—zones, man-to-man, pick and roll, even the alley-oop. For me, this is the best game off the court." Is Aston's presentation an endorsement? Should the FTC consider a complaint if Dimento uses this strategy? What would you need to know to determine if you are safe from a challenge of misleading advertising?

2. A pharmaceutical company has repackaged a previously developed drug that addresses the symptoms of a scientifically questionable disorder affecting approximately 5 percent of women. While few women are affected by the "disorder," the company's advertising strategy is comprehensive, including dozens of television, radio, and magazine ads. As a result, millions of women with symptoms similar to those of the disorder have sought prescriptions for the company's drug. In turn, the company has made billions of dollars.

What, if any, are the ethical implications of advertising a remedy to a mass audience when the affected group is small? Is the company misrepresenting its drug by conducting a "media blitz"? Why or why not?

3. *Three-Minute Debate* Zack Wilson is the advertising manager for the campus newspaper. He is looking over a layout for a promotion for a spring break vacation package. The headline says, "Absolutely the Finest Deal Available This Spring—you'll Have the Best Time Ever if You Join Us in Boca." The newspaper has a solid reputation for not running advertising with questionable claims and promises. Should Zack accept or reject this ad? Organize into small teams with pairs of teams taking opposing sides. In class, set up a series of three-minute debates in which each side has 1½ minutes to argue its position. Every team of debaters must present new points not covered in the previous teams' presentations until there are no arguments left to present. Then the class votes as a group on the winning point of view.

Take-Home Projects

1. *Portfolio Project* Check the websites of three big-name companies such as:
   - McDonald's (*www.mcdonalds.com*)
   - Avon (*www.avon.com*)
   - Ben & Jerry's (*www.benjerry.com*)
   - Starbucks (*www.starbucks.com*)
   - Body Shop (*www.thebodyshop.com*)
   - Target (*www.target.com*)

   Write a two- to four-page report on their efforts to be socially responsible. How is the company's social responsibility position reflected in its advertising?

2. *Mini-Case Analysis* Imagine that you are now working for Häagen-Dazs. What did the company do that provides evidence that it is socially and environmentally responsible? What other ways can you think of for the company to expand these efforts?

Team Project: The BrandRevive Campaign

For your BrandRevive project, identify ethical issues you may face as you develop your campaign. Make a list of those issues for your reference as you proceed through this project. Create your list in a one-page report and a Power Point presentation that is no longer than three slides.

- How might this campaign have a social impact?
- What are the key ethical issues you may encounter?
- What are the legal issues you should watch for?

Hands-On Case

The Century Council

Read the Century Council case in the Appendix before coming to class.

1. Should advertising of alcoholic products be limited on college campuses where the majority of students are under the legal drinking age?

2. Should the major beer and liquor companies funding the Century Council put their logos on the bottom of "The Stupid Drink" campaign? Why or why not?

3. Doesn't "The Stupid Drink" campaign actually promote underage drinking? Why or why not?

PRINCIPLE: BE TRUE TO THY BRAND

Part 1 introduced the basics of advertising and marketing practice. Part 2 focuses on how marketing communication works, how consumers make decisions, and how strategy reflects the way consumers think and feel.

No matter how much advertising and marketing communication change, a basic principle is that brands should be true to themselves—and to the consumers who buy them. Regina Lewis, vice president of consumer insights for the InterContinental Hotel Group, explains that principle in her essay about the true nature of brand loyalty—how branding, which we introduced in Chapter 2, intersects with consumers' feelings and self-images.

Consumers Are Not Loyal to Brands . . . They Are Loyal to Themselves

As I, along with my marketing and advertising agency colleagues, strive to reignite consumers' emotional bond with the Holiday Inn power brand, I think back to a basic fact about consumers. This is that consumers demonstrate loyalty to certain brands because those brands say something about them, as human beings, that they like.

Consumers who are loyal to Dunkin' Donuts, which is a down-to-earth, approachable brand, relish the fact that carrying a Dunkin' cup says to others that they, personally, are down to earth and approachable.

Consumers who are loyal to Jeep Wrangler, which may symbolize an unconventional attitude and a sense of adventure, love the fact that driving a Wrangler informs others that they, too, are unconventional and adventurous.

When a brand fails to convey a soul or essence that matches personal characteristics that consumers value, a brand lacks meaning; in the competitive marketplace, it blends in with all other bland brands that lack charisma. On the other hand, when a brand becomes a badge that consumers are proud of displaying, that brand becomes interwoven into consumers' everyday lives.

Holiday Inn is a power brand for many reasons. Perhaps most importantly, it is a brand that is comfortable in its own skin . . . a brand that doesn't need to be showy, but that celebrates the joys of travel, work, and family in practical ways. Holiday Inn is a place where people can be themselves, where people can live their lives while away from home with the feeling of comfort that home provides. For people who are unpretentious, Holiday Inn offers "real-world" lodging with genuine service.

Regina Lewis, Vice President of Consumer Insights for the InterContinental Hotel Group.

As I, along with my marketing and advertising agency teams, ensure that Holiday Inn retains its place in the hearts and minds of guests, I heed the following set of principles:

1. *Feel* Because all human decisions involve some emotional component, no purely rational advertising approach can offer sustainable advantage. An advertisement must make folks "feel" something!

2. *Connect* All advertising must not only contain an emotional component, it also must get that emotion right. It must nail a way in which folks want to see either their world or themselves.

3. *Identify* While all consumers are individuals, we also can identify groups of consumers who think and feel the same way; identifying and understanding these groups is at the root of strategic planning.

4. *Understand* To effectively deliver emotion through advertising, we must avoid "group think"; sometimes, the most powerful idea can come from one consumer's story . . . and the most powerful message can be imagined by one brilliant creative mind that understands the minds of the target audience.

5. *Smile* While economic times are tough at the time I am writing this essay, it is critical to remember that people want to feel happy! Just as songs that made people smile were celebrated during the Great Depression, advertising that makes people smile will always be meaningful when life feels difficult.

These principles will be explained further in the chapters that make up Part 2. Chapter 4 answers the big picture question of "How does advertising and other marketing communication work?" Effectiveness factors are spelled out using the Facets Model of Effects. Building on that discussion as a foundation, Chapter 5 introduces the consumer audience and discusses how targeting works. Chapter 6 introduces the basics of research used to understand consumers and the marketplace. Finally, Chapter 7 explains that ideas about how advertising works, as well as how consumers think and behave, come together in a strategic plan.

How Marketing Communication Works

It's a Winner

Campaign:	Company:	Agency:	Award:
"Ford SYNC"	*Ford*	*Zubi Advertising Services*	2009 Silver Effie, Category: Hispanic

1. How does marketing communication work both as a form of mass communication and interactive communication?

2. How did the idea of advertising effects develop, and what are the problems in traditional approaches to advertising effects?

3. What is the Facets Model of Effects, and how does it explain how marketing communication works?

Ford in Sync with Hispanic Audience

We're all experts on advertising, aren't we? But have you ever stopped to think about what makes some ads work and others seem ineffective? The story behind Ford's campaign for its new SYNC technology will give you some insights about how effective advertising works.

Ford faced a significant challenge as it tried to convince potential consumers of its small to medium-sized Focus and Edge vehicles that the vehicles had some technological advantages. First, Ford is known for its tough, dependable trucks, not as a technology leader. Consumers perceived competitors like Nissan Sentra, Honda Civic, Scion, Toyota Corolla, and VW Rabbit or Jetta as being technologically superior. Second, not only did Ford need to overcome the perception that foreign-made automobiles were more technologically advanced, it needed to make the audience aware of its new innovation, which was practically invisible. About all Ford had to show potential buyers was a button on the steering wheel and a SYNC logo on the dashboard.

Before we get into a detailed analysis about how the advertising worked, let's look at Ford's innovative technology. At the touch of a button or a simple voice command, drivers could use Ford's SYNC technology, developed by Microsoft, to play music from their digital music players and to make phone calls. What differentiates this technology from the competition is SYNC's ability to understand various dialects of Spanish, which is particularly important to voice-activated commands from a diverse U.S. Hispanic market. Ford knew that those who experienced this system in demos and focus groups gave it rave reviews.

Wanting to capitalize on the SYNC technology, Ford sought a campaign targeting the 18- to 49-year-old Hispanic market that would accomplish two objectives: generate consumer awareness of SYNC by educating consumers, and get hand-raisers (those who indicate interest by responding online) to register for sweepstakes and to opt in for future Ford communications.

Ford hired Zubi, an Hispanic agency, to create a campaign. Zubi recognized that Ford needed to get the attention of its audience before it could accomplish the goals of making people aware of this great new technology and persuading them that they ought to own it. Here's how they did it.

The campaign's Big Idea centered on the notion that Ford's SYNC—the ability to control cell phones and MP3 players—was available at the driver's command. Audience research showed that members of the Hispanic target market are technologically savvy. They count on their MP3 players to help them during long commutes. To successfully introduce SYNC in fuel-efficient Fords, the campaign message needed to align the technology with consumers' lifestyles in a fun way that would grab their attention. The slogan, "SYNC: At Your Command" (SYNC: A Tus Ordenes"), captured the heart of the message.

Zubi identified a spokesperson for SYNC who would be believable. That person was the popular Colombian singer, songwriter, and multiple Grammy award-winner Juanes. As a major sponsor for Juanes's World Tour, Ford was able to reach members of the Hispanic target market and educate them about SYNC. Every concert featured a SYNC Zone, where people could see SYNC demonstrations and participate in giveaways. Potential consumers could visit a SYNC Juanes destination website highlighting video content. They could enter an online sweepstakes with a Juanes VIP concert experience as a grand prize. (Note the opportunity to capture the hand-raisers, build Ford's database, and offer incentives for test drives.) The campaign used display banner ads, video banners, paid search (a fee given to get a sponsor's website results shown near the top of search engine results pages), a widget such as a clock or temperature gauge, and publisher-driven e-mail blasts online. Magazine and newspaper advertising and radio spots helped publicize the concert and online activities. Talking billboards and text messaging attracted even more attention. Consumers walking by key talking billboards in high pedestrian-traffic areas triggered a motion detector, which in turn generated Juanes' voice talking about SYNC to passersby.

What made this campaign successful in part according to Dave Rodriguez, multicultural marketing communication manager for Ford Motor Co., was this: "This campaign is not necessarily the standard 'Let's sponsor a concert.' Juanes is very much part of the creative messaging, and a lot of that is going live online because that's where the consumer is going." The target audience already liked Juanes, and the concerts and Internet were used as opportunities to help consumers learn about and experience the benefits of SYNC. Advertising lesson: a fit between a spokesperson and the target audience can generate awareness and create synergy.

To see just how successful this campaign has been in achieving its objectives, turn to the *It's a Wrap* feature found at the end of this chapter.

Sources: "Ford SYNC Integrated Marketing Program," Effie Awards Brief of Effectiveness and Press Release, *www.nyama .org*; *www.syncmyride.com*; Karl Greenberg, "Ford Campaign for SYNC Centers on Singer Juanes," October 26, 2007, *www.mediapost.com*; "The Perfect Sound: Juanes and Ford Give Power to Your Voice," October 27, 2007, *www .hispanicprwire.com*; "Ford Gets a Latin Beat," October 25, 2007, *www.ford.com*.

How does marketing communication affect you? What ads can you remember seeing? Do you remember to buy a new product in the store after you've see some advertising that intrigues you? Do you have favorite ads? These are all important questions to advertising professionals, as well as to students, professors, and critics of advertising. In this chapter we'll try to answer these questions about how advertising and other marketing communications work by looking at the *effects* behind the concept of *effectiveness*. We are introducing effectiveness now because understanding how marketing communication works is a foundation for discussions in the following chapters on consumer behavior, consumer research, and strategic planning. It's our view that you can't make intelligent decisions in those areas unless you have some understanding of how marketing communication works.

In this chapter we'll first consider advertising as communication. Then we'll look at various types of consumer responses to messages to identify the key effects, which we organize and present as the Facets Model of Effects. This chapter, then, lays the groundwork for our explanation of effectiveness, which is an important theme in this book.

DOES ADVERTISING WORK?

Would it surprise you to know that a lot of professionals, as well as academics, are really not sure how advertising works—or even if it works well at all? This is even more of a problem for the new digital media and other forms of marketing communication.

This classic quote attributed to Philadelphia department store baron John Wanamaker in the early 1900s sums up the issue: "I know half my advertising is wasted, but I don't know which half." (You can find his quotes and others about the impact of advertising on the Advertising Hall of Fame website, *www.advertisinghalloffame.org/members*.)

Wanamaker is more positive than some advertising experts. The chairman of a British promotions company estimated that only about 1 percent of the average campaign spending actually works because few people are aware of ad messages, and of those who are aware, few actually do anything in response.[1] Research by retired Syracuse University professor John Philip Jones, who worked for many years at the J. Walter Thompson advertising agency, led him to conclude that only 41 percent of advertising actually works in terms of producing sales.[2]

Of course, many professionals, including the managers of big global brands and big advertising agencies, absolutely believe that advertising works both in the short term to create sales and in the long term to build brands. After all, advertising is an $80 billion industry[3]—even larger when you consider all of the various related areas of marketing communication.

The problem is that a lot of poorly executed advertising doesn't communicate well to its intended audience or have the impact its creators desired. So let's begin our discussion of how advertising and marketing communication* work by looking in more depth at its communication role.

HOW DOES MARKETING COMMUNICATION WORK?

Advertising and other forms of marketing communication are first of all a form of communication, messages that are designed to have some type of impact. In a sense, effective advertising is a message to a consumer about a brand. It gets attention and provides information, sometimes even a bit of entertainment as the Ford SYNC campaign demonstrated. It is purposeful in that it seeks to create some kind of response, such as an inquiry, a sale, a visit to a website, or in the case of Ford's SYNC, a test drive.

The legendary David Ogilvy would like to see advertising as relevant as a personal conversation.[4] He pretends he is at a dinner party and the woman next to him asks for advice. He explains, "I give her the facts, facts, facts. I try to make it interesting, fascinating, if possible, and personal—I don't write to the crowd."

In reality, however, most traditional advertising is not as personal or as interactive as a conversation because it relies on mass communication. Although other forms of marketing communication, such as personal selling and telemarketing, can deliver the personal contact of a conversation, Ogilvy's comparison ignores the challenge of getting the attention of a largely disinterested audience when using mass communication. So let's look first at how *communication* works in general and then we'll apply that analysis to mass media advertising and finally to the broader arena of brand communication.

*Note: It's simpler to just say "advertising," but in this chapter we are referring to advertising as well as the more general area of marketing communication.

Nyack College
Wilson Library

A Basic Communication Model

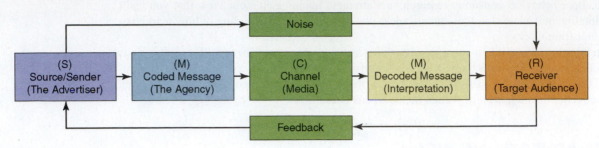

FIGURE 4.1A

A Basic Mass Communication Model

The Mass Communication Approach

Mass communication is a process, as depicted in the model in Figure 4.1a, which outlines the important players and steps. The **SMCR model** diagrams how mass communication works: It begins with a **source** (S), a sender who encodes a **message** (M), or puts it in words and pictures. The message is presented through **channels of communication** (C), such as a newspaper, radio, or TV. The message is decoded, or interpreted, by the **receiver** (R), who is the reader, viewer, or listener. **Feedback** is obtained by monitoring the response of the receiver to the message. The entire process is complicated by what we refer to as **noise,** things that interrupt the sending and receiving of the message, such as a bad connection or words with unclear meanings.

Advertising as Mass Communication

To translate the SMCR model to advertising using the Ford SYNC example, consider that the *source* typically is the advertiser (Ford) assisted by its agency (Zubi) who encodes the information—that is, advertising professionals turn the marketer's information (voice-recognition technology) into an interesting and attention-getting message (SYNC: At Your Command—a message delivered through music by spokesperson Juanes). Together they determine the *objectives* for the message— an advertisement or campaign—in terms of the effects they want the message to have on the *consumer audience (receiver)*. If the communication process fails to work and the consumer does not receive the message as intended by the advertiser, then the communication effort is ineffective. The advertising communication model shown in Figure 4.1b describes how this communication process works.

FIGURE 4.1B

An Advertising Communication Model

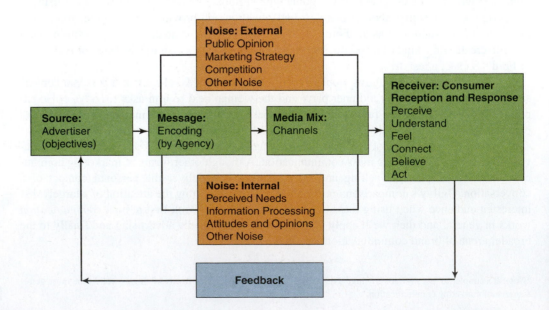

The *message*, of course, is the advertisement or other marketing communication, such as a press release, store banner, brochure, video, or Web page. The message may be spelled out in the words, but in most advertising the visual elements also carry meaning. In fact, some advertising messages, such as the 1984 commercial for the Macintosh discussed in Chapter 1, are primarily visual.

The *medium (channel)* is the vehicle that delivers the message (TV commercials, website, flyers, Twitter tweets, events, in-store displays). In advertising, that tends to be newspapers and magazines in print, radio and TV in broadcasting, the Internet, and other forms of out-of-home vehicles, such as outdoor boards and posters. Other media include the phone, fax, specialty items (mugs, T-shirts), in-store signs, brochures, catalogs, shopping bags, inflatables, even sidewalks and toilet doors. The latest entry in the medium of marketing communication is the cell phone, which has become a major personal communication technology. With instant messaging, **podcasting,** movie downloads, photo transmission, Web surfing and tweeting, the cell phone is the newest "must-have" communication device.

External noise, which hinders the consumer's reception of the message, includes technical and socioeconomic trends that affect the reception of the message, like the economic downturn. Health trends, for example, often harm the reception of fast-food messages. Problems with the brand's marketing mix (product design, price, distribution, and marketing communication) can also have an impact on the consumer's response.

External noise can also be related to the advertising media. It can be as simple as bad broadcast or cell phone reception. A more likely cause of noise is **clutter,** which is the multitude of messages all competing to get consumers' attention. More specifically, clutter is all the ads in a magazine or newspaper, or all the commercials you see on television when watching a program or listening to your favorite radio station. It can even include any of the 3,000 or so commercial messages you see in your daily environment, such as outdoor boards and brand names on T-shirts, as well as in unexpected places, such as painted messages on sidewalks.

Internal noise includes personal factors that affect the reception of an advertisement, such as the receiver's needs, language skills, purchase history, information-processing abilities, and other personal factors. If you are too tired to listen or your attention is focused elsewhere, then your fatigue or disinterest creates noise that hinders your reception of the message. Distraction from competing brand messages can also create internal noise, such as doubt or confusion.

Feedback is the reaction the audience has to a message. It can be obtained through research or through customer-initiated contact with the company, which are important tests of the effectiveness of marketing communication messages.

The end point of the communication process is the *receiver,* or in advertising terms the consumers who make up the audience. How the consumer responds to the message determines the effectiveness of the advertising. Consumer response is the focus of the rest of this chapter.

A really important thing to remember is that this process is not foolproof or even dependable. You can't be sure the receiver will understand and interpret your message as you intended. Remember the childhood "telephone" game where you stand in a circle and whisper a message from person to person—and the last message rarely comes out sounding like the initial message. That's why feedback research is so important in marketing communication.

Adding Interaction to Marketing Communication

Mass communication is traditionally seen as a one-way communication process with the message depicted, as in Figures 4.1a and b, as moving from the source to the receiver—from an advertiser to a target audience. However, **interactive communication** such as Ogilvy's idea of advertising as personal conversation, is two-way communication—a dialogue or conversation—and marketing communication is moving in that direction. The difference between one-way and two-way communication is that two-way communication, is interactive, and the source and receiver change positions as the message bounces back and forth between them (think ping-pong)—the source becomes the listener and the receiver becomes the sender. Figure 4.2 is a model of how two-way communication works.

The interest in *buzz marketing* is an indication of an important trend in marketing communication strategy that is moving beyond two-way communication. In social marketing there are multiple conversations occurring in the network. In terms of the old notion of source and receiver, interactive communication means people are contacting companies through the Web or by phone,

An Interactive Communication Model

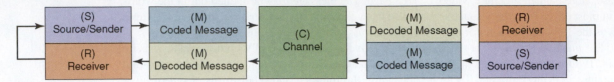

FIGURE 4.2

An Interactive Communication Model

The basic communication model is modified here to show how interactive communication works as a conversation or dialogue. Note how the source and receiver change positions as the message bounces back and forth between them.

and they are talking to one another in a circle of comments about products and brands. As one expert in interactive telecommunication explained, "We're living through the largest expansion of expressive capability in the history of the human race."[5] Inevitably, that means advertising must change to also become more interactive.

Interactivity is important because, in addition to a purchase, consumers today can react to a marketing communication message in many other ways: by responding with comments, phone calls, and e-mail inquiries to sales personnel and customer service. They initiate communication, as well as receive it. If advertisers want to overcome the impersonal nature of mass communication, they need to learn to receive (i.e., *listen to*) as well as send messages to customers. *Permission marketing* reflects this desire for more interactive and sensitive communication. The idea behind permission marketing is that you ask people if it is okay to contact them or you rely on them to contact you first in order to open the door for follow-up conversation.

Dialogue creates new ways to listen to customers. In the traditional communication model, customers' responses, or *feedback,* are gathered primarily through research, but in newer approaches to communication, feedback occurs in a real-time environment of ongoing communication. This feedback is achieved by using more interactive forms of marketing communication (personal selling, customer service, online marketing) and monitoring the responses and customer-initiated dialogue that comes through response devices such as toll-free numbers and e-mail addresses.

More than capturing feedback, some companies are designing programs specifically to solicit ideas from customers and even get them involved in product design using their own websites, blogs, Facebook, and even Twitter. UserVoice is a San Francisco–based company that sets up forums on clients' websites that encourage customers to contribute and vote on ideas.[6] (Check out *https://uservoice.com.*)

In addition to listening and generating feedback, the Internet has also changed our conversations in ways David Ogilvy would never have dreamed. For example, texting uses a shorthand code with an entirely new set of spelling codes. Twitter limits conversation to 140 characters and has made brevity cool. And now **hashtags,** which are mashed-together phrases marked with a hash symbol (the pound sign) that indicates what topic the tweet addresses, have created a new way of organizing information. The hashtag is like a pause in a conversation where the speaker says, "what we're talking about here is the future of newspapers (#futureofnewspapers). The hashtag is also a link that makes it possible to instantly search the Internet for other comments on that topic.[7]

Two-way communication is one of the objectives of an integrated marketing communication (IMC)-focused program because it helps create long-term customer relationships with a brand. The growth of *permission marketing,* a practice that invites consumers to sign up for messages or self-select themselves into a brand's target market, mirrors the shift from one-way to two-way communication. It's a way to build a respectful relationship with a customer.

WHAT ARE THE EFFECTS BEHIND EFFECTIVENESS?

What are the effects that make an advertisement effective? Consider your favorite commercials— do they grip you emotionally? (Think Hallmark and Dove soap.) Do they have a compelling message? (The "1984" commercial we introduced in Chapter 1 is a good example.) How about learning something—do you think about things because of something you heard or read in an ad?

(Think the Wii campaign.) Does an ad need to be entertaining to work? (Think the Burger King "Whopper Freakout" campaign.)

The theme of this book is that good advertising—and marketing communication—is effective when it achieves the advertiser's desired response. The message is effective to the degree that it achieves this objective. Thus, understanding what kinds of effects can be achieved with a marketing communication message is essential to anyone engaged in planning advertising and all other forms of marketing communication.

Principle
The intended consumer response is the message's objective, and the message is effective to the degree that it achieves this desired response.

Traditional Approaches

When we ask how it works, we are talking about the **impact** communication has on receivers of the message—that is, how they respond to the message. What are the effects that determine whether an advertisement works or not? Over the years, professionals have used several models to outline what they believe is the impact of an advertisement on its audience:[8]

- *AIDA* The most commonly used explanation of how advertising works is referred to as **AIDA,** which stands for **a**ttention, **i**nterest, **d**esire, and **a**ction. This concept was first expressed around 1900 by an advertising pioneer named St. Elmo Lewis. Because AIDA assumes a predictable set of steps, it also is referred to as a **hierarchy of effects** model. Numerous other hierarchical models have been developed over the years to help advertisers plan their advertising.[9]
- *Think/Feel/Do* Another relatively simple answer to how advertising works is the **think/feel/do model** developed in the 1970s. Also referred to as the *FCB model* in honor of the agency where it was developed as a strategic planning tool, the idea is that advertising motivates people to think about the message, feel something about the brand, and then do something, such as try it or buy it.[10] That view is supported by recent research by Nyilasy and Reid into what professionals in advertising know and believe about how advertising works. Their in-depth interviews found that "agency practitioners strongly believe that exposure to ads causes changes in human cognition, emotions, and behavior"—or think/feel/do.[11]
- *Domains* A different approach that attempted to solve the problem of linear steps is found in Moriarty's domains model. It is based on the idea that messages have an impact on consumer responses, not in steps, but simultaneously. The three key effects, or domains, identified in this approach are (1) perception, (2) learning, and (3) persuasion. The idea is that a message can engage consumers' perceptions (attention, interest), educate them (think, learn), and persuade them (change attitude and behavior) all at the same time.[12] The Port of Vancouver ads are an example of how these effects interact. Even though the ads are in the business-to-business (B2B) category, the ads get the attention of their audience with dramatic headlines and visuals: "We have room to fulfill your vision" and the "Vacancy" sign, for example. The "Vacancy" ad is an educational message as the rest of the headline explains ("858 acres to be exact"), but also persuasive in that it makes the argument that the Port of Vancouver has room to grow and provide space to meet the needs of its customers.

How do we make sense of all of these ideas about how advertising works in order to create a reasonable approach to use in planning and critiquing advertising? One goal of this book is to organize all of these effects so they are useful for setting objectives and, ultimately, evaluating effectiveness. But how to do it? That's the question at the heart of this chapter and we'll answer with our model of how advertising and marketing communication work, a model that we think you will find to be simple and easy to use in explaining the impact of a message.

What Effects Are Critical?

Advertising professionals learn from their experiences producing marketing communication that works—and sometimes doesn't work very well. The practitioners interviewed by Nyilasy and Reid identified four building blocks as essential to effective advertising. They are attention, brand awareness, attitudes, and behavioral responses.[13]

Attitudes are both rational and emotional. The rational element is confirmed by David Ogilvy, who says in his classic little book, *Confessions of an Advertising Man,* "Very few advertisements contain enough factual information to sell the product." He was also quoted on the Advertising Hall of Fame website as saying that it needs to be informative to be persuasive.[14]

WE HAVE ROOM TO FULFILL YOUR VISION.
(858 ACRES TO BE EXACT.)

Unlike other ports, the Port of Vancouver has room to grow. That's thanks to our available and developable land, which gives us space for staging and managing cargo and room to meet new customer needs without compromising the demands of current customers. At present, we have plans to develop 216 acres at our new Terminal 5. To the north we have 108 acres set aside for light industrial development. Additionally, we have 534 acres available for future development at Columbia Gateway. With so much land yet to be developed along with our already expansive storage, warehousing and transit facilities, we're truly the port of possibilities. Give us a call or send us an email today to discuss your needs and learn how we can help.

THE PORT OF POSSIBILITY

Port of Vancouver USA
portvanusa.com

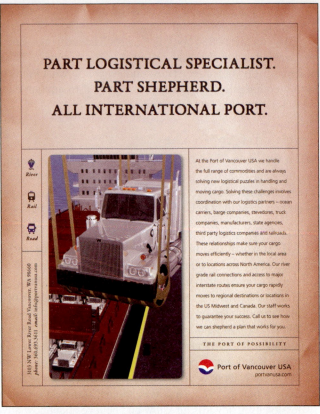

PART LOGISTICAL SPECIALIST.
PART SHEPHERD.
ALL INTERNATIONAL PORT.

At the Port of Vancouver USA we handle the full range of commodities and are always solving new logistical puzzles in handling and moving cargo. Solving these challenges involves coordination with our logistics partners — ocean carriers, barge companies, stevedores, truck companies, manufacturers, state agencies, third party logistics companies and railroads. These relationships make sure your cargo moves efficiently – whether in the local area or to locations across North America. Our river grade rail connections and access to major interstate routes ensure your cargo rapidly moves to regional destinations or locations in the US Midwest and Canada. Our staff works to guarantee your success. Call us to see how we can shepherd a plan that works for you.

THE PORT OF POSSIBILITY

Port of Vancouver USA
portvanusa.com

EVEN TODAY,
WIND BRINGS SHIPS
TO US.

It's not just a question of might. We have it: two 140-ton Liebherr mobile harbor cranes (the second is expected in early 2009). Nor is it a case of endurance. We have that, too. Our determination is where we excel. Even before offloading our first wind power components, we were developing operations and logistics with one thing in mind: becoming the West Coast's premier port for handling and transporting wind turbines. To date, we've handled more than 2,000 MW of turbines and hundreds of towers, many of which are destined for the Midwest, or Canada, via our on-terminal rail loading facilities – and that's just the beginning. We're increasing capacity, dedicating more space for staging and working harder than ever to keep wind power moving, truly making us your port of possibilities.

THE PORT OF POSSIBILITY

Port of Vancouver USA
portvanusa.com

SHOWCASE

This campaign is aimed at professionals in the transportation industry. These are three in a series of six ads that explain what services the Port of Vancouver offers its customers.

This campaign was contributed by Karl Schroeder, copywriter at Coates Kokes in Portland, Oregon. A graduate of the University of Oregon advertising program, his work was nominated for inclusion in this book by Professor Charles Frazer.

Ogilvy's advice comes from the traditional school that prizes rational decision making. Information and rational *information processing* are definitely important to certain types of ads. Consider, for example, the Canadian government's new Citizenship Act, which is designed to restore citizenship to thousands of unsuspecting foreigners, many of them Americans, who were forced to renounce their Canadian citizenship when they became citizens of another country. Canada uses ads on YouTube titled "Waking Up Canadian" to explain the situation.[15] (Check them out at *www.youtube.com/watch?v=eDeDQpIQFD0*)

Ogilvy's views and most of the traditional models, however, leave out a very critical factor that helps explain how advertising works and that is *emotion,* which Nyilasy and Reid's practitioners believe is just as important as information in the formation of attitudes. Some experts even believe emotion is more important than logical thinking in consumer decision making.

Ogilvy also recognizes *persuasion* as an important function and Nyilasy and Reid's professionals point to attitudes as critical—attitude formation and change being an important result of persuasive communication. (For other quotes and insights into how advertising works—or should work—visit *www.advertisinghalloffame .org/members.*)

The traditional approaches to defining the effects of advertising pose two problems: (1) the presumption of a set of steps as a predictable pattern of response—as in the old hierarchy of effects models—and (2) missing effects. The problem with the step-based (hierarchical and linear) models is that advertisers now realize people don't always respond in such a predictable fashion. This was confirmed by the opinions of the practitioners interviewed by Nyilasy and Reid who insist that "effects beyond getting attention can occur in any order, or even simultaneously."[16]

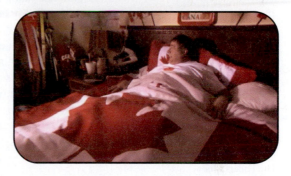

Ogilvy's focus on persuasion illustrates the problem that effects models don't always cover the essential facets of marketing communication impact. This problem is also particularly apparent when we look at research techniques used to evaluate effectiveness. Consider, for example, that the model of television advertising the Ameritest research company (*www.Ameritest.net*) developed to test commercials is based on three factors—attention, brand linkage, and motivation—and two of these—brand linkage and motivation—aren't mentioned in the traditional formulas we just discussed.[17] How can a major company that specializes in measuring effectiveness use an approach that is so different from the models professionals use in planning the advertising? As Chuck Young, the founder of Ameritest, emphasizes, "In all acts of perception and communication, emotion comes first, and thought comes second."[18]

An unsuspecting but newly recognized Canadian citizen wakes up to find his bedroom has become a center of Canadian symbols.

Another important area missing from the traditional models, but not from the Ameritest approach, is brand communication. As an indication of its importance to the professional community, consider that Ogilvy & Mather (O&M) makes brand communication the foundation of the agency's 360° Brand Stewardship philosophy. On its website (*www.Ogilvy.com*), the agency says, "We believe our job is to help clients build enduring brands that live as part of consumers' lives and command their loyalty and confidence." To accomplish that aim, O&M describes its role as:[19]

Creating attention-getting messages that make a promise consistent and true to the brand's image and identity. And guiding actions, both big and small, that deliver on that brand promise. To every audience that brand has. At every brand intersection point. At all times.

WHAT ARE THE FACETS OF IMPACT?

Our objective in this chapter is to present our Facets Model of Effects that does a more complete job than previous models of explaining how advertising creates impact in terms of various types of consumer responses. Ultimately, we are guided by the kind of thinking that Regina Lewis expressed in the Part 2 opener: that consumers are loyal to brands that say something about them as human beings. Effective marketing communication speaks to us about things that we want to know in ways that we like.

The simplicity of think/feel/do makes it a good starting point, since all three of these effects are generally recognized as critical consumer responses to advertising. Several of the models begin with terms like *attention, awareness,* and *exposure,* concepts that recognize there is a *perceptual dimension* to advertising impact, as Moriarty's domains model suggests. Another missing area we've noted is *persuasion,* which explains how beliefs and attitudes are created or changed and conviction is established. Since persuasion relies on both think and feel responses, it doesn't fit at all in the hierarchical models and falls between the cracks if you are trying to use the think/feel/do approach as a model for objectives. Another of the areas missing from most models is *association,* which Preston and Thorson use to explain how brand communication works in general.[20] In recognition of its importance to brand communication, this category is also called *brand transformation* or *brand linkage.*

The solution, then, to our search for a new model is to build on the effects identified in the think/feel/do approach and add the missing categories. It is interesting that the missing areas we just identified—perception, brand association, and persuasion—are also related to the three areas that the Ameritest research company uses in evaluating effective commercials.

Thus, we propose a six-factor model that should be useful both in setting objectives and evaluating the effectiveness of advertising. Our answer to the question of how advertising works is to propose that effective advertising creates six types of consumer responses: (1) see/hear, (2) feel, (3) think/understand, (4) connect, (5) believe, and (6) act/do—all of which work together to create the response to a brand message. These six consumer responses and the categories of effects to which they belong are represented in Figure 4.3.

Think, of these six effects as facets—polished surfaces like those of a diamond or crystal—that come together to make up a unique consumer response to an advertising message. The effects are holistic in the sense that they lead to an impression, or what Preston calls an "integrated perception."[21] An effective message has a diamond-like quality that represents how the message effects work together to create the desired consumer response. The effects can vary in importance with some advertising campaigns more focused on one or several of the facets.

FIGURE 4.3
The Facets Model
of Effects

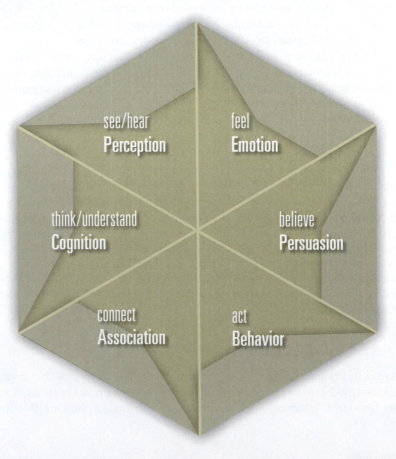

Here is a table to help you analyze the impact of an advertisement in terms of the type of objective the ad is trying to achieve and how that will be apparent in the way consumers respond to the message. The final column lists factors that can be measured to determine if you achieved the desired type of impact.

Communication Objective	Consumer Response	Factors That Drive a Response
Perception	See/Hear	Exposure, selection and attention, interest, relevance, curiosity, awareness, recognition
Emotional/Affective	Feel	Wants and desires, excitement, feelings, liking, resonance
Cognition	Think/Understand	Need, cognitive learning, comprehension, differentiation, recall
Association	Connect	Symbolism, conditioned learning, transformation
Persuasion	Believe	Motivation, influence, involvement, engagement, conviction, preference and intention, loyalty, believability and credibility
Behavior	Act/Do	Mental rehearsal, trial, buying, contacting, advocating and referrals, prevention

Let's now explore these six categories of effects in more detail. We'll start with perception, which is where the consumer response to an advertisement begins.

The Perception Facet: See/Hear

Every day we are bombarded with stimuli—faces, conversations, scents, sounds, advertisements, news announcements—yet we actually notice only a small fraction of those stimuli. Why?

The answer is perception. **Perception** is the process by which we receive information through our five senses and assign meaning to it. If an advertisement is to be effective, first of all, it must get noticed. It has to be seen or heard, even if the perception is minimal and largely below the level of awareness. We "see" ads in magazines even if we page through the publication without stopping to read them; we "see" commercials on TV even as we zip through a recorded program. The challenge is to create breakthrough advertising, messages that get attention and stick in the mind.

Our minds are full of impressions that we have collected without much active thought or concentration. Of course, on occasion we do stop and read an ad or watch a commercial all the way through, so there are various degrees and levels of perception. The Burger King "Freakout" ads were particularly effective at breaking through inattention and building awareness. Breakthrough advertising, then, is advertising that breaks through the perceptual filters and makes an impression on the audience.

Principle
For an advertisement to be effective, it first has to get noticed or at least register on some minimal level on our senses.

Factors That Drive the Perception Response   Consumers select messages to which they pay attention, a process called **selective perception.** Here's how perception works: Some ads for some product categories—personal hygiene products, for example—battle for attention because people don't choose to watch them. However, if the message breaks through the disinterest and is selected and attended to, then the consumer may react to it with interest if it is relevant. The result is awareness of the ad or brand, which is filed in memory at least to the point that the consumer recognizes the brand or ad.

The key factors driving perception, then, are exposure, selection and attention, interest, relevance, curiosity, awareness, and recognition. Here is a brief review of these terms and how they relate to advertising impact:

- *Exposure* The first test of perception is whether a marketing communication message is seen or heard. In advertising, this is called **exposure,** which is an important goal of media planners who try to find the best way to reach consumers with a message.

- *Selection and Attention* The next factor that drives perception is **selective attention,** the process by which a receiver of a message chooses to attend to a message. Amid all the clutter in the media environment, selection is a huge problem. The ability to draw attention that brings visibility to a brand is one of advertising's greatest strengths. Advertisements, particularly television commercials, are often designed to be **intrusive,** which means they intrude on people's perception in order to grab attention.
- *Interest* A factor in crossing the selection barrier is **interest,** which means the receiver of the message has become mentally engaged in some way with the ad and the product. Ad messages are designed not only to get attention, but also to hold the audience's interest long enough for the audience to register the point of the ad. That level of interest and attention is sometimes referred to as **stickiness,** particularly for websites.
- *Relevance* One reason people are interested in something is **relevance,** which means the message, such as the accompanying example for the Peace Corps, connects on some personal level. The Peace Corps launched a national recruiting campaign with the theme "Life is calling. How far will you go?" It was designed to address more relevant personal issues for potential volunteers and tell them how the volunteer experience would enrich their lives.
- *Curiosity* Another reason people pay attention is curiosity, which results from questioning, wanting to know more, or being intrigued by something. Curiosity also may be a problem for certain types of campaigns, such as antidrug and anti-smoking efforts, as Ohio University Professor Carson B. Wagner found out in his research on the government's "Just Say No" campaign. He explains:

Would you stop to give someone directions?
If you were walking that way,
would you guide them?
What if it was out of your way?
One mile.
Two miles.

Two thousand miles,
directly inland from the Skeleton Coast,
to a one-room schoolhouse in the foothills of Namibia.
What if you were the teacher in that schoolhouse?
Would you travel that far to teach someone?
To learn something yourself?

Peace Corps.
Life is calling. How far will you go?

Call 800.424.8580 | Visit peacecorps.gov

Messages that are relevant speak to a consumer's special interests.

One weekend, my father, who is an advertising executive, and I got into a conversation about how it seemed every time a news story aired about illicit drugs, a small epidemic of drug use would ensue. Of course, there's been a lot of research done about the ways media can encourage drug use, but most of that is about popular media such as movies and music. We'd presume that news programs and antidrug ads that are meant to show illicit drugs in a negative light shouldn't lead people toward drugs. But, as almost any student of communication has learned, media don't tell us what to think; they tell us what to think about.

So, I decided to test the idea on antidrug ads—the most counterintuitive possibility—in a small experiment for my master's thesis. I scoured prior research, but I couldn't find anything suggesting that antidrug ads might lead to drug use. Almost all studies showed that drug attitudes became more negative. But, the psychology-of-curiosity literature suggested something else: If antidrug ads make people think drug use is widespread, they might become curious about experimenting themselves. My study found that the curiosity literature was correct.

Wagner's counterintuitive results were so compelling that he found himself on talk shows and featured in news and wire stories. He also presented his findings to Congress. Since then, a large-scale government-sponsored survey examining the first five years of the government's "Just Say No" campaign uncovered similar relationships between antidrug advertising and drug use. Unfortunately it doesn't seem to have gotten any better reception than Wagner's study did. It's hard to convince some experts that even negative attention is still attention.

- *Awareness* When you are aware of something, you know that you have seen it or heard it before. In other words, **awareness** results when an advertisement makes an impression—when something registers. New product campaigns, for example, seek to create high levels of brand awareness. Brand reminder ads on billboards and Web pages are also designed to maintain a high level of awareness of familiar brands, as are logos on clothing.
- *Recognition* Advertisers are interested in two types of memory: **recognition** which means people remember seeing the ad, and **recall,** which means they remember what the ad said. Recognition is a measure of perception and is used to determine awareness. Recall is a measure of understanding, which we will talk about in a later section on cognitive effects. Recognition relies on simple visuals that lock into memory, such as logos (Nike's swoosh), as well as colors (IBM's blue), jingles and sounds (Gershwin's "Rhapsody in Blue" for United Airlines), characters (the Energizer bunny), key visuals (Polo's pony, the disbelieving look of the Aflac duck), and slogans (Altoids, "The Curiously Strong Mints"). Memory depends heavily on repetition to anchor an impression in the mind.

The Synergy Requirement We mentioned earlier Preston's idea that the end result of effective advertising and marketing communication is an integrated perception. We call that a brand. In campaigns that use an IMC approach, marketers coordinate all the marketing communication messages to create **synergy,** which means individual messages have more impact working jointly to promote a product than they would working on their own.[22] The reason is that people automatically integrate the messages and experiences they have with a brand to create their own personal brand perception. This happens whether or not the marketer plans for integrated communicated. That's just how perception works. Sophisticated managers understand this and try to manage their communication programs so all the messages work together to create Preston's coherent brand perception.

The Subliminal Issue Before we leave the perception category, let's consider the controversial area of subliminal effects. **subliminal** effects are message cues given below the threshold of perception. In other words, they don't register. As Professor Sheri Broyles explains in the *A Matter of Principle* feature, "By definition, *subliminal* means the stimulus is below your threshold of consciousness. The first thing to know is if you can see something, then it isn't subliminal." The idea is that subliminal messages are designed to get past your perceptual filters by talking directly to your subconscious. People who believe in subliminal advertising presume such messages to be intense enough to influence behavior and they consider it to be unfair manipulation of unaware viewers. Broyles describes the research and thinking about the idea that unseen messages can be communicated in advertising in the *A Matter of Principle* feature.

> **Fifth Principle of IMC**
> People automatically integrate brand messages and experiences. Synergy occurs when all of the messages work together to create a coherent brand perception.

The Emotional or Affective Facet: Feel

Do you have favorite brands that you like—and did advertising have anything to do with why you like that brand? Can you remember any ads that you liked and why you liked them? **Affective responses** mirror our feelings about something. The term *affective* describes something that stimulates wants, touches the emotions, establishes a mood, creates liking, and elicits feelings.[†]

In the Part 2 opener, Regina Lewis emphasized the importance of emotional connections for successful brands. A lesson learned from the recent economic downturn is that positive brand communication is important. She explains, "During tough times, brands that are able to lift the mood through their communications are rewarded." But it's more than just cheery messages; she also notes that certain types of emotional messages have more resonance: "Nostalgic brands that give people a sense of tradition and security tend to thrive."

Feelings and emotions can be positive—or negative. Generally, marketing communication seeks to wrap a positive halo around a brand and a purchase decision. Kevin Roberts, CEO of

---

[†]*Affective* refers to emotional responses; *effective* refers to how well something works.

A MATTER OF PRINCIPLE

Ice Cubes, Breasts, and Subliminal Ads

Sheri Broyles, *Associate Professor, University of North Texas*

For 50 years people have been looking for secret little subliminal messages carefully hidden in advertising we see every day.

It began in 1957 in a movie theater experiment when James Vicary subliminally suggested people "eat popcorn" and "drink Coca-Cola" by projecting those words at 1/3,000th of a second on the screen during a movie. News media at the time widely reported his claims that sales of popcorn and soda increased as a result. Though he later admitted these results were a hoax, it was as if Pandora had let subliminal advertising out of her box. A large majority of people have repeatedly said that they have heard of subliminal advertising (74 to 84 percent), they believe advertisers use this technique (68 to 85 percent), and they think it is effective (68 to 78 percent). Obviously, subliminal advertising continues to be an issue today.

Subliminal also has been misused to mean "suggestive" or "sexual." In the 1970s and 1980s Wilson Bryan Key popularized this view in his books *Subliminal Seduction, Media Sexploitation*, and *The Clam-Plate Orgy*. He suggested that photographs were embedded (that is, manipulated by airbrushing) with sexual or arousing images in ambiguous portions of the picture. He maintained that products ranging from alcoholic beverages to Ritz crackers used these sexual embeds. Key's self-proclaimed disciple, August Bullock, makes similar statements in his more recent book *The Secret Sales Pitch*.

There's been a continuing debate over the years about whether subliminal advertising actually exists. However, it's impossible to convince devout believers in subliminal advertising that what they *think* they see isn't there. Even more troubling is their assumption that presence implies effectiveness. Their belief is that because subliminal advertising exists—at least in their minds—it must be effective; otherwise, it wouldn't exist. Perhaps the more important question isn't whether subliminal advertising exists, but whether or not it's an effective advertising tool. It should be noted that neither Key nor Bullock offers documentation that subliminal advertising actually works in any of the many examples in their books.

Several studies followed Vicary's theater experiment that explored whether subliminal advertising had an effect on consumers. Many different methodologies were used to test the effectiveness of subliminal stimuli. One 1959 study used early television to test subliminal

A liquor advertising campaign showed ice cubes with shapes in them and deliberately called attention to these supposedly "subliminal" messages. Of course, they weren't subliminal because you could see the images. The whole campaign was a spoof on Key's theories.

persuasion. Another used a slide projector to subliminally superimpose a message. Others placed embeds in print ads. Most experiments showed no effect. Those that did either could not be replicated by the researchers or the effect was so weak that it would be canceled out by competing stimuli for the consumer's attention if it were not in a laboratory setting. There is no evidence to suggest that subliminal advertising would persuade real consumers to buy real products.

If subliminal advertising isn't effective, why are we still talking about it 50 years later? While research has repeatedly shown that subliminal advertising doesn't work, the general public hasn't been persuaded, perhaps because they haven't been exposed to the decades of research. Subliminal advertising is like an urban legend or a good conspiracy theory—it's something that people want to believe. However, whether valid or not, it does affect the public's perception of advertising. That, in turn, reduces the credibility of advertisers and their agencies. And that's a concern for everyone in the advertising industry.

Saatchi & Saatchi, describes the passion that loyal customers feel for their favorite brands with the term *lovemarks*. You can read about lovemarks in his books (*Lovemarks: The Future beyond Brands* and *The Lovemarks Effect: Winning in the Consumer Revolution*) and on the website: *www.lovemarks.com.* Check out the case studies on this website to understand how businesses can inspire love for their brands.

Sometimes, however, a brand message arouses different emotions—fear or dislike, for example. Some ads are designed to make you feel negative about something (smoking, bugs in your home, a political candidate). In the case of irritating advertising, you may even respond by disliking a brand or an ad, which may be a sign of a failed campaign. Have you ever seen an ad that you positively disliked? How did that affect your attitude toward the brand?

Look back at the Facets Model of Effects in Figure 4.3. Notice how *perception* and *feel* sit side by side at the top of the model. Although this isn't a linear process model, the perceptual process begins with perception if a message registers at all. That also means emotion is a driving factor because it is so closely related to perception. Erik du Plessis, the CEO of a global advertising research firm, makes the argument in his book *The Advertised Mind* that attention is driven by emotion.[23] He says our emotional responses to a message determine whether or not we pay attention. The key task of an ad, then, is initially to evoke an emotional response.

This view is supported by recent research in the neurosciences, which advertising professor Ann Marie Barry says "acknowledges the primacy of emotions in processing all communication."[24] She explains further that "Perception, the process by which we derive meaning from what we see, is an elaborate symphony played first and foremost through the unconscious emotional system." The important role of emotion in directing perception also structures our responses to brand messages, particularly those that engage us on a personal level. For more on this subject, check out Barry's comments on thinking versus feeling in the *A Matter of Practice* feature.

Factors That Drive the Emotional/Affective Response
Emotional responses are powerful, not only because they drive perception, but also because, as du Plessis explains, they determine whether our unconscious reaction becomes conscious—in other words, the ad breaks through disinterest. Furthermore, he suggests that positive emotional responses drive memory as well.

The affective response drivers are wants and desires, excitement, feelings, liking, and resonance. Emotion, then, causes us to "feel" something. Another classic commercial that has generated positive responses for more than 40 years is the Coca-Cola "Hilltop" commercial, which shows a multi-ethnic group of young people singing "I want to teach the world to sing in perfect harmony." A product of the anti-war, Peace Movement, Woodstock generation, the 1972 commercial touched nerves, as well as hearts, and continues to get airtime, particularly on holidays. (Check it out at *www.youtube.com/watch?v=6mOEU87SBTU*.)

- **Wants and Desires** "I want something" implies desire. **Wants** are driven by emotions and based on wishes, longings, and cravings—such as teaching the world to sing, which is a metaphor for peace. Impulse buying is a good example of the motivational power of wants. When you are standing in line at a store and see a display of candy bars, you may want one, but that doesn't mean you need it. It's strictly desire, and desire is driven by emotion. Consider Axe, which pioneered the new category of body spray for men in 2002. Now it boasts an astonishing $150 million in annual sales. Did guys know before 2002 that they would want scented body spray?

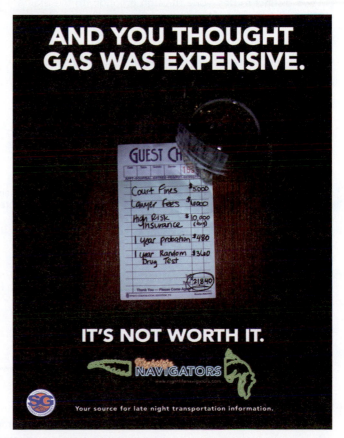

SHOWCASE

The "expensive gas" poster from the Nightlife Navigators campaign intends to create a negative feeling about the financial impact of a DUI ticket. This is one of a series of ads about drinking and driving by the Adwerks student advertising agency at the University of Florida.

A MATTER OF PRACTICE

Thought vs. Feeling

Ann Marie Barry, *Associate Professor, Boston College*

Building a brand identity that fits the preferred self-image of the target market is a matter of designing advertising messages so that they are fully in tune with the self-identity of the consumer. To do this, advertisers need to understand basically how the mind functions, beginning with the fundamental relationship between thought and feeling.

Rational thought takes place in the *neocortex*, the most evolved and "highest" part of the brain, but feelings emanate from the *limbic system*, the cerebellum and brainstem, the most primitive part of the brain.

When we see something, the sensory path follows two distinct routes—one through emotion (to the brain's *amygdala)* and the other up to thought (the brain's neocortex). The emotional route is very fast and is geared toward survival, sending reaction signals to other parts of the brain and the rest of the body, well before the neocortex has had the chance to form a conscious thought. Emotion is the first path that perception takes. It is also the fastest, and most significant factor in perception. The whole process might be diagrammed this way:

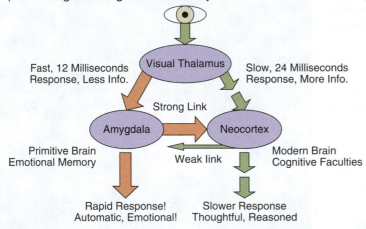

Not only do we feel before we think, but we need to feel in order to think. Unconscious emotional processing sets up thinking by producing a definite attitude. This attitude uses the memory of past experience to prepare thoughts and actions before we are even consciously aware of reacting at all. In fact, most of what we call the *thought process* in making decisions is actually trying to rationalize what we have already concluded through our emotional system. Marketers know that if they can convince us emotionally, we can rationalize away any objections by ourselves.

Descartes professed "I think therefore I am." Today's neurologists, however, concur that we think because we feel. Advertising images can connect with consumers' self-image on a deep emotional level because neurons come together in the mind as circuits that form mental meaning, in what might best be described as a story. When you buy an Apple computer or an iPod, for example, you buy more than electronics; you buy a message about a product user that confirms you as a person. This is the story implicit in Apple's commercials—that its customers are nonconformist and very hip. It is this attitude that resonates with us emotionally when we think of Apple products and that sets up our rational decision making.

Every brand that we use in effect advertises who we are when we wear it or use it, telling people a little bit about us, or just reinforcing how we feel about ourselves (or would like to feel). If the emotional appeal is missing, however, we lose a personal connection with the product or service. If the rational benefit is missing, we may not find enough reason to purchase an item where elements such as price, ease of use, or technological advantages play a major role. For an advertisement to be truly effective, the visual story implicit in it must seamlessly bring together both consumer image and brand image in a perfect integration of both thought and feeling.

- *Excitement* A step above interest in terms of intensity of response (see the perception discussion) is excitement, which means our emotions or passions are aroused. If we are excited about something, we are agitated or energized and more willing to participate or make a commitment.
- *Feelings* Our passions and feelings are addressed in a number of ways in advertising, such as humor, love, or fear. Ads that rely on arousing feelings are referred to as using **emotional appeals.** The idea that emotional appeals may have more impact than rational approaches on both attitudes and behavior was supported by a University of Florida study that analyzed 23,000 consumer responses and found that the emotional response is more powerful than cognition in predicting action.[25]

- *Liking* Two important affective responses to a message are liking the brand and liking the ad. **Liking** reflects the personality of the brand or the entertainment power of the ad's execution. The assumption is that if you like the ad, then that positive feeling will transfer to the brand and if you feel positive about the brand, you will be more likely to buy it. A classic study of advertising testing methods by the Advertising Research Foundation (ARF) found that liking—both the brand and the ad—was the best predictor of consumer behavior.[26]

  On the opposite side of liking is *aversion,* which means people avoid buying a brand because they don't like the ads or what they associate with the brand. We don't like to see condom ads, so they aren't often found in the mass media. Negative political ads demonstrate the flip side of liking. They are an example of an affective strategy that seems to work by putting opponents on the defensive. They may work through the power of suggestion, but most people say they dislike these ads because they sometimes seem unfair or mean spirited.

- *Resonance* Effective advertisements sometimes create **resonance,** or a feeling that the message "rings true." Like relevance, messages that resonate help the consumer identify with the brand on a personal level. Resonance is stronger than liking because it involves an element of self-identification. These sympathetic vibes amplify the emotional impact by engaging a consumer in a personal connection with a brand.

Principle

A positive response to an ad is important because advertisers hope that liking the ad will increase liking the brand.

The Cognition Facet: Think/Understand

How many ads that you have seen on television or noticed in print caused you to stop and think about the brand? Can you recall any instance where you learned something new about a product from an ad? Have you ever seen an ad you liked and then can't remember the name of the advertiser? Although perception and its partner, emotion, are the first effects of an advertising message, an advertisement may generate any of the other responses—cognition, association, persuasion, and behavior—next. For this discussion, we'll talk first about cognitive impact.

Cognition refers to how consumers search for and respond to information, as well as how they learn and understand something. It's a rational response to a message. Some call this a left-brain approach, based on the left–right brain ways of thinking that evolved from brain hemisphere research. Right-brain thinking is presumed to be more emotional and creative. The American Airlines ad uses the left–right brain metaphor to demonstrate the difference between a cognitive and an emotional advertising message.

Factors That Drive the Cognitive Response
With a cognitive response a consumer may need something or need to know something, and the information gathered in response to that need leads to understanding. The information is filed in memory but can be recalled when needed. Advertising and other marketing communication often provide information about products, usually facts about product performance and features, such as size, price, construction, and design. Many consumers seek out and value this kind of information. The Yankelovich research company, for example, found that consumers say they want

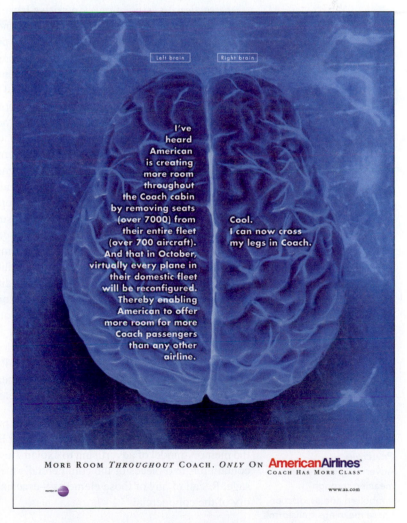

To creatively communicate its new seating in coach, American Airlines used a picture of a brain with the left side representing cognitive thinking and the right brain illustrating an affective response.

more nutrition information on food labels as well as guidelines on packages. (Check out www.yankelovich.com.) The informative nature of advertising is particularly important for products that are complex (e.g., appliances, cars, insurance, computers, software) or that involve a high price or high risk (e.g., motorboats, vacations, medical procedures).

The key drivers of a consumer's cognitive response are need, cognitive learning, comprehension, differentiation, and recall.

- *Need* Advertisers talk a lot about consumer needs and wants. Generally, **needs** are basic biological motivations but they are also something you think about; wants tend to be based more on feelings and desires. In other words, when we refer to needs, we are usually talking about a message that describes something lacking in consumers' lives and that often stimulates a cognitive response. Advertisers address consumer needs through informational ads that explain how a product works and what it can do for the user—the benefits it offers to the user. For example, consumers need a virus protection program for their personal computers, but they also may need an explanation of how the program works. Complicating our understanding of needs and wants is the impact of a major event, such as the recent recession. A *Wall Street Journal* article analyzed the auto industry in terms of the tug between want (a Cadillac Escapade specially designed on GM's website to a customer's order) and need (a used car that offers the best value in terms of miles and price) or a need that's simply postponed because it's of less significance that other more compelling needs.[27]
- *Cognitive Learning* Consumers learn about products and brands through two primary routes: cognitive learning and conditioned learning. (We'll talk about conditioned learning in the section on association.) **Cognitive learning** occurs when a presentation of facts, information, and explanations leads to understanding. Consumers who are trying to find information about a product before they buy it are taking the cognitive learning route. This typically applies to large purchases, such as cars, computers, and major appliances. Learning is also a part of new product introductions—in recent years, we have had to learn to use computers, VCRs, the Internet, TiVo, and the iPod, and marketing communication is the key tool used by marketers to teach prospective customers about these products and product innovations.
- *Comprehension* **Comprehension** is the process by which people understand, make sense of things, and acquire knowledge. Confusion, on the other hand, is the absence of understanding and is usually the result of logic problems. For example, it's difficult for consumers to understand why an outdoor board for the gas-guzzling Hummer would use a green marketing strategy. The headline "Thirst for adventure. Not gas" suggests a gas-efficient Hummer and the logic doesn't follow from what people commonly know about this vehicle.
- *Differentiation* **Differentiation** is the consumer's ability to separate one brand from another in a product category. Distinguishing between competing brands is what happens when consumers understand the explanation of a competitive advantage. In a historic but still important study of effective television commercials, researchers concluded that one of the most important effectiveness factors is a brand-differentiating message.[28]
- *Recall* We mentioned earlier that recognition is a measure of perception and recall is a measure of learning or understanding. When you recall the ad message, you not only remember seeing the ad and hopefully the brand, you also remember the copy points, or the information provided about the brand. To recall information presented in the ad, however, you must have concentrated on it and thought about it either as the information was being presented or afterward. Thinking about it—similar to mentally rehearsing the key points—is a form of information processing that helps anchor ideas in memory and makes recall easier.

Even though this section is on cognitive processing, note that feeling and thinking work together. Psychologist and advertising professor Esther Thorson and her colleagues have developed the memory model of advertising to explain how commercials are stored in memory as traces that contain bits and pieces of the commercial's message, including the feelings elicited by the message. Recall of any of those elements—especially feelings—can serve as a cue to activate memory of the commercial.[29]

The Association Facet: Connect

What do you think of when you see an ad for Nike, Viagra, or Mountain Dew? The things that come to your mind, such as athletes for Nike, older men for Viagra, and teenage guys having fun

Principle

Advertising creates brand meaning through symbolism and association. These meanings transform a generic product into a specific brand with a distinctive image and personality.

for Mountain Dew, are the brands' associations. **Association** is the technique of communicating through symbolism. As such, it is the primary tool used in brand communication. It is the process of learning to make symbolic connections between a brand and desirable characteristics and qualities, as well as people, situations, and lifestyles that cue the brand's image and personality.

You see association at work in advertising in the practice of linking a brand with a positive experience, or a lifestyle, such as Axe with cool young men or Coke with a mountaintop experience. The idea is to associate the brand with things that resonate positively with the customer. It's a three-way process: the (1) brand relates to (2) a quality that (3) customers value. Brands take on symbolic meaning through this association process. Professor Ivan Preston, in his association model of advertising, believes that you can explain how advertising works by understanding association.[30]

Factors That Drive the Association Response   The goal of association is to use symbolic connections to define the brand and make it distinctive. **Brand linkage** reflects the degree to which the associations presented in the message, as well as the consumer's interest, are connected to the brand. For example, an ad for Bisquick HeartSmart mix shows a pancake in the shape of a heart. In this case, the brand name—Bisquick HeartSmart—is easily associated with the product use—your heart and healthy pancakes. The association drivers we discuss here are symbolism, conditioned learning, and transformation:

- *Symbolism* Through association a brand takes on a **symbolic meaning,** which means the brand stands for certain qualities. It represents something, usually something abstract. Bisquick's pancakes shaped like hearts convey the heart-healthy message symbolically. The Port of Vancouver B2B ads use symbolism to catch attention and tell a story, such as the vacancy sign in the ad analyzed earlier. Symbolism is also used in the other ads, where one refers to cargo handling as shepherding and the other references wind power both as a cargo and as a source of movement for ships.

- *Conditioned Learning* Although advertisements sometimes use a cognitive strategy, they frequently are designed to elicit noncognitive associations through **conditioned learning,** the process by which a group of thoughts and feelings becomes linked to the brand through repetition of the message. Beer advertising directed at a young male audience, for example, often uses images of sporting events, beach parties, and good-looking young women. People also learn by watching others, which is called **social learning.** We learn about fashion by watching how others dress and about manners by watching how other people interact. We connect their appearance and manners to certain situations reflected in the ads.

- *Transformation* The result of the brand association process is transformation. **Transformation,** as originally explained by former DDB research director Bill Wells, is what happens when a product takes on meaning and is transformed from a mere product into something special. It becomes differentiated from other products in the category by virtue of its brand image symbolism and personality cues. Bisquick HeartSmart is more than just flour; it rises above the average product in the category and stands out as something unique and healthy. That transformation in a consumer's mind is a perceptual shift created by the associations cued through advertising messages.

A dramatic photo of Mount McKinley captures the attention of Coke drinkers visiting Alaska's Denali National Park. It associates drinking Coke with an enduring and majestic mountaintop.

Association Networks   You probably had a number of associations when we asked you to think about Nike. Athletes come to mind, but also shoes, engineering, design, the Swoosh logo, competition, sporting events, maybe even a fun retail experience if you have ever visited a Nike store. The association process is built on a **network of associations,** called a **knowledge structure.** Solomon in his book on consumer behavior describes these networks as spider webs[31] where one thought cues other thoughts. Your thoughts and feelings about the Nike brand are elements linked in your own individual pattern of associative thinking. You might say that these association networks explain how our memories work. Researchers seeking to determine the meaning of a brand will ask people to talk about their associations with a brand and to re-create these association networks in order to understand how a brand's meaning comes together as an impression in people's minds.

The Persuasion Facet: Believe

When you see ads from the "Got Milk?" campaign with celebrities sporting a milk mustache, what do you think is the objective of the advertising? Is it providing information about milk? Is it trying to connect with you on an emotional level through fear, love, envy, hunger, or some other feeling? Is it trying to get you to run down to the store and load up on milk? The real objective of these ads is to change your attitude toward milk. It aims to convince you that milk isn't just for kids and that attractive, interesting adults drink it, too.

Persuasion is the conscious intent on the part of the source to influence or motivate the receiver of a message to believe or do something. Persuasive communication—creating or changing attitudes and creating conviction—are important goals of most marketing communication. An **attitude** is a state of mind—a tendency, inclination, or mental readiness to react to a situation in a given way. Since advertising rarely delivers immediate action, *surrogate* effects, such as changing an attitude that leads to a behavior, are often the goal of advertising. Attitudes are the most central factors in persuasion.

Attitudes can be positive, negative, or neutral. Both positive and negative attitudes, particularly those embedded in strong emotions, can motivate people to action—or away from action. A negative attitude toward smoking, for example, may keep teenagers from trying cigarettes, and creating that negative attitude was the objective of the *truth®* campaign discussed in Chapter 1.

When people are convinced of something, their attitudes are expressed as **beliefs.** Sometimes attitude strategies attempt to extinguish beliefs—for example, that getting drunk is a badge of masculinity, overeating is acceptable, or racist and sexist comments are funny. Attitude change strategies often use the tools of logic and reasoning, along with arguments and counterarguments, to intensify the feelings on which beliefs are built.

Persuasion, in other words, is an area where cognitive and affective factors are interrelated—persuasion works both through rational arguments and by touching emotions in such a way that they create a compulsion to act. Persuasive strategies can be used to touch both the head and the heart. As discussed in the *A Principled Practice* feature, negative advertising, or attack ads, is a good example of how people form opinions at the same time as they process information that is presented within an emotional frame.

Principle
Advertising employs both rational arguments and compelling emotions to create persuasive messages.

Factors That Drive the Persuasion Response   Persuasion has many dimensions, but advertisers identify the following factors to explain how persuasion affects consumers: motivation, influence, involvement, engagement, conviction, preference and intention, loyalty, and believability and credibility.

- *Motivation* A factor in creating a persuasive message is **motivation.** Underlying motivation is the idea that something, such as hunger or a desire to be beautiful or rich, prompts a person to act in a certain way. How strongly does someone feel about acquiring something or about taking a certain kind of action, such as applying to graduate school or signing up for the Peace Corps? This sets up a state of tension, and the product becomes a tool in achieving that goal and thus reducing the tension. A more current example of the power of motivation cropped up in the development of **carrot mobs,** a technique used by environmentalists to reward companies that support green marketing. It's a reverse boycott that uses positive action—getting large groups of people to shop at eco-friendly stores.[32]

A PRINCIPLED PRACTICE

Does Negative Political Advertising Help or Hinder Citizens?

Marilyn S. Roberts, *Ph.D., Zayed University*

Negative political advertising is not new. One example of a highly negative campaign dates back to the 1828 presidential election between Andrew Jackson and his opponent, John Quincy Adams. Fast forward to 1952, when the televised political advertising era began and brought new concerns. With the combination of sight, sound, and motion, the merits and criticisms of negative television advertising began debates that continue today.

From a practitioner's perspective, an important question is "Do negative ads work?"

Almost in unison political media consultants for major U.S. political parties say, "Yes!" One may find that exception is taken by consultants when referring to what they create as "negative" advertising. Instead, many professionals prefer to use the term *contrast advertising* to underscore the differences between their candidate and his or her opponent.

In seminal research over 40 years ago, Patterson and McClure argued that citizens do learn about issues from spot commercials, a finding that flew in the face of convention at the time. The frequency of attack ads in presidential campaigns has risen steadily over the past decades, regardless of party affiliation.

Today scholars hold widely differing opinions as to the beneficial or detrimental role that negative advertising plays in contemporary campaigning and civil society. Kathleen Hall Jamieson attests that there is a strong association between negativity and deception. Her efforts have influenced how journalists report on campaign advertising and led to increased efforts to check the accuracy of advertising content and claims.

John G. Geer offers reasons to rethink opposition to negativity in political campaigns. He compared the quality of nearly 800 positive and negative political ads by applying the following standards:

- The more issues are discussed, the better.
- The more evidence is presented, the better.
- The clearer the differences between candidates, the better.
- The more relevant the appeal is to governing, the better.

Geer's findings suggest that negative information is more issue oriented than positive ads. Attack ads are more likely to be supported by evidence than self-promotional positive ads. Previous research also supported the notion that negative information is more easily recalled than positive information.

Does negativity in campaigns hurt the democratic process? Many observers worry that it does, while others argue the contrary. Whether one views negativity as good, bad, or mixed, politics is about conflict. As interactive political advertising and blogs play a larger role in contemporary campaigns, the questions and concerns about the rise in negativity will not diminish. Citizens, the news media, and candidates and their consultants must monitor and take responsibility for the tone of campaigns.

Sources: Kathleen Hall Jamieson, *Packaging the Presidency: A History and Criticism of Presidential Campaign Advertising*, 3rd ed., New York: Oxford University Press, 1996; Kathleen Hall Jamieson, *Dirty Politics; Deception, Distraction, and Democracy*, New York: Oxford University Press, 1992; Thomas E. Patterson and Robert McClure, *Unseeing Eye*, New York: Putnam, 1976; John G. Geer, *In Defense of Negativity: Attack Ads in Presidential Campaigns*, Chicago: University of Chicago Press, 2006.

- *Influence* If you think you need to lose weight or stop smoking, how much of that decision is based on your own motivations and how much of your motivation results from messages from others? Some people, known as **opinion leaders,** may be able to influence other peoples' attitudes and convince them of the "right" decision. The idea is that other people—friends, family, teachers, and experts such as doctors—may affect your decision making. Testimonies—from real people, celebrities (the "Got Milk?" campaign), and experts—are often used to change attitudes. **Bandwagon appeals**—messages that suggest that everyone is doing it—are also used to influence people's decisions. **Word-of-mouth** communication

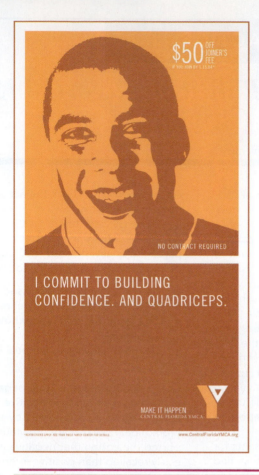

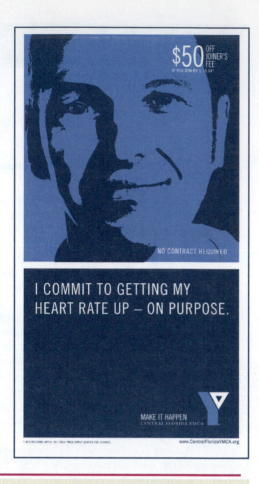

SHOWCASE

For a YMCA membership drive in Orlando, Florida, the objective was not just to get new members, but keep them—and keep them participating. To drive conviction, the FHB agency in Orlando developed a campaign highlighting real members' commitments to mind, body, and spirit. With its bold, graphic look the campaign attracted attention and was positively received.

These ads were contributed by Lara Mann, a graduate of the University of Florida, whose work was nominated for inclusion by Professor Elaine Wagner.

has always been recognized as the most powerful form of persuasion, and that's why strategies that engage influencers are so important.

• *Involvement* Advertisers distinguish between products, messages, and media on the basis of the level of involvement they require from the buyer. **Involvement** refers to the degree to which you are engaged in attending to an ad and the process you go through in responding to a message and making a product decision. Some products, for instance, cosmetics, call for a more involving process than others, say, toothpaste. **High-involvement** products are considered purchases; in other words, purchases for which consumers spend more time and effort searching for information and comparison data before they make decisions. **Considered purchases** includes such products as cars and computers, as well as things you care about a lot like clothes and cosmetics. Examples of **low-involvement** products are aspirin, paper napkins, envelopes, paper clips, milk, and lettuce. The idea is that you think about some products and reflect on the advertising you see for them, but with other products you don't spend much time thinking about them before you buy them. Nor do you pay much attention to their advertising, which you may ignore or file away without much thought.

Some message strategies are more involving than others, such as dramas and humor. Likewise, various types of media are intrinsically more or less involving. Television, for example, is considered to be less involving than print, which demands more concentration from its readers than TV does of its viewers—although a gripping TV drama can be involving because of the power of the storyline. Marketing communication tools, such as sales promotions, events, and brand clubs, are inherently more involving, particularly the ones that allow customers to have more personal contact with the brand.

- *Engagement* The idea of **engagement** is that a consumer is more than just interested in something, that he or she is, in the words of the Advertising Research Foundation committee that investigated engagement, "turned on."[33] Participation strategies, for example, get consumers involved with a brand on a personal level. Engagement cultivates passion.

- *Conviction* Effective persuasion results in **conviction,** which means consumers agree with a persuasive message and achieve a state of certainty—a belief—about a brand. A factor in conviction is the power of the **argument,** which uses logic, reasons, and proof to make a point and build conviction. Understanding an argument is a complex cognitive process that demands the audience "follow through" on the reasoning to understand the point and reach a conclusion.

- *Preference and Intention* When consumers marry belief with a **preference** for, or an **intention** to try or buy, a product, they are motivated by conviction. Intention can be heightened with reward strategies, such as good deals, sale pricing, and gifts. An example of persuasive work designed to create conviction is the Orlando, Florida, YMCA ads. Good intentions are the motivations behind cause marketing and social responsibility. Hewlett-Packard, for example, promotes its computer recycling program to increase preference for HP products by its customers. According to the company's vice president of global branding and marketing communication, the PC recycling program attracts consumers to HP products because the company assumes responsibility for recycling its old products. That's a benefit for customers and leads to higher customer satisfaction and, thus, loyalty to the HP brand.

- *Loyalty* Is there any brand you buy, use, or visit on a regular basis? Do you have a favorite shampoo, restaurant, or beverage? Why is that? What we are referring to when we talk about a "favorite" brand is preference, but also **brand loyalty,** which we mentioned in Chapter 2. Loyalty is an attitude (respect, preference), an emotion (liking), and an action (repeat purchases). It is a response to brand communication that crosses over between thinking, feeling, and doing—a response that is built on **customer satisfaction.** If you try a product and like it, then you will be more likely to buy it again. If you don't like it, is there a return policy or guarantee that frees you from risk when you buy something for the first time? Providing information about warranties, customer service, and technical support for technology products is an important part of brand loyalty strategies. The idea is to reduce risk and put the customer's mind at ease. Incentives are also used in loyalty programs, such as frequent flyer or frequent buyer programs. In addition, social responsibility and cause marketing programs can build trust, respect, and preference that lead to loyalty.

- *Believability and Credibility* An important issue in persuasion is **believability,** which refers to the credibility of the arguments in a message. Puffery or unprovable claims, such as the common phrase "9 out of 10 doctors recommend . . . " can strain believability. Related to believability is **credibility,** which is an indication of the trustworthiness of the source. **Source credibility** means the person delivering the message, such as an expert, is respected, trusted, and believable.

Bob Garfield, respected *Advertising Age* columnist, points out in his recent book, *The Chaos Scenario,* that you trust messages from friends more than from any sort of commercial message—"anything dictated to you by Procter & Gamble channeling its marketing message through Mr. Whipple. . . ."[34] That explains the power of word-of-mouth and viral online communication. Trust is also a factor in media choice. We watch certain television news programs, read newspapers, and subscribe to specific magazines because we trust them as information sources.

Credibility is one of the big advantages of public relations because publicity stories delivered through a supposedly unbiased news medium have higher credibility than advertising, which is seen as self-serving. However, advertising can use a credibility strategy to intensify the believability of its message. After the oil spill off the Louisisan coast, BP used advertising to say that the company was committed to cleaning up the mess. The strategy hinges on the company's credibility. Using data to support or prove a claim, for example, gives consumers a **reason to believe** the advertising.

A highly effective poster designed to create action, this ad was used during World War I to convince young people to join the military. Most modern advertising is more subtle than this, but the motivation to inspire action is still the same.

The Behavior Facet: Act/Do

We introduced loyalty in the previous section on persuasion and noted that it intersects with behavior. Behavior can involve different types of action in addition to trying or buying the product. The goal is to get people to act in various ways—to try or buy the brand, for example, or visit a store, return an inquiry card, call a toll-free number, join an organization, donate to a good cause, or click on a website. The "I Want You" World War I poster by artist James Montgomery Flagg is a classic example of an advertising message that was designed to create action. It's been used many times by other organizations to create that same compelling message.

We must distinguish, however, between **direct action,** which represents an immediate response (cut out the order form and send it back by return mail), and **indirect action,** which is a delayed response to advertising (recall the message later in the store and select the brand). There is also purposeless action, which became a fad in the 2000s when viral e-mail messages would generate a sudden and conspicuous gathering of people. Called **flash mobs,** these public spectacles included a worldwide day of pillow fights in public places in 2008. Flash mobs demonstrate the power of the Internet and buzz to engage people and drive them into action—even if the action is largely meaningless. A faux flash mob was featured in a viral video known as the T-Mobile "Dance" where people walking through London's Liverpool Street Station spontaneously broke out in a 400-person choreographed dance commercial.[35] (Check it out at *www.youtube.com/watch?v=VQ3d3KigPQM* and the making of it at *www.youtube.com/watch?v= uVFNM8f9WnI.*)

Factors That Drive the Behavioral Response   The behavioral response involving action of some kind is often the most important goal of marketing communication, particularly tools such as sales promotion and direct marketing. Factors that drive a behavioral response include mental rehearsal, trial, buying, contacting, advocating and referrals, and prevention.

- *Mental Rehearsal* The **mental rehearsal** of behaviors is made possible by showing visuals of people doing things. As Charles Young explains,[36] one of the functions of advertising is to create virtual memories, in other words, experiences that we can imagine ourselves doing. Visualization is an imagined action, but one that is the predecessor to the behaviors with which the advertiser hopes the consumer will feel comfortable and familiar.
- *Trial* The first step in making a purchase is often to try the product. A **trial** is important for new products and expensive products because it lets a customer use the product without initially committing to a purchase. In other words, the risk is reduced. Sales promotion is particularly good at driving trials through special price deals, sampling, and incentive programs that motivate behavior, such as a free gift when you go to a dealer to test drive a new car.
- *Buying* The objective of most marketing programs is sales. In advertising, sales is sometimes stimulated by the **call to action** at the end of the ad, along with information on where to purchase the product. From a customer perspective, sales means making a purchase. In customer-focused marketing programs, the goal is to motivate people to try or buy a certain brand. But in some marketing programs, such as those for nonprofit organizations, the mar-

keting program may be designed to encourage the audience to sign up, volunteer, or donate. For many managers, however, sales is the gold standard for effective advertising. They feel that, even if they are funny, memorable, or entertaining, ads are failures if they don't help sell the brand. The problem is that it may be difficult to prove that a marketing communication message is the one factor in the marketing mix that delivered the sales. It could be the price, the distribution, the product design and performance, or some combination of the marketing mix elements. Effectiveness programs, such as the London-based Institute of Practitioners Award program (IPA), encourage advertisers to use research to prove that it was, in fact, the advertising that actually drove the sales.

- *Contacting* Trying and buying may be the marketer's dream response, but other actions also can be important measures of an advertisement's behavioral effectiveness. Responding by making contact with the advertiser can be an important sign of effectiveness. Initiating contact is also valuable, particularly in IMC programs designed to maintain brand relationships by creating opportunities for customer-initiated dialogue, such as encouraging customers with a complaint, compliment, or suggestion to contact the company.

- *Advocating and Referrals* One of the behavioral dimensions of brand loyalty is **advocacy,** or speaking out on a brand's behalf and referring to it when someone asks for a recommendation. Contacting other people is a valuable response, particularly when a satisfied customer brings in more business for the brand by providing testimonials to friends, family, and colleagues on behalf of the brand. In terms of the impact of **referrals,** when a satisfied customer recommends a favorite brand, this form of word of mouth can be incredibly persuasive, more so than advertising, which is seen as self-serving. Apple Computer's success is credited to its passionate customers who, as evangelists for the brand, spread the word among their friends and coworkers.

  This *advocacy level*, which Smith and Cross describe in their book, *Customer Bonding*,[37] represents the highest form of a brand relationship. A recommendation to buy a specific brand is the ultimate test of the bond between consumers and their favorite brands. And the opposite—brand aversion—can be disastrous if the dissatisfied customer shares his or her dislike with other people.

- *Prevention* In some social action situations, advertising messages are designed to deter behaviors, such as clean-air campaigns that hope to reduce car use. This is a complicated process that involves counterarguing by presenting negative messages about an unwanted behavior and creating the proper incentives to stimulate the desired behavior. Because the effects are so complicated, the impact of such campaigns is not always clear. Earlier in the perception discussion we mentioned the national "Just Say No" campaign, which claims to have had an impact on teenagers' drug use. However, as Carson B. Wagner discovered, sometimes antidrug advertising can boomerang because it calls attention to the unwanted behavior.

THE POWER OF BRAND COMMUNICATION

The six-factor Facets Model of Effects that we've been describing is our answer to the question of how advertising works. This model is also useful in analyzing the power and impact of advertising messages through the interaction of these effects.

An example of a flash mob employed as a guerilla marketing technique is the T-Mobile "Dance" video that created a spectacle in London.

Interaction and Impact

As we had suggested, these six factors, when they work together, can create a coherent brand perception. You should remember two things about how this model works: (1) the effects are interdependent, and (2) they are not all equal for all marketing communication situations.

In terms of effects interaction, we suggested in the previous discussions that cognitive and emotional responses work together. Consider that memory is a function of both attention (the perception facet) and emotion (the affective facet). As du Plessis explains, "What we pay attention to, we remember."[38] The stronger the emotional hook, the more likely we'll attend to and remember the message. Even informative messages can be made more memorable if they are presented with an emotional story. Furthermore, recent ideas about how advertising memory works suggest that an effective ad helps consumers remember their best moments with a product,[39] so it brings back emotion-laden brand experiences that encompass both feelings and thoughts.

A good example of the interplay between thinking and feeling is found in the public service LATCH campaign, which was designed to build awareness of the child safety problem, but also explain what parents need to do to make their kids safe in a car seat, and carefully engage emotions such as love and the concern that drives protectiveness. *The Inside Story* explains the thinking behind the campaign.

In terms of impact, we recognize that different advertising strategies emphasize different patterns of impact. Sometimes more emphasis in a message strategy needs to be placed on emotion or image building than on reasons and facts. Therefore, a specific strategy for an advertising campaign may be depicted as heavier in one area than another. In such a situation, the actual shape of the facets model can change as the pattern of emphasis is adapted to the marketing situation with emotion and association, for example, or cognition or persuasion increasing in size.

The "strong effects" view of advertising is parodied in this ad by the American Association of Advertising Agencies, which has created a long-running campaign to explain and defend advertising.

Strong and Weak Effects

Some believe that sales is the only true indication of message effectiveness. The power of advertising, in other words, is determined by its ability to motivate consumers to buy a brand. Some even believe advertising is so powerful that it can motivate people to buy things they don't need, as the ad by the American Association of Advertising Agencies (4As) suggests.

Others, including the authors of this textbook, believe communication effects include a wide range of consumer responses to a message—responses that may be just as important as sales because they lead to the creation of such things as liking and a long-term brand relationship. This power is analyzed in terms of "strong" and "weak" effects.[40]

This debate is the source of controversy in the analysis of what advertising effectiveness really represents. The sales-oriented philosophy suggests advertising can move the masses to action. Those who believe in the "strong" theory of advertising reason along these lines:

Advertising increases people's knowledge and changes people's attitudes and, therefore, it is capable of persuading people who had not formerly bought a brand to buy it, at first once and then repeatedly.

In contrast, those who believe in the "weak" theory of advertising, like the British promotions person quoted at the beginning of this chapter, think that advertising has only a limited impact on consumers and is best used to reinforce existing brand perceptions rather than change attitudes:

Consumers are not very interested in advertising. The amount of information communicated is

THE INSIDE STORY

Kids, Cars, and Car Seat Safety

Trent Walters, *Account Director, The Richards Group*

Since its earliest days during World War II, the Ad Council has mirrored and influenced some of the most important social conditions facing our country—think Smoky the Bear and fire prevention. More than half a century later, it continues to take on key issues threatening the nation's welfare—from obesity and financial literacy to Internet safety and high school dropout prevention.

One of these issues is child passenger safety. In 2007, the U.S. Department of Transportation turned to the Ad Council to help get the message out about the importance of the LATCH (Lower Anchors and Tethers for Children) system for keeping children safe in the car. They found that three out of four kids were not as secure in the car as they should be because their car seats were not being used correctly by their parents or caregivers. These were not neglectful people either. They were concerned and caring parents and caregivers who would do everything they could to keep their kids safe in the car—as long as they knew what to do.

To address this issue, The U.S. Department of Transportation teamed up with various companies and organizations that were interested in promoting this cause to create public service advertisements (PSAs). These stakeholders included representatives from the auto industry, car seat manufacturers, and child safety advocacy groups. Together, these groups would help make people aware of the LATCH system. It was already available in most cars and it was an easy way to be certain that a car seat was installed correctly.

The Richards Group was responsible for developing the campaign. The objective was to make parents aware (without frightening them) that they may have installed their car seat incorrectly and understand that the LATCH system would make it easier for them to do it correctly. The Richards Group developed an icon that would help to universally identify the LATCH system in cars and in printed information. Television, radio, print and online PSAs were also developed to inform and educate parents about the importance of the LATCH system and the proper usage.

Since the launch of the campaign in the fall of 2008, we've begun to see changes in behavior. Of those surveyed about their usage of the LATCH system, the percentage of respondents who said they are already using the LATCH system every time they drive with their child increased significantly from the benchmark finding of 58 percent in 2008 to 62 percent in 2009, which represents a very acceptable 6.9 percent change in behavior. For certain demographic subgroups, from 2008 to 2009, there was significant growth among those who said they use the system every time, such as higher income ($50K+) moms in the Northeast.

Trent Walters is a graduate of the University of North Texas and was selected by the American Advertising Federation as one of its "Most Promising Minority Students." He was nominated by Professor Sheri Broyles.

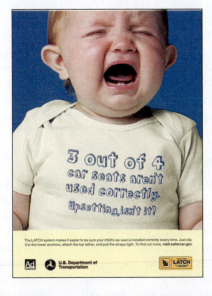

These ads from the Ad Council's LATCH campaign show three cute kids whose faces express emotions and thoughts such as surprise, unacceptable, and upsetting. *The Inside Story* explains the thinking behind the campaign.

limited. Advertising is not strong enough to convert people whose beliefs are different from those in the ad, overcome their resistance, or change their attitudes. Most advertising is more effective at retaining users rather than converting new ones.

These differences explain why some experts believe that the communication effects, such as emotion, knowledge, and persuasion, are merely "surrogate" effects—communication effects that can be measured more easily than sales but are less important to marketing managers. Others believe these communication effects are important in and of themselves because of what they contribute to brand strength.

Complicating the issue is the recognition that the impact of traditional advertising is seldom immediate. When you see an ad for a new product that catches your attention, such as a new music group or CD, and you concentrate on the message, you may think about the ad later when you find yourself walking by a music store. Thus, your memory is involved in recalling not just the ad and the brand, but the content of the message. But memory is unreliable and the impressions may not be embedded sufficiently in memory to elicit this kind of response at a later date.

Principle
Advertising has delayed effects in that a consumer may see or hear an advertisement but not act on that message until later when in a store.

In other words, advertising is a victim of **delayed effects:** messages are seen and heard at one time (at home on the TV, in the car on the radio, in the doctor's office in a magazine ad) and may or may not come to mind at a later date when you are in a purchase situation (in a store, in a car looking for a place to eat). Advertisers must keep the delayed effects problem in mind when relying on consumer attention, interest, motivation, and memory to bring a message to mind days or weeks later.

Does It or Doesn't It?

Considering all that you've learned in this chapter about advertising effectiveness, if you were asked, where would you come down in this debate about the power of advertising—strong or weak effects?

If you are interested in learning more about how advertising and other marketing communication work in order to answer questions like that, then see the *Practical Tips* feature by Professor Sheri Broyles at *www.pearsonhighered.com/moriarty* and consult some of the fascinating books that have been written about this industry, including the new one from Bob Garfield that we mentioned earlier in this chapter, *The Chaos Scenario: Amid the Ruins of Mass Media the Choice for Business Is Stark: Listen or Perish.* An excerpt from this provocative book can be found at the end of the interview transcript at *www.npr.org/templates/story/story.php?storyid=111623614.*

Long-term research by retired Syracuse professor John Philip Jones using extensive industry data proves that there is a link between advertising and consumer behavior and that advertising can trigger sales.[41] The problem has always been understanding *how it works,* and, in many cases, *how it doesn't work.* The facets model takes a step forward in helping the industry create a logical framework for analyzing advertising effects. The important conclusion to the bigger question about how advertising works is that we know that advertising (and other marketing communication) does work when it's carefully planned and executed. It may not work in every situation and every ad may not be equally effective, but if it's done right, then advertising can have impact on consumer responses. That's why the Effie awards, and other award shows that recognize effectiveness, are so valuable.

Looking Ahead

To a great extent, the impact of the recession lies in the emotional facet. Instead of snarly, sarcastic, and cutting responses, researchers have decided that the recession ushered in an Age of Nice—think bright yellow smiley faces. Graceann Bennett, strategic planner at Ogilvy & Mather's Chicago office, explains in a *New York Times* article that her clients frequently critique ad ideas by saying "we don't want mean."[42] Even Pepsi's new logo in 2009 was characterized as looking like the smiley face. Mocking ads worked to the degree that they tapped into people's frustrations over the economy. Earnestness and altruism became the new face of consumer culture—and consumer culture is what we'll talk about in the next chapter.

"I love you, man" and "Have a nice day."

IT'S A WRAP

Pitch Perfect: Ford's in SYNC with Singer/Songwriter

Dave Rodriguez, multicultural marketing communication manager for Ford, summed up the SYNC campaign's ability to reach the Hispanic target audience: "Ford, SYNC and Juanes are just the perfect fit because we're all focused on the importance of being able to connect with people. Staying connected to friends and music while on the go is no longer a trend, it's part of everyday life for our Hispanic target and SYNC brings this power exclusively to Ford drivers."

When advertising is able to connect its audience with a powerful message about a meaningful product, it gets results. It built brand awareness of the new technology through experiential activities, which made the Hispanic target audience aware of SYNC and educated them about its benefits. About 100,000 consumers visited SYNC Zones at the Juanes concerts and almost 200,000 unique visitors visited the syncjuanes.com site.

The campaign successfully engaged significantly more participants than expected—about 63,000 registrations and 30,000 hand-raisers who opted in for future Ford communications. Once the consumers understood and experienced SYNC, they were likely to move closer to a purchase decision. The campaign generated test-drive leads and test drives with a test-drive conversion rate of almost 30 percent (15 times the industry average). For its excellent work, Ford and Zubi won a Silver Effie.

Key Points Summary

1. How does marketing communication work both as a form of mass communication and interactive communication? By analyzing advertising as mass communication, we have a model for explaining how commercial messages work. Consider that the *source* typically is the advertiser assisted by its agency and the *receiver* is the consumer who responds in some way to the message. The *message* is the advertisement or other marketing communication tool. The *medium* is the vehicle that delivers the message; in advertising, that tends to be newspapers and magazines in print, radio and TV in broadcasting, the Internet, and other forms of out-of-home vehicles, such as outdoor boards and posters. In integrated marketing communication, the media are varied and include all points of contact where a consumer receives an impression of the brand. *Noise* is both external and internal. *External noise* in advertising includes consumer trends that affect the reception of the message, as well as problems in the brand's marketing mix and clutter in the channel. *Internal noise* includes personal factors that affect the reception of the message. If the communication process fails to work and the consumer does not receive the message as intended by the source, then the communication effort is ineffective. Interactive communication is two way, such as a dialogue or conversation, and the source and receiver change positions as the message bounces back and forth—the source becomes the listener and the receiver becomes the sender.

2. How did the idea of advertising effects develop, and what are the problems in traditional approaches to advertising effects? The most common explanation of how advertising works is referred to as AIDA, which stands for attention, interest, desire, and action. This model in all of its subsequent forms is described as a hierarchy of effects because it presumes a set of steps that consumers go through in responding to a message. A different approach, referred to as think/feel/do, recognizes that different marketing communication situations generate different patterns of responses. Two problems are inherent in these traditional approaches: (1) the idea of predictable steps and (2) missing effects, particularly those that govern the way people respond to brands.

3. What is the Facets Model of Effects, and how does it explain how marketing communication works? The authors believe that marketing communication works in six key ways: it is designed to help consumers (1) see and hear the message (perception), (2) feel something for the brand (emotional or affective response), (3) understand the point of the message (cognitive response), (4) connect positive qualities with the brand (association), (5) believe the message (persuasion), and (6) act in the desired ways (behavior). All of these work together to create a brand perception. An effective message, then, has a diamond-like quality that represents how the message effects work together to create the desired consumer response.

Words of Wisdom: Recommended Reading

Du Plessis, Erik, *The Advertised Mind: Ground-Breaking Insights into How Our Brains Respond to Advertising,* London UK: Millward Brown, 2005.

Gladwell, Malcolm, *The Power of Thinking without Thinking,* New York: Little, Brown, 2005.

Jones, John Philip, *When Ads Work: New Proof That Advertising Triggers Sales,* 2nd ed., Armonk, NY: M.E. Sharpe, 2007.

Lehrer, Jonah, *How We Decide,* New York: Houghton Mifflin Harcourt, 2010.

Roberts, Kevin, *The Lovemarks Effect: Winning in the Consumer Revolution,* rev. ed., Brooklyn, NY: PowerHouse Books, 2006.

Tellis, Gerard J., *Effective Advertising: Understanding When, How, and Why Advertising Works,* Thousand Oaks, CA: Sage Publications, 2004.

Wasik, Bill, *And Then There's This: How Stories Live and Die in Viral Culture,* New York: Penguin Group, 2009.

Zaltman, Gerald, *How Customers Think: Essential Insights into the Mind of the Market,* Boston: Harvard Business School Press, 2003.

Key Terms

advocacy, p. 121
affective response, p. 109
AIDA, p. 103
argument, p. 119
association, p. 115
attitude, p. 116
awareness, p. 109
bandwagon appeals, p. 117
beliefs, p. 116
believability, p. 119
brand linkage, p. 115
brand loyalty, p. 119
call to action, p. 120
carrot mob, p. 116
channels of
    communication, p. 100
clutter, p. 101
cognition, p. 113
cognitive learning, p. 114
comprehension, p. 114
conditioned learning, p. 115

considered purchase, p. 118
conviction, p. 119
credibility, p. 119
customer satisfaction, p. 119
delayed effects, p. 124
differentiation, p. 114
direct action, p. 120
emotional appeals, p. 112
engagement, p. 119
exposure, p. 107
feedback, p. 100
flash mob, p. 120
hashtags, p. 102
hierarchy of effects, p. 103
high involvement, p. 118
impact, p. 103
indirect action, p. 120
intention, p. 119
interactive
    communication, p. 101

interest, p. 108
intrusive, p. 108
involvement, p. 118
knowledge structure, p. 116
liking, p. 113
low involvement, p. 118
mental rehearsal, p. 120
message, p. 100
motivation, p. 116
needs, p. 114
network of associations, p. 116
noise, p. 100
opinion leaders, p. 117
perception, p. 107
persuasion, p. 116
podcasting, p. 101
preference, p. 119
reason to believe, p. 119
recall, p. 109
receiver, p. 100

recognition, p. 109
referrals, p. 121
relevance, p. 108
resonance, p. 113
selective attention, p. 108
selective perception, p. 107
SMCR model, p. 100
social learning, p. 115
source, p. 100
source credibility, p. 119
stickiness, p. 108
subliminal, p. 109
symbolic meaning, p. 115
synergy, p. 109
think/feel/do model, p. 103
transformation, p. 115
trial, p. 120
wants, p. 111
word-of-mouth, p. 117

Review Questions

1. What are the key components of a communication model, and how do they relate to advertising?

2. Why is it important to add interaction to the traditional communication model?

3. What is a hierarchy of effects model? Give an example.

4. What are the six categories of effects identified in the facets model? What does each one represent in terms of a consumer's response to an advertising message?

5. What is clutter and why is it a problem?

6. Explain the difference between brand responses that involve thinking and feeling.

7. Differentiate between wants and needs. How are both of these concepts used in advertising?

8. What does transformation mean, and why is it important as an advertising effect?

Discussion Questions

1. What is breakthrough advertising? What is engaging advertising? Look through this textbook, find an example of each, and explain how they work. Prepare to explain in class why you evaluated the two ads as you did.

2. This chapter identifies six major categories of effects or consumer responses. Find an ad in this book that you think is effective overall and explain how it works, analyzing the way it cultivates responses in these six categories.

3. Eva Proctor is a planner in an agency that handles a liquid detergent brand that competes with Lever's Wisk. Eva is reviewing a history of the Wisk theme, "Ring around the Collar." In its day, it was one of the longest running themes on television, and Wisk's sales share indicated that it was successful. What is confusing Eva is that the Wisk history includes numerous consumer surveys that show consumers found "ring around the collar" to be a boring, silly, and irritating advertising theme. Can you explain why Wisk was such a popular brand even though its advertising campaign was so disliked?

4. *Three-Minute Debate:* You have been asked to participate in a debate in your office about three different views on advertising effects. Your office has the assignment to introduce a new electric car. A copywriter says informing consumers about the product's features is most important in creating effective advertising. An art director argues that creating an emotional bond with consumers is more important. One of the account managers says that the only advertising performance that counts is sales and the message ought to focus on that. Your client wants to be single minded and tells you to pick one of these viewpoints to guide the new marketing communication. As a team, develop a position on one side or the other. Prepare your point of view in a one-page position paper.

Take-Home Projects

1. *Portfolio Project:* From current magazines, identify one advertisement that has exceptionally high stopping power (attention), one that has exceptionally high pulling power (interest), and one that has exceptionally high locking power (memory). Make photocopies of these ads to turn in. Which of them are mainly information and which are mainly emotional and focused on feelings? Which are focused on building a brand or creating associations? Do any of them do a great job of creating action? Choose what you believe to be the most effective ad in the collection. Why did you choose this one, and what can you learn from it about effective advertising?

2. *Mini-Case Analysis:* We discussed some aspects of the "Ford SYNC" Hispanic campaign in the chapter. Briefly summarize the key decisions behind this campaign. Now apply the facets model to analyze how the campaign worked and explain your conclusions about what did or didn't make this an effective campaign. Write a short analysis (no more than two double-spaced pages) that explains your thinking.

Team Project: The BrandRevive Campaign

For the BrandRevive project, review the six facets of effectiveness and consider how they relate to the marketing of your chosen brand.

- Analyze the brand's situation and decide which effects are most critical for marketing products in your product category.

- Build an effects model that shows the relative importance of the various facets for reenergizing the brand.
- Develop your analysis as a diagram. In a one-page document explain your analysis and why you believe certain effects are more important than others for products in this category. Prepare a PowerPoint of no more than three slides to explain your analysis.

Hands-On Case

The Century Council

Read the Century Council Case in the Appendix before coming to class.

1. Explain how advertising works in the case of "The Stupid Drink" campaign.

2. How could you strengthen the target's participation in the campaign as a solution for binge drinking on college campuses?

3. Analyze "The Stupid Drink" campaign in terms of the Facets Model of Effects. Based on this model, what might be done to strengthen the campaign's desired effect?

Segmenting and Targeting the Audience

It's a Winner

Campaign:	Company:	Agency:	Award:
"SuperModelquins"	*Old Navy*	*Crispin Porter + Bogusky*	*National Retail Federation, "Shoppers' Favorite Holiday Ads" #6 ranking*

CHAPTER KEY POINTS

1. What cultural, social, psychological, and behavioral influences affect consumer responses to advertising?
2. What characteristics are used to segment groups of consumers?
3. How does the consumer decision process work?
4. How does targeting work and how is it different from segmenting?

Old Navy SuperModelquins Reveal Secrets

If sales are slumping, as is the case for many companies including Old Navy during the latest recession, what can be done to reverse the downward trend? What role does branding play in the process, and how does brand communication work?

To answer these questions, let's start with a discussion of Old Navy's "SuperModelquins" campaign. Have you seen it? If not, introduce yourself to the models at *www.oldnavyweekly.com*. You'll discover the mannequins have names, love lives, families, and careers. Here's an excerpt from the introduction video, which highlights Old Navy merchandise as the models reveal their secrets:

Narrator: "The SuperModelquins. They pose. They smile. They pose some more. But what's behind those chiseled good looks and perma-smiles? We'll find out as we meet fashion's hottest new mannequins. Kelly started out as a small town mannequin with big dreams. She was discovered here in the humble window of Wilma's Wearables by a mannequin scout.

Kelly: He offered me a card and a first-class crate to the big city.

Narrator: Kelly was a hit, especially with the soon-to-be men's wear super-star, Josh.

Josh: She was being wheeled by and I just froze.

Narrator: They were soon inseparable. Then a call came in. Old Navy was look-ing for a star and loved Kelly's fresh-faced look. Her life was moving so fast that love couldn't keep up. In the fall 2005 Josh and Kelly split up. Kelly had found herself a fresh start and new friends like Michelle.

Michelle: Being here with Wesley and my kids keeps me grounded. Well, that and my metal stand.

Narrator: Michelle and Wesley met in the spring of 2001 at an auto show. She was working as a minivan display model, he as a crash test dummy. In 2001, they tied the knot in the bridal section of a department store and two months later they became SuperModelquins. But there was one thing missing from the picture: kids.

Wesley: So we filled out a form and three to four business days later our boy was delivered. Christopher arrived on February 28 weighing 57 pounds, 4 ounces.

What do you think? Do you like the quirky campaign with the talking models? What did you like or not like about it? Do you think it was effective advertising? This chapter challenges you to think deeply about what makes brands work to accomplish their business objectives by truly reaching the minds and emotions of their audiences.

First, some background about Old Navy, an offshoot of the Gap. Although Old Navy has long stood for value—low budget and somewhat trendy fashions—recently it has faced fierce competition from Target and Kohl's. Old Navy's sales were down significantly. Sure, part of the downturn is probably due to the economy. But what can be done to reverse the losses?

Old Navy President Tom Wyatt put his finger on part of the problem: the company lost its way when it abandoned the target of moms with young children and focused on teens. A gold-lamé bikini, such as the one featured in a recent ad campaign, is not what a 25- to 35-year-old mom is looking for, said Wyatt. Moms went elsewhere to shop. The first step of Old Navy's strategy called for a renewed focus on young moms.

To appeal to moms, the campaign used 12 mock supermodels with celebrity-worthy stories. They're featured on TV and the Web on Old Navy's website. They've been featured in a flyer patterned after a celebrity magazine. You can follow them on Twitter. These pseudo-celebs have made appearances at an NBA Lakers game, a celebrity party in New York, and a trendy restaurant in Los Angeles. SuperModelquins—some 13,000 of them—may even have made their way to an Old Navy store near you. (Incidentally, you may be interested to know that the campaign's done wonders for Fusion Specialties, the mannequins' maker.)

In your analysis of the campaign's effectiveness, one of the first questions you should ask yourself is "Does this reach the target audience?" Do you think these SuperModelquins "speak" to young moms? A critical lesson is that ads that are based on understanding the consumer market are more likely to speak to their interests. At the end of the chapter, in the *It's a Wrap* feature, you can find out how well Old Navy achieved its goals.

Sources: www.oldnavyweekly.com; Mae Anderson, "Old Navy's New Ad Campaign Heavy on 'Quirky,'" February 2, 2009, www.money.aol.com; Elizabeth Aguilera, "Old Navy's New Ad Campaign Breaks the Mold and Boosts a Broomfield Mannequin-Maker," March 12, 2009, www.denverpost.com; Anne D'Innocenzio, "Gap Earnings Drop 8:3% But Beat Estimates," February 26, 2009, www.USAToday.com; Jennifer Reingold, "Gap Tries Branding to Boost Sales," February 27, 2009, www.cnnmoney.com.

The success of campaigns, such as the Old Navy "SuperModelquins" campaign, hinges on a critical consumer insight that gives direction to the advertising. By recognizing that the store's ads were speaking to the wrong audience, the CP+B team was able to develop a storyline that young mothers would find interesting and fun; at the same time it showcased fashions that were relevant to this audience.

To better understand that connection, this chapter explores influences on consumers' behavior—in other words, what motivates them as they make purchasing decisions—and then discusses how these factors help define groups of people who might profitably be targeted with marketing communication or advertising messages. By studying these influences on consumer decisions, advertisers can better design effective campaigns through careful targeting of the message and the media.

WHAT INFLUENCES CONSUMER DECISIONS?

Think about something you bought last week. How did the purchase process happen? Was it something you needed or just something you wanted? These are the kinds of questions marketers and advertisers ask about their customers. **Consumer behavior** describes how individuals or groups select, purchase, use, or dispose of products, as well as the needs and wants that motivate these behaviors. As we proceed through this chapter, keep asking yourself these questions about your own consumer behavior and that of your friends and family.

As our opening story stressed, marketing communication planners need to understand what appeals to customers and why. Then they need to be able to describe prospective customers using characteristics that help predict the likelihood that they will respond to a brand message and, ultimately, buy the brand.

There are various ways to segment consumers and target a market. One way is to divide them by the type of market they represent—either business or consumer—this leads to *business-to-business* (B2B) or *business-to-consumer* (B2C) marketing strategies. Another way is to refer to them either as (1) those who shop for and purchase the product (purchasers or customers), (2) those who actually use the product (users), or (3) influencers—people who help the buyer make a brand choice (children, trendsetters, family, and friends). This distinction is important because purchasers and users can have different needs and wants. In the case of children's cereals, parents (the purchasers) often look for nutritional value and a decent price. In contrast, children (the users) may look for a sweet taste and a package with a prize inside.

Before we review how consumers make a buying decision, let's consider the various factors that influence them: their cultural affinities, their family and friends, their personal needs, and their experiences with a brand. Figure 5.1 is a general model of consumer behavior. It is also a visual road map for this chapter. We will begin by discussing three types of influences that affect the way consumers make purchasing decisions. Then we'll use that knowledge to explain how audiences are profiled, segmented, and then targeted with specific types of messages.

Principle
Buyers may not be the users and users may not be the buyers. Buyers and users often have entirely different needs and wants.

FIGURE 5.1
Influences on Consumer Decision Making

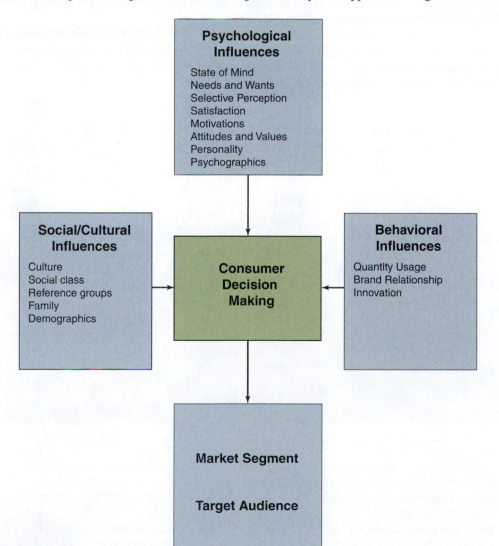

Cultural Influences

CP+B is known for advertising that weaves cultural insights into sometimes off-the-wall advertising messages, as with the Old Navy SuperModelquins. In other words, marketing communication that moves people often builds on or confronts deep-seated cultural values. **Culture** is made up of tangible items (art, literature, buildings, furniture, clothing, and music) and intangible concepts (history, knowledge, laws, morals, customs, and even standards of beauty) that together define a group of people or a way of life. Culture is learned and passed on from one generation to the next.

Generally culture is seen as providing a deep-seated context for marketing communication, but popular culture—what we see on television, sports, fashion, and music among other areas—is dynamic. Lee Clow, chairman and chief creative direct of TBWA/Worldwide, who also created the legendary "1984" Macintosh commercial discussed in Chapter 1, observed that "you have to do advertising at the speed of culture." He was referring to the transformation brought by the Internet and other new forms of digital communication, but his point is that "culture is moving very fast and it's very responsive."[1]

Norms and Values   The boundaries each culture establishes for "proper" behavior are **norms,** which are simply rules we learn through social interaction that specify or prohibit certain behaviors. The source of norms is our **values,** particularly cultural values, which represent our underlying belief systems. In the United States, we value freedom, independence, and individualism; in other countries, particularly some Asian and Latin countries, people value families and groups more than individualism. Of course, there are some universals—most people value good health and most women want to look good. An example of ads that appeal to Americans' nostalgia is the 76 campaign aimed at truckers.

Values are few in number and hard to change. Advertisers strive to understand the underlying **core values** that govern people's attitudes and guide their behavior. An ad's primary appeal aims to match the core values of the brand to the core values of the audience. Here are 10 basic core values that, in many cases, transcend cultural differences:

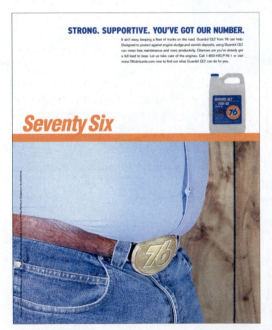

SHOWCASE

These ads for 76 motor oil ran in national trade publications for the trucking industry. The creative team wanted to associate the 76 brand with Americana using a nostalgic appeal. Do you think this imagery speaks to truck fleet owners who authorize the purchase of commodities such as motor oil?

These ads were contributed by Chris Hutchinson, art director at Wieden + Kennedy, who graduated from the advertising program at the University of Oregon.

1. A sense of belonging
2. Excitement
3. Fun and enjoyment
4. Warm relationships
5. Self-fulfillment
6. Respect from others
7. A sense of accomplishment
8. Security
9. Self-respect
10. Thrift

Thrift and frugality were hallmarks of the recession of the late 2000s and a Harris Poll found that Americans tightened their belts, saved more, spent less, and borrowed less.[2] The orientation to spending and saving is discussed in the *A Matter of Principle* feature that investigates the post–9/11 admonition to buy more in order to rebuild consumer confidence.

A MATTER OF PRINCIPLE

Patriotism, Spending, and Saving

Wanhsiu Sunny Tsai, *Assistant Professor, School of Communication, University of Miami*

As an international scholar from an Eastern culture in which saving and long-term financial plans are considered important, I was intrigued by how consumer spending was promoted as an important means of resisting terrorism and rebuilding a prosperous post–9/11 economy in the United States. For example, General Motors explicitly stated in its post–9/11 campaign that purchasing cars was crucial to "Keep America Rolling."

With the ongoing war in Iraq and a slowing economy in 2006, President Bush urged, "As we work with Congress . . . to chart a new course in Iraq . . . we must also work together to achieve important goals for the American people here at home. This work begins with keeping our economy growing . . . and I encourage you all to go shopping more."

But I have to wonder, what about saving? Is putting money aside believed to contribute to the national economy? Do consumers share the publicized viewpoint that individual spending is related to the nation's economic health? And why is shopping so heavily emphasized in American culture?

My interviews with consumers suggest that the marketplace was a significant place in which consumers could reaffirm core American values such as democracy (which informants expressed in terms of an open market free from government intervention), freedom (in the form of consumer choice), independence (embodied in financial independence and consumer sovereignty), and equality (that is, everyone has a chance to pursue the American dream).

Rather than viewing shopping as a form of self-indulgence, the study participants believed that shopping and buying were helping behaviors through which Americans, including corporate advertisers, joined together to overcome economic hardship and adversity. Furthermore, informants believed that it was excessive spending on hedonistic consumer goods or services such as flat-screen televisions or cruise vacations—not everyday necessities or utilitarian products like gas or breakfast cereal—that had a real impact on the national economy since it was indulgent products that were heavily promoted by advertising.

However, when asked how saving contributed to the national economy, informants had a clear sense of difficulty, hesitance, and uncertainty in formulating arguments. Some even suggested that increased rates of saving and the resultant weakness in spending had led to the current economic slowdown: "[By] squirreling away money into savings, you're hurting other people . . . because then there won't be jobs created."

In general, saving money was regarded as a relatively self-centered practice devoid of the positive, collective, and aggregated effects on the nation's economy—unless the purpose was to save for more and bigger spending in the future. But serious ramifications may be involved. One potential consequence of the emphasis on consumption instead of saving is escalation of consumer debt. According to the latest Federal Reserve study, around 43 percent of U.S. families spend more than they earn. It is understandable that advertisers and policy makers want to stimulate the economy, but they also have a duty to encourage sustainable consumption and to advocate financial literacy and improved financial management among consumers.

Corporate Culture   The concept of culture applies to B2B marketing as well as B2C. **Corporate culture** is a term that describes how various companies operate. Some are formal with lots of procedures, rigid work hours, and dress codes. Others are more informal in terms of their operations, office rules, and communication. The same patterns exist in the way businesses make purchasing decisions: some rigidly control and monitor purchases; others are loose and easygoing, and purchases may be less controlled or governed more by friendships and handshakes, as in Japan, than by rules.

The Ogilvy & Mather agency has a statement about its corporate culture on its website. Among others things it sets out these principles: "We are opposed to management by intimidation. We abhor ruthlessness. We like people with gentle manners." Visit *www.ogilvy.com/About/Our-History/Corporate-Culture.aspx* for an inside view of how this agency articulates its view of its own corporate culture.

Social Influences

In addition to the culture in which you were raised, you also are a product of your social environment, which determines your social class or group. Reference groups, family, and friends also are important influences on opinions and consumer behavior and affect many of your habits and biases.

Social Class   The position you and your family occupy within your society is called a **social class,** and it is determined by such factors as income, wealth, education, occupation, family prestige, value of home, and neighborhood. In more rigid societies, such as those of India, people have a difficult time moving out of the class into which they were born. In the United States, although people may move into social classes that differ from their families', the country still has a class system consisting of upper, middle, and lower classes. Marketers assume that people in one class buy different goods for different reasons than people in other classes.

Reference Groups   A **reference group** is a group of people you use as a model for behavior in specific situations. Examples are teachers and religious leaders, as well as members of political parties, religious groups, racial or ethnic organizations, hobby-based clubs, and informal affiliations such as fellow workers or students—your peers.

Brand communities, such as the Harley Owners Group (HOG) for Harley-Davidson, are groups of people devoted to a particular brand. To get a sense of how this group operates, check out *www.harley-davidson.com/wcm/Content/Pages/Owners/Owners.jsp?locale=en_US.* Apple is another company that generates a brand community. One writer described a "Cult of Apple" with "fanboys" and "fangirls" who have Apple stickers on their cars and briefcases, wear Mac or iPod-related clothing, and sport Mac tattoos and shaved Mac heads. He observes that "It's not a brand, it's a lifestyle."[3] You can check out some of this at *www.CultofMac.com* or *http://snurl.com/mactattoo.* The Internet has had a huge impact on the creation of reference groups in the form of online virtual communities that revolve around interests, hobbies, and brands.

For consumers, reference groups have three functions: (1) they provide information, (2) they serve as a means of personal comparison, and (3) they offer guidance. Ads that feature typical users in fun or pleasant surroundings are using a reference strategy. You may be attracted to a particular reference group and want to be like the members of that

Graduates of universities and colleges tend to identify themselves by their school affiliation, as this ad for the Virginia Commonwealth University (VCU) demonstrates. What can you tell about this person's career choice and interests from these bumper stickers?

At Virginia Commonwealth University, we engage a world that's ever evolving. We apply street-smart solutions to local and global challenges. We embrace a deep understanding of a diverse population. We are future scientists, artists and educators; communicators and performers; doctors and business executives; engineers and social leaders; social workers and politicians. **We create change. We move the needle. We make a dent.**

VCU.edu
Virginia Commonwealth University

group out of respect or admiration. Advertisers use celebrity endorsements to tap into this appeal. The Old Navy "SuperModelquins" campaign played with the idea that models and mannequins set fashion and appearance standards.

Sociologist David Reisman describes individuals in terms of their relationships to other people as inner directed (individualistic) or outer directed (peer group and society). Advertisers are particularly interested in the role of peers in influencing their outer-directed friends' wants and desires. On the other hand, inner-directed people are more likely to try new things first.

Family   The family is the most important reference group for many people because of its formative role and the intensity of its relationships. Other reference groups, such as peers, coworkers, and neighbors, tend to change as we age. According to the U.S. Census definition, a **family** consists of two or more people who are related by blood, marriage, or adoption and live in the same household. A **household** differs from a family in that it consists of all those who occupy a dwelling whether they are related or not. The family is responsible for raising children and establishing a lifestyle for family members. **Lifestyle** reflects family situation, values, and income. It determines the way people spend their time and money and the kinds of activities they value.

In the 21st century—for the first time in U.S. history—one-person households outnumber married couples with children. This reflects a growing trend in America during the past 30 years to marry later in life, divorce, or never get married at all. Marketers and their advertisers have been right on top of this trend. Banks have created special mortgages, builders are providing homes and apartments to meet the needs of single occupants, and food marketers have introduced "single" portions.

Psychological Influences

We have analyzed **cultural and social influences** on consumer behavior. Now let's look at the personal characteristics that affect how you respond as an individual. The psychological factors of interest to advertisers include state of mind, needs and wants, motivations, as well as attitudes, personality, and thoughts and thinking patterns.

Perception and State of Mind   Your state of mind affects the way you perceive information. Your past experiences with a brand, as well as what your friends say about it, can color your feelings and make you more or less receptive to a brand message. Other mental states—such as anger, fatigue, hunger, excitement, or lethargy—can also affect your behavior because they create internal noise that gets in the way of your reception of a message or provide the impetus to drive you to buy something.

Needs and Wants   In Chapter 4, we described needs and wants as two different types of responses that lead to different reactions to an advertising message. The basic driving forces that motivate us to do something that reflect basic survival, such as choose a motel (shelter) or restaurant (food) when traveling, are called *needs*. Primary needs (biological) include the need for water, food, air, and shelter. In the case of the needs pyramid developed by psychologist Abraham Maslow (see Figure 5.2), these are called physiological and safety needs.

Needs we learn in response to our culture and environment are called **acquired needs.** These may include the need for esteem, prestige, affection, power, learning, and, yes, beauty. Because acquired needs are not necessary to your physical survival, they are also called secondary needs. Maslow called them social *(belonging), egoistic,* and *self-actualization.* The Old Navy campaign, with its moderate-priced fashion line, builds demand for products that address acquired needs.

A want occurs when we desire or wish for something—we won't die if we don't get it, but it can still provide a strong motivation to try or buy something new. This is particularly true in fashion areas, such as clothing and music. Research has uncovered the power of new and novel. As account planner Susan Mendelsohn explains, "In some cases, we want things just for the sheer fun of newness—think about how many pairs of shoes or the amount of clothes people have."[4]

Desire is the driving force behind demand and successful brands focus more on what we want than on what we need. Brian Martin, the founder of Brand Connections, has built a list of 10 desires that successful brands satisfy:[5]

1. To feel safe and secure
2. To feel comfortable

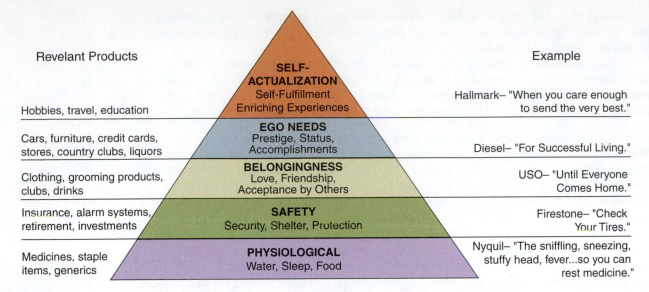

FIGURE 5.2
Maslow's Hierarchy
of Needs

3. To be cared for and connected to others
4. To be desired by others
5. To be free to do what we want
6. To grow and become more
7. To serve others and give back
8. To be surprised and excited
9. To believe there is a higher purpose
10. To feel that they matter

Principle

An item we need is
something we think is
essential or necessary for
our lives; an item we want
is something we desire.

Schwartz describes the power of what he calls "mass desire" in his book *Breakthrough Advertising*. He explains that mass desire is the public spread of a private want; it can't be created by advertising, but advertising can address it and channel it to focus on a particular brand.[6] The trend toward more gas-efficient cars has led to a demand for hybrid cars such as the Prius. If there wasn't a mass desire for this type of vehicle, there would be no market for the Prius. On the other hand, there is also a market for the Cadillac Escalade. Related to needs and wants are satisfaction and dissonance.

- *Satisfaction* A feeling of satisfaction is only one possible response to a brand message or brand experience; more troublesome is dissatisfaction or doubt. People can pay attention to a commercial, then buy a product and be disappointed. One of the reasons is that advertising sometimes raises consumers' expectations too high, in other words, it promises more than it can deliver.
- *Dissonance* **Cognitive dissonance** refers to a conflict between two thoughts—you want to buy a car but don't have the money. That creates a state of tension. Marketers must address the negative side and, in auto marketing, they do that by offering no or low interest plans to reduce the conflict and make it easier to justify or rationalize the decision. Buyer's remorse is another form of tension and it occurs when there are discrepancies between what we thought we would receive and what we actually received. When there is a difference between reality and facts, people engage in a variety of activities to reduce cognitive dissonance. Most notably, we seek out information that supports our decisions—that's why we pay attention to ads for products we have already bought—and ignore and distort information that does not. For example, car makers use testimonials from satisfied customers. An important category of automotive service called "aftermarketing" is designed to keep customers happy after they buy a car.

Motivations   A **motive** is an internal force—like the desire to look good—that stimulates you to behave in a particular manner. This driving force is produced by the tension caused by an unfulfilled want or need. People strive to reduce the tension, as the Airborne ad demonstrates. At any given point you are probably affected by a number of different motives—your motivation to buy a new suit will be much higher if you have several job interviews scheduled next week.

Research into motivation uncovers the "why" questions: Why did you buy that brand and not another? What prompted you to go to that store? Understanding buying motives is crucial to advertisers because the advertising message should reflect consumers' motivations. Unfortunately motivations operate largely at an unconscious level. Some of the reasons may be apparent—you go to a restaurant because you are hungry. But what else governs that choice—is it location, interior decoration, a favorite menu item, or the recommendation of a friend?

In our discussion in Chapter 4 of routine or habit approaches to consumer decision making, we noted the lack of conscious thought about many decisions. That is true also for decisions that are driven by emotions and feelings. Ann Marie Barry described the emerging field of neuroscience in Chapter 4. Applying neuroscience to consumer decision making, **neuromarketing,** the new brain-science approach to how people think, provides a deeper understanding of the way low-attention processing actually works and motivates people into unconscious, intuitive decision making. Ann Marie Barry reports that this neurological research "reveals that visuals may be processed and form the basis of future action without passing through consciousness at all."[7] These studies are particularly useful in describing how emotion is the driving force behind motivations that can lead to largely unconscious brand decisions and behaviors.

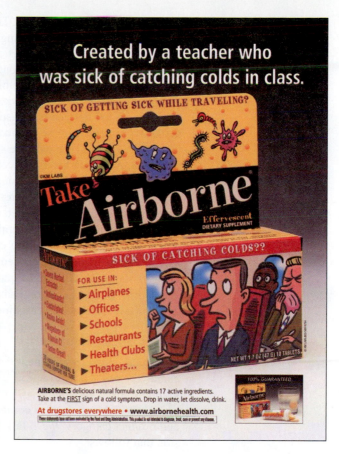

The motivation is obvious for a product that helps you avoid catching a cold when you travel. Do you think it is effective to also feature the motivation of the product's creator?

Principle
Segmenting is efficient and cost effective when it identifies those people who are in the market, but also eliminates those who aren't.

HOW DO WE SEGMENT CONSUMER GROUPS?

Most brands don't have unlimited funds to spread their messages in all directions to all people. Instead, cost efficiency—and effectiveness—demands that marketers (1) segment the market and (2) target the audience group most likely to respond. First let's discuss **segmenting,** which means dividing the market into groups of people who have similar characteristics in certain key product-related areas.

Why do segmenting? Because it's efficient and cost effective. It costs money to reach people with a brand message and most marketers don't want to spend money to reach people who aren't interested in the category or brand. So segmenting does two things: it identifies those people who are in the market, but it also eliminates those who aren't.

Segmentation Strategies

At one point in its history, Coca-Cola viewed the U.S. market for its brand as homogeneous and used general appeals—such as "Coke is it!"—for all consumers, which is considered an **"undifferentiated" strategy.** But even Coke is sold in different types of places, and people hear about Coke through different types of media. Therefore, customers are grouped almost by definition, based on their contact points with the product. Of course, there are also differences in age, for instance, between a long-time adult Coke drinker and a teenager.

Consumer differences, as well as product variations, determine how marketers address people in marketing communication and reach them using media. In other words, few examples of homogeneous markets exist in contemporary marketing, consequently most strategies are based on a **market segmentation** approach that drives marketing communication strategies.

By using a segmentation strategy, a company can more precisely match the needs and wants of the customer with its products. That's why soft drink manufacturers such as Coke and Pepsi have moved away from an undifferentiated approach and introduced product variations to appeal to different consumer segments, such as diet, caffeine-free, diet caffeine-free, and flavored versions of their basic products. This approach also allows a company to target advertising messages by more precisely matching the interests, attitudes, and preferences of consumers in each segment of the soft-drink market.

Although marketing has gone global to reach large markets, many advertisers have moved toward tighter and tighter **niche markets,** which are subsegments of a more general market segment. Individuals in a niche market, such as ecologically minded mothers who won't use disposable diapers, are defined by a distinctive interest or attitude. Instead of marketing to the masses, marketers target narrow segments, such as single women in the international traveler category or pogo-stick riders in the extreme sports category. Although large companies may develop niche strategies, niche marketers are companies that pursue market segments of sufficient size to be profitable although not large enough to be of interest to large marketers. Exploritas, for example, markets to seniors who are interested in educationally oriented travel experiences.

Consumers in niche markets may be more passionate about their favorite brands than general consumer markets. For example, Celestial Seasonings sells one variety called Roastaroma. It is a caffeine-free alternative to coffee. True to Celestial's commitment to herbal ingredients, Roastaroma is made from roasted barley, chicory, and carob, as well as cinnamon, allspice, and Chinese star anise. It's not a popular flavor and has a low sales level, but when Celestial tried to discontinue the line, the company was flooded with letters from irate customers protesting the decision—and Celestial Seasonings gave in to its small band of Roastaroma drinkers.

Types of Segmentation

In general, marketers segment their markets using six broad categories based on key consumer characteristics. The six approaches, illustrated in Figure 5.3, are demographics, life stage, geographics, psychographics, behavior characteristics, and values and benefits sought (needs based). Which approach or combination of approaches is used varies with the market situation and product category. We'll talk about the characteristics behind these segments in the discussion that follows.

• *Demographic Segmentation* divides the market using such characteristics as gender, ethnicity, and income. Age is often the first characteristic to be used in defining a market segment.
• *Life-Stage Segmentation* is based on the particular stage in consumers' life cycle, which includes such categories as children, young people living at home, college students, singles living on their own, couples, families with children, empty nesters, and senior singles living alone. Age is a characteristic of life stage, as is living situation.
• *Geographic Segmentation* uses location as a defining variable because consumers' needs sometimes vary depending on where they live—urban, rural, suburban, North, South. The most important variables are world or global, region, nation, state, city, or zip code. Factors related to these decisions include climate, population density, and urban/rural character. Geography affects both product distribution and marketing communication.

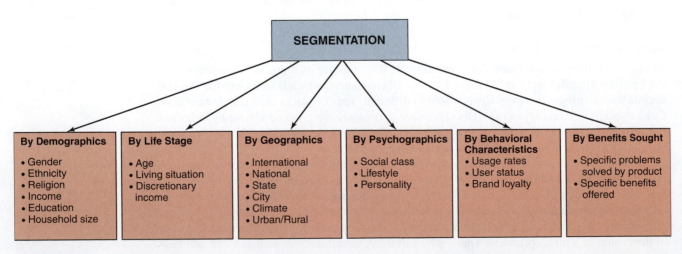

FIGURE 5.3
Market Segmentation Approaches

- *Psychographic Segmentation* is primarily based on studies of how people spend their money, their patterns of work and leisure, their interest and opinions, and their views of themselves. This strategy is considered richer than demographic segmentation because it combines psychological information with lifestyle insights.
- *Behavioral Segmentation* divides people into groups based on product category and brand usage.
- *Values and Benefits-Based Segmentation* groups people based on tangible and intangible factors. Values segmentation reflects consumers' underlying value system—spiritual, hedonistic, thrifty, and so forth. Benefit segmentation is based on consumers' needs or problems. The idea is that people buy products for different benefits they hope to derive. For example, car buyers might be grouped based on whether they are motivated by concerns for safety, gas mileage, durability/dependability, performance and handling, luxury, or enhancement of self-image.

Brand communication, in most cases, is designed to address groups of people who are users of a product or are prospective customers. To describe these groups, planners use a set of terms that represent certain types of cultural, social, and personal characteristics. The idea behind segmenting people is that groups of people to whom advertisers direct their messages can be defined, or profiled, by these key characteristics. Furthermore, those characteristics also define *how* they are different from others who may not be in the market for the product. The four primary categories of descriptive information are demographic, psychographics, behavior, and decision making.

Demographics

The statistical, social, and economic characteristics of a **population,** including such factors as age, gender and sexual orientation, education, occupation, income, family status, race, religion, and geography are called **demographics.** These characteristics serve as the basis for identifying potential audiences, and knowing these factors helps advertisers in message design and media selection for the **target market.** The first place to start when analyzing and compiling demographics is the country's census data. In the United States, the Census Bureau compiles a huge collection of demographic information every 10 years—the most recent census was in 2010.

Age   The most important demographic characteristic used by advertising planners is age. People of different ages have different needs and wants. An advertising message must be geared to the target audience's age group and should be delivered through a medium that members of the group use. But age also determines product choice. How old are you? What products did you use 5 or 10 years ago that you don't use now? Look ahead 10 years. What products might you be interested in buying in the future that you don't buy now?

Table 5.1   U.S. Population Age Breakdowns

Group	In Millions	%
9 and younger	41.1	13.5
10–19	41.6	13.7
20–34	62.0	20.0
35–44	42.5	14.0
45–54	44.4	14.6
55–64	34.0	11.2
65–74	20.1	7.0
75–84	13.0	4.2
85 and older	5.7	1.8

Source: American Fact Finder, U.S. Census Bureau, retrieved September 9, 2009, from http://factfinder .census.gov/servlet/QTTable?_bm=y&-qr_name=PEP_2008_EST_DP1&-geo_id=01000US&-ds_name= PEP_2008_EST&-_lang=en&-format=&-CONTEXT=qt.

Consider the age categories in the following list and the breakdowns in Table 5.1. What is the size of your age group? Which groups are the largest and smallest, and what types of products would they be most interested in buying? An age group often targeted by advertising planners is ages 35 to 54. This group could be generally described as middle aged—how important is it in terms of its size? The following list describes some of the other more common age-related population categories that are used by marketers:

Age-Related Population Categories

- Referred to as the *Greatest Generation* by Tom Brokaw in his book by that name, this generation born in the 1910s through the late 1920s lived through the Great Depression and fought World War II. A small group, these seniors are in their final years. This group opened up college education to the middle class after the war and lived frugal, yet financially satisfying, lives.
- Known as the *Silent Generation* or *traditionalists,* these people born from the late 1920s to the war years are now active seniors. They were described in a national poll as the generation having the most "positive impact" on the American economy for their role in fueling the postwar boom.[8]
- *Baby boomers,* people born between 1946 and 1964, represent the largest age-related category in the United States. The 78 million baby boomer consumers are now in the final years of their careers, having made a huge population bulge as they have moved through the life cycle. While they were growing up, boomers' numbers affected first schools, then the job market, and now retirement programs and health care. This generation has been influenced by significant societal movements and scientific breakthroughs, from the Civil Rights movement to the anti–Vietnam War protests to putting a person on the moon, although the term *boomer* has also become associated with greedy, spoiled, divorced, mega-shoppers who want it all.[9]
- A newly identified subgroup called *Generation Jones* is the younger baby boomers who were born from the mid- to late 1950s through the mid-1960s. The *Jones* reference comes from their continuing need to chase the dream of affluence by trying to "keep up with the Joneses."
- *Gen X,* also known as *Baby Busters,* is the group whose 70 million members were born between 1965 and 1979. Now adults, they have been described as independent minded and somewhat cynical. They are concerned with their physical health (they grew up during the AIDS outbreak) and financial future (the job market became more difficult just about the time they entered).
- Sometimes referred to as the *Me Generation* because of their affluent younger years, those born in the 1970s to early 1990s are characterized as more self-absorbed and narcissistic than their parents, although that changed as they confronted the *dot.com* bust at the end of the 1990s.
- Born between 1980 and 1996, members of *Generation Y* are also known as *Echo Boomers,* as well as the *Me Generation,* because they are the children of baby boomers. They are important to marketers, because they are next in size to the boomer generation with 100 million plus members. This generation is also described as the *Digital* or *Net Generation*[10] because they grew up with computers and are seen as more technologically savvy than their older siblings or parents. This group is now the young adult market that marketers want most to reach because they are in the formative years of their brand relationships. They are the first generation to grow up with e-mail and cell phones.
- *Millennials* encompass those 80 million children born from the late 1990s into the beginning decade of the new century. Also called the *iGeneration,* these folks spend considerably more time texting and using social media than even the older Net Generation. Initially marketers were delighted to find that these kids (and their doting parents) were brand conscious and more willing than their predecessors to wear a brand logo as a badge.[11] But that changed as they became teenagers and had to confront the problems of the recession that dragged down the economy in the late 2000s. They are known as the most environmentally educated generation with 76 percent believing that brands should be ecologically conscious. They are also seen as having outlandish personal expectations and a feeling of entitlement,[12] although the recession may have toned that down a bit.

Age is a key factor in media plans because age usually determines what media you watch, listen to, or read. Note how the radio script for the public service LATCH campaign about child car safety, which we introduced in Chapter 4, plays with the idea of generations. The older the age group, the more likely they are to use media daily or several times a week and the more likely they are to read newspapers. Overall usage patterns for each medium vary by age group. For instance, 88 percent of "mature" audience members watch local broadcast news.[13] Kids ages 8 to 18 now spend more than 7 1/2 hours a day with electronic devices, which include smart phones, computers, televisions and video games, a finding that shocked researchers in 2010 who thought the day couldn't continue to expand to fit in more wired activities.[14]

AD COUNCIL / US DEPARTMENT OF TRANSPORTATION
LATCH Campaign – :60 Radio
ZRAG-11806R
"Generations"
1BON-08-0033
04/30/08 – Produced
07/1/08 – Final Mix
07/15/09 – Expiration Date

VO:	First, there was the "Lost Generation."
SFX:	Music up and under: Jazz Age swing.
VO:	Then came the "Greatest Generation."
SFX:	Battle sounds.
VO:	Followed by the "Silent Generation."
SFX:	Silence.
VO:	The "Me Generation."
SFX:	Acid rock.
VO:	And "Generation X."
SFX:	Video game sounds.
VO:	Now comes the over-scheduled, over-protected, hyper-parented generation…
SFX:	Baby's laugh.
VO:	…three out of four of whom are riding in car seats that aren't being used correctly. The LATCH system is in most cars and makes it easier to be sure your child's car seat is installed correctly. Just clip it to the anchors (CLICK), attach the top tether (CLICK), and pull the straps tight. To find out more, visit safercar.gov.

Anchor. Tether. LATCH. It's the next generation of child safety *(SFX of baby's laugh)*–for the next generation.

A message from the US Department of Transportation and the Ad Council.

SHOWCASE

In Chapter 4 Trent Walters, account director for the Richards Group, explained the thinking behind the U.S. Department of Transportation's LATCH campaign, which is a public service effort by the Ad Council. Here is a radio script from that PSA campaign.

A graduate of the University of North Texas, Trent Walters was nominated by Professor Sheri Broyles.

Age is driving a fundamental shift in U.S. marketing strategy. For 50 years, marketers have focused on reaching young people, not only because they are in the formative years of making brand choices, but also because the youth market during that era was huge in terms of numbers. Now with the boomer bulge moving into retirement, there is tension between the temptation to focus on young people and the realization that wealth and numbers belong to this active senior market. Not only is the senior marketing getting larger, a Pew Research Center study finds a growing generation gap between old and young. Almost 80 percent believe the viewpoints are dramatically different and this shows up in attitudes toward religion, values, morality, lifestyles, manners, and work ethic.[15]

Gender and Sexual Orientation　An obvious basis for differences in marketing and advertising is gender. The fact that interests marketers is that women account for 85 percent of all consumer purchases in the United States.[16] So it's important to know what attracts a female market and how you build brand relationships with them. The Boston Consulting Group spotted the first stages of the United States evolving to a matriarchal society in the mid-2000s.[17] Their research, and more recent studies, point to the increasing percentage of women in college,[18] which also may mean eventual changes in income and occupation patterns.

Many brands are either masculine or feminine in terms of use, as well as brand personality. It is unlikely that men would use a brand of cologne called "White Shoulders." The Gillette Company found that the majority of women would not purchase regular Gillette razor blades, so they introduced brands exclusively for women, such as the Daisy disposable razors. An interesting story is that Marlboro started off as a cigarette marketed to women and was later targeted to men with the cowboy image.

Gender stereotypes have been a problem in advertising for decades and some believe that may be because the majority of the work has been created by men. Jessica Shank, a copywriter at Goodby, Silverstein & Partners, explored that idea and concluded, "If most of the work specifically aimed at women were any indication of modern life, we'd all be at home dancing with our mops and fretting about plastic food storage." She explains, "There's a real disconnect between the lives women lead and the way advertising portrays our daily lives and desires."[19]

During the past decade sexual orientation has also become a marketing issue as gay and lesbian consumers have become serious target markets. Bob Witeck, CEO of Washington, D.C.–based Witeck-Combs Communications, estimates that the buying power of this market is conservatively estimated at $712 billion. He's basing that on a population estimate of approximately 15 million, which would be 6.7 percent of the population.[20] In the *A Matter of Practice* feature at *www.pearsonhighered.com/moriarty,* Witeck explains how this market dealt with the economic downturn.

Education, Occupation, and Income　According to the 2009 Census Report, U.S. males are falling behind females in higher levels of education. Generally, white U.S. consumers attain higher levels of education than blacks and Hispanics. For advertisers, education also tends to correlate with the type of medium consumers prefer. Consumers with lower education are higher users of television, especially cable. Consumers with higher education prefer print media, the Internet, and selected radio and cable stations. Likewise, education dictates the way copy is written and its level of difficulty. Examine ads in *Fortune* or *Forbes* and you will find different words, art, and products than you will in *People* or **tabloid** publications. Advertisers don't make value judgments about these statistics. Their objective is to match advertising messages to the characteristics of the target audience.

Most people identify themselves by what they do. In the United States there has been a gradual trend from blue-collar occupations (manufacturing, for example) to white-collar occupations (management and information). There have also been shifts within white-collar work from sales to other areas, such as professional, technical, and administrative positions. The number of service-related jobs continues to increase, especially in the health care, education, and legal and business service sectors. Much of this transition is a direct result of computer technologies, which have eliminated many labor-intensive, blue-collar occupations. This shift has affected advertising in a number of ways: today, advertisements seldom portray blue-collar jobs, for example.

Another key demographic indicator for many advertisers is income. You are meaningful to marketers to the extent that you have the resources to buy their products or services or contribute to their causes. The patterns of income distribution generally show that the most affluent 20 percent has 50 percent of the total U.S. consumer income; the bottom income groups, which combined include 60 percent of the population, get by on about one-fourth of the total consumer income.[21]

Advertisers track trends in income, especially **discretionary income,** which is the amount of money available to spend after paying for taxes and basic necessities, such as food and shelter. Some industries, such as movie theaters, travel, jewelry, and fashion, would be out of business if people didn't have discretionary income. Discretionary income has been found to be a more reliable predictor of spending than income.[22]

Family Status   Age also relates to family status. The trends during the past 30 years have been for people to increasingly be older when they marry, and the number of families also continues to shrink. Although families dominate American households, they are fewer in number than in 1980. In data reported in 2009, 67 percent of the households were families and 33 percent were singles. The composition of households is particularly important in media planning where many of the decisions are based on reaching households who subscribe or view programs, rather than individuals. That's because the media vehicles generally report their data, and compute their impact (readers, users, viewers) based on household estimates.

Race, Ethnicity, and Immigration   In the United States, ethnicity is a major factor in segmenting markets. According to 2009 Census Bureau data, Hispanics make up 15 percent of the population and have overtaken African Americans at 13 percent as the largest ethnic group. African Americans, however, have seen a dramatic increase of more than 55 percent in their buying power since 2000.[23] Asians are 5 percent. Hispanics are the fastest growing minority, and the U.S. Census Bureau estimates that by 2050 they will make up 30 percent of the total population. These three major categories make up more than a third of the U.S. population, that is, roughly one in every three people are now minorities. All three groups are projected to make up more than half of the U.S. population in 2050.

Multicultural strategies that recognize these trends have been important for a number of years, but will dominate the practice of advertising in the midcentury. According to multicultural analysts, "The U.S. is more multicultural than ever."[24] What changes in advertising would you expect to see as a result of such a dramatic change in the racial profile of the country?

After nearly two years in a recession, the 2009 annual survey found that for the first time in nearly 40 years the foreign-born population declined with fewer low-skilled immigrants from Mexico and elsewhere. However, the survey found continuing increases in high-skilled immigrants from India and other Asian countries.[25] The survey also found that about one in five U.S. residents spoke a language other than English at home—mostly in California, New Mexico, and Texas.[26] In three metro areas—Miami, San Jose, and Los Angeles—more than a third of residents are foreign born. Data from Synovate's Diversity Markets Report, found that of all Hispanics, most were (56 percent) were U.S. born.[27]

This ad for Tide targets the Hispanic culture. The translation is "The salsa is something you dance, not what you wear." If you were on the Tide team, would you recommend using this ad? Why or why not?

Media use differences may also be based on ethnicity. For example, a Nielsen study found that Hispanic viewers are more likely to watch commercials in their entirety than non-Hispanic viewers. Nielsen has found that Hispanic audiences are more influenced by advertising than other U.S. consumers—they are more likely to base their purchasing decisions on advertisements, and they are less cynical about marketing.[28]

Self-identity is also affected by race and ethnicity. This is another reason diversity is so important in advertising—both in the ads themselves but also in the minds of the professionals who create the advertising—a point well made in the *A Principled Practice* feature.

The point is that many marketers are employing multicultural strategies to better serves their customers. McDonald's chief marketing officer, for example, reports that 40 percent of the fast-food chain's customers come from the Hispanic, Asian, and African American markets, and 50 percent of customers under the age of 13 are from those segments. He observes that

Principle
Income is a key demographic factor because consumers are meaningful to a marketer only if they have the resources needed to buy the product advertised.

A PRINCIPLED PRACTICE

Making Blacks Visible

Jason Chambers, *Associate Professor and Assistant Dean College of Media, University of Illinois*

In the early 1990s, Kay Lorraine, a Chicago-based advertising producer, assembled a cast and crew on location to film a commercial for a Cleveland grocery chain. She hired a multiracial cast to reflect Cleveland's diversity, but the client representative, after seeing the black actors at the taping "had a fit and wanted them off the set." Lorraine refused. After several tense moments, he relented. "O.K." he allowed, "they can push the shopping carts around in the back, but make sure they don't touch the food." So Lorraine filmed the commercial with the black actors in the back of the scene and not touching any of the products—quietly pretending that they were not there.

Although Lorraine's encounter with a prejudiced executive took place late in the 20th century, it could have happened in nearly any decade and in any place in America. For much of the century, to include African Americans in a commercial, even one aired in a city with a large black population, was anathema to many executives. Indeed, many of the people who decided the advertising and marketing direction for their companies simply acted as though blacks did not exist as consumers for their products. Therefore, they often gave them no place in their advertising, unless individuals like Lorraine, black consumers, or advocacy groups pressured them to do so.

Lorraine risked losing the account when she openly confronted the representative's prejudice. Advertising is a service business. Agencies exist to meet the needs of clients and those clients have complete power over where their advertising dollars go. That Lorraine, a white woman, took this stand was due in part to the hard work of numerous African Americans in the advertising and media industries. Over the course of several decades, these men and women stood up to the negative and denigrating treatment by advertising agencies and American corporations, and their hard work helped make the black consumer market visible. As this examination of the advertising industry will show, too few others acted with Lorraine's courage to include blacks in advertisements—or as employees in advertising agencies. Yet it was only through this sort of pressure that the advertising industry ever changed at all.

Excerpt from the Introduction to *Madison Avenue and the Color Line: African Americans in the Advertising Industry*, by Jason Chambers, University of Pennsylvania Press, 2009.

---

these "ethnic segments are leading lifestyle trends," and they are also McDonald's most loyal customers.[29]

Religion   One area that connects culture to demographics is religion. Religion is sometimes a useful factor because of the increasing importance of product bans. In terms of demographics, Christianity is the largest religion both in the United States and in the world. Islam is one of the fastest growing faiths in the world and may soon overtake Christianity in numbers worldwide. As an indication of that growth, National Public Radio reported that *Mohammad* has become the top male name in England, many European cities, and also in the world.[30] There is also a large percentage of the population, both in the United States and worldwide, that is secular or unaffiliated with any organized religion.

Some religions forbid certain products. Mormons, for example, avoid tea, coffee, caffeinated soft drinks, alcohol, and tobacco. Muslims also avoid alcohol and both Muslims and Jews avoid pork products, as well as other food products that aren't certified as halal (Muslim) or kosher (Jewish). Most religions celebrate gift giving, such as some Native American faiths and Christianity at Christmastime. Other religions affect people's choice of clothing and adornment. Religion has also become a huge factor in determining political choices and adherence to certain causes. It depends on the product category, but religion can be a key factor in identifying those who are or are not in the market for a good, service, or idea.

Geography   Marketers study the sales patterns of different parts of the country because people residing in different regions need certain products. For example, someone living in the Midwest or the Northeast is more likely to purchase products for removing snow and ice than a Floridian. Differences also exist between urban areas and suburban or rural areas. Swimming pools that sell well in a residential suburban neighborhood would not be in demand in an urban neighborhood filled with apartment buildings.

Another important role for geography is in media planning where a **designated market area (DMA)** is used in describing media markets. A DMA is identified by the name of the dominant city in that area and it generally aligns with the reach of local television signals. The Seattle-Tacoma DMA in Washington, for example, covers some 13 counties in the northwest corner of the state.

Psychographics

Just as demographics relates to social characteristics, psychographics summarizes personal factors. The term **psychographics** refers to lifestyle and psychological characteristics, such as activities, values, interests, attitudes, and opinions.

Sometimes these complex psychographic factors are more relevant in explaining consumer behavior than are demographics. For example, two families living next door to each other with the same general income, education, and occupational profiles may have radically different buying patterns. One family may be obsessed with recycling, while their neighbors rarely bother to even keep their newspapers separate from their trash. One family is into hiking and other outdoor sports; the other watches sports on television. One is saving money for a European vacation; the other is seriously in debt and can barely cover the monthly bills. The differences lie not in their demographics, but in their psychographics—their interests and lifestyles.

Principle
Often differences in consumer behavior lie in psychographics— consumers' interests and lifestyles—rather than in demographics.

Advertisers use psychographics to depict fairly complex consumer patterns. Libraries of psychographic measures can be purchased from research firms, or a company and its advertising agency can create its own set of psychographic measures to fit its particular product. These psychographic measures can then be used to describe customers (such as heavy users of gourmet coffee), their response to advertising message strategies (taste comparison ads), or their media choices (heavy users of the Internet).

Attitudes   An **attitude** is a predisposition that reflects an opinion, emotion, or mental state directed at some object, person, or idea. Advertisers are interested in attitudes because of their impact on motivations. Because attitudes are learned, we can establish them, change them, reinforce them, or replace them with new ones. However, most attitudes are deeply set, reflect basic values, and tend to be resistant to change—you can hold an attitude for years or even decades. Attitudes also vary in direction and strength; that is, an attitude can be positive or negative, reflecting like or dislike, or it can be neutral. Attitudes are important to advertisers because they influence how consumers evaluate products, institutions, retail stores, and advertising.

Principle
Strategies that are designed to affect attitudes focus on establishing, changing, reinforcing, or replacing them.

One trend that depicts changing attitudes is what *Time* magazine editor Richard Stengel called "ethical consumerism," which refers to consumers who buy according to their conscience, whether it be a concern for supporting local businesses and ecology and energy efficiency or boycotting wasteful packaging and sweatshops. The *Time* poll found that 82 percent said they shop local and 40 percent said they purchased a product "because they liked the social or political values of the company that produced it." At the same time, many companies have found that social responsibility attracts investments, as well as customer loyalty. Stengel explains, "With global warming on the minds of many consumers, lots of companies are racing to 'outgreen' one another." This results in business practices that build a positive "triple bottom line": profit, planet, and people.[31]

Lifestyles   Psychographic analysis looks at lifestyles in terms of patterns of consumption, personal relationships, interests, and leisure activities. The DDB advertising agency has been conducting lifestyle research annually in the United States since 1975. The agency surveys 5,000 men and women on nearly 1,000 questions pertaining to such diverse topics as health, financial outlook, raising kids, shopping, religion, hobbies, leisure activities, household chores, politics, even their desired self-image. The survey also asks people about the products they use (from soup to nuts!) and their media habits. This wealth of information makes it possible to paint a vivid,

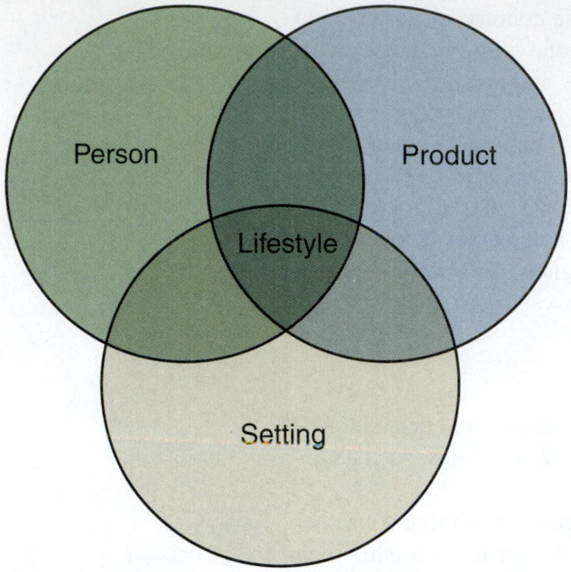

FIGURE 5.4

Lifestyle Components
Products are linked to lifestyles in the way they reflect the interests of people and the settings in which the products are used.

detailed, multidimensional portrait of nearly any consumer segment that might be of interest to a client—and it also lets the agency spot changes and trends in people's lifestyles over time.

Former DDB strategy director Marty Horn says that "DDB believes that advertising—and all other forms of marketing communication—is really a personal conversation between the brand being advertised and the consumer, and the better we know the consumer with whom we are conversing, the more engaging and persuasive our message will be." The agency's Life Style Survey is an important source of information that lets this conversation happen. Horn explains, "The DDB Life Style Survey helps us get a more 'up close and personal' look at who our clients' customers are than what conventional research alone can provide."

Horn describes an example of the use of the Life Style Survey data to segment an audience for the Blood Center of Wisconsin when the center found itself low on donations. The DDB research team was able to describe frequent donors as sociable, doting parents, hard working, information seekers, and community leaders. The communication strategy was refined to appeal to a more professional working people audience and the center saw a turnaround in its level of donations.

Some of the most common lifestyle patterns are described by such familiar phrases as *yuppies* (young urban professionals) and *yuppie puppies* (their children). These terms are group identifiers, but they also refer to a set of products and the setting within which the products are used. For example, yuppies have been characterized as aspiring to an upscale lifestyle, so products associated with this lifestyle might include Cole Haan shoes, Hermes scarves, and BMW cars.

As a result of the recent recession, the idea of sustainable living became more popular, particularly with older boomers who adopted the New Urbanist lifestyle, which means leaving a smaller carbon footprint on the planet by selling their suburban homes, moving to lofts or in-town condos, and selling their second cars so they could drive less and walk more.[32] Figure 5.4 illustrates the interactions between the person, the product, and the setting in which a product is used.

As part of their services to clients, some research firms create lifestyle profiles that collectively reflect a whole culture. We discuss two of these proprietary tools here: the Yankelovich MONITOR's MindBase and the VALS System from SRI Consulting Business Intelligence (SRIC-BI).

The Yankelovich MONITOR™ has been tracking consumer values and lifestyles since 1971. Its MindBase™ tool uses the MONITOR database to identify groups of people with distinctive attitudes, values, motivations, and lifestyles. (Check this company out at *www.yankelovich.com/index.php?option=com_content&task=category&sectionid=21&id=42&Itemid=88.*) Although the database can be used to custom design segments for individual clients, MindBase has identified eight general consumer groups that span the four generations of matures, baby boomers, Generation X, and echo boomers. The eight MindBase categories are as follows:[33]

- *"I Am Expressive"* Lives life to the fullest; not afraid to express my personality; active and engaged; "live in the now" attitude; believes that the future is limitless and I can do anything I put my mind to.
- *"I Am Down to Earth"* Cruising through life at my own pace; seek satisfaction where I can; hope to enhance my life; I like to try new things; I treat myself to novel things.
- *"I Am Driven"* Ambitious with a drive to succeed; self-possessed and resourceful; determined to show the world I'm on top of my game.
- *"I Am Sophisticated"* Intelligent, upstanding with an affinity for finer things; high expectations; dedicated to doing a stellar job, but I balance career with enriching experiences.
- *"I Am at Capacity"* Busy and looking for control and simplification; a demanding and vocal consumer; looking for convenience, respect, and a helping hand; want to devote more of my time to the important things in life.
- *"I Measure Twice"* Mature; like to think I'm on a path to fulfillment; live a healthy, active life; dedicated to a secure and rewarding future.
- *"I Am Rock Steady"* Positive attitude; draw energy from home and family; dedicated to an upstanding life; listen to my own instincts for decisions in life and in marketplace.

- *"I Am Devoted"* Traditional; rooted in comforts of home; conventional beliefs; spiritual and content; like things the way they've always been; doesn't need novelty for novelty's sake or newfangled technology.

The VALS™ system by research firm SRIC-BI is known for its values and lifestyles system, which categorizes consumers according to psychological traits that correlate to purchasing behaviors. Advertisers correlate these VALS groups with their clients' products and use this information to design ads and select media. (Check out this system at *www.sric-bi.com/vals.*)

Figure 5.5 shows the eight VALS groups, as well as their three primary motivations (ideals, achievement, and self-expression) for buying products and services. "Thinkers" and "Believers" are motivated by ideals—abstract criteria such as tradition, quality, and integrity. "Achievers" and "Strivers" are motivated by achievement, seeking approval from a values social group. "Experiencers" and "Makers" are motivated by self-expression and make value purchases that enable them to stand out from the crowd or make an impact on the physical world. The VALS groups on the top half of the figure have more resources—a combination of education, income, energy, innovativeness, and self-confidence—than the groups on the bottom half. You can take the survey yourself and find out your own VALS type at *www.strategicbusinessinsights.com/ vals/presurvey.shtml.*

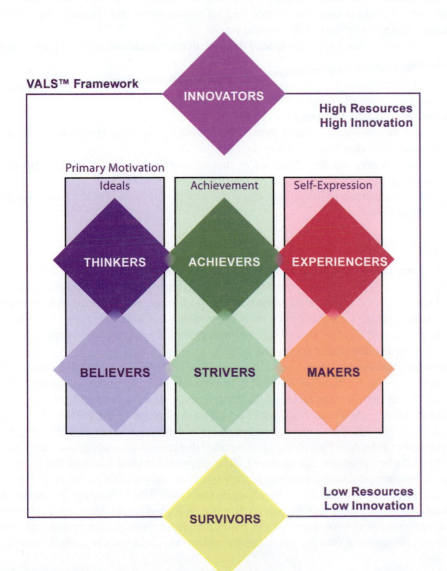

FIGURE 5.5

VALS™ Lifestyle Framework
The lifestyle groups as identified by VALS-BI research. Where would you place yourself? Your parents?

Courtesy of SRI Consulting Business Intelligence (SRIC-BI). All rights reserved. *www.sric-bi .com/VALS*

© SRI Consulting Business Intelligence. All rights reserved.
www.sric-bi.com/VALS

The VALS framework enables advertisers to discover which VALS types buy which products so they can select an appropriate target. VALS also describes the communication styles of each VALS group so the advertiser can design ads using images and copy in a style that will grab the target group's attention. In addition, by using GeoVALS™, the advertiser can place the ad where concentrations of the target live. In addition to the U.S. system, Japan-VALS™ and UK-VALS™ have also been developed.

Sociodemographic Segments   One common approach to demographic segmentation that has entered mainstream vocabulary comes from referring to people in terms of when they were born. Although these categories are age driven and we discussed them in an earlier section, these market segment terms also refer to lifestyle differences. We've talked about the incredible impact baby boomers have had as a market category, so you can understand their importance as a market segment, but savvy marketers recognize the many differences in lifestyles and attitudes among this huge population. Generations X and Y, as well as the echo boomers, are also important demographic segments, but their sociodemographic characteristics may represent more consistent lifestyle differences.

Seniors are also referred to as the *gray market* and divided into two categories: young seniors (ages 60 to 74), called the *Boomer-Plus* group,[34] and older seniors (ages 75 and older). Seniors, both younger and older, comprise a huge market, especially in the United States, and also a wealthy one. As baby boomers move into their retirement years, this senior market will become even larger relative to the rest of the population.

Other fun terms that have been used to describe demographic and lifestyle segments include the following:

- *Dinkies* Double-income young couples with no kids
- *Guppies* Gay upwardly mobile professionals
- *Skippies* School kids with purchasing power
- *Slackers* A recycled term inspired by the 1991 movie *Slacker,* referring to teenagers and young adults who don't care much or do much
- *Bling-Bling Generation* A term coined by rappers and hip hoppers referring to people with a high-rolling lifestyle who flash costly jewelry
- *Ruppies* Retired urban professionals; older consumers with sophisticated tastes and generally affluent lifestyles.

Behavior

The behavioral component of the think/feel/do model that we discussed in Chapter 4 is a key strategic factor used in describing the relationship consumers have with a product category or a brand. That behavioral component, particularly product usage, is often used in segmenting consumers. A recent behavioral economics study in Sacramento, California, found that when people were told how much their neighbors save on their electrical bills, this comparative information motivated them to reduce their energy use as well.[35]

Behavior, however, is often a product of feelings (impulse) or thoughtful search. One area where such behaviors has been investigated is grocery shopping. An observational study by a University of Florida student, Kate Stein, found that grocery shoppers often buy food impulsively and irrationally. (Stein worked with Professor Brian Wansink, director of the Cornell University Food and Brand Lab, and you'll read more about her research experience in the next chapter.) Published as an op-ed piece in the *New York Times,* Stein reported that browsing slowly doesn't necessarily help you pick out the best products. She observed, "The shoppers I studied who took the longest, examining packages, stopping at whatever caught their eye, invariably spent more money." Furthermore, she noticed that these slow and thoughtful shoppers often loaded their shopping carts with unhealthy items that, when questioned, they couldn't give a reason for buying. In other words, the best shoppers use a grocery list, control their instincts, and move quickly through their product selections. For more tips on streamlining your grocery shopping endeavors, check out *www.mindlesseating.org.*[36]

Brand Usage and Experiences   A critical behavior predictor called **usage** refers to how much of a product category or brand a customer buys. There are two ways to classify usage: usage rates and brand relationship, as Table 5.2 illustrates. *Usage rate* refers to quantity of purchase: light,

Table 5.2   Consumer Categories Based on Product Usage

Quantity	Brand Relationship	Innovation
Light users	Nonusers	Innovators
Medium users	Ex-users	Early adopters
Heavy users	Regulars	Early majority
	First-timers	Late majority
	Loyal users	Laggards
	Switchers	

medium, or heavy. Heavy users typically buy the most of a product category or a brand's share of the market. An old rule of thumb called the Pareto rule states that 20 percent of the market typically buys 80 percent of the products. That explains why the heavy-user category is so important to marketers and why planners make special efforts to understand this key customer group. Heavy users and brand loyal buyers are usually a brand's most important customers, and they are the most difficult for competitors to switch away from a brand. **Switchers** are people with low levels of brand loyalty who may be willing to try a new brand.

We mentioned in a previous chapter that experience marketing has become an important idea. You know the old saying that "getting there is half the fun." The experience of shopping, for some women, is as important as, or maybe more important than, what they buy. In a larger sense, our decisions are often based on what our experience has been with the brand—how well it performed, how easy it was to use, how well customer service responded to questions, and so forth.

Innovation and Adoption   Another type of behavior has to do with how willing people are to try something new and how willing they are to risk buying new products. Everett Rogers developed the classification system which he called the *diffusion of innovation curve,* to identify innovation and **adoption** behaviors. This **adoption process** is identified in terms of personal behavior and how the behavior reflects the speed with which people are willing to try something new, such as *innovators, early adopters, early majority, late majority,* and *laggards.*[37] This system is directly related to the willingness of people to try new products, which reflects the speed of **diffusion** of new ideas. See Figure 5.6 for an interpretation of Rogers' Diffusion of Innovation model.

The innovator category, which is the group of brave souls willing to try something new, represents only about 2.5 percent of the population. Obviously this group and the early adopter category are important groups for marketers launching new products. Risk taking is a personality characteristic, but it drives behavior in the area of trying a new product. **Perceived risk** is your view of the relationship between what you gain by trying something new and what you have to lose if it doesn't work out. In other words, how important is the consequence of not making a good decision? Price is a huge barrier for high-involvement products; personal status and self-image may be a risk barrier for a fashion product.

Early adopters have been studied by SRI International, the consulting company behind the VALS segmentation scheme. Its clients often ask for guidance about identifying early adopters of innovative products. Cheri Anderson, an SRI consultant, explains the company has discovered that early adopters:

- Are people involved in unusual activities and whose level of activity will disproportionately affect the behaviors of others
- Have many weak social contacts
- Are masters of their own universes
- Are high media users
- Have a more complex history of personal and sexual relationships

Who are these people? SRI's research has found that "contrary to popular belief, there is no one innovator or early adopter group but adoption patterns vary with the product category. Early adopters are in different strata and roles in society and cannot be identified by demographics

Principle
In many product categories, 20 percent of the users buy 80 percent of the products.

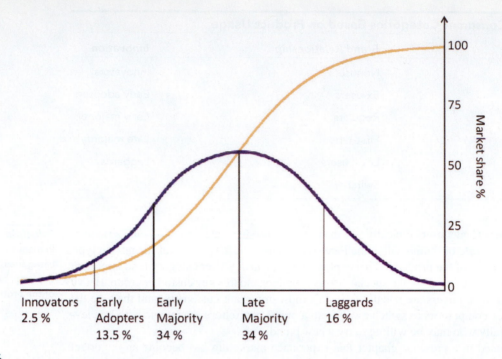

FIGURE 5.6

The Diffusion of Innovation

This version of Rogers' diffusion of Innovation model shows the usual bell curve with data estimating the percentage of people in the standard adaption categories, however, it also presents a percentage line that estimates the cumulative effect of successive groups of consumers adopting a new idea until it eventually reaches a saturation level.

Source: Tungsten, *http://en.wikipedia.org/wiki/Everett_Rogers.* Based on Rogers, E. (1962) Diffusion of innovations. Free Press, London, NY, USA.

alone. Anderson explains why early adopters are important to research firms such as SRI: "By understanding what motivates and de-motivates different early adopter groups, we can help our clients identify targets and steer their brands for successful market entry."

Trends and Fads   The phenomenon of trends and fads is related to lifestyle and psychographic factors, as well as the fascination with choice in a consumer culture. We've seen "acre homes" and fancy bathroom retreats, as well as low-carb diets, healthy food (oat bran, antioxidants), natural products, fitness fads and personal trainers, hybrid cars, carbon trading, simple life (don't buy things), and local products (don't buy things that use a lot of gas in transportation to get to your local store). Even Girl Scout cookies are trying to appeal to people by using new formulations that are low in trans fats.[38]

Young people are particularly involved in trends. For example, the way teenagers dress and talk and the products they buy are driven by a continuing search for coolness. **Trend spotters** are professional researchers hired by advertisers to identify trends that may affect consumer behavior. **Cool hunters** are trend spotters who specialize in identifying trendy fads that appeal to young people. They usually work with panels of young people in key trendsetting locations, such as New York, California, urban streets, and Japan. Loic Bizel, for example, hunts Japanese super trendy fads as a consultant for many Western companies and designers. Through his website (*www.fashioninjapan.com*), you can get a taste of those cool ideas and fashion in Japan's streets and life, such as studded high tops and spray-on stockings.

CONSUMER DECISION MAKING

Another important factor in identifying a brand's potential customers is the way consumers go about making product choices. A complicating factor is the increasing number of choices. Brand variations clutter shelves and media choices seem unlimited. Chicago agency Brandtrust believes the consumer decision process is "a complex alchemy" set in play by product features plus consumers' past experiences with shopping in the product category.[39]

In Chapter 4 we looked at a number of models from a marketer's point of view. Now let's examine them from the consumer's perspective. The traditional view of consumer decision making, which is similar to the more classic AIDA-based models of message impact, is based on a linear, information-processing approach. It suggests that most people follow a decision process with fairly predictable steps: (1) need recognition, (2) information search, (3) evaluation of alternatives, (4) purchase decision, and (5) post-purchase evaluation.

- *Need recognition* can vary in terms of seriousness or importance. The goal of advertising at this stage is to activate or stimulate this need.
- *Information search* can be casual (reading ads and articles that happen to catch your attention) or formal (searching for information in publications such as *Consumer Reports*). Advertising helps the search process by providing information that is easy to find and remember. For low-involvement products this stage may not occupy much time or thought or it may be skipped altogether. Another way to describe consumer behavior in terms of information needs includes such terms as *searchers* and *impulse buyers.* Searchers are driven by a need to know everything they can about a product before making a purchase, particularly major purchases. In contrast, people who buy on impulse generally do so without much thought based on some immediate desire such as thirst or hunger. Usually there's not much at stake, so the risk of making a bad decision is much lower. It is true, however, that even major purchases, such as cars, can be made on the spur of the moment by people who are not dedicated searchers for information.
- *Evaluation of alternatives* is the stage where consumers compare various products and features and reduce the list of options to a manageable number. They select certain features that are important and use them to judge alternatives. Advertising is important in this evaluation process because it helps sort out products on the basis of tangible and intangible features. Even with low-involvement products, there may be what we call an **evoked set** of brands that are all considered permissible. What are your favorite candy bars? The brands you name makes up your evoked set.
- *Purchase decision* is often a two-part decision. Usually, we select the brand first and then select the outlet from which to buy it. Is this product available at a grocery store, a discount store, a hardware store, a boutique, a department store, or a specialty store? Sometimes we select the outlet first, particularly with impulse purchases. In-store promotions such as packaging, **point-of-purchase displays,** price reductions, banners and signs, and coupon displays affect these choices.
- *Post-purchase evaluation* is the last step in the rational process. As soon as we purchase a product, particularly a major one, we begin to reevaluate our decision. Is the product what we expected? Is its performance satisfactory? This experience determines whether we will keep the product, return it, or refuse to buy it again. We referred to *cognitive dissonance* in the discussion of satisfaction and this is also an important factor in the post-purchase evaluation step. Many consumers continue to read information even after the purchase, to justify the decision to themselves. Guarantees, warranties, and easy returns are also important for reducing the fear of a purchase that goes wrong.

This set of steps is hierarchical and suffers from the limitations we discussed in Chapter 4. We know that involvement, for example, is an important variable in consumer decision making and that the involvement level varies with product category, affecting how people make brand decisions. In other words, the process consumers go through in making a purchase varies between low-involvement and high-involvement purchase decisions (see Figure 5.7). Note that with low-involvement situations, there is little or no information search and the decision may be more of an impulse purchase. In contrast, high-involvement products and decisions use the traditional information-processing approach, which invites more information seeking and careful consideration of decision factors, such as quality or price.

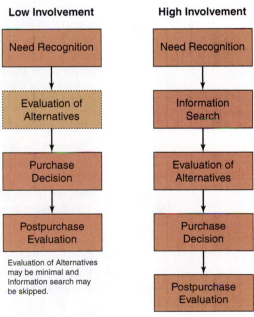

Low Involvement

Need Recognition

Evaluation of Alternatives

Purchase Decision

Postpurchase Evaluation

Evaluation of Alternatives may be minimal and Information search may be skipped.

High Involvement

Need Recognition

Information Search

Evaluation of Alternatives

Purchase Decision

Postpurchase Evaluation

FIGURE 5.7

Low- and High-Involvement Decision Processes
The decision processes people use for low- and high-involvement products are quite different. What have you purchased recently that could be considered low- or high-involvement products? How did your decision process compare to these models?

Table 5.3   Different Paths to a Purchase Decision

Path	Goal	Example	Advertising's Objective
Think—feel—do	Learning, interest	Computer game, CD, DVD	Provide information, emotion
Think—do—feel	Learning, understanding	College, a computer, a vacation	Provide information, arguments
Feel—think—do	Needs	A new suit, a motorcycle	Create desire
Feel—do—think	Wants	Cosmetics, fashion	Establish a psychological appeal
Do—feel—think	Impulse	A candy bar, a soft drink	Create brand familiarity
Do—think—feel	Habit	Cereal, shampoo	Remind of satisfaction

The Paths to a Brand Decision

Given the importance of involvement, let's reconsider the classic information approach to brand decisions. In Chapter 4 we introduced the think/feel/do model of consumer response to a message. That same model is useful in analyzing the many different ways consumers make brand decisions.

The idea is that the path to a decision depends on the type of product and the buying situation. If you're hungry (a feeling drives a purchase decision), you grab a candy bar without much information search. If you try a sample product and like it (behavior is the driver), then you may buy the product without much evaluation of alternatives. In other words, not all responses begin with thinking about a product, nor do they follow the same route to a decision. Table 5.3 illustrates the many ways a purchase decision can be made.

Given all of the different ways consumers go about making a brand choice, you can see why brand planners need to know how this decision process works for a specific product category. Obviously the message would be different for a consumer who is searching for information to buy a computer and considering the differences between brands in comparison to someone who makes an impulse purchase like buying a soft drink. That's why this information becomes an important part of a consumer profile when identifying prospects to target in a campaign.

Influences on B2B Decision Making   Many of the influences that affect consumer buying also are reflected in business-to-business marketing. However, we also know that B2B decision making generally follows the informational route. Emotion may still be important in certain situations (e.g., the buyer wants to impress the boss), but ultimately these decisions usually are more rational than emotional for the following reasons:

- In organizational buying, many individuals are involved in reviewing the options, often with a buying committee making the final decision.
- Although the business buyer may be motivated by both rational and emotional factors, the use of rational and quantitative criteria dominates most decisions.
- The decision is sometimes made based on a set of specifications to potential suppliers who then bid on the contract. Typically in these purchases, the lowest bid wins.
- The decision may span a considerable time period and create a lag between the initial contact and final decision. On the other hand, once a decision is made, it may be in place for a long time and sometimes is supported by a contract.
- Quality is hugely important, and repeat purchases are based on how well the product performs.
- Personal selling is also important in B2B marketing, so advertising is used to open the door and generate leads for the sales force.

TARGETING THE RIGHT AUDIENCE

Traditionally a market is first divided to identify segments, and then potentially profitable segments are selected to be the target audience for a marketing communication effort. Through **targeting,** the organization can design specific communication strategies to match the audience's needs and wants and position the product in the most relevant way to match their interests. Targeting is also the key factor in selecting the right media.

Consider, for example, how Niman Ranch of Bolinas, California, built a luxury brand for its beef. The obvious target would be upscale consumers who value natural food and are willing to pay more for the best. But that's not the route Niman Ranch took. Instead it bypassed consumers and marketed directly to prestigious chefs whose restaurants featured the brand on their menus. By using an innovative targeting strategy, Niman moved from commodity to a cachet brand that has brought huge growth to the little company. More recently with the interest in organic products and local farming, Niman has become a model for knitting together a network of hundreds of small-scale, organic farmers that leverages economies of scale, while at the same time leaving farmers in control of their local operations.[40]

It is important to remember that the changing media environment, with its opportunities for consumer-initiated messages and two-way communication, is creating new approaches to targeting. In the Age of Twitter, targeting is less about aiming an ad than it is about listening and responding.

Profiling the Target Audience

Regardless of whether the marketing communication is using one-way or two-way communication strategies, planners still need some sense of who they are talking to and with. The target is first of all described using the segmentation characteristics that separate a prospective consumer group from others who are not as likely to buy the brand, such as women who buy hair color. The target audience is then profiled using descriptive information based on the demographic and psychographic factors we've discussed in this chapter. For example, what are the target audience members' ages, income, education, geography, and critical psychographics? What motivates them? **Profiles** are descriptions of the target audience that read like a description of someone you know. These are used in personalizing the consumer to develop on-target media and message decisions. Analyze how Clairol appealed to its target market in the classic "Does She or Doesn't She" campaign.

Pretend you're launching a new diaper service. The first consideration is identifying common characteristics of the parents in your target market. What are your brand features and how important are they to parents: price, features, materials, ecological sensitivity, and so forth. In the large market of parents of infants, who cares for the features that are most distinctive for your brand?

You know that mothers are primary caretakers of infants, and you know that mothers are not all alike—but in order to narrow your target, what makes them different? Some are affluent, while others struggle to get by. Are these important factors for the brand (inexpensive or expensive?), or do factors other than income need to be considered? If so, what are they?

You build a profile by starting with the most important characteristic—matching the key brand features to the interests and concerns of the market. In the diaper service example, that would be gender, of course, and then age, let's say women ages 18 to 35. Then you add other factors, such as income, urban versus rural dwellers, education, or whatever factors come up in research as important predictive variables for your brand.

As Figure 5.8 illustrates, each time you add a variable, you narrow the market as you come closer to the ideal target audience. The objective is to get the largest group that can be defined in such a way that you can direct a message that will speak to people in that group and that you can reach with specific media. Once these predictor variables have been sorted out, it should be possible to build an estimate of the size of this target market.

CLASSIC

One of advertising's most familiar slogans moved women who were tired of being told that there are things ladies don't do, such as color their hair. Legendary copywriter Shirley Polykoff understood these emotions and that it was okay to be a little bit naughty as long as you were nice. In 1967 Time magazine reported that the number of women who used hair color increased from 15 to 50 percent after this campaign began in 1956. The campaign also appears as #9 on Advertising Age's list of the Top 100 Campaigns in history. What lesson can you learn from a successful ad like this even if it's 50 years old?

FIGURE 5.8

Narrowing the Target
As descriptors are added to the identification of the target, the number in the middle of the target gets smaller. As this target is defined, the size of the group can be predicted.

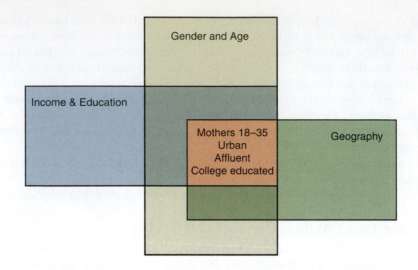

An example of how consumers can be profiled comes from Forrester Research, which uses a research approach called "design personas." Harley Manning, research director for customer experience, describes the concept as "a model of a customer's goals, needs, attitudes, and behaviors distilled from interviewing and observing real people in a market segment." He explains that when you build a "persona," you have a vivid profile of a type of person. For example, he referred to "Stanley," a person used by J.P. Morgan to model its active, savvy investors. He notes that this type of person won't be satisfied with a simple account summary and instead wants advanced portfolio details.

Principle

Each time you add a variable to a target audience definition, you narrow the size of the target audience.

Behavioral Targeting   Although behavioral characteristics have always been important, **behavioral targeting** based on Internet use is getting more attention because of the increasing importance of digital marketing. It's also changing the focus of targeting in general, particularly for brand campaigns that hope to increase customer interactivity. The Internet makes it possible to deliver ads personalized in terms of a customer's own usage patterns.[41] Amazon, for example, has pioneered the practice of promoting books to people based on their past purchases. The idea is that a person who is only known by an ISP number gets a specially targeted ad based on sites visited or purchases made online.

As David Rittenhouse, of Ogilvy & Mather, explains, "Online media have emerged as a preferred channel for behavioral targeting due to the massive amount of data available on Web users' browsing patterns and the dynamic nature of the way ads are delivered." He makes the point in *The Inside Story* that this has opened up new opportunities for marketers to use better targeted and more cost-efficient and relevant messages. Check out his digital agency, neo@ogilvy, at this website: *www.ogilvy.com/About/Network/Neo.aspx*.

Microtargeting

A targeting practice that has emerged from political campaigning is called **microtargeting,** which refers to using vast computer databanks of personal information to identify voters most likely to support one candidate or another. This **data mining** practice, which enables advertisers to direct highly tailored marketing messages to narrow slices of a segment, was refined for George Bush's 2004 reelection campaign and used again in the midterm elections by California Governor Arnold Schwarzenegger, as well as other candidates, both Democrat and Republican, in the 2008 election. From these data banks, political experts can tell what car or cars likely voters will drive, as well as their choices in recreation, leisure time activities, and restaurants.

Microtargeting has applications beyond politics. Several marketers have been able to profile prospects by carefully analyzing data on their regular customers to identify these revealing tendencies and characteristics.

But sometimes it doesn't work. An example of what sounded like a good idea at microtargeting comes from Chevrolet's "Come Together and Worship," a 16-concert tour with top Christian-music performers. The idea was that the Christian-music psychographic reflected a segment of

THE INSIDE STORY

Behavioral Targeting: An Emerging Online Strategy

David Rittenhouse, *Senior Partner and Planning Director, neo@Ogilvy*

It's not a new concept for marketers to observe consumer behavior and use the resulting insights to improve program performance. Advertisers have long led the charge, taking certain types of behavior as indicators of interest, grouping them into segments, and matching ads to them.

What Is Behavioral Targeting?

Behavioral targeting is about matching ads to interests indicated by *recency* and *frequency* of consumer behaviors, collected unobtrusively. For example, imagine a consumer shopping for a car and researching the purchase online. She visits car-related Web pages and reads reviews, sales listings, and other automotive content. She does this four times in a 30-day time span within a network of websites. This type of behavior pegs her as an "auto shopper," a segment comprising type of content plus frequency of recent visits.

A behaviorally targeted ad placement would deliver an impression only after the Web user had met these predefined criteria that put her into the "auto shopper" segment. The ads would not necessarily be delivered in automotive content, but in some cases via the least expensive ad space available.

OgilvyOne was among the first agencies to test behavioral targeting. Our own advertiser case studies have shown that behavioral targeting improves the composition of target audiences, lowers the cost of targeted impressions, and increases responsiveness to advertisements.

An early test run in the United Kingdom with a major technology client showed strong increases in audience composition over more traditional types of online ad placements. Since then, we have run behaviorally targeted placements for other clients across other categories, such as financial services and pharmaceuticals. These tests confirmed our earlier findings, showing decreased impression and response costs. Other marketplace studies have shown behavioral targeting to increase product sales and brand metrics such as brand awareness and preference.

A Word on Privacy

Internet user privacy has been raised as a potential issue with behavioral targeting. When done properly, no personally identifiable information is collected. Ads are not matched to an individual (name, address, date of birth) but to an interest segment (shopping for a car). Behaviorally targeted ads are paid for and served as part of publisher pages, not pop-ups generated by a piece of spyware, so they are controlled to ensure that the relationship with the reader (and the advertiser's brand) is not damaged.

The Internet Advertising Bureau (IAB) and consumer advocates have come out in favor of behavioral targeting in its present form, as long as consumers are informed and given a choice.

A graduate of the University of Colorado where he received a master's degree, David Rittenhouse was nominated by Professor Sandra Moriarty.

Chevy's Americana audience. The Jewish community, however, wondered why Chevy was favoring one religion over others, and influential Christian leaders criticized the idea as "blurring the lines between the commercial and the sacred."[42]

Ethical Issues

In addition to the privacy issue raised in *The Inside Story*, other ethical issues are involved with segmenting and targeting. Let's consider two examples of ethical quandaries surrounding the advertising of potentially unhealthy products to specific segments, such as targeting young black men in inner cities with malt beer ads and children with commercials for sugary foods.

One of the biggest issues in targeting is the emphasis in many advertising programs on targeting young consumers. It started back in the 1950s and ever since then, marketers and advertisers have tried to reach the trendsetting youthful audience. But the growth in the numbers of older consumers has led to some resentment about the continuing emphasis on young people as a general targeting strategy. It's a particular problem in television programming, most of which is aimed at twenty-somethings. With 78 million boomers now in their "power years," advertisers are rethinking their emphasis on youth.

Looking Ahead

In this chapter we've discussed demographic and psychographic characteristics and how they are used in segmenting and targeting. How these characteristics are identified is the topic of the next chapter where we'll discuss the research needed to support these basic strategic planning decisions.

IT'S A WRAP

A Model New Way to Connect with Customers

Reconnecting with a valuable segment of the target audience helped Old Navy improve its fortunes. Attracting value-conscious moms seems to be paying off. As a result of improving the clothing lines, stores, and merchandising and promotional strategies, the brand was able to build and maintain its strong value message, which translated into sales.

The Gap, Old Navy's parent company, posted a 45 percent profit increase in the fourth quarter of 2009, thanks in large part to Old Navy success. Sales at the Old Navy stores that have been open at least a year rose 7 percent.

A key insight about the target audience and a clever campaign using some quirky mannequins that talk helped Old Navy create positive brand perception in the eyes of the target audience: young moms. Old Navy sells more than inexpensive, cool clothes at a good price. Its brand sells fun. Old Navy's President Tom Wyatt said, "There are a lot of people that portray value, but no one portrays value with our quirky spirit."

A J.D. Power study revealed another sign of brand effectiveness. The study evaluated favorable online mentions of retailers by 22- to 29-year-olds and found that value brand Old Navy closely followed some more trendy brands, such as Anthropologie and Bath & Body Works.

Old Navy is starting to receive recognition for its creative work, as well. The National Retail Federation asked more than 9,900 consumers across the nation to name their favorite holiday campaign. "Super-Modelquins" ranked high at number six.

Key Points Summary

1. **What cultural, social, psychological, and behavioral influences affect consumer responses to advertising?** The social and cultural influences on consumer decision making include norms and values, society and subcultures, social class, reference groups, age, gender, family status, education, occupation, income, and race. Psychological influences on consumers include perception, needs and wants, learning, and motivations.

2. **What characteristics are used to segment groups of consumers?** Advertisers identify audiences in terms of demo-

graphics, psychographics, product-related behavior, and decision making. Demographic profiles of consumers include information on population size, age, gender and sexual orientation, education, occupation, income, family status, race, religion, and geography. Psychographic profiles include information on attitudes (activities, interests, opinions) and lifestyles. Behavior profiles emphasize brand usage, as well as innovativeness and risk taking, and participation in trends and fads. Quantity of usage is an important characteristic of a profitable market. The relationship the consumer has with the brand in terms of use and loyalty is also important. Finally, the innovativeness of people in the group in terms of their willingness to try something new is another important behavioral factor in segmentation.

3. **How does the consumer decision process work?** The information-driven decision process involves five stages: need recognition, information search, evaluation of alternatives, purchase decision, and post-purchase evaluation. The paths approach to consumer decision making identifies a multitude of different routes that a consumer may take to reach a purchase decision.

4. **How does targeting work and how is it different from segmenting?** In contrast to segmentation, which involves dividing a market into groups of people who can be identified as being in the market for the product, targeting identifies the group that would be the most responsive to an advertising message about the product. Both segmenting and targeting use social/cultural, psychological, and behavioral characteristics to identify these critical groups of people. But targeting uses this data to build a profile of the ideal person to whom the marketing communication is directed.

Words of Wisdom: Recommended Reading

Anderson, Chris, *The Long Tail: Why the Future of Business Is Selling Less of More,* New York: Hyperion, 2006.

Bogusky, Alex, and Warren Berger, *Hoopla (An Inside Look at Crispen Porter + Bogusky),* Brooklyn, NY: Powerhouse Books, 2006.

Cahill, Dennis, *Lifestyle Market Segmentation,* Binghamton NY: Haworth Publishing, 2006

Chambers, Jason, *Madison Avenue and the Color Line: African Americans in the Advertising Industry,* Philadelphia: University of Pennsylvania Press, 2009.

Gronbach, Kenneth, *The Age Curve: How to Profit from the Coming Demographic Storm,* New York: AMACOM, 2008.

Magnus, George, *The Age of Aging: How Demographics Are Changing the Global Economy and Our World,* New York: AMACOM, 2008.

Key Terms

acquired needs, p. 135
adoption, p. 149
adoption process, p. 149
attitude, p. 145
behavioral targeting, p. 154
brand communities, p. 134
cognitive dissonance, p. 136
consumer behavior, p. 130
cool hunters, p. 150
core values, p. 132
corporate culture, p. 134
cultural and social influences, p. 135

culture, p. 132
data mining, p. 154
demographics, p. 139
designated marketing area (DMA), p. 145
diffusion, p. 149
discretionary income, p. 143
evoked set, p. 151
family, p. 135
household, p. 135
lifestyle, p. 135
market segmentation, p. 137

microtargeting, p. 154
motive, p. 136
neuromarketing, p. 137
niche market, p. 138
norms, p. 132
perceived risk, p. 149
point-of-purchase (PoP) display, p. 151
population, p. 139
profiles, p. 153
psychographics, p. 145
reference group, p. 134

segmenting, p. 137
social class, p. 134
switchers, p. 149
tabloid, p. 142
target market, p. 139
targeting, p. 152
trend spotters, p. 150
undifferentiated strategy, p. 137
usage, p. 148
values, p. 132

Review Questions

1. In what ways does the culture in which you grew up affect your consumer behavior? Describe and explain one purchase you have made recently that reflects your cultural background.

2. What are reference groups? List the reference groups to which you belong or with which you associate yourself.

3. What is the difference between needs and wants? Give an example of something you have purchased in the past week that represents a need and another that represents a want.

4. What are the key behavioral influences on consumer behavior? For example, say you want to go out to eat on Friday.

Analyze your decision about where to go in terms of behavioral factors.

5. What are your key demographic and psychographic characteristics? Build a profile of yourself and give an example of how each one might be used in planning an advertising campaign targeted to someone like you.

6. What are the key steps in the adoption process, and how do they relate to product purchases? Who do you know who might clarify as an early adopter? As a laggard? Profile those two people and identify the key characteristics that make them different in their orientation to new ideas or products.

7. Define targeting. How does it differ from segmenting? Explain how Old Navy approached the segmenting and targeting decision in its SuperModelquins campaign. Do you think this approach is effective? How would you make the targeting more relevant given the opportunities offered by interactive communication?

Discussion Questions

1. Analyze the corporate culture at various agencies and clients. Start with the statement on *www.ogilvy.com/About/Our-History/Corporate-Culture.aspx* for an inside view of how this agency articulates its view of its own corporate culture. Then find at least one other agency or client website that refers to its corporate culture, and compare that statement with Ogilvy's. (Start with the companies whose websites have been mentioned in this chapter or previous chapters.) Where would you prefer to work and why?

2. We discuss inner- and outer-directed personalities in this chapter. Check out the following articles about Reisman's theory on these or other websites and then write a profile for yourself and your best friend. Compare and contrast your orientation toward your peers. *www.helium.com/items/232453-are-you-inner-or-outer-directedfredasadventures.com/everyday-life/are-you-an-inner-or-outer-directed-person*

3. Consider the social factors that influence consumer decisions. Identify two demographic or psychographic factors that you think would be most important to each of these product marketing situations:

   a. Dairy product company (milk, cheese, ice cream) offering an exclusive packaging design that uses fully degradable containers

   b. A new SUV that is lighter in weight, runs on ethanol, and gets better gas mileage than the average SUV

   c. An athletic clothing company that is sponsoring the next Pogopalooza, the world championship of extreme pogo

4. The U.S. Census projects that minorities will grow to 50 percent of the population by 2050. What are the implications? What challenges will this pose for advertisers and marketing communication agencies? Analyze the impact of this demographic change on a product category. First choose a minority group that we discussed in this chapter. Then choose a product category—either car insurance, organic fruits and vegetables, or health clubs. For your product, develop a list of research questions you would like answered that would give you better insight into this group and help you better target this population. What consumer characteristics—demographic factors, psychographics, and buying behavior—are important in segmenting and targeting this group?

5. Analyze the decision making involved in choosing your college:

   a. Interview two classmates and determine what influenced their decision to attend this school.

   b. How did you—and the people you interviewed—go about making this decision? Is there a general decision-making process that you can outline? Where are the points of agreement and where did you and your classmates differ in approaching this decision?

   c. Draw up a target audience profile for students attending your college. How does this profile differ from another school in your same market area?

6. You are working on a new account, a bottled tea named Leafs Alive that uses a healthy antioxidant formulation. The sale of bottled tea, as well as healthy products, is surging. Analyze your market using the following questions:

   a. What consumer trends seem to be driving this product development?

   b. What cultural, social, psychological, and behavioral factors influence this market?

   c. Plot the consumer decision process you think would best describe how people choose a product in this category.

   d. Choose one of the VALS (*www.sric-bi.com/vals/*) or Yankelovich MONITOR's MindBase groups that you think best describes the target market for this product (*www.yankelovich.com/index.php?option=com_content&task=category&sectionid=21&id=42&Itemid=88*). Explain your rationale.

7. *Three-Minute Debate:* One of your classmates argues that the information-driven approach to a consumer decision is absolutely the most important route and that advertising strategies should focus on that type of situation. Two other classmates disagree strongly: One argues that a feeling-driven approach is much more effective in generating a response, and the other says the only thing that counts is driving action, particularly sales.

   In class, organize into small teams with each team taking one of the three positions. Explain your team's position in a short presentation for your classmates.

Take-Home Projects

1. *Portfolio Project:* Choose two VALS and two MindBase categories. Find one print advertisement that appears to be targeted to people in each category. Explain why you think the ad addresses that audience. Do you believe that the categories are mutually exclusive? Can consumers (and ads directed to them) be classified in multiple categories? Why or why not?

2. *Mini-Case Analysis:* Review the chapter opening and closing story about Old Navy's SuperModelquins campaign.

The agency is known as being tuned into cultural trends, so how does this campaign reflect a cultural or social insight? What psychological insight helps explain the thinking behind this campaign? From what is presented in this mini-case, develop a profile of an individual member of this target audience.

Team Project: The BrandRevive Campaign

How do people make decisions to buy your product, whether a good or service, or participate in the case of a nonprofit? For goods, assign your team members to different stores to do unobtrusive "aisle checks" by standing in the aisle and observing shoppers considering purchases. For services and nonprofits, observe customers, if possible, or interview prospects about their decision making in this category. Then, as a team, write up a report that describes how people make decisions about brands in your product category.

- Analyze the decision: Is it a brand decision? A price decision? An emotional decision? Or is it based on some other feature?

- Analyze the information search: Do they study labels, read product literature, go online and search for information, listen to sales pitches, or make a snap decision? How important is information in the decision?

- From what you can observe, what other features are important in decision making in the category?

- Present your findings in a one-page report and a PowerPoint presentation that is no longer than three slides.

Hands-On Case

The Century Council

Read the Century Council case in the Appendix before coming to class.

1. From the case study and your own personal experiences in college, what factors do you believe most strongly encourage binge drinking on college campuses?

2. What efforts to curb underage drinking are you aware of, and do you believe they are successful? Why or why not?

3. You have been asked by the Century Council to develop target market profiles of different types of underage drinkers on college campuses. Write detailed descriptions of these different people with enough detail that we feel as if we know them personally.

Strategic Research

It's a Winner

Campaign:
*"Mischievous Fun
with Cheetos®"*

Company:
Pepsico/Frito-Lay

Agency:
Goodby,
Silverstein &
Partners

Award:
*2009 Grand
Ogilvy Winner*

160

CHAPTER KEY POINTS

1. What are the basic types of strategic research and how are they used?
2. What are the most common research methods used in advertising?
3. What are the key challenges facing advertising researchers?

Cheesy Fun. It's Not Just for Kids.

What do you think of when you think of Cheetos? The crunch and maybe orange fingers? A product that's been marketed to kids for its 60-year history, Cheetos is a brand long-associated with fun.

But it wasn't so funny when competitors Goldfish and Cheez-It started spending double the amount that Cheetos did on media.

The competitive problem was complicated by some social responsibility issues. Growing concerns about childhood obesity and the ethical concern of marketing to kids were serious challenges to Pepsico/Frito Lay, which is Cheetos' parent company. A commitment to be socially responsible led Pepsico to voluntarily sign the Children's Food & Beverage Advertising Initiative in 2007, which restricted advertising of not-so-healthy foods to children under age 12.

The result? Cheetos chose to abandon its position as a favorite kids' snack and target a new audience. That's a scary new strategy for any brand. It started its quest to find a new direction by setting specific objectives to help focus its research efforts:

1. Discover if an alternate adult target could be identified for Cheetos.
2. Develop a better understanding of the Cheetos' consumption experience.
3. Understand the overlaps between kids and the new adult target so that existing brand equities could be carried forward.
4. Develop and evaluate compelling new message strategies for the new target audience.

Findings from this research might surprise you. Even though Cheetos had been marketed as a children's snack, adults ate them too. Several studies revealed fascinating insights that eventually led to a new campaign for adults.

One study investigated attitudes of adults and children (ages 10 to 13) who claimed to be Cheetos brand lovers. Interestingly, both the adults and the kids communicated feelings of stress. A key insight from the research revealed that the playfulness associated with Cheetos could help these consumers escape some of their daily pressures.

Researchers also listened to what Cheetos fans said about the experience of eating Cheetos and watched how they acted when they ate Cheetos. Group members loved eating them and licking their fingers as if to say they were looking for permission *not* to act their age or conform to expected adult behavior.

Cheetos spokes-animal Chester Cheetah related well to kids. But would he appeal to adults? To test this idea, someone dressed up in a Chester Cheetah costume and walked the hot spots in San Francisco. Grown adults embraced the mascot by hugging and posing for pictures with him, proving this icon was up to the job no matter what the age of the Cheetos' fan.

Another study asked 1,000 adults about their attitudes to play. The respondents answered questions about when they played hooky from work and when they last skinny dipped and so on. Findings from this survey were telling. About half of those labeled "very playful" were most likely to eat a lot of Cheetos, and the "least playful" were also least likely to consume the product.

From literature on cultural trends, the agency was able to define an emerging group of people who were likely to be passionate for Cheetos. A book by Christopher Noxon[1] identified a new breed of adults called "rejuveniles." These are the folks who think playing isn't just for kids. Yankelovich, a leading consumer research firm, confirmed the emerging trend of adults who liked being just a tad naughty and child-like regardless of their age. These people identified with brands such as Disney, Wii, Lego, and, not surprisingly, Cheetos.

Cheetos' agency, Goodby, Silverstein & Partners synthesized information from these research efforts and came up with a Big Idea. The new adult target, "rejuveniles," could "bend the rules with mischievous fun." The tone of the campaign was edgy fun for adults rather than the sweet fun that had been used for kids. The big idea played out in a campaign that might not appeal to everyone, but it sure did to the target audience. Three TV spots illustrated how the inner child could be released with pranks involving Cheetos. One spot featured a woman at a laundromat who'd been berated by another woman. To get revenge and encouraged by mascot Chester Cheetah, the young woman put a bag of orange Cheetos in the other woman's white load of wash.

The online component of the campaign, OrangeUnderground.com, encouraged adults to play mischievous pranks with the orange snacks by creating Random Acts of Cheetos. The only rule: the pranks had to be "benign and harmless, never malicious or hurtful." Cheetos partnered with Comedy Central for a promotion that encouraged fans to make mischief, video it, and post it to the website. The interactive website itself features oddball humor with games, the Legend of Cheetocorn, a giant Cheetos pet, and all sorts of crazy stuff.

The ad lessons from this Cheetos story? Sometimes what looks like bad news about your product can lead to new opportunities that research can help you identify. A more important lesson: stay true to your brand. To see if the lessons learned from research paid off, go to the end of the chapter and read the *It's a Wrap* feature.

Sources: "Advertising Research Foundation Case Study: 'Mischievous Fun with Cheetos,'" *http://thearf.org/assets/ogilvy-09*; Bob Garfield, "Cheetos Ads That Promote 'Random Acts' Are Irresponsible," May 26, 2008, *http://adage.com*; Steve Centrillo and Dave Tutin, "Cheetos Offers How-to-Guide for Reaching Look-at-Me Gen," January 28, 2008, *www.brandweek.com*; Eric Newman, "Strategy: Cheetos on the Prowl for Adult Consumers," January 7, 2008, *www.brandweek.com*; Bruce Horovitz, "Don't Worry, Buy Happy: Cheerful Stuff Is Selling Well," March 30, 2009, *www.usatoday.com*.

In our previous chapters on how to plan marketing communication that has a real impact on consumers, we noted that marketers such as Frito-Lay need to do brand, market, and consumer research. This research effort becomes the foundation for objective setting, segmenting the market and targeting the audience, and developing the brand communication plan. So now that we understand the need for research, let's talk about how to do it. This chapter presents some key research concepts, beginning with an explanation of the two most basic categories of research, primary and secondary; the basic categories of research tools, quantitative and qualitative; and the most common research methods used in planning marketing communication. We also discuss the key challenges facing advertising researchers.

HOW DO YOU FIND CONSUMER INSIGHTS?

In the previous chapter we talked about insight—in fact, an effective marketing communication program is totally dependent on consumer insight. Know your customer—and listening is the first step in understanding customers.

What does that mean? It means that brand strategy begins with consumer research—the tools of listening. Consumer research investigates the topics we discussed in the previous chapter on segmentation and targeting, including attitudes, motivations, perceptions, and behaviors. The research findings then lead to planning decisions based on these insights. But first we must understand the principles and practices of advertising research and how to listen effectively to consumers.

In-house researchers or independent research companies hired from outside the company usually handle a client's market and consumer research. The objective at all stages of the planning process is to answer the question: What do we need to know in order to make an informed decision? Here are the various types of research used in planning advertising and marketing communication, such as the Cheetos campaign:

- **Market research** compiles information about the product, the product category, competitors, and other details of the marketing environment that will affect the development of advertising strategy.
- **Consumer research** identifies people who are in the market for the product in terms of their characteristics, attitudes, interests, and motivations. Ultimately, this information is used to decide who the targeted audience for the advertising should be. In an integrated marketing communication (IMC) plan, the consumer research also acquires information about all the relevant stakeholders and their points of contact with the brand.
- **Advertising research** focuses on all elements of advertising, including message development research, media planning research, evaluation, and information about competitors' advertising. **IMC research** is similar, except that it is used to assemble information needed in planning the use of a variety of marketing communication tools. IMC is particularly concerned with the interaction of multiple messages from a variety of sources to present the brand consistently.
- **Strategic research** uncovers critical information that becomes the basis for strategic planning decisions for both marketing and marketing communication. In advertising, this type of research covers all of the factors and steps that lead to the creation of message strategies and media plans. Think of strategic research as collecting all relevant background information needed to make a decision on advertising and marketing communication strategy. The importance of finding an adult target audience who appreciated having fun was important to the Cheetos campaign.

Knowledge about consumers' needs and wants is at the heart of all marketing communication plans. The foundation for all strategic decisions about segmentation, targeting, and positioning is consumer research.

In another example, whether you knew it or not, you were engaged in strategic research when you looked for an

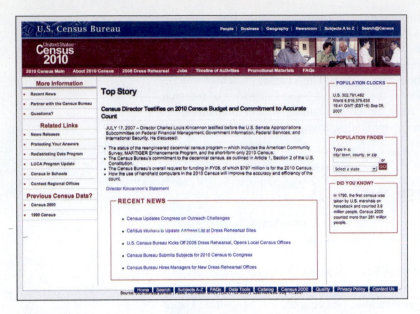

Demographic information, such as that available from the U.S. Census Bureau, is fundamental to marketing and communication planning.

Source: *www.census.gov/2010census.*

acceptable college to attend. You conducted market research (what information is available?), strategic research (what factors are most important in making a decision and how do the schools stack up?), and evaluative research (how will I know I made the best decision?). An advertising plan goes through similar stages of development with research as the first step.

What Are the Basic Types of Research?

New advertising assignments always begin with some kind of informal or formal background research into the marketing situation. This is called *secondary research,* and we'll compare it with *primary research,* which is original research conducted by the company or brand.

Secondary Research   Background research that uses available published information about a topic is **secondary research.** When advertising people get new accounts or new assignments, they start by reading everything they can find on the product, company, industry, and competition: sales reports, annual reports, complaint letters, and trade articles about the industry. They are looking for important facts and key insights. This kind of research is called secondary, not because it is less important, but because it has been collected and published by someone else.

A typical advertising campaign might be influenced, directly or indirectly, by information from many sources, including in-house agencies and outside research suppliers. The use of secondary information for the Cheetos case—finding the information about the "rejuvenile" market in Christopher Noxon's book—underscores the importance of reading widely.

Here are a few of the more traditional sources of secondary information that are available to advertisers doing backgrounding:

- *Government Organizations* Governments, through their various departments, provide an astonishing array of statistics that can greatly enhance advertising and marketing decisions. Many of the statistics come from census records on the population's size, geographic distribution, age, income, occupation, education, and ethnicity. As we explained in Chapter 5, U.S. Census Bureau demographic information of this kind is fundamental to decision making about advertising targets and market segmentation. An advertiser cannot aim its advertising at a target audience without knowing that audience's size and major dimensions. In addition to census information, other government agencies generate reports that help advertisers make better decisions, such as the *Survey of Current Business* from the U.S. Department of Commerce (*www.bea.gov/scb*).

- *Trade Associations* Many industries support trade associations—professional organizations whose members all work in the same field—that gather and distribute information of interest to association members. For instance, the American Frozen Food Institute or the Game Manufacturers Council are both organizations that assist members in conducting their business. The trade associations for marketing communication include the American Association of Advertising Agencies (AAAA), which issues reports that help ad agencies monitor their performance and keep tabs on competitors; the Radio Advertising Bureau publishes *Radio Facts,* an overview of the commercial U.S. radio industry; the Account Planning Group (APG) conducts seminars and training sessions for account planners; and the American Association for Public Opinion Research (AAPOR) serves the professional needs of opinion researchers.

- *Secondary Research Suppliers* Because of the overwhelming amount of information available through secondary research, specialized suppliers gather and organize that information around specific topic areas for other interested parties. Key secondary research suppliers are FIND/SVP, Off-the-Shelf Publications, Dialog Information Services, Lexis-Nexis, and Dow Jones' Factiva.

- **Secondary Information on the Internet** For any given company, you're bound to find a website where you can learn about the company's history and philosophy of doing business, check out its complete product line, and discover who runs the company. These sites offer credible information for account planners and others involved in market research. Other sources of Internet information are blog sites and chat rooms where you can learn about people's reactions to brands and products. There are also many industry-related sites for marketing that report on research, essays, and best practices:

BrandEra (*www.brandera.com*) offers information by product category.

MarketPerceptions (*http://marketperceptions.com*) represents a research company that specializes in health care research. The site has information about its focus group capabilities.

Forrester Research (*www.forrester.com*) provides industry research into technology markets.

Greenbook.org (*www.greenbook.org*) is a worldwide directory of marketing research focus group suppliers.

Cluetrain (*www.cluetrain.com*) publishes new ways to find and share innovative marketing information and ideas.

Primary Research Information that is collected for the first time from original sources is called **primary research.** To obtain primary research, companies and their agencies do their own tracking and monitoring of their customers' behavior. An example of a company that took on its own research is Perdue Farms and its classic "tough man" campaign. In contemporary times, companies usually hire specialized firms to do this type of research.

In another example of a company doing its own primary research, Toyota undertook a huge two-year study of ultra-rich consumers in the United States to better market its upscale Lexus brand. A team of nine Lexus employees from various departments was designated the "super-affluent team" and sent on the road to interview wealthy car buyers about why they live where they do, what they do for enjoyment, what brands they buy, and how they feel about car makes and models. One surprising finding was that these consumers don't just buy a car, they buy a fleet of cars because they have multiple homes and offices.[2]

Primary research suppliers (the firms clients hire) specialize in interviewing, observing, recording, and analyzing the behavior of those who purchase or influence the purchase of a particular good or service. The primary research supplier industry is extremely diverse. Companies range from A.C. Nielsen, the huge international tracker of TV viewing habits, which employs more than 45,000 workers in the United States alone, to several thousand entrepreneurs who conduct focus groups and individual interviews, prepare reports, and provide advice on specific advertising and marketing problems for individual clients.

Many advertising agencies subscribe to large-scale surveys conducted by the Simmons Market Research Bureau (SMRB) or by Mediamark Research, Inc. (MRI). These two organizations survey large samples of American consumers (approximately 30,000 for each survey) and ask questions about the consumption, possession, or use of a wide range of products, services, and media. The products and services covered in the MRI survey range from toothbrushes and dental floss to diet colas, camping equipment, and theme parks.

Both SMRB and MRI conduct original research and distribute their findings to their clients. The resulting reports are intended primarily for use in media planning, but because these surveys are so comprehensive, they also can be mined for unique consumer information. Through a computer program called Golddigger, for example, an MRI subscriber can select a consumer target and ask the computer to find all other products and services and all of the media that members of the target segment use. This profile provides a vivid and detailed description of the target as a person—just the information creative teams need to help them envision their audiences. To give you an idea of what the media data look like, check out Figure 6.1 for a sample MRI report of the types of TV programs adults ages 18 to 34 watch.

CLASSIC

"It takes a tough man to make a tender chicken" was the signature line for a long-running campaign that began in 1971 for Perdue Farms. It featured the owner, Frank Perdue, as the plain-spoken farmer who cared about the quality of his chickens. Scali, McCabe, Sloves was the agency behind the campaign that created the first recognizable brand for an unlikely commodity product—chickens. But the reason the campaign was successful wasn't just the iconic, perhaps ironic, "tough man" line, but rather Frank Perdue's knowledge of his market. When he decided in the 1960s to eliminate brokers and sell directly to stores, he spent months on the road talking to butchers about what they wanted in chickens and identified 25 quality factors. Then he modified his operations to produce chickens that delivered on those 25 factors—a tough man who was obsessed with tender chickens.

Base: Adults	Total U.S. 000	Respondent 18–34 1-Person Household				Respondent 18–34 and Married, no children				Respondent 18–34 and Married, Youngest Child <6				Respondent 18–34 and Married Youngest Child 6+			
		A 000	B % Down	C % Across	D Index	A 000	B % Down	C % Across	D Index	A 000	B % Down	C % Across	D Index	A 000	B % Down	C % Across	D Index
All Adults	184274	5357	100.0	2.9	100	7559	100.0	4.1	100	18041	100.0	9.8	100	4978	100.0	2.7	100
Program-Types: Average Show																	
Adven/Sci Fi/West-Prime	19969	590	11.0	3.0	102	875	11.6	4.4	107	2303	12.8	11.5	118	694	13.9	3.5	129
Auto Racing-Specials	6590	*226	4.2	3.4	118	*242	3.2	3.7	90	634	3.5	9.6	98	*251	5.0	3.8	141
Awards-Specials	16490	397	7.4	2.4	83	514	6.8	3.1	76	1576	8.7	9.6	98	*451	9.1	2.7	101
Baseball Specials	28019	806	15.0	2.9	99	1128	14.9	4.0	98	2671	14.8	9.5	97	*506	10.2	1.8	67
Basketball-Weekend-College	7377	*222	4.1	3.0	104	*244	3.2	3.3	81	531	2.9	7.2	74	*183	3.7	2.5	92
Basketball Specials-College	17096	529	9.9	3.1	106	694	9.2	4.1	99	1459	8.1	8.5	87	*423	8.5	2.5	92
Basketball Specials-Pro.	32470	1057	19.7	3.3	112	1369	18.1	4.2	103	3128	17.3	9.6	98	886	17.8	2.7	101
Bowling-Weekend	16808	312	5.8	1.9	654	744	9.8	4.4	108	1476	8.2	8.8	90	*386	78	2.3	85
Comedy/Variety	26254	930	17.4	3.5	122	1150	15.2	4.4	107	3257	18.1	12.4	127	999	20.1	3.8	141
Daytime Dramas	7621	*192	3.6	2.5	87	*287	3.8	3.8	92	845	4.7	11.1	113	*343	6.9	4.5	167
Daytime Game Shows	7747	*97	1.8	1.3	43	*194	2.6	2.5	61	734	4.1	9.5	97	*235	4.7	3.0	112
Documen/Information-Prime	22514	532	9.9	2.4	81	504	6.7	2.2	55	1739	9.6	7.7	79	*454	9.1	2.0	75
Early Morning News	12226	280	5.2	2.3	79	*429	5.7	3.5	86	1065	5.9	8.7	89	*330	6.6	2.7	100
Early Morning Talk/Info/News	14681	258	4.8	1.8	60	580	77	4.0	96	1291	7.2	8.8	90	*268	5.4	1.8	68
Early Eve. Netwk News-M-F	25946	596	11.1	2.3	79	836	11.1	3.2	79	1822	10.1	7.0	72	*594	11.9	2.3	85
Early Eve. Netwk News-Wknd	11338	*197	3.7	1.7	60	*208	2.8	1.8	45	795	4.4	7.0	72	*187	3.8	1.6	61
Entertainment Specials	19630	408	76	2.1	71	701	9.3	3.6	87	1719	9.5	8.8	89	*494	9.9	2.5	93
Feature Films-Prime	17232	371	6.9	2.2	74	*538	7.1	3.1	76	1209	6.7	70	72	*475	9.5	2.8	102
Football Bowl Games-Specials	13322	369	6.9	2.8	95	*381	5.0	2.9	70	1512	8.4	11.3	116	*245	4.9	1.8	68
Football Pro.-Specials	44804	1471	27.5	3.3	113	1766	23.4	3.9	96	4555	25.2	10.2	104	1104	22.2	2.5	91
General Drama-Prime	19880	581	10.8	2.9	101	571	76	2.9	70	2095	11.6	10.5	108	*555	11.1	2.8	103
Golf	5161	*102	1.9	2.0	68	*152	2.0	2.9	72	*324	1.8	6.3	64	*15	.3	.3	11
Late Evening Netwk News Wknd	5146	*146	2.7	2.8	98	*114	1.5	2.2	54	*293	1.6	5.7	58	*104	2.1	2.0	75
Late Night Talk/Variety	9590	313	5.8	3.3	112	*297	3.9	3.1	75	1009	5.6	10.5	107	*198	4.0	2.1	76
News-Specials	14508	234	4.4	1.6	55	510	6.7	3.5	86	1297	7.2	8.9	91	*212	4.3	1.5	54
Pageants-Specials	22025	439	8.2	2.0	69	952	12.6	4.3	105	2503	13.9	11.4	116	547	11.0	2.5	92
Police Docudrama	23575	726	13.6	3.1	106	1179	15.6	5.0	122	2309	12.8	9.8	100	731	14.7	3.1	115
Pvt Det/Susp/Myst/Pol.-Prime	28183	673	12.6	2.4	82	763	10.1	2.7	66	1739	9.6	6.2	63	*493	9.9	1.7	65
Situation Comedies-Prime	19097	598	11.2	3.1	108	919	12.2	4.8	117	2737	15.2	14.3	146	688	13.8	3.6	133
Sports Anthologies-Weekend	4847	*218	4.1	4.5	155	*232	3.1	4.8	117	*403	2.2	8.3	85	*108	2.2	2.2	82
Sunday News/Interview	5809	*70	1.3	1.2	41	*116	1.5	2.0	49	*214	1.2	3.7	38	*97	1.9	1.7	62
Syndicated Adult General	10444	*271	5.1	2.6	89	462	6.1	4.4	108	766	4.2	7.3	75	*221	4.4	2.1	78
Tennis	10033	338	6.3	3.4	116	380	5.0	3.8	92	826	4.5	8.2	84	*105	2.1	1.0	39

FIGURE 6.1

MRI Consumer Media Report

This MRI report breaks down the 18–34 age market into four market segments based on size of household and age of children, if any, and describes their television viewing patterns. Here's a question: Where would you advertise to reach single adults in the 18–34 category? First look at the Index column under that category heading and find the two highest percentages. Then, for each high rating, look across to column A and determine the size of that group. As a point of comparison, do the same analysis for the Married with the Youngest Child over 6 category. How do the two groups differ in the television viewing patterns?

Source: Mediamark Research, Inc.

Quantitative Research   Primary research can be both quantitative and qualitative. **Quantitative research** delivers numerical data such as number of users and purchases, their attitudes and knowledge, their exposure to ads, and other market-related information. The MRI page is an example of data obtained through quantitative research. It also provides information on reactions to advertising and motivation to purchase, sometimes called *purchase intent*. Quantitative methods that investigate the responses of large numbers of people are useful in testing ideas to determine if their market is large enough or if most people really say or behave in a certain way.

Two primary characteristics of quantitative research are (1) large sample sizes, typically from 100 to 1,000 people, and (2) random sampling. The most common quantitative research methods include surveys and studies that track such things as sales and opinions. Quantitative research is usually designed either to accurately count something, such as **sales levels,** or to predict something, such as attitudes. To be predictive, however, this type of research must follow careful scientific procedures. The Cheetos campaign used a study with a sample of 1,000 adults to find out about their frequency of game playing in order to correlate that information with their levels of Cheetos consumption.

One of the biggest problems in using quantitative methods to study consumer decision processes is that consumers are often unable to articulate the reasons they do what they do because their reasons may not fit into answers provided in a survey. Furthermore, most people aren't tuned in to their own thoughts and thinking process so that they are comfortable saying yes or no or checking a space on a rating scale. Respondents also have a tendency to give the answers that they think the researcher wants to hear. These are all reasons why qualitative research has become much more important in brand communication in the last 20 years. It offers the ability to probe and move beyond the sometimes superficial responses to a survey.

Qualitative Research   The goal of qualitative research methodologies, therefore, is to move beyond the limitations of what consumers can explain in words or in responses to preplanned questions. **Qualitative research** provides insight into the underlying reasons for how consumers behave and why. Common qualitative research methods include such tools as observation, ethnographic studies, in-depth interviews, and case studies. They trade large sample sizes and scientific predictions for greater depth of insight. These exploratory research tools are useful for probing and gaining explanations and understanding of such questions as these:

- What type of features do customers want?
- What are the motivations that lead to the purchase of a product?
- What do our customers think about our advertising?
- How do consumers relate to the brand? What are their emotional links to the brand?

Qualitative methods often are used early in the process of developing a brand communication plan or message strategy for generating insights, as well as questions and hypotheses for additional research. They are also good at confirming hunches, ruling out bad approaches and questionable or confusing ideas, and giving direction to the message strategy. However, because qualitative research is typically done with small groups, researchers cannot project their findings to the larger population.

Rather than drawing conclusions, qualitative research is used to answer the question why, as well as generate hypotheses that can be tested with quantitative methods.[3] As Sally Reinman, worldwide market planner at Saatchi & Saatchi, wrote for this book, research is more than numbers. She explains:

Research processes are more varied and exciting than ever before. Examples include asking consumers to draw pictures, create collages, and produce home videos to show how they use a product.

As consumers around the world become better informed and more demanding, advertisers that target different cultures need to find the "commonalities" (or common ground) among consumer groups from these cultures. Research for Toyota's sports-utility vehicle (SUV), the RAV 4, showed that consumers in all the targeted countries had three common desires: They wanted an SUV to have style, safety, and economy.

To find these commonalities, I work with experts to learn the cultural meaning of codes and symbols that people use to communicate. The experts I work with include cultural and

Principle
Quantitative research investigates the attitudes, opinions, and behaviors of large numbers of people in order to make conclusions that can be generalized to the total population; qualitative research provides insight into how and why consumers think and behave.

Principle
Quantitative research can be used to draw conclusions about how much and how often; qualitative research answers questions about why and generates questions for quantitative methods.

cognitive anthropologists, psychologists, interior decorators, and Indian storytellers. Anyone who can help me understand consumers and the consumer decision-making process is fair game.

Experimental Research   Tightly controlled scientific studies are sometimes used to puzzle out how people think and respond to messages and incentives. **Experimental research** is designed using formal hypothesis-testing techniques that compare different message treatments and how people react to them. The idea is to control for all factors except the one being tested; if there is a change in the results, then the researcher can conclude that the variable being tested caused the difference. Experimental research is used to test marketing factors as well as advertising appeals and executions in such areas as product features and design, price, and various creative ideas.

Do your professors and instructors talk about the research they conduct? Here's an example of one professor's research about cigarette advertising that has practical implications for the tobacco industry and policy makers. It tests the idea that cigarette advertising can prime (or prepare) teens to think that smoking is cool. The *A Matter of Principle* box explains how this researcher used experimental studies to determine the impact of advertising on behavior.

Sometimes in experimental research the measurements are electronically recorded using such instruments as MRI or EEG machines or eye-scan tracking devices. Electrodes can be used to monitor heart rate, pulse, and skin temperature to determine if people have a physical response to a message that they may not be able to put in words. Emotional responses, in particular, are hard to verbalize but may be observable using these types of sensors. Hewlett-Packard Company, for example, wired a group of volunteers with electrodes to see how they reacted to photos of people smiling. The study found that there were obvious differences in brain activity in people looking at photos of smiling people, particularly pictures of children smiling.

A MATTER OF PRINCIPLE

Does Advertising Make Smoking Cool?

Cornelia (Connie) Pechmann, *Professor of Marketing, University of California, Irvine*

In 1991, I began a program of research on tobacco-use prevention through advertising and the mass media. I wondered how often people saw advertisements for products shortly before experiencing the products. It occurred to me that advertising exposure and product experience were perhaps most likely to occur concurrently in the case of cigarette advertising and encounters with smokers. In 1991, cigarette advertising on billboards was ubiquitous and 20 percent of high school seniors smoked daily, so I reasoned that adolescents might see cigarette advertisements and peers smoking concurrently. I also reasoned that encounters with smokers would often be ambiguous.

Looking at the literature, I could find few controlled experiments on cigarette advertising. However, surveys indicated there was a strong association between adolescents' perceptions of smokers and smoking initiation. With the assistance of coauthors, I completed two research projects that documented that cigarette advertisements can prime adolescents' positive beliefs about smokers and thus alter their social encounters with smokers. Specifically, cigarette advertisements serving as primes can favorably bias adolescents' perceptions of peers who smoke and thus increase their intent to smoke. One of our papers on this topic received the Best Paper Award from the *Journal of Consumer Research*. I continue to conduct research in this area.

I am told that my tobacco-related research has been cited by expert witnesses in legal cases such as the federal tobacco case, in legislative hearings, and in U.S. Attorney General meetings. I believe that some academic research should be conducted to inform public policy and that if research is not designed for this purpose, it likely will not have this effect.

Sources: J. A. Bargh, M. Chen, and L. Burrows, "Automaticity of Social Behavior: Direct Effects of Trait Construct and Stereotype Activation on Action," *Journal of Personality & Social Psychology*, 71, No. 2 (1996): 230–244; C. Pechmann and S. J. Knight, "An Experimental Investigation of the Joint Effects of Advertising and Peers on Adolescents' Beliefs and Intentions about Cigarette Consumption," *Journal of Consumer Research*, 29, No. 1 (2002): 5–19; C. Pechmann and S. Ratneshwar, "The Effects of Antismoking and Cigarette Advertising on Young Adolescents' Perceptions of Peers Who Smoke," *Journal of Consumer Research*, 21, No. 2 (1994): 236–251.

The Uses of Research

Agencies and clients use research to make strategic decisions, as we have just discussed, but agencies rarely *conduct* research. Most research has become so specialized that separate research companies, as well as in-house client research departments, are the most likely research sources. These firms and departments collect and disseminate secondary research data and conduct primary research that ultimately finds its way into brand communication efforts. DDB is one of the few large agencies that still does its own in-house research. Its annual Life Style Survey, which we discussed in Chapter 5, is a major source of consumer information.

As markets have become more fragmented and saturated, and as consumers have become more demanding, the need for research-based information in advertising planning has increased. Figure 6.2 summarizes the seven ways research is used in marketing communication planning:

1. Market information
2. Consumer insight research
3. Brand information
4. Media research
5. Message development research
6. Advertising or IMC plan
7. Evaluation research

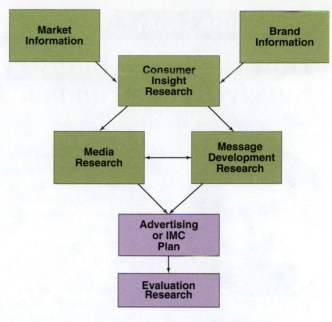

FIGURE 6.2

The Use of Research in Marketing Communication Planning

Market Information   Formal research used by the marketing department for strategic planning is called **marketing research.** It includes surveys, in-depth interviews, observational methods, focus groups (which are like in-depth interviews with a group rather than individuals), and all types of primary and secondary data used to develop a marketing plan and ultimately provide information for a brand communication plan. A subset of marketing research, *market research* is research used to gather information about a particular market.

An example comes from Iceland, a country hard hit by the global economic downturn that started in 2007. As explained by Ingvi Logason, principal in his own advertising firm in Reykjavik, "Iceland, with its overexpanded banking sector, was hit worse than any other Westernized country." With all of its banks except one going into bankruptcy or only barely being saved by serious rescue activities by the government, national debt outweighed gross national production by 2 to 1. Iceland was on the brink of national bankruptcy. *The Inside Story* details how Logason and his agency guided his client, the lamb industry, through this difficult time.

Market information includes everything a planner can uncover about consumer perceptions of the brand, product category, and competitors' brands. Planners sometimes ride with the sales force and listen to sales pitches, tour manufacturing plants to see how a product is made, and work in a store or restaurant to evaluate employee interaction with customers. In terms of marketing communication, planners test the brand's and its competitors' advertisements, promotions, retail displays, packaging, and other marketing communication efforts.

Brand information includes an assessment of the brand's role and performance in the marketplace—is it a leader, a follower, a challenger, or a subbrand of a bigger and better known brand? This research also investigates how people perceive brand personalities and images. Here are some common methods used to gather information about a brand and the marketplace:

- *The Brand Experience* When an agency gets a new client, the first thing the agency team has to do is learn about the brand through brand research. That means learning where the brand has been in the past in terms of the market, its customers, and competitors, as the Cheetos campaign demonstrated. Also important is eliciting the corporate point of view regarding the brand's position within the company's line of products, as well as corporate goals and plans for the brand. Another critical area of brand research is the brand's relationships with its customers. Researchers, for example, may go through all of the experiences

THE INSIDE STORY

How the Lamb Industry in Iceland Survived the Economic Downturn

Ingvi Logason, *Principal, H:N Marketing Communication, Reykjavik, Iceland*

In 2009 (when this was written) the whole world was facing probably its greatest economic crisis since the early 20th century. This recession hit the Icelandic public suddenly and it hit hard—obliterating purchasing power. Overnight the situation changed the way Icelanders search and shop, as well as what they want from their brands. In this market planners had to truly understand the role a brand plays in the lives of its target audience clarifying "what's in it for me" in all communication.

One brand that my marketing communication firm has handled and had to adapt to the changed market is Icelandic Lamb. Traditionally lamb had been around a 29 percent share of Icelandic meat consumption with heavy and almost exclusive emphasis on the prime (and more expensive) parts of the lamb. That left farmers with a high percentage of the lamb unsold. Now lamb was down to a 26 percent share and falling.

Anyone could see that this was not a good situation with the sharp decrease in purchasing power leading to fewer sales in luxury and expensive food items. Furthermore, sales figures showed that consumers were not going for the less expensive cuts of lamb, but rather opting for other cheaper meat products. Although we were quick to catch the trend and see the possible sales decline, we were not sure why sales hadn't moved to less expensive lamb cuts.

We assembled focus groups to determine the underlying problem. With clever probing, the main problem became clear: consumers simply did not know how to prepare the less costly parts—it was a forgotten art. Lamb had become such a luxury item that it was easier for our target group to increase their consumption of less costly meat than learn new recipes. Our extensive consumer research showed that:

- Our target group liked lamb meat but didn't know how to cook it.
- Lamb meat had the highest top-of-mind (TOM) awareness of all meat products in Iceland.
- Our target group was always looking for ways to find economic and quick solutions to the question "What's for dinner?"
- Our research also found up to 25 percent better engagement in food advertising when recipes were included.

So how do you connect with your target group and teach time-pressed people new tricks in a world with ever-expanding media options and less time for anything domestic like cooking?

We developed a strategy to counter the trend away from lamb. Fast dissemination of information for a fast-moving world became our goal.

The big idea we developed was "micro-cooking" shows—we would teach you to cook in 90 seconds or less. The recipes were tasty, simple, and easy. In addition, the lamb website carried the cooking shows, which also became viral ads. We created and recruited a Facebook group interested in lamb who passed the shows on, extending their reach to new customers.

By researching and understanding the role that our brand played in the lives of our target group, we were able to come up with a campaign that matched our target group's needs and pace of life. These insights resulted in a strategy that connected with consumers and delivered the sales figures we needed to help the lamb industry survive the downturn.

---

that a typical consumer has in buying and using the product. If you were taking on a pizza restaurant account, for example, you might work in the store or visit it as a customer. Brand buying is also a form of commitment to the client: the parking lots of agencies that have automotive accounts are usually full of cars made by their clients.

- *Competitive Analysis* It's also important to do a competitive analysis. If you handle a soap account, you obviously want to use that brand of soap, but you may also buy the competing brands and do your own comparative test just to add your experiences to your brand analysis.
- *Marketing Communication Audit* Either formally or informally, most planners will begin an assignment by collecting every possible piece of advertising and other forms of marketing communication by the brand, as well as its competitors and other relevant categories that may have lessons for the brand. Often these pieces are attached to the walls in a "war room" where team members can immerse themselves in messages to stimulate new ideas. This includes compiling a historical collection as well. There's nothing more embarrassing than proposing a great new advertising idea only to find out that it was used a couple of years ago by a competitor or, even worse, by your client.
- *Content Analysis* The marketing communication audit might include only informal summaries of the slogans, appeals, and images used most often, or it might include more formal and systematic tabulation of competitors' approaches and strategies, called a **content analysis.** By disclosing competitors' strategies and tactics, analysis of the content of competitive advertisements provides clues about how competitors are thinking and suggests ways to develop new and more effective campaigns. Planners also try to determine what mental territories or positions competitors claim and which are still available and relevant to the brand.

Consumer Insight Research   A basic principle in this book is that effective marketing communication rests on truly understanding the consumer. As Regina Lewis, a member of this book's Advisory Board, explained in the Part 2 opener, brands have to be true to the consumers who buy them. Consumers, even brand loyal ones, are more loyal to themselves and their own interests than they are to brands. Both the creative team members (who create messages) and the media planners (who decide how and when to deliver the messages) need to know as much as they can, in as much depth and detail as possible, about the people they are trying to reach. That's the point of *The Inside Story* about selling Icelandic lamb during the recession. To turn the sales pattern around, the agency had to really know how its target market was adapting to the new economic situation.

We mentioned in the discussion of the communication role of marketing communication that feedback can be obtained from customers as a part of a research program that uses customer contact as an information source—systematically recording information from customer service, technical service, inbound telemarketing calls, and online sites. Some businesses use the Internet to involve customers in making decisions about product design, distribution, price, and company operations using online surveys, blogs, online communities, and other social media.

You've probably heard the phrase "This call may be monitored for quality assurance." These recordings are used for training, but they also can be analyzed for marketing intelligence.[4] If customers say they are confused or ask the representative to repeat a phrase, then it could indicate that the sales offer or technical explanation isn't working right. These calls can provide instant feedback about the strength of a brand's offering as well as competitors' offers. Specific questions such as "Where did you hear about this?" are used to monitor brand contact points and media performance.

Principle
Do your homework about your brand. There's nothing more embarrassing than proposing a great new advertising idea only to find out that it was used a couple of years ago by a competitor or, even worse, by your client.

More importantly, as we explained in Chapter 5, researchers try to determine what motivates people to buy a product or become involved in a brand relationship. But a note of caution, sometimes the biggest consumer research projects may not give reliable results. A classic example is the New Coke reformulation introduced in 1985 after some 200,000 consumers participated in blind taste tests. Based on this huge $4 million research effort, Coke managers decided to dump the old Coca-Cola formula, which had been in use since 1886, because researchers concluded that Coke drinkers preferred a new sweeter taste. The reaction was overwhelming from loyal Coke drinkers who wanted the "Real Thing," an emotional bond that wasn't revealed in the consumer research.

Principle

Insight research is designed to uncover the whys of the buys, as well as the why nots.

The objective of **consumer insight research** is to puzzle out a key consumer insight that will help move the target audience to respond to the message. Insight research, in other words, is basically about asking and listening, and then asking more questions to probe deeper into thoughts, opinions, attitudes, desires, and motivations.

Researchers often try to uncover the *whys of the buys,* but insight research may also uncover reasons why people don't want to try or buy a product. For example, Dunkin' Donuts found in its consumer research several reasons why its customers were uncomfortable ordering fancy coffee drinks. Mostly they were intimidated by the whole "barista" thing and the fancy coffee names.

The DDB agency regularly conducts "Barriers to Purchase" research[5] realizing that these barriers often create an opportunity for advertising messages to present information or change perceptions. The American Dairy Association, for example, asked DDB to find out why cheese consumption was declining. A study identified one barrier that was most easily correctable through a marketing communication effort: the absence of simple cheese recipes for home cooks. Ads and the association's website (*www.ilovecheese.com*) offer many such recipes.

Emotions are elicited by asking consumers what they think people in various photos and situations are feeling. Associations are investigated by asking people what comes to mind when a word or brand is mentioned. In **association tests,** people are asked what they think of when they hear a cue, such as the name of a product category or a brand. They respond with all of the things that come to mind, and, as we have said, that forms a **network of associations.** Brand perceptions are tested this way to map the structure and logic of these association networks, which lead to message strategies. For example, what do you think of when you think of Taco Bell? Wendy's? Arby's? Each restaurant should bring to mind some things in common (fast food, cheap food), but they also have distinct networks of associations based on type of food (Mexican, hamburgers, roast beef), restaurant design, logo and colors, brand characters, healthfulness, and so forth. Each restaurant, then, has a distinctive profile that can be determined from this network of associations.

To get inside consumers' minds to see what they are really thinking, marketers have turned to the tools of neuroscience, which uses highly technical equipment to scan the brain as it processes information and makes decisions. Neuromarketing, which we have mentioned in previous chapters, is the application of this research technology to consumer behavior. One study by a UCLA researcher, for example, mapped how viewers responded to Super Bowl ads below the level of their awareness. In the *A Principled Practice* feature at *www.pearsonhighered.com/moriarty,* Professor Ann Marie Barry explains how this research works and raises some ethical questions about just how private our thinking should be.

Campbell's Soup used neuromarketing and biometrics to analyze consumer responses to brand communication. As part of a major two-year study and

The DDB agency found that a barrier to purchasing cheese was the lack of good recipe ideas using cheese products. The American Dairy Association responded by getting more recipes distributed through advertising and its website.

redesign of the labels on its iconic red and white soup cans, Campbell's used neuromarketing techniques to see how consumers reacted to everything from pictures of bowls, to the use of a spoon, and other graphic cues, such as steam rising from the bowl. The objective was to find ways to help consumers connect on a deeper and more emotional level with the brand. Changes included color coding the different varieties; depict steam to make the soup in the picture look warm; remove the spoon, which consumers said served no purpose; update the look of the bowl; and move the Campbell's logo to the bottom in order to better identify the varieties.[6]

Media Research   Media planning begins with consumer research and questions about media behavior that help with the media selection decision. Media planners often work in conjunction with the information account planners uncover to decide which media formats make the most sense to accomplish the objectives. The goal is to activate consumer interest by reaching them through some medium that engages their interest.

Next, **media research** gathers information about all the possible media and marketing communication tools that might be used in a campaign to deliver a message. Media researchers then match that information to what is known about the target audience. The MRI data shown earlier in Figure 6.1 illustrates the type of information media researchers consult to develop recommendations.

Message Development Research   As planners, account managers, and people on the creative team begin to develop a message strategy, they involve themselves in various types of informal and formal **message development research.** They read all of the relevant secondary information provided by the client and the planners to become better informed about the brand, the company, the competition, the media, and the product category. As Jackie Boulter,[7] head of planning at the London-based Abbott Mead Vickers-BBDO agency, explained, creative development research is focused on refining message ideas prior to production. It uses qualitative research to predict if the idea will solve the business problem and achieve the objectives.

Sometimes called **concept testing,** it can help evaluate the relative power of various creative ideas. It's a "work-in-progress" type of evaluation. The idea is to test the big idea that communicates the strategy behind the message—or various types of *executions* of the concept. These interviews are often conducted in malls and downtown areas where there are lots of people who can be asked to look at a rough sketch of the idea or ad and respond to it. They can also be conducted over the phone, by mail, or online.

As writers and art directors begin working on a specific creative project, they almost always conduct informal research of their own. They may do their own personal observational research and visit retail stores, talk to salespeople, and watch customers buy. They may visit the agency information center or library, browse through reference books, and borrow subject and picture files. They will look at previous advertising, especially that of competitors, to see what others have done, and in their hearts they will become convinced that they can create something better than, and different from, anything that has been done before. This informal, personal research has a powerful influence on what happens later in the message development process.

Another technique used to analyze the meaning of communication is **semiotic analysis,** which is a way to take apart the signs and symbols in a message to uncover layers and types of meanings. The objective is to find deeper meanings in the symbolism that might be particular to different groups of consumers. Its focus is on determining the meanings, even if they are not obvious or highly symbolic, that might relate to consumer motivations.

For example, the advertising that launched General Motors' OnStar global positioning system (GPS) used a Batman theme. By looking at this commercial in terms of its signs and symbols, it was possible to determine if the obvious, as well as hidden, meanings of the message are on strategy. For example, the decision to use a comic book hero as the star created a heroic association for OnStar. However, Batman is not a superhero, but rather more of a common person with a lot of great technology and cool gadgets—remember Jack Nicholson as the Joker and his famous comment: "Where does he get all those wonderful toys?" The "bat beacon" then becomes OnStar for the average person. Batman is also ageless, appealing to young people who read comic books and watch movies today as well as older people who remember

Batman from their youth.[8] A highly successful effort, this Batman OnStar campaign won a David Ogilvy Research Award.

Evaluation Research Concept testing is actually the first level of evaluation. After an advertisement or other type of marketing communication (marcom) message has been developed and produced, it can be evaluated for its effectiveness both before and after it runs as part of a campaign. **Pretesting** is research on an execution in its finished stages but before it appears in media. While creative development research looks at the power of the advertising idea, pretesting looks at the way the idea is presented. The idea can be strong, but the target might hate the execution. This type of test elicits a go or no-go decision for a specific advertisement. Sometimes pretesting will also call into doubt the strength of the advertising idea, forcing the creative team to rethink its strategy.

Evaluative research, often referred to as **copytesting,** is done during a campaign and afterward. If it's used during a campaign, the objective is to adjust the ad to make it stronger. Afterward, the research determines the effectiveness of the ad or campaign.

We will explore many different types of evaluation methods in Chapter 19, but let's just mention two common forms here. Memory can be measured using **aided recognition** (or recall). A researcher might page through a magazine (or use some other medium) and ask respondents whether they remember seeing a particular ad. **Unaided recognition** (or recall) means respondents are asked to tell what they remember without being prompted by seeing the magazine (or other medium) to refresh their memories. These tools are used both in developmental research and also in evaluation. Strategic, developmental, and evaluative research share some common tools and processes and we briefly describe some of these in the following section.

WHAT ARE THE MOST COMMON RESEARCH METHODS?

This section focuses on the types of research used in message development and the research situations where these methods are typically used.

Ways of Contact: Quantitative Methods

Consumer research methodologies are often described in terms of the ways researchers contact their respondents. The contact can be in person, by telephone, by mail, through the Internet or cable TV, or by a computer kiosk in a mall or store. Most quantitative research in marketing communication is survey based, however, consumers can also be contacted in malls where they are invited to participate in experimental research.

Principle
Careful scientific procedures are used in survey research to draw a representative sample of a group in order to accurately reflect the population's behavior and attitudes.

Survey Research In a survey, questionnaires are used to obtain information about people's attitudes, knowledge, media use, and exposure to particular messages, and this was an important part of the Cheetos retargeting campaign. **Survey research** is a quantitative method that uses structured interviews to ask large numbers of people the same set of questions. The questions can deal with personal characteristics, such as age, income, behavior, or attitudes. The surveys can be conducted in person, by phone, by mail, or online. There are two big questions to consider: how to build a representative sample of people to be interviewed and what method is best to collect the data.

Sampling is used because in most cases, it is cost prohibitive to try to interview everyone in the population or target market. Instead the people interviewed are a representative **sample** of the larger group, a subset of the population that is representative of the entire population.[9] For survey research to be an accurate reflection of the population, those who participate must be selected at random, which means every person who belongs to the population being surveyed has an equal likelihood (probability) of being chosen to participate. For a classic example of how nonrandom sampling can create inaccurate results, consider the *Literary Digest* presidential election polling of Landon versus Roosevelt in 1936, which produced incorrect results for the presidential election, even though it had a sample size of more than 2 million households. Why? Analysis of the poll results indicates that both the magazine's sample and the response were biased and did not accurately predict voter behavior.[10]

Incentives are important when doing surveys. As Karl Weiss, a member of this book's Advisory Board and president of a marketing research company explains, choose an incentive that

Survey research can be conducted in person and is often conducted in malls, supermarket aisles, or other public places.

Phone surveys are commonly used. Often they come from commercial call centers where many people hired by a research company staff a bank of phones. In recent years the contact is made through electronic dialing and when respondents answer, the call is transferred to an interviewer.

is appropriate for your audience—perhaps $5 or $10 in cash, a drawing for a Wii or iPhone, or even a summary of the results. Different audiences have different interests so make your incentive appealing to them. Be careful, however, not to bias your results in the process. If you are studying airline travel behavior and your incentive is a PlayStation, don't be surprised to find that most of those who complete the survey are males under 35 years old.

Since survey research first began, the way researchers have gone about collecting data from respondents has seen almost constant change as new technologies have made such research more cost efficient:

- *Door-to-Door Interviews* In the 1950s and 1960s, marketing researchers literally roamed the streets knocking on people's doors with clipboards in hand in order to gather their survey data. Following complex sampling strategies, they made their way through everything from apartment buildings to rural farm areas, with their sampling road map designed to maximize the randomness and representativeness of the population they studied. It wasn't surprising to see this laborious and oftentimes even dangerous approach to collecting survey data replaced by telephone interviewing by the 1970s.
- *Phone Interviews* As access to telephones increased after World War II, calling soon became the survey mode of choice, as it was much less expensive and far less invasive than sending interviewers out to people's homes. The listing of phone numbers in phone directories gave researchers the perfect source from which they could draw a **random sample,** which means each person in the population has an equal chance of being selected to be in the sample. Although telephone interviewing was more practical than going from door to door, researchers lost the ability to interact directly with their participants when communicating just by telephone, especially when there was a need to show pictures or samples of what they were evaluating. However, telephone surveys were not only more cost effective but necessary as people stopped answering their doors due to solicitation efforts (door-to-door sales were very common at that time) and concerns over personal safety.

But over time, telephone interviewing too faced its challenges. In the late 1980s and early 1990s, telemarketing efforts became so pervasive that consumers sought ways to make it stop, from the use of call-screening devices such as answering machines and Caller ID to signing up on the National Do Not Call Registry, which put legal ramifications behind unsolicited phone calls. Although marketing research calls were exempt from this legislation, because nothing is being sold, research calls were screened out with the rest as consumers fortified their privacy efforts. Today it is not uncommon for up to 60 percent of households to not answer their phones when called for a survey. Just as door-to-door surveying met its end as more cost-effective and acceptable alternatives became available, researchers once again need to look for new alternatives for gathering survey data.

• *Mail Surveys* As household addresses became readily available after the Second World War, mail surveys increased in use because researchers could pull addresses from city directories. Specialized research companies sold lists of addresses to direct marketers and these lists also were used by researchers. Mail surveys were popular because they didn't use live interviewers and thus were even less expensive than telephone surveys. In terms of survey design, the mail surveys have to be extremely easy to understand and all of the questions need to be carefully tested because an interviewer won't be present to clarify respondents' questions. Many variables determine the response rate, such as the interest level of the topic to the respondent, personalization of the message, the quality of the paper, the design of the envelope, and the inclusion of a prepaid return envelope. In spite of all the testing that has been done on mail survey design, the problem continues to be a low return rate, in addition to the loss of direct contact with the respondent.

• *Internet Surveys* Today, the world of data collection is changing again. Landline telephones are on the decline as cell phones become more popular and are beginning to be used for research. Unlisted phone numbers are becoming more common. Mail surveys have become largely ineffective, with response rates sometimes as low as the 1 to 3 percent range, which can fail to meet the statistical criteria necessary for valid random sampling. Researchers have been forced by these changes to find new ways to collect data from respondents. Telephone and mail surveys are gradually being replaced by online survey methods.

The Internet has opened up new opportunities for collecting data (see the *A Matter of Practice: Part 1* feature). In Chapter 7 you'll read about the Billings, Montana, rebranding campaign in which the campaign was launched with an online survey of more than 1,000 people. We have printed here the screen download, "Take the Survey," from this effort.

In addition to survey research, the Internet can also be a useful tool for monitoring online behavior. Jason Cormier, cofounder of social-media agency Room 214, explains that marketing communication research can be based on the data provided by members of social networks such as Facebook. One example of this type of research is pay per click. In this method, when a user clicks on an ad in Facebook, the advertiser is charged a fee based on each click of the ad. This method is extremely targeted due to the volumes of data being collected.

The rebranding campaign for Billings began with a broad survey of people involved in the business of supporting the city. For online surveys to work, they need to be supported by an invitation to participate that showcases the easy-to-use message.

Ways of Contact: Qualitative Methods

Various types of surveys are the most common quantitative research methods, but certain types of surveys can also be used for probing and to gather more insightful responses.

In-Depth Interviews One qualitative method used to survey consumers is the **in-depth interview,** which is conducted one-on-one using **open-ended questions** that require respondents to generate their own answers. In a personal interview the researcher asks questions to the consumer directly. The primary difference between an interview and a survey is the interviewer's use of a more flexible and unstructured questionnaire. This is the type of research method used by the Lexus "super-affluent team" we discussed earlier. Interviewers use a discussion guide, which outlines the areas to be covered during the session.

The discussion guides tend to be longer than surveys with questions that are usually very broad. Examples include "What do you like or dislike about this product?" and "What type of television programs do you like to watch?" Interviewers probe by responding to the answer with "Why do you say that?" or "Can you explain in more detail?" Interviews are considered qualitative because they typically use smaller sample sizes than surveys, their results cannot be generalized, and they are subjected to statistical tests.

A MATTER OF PRACTICE: PART 1

Online Survey Research

Karl Weiss, *President/CEO, Market Perceptions Inc., Denver, CO*

Without a doubt, the Internet has forever changed the world in which we live, and the way in which we do marketing research. Online surveys are much less intrusive than phone surveys, allowing participants to complete them whenever they like. Also, the self-administered approach provides a greater sense of privacy than answering these questions with a stranger over the phone (or in your home!).

In their most basic form, online surveys look and feel pretty much like paper-based surveys, with radio buttons or check boxes for people to click or check instead of filling in a bubble on a computer-readable form. But the online environment allows researchers to do much more. They can not only ask questions and request answers, but they can share sound, pictures, video, and even other websites with the participant. Photos or images can be dragged and dropped into various categories or "buckets" to indicate preference, scales can be continuous sliders, and written product descriptions can be replaced or enhanced with video, audio, and images. If desired, a live interviewer can even "join" the survey midstream or at the end to ask additional questions based on the participant's responses.

Of course, the Internet has not proven to be a replacement for phone and mail surveys because two concerns still limit this approach. First, not everyone has a computer and access to the Internet, and those who do not are demographically different from those who do, making online results skewed to the more educated and affluent. Although the digital divide is shrinking every day, the bigger problem remains—that of obtaining a random sample. With telephone and mail surveys, it is possible to obtain listings of almost everyone with a physical address or to use random digit dialing to include every possible phone number.

For online surveys, however, we must reach our participants by e-mail (exceptions are panels of prerecruited respondents and survey solicitation through online banner ads or even print ads to sign up to do research surveys on a website), but there is no universal listing of e-mail addresses like there is of physical addresses. Furthermore, even when a list of a population can be obtained (such as a customer database of e-mail addresses), typically more than 90 percent of the e-mail survey requests are deleted or ignored by the user, or never make it to the user's in-box because of spam or junk mail filters. So, although Internet surveys are even more cost effective than telephone and mail surveys, the lack of representativeness of those who participate leaves us uncertain as to whether the results are projectable to the population or just to those who like to do surveys.

Online surveys can be created easily using free services such as SurveyMonkey.com and SurveyGizmo.com. But just because these services are free (or very low cost) and easy to use, that should not be a license to send out questionnaires every time a question arises or to spend less time thinking about the quality or necessity of questions. Survey participants are not an easily renewable resource. Overuse them, especially with poorly constructed questionnaires, and participants won't help again when you might really need them.

Boring surveys equal poor results. One of the greatest challenges with online surveys is getting quality data. Most people today do online surveys to get something, from cash to frequent flyer miles to a chance to win something. Their goal is less about giving you the best answers they can and more about finishing the task at hand to get to the carrot at the end of the stick. Long online surveys, especially those with long lists of attributes to rate on the same scale (such as "Extremely Important" to "Not At All Important") are easy sections to randomly pick answers without reading the questions. Make your surveys interesting so that participants *want* to read them and provide the best answers.

Check your online data for speeders and cheaters. Look at how long it took to complete the survey and discard those that were done so quickly that you know they probably didn't really give the questions much attention. Let people know you are watching for speeders by asking them to provide a certain response to a question to make sure they are paying attention. For example, a question early in the survey could be, "To make sure only real people are completing this questionnaire and that they are paying attention, please mark "Somewhat Agree" to this question."

Focus Groups   Another qualitative method is a **focus group**, which is a group interview of 6 to 10 users and potential users of a product who are gathered around a table to have a discussion about some topic, such as the brand, product category, or marketing communication. The objective is to get participants talking in a conversational format so researchers can observe the dialogue and interactions among the group. It's a directed group interview. A moderator supervises the group, providing direction through a set of carefully developed questions that stimulate conversation and elicit

In-depth interviews are conducted one on one with open-ended questions that permit the interviewee to give thoughtful responses. The informal structure of the questions allows the interviewer to follow up and ask more detailed questions to dig deeper into attitudes and motivations.

Focus groups are conducted around a conference table with a researcher serving as the moderator working from a list of prepared discussion questions. The session is usually held in a room with one-way glass so the other team members from the agency and client can observe the way respondents answer the questions.

the group members' thoughts and feelings in their own words. Other qualitative tools can also be used with groups such as asking participants to create posters, diaries, or poems or complete exercises in day mapping or memory associations (what comes to mind when you think of something, such as a brand, situation, or location).

Focus groups can be used at any step in the planning process, but they are often used early in information gathering to probe for patterns of thought and behavior that are then tested using quantitative research tools, such as surveys. For example, the Cheetos team conducted focus groups with adult heavy-users of Cheetos. Information from focus groups can uncover, as it did in this case, answers to "how" and "why" questions. The Cheetos participants said they gave themselves permission to lick their fingers and not act like adults. Focus groups are also useful in testing creative ideas or exploring various alternatives in message strategy development.

A **friendship focus group**[11] takes place in a comfortable setting, usually a private home, where the host has recruited the participants. This approach is designed to break down barriers and save time in getting to more in-depth responses. For example, one study of sensitive and insensitive visuals used in advertising directed to black women found that a self-constructed friendship group was easier to assemble and yielded more honest and candid responses than a more traditional focus group where respondents are recruited by a research company.[12]

The Web is not only a tool for online surveys, but also for online focus groups based on the idea of getting a group of brand loyalists together as a password-protected online community. Online research company Communispace has created some 225 online communities for marketers, including Kraft Foods, Unilever for its Axe brand, and Charles Schwab. You can read more about this technique at *www.communispace.com*. In the *A Matter of Practice: Part 2* feature, Karl Weiss continues his discussion of the various ways the Internet can be used to conduct qualitative research.

A broad-based approach to online focus groups is available through the new practice called **crowdsourcing**, a term coined by Jeff Howe in *Wired* magazine in 2006.[13] It refers to aggregating the wisdom of Internet users in a type of digital brainstorming. In a search for "collective intelligence," crowdsourcing collects opinions and ideas from a digital community.

Suggestions and Comments   Informal feedback has always been available in stores through suggestion boxes and customer satisfaction cards. Target took that idea online by publishing an ad in the *Wall Street Journal* asking customers to "Tell us what more we can do for you." Some 627 respondents e-mailed suggestions. Target then published the suggestions and the company's responses to them in two-page ads. It was a novel way of eliciting comments, listening to them, and

A MATTER OF PRACTICE: PART 2

Online Qualitative Research

Karl Weiss, *President/CEO, Market Perceptions Inc., Denver, CO*

Qualitative research methods have benefited from the new technologies of the Internet, allowing researchers and respondents to see one another using webcams, and online focus groups provide a way for people across the state or globe to easily come together to discuss a topic.

But the Internet has provided the marketing research community with more than just a new method for collecting and reporting data; its mark on the industry is truly much more profound. With the massive explosion of the Internet and all that we can do on it, researchers now have a new *kind* of data, data that they can obtain without asking a single question. This shift is far more significant than the transition from telephone to online surveying.

The Internet allows today's researchers to observe consumer behavior in many ways previously not only unimaginable but impossible. The most obvious of these are Web surfing patterns, seeing where people go on the Web, what they are looking for, and what they choose to buy and not buy. But that's really just scratching the surface. With social media networking sites such as Facebook, Twitter, MySpace, and LinkedIn, not to mention other user-generated content through blogs, **vlogs,** podcasts, wikis, forums, chats, and discussion boards, researchers are now able to "listen" to what people are saying and see how consumers might be reacting to a competitor's new product or even what they are saying about a television ad. They can troll through millions of pages of blogs and discussion groups in seconds to find key words or phrases and perform content analysis to even classify the age and gender of the author.

Combining the data of the Internet with other electronic forms of information, such as credit card transactions, phone call records, and even GPS tracking, the amount of knowledge that can be surmised about *individuals* provides a whole new playing field for marketers, not to mention a growing area of concern for privacy organizations.

We don't need to look too far into the future to imagine how easy it would be to learn that Chris, a 19-year-old male college student who holds a season pass to an area ski resort, has been researching different brands of snowboards although has yet to purchase one. We could even know from the GPS information transmitted from his cell phone that he is about to walk past a ski and snowboard shop that just happens to be having a sale on one of the boards he has been considering. A message to his phone with a photo of the board, address of the store, and the sale price of the product he was considering, reaching him at exactly the right time, completely redefines "target marketing."

While privacy concerns certainly come to mind (not to mention that it's a bit creepy to have someone, even a computer, know that much about us), these types of systems are already in development and in some shape or form will become a significant piece of marketing research of the future. (For more on this topic, see *The Numerati* by Stephen Baker listed In the Recommended Readings section at the end of this chapter.)

But for now, the Internet provides us with a new way of surveying people, a new way of reporting back results to those who need them, and endless possibilities for making research less like a test laboratory and more like the real world.

then responding. Starbucks, and many other companies, use an online suggestion box incorporating the practices of *crowdsourcing*. MyStarbucks Idea is a website for Starbucks customers to contribute ideas, join the discussion, and vote on the ones they like best. Check it out at *http://mystarbucksidea.force.com/ideaHome.*

The Internet has made it even easier to track comments about a brand. Many marketers, such as IBM and Microsoft, monitor chats and blogs, and also do more general scanning for key words to find out what people are saying about their brands and products. These findings can be incorporated back into other methods, such as focus groups, to verify and explain the sentiments expressed online.[14]

Panels An **expert panel** gathers experts from various fields into a focus group setting. This research tool can stimulate new ways of looking at a brand, product, or customer pattern. More commonly, however, a marketing or **consumer research panel** is an ongoing group of carefully selected people interested in a topic or product category. A standing panel can be maintained over time by a marketer as a proprietary source of information or by a research company whose clients provide topics for the panel members' consideration. Panels can gather in person or be contacted by phone, mail, or the Internet. An example of this type of research comes from cool hunters and trend watchers who may use proprietary panels to track fashions and fads.

A DAY IN THE LIFE

A Stopwatch, Codesheet, and Curiosity

Kate Stein, *University of Florida*

I interned as a consumer-behavior researcher in grocery stores for Brian Wansink, director of the Cornell University Food and Brand Lab, and got an eyeful of insight about how people select the products they buy. I observed shoppers in the aisles as they checked the freshness of produce, compared prices, and read package labels.

Collecting data and running studies like these require observing thousands of supermarket customers in situ as they complete their shopping expeditions. The goal is to collect data that will be descriptive of reality without interfering with it. So I'm a participant, as well as a researcher.

My observations were made across several different types of grocery stores to obtain data about a wide variety of shopper types and of products available to select. I spent between 5 and 10 hours a day in grocery stores, pacing the tiled floors as I conducted my research. Setting up a study requires creating a detailed map of the grocery store, complete with measurements of the width of the grocery aisles.

To remain unnoticed and observe real behavior, researchers must appear to be supermarket shoppers themselves, blending in with their surroundings as just another innocuous grocery store patron. Using a cart and pretending that your data sheet is a grocery list are two useful measures to enhance the credibility of an undercover researcher.

Much like people watching in an airport, the appeal of observational research is easy to understand. One can feel like a true spy as you attempt to blend in with the surroundings and pose as a neutral participant in an environment where you are actually conducting research.

Observational research requires a sharp eye and a curiosity into the actions of others. Anyone with a natural interest in human nature should find consumer behavior research to be a rewarding pursuit. For more on this study, check out Professor Wansink's website: *www.mindlesseating.org*.

When this research project was undertaken, Kate was a finance and mass communication major at the University of Florida and a student of Professor Richard Lutz.

Observation Research   Like anthropologists, observation researchers study the actual behavior of consumers in settings where they live, work, shop, and play, acting as what Shay Sayre refers to as "professional snoops."[15] Direct **observation research** is closer and more personal than most other types of research. Researchers use video, audio, and disposable cameras to record consumers' behavior at home (with consumer consent), in stores, or wherever people buy and use their products. A marketer may rely on observation in the aisles of grocery, drug, and discount stores to watch people as they make product selections. Grocery shopping might seem like a mundane, mechanical activity, but look around next time you're in a store and watch how your fellow shoppers make their product choices. An example of this type of experience comes from a *New York Times* article written by Kate Stein, a University of Florida student, who describes what it's like to participate in observational research.

Cool watchers, researchers who keep tabs on trends, also use observational research when visiting places and events where their target market gathers. The Cheetos team used observational research to discover how adults respond to Chester Cheetah, the brand's character. They determined that Chester still appealed to adults because when he showed up on the street in big cities such as San Francisco, adults came up to him and gave him hugs or had their pictures taken with him.

The Consumer Behavior Odyssey was a classic observational research project that opened the door for this type of research in marketing. The Odyssey put a team of researchers in a Winnebago on a trip from Los Angeles to Boston. Along the way, the researchers used a variety of observational techniques to watch and record people behaving as consumers.[16]

A variation on observational research is **participant observation.** In this research method, the observer is a member of the group being studied. For example, research into television viewing behaviors sometimes uses friendship groups of the researcher who unobtrusively records his or her friends' behavior as part of the viewing session. The idea is that by immersing themselves in the activity, observers have an inside view—perhaps a more empathetic view—of their groups' experiences.

Ethnographic Research   Related to observation, **ethnographic research** involves the researcher in living the lives of the people being studied. Ethnographers have elevated people watching to a science. In ethnographic research, which combines anthropology and marketing, observers immerse themselves in a culture to study the meanings, language, interaction, and behavior of the people in the group.[17] The idea is that people's behavior tells you more than you can ever get in an interview or focus group. This method is particularly good at deriving a picture of a day in the life of a typical consumer. An example comes from a Walgreen's vice president who wore glasses that blurred his vision, taped his thumbs to his palms, and wore shoes containing unpopped popcorn. The exercise was designed to help him and other retail executives understand the difficulties facing elderly shoppers—confusing store layouts, eyesight problems, arthritis, and the inability to reach or stoop.[18]

Major companies like Harley-Davidson and Coca-Cola hire marketing experts trained in social science research to observe and interpret customer behavior. These participant observers then meet with the company's managers, planners, and marketing staff to discuss their impressions.[19] The case of Eight O'Clock coffee is an example of the use of a videotaped ethnographic study. The brand's agency, New York–based Kaplan Thaler, got 14 families in Pittsburgh and Chicago to use video cameras to record their typical mornings in order to identify the various roles that coffee played in their morning rituals.[20]

Direct observation and ethnographic research have the advantage of revealing what people actually do, as distinguished from what people say they do. It can yield the correct answer when faulty memory, a desire to impress the interviewer, or simple inattention to details would cause an interview answer to be wrong. The biggest drawback to direct observation is that it shows what is happening, but not *why*. Therefore, the results of direct observation often are combined with personal interviews afterward to provide a more complete and more understandable picture of attitudes, motives, and behavior.

The McCann agency is dedicating a $2.5 million research effort to understanding the lives of low-income Latinos from Mexico to Chile.[21] A new division named "Barrio" studies the marketing efforts of its clients, such as Nestlé and Danone. It has transformed conference rooms into "bodegas" (corner grocery shops) and sent employees to live with families amassing some 700 hours of video recordings. The reason is that practical insights into low-income groups are hard to find, yet these people are consumers, too, and marketers need to understand their needs as emerging economies bring new lifestyles to the disadvantaged.

Diaries   Sometimes consumers are asked to record their activities through the use of diaries. These **diaries** are particularly valuable in media research because they tell media planners exactly what programs and ads the consumers watched. If comment lines are provided, then the activities can also be accompanied by thoughts. *Beeper diaries* are used as a way to randomize the recording of activities. Consumers participating in the study are instructed to grab the diary and record what they are doing when the beeper goes off. Diaries are designed to catch the consumer in a more realistic, normal life pattern than you can derive from surveys or interviews that rely on consumers to remember their activities accurately. This can also lead to a helpful reconstruction of a typical day in the life of a consumer.

An example comes from Dunkin' Donuts. Regina Lewis, formerly vice president of consumer and brand insights, explained that she used a young adult diary study to determine when this target audience starts drinking coffee. She recruited 20 people in five cities. From their records, Lewis and her team had hundreds of points of observations. At research centers, the participants were then asked to explain what was going on when they thought about having coffee—what day, what time, why are they thinking about coffee, and so forth. From that research, the team learned that many young adults want "chuggable" coffee, particularly because they want an immediate caffeine hit. As a result, they drink iced coffee because hot coffee is too hot and they can't get their caffeine shot fast enough. Dunkin' responded with "Turbo Ice" coffee with an extra shot of espresso.[22]

Principle
Direct observation and ethnographic research methods reveal what people actually do, rather than what they say they do, but they also lack the ability to explain *why* these people do what they do.

Other Qualitative Methods   Marketing communication planners are always probing for reasons, feelings, and motivations behind what people say and do. To arrive at useful consumer insights, they use a variety of interesting and novel research methods. In particular, they use stories and pictures. Cognitive psychologists have learned that human beings think more in images than in words. Most research continues to use words to ask questions and obtain answers, but recent experiments with visual-based research opens up new avenues of expression that may be better able to uncover people's deep thoughts.

Researchers use pictures, as well as other tools to uncover mental processes that guide consumer behavior. Professor Larry Soley refers to these methods as **projective techniques,** which means they ask respondents to generate impressions rather than respond to more controlled quantitative surveys and rating systems. He describes projective techniques as psychoanalytic.[23]

Harvard Business School professor Gerald Zaltman believes that the conventional wisdom about consumer research, such as using interviews and focus groups that rely on talking to people and grilling them about their tastes and buying habits, is only good for getting back predictable answers. If you ask people what they think about Coke, you'll learn that it is a "high-energy, thirst-quenching, fun-at-the-beach" kind of drink. But that may not be an adequate description of how people really feel about the soft drink.[24]

Here is a collection of some of the more imaginative ways qualitative researchers use projective techniques as games to gather insights about people's relationships with the brands they buy:

- *Word association* is a projective technique that asks people to respond with thoughts or other words that come to mind when they are given a stimulus word. The idea is to uncover the networks of connections in their thought patterns. These are used to test brand personalities, as well as other types of meanings that govern consumer behavior.
- *Fill in the blanks* is a form of attitude research in which people literally fill in the blanks in a story or balloons in a cartoon. Perceptions can come to the surface in the words participants use to describe the action or situations depicted in the visuals.
- *Sentence completion* tests give respondents the beginning of a sentence and ask them to finish it. These are good at eliciting descriptions, causes, results, as well as the meanings in personal experiences.
- *Purpose-driven games* allow researchers to see how people solve problems and search for information.[25] Games can make the research experience more fun and involving for participants. They also uncover problem-solving strategies that may mirror the participants' approach to information searching or the kinds of problems they deal with in certain product situations.
- *Theater techniques* use games in a theater setting where researchers have people experience a variety of exercises to understand how they think about their brand. Some of these games have people tell stories about products or simulations where they have to convince others to use a brand.
- *Sculpting and movement techniques,* such as positioning the body as a statue, can be a source of insight in brainstorming for creative ideas and new product ideas. Sculpting involves physically putting product users in static positions that reflect how they think about or use a brand. Physical movements, such as dance movements and martial arts, can be added to increase the range of insight.
- *Story elicitation* asks consumers to explain the artifacts of their lives, such as the photos displayed in their homes and the objects they treasure. These stories can provide insights into how and why people use or do things.
- *Artifact creation* is a technique that uses such ideas as life collages, day mapping (tracking someone's activities across a day), and the construction of instruction books as ways to elicit stories that discuss brands and their role in daily life. These projects are also useful later in explaining to others—clients, the creative team, or other agencies—the triggers behind consumer insights.[26]
- *Photo elicitation* is similar to artifact research except it uses visuals to elicit consumer thoughts and opinions. A form of photo-based interviewing, consumers are asked to look at a set of visuals or instructed to visually record something with a camera, such as a shopping trip. Later in reviewing the visuals, they are asked to explain what they were thinking or doing.

- *Photo sorts,* which is yet another visual technique, asks consumers to sort through a deck of photos and pick out visuals that represent something to them, such as typical users of the product or situations where it might be used. In identifying typical users, they may be asked to sort the photos into specific piles, such as happy, sad, angry, excited, or innovative people.
- *Metaphors* is a tool used by researchers to enrich the language consumers use to talk about brands. (Remember your grammar: A **metaphor** compares one thing to another without using the actual words *like* or *as.*) The Evian ad, for example, uses a strong metaphor to define its product. The insight into how people perceive brands through such connections comes from exploring the link between the two concepts. Metaphor games are used in creativity to elicit new and novel ideas, but they can also be used to analyze cognitive patterns in people's thinking.

L'original

These methods can be combined. Harvard professor Zaltman is the creator of ZMET (pronounced ZEE-MET), the Zaltman Metaphor Elicitation Technique, which uses metaphors and visual images to uncover patterns in people's thinking. For a typical session, the respondents bring images that they think relate to the product category or brand being studied. Then they make up stories that describe their feelings about the product or brand.[27] The Cheetos research team used the ZMET and uncovered the unexpected finding about stress and how Cheetos was an escape from those pressures.

This metaphoric ad equating Evian sparkling water with a mermaid tries to add a touch of originality, as well as meaning, to the Evian brand image.

For Coca-Cola in Europe, Zaltman asked volunteers to collect at least a dozen pictures that captured their feelings about Coca-Cola. Then they discussed the images in personal interviews. Finally, the volunteers created a summary image—a digital collage of their most important images and recorded a statement that explained its meaning. The ZMET team found that Coke is not just about feelings of high energy and good times; it also has an element of calm, solitude, and relaxation.[28]

Choosing a Research Method

Determining the appropriate research method to use is an important planning decision. It might help to understand two basic research criteria, validity and reliability, that are derived from what researchers call the "scientific method." **Validity** means that the research actually measures what it says it measures. Any differences that are uncovered by the research, such as different attitudes or purchasing patterns, really reflect differences among individuals, groups, or situations. **Reliability** means that you can run the same test again and get the same answer.

Quantitative researchers, particularly those doing experiments and surveys, are concerned about being faithful to the principles of science. Selecting a sample that truly represents the population, for example, increases the reliability of the research. Poorly worded questions and talking to the wrong people can hurt the validity of surveys, as well as focus groups. The problem with experiments is twofold: (1) experiments are limited by a small number of people in the experimental group, and (2) they are conducted under artificial conditions.

The information you get from surveys of a broad cross section of a population is limited to your ability to develop good clear questions that everyone can understand and answer. This tight control makes it harder to ask questions around the edges of a topic or elicit unexpected or unusual responses. On the other hand, focus groups and in-depth interviews that permit probing are limited by small numbers and possible problems with the representativeness of the sample.

Generally, quantitative methods are more useful for gathering data (how many do this or believe that?), and qualitative methods are better at uncovering reasons and motives (why do they do or believe?). For these reasons, most researchers use a variety of research methods—quantitative and qualitative and occasionally experimental designs. Which method should you choose when you conduct research? The answer depends on what questions you need to answer.

RESEARCH TRENDS AND CHALLENGES

Marketing communication researchers face a number of challenges: **globalization** and new media technology are reshaping the industry. Practices are also changing as the industry searches for ways to more naturally embed research as feedback, as well as gain more insightful analysis and move into IMC planning. Let's examine each challenge briefly.

Global Issues

The key issues that global researchers face include how to manage and communicate global brands in widely different localities and how to shift from studying differences to finding similarities around the world. The biggest problem is cross-cultural communication and how to arrive at an intended message without cultural distortions or insensitivities. Researchers are becoming more involved in puzzling out cultural meanings and testing marketing communication messages for cultural sensitivity in different countries. They struggle to determine how other cultures will interpret the elements of a campaign so that they convey the same brand message across cultures. Cultural differences complicate planning as account planner Susan Mendelsohn, who is a member of this book's Advisory Board, discovered in planning for a new analgesic that contained caffeine. In test markets the agency discovered that perceptions about caffeine vary positively and negatively in different cultures.

IMC Research Challenges

The deluge of data is only complicated by IMC planning, which requires research into many stakeholder groups and contact points. Instead of campaign planning where messages are tweaked slightly to fit different media, *strategic consistency* in IMC planning suggests that different audiences, as well as media, need different messages. Susan Mendelsohn calls this a more radical trend in planning research and points to "companies that are experimenting with multimessage strategies that fit each vehicle uniquely and yet might be radically different from each other." She cautions that the company needs to be clear about the goals for its brand, recognizing that there might be multiple goals—a set of integrated goals—rather than one big underlying goal and that suggests multiple measurements of effectiveness, as well.

Planning for Feedback

Learning how to better listen to consumers has become an important factor in effective marketing communication. Earlier we mentioned the use of customer contact to elicit feedback; there are also ways to structure feedback into message strategies. In **embedded feedback research,** the research method is built into the response, including the contact point, purchase activity, and use situations. Campaigns that encourage interested prospects to contact a company, for example, are setting up response monitoring as part of the message strategy. *Call centers*, both inbound (customer calls to complain or get assistance) and outbound (telemarketing), can also be used as research centers to gain real-time feedback about the brand and its marketing and advertising strategies. In other words, whenever a call is made, for whatever purpose, that contact provides an opportunity to ask a brand-related question. Marketers also monitor blogs, chat rooms, and social media (Facebook, MySpace, Twitter) for clues about what people are saying about a brand.

An example of a structured feedback program comes from Nordstrom's Personal Touch Program, which uses a team of *personal shoppers* who are fashion consultants on one level but on another level are trained to gather information from their clients to feed back into the company's business planning and marketing.

Looking Ahead

Research, analysis, and new techniques such as crowdsourcing, lead to marketing communication plans and strategic decisions, which will be the topic of the next chapter. The research findings also lead to message strategies, which we introduce in Part 3, and media strategies, which will follow in Part 4.

IT'S A WRAP

Comfort Food for Thought

Cheetos' research shifted the focus of its strategy from kids to "rejuvenile" adults as a target audience. Key insights from research efforts shaped the creative direction to create edgy humor that spoke to those current and would-be Cheetos lovers. The message became "It's all about fun"—and that appealed to a certain segment of the adult audience, who just happened to be fans of Cheetos.

Consultant Howard Papush, aka Dr. Play, said, "When we're stressed, we revert back to the things that comforted us as kids. We want to play our way through stress." It seems to be a universal truth, at least for some of us, that comfort food, aka Cheetos, can occasionally be a good way to relieve stress. And orange fingers are fun.

Interestingly, little in the campaign speaks about the product. Yet, the campaign seems to succeed, maybe because the audience it seeks rejects a direct push about the product. Besides, who doesn't know what Cheetos are? Did the campaign work to accomplish the objective of repositioning the brand for a new target market? Several indicators suggest the success of the Cheetos campaign.

First, and most importantly, Cheetos' sales rose significantly, almost doubling the targeted rate. In a tracking study about the best-regarded snack brands, Cheetos improved from 41st position to 34th, and this improvement was mainly from households without children.

The repositioning strategy created energy for the brand by connecting the message that this snack could help consumers lighten up with its audience in a variety of traditional and digital media. Disregarding your mother's admonition not to play with your food, this campaign tells you it's okay in ways that speak effectively to the target audience. The new Cheetos campaign created more than mischievous fun. It made award-winning advertising communication. In 2009 the Advertising Research Foundation awarded this campaign its best of show, the Grand Ogilvy Winner.

Key Points Summary

1. **What are the basic types of strategic research and how are they used?** Secondary research is background research that gathers already published information, and primary research is original research findings collected for the first time from original sources. Quantitative research is statistical and uses numerical data to investigate how people think and behave; qualitative research is exploratory and uses probing techniques to gain insights and identify questions and hypotheses for further quantitative research. Experimental research tests hypotheses using carefully designed experiments.

   Research is used to (1) develop an analysis of the marketing situation, (2) acquire consumer information and insights for making targeting decisions, (3) identify information about available media to match the media to the target audience, and (4) develop message strategies and evaluate their effectiveness.

2. **What are the most common research methods used in advertising?** Survey research is used to amass quantities of

responses from consumers about their attitudes and behaviors. In-depth interviews probe the reasons and motivations consumers give to explain their attitudes and behavior. Focus groups are group interviews that operate like a conversation directed by a researcher. Panels are long-running consumer groups that permit tracking of attitude and behavior changes. Observation research happens in the store or home where researchers watch how consumers behave. Ethnographic research is an anthropological technique that involves the researcher in participating in the day-to-day lives of consumers. Diaries are records of consumers' behavior, particularly their media use. A number of other qualitative methods are used to creatively uncover patterns in the way consumers think and act.

3. **What are the key challenges facing advertising researchers?** Globalization complicates the way research is conducted for global products because it adds a cultural dimension and varied legal restrictions. Media fragmentation and convergence complicate the process of

determining media effects. New research techniques are being created as a result of new media technology as well as the Internet, which offers opportunities for virtual interviews. Embedded research is a way to get immediate feedback that comes from the process of buying or using the product. Beyond the accumulation of numbers and information, the search for insight is a driving force in advertising research.

Words of Wisdom: Recommended Reading

Baker, Stephen, *The Numerati,* New York: Houghton Mifflin, 2008.

Edmunds, Holly, *Focus Group Research Handbook,* New York: McGraw-Hill, 2000.

Howe, Jeff, *Crowdsourcing,* New York: Crown Business, 2008.

Hubbard, Douglas, *How to Measure Anything: Finding the Value of "Intangibles" in Business,* Hoboken, NJ: John Wiley, 2007.

Jones, John Philip (Ed.), *How Advertising Works: The Role of Research,* Thousand Oaks, CA: Sage, 1998.

Morrison, Margaret, Eric Haley, Kim Sheehan, and Ronald Tayler (Eds.), *Using Qualitative Research in Advertising: Strategies, Techniques and Applications,* 2nd ed., Thousand Oaks, CA: Sage, 2008.

Sayre, Shay, *Qualitative Methods for Marketplace Research,* Thousand Oaks, CA: Sage, 2001.

Young, Charles, *The Advertising Research Handbook,* Seattle, WA: Ideas in Flight, 2005.

Key Terms

advertising research, p. 163
aided recognition, p. 174
association tests, p. 172
concept testing, p. 173
consumer insight research, p. 172
consumer research, p. 163
consumer research panel, p. 179
content analysis, p. 171
copytesting, p. 174
crowdsourcing, p. 178
diaries, p. 181
embedded feedback research, p. 184

ethnographic research, p. 181
evaluative research, p. 174
experimental research, p. 168
expert panel, p. 179
focus group, p. 177
friendship focus group, p. 178
globalization, p. 184
IMC research, p. 163
in-depth interview, p. 176
market research, p. 163
marketing research, p. 169
media research, p. 173

message development research, p. 173
metaphors, p. 183
network of associations, p. 172
observation research, p. 180
open-ended questions, p. 176
participant observation, p. 181
pretesting, p. 174
primary research, p. 165
projective techniques, p. 182
qualitative research, p. 167
quantitative research, p. 167

random sample, p. 175
reliability, p. 183
sales levels, p. 167
sample, p. 174
secondary research, p. 164
semiotic analysis, p. 173
strategic research, p. 163
survey research, p. 174
unaided recognition, p. 174
validity, p. 183
vlogs, p. 179

Review Questions

1. Explain the difference between primary and secondary research and between quantitative and qualitative research.

2. What are the four uses of research in advertising? Give an example of each one.

3. How many different ways are there to contact people to gain information for use in advertising planning?

4. What is survey research and how is it conducted? How do in-depth interviews differ from surveys?

5. Explain when to use the following research methods: focus group, in-depth interviews, observational research, ethnographic research, and diaries.

6. Explain the difference between validity and reliability and explain how these concepts affect advertising research.

7. What are two ways to gather feedback? Explain how to acquire this information and why feedback is important.

Discussion Questions

1. Suppose you are developing a research program for a new bookstore serving your college or university. What kind of exploratory research would you recommend? Would you propose both qualitative and quantitative studies? Why or why not? What specific steps would you take?

2. Consult the MRI data reproduced on p. 166 and do the following analysis: Look first at the four Index columns and find the highest viewing category of late evening weekend news and compare that with the highest viewers of early evening weekend news. If you were advertising a new hybrid car, which category and time slot would deliver the greatest *percentage* of viewers who might be in the market? Now analyze the size of the category to determine which of the high viewing categories delivers the greatest *number* of viewers.

3. Bottled water is an outgrowth of the health and fitness trend. It has recently moved into second place in the beverage industry behind wine and spirits, beating out beer and coffee. The latest twist on bottled water is the "enhanced" category with designer waters that include such things as extra oxygen, vitamins, or caffeine. You have a client with a product that fits this new category. Go online and find secondary data about this market. Indicate how you would use this information to design a branding program for this product.

4. *Three-Minute Debate* You have been hired to develop and conduct a research study for a new upscale restaurant chain coming into your community. Your client wants to know how people in the community see the competition and what they think of the restaurant's offerings. It uses an unusual concept that focuses on fowl—duck, squab, pheasant, and other elegant meals in the poultry category. A specialty category, this would be somewhat like a seafood restaurant. One of your colleagues says the best way to do this study is with a carefully designed survey and a representative sample. Another colleague says, no, what the client really needs is insight into the market; she believes the best way to help the client with its advertising strategy is to use qualitative research. As a team, choose one side in this debate and identify its strengths in terms of this campaign problem. Prepare your point of view and a brief presentation to your class that will convince them.

Take-Home Projects

1. *Portfolio Project* Assume you are working for Gerber Baby Foods. You have been asked to identify the relevant trends that are forecasted for U.S. birth rates between 2012 and 2015. Identify Internet sources that would provide that information. Gather as much information as you can from these sites and write a one-page report on the trends you find.

2. *Mini-Case Analysis* What were the key research findings that led to the Cheetos repositioning campaign? You have just been assigned to the Cheetos team for the next year of the campaign. What research would you want to do before planning the next year's efforts? Identify a list of key research questions that have to be answered before the campaign can move forward.

Team Project: The BrandRevive Campaign

For the BrandRevive campaign, we need to know what people interested in this category think about the brand. All team members should identify friends and family members who would be willing to be interviewed. Identify those among your pool of interviewees who are users of your brand or the category. Also identify those in your group category users who are *not* users of your brand. (For Avaya, consider the category to be business hardware and software, similar to IBM offerings.)

• Interview both groups about their attitudes to the category and specific brands. Build a profile of the brand users—what characteristics distinguish them from the nonusers?

• What are their perceptions of the brand (of both users and nonusers)?
• What brands compete with your brand in the minds of your interviewees?
• What other research would you propose doing to better understand this market and brand?
• Present your findings in a one-page report and a PowerPoint presentation that is no longer than three slides.

Hands-On Case

The Century Council

Read the Century Council case in the Appendix before coming to class.

1. How did "The Stupid Drink" campaign team use research to better understand the problem they were trying to solve?

2. How did "The Stupid Drink" campaign team use research to inspire a creative solution to the problem of underage binge drinking on college campuses?

3. What other methodologies would you recommend to the team to better understand the success of its program in the market?

Strategic Planning

It's a Winner

Campaign:	Company:	Agencies:	Award:
"Coke/Coke Zero Taste Infringement"	Coca-Cola	Crispin Porter + Bogusky, Mediavest USA	2009 Silver Effie Winner

CHAPTER KEY POINTS

1. What is the difference between objectives, strategies, and tactics in strategic planning and how are the three levels of planning connected?
2. How is a campaign plan constructed, and what are its six basic sections?
3. What is account planning, and how is it used in advertising?
4. In what ways does an IMC plan differ from an advertising plan?

How to Sell Diet Drinks to People Who Don't Like the Idea of Diet Drinks

How many guys do you know who admit they are on a diet? Probably not many. Diets are kind of a girl thing. So you can imagine the job Coca-Cola had when it wanted to convince young men ages 18 to 34 to try its no-calorie Coke Zero. The very dudes Coca-Cola wanted to appeal to said that diet sodas tasted bad and were far too feminine for them.

Although Coke Zero had been around for three years and was gaining acceptance, Coca-Cola wanted to grow its share of market by adding the 18- to 34-year-old male demographic. This wouldn't be an easy sell. Enter Crispin Porter + Bogusky (CP+B), an agency that has made its award-winning reputation on edgy work that reaches the target market.

CP+B knew from Coca-Cola's research that these guys liked the taste of regular sugary sodas, but as they aged they began to drink more lower calorie options like energy drinks, water, or sports drinks and less pop. To accomplish the client's three main objectives—increase brand awareness, motivate the target audience to try Coke Zero, and convince men 18–34 that Coke Zero tastes like Coke—CP+B relied on consumer research, which indicated that those who tried Coke Zero really thought it tasted like Coke.

Knowing that young men had a negative perception of anything "diet," CP+B proposed to the client that the advertising should focus on the taste similarity of the two products in a funny campaign that would appeal to the skeptical audience. CP+B thought Coke Zero would be a great alternative if, and it's a big if, these young 18–34 men could be convinced it tasted as good as regular Coca-Cola. CP+B's strategy then was to convince guys that calorie-free (note they don't say "diet") Coke Zero was as good as "the real thing." But how?

The communication strategy focused on appealing to the male target through wide-reaching media such as out-of-home media and cinema (a whopping 87 percent of all U.S. theaters) to build awareness, and print, TV, digital, and radio to encourage product trial. Where Coke had big brand presence, such as with NASCAR, the NCAA, and Fantasy Football, there too went Coke Zero. And why there?

The creative strategy was based on the self-deprecating humor you recognize from *The Daily Show* and *The Office*. The gist of the big idea was that the legal department from Coca-Cola wanted to sue Coke Zero for taste infringement. The company made fun of itself proposing imaginary lawsuits and provided a non-traditional campaign for Coke Zero. In one commercial, an unsuspecting real attorney warns actors portraying Coke Classic executives not to sue Coke Zero, lest the suit be dismissed and they be utterly humiliated.

So where you might expect to see a Coke message, you might also see the lawyers ranting about Coke Zero stealing its taste. Here's a fun example. At the NCAA Final Four event in San Antonio, passersby could see a "Stop Coke Zero" rally and sample the taste similarity, providing an opportunity to prove to the targeted males that Coke Zero really did taste like Coke. CP+B even created an advergame, called *Rooftop Racer*. The object of this NASCAR game was to invite players to step into a virtual car and race with other fellow drivers to the finish line while balancing a Coke Zero bottle on top of their car. Visitors to the CokeZero.com site could "Sue a Friend."

This campaign signifies a shift in thinking about media strategy for Coca-Cola products, according to Katie Bayne, senior vice president for Coco-Cola brands in North America at Coca-Cola in Atlanta. "It's not just about a television spot," she said. That is especially true for Coke Zero as we look at where we need to be to connect with the target audience. So what lesson do we learn from Coke Zero? Sometimes you've got to take calculated risks, and sometimes they pay off, especially when you use well-conceived message and media strategies to connect with a carefully targeted audience.

To see more of this campaign, check out the Coke Zero website, *www.cokezero .com*. To see how well this oddball campaign connected with young males, turn to the end of this chapter and read the *It's a Wrap* feature.

Sources: "Coke/Coke Zero Taste Similarity," Effie Awards Brief of Effectiveness, *www.nyama.org*; Stuart Elliott, "Can't Tell Your Cokes Apart? Sue Someone," March 5, 2007, *www.nytimes.com*; Paul van Veenendaal, "CP+B Launches Rooftop Racer for Coke Zero," *www.viralblog.com*; "Coke v. Coke Zero: A Winning Case," *www.adforum.com*.

Marketing and advertising strategies are chosen from an array of possible alternatives. In most cases, there is no one completely right way to do anything in advertising, but if you understand how advertising works, you may be able to identify the best strategy to accomplish the objectives. This chapter explains the concept of strategic planning as it is used in business, marketing, and advertising and integrated marketing communication (IMC) plans. It covers key planning decisions, such as identifying critical problems and opportunities, targeting the right audience, positioning or repositioning the brand against the competition, and making implementation decisions. It also introduces the concept of account planning and explains its critical role in determining the consumer insights that lead to message and media strategies.

WHAT IS STRATEGIC PLANNING?

For marketing communication, **strategic planning** is the process of identifying a problem that can be solved with marketing communication, then determining **objectives** (what you want to accomplish), deciding on **strategies** (how to accomplish the objectives), and implementing the **tactics** (actions that make the plan come to life). This process occurs within a specified time frame. Objectives are usually long-term propositions, strategies are more medium term in focus, and tactics are more short term.

Even those experienced in advertising sometimes have a hard time telling the difference between an objective and a strategy. Remember, an *objective* is a goal to be accomplished; in advertising, objectives are determined by the effects you want to achieve. A *strategy* is the means, the design or plan, by which the objective is accomplished—the advertising message and media strategies, for example. In advertising, *tactics* are the way the ads and other marketing communication efforts are executed—how they are designed and what they say.

In the Coke Zero case, the objective was to position Coke Zero as tasting like regular Coke. The strategy was to use taste tests so the young male target could experience how similar the tastes were. The tactic was to use the idea of "taste infringement" complete with lawyers, actors, and imaginary lawsuits.

We talk a lot about creativity in this book and we'd like to emphasize that strategic thinking is just as creative as coming up with a Big Idea for a marketing communication campaign. Both processes involve searching for ideas to solve problems, whether they are found in marketing situations or communication challenges. Pat Fallon and Fred Senn, cofounders of the legendary agency Fallon Worldwide, explain that principle in their book, *Juicing the Orange: How to Turn Creativity into a Powerful Business Advantage*. They have identified seven principles that link creative thinking and strategic planning to business results[1]:

Pat Fallon (top) and Fred Senn were cofounders of Fallon Worldwide, the agency behind NBC, Holiday Inn Express, Travelers Insurance, Sony, and many other major brands.

1. ***Always Start from Scratch*** Simplify the problem. You know too much. There's a good chance that you know so much that you can't see how the problem could be solved in a fresh way.
2. ***Demand a Ruthlessly Simple Definition of the Business Problem*** Smart people tend to make things too complicated. Be a relentless reductionist. Einstein said, "Make things as simple as possible, but no simpler."
3. ***Discover a Proprietary Emotion*** The key component of any communication program is a powerful consumer insight that leads to a ruthlessly smart strategy executed brilliantly across all platforms. It all starts with the insight, which is the central truth of what you are going to say and how you are going to operate. Once you find an emotional truth, you can make it proprietary through execution.
4. ***Focus on the Size of the Idea, Not the Size of the Budget*** It's our credo that it's better to outsmart than outspend.
5. ***Seek Out Strategic Risks*** Understand the benefits of prudent risk. Great big ideas in the early stages are often scary ideas. When Darwin taught us about the survival of the fittest, he didn't mean the strongest. He meant that it's the most nimble—the quickest to adapt to a changing environment—who prosper both in nature and in a capitalist economy.
6. ***Collaborate or Perish*** This is more than "getting along"; it is about recognizing that the rules of engagement have changed. We live in an era in which victory goes to the best collaborators. This means teams from different disciplines and different corporate cultures will be working together. Teams that are aligned and motivated can make history.
7. ***Listen Hard to Your Customers (Then Listen Some More)*** Listening is often step Number One on the road to understanding. Listening often yields that precious insight that gives you a competitive advantage; something your competitors have overlooked.

The Business Plan

Strategic planning is a three-tiered process that starts with the business plan and then moves to functional areas of the company such as marketing where a marketing plan is developed that outlines objectives, strategies, and tactics for all areas of the marketing mix. As illustrated in Figure 7.1, both the business plan and the marketing plan provide direction to specific plans for specialist areas, such as advertising and other areas of marketing communication.

A business plan may cover a specific division of the company or a **strategic business unit (SBU),** which is a line of products or all the offerings under a single brand name. These divisions, or SBUs, share a common set of problems and factors. Figure 7.2 depicts a widely used framework for the strategic planning process in business. The objectives for planning at this level tend to focus on maximizing profit and **return on investment (ROI).** ROI is a measurement that shows whether, in general, the costs of conducting the business—the investment—are more than matched by the revenue produced in return. The revenue above and beyond the costs is where profit lies.

FIGURE 7.1

Strategic Planning from Top to Bottom
Business planning involves a set of cascading objectives and strategies. Corporate objectives and strategies are achieved through planning at the level of marketing (and other areas, such as production), and marketing objectives and strategies give direction to marketing communication programs.

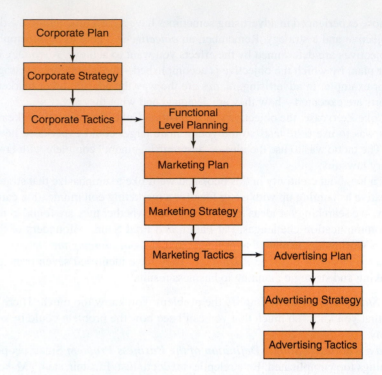

Note that the business planning process starts with a business **mission statement,** a concise expression of the broad goals and policies of the business unit. The mission statement is unique, focused, and differentiating. Tom's of Maine states its mission clearly on its website:

> "Through the years, we have been guided by one simple notion—do what is right, for our customers, employees, communities, and environment. We call this Natural Care—a philosophy that guides what we make and all that we do."

The Marketing Plan

A **marketing plan** is developed for a brand or product line and evaluated annually, although sections dealing with long-term goals might operate for a number of years. To a large extent, the marketing plan mirrors the company's business plan and contains many of the same components, although they are focused on a specific brand rather than the larger organization or corporation. Figure 7.3 illustrates the steps involved in creating a marketing plan.

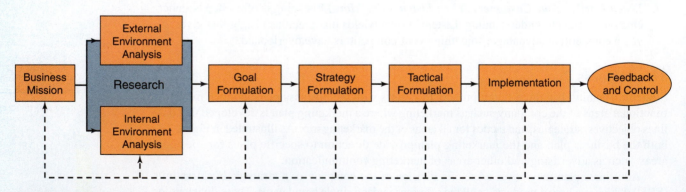

FIGURE 7.2

Steps in the Development of a Business Plan
The business planning process begins with a mission statement and moves through research, goal setting, strategy statements, identifications of tactics, implementation processes, and controls (meeting the budget and quality standards, for example). The entire process is monitored through feedback.

Source: Philip Kotler, *Marketing Management*, 13th ed., Upper Saddle River, NJ: Prentice Hall, 2009: 48. Reproduced by permission of Pearson Education, Inc., Upper Saddle River, NJ.

A *market situation analysis* is based on extensive market research that assesses the external and internal environments that affect marketing operations—the company's history, products, and brands, as well as the competitive environment, consumer trends, and other marketplace trends that have some impact on the product category. A set of "what's going on" questions helps structure this market analysis. Answers to these questions help define the key marketing problem and, ultimately, the SWOTs, which stands for strengths, weaknesses, opportunities and threats:

- What is happening with the brand and the category?
- How is it happening?
- Where is it happening?
- When is it happening?
- To whom is it happening?

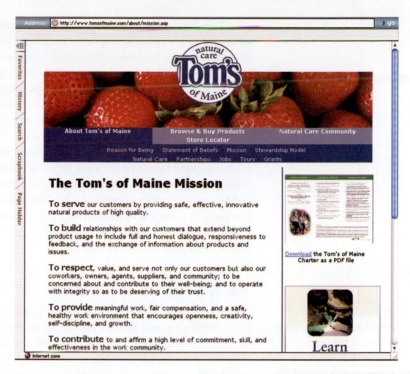

This mission statement for Tom's of Maine helps its managers develop specific business objectives and goals. It also guides all of the company's marketing communication efforts.

We could answer those questions for Coke Zero by summarizing the market situation and the key problem facing Coke Zero as a marketplace for diet drinks that appealed primarily to women, thus leaving out the large number of young male pop drinkers who make up the largest portion of the soft drink market.

The objectives at the marketing level tend to be focused on sales levels and **share of market,** measurements referring to the percentage of the category purchases that are made by the brand's customers. Other objectives deal with specific areas of the marketing mix, such as distribution, where an objective might detail how a company will open a new territory.

For marketing communication (marcom) managers, the most important part of the marketing plan is the *marketing mix strategy,* which includes decisions about the target market, brand position, product design and performance, pricing, and distribution, as well as marketing communication. Product design and formulation decisions are sometimes responses to consumer trends, such as the increase in the number of packaged foods making high-fiber claims (think Fiber One with its expanded line of cereals and snack bars). Other challenges to marketing planners came from the competition. When McDonald's began advertising its Angus burger in 2009, the Hardee's and Carl's Jr. chains responded with taste challenges, mail-in refund promotions, and parodies of Big Mac advertisements.[2]

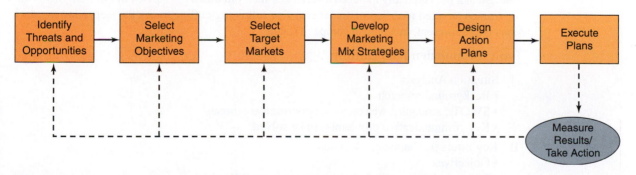

FIGURE 7.3

Steps in the Development of a Marketing Plan

A marketing plan begins with an analysis of the marketing situation in terms of strengths, weaknesses, opportunities, and threats. Setting objectives is the next step. Target markets are selected and marketing strategies are developed, as well as action plans and specific executions of ideas and programs. The plan is evaluated and that information feeds back into the next generation of planning.

This marketing analysis—and the marketing mix strategy derived from it—link the overall strategic business plan with specific marketing programs, including advertising and other IMC areas. Whether to use a frequency club, an advertising campaign, or a sales promotion strategy to increase brand loyalty, for example, are marketing communication decisions that support marketing strategies.

A new contributor to this process is crowdsourcing, which we mentioned in the previous chapter. This practice mobilizes a digital crowd to provide collective intelligence. For example, consider how Wikipedia operates with experts contributing and reviewing entries. In a marketing environment, crowdsourcing can be used to channel the latent wisdom of online crowds including experts as well as average citizens. John Fluevog Open Source Footwear is a company that invites anyone to contribute ideas for shoes. Decisions about the best ideas are made through peer voting, feasibility, and admittedly what the owner John Fluevog likes. The design ideas become public domain but the company adds the winners to its line of shoes. Check out this interesting company at *www.fluevog.com/files_2/os-1.html*. Procter & Gamble uses InnoCentive.com, a digital think tank for innovation, to engage some 140,000 scientists and engineers worldwide to help with its research and development.[3]

The Advertising or IMC Plan

Principle

An advertising plan seeks to match the right audience to the right message and present the message in the right medium to reach that audience

Advertising and marketing communication planning operates with the same concern for objectives, strategies, and tactics that we've outlined for business and marketing plans. It outlines all of the communication activities needed to deliver on the business and marketing objectives in terms of communication objectives, strategies, tactics, timing, costs, and evaluation. In general, an advertising plan seeks to match the right audience to the right message and present the message in the right medium to reach that audience. These three elements—audience insight, message, and medium—are at the heart of an advertising plan.

An example of how all of these elements come together in a plan comes from a brand identity campaign for the city of Billings, Montana. *The Inside Story* feature gives you a look inside the planning of a branding campaign for a place. Pay particular attention to the "Brand Standards" online guidebook at the website *www.brandbillings.com*. This online guidebook explains how the campaign is designed to create a unified voice for the community with a consistent image and message, one that reinforces Billings' unique geography, resources, and heritage.

Let's now look at how an advertising or marketing communication plan is developed. The following discussion outlines the basic steps in planning a campaign, as well as the critical strategic decisions planners must make.

WHAT'S IN A CAMPAIGN PLAN?

In addition to or instead of an annual marketing plan, a firm may develop a **campaign plan** that is more tightly focused on solving a particular marketing communication problem in a specified time. Such a plan typically includes a variety of marcom messages carried in different media and sometimes targeted to different audiences. The following outline traces the steps, and the decisions they represent, in a typical campaign plan.

Typical Campaign Plan Outline

I. Situation Analysis
- Background research
- SWOTs: strengths, weaknesses, opportunities, threats
- Key communication problem(s) to be solved

II. Key Strategic Campaign Decisions
- Objectives
- Target audience (or stakeholder targets in an IMC plan)
- Brand position: product features and competitive advantage
- Campaign strategy: key strategic approach and marcom tools

III. Media Strategy (or Points of Contact in an IMC Plan)
- Media objectives
- Media selection

Branding Billings

John Brewer, President & CEO, Billings (Montana) Chamber of Commerce/Convention & Visitors Bureau

What do you think of when you think of Montana? Big Sky, right? That's an example of an incredibly successful branding campaign for a place.

What do you think of when you think of Billings, Montana? . . . uh . . . , probably not much, right?

That's the problem I faced in 2007 when our steering committee took on the problem of branding Billings. So this is a story of our two-year effort to create a brand identity campaign for the city.

You can check out the results of this plan at the website *www.brandbillings.com*. In addition to beautiful scenery, the first thing you may notice on the site is a logo with the slogan: "Billings—Montana's Trailhead." Here's how the city arrived at that theme line.

The campaign began with research including more than a thousand online surveys, community workshops, and presentations to clubs and service groups followed by countless hours of strategic envisioning sessions. The research and analysis determined that Billings is a very special place that merges its location with an attitude—a position that combines "open space" and "western pace."

The important brand characteristics begin with its location—shaped by the Yellowstone River and sheltered by the Rims geographic formation. The community is progressive and a regional center for finance, health care, transportation, arts and culture, and diverse educational opportunities. Its hard-working citizens have a unique Montana perspective that combines warmth with an appreciation of scenery and history. But what also defines them most is a lifestyle that loves the adventure of an untamed wilderness right outside the door.

Those characteristics translated into a statement of Billings brand essence as "Montana's city connects you to the authentic historical west." The "trailhead" idea springs from the recognition that Billings is a starting point for business growth and development, as well as a gateway for opportunities to explore the wonders of Montana. The starting point idea was supported in the "trail" graphic with its "X marks the spot" symbol. The "Where Ya Headin'?" tagline expresses the idea that Billings is the gateway for adventure.

The campaign's objective was to create a position that expresses this brand essence and to create a consistent and cohesive brand message that unifies the city's efforts to encourage business and workforce development, individual and family relocation, tourism, and community pride.

An ongoing identity development project, the campaign is spreading out to local businesses and community events. For example, the airport etched the brand logo into its five main terminal entryways. Newspaper ads by local merchants proclaimed billings as the trailhead for great shopping. The local Walmart carries Trailhead apparel with the new logo. Pepsi branded half a million Pepsi cans with a picture of Trailhead hats for a joint promotion with the Chamber of Commerce.

To sustain the campaign, a Trailhead Marketing Committee meets regularly. Using the brand standards website and tool kit as a guide, this committee encourages:

1. Businesses to adopt the brand
2. General local awareness
3. Individual and family relocation
4. Community pride through public relations and other marketing opportunities.

Success will be determined on an annual basis from media clips, and the increased number of businesses that are using the brand in their messaging and the frequency of that use. In terms of results as of this writing, in the first eight months of the campaign following the brand launch, the site (*www.brandbillings.com*) has had 7,913 visitors and a daily average total of 33 per day.

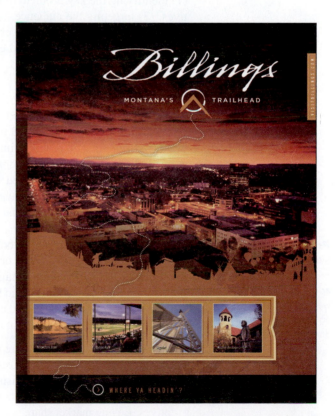

The Travel Planner is the primary piece sent to visitors by the Billings Chamber of Commerce/Convention & Visitors Bureau. Its cover uses an appealing photo of Billings, as well as the new logo and Trailhead slogan, and the "trail" graphics.

  - Media planning and buying:
    - Vehicle selection
    - Budget allocation
    - Scheduling
IV. Message Strategy
  - Key consumer insight (brand relationship insight in IMC)
  - Message objectives
  - Selling premise
  - Big idea
  - Message design and executions
V. Other Marcom Tools Used in Support
  - Public relations
  - Direct marketing
  - Sales promotion
  - Personal selling
  - Sponsorships
  - Merchandising, packaging, point-of-purchase
  - Integration strategy (maximize synergy)
VI. Campaign Management
  - Evaluation of effectiveness
  - Campaign budget

This outline is useful as a guide for the planning document, but more importantly, it identifies the key strategic decisions that guide various sections of a campaign plan. Decisions include (1) identifying the key problem to be solved based on analysis of the SWOTs, (2) stating objectives, (3) targeting the audience, (4) creating or reinforcing a position, (5) identifying the key strategic approach that will deliver the objectives, and (6) using management controls to determine efficiency in budgeting and effectiveness through evaluation. Let's look at these strategic planning decisions in more detail.

Situation Analysis

The first step in developing an advertising plan, just as in a marketing plan, is not planning but *backgrounding*—researching and reviewing the current state of the business that is relevant to the brand and gathering all pertinent information. After the research is compiled, planners try to make sense of the findings, a process sometimes referred to as a **situation analysis.** The goal is to identify a problem that can be solved with communication. As Fallon and Senn explained in their "Juicing the Orange" list, you have to start by simplifying the problem. The information collection will probably be huge, but the problem statement should simplify the task.

Principle
SWOT analysis is the process of finding ways to address a brand's weaknesses and threats and leverage its strengths and opportunities.

SWOT Analysis The primary tool used to make sense of the information gathered and identify a key problem related to a brand or product is a **SWOT analysis,** which, as we have said, stands for strengths, weaknesses, opportunities, and threats. The strengths and weaknesses are *internally focused,* and the opportunities and threats lie in the *external* marketing environment. In strategic planning the idea is to *leverage* the strengths and opportunities and *address* the weaknesses and threats, which is how the key problems and opportunities are identified.[4]

- The *strengths* of a business are its positive traits, conditions, and good situations. For instance, being in a growth industry is a strength. Planners ask how they can leverage this strength in the brand's advertising.
- The *weaknesses* of a business are traits, conditions, and situations that are perceived as negatives. Losing market share is a weakness. If this is an important weakness, then planners ask how they can address it with advertising.
- An *opportunity* is an area in which the company could develop an advantage over its competition. Often, one company's weakness is another company's opportunity. Planners strive to identify these opportunities and leverage them in the brand's advertising.
- A *threat* is a trend or development in the environment that will erode business unless the company takes action. Competition and economic downturns are common threats. Advertis-

ing planners ask themselves how they can address a threat if it is a critical factor affecting the success of the brand.

In the Coke Zero case, the strength of the brand lies with the Coca-Cola tradition as "the real thing." The opportunity existed to transfer that Coke magic to a calorie-free version of the flagship brand. The weakness is the association of diet drinks with women. The threat lies with the idea that "diet drinks" have an unpleasant taste.

Key Problem(s)   The key word in the title of this section is *analysis,* or making sense of all the data collected and figuring out what the information means for the future success of the brand. Advertising planners must analyze the market situation for communication problems that affect the successful marketing of a product, as well as opportunities the advertising can create or exploit. Analyzing the SWOTs and identifying any problems that can be solved with an advertising message are at the heart of strategic thinking. An example of locating a timing opportunity is illustrated by the Special K "2-Week Challenge" that capitalized on consumers' goals to lose weight after the holidays.

Advertising can solve only message-related problems such as image, attitude, perception, and knowledge or information. It cannot solve problems related to price, availability, or quality, although it can address the perception of these marketing mix factors. For example, a message can speak to the perception that the price is too high, or it can portray a product with limited distribution as exclusive. In other words, advertising can affect the way consumers perceive price, availability, and quality. The advertiser's basic assumption, however, is that the campaign works if it creates an impression, influences people to respond, and separates the brand from the competition.

Principle
Advertising can only solve message-related or perception problems.

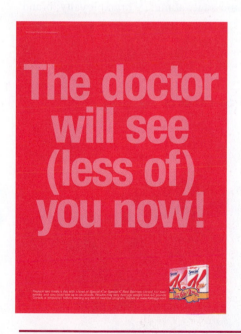

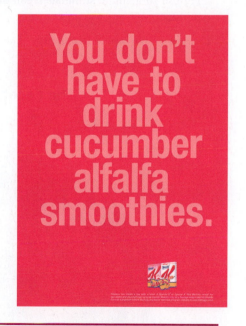

SHOWCASE

This two-week Kellogg's Special K challenge promises customers they will lose up to six pounds in two weeks by replacing two meals a day with Special K and eating a sensible third meal. Reaching consumers at the moment they are in need of a weight-loss solution and delivering a simple diet in the context of their environment—in this case posters in department store dressing rooms, health clubs, doctor's offices, hair or nail salons, and bridal salons—was very effective. Business results included an overall increase in the poster markets of 20 percent over nonposter markets.

These two posters for Special K were contributed by Amy Hume, communications consultant in the Integrated University Communications office at the University of Colorado–Denver. Hume is a graduate of the University of Colorado–Boulder and was an associate media director at Starcom Worldwide where she handled this mini-campaign for Special K. She and her work were nominated for inclusion in this book by professor Tom Duncan.

Objectives

After planners have examined the external and internal environments and defined the critical areas that need to be addressed, they can develop specific objectives to be accomplished during a specified time period. Objectives are formal statements of the goals of the advertising or other marketing communication. They outline what the message is designed to achieve in the long term and how it will be measured.

Main Effects and Objectives   Remember from Chapter 4 the six categories in The Facets Model of Effects: perception, emotion, cognition, persuasion, association, and behavior. These main effects also can be used to identify the most common consumer-focused objectives. For example, here are some sample objectives for each category, as well as sample ads and campaigns that we have discussed in this or previous chapters:

- *Perception Objectives* Grab attention; create awareness; stimulate interest; stimulate recognition of the brand or the message; create brand reminder.

  Example: "1984" ad for Macintosh launch

- *Emotional/Affective Objectives* Touch emotions; cue the psychological appeal; create brand or message liking; stimulate brand loyalty; stimulate desire.

  Example: Burger King "Whopper Freakout" campaign

- *Cognition Objectives* Establish brand identity; establish or cue the brand position; deliver information; aid in understanding features, benefits, and brand differences; explain how to do or use something; stimulate recall of the brand message; stimulate brand loyalty; brand reminder.

  Example: "Wii would like to play" launch

The Facets Model of Effects

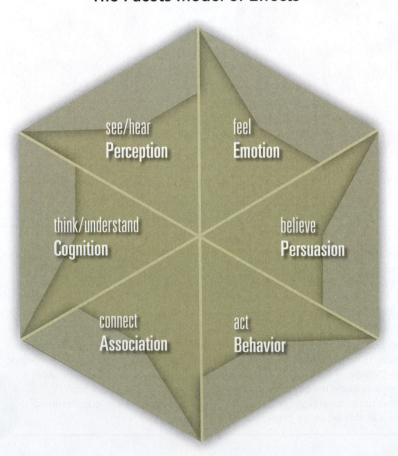

see/hear
Perception

feel
Emotion

think/understand
Cognition

believe
Persuasion

connect
Association

act
Behavior

- *Association Objectives* Establish or cue the brand personality or image; create links to symbols and associations; connect to positive brand experiences.

  Examples: Ford's "SYNC" campaign for Hispanics, Old Navy's "SuperModelquins"

- *Persuasion Objectives* Stimulate opinion or attitude formation; change or reinforce opinion or attitude; present argument and reasons; counterargue; create conviction or belief; stimulate brand preference or intent to try or buy; reward positive or desired response; stimulate brand loyalty; create buzz or word of mouth; energize opinion leaders; create advocacy and referrals.

  Example: Coke Zero "Taste Infringement"

- *Behavior Objectives* Stimulate trial, sample, or purchase; generate other types of response (coupon use, attendance, test drive, visit store or dealer, volunteering, sign up, call in, visit website, clicks, attend, participate); create word-of-mouth buzz; create advocacy and referrals.

  Example: Special K "2-Week Challenge," campaigns encouraging participation in the 2010 census

Given the huge amounts of money spent on advertising, it is important for advertisers to know what to expect from a campaign or ad. Although a rule of thumb for advertising is that it should be single minded, we also know from Chapter 4 that multiple effects are often needed to create the desired impact. Some ads may use an emotional strategy while others are informational, but sometimes the message needs to speak to both the head and the heart. That was particularly true for the Coke Zero campaign: customers needed to understand that the taste of Coke Zero was similar to regular Coke but it had to do it with a style and attitude that twenty-something males would like.

Although some objectives are tightly focused on one particular effect, others, such as brand loyalty, call for a more complex set of effects. To create brand loyalty, for example, an advertising campaign must have both cognitive (rational) and affective (emotional) effects, and it must move people to repeat buying. That's one reason brand loyalty is considered a type of long-term impact developed over time from many experiences that a consumer has with a brand and brand messages.

Note also that communication objectives may be important, even if they aren't focused directly on a sale. For example, Expedia.com, a travel consulting company, views its advertising as a way to draw attention to itself, create name recognition, and create understanding of the products and services it sells.

Measurable Objectives   We cannot overstate the importance of writing focused and measurable advertising objectives. Every campaign, and the ads in it, must be guided by specific, clear, and measurable objectives. We say *measurable objectives* because that's how the effectiveness of advertising is determined. It is also critical that an objective be **benchmarked,** which means the planner uses a comparable effort, such as a similar product or prior brand campaign, to predict a logical goal. A measurable objective includes five requirements:

1. A *specific effect* that can be measured
2. A *time frame*
3. A *baseline* (where we are or where we begin)
4. The *goal* (a realistic estimate of the change the campaign can create; benchmarking is used to justify the projected goal)
5. *Percentage change* (subtract the baseline from the goal; divide the difference by the baseline).

A hypothetical objective, then, would read like this: *The goal of this campaign is to move the target's awareness of Coke Zero's taste similarity with regular Coke from 18 to 23 percent within 12 months, an increase of 28 percent.*

Targeting

We discussed targeting and segmenting in Chapter 5, which are strategic decisions made possible because of a deep knowledge of consumers. In particular, this research-based knowledge identifies what makes specific groups of consumers different from people in other groups. These characteristics also identify how consumers are similar to others in ways that characterize a specific type of viewpoint or lifestyle, such as the student partying lifestyle on many campuses, a problem addressed by the Navigators' posters.

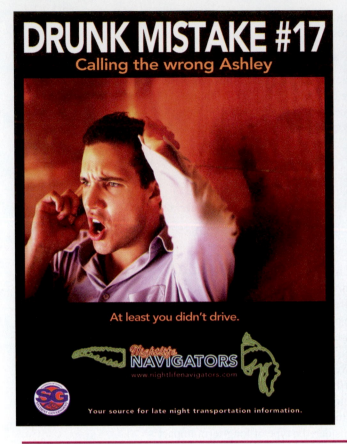

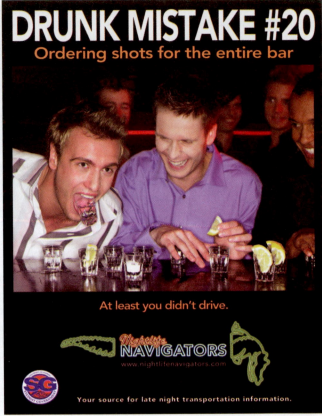

SHOWCASE

These anti–drunk driving posters were used in the Nightlife Navigators campaign at the University of Florida. They were created by the Adwerks student-run advertising agency.

As we discussed in Chapter 5, segmenting and targeting are important because marketing communication strategy is based on accurately targeting an audience that will be responsive to a particular type of message, one that will deliver the objectives.

There is more to targeting than just identifying and profiling a possible audience. How does the target audience relate to the brand? General Mills, for example, during the recent recession was able to maintain significant marketing increases by concentrating on its big-name brands, but also on its multicultural consumers, which the marketer saw as a "high ROI area."[5] Advertising planners also want to know what's going on in people's heads and hearts—what motivates them to attend to a message and respond to it. Getting deeper insight into consumers is the responsibility of the account planning function. We'll return to that role later in this chapter.

We want to emphasize that understanding a target audience demands an appreciation of diversity—and the empathy that results from such an appreciation. Professor Peggy Kreshel defines diversity as "the acknowledgment and inclusion of a wide variety of people with differing characteristics, attributes, beliefs, values, and experiences." In advertising, diversity tends to be discussed primarily in terms of *representations of gender, race,* and *ethnicity in advertising content,* although as she points out in the *A Principled Practice* feature, diversity goes beyond the images used in ads. This is the heart of the issue raised in the excerpt in Chapter 5 from *Madison Avenue and the Color Line* by historian Jason Chambers, which Kreshel references in her essay.

In recognition of the importance of this diversity issue, the American Advertising Federation (AAF) sponsors multicultural programs such as the Most Promising Minority Students and the AAF Mosaic Awards. The leader of those programs, Constance Cannon Frazier, is on this book's Advisory Board and the work of some of the Most Promising Minority Students are featured in this book. Another effort is the AdColor Industry Coalition and its AdColor

A PRINCIPLED PRACTICE

What Is Diversity and Why Is It Important?

Peggy Kreshel, Associate Professor, Department of Advertising, University of Georgia

Sometimes we forget that diversity isn't only about gender, race, and ethnicity. Consider, for example, language use, spiritual practices, sexual orientation, socioeconomic status, and age. Nor is diversity simply about images. Certainly ads and the professionals who create them frequently are criticized for lack of inclusiveness and reliance on denigrating stereotypes. However, diversity affects every aspect of the advertising profession: professional culture, production of content, content itself, the manner in which that content is placed and received, and the ways in which the profession is regulated.

One of the most visible barometers of diversity in the advertising industry is hiring and promotion practices. In *Madison Avenue and the Color Line*, historian Jason Chambers examines African American participation in the advertising industry. He found that African Americans positioned themselves as experts on the black consumer market and worked from *outside* the industry because the doors to most advertising agencies were closed to them. A 1978 New York City Commission on Human Rights report concluded that minority employees continued to be excluded from significant participation in advertising jobs. Nearly thirty years later, the commission again challenged the industry's record of minority hiring, calling it "an embarrassment for a diverse city."[6]

The advertising industry has attempted to address the diversity problem in a variety of ways. In 2005, the AdColor Industry Coalition of advertisers, agency professionals, and trade associations was formed to increase diversity in the industry and celebrate the accomplishments of diverse role models and leaders. The AAAA has partnered with Howard University's School of Communication to create a professional development and research center at that historically black university. The industry has made progress, but diversity in hiring and retention remains a highly charged issue.

Who creates the ads we see? The industry's troubled, largely unsuccessful efforts to create a racially and ethnically diverse workplace tell part of the story. Minority-owned advertising agencies provide opportunities for diversity but are frequently viewed as being capable of speaking only to minority audiences. Women comprise the majority of the advertising workforce, yet an *Adweek* study a few years ago found only four female creative directors in the top 33 advertising agencies. We can only guess at the impact, knowing that creative directors are chiefly responsible for an agency's output.

Content reflects those who create it and their perceptions of audiences. Advertisers' persistent emphasis on 18- to 34-year-olds, a group they view to be impressionable trendsetters who haven't yet formed brand loyalties, has occurred largely to the exclusion of other demographic groups. This preoccupation shapes our business (which constructs itself as youthful, rebellious, and cutting edge), media (where reality programming, the "entertainmentization" of news, and technological wizardry target 18- to 34-year-olds), and culture (reinforcing our celebration of the young, beautiful, and white).

Similarly, marketers routinely define the Hispanic market primarily as "Spanish speaking." The richness and diversity of the many cultures that comprise that group—from Puerto Rico, to Mexico, to Central and South America—have been lost in the desire to construct a homogeneous market large enough to be economically viable. It is only recently that a conversation about the complexity of the Latino market—a complexity that goes beyond merely language or ethnic predilections—has begun to appear in the trade press.

As our lives, professional and personal, become increasingly global, diversity will continue to develop and its influence will be experienced in increasingly complex, sometimes tangled ways. It is essential that advertising professionals adopt broad interpretations of advertising's impact on diversity, and diversity's impact on advertising. Creating an inclusive advertising industry is not only a social responsibility; it is a social and economic necessity.

Awards,[7] which are sponsored by the Association of National Advertisers (ANA), the Advertising Club of New York, the American Association of Advertising Agencies (4As), Arnold Worldwide, Omnicom Group, and AAF. In addition to the AAF and AdColor programs, many local advertising and marketing groups are sponsoring diversity programs in their communities.

Positioning

Principle

The goal of positioning is to locate a product in the consumer's mind based on its features and advantages relative to its competition.

Another reason we revisit targeting here is because understanding the target is the first step in understanding the brand's position within the competitive marketplace. The objective is to establish in the consumer's mind what the brand offers and how it compares with the competition. A **position,** then, is how consumers define the product or brand in comparison to its competitors. A position is based on two things: first, a particular feature or attribute—Coke Zero is low calorie but tastes like regular Coke. The feature also can be psychological, such as heritage (Kodak or Hallmark). Secondly, that feature must be important to the consumer.

A classic example of positioning is the campaign for Avis, which used the line "We Try Harder" to describe how it competes against category leader Hertz. The line was not only a good positioning statement, it also was named as one of the Top 10 Slogans of the 20th Century. The campaign was described by the fathers of positioning, Jack Trout and Al Ries, in their groundbreaking book *Positioning: The Battle for Your Mind.*[8]

A position is based on some notion of comparison. Is the brand more expensive or less; is it a status product or a symbol of frugality; is it sporty, functional, safe or extremely risky? Walmart's position, for example, is encompassed in its slogan, "Always Low Prices." Positioning, then, is about locking the brand in consumers' minds based on some quality relevant to them where the brand stands out. Compare the positioning strategies of the various arms of the U.S. military as they represent themselves in their ads.

Positions are difficult to establish and are created over time. Once established, they are difficult to change, as Kodak discovered with its ownership of the film category when the market moved to digital pictures. Category dominance is important, as Al Ries, one of the founders of the positioning concept, argues, but sometimes the category changes and the brand has to change as well or get left behind. To better understand positioning strategy, let's consider related concepts used to define the competitive situation—product features and attributes, differentiation, and competitive advantage. Then we'll return to how advertising establishes a position in a competitive marketplace.

Principle

Positioning identifies the features that make a brand different from its competitors and relevant to consumers

Product Features and Attributes   An initial step in crafting a position is to identify the **features** of the brand, as well as those of the competition, to determine where the brand has an advantage over its competitors. A marketer carefully evaluates the product's tangible features (such as size, color, design, price, and ease of use) and other intangible attributes (such as quality, status, value, fashion, and safety) to identify the dimensions of the product that are relevant to its customers and that make it different from its competitors.

An interesting twist on features developed when the electric hybrid cars, such as GM's Volt, were introduced to the market. The standard MPG estimate of fuel efficiency was turned upside down with projections of 230 MPG for Volt and 367 MPG for the Nissan Leaf. Of course, these cars use very little gas as long as they are running on their batteries—gas is only used when the charge runs out. If you only use the car to run around town, theoretically you could get unlimited gas mileage.[9] So what does this changing standard do to traditional car-buying marketing and decision making?

Differentiation and Competitive Advantage   Most markets involve a high level of competition. How does a company compete in a crowded market? It uses **product differentiation,** a strategy designed to focus attention on product differences that are important to consumers and that distinguish the company's product from that of its competitors. We refer to products that really are the same (examples include milk, unleaded gas, and over-the-counter drugs) as undifferentiated or **parity products.** For these products marketers often promote intangible, or psychological, differences, particularly through branding.

The creation of a unique brand image for a product (think Swatch) is the most obvious way to differentiate one product from another. Internet-based Mozilla and Craigslist are small companies but big brands that are strong because they have the support of dedicated users. This strong customer–brand relationship reflects a leadership position—a brand that has defined or created

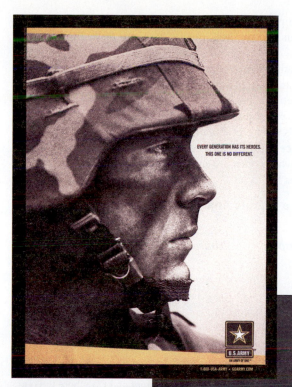

In these four ads for the Navy, Army, Air Force, and Marines, can you perceive a difference in their positioning strategies? How do they communicate their positions in the style, copy, and graphics? Which do you think would be most effective in recruiting volunteers?

its category. But it's not just hot Internet companies that have achieved this type of leadership—McIlhenny's Tabasco Sauce, which was launched in 1868, created and still owns the hot sauce category.

A technique called **feature analysis** helps structure an assessment of features relative to competitors' products to identify where a brand has an advantage. To conduct a feature analysis, first, make a chart of the product and competitors' products, listing relevant features, as the following table illustrates. Then evaluate how well the product and the competitors' products perform on those features. What are the brand's strong points or weak points? Next, evaluate how important each feature is to the target audience using opinion research. In other words, how much do consumers care about various features (which ones are most important to them) and how do the various brands compare on these features?

How to Do a Feature Analysis

		Product Performance			
Feature	*Importance to Prospect*	*Yours*	*X*	*Y*	*Z*
Price	1	+	−	−	+
Quality	4	−	+	−	+
Style	2	+	−	+	−
Availability	3	−	+	−	−
Durability	5	−	+	+	+

Using the two factors of importance and performance, **competitive advantage** is found where (1) the product has a strong feature (2) in an area that is important to the target and (3) where the competition is weaker. The product in the preceding table would compete well on both price and style against X, on price against competitor Y, and on style against competitor Z. Competitor X seems the most vulnerable on two features, price and style, that consumers rate as the most important decision points.

An example of a product launch that was built on a competitive advantage strategy was Sprint's Palm Pre, which was launched in direct competition with Apple's iPhone. The Pre's advantage was multitasking, especially the ability to switch between several open applications and websites.

Locating the Brand Position Let's return now to the concept of a position to see how it is created. In addition to specific product attributes, a number of factors can be used to locate a position for a brand including the following:

• *Superiority Position* Jack Trout suggests that positioning is always easy if something is faster, fancier, safer, or newer.
• *Preemptive Position* Being first in the category often creates category leadership and dominance.
• *Value Position* Walmart's "Always Low Prices" is the epitome of offering good value for the money. Hyundai rode that position through the economic downturn and picked up market share faster than its competitors, passing both Honda and Ford to become the 4th largest automaker in the world.[10]
• *Psychological Position* Often brands are designed around nonproduct differences. For psychological positions, consider these examples: Volvo owns the safety position, Coke owns a position of authenticity for colas ("It's the real thing"), and Hallmark a quality position ("When you care enough to send the very best").
• *Benefit Position* How does the product help the consumer?
• *Usage Position* How, where, and when is the product used and who is using it?
• *Competitor's Strategy* How can the product go head to head with or move completely away from the competition?
• *Category Factors* Is the competition coming from outside the category and, if so, how does the brand compare to these other categories and how does that change the analysis of strengths and weaknesses?

Principle
Strong brands are known for one thing—the test is "What do you think of when you mention the brand's name?"

As we've mentioned the differences have to be distinctive to the brand, as well as important to the consumer. The point is that strong brands become well known for one thing. When you think of Google or eBay, what's the first thing that comes to mind? (Google = search engine; eBay = online auctions.)

James Stengel, former global marketing chief at Procter & Gamble, has developed a new positioning approach that he calls "purpose-based marketing." He points to P&G's Pampers brand, which moved from just keeping babies' bottoms dry to a higher purpose—helping moms nurture healthy, happy babies. The company created new programs offering parenting advice and conducted research on infant-related problems such as sleeping that led to product redesigns.[11]

Many ad campaigns are designed to establish the brand's position by giving the right set of cues about these decision factors to help place the brand in the consumer's mind. If a position is a point in a consumer's mind, planners can map that—in fact, the way planners compare positions is by using a technique called a **perceptual map** that plots all of the competitors on a matrix based on the two most important consumer decision factors. Figure 7.4 illustrates how positions can be mapped for automobiles.

Repositioning Positions are difficult to establish and take years of marketing communication but experts Al and Laura Ries recommend the difficult challenge of **repositioning** when the market changes. Kodak, for example, has always stood for pictures and over the years has owned the moment of capturing an image with a photo: "the Kodak moment." But Kodak also stands for film (think yellow box) and that was the reason for its recent marketplace problems as the camera industry moved to digital formats. Kodak's agency, Ogilvy, developed a repositioning strategy to adapt Kodak's position from "the Moment" to "the gallery"—a place where pictures are kept. This place, of course, can be a digital photo album and that builds on Kodak's tradition and understanding of the importance of pictures in people's lives.

Repositioning, in the view of the Ries's, can only work if the new position is related to the brand's core concept. They are wary of Kodak's move and wonder if the link between the Kodak brand and film is too strong to stretch to digital products. Instead, they recommend using a new brand name for the line of digital products.[12] It will be interesting to see how this repositioning strategy turns out and if Kodak's position can be redefined as galleries of pictures rather than film and photo albums.

For an example of an effective repositioning effort, Ries and Ries point to IBM as a company that repositioned itself from a computer manufacturer to a provider of services. Even though the market for mainframe computers has been declining, they observe that the connection with IBM's brand essence is still there in IBM's new position as a global computer service company. An example comes from China where IBM is marketing an urban-planning tool called Smart City that connects public services and infrastructure projects through information technology. IBM sees China, with its huge public sector and infrastructure projects, as a huge market for its services.

Advertising may express the position, but personal experiences anchor it in the target audience's mind. The role of the brand communication strategy, then, is to relate the product's position to the target market's life experience and associations. The principle in repositioning is to move ahead while at the same time retaining the brand essence. A classic example of an effective repositioning campaign that retains the brand essence as it carves out a new location in consumers' minds is 7-Up, which is described in the *A Matter of Principle* feature.

But sometimes the repositioning strategy may not work. How will it work, for example, when Rolls-Royce unveils an economy car, or at least one that costs a third less than its $380,000 flagship Phantom. Can Rolls use a cheaper car to pump up volume sales or will that strategy dilute the brand's exclusive image?

Brand Communication Strategy

After the objectives, targeting, and positioning have been stated, the next step is to decide the key strategic approach that will deliver the objectives. We'll discuss this in more detail later in this chapter as we explain the "communication brief" created by the account planner to give direction to the creative team. It will also be discussed in more depth in the Chapter 8 on message strategy.

For now, however, consider that the six main effects outlined in the Facets Model all lead to different communication objectives and, therefore, to different strategies. Let's just consider the two

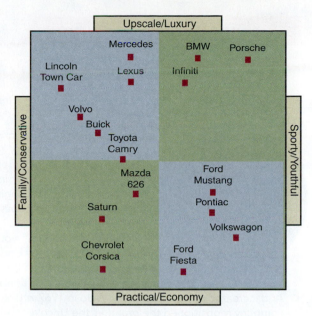

FIGURE 7.4

Perceptual Map

Perceptual maps illustrate the positions occupied by competitors relative to important decision factors. These positions are determined by research into the perceptions of the target market.

A MATTER OF PRINCIPLE

7-Up: The Uncola Story

Bill Barre, *Lecturer, Department of Communication/Journalism, University of Wisconsin-Eau Claire*

How do you turn what was originally a medicinal product (intended to cure hangovers) and then a mixer with whisky into a soft drink without changing anything about the product or its packaging?

If you said "magic," you'd be correct. But it's not the kind of magic you might think. This is branding magic. It's called positioning. And it created magical results for 7-Up in 1967 when the company repositioned the brand as the Uncola.

Preceding 1967, during the first 37 years that 7-Up was marketed, consumers didn't think of 7-Up as a soft drink, just as we don't think of club soda and tonic water as soft drinks. In 1967, a soft drink was a cola, and a cola was a soft drink.

Four people were in the room when the term "uncola" was first uttered. Three of them are deceased—Orville Roesch, 7-Up's ad manager; Bill Ross, creative director at JWT; and Bob Taylor, senior art director at JWT. Charlie Martell was the fourth person and just a young writer at JWT at the time of the meeting.

"I remember the meeting to this day," recalls Martell. "We realized that we had to be a lot more specific if we hoped to change people's minds about 7-Up. We had to find a way to pick up that green bottle (7-Up), pick it up mentally in consumers' minds, and move it over to here, where Coke and Pepsi were. And until we did that, anything we did that smacked of soft-drink advertising was going to be rejected by consumers."

The objective was clear, yet getting there proved to be completely perplexing. "They had to find a way to attach the word *cola* to 7-Up. Nobody had ever done that before. This was before the word *positioning* was even used in advertising and marketing," says John Furr, a management supervisor at JWT at the time.

Martell remembers that the strategy meeting started as it always started for 7-Up. "We got to talking about how to get somebody to move this green bottle from here to there. And I think Orville said something like we had to associate ourselves with the colas. And Bill Ross started talking about, 'Well, how about, maybe, we call ourselves the non-cola.' And Orville nodded. Thought that sounded good. And I chimed in with 'Maybe we could call it the uncola.' And everyone nodded and said that was an interesting thought. Didn't blow anybody away at that point. They filed it away in their collective consciousness. Few days later, came back and said, 'Maybe we just got something here.' Uncola—it did everything we had been wanting to do. In one word, it did it all. It positioned 7-Up as a cola, yet not a cola. We said, 'Hey . . . let's make some advertising.'"

Today, the 7-Up Uncola campaign is regarded as perhaps the classic example of brand repositioning—and a classic example of how the right brand positioning can lead to marketing magic.

---

most basic approaches, which we sometimes refer to as appealing to the head or the heart. **Hard-sell approaches** use reasons to *persuade* consumers, whereas **soft-sell approaches** build an *image* for a brand and touch consumers' emotions. An ad trumpeting a special reduced price on a tire or claims about its performance is an example of a hard-sell approach. On the other hand, the long-running Michelin ad campaign that shows a baby sitting inside a tire is a soft sell; it symbolizes the brand's safety and reliability with an image that touches your emotions. Go back to the four military ads in the positioning discussion and decide which are hard sell and which are soft sell.

In addition to brand position, let's also consider how a consumer response to messages creates a brand perception. Brand managers use many terms to explain how they think branding works, but they all relate in some way to communication. To better understand how a brand can be linked to a perception, we propose an outline of the communication dimensions of branding using the same six effects we presented in the Facets Model in Chapter 4:

Advertiser's Brand Objective	Consumer's Response
Create **brand identity**	**See/Hear**
Cue **brand personality, liking**	**Feel**
Cue **brand position, understanding**	**Think/Understand**
Cue **brand image**	**Connect**
Create **brand promise, preference**	**Believe**
Inspire **brand loyalty**	**Act/Do**

- *Brand Identity* A brand identity must be distinctive. In other words it only represents one particular product within a category, and it must be recognizable and, therefore, memorable. Recognizing the brand means that the consumer knows the brand's identification markers—name, logo, colors, typeface, design, and slogan—and can connect those marks with a past experience or message. All of these can be controlled by the advertiser. The Billings brand identity campaign described earlier in *The Inside Story* included brand reminders in places, as well as conventional marketing communication materials.

- *Brand Personality and Liking* Brand personality—the idea that a brand takes on familiar human characteristics, such as loving (Hallmark, Kodak), competent (IBM), trustworthy (Volvo, Michelin), or sophisticated (Mercedes, Hermes, Rolex)—contributes an affective dimension to the meaning of a brand. Green Giant, for example, built its franchise on the personality of the friendly giant who watches over his valley and makes sure that Green Giant vegetables are fresh, tasty, nutritious, and appealing to kids. Larry Kelley and Donald Jugenheimer explain in their account planning textbook that it is important to measure the way these personality traits are associated with a brand or a competitor's brand. They observe, "Sometimes it is as important to understand what your brand isn't as much as what it is."[13] The point is to profile the brand as if it were a person, someone you like.

The Billings airport used the new "Trailhead" identity campaign in its interior architecture as a welcome to the community and a statement of the Billings brand identity.

- *Brand Position and Understanding* What does it stand for? Brand strategists sometimes focus on the *soul* or *essence* of the brand. This is related to position, but it goes deeper into the question of what makes the brand distinctive. As Jack Trout explained, "You have to stand for something," and it has to be something that matters to consumers.[14] Kodak is a classic example of a brand with a soul, one deeply embedded in personal pictures and memories. Hallmark's soul is found in the expression of sentiment. Brand essence is also apparent when a brand dominates or defines its category. Category leadership often comes from being the first brand in the market—and with that comes an ownership position. ESPN, for example, owns sports information, Silk is *the* soy milk drink, Starbucks created the high-end coffeehouse, and eBay owns the world of online auctions.

- *Brand Image* Understanding brand meaning involves understanding the symbolism and associations that create **brand image,** the mental impression consumers construct for a product. The richness of the brand image determines the quality of the relationship and the strength of the associations and emotional connections that link a customer to a brand. Advertising researchers call this **brand linkage.**

- *Brand Promise and Brand Preference* A brand is sometimes defined as a promise because it establishes an expectation based on familiarity, consistency, and predictability. And believing the brand promise leads to brand preference and intention to buy. That's what has driven McDonald's to its position as a worldwide leader in the fast-food category. You know what to expect when you walk into a McDonald's anywhere in the world—quality fast food at a reasonable price.

- *Brand Loyalty* A personal experience with a brand can develop into a brand relationship, which is a connection over time that results in customers preferring the brand—thus brand loyalty—and buying it over and over. People have unique relationships with the brands they buy and use regularly, and this is what makes them brand loyal. The company's attitude toward its customers is another factor in loyalty.

To put all this together, a brand perception is created by a number of different fragments of information, feelings, and personal experiences with a brand. You could say that a brand is an *integrated perception*[15]—in other words, all of these different aspects of brand communication work together to create brand meaning. In the best of all worlds, these meanings would be

Principle
A brand is an integrated perception that includes fragments of information, feelings, and personal experience, all of which come together to give the brand meaning.

ALLY's ALLEY.

Carl Ally. Tough manager, persuasive salesman, creative rebel. Founder of Carl Ally, Inc., an agency noted for clear and to-the-point advertising that works with devastating effectiveness. Here, from a recent interview, are some verbal ten-strikes that went rolling right down Ally's alley.

On ad effectiveness:

"You have to satisfy three groups of people if you want an ad to work. The people who make the ad. The people who pay for the ad. And the people who read the ad. If you aren't smart enough to satisfy all three groups, the whole thing will be a bummer."

On what makes a great agency:

"Great clients make great agencies, not vice-versa. If you have an agency that produces great work, but the clients won't publish the work, you're not going to get anywhere. We've been lucky. We've had some very bright, very tough, very talented, very daring clients. They've given us our head. And that's what's made us. Clients make agencies -- good or bad. It's easy for some agency guy to come up with a wild idea. If it bombs, he can go and get another job. But it takes a lot of courage for a client to put his money behind that idea. Because if it bombs, the whole company can go down the drain."

On manipulation:

"Advertising doesn't manipulate society. Society manipulates advertising. Advertisers respond to social trends. Agencies respond to advertisers. It's that simple. The advertising business only reflects the moods of advertisers -- and their moods only reflect the moods of the people they want to sell."

On making great ads:

"Look, it's easy to say water is wet and fire is hot. But it takes something special to figure out that if you put water on fire, the fire will go out. That's what I really enjoy about this business, the whole thing of figuring out what you can do that will make a real difference. Then there's execution, the technical stuff. We're great, technically -- but so are a lot of people. The real trick is figuring out what the substance of an ad should be, and then in handling that substance in the best way possible."

On budgets:

"Good work begets good results. Results beget bigger budgets. Federal Express started with us at $300,000. This year, they'll spend $3 million. Next year, maybe $5 million. Why? Because they know that the money they put into advertising comes back to them multiplied. That's what the advertising business is all about."

On greatness:

"There's a tiny percentage of all the work that's great. And a tiny percentage that's lousy. But most of the work -- well, it's just there. That's no knock on advertising. How many great restaurants are there? Most aren't good nor bad, they're just adequate. The fact is, excellence is tough to achieve in any field. But you have to try."

On The Wall Street Journal:

"I'm a writer, a wordsmith. I started as a copywriter. I was a creative director. I began by writing tons -- literally -- tons of copy. So I like The Journal because it is great copy. I use The Journal because I'm in business. And if you're trying to run a business, make it grow, you need The Journal. I put a lot of advertising in The Journal because I know advertising has to make things happen. The Journal gives me the kind of platform I need. The kind of advertising we do -- plain, honest, no nonsense, but with flair and imagination -- works like crazy in The Journal. The Journal's helped us build an advertising agency because it's helped us build the business of the people for whom we work."

CLASSIC

This ad that features Carl Ally is one in a campaign series that the *Wall Street Journal* placed in advertising trade publications. The long-running campaign began in 1975 and featured leaders in advertising explaining their views on how advertising works and why the *Wall Street Journal* is a good medium in which to advertise.

consistent from one customer to another, but because of the vagaries of personal experience, different people have different impressions of a brand.

Emotional branding is one way to anchor a brand perception. As we have said, emotion is a powerful tool in marketing communication and brand liking leads to trust and loyalty. Branding expert John Williams explains, "Research shows that reason and emotions differ in that reason generates conclusions but not necessarily actions, while emotions more frequently lead to actions."[16] Brand liking is the most powerful differentiator.

The challenge to advertisers is to manage their communication efforts so the fragments fit together to form a coherent and integrated brand impression. An example of creating a brand meaning that connects with its audience is the classic *Wall Street Journal* campaign that ran for 25 years in advertising trade publications and established the *Journal* as a premier medium for advertising. You can find many of the ads from this campaign at *www.aef.com/industry/careers/2026.*

Campaign Strategies and Management

Once the situation has been analyzed and the objectives stated, planners decide *how to achieve* the objectives. That calls for a general statement of strategy. The general strategy that guides a campaign can be described in several ways. For example a strategy can focus on branding, positioning, countering the competition, or creating category dominance. Maybe the strategy is designed to change consumers' perception of the brand's price or price–value relationship. The strategy may also seek to increase the size of the market or what marketers call **share of wallet,** the amount customers spend on the brand. Other marketing efforts might involve launching a new brand or a brand extension or moving the brand into a new market.

The important thing to remember, as marketing professor Julie Ruth explains,[17] is that planners have to first analyze the situation to arrive at a great strategy before racing ahead to think about tactics. The decision to expand the market (strategy) by increasing share of wallet (objective) is implemented through promotional tactics ("buy four and get one free").

Another factor in the brand communication strategy is determining the role and importance of the brand's competitive position and how to respond to competitor's messages. During the recession, for example, a number of major brands, such as Dunkin' Donuts, Burger King, and Campbell's Soup developed highly competitive advertising. Domino's Pizza, for example, used an aggressive campaign comparing its oven-baked sandwiches as tasting better than Subway's hoagies. This is a strategy often seen in economic downturns, which analysts describe as "a dogfight" for market share.[18]

Other strategy decisions involve the use of a celebrity spokesperson who becomes the face of the brand. A crisis in emotional branding happened when celebrity superstar Tiger Woods was caught up in a sex scandal. That event moved him from one of the most respected celebrity endorsers to a flawed figure with questionable integrity. His sponsors, including Nike and Accenture, among others, had to decide how to relate their brands not only to his long-time dominance of golf, but also his loss of honor. It's not just the brand images that were threatened by Tiger's infidelities; economists estimate the loss to shareholders of his nine corporate sponsors as close to $12 billion.[19]

For another example, American Express sponsored a four-minute humorous online commercial featuring comedian Jerry Seinfeld and an animated Superman that was designed to create *brand liking.* The two sidekicks play the role of neurotic New Yorkers complaining about such earth-shaking topics as the amount of mayonnaise on their tuna sandwiches. They also relate the benefits of using an American Express card. The message is soft sell and embedded in a gag, which makes the commercial feel more like cinema than advertising. Seinfeld jokes that it isn't going to be interrupted by a commercial because it is a commercial.[20]

Once the strategies have been identified, the next step is implementation. Next we discuss the budgeting and evaluation aspects of implementation. The budget is a critical part of planning an advertising campaign.

An online mini-film commercial for American Express featuring Jerry Seinfeld was designed to entertain and create brand liking. It also generated buzz, which extended its impact through the power of word of mouth.

Budgeting   A $50,000 budget will only stretch so far and probably will not be enough to cover the costs of television advertising in most markets. Microsoft, for example, used a $300 million ad blitz to launch its Windows 7 operating system in 2009. The budget also determines how many targets and media plans a company or brand can support and the length of time the campaign can run.

Determining the total appropriation allocated to advertising is not an easy task. Typically, a dollar amount, say $370,000, is budgeted for advertising during the budget planning process (just before the end of the fiscal year). The big budgeting question at the marketing mix and marketing communication mix level is: How much do we need to spend? Let's examine five common budgeting methods used to answer that question:

- *Historical Method* Historical information is the source for this common budgeting method. A budget may simply be based on last year's budget, with a percentage increase for inflation or some other marketplace factor. This method, although easy to calculate, has little to do with reaching advertising objectives.
- *Objective-Task Method* The **objective-task method** looks at the objectives for each activity and determines the cost of accomplishing each objective. For example, what will it cost to make 50 percent of the people in the market aware of this product? This method's advantage is that it develops the budget from the ground up so that objectives are the starting point.
- *Percentage-of-Sales Method* The **percentage-of-sales method** compares the total sales with the total advertising (or marketing communication) budget during the previous year or the average of several years to compute a percentage. This technique can also be used across an industry to compare the expenditures of different product categories on advertising. For example, if a company had sales of $5 million last year and an advertising budget of $1 million, then the *ratio* of advertising to sales would be 20 percent. If the marketing manager predicts *sales* of $6 million for next year, then the ad budget would be $1.2 million. How can we calculate the percentage of sales and apply it to a budget? Follow these two steps:

  Step 1: $\dfrac{\text{Past advertising dollars}}{\text{Past sales}} = \%\text{ of sales}$

  Step 2: $\%\text{ of sales} \times \text{Next year's sales forecast} = \text{New advertising budget}$

- *Competitive Budgets* This method uses competitors' budgets as benchmarks and relates the amount invested in advertising to the product's share of market. This suggests that the advertiser's share-of-advertising voice—that is, the advertiser's media presence—affects the share of attention the brand will receive, and that, in turn, affects the market share the brand can obtain. Here's a depiction of these relationships:

  $$\frac{\text{Share of}}{\text{media voice}} = \frac{\text{Share of}}{\text{consumer mind}} = \frac{\text{Market}}{\text{share}}$$

  Keep in mind that the relationships depicted here are only a guide for budgeting. The actual relationship between *share-of-media voice* (an indication of advertising expenditures) and **share of mind** or share of market depends to a great extent on factors such as the creativity of the message and the amount of clutter in the marketplace.

- *All You Can Afford* When a company allocates whatever is left over to advertising, it is using the "all you can afford" budgeting method. It's really not a method, but rather a philosophy about advertising. Companies using this approach, such as high-tech start-ups driven by product innovation, don't value advertising as a strategic imperative. For example, a company that allocates a large amount of its budget to research and has a superior product may find the amount spent on advertising is less important.

Evaluation: Determining Effectiveness   Evaluation is an important part of an advertising plan because it is the process of determining the effectiveness of a campaign. Evaluation is impossible if the campaign has not established measurable objectives, so this part of the campaign plan specifies how exactly those objectives will be measured. In effect, it is a research proposal. All of these procedures and techniques for post-campaign evaluation will be discussed in more detail in Chapter 19. A tool for setting these measurable objectives is account planning, which provides information about what consumers think and feel in order to determine what the plan needs to do to have impact on the market.

ACCOUNT PLANNING: WHAT IS IT?

As Fallon and Senn outlined in one of their principles earlier in this chapter, the key to effective advertising is a powerful consumer insight, a central emotional truth about a customer's relationship with a brand.

When the Eight O'Clock coffee brand, for example, wanted to know more about its audience to better target its message, it used videotaped observational research to identify key insights into how people relate to coffee. Rather than a rosy sunrise, the tapes showed that it was a struggle to get moving. "In real life," the strategic planner concluded, "people stumble around, trying to get kids out of bed. Coffee is the fuel that gets them dressed, fed, and out the door." On other tapes, it also showed that coffee was the reward for mom after the kids are out the door. "I have my cup of coffee when the kids leave," one mom observed. "It's my first moment to take a breather. And it gives me energy."[21]

Account planning is the tool that analyzes the research to uncover these consumer insights. Insight—that's what happens when the light bulb goes off and the planner sees something in a new way. As in the Eight O'Clock coffee example, the planner struck gold by finding out that coffee is the fuel that gets adults, particularly moms, through the morning rush—and it's also the reward for surviving that busy routine. From this insight come clues about how and when to reach the target audience and what to say to her. Here's the planner's mission:

- *Who?* Who are you trying to reach and what insight do you have about how they think, feel, and act? How should they respond to your advertising message?
- *What?* What do you say to them? What directions from the consumer research are useful to the creative team?
- *Where?* How and where will you reach them? What directions from the consumer research are useful to the media team?

Account planning is the research and analysis process used to gain knowledge of the consumer that is expressed as a key *consumer insight* about how people relate to a brand or product. An **account planner,** then, is a person in an agency who uses a disciplined system to research a brand and its customer relationships to devise advertising (and other marketing communication) message strategies that are effective in addressing consumer needs and wants. Account planning agencies are based in research but focus on deriving meanings about consumers. Hall & Partners, for example, has noted that with the new social media, the walls between private life and public life have been breached. (Check the company out at *www.hall-and-partners.com.*) In case you're interested in account planning as a career, here is an actual job description for a vice president for global consumer insights for a major apparel company:

The role of the VP, Global Consumer Insights, is to create competitive advantage by delivering fact-based consumer/customer understanding and insights that facilitate speed and accuracy of strategic and tactical decision-making across all critical parts of the organization. In short, turning data into Insights, and then into Action. The planner will accomplish this by placing consumers first, integrating their "voices" into the planning process, and creating sustaining value at the corporate and brand levels.

As the job description suggests, the account planning function develops the marketing communication strategy with other members of the client and agency team and guides its implementation in the creative work and media planning. Here's an example from Dunkin' Donuts of how account planning works to uncover, in this case, the barriers to purchasing fancy coffee drinks. This mini-case was provided by Regina Lewis, a member of this book's Advisory Board and former vice president of consumer and brand insights at Dunkin':[22]

We found through our research that people wanted to try espresso drinks like lattes and cappuccinos, but they were intimidated and thought such fancy coffee drinks were an ordeal to order. Dunkin' Donuts, of course, is known for its coffee and we felt that to be a great coffee player, we had to have an espresso line. But our brand has always been hot regular coffee for average Joe. What we realized was that there was a place in the marketplace for espresso-based drinks for everybody. It doesn't have to be a fancy treat. We learned that a lot of people like the milky steamed beverages, but they were intimidated by whether they would know how to order them.

When we launched our new line, we used the positioning umbrella of the *democratization of espresso*. We dramatically changed the way our customers view a latte and eliminated the whole barista thing. With push-button machines, we created a world where you can get espresso through the drive-through in less than two minutes. We made espresso available for everybody and we also priced our drinks under Starbucks. We launched with a big public relations campaign titled "The Espresso Revolution—a Shot Being Fired in New England."

In contrast to account managers who are seen as the voice of the client, account planners are described as the voice of the consumer. As London's Account Planning Group (APG) explains it, "The job is to ensure that an understanding of consumer attitudes and behavior is brought to bear at every stage of communications development via continuous involvement in the process."[23]

Account planners don't design the creative strategy for an ad, because this is usually a team process with the participation of the creative people. Rather, the planner evaluates consumers' relationships with the brand to determine the kind of message to which they might respond. Ultimately, the objective is to help the creative team come up with a better idea—making their creative process easier and faster. Susan Mendelsohn, a leader in the U.S. account planning industry and another member of this book's Advisory Board, explains the account planner's task as the following[24]:

1. Understand the meaning of the brand.
2. Understand the target audience's relationship to the brand.
3. Articulate communication strategies.
4. Prepare creative briefs based on an understanding of the consumer and brand.
5. Evaluate the effectiveness of the communication in terms of how the target reacts to it (so that planners can keep learning more about consumers and brand communication).

The Research Foundation

As we said at the beginning of this chapter, understanding begins with consumer research, which is at the core of account planning. Some advertisers, such as Johnson & Johnson, insist that consumer researchers and creative teams need to work closely together.[25] That is the role, if not the goal, of most account planners.

Planners use a wide variety of research tools to do "insight mining." In a sense they are social anthropologists who are in touch with cultural and social trends and understand how they take on relevance in people's lives. To do that, the account planner is an *integrator* (who brings all of the information together) and a *synthesizer* (who expresses what it all means in one startlingly simple statement). The *A Matter of Practice* feature about anti-smoking campaigns provides insight about the role research plays in strategic decision-making for campaigns.

Principle

The account manager is seen as the voice of the client, and the account planner is seen as the voice of the consumer.

A MATTER OF PRACTICE

"Just Give Me My One Vice:" Collegea Students and Smoking

Joyce M. Wolburg, Professor and Associate Dean, Marquette University

A few years ago, I asked the students in my research class to bring in samples of magazine ads. One student came with anti-smoking messages, which prompted a classmate to say defiantly, "Those ads make me so mad, they just make me want to light up a cigarette." One ad was from the Lorillard Tobacco Company's Youth Smoking Prevention Program and used the slogan, "Tobacco is Whacko." The other was from the American Legacy Foundation's "truth" campaign and told readers, "Your pee contains urea. Thanks to tobacco companies, so do cigarettes. Enjoy." The student's response made me realize that if this reaction is common among other college students, millions of dollars devoted to changing attitudes and behavior toward smoking are missing the mark. As a qualitative researcher, I wanted to find out and decided to investigate what's going on.

Using individual interviews among students, my first revelation was that college student smokers and non-smokers have dramatically different views of anti-smoking messages. Among other findings, non-smokers championed the ads—in fact, the more insulting the better. Many expressed feelings that they have suffered the effects of cigarette smoke long enough, and "it's about time someone took responsibility for the deadly addiction that kills so many people." Anti-smoking messages also reinforced their decision not to smoke. Smokers, on the other hand, rarely championed the ads and frequently showed defiance toward the ads. "I am going to die from something someday, so why shouldn't this be my cause of death?" Students also felt a sense of entitlement toward smoking. "All I'm doing is smoking. I'm not doing heavy drugs or robbing banks or murdering people. This is as bad as I get. Let me have my cigarette. "

Psychologists have long known that when people are told to change their behavior, they will dig in their heels and resist change if they feel their freedom is at stake. And initiatives against smoking and binge drinking have been known to backfire—the so-called "dark side" of social marketing campaigns. Although many smokers believe that the messages are effective for others, the fact that they started smoking proves to them that anti-smoking messages don't work. When they started smoking, they were well aware of the health risks—"you would have to be a moron to not know that it kills"—and they didn't find the ads persuasive—"there isn't an ad out there that would get me to quit." Two things they didn't count on were how addictive smoking is and how quickly people become addicted.

I was convinced that anti-smoking messages were not connecting with this audience and special cessation strategies were needed. I began to wonder how students who have succeeded in quitting were able to accomplish the task. A second qualitative study explored their decisions about quitting and examined the strategies that worked versus those that failed. By far the most common reason for quitting was a personal health scare, which convinced them that they were vulnerable to the risks after all; however, others quit because they no longer identified with smokers or were afraid they were losing control to nicotine. Unfortunately, they were so optimistic that quitting would be easy that they weren't prepared for failure. Every student interviewed made multiple attempts before eventually succeeding

Every student also had a quit date in mind—"by my next birthday, by the time I graduate, by the time I get my first job, by the time I get married, by the time I have children . . . " But they didn't have a plan for how to do it. One of the most common problems was not anticipating the times and places that triggered smoking, and bars seemed to be at the top of everyone's list of places that triggered the impulse to smoke. The association between drinking and smoking was so strong that more than one student had to avoid bars for a period of time until they could handle the temptation.

Most students wanted to quit "cold turkey" without any help from others because they saw it as a badge of honor. However, this strategy only worked for a few. Other students sought support from various sources including the campus health facility. One met regularly with a physician's assistant, who provided support and held him accountable. "Once a week, I would go see this guy and it gave me a sense of accountability. I knew that if I smoked,

I would have to tell him. Not only would I disappoint myself, but I would disappoint him."

Given these insights, I began to wonder if existing cessation programs are addressing the needs of students. I examined various online cessation programs—one from a non-profit organization, one from a government organization and one from the tobacco industry—and found that most offered tips based on the same strategies that worked with these students, but few communicated in a style that students could relate to. Many used testimonials from older smokers, who quit for reasons that were not relevant to most students, such as wanting to avoid exposing their children to secondhand smoke. One program offered targeted materials to groups including smokers over the age of 50, recent quitters, African-American smokers, and Hispanic smokers, but not college students.

So why do college students need a campaign specifically designed for them? One reason is that they operate on a different calendar than others.

Holidays, such as Halloween and St. Patrick's Day, are heavy drinking occasions on most campuses, and with heavy drinking comes heavy smoking. Events that could encourage them to quit smoking are not well timed either. The Great American Smokeout traditionally takes place on the third Thursday in November, days before they are leaving campus to go home for the Thanksgiving holiday.

So, what's the next step? Certainly, it is to implement these findings into a campus-wide campaign. I don't yet know the exact message, but the strategy will have to include storytelling about what worked and what didn't to engage students' interest. Messages must also originate from students in order to achieve relevance and gain credibility.

Sources: Joyce Wolburg, 2006, "College Students' Responses to Antismoking Messages: Denial, Defiance, and Other Boomerang Effects," *Journal of Consumer Affairs,* 40 (2) 294-323; Joyce Wolburg, 2009, "Misguided Optimism among College Student Smokers: Leveraging their Quit Smoking Strategies for Smoking Cessation Campaigns," *Journal of Consumer Affairs,* 43 (2) 305-331)..

Consumer Insight: The Fuel of Big Ideas

Advertising is sometimes thought to be an idea factory, but account planners look at advertising as an insight factory. As Mendelsohn says, "Behind every famously great idea, there is a perhaps less flashy, but immensely powerful insight." Insights are the fuel that fires the ideas. A great insight always intersects with the interests of the consumer and the features of the brand by identifying the value that the brand has for the consumer.

Through the process of strategic and critical thinking, the planner interprets consumer research in terms of a key consumer insight that uncovers the relevance factor—the reason why consumers care about a brand message. Consumer insights reveal the inner nature of consumers' thinking, including such things as mind-sets, moods, motivations, desires, aspirations, and motives that trigger their attitudes and actions.

Finding the "a-ha" in a stack of research reports, data, and transcripts, which is referred to as **insight mining,** is the greatest challenge for an account planner. The Account Planning Group (APG) association describes this process on its website (*www.apg.org.uk*) as "peering into nooks and crannies without losing sight of the big picture in order to identify a key insight that can transform a client's business."

Mendelsohn describes insight mining as "a deep dive" into the meaning of a brand looking for "major truths." She explains that the planner engages in unearthing the relationship (if there is any) that a target audience has with a brand or product and what role that brand plays in their lives. Understanding the brand/consumer relationship is important because account planners are taking on the position of the agency's brand steward. As Abigail Hirschhorn, chief strategic planning officer at DDB explains, "Our work puts our clients in touch with the souls of their brands."[26]

The account planning tool kit is made up of questions that lead to useful insights culled from research. Here is a set of questions that can lead to useful insights:

- What is a realistic response objective (perception, knowledge, feelings, attitudes, symbolic meanings, behavior) for this target group?
- What are the causes of their lack of response?
- What are the barriers to the desired response?
- What could motivate them to respond in the desired way?
- What is the role of each element in the communication mix to motivate them or remove a barrier?

Principle
A great insight intersects with the interests of the consumer and the features of the brand.

Here's an example of how data analysis works: Imagine you are working on a cookie account. Here's your brand share information:

	2009 Share (%)	2010 Share (%)
Choco Nuts (your brand)	50	40
Sweet 'n Crunchy (your main competitor)	25	30

What's the problem with this situation? Obviously your brand is losing market share to your primary competitor. As a result, one of your goals might be to use a marketing communication mix to drive higher levels of sales. But that goal is so broad that it would be difficult to determine whether communication is sufficient to solve the problem. Let's dig deeper and consider another set of data about household (HH) purchases in a year.

	2009 HH Purchases	2010 HH Purchases
Choco Nuts	4	3
Sweet 'n Crunchy	2.5	3

What problem can you identify here? It looks like your loyal brand users are reducing their purchases at the same time Sweet 'n Crunchy customers are increasing their purchases. It may even be that some of your customers are switching over to Sweet 'n Crunchy. A strategy based on this information might be to convince people that your brand tastes better and to remind your loyal customers of the reasons they have preferred your brand. Those goals can be accomplished by marketing communication.

When you combine the two pieces of information and think about it, another insight might explain this situation. Perhaps people are simply eating fewer cookies. If that's a problem, then the communication opportunity lies in convincing people to return to eating cookies. That is more of a *category sell* problem (sell cookies) rather than a *competitive sell* (set the brand against the competition). In the Choco Nuts example, it would take more research to know which situation applies here. Here's a summary of these two different strategic approaches.

	Competitive/Brand Sell	Category Sell
What?	Challenger brand	Leader brand
Who?	Loyal buyers	Medium/light/lapsed buyers
What effect?	Compare cookie brands	Compare against other snacks
Objective?	Increase share of wallet	Increase total category sales
Message?	"Our cookies are better than theirs"	"Cookies are better than candy or salty snacks"

The important dimensions account planners seek to understand in planning brand strategies include relationship, perceptions, promise, and point of differentiation. Most importantly, planners are looking for clues about the brand's *meaning,* which is usually phrased in terms of the brand essence (core, soul), personality, or image, as the SeaPort outdoor boards illustrate.

The Communication Brief

The outcome of strategic research usually reaches agency creative departments in the form of a strategy document called a **communication brief** or **creative brief,** which explains the consumer insight and summarizes the basic strategy decisions. Although the exact form of this document differs from agency to agency and from advertiser to advertiser, the brief is an outline of the message strategy that guides the creative team and helps keep its ideas strategically sound. As the planner's main product, it should be clear, logical, and focused. Here is an outline of a typical communication brief:

• *Problem* What's the problem that communication can solve? (establish position, reposition, increase loyalty, get people involved, increase liking, etc.)
• *Target Audience* To whom do we want to speak? (brand loyal, heavy users, infrequent users, competition's users, etc.)

WELCOME TO THE FAST CLASS. **SEA✦PORT** AIRLINES

DEPART FROM THE HASSLE. **SEA✦PORT** AIRLINES

SHOWCASE

These outdoor boards are for SeaPort Airlines, which serves Seattle, Juneau, Portland, and other West Coast cities. They make a statement about the SeaPort target audience—influential business travelers—and their lifestyle.

These ads were contributed by Karl Schroeder, copywriter at Coates Kokes in Portland, Oregon. A graduate of the University of Oregon advertising program, he was nominated by Professor Charles Frazer.

- *Consumer Insights* What motivates the target? What are the "major truths" about the target's relationship to the product category or brand?
- *Brand Imperatives* What are the important features? What's the point of competitive advantage? What's the brand's position relative to the competition? Also, what's the brand essence, personality, and/or image. Ogilvy & Mather says, "What is the unique personality for the brand? People use products, but they have relationships with brands."
- *Communication Objectives* What do we want customers to do in response to our messages? (perception, knowledge, feelings, symbolic meanings, attitudes and conviction, action)
- *The Proposition or Selling Idea* What is the single thought that the communication will bring to life in a provocative way?
- *Support* What is the reason to believe the proposition? Ogilvy & Mather explains, "We need to give consumers 'permission to believe'—something that allows them to rationalize, whether to themselves or others, what is in reality an emotionally driven brand decision. The support should be focused on the insight or proposition, the truths that make the brand benefit indisputable."
- *Creative Direction* How can we best stimulate the desired response? How can we best say it?
- *Media Imperatives* Where and when should we say it?

Source: This outline was compiled from one contributed by Susan Mendelsohn, as well as from the creative brief outline developed by the Ogilvy agency and presented on its website (*www.ogilvy.com*).

The brief is strategic, but it also should be inspirational. It is designed to ignite the creative team and give a spark to their idea process. A good brief doesn't set up limitations and boundaries but rather serves as a springboard. It is the first step in the creative process. Charlie Robertson, an account planner and brand consultant, likens the brief to a fire starter: "The match is the brief, the ignition is the inspiring dialogue [in the briefing], and the flare is the creative."[27]

PLANNING FOR IMC CAMPAIGNS

An IMC plan follows the same basic outline as an advertising plan. The difference, however, lies with the scope of the plan and the variety of marketing communication areas involved in the effort. The more tools used, the harder it is to coordinate their efforts and maintain consistency across a variety of messages. The objective in IMC planning is to make the most effective and consistent use of all marketing communication functions and to influence or control the impact of other communication elements. Account planner Susan Mendelsohn, who is also a member of this book's Advisory Board, explains the intersections of IMC and account planning in the *A Matter of Practice* feature.

IMC Campaign Planning

Effective IMC plans lead to profitable long-term brand relationships. The emphasis on brand building is one reason account planning is moving beyond advertising and being used in IMC campaign planning. Jon Steel, author of a book on advertising and account planning, says planning works best as it is integrated into the entire communication mix.[28] The three main areas where an IMC plan differs from an advertising plan are objectives, stakeholders, and contact points.

Objectives   IMC objectives are tied to the effects created by the various forms of marketing communication. All marketing communication tools have strengths and weaknesses. You use public relations, for example, to announce something that is newsworthy, whereas you use sales promotion to drive immediate action. Therefore, an IMC plan operates with a set of interrelated objectives that specify the strategies for all of the different tools. Each area has a set of objectives similar to those outlined earlier for advertising; these will be presented in more detail in chapters later in the book that relate to those areas. For discussion at this point, however, the following list presents the main IMC areas in terms of their primary effects:

- *Public Relations* Announce news; affect attitudes and opinions; maximize credibility and likability; create and improve stakeholder relationships.
- *Consumer Sales Promotion* Stimulate behavior; generate immediate response, intensify needs, wants, and motivations; reward behavior; stimulate involvement and relevance; create pull through the channel.
- *Trade Sales Promotion* Build industry acceptance; push through the channel; motivate cooperation; energize sales force, dealers, distributors.
- *Point-of-Purchase* Increase immediate sales; attract attention at decision point; create interest; stimulate urgency; encourage trial and impulse purchasing.
- *Direct Marketing* Stimulate sales; create personal interest and relevance; provide information; create acceptance, conviction.
- *Sponsorship and Events* Build awareness; create brand experience, participation, interaction, involvement; create excitement.
- *Packaging* Increase sales; attract attention at selection point; deliver product information; create brand reminder.
- *Specialties* Reinforce brand identity; continuous brand reminder; reinforce satisfaction; encourage repeat purchase; reward loyal customers.

Stakeholders   We introduced the concept of stakeholders in the IMC introduction in Chapter 2, but let's look a little deeper into this concept. The target in an IMC plan includes more than just consumers. The term **stakeholder** refers to any group of people who have a stake in the success of a company or brand. These audiences include all those who might influence the purchase of

A MATTER OF PRACTICE

The Crossover between Account Planning and IMC

By Susan Mendelsohn, Ph.D., President, Susan Mendelsohn Consultants

The distinction between account planning and IMC is becoming blurred. In today's multifaceted business world, account planners have to become immersed in all aspects of a client's business in order to address their numerous stakeholders, not just their consumers. To accomplish this, account planners first need to learn about most aspects of a company as possible using the techniques described earlier in this book. Second, planners must address every part of a business that could influence and impact the brand/product. Finally, the planner must craft meaningful communication messages and programs for each constituent.

Getting to know the unique components of each business and then understanding the interplay of these components is the account planners' new challenge. The planner must use multiple sources to uncover useful brand/product information about each business.

Example one: with nonprofits such as a museum, an account planner might need to examine the appropriate scientific community, government agencies and foundations, donors/board of trustees/friends of the museum, and the public. It might be necessary to alter the communication messages for these different groups from the overarching main message of the museum in order to address the needs of each individual constituent.

Example two: when working with packaged-good companies, planners have to address industry specific business issues and develop an appropriate contact point mix. Here, the account planner typically considers the different needs and perspectives of consumer brands, marketing, cafés/kiosks, retail, sales force, and food service (restaurants, hotels, convenience stores).

Example three: addressing insurance or financial institutions, the mix changes again. Planners in the insurance area often examine consumers (current and prospective policy holders), corporate decision makers, sales agents, stockholders, and the financial community (including Wall Street).

It's an exciting time to be involved in the field of account planning. The planner's role is expanding and becoming more complex is order to address the new challenges of of business, branding, and fragmented communication.

---

products and the success of a company's marketing program, as the table below shows. Employees are particularly important and their support or buy-in for marketing, advertising, and marketing communication programs is managed through an activity called **internal marketing.** Susan Mendelsohn, for example, describes the targets for one of her snack clients as brand marketing consumers, café and kiosk customers, food service operations, and sales staff.

Types of Stakeholder Audiences

Corporate Level	*Marketing Level*	*Marcom Level*
Employees	Consumers	Target audiences
Investors, financial community (analysts, brokers, and the financial press)	Customers	Target stakeholders
	Stakeholders	Employees
	Market segments	Trade audiences
Government bodies and agencies	Distributors, dealers, retailers, and others in the distribution channel	Local community
Regulatory bodies	Suppliers and vendors, including agencies	Media (general, special interest, trade)
Business partners	Competitors	Consumer activist groups
		General public
		Opinion leaders

An important thing to remember is that people don't simply line up in one box or another. Here's a new principle: the **Sixth Principle of IMC,** which states that *stakeholders overlap*. Not

Sixth Principle of IMC
Stakeholders overlap.

only do they play different roles, they also talk to one another. Employees, for example, may also be customers, shareholders, and members of the local community, perhaps even elected officials. Their primary medium is word of mouth, which is another reason why this type of communication is so important in IMC programs. The fact of overlapping membership complicates message strategy and demands that there be a certain core level of consistency in all brand messages both from a company but also within stakeholder conversations.

Contact Points   IMC programs are designed to maximize all the contacts that a consumer and other stakeholders might have with a brand. As we explained in Chapter 2, **contact points,** also called **touch points,** are all the ways and places where a person can come into contact with a brand, all the points where a message is delivered about the brand. Contact points can be advertising and traditional marketing communication messages, but they can also include all of the other ways a brand communicates through personal experiences. This leads to the **Seventh Principle of IMC:** *all contact points deliver brand messages.* These messages can be both good and bad, creating positive or negative feelings. Marcom managers hope to maximize and leverage the good ones and minimize the bad ones.

Seventh Principle of IMC

All contact points deliver brand messages.

Synergy and Strategic Consistency

Given that an IMC plan involves a lot of messages delivered through multiple media at many different contact points, as well as interactive communication, the marcom planner's biggest concern is creating consistent messages. The ultimate difference between an advertising campaign and an IMC campaign is the creation, development, delivery, and evaluation of multiplatform messages. For that reason, IMC planners are looking for ways to intensify the synergy of the messages so that the brand impact is greater than what can be delivered by any one type of message. This leads to the **Eighth Principle of IMC:** *consistency drives synergy.*

Eighth Principle of IMC

Consistency drives synergy.

Synergy is particularly important for marketers concerned about the efficiency of their marketing communication who are looking for ways to maximize the cost efficiency of their budgets. Andy Polansky, president of the Weber Shandwick agency, cautions managers to be efficient by making all communication efforts align with audience interests "so there is strategic consistency across how you are marketing online, in-person and in traditional media."[29]

The problem is that we know various stakeholders have different types of bonds with a brand, so the message, by necessity, will be different for different audiences. Kellogg's doesn't talk to moms the same way it talks to kids about a kid's cereal, such as Froot Loops. And it certainly has a different message for regulators at the Food and Drug Administration and activists concerned about children's health, as well as those messages for the investment community including its own shareholders. It isn't that the messages are inconsistent, they are just different in that they address different concerns and issues of the various stakeholder audiences. What is common, however, is faithfulness to the brand image and position. That's what we mean by **strategic consistency**—messages vary with the interest of the stakeholder but the brand strategy remains the same.

Synergy is an organizational problem, one that calls for **cross-functional planning.** In other words, everyone involved in delivering messages or responding to consumer messages needs to be involved in planning the campaign so no off-strategy messages undercut the consistency of the effort.

Looking Ahead

Strategic consistency is the result of carefully researched marketing communication plans. The actual messages that bring the strategy to life are also a result of strategic planning, but also creative thinking. Part 3 of this book will review the creative side of marketing communication beginning with Chapter 8, which continues the strategy discussion in terms of message strategy.

IT'S A WRAP

Winning the Coke Zero Infringement Case

So how well did the Coke Zero campaign strategies work in exciting the interest of young males in a lower calorie soft drink and delivering the message that Coke Zero tastes similar to real Coke?

To evaluate the effectiveness, return to the three measurable objectives: increase brand awareness, motivate the target audience to try Coke Zero, and convince men ages 18 to 34 that Coke Zero tastes like Coke. Within a year Coke Zero's overall brand awareness far exceeded the goal, achieving awareness with more than 90 percent of its target audience. It succeeded in not only getting the men to know about Coke Zero, nearly half of the target audience of young men 18–34 tried it, too. The campaign was able to increase consumer recognition of the taste similarity message. Four out of 10 people who were interviewed recognized the message that Coke Zero tastes like Coke. The success of achieving the campaign goals is evident.

You might ask if this campaign was beneficial for the Coca-Cola company overall. Could it be that it cannibalized its audience by shifting Coke drinkers to Coke Zero drinkers? John D. Sicher, Jr., editor and publisher at *Beverage Digest*, believes the campaign's effects have been positive. He said, "Forty-five percent of Coke Zero sales are incremental rather than borrowed from Diet Coke."

Based on the evidence, this nontraditional campaign, and its unconventional message, Coke Zero was awarded a Silver Effie for effectiveness.

Case closed.

Key Points Summary

1. **What is the difference between objectives, strategies, and tactics in strategic planning and how are the three levels of planning connected?** Objectives are what you want to accomplish, or goals; strategies are how you will accomplish the objectives, or the design or plan; and tactics are the ways in which you implement the strategies, or the execution. The three-tiered process of strategic planning involves a set of cascading objectives and strategies. Corporate objectives and strategies as spelled out in a business plan are achieved through planning at the level of marketing (and other business areas, such as production), and marketing objectives and strategies give direction to marketing communication programs including advertising.

2. **How is a campaign plan constructed, and what are its six basic sections?** An advertising or IMC plan summarizes the strategic decisions in the following areas: situation analysis (background research, SWOTs, key communication problem), objectives, targeting, positioning (features, attributes, differentiation, competitive advantage), strategic approach (branding, positioning, category dominance, marketing mix support, consumer response), and campaign management (budgeting, evaluation).

3. **What is account planning, and how is it used in advertising?** Account planning matches the right message to the right audience and identifies the right media to deliver that message. The three key factors are consumer insight, message strategy direction, and media strategy direction.

4. **In what ways does an IMC plan differ from an advertising plan?** The three additional factors you find discussed in an IMC plan are the stakeholders, the contact points, and a wider set of objectives that identify the interwoven effects of the various marketing communication tools.

Words of Wisdom: Recommended Reading

Avery, Jim, *Advertising Campaign Planning*, Chicago: The Copy Workshop, 2000.

Fallon, Pat, and Fred Senn, *Juicing the Orange: How to Turn Creativity into a Powerful Business Advantage*, Boston: Harvard Business School Press, 2006.

Kelley, Larry, and Donald Jugenheimer, *Advertising Account Planning,* Armonk, NY: M.E. Sharpe, 2006.

Parente, Donald, *Advertising Campaign Strategy: A Guide to Marketing Communication Plans,* 4th ed., Florence, KY: South-Western, 2005.

Ries, Al, and Jack Trout, *Positioning: The Battle for Your Mind,* New York: McGraw-Hill, 1981 (20th anniversary ed., 2000).

Schultz, Don, and Beth Barnes, *Strategic Advertising Campaigns,* 4th ed., Lincolnwood, IL: NTC, 1995.

Steel, Jon, *Truth, Lies and Advertising: The Art of Account Planning,* Hoboken, NJ: Wiley, 1998.

Weichselbaum, Hart (Ed.), *Readings in Account Planning,* Chicago: The Copy Workshop, 2000.

Key Terms

account planner, p. 210
account planning, p. 210
benchmarked, p. 199
brand image, p. 207
brand linkage, p. 207
campaign plan, p. 194
communication brief, p. 214
competitive advantage, p. 204
contact points, p. 218
creative brief, p. 214
cross-functional planning, p. 218
feature analysis, p. 204

features, p. 202
hard-sell approaches, p. 206
insight mining, p. 213
internal marketing, p. 217
marketing plan, p. 192
mission statement, p. 192
objectives, p. 190
objective-task method, p. 209
parity products, p. 202
percentage-of-sales
   method, p. 209

perceptual map, p. 205
position, p. 202
product differentiation, p. 202
repositioning, p. 205
return on investment
   (ROI), p. 191
share of market, p. 193
share of mind, p. 209
share of wallet, p. 208
situation analysis, p. 196

soft-sell approaches, p. 206
stakeholder, p. 216
strategic business unit
   (SBU), p. 191
strategic consistency, p. 218
strategic planning, p. 190
strategies, p. 190
SWOT analysis, p. 196
tactics, p. 190
touch points, p. 218

Review Questions

1. Define objectives, strategies, and tactics, and explain how they differ.

2. What information does an advertising plan derive from the business plan? From the marketing plan?

3. What is a situation analysis, and how does it differ from a SWOT analysis?

4. What are the requirements of a measurable objective?

5. Explain how the facets model of advertising effects can be used to structure a set of advertising objectives.

6. What is a position, and how is it established?

7. What is account planning, and what does the account planner bring to an advertising plan?

8. What are the key differences between an advertising plan and an IMC plan?

Discussion Questions

1. Think of a product you purchased recently after seeing an advertisement. Which strategies can you discern in the advertising? Did the advertising help to convince you to purchase the product? How did that work?

2. Luna Pizza is a regional producer of frozen pizza. Its only major competitor is Brutus Bros. The following is a brief excerpt from Luna's situation analysis for the next fiscal year. Estimate the next year's advertising budgets for Luna under each of the following circumstances:

   a. Luna follows an historical method by spending 40 cents per unit sold in advertising, with a 5 percent increase for inflation.

   b. Luna follows a fixed percentage of projected sales method, using 7 percent.

   c. Luna follows a share-of-voice method. Brutus, the primary competitive pizza brand, is expected to use 6 percent of sales for its advertising budget in the next year.

	Actual *Last Year*	*Estimated* *Next Year*
Units sold	120,000	185,000
$ sales	420,000	580,000
Brutus $ sales	630,000	830,000

3. The owners of the Vico brand of organic coconut water believe that it is the next big trend in the bottled water category, except it uses the clear liquid inside young, green coconuts (not coconut milk that is derived from pressing the coconut pulp). Healthy and natural, the product is popular in South America and is becoming a niche market in New York City and other cities with South American immigrant populations. Outline a preliminary situation analysis, objectives, targeting, positioning, and branding strategies. In each section, explain what other information you would need to fully develop this plan.

4. *Three-Minute Debate* You are in a meeting about the strategy for an automotive client who is proposing a new upscale luxury version of an electric car. One of your team members says positioning is an old strategy and no longer useful for modern products because the market is so complex and changes so fast. Another person argues strongly that you need to understand the position in the consumer's mind before you can even begin to develop an advertising strategy. As a team, take one side of this issue, for the launch of this new product and develop your position to present and defend in a class debate.

Take-Home Projects

1. *Portfolio Project* Examine the following websites: *www .lexus.com, www.infiniti.com,* and *www.mercedes-benz .com.* Based on what you find on these sites, compare the positioning strategies for these top-of-the-line SUV models. Analyze the product features, competitive advantage, and points of differentiation.

2. *Mini-Case Analysis* Review the "Coke/Coke Zero Taste Infringement" case that opened and closed this chapter. Assume you are working on this account and have been asked to pull together a presentation for the brand team for the next year of this campaign. What research would you recommend conducting in order to decide if the campaign should be continued? What do you need to find out in order to make this decision?

Team Project: The BrandRevive Campaign

After compiling as much information as you can for your BrandRevive campaign on your brand, the category, and consumers, the next step is to draft a campaign plan for the brand's revitalization.

• Review your research and develop a set of SWOTs and from that analysis the key communication problem to be solved with this campaign.

• Develop a set of objectives for this campaign and explain them.

• Identify the target audience for your campaign and explain your decision.

• Develop a brand positioning strategy for your brand and explain it. In particular, consider the wisdom and feasibility of a repositioning effort.

• Identify the key insight(s) that would make your brand more relevant and explain how you arrived at that conclusion. Summarize your findings about the target market in a creative brief.

• Present your findings in a two-page report and a PowerPoint presentation that is no longer than four slides. In the presentation explain and justify your recommendations.

Hands-On Case

The Century Council

Read the Century Council case in the Appendix before coming to class.

1. Create an outline of what you believe "The Stupid Drink" campaign plan looked like based on this chapter and the case study. Keep it to one page.

2. Develop at least three business objectives and strategies, three communications objectives and strategies, and three media objectives and strategies based on the case study.

3 PRACTICE: WHERE IS CREATIVE HEADED?

The advent of the new century found companies facing unprecedented competition for the attention of customers. It also created a huge challenge for marketing communication creatives who have to create breakthrough messages that will not get lost in the media explosion of the 21st century. The problem is that the more messages that appear, the less effective they are. Overwhelmed consumers often respond by avoiding advertisements and other marketing communication.

The creatives' challenge is to create clutter-busting messages that engage and involve and touch the hearts and minds of the audience. The ads accomplish this by delivering messages that people want to watch, hear, and read. As clutter continues to increase and people take more of the message control into their own hands, the creative stakes get higher. As Professor Karen Mallia explains: "Words and pictures—those are the weapons the creative team uses to produce communication that breaks through indifference and inattention."

The Tools in the Creative Toolbox

Karen L. Mallia,
Assistant Professor, University of South Carolina, and former copywriter/creative director.

Every time media evolve, doomsayers predict the death of the current form. Today, some pundits say the Internet will kill the print medium; others argue we will always have words on paper. Still others look at the growing domination of visual media and predict the utter demise of the written word, frequently with the old saw "a picture is worth a thousand words." (Hmm, that argument is made of words, isn't it?)

As long as human beings use language to think and communicate, words aren't likely to disappear from advertising. Remember, the advent of acrylic didn't stop artists from using watercolors, and television didn't kill radio. And while styles come and go (modern, retro, skinny ties, wide ties, high waists, low rise), the tools in the advertising toolbox will all remain there for the deft to create magical things.

There's no doubt that most marketing communication has moved from a verbal argument to a more emotive, visually based mode of persuasion. Look at historic ads on a timeline, and the average word count drops with each decade.

Great advertising has always been found at the point where the visual and verbal perfectly intersect. Think of the headline on one of DDB's iconic 1960s VW ads: "Lemon." Without that one essential word, you'd have just a picture of a car. Without the summation in "Priceless," the logic of the MasterCard campaign would be lost. Inevitably, the power in the greatest creative work comes from the synergy between words and pictures. Together, an ad's impact increases exponentially.

Take the 2005 Nike women's campaign celebrating body parts ("My butt," "My hips," "My shoulders"). It's visually striking—yet verbally driven. Study every word, and how visual and copy together create an unmistakable brand voice.

No matter what "most" people are doing, there will always be glorious exceptions proving that great creative work solves problems in an unexpected way. ("Zig when others zag." Remember that—always.) In a time of visual dominance, words underpin Mars' "Snacklish" campaign from creative powerhouse TBWA/Chiat/Day. The campaign began with billboards and transit posters using fabricated words in the telegraphic Snickers logotype and coloring: "Hungerectomy," "Peanutopolis," and "Substantialiscious." By 2009, the wordplay had evolved into an entire "language" taught at a viral "university" and featured an online translator.

Even video needs well-chosen words. Writing dialogue for film and video is a particular kind of writing with a style and rules all its own. But the role of copy in video isn't always that obvious. Consider YouTube's most-watched brand video from 2009, Evian's "Skating Babies." (You can view it at *www.youtube.com/watch?v=_PHnRIn74Ag.*) At first you might not see the imprint of the writer, but it's there—in a title card stopping viewers in the middle, and a super at the end. Without that copy, would the video be as meaningful? How would the brand and the story connect? The same is true for the award-winning Cadbury gorilla spot from the United Kingdom. (View it at *www.youtube.com/watch?v=Ow_o78zjo14.*) It wouldn't make any sense without being anchored by the brand's tagline, "A glass and a half full of joy." It wouldn't be advertising, either—just a Phil Collins music video. Creating successful integrated communication means using every weapon in your arsenal. Sometimes the answer is visual; sometimes the sharpest tool is a word. Let's not forget three of the most persuasive words in the English language, and what they can get people to do: "I love you." I dare you to find the picture that says it better.

How do agencies organize, motivate, and inspire their creative people to produce breakthrough marketing communication that engages its target audience? The three chapters in this part will help you better understand how the creative side works.

8

The Creative Side

LIVE

Aaron Knauer
DIA Correspondent

BREAKING NEWS

FLIPTOMEXICO.COM ACTIVIST FAITH MELTZER CALLS HODAS' STATEMEN

It's a Winner

Campaigns:	Company:	Agency:	Awards:
"Still the One," "Flip to Mexico," "Leather Seats"	Frontier Airlines	Grey Worldwide	Gold Effie (for sustained success), Silver Clio, Silver Effie, Gold Mobius ("Best of Show" Nomination) for "Flip to Mexico"

CHAPTER KEY POINTS

1. How do we explain the science and art of creative strategy, as well as the important parts of a creative brief?
2. What are some key message strategy approaches?
3. Can creative thinking be defined, and how does it lead to a Big Idea?
4. What characteristics do creative people have in common, and what is their typical creative process?
5. What issues affect the management of creative strategy and its implementation?

Frontier: A Whole Different Animal

When low-cost carrier Frontier Airlines started up in 1994, it took off with animals emblazoned on the tails of its planes. Frontier's distinctive aircraft tails, all of which depict a variety of different wildlife, have made Frontier's brand name synonymous with the airline's Western heritage. Years of award-winning advertising have firmly established the airline with its talking animals on the planes' tails as a favorite of consumers in the Denver market and beyond.

The economic downturn of 2008 and 2009, however, grounded much of Frontier's advertising as the airline was forced into bankruptcy because of a cash-flow problem. Luckily, it emerged from the downturn with a new owner who recognized the value of the brand and its award-winning advertising.

Frontier's agency, Grey Worldwide, realized that Denverites were elated that their hometown airline and its beloved animals would live to see another day. A narrow window to celebrate this great news emerged. And once again, Creative Directors Shawn Couzens and Gary Ennis turned to Larry, Jack, Flip, and the rest of the gang for the perfect solution. The campaign had to be written and produced quickly and affordably—so it could air while the news was still fresh. And so, in just a few short weeks, the "Still the One" campaign was born.

This is just one example of how nimble the Frontier campaign is. No matter what the message, or how quick the turnaround, the animals can always deliver it in a way that's engaging and relevant. In fact, the animals have proven so popular, they may end up being the airline's single most important asset when it comes to the brand's ultimate survival.

So how did it all start? In 2003, Grey Worldwide brought the tail animals to life by creating a likable cast of characters—each different and unique in its own way. The humorous ad campaign broke away from the buttoned-up approach used by most airlines by creating an "episodic sitcom" much like *Seinfeld* or *Cheers*. As a result, consumers built an emotional attachment to the brand and its spokes-animals. And with each new commercial, that connection grew stronger as Frontier continued to evolve the campaign.

"Flip to Mexico"

In 2006, when rival airline United emerged from bankruptcy with a multi-million dollar ad campaign, Frontier decided to steal the spotlight by creating a diversion. Couzens said, "We wanted to promote our increased service to Mexico. For years, Flip the Dolphin had been dying to travel to a warm, tropical climate. But we always sent him to the cold Windy city of Chicago. It was a long-running joke in our campaign. Well, Flip had had enough. He decided to offer Frontier an ultimatum: Either they send him to Mexico, or he would quit."

Couzens and Ennis conceptualized the commercials as a news story which would unfold and evolve in real time. The "Flip to Mexico" campaign featured ads with Flip, fake news spots on Flip's demand that he be allowed to fly to Mexico, staged protests, podcasts, blogs, Flip's anthem on iTunes, and a Flipmobile that was conspicuous around Denver to generate awareness. Fans caught the spirit and started demonstrating on Flip's behalf. The four-week campaign culminated in an ad that played during the Super Bowl announcing that Flip was finally going to Mexico.

"Leather Seats"

Another commercial shows how the concept was extended with different types of messages the airline wanted to deliver. Jack the Rabbit and Larry the Lynx announce new aircraft, new destinations and new seats in one commercial. The brilliant copy captivates the audience, as these two characters ponder why there are not any cows on the tails of the airplanes. They conclude tails with cows probably would not be appropriate, given the new leather seats.

You will read another campaign that demonstrates the extendability of the talking animal concept in the case opener for Chapter 16, which illustrates a great award-winning special promotion to get passengers to book their Frontier flights on-line.

What can you learn from talking animals? Ad Lesson: Bad economic times can sometimes make great opportunities for advertising, especially when a strong brand has been created. For more information about how Grey's work helped Frontier on the next leg of its flight, see *It's a Wrap* at the end of the chapter.

Sources: Shawn M. Couzens interview, October 23, 2009; "Still the One," www.FrontierAirlines.com; "Leather Seats" www.youtube.com/watch?v=oyZYi7WZz-U; Shawn M. Couzens and Gary Ennis interview, February 21, 2007; "Frontier Airlines Documentary: How Flip Got to Mexico," www.youtube.com/watch?v=I-NC8UtLJCA; www.frontierairlines.com; www.fliptomexico.com/visitor.

Effective advertising is both an art in its creativity and a science in its strategy. This chapter explores how the two dimensions come together as creative strategy—the logic behind the message. We also examine how the strategy works with creative ideas to deliver a message's objectives. This includes a discussion of a planning tool called a *creative brief,* which provides direction for the execution of the Big Idea and for the evaluation of the creative strategy. We discuss the characteristics of creative people and the process of creative thinking, with the aim of showing how you can be a more creative thinker. The chapter ends with a discussion of the implementation of creative strategy.

SCIENCE AND ART?

Effective advertising is successful because the right media delivers the right message to the right target audience at the right time. In Part 2 we concentrated on how marketing communication works and how it's planned, and in Part 4 we'll consider the media and how a message is delivered. In Part 3—the next three chapters—we'll concentrate on how the message is created. It's important to keep in mind, however, that like two hands clapping, media and message need to work together to create effective communication. In fact, planning the message usually happens simultaneously with planning the media. Figure 8.1 diagrams this relationship.

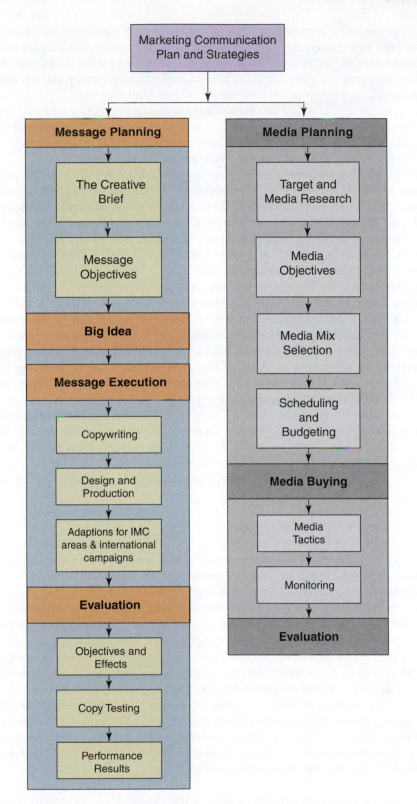

FIGURE 8.1
Media and Message
Strategy Work in Parallel

Effective marketing communication is not only focused on media and messages, it's also a product of both logic and creativity. The message plan, for example, is a rational analysis of a problem and what's needed to solve that problem. The advertisement itself translates the logic of the planning decisions into a creative idea that is original, attention getting, and memorable, such as the idea of talking animals as "spokes-characters" for Frontier airlines.

Beyond originality, Stuhlfaut and Berman say that creativity is not an open-ended process—it is directed at achieving objectives. They also emphasize that creative strategy is a problem-solving process,[1] and problem solving demands creative thinking—the mental tool used in figuring things out. Big Ideas and Big Plans both call for creative thinking.

In their book *Creative Strategy in Advertising,* Drewniany and Jewler say that an ad "needs to contain a persuasive message that convinces people to take action." To be creative, however, they suggest that the message must connect the target audience to the brand in a relevant and unexpected way. They explain, "Great advertising starts with a problem from the client and ends with a solution for consumers."[2] This description of creative advertising supports the principle that advertising is both a science—in the way a message is designed to be persuasive—and an art—in presenting an original and unexpected idea.

The creative element is the most visible—and, in some respects, the most important—dimension of marketing communication. As Professor Sheila Sasser, who is an expert on creativity and a regular contributor to this textbook, has explained, "Many advertisers openly claim they actively seek out new advertising agencies to achieve stronger or better creative work." What they are looking for is new ideas—new ways to present and deliver messages that have an impact.

Sometimes the new way to present a message demonstrates creativity in the use of media as much as it does in the design of the message. The nature of creative ideas has changed with the development of new, more engaging media. For example, you may remember that in Chapter 6 we introduced the Icelandic lamb case study. In it, Ingvi Logason and his Reykjavik agency redefined the meaning of "advertising media." He explains, "We created 'advertising' in the form of a series of traditional cooking shows designed to teach new and traditional recipes, but the shows would be only 40 to 90 seconds long. The execution of the campaign was ten cooking-show 'ads' that we strategically ran on various stations followed by viral distribution of the same micro-cooking shows through Facebook."

Principle
Effective advertising is a product of both science (persuasion) and art (creativity). Big Ideas and Big Plans both call for creative thinking.

Who Are the Key Players?

All agencies have copywriters and art directors who are responsible for developing the creative concept and crafting the execution of the advertising idea. They often work in teams, are sometimes hired and fired as a team, and may work together successfully for several years. Broadcast producers can also be part of the team for television commercials. The **creative director** manages the creative process and plays an important role in focusing the strategy of ads and making sure the creative concept is strategically on target. Of course, the account planner has helped put the strategy together in the form of a creative brief, so that person may also be involved in providing both background and direction to the creative team. Because advertising creativity is a product of teamwork, copywriters and art directors work together to generate concept, word, and picture ideas. Their writing or design specialties come into play in the execution of the idea.

The agency environment is particularly important. As Sasser explains, advertising agencies represent the perfect "think tank" to inspire creativity and research into creative thinking. Her research has found that agencies are natural incubators in terms of the 3 Ps of innovation: Place, Person, and Process. She explains these themes as follows:

Sheila Sasser is professor of advertising, IMC, and marketing at Eastern Michigan University College of Business.

- *Place* Environment research focuses on areas of the agency, office, or workspace setting that impact on creativity, such as image, structure, culture, integration, and communication. Creative boutique agencies have playful offices to stimulate their creative team's ideas. Colorful, artistic, and evocative creative department spaces exist even within the most conservative agency.
- *Person* Individual research provides insight into what makes individuals creative. These insights focus on how creative people think and behave in various ways to prompt their creative juices. Personality and motivation, also known as the passion to create, occupy key roles in stimulating individual creativity. Everyone has some level of internal creativity.

A DAY IN THE LIFE

What's in a Title?

Michael Dattolico, *Musion Creative, LLC*

If only I could sum up in a few words what I do each day, I would finally have a title for my office door. But the fact is, I can't decide on a title like some people can't pick a brand of laundry detergent. Each job I perform, each professional hat I wear, each skill set I practice has a specific benefit to whatever project I might be working on. I pride myself—and my company—on this diversity. A fusion of inspiration and execution through a diverse melding of design, creativity, and strong-minded marketing strategy. The tricky part is knowing how much to add to what load.

Each day I get up, commute to work, and turn on some tunes. I try to keep myself in a flexible, stimulating, creative environment where I can focus but stay lucid enough to lure creativity into my head. Music does that for me, but different people prefer different things to keep them going in a creative job. It's like deciding between lemon fresh or mountain scent detergent; who really cares how you do it, just get the job done.

By morning I usually already have a few briefs slated for the day, but I check my morning e-mails to see if anything pressing has come in. Since I do have a large list of professional hats to sift through, sometimes my days involve detailed ASP scripting (Microsoft Active Server Pages, a tool used in the design of Web pages), sometimes I get to doodle on my sketchpad trying to come up with a solid creative idea. The hardest part of my job is switching gears without grinding them. It can be difficult to switch mind-sets so drastically, but I thrive on challenges, so no worries.

Once I finally have that brief in front of me, I brainstorm. I strategize a plan of action, how I plan on tackling the brief, how conservative the client is. Every ad, every client is not looking for a One Show winner. You have to feel out what they're looking for, get inside their head as well as the target market. I think that was one of the major misconceptions I took away from college. You're not just creating, you're selling. You have to create something the client wants, whether it's a sweet creative idea or a starburst-heavy flyer. Because if not, you risk them taking their work to another laundromat next time.

After I map out a design and approach, I dive into the professional software I need. A computer can be your savior, but if you jump in too early it can actually hinder your work. Sometimes starting out with a pad and pencil helps weed out dozens of weak ideas and layouts that would take hours on a PC. A weak idea will never become stronger no matter how spectacularly you dress it. Some things need to be pretreated before you throw them in the wash.

By now, I should have something I'm happy with. Usually I come up with a few options to show the client, a left-field creative version and a right-field conservative option. This way if they love the creativity we can go with that, but if they want to stay conservative, at least they have something already done we can work on. This is the best way to push the creative envelope a little bit with the client, show them your capabilities while not missing a deadline. I've found that the client almost never picks the creative idea on the first project, but it plants the seed for the second or third project. It helps grow the relationship into something you will both be happy with.

That's it. Rinse and repeat.

Owner of his own design studio, Musion Creative LLC (*www.musioncreative.com*), Michael Dattolico graduated from the advertising program at the University of Florida and a creative advertising program in England at the University College of Falmouth. His work was nominated for inclusion in this book by Professor Elaine Wagner.

• ***Process*** Output research focuses on the creative product, the actual campaign. Although there is some reluctance to say what is creative, most people have their own definition, which includes such dimensions as originality, appropriateness, and artistry.

Although agencies offer an environment designed to stimulate creative thinking, professionals working on their own find that the varied nature of their assignments and projects create their own challenges, as Michael Dattolico describes in his *A Day In the Life* feature.

What Is the Role of Creativity?

Creativity is a special form of problem solving, and everyone is born with some talent in that area. Media planners, market researchers, copywriters, and art directors are all searching for new ideas. Ty Montague, former chief creative officer and co-president at JWT New York, made this point in a speech at the Effie Awards presentation. He said that even though the word *creative* is attached to his job, that doesn't mean its use is limited to the creative side. Montague noted that "every client I have ever worked with desperately wants every facet of the development of a product and its marketing to be infused with as much creativity as possible."[3]

Montague points to Apple CEO Steve Jobs who, in his opinion, is "the current world heavy-weight champion in the marketing world and who makes sure that the entire Apple brand stands for creativity." In other words, when Apple launched iPod, "the creativity begins with the way the product looks, works, and feels." And everything else is a creative challenge—packaging, distribution, PR, the events, the business model—it's all creative. "Creativity was baked into the iPod way before the agency got involved."

Highly creative people range from Henry Ford, the father of the Model T, to Steven Jobs, the cofounder of Apple Computer, to Lucille Ball of *I Love Lucy* fame. They are idea people, creative problem solvers, and highly original thinkers. Creative people are found in business, science, engineering, advertising, and many other fields. But in advertising, creativity is both a job description and a goal. Figure 8.2 contains a mini-test to evaluate your own creative potential.

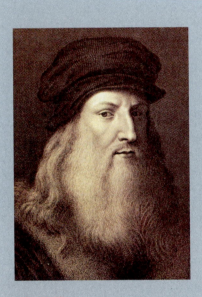 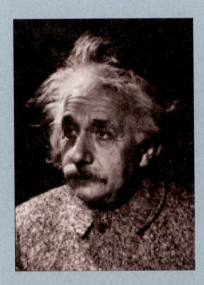 

■ ■ ■
Leonardo DaVinci, Albert Einstein, and Georgia O'Keefe excelled in different fields, but all three qualify as creative geniuses.

How Creative Are You?

By Sheri Broyles, *University of North Texas*

Do you ever wonder whether you are creative? Does creativity have anything to do with your personality? Your personality is your own distinctive and consistent pattern of how you think, feel, and act. You may not be a creative genius but still you may have creative abilities that can be nurtured and developed.

A current view of creativity suggests that the area of personality most related to creativity is how open you are to new experiences. According to researchers, how open you are to new experiences can be measured by survey questions that ask if you agree or disagree with statements like the following:

1. "I enjoy working on mind-twister-type puzzles."
2. "Once I find the right way to do something, I stick to it."
3. "As a child I rarely enjoyed games of make-believe."
4. "I enjoy concentrating on a fantasy or daydream and exploring all its possibilities, letting it grow and develop."

Which ones do you believe may predict a creative personality? Explain why. What can you do to expand your talents in those areas?

FIGURE 8.2
The Creative Personality

Source: Sheri J. Broyles, University of North Texas Department of Journalism, P.O. box 311277, Denton, TX 76203 sbroyles@unt.edu. Also based on R. R. McCrae and P. T. Costa Jr., "Openness to Experience" in *Perspectives in Personality,* Vol. 1, ed. R. Hogan and W. H. Jones (Greenwich, CT: JAI Press, 1985): 145–172.

The next section reviews creative message strategy and then comes back to an analysis of Big Ideas and explanations of how creative thinking works. It will help you understand how you can be a more creative problem solver.

The Creative Brief

The art and science of advertising come together in the phrase *creative strategy*. A winning marketing communication idea must be both *creative* (original, different, novel, unexpected) and *strategic* (right for the product and target; meets the objectives). It's not just about coming up with a novel idea that no one has thought of before, but rather advertising creativity is about coming up with an idea that solves a communication problem in an original way.

The *Road Crew social marketing campaign* is an example of creative problem solving for a good cause. We'll be using the Road Crew campaign throughout this chapter to illustrate different aspects of message strategy. The problem was to get young men in Wisconsin small towns who drink and drive to use a ride service. The objective was to reduce the incidence of alcohol-related car crashes by 5 percent. The breakthrough creative concept was to use the idea of a road crew for a group of young partiers who needed a ride on their big night out.

People who create advertisements also make a distinction between creative strategy and creative executions. **Creative strategy,** or **message strategy,** is *what* the advertisement says; **execution** is *how* it is said. This chapter focuses on creative strategy, and the two chapters that follow explore the writing, design, and production of advertising executions.

The creative strategy and the key execution details are spelled out in a document called a **creative brief** (or **creative platform,** *worksheet,* or *blueprint*). The brief is the document prepared by the account planner to summarize the basic marketing and advertising strategy that we briefly introduced in Chapter 7. It gives direction to creative team members as they search for a creative concept. The following outline summarizes the key points in a typical brief:

- *Problem* that can be solved by communication
- *Target audience* and key *insights* into their attitudes and behavior
- *Brand position* and other branding decisions, such as *personality* and *image*
- *Communication objectives* that specify the desired response to the message by the target audience
- *Proposition* or *selling idea* that will motivate the target to respond
- *Media considerations* about where and when the message should be delivered
- *Creative direction* that provides suggestions on how to stimulate the desired consumer response. These aren't creative ideas but may touch on such execution or stylistic direction as the ad's **tone of voice.**

Different agencies use different formats, but most combine these basic advertising strategy decisions. The briefs typically are in outline form, to be filled in by account planners and given to the creative team. The point is that advertising planning—even planning for the creative side—involves a structured, logical approach to analysis, which may leave out the intuitive, emotional message effects. The Crispin Porter + Bogusky agency, for example, designs its advertising by looking for what it calls "tension points." Its brief asks planners to consider: "What is the psychological, social, categorical, or cultural tension associated with this idea?"

The Road Crew campaign planning began with a creative brief. The ultimate goal was to encourage guys who like to party and visit bars to rely on a limousine ride service rather than trying to drive home themselves. Here is the creative brief that shows the thinking behind the campaign:

- *Why are we advertising at all?* To create awareness for an evening alternative ride service.
- *What is the message trying to do?* Make the new ride service appealing to men in order to reduce the number of alcohol-related crashes.
- *What are their current attitudes and perceptions?* "My car is here right now. Why wait? There are few options available anyway. I want to keep the fun going all night long."
- *What is the main promise we need to communicate?* It's more fun when you don't have to worry about driving.
- *What is the key moment to which we tie this message?* "Bam! The fun stops when I need to think about getting to the next bar or getting home."

- *What tone of voice should we use?* The brand character is rugged, cool, and genuine. We need to be a "straight-shooter" buddy on the barstool next to the target. They do not want to be preached to or told what to do. We need to communicate in a language to which they can relate. (Words like *program* may cause our audience to tune out.)

Message Objectives   In planning creative strategies, what do you want the message to accomplish? What message objectives would you specify for the Road Crew campaign in order to meet the goal of reducing alcohol-related crashes by 5 percent?

Some experts say advertising's role is to create awareness or announce something; others say it is to inform or persuade.[4] Hard-nosed businesspeople say the only real objective is to create sales. In some cases, the objective is to build or change demand for a brand. In Chapters 4 and 7, we introduced the concept of the *Facets Model of Effects* (Figure 8.3). Here is a review of some common advertising objectives that relate to the most critical facets of effectiveness:

- *See/hear* Create attention, awareness, interest, recognition.
- *Feel* Touch emotions and create feelings.
- *Think/Understand* Deliver information, aid understanding, create recall.
- *Connect* Establish brand identity and associations, transform a product into a brand with distinctive personality and image.
- *Believe* Change attitudes, create conviction and preference, stimulate trust.
- *Act/Do* Stimulate trial, purchase, repurchase, or some other form of action, such as visiting a store or website.

Of course, these effects are also driven by the demands of the marketing situation, target audience insights, and the needs of the brand. We mentioned that the primary goal of the Road Crew campaign was to reduce the number of alcohol-related crashes. Other objectives involved creating awareness of the ride service program and positive attitudes toward it and establishing a cost-

FIGURE 8.3

Facets Model of Effects

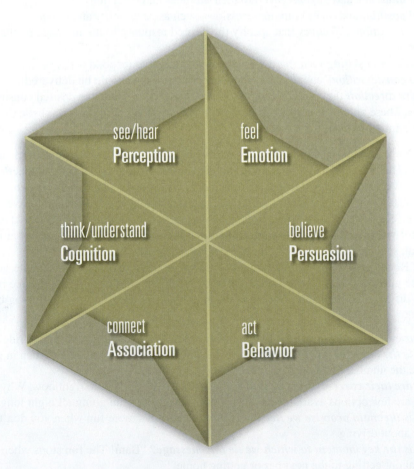

efficient level of rides in the first year of operations, which involved fund-raising, the solicitation of volunteers, and other community support. The heart of the problem uncovered by the Road Crew research, however, was a gap between *awareness* (don't drink & drive), *attitudes* (risky, scary, potentially dangerous), and *behavior* (get someone else to drive). The campaign was designed to address this gap and encourage the target audience's behavior to change in accordance with their attitudes and awareness.

Targeting   The target decision is particularly important in planning a message strategy. For example, we mentioned in the media chapters that advertisers have a difficult time reaching young men. New cable TV programs, as well as Web and cell phone opportunities, are developing to deliver this critical demographic, but what should the message say in these new media formats?

The target audience for the Wisconsin Road Crew campaign was identified as 21- to 34-year-old single men with a high school education and employed in blue-collar jobs. They were the primary target for the ride service because research found that this group is responsible for the most alcohol-related crashes, they kill more people than any other age group, and they themselves are most likely to die in an alcohol-related crash. What moves this group? Research found that many of these guys tended to worry about driving home drunk as the end of the evening approached and this worry took the edge off an otherwise delightful end of the evening. So the ride service made their evening more fun because it reduced their worry.

Branding and Positioning   The demands of the brand are also important considerations. Brand positions and brand images are created through message strategies and brought to life through advertising executions. Finding the right position is difficult enough, but figuring out how to communicate that position in an attention-getting message that is consistent across multiple executions and various media is difficult. The classic "Think Small" campaign that launched the VW Beetle is an example of advertising that created a powerful brand at the same time it carved out a unique position in a cluttered automobile market.

Brand communication creates symbols and cues that make brands distinctive, such as characters, colors, slogans, and taglines, as well as brand personality cues. Burger King has taken on market leader McDonald's by being cool, as evidenced by the power of its icon with an attitude—the Burger King king, which is only one of a group of brand icons that lend personality, emotion, and stories to their brands. The Geico Gecko and Frontier's talking animals are brand-savvy characters that are making the earnest Mr. Clean, Pillsbury Doughboy, and Jolly Green Giant look like dinosaurs. The difference is that these new-age characters are self-aware and even a little self-mocking, and they speak to the ad resistance of today's consumers with irony and inner conflict.[5]

Advertising and other forms of marketing communication are critical to creating what brand guru Kevin Keller calls *brand salience*[6]—that is, the brand is visible and has a presence in the marketplace, consumers are aware of it, and the brand is important to its target market. For example, Hewlett-Packard, a leader in the computer industry, has always been a follower in brand image behind the more creative Apple. To drop its stodgy image and imbue the brand with a sense of cool, a website (*www.fingerskilz.tv*) uses what appears to be fingers doing soccer tricks on a desk with a wadded-up paper ball. Later revealed to be an HP "viral" ad, the site attracted more than 180,000 visitors and lit up discussions on blogs and chat rooms.[7]

In addition to brand salience—measured as *top-of-mind awareness*—another objective for branding and positioning campaigns is to create trust. We buy familiar brands because we've used them before

Lemon.

CLASSIC

In an era of big cars and huge tail fins, Volkswagen launched its unimposing little Beetle in the 1960s. Other car ads were in full color with mansions in the background and beautiful people in the foreground. In the classic "Think Small" campaign, the Beetle was shown in black and white with a simple headline, "Lemon," in contrast to the bombastic promises of its competitors. Why "Lemon"? The copy explains that this little car had a quality problem with a chrome strip on its glove compartment, and it needed to be replaced. The ad stated that VW's inspectors found no detail too small to overlook, assuring consumers that their cars would last longer than other cars. Advertising Age recognized VW's "Think Small" campaign as number one on its list of the Top 100 advertising campaigns in history.

Fade in on *Jack the Rabbit* pulling into the gate.

Jack: I'll tell ya Larry, the tarmac never looked better.

He sees his pal *Larry the Lynx* and the two banter throughout . . .

Larry: I'll say.

Jake: New planes, new cities, new leather seats.

Larry: Pretty exciting stuff, huh?

Jake: Hey Larry, what's leather made from?

Larry: Cowhide

Jack: Ohhhh—so *that's* why there are no cows on the tails of our planes.

Larry: It's creepy.

Cut to supers . . .

MUSIC: Frontier music under staged

SUPER: New planes. New cities. New leather seats.

SUPER: A whole different animal. FRONTIER

Cut back to the tarmac for a quick button . . .

The "moment of silence" is ridiculously short . . .

. . . and they quickly turn their attention toward lunch

Larry: Wanna do do a moment of silence for cows?

Jack: Sure

SFX: *Slight pause* . . .

Jack: That's enough–wanna grab a burger?

Larry: I'm starving.

Frontier's "Leather Seats" commercial, which is part of the long-running "A Whole Different Animal" campaign, was carefully planned to deliver the brand personality conveyed through its menagerie of high-flying characters.

and we trust them to deliver on their promises. One category where trust is absolutely critical is pharmaceuticals. Another category is riding in automobiles, particularly GM and Chrysler after their governmental bailouts and Chrysler's bankruptcy. Both companies subsequently turned to strategies that reassured consumers that the companies would exist and their cars would continue to excel in quality.

MESSAGE STRATEGIES

Once you have an objective or set of objectives to guide the advertising message, how do you go about translating those goals into strategies? Remember, there is no one right way to do advertising—in most cases there are a number of ways to achieve a communication objective. If you were creating the advertising for a hotel, for example, what would you emphasize—speed of check-in, size of the room, hair dryers, mints on the pillow? Rather than tangible features like these, Sheraton decided to emphasize the emotional side of traveling and shows people greeting one another. Since it's a global company, the greetings include hugs, bows, and kisses on both cheeks. The company believes that its customers worldwide like to be welcomed, appreciated, and made to feel at home.

Planners search for the best creative strategy—the approach that makes the most sense given the brand's marketing situation and the target audience's needs and interests. But how do you talk about the various strategic approaches you might consider? In other words, how do you put strategies into words?

The Strategic Approach

First let's review some simple ways to express a strategic approach—head or heart and hard or **soft sell.** Then we'll look at some more complex models that get a little deeper into the complexities of message strategy.

Head and Heart   In the Facets Model the cognitive objectives generally speak to the head, and the affective objectives are more likely to speak to the heart. Sometimes, however, a strategy is designed to inform the mind as it touches the emotions. For example, in a strategy statement for Volkswagen's "Drivers Wanted" campaign, the agency identified both rational and emotional dimensions to the VW brand:

VW's rational brand essence:

"The only brand offering the benefits and 'feeling' of German engineering within reach."

VW's emotional brand essence:

- *Exciting*
- *Different driving feeling*
- *Different way of living*
- *More feeling, fun, alive, connected.*

Another way to refer to head and heart strategies are hard- and soft-sell approaches. A **hard sell** is an informational message that is designed to touch the mind and create a response based on logic. The assumption is that the target audience wants information and will make a rational product decision. A soft sell uses emotional appeals or images to create a response based on attitudes, moods, and feelings. The assumption with soft-sell strategies is that the target audience has little interest in an information search and will respond more favorably to a message that touches their emotions or presents an attractive brand image. A soft-sell strategy can be used for hard products. NAPA auto parts ran an emotional ad that showed a dog sitting at a railroad crossing, forcing a truck to brake hard to avoid hitting him as a train bears down on the scene. The slogan puts the heart-stopping visual story into perspective: "NAPA, because there are no unimportant parts."

But there are also examples of ads designed to stir emotions that didn't work because they were too manipulative or raised inappropriate emotions—think sexy calendars for car parts. It is possible to manipulate emotions in a way that viewers and listeners resent. For example, a billboard for a pest control company located in the heart of downtown that depicted a huge scary bug looming over the sidewalk elicited many complaints from pedestrians as well as drivers.

Sometimes, however, high emotion works. A 30-minute public service announcement referred to as "COW" was designed to teach Welsh schoolchildren about the dangers of texting while driving using a strong fear appeal. "COW" features Cassie Cowan, a nice girl from a nice Gwent valleys family—who kills four people on the road because she used her mobile and lost her concentration for a few seconds. It starts with three girls in a car with Cassie, the driver, texting while driving. The next scene is a horrifying slow-motion three-car accident with the girls being thrown around inside the car followed by images of blood, wounds, and the seriously injured girls, as well as the the horror and fear of the driver who survives with minor injuries. In the other cars there is a middle-age driver who is motionless and two unconscious adults in the third car with an infant and 2-year-old girl who keeps saying, "Mommy, Daddy, wake up." Bob Garfield, *Advertising Age's* critic, says that usually such graphic displays turn off the audience but he suspects this one may force people "to confront the consequences of a few moments of driver inattention"—presumably the death of four people. He explains, "We can't help but put our stupid selves in Cassie's flip-flops."[8] You can see the video online at *www.gwent.police.uk/leadnews.php?a=2172.*

Systems of Strategies   Head or heart, hard sell or soft sell—these terms all refer to some basic ideas about message strategy. But these are simple concepts, and creative strategy is more complex. We'll look at two of approaches that address other aspects of advertising strategy: Frazer's six creative strategies and Taylor's strategy wheel.

University of Washington Professor Charles Frazer proposed a set of six creative strategies that address various types of message situations.[9] Although not comprehensive, these terms are useful to identify some common approaches to message strategy. The strategies are described as follows:

Frazer's Six Creative Strategies

Strategy	Description	Uses
Preemptive	Uses a common attribute or benefit, but brand gets there first—forces competition into "me too" positions.	Used for categories with little differentiation or new product categories.
Unique selling proposition	Uses a distinct difference in attributes that creates a meaningful consumer benefit.	Used for categories with high levels of technological improvement and innovations.
Brand image	Uses a claim of superiority or distinction based on extrinsic factors such as psychological differences in the minds of consumers.	Used with homogeneous, low-tech goods with little differentiation.
Positioning	Establishes a place in the consumer's mind relative to the competition.	Used by new entries or small brands that want to challenge the market leader.
Resonance	Uses situations, lifestyles, and emotions with which the target audience can identify.	Used in highly competitive, undifferentiated product categories.
Affective/ anomalous (or ambiguous)	Uses an emotional, sometimes even ambiguous message, to break through indifference.	Used where competitors are playing it straight and informative.

The preemptive strategy shows up in competitive advertising where one competitor tries to build a position or lay a claim before others enter the market. An example comes from the Coffee Wars between Starbucks and McDonald's that erupted when McDonald's announced its McCafe line of fancy coffees at lower prices. In anticipation of the McCafe advertising blitz, Starbucks began its first-ever branding campaign. Designed with burlap-sack backgrounds that are reminiscent of roasted coffee bags, the ads have hard-hitting headlines like, "Starbucks or nothing. Because compromise leaves a really bad aftertaste" and "If your coffee isn't perfect, we'll make it over. If it's still not perfect, you must not be in a Starbucks." The campaign is designed to separate the Starbucks' experience from the mass-market approach of McDonald's and Dunkin' Donuts.

University of Tennessee professor Ron Taylor developed a model that divides strategies into the *transmission view,* which is similar to the more rational "head" strategies, and the *ritual view,* which is similar to the more feeling-based "heart" strategies. He then divides each into three segments: ration (rational), acute need, and routine on the transmission side; and ego, social, and sensory on the ritual side.[10] He explains the principles behind this model, as well as its application in a problem-solving context, in the *A Matter of Principle* feature.

Strategic Formats

Even though advertising is a constant search for a new and novel way to express some basic truth, there are also some tried and true formats that have worked over the years. We'll talk about these options from a literary, psychological, and sales viewpoint.

The ads and slogan, "It's not just coffee. It's a Starbucks," tell the brand's quality story and counters the McDonald's McCafe campaign.

Lectures and Dramas   Most advertising messages use a combination of two basic literary techniques to reach the head or the heart of the consumer: lectures and dramas.[11] A lecture is a serious instruction given verbally. The speaker presents evidence (broadly speaking) and uses a technique such as an argument to persuade the audience. The advantages of lectures are many: They are relatively inexpensive to produce and are compact and efficient. A lecture can deliver a dozen selling points in seconds, get right to the point, and make the point explicitly. In advertising we use the phrase *talking head* to refer to an announcer who delivers a lecture about a product. This can also be a celebrity spokesperson or an authority figure, such as a doctor or scientist.

Drama, however, relies on the viewer to make inferences about the brand. Sometimes the drama is in the story that the reader has to construct around the cues in the ad. Through dramas, advertisers tell stories about their products; the characters speak to each other (Frontier's talking animals), not to the audience. Like fairy tales, movies, novels, parables, and myths, advertising dramas are essentially stories about how the world works. They can be funny as well as serious. Viewers learn from these commercial dramas by inferring lessons from them and by applying those lessons to their everyday lives. The Leo Burnett agency built a creative philosophy around "Inherent Drama," which describes the storyline built into the agency's archetypal brand characters, such as the Marlboro Man, Charlie the Tuna, the Jolly Green Giant, and Tony the Tiger.

Psychological Appeals   The psychological appeal of the product to the consumer is also used to describe a message that appeals primarily to the heart. An **appeal** connects with some emotion that makes the product particularly attractive or interesting, such as security, esteem, fear, sex, and sensory pleasure. Although emotion is at the base of most appeals, in some situations, appeals can also have a logical dimension, such as saving money for retirement (relief based on knowledge). Appeals generally pinpoint the anticipated response of the audience to the product and the message. For example, if the price is emphasized in the ad, then the appeal is value, economy, or savings. If the product saves time or effort, then the appeal is convenience. Advertisers use a status appeal to establish something as a high-quality, expensive product. Appetite appeal using mouth-watering visuals is used in food advertising, such as the Quaker Trail Mix Bar ad.

The appetite appeal of the trail mix bar is dramatized by an extremely close-up visual that shows all the nuts and raisins larger than life.

Six Message Strategies in Six Minutes

Ronald E. Taylor, *University of Tennessee*

It's crunch time. You've got to generate several different message strategies to discuss with your boss for a new business pitch. She's meeting with a regional bottler who plans to add bottled water to her product line. Your boss wants to hear your ideas over lunch. Problem is, this bottled water is no different from all the other brands of bottled water.

You head out to meet your boss, a six-minute trip away from your office. You've got to enter the restaurant with the strategies in your head. You remember a strategy device from your advertising class in college: the six-segment strategy wheel (Figure 8.4). It was designed primarily to generate strategies, to create several to choose from. You remember that it had two broad divisions—transmission and ritual—and three segments under each division. You mentally work your way counterclockwise around the wheel to think about ways to promote the product.

1. *Ration Segment* Ration strategies are based on rational thought and logic. They represent the classic reason-why, product-focused message strategies. You think "Brand X Water, the economical, convenient, portable beverage."

2. *Acute Need Segment* Acute need, or special need, strategies are based on consumers' unanticipated need for the product or service, like appliance repair or medical surgery, or special occasions, like the need for a tuxedo or dress for a formal occasion. But when do you have an acute need for water? When traditional supplies aren't available! "Stock up on Brand X Water for the hurricane season."

3. *Routine Segment* Routine strategies attempt to routinize everyday behavior. You remember that drinking multiple glasses of water a day is good for you, so you think "Brand X Water, A Great Beverage with Every Meal Every Day."

You've moved down the left-hand side of the wheel and the amount of time consumers spend deliberating on choices has been reduced in each segment. Now you are mentally crossing over the vertical line to the ritual, or emotional side, and the importance of the item and emotional connection will increase as you move up the right-hand side of the wheel—and you're halfway to lunch with the boss.

4. *Sensory Segment* Sensory strategies are based on one of the five senses: sight, touch, hearing, smell, taste. You think "Refreshing, clear taste. Brand X Water."

5. *Social Segment* Many social strategies are based on establishing, maintaining, or celebrating relationships with others. You think "Get noticed. Drink Brand X Water" or "Share Brand X Water with someone you love."

6. *Ego Segment* Ego strategies are based on images that consumers have of themselves. Brands say to consumers "This is who you are." Active people who eat healthy foods and exercise regularly like reinforcement that they are doing the right thing. You think "Brand X Water, the bottled water for people who care about their health."

The wheels are turning now. You've arrived at the parking lot and you start combining strategies.

7. Serve refreshing (sensory) Brand X water to your family (social) every day (routine).

8. Clear refreshment (sensory) in an unbreakable (ration), portable (ration) container.

Your boss is impressed with your ability to generate strategies. Most advertising professionals generate two or three and then do multiple executions within a single strategy. But you are not so limited. In fact, your boss has invited you to lunch again tomorrow to discuss the pitch for a national pizza chain. How many strategies can you generate?

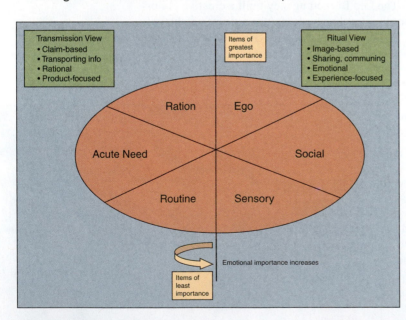

FIGURE 8.4

Taylor's Six-Segment Strategy Wheel

Source: Ronald E. Taylor, University of Tennessee *http://web.utk.edu/~retaylor/six-seg.htm*

Source: http://web.utk.edu/~retaylor/six-seg.htm.

Selling Strategies   Advertising has developed a number of strategic approaches that speak to the head with a sales message. A **selling premise** states the logic behind the sales offer. A premise is a proposition on which an argument is based or a conclusion is drawn. This type of message strategy is usually a rational approach, an appeal to the head.

A basic selling premise is designed to sell a product based on tested principles, or selling premises, that, as Edd Applegate reminds us in his book, *Strategic Copywriting,* have been shown to work time after time.[12] To have a practical effect on customers, managers must identify the product's **features** (also called **attributes**) in terms of those that are most important to the target audience. Another type of selling premise is a **claim,** which is a product-focused strategy that is based on a prediction about how the product will perform. Health claims on food products like oatmeal, for example, suggest that the food will be good for you.

A rational, prospect-centered selling premise identifies a reason that might appeal to potential customers and motivate them to respond. Here is a summary of these rational customer-focused selling premises:

- A *benefit* emphasizes what the product can do for the user by translating the product feature or attribute into something that benefits the consumer. For example, a GM electric car ad focuses on the product feature (the car doesn't use gas) and translates it into a benefit: lack of noise (no pistons, valves, exhaust).
- A *promise* is a benefit statement that looks to the future and predicts that something good will happen if you use the product. For example, Dial soap has promised for decades that if you use Dial, you will feel more confident.
- A *reason why* emphasizes the logic behind why you should buy something, although the reason sometimes is implied or assumed. The word *because* is the key to a reason-why statement. For example, an Amtrak ad tells you that train travel is more comfortable than flying because Amtrak is a more civilized, less dehumanizing way to travel.
- A *unique selling proposition (USP)* is a benefit statement that is both unique to the product and important to the user. The USP is a promise that consumers will get this unique benefit by using this product only. For example, an ad for a camera states, "This camera is the only one that lets you zoom in and out automatically to follow the action."

Principle
In the comparison approach, as with a demonstration, seeing is believing, so the objective is to build conviction.

Most selling premises demand facts, proof, or explanations to support the sales message. Proof statements that give the rationale, reasoning, and research behind the claim are used to substantiate the premise. The proof or **substantiation** needed to make a claim believable is called **support.** In many cases this calls for research findings. With claims, and particularly with comparisons, the proof is subject to challenge by the competitor as well as industry review boards.

Other Message Formulas   In addition to the basic categories of selling premises, some common message formulas emphasize different types of effects. The planner uses these terms as a way to give direction to the creative team and to shape the executions. Here are some common formats:

- A *straightforward* message, which is factual or informational, conveys information without any gimmicks, emotions, or special effects. For example, in an ad for *www.women.com,* the website advertises that "It's where today's educated, affluent women are finding in-depth coverage on issues they care about" and that more than 2 million women visit each month.
- A *demonstration* focuses on how to use the product or what it can do for you. For example, an ad for Kellogg's Special K and Smart Start uses cereal bowls to demonstrate how a daily regimen of healthy cereal would help a dieter lose six pounds.

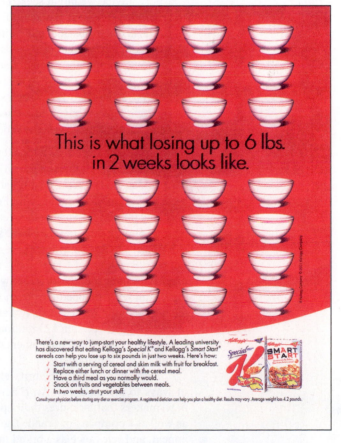

This is what losing up to 6 lbs. in 2 weeks looks like.

The Kellogg's Smart Start ad uses 28 cereal bowls to demonstrate the amount that Special K and Smart Start equal in weight loss.

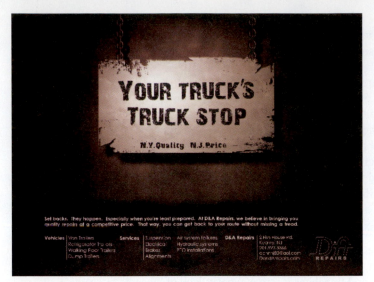

SHOWCASE
The "Truck Stop" headline for D&A uses a twist to make the repair shop the hero. This ad was contributed by the Boston University AdLab.

- A *comparison* contrasts two or more products to show the superiority of the advertiser's brand. The comparison can be direct, with competitors mentioned, or indirect, with just a reference to "other leading brands." In the comparison approach, as with a demonstration, seeing is believing, so the objective is to build conviction. When people see two products being compared, they are more likely to believe that one is better than the other.

- In a *problem solution* message, also known as **product-as-hero,** the message begins with a problem and then showcases the product as the solution. A variation is the **problem avoidance message** format, in which the product helps the consumer avoid a problem.

- **Humor** can be a useful creative strategy—using a comedian such as Jerry Seinfeld as the star, for example (see Chapter 7, p. 209)—because it grabs attention and is memorable. Planners hope people will transfer the warm feelings of being entertained to the product.

- The *slice-of-life* message is an elaborate version of a problem solution staged in the form of a drama in which "typical people" talk about a common problem and resolve it.

- In the **spokesperson** (also **spokes-character, brand icon**) or **endorser** format, the ad features celebrities we like (Michael Jordan), created characters (the Aflac duck, the Geico Caveman), experts we respect (the Maytag repairman, doctors), or someone "just like us" whose advice we might seek. The spokesperson speaks on behalf of the product to build credibility. A recent change in FTC rules now makes endorsers, as well as advertisers, liable for false or unsubstantiated claims, so spokespersons have to be very careful about what they say about any product they advertise.

- **Teasers** are mystery ads that don't identify the product or don't deliver enough information to make sense, but they are designed to arouse curiosity. These are often used to launch a new product. The ads run for a while without the product identification and then when curiosity is sufficiently aroused, usually at the point when the product is officially launched, a concluding ad runs with the product identification.

The use of celebrities as spokespersons, endorsers, or brand symbols is an important strategy because it associates the brand with a famous person and qualities that make that person important. Michael Jackson is credited with starting a new era of celebrity advertising when he signed a record-breaking $5 million contract with Pepsi in 1984. Before that time, celebrities were often reluctant to appear for a brand because they feared it might tarnish their image. More recently advertisers have worried about celebrities they have signed who might tarnish the brand's image. A classic example is Michael Phelps, the winner of eight gold medals in the Beijing Olympics, who appeared in the famous "Breakfast of Champions" series on Corn Flakes packages. After the swimmer was suspended for three months by USA Swimming for a photo that showed him inhaling from a marijuana pipe, Kellogg's dropped him from the package. In another example, many companies distanced themselves from Tiger Woods following disclosure of his personal problems. One source estimates that Woods lost between $23 million and $30 million in endorsements with companies such as Accenture and AT&T.[13] Temperamental stars, drug and driving arrests, assaults, and loose tongues are a nightmare for marketers.

Another aspect of celebrity effectiveness is their appeal or influence. There are a number of ways to measure this. An *E Score* is a system of ratings for celebrities, athletes, and other newsmakers that measures their appeal. A *Q Score* is a measure of the familiarity of a celebrity, as well as a company or brand. The *Davie Brown Index (DBI)* measures a celebrity's awareness, appeal, and relevance as a brand image. It also evaluates the influence of the celebrity on buying behavior.

Matching Messages to Objectives

We talked earlier about message planning, including objectives, and then moved to a discussion of various types of message strategies. Now, let's try to bring those two together. What types of messages deliver which objectives? What approach can best overcome a weakness or solve a problem? If it's a credibility problem, for example, you might want to think about a testimonial, a demonstration of proof, a reason why, or even a press release with the built-in believability of a news story. The Facets Model can be helpful in thinking through objectives and their related strategies:

- *Messages That Get Attention* To be effective, an advertisement needs to get exposure through the media buy and get attention through the message. Getting consumers' attention requires stopping power. Creative advertising breaks through the old patterns of seeing and saying things—the unexpectedness of the new idea (the Geico Caveman) creates stopping power. Ads that stop the scanning and break through the clutter can also be high in personal relevance. Intrusiveness is particularly important in cluttered markets. Many clutter-busting ads are intrusive and use loud, bold effects to attract viewer attention—they work by shouting. Others use engaging, captivating ideas, curiosity/ambiguity, or mesmerizing visuals. Curiosity is particularly important for teaser strategies.

- *Messages That Create Interest* Getting attention reflects the stopping power of an advertisement; keeping attention reflects the ad's pulling power. An interesting thought keeps readers' or viewers' attention and pulls them through to the end of the message. One way to intensify interest is through curiosity, such as using a teaser campaign where the message unfolds over time. Ads that open with questions or dubious or ambiguous statements are designed to create curiosity.

- *Messages That Resonate* Ads that amplify the emotional impact of a message by engaging a consumer in a personal connection with a brand are said to resonate with the target audience. The women's campaign for Nike, for example, does a good job of speaking to women in a way that addresses their concerns about personal achievement, rather than the competitive theme of the more traditional men's campaign. If a woman identifies with this message, then it is said to resonate for her.

- *Messages That Create Believability* Advertising sometimes uses a credibility strategy to intensify the believability of a message. Using data to support or prove a claim is critical. The use of brand characters such as Colonel Sanders for KFC, who was a real person and the creator of the famous chicken recipe ("11 herbs and spices"), is designed to give consumers a *reason to believe* in a brand by cementing conviction.

- *Messages That Are Remembered* Not only do messages have to *stop* (get attention) and *pull* (create interest), they also have to *stick* (in memory), which is another important part of the perceptual process. Most advertisements, for example, are carefully designed to ensure that these memory traces are easy to recall. In Chapter 4 we explained that much of advertising's impact lies in its delayed effects, hence memorability is a huge factor in effectiveness. Ads use catchy headlines, curiosity, and intriguing visuals to make this recall process as easy as possible and lock the message in memory.

Principle
A message needs to *stop* (get attention), *pull* (create interest), and *stick* (be memorable).

Repetition is used both in media and message strategy to ensure memorability. Jingles are valuable memorability devices because the music allows the advertiser to repeat a phrase or product name without boring the audience. Advertising psychologist Esther Thorson says asking the consumer to make a moral or value judgment also anchors the copy point in memory, such as relating the point to a good cause.[14]

Clever phrases are useful not only because they grab the consumer's attention, but also because they can be repeated to intensify memorability. Marketing communication uses **slogans** for brands and campaigns, such as "Get Met. It Pays" (MetLife) or Nike's slogan, "Just Do It." **Taglines** are used at the end of an ad to summarize the point of the ad's message in a highly memorable way, such as "Nothing outlasts the Energizer. It keeps going and going and going." In addition to verbal memory devices, many print and interactive messages and most television commercials feature a *key visual*. This visual is a vivid image that the advertiser hopes will linger in the viewer's mind. Color can be a memory cue. Wrigley's Doublemint gum uses green and Juicy Fruit uses yellow.

REFRESCANTEMENTA DURADERO

UNPEQUEÑOPLACER Y NADA MAS

SHOWCASE

The familiar Doublemint green anchors the brand's identity even when the campaign is aimed at Hispanics and the ads are written en Español.

These ads were contributed by Sonia Montes Scappaticci, who is partner and new business director at Catmandu Branded Entertainment. A graduate of Michigan State University's advertising program, she was also named one of AAF's Most Promising Minority Students. She was nominated by Professor Carrie La Ferle.

• *Messages That Touch Emotions* Emotional appeals create feeling-based responses such as love, fear, anxiety, envy, sexual attraction, happiness and joy, sorrow, safety and security, pride, pleasure, embarrassment, and nostalgia. Appetite appeal uses mouth-watering food shots to elicit feelings of hunger and craving, like the photo in the Quaker Trail Mix Bar print ad. Hallmark has used an emotional appeal for years in its advertising to tie the sentiment in greeting cards with the moving experiences in our lives. Home Depot targeted women with uplifting tales of what women customers can do to help themselves become do-it-yourselfers. The customers even tear up as they speak and hug the employees who helped them in a style reminiscent of reality TV.[15] A more general emotional goal is to deliver a message that people like in order to create liking for the brand.

• *Messages That Inform* Companies often use news announcements to provide information about new products, to tout reformulated products, or even to let consumers know about new uses for old products. The news angle, which is often delivered by publicity stories, is information focused. Sometimes this means following a press release with a long-copy print ad or an infomercial in television. Informative ads and brochures that focus on features and attributes seek to create understanding about a product's advantages. Comparison ads are often heavy on information and used to explain a product's point of difference and competitive advantage. Attributes can be both tangible and intangible (see Figure 8.5). The ads for Sunkist oranges and Harley-Davidson focus on tangible and intangible features.

• *Messages That Teach* People learn through instruction so some advertisements are designed to teach, such as demonstrations that show how something works or how to solve a problem. Educational messages are sometimes designed to explain something, such as why it is important to brush your teeth or get involved in local politics. Learning also is strengthened through repetition, as in the famous Pavlovian experiment where the dog learned to associate food with the sound of a bell. That's why repetition is such an important media objective.

Principle
When advertising gives consumers permission to believe in a product, it establishes the platform for conviction.

• *Messages That Persuade* Persuasive messages are designed to affect attitudes and create belief. Strategies that are particularly good are *testimonials* and messages that generate word of mouth about the product. Endorsements by celebrities (the Seinfeld commercial mentioned in Chapter 7) or experts are used to intensify conviction. Selling premises that focus on how the product will benefit the consumer, state a reason why, or explain a unique selling proposition (USPs) are persuasive, particularly if they provide proof or support. Torture tests, comparisons, and before-and-after demonstrations also are used to prove the truth of a claim. Conviction is often built on strong, rational arguments that use such techniques as test results, before-and-after visuals, testimonials by users and experts, and demonstrations to prove something. Celebrities, product placements, and other credibility techniques are used to give the consumer **permission to believe** a claim or selling premise.

• *Messages That Create Brand Associations* The transformative power of branding, where the brand takes on a distinctive character and meaning, is one of marketing communication's most important functions. **Image advertising,** in particular, is used to create a representation of a brand, an image in a consumer's mind, through symbolism. Advertising's role is to provide the cues that make these meanings and experiences come together in a coherent brand image. The Sunkist ad associated oranges with candy to convey the message of sweetness.

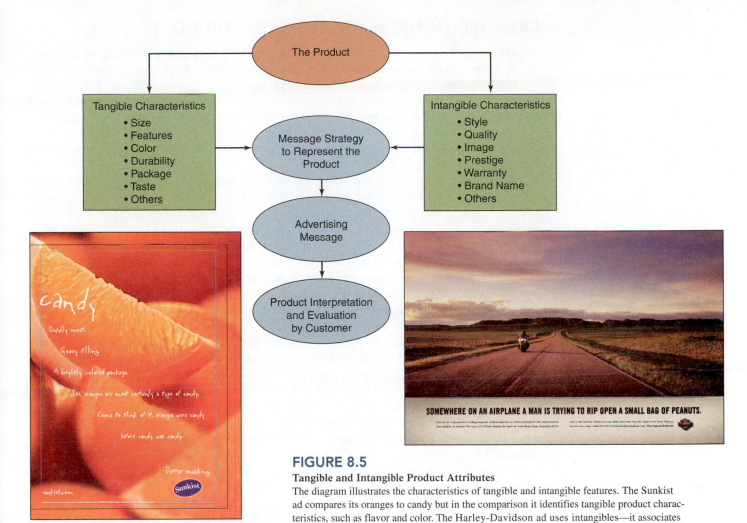

FIGURE 8.5

Tangible and Intangible Product Attributes

The diagram illustrates the characteristics of tangible and intangible features. The Sunkist ad compares its oranges to candy but in the comparison it identifies tangible product characteristics, such as flavor and color. The Harley-Davidson ad uses intangibles—it associates the Harley brand image with the personality of people who ride on the edge of life.

An association message strategy delivers information and feelings symbolically by connecting a brand with a certain type of person or lifestyle. This link is often created through visuals. A consumer gets a feeling about the product—who uses it and how and where they use it—through these symbolic cues. Some advertising strategies want you to identify with the user of the product or see yourself in that situation. Fashion and cosmetic products invite you to project yourself into the ad and make a fashion statement when you wear or use the product.

• *Messages that drive action* Even harder to accomplish than conviction is a change in behavior. It often happens that people believe one thing and do another. The Road Crew campaign was designed to overcome a gap between attitudes and behavior. Sometimes an advertising message can drive people to act by offering something free or at a discounted sales price. Sales promotion, for example, works in tandem with advertising to stimulate immediate action using sampling, coupons, and free gifts as incentives for action.

Most ads end with a signature of some kind that serves to identify the company or brand, but it also serves as a **call to action** and gives direction to the consumer about how to respond, such as a toll-free phone number, website URL, or e-mail address. Marketing communication can drive people to a website or to a toll-free number to call a company. Similar to the Road Crew campaign, another form of action is to discourage or extinguish actions such as smoking, drug use, or driving drunk.

Ultimately, marketers want loyal customers who purchase and repurchase the product as a matter of habit or preference. **Reminder advertising,** as well as distributing coupons or introducing a continuity program (such as a frequent flyer program), is designed to keep the brand name in front of customers to encourage their repeat business.

CREATIVE THINKING: SO HOW DO YOU DO IT?

Given how much we've been talking about creativity, perhaps a definition might be appropriate. In a research review of creativity in advertising education, Mark Stuhlfaut identified the significant elements, which begin with novelty but include appropriateness. He says that "among advertising professionals, creativity requires singularity, uniqueness, adaptability, and revelation of truth (the 'aha' moment), which implies authenticity and relevance." Stuhlfaut adds that if it's creative, it is also often generative; in other words, it leads to other new ways of thinking.[16] So creativity can be defined as generating novelty and uniqueness that makes something ring true.

Marketing communication and advertising are creative idea businesses. But what do we mean by an idea? An **idea** is a thought or a concept in the mind. It's formed by mentally combining pieces and fragments of thoughts into something that conveys a nugget of meaning. It's a form of construction—a mental creation. Advertising creatives sometimes use the term **concepting** to refer to the process of coming up with a new idea, such as the famous "Got Milk?" campaign. There's even a book called *Concepting* by Jan Rijkenberg that explains how concept branding leads to ideas that mean something to consumers and create identification with the brand.[17]

We have tried to define creativity and creative ideas, but to understand what it is, it may be helpful to think about what it isn't. What's the opposite of creative? In advertising, **clichés** are the most obvious examples of generic, nonoriginal, non-novel ideas. An example of an industry immersed in clichés is hospitals—where advertising conventions typically feature skilled doctors and caring nurses working together as teams in new high-tech buildings with incredibly new equipment. Hospitals, along with banks, are filled with friendly staff and we are often reminded how much they care. In contrast, an innovative campaign for the Akron Children's Hospital has been showcased for its new approach. Its commercials are unscripted and use patients and their families, who talk about how they are coping. The idea is that hospitals are dramatic places and the challenge was to present the inherent drama in the hospital situation by focusing on real people. When the New York–based DeVito/Verdi agency was hired by the Mount Sinai hospital to also break away from the clichés, the agency drafted a list of commandments: No pictures of doctors, no smiling people, no fancy machinery, no overpromises about medical care, no complicated medical terminology.[18]

To help you understand how creative people think about strategy and advertising ideas, consider the 10 tips offered in the *Practical Tips* box by Professor Tom Groth, whose students consistently win awards. These are suggestions about how professionals approach creative assignments, but they also provide you with a road map for your own personal growth as a creative person.

Creative Big Ideas

What we call a **Big Idea**, or **creative concept**, becomes a point of focus for communicating the message strategy. The Marlboro Man with its connotation of Western independence and self-reliance is a Big Idea that has been worth millions, maybe billions, of dollars in brand equity over the years. It's ranked number three in *Advertising Age*'s Top 100 advertising campaigns of the century.[19]

But Big Ideas can be risky because they are different and, by definition, untested. The "SuperModelquins" campaign by Crispin Porter & Bogusky described in Chapter 5 was a risky strategy because it was so unexpected. CP&B has had trouble with some of its other edgy ideas, such as the creepy Burger King. To be fair, the agency was recognized for its cutting-edge work and named Agency of the Year at the CLIO's 50th anniversary show in 2009. The agency, however, lost VW as a client because its brassy taglines and quirky situations departed too much from VW's "heritage of tasteful wit." The ads, some of which alienated VW's independent dealers, featured a lab-coated Helga, a soccer mom who mocked Brooke Shields, and a VW Bug with a heavy Teutonic accent hosting a late-night talk show.[20] So risky is good for edgy Big Ideas, but how far on the edge is a difficult question.

Where do big ideas come from? As advertising legend James Webb Young, a founder of the Young & Rubicam agency, explained in his classic book on creative thinking, an idea is a new or unexpected combination of thoughts. Young claims that "the ability to make new combinations is heightened by an ability to see relationships."[21] An idea, then, is *a thought that comes from placing two previously unrelated concepts together* as the Harley "Steak for Your Ears" ad demonstrates.

Principle
Big Ideas are risky because they are by definition new, unexpected, and untested.

Ten Creative Tips

By Tom Groth, *University of West Florida*

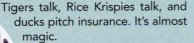

Tigers talk, Rice Krispies talk, and ducks pitch insurance. It's almost magic.

Who thinks of this stuff? Creatives! Art directors, copywriters, and, of course, creative directors—innovative, artsy, eccentric, nonconformist, and soooo cool. How do they come up with fresh ideas seemingly out of thin air? In an ever-changing world, creativity is the fundamental skill for success.

Too bad there isn't a pull-down menu on your computer for creativity. Until then, try these 10 creative tips. Soon your classmates might be asking, "How did you come up with that?"

Creative Tip 1

Live big. Prepare. Be smart. Work hard. Don't be lazy. Laugh.

Often an ad is dull and boring simply because its creator is dull and boring. The only thing that you can put into an ad is yourself. Nothing more.

- Dig into life. Immerse yourself in art, music, pop culture, books, advertising, the Internet, your client, your product, and most of all, your prospect.
- Breakthrough creative is not in the research or on the Internet—it is within you.

Creative Tip 2

The right answer is the wrong answer.

Too often we are looking for "the correct answer," the safe answer, the answer the teacher or client expects. The expected solution is not a solution. It is often a rut, a cliché. Think dull, boring, been-there-done-that.

Education = apple
5 × 5 = 25
Sky = blue
Insurance = a duck!

"I never thought of it that way!"
- Creativity forgets the way things are supposed to be!

Creative Tip 3

What do you want to say?

Discover the core message about your brand before you ever pick up a pencil. Have a clear strategy.
- You cannot communicate a message if you don't know what the message is.

Creative Tip 4

Warning! Do not use a computer to create.

A computer immediately thrusts you into your left brain.

Which font?
Which point size?
Which program?
Where do I get a picture of a giraffe smiling?

- Always carry a notepad. Ideas may come in the shower, in the middle of the night, on a date, or at a stoplight. Oh, that breakthrough concept can vanish in a heartbeat. Get it down fast.

Creative Tip 5

Use the power of play. You remember how to play, don't you?

Try free play. Recess. No rules, no coach—shut down your adult, left brain, and all the tired baggage that comes with it. Start with lots and lots and lots of thumbnails. All ideas are valid now. Don't evaluate yet. Wait. Pick your winner another day.

Creative Tip 6

Play the what if game.

What if . . . a pink bunny sold batteries?
Pretend . . . a green giant raised peas!
Suppose . . . a clown with red hair pitched burgers.
Imagine . . .

- Give yourself permission to suspend reality! Look beyond the facts to what might be. Imagine the possibilities!

Creative Tip 7

Don't play scared.
Fear says, "There already exists one answer and you'd better find it." Creativity says, "The world is not done. There are more pages possible!"
- Fear kills creativity. Fear of ridicule. Fear of being a fool. Fear of being fired. Fear it won't be perfect.
- Perfection kills ideas. Take a risk. Be brave. Be braver.

Creative Tip 8

Think of it as. . .

- Use associations. This is how your brain works and how great ads work too.

(continued)

A pet is a . . . *date magnet.*
A crayon is a . . . *power tool.*
Cough syrup is a . . . *silent night.*
* Just link two previously unrelated ideas. This breaks the boredom barrier and dramatizes your brand's benefit!

Creative Tip 9

Set-up and punch line.

Set-up: Two antennas meet on a roof, fall in love, and get married.
Punch line: The ceremony wasn't much, but the reception was brilliant.
* Bad joke; but a review of any awards annual will reveal this approach is the basis of many killer ads! Here's how it works.

Step 1   The *set-up* creates a question through curiosity. (It shows or says something that disrupts expectation.)

Step 2   The *punch line* answers the question and reveals the core brand message.
* Set-Up: *By the end of this sentence you'll be thinking of a turkey with a green beak.*

Creative Tip 10

Have fun!

People like to work with people who have a sense of humor. People buy brands from ads they like. A sense of humor wins accounts, makes friends, sells brands, and turns good creative into great creative.

The name Road Crew was the defining element of that campaign's Big Idea. It was supported with a slogan—"Beats driving"—that conveyed the benefit of the program in the language of the target audience. The logo was in the style of the Harley-Davidson logo. The Road Crew planners realized that a Big Idea that reflects the lifestyle of the target audience in appealing language and tone can motivate behavior and change attitudes, and Harley connects with the attitude of the young male audience the campaign wanted to reach.

Principle
An idea can be creative for you if you have never thought of it before, but to be truly creative it has to be one that no one else has thought of before.

The ROI of Creativity
A Big Idea is more than just a new thought because in advertising it also has to accomplish something—it has a functional dimension. According to the DDB agency, an effective ad is *relevant*, *original*, and has *impact*—which is referred to as **ROI of creativity.** That formula sounds like the way a businessperson would talk metaphorically about creativity in terms of "return on invest-

The Road Crew creators wanted to create a design in the spirit of the Harley image, realizing that members of the target audience were all Harley fans.

This Harley-Davidson ad equates the taste of a steak with the throaty roar of a Harley engine.

ment."[22] But it has a different meaning here. According to DDB's philosophy: Ideas have to be **relevant** and mean something to the target audience. **Original** means one of a kind—an advertising idea is creative when it is novel, fresh, unexpected, and unusual. Because it is novel, it is surprising and gets your attention. To be effective, the idea also must have **impact,** which means it makes an impression on the audience.

But how do you know if your idea is creative? Any idea can seem creative to you if you have never thought of it before, but the essence of a creative idea is that *no one else has thought of it either*. Thus, the first rule is to avoid doing what everyone else is doing. In an industry that prides itself on creativity, **copycat advertising**—that is, using an idea that someone else has originated—is a concern. Advertising expert John Eighmy estimates that about 50 percent of the advertising in the United States falls into this category.[23]

The importance of originality may be obvious, but why is relevance important to an advertising Big Idea? Consider the award-winning California Milk Board campaign "Got Milk?" The consumer insight is that people drink milk with certain foods such as cupcakes. If milk is unavailable to drink with those foods, people are—to say the least—frustrated. Thus, associating these products with milk is a highly relevant idea.

Likewise, why is impact important? We know that many advertisements just wash over the audience. An idea with impact, however, breaks through the clutter, gets attention, and sticks in memory. A *breakthrough ad* has stopping power and that comes from an intriguing idea—a Big Idea that is important, interesting, and relevant to consumers.

The idea that some moments, such as when eating cupcakes and cookies, require a glass of milk is the creative concept behind the award-winning "Got Milk?" campaign. The creative concept is expressed both in words and pictures in this ad.

The Creative Leap

We all use different ways of thinking in different situations. For example, the term **divergent thinking** is used to describe a style of thinking that explores multiple possibilities rather than using rational thinking to arrive at the "right" or logical conclusion. The heart of creative thinking, divergent thinking uses exploration (playfulness) to search for alternatives. Another term for divergent thinking is **right-brain thinking,** which is intuitive, holistic, artistic, and emotionally expressive thinking in contrast to **left-brain thinking,** which is logical, linear (inductive or deductive), and orderly. How can you become a more creative thinker—someone who uses the right brain for divergent explorations?

First, think about the problem as something that involves a mind shift. Instead of seeing the obvious, a creative idea looks at a problem in a different way, from a different angle. That's referred to as *thinking outside the box*. It doesn't matter how dull the product might appear to be, there is always an opportunity to move it beyond its category limitations through a creative Big Idea.

For example, as Frontier restructured its operations during the economic downturn of the late 2000s, like other airlines, it raised prices on checked luggage. However the creative team at Grey deftly asked consumers to think about this in another way—instead of thinking of baggage charges as additional costs, it asked passengers to pay only for what they used. The agency repositioned the practice to show that now passengers had the freedom of choice to pay only for services if they use them.

Second, put the strategy language behind you. Finding the brilliant creative concept entails what advertising giant Otto Kleppner called the *creative leap*[24]—a process of jumping from the rather boring business language in a strategy statement to an original idea. This Big Idea transforms the strategy into something unexpected, original, and interesting. Since the creative leap means moving from the safety of a predictable strategy statement to an unusual idea that hasn't been tried before, this leap is the *creative risk*.

A classic example of out-of-the-box thinking is Michelin's tire advertising, which is driven by the strategic idea that the tire is durable and dependable—language that would make a pretty boring ad. The creative idea, however, comes to life in the long-running campaign that shows a baby sitting in a tire. The visual is reinforced by the slogan, "Because so much is riding on your

Principle

To get a creative idea, you must leap beyond the mundane language of the strategy statement and see the problem in a novel and unexpected way.

Another safe delivery.
Michelin. Because so much is riding on your tyres.

Michelin's dependability and durability surround and protect a car's precious cargo.

Principle
Getting a great advertising idea that is also on strategy is an emotional high.

tires." The creative concept "leaps" from the idea of a durable tire to the idea of protecting your family, particularly precious members like tiny children, by surrounding them with the dependability of a Michelin tire.

All creative ideas in advertising involve this element of risk. Alex Bogusky, chief creative officer at Crispin Porter + Bogusky, one of the country's hottest creative agencies, says he welcomes over-the-top work (think the Subservient Chicken and the Burger King king) because it gets talked about. "I don't mind spectacular failure or spectacular criticism," he says, because those ideas make headlines, which means everybody's talking about them. "There's so much advertising that nobody knows even exists," he adds. "That's the stuff that I worry about making."[25]

Dialing Up Your Creativity

How creative are you? You probably know people who are just naturally zany, who come up with crazy, off-the-wall ideas. As Sasser reminds us, "everyone has some level of internal creativity." Creative advertising people may be weird and unconventional, however they can't be totally eccentric. They still must be purpose driven, meaning they are focused on creating effective advertising that's on strategy.

Coming up with a great idea that is also on strategy is an emotional high. Advertising creatives describe it as one of the biggest emotional roller coasters in the business world. One copywriter explained that when the ideas aren't flowing, you feel like fleeing the country. But when it's a good idea, there's nothing better. It's a real high. In *The Inside Story* at *www.pearsonhighered.com/moriarty,* Ingvi Logason explains how he got the idea for a campaign for a recycling center in Iceland.

Research by the Center for Studies in Creativity in Buffalo, New York, has found that most people can sharpen their skills and develop their creative potential. Research indicates that creative people tend to be independent, assertive, self-sufficient, persistent, and self-disciplined, with a high tolerance for ambiguity. They are also risk takers with powerful egos that are internally driven. They don't care much about group standards and opinions and typically have inborn skepticism and strong curiosity. Here are a few of the key characteristics of creative people who do well in advertising:

- *Problem Solving* Creative problem solvers are alert, watchful, and observant and reach conclusions through intuition rather than through logic.
- *Playful* Creative people have fun with ideas; they have a mental playfulness that allows them to make novel associations.
- *The Ability to Visualize* Most of the information we accumulate comes through sight, so the ability to manipulate visual images is crucial for good copywriters as well as designers. They can see products, people, and scenes in the mind's eye, and they can visualize a mental picture of the finished ad while it is still in the talking, or idea, stage.
- *Open to New Experiences* As we said earlier, one characteristic that identifies creative people is that they are open to new experiences. Over the course of a lifetime, openness to experience may give you many more adventures from which to draw. Those experiences would, in turn, give a novelist more characters to write about, a painter more scenes to paint, and the creative team more angles from which to tackle an advertising problem.[26]
- *Conceptual Thinking* It's easy to see how people who are open to experience might develop innovative advertisements and commercials because they are more imaginative.[27] Such imagination led to a famous Nike commercial in which Michael Jordan and Larry Bird play an outlandish game of horse—bouncing the ball off buildings, billboards, and places that are impossible to reach.

PRACTICAL TIPS

Exercise Your Creative Muscles

Linda Conway Correll, *Assistant Professor, Southern Illinois University*

Developed by Linda Conway Correll, Creative Aerobics is a four-step, idea-generating process that is explained here in terms of finding a creative idea for a hypothetical client—oranges:[29]

1. *Facts* The first exercise is left brain and asks you to come up with a list of facts about a product (an orange has seeds, is juicy, has vitamin C).
2. *New Names* In the second exercise you create new "names" for the product (Florida, a vitamin supplement, a kiss of sunshine).
3. *Similarities* The third exercise looks for similarities between dissimilar objects. (What are the similarities between the new names and the product? For in-

stance, Florida sunshine and oranges both suggest warmth, freshness, sunshine, the fountain of youth.)

4. *New Definitions* The fourth exercise, a cousin of the pun, creates new definitions for product-related nouns. Peel (face peel, peel out), seed (seed money, bird seed), navel/naval (naval academy, contemplating one's navel), pulp (pulp fiction), C/see/si/sea (C the light).

Headlines derived from those definitions might be: "Seed money" (the money to purchase oranges), "Contemplating one's navel" (looking at oranges), "Peel out" (when your grocer is out of oranges), "Navel intelligence" (information about an orange), "Pulp fiction" (a story about an orange), "C the light" (the orange is a low-calorie source of vitamin C). These new definitions stimulate the flowering of a new Big Idea.

As important as creative thinking is for advertising professionals, strategic thinking is just as important. In taking a peek into the minds of those who hire new creative people, researchers found repeated verbatim comments from creative directors concerning the importance of strategic Big Ideas. "Emphasize concept," said one creative director. "Teach them to think first and execute later."[28]

Principle
Emphasize concepts. Worry about their execution later.

The Creative Process: How to Get an Idea

Only in cartoons do light bulbs appear above our heads from out of nowhere when a good idea strikes. In reality, most people who are good at thinking up new ideas will tell you it is hard work. They read, study, analyze, test and retest, sweat, curse, and worry. Sometimes they give up. The unusual, unexpected, novel idea rarely comes easily—and that's as true in science and medicine as it is in advertising.

But most experts on creativity realize that there are steps to the process of thinking up a new idea. One approach called *creative aerobics* is a thought-starter process detailed in the *Practical Tips* feature that works well in advertising because it uses both the head and the heart.

The creative process usually is portrayed as a series of steps. English sociologist Graham Wallas was the first to outline the creative process, but others followed, including Alex Osborn, one of the founders of the BBDO agency and the Creative Education Foundation.[30] Let's summarize this classic approach in the following steps:

Step 1. **Immersion** Read, research, and learn everything you can about the problem.

Step 2. **Ideation** Look at the problem from every angle; develop ideas; generate as many alternatives as possible.

Step 3. **Brainfag** Don't give up if—and when—you hit a blank wall.

Step 4. **Incubation** Try to put your conscious mind to rest to let your subconscious take over.

Step 5. **Illumination** Embrace that unexpected moment when the idea comes, often when your mind is relaxed and you're doing something else.

Step 6. **Evaluation** Does it work? Is it on strategy?

Carlsberg Sport Drink used a number of creative techniques in this commercial including the unexpected (squirrel playing soccer after sipping the drink) and exaggeration.

Brainstorming

As part of the creative process, some agencies use a thinking technique known as **brainstorming** where a group of 6 to 10 people work together to come up with ideas. One person's idea stimulates someone else's, and the combined power of the group associations stimulates far more ideas than any one person could think of alone. The group becomes an idea factory.

That's how the Road Crew concept was developed. This Big Idea evolved out of many brainstorming sessions with the project leadership team, as well as with people in the communities where the team was working with local leaders to build coalitions to sponsor the effort. A list of names for the project was compiled and guys in bars who fit the target audience profile voted on the winner, which turned out to be Road Crew. The slogan "Beats driving" was developed using the same process.

The term *brainstorming* was coined by Alex Osborn, founder of the advertising agency BBDO and explained in his book *Applied Imagination*. The secret to brainstorming is to remain positive and defer judgment. Negative thinking during a brainstorming session can destroy the informal atmosphere necessary to achieve a novel idea.

To stimulate group creativity against a deadline, some agencies have special processes or locations for brainstorming sessions with no distractions and interruptions, such as cell phones and access to e-mail, and walls that can be covered with sheets of paper on which to write ideas. Some agencies rent a suite in a hotel and send the creative team there to get away and immerse themselves in the problem. When the GSDM agency was defending its prized Southwest Airlines account, the president ordered a 28-day "war room/death march" that had staffers working around the clock, wearing Rambo-style camouflage, and piling all their trash inside the building to keep any outsiders from rummaging around for clues to their pitch.

The following list builds on our previous discussion of creative thinking. It can also be used as an outline for a brainstorming session.

To create an original and unexpected idea, use the following techniques:

- ***What if?*** To twist the commonplace, ask a crazy *what if* question. For example, what if wild animals could talk? That question is the origin of Frontier's talking animals campaign.
- ***An Unexpected Association*** In **free association** you think of a word and then describe everything that comes into your mind when you imagine that word. If you follow a chain of associations, you may come up with an idea that sets up an unexpected juxtaposition with the original word or concept. An ad for Compaq used a visual of a chained butterfly to illustrate the lack of freedom in competitors' computer workstations.
- ***Dramatize the Obvious*** Sometimes the most creative idea is also the most obvious. That's true for the Voodoo Doughnuts campaign. One of our Showcase contributors, Karl Schroeder, explained that the idea of magical power residing in a doughnut is new, but the black magic idea comes directly from the name of the product.
- ***Catchy Phrasing*** Isuzu used "The 205 Horsepower Primal Scream" for its Rodeo headline.

- *An Unexpected Twist* An ad for Amazon.com used the headline "460 books for Marxists. Including 33 on Groucho." A road crew usually refers to highway construction workers or the behind-the-scenes people on a concert tour, but for the Road Crew campaign, the phrase was twisted to refer to limo drivers who give rides to people who have had too much to drink.
- *Play on Words* Under the headline "Happy Camper," an ad for cheese showed a picture of a packed sports utility vehicle with a huge wedge of cheese lashed to the rooftop.
- *Analogy and Metaphor* Used to see new patterns or relationships, metaphors, and **analogies** that by definition set up juxtapositions. Harley-Davidson compared the legendary sound of its motorcycles to the taste of a thick, juicy steak.
- *Familiar and Strange* Put the familiar in an unexpected situation: UPS showed a tiny model of its familiar brown truck moving through a computer cord.
- *A Twisted Cliché* They may have been great ideas the first time they were used, but phrases such as "the road to success" or "the fast track" become trite when overused. But they can regain their power if twisted into a new context. The "Happy Camper" line was twisted by relating cheese to an SUV.
- *Twist the Obvious* Avoid the predictable, such as a picture of a Cadillac on Wall Street or in front of a mansion. Instead, use an SUV on Wall Street ("fast tracker") or a basketball hoop in front of a mansion ("slam dunk").
- *Exaggeration* Take a common situation or item and exaggerate it until it becomes funny (an unbreakable kiss with the lovers totally unresponsive to over-the-top attempts to break them apart).

To prevent unoriginal ideas, avoid or work around the following:
- *The Look-Alike* Avoid copycat advertising that uses somebody else's great idea. Hundreds of ads for escape products (resorts, travel, liquor, foods) have used the headline "Paradise Found." It's a play on "paradise lost" but still overused.
- *The Tasteless* In an attempt to be cute, a Subaru ad used the headline, "Put it where the sun don't shine." An attempted twist on a cliché, but it doesn't work.

Getting the Big Idea for marketing communication campaigns has always been the province of creative teams in agencies. Recently, however, with the development of new crowdsourcing practices, marketers are finding ways to enlist the collective ideas of thousands to come up with great ideas. Doritos has held "Crash the Super Bowl" competitions that invite consumers to create ads to run during the Super Bowl.

MANAGING CREATIVE STRATEGIES

We've talked about creative strategy and how it is developed, along with the types of effects advertising creates and the message strategies that deliver on these objectives. Let's now look at management issues that affect the formulation of creative strategies and campaigns: extension, adaptation, and evaluation.

Extension: An Idea with Legs

One characteristic of a Big Idea is that it gives *legs* to a campaign. By that we mean that the idea is strong enough to serve as an umbrella concept for a variety of executions in different media talking to different audiences. It can be endlessly extended.

Extendability is a strength of Frontier's talking animals campaign as well. The logic and structure of the concept is explained by the campaign's creators in the *A Matter of Practice* box.

Adaptation: Taking an Idea Global

The opportunity for standardizing the campaign across multiple markets exists only if the objectives and strategic position are essentially the same. Otherwise, a creative strategy may call for a little tweaking of the message for a local market or even major revision if there are a great deal of cultural and market differences.

In the case where the core targeting and positioning strategies remain the same in different markets, it might be possible for the central creative idea to be universal across markets. Although

A MATTER OF PRACTICE

A Campaign with Legs (and Flippers)

Shawn Couzens and Gary Ennis, *Creative Directors, Grey Advertising*

When Frontier has something to sell—whether it's a new city, a website, or the frequent flyer program—we let the animals deliver the message in a fun, humorous way. Certain characters are better suited for certain messages than others.

Flip, for example, is the lovable loser who never gets a break. For years, he's been dying to fly to a warm, tropical climate, such as Florida. But instead, he always gets sent to Chicago. This has been a recurring theme in several commercials. So, when Frontier expanded its service to Mexico, this was the perfect opportunity to build on Flip's storyline. Hence, "Flip to Mexico."

The point is that the campaign has always been episodic, like a situation comedy. With 10-plus TV spots a year, we needed a structure that allowed us to build on the characters and their storylines.

If our base-brand campaign were a sitcom, then *Flip to Mexico* would be a spin-off. The idea was to blanket the city with the "news" that Flip would quit unless he went to Mexico—and he needed the public's help to get there. We wanted the community to be an active participant in the story. To facilitate this, we launched a series of mock newscasts covering Flip's evolving storyline. We hired "activists" to hold placards and distribute leaflets, and we created an elaborate underground website with lots of interactive content. We even involved real Frontier employees, like CEO Jeff Potter, to help blur the line between reality and fiction. Consumers enjoyed the interplay, and they happily rallied for Flip. The story really captivated the city of Denver. It was all over the news. And it deepened the bond between Frontier and the community at a time when other airlines were trying to eat into Frontier's home turf.

But it's no longer about just TV, print, and radio. An idea has to perform across multiple platforms, and new media is a big part of that. Brands will have to find other ways to connect with consumers—like podcasts, interactive websites, YouTube Contests, branded entertainment, product placement, long-format digital content, and more. Some brands are creating their own TV shows or Web channels with original programming. The media landscape will continue to change. What won't change is the need for talented writers and art directors who can think outside the parameters of traditional media and make the brand story relevant and entertaining across all of these different media and formats.

A campaign is an evolving story, so you can't rest on your awards. When you launch a successful campaign, and everyone likes it, you've set the creative bar pretty high. Everyone's waiting to see what you'll do next. Your job is to keep surprising them, keep raising the bar—because if you don't do it, someone else will.

There's a saying in the industry, "You're only as good as your last ad." It's kind of true. One week, you're being praised for an ad or campaign. But the next week, you have a new creative brief in your hand, and you have to prove yourself all over again.

---

the implementation of this idea may vary from market to market, the creative concept is sound across all types of consumers. Even if the campaign theme, slogan, or visual elements are the same across markets, it is usually desirable to adapt the creative execution to the local market, as we explained in the discussion of cultural differences in Chapter 5.

An example of a difficult adaptation comes from Apple's series of "Mac vs. PC" ads that show a nerdy PC guy who can't keep up with the activities of a laid-back Mac guy. It uses delicate humor and body language to make subtle points about the advantages of the Mac system. In moving the campaign to Japan, Apple's agency, TBWA/Chiat/Day wrestled with the fact that in Japanese culture, direct-comparison ads are considered rude. The Japanese version was tweaked to make the Apple more of a home computer and the PC a work tool, so the differences were focused more on place than person.[31] The point is that cultural differences often require nuanced and subtle changes in ads if they are to be acceptable beyond the country of their origin.

Evaluation: The Go/No-Go Decision

How do you decide if the creative idea is strong enough to justify the expense of creating a campaign based on it? Whether local or global, an important part of managing creative work is evaluation, which happens at several stages in the creative process. Chapter 19 focuses on evaluation, but we'll introduce some basics here to help you understand this important final step in the creative process.

A new book on Bill Bernbach and the golden age of advertising, *Nobody's Perfect* by Doris Willens,[32] analyzed the brilliant advertising his creative team at DDB produced during the 1960s. In commenting on the book, positioning guru Al Ries observed that Bernbach was a true creative genius because he had the ability to sort good ideas from bad. Ries concluded, "It's a trait that's extremely rare."[33]

So nobody starts off being a Bernbach, but everyone can learn to be more critical about the advertising they see. The first question is: Is it on strategy? No matter how much the creative people, client, or account executive may like an idea, if it doesn't communicate the right message or the right product personality to the right audience at the right time, then it is not effective. That's the science of advertising.

Structural Analysis   The Leo Burnett agency has an approach for analyzing the logic of the creative strategy that goes beyond just evaluating the strategy. The Burnett creatives use it to keep the message strategy and creative concept working together, along with the head and heart appeals. This method, called **structural analysis**, relies on these three steps:

1. Evaluate the *power of the narrative* or story line (heart).
2. Evaluate the *strength of the product claim* (head).
3. Consider *how well the two are integrated*—that is, how the storyline brings the claim to life.

Burnett creative teams check to see whether the narrative level is so high that it overpowers the claim or whether the claim is strong but there is no memorable story. Ideally, these two elements will be so seamless that it is hard to tell whether the impact occurs because of the power of the story or the strength of the claim. Such an analysis keeps the rational and emotional sides of an advertisement working together.

Copytesting   A formal method to evaluate the effectiveness of an ad, either in draft form or after it has been executed, is called **copytesting**. Remember: To evaluate the results, the objectives need to be measurable, which means they can be evaluated to determine the effectiveness of the creative strategy. Copytesting uses a variety of tools to measure and predict the impact of the advertisement. Chapter 19 explains these tools in more detail.

A particular problem that Big Ideas face is that the message is sometimes so creative that the ad is remembered but not the product. That's called **vampire creativity,** and it is one reason some advertisers shy away from really novel or entertaining strategies. That's also why it is important to copytest the effectiveness of the ad's creative features while still in the idea stage to determine if there is brand linkage and memorability.

Looking Ahead

That's a brief review of the changes in message strategy prompted by the economic downturn. The next step in learning about the inner workings of the creative side is to move to the execution of message—both copy and design. We'll talk first about copywriting in Chapter 9 and then visual communication in Chapter 10.

IT'S A WRAP

Frontier's Still the One

Frontier Airlines and Grey Worldwide sent an unmistakable message that airline advertising doesn't need to be stuffy. Talking and singing animals broke through the clutter demonstrating another lesson: You can sell your audience and entertain them simultaneously, but accomplishing the client's business goals is central to success. Maybe the most important lesson of this work is that a strong brand and a good story can even help a company survive bankruptcy.

Over time the animals and their quirky personalities made an emotional connection with would-be travelers. A campaign about sending an animal to a warm weather destination is much more fun than a plain vanilla announcement that an airline now has a route to Mexico. Animals that sing a spirited rendition of "You're Still the One" show that, in spite of hard times, Frontier is "Still a Whole Different Animal" and a brand worth celebrating.

Frontier's campaigns demonstrate both the art and science of advertising. At the same time the message strategies for these campaigns resulted in a hard-nosed, business-building effort, the creative ideas also captivated consumers. The advertising works not only because it delivers on the brand promise, but also because customers like the airline more because of the campaign and are engaged enough with the Frontier brand to follow the stories of its cast of characters.

Frontier's advertising has been recognized with a hangar full of awards. Frontier was nominated for "best of show" at the International Mobius awards for two years in a row. Frontier was awarded a Silver Clio for the prestigious "content & contact" category. Frontier won coveted Effie awards as well, including a gold Effie in the category of sustained success.

Key Points Summary

1. **How do we explain the science and art of creative strategy, as well as the important parts of a creative brief?** From the advertising strategy comes the problem statement, the objectives, the target market, and the positioning strategy. The message strategy decisions include the appropriate type of creative strategy, the selling premise, and suggestions about the ad's execution, such as tone of voice.

2. **What are some key message strategy approaches?** Creative strategies are often expressed as appeals to the head, the heart, or both. More complex systems of strategies have been proposed by Frazer and Taylor. Creative strategy formats include lectures, dramas, psychological appeals, and selling strategies. Different formulas have evolved that deliver these strategies and guide the development of executions.

3. **Can creative thinking be defined, and how does it lead to a Big Idea?** To be creative, an ad must make a relevant connection with its audience and present a selling idea in an unexpected way. There is both a science (the way a message is persuasive, convincing, and relevant) and an art (the

way a message is an unexpected idea). A Big Idea is a creative concept that makes the message attention getting and memorable.

4. **What characteristics do creative people have in common, and what is their typical creative process?** Creative people tend to be independent, assertive, self-sufficient, persistent, and self-disciplined, with a high tolerance for ambiguity. They are also risk takers with powerful egos that are internally driven. They don't care much about group standards and opinions and typically have inborn skepticism and strong curiosity. They are good problem solvers with an ability to visualize and do conceptual thinking. They are open to new experiences. A typical creative process involves immersing yourself in background research; developing alternatives through ideation; getting past brainfag, where you hit the wall and can't come up with anything; and embracing illumination of the great idea.

5. **What issues affect the management of creative strategy and its implementation?** Those working on the creative

side of advertising must do so within the parameters of the business context. Some factors that have an impact on the development of creative strategy and its implementation are extension, adaptation, and evaluation. A concept is extendable if it can serve as an umbrella idea for other communication. A campaign is adaptable if the idea can be used in another context such as a global application. Evaluation is a critical management issue because it is important to test whether a concept communicates the intended message to the target audience.

Words of Wisdom: Recommended Reading

Alstiel, Tom, and Jean Grow, *Advertising Creative: Strategy, Copy and Design,* 2nd ed., Sage Publications, 2009.

Barry, Pete, *The Advertising Concept Book: A Complete Guide to Creative Ideas, Strategies, and Campaigns,* London: Thames & Hudson, 2008.

Bendinger, Bruce, *The Copy Workshop Workbook,* Chicago: Copy Workshop, 2009.

Drewniany, Bonnie L., and A. Jerome Jewler, *Creative Strategy in Advertising,* 10th ed., Boston: Wadsworth, Cengage Learning, 2011.

Griffin, W. Glenn, and Deborah Morrison, *The Creative Process Illustrated: How Advertising's Big Ideas Are Born,* Cincinnati, OH: F&W Media/HOW Design, 2010.

Pricken, Mario, *Creative Advertising: Ideas and Techniques from the World's Best Campaigns,* London: Thames & Hudson, 2008.

Sullivan, Luke, *Hey, Whipple, Squeeze This: A Guide to Creating Great Advertising,* Adweek Series, Hoboken, NJ: Wiley, 2008.

Key Terms

analogies, p. 251
appeal, p. 237
attributes, p. 239
benefit, p. 239
Big Idea, p. 244
brainfag, p. 249
brainstorming, p. 250
brand icon, p. 240
call to action, p. 243
claim, p. 239
clichés, p. 244
comparison, p. 240
concepting, p. 244
copycat advertising, p. 247
copytesting, p. 253
creative brief, p. 231
creative concept, p. 244

creative director, p. 228
creative platform, p. 231
creative strategy, p. 231
demonstration, p. 239
divergent thinking, p. 247
endorser, p. 240
execution, p. 231
features, p. 239
free association, p. 250
hard sell, p. 235
humor, p. 240
idea, p. 244
ideation, p. 249
illumination, p. 249
image advertising, p. 242
immersion, p. 249
impact, p. 247

incubation, p. 249
left-brain thinking, p. 247
message strategy, p. 231
original, p. 247
permission to believe, p. 242
problem avoidance
  message, p. 240
problem solution
  message, p. 240
product-as-hero, p. 240
promise, p. 239
reason why, p. 239
relevant, p. 247
reminder advertising, p. 243
right-brain thinking, p. 247
ROI of creativity, p. 246
selling premise, p. 239

slice-of-life message, p. 240
slogans, p. 241
soft sell, p. 235
spokes-character, p. 240
spokesperson, p. 240
straightforward
  message, p. 239
structural analysis, p. 253
substantiation, p. 239
support, p. 239
taglines, p. 241
teaser, p. 240
tone of voice, p. 231
unique selling proposition
  (USP), p. 239
vampire creativity, p. 253

Review Questions

1. This chapter argues that effective advertising is both a science and an art. Explain what that means and give examples of each.

2. How do various strategic approaches deliver on the objectives identified in the Facets Model of Effects?

3. What is an appeal? How do advertisements touch people's emotions? Describe two techniques.

4. Explain the four types of selling premises.

5. What is a Big Idea, and what are its characteristics?

6. When a creative director says your idea needs to make a "creative leap," what does that mean?

7. Describe the five steps in the creative process.

8. Explain how brainstorming is used in advertising.

9. Give an example of a technique you might use as a thought starter to stimulate a creative idea.

10. List five characteristics of creative people. How do you rate yourself on those factors?

11. Explain structural analysis and copytesting and how they are used in evaluating the creative strategy.

Discussion Questions

1. Find the ad in this book that you think is the most creative.

   • What is its Big Idea? How and why does it work?

   • Analyze the ad in terms of the ROI formula for evaluating effective creative advertising.

   • Re-create the creative brief that would summarize the ad's message strategy.

2. Divide the class into groups of 6 to 10 people and discuss this problem: *Your community wants to encourage people to get out of their cars and use alternative forms of transportation.* Brainstorm for 15 minutes as a group, accumulating every possible idea. How many ideas are generated?

   Here's how to run this brainstorming group:

   • Appoint one member to be the *recorder* who lists all the ideas as they are mentioned.

   • Appoint another member to be the *moderator* and suggest techniques described in this chapter as idea starters.

   • Identify a *cheerleader* to keep the discussion positive and find gentle ways to discourage critical or negative comments.

   • Work for 15 minutes generating as many different creative concepts as your team can come up with, regardless of how crazy or dumb they might initially sound.

   • Go back through the list as a group and put an asterisk next to the 5 to 10 ideas that seem to have the most promise.

   When all of the groups reconvene in class, each recorder should list the group's best ideas on the blackboard. As a class, pick out the three ideas that seem to have the most potential. Analyze the experience of participating in a brainstorming group and compare the experiences of the different teams.

3. *Three-Minute Debate* Here's the topic: *Is entertainment a useful objective for an advertising campaign?* This is an issue that advertising experts debate because, although entertainment may get and keep attention, some experts believe the focus should be on selling products not entertaining consumers. Build a case for your side—either pro or con on the effectiveness of entertaining ads.

Take-Home Projects

1. *Portfolio Project* Find at least two newspaper or magazine advertisements that your team believes are bland and unexciting. Rewrite them, first to demonstrate a hard-sell approach and then to demonstrate a soft-sell approach. Explain how your rewrites have improved the original ad. Also explain how the hard-sell and soft-sell appeals work. Which do you believe is the most effective for each ad? If you were a team of professionals working on these accounts, how would you go about evaluating the effectiveness of these two ads? In other words, how would you test your intuitive judgment of which one works best?

2. *Mini-Case Analysis* Summarize the creative strategy behind Frontier's "Whole Different Animal" campaign. Explain how the Big Idea works and what makes it creative. How does the "Leather Seats" commercial relate to the "Whole Different Animal" campaign? Brainstorm on an idea for a new commercial that would extend the campaign's theme and develop this new Big Idea as a proposal to present to your instructor.

Team Project: BrandRevive Revitalization Campaign

Based on the BrandRevive campaign plan that your team developed in the preceding chapter, now put together a message strategy for this campaign. First review the Creative Brief then outline a creative strategy to bring this fading or unknown product back to life or create a stronger consumer presence for the brand.

- Decide the strategic approach—head/heart or some other approach from the Frazer or Taylor models and explain why you believe that approach would work.

- Decide the appeal and/or selling strategy and explain why.
- Brainstorm for a Big Idea. Explain the best of the ideas you developed and how you decided on one as your Big Idea.
- Present your findings in a one-page report and a PowerPoint presentation that is no longer than three slides. In the presentation explain and justify your recommendations.

Hands-On Case

The Century Council

Read the Century Council case in the Appendix before coming to class.

1. What is the Big Idea in The Century Council case study? Write a one-page summary of why you think it is a good or bad idea.

2. Write the creative brief for The Century Council case study.

3. Once the target understands the concept of The Stupid Drink, they seem to understand it. How would you evolve the campaign in its second year?

9

Copywriting

It's a Winner

Campaign:	Company:	Agency:	Awards:
"Eat Mor Chikin"	Chick-fil-A	The Richards Group	Silver Effies in Sustained Success Campaign and Restaurant Categories, Obie Hall of Fame (Outdoor Advertising Association of America), Silver Lion at Cannes International Advertising Festival

258

CHAPTER KEY POINTS

1. What basic style of writing is used for advertising copy?
2. Which copy elements are essential to a print ad?
3. How can we characterize the message and tools of radio advertising?
4. What is the best way to summarize the major elements of television commercials?
5. How is Web advertising written?

Chick-fil-A Gets Creative with Renegade Cows

You gotta hand it to the cows. While the renegade cows do not know how to spell, they sure know how to sell "chikin" sandwiches for Chick-fil-A. And they've been doing it for more than 14 years in the award-winning "Eat Mor Chikin®" campaign created by The Richards Group.

Behind the successful cow campaign are copywriters who are responsible for generating the creative concept and writing the copy, or text, for ads. They understand this ad lesson: At the heart of every piece of memorable advertising is a great concept. These creatives know that good copywriting is an art that sells. It's the job of copywriters to marry visual with the words to bring the concept to life. They distill a promotional idea to its very essence and communicate it through their art. The really great ideas like Chick-fil-A's renegade cows have sticking power because they memorably connect with the audience.

As you analyze the "Eat Mor Chikin" campaign for Chick-fil-A, ask yourself why it has been effective for so many years. Let's take a closer look.

Chick-fil-A started with a significant challenge: It had to persuade people to eat chicken sandwiches when everybody else in the world seemed to be eating hamburgers. Chick-fil-A is not your typical quick-service restaurant chain, and neither is its advertising. Truett Cathy founded Chick-fil-A with the vision that his chicken sandwich company would be a leader in the quick-service restaurant industry. Chick-fil-A has become just that, in part by understanding how to put advertising to work to attract consumers' attention and generate a response at the restaurants.

Here's another important ad lesson: You do not have to be a big brand with millions of dollars to have great advertising. The Chick-fil-A "Eat Mor Chikin" campaign is a great example. Chick-fil-A competes in the fast-food category, one of the largest and most competitive industries. It is outnumbered 4 to 1 in store count and outspent 10 to 1 in media by the likes of McDonald's, Burger King, and Wendy's.

Faced with these disadvantages in the marketplace, Chick-fil-A and its advertising agency set out to develop a brand campaign that would increase top-of-mind awareness, increase sales, and earn Chick-fil-A a spot in consumers' consideration list of fast-food brands. To do this effectively, the campaign positioned Chick-fil-A chicken sandwiches as the premium alternative to hamburgers.

Chick-fil-A defines its brand: "To choosy people in a hurry, Chick-fil-A is the premium fast-food restaurant brand that consistently serves America's best-loved chicken sandwiches." The copywriters crafted a campaign to communicate the brand's promise. And they did so by creating the beloved bovines that could do the selling for them.

The company couldn't outspend the competition. It couldn't even afford a national campaign on television, which is where most of its competitors were advertising. So it decided to advertise where its competitors weren't—on billboards. Copywriters kept the idea simple and fun (after all, they are selling chicken sandwiches) and the copy to a minimum.

For Chick-fil-A and its agency, overcoming the challenge turned out to be easier than expected. Chick-fil-A's "Eat Mor Chikin" three-dimensional billboard campaign helped break the fast-food hamburger pattern. The witty use of Holstein cows encouraging the target audience to "Eat Mor Chikin" instead of beef provided a bold brand personality that broke through industry clutter. Why? The message and execution were simple, the cows were funny, the creative idea was unexpected, and the call to action was powerful.

In this chapter you will learn what it takes to write effective copy. You will read about different techniques for a variety of media. You will also learn what it takes for companies such as Chick-fil-A to create memorable advertising that works.

Did the charming cows successfully moo-ve consumers to eat more Chick-fil-A? Hoof it to the end of the chapter to see the results.

Sources: www.chick-fil-a.com; information courtesy of Mike Buerno, The Richards Group, "Winners Showcase," www.effie.org; www.lamaroutdoor.com/outdoorfiles.

Words and pictures work together to produce a creative concept. However, the idea behind a creative concept in advertising is usually expressed in some attention-getting and memorable phrase, such as "Curiously Strong Mints" for Altoids or "Eat Mor Chikin." Finding these "magic words" is the responsibility of copywriters who search for the right way to warm up a mood or soften consumer resistance. They begin with the strategy outlined in the previous chapter, which is usually summarized in a creative brief. Then, working with an art director, and perhaps a creative director, the creative team searches for Big Ideas, in the form of magic words and powerful visuals that translate the strategy into a message that is attention getting and memorable. This chapter describes the role of the copywriter as part of this team and explains the practice of copywriting in print, broadcast, and Internet advertising.

WHAT IS THE LANGUAGE OF COPYWRITING?

Some creative concepts are primarily visual, but intriguing ideas can also be expressed through language; and a truly great Big Idea will come to life in the interaction between the words and pictures. For example, a long-running campaign for the NYNEX Yellow Pages illustrates how words and pictures work together to create a concept with a twist. The campaign used visual plays on words to illustrate some of the headings in its directory. Each pun makes sense when the visual is married with the heading from the directory but neither the words or the pictures would work on their own. One commercial in the series included three train engineers with overalls, caps, and bandannas sitting in rocking chairs in a parlor and having tea to illustrate the "Civil Engineering" category; a picture of a bull sleeping on its back illustrates the category "Bulldozing."

Although advertising is highly visual, words are crucial in four types of advertisements:

1. **Complex** If the message is complicated, particularly if it is making an argument, words can be more specific than visuals and can be read over and over until the meaning is clear.
2. **High Involvement** If the ad is for a high-involvement product, meaning the consumer spends a lot of time considering it, then the more information the better. That means using words.
3. **Explanation** Information that needs definition and explanation, like how a new wireless phone works, is best delivered through words.
4. **Abstract** If a message tries to convey abstract qualities, such as justice and quality, words tend to communicate these concepts more easily than pictures.

The Copywriter

The person who shapes and sculpts the words in marketing communication is called a **copywriter.** *Copy* is the text of an ad or the words people say in a commercial. A successful advertising copywriter is a savvy marketer and a literary master, sometimes described as a "killer poet." Many copywriters have a background in English or literature. They love words and search for the clever twist, the pun, the powerful description, the punch, the nuance, as well as the rhyme and rhythm of speech. They use words that whip and batter, plead, sob, cajole, and impress. They know the meanings, derivations, moods, and feelings of words and the reverberations and vibrations they create in a reader's mind. A classic ad, titled "The Wonderful World of Words," expresses this fascination. A house ad for the business-to-business agency Marsteller Inc., it was written by Bill Marsteller, another advertising legend. He also was co-founder of public relations agency Burson-Marsteller. Here is an excerpt from this ad:

> "Human beings come in all sizes, a variety of colors, in different ages, and with unique, complex and changing personalities.
>
> So do Words.
>
> There are tall, skinny words, and short, fat ones, and strong ones and weak ones, and boy words and girl words.
>
> For instance, title, lattice, latitude, lily, tattle, Illinois, and intellect are all lean and lanky. While these words get their height partly out of t's and l's and i's, other words are tall and skinny without a lot of ascenders and descenders. Take, for example, Abraham, peninsula and ellipsis, all tall.
>
> Here are some nice short-fat words: hog, yogurt, bomb, pot, bon-bon, acne, plump, sop and slobber."

In addition to having an ear for the perfect phrase, copywriters listen to the way people talk and identify the tone of voice that best fits the target audience and the brand. An example comes from an all-copy ad for British Airways. Set up like a poem with definite rhythm and alliteration, the copy block begins and ends with the airlines initials, but in between it lyrically interprets what "upgrading" to BA means to a passenger:

Be a guest not a
passenger. We believe
The way you fly is
just as important
as where you fly.
It's not simply
about getting

a seat, it's about
getting service.
Not just food
but a meal. Not
just something
to watch but
something worth

watching. In short,
it's about upgrading
flying for every
passenger on
every plane. Now
there's an ideA.

Source: Courtesy of British Airways plc.

Our book gives advertisers reason to smile.

▶ **Amusement Devices**

LEE'S MOON TRIP

The NYNEX Yellow Pages is constantly working to help our advertisers make some serious money. Its reach far exceeds its rivals. Last year alone, when referring to the yellow pages, the NYNEX directory was used by over 87% of the NYNEX region. And 50% of those who referred to our book ultimately made a purchase. As you would expect, such reach and consumer response make advertising in the NYNEX Yellow Pages a pleasure. **NYNEX Yellow Pages**

CLASSIC
The NYNEX ads feature puns based on Yellow Pages category headings. This ad, which is directed to media buyers, uses that same creative Big Idea with a visual pun on the heading "Amusement Devices" in the directory.

Like poets, copywriters may spend hours, even days, crafting a paragraph. After many revisions, others read the copy and critique it. It then goes back to the writer, who continues to fine-tune it. Copywriters must have thick skins as there is always someone else reading their work, critiquing it, and asking for changes. Versatility is a common trait of copywriters. They can move from toilet paper to Mack trucks and shift their writing style to match the product and the language of their target audience.

As Professor Mallia suggested in the Part III opener, copywriters can rejoice because the power of words remains strong even with new visual media. She says, "The power of words doesn't rest in their volume, but in their clever combination. In fact, the fewer the words, the more important every single one becomes—and the more critical copywriting talent becomes." The skill, she explains, is to "distill a thought down to its most concise, precise, and unexpected expression. That's the reason the craft isn't about to disappear anytime soon, and great copywriters will always be in demand. Think 'Got Milk?' and 'Think different' and see true mastery of the craft. Each tagline is just two words but rich in meaning and power."

The Art and Science of Names

The most important word selection in marketing communication is the brand or corporate name. Low-cost airline JetBlue was originally founded in 1999 as New Air but its founders realized it needed a more distinctive name. They considered naming it Taxi and painting the planes yellow, but backed off because of negative associations with New York City taxis and questionable service. JetBlue has been a good choice because it states the business (jet = airlines), as well as sky (blue) with its calming connotations.

Many brand names are made up, but it's not just names that are created by marketing communicators. The "uncola" position was created for 7-Up and more recently the True Value hardware chain has proclaimed itself "masters of all things hardwarian," a phrase that suggests mastery of a traditional art or skill.

There is a science to letters, as well as words. Research has determined that letters with a hard edge like T or K suggest effectiveness (Kodak, Target, Tide); X and Z relate to science (Xcel, Zantac, Xerox) ; C, L, R, P, and S are calming or relaxing (Cialis, Lexus, Puffs, Revlon, Silk); and Z means speed (Zippo, Ziplock, *Zappos.com*). In the erectile dysfunction category, Lilly's drug Cialis is derived from *ciel,* the French word for sky and was chosen because it is a smooth, soft sound that connotes a sense of intimacy. In contrast, Pfizer's Viagra evokes the power of Niagara Falls.[1]

Advertising Writing Style

In almost all situations, advertising has to win its audience, no small task given that it usually competes in a cluttered environment and the audience is generally inattentive and uninterested. For that reason, the copy should be as simple as possible—think "Eat Mor Chikin." Chick-fil-A's single line of copy is succinct and single-minded, meaning that it has a clear focus and conveys only one selling point.

As the YMCA ad demonstrates, advertising writing is tight. Every word counts because both space and time are expensive. Ineffective or overused words and phrases—such as *interesting, very, in order to, buy now and save, introducing, nothing less than*—waste precious space.

Copy is usually written in a conversational style using real people language. The legendary David Ogilvy, founder of the advertising agency that bears his name, Ogilvy & Mather (O&M), explained his view many years ago of advertising as conversation:

I always pretend that I'm sitting beside a woman at a dinner party, and she asks me for advice about which product she should buy. So then I write down what I would say to her. I give her the facts, facts, facts. I try to make it interesting, fascinating, if possible, and personal—I don't write to the

SHOWCASE

Part of a membership drive campaign, this ad demonstrates how a copywriter plays with language to deliver a selling point succinctly and with style.

Copywriter Lara Mann is a graduate of the University of Florida advertising program. Her work was nominated for inclusion in this book by Professor Elaine Wagner.

crowd. I try to write from one human being to another. . . . And I try not to bore the poor woman to death, and I try to make it as real and personal as possible.[2]

(You can listen to David Ogilvy talking about his views on advertising at *www.youtube.com/watch?v=0kfsnjcUNiw*)

Copywriters try to write the way the target audience thinks and talks. That often means using personal language and direct address. For example, an ad for Trojan condoms makes a pointed argument on a touchy subject for its young, single target audience. Combining headline with body copy, it reads as a dialogue:

> *I didn't use one because I didn't have one with me.*
> *Get real.*
> *If you don't have a parachute, don't jump, genius.*

How to Write Effective Copy

Copywriters revise copy seemingly a hundred times to make it as concise as possible. The tighter the writing, the easier it is to understand and the greater its impact. Simple ads avoid being gimmicky, full of clichés, or too cute; they don't try too hard or reach too far to make a point. The following list summarizes some characteristics of effective copy:

Principle
Effective copy is succinct, single-minded, and tightly focused.

- **Be Succinct** Use short, familiar words, short sentences, and short paragraphs.
- **Be Single-Minded** Focus on one main point.
- **Be Specific** Don't waste time on generalities. The more specific the message, the more attention getting and memorable it is.
- **Get Personal** Directly address your audience whenever possible as "you" rather than "we" or "they."
- **Keep a Single Focus** Deliver a simple message instead of one that makes too many points. Focus on a single idea and support it.
- **Be Conversational** Use the language of everyday conversation. The copy should sound like two friends talking to each other, so don't shy away from incomplete sentences, thought fragments, and contractions.
- **Be Original** To keep your copy forceful and persuasive, avoid stock advertising phrases, strings of superlatives, brag-and-boast statements, and clichés.
- **Use News** News stories are attention getting if . . . if . . . they announce something that is truly newsworthy and important. (In contrast, Post Shredded Wheat ran an ad with the headline "Beware of New" in which it bragged about its original recipe that it had been using for 117 years.)
- **Use Magic Phrases** Phrases that grab and stick add power and memorability. In comparing its paper towels with the cheaper competition, Bounty asked "Why use more when you can use less?"
- **Use Variety** To add visual appeal in both print and TV ads, avoid long blocks of copy in print ads. Instead, break the copy into short paragraphs with subheads. In TV commercials, break up television monologues with visual changes, such as shots of the product, sound effects, and dialogue. The writer puts these breaks in the script while the art director designs what they will look like.
- **Use Imaginative Description** Use evocative or figurative language to build a picture in the consumer's mind.
- **Tell a Story—with Feeling** Stories are interesting and they have a structure that keeps attention and builds interest. But most importantly, they offer an opportunity to touch emotions. An ad about two brothers, one with cancer and the other who became inspired to become a radiation oncologist, told their story as they confronted the rare cancer and turned to the Memorial Sloan-Kettering Cancer Center to help defeat the illness.

Tone of Voice   To develop the right **tone of voice,** copywriters write to the target audience. If the copywriter knows someone who fits the audience profile, then he or she may write to that person as if they were in a conversation as the Trojan ad demonstrated. If the writer doesn't know someone, one trick is to go through a photo file, select a picture of the person who fits the description, and write to that "audience member."

So You Think You Want to Create a Funny Ad?

Fred Beard, *Professor, Gaylord College of Journalism and Mass Communication, University of Oklahoma*

These parting words of British actor Sir Donald Wolfit should give anyone thinking of creating a funny ad second thoughts: "Dying is easy, comedy is hard."

Writing a funny, effective ad is especially hard when you consider that the ad must make people laugh at the same time it accomplishes an advertising objective—an increase in attention, recall, favorable attitudes, or an actual purchase. If you're still not deterred, keep in mind that funny ads work best when the following circumstances apply:

1. *Your goal is to attract attention.* Decades of research and the beliefs of advertising creative professionals match up perfectly on this one.
2. *Your goal is to generate awareness and recall of a simple message (think Aflac).* Most advertising creatives agree that humor works best to encourage recall of fairly simple messages, not complex ones.
3. *Your humor is related.* Did you ever laugh at an ad and forget what it was advertising? Creatives will tell you humor is a waste of money if it isn't related to a product's name, uses, benefits, or users.
4. *Your goal is to get the audience to like your brand.* Research shows people often transfer their liking of funny ads to the brand.

5. *You expect the audience to initially disagree with your arguments.* An ad's humor can distract people from arguments they disagree with, encouraging them to lower their perceptual defenses, accept the message, and be persuaded by it.
6. *Your target audience is men, especially young ones.* Creative professionals say younger male audiences respond best to humor, and research confirms men favor more aggressive humor.
7. *Your audience has a low need for cognition (NFC) or a high need for humor (NFH).* People with a low NFC don't enjoy thinking about things—they prefer emotional appeals like humor. People with a high NFH seek out humor. If your audience is low NFC and high NFH, you can't miss.
8. *You have good reasons for using the broadcast media.* By far, the majority of creatives believe humor works best in radio and TV ads.
9. *You're advertising a low-involvement/low-risk product or service.* Academic researchers and creative professionals agree funny ads seem to work best for routine purchases people don't worry about too much.
10. *Your humor is definitely funny.* Research shows if an ad's humor fails, not only will there be no positive outcomes, it could even produce negative responses.

Molson Beer won awards for a commercial it created, called "The Rant," which mirrors the attitude of many Canadians. The commercial starts softly with an average Joe character disassociating himself from Canadian stereotypes. As he talks, he builds up intensity and at the end, he's in a full-blown rant ending with the line *"My name is Joe, and I am Canadian"* at the top of his voice. The commercial was so successful it was played at events all around the country.

Humor is a type of writing that copywriters use to create entertaining, funny ads. The idea is that, if the humor works, the funny copy will lend a positive aura to a brand. It's particularly important to master funny writing if you are trying to reach an audience that's put off by conventional advertising, such as young males. The *Practical Tips* box provides some suggestions on how to use humor in advertising copy.

The newest game in choosing a tone of voice is for brand avatars. If you were to talk with eBay or MTV, what would that brand's avatar sound like? You get computerized voices when you call most companies, but some organizations have moved away from the easily recognized computer voice to a voice that better reflects the brand's personality. So think about the way your brand sounds to customers as another dimension of styling the tone of voice for a brand or company.

Grammar and Adese Copywriters also are attuned to the niceties of grammar, syntax, and spelling, although sometimes they will play with a word or phrase to create an effect, even if it's grammatically incorrect. The Apple Computer campaign for the Macintosh that used the slogan "Think different" rather than "Think differently" caused a bit of an uproar in Apple's school market. That's why copywriters think carefully about playing loose with the language even if it sounds right.[3]

In contrast to the good practices in copywriting we've been describing, there are also some things to avoid. Meaningless words (*really, very, that, a lot*) or words made meaningless by overuse (*free, guarantee, opportunity*) are to be shunned in business writing and advertising according to a feature on advertising writing on MSNBC.[4]

Formulaic advertising copy is one problem that is so obvious that comedians parody it. This type of formula writing, called **adese,** violates all the guidelines for writing effective copy that we've been describing. It is full of clichés (as easy as pie), superlatives and puffery (best in class), stock phrases (buy now; free trial offer), and vague generalities (prices too low to advertise). For example, consider this copy; can you hear yourself saying something like this to a friend?

> *Now we offer the quality that you've been waiting for—at a price you can afford. So buy now and save.*

For more advertising clichés, check this website: *www.the-top-tens.com/lists/most-overused-advertising-cliches.asp*.

The pompous overblown phrasing of many corporate statements doesn't work—it doesn't get attention; it's not memorable; it doesn't get read. We call it **your-name-here copy** because almost any company can use those words and tack a signature on the end. For example, a broadband company named Covad started off an ad like this:

> *Opportunity. Potential. These are terms usually associated with companies that have a lot to prove and little to show for it. But on rare occasion, opportunity can be used to describe a company that has already laid the groundwork, made the investments, and is well down the road to strong growth.*

It's all just platitudes and clichés—and any company could use this copy. It isn't attention getting and it doesn't contribute to a distinctive and memorable brand image. That's always a risk with company-centered copy, which doesn't say anything that relates to the customer's needs, wants, and interests. It just doesn't work.

Another type of adese is **brag-and-boast copy,** which is "we" copy written from the company's point of view with a pompous tone, similar to the Covad ad. Consider a print ad by Buick. The ad starts with the stock opening, "Introducing Buick on the move." The body copy includes superlatives and generalities such as "Nothing less than the expression of a new philosophy," "It strikes a new balance between luxury and performance—a balance which has been put to the test," and "Manufactured with a degree of precision that is in itself a breakthrough." Because people are so conditioned to screen out advertising, messages that use this predictable style are easy to ignore—or parody if you're a comedian.

The Strategy Imperative   We said in the beginning of this chapter that the creative team begins with the strategy statement from the client or the creative brief from agency planners. That means even beautiful writing has to also make the strategy sing. As Susan Gunelius, author of *Kick-Ass Copywriting in 10 Easy Steps* explains, "Copywriting is about creating perceived needs among a specific audience."[5] If it doesn't move the audience and deliver on the objectives, then it's not effective copywriting.

Furthermore, the writing not only has to be strategic, the claims also have to be tested and meet basic requirements of truth, as the *A Principled Practice* feature explains.

HOW IS COPY CREATED FOR PRINT?

A print piece, such as an advertisement or brochure, is created in two pieces: a copy sheet and a layout. Even though they work together to create a creative concept, we'll discuss copy in this chapter and layout in the next chapter.

The two categories of copy that print uses are display copy and body copy (or text). **Display copy** includes all elements that readers see in their initial scanning. These elements—headlines, subheads, call-outs, taglines, and slogans—usually are set in larger type sizes than body copy and are designed to get attention and to stop the viewer's scanning. **Body copy** includes the elements that are designed to be read and absorbed, such as the text of the ad message and captions.

A PRINCIPLED PRACTICE

Check Those Claims

You should be able to believe the advertising from trusted major brands such as General Mills and Kellogg's.

A high-profile case made headlines in 2009 when the Food and Drug Administration challenged Cheerios' long-running cholesterol-reduction claims. For years, Cheerios boxes have included the lines *"You can Lower Your* Cholesterol *4% in 6 weeks"* and *"Clinically proven to lower cholesterol."* The FDA believes this is a claim that puts it in the drug category. The FDA allows the more general claim of reduced heart disease but doesn't allow specific rates of risk reduction, which is more appropriate for drugs. If the FDA prevails, General Mills may face enormous marketing and packaging costs to rectify the questionable claim. There's even an issue with the language on the brand's website.

In defense of the Cheerios' claim, General Mills responded that "the clinical study supporting Cheerios' cholesterol-lowering benefit is very strong." General Mills points to 25 years of clinical proof that Cheerios can help lower cholesterol and, therefore, is heart healthy. The FDA, in fact, in 1997 granted Cheerios the first food-specific health claim for the fiber in oatmeal and its heart-healthy benefits.

Kellogg's was challenged by the Federal Trade Commission in 2009 for television advertising that said children's attentiveness improved nearly 20 percent for those who ate Frosted Mini-Wheats compared to those who skipped breakfast. It's probably true that kids who eat breakfast pay more attention in school, but the FTC said that only half of the children studied showed more attentiveness and of those only

11 percent had an improvement of 20 percent in their attentiveness. Kellogg's agreed to settle the charges.

Kellogg's Coca Krispies has been challenged for bragging on the package that the sugary cereal "helps support your child's immunity." San Francisco's city attorney wrote to Kellogg's demanding the claim be substantiated. He says, "I am concerned that the prominent use of the immunity claims to advertise a sugar-laden, chocolate cereal like Cocoa Krispies may mislead and deceive parents of young children."

Similarly a drink mix enhanced with vitamins A, C, and E claims that it will help "maintain a healthy immune system," even though the *Chicago Tribune* says there is no scientific evidence to back up this claim.

So are consumers being led astray by health claims on food packages, websites, and advertising? Should health claims for packaged foods be banned? And what is a copywriter to do if a marketing director asks for health claims. What kind of support would you like to see before you are comfortable writing this kind of copy?

Sources: Julie Deardorff, "Should Health Claims on Food Be Banned?" *www.pressofAtlanticCity.com,* October 26, 2009; Dan Mitchell, "San Francisco Goes after Crazy Cereal Health Claims," The Big Money website, October 30, 2009, *www.thebigmoney.com;* "Kellogg to Settle FTC Charges of False Advertising," *The New York Times,* April 20, 2009, *www.nytimes.com;* Donna Byrne, "When Is Breakfast Cereal a 'Drug?' When It's Cheerios," Food Law Prof Blog, May 13, 2009, http://lawprofessors.typepad.com/foodlaw/ health_claims/; "FDA Warns General Mills: Cheerios Is a Drug," *The Wall Street Journal,* May 12, 2009, http://blogs.wsj.com; "Quaker Celebrates 25 Years of Clinical Proof," *PR Newswire,* November 17, 2008, *www.prnewswire.com.*

We have suggested that ad copy should be succinct but some respected copywriters, such as David Ogilvy and Howard Gossage, were successful in writing long copy ads that intrigued their audiences. Gossage, a legendary San Francisco ad man played with humorous ideas, as well as words. One ad for Eagle Shirtmakers asked, "Is this your shirt?" A following line said, "If so, Miss Afflerbach will send you your [Eagle logo picture] label." The idea, which is explained in the body copy, is that Eagle makes shirts for various shirtmakers, so you can contact "Miss Afflerbach" for the official logo to add to your shirt. If you're interested in more of Gossage's tongue-in-cheek ads, check a collection compiled by the LA Creative Club at *www.lacreativeclub.com/ gossage.html* or get his book, *The Book of Gossage* from the Copy Workshop (*www.adbuzz.com/ copyworkshop_catalog.pdf*).

No one ad uses all of the copy elements; however, they are all used in different ads for different purposes. The most common tools in the copywriter's toolkit are listed in Table 9.1.

How to Write Headlines

The **headline** is a key element in print pieces. It conveys the main message so that people get the point of the message. It's important for another reason. The headline works with the visual to get

Table 9.1   The Copywriter's Toolkit

- *Headline* A phrase or a sentence that serves as the opening to the ad. It's usually identified by larger type or a prominent position and its purpose is to catch attention. In the Corporate Angel Network ad, for example, the headline is "Cancer Patients Fly Free."

- *Overlines* and *Underlines* These are phrases or sentences that either lead into the headline or follow up on the thought in the headline. They are usually set in smaller type than the headline. The purpose of the overline is to set the stage, and the purpose of the underline is to elaborate on the idea in the headline and serve as a transition to the body copy. The underline leads into the body copy as demonstrated in the DuPont ad: "Find food that helps prevent osteoporosis."

- *Body Copy* The text of the ad. It's usually smaller-sized type and written in paragraphs or multiple lines. Its purpose is to explain the idea or selling point.

- *Subheads* Used in longer copy blocks, subheads begin a new section of the copy. They are usually bold type or larger than the body copy. Their purpose is to make the logic clear to the reader. They are useful for people who scan copy and they help them get a sense of what the copy says. The Corporate Angel Network ad uses subheads.

- *Call-Outs* These are sentences that float around the visual, usually with a line or arrow pointing to some specific element in the visual that they name and explain. For example, Johnson & Johnson once ran an ad that used call-outs as the main pieces of the body copy. The head read: "How to bathe a mommy." Positioned around a picture of a woman are short paragraphs with arrows pointing to various parts of her body. These call-outs describe the good things the lotion does for feet, hands, makeup removal, moisture absorption, and skin softening.

- *Captions* A sentence or short piece of copy that explains what you are looking at in a photo or illustration. Captions aren't used very often in advertising because the visuals are assumed to be self-explanatory; however, readership studies have shown that, after the headline, captions have high readership.

- *Taglines* A short phrase that wraps up the key idea or creative concept that usually appears at the end of the body copy. It often refers back to the headline or opening phrase in a commercial. For example, see the line, "Need a lift? Just give us a call. We'll do the rest," in the Corporate Angel Network ad.

- *Slogans* A distinctive catch phrase that serves as a motto for a campaign, brand, or company. It is used across a variety of marketing communication messages and over an extended period of time. "What happens in Las Vegas stays in Las Vegas" is a tourism slogan that hints at the pleasures you don't enjoy at home.

- *Call to Action* This is a line at the end of an ad that encourages people to respond and gives information on how to respond. Both ads—Corporate Angel Network and DuPont—have response information: either an address, a toll-free phone number, an e-mail address, or Web address.

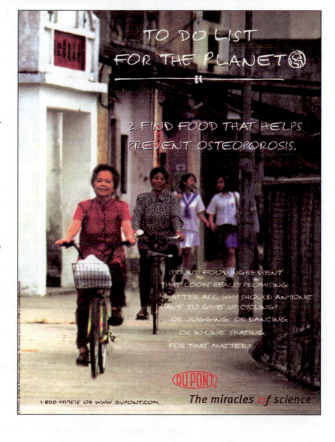

attention and communicate the creative concept. This clutter-busting Big Idea breaks through the competitive messages. It comes across best through a picture and words working together, as the DuPont ad illustrates. The headline carries the theme ("To Do List for the Planet") and the underline ("Find food that helps prevent osteoporosis") makes a direct connection with the visual.

People who are scanning may read nothing more, so advertisers want to at least register a point with the consumer. The point has to be clear from the headline or the combination of headline and visual. That's particularly true with outdoor boards. Researchers estimate that only 20 percent of those who read the headline in advertising go on to read the body copy, so if they take away anything from the ad, it needs to be clear in the headline.

Principle
Good headlines interrupt readers' scanning and grab their attention.

Headlines need to be catchy phrases, but they also have to convey an idea and attract the right target audience. Tobler has won Effie awards for a number of years for its clever headlines and visuals. For Tobler's Chocolate Orange, the creative concept showed the chocolate ball being smacked against something hard and splitting into orange-like slices. The headline was "Whack and Unwrap." The next year the headline was "Smashing Good Taste," which speaks to the candy's British origins and to the quirky combination of chocolate and orange flavors. The headline and visual also tell consumers how to "open" the orange into slices—by whacking it.

Agencies copytest headlines to make sure they can be understood at a glance and that they communicate exactly the right idea. Split-run tests (two versions of the same ad) in direct mail pieces have shown that changing the wording of the headline while keeping all other elements constant can double, triple, or quadruple consumer response. That is what experts, such as ad legend David Ogilvy, state that the headline is the most important element in the advertisement.[6] Because headlines are so important, some general principles guide their development and explain the particular functions they serve:

- *Target* A good headline will attract only those who are prospects—there is no sense in attracting people who are not in the market. An old advertising axiom is "Use a rifle, not a shotgun." In other words, use the headline to tightly target the right audience.
- *Stop and Grab* The headline must work in combination with the visual to stop and grab the reader's attention. An advertisement by Range Rover shows a photo of the car parked at the edge of a rock ledge in Monument Valley with the headline, "Lots of people use their Range Rovers just to run down to the corner."
- *Identify* The headline must also identify the product and brand and start the sale. The selling premise should be evident in the headline.
- *Change Scanning to Reading* The headline should lead readers into the body copy. For readers to move to the body copy, they have to stop scanning and start concentrating. This change in mind-set is the reason why only 20 percent of scanners become readers.

Headlines can be grouped into two general categories: direct action and indirect action. **Direct-action headlines** are straightforward and informative, such as "Keep Your Body Strong," which is one in a series of "Healthy People" posters for Johnson & Johnson. The copy associates the health of your body with the health of nature. It closes with a line that pulls these two thoughts together: "Your body is just like nature. Keep it strong with daily physical activity and bring your planet to balance." Note how this structure of the message is consistent in the "Mind" and "Spirit" posters.

Direct-action headlines are highly targeted, but they may fail to lead the reader into the message if they are not captivating enough. **Indirect-action headlines** are not as selective and may not provide as much information, but may be better at drawing the reader into the message and building a brand image.

Here are some common types of direct-action headlines:

- *Assertion* An assertion is a headline that states a claim or a promise that will motivate someone to try the product.
- *Command* A command headline politely tells the reader to do something.
- *How-to Heads* People are rewarded for investigating a product when the message tells them how to use it or how to solve a problem.
- *News Announcements* News headlines are used with new-product introductions, but also with changes, reformulations, new styles, and new uses. The news value is thought to get attention and motivate people to try the product.

SHOWCASE
Michael Dattolico designed a series of posters for Johnson & Johnson to use in promoting its "Healthy People" initiative. These two advise you to keep "your mind flowing" and "your spirit pure."

A graduate of the University of Florida, Dattolico's work was nominated for inclusion in this book by Professor Elaine Wagner.

Here are some common types of indirect-action headlines:

- *Puzzles* Used strictly for their curiosity and provocative power. Puzzling statements, ambiguities, and questions require the reader to examine the body copy to get the answer or explanation. The intention is to pull readers into the body copy.
- *Associations* These headlines use image and lifestyle to get attention and build interest.

An ad for the Motorola Talk About™ two-way radio demonstrates the problem of bad reception in the headline: "Help, I Think I Need a Tourniquet!" That headline then draws us into the underline which makes the point that, if the reception isn't clear, the headline can sound like "Well, I think I'll eat a turnip cake!" This headline, which played with the similar sounds of words, and other curiosity-provoking lines are provocative and compel people to read on to find out the point of the message. Sometimes these indirect headlines are called "blind headlines" because they give so little information. A **blind headline** is a gamble. If it is not informative or intriguing enough, the reader may move on without absorbing any product name information, but if it works as an attention getter, it can be very effective.

How to Write Other Display Copy

Next to the headline, **captions** have the second highest readership. In addition to their pulling power, captions serve an information function. Visuals do not always say the same thing to every person; for that reason, most visuals can benefit from explanation. In addition to headlines, copywriters also craft the **subheads** that continue to help lure the reader into the body copy. Subheads are considered display copy in that they are usually larger and set in different type (bold or italic) than the body copy. Subheads are sectional headlines and are also used to break up a mass of "gray" type (or type that tends to blur together when one glances at it) into a large block of copy.

Taglines are short catchy phrases and particularly memorable phrases used at the end of an ad to complete or wrap up the creative idea. An ad from the Nike women's campaign used the headline "You are a nurturer and a provider. You are beautiful and exotic" set in an elegant script. The tagline on the next page used a rough, hand-drawn, graffiti-like image that said, "You are not falling for any of this."

Slogans, which are repeated from ad to ad as part of a campaign or a long-term brand identity effort, also may be used as taglines. To be successful, these phrases have to be catchy and memorable, although many corporate slogans fall back into marketing language or clichés and come across as leaden ("Total quality through excellence," "Excellence through total quality," or "Where quality counts"). Wells Fargo, for example, uses "Together we'll go far," which is not distinctive, could be used by any company, and says nothing about Wells Fargo or its business. Accenture uses "High performance. Delivered." which also is nondistinctive and not very memorable.

The best ones have a close link to the brand name: "With a name like Smucker's, it has to be good," "America runs on Dunkin'," and "Ford Tough." "Finger lickin' good" for KFC doesn't use the brand name, but still is highly recognizable because it connects with the product (fried chicken) and has been in use since 1952. That's another characteristic of a good slogan, it is enduring—slogans are rarely changed. A true classic, Maxwell House's "Good to the last drop," has been used since 1915 and Morton Salt's "When it rains, it pours" has been around since 1914.

Of course, they also have to be original as Wisconsinites found out when the official state slogan was changed to "Live Like You Mean It." The state spent some $50,000 on the new slogan and then later discovered that it had previously been used as the tagline in a Bacardi Rum campaign.[7]

Consider the distinctiveness and memorability of the following slogans

TEST YOURSELF

Match the Company with Its Slogan:

1. Together we can prevail		a.	Merck
2. Imagination at work*		b.	Bristol-Myers Squibb
3. A mind is a terrible thing to waste*		c.	Hallmark
4. Know How		d.	Swatch
5. A business of caring		e.	Hitachi
6. Melts in your mouth, not in your hands*		f.	Verizon
7. Always surprising		g.	Cigna
8. We deliver for You*		h.	FedEx
9. Inspire the next		i.	Diesel
10. When you care enough to send the very best*		j.	UPS
11. Where patients come first		k.	Canon
12. Can you hear me now?*		l.	Chrysler
13. For successful living		m.	U.S. Postal Service
14. Inspiration comes standard		n.	M&Ms
15. When it absolutely, positively has to be there overnight*		o.	United Negro College Fund
16. What can brown do for you?*		p.	GE

Answers to Companies: 1:b Bristol-Myers Squibb; 2:p GE*; 3:o United Negro College Fund*; 4:k Canon; 5:g Cigna; 6:n M&Ms*; 7:d Swatch; 8:m USPS*; 9:e Hitachi; 10:c Hallmark*; 11:a Merck; 12:f Verizon*; 13:i Diesel; 14:l Chrysler; 15:h FedEx*; 16:j UPS.*

Study the slogans in the matching activity. Which ones did you get and which ones stumped you? Note that eight of the companies are identified with an asterisk. Those eight have been recognized by *Adweek* as winning slogans and have been celebrated as part of the magazine's annual Advertising Week. In your view, why were they selected for this honor, and what makes them different from the others on the list that have not been honored in this way?

One of America's favorite slogan winners according to *Adweek* is the "Don't Mess with Texas" anti-litter slogan. Created in 1986 by Austin-based GSD&M for the Texas Department of Transportation, the award-winning social-marketing campaign built around this slogan features billboards, print ads, radio and TV spots, and a host of celebrities (Willie Nelson, Stevie Ray Vaughan, Matthew McConaughey, George Foreman, and LeAnn Rimes, among others) who take turns with the tough-talking slogan that captures the spirit and pride of Texans. One billboard, for example, warns, "Keep Your Butts in the Car." The *dontmesswithtexas.org* website, where you can see all these ads, including the commercials, also has been featured by *Adweek* as a "Cool Site."

Copywriters use a number of literary techniques to enhance the memorability of subheads, slogans, and taglines. These are other techniques copywriters use to create catchy slogans:

- *Direct Address* "Have it your way"; "Think small."
- *A Startling or Unexpected Phrase* Twists a common phrase to make it unexpected, as in the NYNEX campaign: "If it's out there, it's in here."
- *Rhyme, Rhythm, Alliteration* Uses repetition of sounds, as in the *Wall Street Journal*'s slogan, "The daily diary of the American Dream."
- *Parallel Construction* Uses repetition of the structure of a sentence or phrase, as in Morton Salt's "When it rains, it pours."
- *Cue the Product* Folgers' "Good to the last drop"; John Deere's "Nothing runs like a Deere"; Wheaties' "Breakfast of Champions"; "Beef. It's What's for Dinner."
- *Music* "In the valley of the Jolly, ho-ho-ho, Green Giant."
- *Combination* "It's your land, lend a hand," which is the slogan for Take Pride in America. (*Rhyme, rhythm, parallel*)

How to Write Body Copy

The body copy is the text of the ad, and its primary role is to maintain the interest of the reader. It develops the sales message, states the argument, summarizes the proof, and provides explanation. It is the persuasive heart of the message. You excite consumer interest with the display elements, but you win them over with the argument presented in the body copy, assuming the ad uses body copy or an overt selling premise.

Consider the way the copy is written for this classic ad that comes from the award-winning Nike women's campaign. Analyze the argument the copywriter is making and how the logic flows to a convincing conclusion. The *A Matter of Principle* box explains the logic and message strategy behind the Nike's women's campaign, which focuses on self-awareness.

A magazine is not a mirror. Have you ever seen anyone in a magazine who seemed even vaguely like you looking back? (If you have, turn the page.) Most magazines are made to sell us a fantasy of what we're supposed to be. They reflect what society deems to be a standard, however unrealistic or unattainable that standard is. That doesn't mean you should cancel your subscription. It means you need to remember that it's just ink on paper. And that whatever standards you set for yourself, for how much you want to weigh, for how hard you work out, or how many times you make it to the gym, should be your standards. Not someone else's.

The "Let Me Play" ad is a more recent version of the sentiment expressed in the "Mirror" ad copy. Nike launched the Let Me Play Fund in support of this campaign after racist and sexist comments about the Rutgers University women's basketball team by radio shock jock Don Imus. In response to his offensive comments, Nike ran a full-page ad in *The New York Times* than opened with "Thank you, ignorance" followed by "Thank you for moving women's sports forward."

A MATTER OF PRINCIPLE

The Principle of Truth

Jean Grow, *Associate Professor, Marquette University*

"It wasn't advertising. It was truth. We weren't selling a damn thing. Just the truth. And behind the truth, of course, the message was brought to you by Nike."
—Janet Champ, *Nike*

The creatives who produced early Nike women's advertising (1990–1997) were an amazing trio of women (Janet Champ, copywriter, and Charlotte Moore and Rachel Manganiello, art directors). Their work was grounded in the principle of truth, fueled by creativity, and sustained by nothing less than moxie.

"Nike in 1990 was not the Nike of today," Manganiello said. There was always this "political stuff about big men's sports. And, you know, (it was like we were) just kind of siphoning off money for women. So, in some ways we couldn't be as direct as we sometimes wanted to be." However, being direct and being truthful are not always the same thing. And truth for the Nike women's brand, and for themselves, was what these women aspired to.

Living the principle of truth, and trusting their gut, is what defined their work ethic and ultimately the women's brand. Moore explained, "I would posit that market research has killed a lot of advertising that was based on effective human dialogue, because it negates faith in intuition. Guts. Living with your eyes open."

To launch the women's brand within the confines of the male parent brand was no easy assignment. The creative team members began with their "gut" and with their "eyes open." They created campaign after campaign that moved the needle, but each time the approval process was a test of their principles, with meetings that were more than tinged with gender bias.

"We were almost always the only women in the room, and they killed the stuff because it scared them," said Champ. "But we always came back. And they let us do what we wanted, as long as we didn't 'sully' the men's brand . . . and as long as women's products kept flying off the shelves, they were happy."

As time went on, their instincts and principles earned them respect. According to Champ, "We told them, pretty much, that we believed in it and they had to run it and trust us, and they sighed, once again. They were soooooo tired of hearing me say that. And they ran it and they were SHOCKED at what a nerve it touched."

In trusting their guts—in telling the truth—they created award-winning campaigns and exceeded marketing expectations. "As creative people," Moore said, "we had found our home and our voice, and we'd found the most fertile ground for the brand."

In the end, truth and the willingness to "trust your gut" are what make great brands and create fertile ground for others. When you consider the terrifically truthful Dove campaign, I suggest we owe a debt of gratitude to the women of early Nike women's advertising, who stood for truth nearly 20 years ago. I only wish we would see more truthful work. That however might take a truthful acknowledgment that women still make up less than a quarter of all advertising creative departments. In the end, truthful work depends on making a commitment to increasing the number of women in creative departments. To have guts. To live with ones eyes wide open.

There are as many different kinds of writing styles as there are product personalities, but there are also some standard approaches:

- *Straightforward* Factual copy usually written in the words of an anonymous or unacknowledged source.
- *Narrative* Tells a story in first person or third person.
- *Dialogue* Lets the reader "listen in" on a conversation.
- *Explanation* Explains how something works.
- *Translation* Technical information, such as that written for the high-tech and medical industries, which must be defined and translated into understandable language.

Two paragraphs get special attention in body copy: the **lead paragraph** and the **closing paragraph.** The lead, the first paragraph of the body copy, is another point where people test the message to see whether they want to read it. Notice in the copy from the Nike women's campaign how the first lines work to catch the attention of the target audience: "A magazine is not a mirror."

Closing paragraphs in body copy serve several functions. Usually, the last paragraph refers back to the creative concept and wraps up the Big Idea. Direct action messages usually end with a **call to action** with instructions on how to respond. A Schwinn bicycle ad that is headlined "Read poetry. Make peace with all except the motor car," demonstrates a powerful and unexpected ending, one that is targeted to its youthful audience:

Schwinns are red, Schwinns are blue.
Schwinns are light and agile too.
Cars suck. The end.

Print Media Requirements

The media in the print category—from newspapers and magazines to outdoor boards and product literature—all use the same copy elements, such as headlines and body copy. However, the way these elements are used varies with the objectives for using the medium.

Newspaper advertising is one of the few types of advertising that is not considered intrusive because people consult the paper as much to see what is on sale as to find out what is happening in City Hall. For this reason, the copy in newspaper advertisements does not have to work as hard as other kinds of advertising to catch the attention of its audience. Because the editorial environment of a newspaper generally is serious, newspaper ads don't have to compete as entertainment, as television ads do. As a result, most newspaper advertising copy is straightforward and informative. The writing is brief, usually just identifying the merchandise and giving critical information about styles, sizes, and prices.

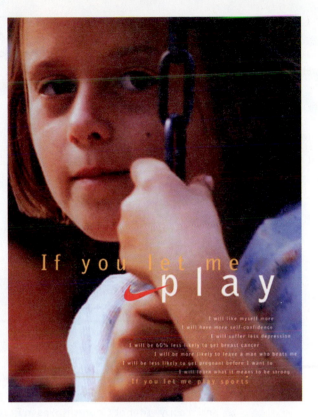

This ad from the "Let Me Play" campaign ad reflects Nike's strategy of talking to women about sports in a way that reflects their attitudes and feelings.

Magazines offer better quality ad production, which is important for brand image and high-fashion advertising. Consumers may clip and file advertising that ties in with the magazine's special interest as reference information. This type of magazine ad can be more informative and carry longer copy than do newspaper ads. Copywriters also take care to craft clever phrasing for the headlines and the body copy, which, as in the Nike women's campaign, may read more like poetry.

Directories that provide contact information, such as phone numbers and addresses, often carry display advertising. In writing a directory ad, copywriters advise using a headline that focuses on the service or store personality unless the store's name is a descriptive phrase such as "Overnight Auto Service" or "The Computer Exchange." Complicated explanations don't work well in the Yellow Pages either, because there is little space for such explanations. Putting information that is subject to change in an ad can become a problem because the directory is published only once a year.

Posters and outdoor boards are primarily visual, although the words generally try to catch consumers' attention and lock in an idea, registering a message. An effective poster is built around a creative concept that marries the words with the visual. For the Coffee Rush chain, Karl Schroeder created a series of posters to change consumers' perceptions that the shop was merely a drive-through for fast, cheap coffee. Schroeder's team did this by promoting a line of cold drinks with captivating names such as Mango Guava and Wild Berry.

One of the most famous billboard campaigns ever was for a little shaving cream company named Burma Shave. The campaign used a series of roadside signs with catchy, cute, and sometimes poetic advertising copy aimed at auto travelers. Some 600 poems were featured in this campaign, which ran for nearly 40 years, from 1925 to 1963, until the national interstate system and fast roads made the signs obsolete.[8] (To read more about Burma Shave, go to *www.eisnermuseum.org/ _burma_shave/signs_of_the_times.html* or check the collection at *www.sff.net/people/teaston/ burma.htm*.) On the Burma Shave signs the product was always a hero:

If you think	*My job is*
she likes	*keeping faces clean*
your bristles	*And nobody knows*
walk bare-footed	*de stubble*
through some thistles	*I've seen*
Burma Shave	*Burma Shave*

SHOWCASE

These posters for the Coffee Rush group of small, drive-through coffee shops, told newcomers that Coffee Rush sold more than just "a cup of joe." The copy, which had to be simple to be read by people in a car, was designed to tease people into tasting these fun drinks.

These posters were contributed by Karl Schroeder, a graduate of the University of Oregon and a copywriter at Coates Kokes in Portland, Oregon. He was nominated by Professor Charles Frazer, University of Oregon.

More recently, the city of Albuquerque used the Burma Shave format to encourage drivers to reduce their speeds through a construction zone. Today, a construction zone is about the only place where traffic moves slowly enough to use a billboard with rhyming copy.

Through this maze of machines and rubble
Driving fast can cause you trouble
Take care and be alert
So no one on this road gets hurt.

In contrast to the Burma Shave signs, the most important characteristic of copywriting for outdoor advertising is brevity. Usually, a single line serves as both a headline and product identification. Often the phrase is a play on words. A series of black-and-white billboards in the Galveston-Houston area, recruiting priests for the Roman Catholic diocese, features a Roman collar with witty wording such as "Yes, you will combat evil. No, you don't get to wear a cape." Others are more thoughtful: "Help wanted. Inquire within yourself." Some experts suggest that billboard copywriters use no more than six to seven words. The copy must catch attention and be memorable. For example, a billboard for Orkin pest control showed a package wrapped up with the word Orkin on the tag. The headline read, "A little something for your ant."

Sometimes called **collateral materials** because they are used in support of an advertising campaign, product literature—brochures, pamphlets, flyers, and other materials—provides details about a product, company, or event. They can be as varied as hang tags in new cars or bumper stickers. Taco Bell's little messages on its tiny taco sauce packages are an example of clever writing in an unexpected place with messages like: "Save a bun, eat a taco," "Warning! You're about to make a taco very happy," and "My other taco is a chalupa."

Typically, product literature is a heavy copy format, or at least a format that provides room for explanatory details along with visuals; the body copy may dominate the piece. For a pamphlet with folds, a writer must also consider how the message is conveyed as the piece is unfolded. These pieces can range from a simple three-panel flyer to a glitzy multipage, full-color brochure.

HOW IS COPY WRITTEN FOR RADIO?

Ads that are broadcast on either radio or television are usually 15, 30, or 60 seconds in length, although 10- and 15-second spots may be used for brand reminders or station identification. This short length means the commercials must be simple enough for consumers to grasp, yet intriguing enough to prevent viewers from switching the station. That's why creativity is important to create clutter-busting ads that break through the surrounding noise and catch the listener's attention.

Because radio is a transitory medium and listeners are often in the car or doing something else, the ability of the listener to remember facts (such as the name of the advertiser, addresses, and phone numbers) is difficult. That's why copywriters repeat the key points of brand name and identification information, such as a phone number or address. Radio is pervasive in that it surrounds many of our activities, but it is seldom the listener's center of attention and is usually in the background. Radio urges the copywriter to reach into the depths of imagination to create a clutter-busting idea that grabs the listener's attention or a catchy tune that can be repeated without being irritating.

Radio's special advantage, referred to as **theater of the mind,** is that in a narrative format the story is visualized in the listener's imagination. Radio copywriters imagine they are writing a musical play that will be performed before an audience whose eyes are closed. The copywriter has all the theatrical tools of voices, sound effects, and music, but no visuals. How the characters look and where the scene is set come from their listeners' imaginations.

As an example of theater of the mind, consider a now-classic commercial written by humorist Stan Freberg for the Radio Advertising Bureau. The spot opens with an announcer explaining that Lake Michigan will be drained and filled with hot chocolate and a 700-foot mountain of whipped cream. The Royal Canadian Air Force will fly overhead and drop a ten-ton maraschino cherry, all to the applause of 25,000 screaming extras. The point is that things that can't be created in real life can be created by radio in the imagination of listeners.

The Radio Advertising Bureau has used the slogan "I saw it on the radio" to illustrate the power of radio's ability to evoke rich images in the listener's mind. Research indicates that the use of imagery in radio advertising leads to high levels of attention and more positive general attitudes toward the ad and its claims.[9] Even though we're talking about imagery, it is produced by the copywriter's masterful use of the tools of audio as discussed next.

Tools of Radio Copywriting

Print copywriters use a variety of tools—headlines, body copy, slogans, and so forth—to write their copy. In radio advertising, the tools are the audio elements the copywriter uses to craft a commercial: voice, music, and sound effects.

Voice　The most important element in radio advertising is the human voice, which is heard in songs, spoken dialogue, and announcements. Most commercials use an announcer either as the central voice or at the closing to wrap up the product identification. The voices the copywriter specifies help listeners "see" the personalities in the commercial. The copywriter understands that we imagine people and what they are like based on their voices. Dialogue uses character voices to convey an image of the speaker: a child, an old man, an executive, a Little League baseball player, a rock singer, and so forth. Copywriters specify voices for commercials based on the evocative qualities they contribute to the message. Chicago radio announcer Ken Nordine's voice was once described as sounding like warm chocolate; singer Ray Charles was described as having a charcoal voice.

Radio advertising relies on conversational style and vernacular language. A good radio copywriter also has an ear for distinctive patterns of speech. Two of the most famous jingles ever written used children singing about Oscar Mayer meats. The "Bologna Song" used a little child singing: "My bologna has a first name, it's O-S-C-A-R. My bologna has a second name, it's M-A-Y-E-R." The second big hit also used kids singing: "Oh I wish I were an Oscar Mayer Weiner. That is what I'd truly like to be. 'Cause if I were an Oscar Mayer Wiener, everyone would be in love with me."

Spoken language is different from written language. We talk in short sentences, often in sentence fragments and run-ons. We seldom use complex sentences in speech. We use contractions that would drive an English teacher crazy. Slang can be hard to handle and sound phony, but copy that picks up the nuances of people's speech sounds natural. In radio advertising, speaking style should match the speech of the target audience. Each group has its own way of speaking, its own phrasing. Teenagers don't talk like 8-year-olds or 50-year-olds.

Principle
Radio copywriters try to match their dialogue to the conversational style of the target audience.

Music Similar to movie scriptwriters, radio copywriters have a sense of the imagery of music and the role it plays in creating dramatic effects. Music can be used behind the dialogue to create mood and establish the setting. Any mood, from that of a circus to a candlelit dinner, can be conveyed through music. The primary use of music is a **jingle,** which is a commercial in song, like the Oscar Mayer songs. Radio copywriters understand the interplay of catchy phrases and "hummable" music to create little songs that stick in our minds. Anything consumers can sing along with helps them remember and get involved with the message.

Advertisers can have a piece of music composed for a commercial or borrow it from previously recorded songs. Numerous music libraries sell *stock music* that is not copyrighted. A custom-made jingle created for a single advertiser can cost $10,000 or more. In contrast, many *jingle houses* create "syndicated" jingles made up of a piece of music sold to several different local advertisers in different markets around the country for as little as $1,000 or $2,000.

One of the most famous jingles of all time was the song "I'd like to teach the world to sing" produced for Coca-Cola in 1969 by its agency, McCann-Erickson. A great example of a jingle that was an instant hit worldwide, it later was recorded as a pop song without the Coke reference and sold millions of copies. Called "Hilltop," the TV commercial shows young people singing "I'd like to buy the world a Coke" on a hilltop in Italy. Surveys continue to identify it as one of the best commercials of all time. It is still run by Coke on special occasions and the sheet music continues to sell more than 30 years after the song was first written. You can read more about this famous commercial on *www.thecoca-colacompany.com/heritage/cokelore_hilltop.html.* Click through to "Hilltop" to hear the commercial.

Sound Effects The sound of seagulls, automobile horns honking, and the cheers of fans at a stadium all create images in our minds to cue the setting and drive the action. The Freberg "Lake Michigan" commercial for the Radio Advertising Bureau used **sound effects (sfx)** to make a commercial attention getting and memorable. In the original commercial, which demonstrated the power of the "theater of the mind," listeners were asked to imagine the draining of Lake Michigan, which then is filled with hot chocolate and a 700-foot mountain of whipped cream. Then imagine the Royal Canadian Air Force flying overhead and dropping a ten-ton cherry to the applause of 25,000 screaming extras. All of this was conveyed through sound effects and an announcer telling the story. The point is that radio is more powerful than television in creating images in your mind. Sound effects can be original, but more often they are taken from *sound-effects libraries* available on CDs or online.

The Practice of Radio Copywriting

The following guidelines for writing effective radio commercials address the distinctive characteristics of radio advertising:

- *Keep It Personal* Radio advertising has an advantage over print—the human voice. The copy for radio ads should use conversational language—as if someone is "talking with" the consumer rather than "selling to" the consumer.
- *Speak to Listeners' Interests* Radio offers specialized programming to target markets. Listeners mostly tune in to hear music, but talk radio is popular, too. There are shows on health, pets, finance, politics—whatever interests people. Copywriters design commercials to speak to that audience interest and use the appropriate music and tone of voice.
- *Wake Up the Inattentive* Most people who are listening to the radio are doing something else at the same time, such as jogging, driving, or fixing breakfast. Radio spots are designed to break through and capture attention in the first three seconds with sound effects, music, questions, commands, or something unexpected.
- *Make It Memorable* To help the listener remember what you are selling, commercial copy should mention the name of the product emphatically and repeat it. An average of three mentions in a 30-second commercial and five mentions in a 60-second commercial are recommended, as long as the repetition is not done in a forced and/or annoying manner. Copywriters use taglines and other key phrases to lock the product in consumers' memories.
- *Include Call to Action* The last thing listeners hear is what they tend to remember, so copywriters make sure the product is it. In radio that's particularly important since there is no way to

show a picture of the product or the label. Those last words communicate the Big Idea in a way that serves as a call to action and reminds listeners of the brand name at the close of the commercial. "Got Milk?" is not only a highly memorable slogan, it's also a strong call to action.

- *Create Image Transfer* Radio advertisements are sometimes designed to link to a television commercial. Called **image transfer,** the visuals from the TV version are re-created in a listener's mind by the use of key phrases and ideas from the TV commercial.

Planning the Radio Script

Copywriters working on a radio commercial use a standard **radio script** format to write the copy to certain time blocks—all of the words, dialogue, lyrics, sound effects, instructions, and descriptions. The instructions and descriptions are to help the producer tape the commercial so that it sounds exactly as the copywriter imagined. The script format usually has the source of the audio written down the left side, and the content—words an announcer reads, dialogue, and description of the sound effects and music—on the right. The instructions and descriptions—everything that isn't spoken—are typed in all-capital letters. You may also see a script written in paragraph form with the instructions in parentheses. Note how the tools of radio are used in the LATCH child safety commercial.

HOW TO WRITE TELEVISION COPY

Television copywriters understand that it is the moving image—the action—that makes television so much more engaging than print. The challenge for the writer is to fuse the images with the words to present not only a creative concept, but also a story, as the Frontier Airlines commercials discussed in the previous chapter do so well.

One of the strengths of television is its ability to reinforce verbal messages with visuals or reinforce visuals with verbal messages. As Ogilvy's Peter Hochstein explains,

> The idea behind a television commercial is unique in advertising. The TV commercial consists of pictures that move to impart facts or evoke emotion, and selling words that are not read but heard. The perfect combination of sight and sound can be an extremely potent selling tool.[10]

Viewers watching a program they enjoy often are absorbed to a degree only slightly less than that experienced by people watching a movie in a darkened theater. Storytelling is one way that copywriters can present action in a television commercial more powerfully than in other media. Television's ability to touch our emotions and to show us things—to demonstrate how they look and work—make television advertising highly persuasive. Effective television commercials can achieve this level of audience absorption if they are written to maximize the dramatic aspects of

---

AD COUNCIL / US DEPARTMENT OF TRANSPORTATION
LATCH Campaign – :60 Radio
ZRAG-11804R
"Bookstore"
1BON-08-0033
04/30/08 – Produced
07/1/08 – Final Mix
07/15/09 – Expiration Date

Checker:	I can help the next customer over here.
Woman:	Oh… thank you…hi.
Checker:	Wow, that's a lot of books! Let's see…"*How To Keep Your Child Safe.*"(beep) "*Child-Proofing Your Home.*" (beep) "*Child-Proofing Your Yard.*" (beep) "*Child-Proofing Your In-Laws' Home and Yard.*" (beep) I'm guessing you have a little one at home?
Woman:	Yeah.
Checker:	Well, it looks like you must take good care of her.
Woman:	Oh. Thank you.
Checker:	Now let's see… "*Parent's Guide To Safe Toys*" (beep) That's a really good one. "*Parent's Guide To Safe Foods.*" (beep) "*Parents Guide To Safe Safety Products.*" (beep) "*Parents' Guide To Parenting Guides*" (beep) … "*Don't Throw The Baby Out With The Bath Water And Other Safety…*"(continues under.)
VO:	Of all the things you can read about keeping your child safe, the most important is attached to the back of their car seat. Read the instruction manual and learn to use the LATCH system. It makes it easier to be sure your child's car seat is installed correctly.
Checker:	"*Parent's Guide To Telling Other Parents How To Raise Their Kids*" (beep)…
VO:	To learn more, go to safercar.gov. Anchor. Tether. LATCH. The next generation of child safety. A message from the US Department of Transportation and the Ad Council.

SHOWCASE

In his *The Inside Story* in Chapter 5, Trent Walters explained the strategy behind the LATCH campaign for car-seat safety. This commercial uses a sound effect—the beep of the cash register—to punctuate the idea that parents are highly concerned about the safety of their children.

Walters is a graduate of North Texas State University and he was nominated by Professor Sheri Broyles.

Principle

In great television commercials, words and pictures work together seamlessly to deliver the creative concept through sight, sound, and motion.

moving images and storytelling. These are just a few of the techniques used in television advertising. Here are more:

Technique	*Message Design*
• *Action* When you watch television, you are watching a walking, talking, moving world that gives the illusion of being three dimensional.	• Good television advertising uses the effect of action and motion to attract attention and sustain interest. Torture tests, steps, and procedures are all actions that are easier to present on TV than in print.
• *Demonstration* Seeing is believing. Believability and credibility—the essence of persuasion—are high because we believe what we see with our own eyes.	• If you have a strong sales message that lends itself to demonstration, such as how-to messages, television is the ideal medium for that message.
• *Storytelling* Most of the programming on television is narrative, so commercials use storytelling to take advantage of the medium's strengths.	• TV is our society's master storyteller because of its ability to present a plot and the action that leads to a conclusion in which the product plays a major role. TV can dramatize the situation in which a product is used and the type of people using it.
• *Emotion* The ability to touch the feelings of the viewer makes television commercials entertaining, diverting, amusing, and absorbing. Real-life situations with all their humor, anger, fear, pride, jealousy, and love come alive on the screen. Humor, in particular, works well on television.	• Emotional appeals are found in natural situations with which everyone can identify. Hallmark has produced some tear-jerking commercials about the times of our lives that we remember by the cards we receive and save. Kodak and Polaroid have used a similar strategy for precious moments that are remembered in photographs.

Tools of Television Copywriting

Television copywriters have two primary toolkits: visual and audio. Both words and pictures are designed to create exactly the right impact. Because of the number of visual and audio elements, as well as the many ways they can be combined, a television commercial is one of the most complex of all advertising forms. It is also an ideal form for storytelling. Copywriters who write scripts for television commercials are masters of the emotional moment as researcher Charles Young explains in the *A Matter of Practice* feature.

Video and Motion   When we watch a commercial, we are more aware of what we're seeing than anything else. Copywriters keep in mind that visuals and motion, the silent speech of film, should convey as much of the message—the Big Idea—as possible. Likewise, emotion, which is the effect created by storytelling, is expressed convincingly in facial expressions, gestures, and other body language. Because television is theatrical, many of the copywriter's tools, such as characters, costumes, sets and locations, props, lighting, optical and computerized special effects, and on-screen graphics, are similar to those you would use in a play, television show, or movie.

Audio   As in radio, the three audio elements are music, voices, and sound effects, but they are used differently in television commercials because they are connected to a visual image. The copywriter may have an announcer speak directly to the viewer or engage in a dialogue with another person, who may or may not be on camera. The copywriter writes the words they will say and blocks out on paper how this "talk" happens. A common manipulation of the camera–announcer relationship is the **voice-over,** in which an announcer who is not visible describes some kind of action on the screen. Sometimes a voice is heard **off camera,** which means you can't see the speaker and the voice is coming from the side, behind, or above.

A MATTER OF PRACTICE

How the Emotional Pivot Works in a Story

Charles Young, *Founder and CEO, Ameritest*

To investigate the power of emotional engagement in a video, we studied the structure of a six-minute film of Susan Boyle, who turned in a surprising 2009 performance on *Britain's Got Talent.* Employing the same research techniques we use to analyze television commercials, we found that this YouTube video is built on a standard dramatic structure that we commonly see in advertising, one that we call an "emotional pivot." (You can watch it on YouTube at *www.youtube.com/watch?v=9lp0IWv8QZY.*)

Good storytellers understand that with a pivot structure, the emotional impact is particularly strong because the valence of the emotion changes from initially negative to positive, which creates the strongest possible contrast between what the audience feels at the beginning of the story and what they feel at the end.

Here's how we identified the emotional pivot in the *Britain's Got Talent* video featuring a rather frumpy Scottish woman named Susan Boyle. Using a photo sort of still frames from the video, we track the flow of emotion throughout the six-minute video. In the graph, you can see strong negative emotions at the beginning of the video shown with strong spikes in the red line. This reflects the entrance on stage of this rather overweight and middle-aged Scottish woman. The rolled eyes and sideway glances of disbelief from the lead judge Simon Cowell reinforce this negative first impression.

Then toward the middle, the green (positive) line begins to rise rapidly and the red (negative) line fades away as emotions turn, or pivots, on frame 18 as Susan begins to sing. As her beautiful voice fills the room, the judges and the audience are transformed.

Finally, positive emotions rise to a sustained, high volume of intensity for the rest of the video. It ends with the entire studio audience—and even one of the judges—on their feet cheering wildly.

At the pivot point—the boundary between these two states of emotion—lies the most dramatic, brand-creating moment of this piece of film. So in frame 18 when Susan first begins to sing, we are able to pinpoint the actual moment of a birth of a new star—or brand, in advertising terms.

In storytelling, this is the moment when a gap opens up in the mind of an audience—a break between what the audience expected to see, and what just happened. The mind of the audience is forced to turn in a new direction. As their personal interpretations of the event are recalculated, audience members build a new mental model of realty to make sense of what they are seeing. Unexpectedly, the ugly duckling just turned into a swan!

Interestingly, when we tested a shorter version of the video with the "negative set-up" removed, we found the emotional response to the singing was just as positive, but when we interviewed respondents, it was obvious that something was lost. This shorter version was much less likely to be rated as "unique," "involving," "entertaining," or "inspirational." In other words, changing the narrative to an uninterrupted flow of positive emotions diminished the impact. Ironically, the Susan Boyle story would be different—and she might not be a star—without Simon Cowell's display of cynicism at the beginning.

You can watch this video on YouTube. Search for "Susan Boyle I dreamed a Dream."

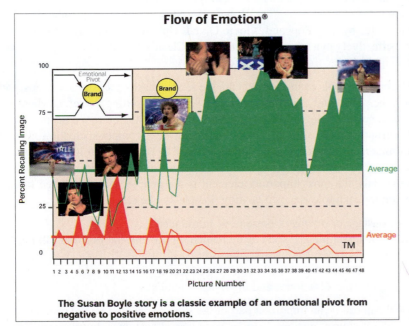

The Susan Boyle story is a classic example of an emotional pivot from negative to positive emotions.

Dialogue, both in radio and television, is an interesting challenge for copywriters who try to keep the words natural and the interaction interesting. In the Frontier Airlines talking animals commercials, for example, the repartee between the characters is as important to the message as the words themselves. Note how the dialogue between Jack the Rabbit and Larry the Lynx bounces back and forth in the "Leather Seats" commercial. Also note the brand identity text in the middle. This structure is called a "donut" because it uses an attention-getting idea to open and close with brand copy embedded in the middle.

Jack the Rabbit:	I'll tell you, Lar, the tarmac never looked better.
Larry the Lynx:	I'll say.
Jack:	New planes. New cities. New leather seats.
Larry:	Pretty exciting stuff, huh?
Jack:	Hey, uh, Larry, what's leather made from?
Larry:	Cowhide.
Jack:	Oh. So that's why there are no cows on the tails of our planes.
Larry:	It'd be creepy.
GRAPHIC:	New planes. New cities. New leather seats.
[MUSIC UNDER]	A whole different animal. *FrontierAirlines.com*. Frontier.
Larry:	Wanna moment of silence for the cows?
Jack:	Sure.
Both:	That's enough.
Jack:	Wanna grab a burger?
Larry:	I'm starving.

Source: Courtesy of Frontier Airlines and Grey Worldwide.

Music is also important in most commercials. Sometimes it is just used as background; at other times, the song is the focus of the commercial. In recognition of the role of music in advertising, Universal Music released a CD in 2001 called "As Seen on TV: Songs from Commercials," a collection of tunes that have become popular—or resurrected—thanks to their use in TV commercials. Included among the 20 songs are "Mr. Roboto" by Styx, "Right Here, Right Now" by Fatboy Slim, "Lust for Life" by Iggy Pop, and "Got to Give It Up" by Marvin Gaye. All of these songs have been used effectively in a television commercial. Clash's "London Calling" song became the theme for a highly successful sales event for Jaguar.

Other TV Tools   The creative tools examined next are the setting, casting, costumes, props, and lighting—all of which the copywriter must describe in the script. The setting, or **set,** is where the action takes place. It can be something in the studio, from a simple tabletop to a constructed set that represents a storefront or the inside of a home, or it can be a computer creation layered behind the action. Commercials shot outside the studio are said to be filmed **on location,** which means the entire crew and cast are transported somewhere away from the studio.

For many commercials, the most important element is the people, who are called **talent.** Finding the right person for each role is called **casting.** People can be cast as:

- *Announcers* (either onstage or offstage), presenters, introducers.
- *Spokespersons* (or "spokes-animals," such as the Geico Gecko and the Frontier talking animals).
- *Character Types* (old woman, baby, skin diver, police officer).
- *Celebrities,* such as Catherine Zeta-Jones and the Black Eyed Peas.

Costumes and makeup can be an important part of the story depending on the characterizations in the commercial. Of course, historical stories need period costumes, but modern scenes may also require special clothing such as golf outfits, swimsuits, or cowboy boots. Makeup may be important if you need to change a character from young to old. The copywriter must specify all of these details in the script. The director usually manipulates the lighting, but the copywriter might specify special lighting effects in the script. For example, you might read "Intense bright light as though reflected from snow" or "Light flickering on people's faces as if reflecting from a television screen."

Copywriters might also have to specify the commercial's **pace**—how fast or slowly the action progresses. Some messages are best developed at a languid pace; others work better when presented at an upbeat, fast pace. Research has found that the pace of TV commercials has been steadily getting faster since the mid-20th century. Why do you suppose that might be?

Planning the TV Commercial

Copywriters must plan how long the commercial will be, what shots will appear in each scene, what the key visual will be, and where and how to shoot the commercial. Other key decisions the copywriter must consider in planning a commercial are the length, number of scenes, and key frames. The common lengths of TV commercials are 10, 15, 20, 30, and 60 seconds. The 10-, 15-, and 20-second lengths are used for reminders and product or station identification. The 60-second spot, which is common in radio, has almost disappeared in television because of the increasing cost of airtime. The most common length for a TV commercial is 30 seconds.

Scenes and Key Frames   A commercial is planned in **scenes**—segments of action that occur in a single location. A scene may include several shots from different angles. A 30-second commercial usually is planned with four to six scenes, but a fast-paced commercial may have many more. Because television is a visual medium, the message is often developed as a **key visual** that conveys the heart of the concept. The **key frame** is the shot that sticks in the mind and becomes the image viewers remember when they think about the commercial. Copywriter Lara Mann describes a campaign she worked on for the Florida Film Festival. The campaign used television commercials but they were supported by posters with key frames from the commercials. The TV tagline "Where Will It Take You?" appears on the posters to express the thought that the Film Festival takes you to some exotic locations.

Copywriters need to answer many questions when planning a television spot. How much product information should there be in the commercial? Should the action be fast or slow? Is it wise to defy tradition and create unusual, even controversial ads as Crispin Porter + Bogusky did with Old Navy's SuperModelquins? How intrusive should the ad be?

Every producer and director will respond to these questions differently, depending on personal preferences and the advertising objectives. Nevertheless, these general principles as outlined by Drewniany and Jewler in their creative strategy book and earlier editions of their book are relevant for most effective television commercials:[11]

- *What's the big idea* you need to get across? In 30 seconds you barely have time to do much more than that. Alternative concepts are also tested as key visuals in developing the idea for the commercial. For each idea, a card with the key visual drawn on it is given to a respondent, along with a paragraph that describes the concept and how it will be played out in the commercial.
- *What's the benefit* of that big idea, and who does it benefit? Connect the big idea back to the target audience.
- *How can you turn that benefit into a visual element?* This visual is what sticks in people's minds.
- *How can you gain the interest* of viewers at the beginning? The first three seconds are critical.
- *How can you focus on a key visual,* a scene that encapsulates your entire selling message into one neat package?
- *Is the commercial single-minded?* Tell one important story per commercial. Tell it clearly, tell it memorably, and involve your viewer.
- *Is the product identified and shown* in close-up at the end?

Scripts, Storyboards, and Photoboards   Two documents are used to plan commercials: a television script prepared by the copywriter and a storyboard drawn by the art director. Similar to a radio script, a **television script** is the written version of the commercial's plan. It contains all the words, dialogue, lyrics (if important to the ad message), instructions, and descriptions of the details we've been discussing—sets, costumes, lighting, and so forth. For television commercials that use dialogue, the script is written in two columns, with the audio on the right and the video on the left.

The key to the structure of a television script is the relationship between the audio and the video. The dialogue is typed as usual, but the instructions and labels are typed in all-capital letters. The video part of the script includes descriptions of key frames, characters, actions, and camera movements in the commercial. Sometimes the script is in a two-column format with the video instructions on the left and the audio in the right column.

A **storyboard,** which is a visual plan or layout of the commercial, is drawn (by hand or on the computer) to show the number of scenes, composition of the shots, and progression of the action. The script information usually appears below the key images. Its purpose is to guide the filming. A **photoboard** uses photographic stills instead of art to illustrate the progression of images. It's created from the still photos or frames from the filming and is used to present to clients. (See the Frontier commercial in Chapter 8.)

HOW DIFFERENT IS COPYWRITING FOR THE INTERNET?

The Internet is more interactive than any other mass medium. Not only do viewers initiate the contact, they can send e-mail on many websites. This makes Web advertising more like two-way communication, and that's a major point of difference from other advertising forms. As a result, the Web copywriter is challenged to attract people to the site and to manage a dialogue-based communication experience. In addition to targeting messages to audiences, Web advertisers have to be prepared to listen and respond to those audiences. That's a major shift in how Web marketing communicators think about advertising.

Principle

To write great copy for the Web, copywriters must think of it as an interactive medium and open up opportunities for dialogue with the consumer.

It is true, however, that there are forms of Internet advertising that look like more traditional ads, such as **banners,** sidebar ads, and pop ups. E-mail and video ads, as well as mobile ads on smart phones, all require variations of traditional copywriting techniques. Most of these formats end with a link to the sponsor's website where the user can participate in a more interactive experience.

In this complicated, fast-changing medium, there aren't a lot of rules. In fact, marketing communication that uses text messaging and Twitter may even throw out the rules of spelling with vowel-free words. Cell-phone company Motorola follows that trend in naming new products such as RAZR, PEBL, and RCKR.

For banners and other formats that look like advertising and seek to attract someone to a company's website, verbosity is a killer. In that situation, no one wants to read a lot of type online. That means Web copywriters have to be able to write everything from catchy phrases for banners to copy that works like traditional advertisements, brochures, or catalogs. A basic principle, however, is that good writing is good writing, whether it is being done for traditional advertising media or for the Web.

Websites

The challenge for Web advertisers is to understand the user's situation and design messages that fit their needs and interests. However, the Web is an information medium and users come to it, in some cases, for reference information—formats that look a lot like catalogs, or even encyclopedias. Corporate or organizational websites are designed to provide information, as well as image cues, so strategies that organize information and package it for easy accessibility are important. **Key words** are used to help *visitors or surfers* (rather than readers, listeners, or viewers) search for the site online, as well as within the site for the information they need.

Creativity is also valued both to entice visitors, but also to keep them actively involved with the site. For example, the "Don't Mess with Texas" anti-litter website mentioned early as an *Adweek* favorite invites visitors into the campaign with advertising materials, testimonials, letters, special events, and involvement programs. It uses colorful animation to create action and spark interest. The language reflects the tough-talking slogan. For example, one section asks, "Who wants to live in a pig sty?" and "Why swim in an ashtray?" Check it out at *http://dontmesswithtexas.org*.

Banners

The most common form of online advertising is small banner ads containing text, images, and perhaps motion **(animation).** Banners in this small format have to be creative to stand out amidst the clutter on a typical Web page and, similar to outdoor advertising, they have to grab the surfer's attention with few words. Effective banners arouse the interest of the viewer, who is often browsing through other information on the computer screen. The key to stopping surfers is vivid graphics, motion, and clever phrases. It is critical to make the site easy to navigate. In general, the copywriter uses these strategies for grabbing surfers and turning them into longer-staying visitors:[12]

1. *Offer a deal* that promises a discount or a freebie as a prize.
2. *Use an involvement device* such as a challenge or contest.
3. *Change the offer frequently,* perhaps even daily. One of the reasons people surf the Internet is to find out what's happening now. Good ads exploit "nowness" and "newsiness."
4. *Keep the writing succinct* because most surfers have short attention spans and get bored easily.
5. *Focus surfers' attention* by asking provocative questions or offering knowledge they can use.
6. *Use the advertisement* to solicit information and opinions from users as part of your research. Reward surfers for sharing their opinions with you by offering them three free days of a daily horoscope or something else they might find fun or captivating.

Sometimes banners provide brand reminder information only, like a billboard, but they usually also invite viewers to click on the banner to link to an ad or the advertiser's home page. The effectiveness of such efforts is monitored in part by the number of **click-throughs.** Their creators make banners entertaining by using multimedia effects such as animation and sound, interactivity, emotional appeals, color, and provocative headlines. One mistake copywriters sometimes make, however, is to forget to include the company name or brand in the banner or ad. Surfers should be able to tell immediately what product or brand the banner is advertising. Effective banner ads satisfy the need for entertainment, information, and context (a link to a product), and often use promotional incentives, such as prizes or gifts, to motivate visitors to click through to the sponsor's website[13] to drive action.

Internet Ads

Similar in some ways to traditional advertising, Internet ads are designed to create awareness and interest in a product and build a brand image. In terms of creating interest, good copywriting works well in any medium, including the Internet. The "Ocean Speaks" ads in *The Inside Story* at *www.pearsonhighered.com/moriarty* illustrates how the same writing style can transfer from print to the Internet and maintain a consistent brand personality. The scuba diving industry wanted to revive interest in the sport of scuba, both with current divers and potential newcomers. The objective of this striking campaign was to move people from print to the company's website.

Art director Chris Hutchinson explains, "We created a campaign in the literal voice of the ocean. The Ocean irreverently compares itself to the dull world up above and invites people to come down for a visit. Instead of using traditional beauty shots of scuba diving, we commissioned surreal organic underwater scenes." The ads were featured in *Archive,* an international collection of the best advertising, television, and poster images.

In contrast to the Ocean speaking campaign, Burton Snowboards uses copy that speaks in the voice of the product's user, but the copy also creates an association with a distinctive brand and user personality.

It also uses its corporate mission statement as copy that speaks in the same tone of voice. This is another creative website. Check it out at *www.burton.com.*

LESSONS ABOUT COPYWRITING

As discussed throughout this chapter, the copywriter's job is to find a memorable way to express the creative concept. All of a copywriter's talent will do no good if the audience cannot understand the "magic words." Understanding the words, as well as the creative idea, is particularly complicated in global brand communication.

Writing for a Global Brand

Language affects the creation of the advertising, which is a problem for global campaigns. English is more economical than many other languages. This creates a major problem when the space for copy is laid out for English and one-third more space is needed for French or Spanish. However, English does not have the subtlety of other languages such as Greek, Chinese, or French. Those languages have many different words for situations and emotions that do not translate precisely into English. Standardizing the copy content by translating the appeal into the language of the foreign market is fraught with possible communication blunders. It is rare to find a copywriter who is fluent in both the domestic and foreign language and familiar with the culture of the foreign market.

Headlines in any language often rely on humor or a play on words, themes that are relevant to one country, or slang. Because these verbal techniques don't cross borders well, copywriters remove them from the advertising unless the meaning or intent can be re-created in other languages. For this reason, international campaigns are not literally translated word by word. Instead, a copywriter usually rewrites them in the second language. An ad for a Rome laundry shows how a poor translation can send the wrong message: "Ladies, leave your clothes here and spend the afternoon having a good time."

Although computer words and advertising terms are almost universally of English derivation, some languages simply do not have words equivalent to other English expressions. Since 1539 the French have had legislation to keep their language "pure" and now have a government agency to prevent words, especially English words, from corrupting the French language. The words *marketing* and *weekend,* unacceptable to the French government agency, are translated literally as "study the market" (or "pertaining to trade") and "end of the week," respectively.

Experience suggests that the most reasonable solution to the language problem is to use bilingual copywriters who understand the full meaning of the English text and can capture the essence of the message in the second language. It takes a brave and trusting international creative director to approve copy he or she doesn't understand but is assured is right. A **back translation** of the ad copy from the foreign language into the domestic one is always a good idea, but it seldom conveys a complete cultural interpretation.

The most recent announcement on the global stage is the opening up of the Internet to non-Roman letters, such as those used in Chinese, Korean, and Arabic. It's a challenge to develop translations for these languages so that a posting can be read in its original language, as well as in Roman letter alphabets, but the technology is making that possible.

Looking Ahead

The most important enduring principle is that in a Big Idea the meaning emerges from the way the words and images reinforce one another. We've explored the practices and principles of copywriting. In the next chapter we'll introduce the role of the art director and explain the important role of visual communication.

IT'S A WRAP

Cows Build Moo-Mentum for Chick-fil-A

Chick-fil-A and its advertising agency, The Richards Group, developed one of the most successful integrated brand campaigns in the fast-food industry, one that has been executed across all media over many years. The strategy is expressed in the line used by wacky cows who demand that we "Eat Mor Chikin," rather than hamburger.

After the initial rollout as a three-dimensional billboard, the campaign continued to evolve and make its way into every point of contact with the customer. A standup cow became part of the in-store kit, along with banners, table tents, cups, bags, and register toppers. The campaign has added direct mail and ads, promotions, events, TV, radio, the Internet, clothing, and merchandise. Calendars have been so popular that production numbers have topped 2.4 million. Anyone brave enough to show up at one of the chain's restaurants dressed as a cow on the annual Cow Appreciation Day gets a free Chick-fil-A meal.

The iconic cows and their quirky antics have become such a key symbol of Chick-fil-A's marketing communication that they were recognized as one of America's most popular advertising icons in a public vote sponsored by *Advertising Week*. They even earned a spot on New York's Madison Avenue Advertising Walk of Fame.

Chick-fil-A's lighthearted, unconventional campaign has helped increase sales every year. Sales have increased almost 600 percent since the campaign's launch. Same-store sales more than tripled the precampaign levels. Sales percentage increases beat the competition hoofs down.

Oh yes, the campaign also won a herd of awards, including induction into the Outdoor Advertising Association of America's Obie Hall of Fame, a Silver Lion at the Cannes International Advertising Festival, and two Effies, including one for its sustained success. That's one way to milk the cows for all they're worth.

Key Points Summary

1. **What basic style of writing is used for advertising copy?** Words and pictures work together to shape a creative concept; however, it is the clever phrases and "magic words" crafted by copywriters that make ideas understandable and memorable. Copywriters who have an ear for language match the tone of the writing to the target audience. Good copy is succinct and single-minded. Copy that is less effective uses adese to imitate a stereotyped style that parodies advertising.

2. **Which copy elements are essential to a print ad?** The key elements of a print ad are the headlines and body copy. Headlines target the prospect, draw the reader's attention, identify the product, start the sale, and lure the reader into the body copy. Body copy provides persuasive details, such as support for claims, as well as proof and reasons why.

3. **How can we characterize the message and tools of radio advertising?** Radio commercials are personal and play to consumers' interests. However, radio is primarily a background medium. Special techniques, such as repetition, are used to enhance retention. The three audio tools are voice, music, and sound effects.

4. **What is the best way to summarize the major elements of television commercials?** The elements of TV commercials are video and audio tools. Television commercials can be characterized as using action, emotion, and demonstration to create messages that are intriguing as well as intrusive.

5. **How is Web advertising written?** Internet advertising is interactive and involving. Online advertising has primarily focused on websites and banners, although advertisers are using new forms that look more like magazine or television ads. Banners and other forms of online advertising have to stand out amid the clutter on a typical Web page and arouse the viewer's interest. Good writing is still good writing, even online.

Words of Wisdom: Recommended Reading

Applegate, Edd, *Strategic Copywriting,* New York: Rowman & Littlefield, 2005.

Bayan, Richard, *Words that Sell: The Thesaurus to Help You Promote Your Products, Services, and Ideas*, rev. ed., New York: McGraw-Hill, 2006.

Bly, Robert, *The Copywriter's Handbook*, 3rd ed., Sand Springs, OK: Holt, 2006.

Gossage, Howard, *The Book of Gossage*, Chicago: The Copy Workshop, 2006.

Gunelius, Susan, *Kick-Ass Copywriting in 10 Easy Steps*, Irvine, CA: Entrepreneur Press, 2008.

Higgins, Denis, *The Art of Writing Advertising: Conversations with Masters of the Craft*, New York: McGraw-Hill, 2003.

Klauser, Anne Henriette, *Writing on Both Sides of the Brain: Breakthrough Techniques for People Who Write*, New York: Harper-Collins, 1987.

Shaw, Mark, *Copywriting: Successful Writing for Design, Advertising, and Marketing*, London, UK: Laurence King Publishing, 2009.

Sugarman, Joseph, *The Adweek Copywriting Handbook: The Ultimate Guide to Writing Powerful Advertising and Marketing Copy from One of America's Top Copywriters*, Hoboken, NJ: Wiley, 2006.

Key Terms

Review Questions

1. What is adese, and why is it a problem in advertising copy?

2. Describe the various copy elements of a print ad.

3. What is the difference between direct-action and indirect-action headlines? Find an example of each and explain how it works.

4. What qualities make a good tagline or slogan?

5. What is the primary role of body copy, and how does it accomplish that?

6. One principle of print copywriting is that the headline catches the reader's eye, but the body copy wins the reader's heart and mind. Find an ad that demonstrates that principle and explain how it works.

7. Explain the message characteristics of radio advertising. What does "theater of the mind" mean to a radio copywriter? What are the primary tools used by the radio copywriter?

8. What are the major characteristics of TV ads? Describe the tools of television commercial copywriting.

9. Discuss how Internet advertising is written.

Discussion Questions

1. Creative directors say the copy and art must work together to create a concept. Consider all of the ads in this chapter and the preceding chapters and identify one that you believe best demonstrates that principle. Explain what the words contribute and how they work with the visual.

2. A principle of TV message design is that television is primarily a visual medium. However, very few television commercials are designed without a vocal element (actors or announcers). Even the many commercials that visually demonstrate products in action use an off-screen voice to provide information. Why is there a need to use a voice in a television commercial?

3. What do we mean by *tone of voice,* and why is it important in advertising? Find a magazine ad that you think has an appropriate tone of voice for its targeted audience (the readers of that particular magazine) and one that doesn't. Explain your analyses of these two ads.

4. Select a product that is advertised exclusively through print using a long-copy format. Examples might be business-to-business and industrial products, over-the-counter drugs, and some car and appliance ads. Now write a 30-second radio and a 30-second TV spot for that product. Present your work to the class, along with an analysis of how the message design changed—and stayed the same—when you moved from print to radio and then to TV.

5. Critique the following (choose one):

   a. Jingles are a popular creative form in radio advertising. Even so, there may be as many jingles that you don't want to hear again as there are ones that you do. As a team, identify one jingle that your group really dislikes and another one that you like. Analyze why these jingles either work or don't work and present your critique to your class.

   b. As a team, surf the Web and find one banner ad that you think works to drive click-throughs and one that doesn't. Print them out and prepare an analysis that compares the two banner ads and explains why you think one is effective and the other is not. Present your critique to your class.

6. *Three-Minute Debate:* Your professor has set up a debate between the advertising sales director of the campus news-

paper and the manager of the campus radio station, which is a commercial operation. During the discussion the newspaper representative says that most radio commercials sound like newspaper ads, but are harder to follow. The radio manager responds by claiming that radio creativity works with the "theater of the mind" and is more engaging than newspaper ads, which mostly feature price copy and sales. In a team of two or three, pick one of these positions, and build your case by finding examples of ads in both print and radio that support your viewpoint.

Take-Home Projects

1. *Portfolio Project:* In Chapter 6's Three-Minute Debate, your team was asked to consider the research needed for a new upscale restaurant chain that focuses on fowl—duck, squab, pheasant, and other elegant meals in the poultry category. Now your creative team is being asked to develop the creative package for the restaurant chain. A specialty category, this would be somewhat like a seafood restaurant. You have been asked to develop the creative package to use in launching these new restaurants in their new markets. Develop the following:

   • The restaurant's name
   • A slogan for the restaurant chain
   • A list of five enticing menu items

   • A paragraph of copy that can be used in print to describe the restaurant
   • The copy for a 30-second commercial to be used in radio.

2. *Mini-Case Analysis:* The Chick-fil-A "Eat Mor Chikin" campaign has been successful for many years. Explain how the concept works. Also explain how the theme line defines the brand and reinforces the brand position. What other factors have made it a winner? Pretend you are assigned to this account and you need to come up with an idea for a new outdoor board execution. Describe your idea in a one-page proposal to turn in to your instructor.

Team Project: The BrandRevive Campaign

Review the message strategy you created in the last chapter for your BrandRevive campaign, as well as the Big Idea you developed as a team. The next step is to translate that strategy and Big Idea into copy. Normally you would be working in a copywriter and art director team, but because we have to introduce first one—copywriting—then the other—art direction, we'll focus in this step of the project on the language.

• Develop a slogan to use with your campaign, one that delivers on your strategy, but at the same time is attention getting and memorable—something that has the potential to move into popular culture.
• Write the copy for a print ad that would run in a magazine targeted to the audience you have selected.
• Write the copy for a radio spot that uses "theater of the mind" techniques.
• Write the copy for a television commercial that uses dialogue.
• Present your copy package in a two-page handout for your class and a PowerPoint presentation that is no longer than three slides. In the presentation explain and justify your copy decisions.

Hands-On Case

The Century Council

Read the Century Council case in the Appendix before coming to class.

1. The case briefly discusses the tonality of the communications. Write a one-page direction to the creative team explaining what the tonality should be and giving rationale for your recommendation. Keep in mind the target audience, your client (The Century Council) and the potential seriousness of the consequences of binge drinking on college campuses.

2. Write a one page instruction for finding your personal stupid drink that you would give to all freshmen arriving on campus.

Visual Communication

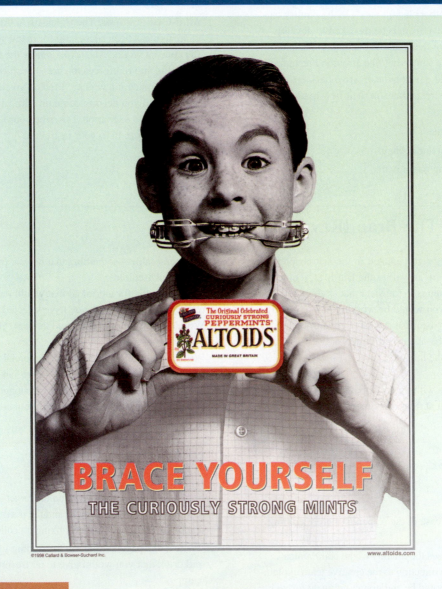

It's a Winner

Campaign:
"Curiously Strong Mints"

Company:
Kraft Foods; Wm. Wrigley Jr. Co. (which became a subsidiary of Mars)

Agencies:
Leo Burnett, Publicis & Hal Riney, BBDO Chicago

Awards:
Two Kelly Awards, including the Grand Prize, two One Show prizes, three Clios, the New York Festival Grand Prix

288

CHAPTER KEY POINTS

1. What is the role of visual communication in marketing communication messages?
2. How can we define *layout* and *composition*, and what's the difference between the two?
3. How are art and color reproduced in print media?
4. What are the steps in planning and producing video?
5. What are the basic techniques of Web design?

A Strong Mint with a Curious Past

Shortly after the United States fought for its independence from England, Smith Kendon created in 1780 a revolutionary British product designed to relieve intestinal discomfort. It's name: Altoids. Today we know Altoids as a "curiously strong mint" designed to fight bad breath. The story about how Altoids came to be the top-selling mint in the United States parallels the evolution of its brand personality.

Advertising as far back as the 1920s plugged the "curiously strong" mint-flavored lozenges, but Altoids was largely unknown in the United States until Kraft Food purchased it in 1995 and turned its advertising over to the Leo Burnett agency.

Kraft inherited a product that came in a distinctive, Old World–looking red-and-white metal tin emblazoned with the slogan, "The Original Celebrated Curiously Strong Peppermints." The Burnett creatives adapted that phrase and captured the brand essence with its campaign's wry slogan: "The Curiously Strong Mint."

The campaign tone features a type of amusing, rather British self-deprecation, as if the brand doesn't take itself seriously. That approach struck a nerve with the largely cynical, sometimes sarcastic Generation X and Y males who have been the brand's most loyal fans.

Burnett's memorable ads from this classic campaign have featured a muscle builder with the line "Nice Altoids," a 1950s teenager with oversized braces and the headline "Brace Yourself," and a stern-looking nurse carrying the little red-and-white Altoids tin with the headline "Now This Won't Hurt a Bit." Another ad proclaimed, "No Wonder the British Have Stiff Upper Lips."

As you probably know, the Altoids brand has expanded to include new flavors, from cinnamon and wintergreen to ginger and sours (in a round tin), as well as gum and strips. No longer do we think of Altoids for its medicinal qualities.

Change is an inevitable fact of life. Not only did the product come to mean something different to consumers over time, brand ownership has changed hands and so have the agencies that manage the marketing communication.

Altoids was a winner for Kraft, so much so that it sold the brand in 2004 to Wm. Wrigley Jr. Co. for the minty fresh sum of $1.46 billion. The new owner then awarded the Altoids advertising account to Publicis & Hal Riney. In late 2008, Mars bought Wrigley, and moved the account to BBDO Chicago. How does a brand maintain a consistent personality amid changing ownership and agencies?

The success of a brand's advertising is based on more than the humor of a single campaign—especially as ownership of a brand shifts. Altoids ads have an iconic look. Most feature an intriguing headline that is only a few words long in all capital letters and a drop shadow outline. Many of the ads are laid out on a plain, mint green background with a double rule border—a great retro look that reflects the package design, which reinforces the brand identity.

Although BBDO Chicago has recently dropped the "Curiously Strong" theme, replacing it with "A Slap to the Cerebellum," it kept some of the elements from the previous campaign. Steffan Postaer, one of the Leo Burnett creatives whose ideas resulted in Altoids award-winning work, did not agree entirely with the approach that BBDO took. But he said this of the new campaign: "You can still see the brand's DNA in the language and typography as well as in the tone and manner." Other efforts include "Brainstorm," a branded entertainment collaboration with Fox Mobile Studios.

See for yourself what you think gives a campaign continuity by looking at past and current advertising at *www.altoids.com/ad-gallery.do*. Then in the *It's a Wrap* section at the end of the chapter, see how well the advertising has performed over time for this intense, extreme, and curiously strong mint.

Sources: www.wrigley.com; www.altoids.com; http://godsofadvertising.wordpress.com/2008/03/13/my-altoids-can-beat-up-their-altoids; Rita Chang, "Altoids Pokes Fun at Itself with 'Brainstorm,'" www.adage.com, September 21, 2009.

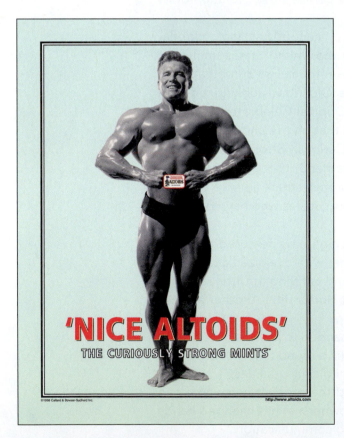

This ad offers a visual pun, playing on the product name and the slang "nice 'toids." Pairing the unexpected—the hunk's deltoid muscles and the product—helps create a memorable association.

The visual consistency and wry humor in the Altoids campaign go far beyond the ability of words to describe things. The quirky images communicate ideas about the brand personality, as well as the feelings and sense of humor of the brand's target market. This chapter is about the visuals used in advertising—how they are designed and what they contribute to the meaning of the ad. First we review some basic ideas about visual impact, both in print and broadcast, and the role of the art director. Then we consider print art production and video production and end with a discussion of the design of Internet advertising.

WHY IS VISUAL COMMUNICATION IMPORTANT?

What makes Altoids so visually remarkable? Does the product grab your attention? How does the visual build brand personality? Is it interesting? Do you remember it?

The success of Altoids breath mints is primarily a result of the consistent graphic presentation of the brand in its marketing communication. The visual consistency is not only apparent in the design of the package and the ads; it also reflects the history of the brand as a quirky old British lozenge.

The Altoids ads use association to create curiosity, but also to reflect the meaning of the slogan. "Nice Altoids" builds on a unique connection between the sound of "deltoids" and the brand name. We've also reproduced an ad used to launch the Altoids Cinnamon line, which continues to build on the brand position but modifies it slightly to read "curiously hot" rather than "curiously strong." A firewalker tiptoeing across a patch of the little white mints visually reinforces a truth about the product—the Cinnamon Altoids are hot enough to tickle your toes.

In effective advertising, both print and television, it's not just the words that need to communicate the message—the visuals need to communicate, too. The visuals normally work with the words to present the creative concept. An example of a simple story told totally through the visuals is the Best of Show award for a One Show competition that showcased a British campaign for Volkswagen. It featured a gently humorous 30-second commercial built around the low price of the VW Polo. Bob Barrie, when he was president of The One Club, an association for people in the creative side of advertising, explained that it was possibly the quietest, most understated TV spot entered in the show. The idea was simple: A woman sits at her kitchen table. Her scanning of the newspaper—and her hiccups—stop abruptly as she discovers an ad for the VW Polo with its "surprisingly ordinary" price.[1]

Visuals do some things better than words, such as demonstrate something. How would you demonstrate, for example, the smallness of a computer chip or a new miniature hard drive? IBM did it through a visual analogy—showing its hard disk drive inside half an eggshell next to a newborn chick.

Even radio can evoke mental pictures through suggestive or descriptive language and sound effects. The effective use of visuals in advertising can be related to a number of the effects we have outlined in our Facets Model of Effects:

1. **Grab Attention** Generally visuals are better at getting and keeping attention than words.
2. **Stick in Memory** Visuals persist in the mind because people generally remember messages as visual fragments, or key images that are filed easily in their minds.
3. **Cement Belief** Seeing is believing, as the IBM chick ad demonstrates. Visuals that demonstrate add credibility to a message.
4. **Tell Interesting Stories** Visual storytelling is engaging and maintains interest.
5. **Communicate Quickly** Pictures tell stories faster than words, as the IBM chick visual illustrates. A picture communicates instantly, while consumers have to decipher verbal/written communication word by word, sentence by sentence, line by line.
6. **Anchor Associations** To distinguish undifferentiated products with low inherent interest, advertisers often link the product with visual associations representing lifestyles and types of users, as the "Nice Altoids" ad demonstrates.

ALTOIDS CINNAMON
THE CURIOUSLY STRONG MINTS®

curious? altoids.com

SHOWCASE

This ad for Altoids Cinnamon shows a firewalker tiptoeing across a patch of the mints. This Altoids "Cinnamon" ad builds on a truth about the product. The cinnamon candies are curiously hot. Just stepping on them would be an experience. You see the ad. You smile. You associate the message with a product attribute. Just maybe you remember the brand when you're in the checkout line.

This Altoids "Cinnamon" ad, which won a Gold Pencil from the One Show, was submitted by the Leo Burnett copywriter and art director team of Andy Dao (top) and Matt Miller, both of whom graduated from the advertising program at the University of Colorado. Their work was nominated for inclusion in this book by Professor Brett Robbs.

Visual Impact

In most marketing communication, the power to get attention primarily lies with the visual. The excitement and drama in a television commercial is created through moving images. But it is an intriguing idea that grabs attention and remains in memory. This is particularly so for larger impact formats, such as posters and outdoor boards.

A provocative outdoor board for the Italian women's apparel firm, No-l-ita, certainly got people's attention, but it also raised ethical issues. The billboard raised a furor in Italy because

Principle
The visual's primary function in an advertisement is to get attention.

IBM used a chick and an egg to demonstrate the smallness of its hard disk drive, which is about the size of a large coin.

it showed shocking pictures of a naked anorexic woman. The image was shot by Oliviero Toscani, the former photographer/art director for Benetton, who stirred up emotions over his photos for that clothing brand by depicting a dying AIDS victim, death-row inmates, and a nun and priest kissing. Professor Edoardo Brioschi explains the issues with these images of anorexia in the *A Principled Practice* feature.

In general, print designers have found that a picture in a print ad captures more than twice as many readers as a headline does. Furthermore, the bigger the illustration, the more the message grabs consumers' attention. Ads with pictures also tend to pull more readers into the body copy; initial attention is more likely to turn to interest with a strong visual. People not only notice ad visuals, they remember ads with pictures more than those composed mostly of type. Both the believability factor and the interest-building impact of a visual story are reasons why visuals are anchored so well in memory.

Big Ideas that capture attention can be puzzling, shocking, or funny. An example is found in the "Welcome" doormat poster used with a twist by Columbia Sportswear. A Vonage campaign for its Web-based phone service uses videos of people doing silly things to illustrate its message: "That people do really stupid things. Like pay too much for home phone service." The commercials show a man cutting down a tree that falls on his car and a man on a treadmill who loses his footing and falls off. The stunts seem to defy credibility but, in fact, they are actual footage from the reality TV show *America's Funniest Home Videos*.[2] Attention, interest, memorability, believability—these factors help explain the visual impact of advertising messages.

Visual Storytelling

In visual storytelling the images set up a narrative, as the YMCA ad demonstrates, that has to be constructed by the reader or viewer. In television, for example, the commercial begins and ends with visual elements that establish the scene and the conclusion. Visual storytelling is important even for abstract concepts such as "empowered," "inspired," and "inventive," which were the focus of commercials in the PBS "Be More Inspired" campaign. In the "Be more empowered" commercial, a goldfish makes its escape from its little round bowl in an apartment and jumps from a puddle to a bottle to a river where it works its way upstream accompanying giant salmon who are leaping up waterfalls in their annual migration.

In another commercial in the series titled "Be more inspired," a composer agonizes over the right notes and eventually hits a point of total frustration. As he looks out the window, he sees a group of birds sitting on a set of five power and telephone wires that are conveniently aligned to look like a music staff. From the bird's positions he crafts a tune that becomes the theme for his composition. PBS used these clever little visual stories to present itself as a creative force that inspires people to use their imaginations.

The point is that creative people and art directors in particular design images that tell stories and create brand impressions. The art—the image or visual elements—in a marketing communication message can touch emotional buttons. Research by professor Karen Mallia, a regular contributor who wrote an essay for our Part 3 opener, suggests that not only are images moving, they also are becoming increasingly dramatic and controversial. She has studied the use of religious imagery in marketing communication and observes that "the change in tenor is best illustrated with the use of priests in advertising."

In 1975, Xerox's "Brother Dominick" spot starred a sweet, earnest monk invoking a "miracle" in duplicating 500 illuminated manuscripts. Fast-forward to 1991, when Benetton shocked the world with a priest and nun kissing. In 2005, Stella Artois' "Skating Priests" award-winning spot used surreal, almost sinister humor as you realize that a group of priests would rather see their fellow priest drown than lose a beer. In 2006, Pirelli tire launched a worldwide campaign with "The Call," a 20-minute Web film starring John Malkovich as a priest called upon to exorcise a car, and Naomi Campbell as the devil.

Mallia concludes that "The Call" with its dramatic tone brings a new level of darkness to advertising featuring priests. What do you think? Are images like these effective? Should religious images be avoided or are there times when they are relevant or appropriately dramatic?

A PRINCIPLED PRACTICE

An Imperative: Respect the Dignity of the Person

By Edoardo Teodoro Brioschi, *Università Cattolica del Sacro Cuore, Milan, Italy*

I believe that there exist certain ethical principles that apply to business activities and those include principles for marketing communication activities. Specifically I'm concerned about the protection of the dignity of the person. A case in obvious conflict with this principle is the use in an advertisement of an image of a woman suffering from an illness: acute anorexia. This is the case in the "No-Anorexia No-l-ita" campaign for an Italian brand of youth apparel.

The woman we see presented in the ad is, in fact, practically a living skeleton. The message shows the image of a naked woman suffering from anorexia posing with her gaze turned to the observer. (The model is 27-year-old French actress named Isabelle Caro who is five feet, five inches tall and weighs 70 pounds.) Both front and back views of her poses were used on outdoor boards and in the daily press during Milan fashion week, as well as in other big cities such as Rome and Naples.

The advertiser claimed that by presenting the images in this way it sought to make specific reference to a drama experienced by young women: anorexia: "We want to keep young people informed about this terrible illness so that, by seeing the effects, the young will not take the same risk."

The body that self-regulates the advertising industry in Italy (Istituto di Autodisciplina Pubblicitaria—the Italian Self-Regulation Institute) examined the No-l-ita "No Anorexia" campaign and judged this message to be in conflict with its Code of Self-Regulation. It summoned the advertiser, Flash & Partners, producer of the No-l-ita brand, for a specific hearing to discuss the case.

As a number of experts testified, anorexia is a complex illness. It follows that, whatever the factor causing the pathology, the behavior at risk is not due to ignorance of its effect. Hence the principle "If you know the results you will avoid them" is not valid. In fact, this pathology unfortunately derives from deep drives, probably including biochemical imbalances, which cannot be overcome or rectified by an advertisement that simply displays its devastating effects.

Therefore, this advertising was banned. In fact, the message in question uses the physical devastation of the naked body of a young woman for commercial purposes—for the purpose of marketing the firm's products—and in so doing it offends her dignity and debases the personal and social drama caused by this type of pathology.

On this question there was a more general observation by this jury, the highest judicial organ of the Italian Self-Regulation Institute. It notes that promotional campaigns dealing with such delicate areas as health and prevention call for extreme caution in their conduct, requiring scientific preparation and justifying a preventive screening by the bodies responsible for advertising self-regulation.

Brand Image

We've talked in previous chapters about the important role marketing communication plays in the creation of a brand image. Much of that contribution comes from the visual elements—the symbolic images associated with the brand and the elements that define the brand, such as the trademark and logo. A classic brand symbol, for example, is the target graphic used by the Target store. The association with the brand name is immediately clear and the brand meaning, that Target is a store where you can go to get what you are looking for, also adds to the identity of the retailer.

SHOWCASE

This award-winning poster for Columbia Sportswear twists the welcome concept and welcomes you to come out rather than in.

Jeremy Boland, art director and photographer at Borders Perrin Norrander in Portland, Oregon, is a graduate of the University of Colorado. He was nominated by Professor Brett Robbs.

SHOWCASE

This commercial for the YMCA tells a simple story of a teenager using a lawnmower to make a statement about his intention to go to the Y.

Lara Mann, copywriter at *DraftFCB* in Chicago, graduated from the University of Florida and was nominated by Professor Elaine Wagner.

A **logo,** which is the imprint used for immediate identification of a brand or company, is an interesting design project because it uses typography, illustration, and layout to create a distinctive and memorable image that identifies the brand. Think of the cursive type used for Coca-Cola, the block letters used for IBM, and the apple with a bite out of it (in both rainbow stripes and white) for Apple computers. Also check out the logo designs by Michael Dattolico.

Brand icons are characters associated with a brand, such Mr. Peanut, Chester the Cheetah, Uncle Ben, and Ronald McDonald. If they are effective, they become an enduring symbol of the brand. Initially the character is designed to reflect the desired brand personality. The Jolly Green Giant is an imaginary and kind friend who encourages kids to eat their vegetables. Over time, however, they may need to be updated as the Betty Crocker image has been a number of times. The trade magazine *Adweek* celebrates brand icons and annually inducts winners into its Madison Avenue Advertising Walk of Fame event every fall. Check these out at *www.adweek.com.*

Package design is another area where brand image is front and center. Sometimes the brand link is in the shape of the packaging as in the distinctive grandmotherly Mrs. Butterworth syrup bottles (see an example at *www.mrsbutterworthsyrup.com*). It may also be in the stylistics as we have shown with Celestial Seasonings tea boxes (see Chapter 2). The package design also accommodates strategic elements with positioning statements, flags that reference current campaigns, recipes, and pricing announcements. During the Great Recession, a number of manufacturers found that new packaging with retro designs appealed to consumers. Check out the Ritz crackers, Oreo cookies, and Corn Flakes brands, among others.

There's always a tension in advertising between doing something over the top that's creative and attention getting and being responsible to the brand image, the strategy, and society. The acceptability of a wacky image in an ad depends, in part, on its targeting, but it also depends on judgment and intuition. Our ethics discussions in this book often focus on the appropriateness of an image and how it reflects on the brand.

For example, an ad for Vaseline Intensive Care Lotion shows a conference room with a speaker and a group of businesspeople—both men and women—paying careful attention to the presentation. In the foreground is a happy woman in a business suit with her back to the speaker and her colleagues. Her legs are up on the table and she's caressing them. Unfortunately she's also a black woman. The headline reads: "Nothing keeps you from handling your business." So does Vaseline Intensive Care want us to know that if black women use their product, they become totally clueless in a business meeting? The point is that what appears to the creative team to be a dynamite visual may, on reflection, send a number of contrary messages.

Environmental Design

Remember we have said that everything communicates and that includes the design of the environment in which goods and services are offered for sale. The architectural design and interior ambiance of a store contribute to its brand personality. If you have been in a Polo store or Polo

SHOWCASE

These logos were designed by Michael Dattolico, who owns his own design studio, MusionCreative LLC (*www.musioncreative.com*).

A graduate of the University of Florida advertising program, Michael Dattolico was nominated by Professor Elaine Wagner.

section in a department store, you might remember some of the details of the environment that make the space different from, say, a Sears department, not to mention a Nike or Patagonia store. Nike stores have even been described as retail theater with displays and spaces that showcase not only the shoes and apparel, but also the sports with which they are associated.

Think about the last time you went to a sit-down restaurant versus your experiences in fast-food places. What's the difference in the way these spaces are designed both inside and outside? Think about the colors and surfaces and types of furniture. Graphic designer Amy Niswonger has been following the redesign of McDonald's interiors and explains what she has observed in *The Inside Story*.

WHAT IS ART DIRECTION?

The person most responsible for creating visual impact, as well as the brand identification elements, is the art director. The art director is in charge of the visual look of the advertisement, both in print and TV, and how it communicates mood, product qualities, and psychological appeals. The art director and copywriter team usually work together to come up with the Big Idea, but the art director is responsible for bringing the visual side of the idea to life.

Specifically, art directors make decisions about whether to use art or photography in print and film or animation in television and what type of artistic style to use. They are highly trained in graphic design, including art, photography, typography, the use of color, and computer design software. Although art directors generally design the ad, they rarely create the finished art. If they need an illustration, they hire an artist. Newspaper and Web advertising visuals are often **clip art** or **click art,** images from collections of copyright-free art that anyone who buys the clip-art service can use.

In addition to advertising, art directors may also be involved in designing a brand or corporate logo, as well as merchandising materials, store or corporate office interiors, and other aspects of a brand's visual presentation, such as shopping bags, delivery trucks, and uniforms. Karl Schroeder's team at Coates Kokes in Portland, Oregon, even designed an ad to be painted on the wall of a building using the distinctive artwork in the SeaPort Air campaign, which we showcased in Chapter 7.

The Designer's Toolkit

One of the most difficult problems that art directors—and those who work on the creative side of advertising—face is to transform a creative concept into words and pictures. During the brainstorming process, both copywriters and art directors are engaged in **visualization,** which means they are imagining what the finished ad might look like. The art director, however, is responsible for translating the advertising Big Idea into a visual story. To do this, the art director relies on a toolkit that consists of illustrations or animation, photos or film shots, color, type, design principles, layout (print), and composition (photography, video, or film), among other visual elements.

SHOWCASE

The distinctive illustration style from the SeaPort Air campaign was used to paint an ad on the side of a multistory building in Tillamook, Oregon.

A graduate of the University of Oregon advertising program, Karl Schroeder was nominated by Professor Charles Frazer.

Illustrations and Photos   When art directors use the word *art*, they usually mean photographs and illustrations, each of which serves different purposes in ads. For instance, photography has an authenticity that makes it powerful. Most people feel that pictures don't lie (even though they can be altered). For credibility, then, photography is a good medium.

The decision to use a photograph or an illustration is usually determined by the advertising strategy and its need for either realism or fanciful images. Generally a photograph is more realistic and an illustration (or animation in television) is more fanciful, as the Sony illustration shows. Illustrations, by definition, eliminate many of the details you see in a photograph, which can make it easier to understand their meaning since what remains are the "highlights" of the image. This ease of perception can simplify the visual message because it can focus attention on key details of the image. Illustrations

THE INSIDE STORY

Loving McDonald's New Look

Amy Niswonger, *President, Little Frog Prints*

McDonald's has a new look these days. Long gone is the bright red and yellow accented mansard roof. In its place are softer, subtler lines and features, bringing this fast-food giant's image in line with today's discriminating consumer's palette.

With the addition of a new design and set of healthier food choices, McDonald's is updating its image from kiddy classic to a destination for all ages. In the past few years, the company has achieved success both in updating its look and feel and expanding its target market without losing core customers. How is this possible you might ask? BRAND EQUITY.

Without hesitation, most people in any country in the world can recognize a McDonald's sign instantly from a great distance. The Golden Arches are an icon, with enormous brand equity attached. For more than fifty years the red and yellow color scheme has been a mainstay among the 30,000+ worldwide locations, and not until recently has it strayed from this design.

Due to its overwhelming worldwide presence through advertisements, endorsements, and other marketing venues, McDonald's has built such a powerful brand—and volume amount of brand equity—that it could dramatically alter its environmental design without taking a hit to its market share. You, as the customer, inherently understand that the Big Mac is still the Big Mac; it's just served now in a hipper, cooler location.

Brand equity, it's a powerful tool. Those who have it love it. Those who don't strive desperately to achieve it.

When you walk into the new McDonald's, you will immediately notice plasma screen TVs, pendant lighting, comfortable armchairs, and perhaps the boldest new feature: WiFi Internet access. At first, you might even mistake the place for a Starbucks or even Panera Bread. That's part of the strategy, as McDonald's is now focusing on creating a specific type of customer experience, not just offering a convenient grab 'n go meal.

The new meaning of "I'm lovin' it" means more than a happy meal. It's an invitation to the customer to come in, eat, enjoy the environment, and stay for a while.

Note: Amy Niswonger is a graphic designer and professor who owns her own design studio. A graphic design and marketing graduate of Miami University in Oxford, Ohio, she was named Most Promising Minority Student by the American Advertising Federation (AAF). She was nominated by Connie Frazier, AAF chief operating officer.

also use artistic techniques to intensify meanings and moods, making illustrations ideal for fantasy (think about comic books and animated films). Photos convey a "seeing is believing" credibility. Photographs, of course, can also evoke fanciful images. For example, the Maxell "500 Plays" ad uses visual symbolism to represent a blast of sound.

It is also possible to manipulate a photograph and turn it into art, a technique that brought recognition to Andy Warhol, among others. This practice has become popular with the advent of the Internet and the availability of easy-to-find digital images, some of which are copyrighted.

CLASSIC
Sony's "Full-Color Sound" campaign used the Big Idea that sound relates to colors. This campaign by Milt Glaser is one of the few signed by the art director. The original is in the permanent collection of the Metropolitan Museum of Art.

CLASSIC
The experience of being "blown away" by a blast of sound was depicted in this Maxell ad from the 1970s.

Recently that technique was used to create a political poster and, at the same time, a legal nightmare for the artist, Shepard Fairey, as discussed in the *A Matter of Principle* feature. Recognized as one of the most important political images of recent years, the Obama HOPE poster raises questions about fair use of manipulated images, something everyone has to think about when they find images online and want to reuse them in marketing communication projects.

Another issue involving digitized images in a global environment revolves around the ability of software programs, such as Photoshop, to manipulate specific content within a photo. Microsoft fell into a hole in 2009 when its website in Poland used a clumsy Photoshop application to turn a black man white. The original image had been used on Microsoft's U.S. website and featured diverse genders and people of many colors. However, on the Polish website where, presumably, there are fewer people of color, the artist chose to paste a white man's head on the body of a black man. Microsoft has apologized, of course, but the fiasco ran wild on news sites and blogs.[3]

Color   In addition to photos and illustrations, another important visual element that art directors manipulate is color, as the Sony ad shown earlier illustrates. Color attracts attention, provides realism, establishes moods, and builds brand identity. Art directors know that print ads with color, particularly those in newspapers, get more attention than ads without color. Most ads—print, broadcast, and Internet—are in full color, especially when art directors use photographs.

Color is particularly important in branding. An example comes from Pepsi's rivalry with Coke in China. Coke, of course, has always used a red can and logo and Pepsi traditionally uses a blue can. For the Beijing 2008 Olympics, Pepsi, which is an official Olympics sponsor, brought out a

A MATTER OF PRINCIPLE

Obama's HOPE Poster Hangs on a Question of Fair Use

Graphic designer, illustrator, and graffiti street artist Shepard Fairey got more attention than he intended when his widely recognized Barack Obama "HOPE" poster from the 2008 presidential election was challenged for illegal use. The posters were seen everywhere including a painted version on the side of a building in Denver, Colorado, where Obama received his Democratic nomination. In 2009, the U.S. National Portrait Gallery added the original HOPE poster to its permanent collection.

Fairey claims he found the original Obama photo using a Google Image search. The problem is that the iconic portrait with its social realism style was eventually found to have been constructed from a copyright-protected image taken by Mannie Garcia while on assignment for the Associated Press. AP claims ownership of the image and wants credit, as well as compensation. The complication is that Garcia also believes he owns the copyright and supports Fairey's use of the image. Fairey believes his use of the image follows the legal definition of fair use and doesn't infringe on AP's copyright.

In U.S. copyright law, *fair use* permits limited use of copyrighted material to advance knowledge or criticism. A creative use is permitted if it transforms the original to advance art. Fair use means, however, the original image can't simply be copied and questions arise if the new image is criticized as derivative, rather than as a new artistic statement.

This artistic requirement is the source of the conflicting interpretations that surround the Obama HOPE poster. Fairey, who has built his career on recycling familiar images, claims that he dramatically changed the original image; AP and even some art critics say the manipulation isn't dramatic enough to be considered a new work of art.

So is it plagiarism, a blatant copy, or is it a street-culture conversion that transforms the original image into an important piece of political art? What do you think? And what principles would you recommend to help art directors avoid fair use issues, particularly with the easy availability of digital images?

Sources: "Shepard Fairey, Obama Poster Artist in Legal Battle with AP, Makes Major Admissions in Case," *Editor & Publisher,* October 16, 2009, www.editorandpublisher.com; "Protecting AP's Intellectual Property: The Shepard Fairey Case," Associated Press, October 20, 2009, www.ap.org/prights/fairey.html; "The Shepard Fairey-AP Case: A Clearer Picture," *Los Angeles Times,* November 1, 2009, www.latimes.com.

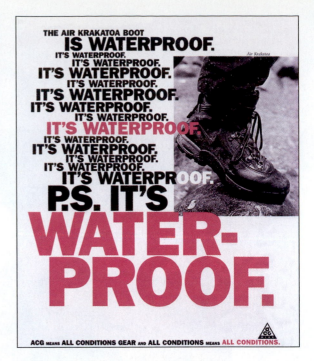

The layout for the Dunham boot ad shown here speaks in a quiet voice about the beauty of nature. Even though it's a boot ad, it projects an elegance that reflects an appreciation for nature and a serene outdoor scene (footprints in the snow). The ACG "Air Krakatoa" ad with an asymmetrical layout uses spot color effectively in the copy. Note how the layout "shouts," in contrast to the soft tone of the Dunham boot ad.

red can. The marketer defended itself saying the new can was more appealing to Chinese consumers and mirrors the color of the country's flag. Critics wonder if the dueling cans will just cause confusion among Chinese consumers who are slowly building loyalty to these Western brands.[4]

The use of black and white is also an important choice in image design because it lends a dignity and sophistication to the visual, even if it's a boot as the Dunham ad demonstrates. A historical effect can be created by shooting in black and white or by using a sepia tone, which can make the images look like old prints that have been weathered by time. When realism is important to convey in an ad, full-color photographs may be essential. Some products and ad illustrations just don't look right in black and white—pizza, flower gardens, and nail polish, for instance.

In print, designers also use **spot color,** in which a second color in addition to black (a black-and-white photo or illustration with an accent color) is used to highlight important elements. The use of spot color is highly attention getting, particularly in newspaper ads. The ACG ad uses red spot color to accent the product and key words.

Color also can help an ad convey a mood. Warm colors, such as red, yellow, and orange, convey happiness. Pastels are soft and often bring a friendly tone to a print ad. Earth tones are natural and no-nonsense. Cool colors, such as blue and green, are aloof, calm, serene, reflective, and intellectual. Yellow and red have the most attention-getting power. Red may symbolize alarm and danger as well as warmth. Black communicates high drama and can express power and elegance. Note that these color associations are culturally determined and uses like these are common in Western countries, but may not be effective in other cultures. White, for example, is the color of death in many Asian countries.

Principle

Type has a functional role in the way it presents the letters in words so they can be easily read, but it also has an aesthetic role and can contribute to the meaning of the message through its design.

Typography   Not only do art directors carefully choose colors, they also specify the ad's **typography**—the appearance of the ad's printed matter. In most cases, good typesetting does not call attention to itself because its primary role is functional—to convey the words of the message. Type or lettering, however, also has an aesthetic role, and the type selection can, in a subtle or not so subtle way, contribute to the impact and mood of the message, as the ACG boot ad demonstrated.

Ad designers choose from among thousands of typefaces to find the right one for the ad's message. Designers are familiar with type classifications, but it is also important for managers and other people on the creative team to have some working knowledge of typography to understand what designers are talking about and to critique the typography and make suggestions. Figure 10.1 summarizes many of the decisions an art director makes in designing the type, such as these:

• The specific typeface, or **font**
• The way capitalization is handled, such as all caps or lowercase

a)

A Font

14 pt

ABCDEFGHIJKLMNOPQRSTUV
abcdefghijklmnopqrstuvwxyz
1234567890

Serif (top) and Sans Serif (bottom)

ABCDEFGHIJKLMNOPQRSTUVWXYZ ABCD
ABCDEFGHIJKLMNOPQRSTUVWXYZ ABCD

All caps (top), lower case (middle), and u&lc (bottom)

THIS IS TIMES ROMAN IN ALL CAPS.
this is times roman in lower case.
This is Times Roman in Upper and Lower Case.

Typeface variations

This is set in a light typeface.
This is set in a normal weight.
This is set in a boldface.
This is set in italic.
This is set in an expanded typeface.
This is set in a condensed typeface.

Type has an aesthetic role in an ad. Art directors choose a serif or sans serif font, as well as a font's size and style, to support the tone of the advertising message.

b)

This is justified text. This is justified text. This is justified text. This is justified text. This is justified text. This is justified text. This is justified text. This is justified text. This is justified text. This is jus-tified text.

This is centered text. This is
centered text.

This is left aligned text. This is
left aligned text.

This is right aligned text. This
is right aligned text.

Where the type sits on the ad and how it relates to the margin has an effect on the ad's overall look.

c)

6 Point
ABCDEFGHIJKLMNOPQRSTUVWXYZABCDEFGHIJKLMNOPQRSTUVWXYZABCDEFGHIJKLMNOPQRSTUVWXYZABCDEFG
abcdefghijklmnopqrstuvwxyzabcdefghijklmnopqrstuvwxyzabcdefghijklmnopqrstuvwxyzabcdefghijklmnopqrstuvwxyz   1234567890

12 Point
ABCDEFGHIJKLMNOPQRSTUVWXYZABCDEFGHIJKLMNOPQ
abcdefghijklmnopqrstuvwxyzabcdefghijklmnopqrstuvwx 1234567890

18 Point
ABCDEFGHIJKLMNOPQRSTUVWXYZAB
abcdefghijklmnopqrstuvwxyzabc 1234567890

Here is a set of different sizes for the Times Roman typeface.

d)

THIS IS CAPITAL LETTERS.   This is reverse type letters.

This is ornamental type letters.

This is type surprinted over something highly patterned.

Research has shown that some typography presentations, such as those shown here—all cap letters, reverse type, overly ornamental type, and surprinted type—can hinder the reading process, which creates a legibility problem.

FIGURE 10.1
The Art of Type

- Typeface variations that come from manipulating the shape of the letterform
- The edges of the type block and its column width
- The size in which the type is set (vertical height)
- **Legibility,** or how easy it is to perceive the letters.

Generally speaking logos are designed to last for a long time, but sometimes brands change the design and typography in an attempt to modernize the look or match the mood of the country. An example comes from the Great Recession period when a number of major brands, such as Kraft and Walmart, among others moved from their all-cap presentations to lower case. The idea was to make their logos look softer and less stiff.[5]

Design Principles

The arrangement of the pieces in a print ad or video shot is governed by basic principles of design. The design has both functional and aesthetic needs—the functional side makes the visual message easy to perceive; the aesthetic side makes it attractive and pleasing to the eye.

These design principles guide the eye by creating a visual path that helps the viewer scan the elements. For example, dominant elements that are colorful or high in contrast (big versus small, light versus dark) catch the viewer's attention first. How all of the elements come together is a function of the unity and balance of the design. Direction or movement is the way the elements are positioned to lead the eye through the arrangement. Simplicity is also a design principle, one that is in opposition to visual clutter. In general, the fewer the elements, the stronger the impact, an idea expressed in the phrase "less is more." Another saying is KISS, which stands for "Keep It Simple, Stupid." The Frontier "Caribou" ad is a powerful image because of its use of a simple horizontal photo across a two-page spread.

Let's look at how these design principles are used in print layout and in the composition of a picture or photograph.

Principle

Design is usually improved by simplifying the number of elements. Less is more.

With over 300 non-stops daily, crossing the country has never been easier.   FRONTIER. A whole different animal.

Sometimes the most powerful images are the simplest in structure—just a wide horizontal landscape with a swimming caribou leaving a trail in the water and a plane flying above him. Notice how the antlers point to the Frontier plane with a caribou on its tail. The whole composition is designed to pull your eye to the right and then up.

Print Layout

For print advertising, once art directors have chosen the images and typographic elements, they manipulate all of the visual elements on paper to produce a layout. A **layout** is a plan that imposes order and at the same time creates an arrangement that is aesthetically pleasing.

Different layouts can convey entirely different feelings about a product. For example, look at the two ads for work boots. The ACG "Air Krakatoa" boot ad screams "waterproof!" signaling the boots' ability to stand up to the most serious weather conditions. In contrast, the ad for the Dunham boot looks like a work of fine art. The difference between the two campaigns clearly lies with the visual impact that comes from the layouts as well as the imagery.

Types of Layouts Here are some common types of ad layouts an art director might use:

- *Picture Window* A common layout format is one with a single, dominant visual that occupies about 60 to 70 percent of the ad's space. Underneath it is a headline and copy block. The logo or signature signs off the message at the bottom. The Altoids ads are of this style.
- *All Art* The art fills the frame of the ad and the copy is embedded in the picture. The Frontier "Caribou" ad is an example.
- *Panel or Grid* This layout uses a number of visuals of matched or proportional sizes. If the ad has multiple panels all of the same size, the layout can look like a window pane or comic strip panel. The Dunham boot ad uses two side-by-side panels.
- *Dominant Type or All Copy* Occasionally, you will see layouts that emphasize the type rather than the art, or even an all-copy advertisement in which the headline is treated as type art, such as the ACG ad. A copy-dominant ad may have art, but it is either embedded in the copy or placed in a subordinate position, such as at the bottom of the layout.
- *Circus* This layout combines lots of elements—art, type, color—to deliberately create a busy, jumbled image. This is typical of some discount store ads or ads for local retailers, such as tire companies.
- *Nonlinear* This contemporary style of layout can be read starting at any point in the image. In other words, the direction of viewing is not ordered, as in the "What a Ride" ad for Schwinn. This style of ad layout works for young people who are more accustomed to nonlinear forms.

This ad for Schwinn bicycles uses a plumbing drain motif to convey the industrial-strength features of the bike. It is a nonlinear design in that it doesn't matter where you start reading and what you read next. The text is carried in callouts that point to different visual elements in the layout.

Layout Stages   The stages in the normal development of a print ad may vary from agency to agency or from client to client. Figure 10.2 shows the six-stage development of an Orly nail polish ad. This ad went through **thumbnail sketches,** which are quick, miniature preliminary sketches; **rough layouts,** which show where design elements go; **semicomps** and **comprehensives,** which are drawn to size and used for presentation either in house or to the client; and **mechanicals,** which assemble the elements in their final position for reproduction. The final product that is used for actual production of the ad is a high-resolution computer file.

Composition

We've been talking about layout, which is a term used to describe how the elements in print (headline, art, tagline, etc.) are arranged. **Composition** refers to the way the elements in a picture are

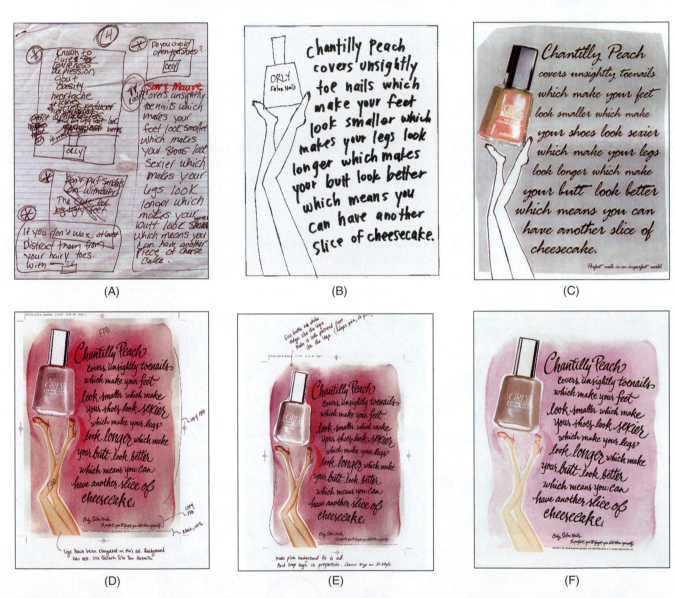

(A)   (B)   (C)

(D)   (E)   (F)

FIGURE 10.2

Orly "Chantilly Peach" Creative Process
(A) Thumbnail Sketches These ideas for Orly were developed by the creative team late at night over Diet Coke and Chinese chicken salad. **(B) Rough Layout** Transitioning to legs and painted toenails, the layout begins to give some glamour and personality to the product. **(C) Semicomps** Type, color, and tagline are still not finalized, but layout is more complete. **(D) Comprehensives** Tagline approved. The illustrator has added more glitz to the layout. **(E) Mechanicals** The digital file before retouching. Client still made small changes at this stage, but had approved the ad's layout and copy. **(F) Final High-Resolution Film** The film house had to retouch, creating separate files for the legs and background image so that the proportion of the leg illustration would be correct.

arranged (think a still-life painting) or framed through a camera lens (think a landscape photo or movie scene). Photographers and **videographers** (people who shoot a scene using a video camera) handle composition in two ways: (1) they may be able to place or arrange the elements in front of their cameras and (2) they may have to compose the image by manipulating their own point of view if the elements can't be moved. In other words, they move around to find the most aesthetic way to frame an image that isn't movable, such as a scene or landscape, as well as to catch different lighting situations, such as bright sun and shade or shadow.

Similar to the way layouts are developed by using sketches, video images are also drawn and presented as **storyboards,** which are sketches of the scenes and key shots in a commercial. The art director imagines the characters and setting as well as how the characters act and move in the scene. The art director sketches in a few key frames the visual idea for a scene and how it is to be shot and how one scene links to the scenes that follow. In addition, the storyboard sketches also reflect the position and movement of the cameras recording the scene, a description of which is spelled out both in the script and on the storyboard. The "Coffee Ambush" storyboard details the action in a commercial for McDonald's new McCafé line of specialty coffees. We'll explain more about the commercial in the production section that follows.

WHAT DO YOU NEED TO KNOW ABOUT PRODUCTION?

Art directors need to understand print media requirements and the technical side of production because these factors affect both the look of the printed piece and its cost. Marketing communication managers also need to understand some of these basics in order to critique ideas and evaluate them in terms of cost and feasibility.

Print Media Requirements

Different media put different demands on the design and production of advertising. Newspapers and directories, for example, are printed at high speed on an inexpensive, rough-surfaced, spongy paper called **newsprint** that quickly absorbs ink on contact. Newsprint is not a great surface for reproducing fine details, especially color photographs and delicate typefaces. Most newspapers offer color to advertisers, but because of the limitations of the printing process, the color may not be perfectly **registered** (i.e., all of the color inks may not be aligned exactly, creating a somewhat blurred image). For that reason, ads such as the Oklahoma City ads are specifically designed for high-contrast, black-and-white printing. These work well for both newspaper and directory ads.

Magazines have traditionally led the way in graphic print production because their glossy paper is a higher grade than newsprint. Excellent photographic and color reproduction is the big difference between newspapers and magazines. Magazine advertisements are also able to take advantage of more creative, attention-getting devices such as pop-up visuals, scent strips, and computer chips that play melodies when the pages are opened. An Altoids ad that launched Altoids chewing gum, for example, ran in magazines with a novel print production technique. It showed a box of Altoids chewing gum on one page, and a singed logo burnt onto the cartoon on the opposite page.

The key to an effective poster or outdoor board is a dominant visual with minimal copy. Because billboards must make a quick and lasting impression from far away, their layout should be compact with a simple visual path. The Institute for Outdoor Advertising (IOA) recommends these tips for designers:

- *Graphics* Make the illustration an eye-stopper.
- *Size* Images in billboards are huge—a 25-foot-long pencil or a 43-foot pointing finger. The product or the brand label can be hundreds of times larger than life.
- *Colors* Use bold, bright colors. The greatest impact is created by maximum contrast between two colors such as dark colors against white or yellow.[6]

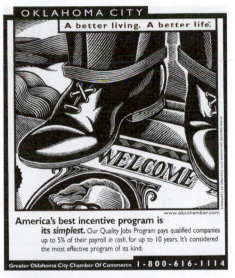

High-contrast graphics are the key to good reproduction in a newspaper. The art in these ads simulates an old wood engraving.

- *Figure/Ground* Make the relationship between foreground and background as obvious as possible. A picture of a soft drink against a jungle background is hard to perceive when viewed from a moving vehicle at a distance. The background should never compete with the subject.
- *Typography* Use simple, clean, uncluttered type that is easy to read at a distance by an audience in motion. The industry's legibility research recommends avoiding all-capital letters, fanciful ornamental letters, and script and cursive fonts.
- *Product Identification* Focus attention on the product by reproducing the label or package at a huge size.
- *Extensions* Extend the frame of the billboard to expand the scale and break away from the limits of the long rectangle.
- *Shape* For visual impact, create the illusion of three-dimensional effects by playing with horizons, vanishing lines, and dimensional boxes. Inflatables create a better 3-D effect than most billboards can, even with superior graphics. Made of a heavyweight, stitched nylon, inflatables can be freestanding, or they can be added to outdoor boards as an extension.
- *Motion* Add motors to boards to make pieces and parts move. Disk-like wheels and glittery things that flicker in the wind create the appearance of motion, color change, and images that squeeze, wave, or pour. Use revolving panels, called *kinetic boards*, for messages that change.

Print Art Reproduction

In general, there are two types of printed images: line art and halftones. A drawing or illustration is called **line art** because the image is solid lines on a white page, as in the Oklahoma City ads. Photographs, which are referred to as **continuous tones** or **halftones,** are much more complicated to reproduce because they have a range of gray tones between the black and white, as shown in Figure 10.3.

FIGURE 10.3

Line Art and Halftone Art

An example of a figure reproduced as line art (left) and as a halftone (right).

FIGURE 10.4
Screen Values and Tint Blocks
This shows the range of tint values that can be produced by different screens that represent a percentage of the color value.

Printers create the illusion of shades of gray in converting photos to halftones by shooting the original photograph through a fine **screen,** which converts the image to a pattern of dots that gives the illusion of shades of gray—dark areas are large dots that fill the screen and light areas are tiny dots surrounded by **white space.** The quality of the image depends on how fine the screen is: Newspapers use a coarse screen, usually 65 lines per inch (called a 65-line screen), whereas magazines use fine screens, which may be from 120 up to 200 or 300 lines per inch.

Screens are also used to create **tint blocks,** which can either be shades of gray in black-and-white printing or shades of color. A block of color can be printed solid or it can be screened black to create a shade. These shades are expressed as a range of percentages, from 100 percent (solid) down to 10 percent (very faint). Figure 10.4 gives examples of screens in color.

Color Reproduction   It would be impossible to set up a printing press with a separate ink roller for every hue and value in a color photo. How, then, are these colors reproduced?

Full-color images are reproduced using four distinctive shades of ink called **process colors,** in order to produce **four-color printing.** These colors are *magenta* (a shade of pinkish purple), *cyan* (a shade of bright blue), *yellow,* and *black.* Printing inks are transparent, so when one ink overlaps another, a third color is created and that's how the full range of colors is created. For example, red and blue create purple, yellow and blue create green, yellow and red create orange. The black is used for type and, in four-color printing, adds depth to the shadows and dark tones in an image. The process printers use to reduce the original color image to four halftone negatives is called **color separation.** Figure 10.5 illustrates the process of color separation.

Digitization   If an ad is going to run in a number of publications, there has to be some way to distribute a reproducible, duplicate of the ad to all of them. The duplicate material for **offset printing** is a slick proof of the original mechanical. More recently, **digitization** of images has been used to distribute reproducible images. This is also how computers now handle the color reproduction process. These digitized images can be transmitted electronically to printers across a city for local editions of national newspapers, or by satellite for regional editions of magazines and newspapers such as *USA Today.* Agencies also use this method for transmitting ad proofs within the agency network and to clients.

Digitization makes it possible to create some spectacular effects in out-of-home advertising. Some outdoor boards have become digital screens complete with changing and moving images. A new technique in transit advertising comes from Atlanta where the city's buses are wrapping their sides with something called "glow skin." The ads use electroluminescent lighting to make the ads glow at night and appear to jump off the sides of the buses.[7]

Binding and Finishing

Art directors can enhance their ads and other printed materials by using a number of special printing effects. For example, USRobotics, a maker of minicomputers, once used a small brochure the actual size of a Palm Pilot to demonstrate its minicomputer's size. The shot of the Palm Pilot was glued to a photo of a hand. As the ad unfolded, it became a complete product brochure that visually demonstrated the actual size of the minicomputer.

Other mechanical techniques include:

- *Die Cutting* A sharp-edged stamp, or die, is used to cut out unusual shapes. A common **die-cut** shape you're familiar with is the tab on a file folder.

FIGURE 10.5

The Color Separation Process

These six photos illustrate the process of creating four-color separations: (A) Yellow plate. (B) Magenta plate.
(C) Yellow and magenta combined plate. (D) Cyan plate. (*Note:* After cyan is added, there would also be combined
plates showing cyan added first to yellow, then to magenta, then to the combined yellow and magenta plates. These
steps were left out to simplify the presentation.) (E) Black plate. (F) Finished art with all four process colors combined.

- *Embossing or Debossing* The application of pressure to create a raised surface (**embossing**) or depressed image (**debossing**) in paper.
- *Foil Stamping* The process of **foil stamping** involves molding a thin metallic coating (silver, gold) to the surface of an image.
- *Tip-Ins* A **tip-in** is a separate, preprinted ad provided by the advertiser that is glued into a publication as the publication is being assembled or bound. Perfume manufacturers, for example, tip in samples that are either scratch-and-sniff or scented strips that release a fragrance when pulled apart.

Another example of a nifty production trick is illustrated in the ad for Specialized Bikes using a "see-through" technique. The graphic elements are separated and printed on the front and

SHOWCASE

Contributed by Aaron Stern, who worked on this ad for Specialized Bikes when he was at Goodby, Silverstein and Partners in San Francisco, the ad shows a creative use of the "see-through" capability of print.

A graduate of the University of Colorado, Stern is now in New York finishing an MFA in creative writing at New York University. He was nominated by Professor Brett Robbs.

back of a page. When you look at the ad you see people in the foreground going about their business but in the background a faint image shows a daredevil bike rider jumping from one building to another or riding on a handrail going down the middle of a set of steps.

WHAT DO YOU NEED TO KNOW ABOUT VIDEO PRODUCTION?

Where does an art director start when putting together a video for a commercial, a video news release, or some other kind of corporate film or video? Lara Mann gives you a look inside the production of a television commercial in the *A Day in the Life* feature.

Obviously the first consideration is the nature of the image. The art director can arrange for filming on a constructed set or in a real location or choose to use **stock footage**—previously recorded images, either video, still slides, or moving film. Typical stock footage files are shots from a satellite, historical scenes such as World War II battles, or a car crash. Animation, stop motion, and 3D are other film production techniques that can be used instead of using stock footage or live filming.

Working within the framework of the creative strategy, art directors create the look of the TV commercial. The look of the award-winning "Cat Herders" commercial that the Fallon agency created for Electronic Data Systems (EDS) was a parody of the American West, much like a John Ford movie, with horses, craggy-faced cowboys who acted as cat wranglers, and stampeding animals (the cats).

A Copywriter's View of TV Production

Lara Mann, *Senior Copywriter, Draft FCB*

As a copywriter at an ad agency, a typical day for me involves a few meetings, a little presenting, a fair amount of concepting, some writing, and more than one trip to the coffee bar. Some of it's challenging. All of it's exciting. But once I've sold a campaign to a client, that's when the real fun begins.

Just between you and me, when I first started out I didn't even know shooting television was part of my job description. They never covered that in school. Director reels? Location scouting? Huh?

Now that I've been around the block (on a tricycle), I can confidentially tell you that coming up with ideas is only half of a copywriter's job. The members of the creative team have to shepherd their idea through all stages of production to make sure their vision is fully realized—or something like that.

First, we're assigned a producer, who will send us director's reels. We pick a director, pack our bags, and grab the next plane out of town. Once on location, we spend the next few days scouting scenes, casting the talent, selecting wardrobe, finding props, and reviewing the director's shooting boards. These tend to be long days, followed by long nights at the hotel watering hole.

Then the shoot begins. My partner and I will either sit in "video village" along with our client and account team, or off to the side with our own little monitor so we can keep track of the action. Should we see an issue (and there are sure to be many), we grab the ear of our producer, who will then tell the line producer, who will then tell the director. This is called the "chain of command" and helps the shoot run smoothly.

After the shoot has wrapped (yes, someone will yell, "That's a wrap!"), we pack up and head back to town, where we will then begin putting the footage together with the help of a talented editor. And so ends another exciting day in the world of advertising.

That's a wrap.

Note: Lara Mann, a graduate of the University of Florida, works for DraftFCB in Chicago. She was nominated by Professor Elaine Wagner.

Other graphic elements such as words, product logos, and still photos are digitized or computer generated right on the screen. A **crawl** is a set of computer-generated letters that appear to be moving across the bottom of the screen. All of these effects are designed or specified by the art director.

Sophisticated computer graphics systems, such as those used to create the *Star Wars* special effects, pioneered the making of artistic film and video advertising on computers. Computer graphic artists brag that they can do anything with an image. They can look at any object from any angle or even from the inside out. One of the most creative video techniques is called **morphing,** in which one object gradually changes into another. Photographs of real objects can change into art or animation and then return to life. Computer graphics specialists use computer software to create, multiply, and manipulate video images. (That's how 50 cats can be made to look like hundreds in the EDS "Herding Cats" commercial.)

Filming and Editing

Most local retail commercials are simple and inexpensive, and they are typically shot and taped at the local station. The sales representative for the station may work with the advertiser to write the script, and the station's director handles the taping of the commercial.

Creating a national TV commercial is more complex and requires a number of people with specialized skills. The ad agency crew usually includes the copywriter, art director, and producer. The producer oversees the production on behalf of the agency and client and is responsible for the budget, among other things. The director, who is the person responsible for filming the commercial, is usually someone from outside the agency. This person takes the art director's storyboard and makes it come to life on film.

The producer and director make up the core of the production team. The commercial's effectiveness depends on their shared vision of the final commercial and the director's ability to bring it to life as the art director imagined it. In the case of the "Cat Herders" commercial, the director was chosen by the agency because of his skill at coaxing naturally humorous performances from nonprofessional actors. In this commercial he worked with real wranglers on their semi-scripted testimonials about their work with kitties.

The following list summarizes the responsibilities of broadcast production personnel:

Who Does What in Broadcast Production?

Copywriter	Writes the script, whether it contains dialogue, narrative, lyrics, announcements, descriptions, or no words at all.
Art Director	In TV, develops the storyboard and establishes the look of the commercial, whether realistic, stylized, or fanciful.
Producer (can be an agency staff member)	Takes charge of the production, handles the bidding and all production arrangements, finds the specialists, arranges for casting talent, and makes sure the expenses and bids come in under budget.
Director	Has responsibility for the actual filming or taping, including how long the scene runs, who does what, how lines are spoken, and how characters are played; in TV determines how the camera is set up and records the flow of action.
Composer	Writes original music and sometimes the lyrics as well.
Arranger	Orchestrates music for the various instruments and voices to make it fit a scene or copy line. The copywriter usually writes the lyrics or at least gives the arranger some idea of what the words should convey.
Editor	Puts everything together toward the end of the filming or taping process; evaluates how to assemble scenes and which audio elements work best with the dialogue and footage.

The Process of Producing Videos

As we said earlier there are a number of ways to produce a message for a video, such as a television commercial. Let's look at these production choices.

Typically the film is shot on 35-mm film or videotape and then digitized, after which the editor transfers the image to videotape for dissemination, a process called **film-to-tape transfer.** Digital technology is changing the process. Eventually films will transfer to hard drives, eliminating the use of videotape. Art directors work closely with editors who assemble the shots and cut the film to create the right pacing and sequence of images as outlined in the storyboard.

Obviously the Big Idea for the "Cat Herders" ad created some real production challenges. In the spot, the Fallon art director decided that the metaphor of herding cats meant that the cats had to swim across a river, but was that even possible? Here's how it was done: The trainers taught a few cats that weren't adverse to water to swim by starting them out in one-quarter inch of water in a child's swimming pool and then gradually adding water to the pool until it was deep enough for the cats to swim. The "river" was actually a small pool warmed by a portable heater—Art Director Dean Hanson described it as "a little kitty Jacuzzi." Multiple copies of the swimming kitties were made and manipulated using computer graphics until an entire herd had been created. And that's how this famous scene came about—a creation of Hanson's unlikely vision of a herd of cats swimming across river.

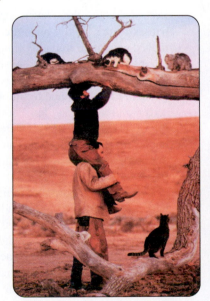 

The Fallon agency was given the impossible task of creating a commercial that illustrated the EDS positioning statement: "EDS thrives on defeating complexity." It translated that language into a popular phrase used in the Silicone Valley culture— "It's like herding cats." To bring that idea to life, the Fallon team filmed a team of rugged cowboys herding thousands of cats.

SHOWCASE

Karl Schroeder says he really hadn't considered stop motion before but it was perfect for this assignment for Metro Recycling and arguably the only solution for this recycling concept. Everything was shot in a studio and composited in the computer.

A graduate of the University of Oregon advertising program, Karl Schroeder was nominated by Professor Charles Frazer.

Animation　The technique of **animation** traditionally meant drawing images on film and then recording the images one frame at a time. Cartoon figures, for example, were sketched and then resketched for the next frame with a slight change to indicate a small progression in the movement of an arm or leg a facial expression. Animation is traditionally shot at 16 drawings per second. Low-budget animation uses fewer drawings, so the motion looks jerky. The introduction of computers has accelerated the process and eliminated a lot of the tedious hand work.

Animation is similar to illustration in print in that it abstracts images and adds a touch of fantasy and/or mood to the image. As Karl Schroeder, a copywriter with Coates Kokes in Portland, Oregon, explains about a project his team worked on for a recycling center: "What was nice about it, when you consider that the spots needed to appeal to EVERYONE who recycles in the area, was that it [animation] got us away from casting racially ambiguous, hard-to-pin-an-age-on talent."

Animation effects can also be used to combine animated characters, such as the little green Geico Gecko, with live-action figures, or even with other animated characters. The famous Aflac duck was created as a collaboration between Warner Brothers and the Aflac agency, the Kaplan Thaler Group in New York. More advanced techniques, similar to those used in movies like *Avatar*, *Up*, and the *Shrek* series, create lifelike images and movement. A technique called "mental ray" was used in a Levi Strauss ad featuring 600 stampeding buffalo. Mental ray is so good it not only created lifelike images but even added realistic hair on the animals.[8]

Stop Motion　A particular type of animation is **stop motion,** a technique used to film inanimate objects like the Pillsbury Doughboy, which is a puppet. The little character is moved a bit at a time and filmed frame-by-frame. Schroeder describes how he and his art director settled on the stop-motion technique for two commercials that changed residential recycling behavior in his community. He says that in developing a concept for commercials, he'll usually think of live-action film first. When he does consider animation, it's usually achieved with computer graphics or illustrations. But for these two recycling spots, here's how the stop-action effects were created:

Both spots have three layers. All of the foreground elements, from the glass bottles to the yellow bins, are actual objects. The animator painstakingly moved each item frame by frame. Furthermore, each frame was shot twice. Normally you'd only need to shoot each frame once. But because we were shooting in front of a green screen and because we were using glass bottles (which reflect), we had to shoot each frame twice, one in front of the green screen and the second in front of a "natural background." So now with two sets of images (as if all this weren't enough work), next up was to clip out the bottles that had the alien green reflection (from the green screen) and drop in the bottles that sported the natural reflections from the other shots, again frame-by-frame.

The next layer is more straightforward, featuring the house and yard. The third layer has the sky and clouds (which move if you look closely). Since the plastic bag spot didn't have glass, it was a little simpler but otherwise followed the same process. Lastly, we didn't want the logo, tag, and info to be tacked on at the end against a black background. Instead, we integrated the information by animating it against a tight shot of our yellow bin. The effect is much less jarring and better unites the "business" with the rest of the spot.

The same technique is used in **claymation,** which involves creating characters from clay and then photographing them one frame at a time. Both have been popular with art directors who create advertising where fantasy effects are desired, although new computer effects also are simplifying these techniques.

3-D Filming　3-D is a type of film production that creates the illusion of depth using a special motion picture camera and projection hardware. Viewers also have to wear special glasses. The 3-D technique has been around for many years but only with the big success of the movie Avatar did it achieve wide popularity. ESPN launched a 3-D Channel in 2010 for the World Cup broadcast and persuaded major advertisers such as Procter & Gamble and Sony to experiment with 3-D spots on the new channel.

Music and Action   Specifying the music is usually done as part of the copywriting; however, matching the music to the action is an art director or producer's responsibility. In some cases, as in high- production song-and-dance numbers, the music is the commercial. Other times, it is used to get attention, set a mood, and lock the commercial into memory.

For example, a recent JanSport commercial for its Live Wire Euphonic Pack, a backpack with built-in earphones and volume controls, cries out for a musical demonstration. The unlikely song picked for the spot, which targets the MTV crowd, was "Do-Re-Mi" from the 1959 *Sound of Music* musical. You might wonder why the creative team at the DDB Seattle agency would choose such a piece. Actually the rendition is not from the early recording but rather an ethereal, techno-pop version. The stick-in-the-head lyrics match the action on screen in a contemporary version of the classic story boy meets girl, boy loses girl, boy finds girl.[9]

The TV Production Process

For the bigger national commercials, the steps in the TV production process fall into four categories: message design, preproduction, the shoot, and postproduction. Figure 10.6 shows the steps in the process.

Preproduction   The producer and staff first develop a set of **production notes,** describing in detail every aspect of the production. These notes are important for finding talent and locations, building sets, and getting bids and estimates from specialists. In the "Cat Herders" commercial, finding the talent was critical. Some 50 felines and their trainers were involved in the filming. Surprisingly, different cats have different skills—some were able to appear to be asleep or motionless on cue, while others excelled as runners or specialized in water scenes.

Once the bids for production have been approved, the creative team and the producer, director, and other key players hold a **preproduction** meeting to outline every step of the production process and anticipate every problem that may arise. Then the work begins. The talent agency begins casting the roles, while the production team finds a location and arranges site use with owners, police, and other officials. If sets are needed, they have to be built. Finding the props is a test of ingenuity, and the prop person may wind up visiting hardware stores, secondhand stores, and maybe even the local dump. Costumes must be made, located, or bought.

The Shoot   The director shoots the commercial scene by scene, but not necessarily in the order set down in the script. Each scene is shot, called a **take,** and after all the scenes in the storyboard have been shot they are assembled through editing. If the director films the commercial on videotape, it is played back immediately to determine what needs correcting. Film, however, has to be processed before the director can review it. These processed scenes are called **dailies. Rushes** are

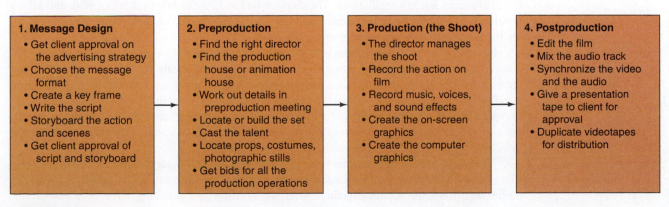

1. Message Design	2. Preproduction	3. Production (the Shoot)	4. Postproduction
• Get client approval on the advertising strategy • Choose the message format • Create a key frame • Write the script • Storyboard the action and scenes • Get client approval of script and storyboard	• Find the right director • Find the production house or animation house • Work out details in preproduction meeting • Locate or build the set • Cast the talent • Locate props, costumes, photographic stills • Get bids for all the production operations	• The director manages the shoot • Record the action on film • Record music, voices, and sound effects • Create the on-screen graphics • Create the computer graphics	• Edit the film • Mix the audio track • Synchronize the video and the audio • Give a presentation tape to client for approval • Duplicate videotapes for distribution

FIGURE 10.6
Video Production Process
In general, there are three steps in the production of a video after agreement is obtained on the message strategy.

rough versions of the commercial assembled from **cuts** of the raw film footage. The director and the agency creative team, as well as the client representative, view them immediately after the shoot to make sure everything's been filmed as planned.

The film crew includes a number of technicians, all of whom report to the director. For both film and video recording, the camera operators are the key technicians. Other technicians include—and you've probably seen these terms in movie credits—the **gaffer,** who is the chief electrician, and the **grip,** who moves props and sets and lays tracks for the dolly on which the camera is mounted. The **script clerk** checks the dialogue and other script details and times the scenes. A set is a busy crowded place that appears, at times, to be total confusion and chaos.

The audio director records the audio either at the time of the shoot or, in the case of more high-end productions, separately in a sound studio. If the sound is being recorded at the time of shooting, a **mixer,** who operates the recording equipment, and a *mic* or *boom* person, who sets up the microphones, handle the recording on the set. In the studio audio is usually recorded after the film is shot so the audio has to be synchronized with the footage. Directors often wait to see exactly how the action appears before they write and record the audio track. However, if the art director has decided to set the commercial to music, then the music on the audio track may be recorded before the shoot, as in the "Do-Re-Mi" audio track, and the filming done to the music.

Occasionally the footage will be shot live to catch natural reactions by the participants, such as the Burger King "Freak Out" commercials described in the opening story for Chapter 1. Another example comes from Boston University where an advertising class starred in a McDonald's McCafé spot called the "Coffee Ambush," as described in the *A Matter of Practice* feature.

In some rare cases, an entire commercial is shot as one continuous action rather than individual shots edited together in postproduction. Probably the most interesting use of this approach is "Cog," an award-winning commercial for the Honda Accord that shows the assembly of pieces of the car piece by piece. It begins with a rolling transmission bearing, and moves through valves, brake pedals, tires, the hood, and so forth, until the car drives away at the end of the commercial. It's tempting to think it was created through computer animation, but the Honda "Cog" commercial was filmed in real time without any special effects. It took 606 takes for the whole thing to work—that's 606 run-throughs of the sequence! One of the most talked-about spots ever made, the publicity given to the commercial was probably even more valuable than an advertising buy. The "Cog" commercial won a Grand Clio (a creative award show), as well as a Gold Lion at the Cannes Advertising Festival. Altogether, it picked up no fewer than 20 awards from various UK and international organizations. The spot can be seen at *www.ebaumsworld.com/flash/play/734.*[10]

Postproduction   For film and video, much of the work happens after the shoot in **postproduction**—when the commercial begins to emerge from the hands and mind of the editor. The objective of editing is to assemble the various pieces of film into a sequence that follows the storyboard. Editors manipulate the audio and video images, creating realistic 3-D images and combining real-life and computer-generated images. The postproduction process is hugely important in video because so many digital effects are being added to the raw film after the shoot. In the "Cat Herders" commercial, Fallon could not film the cats and horses at the same time because of National Humane Society regulations. The director had to film the horses, background, and kitties separately. An editor fused the scenes together during postproduction, editing seamlessly to create the illusion of the elaborate cat drive.

Another goal of **video editing** is to manipulate time, which is a common technique used in commercial storytelling. Condensing time might show a man leaving work, then a cut of the man showering, then a cut of the man at a bar. The editor may extend time. Say a train is approaching a stalled car on the tracks. By cutting to various angles it may seem that the train is taking forever to reach the car—a suspense tactic. To jumble time, an editor might cut from the present to a flashback of a remembered past event or flash forward to an imagined scene in the future. All of these effects are specified by the art director in the storyboard.

The result of the editor's initial work is a **rough cut,** a preliminary edited version of the story that is created when the editor chooses the best shots and assembles them to create a scene. The editor then joins the scenes together. After the revision and reediting have been completed, the editor makes an **interlock,** which means the audio and film have been assembled together. The final version with the sound and film mixed together is called an **answer print.** The answer

A MATTER OF PRACTICE

BU Ad Class Ready for Its Close-Up

Tom Fauls, *College of Communication, Boston University*

It can be quiet, even sleepy, during summer term. So it's no surprise students cue up for caffeine before class. But in August 2009, some Boston University (BU) College of Communication advertising students had a different kind of coffee encounter.

It started a few weeks earlier when Redtree Productions contacted BU officials and later BU professors Judy Austin and Tom Fauls. Working with agency Arnold Worldwide, Redtree was planning a TV shoot for McDonald's McCafé brands.

The concept was developed by Arnold creatives, including a BU alumna. It required a theatre-style hall filled with students expecting a cognitive anthropologist speaking on consumer-brand relationships. After a preproduction meeting at Redtree, Austin and Fauls, both of whom had worked on McDonald's ads at different agencies, invited their students to attend an optional 9 a.m. lecture by Robert Deutsch.

They didn't mention that the lecture would be (1) intentionally boring, (2) interrupted after 10 minutes by uniformed McDonald's workers with McCafé drinks, and (3) entirely captured on tape by cameras hidden behind a faux blackboard.

On the way in, signs said the lecture would be taped and no non-water drinks were allowed. The room was already partially filled with other students who were really paid extras. But the unsuspecting real students were asked to fill the front rows.

Minutes after the coffee was distributed, Arnold and Redtree producers emerged to reveal all and ask students to stay for close-ups and product hero shots, pictures of the products being marketed. Students then toured the substantial mobile production facilities in the alley behind the auditorium.

The final edit opens with a sleepy lecture hall shifting dramatically with up-tempo music as stunned ad students perk up to McCafé lattes and the realization they're in the middle of a real TV shoot.

In the end, students involved in the "Coffee Ambush" spot learned a little cognitive anthropology and a whole lot about broadcast campaigns and video production.

These photos provided by Professor Fauls record the experience of shooting the McDonald's "Coffee Ambush" ad in class. After the initial surprise entrance of the McCafé servers (you can see them on the right), this photo shows the Redtree crew emerging to capture close-ups. This second shot shows how the normal blackboard was replaced with a version modified to let cameras shoot through one-way mirror panels.

print is the final version printed onto a piece of film. For the commercial to air on hundreds of stations around the country, the agency makes duplicate copies—a process called **dubbing**. The dubbed copies are called **release prints.**

WHY STUDY WEB DESIGN?

Web design includes creating ads that run on the Web as well as the website itself. Banner ads are designed more like outdoor boards than conventional print ads because their small space puts intense requirements on the designer to make the ad communicate quickly and succinctly, and yet attract attention and curiosity to elicit a click-through response. You can check out banner ads online at *http://thelongestlistofthelongeststuffatthelongestdomainnameatlonglast.com/banner.html*.

Designers know that Web pages, particularly the first screen, should follow the same layout rules as posters: The graphics should be eye catching without demanding too much downloading time; type should be simple, using one or two typefaces and avoiding ALL CAPs and letter spacing, which can distort words. Because there is often a lot to read, organizing the information is critical. In terms of legibility, black type on a high-contrast background usually is best; all of the design elements—type and graphics—should be big enough to see on the smallest screen.

What makes Web design different from print designs is the opportunity to use motion, animation, and interactive navigation. While attention getting, these can also be irritating. Professor Mallia, who wrote the Part III opener, reminds us that online ads can succeed or fail because of their design, as well as their copy. She explains, "Visual tactics like rollovers and motion often annoy more than attract." She also points out that copy is important in Web design, "Experts find it's the copy that often gets the clickthrough—because it offers something the reader wants to *read* more about." So even in the highly visual online world, it's still important for the art and copy to work together to attract attention and build interest.

A fascinating website was created for a get-out-the-vote site aimed at young people during the 2008 election. Check out this website at *www.thingsarefine.org* and watch how the American flag falls apart on the opening page followed by the cynical admonition: "Don't vote. Things are fine just the way they are." The site also has great posters that viewers can download for free, companion public service commercials, and links to sites that a committed viewer could use to remind friends to vote and invite them to visit the site.

Usually the illustrations are created by artists but sometimes for low-budget projects, the illustrations and photos are obtained from clip-art services, or rather click art, such as that provided by *www.dreamstime.com* or *www.1StopPictures.com*. Actually, any image can be scanned and manipulated to create a Web image, which is causing copyright problems for artists and others who originally created the images, as explained with the Obama HOPE story earlier in the chapter. Because of the magic of digitizing, Web pages can combine elements and design styles from many different media: print, still photography, film, animation, sound, and games.

The combination of interactive navigation, live streaming video, online radio, and 360-degree camera angles creates Web pages that may be more complex than anything you see on TV, which is why ease of use is a factor in website design. The following discussion in the *Practical Tips* feature describes research on the best and worst site design practices conducted by Forrester Research, a company that specializes in monitoring the effectiveness of Internet marketing communication.

Web designers use a completely different toolbox than other types of art directors. Animation effects, as well as sophisticated navigation paths, are designed using software programs such as Flash, Silverlight, Director, Blender, Squeak,

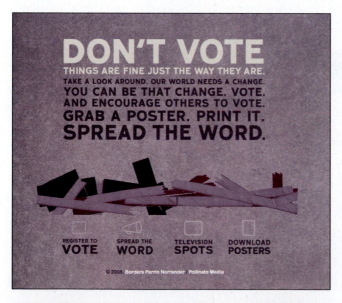

SHOWCASE

The "Things Are Fine" campaign to get out the youth vote had a huge impact. It won a number of industry awards including the One Show award and was featured in *Communication Arts*, *Adweek*, and *Advertising Age's* Ad Critic.

A graduate of the University of Colorado advertising program, Jeremy Boland, art director at Borders Perrin Norrander, was nominated by Professor Brett Robb.

PRACTICAL TIPS

The Best and Worst Website Designs

Harley Manning, *Vice President and Research Director, Customer Experience, Forrester Research, Inc.*

Over the years Forrester has graded the quality of user experiences on over 1,300 websites with a technique called *heuristic evaluation*. Today, variations on this methodology are used by virtually every interactive design agency and testing lab to judge the effectiveness of sites. It's also used in house by many companies, including UPS and Johnson & Johnson.

To identify some of the best and worst examples of Web design each year, we grade sites in each of four industries. Most recently we graded the sites of the four largest auto insurers, discount retailers, running shoe manufacturers, and online travel agencies. When we published the results we kicked up quite a storm because we named names. Here are two key results from Forrester's research into the best and worst of site design in 2009:

- The online travel agency category came out best overall, earning the highest high score (Expedia) and ending up with the highest average score. What's more, three of the four sites received positive grades while only one (Priceline.com) earned a negative score.
- The footwear manufacturer sites we graded laid claim to the cellar, with both the lowest high score

(New Balance) and the lowest low score (Puma). In contrast to the online travel agencies, only one site received a positive grade.

So what explains the relatively poor showing of footwear manufacturer sites versus travel agency sites?

One reason is that online travel agencies' business success ties directly to the quality of customer experience on their sites: When customers can't easily plan and book a trip, it shows up immediately in lost sales. This feedback loop drives industry site designers to quickly find and fix problems like inadequate product information, confusing menus, and poor reliability.

In contrast, managers of footwear manufacturer sites have a conflicted agenda: they simultaneously seek to build the softer aspects of brand, drive store traffic, and enable online sales (which remains a small part of their business). This results in a disjointed and often confusing array of micro sites with inconsistent navigation and information, capped off by overly stylized text and graphics that add to shopper frustration. So when Web traffic logs show visitors wandering aimlessly around their sites, it's hard to tell whether the prospects are fascinated or just plain lost.

Check out Forrester's website at *www.forrester.com*.

Note: The information was contributed by Harley Manning, a master's degree graduate of the advertising program at the University of Illinois. He was nominated by the late Kim Rotzell, former dean of the College of Communication.

---

and nonlinear editing tools such as Premier, FinalCut, and AfterEffects. It's such a rapidly changing design world that it's difficult to keep track of the most recent innovations in Web design software. The use of animation effects and streaming video has made websites look more like television and film. The *A Matter of Practice* box explains how this tool is best used.

An example of a good website design is *www.crewcuts .com*, which was designated as the Best Website by the Internet Professional Publishers Association. It's hard to convey here why the site is effective because of the animation, so check out *www.crewcuts.com*. For more examples of excellence in website design and reviews of the top websites, check out:

www.webaward.org

www.worldbestwebsites.com

www.100bestwebsites.org

www.imarvel.com

www.topsiteslinks.com

www.time.com (look for "50 Best Websites" annual review)

www.webbyawards.com

www.clioawards.com

www.oneclub.com

Action and Interaction

Web advertisers are continuing to find ways to bring dramatic action to the small screen to make the imagery more engaging. For example, Ford used a banner on the Yahoo! home page with the familiar Ford oval and a bunch of little black birds on a wire. Then three of the birds flew down to the middle of the page and started pecking at what looked like birdseed, uncovering an image of the new Explorer. The link read: "Click to uncover the next territory." Those who did click probably expected a pop-up image, but instead the page shook, the birds scattered, and a big red Ford Explorer drove up to the front of the screen, replacing most of the content. It was a surprising, highly involving, and effective announcement of the vehicle.

Because users can create their own paths through the website, designers have to make sure that their sites have clear **navigation.** Users should be able to move through the site easily, find the information they want, and respond. Navigation problems can really turn off viewers. Eye-tracking research (studies that use a camera to follow eye movement when looking at a page or screen) has found that if the navigation is cluttered or unclear, viewers will give up and move on to some other site.[11] Ideally, users who visit a site regularly should be able to customize the site to fit their own interests and navigation patterns.

Online video has also expanded the avenues for action on the small screen on minicomputers, personal digital assistants, and cell phones. Web video is becoming a new business opportunity for businesses that want to use videos to display their products. The secret is to plan these videos specifically for a small screen and not just try to use regular television or film images because the screen is just a fraction of the size of a television and a lot of the detail in an image can get lost.[12]

If a site is well designed, people may want to interact with the organization sponsoring the site. For example, Texture/Media, a Boulder, Colorado, Web design firm, created a seven-episode series over five months that detailed the journey of two men attempting to climb the Meru Sharksfin summit in India, for client Marmot Mountain Works. Called ClimbMeru.com, it chronicled the team's training and trip and hosted contest giveaways that helped gather information about Marmot's customers. Texture/Media's objective with its award-winning websites is to make the consumer a participant in its brand stories.

Looking Ahead

This is the last chapter in Part 3 on the design of the message. We introduced creative thinking and the creation of creative briefs; then we discussed copywriting and in this chapter we have provided you with a brief introduction to art direction and design. Next we turn to Part 4 and the chapters that discuss how messages are delivered—both to and from the target audience and other key stakeholders.

ALTOIDS®

IT'S A WRAP

Keeping the Altoids Brand in Mint Condition

As a product's owners change hands, the new owners are smart to recognize the value of the brand's heritage. The Altoids campaign has a strong, consistent look strengthened by the continuing presence of the distinctive Altoids tin. Repetition of the look is the key to brand recognition.

The brand is recognizable because it builds on the principle that the more times viewers see an ad with a consistent format, the more likely they are to remember the product. Another lesson to be learned from the curiously strong mint: Even though campaigns change, sometimes brands have accrued valuable equity in the previous work that needs to be maintained and protected.

The "Curiously Strong Mints" campaign is one of the most awarded and successful campaigns. The advertising has garnered multiple awards, including a long string of Kelly Awards for magazine advertising, One Show creative prizes, and multiple Clios. It won an international effectiveness award when it received the New York Festival's Grand Prix award. The Magazine Publishers of America (MPA) bestowed its $100,000 Grand Prize Kelly Award for outstanding magazine advertising for the Altoids "Burn Through" campaign, which launched Altoids gum.

The low-cost, edgy campaign has also been a business builder. The brand had virtually no presence in 1995 when Kraft bought it, but by 2000 it dominated the extreme mint market with a 25 percent share. Altoids now is the number one selling mint in the United States. Although it is difficult to predict how the current generation of edgy campaigns will fare, the "Brainstorm" branded entertainment effort shows promise. The trailer alone was viewed more than 100,000 times. Its creators expect to attract 2.5 million views over a six-month period.

What makes Altoids advertising a winner? The memorability and extendability of a curiously strong idea.

Key Points Summary

1. **What is the role of visual communication in marketing communication messages?** Visual communication is important in advertising because it creates impact—it grabs attention, maintains interest, creates believability, and sticks in memory. It also tells stories and creates brand images.

2. **How can we define *layout* and *composition*, and what's the difference between the two?** A layout is an arrangement of all of a print price's elements. It gives the reader a visual order to the information in the layout; at the same time, it is aesthetically pleasing and makes a visual statement for the brand. Principles that designers use in print advertising include direction, dominance, unity, white space, contrast, balance, and proportion. Composition is the way the elements in a picture are arranged, either through placement or by manipulating the photographer's viewpoint.

3. **How are art and color reproduced in print media?** Illustrations are treated as line art and photographs are reproduced through the halftone process by using screens to break down the image into a dot pattern. Full-color photos are converted to four halftone images, each one printed with a different process color—magenta, cyan, yellow, and black—through the process of color separation.

4. **What are the steps in planning and producing video?** Videos are planned using scripts and storyboards. TV commercials are shot live, shot on film or videotape, or created "by hand" using animation, claymation, or stop action. There are four stages to the production of videos—message design (scripts and storyboards), preproduction, the shoot, and postproduction.

5. **What are the basic techniques of Web design?** Web advertising can include ads and banners, but the entire website can also be seen as an advertisement. Art on Web pages can be illustrations or photographs, still images as well as moving ones, and may involve unexpected effects such as 360-degree images. When designers plan a Web page, they need to consider navigation—how people will move through the site. They also need to consider how to incorporate elements that allow for interaction between the consumer and the company that operates the site.

Words of Wisdom: Recommended Reading

Alessandri, Susan W., *Visual Identity,* Armonk, NY: M. E. Sharpe, 2009.

Beaird, Jason, *The Principles of Beautiful Web Design*, Melbourne, Australia: Sitepoint Books, 2007.

Cyr, Lisa L., *Innovative Promotions That Work: A Quick Guide to the Essentials of Effective Design,* Glouster, MA: Rockport, 2006.

Golombisky, Kim, and Rebecca Hagen, *White Space Is Not Your Enemy*, Burlington, MA: Elsevier, 2010.

Landa, Robin, *Advertising by Design: Creating Visual Communications with Graphic Impact,* Hoboken, NJ: John Wiley, 2004.

Morioka, Noreen, and Sean Adams, *Logo Design Workbook: A Hands-On Guide to Creating Logos,* Gloucester, MA: Rockport, 2004.

Samara, Timothy, *Design Elements: A Graphic Style Manual*, Glouster, MA: Rockport, 2007.

White, Alex, *Advertising Design and Typography*, New York: Allworth Press, 2007.

White, Alex, *Thinking in Type: The Practical Philosophy of Typography,* New York: Allworth Press, 2005.

Williams, Robin, *The Non-Designer's Design Book: Design and Typographic Principles for the Visual Novice,* 3rd ed., Berkeley, CA: Peachpit Press, 2008.

Williams, Robin, and John Tollett, *The Non-Designers Web Book*, 3rd ed., Berkeley, CA: Peachpit Press, 2006.

Key Terms

Review Questions

1. Explain why visual impact is so important in advertising.

2. What are the responsibilities of an art director?

3. Compare the use of black and white, spot color, and full color in terms of visual impact.

4. Explain the aesthetic role of typography. Find an ad that illustrates how type can add meaning to the message.

5. List the design principles and explain each one.

6. What's the difference between line art and halftones?

7. What does the phrase *four-color printing* mean? What are the four process colors? What does the phrase *color separation* mean, and how does that work?

8. Explain the following video terms:
   • stock footage
   • crawl
   • morphing
   • animation
   • stop motion
   • claymation

9. Explain the four steps in the video production process.

10. Draw up a list of guidelines to use in designing a website.

Discussion Questions

1. One of the challenges for designers is to demonstrate a product whose main feature cannot be seen by the consumer. Suppose you are an art director on an account that sells shower and bath mats with a patented system that ensures that the mat will not slide (the mat's underside is covered with tiny suction cups that gently grip the tub's surface). Brainstorm some ways to demonstrate this feature in a television commercial. Find a way that will satisfy the demands of originality, relevance, and impact.

2. One approach to design says that a visual image in an ad should reflect the image of the brand. Find a print ad that you think speaks effectively for the personality of the brand. Now compare the print ad with the brand's website. Does the same design style continue on the site? Does the site present the brand personality in the same way as the print ad?

3. Working in a team choose one of the following design critique problems:

   a. **Print** What principles govern the design of a magazine ad? Collect two sample ads, one you consider a good example of effective design and one that you think is not effective. Critique the two ads and explain your evaluation based on what you know about how design principles work in advertising layouts. Make suggestions for how the less effective ad could be improved.

   b. **Television** As a team, find a television commercial that you thought was creative and entertaining. Then find one that you think is much less creative and entertaining. Analyze how the two commercials work to catch and hold your attention. How do the visuals work? What might be done to make the second commercial more attention getting? You can also use online sources to find commercials at *www.adcritic.com* and at *www.badads.org*.

4. You have been asked to design a Web page for a local business or organization (choose one from your local community). Go to *www.flickr.com* or *www.1StopPictures.com* and choose a visual to illustrate the website by trying to match the personality of the organization to a visual image. Then

identify the primary categories of information that need to be included on the page. Develop a flowchart or map that shows how a typical user would navigate through the site. What other image could you find at *www.1StopPictures.com* that might be used on inside pages to provide some visual interest to this business's online image? Now consider interactivity: How could this site be used to increase interactivity between this company and its customers? Create a plan for this site that includes the visual elements and a navigation flowchart.

5. ***Three-Minute-Debate*** Your team is assigned to a new client who has a new hand lotion for men, one that is designed to help men whose hands take a beating in their jobs.

One of your colleagues, a photographer, believes the only way to visualize the product and its use in an ad is through photography. Another colleague, an artist, argues that there are times when art is a much better way to illustrate a product than photography and that this production is a good example. Analyze the differences between using an illustration and using a photograph. What are their roles, and how do they create different types of effects? Are there certain product categories where you would want to use an illustration instead of a photograph and vice versa? Which would work best for this new product? Develop a quick presentation for your class that explains which approach you would use for this assignment.

Take-Home Projects

1. ***Portfolio Project:*** Select a product that is advertised exclusively through print. Examples of such products are business-to-business and industrial products, school supplies, many over-the-counter drugs, and some food items. Your objective is to develop a 30-second television spot for this product. Develop a creative brief (see Chapter 8) to summarize the ad's strategy. Brainstorm about ways to develop a creative idea for the commercial. Then write a script and develop a storyboard to present your idea for this product. In the script include all the key decisions a producer and director would make.

2. ***Mini-Case Analysis:*** Summarize the creative strategy behind Altoid's "Curiously Strong Mints" campaign. Explain the critical elements of both the copy and the visuals. The brand management team has proposed developing a new (sugar-free) line of cough drops. How would you adjust this strategy to appeal to this new market? Design a launch ad that presents your copy ideas and a new visual. Accompany the ad with a statement that explains your thinking.

Team Project: The BrandRevive Campaign

Visit once again the BrandRevive message strategy your team created for Chapter 8, as well as your copy ideas that you developed in Chapter 9. Go online and review the advertising and package/store design (if appropriate) for your brand. Now consider how to marry the strategy and words with a new visual image. Should it be retro or use some other stylistic cues? Describe the new "look" you propose in a strategy statement. If you are unable to illustrate the look, then compile similar images and styles either from other print media or online to use as examples to help explain what you propose.

- Mock up, as best you can, a prototype product package, store, shopping bag, or other signature item that conveys the new look.

- Develop a series of thumbnails for a launch ad for your new campaign. Then choose the best idea and develop, as best you can, a full-page magazine ad for this launch.
- Design the accompanying website—or at least the home page—that takes your new look online.
- For each of these three pieces, write a paragraph that describes the impression you intend to create.
- Present and explain your new look in a two-page document and in a PowerPoint presentation that is no longer than three slides.

Hands-On Case

The Century Council

Read the Century Council case in the Appendix before coming to class.

1. Write a design memo that describes the "look" of The Stupid Drink campaign. What elements would you make mandatory

(e.g., typeface, colors, etc.) and which would you allow individual campuses to personalize in their own colors?

2. The Century Council is never identified as a sponsor of The Stupid Drink campaign. Is that the right thing to do? Why or Why not?

PRACTICE: WHERE ARE MEDIA HEADED?

We talked about creating messages in Part 3. In Part 4, we're turning to the delivery of the message and we'll look at media planning.

Please note that creative and media planning are parallel and simultaneous processes that are completely interdependent. Even though we started first with creative, remember that because of the dynamic media environment, more and more the creative challenge has become to pick the perfect place to deliver—or encounter—a brand message. In fact, media planning is just as creative as message planning.

A crucial point is that the media side of advertising is probably the area that has been challenged the most in terms of changes in the media landscape, as well as media planning practices. To underscore the importance of this dynamic media environment, Larry Kelley, partner and media director at FogartyKleinMonroe, professor at the University of Houston, and author of many articles and books on media, identifies the four most important trends in the practice of media planning.

Out of Disruption

Comes Opportunity

Disruption is the key word to describe the media business today. Everywhere you turn, new technologies, new consumer attitudes, and new methodologies are challenging the conventional wisdom of media companies and media planners.

As we move forward into this brave new media world, there will be some fundamental changes. The first is that media content companies (online and offline publishers and broadcasters) may not be able to rely on advertising to carry their financial load. Historically, media companies largely gave away content for distribution but will that model hold up going forward?

Larry Kelley
Larry Kelley is Professor of Advertising at the University of Houston and partner, Chief Planning Officer at the Houston-based FKM agency.

The second is the consumer attitudes toward media of a new generation who grew up with the Internet. The idea of looking at media as a consumer engagement rather than a pure interruption will challenge media planners and advertisers alike.

The third is digital convergence. All media will likely have some form of digital and interactive component, making media selection even more challenging as the lines between various media blur.

The final change is in the methodology of measurement. Impressions will not be the currency or the method of choice for media selection. In the future we will move from OTS or "opportunity to see" to OFB or "opportunity for behavior" as the critical metric.

For those who are considering media as a career, there is no better time to enter a business than when it is in a disruptive state. Out of disruption comes opportunity.

The media world has been in a state of incredible change from old traditional mass media to new interactive social media; from marketers' control of media placement to consumers' control of media use; and from media targeting to media engagement. In this section, Chapter 14 presents an introduction to the basics of media strategy and the changes in the media industry. Subsequent chapters focus on print and broadcast advertising and the Internet. The final chapter in this part discusses media planning and buying, which is the process by which message strategies are translated into decisions about the appropriate media to use to best reach specific target audiences.

Media Basics

It's a Winner

Campaign:	Company:	Agencies:	Award:
"Axe Detailer: The Manly Shower Tool"	Unilever	Bartle Bogle Hegarty with Mindshare and Edelman Integrated Marketing Services	Gold Effie Winner, New Product or Service Category

CHAPTER KEY POINTS

1. How do media work in marketing communication and how is the industry organized?
2. How would you describe the key strategic media concepts?
3. Why and how is the media landscape changing?

Getting Dirty Boys Cleaner

Let's start with the problem. You have a great product, but you need to reach an audience that's reluctant to be persuaded by traditional advertising techniques. How do you convince more young guys who like Axe products to throw away their bars of soap and start using Axe Shower Gel?

A little background first. Unilever's personal care brand Axe led the way in getting young men to use scented body sprays. Launched in 2002 in the United States, Axe deodorant body sprays captured the attention of its audience and soon became the top male deodorant brand in the country. (Did guys even know they needed scented body sprays before then?)

Expanding its line in men's grooming products with the shower gel represented a great opportunity for Unilever, who, along with its ad agency, Bartle Bogle Hegarty, wanted to grab the attention of the 18- to 34-year-old male audience. It ran the successful and award-winning "How Dirty Boys Get Clean" campaign, which you may have seen.

Axe reached its core audience with that campaign by creating an emotional approach that worked particularly well in the broadcast media. The big idea behind the campaign was that Axe Shower Gel would do more than clean guys physically; it would help clean their spirits as well. The campaign's creative work communicated the "dirty message." The agency chose media to reach and captivate the audience, amplifying the message in situations where guys might be having "dirty thoughts."

To reach these guys, TV commercials ran on programs like *Baywatch*, *The Real World*, and *Aqua Teen Hunger Force*. Print ads were placed in *Maxim*, *Playboy*, and the *Sports Illustrated* swimsuit issue. Axe also turned up at two of the largest spring break destinations for college guys where they encountered shower gel messages everywhere—on bar posters, hotel shower curtains, floor stickers, and bus wraps. The *www.theaxeeffect.com* website also entertained the guys.

After that campaign had run its course, Axe realized it needed to figure out how to get more of the target 18- to 34-year-old guys to switch from bars to shower gel. The "Aha!" moment for the next campaign emerged from research that indicated a correlation between using a loofah and satisfaction with shower gel's cleansing power. Without a scrubber, they just weren't using the shower gel, and although they said they used loofahs, shower ethnography (a bit tricky, don't you imagine?) showed that in reality, they were using fluffy, soft, girlie poufs. Not the macho image you'd expect.

The key to this campaign was to create a new shower tool soft enough for the guys' private parts and tough enough for them to feel clean for their women. Axe brilliantly created a scrubber that looked like a car tire and drawing from car culture, gave it a cool, masculine name, the Detailer. Carrying the idea to the max, the idea developed into a concept that appealed to the target audience: Guywash.

To demonstrate Guywash to the target audience, BBH used the storytelling power of cinema and TV. Furthermore, they capitalized on the interactivity of digital media to let guys try the Detailer. The "Dirty Night Determinator" on the website prescribed a personalized scrub routine for whatever dirty situations the guys might encounter. Girls could use Facebook to send a "gift" to "dirty" guys. Free Detailers were sent to anyone who requested one on the brand page. These media were supported by local-area promotions, in-store Detailer "technicians" who guided them to the section of the store, and point-of-purchase efforts that turned shopping into an experience.

You will find more about the marketing effects of Axe's shower gel campaign at the end of the chapter in the *It's a Wrap* section.

Sources: "Axe Detailer: The Manly Shower Tool," Effie Awards Brief of Effectiveness, www.nyama.org; "How Dirty Boys Get Clean," www.nyama.org; Michael Bush, "Unilever Wins Two Awards for Axe, Dove Media Campaigns," April 20, 2009, www.adage.com; "Mindshare Wins Bet Localisation at Valencia Festival of Media," April 20, 2009, www.mindshareworld .com; www.theaxeeffect.com.

The lesson that the Axe campaign teaches about media is that smart marketing requires creative thinking about how to connect with the audience in this complex media environment. What else has Axe done to reach guys? Read how Axe has made use of branded entertainment in *The Animated Axe Effect in City Hunters* later in this chapter (p. 345). This chapter and the three that follow explain the media side of marketing communication—the story you don't see, the backstory about how various ways to deliver a message are selected.

WHAT DO WE MEAN BY MEDIA?

When we talk about **media,** we are referring to the way messages are delivered to target audiences and, increasingly, back to companies, as well as among audience members themselves. Media is the go-between[1] step in the communication model—the way messages are sent and returned by the source and receiver, that is, the company or brand and its customers.

It's helpful to remember that the basis for most media historically was as a way to present the news to the public—and advertising made presenting the news possible because it supported the costs of producing and distributing print or broadcast media. Of course, some revenue is derived from subscriptions, but in the United States the bulk of the media revenue comes from advertising.

As a result, over the years the word *media* has been associated with advertising, leading many to think that media are used only or primarily for advertising. Nothing could be further from the truth! As Kelley pointed out in the Part 4 opener, advertising may not provide adequate financial support for the new media forms and all media are looking for new revenue streams in order to stay in business.

Media Classifications

The plural noun *media* is an umbrella term for all types of print, broadcast, out-of-home, and Internet communication. The singular noun *medium* refers to each specific type (TV is a medium, for example). A **media vehicle** is a specific TV program (*60 Minutes, The Simpsons*), newspaper (*The Washington Post, Chicago Tribune, El Nuevo Herald*), magazine (*Woman's Day, GQ*), or radio station or program (NPR's *All Things Considered*, Rush Limbaugh's talk show). When a company "buys media," it is really buying access to the audiences of specific media vehicles. The form that those "buys" take is "space" (print, outdoor boards, Internet) and "time" (radio and TV).

Media, particularly those used in advertising, are referred to as **mass media,** the communication channels through which messages are sent to large, diverse audiences. A mass medium reaches many people simultaneously and it uses some technological system or device to reach them (as opposed to personal communication). The size of the audience is the reason why we refer to radio and television as **broadcasting media**—they cast their audio and visual signals broadly to reach mass audiences.

In contrast, **niche media** are communication channels through which messages are sent to niche segments—identifiable groups of people with a distinct common interest, such as the Hispanic market served by *El Nuevo Herald. Advertising Age* and *Adweek,* for example, are a subsegment of the more general business magazine category. They reach the professional advertising industry niche. The distinction between mass and niche is not based necessarily on size. The *AARP Magazine,* for example, which targets baby boomers age 50+, is a niche publication and yet it is the world's largest circulation magazine.[2]

Two other categories of media refer to the way the media transmit the messages. **Addressable media,** such as the Internet, mail, and the telephone, are used to send brand messages to specific geographic and electronic addresses. They are particularly helpful in keeping in touch with current customers or with brand communities. *Interactive media,* such as the phone and Internet, allow two-way communication between companies and customers, as well as between and among consumers.

Another term you'll see in media plans is **measured media,** which refers to the ability of media planners to analyze the cost of a media buy relative to the size of the medium's audience. Metrics are available for traditional media either from the medium itself or from external auditing agencies, but these figures are much harder to find for new and nontraditional media because the auditing procedures for these new media have yet to be developed.

The media landscape, according to TNS Media Intelligence, a reporting service that tracks advertising spending, uses the following categories:[3]

- *Television* network, cable, syndication, spot (local), Hispanic
- *Radio* network, national spot, local
- *Newspapers* national, local, Hispanic
- *Magazines* consumer, B2B, Sunday, local, Hispanic, international
- *Internet*
- *Outdoor*
- *Branded Entertainment*

All marketing communication messages other than personal conversations are carried by some form of media. In other words, media are not just a concern of advertising planners. Integrated marketing communication (IMC) media convey messages, such as brand publicity and sales promotion offers, as well as direct-response messages and loyalty incentive programs. Furthermore, these messages are two way in that they are carried to and from companies and consumers.

All of this means that the face of mass media is changing. Professor Don Jugenheimer in the *A Matter of Principle* feature analyzes the principles of change that are remaking the media landscape.

In South Florida, journalistic excellence in *español* means...

El Nuevo Herald is proud to be recognized as the best Spanish-language newspaper in the United States, reaching more than a half million readers over the course of a week.

Your advertisement in any of our award-winning sections is the sure way to be on the spotlight of the nation's third and most affluent Hispanic market with a whopping buying power of $13 billion plus a year!

The fact is, no other daily newspaper has a higher penetration in a Hispanic market nationwide!

For current rates and information call our **Advertising Department at (305) 376-4951.**

Ethnic media are a type of niche media. *El Nuevo Herald* is an example of a successful newspaper targeted at an ethic group, in this case the Spanish-speaking consumers in Miami and South Florida.

Principle

All marketing communication messages, other than personal conversations, are carried by some form of media.

A MATTER OF PRINCIPLE

The Dynamics of the Changing Media Environment

Donald Jugenheimer, *Principal and Partner, In-Telligence Inc.*

Mass media are changing rapidly. Several trends that are in operation simultaneously are dramatically reshaping the face of mass media:

1. **Convergence** involves the digitization of the media, in which all of the mass media save and transmit information through the same digital forms, as well as the integration of the media to work through and with each other.
2. **Interactivity** means that audience members can send messages back and forth to the media and to each other.
3. **Engagement,** or holding onto the audience through the media using give-and-take messaging, also involves interactivity.
4. Commoditization results when many types of products are similar. Customers think that most airlines are pretty much alike, and most banks offer the same services and hours of operation. The advertising media are similar, too, with broadcast television, cable television, TiVo, and DVD programming all regarded alike by viewers.
5. Cadence reflects the pace of today's life. Things move ever faster, attention spans are shorter, and audiences want to spend less time with advertisements.
6. **Personalization** allows advertisers and others to appeal directly to an individual's interests and needs.
7. Networking brings related messages and offers to audience members, based on their past and present behavior.

What happens when we all get all of our news, entertainment, and information exchanges through our cell phones or over the Internet? What will be the role of the "older" media? What is coming next? Few saw the Internet coming, and there are bound to be significant changes in future media as well.

What Do Media Do?

All marketing communication areas, such as sales promotion, public relations, and direct marketing, use a variety of media to deliver messages to customers. We know from the communication model presented in Chapter 4 that messages move through *channels of communication.* So in this sense, media *deliver* messages. In traditional mass media this is a one-way process from the source (the advertiser) to the receiver (consumers).

In another sense, media are *interactive* because they offer opportunities for dialogue and two-way conversation. The media of marketing communication deliver messages to and from customers and move messages back and forth through channels. This refines the concept of delivery to include receiving and listening, as well as delivering messages. Jugenheimer explains further, "Now we can respond, ask questions, and even place orders for products or services. This interactivity can involve more than the Internet; we can gain interactivity on the telephone, through text messaging on cell phones, and while playing video games."

Media also offers opportunities for *engagement,* a media buzzword that refers to the captivating quality of media that the audience finds engrossing, such as the "wire dancers" on the Windows Vista outdoor board. Certainly this can apply to television commercials and cinema advertising, but it can also be applied to print and Internet ads—anything on which readers concentrate. Media experts describe engagement as the closeness of fit between the interests of viewers and the relevance of the media content.[4] This is how media open the door of the critical "perception" step in the Facets Model of Effects that we introduced in Chapter 4.

Media are also contact points in that they *connect* a brand with the audience and ultimately *touch* their emotions, as well as *engage* their minds. The difference between delivery and connection is significant. To deliver means "to take something to a person or place"; to connect means "to join together." Delivery is the first step in connecting: it opens the door to touching a customer in a meaningful way with a brand message. Beyond conventional mass media, IMC connection media also include personal experiences with events, salespeople, and customer service, as well as word-of-mouth messages from people who influence us—all of which may become imbued with emotions leading to strong personal feelings about a brand.

The Evolution of Media Roles

People in our contemporary society live in a world of media-delivered news and information, which traditionally has been supported by advertising. Over several hundred years, media have evolved from print, to radio, then television, and now the Internet. Newspapers, magazines, and posters provided the visual dimension of communication; radio added an audio dimension. Television enabled messages to be heard and seen with moving images. Today we have the Internet, which has basically combined television and the computer, thus providing the added dimension of interactivity. We can summarize these changes in technology as eras:

The Print Era Ink and print images reproduced as newspapers, magazines, and posters.

The Broadcast Era Visual and audio information in the form of radio and television programs originally transmitted through air waves but now also distributed by cable and satellite.

The Digital Era Electronic information transmitted through the Internet but, like broadcasting, now also distributed through cable and satellite.

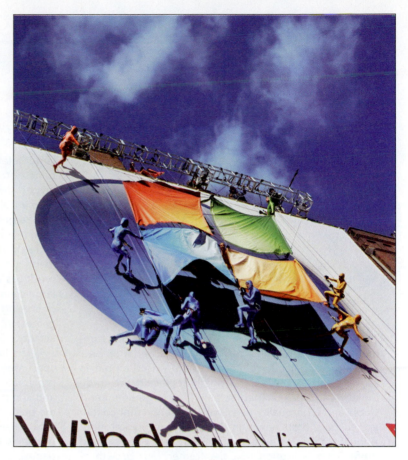

Wire dancers on an oversized billboard brought the Microsoft logo to life for the launch of the Vista operating system—an example of a highly engaging use of outdoor advertising.

It's useful to remember that this Digital Era is quite recent. The first website went on line in 1991; the social networking sites of MySpace and Facebook went on line in 2003 and 2004, respectively; and Twitter only arrived in 2006. In contrast, the first newspaper ad appeared in the early 1700s, the first radio station went on the air in 1897, and television became popular in the United States in the 1940s.

Every technological advance has threatened the older media whose managers feared their medium was on the edge of extinction. In fact, the media adjusted to their new circumstances by emphasizing what they do best—newspapers and magazines deliver information in depth, radio delivers music and other programs tailored to listeners' tastes, and television brings entertainment to the living room. The new media take on some of the characteristics and roles of the old at the same time that they add to the richness of the communication experience. Television, for example, has news shows and advertising that sound a lot like radio news programs and both radio and television use news formats—and advertising—that they adopted from print.

A more serious shift, however, is occurring in the 21st century as computers and the Internet personalize media and bring changes unlike any ever encountered in the history of media. Internet-based communication can do everything that the traditional media identified as their distinctive features and offers most of the communication dimensions of its media ancestors.

The only "medium" that is even more multidimensional than the Internet is personal selling. A salesperson can not only show, tell, and interact, but most importantly, can instantly create customized content. Internet sites can quasi-create content by compiling customer data from which information can be computed, such as creating a selection of customer preferences (Amazon's suggested books) or provide predetermined answers to FAQs (frequently asked questions).

Personalization is the answer to the commoditization point Jugenheimer included in his list of media trends. Another medium that delivers personalization is **word-of-mouth,** which

Principle
Every technological advance has threatened older media, and every new medium is launched in the footprints of its predecessor media.

Principle
Word of mouth delivers personalization, as well as a high level of persuasion.

A MATTER OF PRACTICE

People Really Enjoy Their Large-Screen Televisions

Michael McNiven, *Assistant Professor, Rowan University and* Dean Krugman, *Professor, University of Georgia*

Televisions with screens of 40 inches or more are commonly referred to as large-screen TVs. The larger sets with a rectangular 16 × 9 aspect ratio—used on movie screens and in DVDs—are rapidly replacing the traditional 4 × 3 box-shaped screen. The large sets are a viable and high-quality television innovation that continues to gain prominence in the television marketplace. Annual total sales exceed 30 million sets per year and there is no indication that the tremendous growth of large-screen television adoption will decline. Projected worldwide unit sales for large-screen TVs in 2010 was close to 61 million units.

Larger wide-screen televisions coupled with digital reception represent a significant change from the past in how television fare is delivered to viewers. The combination of digital programming, wider screens, and larger television displays marks a historic and pivotal entrance into the new era of the 21st-century television industry. People report that the changes in television dramatically improve the viewing process.

Large-screen owners are more likely to be married, have teenagers and older children in the home, live with more people, and earn more money. Family entertainment is a major reason for purchasing the sets, which produces a larger, fuller family experience. In addition, large-screen owners are more likely to view event programming (such as sports and movies) and to play video games, which has become a family and/or multiplayer activity.

The large-screen television experience is found by consumers to be enjoyable, easy to watch, and to approximate a theater-like atmosphere. Lifelike pictures and compelling sound often help viewers feel like they are being transported to the location of the content. In most cases large-screen televisions are part of a cluster of television technologies including such items as video games, digital video recorders (DVRs), and cable/satellite distribution.

The synergies of the home television cluster provide dramatically enhanced viewing and entertainment experiences. The increased viewing experience has a social component. In addition to more family viewing, larger screen televisions are used for friend and visitor entertaining, providing an important social component.

---

has emerged as a powerful new force in marketing communication because of its inherent persuasiveness—you tend to believe what you hear from a friend, family member, or other important influencer in your life.

Although new media tend to launch themselves by adapting the forms of the media that preceded them, the older media also adapt by adopting some of the advances of new media. Nearly every media vehicle, for example, now has one or more (most have more) websites—and that creates *convergence*. Jugenheimer notes, "Newspapers have websites, advertisements can be transmitted by e-mail, and television programs can be downloaded into iPods." Furthermore, catalogs are on line, radio is on line, video is on computers, and cell phones and books are electronic.

Television, for example, is not just limited to viewing programs, but has become the center of the digital living room with viewers enjoying new experiences, such as games and exercise via their Wii players and other video games that now can be seen on the TV screen. The *A Matter of Practice* feature explains how consumers are converting their TVs into new multimedia centers.

The Media Industry

The modern media landscape includes up to 200 television channels in some markets, a huge number of special-interest publications, millions of websites, and new and novel media forms that weren't even imagined 20 years ago, such as ads on conveyer belts at airports or brands stamped into the sand at the beach. The Jeep trailer shows how designer Michael Dattolico designed a painted vehicle for one of his clients.

JEEP GRAPHICS
GRAPHIC AREA ☐ JEEP COLOR ■
GRAPHIC COLORS ■ ☐ ☐
SCALE: TBD

Driver's Side

Passenger's Side

SHOWCASE

The Jeep graphics designed by Michael Dattolico for a technology client turned a vehicle into a moving billboard.

Dattolico graduated from the advertising program at the University of Florida and was nominated by Professor Elaine Wagner.

Traditional mass media advertising is a huge industry with almost $141 billion in advertising spending.[5] Media research organization Kantar Media monitors advertising expenditures and provided the data used in Figure 11.1 Although advertising expenditures declined as a result of the Great Recession of the late 2000s, the greatest growth was in online advertising.

The recession, combined with the explosion of online media, seriously hurt traditional media. Even though they still dominate in terms of dollars, all traditional media saw decreases in their ad revenues. This was partly because of an overall decline in media advertising but also because marketers were increasingly turning to the Internet for visibility at less cost.

Newspapers were the biggest losers because of the shift of classified advertising to online sites and the ease with which readers could get news online. Many major papers closed; others were reduced in size, staff, and news coverage. Magazines suffered, as well. Revenues for broadcast were down with traditional radio and television companies seeing red ink. The bright spot during the recession was the cable television sector. *Advertising Age* reported at the end of 2009 that 11 of the top 100 media firms had filed for bankruptcy during the year with print dominating the list.[6]

Key Media Players

In terms of jobs and career opportunities in media, there are professionals who both sell and buy media. It is important that you understand the difference. First let's look at the professionals who sell space or time in media.

• **Media salespeople** work for a specific vehicle, such as a magazine or local television station, with the objective of building the best possible argument to convince media planners to use the medium they represent. A media salesperson is responsible for assembling packets of information, or **sales kits,** on the medium he or she represents, which usually means compiling profile information about the people who

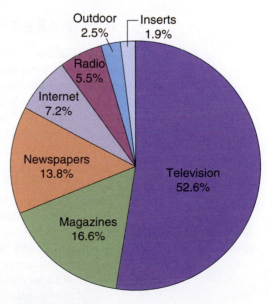

FIGURE 11.1
The Media Landscape

Source: Kantar Media. Based on January–March 2010 (% Share). Used with permission.

watch, listen, or read the medium, along with the numbers describing audience size and geographical coverage. Currently media conglomerates prevail. CBS, for example, created a coordinated ad-selling division, called CBS RIOT, which stands for radio, Internet, outdoor, and television. The new division was designed to serve primarily local markets and offers **cross-media** (also called **multichannel**) integrated deals. Disney is reorganizing its ad sales to deliver a similar cross-media ad sales program for its kids' media properties.[7]

• **Media reps** or **brokers** are people (or companies) who sell space (in print) and time (in broadcast) for a variety of media. If an agency wants to buy space in all of the major newspapers in the West, for example, the agency's buyer could contract with a media rep firm whose sales rep and brokers handle national sales for all those newspapers. This allows the media buyer to place the buy with one order.

On the buying side, media planners, buyers, and researchers work primarily for agencies, although they can also be found working for marketers who handle their own media work in house. Their challenge is to determine the best way to deliver a message, which is called **media planning.** The job functions are as follows:

• **Media researchers** compile audience measurement data, media costs, and availability data for the various media options being considered by the planners.
• **Media planners** develop the strategic decisions outlined in the media plan, such as where to advertise geographically, when to advertise, and which type of media to use to reach specific types of audiences.
• **Media buyers** implement the media plan by contracting for specific amounts of time or space. They spend the media budget according to the plan developed by the media planner. Media buyers are expected to maintain good media supplier relations to facilitate a flow of information within the fast-changing media marketplace. This means there should be close working relationships between planners and buyers, as well as media reps, so media planners can tap this source of media information to better forecast media changes, including price and patterns of coverage.
• Media buying companies, mentioned briefly in Chapter 1, are independent companies that specialize in doing media research, planning, and buying. They may be a spin-off from the media department in an advertising agency, but because they are now independent companies, they work for a variety of clients. They consolidate media buying to get maximum discounts from the media for the volume of their buys. They then pass on some of this saving to their clients.

WHAT ARE THE FUNDAMENTALS OF MEDIA STRATEGY?

Media placement is often the largest single cost item in a marketing communication budget, especially for consumer goods and services. Procter & Gamble, for example, spent more than $2 billion on measured media in 2009, although for the first time P&G lost its leadership position as the top U.S. advertiser to Verizon, the telecom giant, which suffered less during the Great Recession than P&G.[8] Because of the huge amount of money spent on measured media, as well as nontraditional media, decisions about how the money is to be spent are carefully analyzed and justified in the media planning process.

The Media Plan

Principle
The goal of media planning is to maximize impact while minimizing cost.

The challenge marketing communicators face is how to manage all of the media opportunities and yet maximize the efficiency of budgets that are inevitably too small to do everything the firm would like to do to reach every current and potential customer. All of this decision making comes together in a **media plan,** which identifies the best media to use to deliver an advertising message efficiently to a targeted audience. The goal is to balance message impact and cost—maximizing impact while minimizing cost.

The media plan is a subsection within a marcom plan and has its own objectives, strategies, and tactics. It is also developed in tandem with message planning, the topic of Chapter 8. Figure 11.2 shows these relationships, but this time with an emphasis on media planning. We'll introduce

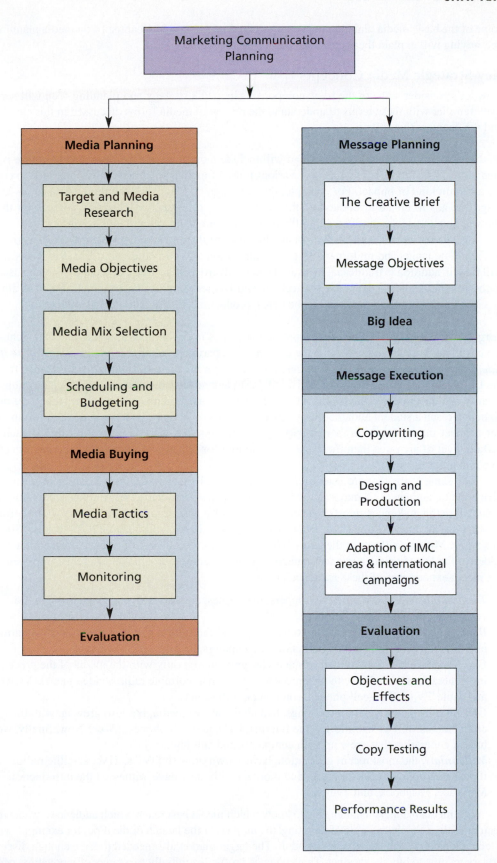

FIGURE 11.2

Marketing Communication Planning

Media and message planning activities are interrelated and work in parallel.

some of the basic media planning concepts here in this chapter but Chapter 14 on media planning and buying will explain these activities in much more detail.

Key Strategic Media Concepts

Now let's consider some of the basic components in media strategy and planning. You will need to be familiar with these terms to understand the review of media forms discussed in this chapter and the chapters that follow.

Media Mix   In most cases a media plan will include more than one medium, and therefore is a *media mix*. This **media mix** is the way various types of media are strategically combined to create a certain kind of impact. For example, the campaign that launched the iPod used posters and magazine ads to create awareness of the new product, followed by television advertising that showed how to use the product, and billboards that reminded people to look for it in stores.

Because of the breadth of IMC plans, the term **multiplatform** has become popular to describe multichannel and multimarketing communication areas. In other words, in IMC plans you will find, in addition to traditional measured media advertising, a variety of other tools being used, such as events, social media (such as Facebook and Twitter), branded entertainment (such as films or video games in which the brand is the hero), product placement, and guerilla marketing.

Targets and Audiences   One of the biggest challenges in developing a media plan is matching the advertiser's target audience with the audience of a particular medium. As discussed in *The Inside Story* feature at *www.pearsonhighered.moriarty*, an example of tight targeting comes from the University of Florida where the university's student advertising agency, Adwerks, developed a campaign for the university's student travel program based on posters and flyers that were designed to reach a student audience. The Adwerks team's objective was to increase sign-ups in order to meet the required number of participants. If trips that were close to full didn't reach a certain level of sign-ups then there was the potential for unhappy participants, creating a negative image for the program.

Principle
Media planners match the target audience with the audience of a particular medium.

The same terms that are used to describe target audiences in Chapter 5 can be used to describe media audiences. A major study by the Newspaper Association of America, for example, grouped media audiences into four useful categories by generation: traditionalists (born before 1946), baby boomers (born 1946–1964), Gen X (1965–1976), and Gen Y (1977–1994).[9] Since this study, Millenials (born in the late 1990s into the first decade of 2000) have been commonly added to the list of media audiences categorized by generation. Dramatic differences are seen in the media experiences of these audience groups:

- *Traditionalists* grew up with newspapers, magazines, and radio. (*Note:* No television; no cell phone, computers, or Internet.)
- *Boomers,* who are in their 50s and 60s, always had those three types of media, but also grew up with television (but still no cell phones, computers, or Internet).
- *Gen Xers,* who are now in their 30s and 40s, grew up not only with the media of the preceding generations, but also with tape recorders, Walkman portable radios, video games, VCRs, and cable TV (still no cell phones, computers, or Internet).
- *Gen Yers,* who are twenty-somethings, had all the above media, but also grew up with the computer, as well as satellite TV, the Internet, CDs, and cell phones. (*Note:* Now, finally, we have a generation that grew up with computers and cell phones.)
- *Millennials,* the most recent generation, have grown up with DVDs, TiVo, satellite radio, iPods, smart phones, Second Life, and more recently they have witnessed the introduction of MySpace, Facebook, and Twitter.

The media planners' challenge is to know which media best reach which audiences, whatever their ages. In a classic example of targeting, the market for the launch of the iPod, for example, was a technologically sophisticated young adult. The target market also needed to have enough discretionary income to buy the product. That audience profile led initially to a target of innovators, people who are into cool gadgets and who love music. Now where do you find those people? One place to start was with posters in subways and other urban sites. The campaign also used outdoor boards, print media, and TV commercials in ways that would generate buzz. A key strategy was to get people talking about this new gadget. Eventually the price dropped and the market widened to include both college and high school students after the initial launch.

The Basis for the Buy

Decisions about which media to use are based on the profile of the audience that reads, views, listens, or visits a medium. Media sales reps provide their own data, but research by account planners also uncovers media use patterns that help make these decisions.

Media planners use a variety of terms to identify and measure audiences. The terms are easy to confuse, so let's explain some here before we begin talking about specific characteristics of traditional media forms in the following chapters.

- *Exposure* Media effects all begin with **exposure.** We know from the discussion in Chapter 4 that the first step in making an impact is perception—you have to be exposed to a message before any other effect is possible. Exposure is similar to circulation for television in that it's a rough estimate of the number of households watching a program. However, just because the television is on doesn't mean you are paying any attention to the program, let alone the advertising that surrounds it. Exposure, in other words, doesn't equate to readership or viewership. At the most basic level, however, media planners estimate the number of exposures delivered by a media mix.
- *Impressions* An **impression** is one person's opportunity to be exposed one time to an ad in a specific vehicle. Impressions can be added up as a measure of the size of the audience either for one medium (one insertion in print) or for a combination of vehicles in a media mix.
- *Circulation* Impressions are different from **circulation,** because impressions (at least in print) estimate the readership or rather the opportunity to be exposed (delivery to the household or a newsstand purchase), rather than just the circulation, which refers to copies sold.
- *Gross Impressions* Circulation doesn't tell you much about the actual exposure of a print ad. A magazine may have a circulation of 1 million, but it might be read on average by 2.5 people per issue. This means impressions for that issue would be 2.5 million. If the ad ran in three consecutive issues, then the estimate of total impressions, called **gross impressions,** would be 7.5 million. Similarly, the number of viewers watching a program might be greater than the number of households reached since there may be more than one viewer watching and the commercial may be repeated several times in a program. Media planners add up all those watching and multiply that times the number of placements to estimate gross impressions for TV.
- *Ratings* Gross impression figures become very large and difficult to work with, which is why the television and radio industries use **ratings** (percentage of exposure), which is an easier measurement to work with because it converts the raw figure to a percentage of households. When you read about a television show having a rating of 20.0 that means that 20 percent, or one-fifth of all the households with televisions, were tuned in to that program. *Note:* One rating point equals 1 percent of the nation's estimated 1,114,000 TV homes; that's why planners describe this program as having 20 **rating points,** or percentage points. A 20 rating is actually a huge figure, since the fragmentation of cable has diversified television watching and made it very difficult to get 20 percent of the households tuned to any one program.
- *Share* A better estimate of impressions might be found in a program's **share of audience,** which refers to the percent of viewers based on the number of sets turned on. The share figure is always larger than the rating, since the base is smaller. For example, the 2010 Super Bowl got a rating of 45 (45 percent of all households with television), but its share was 68, which means 68 percent of all televisions turned on were tuned to the Super Bowl.[10]

Reach and Frequency The goal of most media plans is to reach as many people in the target audience as often as the budget allows. **Reach** is the percentage of the media audience exposed at least once to the advertiser's message during a specific time frame. When we say that a particular media vehicle, such as the Super Bowl, has a wide reach, we mean that a lot of people are watching the program. When we say it has a narrow reach, such as the *El Nuevo Herald,* we mean that a small percentage of the newspaper audience is reading that publication. The idea for the iPod launch was to reach not just everyone who likes music, but specifically to target technologically sophisticated people who are also opinion leaders (whose thoughts on innovations like the iPod would influence many others).

Equally as important as reach is **frequency,** which refers to the number of times a person is exposed to the advertisement. There's a rule of thumb that you have to hear or see something three times before it makes an impact. That's the reason frequency of repetition is so important in many

Principle
Exposure doesn't equate to readership or viewership; just because the television is on doesn't mean anyone is paying attention to it.

Principle
The goal of most media plans is to reach as many people in the target audience as often as the budget allows.

advertising campaigns. Different media have different patterns of frequency. Radio commercials, for example, typically achieve high levels of frequency because they can be repeated over and over to achieve impact. Frequency is more difficult to accomplish with a monthly magazine because its publication—and an ad's appearance in it—is much more infrequent than a radio broadcast.

Most media plans state both reach and frequency objectives and the media mix is designed to accomplish both of those goals. You may remember the discussion in Chapter 6 of the lamb market in Iceland. The objective was to reposition lamb to meet the budget concerns of recession-stressed consumers. Let's revisit that case with more information about the campaign's media plan, which demonstrates how different media are chosen based on consumer use and the ability of the various media to deliver either reach or frequency.

You may remember that focus groups were used by the H:N Marketing Communication agency in Reykjavik, Iceland to uncover key consumer insights about lamb—principally that consumers were not buying pricey prime lamb cuts and didn't know how to cook the more budget-priced cuts. Other information uncovered in that research was useful in identifying key media characteristics of the target market. In particular, Ingvi Logason's research found the following:

- The target group members are the largest consumers of TV in the country.
- Close to 100 percent of the target group has high-speed Internet access and are frequent users of the Internet at work and at home.
- Iceland most likely has the highest penetration of Facebook users in the world: 94 percent of the population in the age group of 25- to 40-year-olds (the lamb industry's target group) have Facebook accounts.

Logason explained that his agency created "an interactive media plan that would connect with our target group in settings where they could be engaged in the ads. We would connect with them on their leisure time where they worked, at home, and in social settings." The plan used both television and Facebook. He explains, "The strength of self-dissemination and friend referrals on Facebook made sure the ad recipes traveled far and wide with recommendation that the person posting the recipe liked it. A strong connection was created between viral ads, the Lamb industry's website, and a Facebook group interested in lamb."

Traditional media, such as television, were also used but the interactive media "allowed us to focus on reach in the TV media buy while we were able to obtain high frequency through viral media." Additional activities included sponsoring TV cooking shows, placing the product in TV shows (cooking and other), and gathering various lamb recipes already online and linking them to the Facebook site. Logason reported that media measurements showed that the unorthodox media mix reached its target for both reach (mostly through TV) and frequency (mostly through viral activities).

Intrusiveness   Because of the high level of commercial message clutter, companies in the past have valued all of the help they can get in attracting attention to their messages. **Intrusiveness**—the ability of a medium to grab attention by being disruptive or unexpected—is the primary strategy for countering clutter. Kelley in the Part 4 opener pointed out that in the new media world, engagement will replace interruption. But still, most media use intrusiveness to some degree as a way to grab the attention of inattentive media consumers.

Principle
The more intrusive a medium, the more it can be personalized, but also the more costly it is to use.

Media, as well as messages, vary in their degree of intrusiveness. The most intrusive medium is personal selling because the sales representative's presence demands attention. Likewise a phone call is also demanding and a loud voice or sound on television can be irritating. The least intrusive media are print media because users choose when and to what extent to use these media and attend to them. The more intrusive a medium, generally speaking, the more it can be personalized, but also the more costly it is to use, which is why personal selling is so much more costly than mass media. Admittedly, the word *intrusive* has negative connotations. If a message is too disruptive or irritating, it may not help build a positive brand relationship.

There are ways to minimize intrusiveness. One is to choose media whose target audience is intrinsically interested in the product category. Research has shown that one of the benefits of specialized magazines is that readers enjoy learning about new products from the advertising. To have visibility without being intrusive is one of the reasons why product placements and events are popular. Giving customers opt-in or opt-out options for receiving brand information digitally means that when messages are sent, they are not unexpected and therefore less likely to be seen as intrusive.

HOW IS THE MEDIA ENVIRONMENT CHANGING?

As we said at the beginning of this chapter, marketing communication media are in an incredible state of flux, partially because of the introduction of the computer and the Internet, but also because of the way people choose to spend their time. Bruce Bendinger, formerly a creative director and now publisher of advertising books, analyzes the changing media environment in the *A Matter of Practice* feature.

IMC and Media

We have talked about the connection role of media. A dimension that is particularly important in IMC is creating, sustaining, and strengthening brand *relationships* over time. Relevant messages delivered through media that drive positive experiences create value for consumers. This value adds up over time and emerges as loyalty—the ultimate goal of relationship marketing programs.

Relationship marketing, a concept that originated with public relations, shifts the focus from the objective of getting a one-time purchase by a target to the maintenance of long-term involvement from all of the firm's critical stakeholders, whether employees, distributors, channel members, customers, agencies, investors, government agencies, the media, or community members. All stakeholders are seen as communicators who can send either positive or negative messages about the brand; therefore, it is important to keep in contact with them and keep them informed about brand programs (see Figure 11.3).

Channels to Contact Points

We have used the term *traditional media* in several places in recognition of the fact that the definition of media is changing. We've also mentioned *contact points*. These redefinitions are derived from technological change, from new patterns of consumer media use, and from changing business practices, particularly the introduction of the IMC perspective in marketing communication planning.

The thinking about contact points is an IMC-based idea that has redefined and broadened our understanding of media as a message delivery system. **Contact points** are the various ways

A MATTER OF PRACTICE

Thoughts about Media Evolution and Revolution

Bruce Bendinger, *Owner, The Copy Workshop*

The economic and recession issues aside, what's going on, simply put, is the evolution of our media—and our media usage. Marshall McLuhan offered some insights—as does history.

When we shifted to books, we had more than an increased appetite for ink and paper. We had the Reformation, the 30 Years' War, and a few years later, the American Revolution—all driven by the printing press. It's no accident that one of the most important (and most successful) individuals in the Colonies was a printer —Benjamin Franklin.

Moving right along, in *The World Is Flat*, Thomas Friedman quotes somebody who said "the printing press turned us into readers, the Xerox turned is into publishers. Television turned us into viewers, the Internet is turning us into broadcasters."

The change in media usage in society is profound. It isn't just broken business models (my father was classified ad manager for a newspaper, a major cash cow, now gone to electronic pastures), it's brand new behaviors, and maybe more.

In that context, a Media Revolution, everything that's going on is . . . well, no surprise.

For you students, you're living in the middle of a recession/depression. But don't get recessed and depressed.

Rather think that you're living in the middle of a Media Revolution—and get excited—and start thinking the kinds of thoughts we'll all need to be having as we work our way into a rather interesting new age.

Long Live the Media Revolution!

FIGURE 11.3
The Roles of IMC Media

Principle
Everything that delivers a message to a stakeholder about a brand is a contact point.

a consumer comes in contact with a brand. This view of media moves from traditional advertising media (print, broadcast, outdoor) and the media of various marketing communication functions (press releases, events, promotional materials, sponsorships) to experiential contacts that in previous advertising-dominated media plans weren't generally considered to be media, such as word of mouth and customer service.

These opportunities are found in a huge variety of vehicles including everything from the traditional advertising media—newspapers and magazines, outdoor boards and posters, radio, and television—but also the Internet, telephone, directories, packages and labels, signs and building designs and ads painted on buildings, company trucks and cars, corporate letterhead and business cards, as well as all of the media of promotion, such as inflatables and airplane banners, and specialty items, such as calendars, coffee mugs, T-shirts, pens, refrigerator signs, and mouse pads, to name a few. The list is endless and can only be identified by studying the lives of customers to spot the points where they come in contact with a brand—or an opportunity for a brand experience or brand conversation.

In Chapter 7 we introduced the seventh principle of IMC: *All contact points deliver brand messages.* Another way to express the contact point idea in terms of our discussion here is: *Everything that delivers a message to a stakeholder about a brand is a contact point.* Contact point management, then, becomes the new way marketing communication planners develop systems of message delivery—and that includes both to and from all key stakeholders.

We also call them brand **touch points** in recognition of the impact these personal experiences can have on stakeholder feelings about a brand. A touch point is a brand experience that delivers a message that touches emotions leading to positive and negative judgments. A **critical touchpoint (CTP)** is one that connects the brand and customer on an emotional level and leads to a yes or no decision about a brand relationship.[11] The SAS lighted board placed in airports to reach SAS's business clients highlights the importance of these new brand connection opportunities.

Sometimes referred to as **experiential marketing,** touch-point strategies and programs use events and store design, among other means, to engage consumers in a personal and involving way. Some would argue that every brand contact is an experience; however, in experiential marketing the goal is to intensify active involvement beyond the more passive activity of reading, viewing, and listening to traditional media. The idea is to connect with consumers in ways that create higher levels of engagement, as well as lasting bonds with a brand.

Packaging   It's not a new function, but **packaging** is receiving increased attention as a key contact point. A package is both a container and a communication vehicle, and it works in the store and in the home or office. In particular, it is the last ad a customer sees before making the decision to buy a brand, as the Pepperidge Farm shelf photo illustrates. Although the focus of this discussion is primarily on packaging for goods, don't forget that services also are packaged in terms of such things as uniforms, other aspects of personal appearance, décor, and delivery vehicles.

The package is an important communication medium. Even if you can't afford a big advertising budget, you've got a chance to grab shopper attention if your product has a compelling image on the shelf." In an attempt to win over undecided consumers at the point of purchase, many manufacturers create innovative, eye-catching packages. Although the industry has never developed a standard for measuring impressions from a shelf, advertisers are aware of the billboarding effect of a massed set of packages, a practice that Pepperidge Farm uses to good effect. Once on the shelf at home or in the office, it is a constant brand reminder.

When the package works in unison with other marketing communication, it not only catches attention and presents a familiar brand image, it can communicate critical information and tie back to a current campaign. The package serves as a critical reminder of the product's important benefits at the moment the consumer is choosing among several competing brands.

Sometimes, the package itself is the focus of the advertising, particularly if there is a new size or innovation, such as Coca-Cola's introduction of a new bottle made from plant materials that is more compostable than plastic.[12] In sum, packaging is a constant communicator, an effective device for carrying advertising messages, and a strong brand reminder.

Packages can also deliver customer benefits. For example, recipes for Quaker Oats' famous Oatmeal Cookies, Nestlé's Tollhouse Cookies, Chex Party Mix, and Campbell's Green Bean Bake all started as promotional recipes on the product's packaging and turned into long-time favorites in homemakers' recipe boxes. There is even a website for these classic recipes (*www.backofthebox.com*) that features more than 1,500 recipes found on packaging.

Another use of packaging is found on milk cartons where cause-marketing campaigns, as well as other cross-promotions, have appeared. Missing children have been featured since the 1980s, but more recently ads on the half-pints given to school children act as tiny billboards promoting children's products such as kids movies. Larger milk cartons sold in stores promote local brands and sports teams, cereals, cookies, Honey Maid graham crackers, and Duncan Hines brownies.[13]

Packaging offers a way to deal with an ethical issue that bedevils some marketers—product ingredient and health effects labeling. A number of categories, such as household cleaners, have been challenged by consumers about the chemicals in their products. Steve Israel, a New York legislator, believes the problem can be addressed with mandatory labeling legislation. Tobacco companies are also being targeted, particularly in Europe where they are required to use a large part of the package for warning labels. Legislation has proposed that warning labels cover the top half of the front and back of cigarette packs and include frightening images, such as diseased lungs.[14]

Word of Mouth   Buzz is important because it means people are talking about a brand. This buzz may be the most important factor in consumer decision making because the recommendations of others are highly persuasive—more so than any advertisement. Given the engaging work of its agency, Crispin Porter + Bogusky, Burger King is often lauded as the "king of buzz." Tia Lang, interactive director at BK, says "Social media is very important in today's environment and we think generating buzz is a positive result in and of itself."

Pepperidge Farm, with its consistent design and distinctive brand image, dominates cookie shelves because of the power of its consistent design across all the brand's variations.

Improve the customer experience across all touch points

▶▶ **Click here to Download Report**

§.sas.
THE POWER TO KNOW.

The SAS business analytics software company connects its products and services to the potential reader by staying in touch with customer experiences and needs.

Principle
A package is the last ad a customer sees before making a decision on which brand to buy.

Principle
The goal of buzz-builder strategies is to get the right people saying the right things about the brand.

She explained that "We have done some innovative campaigns that have helped lead to 20 consecutive quarters of positive sales."[15]

A study of media use by the BIGresearch firm that polled 15,000 consumers found that the most influential form of media is word of mouth.[16] The goal is to get the right people talking about the brand and having them say things in support of the brand strategy. Some media plans are specifically designed to generate excited talk about something new, particularly if the strategies can reach influential or early adopters whose opinions are valued by others. One idea is that buzz is best generated by disrupting common patterns of thinking, or schemas. In other words, we talk about things that surprise and don't fit into our standard mental models.[17]

Viral Communication   An online version of buzz, viral communication describes the way a message spreads on the Internet. **Viral marketing** strategies are designed to create a groundswell of demand for a brand. However, the spread of messages depend totally on consumers creating buzz through their own e-mails and mentions on blogs, Facebook, YouTube, and Twitter. Brands can instigate the viral process, but not control it. An example comes from a McDonald's Filet-O-Fish special promotion that runs every year during Lent. In a parody of the "Big Mouth Billy Bass" gag gift, a fish hanging mounted on a plaque in a garage sings, "Give me back that Filet-O-Fish." The outlandish video has been viewed on YouTube more than a million times and has spawned ads and even a ring tone.[18]

One of the first viral hits was Burger King's "Subservient Chicken" which would respond to commands to do things like tap dance or do exercises. The site urged visitors to "tell their friends." Praised as possibly the most popular marketing website of all time, the site quickly registered half a billion hits in the first couple of weeks, as well as a big increase in sales of BK's chicken sandwiches. The creative team explained that BK's advertising was generally seen as boring and the "Subservient Chicken" was intended to make BK more edgy and fun. See the site and the story behind its complicated execution at *www.barbariangroup .com/portfolio/burger_king_subservient_chicken.*

A worry for planners is that viral messages can also spread negative stories or even be used to organize a boycott against a brand. As Simon Clift, Unilever's chief marketing officer, explains, "No matter how big your advertising spending, small groups of consumers on a tiny budget might hijack the conversation."[19]

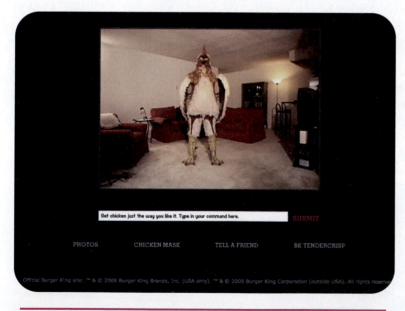

Get chicken just the way you like it. Type in your command here.   SUBMIT

PHOTOS   CHICKEN MASK   TELL A FRIEND   BK TENDERCRISP

Official Burger King site: ™ & © 2009 Burger King Brands, Inc. (USA only). ™ & © 2009 Burger King Corporation (outside USA). All rights reserved.

CLASSIC
With the line, "Get chicken just the way you like it," Burger King's agency, Crispin Porter + Bogusky, launched the "Subservient Chicken" interactive video website for Burger King. Play with the "Subservient Chicken" (*www.cpbgroup.com/awards/subservientchicken.html*) and see if you think it is captivating. Why would it have been so popular at the time it was introduced?

Customer Service   It's not a new business function, but it is new to marketing communication planners who, in the past, were seldom involved in planning or monitoring this critical connection with customers. **Customer service** represents a company's attitude and behavior during interactions with customers. These interactions send some of the most impactful brand messages that customers receive. If the interactive experience is positive, it will strengthen the customer relationship; if it is negative, it can weaken or even destroy a customer's brand relationship.

The importance of customer service as a contact point that delivers positive (or negative) brand experiences is reflected in a campaign by online retailer Zappos.com that demonstrates to customers how its customer service representatives make it easy to order or return merchandise. Called "zappets," the puppet-like characters in the ads are based on actual Zappos.com employees, whom the company calls its "customer loyalty team."

Because customers have so many choices of brands and shopping outlets, how a company treats customers can be the major reason for choosing one over the others. Why has Southwest Airlines been so successful when competitors have faced bankruptcy? The primary reason is customer service. Marketing communication planners don't "manage" customer service in most companies, but they can monitor the messages that are being sent at this critical touch point.

New Consumer Media Use Patterns

Consumers' use of media is changing as fast as the technology. It used to be that most American audiences were involved with three television networks, a newspaper, and one or two magazines. The modern media landscape includes up to 200 television channels in some markets, a huge number of special interest publications, millions of websites, and new and novel media, such as Kindle, iPad, and Twitter, that hadn't even been imagined five years ago. Here are other trends:

- Media consumers are active, in control, and entertained.
- Lives are media focused.
- Personal life has become public.
- Global has become local.

Rather than controlling media choices, consumers are much more in control of their own media and designing their own media landscapes—from video games to Twitter. The people formerly known as "audiences" are creating their own content, a practice we have referred to as *consumer-generated content,* such as the homemade videos and commercials seen on YouTube and personalized audio listening courtesy of the iPod and other MP3 players. Entertainment has become as much of a driving force for modern digital media as news was for traditional media.

Two major changes in media use patterns are media-driven lives and media multitasking. In their youthful days the traditionalists' and baby boomers' lives were dominated by work and family activities. In contrast, more recent generations spend more time with media of all kinds, and those channels are more intertwined with their family, work, and leisure time. People not only spend more time with media, they use more than one medium at a time.[20]

Traditionally most media involved a solitary experience—reading a paper or listening to radio, for example, but another transformation is the creation of truly social media. First there were blogs, then MySpace and Facebook, then Twitter—all of which made personal space public. The immediacy and intimacy of a phone conversation has exploded into millions of interactions via Twitter. (Think about this: if you can send 1 million tweets, are you broadcasting? You probably don't know the 1 million recipients—so has Twitter become a form of mass media?)

It used to be that global media were limited in number and generally media were limited by national boundaries—most media, particularly newspapers, radio, and television, were primarily local. The Internet changed all that. You can be on an island in Indonesia and still text about your experiences to friends back home. Most travelers from Western countries are connected to their media wherever they are in the world. Some countries, such as China, try to control the Internet access of their citizens, but most people are able to travel the world of the Web logging into sites without consideration of where they are or where the site comes from.

New and Alternative Forms of Contact

This is the most creative time in the history of commercial media. We talk about new, converging, and emerging media—older media are converging with new media and new forms are being created faster than we can learn how to use them. We also use the term *nontraditional media* to refer to alternative forms of contact, such as product placement, video games, and guerilla marketing. Melissa Lerner, a specialist

Principle

If an interaction is positive, it can strengthen a customer–brand relationship; if negative, it can weaken or destroy a brand relationship.

Principle

Entertainment is as much of a driving force for modern digital media as news was for traditional media.

ACTUAL CALL WITH ZAPPOS.COM

Zappos.com celebrates its customer service representative in a campaign that reiterates the company's value propositions, "Happy to help. 24/7" by showing how its employees—albeit in sock puppet form—interact with customers.

Place/Affinity Based	Alternative/Guerrilla
Place-Based Broadcast: Airport TV In-Store TV/Radio Mall TV Physician/Pharmacy TV Theatre Radio	**Alternative:** Aerial Media Custom Media Event Sponsorships Experiential Media Interactive Kiosks Naming Rights Projection Media Sampling Specialty Media Sports Sponsorship Travel Affinity Sponsorships New Technology

Affinity-Based:
Bar/Restaurant Media
Cinema
C-Store Media
College Media
Day Care Center Media
Gas/Service Station Media
Golf Media
Health Club Media
In-Flight Media
In-Office Building Media
In-School Media
In-Stadium Media
In-Store Media
Leisure Media
Physician Media
Ski Media
VIP Airline Lounge Media
Wild Posters

Guerilla Media:
Coffee Cups/Sleeves
Graffiti Murals
Mobile Media (i.e. AdVans)
Pizza Boxes
Street Teams
Umbrellas
Deli Bags

FIGURE 11.4

Nontraditional Media

New-media specialist Melissa Lerner says, "Clients are demanding more unique plans and ideas than ever before because impact and engagement help them to become trendsetters in their respective industries." She describes these as exciting "never done before" campaigns.

Lerner earned a B.S. in Business and Economics from Lehigh University.

Principle

The media side with its search for innovative points of contact can be just as creative as the creative side of advertising.

in new-media planning who formerly worked at WOW, a division of Kinetic Worldwide, described nontraditional media as including merging media and digital enhancements, place-based, branded environments, and guerilla executions (see Figure 11.4). She observes, "There is nothing better than working on a nontraditional media concept that comes to fruition and generates exciting PR and buzz within a marketplace."

The search for nontraditional media—that is, new ways to reach target audiences—is particularly important for advertisers trying to reach the elusive youth market, since teens are often the first to experiment with new media forms. In some ways, this search for innovative ways to deliver messages is just as creative as the message concepts developed on the creative side of advertising. That's why one of the principles of this book is that the media side can be just as creative as the creative side of advertising.

Guerilla Marketing   A really hot area of alternative marketing communication is **guerilla marketing,** which uses the power of involvement to create memorable brand experiences. This place-based strategy creates unexpected personal encounters with a brand, such as painted messages on streets or costumed brand characters parading across a busy intersection creating excitement, as well as buzz about a brand.

The idea is to use creative ways to reach people where they live, work, and walk to create a personal connection and a high level of impact. If it works, the encounter gets talked about, creating a buzz moment. Sears used computer-equipped Segways on Michigan Avenue in Chicago to launch its online layaway program. Wireless carrier Vodaphone used holographic ads featuring Portuguese soccer players dribbling balls for the opening of one of its concept stores in Portugal.

A form of guerilla marketing you're probably familiar with are the sign holders hired by local businesses to promote their stores or special marketing events. Most sign holders simply stand and wave or do little dances to catch drivers' attention, but there is an art form in sign spinning, similar to break dancing, that calls for athletic prowess and dramatic moves to present an involved choreography. Also called "human directionals," they specialize in street corner advertising.

More about matching wits than matching budgets, guerilla marketing has limited reach but high impact. For example, Sony Ericsson Mobile Communications Ltd. hired actors to create buzz about a new mobile phone that is also a digital camera. The actors pretended to be tourists who wanted their picture taken, thus allowing consumers to try the product. As a typical guerilla marketing campaign, it only reached those who encountered the actors. Sometimes a guerilla marketing campaign will generate publicity that extends the impact.

Product Placement   For years we have been exposed to **product placement,** in which a brand appears in a television program, movie, or even in print as a prop. With product placement, a company pays to have verbal or visual brand exposure in a movie or television program. George Clooney's movie *Up in the Air,* for example, prominently features American Airlines and Hilton Hotels as "integrated marketers." Media analysts estimate that Apple Computer and Pontiac each received over $25,000 in media value through placements in the television series *24.*[21]

Product placement has become important because it isn't as intrusive as conventional advertising, and audiences can't zap the ads, as they can for television advertising using the remote control or a DVR. At the same time, it may make the product a star—or at least be associated with a star. Sometimes the product placement is subtle as when a particular brand of aspirin is shown in a medicine chest or a character drinks a particular brand of beverage. In other cases, the brand is front

These painted stairs at the Denver Pavilions and the entertainment complex in downtown Denver is an example of guerilla marketing. It is also a "captive ad" because it is unavoidable for people walking up the stairs.

and center. That happened with the prominent role of a BMW Z28, which became a star in the James Bond movie *The World Is Not Enough.* The movie placement, in fact, was the car's launch vehicle.

Television programs have also gotten into the product placement game. Both the Coca-Cola brand and the Ford Motor brand have been embedded into the successful talent show *American Idol,* and the Target bulls-eye is frequently seen as part of the action sets and props on *Survivor.*

The greatest advantage of product placement is that it demonstrates product use in a natural setting ("natural" depending on the movie) by people who are celebrities. It's unexpected and, if it's an obvious use, may catch the audience when their resistance to advertising messages may be dialed down. It's also good for engaging the affections of other stakeholders, such as employees and dealers, particularly if the placement is supported with its own campaign.

The biggest problem is that the placement may not be noticed. There is so much going on in most movies that unless you can overtly call attention to the product, its appearance may not register. A more serious problem occurs when there is not a match between the product and the movie or its audience. Another concern is that advertisers have no idea whether the movie will be a success or failure as they negotiate a contract for the placement. If the movie is a dud, what does that do to the brand's image?

Another problem is an ethical one—when is a product placement inappropriate? For example, some pharmaceutical marketers have found that a product "plug" can be a way around the FDA's requirements on the disclosure of side effects. Public policy critics warn that it's not just drugs; the problem exists for weapons, alcohol, tobacco, and gambling, among other product categories that raise social concerns. Product placement has been called "stealth advertising," by the Writers Guild of America who argued that "millions of viewers are sometimes being sold products without their knowledge . . . and sold in violation of governmental regulations."[22] What do you think? Should there be more controls over product placement?

Video Games Marketers and media planners have been frustrated trying to reach young people with traditional ads on mainstream media. That has led to an increased focus on Internet advertising, but also on unusual media that are clearly the province of young people, such as video games. Now a global multibillion-dollar industry, the video game business is developing as a major new medium for advertisers to target 12- to 34-year-old males, although girls are getting into the act as well, and Wii is bringing in an older adult audience of both men and women with its sports and exercise programs. The iPad made the video game market mobile. Video games offer opportunities for advertising, but also for product placement.

Guitar Hero: Smash Hits is an Activision video game released in 2009. The game basically has the same content as the older versions of *Guitar Hero,* except that it only has songs

SHOWCASE

The Guitar Hero: Smash Hits video game was launched with a website and banners. The purpose of the site was to create hype for the game by allowing Guitar Hero fans to vote for their favorites songs from the game. Once the voting was over, one out of those 48 songs would become a legend by being voted the best song ever on Guitar Hero. After the vote, the message became:" Play the winners and all 48 nominees on one collection, Guitar Hero: Smash Hits." Similar to the category videos, the banners announced the Music Awards, the categories, and ended with an explosion graphic and opportunity to vote on the website and preorder the game.

Diego Contreras graduated from Southern Methodist University with a degree in creative advertising and business. He and his work were nominated for inclusion in this book by Professors Glenn Griffin and Patty Alvey.

released on previous *Guitar Hero* games that are supposed to be fan favorites and the most fun to play, so in that way *Smash Hits* is like the video game version of a "Greatest Hits" album. Diego Contreras, interactive art director at Crispin Porter + Bogusky explained the thinking behind an online promotion for *Smash Hits:* "We divided the songs in nine categories such as Best Scream, Best Shred (guitar solo), and Song of the Year. On the site, each category had a fun video with humorous voice-overs calling out the nominees, in the same fashion as the Oscars or the MTV Music Awards." Check out the site at *http://smashhits.guitarhero.com.*

Marketing communication opportunities will be mined both by creating online games as well as placing products within games. For example, games feature product placements for Puma athletic shoes, Nokia mobile phones, and Skittles candies, among others. Volkswagen of America bought a placement on Sony Computer Entertainment's *Gran Turismo 3* car-racing game. These questions remain: How are game players responding to ads in games and when does it make sense to incorporate branded content in games? Are some brands more acceptable or appropriate than others?

Branded Entertainment   Similar to product placement, the use of the media of entertainment to engage consumers with brands is referred to as **advertainment** or **branded entertainment.** In some cases, companies may produce films for the Internet where the brand is integrated into the storyline, such as an award-winning and ground-breaking series of mini-films for BMW, titled "The Hire." You may remember Geico's popular cavemen characters who became a television program.

We introduced the Altoids story in the last chapter. Primarily a print campaign in the past, Altoids has also moved with the times and created a video series of branded entertainment called "Brainstorm," created in conjunction with Fox Mobile Studios. Targeted at young, hip, urban audiences, these edgy videos are about an advertising agency as it tries to develop a new campaign for the curiously strong mint. Time will tell how successful this effort is as it puts the story behind Altoids on the small screen.

Similar to television programs with recurring episodes in a developing story, **webisodes** have created a new form of Web advertising. Fallon Worldwide created the original experiment in this new format for its client BMW. Known as the "BMW films," the series consisted of high-action mini-movies by well-known action movie directors (John Woo, Guy Ritchie, and Ang Lee), all of which featured various BMW models in starring roles. This practice has become particularly popular in China where increasingly marketers are building plots around their products, particularly lifestyle products that expose viewers to visions of how the newly rich should enjoy their healthy incomes.[23]

An example of branded entertainment is described in *The Inside Story* feature, which explains how an animated program was created for the male-grooming brand Axe. It took almost three years and more than 100 people in four different continents to produce the program titled *City Hunters*. The creative team was composed of award-winning screenwriters, novelists, and creatives under the direction of the Catmandu Branded Entertainment company. The integrated launch campaign featured a special edition package with *City Hunters* characters. The 360-degree promotional effort for the show included:

THE INSIDE STORY

The Animated Axe Effect in City Hunters

Sonia Scappaticci, *New Business Director, Catmandu Branded Entertainment*

Branded entertainment has become something of a buzzword. Perhaps because global marketers are beginning to understand that the 30-second spot is not the whole answer to creating brand positioning and value.

Unilever's Axe brand has consistently created adventurous advertising that has helped position it as the world's top male-grooming brand. When Unilever launched into the branded entertainment realm in Latin America, it was very specific in its goal: to create a TV show for the Axe brand that was fresh, attractive, relevant, and, most important of all, that would help the brand's positioning to go even further. It had to be unlike anything ever seen before. High ratings at any cost were not the objective, but rather creating a show that would be watched by the right target and would live up to the Axe brand standards.

The result was *City Hunters,* an animated show that launched on the Fox Network in Latin America. Because Axe is about the mating game, the show had to be created in a universe where sensuality and seduction were always in the air. Character designs where commissioned to legendary Italian comic artist Milo Manara, famous for his sexy female drawings. It is the story of a master, an apprentice, and a secret society called the "X Lodge," whose members are experts in the art of seduction. The main characters are Dr. Lynch, a retired bon vivant rumored to have been one of the inventors of the original Axe fragrance in the 1970s, and Axel, a street-smart young man who doesn't have trouble meeting women—just understanding them. According to the story, "The Axe Effect" is the compilation of more than 2,000 years of the study of women.

Until not so long ago, it would have been unimaginable to believe a network was going to pay the advertiser in order to co-produce a branded entertainment show. However, when we approached Fox with the *City Hunters* project, it was an instant match. For starters, the show was an animation, enabling it to be easily adaptable to different markets. Second, the format of the show made sense. The series of 10 short films could be aired in sets of two as a regular half-hour show, but could also be broadcast individually if needed.

In terms of results, *City Hunters* premiered as a weekly show in Argentina, where is was first aired, as Fox's number one show of the year (male viewers ages 18 to 24), reaching similar ratings as hit shows like *24* and *Nip/Tuck*. It was then aired in all of Latin America to similar top rating results. There are thousands of blog postings about the show. We also received a lot of media coverage from consumer magazines that index heavy with our target market, like *Rolling Stone* and *Playboy*. However, most importantly, the special-edition *City Hunters* packaging was a success and sold out immediately, even though it was priced higher that the regular product.

Sonia Scappaticci graduated from Michigan State University in 2000 with a B.A. in advertising. While at MSU, she was named one of the 25 Most Promising Minority Students in Communication by AAF and Advertising Age. She was nominated by Professor Carrie La Ferle.

- *Launch Parties* Celebrities and models depicted the show's characters.
- *Website* A dedicated website featured all of the show's info.
- *Text Messaging* Mating game tips were sent by the show's main character.
- *Interactive Billboards* Consumers could text a message that would change the image in the billboards.
- *In-Store Video Trailers* Special displays and flat screens were used to promote the show.
- *Sweepstakes* Prizes such as iPods were given away with a complete *City Hunters* season, merchandising, etc.

Mobile Marketing The phone is the classic example of how media are shape shifting. Telephones, of course, started as a hard-wired home and office device connected by phone lines. With the development of satellite-based and broadband telecommunication, the cell phone has become the all-purpose personal communication tool. **Smart phones,** such as BlackBerry, the iPhone, and Google's Nexus One, are high-end cell phones that have computing and photographic capabilities and can access the Internet, as well as do all of the old telephone functions. The iPad is a hybrid that has some of the capabilities of smart phones. It combines some of the features of a laptop or notebook computer, with an e-reader (books, newspapers, magazines), a video viewer, and a video game player.

The most versatile of all media, the smart cell phones provide music, movies, photography, video games, personal conversation, shopping, and access to all the news and information available on the Internet. The leaders in the development of these new tools have been Scandinavian countries and Japan; the United States is just catching up with these high-tech countries that have been using smart phones for years.

Messages on mobile phones usually look like small banners tucked into the corner of a Web page or text messages that can resemble spam. Mobile marketing agency AdMob and Google have designed more visual ads, some even showing maps with a retailer's location or apps that allow users to watch a commercial between levels in a video game.[24]

Cell phones also launched new product lines such as graphic faceplates and specialty ring tones. Female teenagers were leaders in exploring **text messaging (TM)** on their cell phones and teaching others (their parents, older siblings, teachers). **Instant messaging (IM),** in which two people chat via their computers, has been used more for business, as has the Bluetooth technology, which keeps businesspeople in touch with their companies and clients wherever they are.

In addition to becoming essential communication, information, and entertainment tools in most people lives, cell phones also open up new avenues for commercial communication. **Mobile marketing** is the strategy based on reaching people on the run via their cell phones. It refers to the use of wireless communication (WiFi) and GPS locational devices to reach people on the move with geotargeting capabilities. The Mobile Marketing Association (MMA) defines *mobile marketing* as the use of wireless media, primarily cellular phones and personal digital assistants (PDAs), such as RIM's BlackBerry. But mobile marketing is more than just cell phones and PDAs; it also includes laptop computers and even portable game consoles as vehicles that can deliver content and encourage direct response within a cross-media communication program. Mobile marketing includes instant messaging, video messages and downloads, and banner ads on these mobile devices. The MMA reported that U.S. advertising expenditures on mobile marketing increased by more than 20 percent in 2009 and predicted similar increases during the 2010s.[25]

It is possible, for example, to send text messages or voice mail with news about special sales to people's cell phones or PDAs that use wireless technology (such as Bluetooth) when these customers are in the vicinity of a favorite store or restaurant. If a cell phone user, for example, registers with a favorite store, then that store can contact the user when he or she is in the neighborhood. These calls can announce special deals or invite the customer in for a taste test or some other type of promotion. If the call is not an opt-in message, then it can be intrusive and irritating. The phones can also be used to contact a store. Pizza Hut and Papa John's customers, for example, can use their smart phones to place orders and, by dragging and dropping toppings onto virtual pizzas, they can create their own personal pizza. Domino's features a simulated photographic version on its website that can be customized.[26]

Although IM/TM advertising—primarily in the form of product notices—is big in Japan, it's still seen as an invasion of privacy in the United States. Even with the huge increase in texting, particularly by 18- to 24-year-olds (95 percent use texting), it's a puzzle for marketers because, as *Advertising Age* reported, "it is very much a permission-based channel of communication."[27]

As in other forms of advertising, the way to be less intrusive is to be more relevant and offer opt-in options. Teens may permit advertising if it offers them information they want, such as news about music, games, sports, cosmetics, and fashion. In Japan, a bar code can be sent for a free sample or some other promotion. Like a free coupon, it can be redeemed when a cashier scans the code.

The emerging area of mobile marketing helps companies connect with customers in new ways and new places.

Branded Apps   An *app,* short for *application,* is a piece of software than runs on your computer, cell phone, or social networking site. Thousands of apps are available that serve as links to other sites or provide some kind of immediate service, such as weather reports or current news. The number of iPhone apps now exceeds 100,000. The Google Droid operating system was launched with a Google Map app as a point of competitive advantage.

Marketers are particularly interested in **branded apps,** which are generally free but prominently linked to a brand. For example, REI has an app for snow reports. Zippo has a free virtual lighter for iPhones that looks and acts like a real lighter. You can jerk the phone to open or close the Zippo and a little button let's you light it with a simple flick. The point is strictly brand identification but there is a bit of utility in using a cell phone for that Zippo moment in concerts when people hold up their lights—in this case, images of a Zippo on their iPhones. It's almost a toy but the engagement with the brand has made the Zippo app one of the more popular ones.[28]

Other apps offer more utility. Banks, for example, let you check balances, pay bills, make transfers, and locate branches—and with the GPS navigation capability in some smart phones, the app can even plot a route. A Starbucks app features a Starbucks location finder. Kraft's app, iFood Assistant, which is one of the few that comes with a price tag, provides recipes, cooking instruction videos, meal shopping lists, and store locators. CNN also offers a functional app that provides a 24-hour news feed with video for a one-time fee of $1.99.

The launch of Apple's App Store propelled the development of thousands of branded apps. The concept is showcased in some of Apple and AT&T's full-page ads in publications that show the iPhone with a suite of apps accompanied by callouts that explain what the apps do. You can check out the App Store at *www.apple.com/iphone/apps-for-iphone/phone.*

Other New Media   We have said before that media needs creative ideas just as much as the creative side does. There is a continual search for a novel way to get consumers engaged with a brand.

As we mentioned in the discussion of mobile marketing, **streaming videos** from professional media companies—including television programs and movies—are joining homemade creations like those from YouTube and appear not only on personal computers, but also on smart phones, such as iPhones. Nintendo is now adding Netflix as streaming video to its Wii video game console.[29] These creations can be as engaging as anything on conventional television. For example, CBS has created a cell phone app video game of *America's Next Top Model* where viewers can play with animated versions of the show, pick dresses, and experiment with the stars' makeup. (See it at *http://topmodel.pressokentertainment.com.*) Skype software has continued to innovate with international Internet-based phone service.

Another innovation using streaming video is the **viral video.** Technology has made it possible for interesting videos from a variety of sources (ads, films, YouTube) to be sent from one friend to another in a vast network of personal connections. *Advertising Age* keeps track of the most watched viral videos, such as the various episodes in the Mac vs. Microsoft battle of operating systems. *AdAge* reports that one of the more entertaining videos is for an unlikely company name Microbilt, which provides a risk management service for small and medium businesses. Rhett & Link is a team of YouTubers who created a microsite, *www.ilovelocalcommercials.com,* to promote themselves as ad creators. They sponsored a contest to get nominations for other local businesses who would then win equally engaging videos created by this geek team. Check out the site to see their self-promotion, as well as some of their creations, all of which have been distributed as viral videos.[30]

But innovation isn't focused only on digital forms. A YouTube video that captured a lot of attention showed tiny banners on flies that flitted around with their miniscule billboards—probably the ultimate in guerilla marketing. This Big Media Idea came from the German agency Jung von Matt. Check it out at *www.youtube.com/watch?v=nVxTAz67SAI.*

Flies are the most unlikely of all media, but they were enlisted by German publisher Eichborn as a form of flying banners at the annual Frankfurt Book Fair.

Other new media include ads by Visa on stadium trays used at the Super Bowl concession stands, opening the door for a whole new medium.[31] Here's a review of the advantages and limitations of some of the new and nontraditional media we've discussed in this chapter.

Nontraditional Media Advantages and Limitations

Medium	Advantages	Limitations
Packaging	Stimulates point-of-purchase decision making Last ad a potential customer sees In-home is brand reminder on shelf Billboarding effect can dominate shelf Reinforces brand advertising Delivers product information Packaging costs are required, conveying promotional message is a bonus	Cluttered environment Shelf space may be limited Can get inconvenient placement—such as bottom shelf Limited space needs simple message Needs system for ROI evaluation
Guerilla Marketing	Engages people at unexpected places Highly involved Creates high level of excitement Generates buzz	Small reach Needs publicity
Product Placement	Harder to dismiss as advertising Opportunity for high visibility in natural setting Opportunity for brand reminder	May be overlooked Vehicle may not match the brand's positioning Not as much control over brand's presentation Hard to control targeting Hard to measure effectiveness
Branded Entertainment	The program or game is a vehicle for the brand Can reach new-media savvy audiences Harder to dismiss than advertising Takes advantage of power of film and engaging storylines More control over brand presentation than product placement More time to develop brand personality Opportunity for repetition	Viewers may resent the commercialization of programs/games Needs marketing support Effectiveness measures are still in development
Mobile Marketing	Goes everywhere the target goes Opportunity for location-based message The most personal of all media—also the most social Reaches the technologically savvy	Small screen Unwanted messages can be irritating Hard to type messages on small keyboard Effectiveness measures are still in development Needs technological literacy
Branded Apps	Opportunity for continuing brand contact Engages attention Links social media and their users to brands Provides utility functions for brands Strictly opt-in	Started free, but now some are charging which creates irritation On cell phone, limited by small screen size Opportunity for tracking use

Looking Ahead

We started out by noting that the media environment is going through lots of shifts and we ended by detailing some of those changes. With this brief introduction to the basics of marketing communication media, as well as the new and nontraditional forms of media, we turn now in the next chapter to a review of traditional media—print, outdoor, and broadcast—and the characteristics that make them different from other media forms.

IT'S A WRAP

Axe Cleans Up

As you read throughout this chapter, reaching consumers in a complex and rapidly changing media environment challenges advertisers to think creatively. Those who will be successful in advertising break through the clutter and deliver messages that are relevant to the consumer. The Axe campaigns you read about in the case opener, "How Dirty Boys Get Clean" and "Axe Detailer: The Manly Shower Tool," demonstrate how marketing contributed to making Axe the top male shower brand in the United States.

After the Detailer was introduced, sales exceeded expectations. For example, the number of units sold per Walmart store per week more than doubled that of other shower gel products. The campaign was so successful, many stores had trouble keeping Axe Shower Gel on the shelves. Share of market increased as well, peaking with the communication activity. Tracking studies indicated that the Detailer campaign achieved the goals of communicating the correct branding and teaching something about the product.

Demonstrating another way to clean up, Axe has won many advertising awards, including an Effie and two Bronze Lions from the Cannes International Advertising Festival.

If you read "The Animated Axe Effect in *City Hunters*" in this chapter you realized that Axe is a global brand. You read about Axe's efforts to create branded entertainment. Other award-winning work is occurring across the globe. Mindshare won "best localization" for its multinational work at the Valencia Festival of Media in Spain for a campaign that centered around the concept that "men should be as irresistible as chocolate" to women. To give you an idea about how this worked, French girls gave guys "nibbles and licks" on a social networking site, while in Belgium, luxury chocolate love tokens were distributed. Portuguese guys were coaxed into buying chocolate, seducing girls, and possibly winning a visit to the Chocolate Pleasure Mansion. These sparkling efforts show the extent to which creative ideas can be applied to a variety of media and contexts, all to achieve the same effect—to sell the product.

Key Points Summary

1. **How do media work in marketing communication and how is the industry organized?** Media send and return messages to and from the company or brand and its customers—in other words, they make connections. Media deliver messages and also offer opportunities for interaction; they also touch emotions, engage minds, and build brand relationships. Media has evolved technologically from print to broadcasting and now the Internet. Marketing communication is evolving to include more Internet-based media. Types of media include mass and niche media, as well as addressable, interactive, and measured media. Key players both sell and buy media space and time; they include media salespeople and reps, media researchers, media planners, and media buyers.

2. **How would you describe the key strategic media concepts?** A media plan, which is prepared by a media planner, is a document that identifies the media to be used to deliver an advertising message to a targeted audience both locally and nationally. A media mix is the way various types of media are strategically combined in an advertising plan. Reach is the percentage of the media audience exposed at least once to the advertiser's message during a specific time frame, and frequency is the number of times a person is exposed to the advertisement.

3. **Why and how is the media landscape changing?** More media are available to today's audience as the concept of media channels is redefined to mean contact points and touch points, which include experiences, word of mouth, viral communication, and customer service, in addition to traditional media. Media use is changing with consumers spending a lot more time with media and multitasking more as they are engaged with media. As media have become more social, people's personal lives have gone public and global is the new local. Media forms are also changing with new ways to reach people being included in marketing communication plans, such as packaging, product placement, guerilla marketing, video games, branded entertainment, mobile marketing, branded apps, and a variety of other new media.

Words of Wisdom: Recommended Reading

Azzaro, Marian, *Strategic Media Decisions,* 2nd ed., Chicago: The Copy Workshop, 2008.

Davis, Scott, and Philip Kotler, *The Shift: The Transformation of Today's Marketers into Tomorrow's Growth Leaders,* San Francisco CA: John Wiley & Sons, 2009.

Garfield, Bob, *The Chaos Scenario,* Nashville, TN: Stielstra Publishing, 2009.

McConnell, Ben, and Jackie Huba, *Citizen Marketers: When People Are the Message,* Chicago: Kaplan Publishing, 2007.

Warner, Charles, and Joseph Buchman, *Media Selling: Broadcast, Cable, Print, and Interactive,* Ames: Iowa State Press, 2004.

Key Terms

addressable media, p. 327
advertisement, p. 344
branded apps, p. 347
branded entertainment, p. 344
broadcasting media, p. 327
brokers, p. 332
circulation, p. 335
contact points, p. 337
convergence, p. 328
critical touchpoint
   (CTP), p. 338
cross-media, p. 332
customer service, p. 340
engagement, p. 328

experiential marketing, p. 338
exposure, p. 335
frequency, p. 335
gross impressions, p. 335
guerilla marketing, p. 342
impression, p. 335
instant messaging (IM), p. 346
interactivity, p. 328
intrusiveness, p. 336
mass media, p. 327
measured media, p. 327
media, p. 326
media buyer, p. 332
media mix, p. 334

media plan, p. 332
media planners, p. 332
media planning, p. 332
media reps, p. 332
media researchers, p. 332
media salespeople, p. 331
media vehicle, p. 327
mobile marketing, p. 346
multichannel, p. 332
multiplatform, p. 334
niche media, p. 327
packaging, p. 338
personalization, p. 328
product placement, p. 342

ratings, p. 335
ratings points, p. 335
reach, p. 335
relationship marketing, p. 337
sales kits, p. 331
share of audience, p. 335
smart phones, p. 345
streaming video, p. 347
text messaging (TM), p. 346
touch point, p. 338
viral marketing, p. 340
viral video, p. 347
webisode, p. 344
word-of-mouth, p. 329

Review Questions

1. Trace the evolution of media forms and explain how the new Digital Era is different from previous media environments.

2. Explain the roles of media salespeople, media planners, media buyers, and media researchers.

3. What is a media mix and how does the mix differ for an IMC campaign?

4. What is the difference between reach and frequency?

5. What is the difference between media channels, contact points, and touch points?

6. In what ways are consumer media patterns changing and how does that affect marketing communication.

7. Why have product placement, guerilla marketing, and branded entertainment become popular?

Discussion Questions

1. You are the media planner for an agency handling a small chain of upscale furniture outlets in a top-50 market that concentrates most of its advertising in the Sunday supplement of the local newspaper. The owner is interested in using new media to reach its upscale target market. What would be your recommendations to the furniture store owner?

2. Since his freshman year in college, Phil Dawson, an advertising major, has waited tables at Alfredo's, a small family-operated restaurant featuring excellent Italian food and an intimate atmosphere. The restaurant has relied on its Yellow Pages ads to generate business. The owner asks Phil for advice on what other contact points are important and how he

should use them in his admittedly low-budget marketing communication plan. What should Phil recommend?

3. ***Three-Minute Debate*** This chapter makes the argument that traditional advertising is declining in importance. A classmate argues that these media are still the most important and largest item in most marketing communication plans. If you are the marketing manager for the Segway personal transportation device, would you devote the largest percentage of your budget to traditional or nontraditional media? Take one side or the other of this argument and work with a small group of your classmates to argue your point of view.

Take-Home Projects

1. *Portfolio Project* Collect a set of three traditional media ads that also have online versions. Compare the original with the online version and analyze the differences. What does the traditional medium offer that is not available online, and what does the online version add to the offerings of the original medium.

   Write a one- or two-page report on how these vehicles might better position themselves as advertising media. What are their strengths and how should they position themselves in a competitive media marketplace?

2. *Mini-Case Analysis* Reread the Axe story at the beginning of this chapter. What was the problem this brand faced and how did that affect the media planning? What were the objectives of both the initial campaign and its follow-up? What was the Big Idea that drove the second campaign and how did that affect the media mix. Do you think this effort was driven by reach or frequency? Considering all of the new media reviewed in this chapter, what other media might Axe use in the next year of this campaign?

Team Project: The BrandRevive Campaign

For your BrandRevive campaign, revisit the research your team did on your brand's category or market and, specifically on the brand's target customer. What did you find out about their media use?

- What more do you need to know in order to develop a comprehensive media plan? What other research would be useful?
- From what you found out in your consumer research, what traditional media do you think are important to deliver this brand's message?

- How many different contact points can you identify for this brand? What are its touch points, the critical experiential points of contact that really affect people's attitudes and feelings about the brand?
- What nontraditional media do you think would be useful? In particular, how can you better engage your brand's customers with the brand?

Present and explain your analysis in a two-page document and a PowerPoint presentation that is no longer than three slides.

Hands-On Case

The Century Council

Read the Century Council case in the Appendix before coming to class.

1. Explain the concepts of reach and frequency in relation to The Stupid Drink Campaign. How did the team attempt to reach their target consumer at the right moment?

2. Which element of The Stupid Drink media plan do you believe would be most impactful on your campus? Why? Which would be least impactful? Why?

3. If you were asked to execute The Stupid Drink campaign on your campus, what advertising medium might you add to strengthen the plan? Why?

Traditional Media

youdontknowquack.com

NAD0938

It's a Winner

Title:	Client:	Agency:	Awards:
"You Don't Know Quack"	American Family Life Assurance Company	Zimmerman Agency of Tallahassee, Florida; previously Linda Kaplan Thaler	Gold Effie; selected by online voters, Aflac duck icon enshrined on Madison Avenue's Advertising Walk of Fame

CHAPTER KEY POINTS

1. What key points should marketers know to make effective decisions about advertising in newspapers and magazines?
2. What factors do marketers consider when making out-of-home media advertising decisions?
3. How do radio and television work as marketing communication media?
4. How do marketers use movies and other video formats for marketing communication?

Quacking through Clutter

Geico. Allstate. Nationwide. Met Life. Many insurance companies are begging for your attention. You've probably never heard of the American Family Life Assurance Co., nor are you likely to be familiar with its primary service: supplemental workplace medical insurance, a type of insurance that is used by people to help cover the many loopholes and deductibles in their primary insurance coverage.

Then again, if you are like 94 percent of U.S. consumers, maybe you *have* heard of the company. In its advertising, it calls itself "Aflac."

Introduced in 2000, the long-running Aflac campaign featuring the quacking duck was the brainchild of the New York agency that bears its owner's name, Linda Kaplan Thaler. Almost all ads feature a white duck desperately screaming "Aflac!" at unsuspecting people who presumably need supplemental insurance. Alas, the duck's audience never quite seems to hear him. Most of the ads contain a fair amount of slapstick, usually at the expense of the duck, whose exasperated-sounding voice originates with former *Saturday Night Live* cast member Gilbert Gottfried.

The campaign has been enormously successful. Since its inception, brand name awareness increased from 12 percent to more than 90 percent. *Ad Age* has named a commercial featuring the duck as one of the most recalled ads in the country. Forbes named Aflac one of the Top 25 Power Brands in the United States in 2004. By 2004, sales of the multibillion-dollar corporation had increased by 20 percent.

What a bargain. By one account, Aflac spent a poultry, scratch that, paltry sum of $45 million on television advertising annually. Compare that to McDonald's $680 million annual ad budget, which supports Ronald McDonald, or Energizer, whose company has plunked down about $1 billion on its Bunny advertising during the past 35 years. So, the duck has been quite a bargain in terms of getting attention.

The spokesfowl is not without his problems, however. It seems that the duck gets all the attention. Everyone knows it as an advertising icon, but customers don't know what it sells. The next generation of ducky advertising is addressing that very problem.

Aflac has switched agencies to Zimmerman in Tallahassee, Florida, part of the Omnicom Group, who is building on the brand's identity by using the duck to transform brand identification into brand education. The agency is using both new and traditional media. If you looked, you would have seen the duck on billboards in Times Square along with this odd Web address: *youdontknowquack.com*. The multimedia campaign featured newspaper ads and television commercials during the Winter Olympics to direct people to another Web address for more information. It also featured full-page ads in newspapers, such as the *Wall Street Journal*.

The ad was a teaser ad in that the sponsor was unidentified (unless the duck gave it away). The ad relied on reader curiosity to get people to visit the Aflac site, which opened with a quiz that tested common knowledge. On television the announcer says, "If all you know about us is . . ." when he's interrupted by the duck quacking, "Aflac!" The announcer then continues, ". . . then you don't know quack. To find out all the ways Aflac's got you covered, visit *knowquack.com*."

The efforts to build the brand continue with variety of 45 elements in addition to the traditional print, outdoor, and TV already mentioned, including a Facebook and YouTube presence, trivia questions on TV, a line of duck clothing, a Quack energy drink, video clips called "duckumentaries," commercials on NBC's Winter Olympics, and a NASCAR race car showing the duck's image and using the "You Don't Know Quack" theme.

Turn to the *It's a Wrap* section at the end of the chapter to learn more about how this effective campaign got consumers to know more about Aflac than quack.

Sources: *Aflac Corporate Citizenship Report 2009*, www.aflac.com/us/en/docs/investors/CSRReport.pdf; Susan Vranica, "Creativity on the Cheap: Aflac Duck's Paddle to Stardom," the *Wall Street Journal*, July 30, 2004; Stuart Elliott, "Not Daffy or Donald, But Still Aflac's Rising Star," the *New York Times*, April 22, 2009, www.nytimes.com; Stuart Elliott, "Aflac Is Leaving Its Agency, and Taking the Duck," the *New York Times*, January 22, 2010, www.nytimes.com; Rupal Parekh, "Brand Awareness Was Only Half the Battle for Aflac," http://adage.com, June 22, 2009; James Wisdom, "Case Study: A Marketing Icon's Facebook Journey," October 13, 2009, imediaconnection.com; Noreen O'Leary, "Aflac Spots 'Quack' Wise," January 22, 2010, www.adweek.com; "Aflac Case Study," March 3, 2010, kaplanthaler.com.

The Aflac campaign has been successful because of its use of television to dramatize a funny situation where the Aflac duck tries to get the attention of people needing supplemental insurance. More recently it has used print and outdoor advertising with strong duck graphics to announce a new strategy that proclaims "You Don't Know Quack" about what Aflac offers. These teaser ads are designed to drive traffic to the website where you can find everything you need to know about supplemental insurance.

In this chapter, we explore the uses, structure, audiences, and advantages and disadvantages of traditional media such as print, which includes newspapers and magazines; out-of-home media; and finally broadcast media, which includes radio and television. We also review film and video formats that are used in campaigns.

WHAT ARE THE KEY PRINT MEDIA CHARACTERISTICS?

Print media vehicles include newspapers, magazines, brochures, and other printed surfaces, such as posters and outdoor boards. Although it is true that magazines and newspapers, especially, have expanded their message delivery online, billions of dollars are still spent on traditional print media. That is what this section is all about.

Principle
Print media generally provide more information, rich imagery, and a longer message life than other media forms.

In terms of impact, print media generally provide more information, rich imagery, and a longer message life than broadcast media. It's an information-rich environment so, in terms of our Facets of Effects Model, print media are often used to generate cognitive responses. If you want someone to read and understand something new, then a newspaper or magazine ad is useful because readers can take as much time as they need.

Consumers also find that reading a print publication is more flexible than watching or listening to broadcast because they can stop and reread, read sections out of order, or move through the publication at their own speed and on their own time. They can also save it and reread. Because the print message format is less fleeting than broadcast and more concrete, people tend to spend more time with print and absorb its messages more carefully. Print can be highly engaging when targeted toward audiences that have a special interest in the publication's content, such as women and women's magazines.

Print has the ability to engage more of the senses than other media because it can be both tactile (different types of paper and other surfaces) and aural (smell). Magazines, for example, have long offered scratch 'n' sniff ads, particularly for perfume, and that's becoming more common in newspapers. Newspapers have announced the availability of aromatic ads, so the smell of coffee may waft from your morning newspaper sometime soon.

Newspaper Basics

Newspapers' primary function is to carry news, which means that marketers with news to announce, such as a special sale or new product, may find newspapers to be a comfortable environment. Studies have consistently found that people consider many ads—that is, commercial information—to be news, too, and they read newspapers as much for the ads as they do for the news stories.

Principle
A basic principle of newspaper publishing is that people read newspapers as much for the ads as they do for the news stories.

Marketers trying to reach a local market use newspapers because most newspapers (other than *USA Today* and the *Wall Street Journal)* are identified by the geography of the city or region they serve. The *New York Times* serves the New York region, but it also has a national circulation, particularly for its Sunday edition. Local papers are struggling to survive but their readers still value them for their coverage of local politics, education, crime, sports stories, local events, church news, and local people features.

Retailers like to place ads and press releases in daily newspapers because their **lead time** (the advance time needed to produce a publication) is short—just a few days. Food stores, for example, can change offers and pricing quickly depending on product availability. Also, because most newspapers are local, retailers aren't paying to reach people who live outside their shopping area.

Newspapers can be categorized according to their publication frequency, such as dailies, weeklies, and Sunday editions. In addition, business and organizational newspapers are available to trade and membership groups.

Although newspapers go to a mass audience, they offer **market selectivity,** which allows them to target specific consumer groups. Examples of market selectivity are special-interest newspapers (e.g., for coin collectors); ethnic editions, such as *El Nuevo Herald;* special-interest sections (business, sports, lifestyle); and advertising inserts delivered only to particular zip codes or zones. Newspapers also exist for special-interest groups, religious denominations, political affiliations, labor unions, and professional and fraternal organizations. For example, *Stars & Stripes* is the newspaper read by millions of military personnel. The *Wall Street Journal* and the *Financial Times* are considered specialty newspapers because they concentrate on financial business.

The Newspaper Industry A $59 billion industry, newspapers remain an important medium, although newspaper readership has been declining for years, particularly among young people. Complicating the readership problem, the recession of the late 2000s brought double-digit percentage declines in advertising that caused a rash of newspaper closures.

A beautifully designed illustration using painted hands illustrates the idea of worldwide coverage for telecom giant AT&T.

Newspapers are third to television in terms of advertising revenue. The two largest U.S. newspapers, *USA Today* and the *Wall Street Journal,* continue to be leaders, although circulation has eroded for them, as well as for many local newspapers. To balance the budget, Dow Jones, the owner of the *Wall Street Journal,* has sold six newspapers, cut *WSJ* staff and costs, including reducing the page size, and increased its emphasis on its other media and Internet publishing opportunities to reduce its dependence on print ad revenue. The *WSJ,* however, is one of few newspapers to gain circulation during the recession.[1] *USA Today* reported a 17 percent drop in circulation in 2009, which threatens its number one position. The biggest problem it faces is a travel slump, which has hurt *USA Today's* hotel circulation.

Other sources of revenue besides advertising include reader subscriptions and single-copy sales at newsstands. Circulation is the primary way newspapers' reach is measured and compared with the reach of other media. *USA Today's* circulation is different from other daily newspapers in that it is targeted to travelers and its primary sales consist of single-copy sales and bulk sales to hotels, rather than subscriptions. Subscriptions, however, have been a problem as readers have migrated to online versions and dropped their print subscriptions.

Newspapers are chasing revenue in a number of new areas, in addition to online sales. The *New York Times,* for example, sells a variety of classy items in its *New York Times* store. The merchandise is similar to that found in museum stores, such as art glass, music boxes, and old ship models. It has also started the *New York Times* Knowledge Network and offers a variety of online courses for personal and career development.

A more serious change was announced by the *Dallas Morning News* (*DMN*). The changes revolved around a reorganization that would see section editors (sports, entertainment, real estate, automotive, travel, among others) reporting to sales mangers. Die-hard journalists were horrified at the thought of the editorial side being merged with advertising because of implications for news objectivity and independence. The *DMN* executives, however saw it as a way to grow the business by better meeting advertisers' business development needs.[2]

Newspaper Ad Sales   Mirroring the circulation patterns, newspaper advertising can be described as national or local (retail), as well as classified and online. Newspaper advertising is sold based on the size of the ad space and the newspaper's circulation. The charges are published on a **rate card,** which is a list of the costs for advertising space and the discounts given to local advertisers and advertisers who make volume buys. National advertisers pay a higher rate.

Most advertising sales are handled locally by the sales staff of the newspaper; however, newspaper representatives (called "reps") sell space for many different newspapers. This saves an advertiser or its agency from the need to make a multitude of buys to run a national or regional campaign in newspapers. The system is known as **one-order, one-bill.** The Newspaper National Network (*www.nnnlp.com*) is a partnership of newspaper companies that place ads in some 9,000 newspapers. Google has also gotten into this business, allowing advertisers to buy ads in daily newspapers through its website.

Until the 1980s national advertisers shied away from using newspapers, not only because of the buying problem, but also because each paper had its own peculiar size guidelines for ads, making it difficult to prepare one ad that would fit every newspaper. In the early 1980s, the American Newspaper Publishers Association and the Newspaper Advertising Bureau introduced the **standard advertising unit (SAU)** system to solve this problem. The latest version of the SAU makes it possible for newspapers to offer advertisers a great deal of choice within a standard format. An advertiser can select one of the 56 standard ad sizes and be assured that its ad will work in every newspaper in the country.

Another alternative that allows national advertisers to pay the local rate is cooperative (co-op) advertising with a local retailer. **Co-op advertising** is an arrangement between the advertiser and the retailer whereby the retailer buys the ad and the manufacturer pays half—or a portion depending on the amount of space the manufacturer's brand occupies.

Types of Newspaper Advertising   Three types of advertising are found within the local newspaper: retail/display, classified, and supplements—and most of these are found online, as well as in the print form of the newspaper.

- *Display* The dominant form of newspaper advertising is **display advertising.** Display ads, such as the Aflac ads, can be any size and can be placed anywhere in the newspaper except

the editorial page. The *Wall Street Journal* made headlines in late 2006 when it announced it would add a "jewel-box" ad space to the lower right corner of its front page (think an ad the size of a CD case). Display ads can even be found in the classified section. Display advertising is further divided into two subcategories: *local (retail)* and *national (brand).* Advertisers who don't care where their display ads run in the newspaper pay the **run-of-paper (ROP) rate**. If they want more choice over the placement, they can pay the **preferred-position rate**, which lets them select sections in which the ad will appear.

These are examples of business-to-business newspaper display ads for Aflac that ran in the *Wall Street Journal.* They address business managers with a message about making the supplemental insurance available to their employees.

- *Classified* Two types of **classified advertising** include advertising by individuals to sell their personal goods and advertising by local businesses. These ads are arranged according to their interest to readers, such as "Help Wanted" and "Real Estate for Sale." Classified ads have represented approximately 40 percent of total newspaper advertising revenue in the past, but local online services, such as Craigslist, have almost destroyed newspaper classified advertising. That has created a huge bottom-line problem for local newspapers.

- *Supplements* Newspaper **supplements** are magazine-style publications inserted into a newspaper, especially in the Sunday edition, that are either syndicated nationally or prepared locally. Syndicated supplements, such as *Parade* and *USA Weekend,* are provided by an independent publisher that sells its publications to newspapers throughout the country. A **freestanding insert (FSI)** is the set of advertisements, such as the grocery ads, that are inserted into the newspaper. These preprinted advertisements range in size from a single page to more than 30 pages and may be in black and white or full color. This material is often printed elsewhere and then delivered to the newspaper. Newspapers charge the advertiser a fee for inserting a supplement. FSI advertising is growing in popularity with retail advertisers for three reasons: (1) it allows greater control over the reproduction quality of the advertisement, (2) it commands more attention than just another ad in the paper, and (3) advertisers can place FSIs in certain newspapers that are delivered to certain neighborhoods, or even certain people.

Newspaper Readership Measurement   Nearly half of all adults receive home delivery of a Sunday or weekday newspaper; delivery levels are highest in small- and medium-sized cities and lowest in rural locations and larger metropolitan areas. Historically, newspaper reading tends to be highest among older people and people with a higher educational and income level. It is lowest among people in their late teens and early twenties and among lower education and lower income groups.

Newspaper readership tends to be selective, with a greater percentage reading specific sections rather than the whole paper. Business and professional newspapers, such as *Ad Age,* have particularly high readership levels. Newspapers measure their audiences in two ways: circulation and readership. Readership is always a larger number than circulation because when a paper is delivered to a home or office, it is often read by more than one person. This type of information facilitates the media planner's ability to match a certain newspaper's readership with the target audience. Agencies obtain objective measures of newspaper circulation and readership by subscribing to one or both of the following auditing companies:

- *The Audit Bureau of Circulations (ABC)* The ABC is an independent auditing group that represents advertisers, agencies, and publishers. This group verifies statements about newspaper *circulation* and provides a detailed analysis of the newspaper by state, town, and county. ABC members include only paid-circulation newspapers and magazines.
- *Simmons-Scarborough* Simmons-Scarborough Syndicated Research Associates provides a syndicated study that annually measures *readership* profiles in approximately 70 of the nation's largest cities. The study covers readership of a single issue and the estimated unduplicated readers for a series of issues.

Magazine Basics

The more than 6,000 magazines published in the United States appeal to every possible interest. Most magazines aim at niche markets with a focus on a particular hobby, sport, age group, business category, and profession. These special-interest publications generally have small circulations but there are exceptions. The number-one magazine in terms of circulation is *AARP, The Magazine,* which is sent free to anyone over age 50.

The Magazine Publishers Association (MPA) estimates that more than 90 percent of all American adults read at least one magazine per month, and the average reader spends 44 minutes reading each issue. Furthermore, 80 percent of these readers consider magazine advertising "helpful as a buying guide." In general, media planners know that people tend to pay more attention to magazine advertising and stories, including publicity articles, than to television because they are concentrating more on the medium and the messages are generally more relevant to their interests. Readers also spend more time reading a magazine than they do reading a newspaper, so there is a better opportunity to provide in-depth information.

Quality of reproduction is one of the biggest strengths of magazines. It allows the advertiser's products and brand image to be presented in a format superior to the quality of newspapers. Food companies especially like the ability to make their products look appetizing.

Health of the Magazine Industry   The magazine industry hasn't suffered as much from the recession and changing media environment as newspapers have. Although single-copy sales were down at the end of 2009, these sales make up a small slice (2 percent) of magazine circulation. More importantly, circulation from subscriptions was basically stable—down only 1 percent.[3] The "Power of Print" ad by a group of magazine publishers compares the lasting quality of print with the ephemeral nature of Web content.[4]

Despite the high risks associated with the magazine business, new publications continue to emerge, especially those that target business markets and

Principle
Readership is always larger than circulation because a newspaper is often read by more than one person.

Principle
People spend more time with magazines because the ads and articles usually are more relevant to their interests.

In these ⬛ times of ours, you might think that ⬛ don't read magazines. That the overwhelming ⬛ of the online world has swept them right out of ⬛ . But it's not true at all. From through their ⬛ years, folks are reading magazines ⬛ than they were just a few years ago. Sure, there's a ⬛ being spent online. But there's also a lot of ⬛ being spent on magazines, with nearly 300 million paid subscriptions.

MAGAZINES
The Power of Print®

This campaign by a group of magazine publishers makes the case that magazines are an effective advertising medium even in the Age of the Internet.

growing market segments such as computer users, skateboarders, and scrapbookers. But the greatest growth area is in online magazines, called **zines,** and the online versions of traditional printed magazines. For the Oscars, for example, *People* magazine (*www.people.com*), *Vanity Fair* (*www.vanityfair.com*), and *Entertainment Weekly* (*www.ew.com*) dedicated sections of their websites to this event, piggybacking on the immense viewership—second only to the Super Bowl—the Oscars capture.

Given the growth of zines, magazines are trying to figure out their new future with both hard and online copies. One of the most interesting dilemmas is *Wired* magazine, the publication that has been on the cutting edge for the digital community. Owned by Conde Nast, it's a small-circulation publication at the giant magazine publisher; its

Advertisers look at the audience, geographic coverage, demographics, and editorial diversity of magazines as criteria for using them in a media plan.

website, however, is the most popular of all Conde Nast sites. So issues about the digital future sometimes read like arguments for the print magazine's future. The question the editors debate is this: What happens to the website if Conde Nast decides to eliminate the print version?[5]

Meredith, the giant publisher of magazines such as *Better Homes & Gardens* and *Ladies Home Journal,* is searching for new revenue with custom publishing, e-mail, social media, and mobile campaigns for major marketers who are also its advertisers. For Kraft Foods Meredith publishes Spanish-language magazines, designs Kraft's website, and coordinates weekly e-mail blasts that feature recipe ideas. It also built Kraft's iFood Assistant, an app for cell phones that includes recipes, how-to videos, and shopping lists.[6]

Types of Magazines   The focus of audience interest is the main factor used when classifying magazines. The two main types of audiences that magazines target are consumer and business audiences. **Consumer magazines** are directed at people who buy products for personal consumption. Examples are *Newsweek, Time,* and *People,* which are general-interest publications. However, the largest growth area for consumer magazines is for special-interest publications aimed at narrow or niche audiences.

Business magazines target business readers; they include the following types of publications:

- *Trade magazines* aimed at retailers, wholesalers, and other distributors; *Chain Store Age* is an example.
- *Industrial magazines* aimed at manufacturers; an example is *Concrete Construction*.
- *Professional magazines* aimed at physicians, lawyers, and other professionals; *National Law Review* targets lawyers, and *MediaWeek* targets advertising media planners and buyers.
- *Farm magazines* aimed at those working in agriculture; *Farm Journal* and *Feed and Grain* are examples.
- *Corporate publications* are produced by companies for their customers and other stakeholders. Airline magazines are a good example.

Business magazines are also classified as vertical or horizontal publications. A **vertical publication** presents stories and information about an entire industry. *Women's Wear Daily,* for example, discusses the production, marketing, and distribution of women's fashions. A **horizontal publication** deals with a business function that cuts across industries, such as *Direct Marketing*. In terms of vehicle selection, a number of factors influence how media planners fit magazines into their media mix:

- *Geography* Many magazines have a national audience, but some cater to certain sections or regions of the country or have regional editions. The area covered may be as small as a city (*Los Angeles Magazine* and *Boston Magazine*) or as large as several contiguous states (the

Principle

If you want to start a successful magazine, create a special-interest publication aimed at a narrow or niche audience.

southwestern edition of *Southern Living Magazine*). Geographic editions help encourage local retail support by listing the names of local distributors in the advertisements. Most national magazines also offer a zone edition that carries different ads and perhaps different stories, depending on the region of the country.

- *Demographics* Demographic editions group subscribers according to age, income, occupation, and other classifications. Some magazines for example, publish a special "ZIP" edition for upper-income homes sent to subscribers who live in specific zip codes and who typically share common demographic traits, primarily based on income. *Newsweek* offers a college edition, and *Time* sends special editions to students, business executives, doctors, and business managers.
- *Editorial Content* Each magazine emphasizes a certain type of editorial content. The most widely used categories are general editorial (*Reader's Digest*), women's (*Family Circle*), shelter (*House Beautiful*), business (*Forbes*), and special interest (*Ski*).
- *Physical Characteristics* Media planners and buyers need to know the physical characteristics of a magazine because ads containing various elements of words and pictures require a different amount of space. The most common magazine page sizes are 8 1/2 × 11 inches and 6 × 9 inches. Ads running in *Reader's Digest,* which is a 6 × 9 format, allow for fewer visuals and little copy.
- *Ownership* Some magazines are owned by publishing companies (*Glamour, Brides, Vanity Fair,* and *The New Yorker* are owned by Condé Nast), and some are published by organizations such as AARP. Some magazines are published by consumer companies, such as Kraft's *Food & Family,* that sell ads and carry stories and ads for many of their own products.
- *Distribution and Circulation* Magazine revenues come from advertising, subscriptions, and single-copy sales. According to the MPA, advertising in general contributes 55 percent of magazine revenue and circulation is 45 percent (subscriptions 32 percent; single-copy sales 13 percent).[7]

Controlled versus Uncontrolled Circulation   **Traditional delivery,** called **controlled circulation,** is through newsstand purchases or home delivery via the U.S. Postal Service. These are measured media and their circulation or sales can be determined. **Nontraditional delivery,** referred to as **uncontrolled circulation,** means that the magazine is distributed free to specific audiences. Generally speaking, uncontrolled (free) circulation magazines have lower readership and therefore also lower ad costs. They may also be sponsored by a company and sent to key stakeholders as part of a corporate communication program. In addition to mail, other nontraditional delivery methods include hanging bagged copies on doorknobs, inserting magazines in newspapers (such as *Parade* magazine), delivering through professionals' offices (doctors and dentists), direct delivery (company magazines or those found on airplanes), and electronic delivery, which is being used by organizational and membership publications, such as university alumni magazines.

Magazine Ad Sales   Like newspapers, magazine ad costs are based on the size of the ad and the circulation of the magazine. Media planners and buyers analyze a magazine's circulation so they can assess circulation potential and determine whether the audiences that best match a campaign's target will be reached. In deciding in which magazines to place ads, advertisers need to consider factors such as format and technology.

Although the format may vary from magazine to magazine, all magazines share some format characteristics. For example, the inside front and back cover pages are the most costly for advertisers because they have the highest level of exposure compared to all the other pages in a magazine. The inside back cover is also a premium position.

Normally, the largest unit of ad space that magazines sell is the **double-page spread,** in which two ad pages face each other. A double-page ad must jump the **gutter,** the white space running between the inside edges of the pages, meaning that no headline words can run through the gutter and that all body text is on one side or the other. A page without outside margins, in which the ad's ink extends to the very edge of the page, is called a **bleed.** Magazines sometimes offer more than two connected pages (four is the most common number) that fold in on themselves. This kind of ad is called a **gatefold.** The use of multiple pages that provide photo essays is an extension of the gatefold concept.

Another popular format is a special advertising page or section that looks like regular editorial pages but is identified by the word "advertisement" at the top. The content is usually an article about a company, product, or brand that is written by the corporation's publicity department. The idea is to mimic the editorial look in order to acquire the credibility of the publication's articles. Multiple-page photo essay ads are more common in magazines such as *Fortune* and *BusinessWeek;* these magazines may present, for example, a 20-page special section for businesses in a foreign country.

Finally, a single page or double page can be broken into a variety of units called *fractional page space* (for example, vertical half-page, horizontal half-page, half-page double spread, and checkerboard in which an ad is located in the upper left and the lower right of a double-page spread).

Technology   New technologies have enabled magazines to distinguish themselves from one another. For example, *selective binding* and *ink-jet imaging* allow publishers to personalize issues for individual subscribers. Selective binding combines information on subscribers kept in a database with a computer program to produce magazines that include special sections for subscribers based on their demographic profiles. Ink-jet imaging allows a magazine such as *U.S. News & World Report* to personalize its renewal form so that each issue contains a renewal card already filled out with the subscriber's name, address, and so on. Personalized messages can be printed directly on ads or on inserts ("Mr. Jones—check out our new mutual fund today").

Time Inc. and Lexus hoped to revitalize the magazine business with a new venture called *Mine* and a new approach to personalized marketing communication. Its philosophy was customization, similar to what Lexus offers its upscale customers, but in this print publication, it's the ads that are customized—"Hello (name of customer)," as well as the selection of articles from Time Inc.'s portfolio of publications. The idea for the experiment came from Team One, the Lexus agency.

Satellite transmission, along with computerized editing technology, allows magazines to print regional editions with regional advertising. This technology also permits publishers to close pages (stop accepting new material) just hours before press time (instead of days or weeks as in the past) so that advertisers can drop up-to-the-minute information in their ads. Sophisticated database management lets publishers combine the information available from subscriber lists with other public and private lists to create complete consumer profiles for advertisers.

Magazine Readership Measurement   Magazine rates are based on the **guaranteed circulation** that a publisher promises to provide. Magazine circulation is the number of copies of an issue sold, not the readership of the publication (called readers-per-copy). A single copy of a magazine might be read by one person or by several people, depending on its content. *Time* magazine turned the industry upside down when it announced in 2007 that it would trim its rate base (average circulation level) by almost 20 percent to 3.25 million from 4 million. (In July, 2010 it continues to hold circulation at 3.4 million.)[8] More importantly, it also offered advertisers a figure for its *total audience,* which it estimates at 19.5 million.

Several companies attempt to verify the circulation of magazines, along with the demographic and psychographic characteristics of specific readers. As with newspapers, the Audit Bureau of Circulation is responsible for verifying circulation numbers. Created in 1914, the ABC audits subscriptions as well as newsstand sales and also checks the number of delinquent subscribers and rates of renewal. MediaMark, which provides a service called MRI, is the industry leader in magazine readership measurement. MRI measures readership for many popular national and regional magazines (along with other media). Reports are issued to subscribers twice a year and cover readership by demographics, psychographics, and product use. The Simmons Market Research Bureau (SMRB) provides psychographic data on who reads which magazines and which products these readers buy and consume. Other research companies such as Starch and Gallup and Robinson provide information about magazine audience size and behavior.

One problem with these measurement services is the limited scope of their services. MRI, for example, only measures about 210 magazines. That leaves media buyers in the dark regarding who is actually seeing their ads in magazines not covered by MRI's research. Without the services of an objective (outside) measurement company, advertisers must rely on the data from the magazines themselves, which may be biased.

One interesting change in magazine measurement is the move, which is supported by the MPA, to quantify the "experience" of reading the magazine, rather than just the circulation and readers-per-copy. A major study to pilot test this concept was conducted by the MPA, the Northwestern University Media Management Center, and the American Society for Magazine Editors (ASME). The study identified a set of 39 types of experiences that people report having with their magazines. More importantly, the study found that the more engaged people were in the magazine experience, the more impact the advertising had.[9]

Directories

Newspapers and magazines are important print media types, but directory advertising is another form that is particularly effective at driving specific types of consumer responses. Directories are books like the **Yellow Pages** that list the names of people or companies, their phone numbers, and their addresses. In addition to this information, many directories publish advertising from marketers who want to reach the people who use the directory. Corporations, associations, and other organizations, such as non-profits, also publish directories either in print or online that include members, as well as other stakeholders. These are often provided as a service to members as part of a corporate communication program.

Directory advertising is designed to get attention, communicate key information about the organization, reinforce the company's brand image and position, and drive behavior, the hardest of all facets of advertising effects to achieve. The Terminix ads illustrate how this complex set of objectives was accomplished by the winner of a student advertising competition. The Terminix judges commented that Tran's ads were "terrific examples of creating an unexpected visual without distracting from the main message." The judges explained that "this visual coupled with the explicit copy points (all presented in a clean, accessible layout) differentiate (in a very positive way) Terminix from its directory competitors." Tran's package included a large directory ad, a small directory ad, and an Internet directory ad.

One of the biggest advantages of advertising in directories is that if people have taken the initiative to look for a business or service, then the listing is reaching an audience already in the market for something and ready to take action. Directory advertising doesn't have to create a need because it is a number one shopping aid as reflected in the classic Yellow Pages slogan: "Let Your Fingers Do the Walking." That's why directory advertising's biggest advantage is **directional advertising**: it tells people where to go to get the product or service they want. If you are going to move across town and you want to rent a truck, you will consult the local phone book. As the *A Matter of Principle* feature explains, directory advertising is the main medium that prospects consult once they have decided to buy something they need or want.

SHOWCASE

The Yellow Pages Association (YPA) Advertising Challenge provides real-world experience for advertising students. Some 1,400 students participated in the challenge.

Steven Tran, a student of Professor David Koeher at the University of Illinois at Chicago, created the winning ad for the (YPA) competition's client, Terminix.

A MATTER OF PRINCIPLE

Directories: The Medium You Trust the Most

Joel Davis, *Professor, School of Journalism & Media Studies, San Diego State University*

Which advertising medium satisfies all four of the following criteria?: It is specifically designed to reach consumers when they are thinking about a purchase, it is a medium in which consumers voluntarily seek out ads, its monthly reach exceeds the monthly reach of search engines, and it is the most frequently mentioned medium when consumers are asked by the Forrester media research company, "Which media do you trust a lot?"

The answer is the Yellow Pages—both print and online.

The Yellow Pages continue to connect sellers with consumers in its traditional print format. However, as both consumers and media change, the Yellow Pages have expanded their reach through a variety of approaches. Online yellow pages such as Yellowpages.com and Superpages (*www.superpages.com*) reach a broad online population, while other more narrowly focused approaches reach additional consumers, for example:

- AT&T Interactive's partnership with Yahoo allows Yahoo's Yahoo Local division to use advertiser content from Yellowpages.com.
- Superpages' new Twitter channel allows users to receive addresses and phone numbers via tweets.

Regardless of how the Yellow Pages reaches a consumer, the majority of Yellow Pages usage is motivated by consumers' needs, which in turn are the results of commonly and infrequently occurring life events.

There are two types of commonly occurring events: anticipated and unanticipated. Anticipated events are those that occur without surprise in the normal course of daily activities. These events may occur frequently, such as having a car's oil changed or ordering office supplies, or they may occur less frequently, such as the decision to build a fence or order flowers.

Unanticipated events are those that take you by surprise, for example, the need to repair a roof or respond to flood damage. Yellow Pages usage increases whenever one of these events occurs. The relationship between these events and Yellow Pages usage is reflected in the most commonly used headings, which typically relate to these types of events. The most frequently referenced headings include restaurants, physicians, pizza, auto parts and dealers, and plumbing contractors.

Infrequently occurring events also motivate Yellow Pages usage. In any given year, many individuals and families undergo a major life event, such as marriage, birth of children, or change in jobs. Regardless of the nature of the event, the presence of the event itself causes a need for assistance or information, and the Yellow Pages are one source of information individuals turn to in an attempt to satisfy problems that arise as a result of a life-related event. Yellow Pages usage more than doubles when these events occur: child getting married, birth of a child, youngest child leaves home, personal marriage, separation, or divorce. Given that these events occur only once (or a few times) in an individual's life, the Yellow Pages provide an opportunity to reach consumers who have an immediate need to satisfy, but who have not yet developed strong loyalty to businesses or services that can be used to satisfy their need.

The biggest change for this medium is the advent of online directory information, as well as the decline in landline phones because of the growth of cell phone usage. Directories are expensive to print so it is becoming harder for phone companies to justify the costs of community-wide distribution of the residential books. Some directory providers are using an "opt-in" program for those customers who prefer the book to the computer, but the Yellow Pages and business White Pages are still in business.[10]

The key difference between directory advertising and brand-image advertising is this: directory advertising reaches prospects, people who already know they have a need for the product or service, whereas brand-image advertising seeks to create a need and attractive personality for a brand. Almost 90 percent of those who consult the Yellow Pages follow up with some kind of action.

In addition to the Yellow Pages, an estimated 7,500 directories cover all types of professional areas and interest groups. For example, the *Standard Directory of Advertisers and Advertising Agencies* (known as the Red Book) not only lists advertisers and agencies, it also accepts advertising targeted at those who use the directory. *The Creative Black Book,* another directory used by advertising professionals, also takes ads for photographers, illustrators, typographers, and art suppliers. Most of the directories have been transformed into an electronic version accessible through the Internet.

Principle

The principle behind directory advertising is that it is directional—it tells people who already are in the target market where to go to get the product or service they want.

Other Print Media

At this time, we don't know what Kindle and its other e-book siblings will offer to advertisers, although there's sure to be some angle. But books, even in print, have been and are being used as promotional tools. A number of marketing communication agencies have published books, for example, that focus on the thoughts of their founders and the philosophies of their agencies: Crispin Porter + Bogusky and *Hoppla,* Leo Burnett's *Leo,* DDB's *Bill Bernbach Said,* and Ogilvy and Mather's *Ogilvy on Advertising.* More recently a bank in Brazil presented 120 reasons why people should be customers of Banco Bradesco—one reason per page. The book is at the center of the bank's customer acquisition program.[11]

The biggest change, however, may be coming in the form of the iPad, which may turn out to be the electronic savior of newspapers and magazines because its technology permits a larger page layout than ebooks. *Wall Street Journal* ads, for example, helped launch the iPad with an appeal to download the WSJ for iPad from the iTunes App Store. Publishers hoped the new device would restore ad revenue they had lost to online publications.[12]

WHAT ARE THE OUT-OF-HOME MEDIA CHARACTERISTICS?

Out-of-home advertising includes everything from billboards to hot-air balloons. That means ads on public spaces, including buses, posters on building walls (barn roofs in the old days), telephone and shopping kiosks, painted and wrapped cars and semi-trucks, taxi signs and mobile billboards, transit shelters and rail platforms, airport and bus terminal displays, hotel and shopping mall displays, in-store merchandising signs, grocery store carts, shopping bags, public restroom walls, skywriting, in-store clocks, and aisle displays. Even tall, highly visible grain silos have been recycled into huge Coke cans in Emporia, Kansas; a 50-foot fiddle in Green Island, Iowa; and a beer can in Longmont, Colorado. And don't forget blimps and airplanes towing messages over your favorite stadium.

In addition to being one of the most creative vehicles for delivering brand messages, as the LATCH billboard demonstrates, out-of-home media is also a big and growing segment of the media industry. Although total spending on out-of-home media is hard to determine because of the industry's diversity, this category ranks second only to the Internet as the fastest growing marketing communication industry.[13]

Why is it such a growth area? Out-of-home advertising's defining characteristic is that it is situational: it can target specific people with specific messages at a time and place when they may be most interested. A sign at the telephone kiosk reminds you to call for reservations at your favorite restaurant, a sign on the rail platform suggests that you enjoy a candy bar while riding the train, and a bus card reminds you to listen to the news on a particular radio station. As mass media has decreased in impact, *place-based forms,* such as outdoor, have become more attractive to many advertisers.

Principle

Out-of-home advertising is situational in that it targets people at specific locations.

Ad Council   U.S. Department of Transportation

3 OUT OF 4 KIDS ARE NOT AS SECURE AS THEY SHOULD BE.

SAFERCAR.GOV   Anchor. Tether. **LATCH**

SHOWCASE

This outdoor board from the LATCH public service campaign was contributed by Trent Walters, an account director with The Richards Group.

A graduate of the University of North Texas, Trent Walters was nominated by Professor Sheri Broyles.

Outdoor Advertising

One of the growth areas in the out-of-home category is **outdoor advertising,** which refers to billboards along streets and highways, as well as posters in other public locations. Of the nearly $6 billion spent on traditional outdoor advertising, billboard ads accounted for approximately 60 percent; street furniture, such as signs on benches, and transit ads brought in the rest.

An advertiser uses outdoor boards for two primary reasons. First, for national advertisers, this medium can provide reminders to the target audience, as the Olympus sign illustrates. A second use for billboards is directional; it acts as primary medium when the board is in proximity to where a brand is available. The travel and tourism industries are major users of billboards directing travelers to hotels, restaurants, resorts, gas stations, and other services.

Size and Format   In terms of size and format, there are two traditional kinds of billboards: printed poster panels and painted bulletins. **Printed posters** are created by the advertiser or agency, printed, and shipped to an outdoor advertising company. The prepasted posters are then applied in sections to the poster panel's face on location, much like applying wallpaper. They come in two sizes based on the number of sheets of paper used to make the image: 8 sheet (5 × 11 feet) and 30 sheet (12 × 25 feet). The other kind is the **painted outdoor bulletin,** which differ from posters in that they are normally created on site and vary in size or shape, although their standard size is 14 × 48 feet. They can be painted on the sides of buildings, on roofs, and even natural structures, such as the side of a mountain. Designers can add **extensions** to painted billboards to expand the scale and break away from the limits of the long rectangle. These embellishments are sometimes called **cutouts** because they present an irregular shape.

Outdoor LED boards are brightly lit plastic signs with electronic messaging. These signs come in a variety of sizes, colors, and brightness. Another innovation for billboards, electronic posters, and kiosks is the use of **digital displays.** Digital displays use wireless technology, which allows them to be quickly changed to reflect an advertising situation (a tire company could advertise all-weather tires during snowy conditions) or the presence of a target audience member. Mini USA invited some owners of its Mini cars to join a pilot test of a new program called Motorby. The drivers provide some basic information and agree to participate. They are given special key fobs that trigger Mini billboards to deliver personal messages. This was an experiment and discontinued because of costs, but it illustrates the ideas marketers are exploring to reach people on the go.

Outdoor boards are also getting into green marketing. Many are already solar powered. WePower, a clean energy company, is promoting the idea of fitting the approximately 500,000 billboards on U.S. highways with wind turbines. The company estimates these boards could power approximately 1.5 million homes.[14]

SHOWCASE

This innovative outdoor board was designed to dramatize the quality of the LCD screen on the back of the Olympus digital camera. Its designer, Elisa Guerrero, explains, "The idea is that what you see is what you get." Guerrero's plan proposed placing these all over the United States at popular landmarks and beautiful countryside scenes.

A Silver Addy award winner, this Olympus outdoor board was contributed by Texas Christian University (TCU) graduate Elisa Guerrero. Her work was nominated for inclusion in this book by TCU professor Mike Wood.

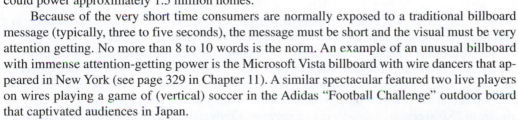

Because of the very short time consumers are normally exposed to a traditional billboard message (typically, three to five seconds), the message must be short and the visual must be very attention getting. No more than 8 to 10 words is the norm. An example of an unusual billboard with immense attention-getting power is the Microsoft Vista billboard with wire dancers that appeared in New York (see page 329 in Chapter 11). A similar spectacular featured two live players on wires playing a game of (vertical) soccer in the Adidas "Football Challenge" outdoor board that captivated audiences in Japan.

The *Practical Tips* box identifies key features of outdoor media and provides suggestions on how to design effective attention-getting messages for this "gigantic canvas." A good example of the power of a strong message comes from the LATCH public service campaign that we introduced in Chapter 4. It demonstrates the key point that a number of young children are not secure in their car seats. How many of the points in the *Practical Tips* box are demonstrated in this outdoor board?

PRACTICAL TIPS

Outdoor: An Effective Brand Communication Medium

James Maskulka, *Associate Professor of Marketing, Lehigh University*

In a recent campaign, the outdoor industry proclaimed, "Outdoor is not a medium. It's a large." In the contemporary view of outdoor, it is not just complementary but an integral part of a multiplatform advertising campaign and a viable alternative for establishing a brand's image, in addition to building brand awareness. Here are some tips on how to plan for and use outdoor advertising for maximum effectiveness:

1. **Frequency of Exposure** The successful execution of a transformational advertising strategy to build brand image requires frequent exposure over an extended time period—a primary benefit of outdoor.
2. **Brand Image Touch-Up** "Great brands may live forever," according to famous adman Leo Burnett, but even great brands may need image updating. This is the area where outdoor may have its greatest relevance to branding. Shifting a brand's image in response to changing consumer lifestyles guarantees that the brand remains relevant. The dynamic imagery of outdoor is an important tool in brand touch-ups.
3. **The Power of the Visual** Certain brand advertisers, such as those handling fashion and food, use visually driven creative as the brand's *raison d'être*. The campaigns must have consistent production values from market to market, a benefit offered by national outdoor campaigns.
4. **A Friend in the Neighborhood** Rather than building a brand on attributes and differentiation, brands with strong philosophies and attitudes build on relationships with consumers. Outdoor delivers consistent exposure of brand personality cues to targeted customers who relate to the brand.
5. **Brand Image Build-Up** The 30-day posting period is long enough so that these exposures can be seen as repositories of long-term brand image leading to favorable consumer attitude accumulation. It's like making a deposit in a bank and watching your wealth grow.
6. **Speaking the Language of Consumers** Brands increasingly serve as a form of consumer communication shorthand. The compact information of outdoor advertising matches consumers' limited processing time. To illustrate, a billboard combined with a vinyl-wrapped car and reinforced by a transit ad or a taxi poster reaches the time-starved consumer with much less investment in personal processing time.
7. **Clarity of Focus** Usually the shorter the outdoor ad copy, the more effective the message. The outdoor message imposes a creative and disciplined brand communication lexicon that ensures ongoing reinforcement of the brand message.
8. **A Gigantic Canvas** Successful outdoor advertisers see billboards as "a gigantic canvas" on which the brand advertiser can create "mega art"[15] that links the brand with relevant icons and symbols. Some of the most important slogans and images in advertising have been captured on billboards.

Source: Adapted from "Outdoor Advertising: The Brand Communication Medium," Outdoor Advertising Association of America (OAAA) special report, November 1999; the original can be found at *www.oaa.org;* Herbert Graf, "Outdoor as the Segue Between Mass & Class," *Brandweek,* July 20, 1999: 19.

Outdoor Ad Sales The cost of outdoor advertising is based on the percent of population in a specified geographical area exposed to the ad in one day. This is typically based on a traffic count—that is, the number of vehicles passing a particular location during a specified period of time, called a **showing**. If an advertiser purchases a "100 showing," the basic standard unit is the number of poster boards in each market that will expose the message to 100 percent of the market population every day. If three posters in a community of 100,000 people achieve a daily exposure to 75,000 people, the result is a 75 showing. Conversely, in a small town with a population of 1,200 and one main street, one board may produce a 100 showing. As you can see, the number of boards required for a 100 showing varies from city to city.

Advertisers can purchase any number of units (75, 50, or 25 showings daily are common quantities). Boards are usually rented for 30-day periods, with longer periods possible. Painted bulletins are bought on an individual basis, usually for one, two, or three years.

On-Premise Signs

Retail signs that identify stores have been with us throughout recorded history and are today the most ubiquitous form of brand communication. Signs are found on small independent businesses, restaurants and chains like Starbucks, hospitals, movie theaters, and other public facilities like zoos and large regional shopping centers. In this complex environment an effective sign may be relatively simple, like McDonald's giant M, or more complex, like those found on the strip in Las Vegas with their large illuminated and animated visual extravaganzas.

Some on-premise signs also act like billboards. American Eagle Outfitters, for example, has a 15,000-square-foot sign above its Broadway store in New York City. The sign has 12 panels and operates 18 hours a day. The company hired ABC Regional Sports and Entertainment to handle sales for the panels.[16]

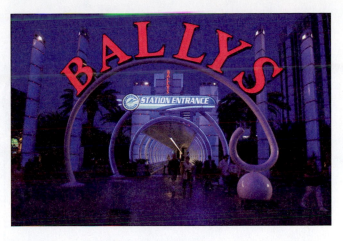

Out-of-home advertising, such as this on-premise sign from Las Vegas, is a highly creative medium, as well as the second fastest growing medium after the Internet. Every building, every store, needs a sign.

Posters

Posters are used on kiosks, bulletin boards, the sides of buildings, and even vehicles. In London, daily hand-lettered posters have been used for centuries to announce newspaper headlines, and the walls of the subway or Tube stations in London are lined with posters advertising all kinds of products, but particularly theater shows. The iPod was launched in London with walls of posters that Tube riders encountered coming up or down the escalators. The walls were papered with the distinctive silhouetted images against their neon backgrounds. The repetition of the images created a strong billboarding effect.

Empty storefronts in prime downtown locations and major thoroughfares have become the latest venue. With their large expanse of window space, these abandoned retail stores have become a frugal way to deliver a big message during the recession. Landlords may charge as little as $500 a month in comparison to comparable spots on a billboard that might cost $50,000.[17]

Special structures called **kiosks** are designed for public posting of notices and advertising posters. Kiosks are typically located in places where people walk, such as a many-sided structure in a mall or near a public walkway, or where people wait. The location has a lot to do with the design of the message. Some out-of-home media serve the same function as the kiosk, such as the ad-carrying bus shelter. The series of posters for Dallas-based Texins Activity Center were contributed by Michael Dattolico.

Transit Advertising

Transit advertising is mainly an urban mass advertising form that places ads on vehicles such as buses and taxis that circulate through the community as moving billboards. Some of these use striking graphics, such as the designs on the sides of the Mayflower moving trucks. Transit advertising also includes the posters seen in bus shelters and train, airport, and subway stations. Most of these posters must be designed for quick impressions, although people who are waiting on subway platforms or bus shelters often study these posters, so here they can present a more involved or complicated message than a billboard can.

There are two types of transit advertising: interior and exterior. **Interior transit advertising** is seen by people riding inside buses, subway cars, and taxis. **Exterior transit advertising** is mounted on the side, rear, and top exteriors of these vehicles, so pedestrians and people in nearby cars see it. Transit advertising is reminder advertising; it is a frequency medium that lets advertisers get their names in front of a local audience who drive a regular route at critical times such as rush hour.

Painted vehicles is another type of transit advertising. It started in 1993, when PepsiCo paid Seattle in return for permission to wrap six city buses with its logo. More recently recession-weary drivers have been tempted to sign up to have their cars and trucks wrapped with ads for brands such as Jamba Juice and Verizon in exchange for monthly payments.

SHOWCASE

These posters for Texins Activity Center were all designed to get the attention of kids and their parents and entice them to enroll in a Spring Break Kids' Camp. The common theme was to "take a break from the digital world" and try such outside activities as photography and tennis.

Michael Dattolico, owner of Musion Creative, is a graduate of the University of Florida. He was nominated by Professor Elaine Wagner.

Using Print and Out-of-Home Media Effectively

This review of print and out-of-home advertising should be helpful in explaining when and why various types of media are included in a media mix. To summarize these key decisions, consider using newspaper advertising for messages that include an announcement of something new. Newspapers are also good for targeting local markets. Magazines are great for targeting people with special interests. They also have great production values and are good for messages that either focus on brand image or need space for a more complete explanation.

Outdoor advertising targets audiences on the move and provides directional information. Outdoor messages are also good for brand reminders. Directory ads catch people when they are shopping. The following table summarizes the advantages and limitations of these various media:

Print and Out-of-Home Media Advantages and Limitations

	Advantages	*Limitations*
Newspapers	Good for news announcements	Short life span
	Good market coverage	Clutter
	Good for comparison shopping	Limited reach for certain groups
	Positive consumer attitudes	Poor production values
	Good for reaching educated and affluent consumers	
	Flexibility—geographic; scheduling	

	Advantages	*Limitations*

Magazines	High production values
	Targets consumers' interests—
	  specialized audiences
	Receptive audience
	Long life span
	Format encourages creativity
	Good for brand messages
	Good for complex or in-depth
	  messages
		Long lead times—limited flexibility
		Lack of immediacy
		High cost
		Sometimes limited distribution

Directories	Directional: Consumers go to
	  directories for shopping
	  information
	Trusted
	Inexpensive
	Good ROI of 1:15—every dollar
	  spent on an ad produces $145
	  in revenue
	Flexible in size, colors, formats
	Long life
		Lack of flexibility—can be a long
		  time before a change can be made
		Competitive clutter and look-alike ads
		Low production quality

Out-of-Home
Media
	Good situational medium
	Directional
	Brand reminder medium
	High-impact—larger than life
	Least expensive
	Long life
		Traffic moves quickly
		Can't handle complex messages—
		  designs must be simple
		May be easy to miss (depending
		  on location)
		Some criticize outdoor ads as
		  "polluting" the landscape
		Transit lacks the size advantage
		  of other outdoor media

WHAT ARE BROADCAST MEDIA CHARACTERISTICS?

When we speak of **broadcast media,** we are discussing media forms that transmit sounds or images electronically. These include radio, television and other video forms, and movie advertising. (The Internet and other digital new media will be discussed in the next chapter.) Print is a static medium bought by amount of space (column inches) and circulation; in contrast, broadcast media are dynamic and bought by amount of time (seconds, minutes) and their audience size. Broadcast media messages are fleeting, which means they may affect the viewer's emotions for a few seconds and then disappear, in contrast to print messages, which can be revisited and reread.

What that means, in terms of our Facets of Effects Model, is that broadcast is more entertaining, using both drama and emotion to attract attention and engage the feelings of the audience. Radio is a talk, news, or music-driven medium, where advertisements can also engage the imagination to create stories in the mind. In contrast, television has movie-like qualities that bring stories to life and create powerful brand imagery. You can see that in the images from the LATCH "Slow Motion" public service commercial. TV can make believers of people who see something demonstrated. Both radio and television use music for emotional impact and to intensify memory of the message through the repetition of tunes and sounds.

Radio Basics

The United States has more than 10,000 commercial radio stations, and most of them, except for the new Internet stations, have a limited geographical reach. In recent years the radio industry's growth has been slow.

The Structure of the Radio Industry   Traditional radio stations are found on the AM/FM dial and most serve local markets. Other options for radio listeners include public radio, cable and satellite

SHOWCASE

The Inside Story behind this LATCH public service campaign was presented in Chapter 4. This commercial, which was contributed by Trent Walters, account director at The Richards Group, features various children filmed in dramatic super-slow-motion who appear to be flying through a weightless environment. Walters explains that the commercial ends with a child landing in her father's arms, in other words arriving safely. But the point made in the narration is that car seats are not always installed correctly and are not as secure as they should be.

A graduate of the University of North Texas, Trent Walters was nominated by Professor Sheri Broyles.

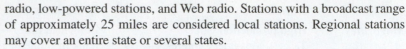

radio, low-powered stations, and Web radio. Stations with a broadcast range of approximately 25 miles are considered local stations. Regional stations may cover an entire state or several states.

Radio networks are groups of affiliated stations. The network system produces programs and distributes them to their **affiliates** who contract with the system. Some of the networks include ABC Radio, Clear Channel Communications, CNN Radio Network, the Fox Sports and Fox News networks, and others that deliver special-interest programming, such as talk radio.

Local **public radio** stations are usually affiliates of National Public Radio (NPR) and carry much of the same programming, although they have to buy or subscribe to the NPR services. For that reason, some local public radio stations might carry a full range of NPR programming, while others that are less well funded may only carry a partial list of NPR programs.

Public radio stations are considered noncommercial in that they rely on listener support for most of their funding. In recent years, however, they have slowly expanded their corporate sponsorship messages. Although public television is losing market share to the many new cable competitors, public radio is growing relative to its competitors. Likewise, corporate underwriting (or sponsorship) has increased along with the audience size because public radio is one of the few media that can deliver an audience of well-educated, affluent consumers.

The radio industry in the United States includes several other broadcast forms:

- *Cable Radio* Launched in 1990, **cable radio** technology uses cable television receivers to deliver static-free music via wires plugged into cable subscribers' stereos. The thinking behind cable radio is that cable television needs new revenue and consumers are fed up with commercials on radio. The service typically is commercial free with a monthly subscription fee.
- *Satellite Radio* The newest radio technology is **satellite radio.** It can deliver your favorite radio stations, regardless of where you are in the continental United States. Sirius and XM satellite radio introduced their systems in 2002. The two companies merged in 2007 as Sirius XM Radio and had some 18 million subscribers in 2009. For a monthly fee, the system allows you to access more than 100 channels.
- *LPFM* If you're a college student, you probably have a **low-power FM (LPFM)** station on your campus. These nonprofit, noncommercial stations serve a small market, with a reach of three to five miles.
- *Web Radio* Web radio provides **webcasting,** which is audio streaming through a website. There are two formats—one is a streaming version of an offline station and the other is Internet-only radio. Web radio offers thousands of stations as well as highly diverse radio shows that play mostly to small select audiences. Radio has been the slowest of all media to make the online version a revenue source with only 2.4 percent of revenue coming from online. In contrast, newspapers get 7 percent and television brings in 3.4 percent of its revenue from online.[18]

Some of the lines between these forms are blurring. For example, some commercial radio networks with special-interest programming, such as the liberal talk radio network Air America, are asking listeners to donate to keep the programs on air, similar to the way public radio is financed.

The Radio Audience   The reason advertisers like radio is that it is as close as we can come to a universal medium. Virtually every household in the United States (99 percent) has at least one radio and most have multiple sets. And almost everybody listens to radio at some time during the day.

A $20 billion industry, radio is tightly targeted based on special interests (religion, Spanish language, talk shows) and musical tastes. In other words, radio is a highly segmented advertising medium. About 85 percent of the radio stations are focused on music. Program formats offered in a typical market are based on music styles and special interests, including hard rock, gospel, country and western, top-40 hits, soft rock, golden oldies, and nonmusic programs such as talk radio and advice, from car repair to finances to dating. Talk radio host Rush Limbaugh is generally acknowledged to have the largest audience with estimates of his audience ranging from 14 million to 25 million.[19]

Principle
Media planners use radio for tight targeting of narrow, highly segmented markets.

Recent research has provided some findings that bode well for radio. One study, for example, found that radio listeners are far less likely to change the dial during ads than are television viewers. An unexpected 92 percent listen through the four- and six-minute commercial pods. The percent is even higher for in-car listeners. The study also found a high level of loyalty among listeners for their favorite station.[20]

Dayparts Advertisers considering radio are most concerned with the number of people listening to a particular station at a given time. Radio audiences are grouped by the time of day when they are most likely to be listening, and the assumption is that different groups listen at different times of the day. The typical radio programming day is divided into five segments called **dayparts** as follows:

Morning Drive Time 6–10 A.M.

Midday 10 A.M.–3 P.M.

Evening Drive Time 3–7 P.M.

Evening 7 P.M.–midnight

Late Night midnight–6 A.M.

The **morning drive time** segment is the period when the most listeners are tuned in to radio. This drive-time audience is getting ready for work or commuting to work, and radio is the best medium to reach them.

Measuring the Radio Audience The radio industry and independent research firms provide several measures for advertisers, including a station's **coverage,** which is similar to circulation for print media. This is simply the number of homes in a geographic area that can pick up the station clearly, whether those homes are actually tuned in or not. A better measure is station or program **ratings,** which measures the percent of homes actually tuned in to the particular station. Factors such as competing programs, types of programs, and time of day or night influence the circulation figure.

The Arbitron Ratings Company estimates the size of radio audiences for more than 250 markets in the United States. Arbitron has been using a seven-day, self-administered diary. A new technology Arbitron is rolling out called the Portable People Meter (PPM) is a pager-size device that detects codes embedded in the audio programming regardless of where the device—whether traditional radio, computer, or cell phone—is located. The device has been found to be quite effective at predicting audience interest, even leading to some major format changes such as when WRFF in Philadelphia switched from a Spanish-language talk show format to alternative rock after new PPM data revealed that rock music was more popular with the WRFF audience.

Radio Advertising The first radio commercials hit the air in 1922 in New York and advertised a real estate firm. These early ads were highly successful for many of the same reasons that keep radio popular today with advertisers. The radio listening experience is unlike that of any other media, creating both challenges and opportunities for radio advertisers. It can be a more intimate experience, because we tend to listen to it alone, particularly for people wearing headphones. In cars, where many people listen to radio, it offers advertisers something close to a captive audience. And it's relatively inexpensive both to produce commercials and buy airtime. Check out the Radio Ranch website, *www.radio-ranch.com* for a look behind the scenes of radio commercial production.

Media planners use radio to deliver a high level of frequency because radio commercials, particularly **jingles**, which are commercials set to music, lend themselves to repetition. Barry Manilow was awarded an Honorary CLIO Award recognizing his long career as a jingle writer. One of his best known is the catchy Band-Ad jingle, "I am stuck on Band-Aid brand cuz Band-Aid's stuck on me." Hear this classic at *www.youtube.com/watch?v=_7MtLNK02lI*.

Radio can also engage the imagination more than other media because it relies on the listener's mind to fill in the visual element. Many radio ads use drama, especially **public service**

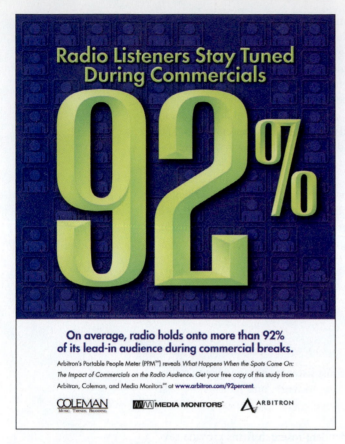

Radio Listeners Stay Tuned During Commercials

92%

On average, radio holds onto more than 92% of its lead-in audience during commercial breaks.

Arbitron's Portable People Meter (PPM™) reveals *What Happens When the Spots Come On: The Impact of Commercials on the Radio Audience*. Get your free copy of this study from Arbitron, Coleman, and Media Monitors℠ at www.arbitron.com/92percent.

COLEMAN   MEDIA MONITORS   ARBITRON

Arbitron is one of several major audience-rating services in the advertising industry. It estimates the size of radio audiences for more than 250 U.S. markets.

Principle

Radio advertising has the power to engage the imagination and communicate on a more personal level than other forms of media.

announcements (PSAs), which are spots created by agencies that donate their time and services on behalf of some good cause. PSAs run for free on radio and TV stations. Check out the Ad Council's website (*www.adcouncil.org*) for a collection of these types of spots. You can also check out the radio spots from the Ad Council's LATCH campaign that we introduced in Chapter 4.

Radio advertising is divided into three categories: network, spot, and local. Network revenues are by far the smallest category, accounting for approximately 5 percent of total radio revenues. Local advertising revenues account for approximately 75 percent, and national spot advertising makes up the remainder. In addition to local, let's consider the categories of national radio buys:

- *Network Radio Advertising* Network advertising can be bought from national networks that distribute programming and advertising to their affiliates. A **radio network** is a group of local affiliates connected to one or more national networks through telephone wires and satellites. The five major radio networks are Westwood One, CBS, ABC, Unistar, and Clear Channel. The largest network by far is Clear Channel, with more than 1,200 stations. Satellite transmission has produced important technological improvements that also make it easier to distribute advertising to these stations. Many advertisers view network radio as a viable national advertising medium, especially for food and beverages, automobiles, and over-the-counter drugs.
- *Spot Radio Advertising* Spot advertising lets an advertiser place an advertisement with an individual station rather than through a network. Although networks broadcast blocks of prerecorded national advertisements, they also allow local affiliates open time to sell spot advertisements locally. (*Note:* National media plans sometimes buy spots at the local level rather than through the network, so it is possible to have a national spot buy that only reaches certain markets.) Thanks to the flexibility it offers the advertiser, **spot radio advertising** makes up nearly 80 percent of all radio advertising. In large cities, 40 or more radio stations may be available. Local stations also offer flexibility through their willingness to run unusual ads, allow last-minute changes, and negotiate rates. Buying spot radio and coping with its nonstandardized rate structures can be cumbersome, however.
- *Syndicated Radio Advertising* This is the original type of radio programming that plays on a large number of affiliated stations, such as the Paul Harvey show, which is broadcast on some 1,200 stations. Program **syndication** has benefited network radio because it offers advertisers a variety of high-quality, specialized, and usually original programs. Both networks and private firms offer syndication. A local talk show may become popular enough to be "taken into syndication." Advertisers value syndicated programming because of the high level of loyalty of its audience.

The growth of network radio has contributed to an increase in syndicated radio, creating more advertising opportunities for companies eager to reach new markets. In fact, syndication and network radio have practically become interchangeable terms.

Using Radio Effectively We have seen that radio is highly targeted and that makes it a great tool for reaching audiences through specialized programming, such as talk shows and musical interests. Radio advertising messages tend to have a higher level of acceptance than television because radio listeners are more loyal to their favorite programs and stations. The Radio Advertising

Bureau (RAB) promotes radio as having a dynamic consumer engagement that can be measured using audience metrics of reach, relevance, and receptivity.

Although radio may not be a primary medium for most businesses, it does have excellent reminder and reinforcement capability and is great about building frequency through repetition, particularly if the message can be delivered through a jingle. It also sparks the imagination because of its ability to stimulate mental imagery through the *theater of the mind*, which uses humor, drama, music, and sound effects to tell a story. It also brings the persuasive power and warmth of a human voice. A good example is the series of Tom Bodett's Motel 6 commercials by the Dallas-based Richards Group. Listen to them at *http://adland.tv/search/node/Motel%206*.

To maximize the impact of a radio spot, timing is critical and depends on understanding the target audience's aperture, which is particularly important in radio with its "drive-time" daypart. **Aperture** means knowing when the target audience is most likely to be listening and responsive. Restaurants run spots before meals; auto dealerships run spots on Friday and Saturday, when people are free to visit showrooms; and jewelry stores run spots before Christmas, Valentine's Day, and Mother's Day. For fast-food franchises, radio buys at the local level supplement national television. Radio acts as a reminder, with spots concentrated during morning drive time, noon, and evening drive time. The messages focus on the location of local restaurants and special promotions. Radio is also flexible and allows for easy changes to schedules. For example, a local hardware store can quickly implement a snow-shovel promotion the morning after a snowstorm.

A disadvantage of radio is that it plays in the background for many of our activities. Although the radio is on, the multitasking listener may not really be listening to or concentrating on the message. Listeners tend to tune in and tune out as something catches their attention, which is why effective radio advertising is designed to "break through" the surrounding clutter. Generally radio ad clutter is lower than television clutter, which averages 15 to 20 minutes per hour of commercials versus 10 to 15 minutes on radio. Also, the lack of visuals on radio can be a problem for products that need to be demonstrated.

Television Basics

Television has become a mainstay of society with, on average, some 280 million sets in use in the United States. Television approaches the universality of radio with 98 percent of American households having one or more television sets. In over half of U.S. households, the TV is on "most" of the time. The U.S. television audience, however, is highly fragmented, tuning in to 100 or more different channels. Nielsen Media Research estimates that the average U.S. household has the set on more than five hours a day.[21]

Television is primarily an entertainment medium although a recent trend, called "behavior placement," is experimenting with moving TV programs into social behavior modification. For example, a segment of *The Office* turned one of the actors into a superhero obsessed with recycling. Scripting positive behaviors into TV shows is seen as a way to model positive behaviors and influence viewers.[22]

Television's use also expanded with the introduction of the Wii, which makes the home TV screen a facilitator in exercise programs, as well as games. As computers begin to use TV screens to project their content, this cross-channel merger will open up entirely new uses for home TVs.

The heavy use of television by children is of concern to parents and early childhood experts. Recent studies found that U.S. children spend an average of nearly four hours a day watching television, DVDs, and videos. Furthermore, three-fourths of sixth graders have a TV in their bedroom. Advertisers are happy to hear that kids haven't totally abandoned TV programming for games and the Web, but these numbers are still worrisome for critics of children's programming and advertising.

Television advertising is embedded in programming, so most of the attention in media buying, as well as in the measurement of television advertising's effectiveness, is focused on the performance of various shows and how they engage their audiences. During the Golden Age of television in the 1950s and 1960s, the three networks virtually controlled the evening viewing experience, but that dominance has shrunk in recent years. The following table shows **prime-time** viewing over the years, as well as the drastic drop in percentage of people watching the leading shows during those years.

Years	Top Show (Percentage of Audience)
1952–53	67 *I Love Lucy* (CBS)
1962–63	36 *Beverly Hillbillies* (CBS)
1972–73	33 *All in the Family* (CBS)
1982–83	26 *60 Minutes* (CBS)
1992–93	22 *60 Minutes* (CBS)
2002–03	16 *CSI* (CBS)
2007–08	16 *American Idol* (Fox)

Source: Adapted from James Poniewozik, "Here's to the Death of Broadcast," Time, *March 26, 2009: 62.*

Principle

Television advertising is tied to television programming and the ad's effectiveness is determined by the popularity of the television program.

Some programs are media stars and reach huge audiences—the Super Bowl is a good example. In 2010 the Saints vs. Colts game became the most watched telecast ever with an average audience of 106.5 million viewers in the United States, and some 51.7 million households tuned in.[23] Others reach small but select audiences, such as *The News Hour with Jim Lehrer* on PBS. As discussed in the *A Matter of Practice* feature, a surprise hit has been the retro *Mad Men* with its stories about the 1950s advertising industry. It's not a huge ratings hit, but is popular with its loyal fan base because of its dramatic power and ability to engage audiences emotionally with the characters, their stories, and the historical period.

In an interesting experiment with television costs and revenue, in early 2010 NBC moved Jay Leno from his late-night time slot to a 10:00 p.m. time (EST) five nights a week. The network gambled that his show would be cheaper to produce than the scripted programs that characterize prime time. Of course, his program would probably also have lower ratings, but the trade-off was worthwhile given the lower program costs. What that decision ignored was the importance of those scripted shows with their higher ratings to the local affiliates who get a share of the revenue from those shows. The lower ratings also hurt their revenue stream from both national and local advertising. Even worse, the Leno show ended up being a weaker "lead-in" for the local stations' 11:00 p.m. newscasts. So what seemed to be a savvy business decision played havoc with the budgets of more than 200 affiliates and six months later the network moved Leno back to his 11:30 p.m. slot. Even though the network made money by saving on production costs, it created a firestorm of complains from affiliates who lost ratings and advertising revenues.[24]

The economic model of broadcast television is generally based on an advertising-supported model, at least for the traditional networks. The model relies on producing programs that attract a large audience that advertisers want to reach. Advertising, plus revenue from the programs that are syndicated after they go off air, has supported network TV since its beginnings, although that model is in serious trouble with the development of cable and the splintering of the viewing audience.

Structure of the Television Industry   To better understand how television works, let's first consider its structure and programming options. Then we'll look at television as an advertising medium, the way it connects with its audience, and its advantages and disadvantages. The key types of television delivery systems include network, subscription (cable and satellite), pay programming, local and public television, and syndication.

Network Television   A **broadcast network** is a distribution system that provides television content to its affiliated stations. Currently, there are four national, over-the-air television networks in the United States: the American Broadcasting Company (ABC), the Columbia Broadcasting System (CBS), the National Broadcasting Company (NBC), and Fox Broadcasting. The big three networks' hold on the viewing audience has dropped from 75 percent in 1987 to less than 30 percent. When Fox is included, networks still only capture less than half of the audience. The networks suffered in the recession except for Fox, which, in 2010 made more money than the evening newscasts of NBC, ABC, and CBS combined.[25]

Each network has about 150 affiliates. The network sells some commercial time to national advertisers and leaves some open for the affiliates to fill with local advertising. Affiliates pay their

A MATTER OF PRACTICE

Mad Men: Advertising at the Intersection of Social Change

Bruce Vanden Bergh, Professor, Michigan State University

Advertising is a fascinating business because it sits somewhat precariously at the intersection of societal change as it constantly adjusts to people's changing desires in an effort to sell products, services, and ideas ostensibly to make their lives better. That is what makes the advertising agency portrayed in the TV drama *Mad Men* such a great prism through which to view one of the most socially tumultuous eras of the 20th century, the 1960s. The show starts in the early 1960s in the New York City office of Sterling Cooper, a small conservative advertising agency inhabited by a caste of iconic characters, each of whom represents his or her own subculture's struggle to find its place and identity in a rapidly changing world.

The central character in the show is Don Draper who, with all of his Hollywood leading-man good looks, is the brilliant creative director of Sterling Cooper. His knack for conjuring up winning ideas just at the point the client is ready to walk out of the room is illustrated by his day-saving idea to say that Lucky Strikes are "toasted" to avoid the federal government's scrutiny of the health hazards of smoking even as he and his colleagues indulge in the habit.

Don Draper is as troubled as he is handsome. His troubles are manifold. He has created a false identity for himself that gives him the freedom to create the life he thinks he wants unfettered by a past. However, this still leaves him empty in ways he cannot fully satisfy by chasing women, drinking, smoking, or making money. He avoids serious commitment like the plague, including working without a contract. Thus, he always has one foot out the door should he want to escape from his responsibilities.

The central cast that surrounds Don Draper presents us with other struggles and changes to come in our country at the time. Joan Holloway is the office manager who knows how to get what she wants from the secretarial pool and the men at the office. However, she is still playing by and manipulating the old rules of power, which for her are based on beauty and sex appeal. Peggy Olson, on the other hand, rises out of the secretarial pool to become a copywriter with a keen sense of the changes going on in society and how to harness them in her copy and ideas. Salvatore Romano is an art director awakening to the fact that he is gay in a world not yet ready to accept that revelation. Peter Campbell is a young, ambitious account executive who never seems quite sure of himself and his relationships at the office, with his parents, or with his wife. Paul Kinsey gives us a glimpse of the impending civil rights crisis by dating a woman of color and participating in the early stages of the movement. Finally, there is Roger Sterling, one of the agency's principals, who marries a 20-year-old as his way of dealing with his senior status and denying his mortality.

Mad Men also is illuminating in the way it uses changes in the advertising agency business itself to demonstrate that change is an opportunity for some really forward-looking thinking and creative problem solving. This is best demonstrated when the ad agency McCann-Erickson is going to buy a British agency, PPL, that also happens to own Sterling Cooper. While PPL has allowed Sterling Cooper to operate somewhat autonomously, the McCann deal threatens to relegate Don and his colleagues to "midlevel cogs." Don, Roger, and others devise a scheme to get fired to void their contracts with McCann so they can start a new agency with key people (Joan, Peggy, Peter, Roger, and others) and clients from the old Sterling Cooper.

All of this happens in December of 1963 against the backdrop of the assassination of John F. Kennedy, which casts a dark cloud over the country and appears to dash the feeling of hope and a new vitality JFK promised the younger generation. Don Draper, who seemed personally unaffected by the assassination, renews his passion for advertising just three weeks later. This renewal comes complete with a new respect for Peggy and Peter because he now realizes that he needs them more than they need him at the new agency.

One of the paradoxes of *Mad Men* is that while the characters indulge in the unhealthy use of tobacco and alcohol, they appear much more secure in their world than we are in ours. Our world has become more complicated and the advertising business has become as fragmented as has our society. We no longer have just three big TV networks that can deliver large audiences for our ads. We no longer smoke as much, but that has been replaced by overeating. Old problems get solved and new ones arise. Creativity, however, has survived the times intact. It appears to be the common denominator that has helped the very flawed characters of *Mad Men* to change and survive.

For recaps on Mad Men episodes and videos, check out the *TV Guide* site, *www.tvguide.com/tvshows/mad-men/289066.*

respective networks 30 percent of the fees they charge local advertisers. In turn, affiliates receive a percentage of the advertising revenue (12 to 25 percent) paid to the national network. This advertising is the primary source of affiliate revenues.

Subscription Television   Cable is the most familiar example of **subscription television,** which means that people sign up for service and pay a monthly fee. Subscription television is a delivery system that carries the television signal to subscribers. **Cable television** is a form of subscription TV. It has grown into a national network of channels that provide highly targeted special-interest programming options. The impact of cable programming has been to fragment the audience and make it difficult to reach a large, mass audience. Cable has become a significant threat to the financial health of the networks. Viewing time for cable also has increased as the quality of the programming has improved and advertisers have found that "narrowcasting," which uses cable's special-interest programs to reach more tightly targeted audiences, can be even more efficient than mass broadcasting. The Cabletelevision Advertising Bureau found that ad-supported cable has taken over the lead from the broadcast networks.[26] Satellite television is similar to cable in that it's just a competing delivery system.

Some of the best programming in recent years, such as the award-winning *Sopranos* show, have been produced by cable channels. Oprah Winfrey rocked the industry when she announced she was leaving NBC to set up her own cable channel that would carry her programs.

Cable programming comes from independent cable networks and independent **superstations.** These networks include Cable News Network (CNN), the Disney Channel, the Entertainment and Sports Programming Network (ESPN), and a group of independent superstations whose programs are carried by satellite to cable operators (for example, WTBS-Atlanta, WGN-Chicago, and WWOR-New York).

Another form of subscription television is **satellite television.** Direct broadcast television services became available in the United States in the 1990s. Dish Network and DirecTV provide the equipment, including the satellite dish, to access some 125 national and local channels. Satellite television is particularly useful for people who live in rural areas without local or over-the-air service.

Pay Programming and On-Demand Programming   Pay programming and on-demand programming are available to subscribers for an additional monthly fee. This type of programming offers movies, specials, and sports under such plans as Home Box Office, Showtime, and The Movie Channel. Pay networks do not currently sell advertising time.

Local Television   Most local television stations are affiliated with a network and carry both network programming and their own programs. **Independent stations** are local stations not affiliated with networks. Costs for local advertising vary, depending on the size of the market and the demand for the programs carried. For example, a major station in Houston may charge local advertisers $2,000 for a 30-second spot during network prime time. This same time slot may cost $50 in a smaller town. Most advertisers for the local market are local retailers, primarily department stores or discount stores, financial institutions, automobile dealers, restaurants, and supermarkets. Advertisers buy time on a station-by-station basis. National advertisers sometimes buy local advertising on a city-by-city basis, using **spot buys.** They do this to align the buy with their product distribution, to "heavy-up" a national schedule to meet competitive activities, or to launch a new product in selected cities. Even some cable channels are attempting to localize their programming

Principle

Cable programming has fragmented the television audience and makes it difficult for advertisers to reach a large, mass audience.

to gain ground in this market. ESPN, for example, which dominates national and international sports viewing, is testing the use of local websites to report on hometown sports teams.

Public Television   Although many people still consider **public television** to be commercial free, the FCC allows the approximately 350 Public Broadcasting System (PBS) stations some leeway in airing commercial messages, called program **underwriting.** The FCC says these messages should not ask for a purchase or make price or quality comparisons. PBS is an attractive medium for advertisers because it reaches affluent, well-educated households. In addition, PBS still has a refined image, and PBS advertisers are viewed as good corporate citizens because of their support for noncommercial TV. Current FCC guidelines allow ads to appear on public television only during the local 2.5-minute program breaks. Each station maintains its own acceptability guidelines. Some PBS stations accept the same ads that appear on paid programming. However, most PBS spots are created specifically for public stations. Some PBS stations will not accept any commercial corporate advertising, but they do accept noncommercial ads that are "value neutral"—in other words, ads that make no attempt to sell a product or service.

Principle
If you want to reach an otherwise difficult-to-reach target—the well-educated, affluent household—one way to do it is to underwrite public television programming.

Syndication   An important revenue stream for networks and cable channels, such as HBO, that produce original programming is syndication. As in radio programming, television syndication refers to content providers that sell their programs to independent firms and other cable channels to replay as reruns. Some of the most popular first-run programs, such as *House* and *Law & Order,* are valuable properties and move quickly into syndication.

New Technology and Innovative Television   New technology is having an impact on programming options, as well as on distribution patterns and systems. Innovations, such as high-definition TV and interactive TV, expand advertising opportunities.

High-definition TV (HDTV) is a type of TV standard that delivers movie-quality, high-resolution images. All over-the-air stations broadcast their programming in an HDTV format. It's been a struggle, however, getting enough HDTV programming broadcast to build demand on the consumer side. As stations upgraded their equipment and moved to HDTV by 2009, the increased availability of HDTV programming made it necessary for consumers to upgrade to HDTV sets.

Say you're watching your favorite program and a commercial comes on for a product that interests you. A button pops up on the screen that you can click with your remote and you are asked questions about whether you want more information, a coupon, or to give some other response. Cable and DVRs are making **interactive television** feasible. The technology requires that advertisers give their ads to TiVo, for example, where codes are embedded. The ads are then distributed to TV and cable networks. When the ad airs, the digital video recorder boxes pick up the coding and turn on the interactive component for that subscriber. Axe used it to show young men how to use its body spray. The ad featured a motocross champion performing a motorbike stunt. While doing a back flip, the star ripped off his shirt and sprayed Axe from armpit to armpit. Viewers were then asked to go to a different channel to learn the move. Other features included videos and Web pages that can be navigated by using the remote control.

Interactive television also opens up the opportunity for **addressable television,** which is a type of television that makes it possible for individual homes to receive targeted and personalized advertising. The ability to address ads to different homes through cable and other subscription services is becoming more feasible. Several cable companies are experimenting with technology that would make addressability feasible, particularly for local video-on-demand programming. Cablevision provides viewers with a remote control they can use to request samples or promotional offers to be sent to their homes. It's also a lead-generation opportunity and the cable company boasts a high conversion rate tracking the number of viewers who click a second time to actually make an order.[27]

A number of researchers are testing the feasibility of bringing **3-D television** to living rooms by improving on current technology and its use of special glasses. One technology involves a set-top box, and 3-D sets are being tested by Japanese and Korean electronics rivals; Sony and ESPN are particularly focused on this new market.[28] British Sky Broadcasting is proposing a special 3-D television channel that will provide content for these new sets. In the United States several 2010 Super Bowl ads were filmed in 3-D. The logistics are difficult but 3-D may finally be on its way to home television sets.

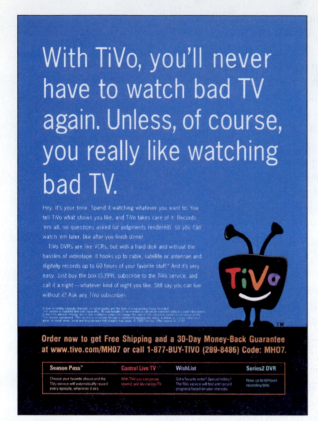

With TiVo, you'll never have to watch bad TV again. Unless, of course, you really like watching bad TV.

Hey, it's your time. Spend it watching whatever you want to. You tell TiVo what shows you like, and TiVo takes care of it. Records 'em all, no questions asked (or judgments rendered), so you can watch 'em later, like after you finish dinner.

TiVo DVRs are like VCRs, but with a hard disk and without the hassles of videotape. It hooks up to cable, satellite or antennae and digitally records up to 60 hours of your favorite stuff.* And it's very easy. Just buy the box ($399), subscribe to the TiVo service, and call it a night—whatever kind of night you like. Still say you can live without it? Ask any TiVo subscriber.

Order now to get Free Shipping and a 30-Day Money-Back Guarantee at www.tivo.com/MH07 or call 1-877-BUY-TIVO (289-8486) Code: MH07.

Season Pass™	Control Live TV	WishList	Series2 DVR
Choose your favorite shows and the TiVo service will automatically record every episode, whenever it airs.	With TiVo you can pause, rewind, and slo-mo Live TV.	Got a favorite actor? Special hobby? The TiVo service will find and record programs based on your interests.	Now, up to 80 hours recording time.

DVR technology poses a challenge for advertisers since it enables consumers to bypass commercials.

Traditional forms of network television are being threatened by **online video.** After Comcast bid to buy NBC, one of the ideas floated by the new management team involved subscription fees for NBC—hoping to make the previously ad-supported network more like premium cable. The new combined media and entertainment company also considered bringing the cable-TV subscription model to the Web and its online video programming.[29]

Another technology that is having a profound effect on television programming and the way people watch television is the **digital video recorder (DVR),** such as TiVo. DVR systems allow users to record favorite TV shows and watch them whenever they like. The technology makes it possible to record the programming without the hassles of videotape, letting users pause, do instant replays, and begin watching programs even before the recording has finished. This capability is known as **time-shifting.**

DVRs are a threat to marketers because it allows consumers to zip past commercials completely. It also is forcing advertisers to rethink the design of their ads, recognizing that they have 3 to 4 seconds, at best, to win the attention of button-happy viewers. It also raises the issue of how advertisers should respond. Some are experimenting with new ways to send messages that immediately engage attention. Coca-Cola and TiVo, for example, have created ads that appear on screen as a small text box when viewers pause a show.[30]

Advertisers and television executives are alarmed over the increasing popularity of time-shifting technology. It calls into question audience measurement numbers: If 20 percent of the audience is recording *24* on Monday night only to watch it Saturday morning commercial free, then is the Monday night measurement accurate? The DVR industry estimates that viewers zip past (fast forward through) about 6 percent of TV commercials—an estimated waste of some $5 billion in ad spending—and predicts that by the end of 2011, about 16 percent will suffer that fate.[31]

A Nielsen study, however, found that viewers are not zipping through commercials as much as advertisers feared. To further understand this pattern, TiVo has also announced that it is considering a service that will provide second-by-second data about which programs the company's subscribers are watching and which commercials they are skipping.

Measuring the Television Audience A great number of advertisers consider television their primary medium. Can television deliver a target audience to advertisers effectively? What do we really know about how audiences watch television? Is it a background distraction? Do we switch from channel to channel without watching any single show? Or do we carefully and intelligently select what we watch on television?

Television viewers are sometimes irritated by the intrusiveness of advertising and are not reluctant to switch channels or zip through commercials on prerecorded programs. Clutter is part of the problem advertisers face and the audience has become very good at avoidance, unless the ads are intrusive or highly engaging. The Super Bowl is one of the few programs where viewers actually watch commercials. Nielsen has found that the average drop in viewing between the game and the commercials was less than 1 percent. CBS says that the typical drop during a normal program is approximately 5 percent.[32]

A. C. Nielsen is the research company that dominates the television measurement industry. **Exposure** is television's equivalent to circulation. Exposure measures households with sets turned on, a population referred to as **households using television (HUT).** But a HUT figure doesn't tell you if anyone is watching the program. Remember from Chapter 11 that we defined an **impression** as one person's opportunity to be exposed one time to an ad. Like print, the impressions from television—the number of viewers exposed to a program—might be greater than the number of households reached since there may be more than one viewer watching and the

Principle

The TV audience has become very good at avoiding commercials unless the ads are intrusive or highly engaging.

commercial may be repeated several times in a program or during a time period. We add all of these impressions up and call them **gross impressions.**

For television programs, the exposure is estimated in terms of number of viewers. The 2010 Super Bowl was watched by 106 million people, making it the most watched telecast ever, surpassing the viewership of the 1983 M*A*S*H final episode. Following those programs, the 1996 Dallas vs. Pittsburgh Super Bowl game drew 97 million viewers and the 2007 Super Bowl featuring the Chicago Bears and Indianapolis Colts, attracted some 93 million viewers.

- *Ratings* These gross impression figures become very large and difficult to work with, which is why the television industry, similar to radio, uses ratings (percentage of exposure) instead. Ratings are an easier measurement to work with because they convert the raw figure to a percentage. When you read about a television show having a rating of 20 that means that 20 percent, or one-fifth of all households with televisions, were tuned in to that program. Note that one rating point equals 1 percent of the nation's estimated 114 million TV homes; that's why planners describe this program as having 20 **rating points,** or percentage points. A 20 rating is actually a huge figure, since the fragmentation of cable has diversified television watching and made it very difficult to get 20 percent of the households tuned to any one program.

- *Share* A better estimate of impressions might be found in a program's **share of audience,** which refers to the percent of viewers based on the number of sets turned on during a specific broadcast period. The share figure for a particular program is always larger than its rating, since the base is smaller. For example, if the Super Bowl gets a rating of 40 (40 percent of all households with television), its share would be 67 if the total HUT was 60 percent. In other words, the Super Bowl has 2/3 (40 divided by 60 = 67) of all households that have their television sets turned on during the Super Bowl.

Independent rating firms, such as A. C. Nielsen, provide the most commonly used measure of national and local television audiences. Nielsen periodically samples a portion of the television viewing audience, estimates the size and characteristics of the audiences watching specific shows, and then makes these data available, for a fee, to advertisers and ad agencies, which use them in their media planning.

Nielsen's calculations are based on audience data from about 5,000 measurement instruments, called **people meters,** which record what television shows are being watched, the number of households that are watching, and which family members are viewing. The recording is done automatically; household members indicate their presence by pressing a button. These are placed in randomly selected households in the 210 television markets in the United States. The company also uses viewer diaries mailed out during the **sweeps** period, which are quarterly periods when more extensive audience data and demographics are gathered. About 1 million diaries are returned each year.

Nielsen continues to add people meters in its top markets to track local viewing patterns. Meters are used only to determine what show is being watched, and not the specific demographics of who is watching it. Demographic data come from diaries. A new locally based meter system would allow Nielsen to identify the age, race, and sex of viewers on a nightly basis. Note that these ratings are based on programs, and are not measures of specific advertisements.

One interesting finding from an analysis of ratings is that even in this age of DVRs, the lead-in show does matter. Fox's *American Idol*, for example, has been a strong lead-in to other Fox shows such as *Fringe*. Another Nielsen finding during the recent recession is the power of ethnic media. For example, the number one TV station in Los Angeles isn't one of the networks, it's Spanish-language KMEX. And it's not just LA's top station, Nielsen ranks it as the number one station in the United States with viewers ages 18 to 49.[33]

Something not measured by all of these metrics is the dedication of a program's superfans. When NBC proposed dropping *Chuck*, fans launched a campaign on Facebook, Twitter, and TV blogs in defense of their favorite program. Realizing the significance of the attachment, Subway jumped in as an ally. To demonstrate the marketing power of ChuckTV.net, a consumer-generated campaign called "Finale & Footlong" urged fans to buy foot-long sandwiches from Subway to eat as they watched the season finale. The effort was successful, and NBC announced it would renew the show.[34]

Television Advertising

The first television commercial aired in 1941 when Bulova bought time on a New York station before a Phillies vs. Dodgers game.[35] Television is used for advertising because it works like the movies—it tells stories, engages the emotions, creates fantasies, and can have great visual impact. Because it's an action medium, it is also good for demonstrating how things work. It brings brand images to life and adds personality to a brand. An example of the dramatic, emotional power of television comes from one of the greatest commercials of all time. Called "Iron Eyes Cody," the Ad Council PSA was created as part of an environmental campaign. It shows a Native American paddling a canoe through a river ruined by trash. A close-up shows a tear from his eye.

Advertising Sales   The first decision in designing a television ad is determining its length, which is usually 10, 15, 30, or 60 seconds. The most common length is 30 seconds because for most advertisers, the 60-second spot is considered too expensive. The 10-second ad is like a billboard and simply announces that a program is "brought to you by . . ." the advertiser. ESPN is experimenting with these "mini-mercials" and offering in-house produced ads that combine an advertiser's message with the lead-in to a show. For example, in an Asics spot, a runner returns home and turns on his TV, which shows the ESPN "SportsCenter" logo with its theme song.[36]

Long-form ads, which are of various lengths, are seen on late-night TV as "infomercials," when the cost of broadcast time is much lower than at other times of day. Late-night infomercials have been the venue for direct-response television with its promise of how-to-do-it tools and vegetable cutters, as well as get-rich investing. An interesting variation is found in rural India where traveling performers present live infomercials from mobile stages to a large and growing population of international brand-focused customers. Late-night informercial products like Snuggies and the Windshield Wonder that clean the insides of car windows are also showing up in retail stores, such as Walmart, Target, and Bed Bath & Beyond.[37]

The actual form of a television commercial depends on whether a network, local, or subscription service schedule is used.

- *Sponsorships* In program **sponsorships,** the advertiser assumes the total financial responsibility for producing the program and providing the accompanying commercials. The *Hallmark Hall of Fame* program is an example of a sponsored program. Sponsorship can have a powerful effect on the viewing public, especially because the advertiser can control the content and quality of the program as well as the placement and length of commercials. However, the costs of producing and sponsoring a 30- or 60-minute program make this option too expensive for most advertisers. Several advertisers can produce a program jointly as an alternative to single sponsorship. This plan is quite common with sporting events, where each sponsor receives a 15-minute segment.
- *Participations* Sponsorships represent less than 10 percent of network advertising. The rest is sold as **participations,** where advertisers pay for 10, 15, 20, 30, or 60 seconds of commercial time during one or more programs. The advertiser can buy any time that is available. This approach, which is the most common one used in network advertising today, provides a great deal more flexibility in market coverage, target audiences, scheduling, and budgeting. Participations do not create the same high impact as sponsorships, however. Finally, the "time avails" (available time slots) for the most popular programs are often bought up by the largest advertisers, leaving fewer good time slots for small advertisers.

CLASSIC

The "crying Indian" image from this famous commercial communicated a strong ecology message. The Indian, played by Iron Eyes Cody, paddled his canoe up a filthy stream and sheds a tear as people in a speeding car throw trash out the window. To read about this "Keep America Beautiful" campaign, go to www.adcouncil.org and choose "Historic Campaigns" from the list on the left; then scan down to the "Pollution: Keep America Beautiful" heading. © 1971. Courtesy of Keep America Beautiful, Inc. (kab.org).

The price of a commercial is based on the rating of the surrounding program (note the rating is for the program, not the commercial). The price is also based on the daypart during which the commercial is shown. The following table shows the Television Standard Dayparts. The most expensive time block is prime time.

- *Spot Announcements* The third form a television commercial can take is the **spot announcement.** Spot announcements are commercials that appear in the breaks between programs, which local affiliates sell to advertisers who want to show their ads locally. Commercials are sold on a station-by-station basis to local, regional, and national advertisers. However, local buyers dominate spot television. PSAs are also distributed to stations for local play based on the station's time availability.

Standard Television Dayparts

Early morning	M–F 7–9 A.M.
Daytime	M–F 9 A.M.–4:30 P.M.
Early fringe	M–F 4:30–7:30 P.M.
Prime access	M–F 7:30–8 P.M.
	M–S 8–11 P.M.
	Su 7–11 P.M.
Late news	M–Su 11–11:30 P.M.
Late night	M–Su 11:30 P.M.–1 A.M.
Saturday morning	Sa 8 A.M.–1 P.M.
Weekend afternoon	Sa–Su 1 P.M.–7 P.M.

Note: All times are Eastern Standard Time (EST).

Media sales operations are trying to encourage advertising through various types of partnerships and cooperative advertising strategies. We have already mentioned ESPN's "minimercials," which embed a brand's reminder ad in the opening of a sports program. Another example comes from Campbell's Soup and CBS, which partnered in an advertising campaign that paired various shows with different types of Campbell soups.

Effectiveness of Television   Television is used because of the reach it delivers. You may remember from our previous discussions of our Facets of Effects Model that one of the most important effects is awareness. A recent study of viewers conducted by the Yankelovich research company for the Television Bureau of Advertising tracked the impact of television from awareness, which it measured at 80 percent, through various decision-making stages for 15 product categories ending at 53 percent for transactions. The study compared TV and the Internet and determined that television had more impact, particularly at the awareness stage.[38]

Television advertising also makes a strong visual and emotional impact. The interaction of sight, sound, color, motion, and drama creates a stronger emotional response than most other forms of advertising media. In Chapter 4 we mentioned *engagement,* which certainly applies to TV. Television is particularly good at creating messages that can be highly engrossing. Even with TiVo, people still sit through advertisements and use online search engines to seek out advertising that is relevant to them.[39] Television is also good for delivering messages that require action, movement, and demonstration, such as the messages created for Avista Utilities in Portland, Oregon. When it comes to energy efficiency, Karl Schroeder explains, every little bit adds up—using energy-efficient bulbs, cleaning the coils on a refrigerator, using Energy Star appliances, and other environmental practices. To spread this idea and empower customers, the messages demonstrate different actions folks can take to improve the efficiency of their home.

Television has drawbacks, as well. The commercial breaks between programs can be difficult time slots for advertisers because there is a great deal of clutter from competing commercials, station breaks, and public service announcements. Commercial breaks also tend to be the time when viewers take a break from their television sets. Research has found that the best position is at the beginning and the end of the commercial break—the spots in the middle have only a quarter of the impact.

The downside of large reach to a mass audience is **wasted reach**—communication directed at an audience that may not fit the advertiser's target market. Cable television is much more

Principle

If you are going to use television, design a message that takes advantage of its visual and emotional impact.

Principle

As the number of commercial messages increases, the visibility and persuasiveness of television advertising diminishes.

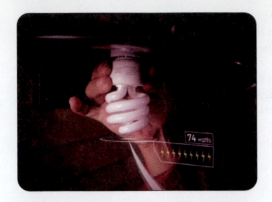

SHOWCASE

An interesting use of computer-created motion graphics demonstrates how different actions create energy efficiency. Copywriter Karl Schroeder was on the Coates Kokes team that created a series of educational videos for Avista Utilities. He explained, "motion graphics were applied to highlight the individual actions and 'connect' the efforts to the rest of the community, expressing the notion that we're all in it together, and together we can make a larger impact."

A graduate of the University of Oregon advertising program, Karl Schroeder was nominated by Professor Charles Frazer.

targeted than network and spot television, so it has less waste. Disinterest is another problem because people are often inclined to **zip** (fast forward) or **zap** (change channels) commercials if they don't have a DVR.

Another big drawback is that television advertising is expensive relative to other media, both for time and production costs. (*Note:* Television is "expensive" in terms of dollar amounts even though it is relatively cheap in terms of gross impressions because its audience is so much larger than that of other media.) A 30-second, prime-time spot averages about $185,000, and most advertisers would want to run a commercial multiple times. That average, however, doesn't mean much because costs vary considerably for a highly rated prime-time show versus a lower rated program. Production costs are higher than ads in other media, as well. They include filming the commercial (several thousand to several hundred thousand dollars) and paying the talent—writers, directors, and actors. When celebrities are used, the price tag can be millions of dollars for the campaign budget.

Another problem is clutter, and its stepchildren, intrusiveness and irritation. In the past, the National Association of Broadcasters (NAB) restricted the allowable commercial time per hour to approximately 6 minutes, but the Justice Department overturned this restriction and the number of commercials has increased significantly (up to 20 minutes per hour of programming). As the number of commercials increases, the visibility and persuasiveness of television advertising diminishes. As clutter has increased, advertisements are becoming more intrusive to grab attention from a disinterested and irritated audience. The high irritation level is what has led viewers to mute and zap commercials.

OTHER VIDEO FORMATS

Radio and television dominate broadcast, but other broadcast forms also carry advertising and marketing communication messages. We'll discuss film trailers and other video formats here.

Movie Trailers and Disc Ads

Movie theaters, particularly the large chain theaters, sell time at the beginning of their film showings for commercials, called **trailers.** Most of these trailers are previews advertising upcoming films, but some are national commercials for brands, ads for local businesses, public service announcements, or other forms of sponsored programs. These messages can be targeted to a certain extent by the nature of the film and the rating, such as G or PG. Some films, such as *Shall We Dance,* draw an audience that is heavily female, while action films, such as the *Matrix* series, draw more males.

Movie trailers are one of the fastest growing types of advertising because of advances in digital technology. According to the Cinema Advertising Council, in-theater advertising is a $500 million industry.[40] The cost of the trailer is based on the number of theaters showing the spot and their estimated monthly attendance. Generally the cost of a trailer in a first-run theater is about the same as the cost of a 30-second television spot in prime time. The reason trailers are valued by marketers is that they play to a captive audience with their attention on the screen, not reading or talking to other people. The attention level is higher for these ads than for almost any other form of commercials. But the captive audience dimension is also the biggest disadvantage of movie advertising because people who have paid $6 to $10 for a ticket resent the intrusion. They feel they paid for the ticket so they shouldn't have to pay with their time and attention to watch commercials.

DVD, Blu-ray, and other video distribution systems also place ads before their movies and on the cases. The targeting strategy is the same as that for theater ads, called *trailers,* where the ad is matched to the movie audience. Unlike the theaters, rental videos tend to carry more brand advertising than movie previews. Even some billboards are now equipped to run mini-movies and ads electronically. The job search company *Monster.com* has been successful with trailers that replay as electronic signboard messages in public spaces—another example of media convergence with video appearing as out-of-home media.

Promotional Videos

Promotional video networks run sponsored programs and commercials, such as the channels you see in grocery stores, doctor's offices, and truck stops that distribute commercials by video or satellites. The pioneer in this arena is Channel M, which markets customized in-store video programming to such companies as Payless Shoes and Kampgrounds of America.

Marketers, such as General Electric and Pepsi, are experimenting with short video clips—both live-action and animated—that can be watched free on the video-on-demand service available to Time Warner cable customers. The shorts can also be seen on the GE website (*www.ge.com/imaginationtheater*), as well as on sites like MySpace, Google Video, and YouTube. Finally, videos and DVDs are used for product literature, as well as in public relations for video news releases (VNRs) to the media.

Using Broadcast and Video Effectively

Now that we have reviewed television and radio media, as well as other film and video formats, we can summarize how to use broadcast media effectively. The following table summarizes advantages and limitations of these media and provides guidelines for broadcast media decisions.

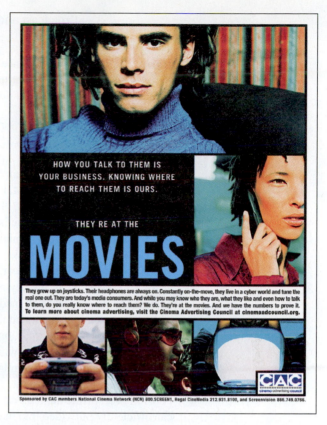

The Cinema Advertising Council (CAC) is an organization devoted to advertising in movies. This ad was placed in *Advertising Age* to reach media buyers and remind them of the power of cinema advertising to target particular groups of moviegoers.

Broadcast and Video Media Advantages and Limitations

	Advantages	Limitations
Radio	• Pervasiveness; in most every home and car • Reaches specialized target audiences • Reaches them at critical apertures (morning and evening drive time) • Offers high frequency; music (jingles) can be repeated more easily than other forms of advertising • Flexible, easy to change • Good for local tie-ins and promos • Mental imagery can be highly engaging • Audience less likely to switch channels when ads come on	• Listener inattentiveness; may just be on in the background • Lack of visuals • Clutter • May have buying difficulties for local buys • Lack of control: talk show content is unpredictable and may be critical
Television	• Pervasiveness; in most every home • High level of viewing • Reaches a mass national audience although can be targeted by programs • High impact: has audio, video, motion, music, color, high drama • Cost efficient	• Clutter—cable offers a large number of channels • High production costs • Wasted reach • Inflexibility; can't easily make last-minute changes • Intrusiveness—some audience resistance to advertising leads to zipping and zapping

Broadcast and Video Media Advantages and Limitations

	Advantages	*Limitations*
Movies	• Captive audience • No need for intrusiveness because audience can't do multitasking • High impact	• Audience resistance is high; hates being a captive audience • Expensive; needs high-value production

Looking Ahead

This chapter has provided an overview of traditional media, their characteristics, and their strengths and weaknesses. But, in truth, traditional media hardly exist any more. An interview on public radio's NPR headlined, "In a 24/7 World, What Is a Magazine?" began with this line: "It's hard to know what a magazine is these days." Is it paper? Is it a website? Martin Sorrell, head of WPP, the world's largest communication company (125 firms including Ogilvy & Mather and JWT advertising agencies) asks: "How do you define a newspaper or a magazine?" He observes, "I doubt free-to-air television or, in particular, newspapers and magazines, will ever be the same again."[41] This is one of the key points of change that Kelley pointed out in his essay in the Part 4 opener. He observes that all media, including the traditional ones, will have some type of digital and interactive component and this will only make media selection more challenging.

Not only are these traditional media formats changing, so are the ads that appear in them. CBS promoted its fall season with ads in the magazine *Entertainment Weekly* that contained video clips of its new programs. Similar to musical greeting cards, the technology used a flexible, thin, plastic screen that was activated when the two-page ad was opened. The videos also included a Pepsi Max ad inside the CBS ad. An executive at Time Warner, publisher of *EW*, observed, "It we can efficiently put video into magazines, think about the possibilities it would open up."[42]

So let's move on to the exciting and equally fast-changing world of digital media, which are generating even more new opportunities for marketing communication. The next chapter will review the dynamic world of online communication.

IT'S A WRAP

Aflac's Duck Spreads Its Wings

How effective is the Aflac duck? The Kaplan Thaler Group succeeded in creating a campaign that led to a 94 percent awareness of Aflac and an increase of 55 percent in U.S. sales during the first three years of the campaign, followed by double-digit growth in the following years. This campaign earned a Gold Effie for the duck who successfully communicated the brand personality as well as the honor of being voted one of the best-known brand icons.

Will the next generation of this ad campaign be as effective as a new agency uses the duck to challenge consumers to find out more about the company? Stay tuned.

In the meantime, you can learn much from these campaigns featuring the celebrated odd duck. This case demonstrates that even in a changing media environment that puts much emphasis on the Web and social media, traditional media are often critical to a campaign's effectiveness. Traditional media helped drive consumers to Aflac's website. All components of the campaign worked together to educate consumers about the brand, to increase brand comprehension, and have a little fun.

Also, you can learn that even as campaigns evolve, it's important to stay true to the brand. According to James Wisdom, senior manager of new media for Aflac, the message in social media, like that in the traditional media, has to "straddle a fine line between lighthearted quips and corporate messaging."

Wisdom said, "We work very hard to stay true to the Aflac Duck as he has been defined in the past, while defining his personality going forward."

As the campaign takes flight, watch as our fine-feathered friend continues to show his plucky, rock star personality and build his vocabulary beyond the one word he knows best, "Aflac."

Key Points Summary

1. **What key points should marketers know to make effective decisions about advertising in newspapers and magazines?** Newspapers are great for announcements of news. They also provide local market coverage with some geographic flexibility, plus an interaction with national news and the ability to reach shoppers who see the paper as a credible source. Magazines reach special-interest audiences who have a high level of receptivity to the message. People read them slowly, and they have long life and great image reproduction. However, magazines require long lead times, have a low level of immediacy and limited flexibility, and generally do not reach a broad mass market.

2. **What factors do marketers consider when making out-of-home media decisions?** Out-of-home media includes everything from billboards to hot-air balloons. A common out-of-home medium is outdoor advertising, which refers to billboards along streets and highways as well as posters. Outdoor is a high-impact and directional medium; it's also effective for brand reminders and relatively inexpensive with a long life. Other forms of out-of-home media include on-premise signs, posters, and transit advertising.

3. **How do radio and television work as marketing communication media?** The traditional radio stations are found on AM and FM and primarily serve local markets. AM and FM are only the beginning of the radio listener's options, which also include public radio, cable and satellite radio, low-powered stations, and Web radio. Radio dramas engage the imagination, but radio is primarily a music-driven medium, which serves audiences defined by their musical tastes. Listeners can have a very intimate relationship with radio and can be quite loyal to their favorite stations, but radio also serves as background.

Television is useful as a marketing communication medium because it works like a movie with story, action, emotions, and visual impact. TV audiences are fragmented, often irritated by advertising, and prone to avoidance. Audiences are measured in terms of ratings and share. TV's greatest advantage is that it is pervasive and cost efficient when reaching a large number of viewers. Because of the special-interest aspect of cable programming, it is good at reaching more narrowly targeted audiences.

4. **How do marketers use movies and other video formats for marketing communication?** Movie theaters sell time for advertisements before their films. Marketing communication messages are also carried on discs, such as DVDs and Blu-ray, as well as in lobbies and other public spaces. Video-generated commercials, sponsored programs, and announcements can also be seen in supermarkets, transit stations, and waiting rooms for professional services such as doctors' offices.

Words of Wisdom: Recommended Reading

Aitchison, Jim, *Cutting Edge Radio: How to Create the World's Best Radio Ads for Brands in the 21st Century,* Upper Saddle River, NJ: Pearson Education, 2002.

Hassett, James, *AdverSelling: How to Build Stronger Relationships,* Burlington, MA: The Avertraining Group, 2005.

Prooth, Victor, and Shelly Ng, *"Radio Advertising Does Not Work." Says Who?* Chicago: American Mass Media Corp, 2006.

Weyland, Paul, *Successful Local Broadcast Sales,* New York: American Management Association, 2008.

Winicki, Michael, *Killer Techniques to Succeed with Newspaper, Magazine, and Yellow Pages Advertising,* Big Noisy Publishing, 2005.

Key Terms

3-D television, p. 377

addressable television, p. 377

affiliates, p. 370

aperture, p. 373

bleed, p. 360

broadcast media, p. 369

broadcast network, p. 374

cable radio, p. 370

cable television, p. 376

classified advertising, p. 357

consumer magazines, p. 359

controlled circulation, p. 360

Review Questions

1. Explain how newspapers vary based on frequency of publication, format and size, and circulation.

2. Explain how newspaper readership is determined and measured.

3. How is magazine readership measured?

4. Explain how advertising impact is measured for outdoor advertising.

5. What is the greatest advantage of outdoor advertising? Directory advertising?

6. How can radio be used most effectively, and what are the advantages and limitations of advertising on radio?

7. How can television be used most effectively, and what are the advantages and limitations of advertising on television?

8. What are trailers and how are they used as an advertising form?

9. How can movie advertising be used most effectively, and what are its advantages and limitations?

Discussion Questions

1. You are the media planner for an agency handling a small chain of upscale furniture outlets in a medium-sized metro market that concentrates most of its advertising in the Sunday supplement of the local newspaper. The client also schedules display ads in the daily editions for special sales. Six months ago a new, high-style metropolitan lifestyle magazine approached you about advertising for your client. You deferred a decision by saying you'd see what reader acceptance would be. Now the magazine has shown some steady increases. If you were to include the magazine on the ad schedule, you'd have to reduce the newspaper advertising somewhat. What would be your recommendation to the furniture store owner?

2. A new radio station is moving into your community. Management is not sure how to position the station in this market and

has asked you to develop a study to help make this decision. What key research questions must be asked and what research methods would you recommend using to get more information about this market and the new station's place in it?

3. You are the media planner for a cosmetics company introducing a new line of makeup for teenage girls. Your research indicates that television advertising might be an effective medium for creating awareness about your new product line. In exploring this idea, how do you design a television advertising strategy that will reach your target market successfully? What programs and times do you choose? Why? Would you consider syndicated television? Why or why not?

4. You have been asked to advise on where advertising should be placed for a new restaurant in town that specializes in

low-fat and low-carb healthy food. Consider newspaper, magazine, outdoor, directory, and local radio and television advertising. Evaluate each medium in terms of its strengths and weaknesses and how well it connects with the people you think would be the target market for this restaurant. What more do you need to know to determine the appropriateness of these media for this restaurant? In your response, begin by stating your advertising goals and your target audience profile, then state what you might or might not accomplish by advertising in each print medium.

5. *Three-Minute Debate* You are a major agency media director who has just finished a presentation to a prospective client in convenience food marketing where you recommend increasing the use of local radio and television advertising in spot markets. During the Q and A period, a client representative says: "We know that network television viewers' loyalty is nothing like it was ten or even five years ago because so many people now turn to cable, VCRs, and the Web. There are smaller audiences per program each year, yet television time costs continue to rise. Do you still believe we should consider commercial television as a primary medium for our company's advertising?" Another member of the client team questions whether broadcast is effective given the clutter on both radio and television with long commercial pods. "Why shouldn't we decrease our use of broadcast advertising?" How would you answer? Working in a team of classmates, develop an argument either in support of increasing or decreasing the use of broadcast advertising for this client. Prepare a presentation to give in class that explains your team's point of view.

Take-Home Projects

1. *Portfolio Project* You have been asked by the director of your school's student union to make a chart of all the traditional media serving your market to use in promoting the center's 50th anniversary events. Develop a profile for each medium giving the key characteristics, such as type of programming (for broadcast), the type of audience reached, the products commonly advertised, and the appropriateness of this medium as an advertising vehicle for the center's special celebration. At the end of your media analysis, identify the top three that you would recommend and explain why.

2. *Mini-Case Analysis* Aflac has been an award-winning campaign for years. Explain how its media use has contributed to its success. In particular, describe the changes in the new strategy and how the media mix has evolved. If you were a member of the team planning the next year's campaign, what changes would you recommend? What other media might be useful?

Team Project: The BrandRevive Campaign

Review the strengths and limitations of the various types of print, out-of-home, and broadcast media discussed in this chapter in terms of your BrandRevive campaign.

- Review your previous audience research to develop some insight into your target's media use.
- Go through the lists of strengths and limitations, as well as the discussions in the text for each traditional medium we discussed in this chapter and analyze if that medium is or isn't appropriate for this BrandRevive project. Give each medium a score of from 1 to 10 with 10 being an excellent medium to use and 1 being the least appropriate.

- From your analysis, make a prioritized list beginning with the medium that you think is the most appropriate. For each of your top two traditional media write a one-paragraph recommendation that explains and justifies your thinking.
- Convert your key findings to a PowerPoint presentation that is no longer than three slides. Prepare and practice to give this presentation to your class.

Hands-On Case

The Century Council

Read the Century Council case in the Appendix before coming to class.

1. Which advertising medium do you believe would be more impactful in The Stupid Drink campaign; television or outdoor stadium boards? Why?

2. The Stupid Drink campaign ignores college radio. Why do you think the media planners thought this was the correct choice? How could they prove it?

3. In choosing colleges to advertise at, The Stupid Drink team choose "ranked" party schools. Do you agree with that methodology of targeting? Why or Why not?

Digital Media

It's a Winner

Campaign:	Organization:	Agency:	Award:
"Virtual Army Experience"	*U.S. Army's Office of Economic & Manpower Analysis*	*Ignited LLC*	*Gold Effie*

CHAPTER KEY POINTS

1. How does the Internet work, and what roles does it play in marketing communication?
2. What are the most common types of online marketing communication?
3. In what ways are Internet practices, issues, and trends evolving?

You're in the (Virtual) Army Now

You may not realize it, but the military has historically been on the frontlines of the digital revolution. In the latter half of the 20th century, the military actively engaged in developing computers and their capabilities. During the Cold War it created a precursor to the World Wide Web, called the Advanced Research Projects Agency Network, better known as ARPANET. So when the U.S. Army wanted to increase its ranks, it was a no-brainer to use digital media for recruiting.

The revolution from analog to digital technology has brought about two fundamental changes facilitated in part by the invention of the personal computer. First, it made it possible to produce and copy information exactly. Second, it became easy to move information between media and to access or distribute it remotely. Interactivity became key.

These abilities have transformed the way people do business. Think about what you can do with your computer. You can buy music, make airline reservations, see how that sweater you're thinking about buying looks in red, or find exotic types of licorice, publish your own blog, participate in social media, and so on—all things that would have been impossible before, say, 1995.

It also means that those who are afraid to embrace the changing media environment are in danger of getting left behind. Clearly the U.S. Army is marching to a different drummer when it comes to recruiting than it did before. Here's what it did to reach its core audience of 17- to 24-year-olds to achieve the goal of recruiting more than 100,000 new soldiers each year.

It used the latest technologies to show the variety of exciting career opportunities available in the U.S. Army. Since the 1980s the U.S. Army's use of media has shifted dramatically away from traditional radio and print media to the Internet.

It also took advantage of the growth of event marketing, unheard of in the 1980s. By 2007, event marketing accounted for about a fifth of the U.S. Army's total marketing budget. The U.S. Army typically has sponsored events such as NASCAR and rodeo bull riding because they shared a common target audience. Realizing they faced the challenging task of recruiting young people in the midst of two wars, both the Army and its agency, Ignited, knew they would need to focus more on the military experience itself if they were to accomplish their goal of interacting with, persuading, and converting prospects into U.S. Army recruits.

The big idea for the campaign? Create an interactive mobile event that would draw the core target audience and engage them in a Virtual Army Experience (VAE). Key to this concept is the use of video games to educate prospects about facts of life in the U.S. Army. Research showed that prospects thought conventional advertising talked at them, rather than to them. So this project was designed to let them hear real-life stories from military personnel and get credible information. The exhibit traveled cross-country, targeting festivals, theme parks, state fairs, and air shows.

The VAE offered a life-size, networked, virtual world using state-of-the-art Army training simulation technology. The exhibit housed more than 70 flat screens and more than 5 miles of data cable. It required more than 75 computers and 260 gigs of processing power to run the experience. Check out its website at *http://vae.americasarmy.com* for more information.

The fast-action, information-rich computer game experience and event immersed participants in the world of soldiering. Prospective recruits viewed videos of actual soldiers decorated for their actions in combat, and received live and recorded briefings from team members to prepare for their virtual combat operation. As they participated in the mission, visitors tested their ability to be a team member who followed rules of engagement, displayed leadership and Army values including integrity and respect, and used high-tech equipment. After completing the mission, participants moved to another area in the exhibit where they were debriefed on their performance. Soldiers guided participants through a review of the experience and stood ready to answer questions about soldiering.

Was the U.S. Army's mission accomplished? You can find out by turning to the end of the chapter to the *It's a Wrap* section.

Sources: "Virtual Army Experience: The U.S. Army's Powerful New Recruiting Tool," *www.effie.org; http://army.mil/-news; http://armyaccessionsnewsroom.com; http://vae.americasarmy.com;* David Centofante, "Virtual Army Hits the Ground at Andrews," *www.washingtontimes.com.*

The U.S. Army is a well-known organization and brand that is using innovative digital and interactive communication media to recruit soldiers. The Virtual Army Experience is a great example of how the new media can be used to engage prospects and persuade them to commit. In this chapter we will discuss a number of interactive media, including the Internet, e-mail, and social media, that connect people in a network of word-of-mouth communication. It's a dynamic and fast-changing media environment that challenges communication planners to not only keep up, but also get ahead of the technological changes that are driving innovation and making this such a creative area of marketing communication.

INTERACTIVE MEDIA: WEB 2.0 AND YOU

Because new technology is exploding, media planners are racing to try to understand the implications of this rapidly changing media landscape for advertising and marketing communication. New hardware offerings such as super-smart phones, netbooks, smart books (like a smart phone with a tablet computer), portable video players, and the next generation of e-readers are stirring the imaginations of early adopters. New operating systems, called *platforms*, include not only the iPhone, which has been the innovative leader, but also Research in Motion's (RIM) Blackberry and Google's Android. MySpace, Facebook, Wikipedia, Craigslist, YouTube, Flickr, and Google are just a few of the sites that provide new tools that permit users to customize messages and interact, which creates new ways of looking at media use by consumers. The Part 4 Introduction by Larry Kelley highlighted the impact of these changes.

The creation of social networking and entertainment sites builds on the interactive power of the Internet with astounding effects. This is a trend referred to as Web 2.0, which calls attention to the shift in control of media from publishers to consumers. As we noted in earlier chapters, users of the Internet are not only viewing and interacting, they are also contributing and taking control of the content. In this more democratic media environment, user-generated content is having a huge impact on both traditional media industries and on advertising. As the authors of *Citizen Marketers* say, "Corporate decision makers are losing even the illusion of control."[1]

Another trend noted in the Part 4 introduction is the convergence and blurring of media forms, a shift that is challenging media planners, and one we'll talk more about at the end of the chapter. The Internet is the ultimate convergence medium because it bridges print and broadcast media and blurs the distinction between them. Newspapers, magazines, and other print forms can be delivered online, and their messages still look like print. Video is moving online and even on to cell phones. We've talked about convergence in previous chapters, but the Internet is driving this trend by creating an increasingly wired and connected world.

The *Budget Travel* website (*BudgetTravel.msnbc.com*) is a partnership between Arthur Frommer's travel magazine and the MSNBC channel and it also offers a free e-mail newsletter. It's an example of the convergence of print, television, and online media. It also invites interaction by letting visitors search for the best travel deals and money-saving ideas. Do you think it would be effective in driving travelers to the website?

These new media forms not only provide access to information, but also encourage more involvement by users and sharing of experiences, both of which lead to more persuasive impact for Web-delivered messages. Before we talk about Internet marketing communication, let's first review the basics of the Internet.

> **Principle**
> The Internet is the ultimate convergence medium because it bridges print and broadcast media and blurs the distinction between them.

Internet Basics

Technically, the **Internet** is a linked system of international computer networks. The **World Wide Web** is the information interface that allows people to access the Internet through an easy-to-use graphical format. However, most people use these terms Internet and Web interchangeably. The thing to remember is that the Internet, which didn't come into common use until the 1990s, is still evolving and driven by innovation. The new applications and technologies are creating a dynamic environment that challenges old ways of doing business. The area seeing the greatest change is media where traditional print and broadcast forms are reshaping themselves for an online presence.

The Internet is an important marketing communication medium because it combines the characteristics of many other media—newspapers and newsletters, magazines, catalogs, directories, television, radio, phones, and film. It is useful for communicating brand information, but that capability is a two-edged sword. Any major problem with a brand can be communicated around the world instantly. Tiger Woods, one of the world's greatest personal brands, found that out when his minor car accident on the street outside his Florida home exploded into a blaze of global communication filled with endless speculation and rumors about his life and loves.

The Internet plays a critical role in both consumer and business-to-business (B2B) customers' brand decisions. Here are some of the reasons why it has become so important to consumers—as well as the marketers who want to reach them—in such a short time:

- *Information* Because of easy searching, Internet users have access to a wealth of information, not only about brands and companies, but also about trends, future developments, and **product reviews.**
- *Choice* The Internet offers more choices and consumers can easily do comparative shopping online. That means they can learn more about brands, not only from a brand's website but also from third parties.
- *Accessibility* The majority of the population has access to computers, and individuals who do not can go online at work or public locations, such as libraries, schools, and Internet cafes.
- *Speed* The Internet has grown to be a medium with unsurpassed speed and widespread coverage. Especially with high-speed connection services, information travels across the Internet almost instantaneously and is carried to almost all parts of the globe.

Online marketers value the Internet for the same reasons, however they also see benefits in some basic business areas:

- *Capital* Opening a business online is far less costly than opening a traditional brick-and-mortar business.
- *Cost Reductions* Selling online and keeping track of customer relationship behavior with real-time data is also less costly than operating a traditional brick-and-mortar business.
- *Location* The Internet reaches beyond local markets, which is important for specialty goods. For example, in Lincoln, NE, a business that specializes in selling licorice would find it hard to thrive if the owners relied solely on people from the area patronizing it. The Internet allows the market to live in the world, not just in a local location.

A number of different "nets" are used in marketing communication beyond the basic Internet. Because it is an interactive "web," the Internet is a relatively inexpensive communication medium that connects a company with all of its stakeholders—employees, investors, and other groups that have a stake in the success of the brand. Companies set up **intranets** for internal communication and **extranets** to connect employees with key external stakeholders, such as marketing communication agencies, suppliers, and distributors.

Here are some other important Internet terms and tools:

- *URLs and Domain Names* A website has an address called a **URL** (Uniform Resource Locator), which is its **domain name,** a global address that identifies a specific location in cyberspace on the Web where a document or website lives.
- *Portals* A **portal** is a site that provides doors, or links, to other websites, such as AOL and MSN. Yahoo!, for example, is a directory, or online guide to the Web. It started as a group of favorite websites compiled by a couple of Stanford University students, who began categorizing the sites as the list grew into the giant library now known as Yahoo! It is considered the top Internet brand and is among the most trafficked websites in the United States. The big three portals—AOL, MSN, and Yahoo!—account for 17 percent of all time spent on the Internet in the United States. On average, MSN users spend 2 hours online daily, AOL users spend 2.5 hours, and Yahoo users spend 3 hours. MSN, however, has the biggest global share of the three and uses that advantage to drive its other products, such as Internet Explorer, Windows, its Silverlight Web design application, and its *Bing.com* search engine.[2]
- *Links* A **link** is an address to another website that can be accessed from the website currently being viewed. Often the links are designed to reflect the topic of the original site. For example, Nike may have a link on a golf site that allows viewers to move back and forth from the golf page to Nike's golf product lines.
- *Search Engines* Google is the biggest **search engine** used to find information and access other sites but it is being challenged by Microsoft's *Bing.com,* which also powers Yahoo's search function. You don't have to know a specific website address; instead, you can type in a **keyword** and the search engine will seek out all sites that provide information on the topic. Most search engines also carry advertising, so they can be considered advertising media. Examples of more specific search sites are *SeenOn.com,* an online shopping guide that lets TV fans find and purchase many of the products they see on TV, and *iLike.com,* which was set up by musicians to help consumers find music they like. Craigslist provides local community-based information: who can repair a radio, where to find supplies for stained glass repairs, how to locate job opportunities, and so on. Craigslist is noncommercial and doesn't accept advertising, but brands sometimes can be found there or searched for on the site.
- *Netcasting* The emergence of new technology that makes it possible to broadcast TV and radio online is a practice called **netcasting.** Blip.tv offers new Web TV series and helps the producers find sponsors and advertisers. The decision by ABC to put previously run episodes of its hit shows online and CBS's experiments with "March Madness on Demand" video streams for the college basketball championships are pushing this technological revolution. MTV is working with Google to move its video content to the Web, and Disney has released some of its movies for use on a video iPod. TV producers are starting to produce shows designed for the tiny 2.5-inch cell phone screen. In a new twist on convergence, a start-up wireless carrier contributed a political parody show it created, the animated *Lil' Bush*, to Comedy Central. This is the first time a U.S. TV network broadcast a show that was

initially produced for cell phones. Netcasting also appeals to advertisers searching for new ways to reach audiences who no longer are sitting in front of televisions.

- *Broadband* The term **broadband** is used to indicate a high-speed connection to the Internet. Slow speeds make it difficult to download large files; higher speed access makes it easier to access complex files, such as **streaming video.** Finland has targeted 2015 as the date when fast Internet connections will be guaranteed to all of its citizens. Other countries have similar plans, but as of 2010 the U.S. Congress was working through the FCC to catch up and develop similar plans.[3] **Bandwidth** is a term used to describe the carrying capacity of an individual's computer connection, that is, how much digital data it can handle.

The Internet Audience

Internet use has expanded over the years from sites appealing to young tech-savvy innovators to sites devoted to just about any age or interest group. The most sought-after audience on the Web continues to be young people, particularly young males who are hard to reach with traditional media. Teens spend more time online—or on their cell phones—than any other age group.

A recent article, however, celebrated new sites, such as *BoomerGirl.com,* that reach women over age 50 with news, blogs, and "tips on health, fashion, family, finances, and fitness." It's not the only site for this population: *Boomerwomenspeak.com* and *eons.com* focus on the concerns of both male and female boomers. In certain markets, such as fashion, 65 percent of online apparel sales is to women over age 35. The fastest growing segment of Facebook users is women over age 55.[4]

In fact, the Internet is the ultimate niche medium in that people turn to it to find out about any topic that interests them. The *A Matter of Practice* feature explains how Toyota used online communication to reach a specific do-it-yourself target audience.

The largest Internet market is China with some 400 million users, 200 million of whom have broadband.[5] China's online users, however, visit the Internet less for purchasing things than for information, game playing, and social contact, although analysts predict that is changing as more big Chinese brands begin to develop websites and offer products online.[6]

Principle
The Internet is the ultimate niche medium because it appeals to people's specific interests.

Internet Marketing

Parallel to the Internet's ability to create new ways to communicate, it also has created new ways to do business. We mentioned the size of the China market; in 2009 online transactions accounted for only 1.2 percent of total retail sales in China compared to 5 percent in the United States, however, most experts predict that the Chinese will dramatically increase their level of Internet purchases during the 2010s.

Most companies have a website that provides information, but many also sell products online, particularly to the B2B market. These business operations also provide ways to track customer behavior and preferences through databases and predictive modeling. *Amazon.com,* for example is able to suggest books to a returning customer based on that customer's previous purchases, as well as search patterns. We referred to this in Chapter 5 as behavioral targeting and it represents one of the innovations resulting from the new technology offered by the Internet.

The online marketer eBay is important because it represents a way of doing business that is different from traditional brick-and-mortar stores as well as a different way of thinking about buying, selling, and advertising—person-to-person commerce. It's also called *re-commerce* because much of its listings are for used items, like an online garage sale. It pioneered a new form of online commerce by linking individuals and small companies who had goods and services to sell with people interested in buying those products. Craigslist has done the same thing for local services and classified advertising.

In a novel experiment, GM tried selling new cars in California on eBay. The program ended after a six-week trial with limited sales success, although GM did report an increase in leads for its dealers. The company found that car retailing with its dealer territories and customer haggling on prices makes an odd fit for Internet transactions.[7]

Amazon.com, eBay, and iTunes exist only as online businesses—they are Internet brands. Others brands, such as Barnes & Noble and Costco, sell their products both online and in stores. Called "clicks and bricks," these merchants and manufacturers have created new ways to serve their customers with stores providing actual experience with the brand or product and the online site providing in-depth and comparative information.

Principle
The Internet has vastly increased person-to-person commerce, in which individuals who have things to sell are connected with people interested in buying.

A MATTER OF PRACTICE

Toyota Taps the DIY Community

Brian Sheehan, *Associate Professor, Syracuse University*

The emergence of the Internet has created innumerable online communities where like-minded people gather around their interests and passions. One such online community is the "do-it-yourself" (DIY) crowd. These are people with an insatiable desire to know how things work: how they can install their own plumbing, rebuild their own computer, and fix their own car. For the launch of Toyota's new V-8 Tundra truck, Toyota realized that many of the full-sized truck buyers are the kind of people who want to do things for themselves and put their truck to the test. Many of them use their big trucks to haul big loads, trailers, or boats.

Toyota and its agency, Saatchi & Saatchi, saw an opportunity to match this audience with their media objective of connecting in-market truck buyers with credible, objective content about their cars. They did it by creating a unique partnership with HowStuffWorks.com (HSW). HSW is true to its name: it explains how everything works. Just put in your subject and it will give you a detailed description of its inner workings. HSW does it so well that they are able to rely on organic search to get to their audience, and their content consistently ends up in the top 10 search results.

Toyota's agreement with HSW was a comprehensive package. There were the usual display ads tied to relevant content. For example, when someone typed in "How to Tow a Boat," HSW would give the answer while displaying an ad about Tundra's powerful, high-torque engine. There were 131 towing-related categories alone! If "How to Brake While Towing" was typed, the ad would be about the truck's huge rotors, which gave better braking performance. In addition, HSW created over 100 pieces of specific Toyota-branded content per month for articles relating to Tundra, as well as Toyota's Prius and Venza.

By tapping into a tight community with relevant, targeted advertising and content, Toyota was able to garner terrific online metrics and improve its image.

After the campaign launched, display ad click-throughs, search engine traffic to Toyota.com, and time spent on the Toyota site all increased. In fact, traffic to the site was up 50 percent, and brand favorability shot up 40 percent.

The online space is noted for its fragmentation. Increasingly, the Internet is dividing into communities of people who congregate around specialized websites and blogs, and insulated social networks. The marketers who succeed online will be the ones, like Toyota, who know how to embed their communications relevantly and seamlessly within the communities most disposed to using their products.

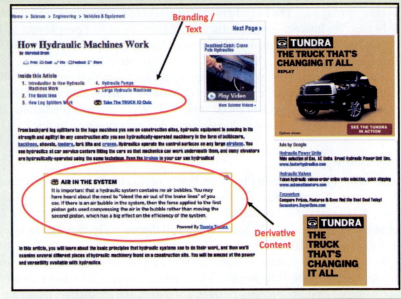

Actual Article and Served Ad

Trade associations, such as those serving realtors, have developed innovative services for their members that make it easy to use online marketing. Local realtors, for example, can sign up for *Realtor.com,* which not only carries online listings, but also provides templates for packaging properties in attractive and accessible formats. The reason realtors value such services is because they realize that more than 80 percent of real estate buyers start their searches on the Internet. Ed Burd, who received the Real Estate Online Marketing Award of Excellence from *Realtor.com,* has found that "print is out of date and there's less response to traditional advertising." He likes the online service because he can provide quick responses to prospects and he gets data tracking information back from the online service.[8]

The Internet as a Marcom Medium

Online marketing communication (marcom) serves five primary purposes. First, it provides a brand reminder message to people who are visiting a website. Second, it works like an ad in traditional media and delivers an informational or persuasive message. The third purpose, however, is critical: it provides a way to entice people to visit the advertiser's website by clicking on a banner or button that links to the website. This is called "driving traffic to the website."

The most important roles from a customer-focus perspective, however, are search and interactivity. These are unique to Internet marketing communication. Search tools, such as Google and Microsoft's *Bing.com,* enable customers to find brands, customer reviews, and other product information. Interactivity makes it possible for consumers to move away from being a "target" and initiate contact with a company or with other customers and have a conversation about a brand.

Early Internet marketing communication sites were either websites providing general information about a company and its brands or an online version of the company's catalog. More recently Internet marketers have begun to move beyond the catalog mentality and are using links, animation, and other technology to bring their products to life. Diego Contreras, art director at Crispin Porter + Bogusky, describes how important online communication has become in his *The Inside Story.* (CP + B, incidentally was named Interactive Agency of the Year at the 2010 Cannes Festival.)

Fashion sites, such as Stylecaster, ShopFlick, Smashing Darling, and Saks, use videos, links to other designers, and wand-based functions that allow visitors to view fashion items from all sides—even the insides of handbags. *MyShape.com* asks customers to type in body measurements and then acts like a personal shopper presenting fashion items specifically chosen to enhance the customer's body shape.

Internet branding is different in some ways from other forms of brand marketing communication. As Web consultant John Williams explains, "The Internet is an interactive channel—one that marries text, movement, sound and design to produce a comprehensive brand personality." He says that this new communication environment is both an opportunity and a challenge because, even though you can create an animated brand presence, "visitors remain completely in charge and competitors are just a click away."[9]

What Are the Functions of Internet Marcom?

Marketers and advertisers are most interested in the **e-business** or **e-commerce** function of the Internet. These terms refer to all of the hardware, software, and computer know-how that provides a platform for businesses that use the Internet to sell products and manage their business operations, such as advertising, customer service, personal sales, internal communication to employees, and external communication to outside stakeholders. In addition to the e-commerce role, other Internet functions that are important to advertisers include the information, entertainment, social, and the word-of-mouth, or dialogue, roles.

The Information Role   The most important advertising-related role that the Internet plays is to provide information for consumer decision making. Beyond shopping on e-business sites, the Internet has developed into a giant online library for consumers of all demographic categories.

Online publishing has contributed to the explosion of digital information. Most traditional media vehicles have websites that adapt the information from their mainline format. Travel sites, such as the one shown earlier for the magazine *Budget Travel*, are particularly popular. Other publications exist solely online. **Zines,** for example, are magazines or newsletters that are only available

Principle
The primary use of the Internet by people of all demographic categories is information searching.

THE INSIDE STORY

Everything Is Going Online

Diego Contreras, *Art Director, Crispin Porter + Bogusky*

Something that I've noticed is that everything is going online.

I barely had any digital pieces on my book after school and relatively no experience in that field. But in the short time I've been here at Crispin Porter, at least 90 percent of my work has been digital. So it's good for students to be up to date with all of the new technologies that are coming out.

Also with the economic recession, a lot of clients are looking for online options because they're cheaper and get higher exposure. With personal blogs, YouTube, Facebook, and now Twitter, digital work spreads out pretty fast, and for free.

When I talk about work getting close to the production phase, which is where I get involved as a Web designer, I mean that the idea is client approved and then we have a meeting where a group of people from Web development, media, content, interaction design, and production departments show up. We talk about budgets and the feasibility of producing an idea in terms of Web development. Sometimes we come up with big ideas that would be impossible to develop or too expensive, so they tell us to scale them back.

Then as an art director, I go back to my original comps and make sure everything looks tight. I create every single element for the website (logos, buttons, navigation bars, backgrounds, color schemes, etc.). On banners, it's kind of a tedious process because you have to create each frame. So every time there's a small change you have to change each frame again, which takes a lot of time.

So there's a lot of planning that goes on for digital.

Diego Contreras graduated from Southern Methodist University with a degree in advertising. He and his work were nominated for inclusion in this book by Professors Glenn Griffin and Patty Alvey.

In this animated banner by Diego Contreras the Windows character "pokes" the Excel character. The idea for the people in costumes who represent the icons comes from Facebook where you "poke" your friends.

Poke-a-thon Storyboard Example

over the Internet. The site *ezinearticles.com* only uses reader-generated content, which offers everyone the opportunity to write magazine-quality articles and publish them online. If not obviously commercial, the site is also an outlet for business-related articles. Many zines are aimed at niche markets. *The Root*, for example, is an online magazine that provides news and culture from a black perspective. You can find it at *www.theroot.com*, and also check out the advertiser that supports this site.

Online encyclopedias, such as Wikipedia, are another huge source of information. Wikipedia publishes contributions from anyone who wants to write and edit entries in a collaborative, open-source system of information collection. The fifth most popular website in the world, it has approximately 325 million visitors a month and 3 million contributors who write and edit the content in 10 languages. The site is so popular that it has spun off a number of other specialized sites that are advertising supported, such as wikiHow, which is a how-to guide (how to cook a brisket, how to fix a garage door opener) built on the same principles as Wikipedia. ShopWiki offers product reviews and Wikitravel provides tourism information. So even encyclopedias are now an advertising medium.

The Entertainment Role   Many users go online for entertainment, such as poker and other games, playing the stock market, and keeping up with fashion, music, and videos. Some of these entertainment opportunities are fun, and some are personally challenging, but they all engage their users either as escape or relaxation, and that also makes them a useful medium in which to advertise because the messages can be associated with positive experiences.

Computer games and video games are, of course, the epitome of digital entertainment. One of the first computer games, Pac-Man, was developed in 1980 by Namco and released for Atari in 1982. Adapted from its arcade game, the movement of the little round yellow icon, which traveled through a maze gobbling up cookies, was controlled by a joystick. Four ghosts impeded his progress and when he encountered one directly he lost his "life" and was reanimated back at the center of the maze to start his quest all over again. You might be interested to know that Pac-Man had a spin-off breakfast cereal. Here's another piece of advertising trivia, in 1983 at age 8 Christian Bale (*Dark Knight*) acted in a Pac-Man cereal commercial. You can watch this classic 1980s song-and-dance extravaganza at *www.youtube.com/watch? v=7jQkBiU_2rg&feature=related.*

Sites that appeal to the coveted demographic of young men, who are so difficult to reach with traditional media, include *Heavy.com*, which attracts viewers to its mix of racy, humorous video programming (animation, music, video games, home movies of weird characters, chicks in bikinis, and pop culture parodies) and keeps their attention with wisecrack commercials. The gorilla of Web entertainment, however, is *YouTube.com*, which is a site that carries consumer-generated film and video clips—teenage video diaries, stupid pet tricks, ad parodies, ideas for TV shows, and actual shows downloaded from TV.

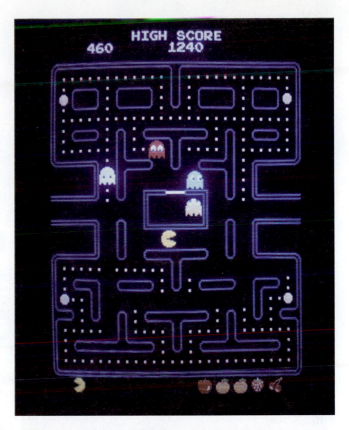

CLASSIC

You can still play Pac-Man; check the game's website at *www .namcogames.com.* Do you think there still might be a market for an updated version of this classic maze game?

The Social Role   We mentioned brand communities in Chapter 5 referring to groups of people who are connected by a favorite brand, such as the Harley-Davidson HOG (Harley Owners Group) fan club which you can check out at the Hog website (*www.harley-davidson.com/ wcm/Content/Pages/HOG/HOG.jsp*). The Internet has created large numbers of **virtual communities** where customers and prospects hang out and discuss brand problems, solutions, and new uses among themselves. Such websites, such as the one featured here for the Smart Car, create opportunities for real-time research into consumer insights and feelings. Many of these sites are not run by companies, but rather by fans, who feel free to express themselves openly. There are also company-sponsored sites that are often controlled and sometimes have rules that limit what can be discussed. The sites that are the most successful are the ones that encourage interaction and networking.[10]

A new category of websites that focus on **social networking** allows users to express themselves, interact with friends, and publish their own content on the Internet. Facebook, MySpace, and Twitter, which you probably know well, are sites that allow users to share personal information with friends. Like the old mall and arcade hangouts, these are places where teens spend hours talking to friends about their joys, crushes, and disappointments.

Hairong Li, a Michigan State professor and contributor to this book, explains that certain characteristics of social media—personal content, user engagement, social relationships, and group dynamics—differentiate social media from conventional mass media. The social engagement helps individuals, particularly young people, develop a sense of self. Li explains that "sharing experience with others is integral to how we construct a coherent yet often fragmented sense of self in a networked society."

The reason these social networking sites are so attractive to marketers is that they engage the power of friendship-based influence. Because of these relationships, network members are more

The official social networking site of smart USA is "smart USA Insider." The site enables owners and enthusiasts of the smart car in the United States to interact and stay connected with the smart brand and each other. The site allows members to create personal profiles and blogs, post videos and photos; participate in forum discussions; join groups and list events. The site also gives members access to exclusive updates directly from smart USA including occasional blog posts from the smart USA president. Check out the "smart USA insider" Web site (*http://www .smartusainsider.com*) and develop a profile of who you think might be a candidate for membership.

likely to respond to messages on the sites, including ads, if they are effective at becoming part of the social context. Professor Li explains that social media are all about relationships:

> Think about your friends in Facebook or MySpace. Some of them are people you first met in person and then continued that relationship online, and some are people with whom you are acquainted only online. Whether you've ever met them in person, some online acquaintances are close friends, some are merely random friends, and the rest are probably in between. Your relationships with these friends will affect how you respond to ads in social media. For example, a close friend of yours may post a comment about a new product she just bought and how she likes it. Wouldn't that make you think about the product after reading her comment?

These social media relationships offer opportunities for marketing communication messages, particularly as people serve as viral marketing agents to take advantage of the social relationships these people have with their network of friends. Professor Li points out that "you may have already seen some movie trailers and album posters on the pages of your friends. These trailers and posters actually represent one of the newest forms of advertising—**user-generated ads.** By user-generated ads, we mean the content of commercial nature that is created or posted on the pages of users in social media that promotes a product, service, or cause."

The Word-of-Mouth Role　In addition to providing information and associating themselves with entertainment and social networking, advertisers are turning to the Internet because it opens up the possibility of two-way communication, as in conversations. This characteristic supports two basic objectives that drive advertisers' use of the Internet: (1) it creates a dialogue with customers and (2) it stimulates a conversation among and between customers and potential customers.

The first objective relates to the interactivity dimension of the Internet. Remember from Chapter 4 that two-way communication is the most persuasive type of communication available to marketers. With interactive media, it is possible for a consumer to contact the company and get a personal answer. The point is that the closer the medium is to a dialogue or the more a user can generate or manipulate the content, the more the marketing communication moves away from traditional advertiser-controlled one-way advertising.

The second objective relates to the power of word-of-mouth communication. Advertising planners have developed a growing respect for media that generate buzz or *word of mouth*. The idea is to get people talking about a brand because we have recognized that the most important factor in consumer decision making is often the opinions of others, such as family and friends. An annual study of media use by the BIGresearch firm, which polled 15,000 consumers, found

Principle

The more interactive a medium and the closer it is to a dialogue, the more personal and persuasive the communication experience.

that the most influential form of media is word of mouth (WoM). The finding was supported by other research that has found WoM to be the most important influence on consumer decision making—considerably more important than traditional media.[11]

Ty Montague, former chief creative officer at JWT, points to his agency's work for JetBlue as a brand built almost entirely on word of mouth. He explains that the airline's advertising "is designed to provide as many ways as possible for fans of the brand to spread the word themselves, from stuff like a high-tech booth where they can literally create their own testimonials, which get run on TV, to things as simple and high touch as prepaid postcards in seat back pockets that they can use to share their experiences."[12]

Japanese marketing communication giant, Dentsu, expresses this idea in its B2C2C concept. A revitalization of the traditional business-to-consumer (B2C) marketing approach, the Dentsu B2C2C strategy proposes that a marcom message emanates from a business then moves to key customers and influencers who then talk about it with other consumers in the target market. Because this is an interactive environment, messages can then move back again from consumers to key customers who are in touch with the business. The important new dimension in this model is the C2C dimension, which recognizes that people today get much of their information from their friends, whether in person or online. Rather than top down, at this level brand messages are flowing side to side, creating a network of shared brand experiences. Although C2C is made easier by all of the new digital media, experts point out that digital marketers can learn a lot from offline word-of-mouth campaigns. The vice president of social media at the Razorfish agency, for example, looks offline to better understand "how the relationship between marketer and influencer is developed and how their influence is measured."[13]

Principle
A B2C2C strategy is designed to move a message from a business to key customers who then talk about it with other consumers—and messages use the same route to come back to the business.

TYPES OF ONLINE MARKETING COMMUNICATION

What kinds of Internet communication are available today to marketers? The industry is moving so quickly that by the time you read this passage, other categories may replace or supplement those we discuss here. Essentially, Internet advertising can be delivered as a traditional ad, just like those you see in a magazine, or it can be presented in a number of other formats such as banner ads, e-mail, brand blogs, and social sites, among other forms.

Websites

You're probably familiar with these terms, but let's review how the Internet is shaping up for marketers. Sometimes called a **home page,** a company's **website** is the online face it presents to the public. The website is a communication tool that blurs the distinction between marketing communication forms, such as advertising, direct marketing, and public relations. In some cases it looks like an online corporate brochure, or it may function as an online catalog. The website can also be an information resource with a searchable library of stories and data about products, product categories, and related topics. It may even deliver sales. In all cases, however, a critical function of a website is to create a brand or organizational identity and reinforce the brand position.

The *Guitar Hero: Smash Hits* website, which we introduced in Chapter 11, is a good example. You heard earlier from Diego Contreras, interactive art director at Crispin Porter + Bogusky, on how he approaches design for online media. We also used some of his *Guitar Hero: Smash Hits* banners in Chapter 11. Let's continue that discussion with comments from him on how he developed the *Smash Hits* website. He explained that Activision had a very small budget for this campaign so they decided to focus their spending online. Here's how the website idea developed according to Contreras:

> At first they wanted us to create a widget or application on their website to slowly reveal the songs that would be featured in the game. We decided to take it further by creating a website from scratch and promoting it with banner ads all over the Web. To add credibility and a bit of a fun factor, we named the campaign the *2009 Guitar Hero Smash Hits Music Awards*.

To see how Web marketing communication agencies promote themselves and establish their own brand identity, check out the Minnesota-based Risdall Advertising website (*www.risdall.net*).

SHOWCASE

The website for *Guitar Hero: Smash Hits* used a music awards theme with visitors voting for what they considered to be the best of *Guitar Hero*'s music.

Diego Contreras graduated from Southern Methodist University with a degree in creative advertising and business. He and his work were nominated by Professors Glenn Griffin and Patty Alvey.

Explore the various divisions described on this website. In particular, look at the page for Risdall Interactive, a division of the marketing communication firm that focuses on designing interactive strategies for Risdall clients.

Whether or not the website is effective depends on several factors—one is **stickiness** and the other is its ease of **navigation.** A "sticky" website is one that encourages visitors to "stick around" instead of bouncing to another site. It has to be interesting and offer meaningful interactivity. The interest level is determined by what's "above the fold," to use a newspaper metaphor. Decisions about whether to leave or stay and investigate the site's content depends on what's visible without scrolling downward. Research has shown that 75 percent of the ads "below the fold" go unnoticed.[14]

To increase its stickiness—in this case value to its customers—Campbell's Soup redesigned its cooking site based on consumer research that indicated cooks were interested in budget meals and recipes that move beyond the casserole. Within the site, *www .CampbellsKitchen.com,* visitors can search for dinner options by mood or flavor, such as chocolaty or cheesy, as well as standard menu categories. The site also has a seven-day meal planning tool, and a section about recipe substitutions and healthy alternatives.

The VW "Truth & Dare" website for its Jetta TDI diesel models (*http://tdi.vw.com*) uses video clips and interactive tools to debunk myths about diesel, such as diesel is dirty or diesel cars don't start in the cold. In "diesel decaf," for example, testers place coffee filters on the exhaust pipes of various cars and then make coffee using them. Of course, the VW diesel filter is so clean there is no residue in the coffee. The site also features a blog forum and tools to compare the VW TDI brands against competitors, such as a Savings Calculator, which compares fuel efficiency and carbon emissions.[15] (To see the "coffee filter" test, check *http://green.autoblog.com/2009/05/04/vw-launches-tdi-truth-and-dare-with-coffee-filter-test.*)

Some people may find a marketer's website after doing a search using a search engine; others may come across the website address in some other communication, such as an ad or brochure. But another way is to encounter a link on a related site usually in the form of an ad with enough impact to entice the visitor to leave the original site and move to this new one. Internet strategists are keenly aware of the difficulty of enticing people to websites.

Like ads, sometimes websites have problems, as Sears found out when a Sears product page carried a product description that proclaimed "Grills to Cook Babies." The problem was that the Sears website was open to editing by anyone who wanted to mess with it. Check out the story on *http://consumerist.com/2009/08/sears-caught-selling-grills-to-cook-babies-thanks-to-poorly-built-website.html.* When Sears tried to get Conde Nast's Reddit site that wrote about the problem to delete the post, the effort blew up and created a hornet's nest of negative publicity for Sears.

E-Mail Communication

One of the attractive features of using e-mail for advertising is that it is so inexpensive. All it takes is a list of e-mail addresses, a computer, and an Internet connection. E-mail is a product of an earlier time in online communication—back in the days when we used to log on and off and check messages in bursts. Some users still operate that way, but with newer forms like instant messaging, Facebook, and Twitter, many users are always online and that has changed the function, as well as the speed, of online connections. The constant stream of information means the inbox is now a river.[16] We'll talk more about e-mail marketing and its evil twin, spam, in Chapter 16, *Direct Response.*

We briefly mentioned viral marketing in an earlier chapter, but it's important to note this e-mail social practice here. Designed to deliver a groundswell of opinion, buzz, or marketplace demand for a product, **viral marketing** uses e-mail, Facebook, and Twitter to circulate a message among family and friends. Depending on public interest in the topic, this practice can distribute a message to an ever-widening network and messages can flash across the Internet like wildfire. Remember "The Diet Coke/Mentos Experiment" that resulted in a geyser of e-mails that exploded again and again on the Internet? That viral advertising was watched by millions, and guess what? Other viewers concocted their own versions and uploaded them on YouTube. Mentos mint sales rose 15 percent. Was that entertainment, or advertising and is its impact on the brand positive or negative? Check out the YouTube version of this story at *www.youtube.com/watch?v= hKoB0MHVBvM.*

Why Is Internet Advertising Growing So Fast?

What makes Internet advertising so exciting and attractive to marketers is that it combines the best aspects of traditional media. You will recall that the major benefit of TV advertising is motion, the benefit of direct response is interactivity, and one of the major benefits of print is its depth of information. An Internet ad provides all of these benefits, and often, at a much lower cost than traditional media.

Although the percentage of most marketing communication budgets spent on Internet advertising is still relatively small, it is growing fast. In 2009, for example, the United Kingdom became the first major economy in which marketers spent more on Internet ads than they did on traditional TV advertising.[17] In the United States analysts announced in 2010 that total U.S. digital advertising was about to surpass print—a major tipping point in the ascendancy of the Internet over more traditional advertising media.[18]

Most forms of online advertising weathered the recent recession better than most other forms of traditional advertising.[19] In fact, media research company ZenithOptimedia reports that the Internet was the only medium to actually attract higher ad expenditures in 2009. The report also predicts that by 2011, Internet advertising will increase from 10.5 percent of all ad expenditures to 15.1 percent.[20]

The greatest percentage of Internet advertising is found on a small group of large, established sites that operate as electronic publishers, such as *www.nytimes.com*, *www.WSJ.com*, and *www.ESPN.com,* as well as on major search engines and service providers, such as Google, AOL, and Yahoo!. These media and search organizations have established reputations, and they know how to sell advertising, so they have been pioneers in the development of Internet advertising.

Even though Internet advertising was less affected by the recession, AOL and Yahoo! suffered from increased competition and both have been trying to rebuild their businesses by experimenting with new models of online content and advertising sales. AOL, for example, is using massive amounts of tracking data to tell what Web search topics are most likely to attract audiences. The system can also predict interest in news stories, which will give direction to its online newsroom. Its new ad model also allows advertisers to partner with AOL creative teams on content development, either articles or videos. AOL and its partners may even mass produce digital content including "advertorials," which are paid articles by advertisers.[21]

One area that is struggling to figure out its Internet advertising policies is pharmaceuticals. Heavily advertised—and regulated—in traditional media, drug manufacturers are unclear about what the U.S. Food and Drug Administration's policies are for online advertising. Even though huge numbers of consumers search the Internet for health information, the pharmaceutical companies have been slow to advertise online because they are not sure what the disclosure requirements might be for this new medium.[22]

When you slice the online advertising pie, advertising on search engines and on the sites they deliver gets the biggest piece at 47 percent, followed by display advertising at 35 percent. Classified advertising gets 10 percent, referrals and lead generation ads 7 percent, and e-mail advertising only 1 percent.[23]

This series of banners for the Zippo lighter develops a message as the banners unfold. The message is a take-off on the blackouts urban areas sometimes experience in the summer when electrical use is high. Do you think this series of banners would entice people to check out the Zippo website? Why or why not?

Banner and Display Ads Small ads on other Web pages that lure visitors to switch pages are called **banner ads.** Visitors can click on them to move to the advertised website, such as the one featured here in a series of animated banner ads for Zippo lighters. Banner ads are easy to create and are usually placed on a website featuring complementary products or related topics.

Although banner ads were very popular when they first appeared and continue to be a major part of online advertising, the overall **click-through** rate has dropped to less than 1 percent. The most successful banner ads achieve 5 to 7 percent click-through and can help build brand awareness even if they don't deliver a high level of response.

The difference in click-through response lies in the creativity and attention-getting power of the banner ad and where it is placed. The more related and relevant a site is to the brand, the more likely it will generate more click-throughs. Entertainment helps, too—for a collection of funny banners, check out the *www.valleyofthegeeks.com* website.

Display ads, like those in print, are larger than banners and include text and images in their designs. The design of other forms of display Internet advertising is constantly changing as the industry advances. Here are some common, as well as novel, formats:

- **Skyscrapers** are the extra-long, skinny ads running down the right or left side of a website. The financial site *CBSMarketWatch.com,* for instance, regularly runs this kind of ad. Response rates for skyscrapers, which began to be used aggressively by more companies in the early 2000s, can be 10 times higher than for traditional banner ads.
- **Pop-ups** and **pop-behinds** burst open on the computer screen either in front of or behind the opening page of the website. Companies like Volvo and GlaxoSmith-Kline (for its Oxy acne medicine) use these forms to present games and product information. However, they are seen as intrusive and annoying, so some Internet advertisers have moved away from this format and some computer software programs block them.
- **Micro-sites** or **mini-sites** are small websites that are the offspring of a parent website, such as the TDI Diesel site on the corporate VW site. For marketing purposes, the micro-site may cover particular products, campaigns, events, or promotions. Micro-sites tend to be more tightly focused than their parent sites and may be transitory because the reason for the site might have a time frame and expire. Another variation allows advertisers to market their products on other branded websites without sending people away from the site they're visiting. General Motors, for example, has used a mini-site on the Shell Oil site, which the viewer can access and enlarge later. This type of advertising generally gets a higher click rate than banners or display ads; the portal *About.com* estimates that 5 percent of the people who see the sites click on them.
- **Superstitials** are thought of as the "Internet's commercial" and are designed to work like TV ads. When you go from one page on a website to another, a 20-second animation appears in a window.
- **Widgets** are tiny computer programs that allow people to create and insert professional-looking content into their personal websites and also onto their TV screens. They include news notes, calculators, weather feeds, stock tickers, clocks, book or music covers, or other Web gadgets that can be a brand name promotional offer. It's a way to get a nonintrusive brand reminder ad on the desktop, website, or blog. Widgets also refer to mini-applications that pull content from some other place on the Web and add it to your site. In addition to getting onto cell phone screens and social media pages, they also can monitor contacts when someone clicks on the feature. Most recently Yahoo! has created TV widgets that allow access to content from new TVs by pushing a remote control button. The founder of *Widgetbox.com* classifies widgets as (1) self-expression tools (photos, clips, games), (2) rev-

enue generators on blogs (eBay categories, favorite DVDs or CDs from *Amazon.com*), and (3) site-enhancement devices (news updates, discussion forums). A fourth type is a marketing communication message.

As advertisers have searched for more effective ways to motivate site visitors to stay longer, they have used animation to become more entertaining with games and contests, interviews with celebrities, even musical performances. Originally Internet ads were jazzed up using relatively simple animation techniques to make elements move. New technologies—including plug-ins, Java script, Flash, Silverlight, and media streaming, both video and audio—provide even more active components. Research generally finds that the click-through rate nearly doubles when motion and an interactive element are added to a banner ad.

We mentioned Sears' problems with a poorly built website, but rogue advertising can also be a problem. For example, an unknown hacker was able to insert a malicious ad that took over the browsers of people visiting The *New York Times* website. The phony ad told visitors that they needed to buy antivirus software, which allowed the advertisers to make a quick buck. Phony ads have become easier to place through the services of ad networkers who aggregate huge volumes of ads from many different advertisers and it's difficult for the host sites to spot these security breaches.[24]

Online Video Ads   Website visitors or viewers watching video downloads also confront a variety of online video ads. Because there are some 30 formats available, advertisers who want to use video are struggling to find the best platform for their ads. The most common are in a *pre-roll* format, which forces viewers to watch a video ad before viewing video clips. Other formats include interactive video ads that drop down over the screen and allow viewers to click for more information, and videos that allow viewers to click on hot spots or buttons within the video to learn more about a product.

The lack of standardization means agencies have higher production costs as they try to adapt to different delivery systems. A recent study led by the giant Paris-based agency Publicis with Microsoft, Yahoo!, CBS, and Hulu, the website portal for streaming TV programming, as partners, tested a number of these formats and concluded that the best way to deliver video ads is through an *ad selector,* a feature that offers a group of ads and invites viewers to choose one. The test found that consumers are more likely to watch and remember video ads if they are able to pick the ones they watch.[25]

Search Advertising   Estimates for the percentage of Internet advertising that goes to sites connected with search advertising range from 50 to 80 percent, which indicates how important the search function is for consumers and the marketers who are trying to reach them.[26]

Search engine advertising is driven by keywords that consumers use to search for information. The reason why the consumer search function is so important is that it provides the marketer with an opportunity to position a brand message adjoining the list of sites (articles, blogs, Wikipedia entries) that is compiled in response to a keyword by search engines. This practice is called **search marketing.** With a credit card and a few minutes, a small business owner can set up a link between his or her brand and a keyword or key terms, such as "chocolate éclairs" or "real estate staging." It's the ultimate in brand linkage and association.

Search providers, such as Google, MSN, and Yahoo!, auction off positions that let advertisers' ads be seen next to specific search results. This has brought a fountain of money to Google over the years. These related ads are priced based on the number of consumer clicks on the ad, with rates averaging around 50 cents per click. To explore how this works, "google" the term *AdWords* and you will find dozens of sites by experts who help businesses construct their search marketing campaigns. Microsoft's *Bing.com* and Google's "Goggles" also offer visual searches that display search results as pictures, rather than words. You can search for pink tennis shoes or titanium tennis rackets and get a response in pictures.

Because consumers initiate the search, the adjoining ads are not perceived to be as intrusive as other forms of advertising. People do hundreds of millions of searches a day, and businesses spend billions to have their ads displayed next to the results. A benefit of online consumer searches is that they leave a trail of clues about products, features, and advertising approaches. This behavior can be mined for insights that lead to new products.

Principle
Search marketing is the ultimate in brand linkage and association because it provides the opportunity to put an ad on a page delivered by a keyword search.

A recent development is Google's foray into *real-time search,* which not only produces the usual search results, but also lets Google supplement the results with updates posted each second on social media, such as Facebook and Twitter.[27] This mix of search and social media will only increase the speed with which brand messages spread and will challenge the ability of companies to monitor their brands' online presence.

Search optimization is the practice of maximizing the link between topics and brand-related websites. Companies try to affect their search engine rankings in order to drive more traffic to their websites. They want their ads to appear as close to the top of the list as possible in order to have maximum visibility. An important first step for marketers in creating a viable website is getting it registered with popular search engines so that it shows up early on the list provided by the search engine.

Classified Ads   A small part of the online advertising piece, classified advertising, whether through local media websites or Craigslist, is still used by local advertisers and organizations. Previously the golden goose for local newspapers, the move to online "want ads" has been a big reason why local newspapers are in trouble financially. Craigslist is a community exchange for people who either want to sell something or are looking for something. Its business model is to operate as a public service. It doesn't accept advertising but does charge for real estate listings and open-job postings.

Craigslist does have a problem with spammers who have automated the mass posting of ads, which has caused grief for customers and led to lawsuits by Craigslist. The company is also suing a San Francisco company that runs a look-alike, "parasite" site called Craigsup. Other legal issues focus on its adult category, which carries explicit sexual-service ads.[28]

Internet Ad Sales   The market for online display ads was estimated at $21 billion a year in 2009. Google has been the most successful at attracting advertising, even during the recession, although Yahoo! draws more traffic.[29] Google also dominates the search ad industry and sells display ads, along with search ads, for thousands of sites.

Selling online advertising space is complicated. Major sites, such as *MSNB.com* and *History.com,* sell ads on their pages charging premium prices because they are on high-traffic sites. They can cost from $10 to $50 per thousand viewings depending on the visibility of the position.[30] Advertisers and their media buyers get access to Internet sites through providers such as DoubleClick, an Internet advertising service owned by Google, that places more than 60 billion online ads per month. DoubleClick provides reports on the placement and performance of these ads to both publishers and advertisers and also helps create ads and widgets.

Middlemen companies act as brokers for online ad space that they aggregate across different sites and package as single buys, in effect setting up an ad network. These ad networkers offer less well designed sites and positions and may sell space for less than a dollar per thousand viewers. They are criticized for flooding the Internet with cheap and sometimes tacky ads. Data-mining companies like Blue Kai and eXelate Media collect data on how visitors move around among sites and then sell access to advertising on groups of sites that attract similar visitors. This is similar to how local newspaper advertising can be purchased through group contracts and makes buying much more efficient.[31]

Google, Microsoft, and AOL have gotten into the ad sales business by setting up ad exchanges that allow advertisers to bid directly

This is a button on the DoubleClick website that lets advertisers create animated widget ads. If you were working for your local campus newspaper, what kind of widget would you design for the publication and where would it be displayed?

on available ad space on large groups of websites. In effect, they are cutting out the middlemen. Other big websites, such as ESPN, Turner Broadcasting, and Forbes magazine, have stopped doing business with the ad networks in order to gain better control over the quality of the content on their sites. The Online Publishers Association, which represents major publishers of Web content, reported on a study that found that ads on portals, as well as ads bought from ad brokers, were significantly less effective than the ads that the premium sites offer. The idea is that the portals and ad networkers' ads may be cheaper but they appear in formats that are less interesting and thus are less likely to connect with visitors.[32]

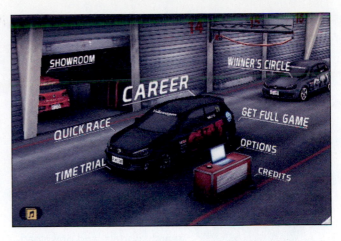

Online games engage potential customers with the brand and help build relationships through positive emotional interactions.

Social Media Tools

Social media marketing refers to the use of blogs, linked social networks (Facebook, Twitter), and online communities (sports and celebrity fans, brand communities) to build relationships with customers. For example, for the launch of its 2010 GTI Hatchback, for example, Volkswagen created a racing game using iPhones and iPod Touch to win a car. Players could send messages on Twitter and post videos of their games on YouTube.

Marketers use these new social media tools to promote brands, engage customers, and create brand relationships—and most of these efforts are free or cheap compared to other forms of marketing communication. They are not only a point of connection—a digital touchpoint—but they also open up a "social web," a network of people connected through the social media site. Social media sites open up a new environment of conversation-based marketing communication, creating opportunities for entirely different forms of nearly instantaneous customer connections. It's word-of-mouth advertising on steroids.

Principle
Conversation-based social media through such sites as Facebook and Twitter is word-of-mouth advertising on steroids.

An example comes from the video game discussion of the *Guitar Hero: Smash Hits* website and banners by art director Diego Contreras in Chapter 11. That promotion was also supported by a "Facebook Connect" function. Here's how Contreras explained this idea:

> Facebook Connect is a reflection of recent Web 2.0 technology and social media trends. It basically allows you to log in to Facebook through the Smash Hits site and voice your thoughts/comments about the site or "trash-talk" others on the comment section. Your comments would also be posted on your Facebook Wall, as well as all of your voting results. So, say I voted for Bon Jovi for Song of the Year, it would show up on my Facebook Wall with a link for my friends to vote for their favorite songs and post them to their profiles too.

In the *A Matter of Principle* feature, David Rittenhouse, who is a media director at Ogilvy's online agency, explains his view of this rapidly growing and changing media environment and the principle of *homophily* that drives online communities and digital associations.

A social media campaign for the Ford Fiesta relaunch invited 100 people, who had been thoroughly vetted by the Fiesta team, to take control of the brand's online message. The Fiesta's manager of brand content calls it courageous and explains, "We had to be credible and stay out of the mix, and that was a tough thing for all of us to do. But by screening all of these people we knew they were going to tell effective and fun stories."[33]

We mentioned that interactivity is one of, if not the, greatest advantage of online marketing communication. It makes conversations possible and brand-related conversations tend to show up in blogs and chat rooms. In this section on social media, we'll discus blogs, social networks, video and image-sharing sites, and social games and virtual communities.

Blogs, Micro-Blogs, and Chat Rooms   A diary-like Web page created by individuals to talk about things that interest them is called a **blog.** Blogs are produced by some 100 million digital essayists worldwide. Historically bloggers used their blogs for creative expression and opinion pieces

A MATTER OF PRINCIPLE

Consumers, Advertisers, and Social Media

David Rittenhouse, *Media Director, Neo@Ogilvy*

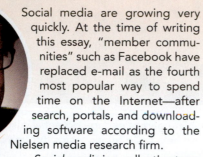

Social media are growing very quickly. At the time of writing this essay, "member communities" such as Facebook have replaced e-mail as the fourth most popular way to spend time on the Internet—after search, portals, and downloading software according to the Nielsen media research firm.

Social media is a collective term for the new media that allows users to connect with friends, network with peers, and organize and share various forms of digital content. Wikis like Wikipedia are social media. Blogs like Boing Boing are social media. Photo-sharing sites like Flickr are social media. Social networks like Facebook are social media.

The content basis for social media is not primarily produced by the media industry. It is not based on films, or television shows, or newspaper articles. Instead it is produced by the users themselves. It is mostly consumer generated. This is why social media is often cited as being "democratized."

Sociologists explain the unique need that social media meets in society with a concept called *homophily*—an impulse common to all people to associate with others like them.

The media industry is watching social media, especially member communities, very carefully because they represent massive new audience potential for their products. News Corp, for example, purchased MySpace, which is now the largest Internet property within the company's entire portfolio.

The challenge facing both advertisers and the media industry is how to put social media to work. No workable advertising revenue model has emerged though several have been tested unsuccessfully—most famously Facebook's trial of "Beacon Ads."

Still Facebook is doing many other things well with users spending 566 percent more of their time on the site from 2007 to 2008, while the overall measure of Internet time spent grew only 18 percent.

With so many people spending so much of their time on the Internet, it won't be long before a model (or a few of them) emerges that allows advertisers and media businesses to participate more fully.

For now, consumers are leading the development of social media. But advertisers are getting more interested—testing different levels of involvement from advertising on social media sites, to developing branded widgets/applications, to hosting discussions on topics of relevance to their brands.

And so are the media companies. Publishers and broadcasters are using social networks as a means through which to distribute their content, and incorporating social media features (such as "share a comment") into their own websites.

for a generally anonymous audience. Some were interested in making money and others were into news or politics. These personal publishing sites also contained links to related sites the bloggers consider relevant. Although these sound like one-way communication tools, most blogs also invite comments that are shared with other readers stimulating conversations, if not debates, among them. Bloggers often have higher levels of credibility than ads or corporate websites, which are seen as self-serving.

Corporations also use blogs in addition to their traditional websites to engage stakeholders of all kinds. Corporate blogs are a way to keep employees and other stakeholders informed, but employees may also be encouraged to have personal blogs. Microsoft has several hundred staffers blogging on personal sites. Sales staffs have found that blogs are changing the sales process by making more experiences with a product available to prospects and keeping customers current with fast-changing technological trends. Small businesses can get help creating blogs—and websites—from software that can be downloaded from *WordPress.org*.

The problem with blogs is that they take a lot of time and many bloggers run out of steam. A survey by a blogger search engine, Technorati, reports that of the 133 million blogs they track, 95 percent are essentially abandoned. Mostly they died because of a lack of reader interest—or of the marketing needed to build them an online presence. Technorati estimates that there are some 7 to 10 million active blogs but probably between 50,000 to 100,000 generate most of the page views.[34] Other bloggers have moved over to social media. A study has found that bloggers are getting older as younger users have moved to Twitter.[35]

Another problem with blogs is that they are sometimes criticized as "stealth advertisers." *Paid posts,* where bloggers plug a product in return for cash or freebies from the company, have caught the attention of the FTC. On a blog for parents, for example, the blogger operator promoted a $135 embroidered baby carrier. The blogger admits the company sent the carrier free. These endorsements are now being addressed by new advertising guidelines that require bloggers to post "clear and conspicuous" disclosures that they have received compensation or freebies.[36]

The concept of a blog with diary and essay postings was reinvented in miniature by Twitter, which permits posts no longer than 140 characters. Called **tweets,** these mini-posts invite users to share their daily doings and immediate thoughts with people who have subscribed, called followers, to the **micro-blog.** Generally the followers are people known to the Tweeter, although in the case of fans, they may approach the size and scale of a large mass audience. Actor Ashton Kutcher, for example, became the first to collect 1 million followers on Twitter narrowly beating CNN's breaking-news feed in a widely publicized race.[37]

Advertising messages also can appear on Twitter as part of a user's stream of messages. As Professor Tom Mueller points out, advertising creatives have always known that short, succinct messages are better, but Twitter forces marcom messages into the tiny format of 140 characters.[38]

A growing group of Tweeters have signed up to allow advertisers to send commercial messages under their name. Sometimes the ads are testimonials embedded in a person's regular stream of Tweets (for example, where to go to find M&Ms that can be customized or custom-label bottles of wine); others turn over their stream to an ad broker that inserts messages for brands and organizations, such as the Make a Wish Foundation. The idea is that people trust what appear to be personal messages. A number of start-up companies are trying to match up brands and topics with influencers who are important within a topical community.

Marketers can create a company account on Twitter that tracks buzz and brand references using a service such as *Summize.com.* An arm of Twitter, Summize tracks news in real time as it searches, filters, and summarizes the huge river of information appearing on Twitter every second.

Groups of people with a special interest can contact one another and exchange their opinions and experiences through **chat rooms,** which are sites located online, sometimes as part of an organization's website, but sometimes completely independent of any company. For example, numerous chat rooms are organized around various computer systems (Linux, Apple, ThinkPad, Sega) and topics (one-to-one marketing, guerilla marketing, virtual marketing). The communication is so fast that announcements, rumors, and criticisms can circulate worldwide within a matter of minutes. Chat rooms also are good information sources about customer experiences as well as competitors' offerings.

Social Networks The idea of an online community is the metaphor for social media sites, such as Facebook, MySpace, and other private or brand-related sites. Social networks link friends, fans, or others who share interest in some topic. But mostly, they are about friends. That's why on Facebook, when you are invited to connect with someone, you are asked to "friend" them. Users can create posts on their own Facebook site but they can also post them on their friends "walls," as well as to other content sites.

The Bloesem "Let's Get Personal" blog is a Dutch-influenced design site by Irene Hoofs, who lives in Kuala Lampur, Malaysia. The blog was selected by *Times.online* as one of its Top 50 design sites. It features all types of design including architecture, interior design, furniture, fashion, and graphics, as well as Irene Hoof's running commentary on the beauty of design. What other blog can you find that you think is interesting? Who do you think follows it and why do you think it works?

MySpace pioneered the social network concept and is still important with some 66 million members; however, it has lost market share to Facebook with its 96 million members, or "friends" in the U.S. Facebook is now an international community of more than 350 million friends around the world.[39] MySpace has evolved as a neighborhood for ethnic and low-income users and others, such as artists, who like its more cluttered and funky but easily personalized look. Facebook has a cleaner, more organized look and appeals to a more mainstream audience. Although some marketers might write off MySpace, it is still a viable medium to reach the difficult lower income and ethnic markets.[40] Research by the BIGresearch firm has also found that Facebook users are slightly older at an average age of 37 years old; MySpace users are younger at an average age of 33.[41]

According to BIGresearch, social media users tend to be younger and female;[42] however, social media have seen the greatest growth in the over-35 market. Forrester Research estimates that four in five online adult users in the United States are involved with social media at least once a month.[43] And new professionally focused interactive sites, such as LinkedIn, are specifically designed to serve the business community.

How are social media involved in marketing communication? Facebook accepts ads and has a section on its site about how to create Facebook advertising (*www.facebook.com/advertising*), as well as techniques to optimize your ads and track their performance. On Facebook advertisers can either pay per click (CPC) or per thousand impressions (CPM).

Companies and brands now have Facebook and MySpace pages with their own brand profiles just like any other member. Facebook fan pages for brands engage consumers who have questions or who are loyal users. P&G, which has set up an office in Silicon Valley to develop social networking sites for its many brands, says that the Pringles fan page has more than 2.8 million global fans.[44] Facebook marketers hope to make friends with interested consumers who visit their sites. These advertisers use video clips, quizzes, downloadable gifts like ring tones and icons, and, of course, links to their own websites. For example, eBay has a special "Student Superstore" page on Facebook called *Half.com,* a discount e-commerce site. Brand personalities, such as the Geico Gecko, are particularly useful as a featured character on Facebook. Check out his page at *www.facebook.com/pages/The-Geico-Gecko/167996161475.* Off-the-Wall, new software by Resource Interactive, makes it possible for companies to sell directly from their Facebook walls, which moves social media into a new dimension of social marketing.

H&R Block reached into the online tax filing space with a campaign that used a Facebook page, as well as a dedicated digital TV spot, blogs, a YouTube channel, apps, and widgets. An army of 1,000 Tweeters will respond to the "Ask a Tax Advisor" buttons on the Block website, as well as answer questions directly and "listen" in on topics being discussed on community forums. Realizing the growing importance of online services, the company hopes to maintain its presence with digital filers, as well as support its stores and encourage filers to consult with its staff of professional tax experts both online and in stores. The H&R Block campaign takes on do-it-yourself competitor Intuit's Turbo Tax, which has a long-standing, devoted online community of users.[45]

Politicians, who have been active users of websites, are also creating MySpace and Facebook profiles with cool and funny things about themselves. Sarah Palin launched her post–Governor of Alaska career from her Facebook page. It is all about connecting on a semi-personal level with a group of like-minded individuals to attract votes, volunteers, and donations.

In terms of marketing communication applications, most of these social media forms also can be set up by organizations to engage stakeholders in brand conversations (employee blogs, for example, or corporate Facebook pages) or, if outside the organization, consulted for buzz, trends, and feedback about brand perceptions. The point is that social media marketing can increase a brand's Web presence and help manage its Internet image.

Video and Image Sharing　One particular type of social media is the community sites where users can post videos (YouTube, Google Video) and photographs (Flickr). YouTube is the Goliath of this genre with all kinds of videos from home shots of babies to parody commercials and brand-sponsored films. Launched in December 2005, the video-sharing service plays more than 100 million clips per day with some 65,000 clips uploaded daily. Visible Measures, which is a research firm that tracks video viewing on YouTube and other video-sharing sites, found that Susan Boyle's version of "Cry Me a River" accumulated a record-breaking 100 million views after her performance on the *Britain's Got Talent* show.[46]

Skype is a video chat service that makes it possible for friends, family members, and colleagues at far distances to talk in real time—like a video phone, but through a computer or smart phone. People can even watch TV together or share other experiences, as long as both have a Skype camera attachment. Online video streaming site Hulu is also developing a real-time interactive video system.

Marketers are experimenting with how best to use this technology. Ski marketers, for example, are using uploaded geotargeted photos and videos to show real-time snow conditions. Sprite is underwriting an interactive Web reality series on YouTube called "Green Eyed World," which will follow British singer-songwriter Katie Vogel as she tries to break into the music world. Similar to the Gecko's Facebook page, the "Itsthegecko" YouTube channel features among others, a video where the Gecko takes a different picture of himself every day for two years. Check it out at *http://www.youtube.com/watch?v= Lw_yEmdisfw.*

Major broadcasters are also joining the YouTube world. BBC was the first global media company to sign a deal with YouTube to provide news and entertainment clips from its broadcasting. These clips also carry advertising. Other broadcasters, however, are challenging YouTube and its owner Google for broadcasting their shows, which are protected by copyright. The media giant Viacom, for example, sued Google in 2007 for videos uploaded by YouTube members, such as *The Daily Show with Jon Stewart.*

Using time-lapse video, the Geico Gecko has a YouTube film where he supposedly takes a picture of himself every day for two years. The images show different postures, expressions, and costumes and project the wacky personality of this well-known brand character. Find another brand that uses YouTube to create a brand personality. Critique the blog's effectiveness.

Popular TV programs, as well as commercials, are uploaded by viewers to their YouTube pages to be shared with the whole YouTube world as a **viral video.** For a viral campaign, which often is a spoof or an irreverent approach to brand marketing that speaks to the under-25 set, experts say that reaching 1 million YouTube viewers is the "magic number." That's generally thought to be the level that generates buzz and delivers significant impressions to create a market response. Some brands and agencies even encourage mock ads cobbled together from clips and amateur video because they are, in some cases, highly creative.

Flip video cameras, which are about the size of a smart phone, are revolutionizing the online video sites. Introduced by Cisco System, the company used video snippets from the lives of real people, as well as celebrities (Lenny Kravitz brushing his teeth) to popularize what Cisco calls "organic moments." Geotags, which add geographical identification to photos, are used to pinpoint locations.

Social Games and Virtual Communities   It started with *Second Life* in 2003. That is the idea that a 3-D virtual world could become a playground for people who wanted to live imaginary lives online by playing **social games.** Sort of a parallel universe, participants created their own **avatars** who were fantasy images of themselves—some even got married and set up housekeeping with another person's avatar. *Second Life* even has a commercial side with its own currency that you use to buy islands of space and create your own place. There are also stores and all kinds of businesses that serve the residents. Interest in *Second Life* peaked in 2007 when some 4 million people joined, but it still continues with about a million people a month logging on. *Second Life* is popular enough that some 1,400 companies and organizations, including IBM, still participate.[47]

In 2009 the action turned to FarmVille, a social game played on Facebook. It's like a computer game but rather than playing alone, you're playing with friends. The idea is to grow crops either through hard work or by buying farmcash by trading and selling crops, exchanging gifts, and accruing capital to expand your farm. The site makes money from ads and virtual goods that people buy (with real money). A third source of income is product come-ons, which are offers like those on website ads, except that if you click on them, you are agreeing to try some product or service.

Social Media Strategies   Marketers are experimenting to find the best ways to use social media and take advantage of the strengths of these new media forms. Marketers who want to use social media see value in conversations and customer relationship-building communication, rather than targeting and promoting to a mass of anonymous consumers.

For example, Coca-Cola undertook an "Expedition 206" campaign in which the soft-drink maker sent three 20-somethings to the 206 countries where Coke is sold. The 275,000-mile journey is documented on its own website (*www.Expedition206.com*), as well as through posts on Facebook and Twitter (@x206), with image and video sharing on Flickr and YouTube. Fans following the journey can send in suggestions for what the trio should do or see in the various countries. Coke will track media impressions created by the undertaking, as well as posts by Facebook and Twitter followers, and website page views. One early success for the campaign came with the internal communication and collaboration in planning between and among the marketing, communication, and public relations teams. The event will also challenge local and regional markets to develop their own supporting social media tools; in some cases they will be using media that were unknown in their previous campaigns.[48]

Principle

Search ads combined with social media campaigns generate the highest level of results.

Research has found that search ads combined with social media campaigns generate higher results than more general search ads on portals and less-well connected websites. Xerox, for example, found a substantial increase in brand-related searches after it launched a promotion about a fake psychological disorder called Information Overload Syndrome. The idea was that Xerox helps manage information, but the spoof video got more than a million hits, generated buzz on blogs and other social networking sites, and delivered a 65 percent increase in brand-related searches.[49]

Principle

Marketers who use social media recognize the value in conversations and customer relationship-building communication.

Social networks were originally designed to be noncommercial; however, brands can enter into the network as both topics and members of the community. They understand that this type of marketing is less about being self-serving and more about serving and service. Social media are also about speed of response—its interaction is much more dynamic than previous media and when questions are asked or complaints are posted, speedy response is essential. Marketers in businesses where last-minute marketing and consumer decision making are important, such as ski resorts, can benefit by providing real-time videos and photos, along with Tweets to skiers.

Understanding the notion of communities is critical. Some form spontaneously around a topic; others already exist. Marketers can help form some communities and help people get together; in other communities they need to maintain a low profile. A basic principle is to know the community rules and respect that everyone is different. An interesting promotion by Fox media used a newspaper ad to reach people who might be interested in joining FoxNation. It's a digital community centered on the *FoxNation.com* website, which includes, videos, blogs, and news stories. The ad enlisted Uncle Sam, or at least his famous image and the "I Want You" pointing finger (see Chapter 4), to help promote the *FoxNation.com*.

The problem with social marketing is that it is changing so fast. MySpace gave way in popularity to Facebook about the same time Twitter appeared on the scene, and they all essentially made chat rooms outdated. The social media we've discussed here are just a few sites in a huge environment. Marketers who want an online presence need to keep up with new technologies and new sites—and know how best to use them.

HOW IS INTERNET MARCOM EVOLVING?

The Internet itself is a catalyst for new thinking about how marcom can be used. New strategies and practices have developed to extend this new world of Web-based marketing communication.

Offline Advertising for Websites

One of the most difficult problems facing Internet marketers is driving traffic to their sites. One way to do this is to use **offline advertising,** which appears in conventional media to drive traffic to a website. In the Chapter 12 opening story, we explained how Aflac used a teaser ad in print media with the headline *"youdontknowquack.com"* to entice readers to check out its site. Once there, readers had a little test on common myths including one that asks about coverage of medical expenses. The answer, of course, argued that everyone needs Aflac to cover all of those other expenses.

Print is particularly useful in offline advertising because it offers the opportunity to present the URL in a format that makes it possible for the reader to note the address. It's harder to present that information in broadcast media where the message is here and gone. Whatever the medium, including URLs in traditional ads does matter to consumers, as the *Practical Tips* box at *www.pearsonhighered.com/moriarty* explains.

E-Media Developments and Applications

As we have said before, convergence is a big challenge, as well as an opportunity, for traditional media industries where the differences between television, print, and the Internet media are blurring. Just to remind you, here are some examples of these changes:

* An online version of the *New York Times Sunday Style* magazine appears as a new website with daily articles and Web-only features.
* *Esquire* magazine is experimenting with technology embedded in its print pages that can trigger real-life video images when the page is held up to a Web camera.
* **Podcasts,** audio shows from the Web that can be downloaded to an MP3 player, are changing the way we listen to radio, as well as music. Walt Disney was one of the first companies to explore the potential of podcasts for promotions when it used a series of them for Disneyland's 50th anniversary celebration.
* TVs and computers are hooking up so you can access the Internet from your TV in your living room or watch your video downloads from your cell phone on your big screen TV, a trend referred to as "tradigital."[50]
* Web TV is stealing market share from network and cable TV and *Hulu.com,* the Internet's most popular streaming video site, is a prize that Comcast acquired when it bought NBC in 2009. Part of that deal was to limit or control the shows available online in order protect cable subscriptions.[51]
* Xbox game players can access Twitter and Facebook from the game's console making it possible for players to tweet their progress, share notes, and compete in real time. Video game viewers will also soon be able to watch streaming TV shows and movies on their video screens. Microsoft hopes its Xbox will take over the role of a cable channel.[52]
* Hulu, an ad-supported content provider sponsored by NBC, ABC, and Fox, can feed streaming video from movies and TV programs to smart phones and gaming consoles, as well as computers. YouTube has more viewers but Hulu offers better quality for long-form video.

The potential of new digital media is that they can combine the advantages of broadcast (high-impact visuals), print (the ability to inform), and the Internet (personalization and interactivity). This hybridization is also creating opportunities in the wireless environment where smart phones have become the Swiss Army knife of media serving as cameras, gaming devices, MP3 players, and video viewers, as well as providing online capability.

The point is that e-media no longer need to look or act like computers. Netbooks pioneered the idea of storing all your files online and using a device simply to access them, a practice called **cloud computing.** A Boston company, Litl, is offering a "webbook," which marries cloud computing with a TV-like viewing experience. It doesn't have memory or run Windows, but instead accesses websites that provide those services.[53]

Tagging, Hashtags, and Tag Clouds   Search marketing is driven by keywords—the concept or thing that you are searching for. In many of the social marketing formats, the posts are categorized by **tags.** Similar to keywords, users of Twitter have created **tagging,** a way to track keywords by inserting a hash symbol (#) before a word in a Tweet. In effect, you have "tagged" that word and it becomes a category. Your note, as well as others with the same **hashtag,** will show

Principle

New digital media combine the advantages of broadcast (high-impact visuals), print (in-depth information), and the Internet (personalization and interactivity).

This tag cloud in the lower right corner from the Phelps Group website illustrates the variety of marketing communication areas involved in the agency's work.

Source: http://blog.thephelpsgroup.com/blogs/thephelpsgroup/default.aspx.

up as posts on *www.hashtags.org*. People tweeting about a brand or company will tag their post with a # symbol plus the company name. Others can follow the tag to see related mentions about the brand or company.

Beyond Twitter mentions, **tag clouds** are visual representations of the use of keywords in searches and tags in social networking. A tag cloud creates a collage of words associated with a certain phrase or name. The frequency of use determines the weight or size of the associated word in the network (or cloud) of associations. Originally popularized by the photo-sharing site Flickr, tag clouds were created from search keywords to help users find photos and videos that had something in common. Tag clouds have been useful in search engine optimization for Web pages. Hashtags and tag clouds have been used by brands and their planners to analyze the network of brand associations referenced on other sites and messages. They give you a quick view of the most talked about topics. For example, study the tag cloud for the Phelps Group (*www.thephelpsgroup.com*), an IMC agency in Santa Monica, California.

Using the Internet across Borders   Because the Internet has a global reach, it offers real strength to global marketers. The Bloesem website (*www.bloesem.blogs.com/bloesem*) mentioned earlier is operated by a Dutch woman living in Malaysia and presented in English to a worldwide audience of people interested in design.

But international business has its challenges. It faces access, legal, linguistic, currency, and technological barriers. First, not everyone around the globe has the access or ability to use the Internet via a computer, but the number of Internet users is growing exponentially. The Internet audience is growing faster internationally than it is in the United States, particularly in developing countries such as China and India.

Advertising and sales promotion laws differ from country to country. Differences in privacy laws between Europe and the United States are expected to force American companies to change the way they collect and share the consumer information they monitor and retrieve from customers' Web behavior. Web censoring is also a problem in certain countries with controlled economies, such as China, Saudi Arabia, Iran, Myanmar, Thailand, Malaysia, and Vietnam. State control of the Internet leads to filtering of political information and suppression of criticism, as well as limitations on marketing communication practices.[54] Even marketing efforts can be censored if they are judged to be undermining the local culture or religious standards.

Language is another factor. Although English is the dominant language on the Internet, some advertisers who want to provide different websites for different countries have trouble ensuring consistency across all sites. Another issue is exchange rates. Companies must decide whether to offer prices in their own currency or in the local currency. For example, one Canadian shopper reported that books on a Canadian website were cheaper than the same books on *Amazon.com*. In addition, some companies make different offers available in different countries.

Marketers must also keep in mind the technological differences among the worldwide Internet audiences. Users in some countries have to pay per-minute charges and therefore want to get on and off quickly, which precludes sophisticated graphics that take a long time to load. In other countries, users have access to fast lines and may expect more sophisticated Internet programming.

Issues in Internet Advertising

Two issues online advertisers continue to study are measuring Internet advertising and privacy concerns.

Measurement The advantages of the Internet as a potential advertising vehicle are tremendous, with rapid, near instantaneous feedback and results chief among them. Rather than wait weeks or months to measure the success of a campaign, marketers can instead run ad tests online, measure meaningful results within days, and quickly invest in the best performers with minimal switching costs. One problem, however, is the question of what to measure—readers, viewers, visitors, repeat visits, responses, sales? And how do such metrics equate to the reach of other media?

Consider **hits** (the number of times a particular site is visited), viewers (the number of viewers to a site), unique visitors (the number of different viewers during a particular time period), and page views (the number of times viewers view a page). These measures track a consumer through a website, but they offer no insights as to motivation, nor do they tell us whether a visitor paid any attention to the surrounding ads.

The primary method currently used to measure consumer response to Internet advertising is click-through (the number of people who click on a banner ad). Many Internet advertisers consider this measure insufficient, and a host of private research providers have emerged to expand on that measure. For example, Denver-based Match Logic identifies for its clients what viewers do next after not clicking on a banner ad.

A recent problem is **click fraud,** which refers to clicks made either to make money for the sponsoring site or to damage a competitor. *NewCars.com* found itself under attack with a large number of clicks coming from Bulgaria, Indonesia, and the Czech Republic. With pay-per-click, the company had to pay a search engine every time a Web surfer clicked on its link. There's even a company, Click Forensics, that specializes in detecting click fraud.[55]

Internet Targeting and Privacy In addition to providing information, e-businesses also capture information and use it to direct their marketing communication efforts to make messages more personal and relevant to consumers. This is true for Internet advertising as well as e-mail advertising and direct marketing, which we will discuss in Chapter 16.

Every time you order something from *Amazon.com,* for example, the company keeps track and starts building a profile of your interests. When you go to Amazon the next time, the site will probably open with an announcement about some new book or CD that might interest you. If you have given Amazon permission, it will also send these announcements to you by e-mail. In other words, companies that collect data about the behavior of their customers can better target them with advertising messages and personalized special promotional offers. We referred to this earlier as behavioral targeting. The Interactive Advertising Bureau (IAB) has an online campaign that addresses the privacy issue.

But there are other tracking mechanisms, such as **cookies,** which are little electronic bugs, that can be placed on your computer by a Web server to track your movements online. They don't do anything bad, like a virus does, but they do report back to their owners what sites you visited and from that they build an online profile about you and your interests. On the good side, cookies let companies store information about your preferences so you don't have to retype everything every time you go to that site.

Are cookies a bad practice or good? Critics say they are an invasion of privacy, but marketers say they are just a way to gather marketing information without the tedious survey or registration process. In fact, many people recognize the trade-off: If they provide a company with information, they will get more personalized service in return. For more information about how you can get your Internet service provider to remove cookies, check out the website *www.webwasher.com.*

Many people have issues with the collection of personal information. Their concern is with how the information is

A public service campaign created pro bono by WPP's Schematic agency, the "Advertising Is Creepy" ads are designed to educate consumers about behavioral targeting and privacy issues.

TRUSTe®

Companies can earn their customers' trust by displaying the TRUSTe seal on their websites. Have you ever seen this seal on a website? Would it make a difference to you?

used and whether its use violates their privacy. AOL, for example, assembles a huge database of customer information, some of which it sells to other direct marketers. It admits this practice in its privacy policy, which is published on its website. It also buys information about its subscribers from other outside database suppliers, which it can use to better target its customers' interests. And that's the primary reason companies collect this type of information: It lets them better target their advertising messages and theoretically be more selective in how they contact customers and prospects.

Many companies try to maintain a responsible position by posting their **privacy policy** on their websites, which details, among other things, how or whether the site is collecting data on its visitors and how those data are used. Sometimes this information is easy to find, sometimes it is buried on the site and difficult to access, and in some instances the website doesn't have any published privacy statement at all. The TRUSTe seal of approval is awarded to sites that meet the oversight body's privacy criteria. A number of consumer activists follow this privacy issue; if you want to learn more about their activities, check the watchdog site Junkbusters (*www.junkbusters.com*). The government also has an Electronic Privacy Information Center (*www.epic.org*), which monitors information-collecting practices and privacy issues.

The FCC reached a settlement in 2008 with Sears over allegations that the retailer failed to adequately inform consumers about how much Sears was tracking their behaviors. Congress is looking into these practices and the industry is trying to head off legal action by taking steps to make their practices more transparent. One proposal, for example, is for an icon that would appear on Web pages to let consumers know that their activity is being tracked.[56] The European Union monitors behavioral targeting practices and even started legal action against the United Kingdom for permitting behavioral targeting without proper notification to consumers or for not requiring opt-out mechanisms.[57]

Advantages and Limitations of Internet Advertising

Internet advertising is growing in popularity because it offers some distinct advantages over other media, in addition to the explosion in its use by consumers. Most notably, it is relatively inexpensive. Advertisers see it as a relatively low-cost alternative to mainstream advertising media. It is also a form that reaches people who aren't watching much television or reading newspapers. Another benefit of Internet advertising is that it is relatively easy to track and reach a highly targeted audience.

Also, advertisers can customize and personalize their messages over the Internet. Thanks to **database marketing,** an advertiser can input key demographic and behavioral variables, making the consumer feel like the ad is just for him or her. Check out *www.classmates.com* for an example. Ads appearing on a particular page are for products that would appeal to a particular age group. Someone who graduated from high school in 1960 would see banner ads for investments that facilitate retirement as opposed to someone graduating in 2000 who might see career ads.

For the B2B advertiser, Internet advertising can provide excellent sales leads or actual sales. Users of a typical B2B site, for example, can access the product catalogs, read the product specifications in depth, request a call from a salesperson, and make a purchase online.

The Internet can level the playing field for small and medium-sized companies that compete against larger organizations. The cost of creating a website, a set of ads, and a database is affordable for virtually every marketer.

Undoubtedly, the most serious drawback is the inability of strategic and creative experts to consistently produce effective ads and to measure their effectiveness. Technological limitations can also cause problems for users with low bandwidth or a lack of computer expertise.

Consider, too, that clutter is just as much a problem with the Internet as it is in other media. In fact, because multiple ads may appear on the same screen—many moving or popping up—the clutter may be even worse.

Looking Ahead

This chapter has described the important developments in digital media and how online media have changed the face of marketing communication. In particular, we've discussed the implications of shape-shifting media and the challenges, as well as opportunities, they create for marketing communication. The next chapter pulls all of these opportunities together and describes how media planning and buying are managed.

IT'S A WRAP

Mission Accomplished

The U.S. Army's traveling Virtual Army Experience effectively reached and built relationships with potential recruits by using media creatively and interactively. In addition to recruiting new soldiers, the VAE attempted to reshape the public perceptions formed in popular culture to teach young people about the hard work and sacrifice soldiers endure in the service to protect our country's freedom each day.

"More than ever before, today's audience is drawn to a brand they can interact and connect with on a more personal level," said Lt. Gen. Benjamin C. Freakley, commanding general of U.S. Army Accessions Command. "We want our prospects to experience the Army brand in a relevant way, so we infuse experiential opportunities into all of our marketing efforts. That way, our prospects can better understand what it's really like to be a soldier and, therefore, make an informed decision about serving our nation in the Army." Sgt. Jason Mike, a Silver Star recipient and one of the "Real Heroes" manning the event at Andrews Air Force Base, said, "I hope that everyone who comes through here leaves with a greater appreciation for the Army and our men and women in uniform."

In the first three years of its operations, the VAE provided a glimpse of soldiering in the U.S. Army to more than 205,000 unique visitors, and has helped identify more than 112,000 qualified prospects to the sales force. It delivered an event cost per lead that was well below its goal. Importantly, it converted leads to U.S. Army contracts. Of all the qualified leads generated through the VAE program, the conversion rate far exceeded the stated goal. According to a 2008 New Recruit Survey Report published by U.S. Army Accessions Command, the VAE became the fifth most attended Army event among new recruits. Pre-event and post-event assessment surveys indicated that negative perceptions of a career in the U.S. Army were significantly dispelled as well. According to the same 2008 survey, U.S. Army Accessions Command also reported that the VAE resulted in the highest percentage of positive change in perception of the top Army event marketing programs.

The operation was deemed a success as a communication campaign. The U.S. Army has been decorated with numerous awards for this project, including a Silver and Gold Effie for Brand Experience and Government/Institution/Recruitment, respectively.

Key Points Summary

1. **How does the Internet work, and what roles does it play in marketing communication?** Most Internet advertising is found on established news media sites that operate as electronic publishers, such as *www.nytimes.com, www.WSJ.com,* and *www.ESPN.com,* as well as on major search engines and service providers, such as Google and Yahoo!. The roles played by Internet communication include providing information and entertainment, connecting people socially, and generating word-of-mouth communication.

2. **What are the most common types of online marketing communication?** Most corporations have websites in which they describe their organization and, in some cases, make it possible to buy products online. E-mail is used by companies to reach customers and prospects with commercial messages and also by customers and other stakeholders to contact the company. The Internet also provides different kinds of advertising opportunities that appear on websites and search en-

gines. Social media offer another way people can stay in touch and that includes companies who use such media as Facebook and Twitter to connect with their customers.

3. **In what ways are Internet practices, issues, and trends evolving?** Important Internet practices that have emerged include the need for offline advertising for websites and new forms of brand experiences on the Web. Convergence has also created new hybrid forms of media involving digital forms of traditional media, and rich media have extended their impact. The Internet is a global medium and that presents both opportunities and problems for marketers. The primary issues are measurement and privacy. The advantages include the Internet's relative inexpensiveness, its ability to reach people who aren't using traditional media, the ability to customize messages, and the ability to track sales leads. Limitations include technological expertise, measurement methods, and clutter.

Words of Wisdom: Recommended Reading

Davis, Scott, and Philip Kotler, *The Shift: The Transformation of Today's Marketers in Tomorrow's Growth Leaders,* San Francisco CA: John Wiley & Sons, 2009.

Halligan, Brian, and Dharmesh Shah, *Inbound Marketing: Get Found Using Google, Social Media, and Blogs (The New Rules of Social Media),* Hoboken, NJ: John Wiley & Sons, 2010.

Harden, Leland, and Bob Heyman, *Digital Engagement: Internet Marketing That Captures Customers and Builds Intense Brand Loyalty,* New York: American Management Association, 2009,

Ryan, Damian, and Calvin Jones, *Understanding Digital Marketing: Marketing Strategies for Engaging the Digital Generation,* Philadelphia, PA: Kogan Page, 2009.

Vollmer, Christopher, and Geoffrey Precourt, *Always On: Advertising, Marketing, and Media In an Era of Consumer Control,* Booz Allen Hamilton (McGraw-Hill), 2008.

Wertime, Kent, and Ian Fenwick, *DigiMarketing: The Essential Guide to New Media and Digital Marketing,* Singapore: John Wiley, 2008.

Zarella, Dan, *The Social Media Marketing Book,* Sebastopol, CA: O'Reilly Media, 2010.

Key Terms

avatars, p. 409	hashtags, p. 411	pop-behind, p. 402	superstitials, p. 402
bandwidth, p. 393	hits, p. 413	pop-up, p. 402	tag clouds, p. 412
banner ads, p. 402	home page, p. 399	portal, p. 392	tagging, p. 411
blog, p. 405	Internet, p. 391	privacy policy, p. 414	tags, p. 411
broadband, p. 393	intranets, p. 392	product reviews, p. 391	tweets, p. 407
chat rooms, p. 407	keyword, p. 392	search engine, p. 392	URL, p. 392
click fraud, p. 413	link, p. 392	search marketing, p. 403	user-generated ads, p. 398
click-through, p. 402	micro-blog, p. 407	search optimization, p. 404	viral marketing, p. 401
cloud computing, p. 411	micro-sites, p. 402	skyscrapers, p. 402	viral video, p. 409
cookies, p. 413	mini-sites, p. 402	social games, p. 409	virtual communities, p. 397
database marketing, p. 414	navigation, p. 400	social media marketing, p. 405	website, p. 399
domain name, p. 392	netcasting, p. 392	social networking, p. 397	widgets, p. 402
e-business, p. 395	offline advertising, p. 411	stickiness, p. 400	World Wide Web, p. 391
e-commerce, p. 395	podcasts, p. 411	streaming video, p. 393	zines, p. 395
extranets, p. 392			

Review Questions

1. What is a website, and how does it differ from other forms of advertising?

2. Describe search engines, chat rooms, and blogs, and explain how they can be used in a company's advertising program.

3. Define and describe a banner ad. Some experts say the effectiveness of banner ads is declining. Is that an accurate assessment? Why or why not?

4. Explain the concept of offline advertising. What is its primary objective?

5. How is the Internet audience measured?

6. What are the advantages and disadvantages of Internet advertising? Of e-mail advertising?

7. What are some of the new forms of alternative media with which advertisers are experimenting? Explain how they work and what advantages they provide.

Discussion Questions

1. One interesting way to combine the assets of print and broadcast is to use the visuals from a print ad or a television commercial in an Internet ad. Why would an advertiser consider this creative strategy? What limitations would you mention? In what situations would you recommend doing this?

2. You are the media planner for a cosmetics company introducing a new line of makeup for teenage girls. Your research

indicates that the Internet might be an effective medium for creating awareness about your new product line. How do you design an Internet advertising strategy that will reach your target market successfully? What websites would you choose? Why? What advertising forms would you use on these sites and why? What other media would you recommend using as part of this campaign and why?

3. Your small agency works for a local retailer (pick one from your community) that wants to create buzz and get people talking about it. The retailer has very little money to use on advertising. Your agency team agrees that using social media might be a solution. Brainstorm among yourselves and come up with a list of at least five ideas for using social media that would get people talking about the store. Write the ideas as a proposal to the store owner and prepare a presentation to share your ideas with the class.

4. *Three-Minute Debate* You are a sales rep working for a college newspaper that has an online version. How would you attract advertising? One of your colleagues says there is no market for online advertising for the paper, but you think the paper is missing an opportunity. Consider the following questions in deciding whether online advertising for the paper makes sense: What companies would you recommend to contact? How can Internet sites like your online newspaper entice companies to advertise on them? What competitive advantage, if any, would Web advertising for your paper provide? Take one side or the other of this debate and prepare a brief presentation of your arguments to give to your class.

Take-Home Projects

1. *Portfolio Project* Examine the various ads found on major portals, such as the *New York Times* (*www.nytimes.com*), the *Wall Street Journal* (*http://online.wsj.com/home-page*), FOX News (*www.foxnews.com*), ABC News (*http://abcnews.go.com/*), the *Washington Post* (*www.washingtonpost.com*), *USA Today* (*www.usatoday.com*), Yahoo! News (*http://news.yahoo.com/*), MSNBC (*www.msnbc.msn.com*), AOL (*www.aol.com*), Yahoo! (*www.yahoo.com*), NPR (*www.npr.org*), and PBS (*www.pbs.org*). Download three ads you find most visually attractive, engaging, and motivating. Write a paragraph for each that explains your evaluations. Which ones do you think could easily be used as television commercials? As radio commercials? Write a one- to two-page report on your assessment of their ability to transfer to other media formats.

2. *Mini-Case Analysis* The Army's traveling Virtual Army Experience was deemed to be effective and won numerous awards. In analyzing the success of this effort, consider the following questions:

- What made the Army's Virtual Army Experience effective in connecting with potential recruits?
- What elements contributed to a change in the negative perceptions of young people about joining the Army?
- What are the limitations of this program and what might the Army do to extend the impact of this program in the following years?

Team Project: The BrandRevive Campaign

You have been working with a brand revitalization campaign throughout the previous chapters. Now let's apply your knowledge of digital media opportunities to your brand.

- Based on your knowledge of your brand's marketing situation and the targeting strategy you have proposed, which

digital media seem most appropriate to use in your revitalization campaign? Explain and justify your selection.
- Develop your ideas for a creative way to employ these media in your brand's revitalization project.

Hands-On Case

The Century Council

Read the Century Council case in the Appendix before coming to class.

1. The Stupid Drink uses very little traditional media in comparison to nontraditional media. Do you think that was a wise decision when attempting to target college students?

2. Name new and even better ways to use the Internet to strengthen The Stupid Drink campaign.

Media Planning and Buying

It's a Winner

Campaign:	Company:	Agency:	Award:
"Campaign for Real Beauty"	Unilever	Unilever	Grand Effie; Grand Prix, Cannes International Advertising Festival, Ad Age's Best Non-TV Campaigns of the Decade, Festival of Media Awards

1. What is a media plan and what is the role of media research in developing media plans?
2. What are the four steps in media planning and why are they important?
3. How do IMC and global marketing affect media plans?
4. What are the responsibilities of media buyers?

Dove Audiences Redefine Beauty

So far you've read a lot about effective brand communication. You've seen how Burger King successfully kept its Whopper in the minds of the hungry, how Wii became a cultural phenomenon, and how Chick-fil-A consistently conveys its quirky "Eat Mor Chikin" message delivered by cows on billboards. As these cases demonstrate, one of the fundamental principles of successful communication is the ability to understand how best to connect with the consumer.

Unilever's campaign for Dove, which won a Grand Effie and Festival of Media Award for "branding bravery," provides another example of great advertising that recognized a truth held by consumers and then connected on a personal level with those consumers. The "Campaign for Real Beauty" touched a nerve and punctured the cultural obsession with stick-thin bodies and Barbie doll images. The Dove campaign was risky because it sought to literally redefine beauty in advertising and to acknowledge a change in the way women see themselves. It could have been a bomb, but it was a winner because it spoke to every woman's need to look and feel her best without promising or reinforcing impossible standards of beauty.

Unilever commissioned research that eventually drove the marketing campaign. Some startling statistics from the study included these findings:

- Only 2 percent of the respondents believed they were beautiful.
- Of the respondents, 68 percent indicated they strongly believed that the media and advertising set an unrealistic standard of beauty most women can't achieve.

Here's how the Dove "Campaign for Real Beauty" unfolded.

Dove recognized it needed to reach every woman, and to do that it strategically placed messages in many different media. The message of the Dove "Campaign for Real Beauty" provided a deliberate contrast with that of the competition in beauty and women's magazines like *Glamour*, *Allure*, and *Vogue*. Heavy emphasis was placed on print rather than television because of print media's ability to stop the audience and make them really look at the models in the ad and contemplate the meaning of beauty.

419

Dove didn't ignore broadcast media, however—they even ran an ad during the Super Bowl. They also established a website (*campaignforrealbeauty.com*), which urges a boost in self-esteem by defying stereotypes that define beautiful as perfect—and skinny. Part of the campaign, a Web video titled *Evolution*, was a viral phenomenon that reached millions.

Spending a fifth of the normal amount for a personal-care product launch, the Dove advertising was concentrated in the top 10 cities where it would have the most immediate impact. Outdoor and transit advertisements were plastered on billboards and buses to generate public debate.

A similar strategy was used in 2007 to launch Dove's *ProAge* line, which continues the counterintuitive strategy by celebrating older women with their silver hair, wrinkles, and age spots. In Canada, the campaign found its voice in *Finding Body and Soul*, a play celebrating beauty through the ages by well-respected Canadian playwright Judith Thompson. Its cast of 12 real women (not actresses) are ages 45 and older, and auditioned by writing a letter that started "Dear Body. . . ." Dove devotees also were invited to host *ProAge* parties, complete with a party kit.

Although we live in a culture that worships physical perfection, Dove is trying valiantly to broaden that definition. At the end of the chapter you'll read about the results of the Dove efforts.

Sources: Effie brief supplied by Ogilvy & Mather; "Dove Campaign for Real Beauty Case Study: Innovative Marketing Strategies in the Beauty Industry," June 2005, *www.datamonitor.com;* Molly Prior, "Most Innovative Ad Campaign: Dove Campaign for Real Beauty," *Women's Wear Daily,* 190, Issue 122, December 9, 2005: 36–39; Ann-Christine Diaz, "Book of Tens: Best Non-TV Campaigns of the Decade," December 14, 2009, *http://adage.com;* Michael Bush, "Unilever Wins Two Awards for Axe, Dove Media Campaigns," April 20, 2009, *http://adage.com.*

As Unilever knows, media planning is a problem-solving process. The problem: How can media choices help meet the marketing and advertising objectives? The ultimate goal is to reach the target audience with the right message in the best possible way at the best possible time in the most efficient way possible. In this chapter, we review how a media plan is developed—how media planners set objectives and develop media strategies. We then explore the media-buying function and explain how media buyers execute the plan.

HOW ARE MEDIA PLANS CREATED?

Media planners are in the connection business, as the Dove case illustrates. Their work connects brand messages with customers and other stakeholders. They identify and activate the points of contact where brand messages touch consumers. The Dove plans included traditional media, particularly print and outdoor, but also websites, Internet videos, viral marketing, a theatrical play, and party hosting. Note that this media plan involved a lot more than advertising, which supports the point we made in Chapter 11 that all forms of marketing communication use media.

Making connections that resonate with the audience is the hallmark of effective marketing communication, wherever that may occur. Think about the U.S. Army's power to connect with recruits using the video game–based experience and event you read about in Chapter 13, as well as the emotional connections created in the Dove "*Real Women*" and "*ProAge*" campaigns. Another example features embedded ads in video games as described in *The Inside Story* feature. Not only was this an interesting ad placement, it also generated great publicity.

We mentioned in Chapter 11 that traditionally, the advertising agency's media department has been responsible for developing the media plan with input from the agency's account and creative teams and the marketer's brand management group. More recently, media-buying companies have moved into the planning stage as well, bringing the expertise of their media researchers and negotiators. Some major agencies have spun off the media function as a separate company; then they contract with that company for their media planning and buying services. Others have

THE INSIDE STORY

Campaign Ads in Video Games

Holly Duncan Rockwood, *Director of Corporate Communications, Electronic Arts*

In the fall of 2008, President Obama made advertising history when his political campaign ran ads in video games. The ads were highly targeted, intended to reach a typically hard-to-reach demographic—males ages 18 to 34—and ran for just a few weeks before the election in a half dozen games from Electronic Arts. The ads were dynamically served via the Internet to gamers who resided in swing states, coveted votes that had the potential to make or break the election. For example, a gamer might drive down a freeway in *Burnout* and pass a billboard advertising that "Early Voting Has Begun" and a similar message could be found inside the stadium of an *NBA LIVE* basketball game. The campaign was considered groundbreaking for several reasons. For starters, it was a first that such a prominent political candidate would build a marketing strategy that included advertising in video games. This type of advertising is an emerging medium for reaching consumers that has frequently been touted as the next big opportunity for marketers. From a corporate communications perspective, the Obama campaign seemed to suggest that video game advertising had finally arrived, and the novelty provoked an unprecedented level of interest from news organizations.

The first media calls we received were simply fact checking that the campaign ads were running and actually real, not a hoax. However, when we received calls from the *New York Times*, the Associated Press, and National Public Radio early on a Tuesday morning, we realized this might be the tip of a major news story. Our corporate message quickly evolved from one of just acknowledging the campaign, to one that proactively supported EA's corporate messaging around in game advertising. We stressed that EA did not side with one party or another, and emphasized the effectiveness of reaching a highly engaged target audience that plays the games that ran the ads.

Like political campaigns, this rapid response approach to corporate communications strategy is not uncommon in video games, an industry that is highly competitive and often in the public eye with topics ranging from mature content and video game ratings to the unveiling of hotly anticipated titles. Corporate communications professionals often act as spokespeople for timely and occasionally controversial issues.

There are many lessons to be found by working in public relations in the video games industry, like being creative in finding opportunities to drive a story when others might shy away. It's exciting to work for a company like EA, and there are a lot of opportunities for the people who speak on behalf of it. There is never a dull moment and it's one of the best jobs I've ever had.

Holly Duncan Rockwood earned her B.S. in advertising from the University of Colorado and an M.S. in integrated marketing communication from Northwestern University.

FIGURE 14.1

The Central Role of Media Research

Media planners look for data from creative, marketing, and media sources. All of this information is used in both media planning and buying.

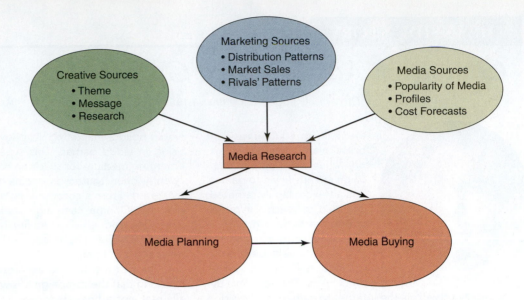

kept the planning in house but contract with an outside media-buying service. Once the media plan is developed, a media-buying unit or team, either in the ad agency or external in a separate media company, executes it.

Given the industry trends, the hot media shops have specialties in new media. For example, the long-established Ogilvy agency launched neo@Ogilvy as a digital-media group to help advertisers figure out how to allocate their ad budgets in the vast array of new media, such as online video, social networking sites, and search advertising. *The Inside Story* by David Rittenhouse in Chapter 5 explained how agencies such as neo@Ogilvy approach the new arena of online behavioral targeting.

Media Research: Information Sources

Some people believe media decisions are the hub in the advertising wheel because media costs are often the biggest element in the marketing communication budget. Not only are media decisions central to advertising planning, media research is central to media planning. That realization stems from not only the large amount of money that's on the line, but also the sheer volume of data and information that media planners must gather, sort, and analyze before media planning can begin. Figure 14.1 illustrates the wide range of media information sources and the critical role media research plays in the overall advertising planning process.

- *Client Information* The client is a good source for various types of information media planners use in their work, such as demographic profiles of current customers (both light and heavy users), response to previous promotions, product sales and distribution patterns, and, most importantly, the budget of how much can be spent on media. Geographical differences in category and brand sales also affect how the media budget is allocated. With consumer goods and services especially, rates of consumption can differ greatly from one region to another.
- *Market Research* Independently gathered information about markets and product categories is another valuable tool for media planners. Mediamark Research, Inc. (MRI), Scarborough (local markets), and Mendelsohn (affluent markets) are research companies that provide this service. This information is usually organized by product category (detergents, cereals, snacks, etc.) and cross-tabulated by audience groups and their consumption patterns. Accessible online for a fee, this wealth of information can be searched and compared across thousands of categories, brands, and audience groups. Although the reports may seem intimidating, they are not that difficult to use. Figure 14.2 is a page from an MRI report showing how to read MRI data. Media planners use MRI data to check which groups, based on demographics and lifestyles, are high and low in category use, as well as where they live and what media they use.
- *Competitive Advertising Expenditures* In highly competitive product categories, such as packaged goods and consumer services, marketers track how much competing brands spend

How to Read an MRI CrossTab

The CrossTab format is a standard research display format that allows multiple variables of related data to be grouped together. Below is a screen capture of an MEMRI² CrossTab, complete with explanations of key numbers. Please note that all the numbers are based on the 2004 Spring MRI study, and that the projected numbers (000) are expressed in thousands.

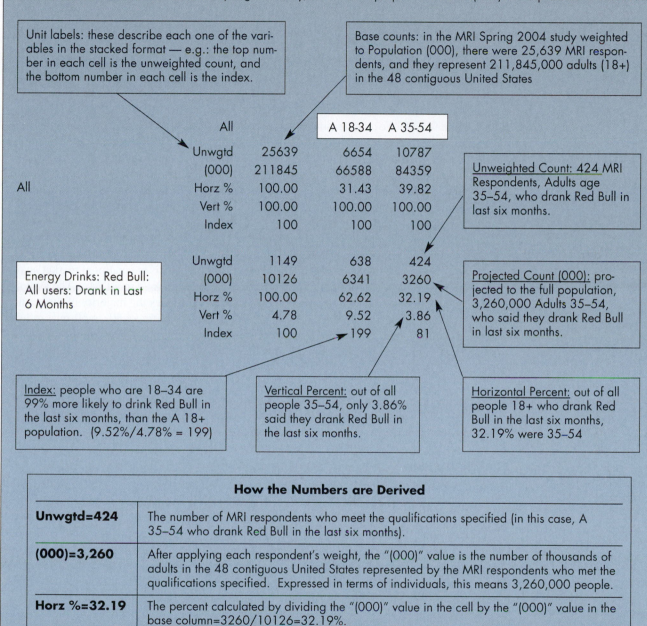

FIGURE 14.2

How to Read MRI CrossTabs

The MRI market research service provides information on 4,090 product categories and services, 6,000 brands, and category advertising expenditures, as well as customer lifestyle characteristics and buying style psychographics.

Source: Courtesy of Mediamark Research Inc. All rights reserved.

on media compared to how much they are spending on their particular brand. This is called **share of voice**. In other words, marketers want to know which, if any, competing brands have louder voices (i.e., are spending more) than they do. For example, if the total spent on airline advertising last year was $200 million, and $50 million of that was spent by United Airlines, UA's share of voice would be 25 percent ($50 \div 200 = 25\%$). Most agencies recommend that a brand's share of voice be at least as high as its share of market. For a new brand, obviously its share of voice needs to be more than its share of market if it wants to grow.

• *Media Kits* The various media and their respective media vehicles provide media kits, which contain information about the size and makeup of their audiences. Although media-supplied information is useful, keep in mind that this is an "inside job"—that is, the information is assembled to make the best possible case for advertising in that particular medium and media vehicle. For that reason, outside research sources, such as media rep companies and the Nielsen reports, are also used. As discussed in previous chapters, Nielsen Media Research audits national and local television, and Arbitron measures radio. Other services, such as the Auditing Bureau of Circulations (ABC), Simmons, and MRI monitor print audiences, and Media Metrix measures Internet audiences. All of these companies provide extensive information on viewers, listeners, and readers in terms of the size of the audience and their profiles.

• *Media Coverage Area* One type of media-related information about markets is the broadcast coverage area for television. Called a **designated marketing area (DMA)**, the coverage area is referred to by the name of the largest city in the area. This is a national market analysis system, and every county in the United States has been assigned to a DMA. The assignment of a county to a DMA is determined by which city provides the majority of the county households' TV programming. Most DMAs include counties within a 50- to 60-mile radius of a major city center. Even though this system is based on TV broadcast signals, it is universally used in doing individual market planning.

• *Consumer Behavior Reports* We mentioned some of the consumer research sources in Chapter 5 that are used in developing segmentation and targeting strategies. They are also useful in planning media strategies. For example, media planners use such services as the Claritas PRIZM system, Nielsen's ClusterPlus system, and supermarket scanner data to locate the target audience within media markets.

The Media Plan

The **media plan** is a written document that summarizes the objectives and strategies that guide how media dollars will be spent. The goal of a media plan is to find the most effective and efficient ways to deliver messages to a targeted audience. Media plans are designed to answer the following questions: (1) who (target audience), (2) what for (objectives), (3) where (the media vehicles used), (4) where (geography), (5) when (time frame), (6) how big (media weight), and (7) at what cost (cost efficiency). The first three are media objectives and the second group represents media strategies. To see where media planning and buying fit into the overall advertising process, see Figure 14.3, which outlines the primary components of a media plan.

When IMC planners develop a media plan, they also take into consideration *contact points*. These include exposure to traditional mass media, as well as word of mouth, place-based media, in-store brand exposures, and the new, interactive media. We'll discuss the IMC dimension of media planning at the end of this chapter. To help you better understand the role of media planners, read the discussion of a week in the life of a media planner in the accompanying feature.

WHAT ARE THE KEY STEPS IN MEDIA PLANNING?

Media planning is more than just choosing from a long list of media options. Traditional **measured media** are chosen based on such metrics as GRPs and CPMs, which are explained later in this chapter, but the new media lack similar metrics and are characterized more by such considerations as the quality of the brand experience, involvement, and personal impact. Old-line advertising media planners are intent on buying reach and frequency, but the problem is that many of their clients are looking for more effective outcomes, such as engaging experiences and brand-

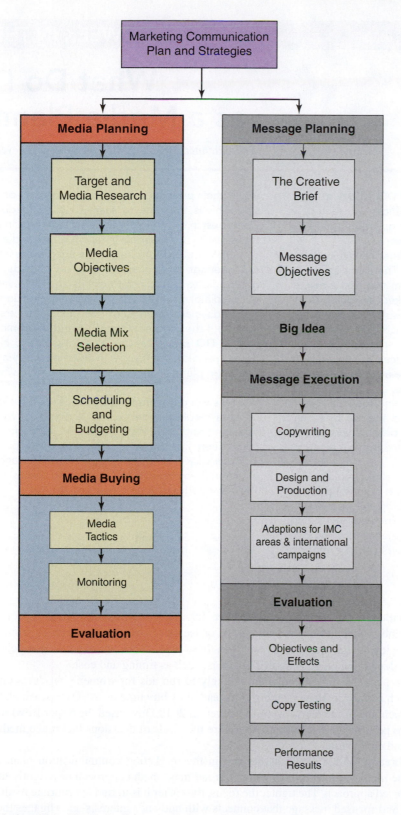

FIGURE 14.3
The Components of a
Media Plan

building relationships. Thus, the framework for making media-planning decisions is changing along with the list of media options.

The four basic steps in media planning are targeting, setting media objectives, developing media strategies, and analyzing the metrics of a media plan.

Step 1: Target Audience

A key strategic decision is identifying a target audience. In media planning, the challenge is to select media vehicles that (1) are compatible with the creative executions and (2) whose audiences

What Do I DO as a Media Planner?

Heather Beck, *Senior Media Planner, Melamed Riley Advertising, Cleveland, Ohio*

People often ask me what it is that I **DO** all day at work. There are 12 media planners in my office, and each of us would have a different answer to that question. But here's a general outline of week's worth of work.

Monday morning there is a conference call involving everyone who works on an account. The client shares information such as sales numbers from the past week, as well as budget changes or which markets are going to run a test campaign. The agency shares results from market research and the status of current projects. During the next couple of hours I **DO** *media research*—requesting and researching information from media sources for new projects.

It's lunch time now! Once or twice a week, media reps either bring in a deli tray for the office, or they take us out for a lunch meeting to pitch their media products. It is the job of the media planner to **DO** *media analysis*, by which I mean analyzing all the options and determining what is best for the client. So we don't let a nice lunch or fancy gift basket sway our judgment.

After lunch, I return phone calls and reply to e-mails. I spend the rest of the day gathering and organizing any information I have received and analyzing the data—that's when I **DO** *media planning*. Actually I do this all week long.

The rest of the week is similar. Tuesday morning conference calls are split up so that groups can talk specifics about their projects with their counterparts on the client side. This is the time to share detailed feedback. What works best in one market might not work well in another so these results are essential in tailoring the media plans.

On Wednesday mornings the agency has informal status meetings or conference calls on Thursday—this is a good time to check in with clients and **DO** *evaluations* of our media plans. Then the day is spent finalizing projects.

Fridays are when all of the agency players on an account put their projects together and determine the best way to **DO** *presentations* of the results to clients. Another typical Friday task is to **DO** *media buying*—that is, place the planned media buys for the following week or month.

This is a generalized example of a typical week in the life of a media planner. Some days you might work until midnight, and other days you'll take long lunch breaks. It might seem like the same thing day to day, but the actual projects vary enough to keep it interesting and challenging. And if you need a break, you can always catch up on the latest issues of *Media Week* or *Ad Age*.

A graduate of the advertising program at Middle Tennessee State, Heather Beck is a media planner at Cleveland-based Melamed Riley Advertising.

best match those of the brand's target audience. In other words, does the group of people who read this magazine, watch this television program, or see these posters include a high proportion of the advertiser's ideal target audience? If so, then these media vehicles may be a good choice for the campaign, depending on other strategic factors, such as timing and cost.

Media planners, for example, are unlikely to run ads for women's products on the Super Bowl, which is skewed 56 percent male; instead, they buy time on the Oscars, which has a much higher percentage of female viewers. However, in 2010 Dove used the Super Bowl to launch its Men+Care personal care products.[1] These are the kinds of decisions that make media planning both fun and challenging.

The breadth of the target, as defined in the marketing communication plan, determines whether the media planner will be using a broad mass media approach or a tightly targeted and highly focused approach. The tighter the focus, the easier it is to find appropriate media to deliver a relevant and focused message that connects with audience interests and engages them personally in a brand conversation.

As you can imagine, every media vehicle's audience is different and therefore varies regarding what percentage of its audience is in the brand's target audience. For example, Mercury Marine, which makes outboard boat motors, targets households (HHs) that own one or more boats. It prefers to advertise in magazines where it can feature beautiful illustrations of its products as well as room to explain the many benefits of its motors. Should it advertise in *Time* or *Boating* magazine? *Time* magazine reaches 4 million HHs, of which 280,000 HHs have boats; in

Principle

The tighter the focus on a target market, the easier it is to find appropriate media to deliver a relevant message.

comparison, *Boating* has only 200,000 HH subscribers. If you said *Time,* sorry, you're not being very cost efficient. This is because even though *Time* reaches 80,000 more boat-owning households, it also reaches 3.7 million HHs that don't own boats. Mercury would have to pay to reach all readers, even those not in its target audience. By advertising in *Boating,* it can pretty well assume that subscribers either own a boat or at least are interested in boating.

In addition to information compiled by the team's media researchers, consumer insight research also is used to identify and analyze the target audience's media use patterns. Industry research helps. For example, in a 2009 study, Harris Interactive Research found that 37 percent of Americans said TV ads are most helpful in making a purchase decision. Newspapers (19 percent) came in second; only 14 percent said Internet search engines were most helpful. In fact, nearly half of the respondents said they ignored Internet banner ads.[2]

This type of research that asks consumers what they think influences their behavior is best used when combined with other consumer behavior findings. Why? Because most consumers don't really know what influences them. (Just ask some of your friends how much advertising impacts what they buy. Most will probably say that "it doesn't" or "just a little.")

For the launch of the Audi A3, the McKinley + Silver media team knew it needed an in-depth understanding of its target audience of young males to develop a media plan that would work for this difficult-to-reach group. From research they found that young males typically don't read or watch traditional media. They're busy and skeptical about commercial messages. From these findings the team came up with a profile of the target, which they described as "intelligent, independent, and innovative" and heavy users of new media. This target audience for this product category is made up of opinion leaders who influence their peers. They are not as interested in buying an entry-level car as they are in getting "what's next."

Step 2: Communication and Media Objectives

Although creative decisions are sometimes made before media planning, this is changing. With the increasing variety of media options available, smart clients and agencies are having up-front cross-functional planning meetings that include creatives, media planners, and account executives. The point is that the media and message strategies are interdependent and decisions in one area affect decisions in the other.

Marketing communication objectives, as you will recall, describe what a company wants target audiences to think, feel, and most importantly, do. **Media objectives** describe what a company wants to accomplish regarding the delivery of its brand messages and their impact on the target audience.

The communication objectives provide guidance to media planners. For example, why would brands want to spend some $3 million to advertise on the Super Bowl unless the buy fits with its brand communication objectives? Pepsi, a long-time Super Bowl advertiser, pulled out in 2010 deciding that expensive brand reminder ads in front of an audience that already knows the brand don't make sense. On the other hand, brands that are building their images, launching new products, or who want to use messages to shape public perceptions on a mass scale—the Super Bowl reaches some 100 million viewers—might see the investment as a good one. Two advertisers during the 2010 Super Bowl illustrate reasons corporations might want to make the investment. Hyundai, for example, wants to change its image from a maker of small, cheap cars to a upscale image and Career Builder believes its job search services are appropriately communicated to a broad population as the United States comes out of a recession.[3]

As we mentioned in Chapter 11, the two basic media objectives are reach and frequency. Let's consider how planners create strategies that deliver on those objectives.

The Reach Objective   The percent of people exposed to a brand message one or more times within a specified period of time is called **reach**. A campaign's success is due in part to its ability to reach as many of the targeted audience as possible within a stated budget and time period. Consequently, many planners feel that reach is the most important objective and that it's the place to start when figuring out a media plan.

Using demographic and lifestyle data, planners can focus on reaching specific types of households (e.g., empty nesters, homes with two+ children under age 18, single-parent households, HHs with incomes over $100,000) or individuals (males ages 25 to 49, people who rent). This enables planners to better match media profiles with the characteristics of the campaign's target audience.

Principle
Reach is the first place to start when setting objectives for a media plan.

Because most media reach large numbers of people who are not in the target market, however, most marketers are more interested in **targeted reach**, which is the percentage of a vehicle's audience that matches the brand's target market. An estimate of targeted reach can be developed assuming the brand's target market can be identified in the vehicle's audience profile. Targeted reach is particularly important to calculate in order to estimate the amount of **wasted reach,** which is the number of people in the vehicle's audience who are neither customers nor prospects. We mentioned this problem in our discussion of network television, which is particularly susceptible to this criticism because of its mass audience.

Assessing the media for target audience opportunities is a major challenge for media planners. The evening news on television, for example, reaches a broad mass-market audience; if your target is women ages 25 to 49, then you have to consider the *targeted reach* of that news program. Obviously both men and women watch news, so you know that your audience would probably be half or less of that, especially since you are targeting a specific age group. Maybe the evening news isn't a good option to reach this target because there would be so much waste. Outdoor, as the *Court TV* posters illustrate, are a location-bound medium and posters are particularly good at targeting a specified population.

The Frequency Objective   As we explained in Chapter 11, **frequency** refers to the repetition of message exposure. You should keep in mind that the frequency number for a media buy is actually the average number of exposure opportunities of those reached.

Because frequency is an *average,* it can be misleading. The range of frequency is often large: Some people see a particular brand message once, while others may see it 10 times within a given period. **Average frequency,** then, can give the planner a distorted idea of the plan's performance because all of those people reached vary in the number of times they have the opportunity to be exposed to a message.

Suppose a media mix includes four magazines and each magazine carries one ad a week for four weeks. The total number of message insertions would be 16 (4 magazines × 1 insertion a

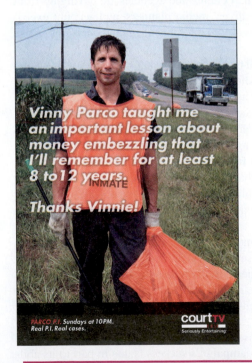

SHOWCASE

These two posters for the *Court TV* television program were created by Aaron Stern when he was an award-winning copywriter at Venables Bell & Partners in San Francisco.

A graduate of the University of Colorado, Stern is now in New York where he recently completed his MFA in Creative Writing at New York University and now works as a freelance copywriter. He and his work were nominated for inclusion in this book by Professor Brett Robbs.

week × 4 weeks = 16 total insertions). It is possible that a small percentage of the target audience could be exposed to all 16 insertions. It is also possible that some of the target would not have the opportunity to be exposed to any of the insertions. In this case the frequency ranges from 0 to 16. Thus, because the average frequency equals 8, you can see how misleading this average frequency number can be.

For this reason planners often use a **frequency distribution** model that shows the percentage of audience reached at each level of repetition. A **frequency quintile distribution analysis** divides an audience into five groups, each containing 20 percent of the audience. Employing media-usage modeling, it is then possible to estimate the average frequency for each quintile as shown in the following table. For example, this table shows that the bottom 20 percent has an average frequency of 1, whereas the top 20 percent has an average frequency of 10. In this hypothetical distribution, the average frequency is 6.

Quintile	Frequency (Average Number of Exposure Opportunities)
Top 20% of universe	10
20%	7
20%	5
20%	3
Bottom 20%	1

If the media planner feels it is necessary that 80 percent of those reached should have an average frequency of 8, then a more intensive media plan would be needed to raise the overall number of exposures; in other words, to shift the average from 6 to 8.

Effective Frequency   Because of the proliferation of information and clutter, there should be a threshold, or minimum frequency level, that produces some type of effect, such as a request for more brand information, a change in attitude toward the brand, or the most desired effect—purchase of the brand.

A standard rule of thumb is that it takes 3 to 10 exposures to have an effect on an audience. Obviously this frequency range is extremely wide. The "right" frequency number is determined by several factors, including level of brand awareness, level of competitive "noise," content of the message, and sophistication of the target audience. Because so many different things can impact a response (i.e., an effect), audience response research is necessary. If the desired effect/response is not achieved, you may need to increase frequency of exposure or change the message. Research diagnostics, such as tracking studies, provide direction. The principle of **effective frequency** is that you add frequency to reach until you get to the level where people respond.

Media Waste   In the discussion of targeted reach we mentioned waste as a result of targeting too wide of a target market. Actually, there are two sides to waste—both reach and frequency. The goal of media planning is to maximize media efficiency, which is to eliminate excessive overlap or too much frequency. Efficiency is achieved, therefore, by reducing media waste. Media professionals use their own experience, as well as audience research and computer models, to identify media efficiency. The point is, when additional media weight ceases to increase the response, it produces waste.

Writing Media Objectives   Given this discussion of the relationship between reach and frequency, it should be clear that usable media objectives would focus on those dimensions ideally including both factors. Here are some examples of media objectives:

1. Reach 60 percent of target audience with a frequency of 4 within each four-week period in which the advertising runs.
2. Reach a maximum percentage of target audience a minimum of five times within the first six months of advertising.
3. Reach 30 percent of the target audiences where they have an opportunity to interact with the brand and users of the brand.
4. Reach category thought leaders and influencers in a way that will motivate them to initiate measurable word of mouth (WOM) and other positive brand messages.

Principle
Effective frequency means you add frequency to reach until you get to the level where people respond.

The first of these objectives is the most common. It recognizes that you can seldom ever reach 100 percent of your target audience. It also acknowledges that a certain level of frequency will be necessary for the brand messages to been seen/heard/read. The second objective would be for a product where the message is more complex; through research (and judgment) it has been decided that prospects need to be exposed to the message at least five times to be effective. In this case frequency is more important than reach. Put another way, it is more important to reach a small portion of the audience five or more times and have them respond than it is to reach a major portion fewer than five times and have little or no response.

Objectives 3 and 4 deal directly with impact. To achieve these objectives, media buyers will have to find media vehicles and contact points, such as events and sponsorships, where interaction with the brand and its users is possible as opposed to using more passive media such as traditional mass media. Note that objective 4 is not measurable as stated.

Step 3: Media Strategies

Strategic thinking in media involves a set of decision factors and tools that help identify the best way to deliver the brand message. Regardless of whether a company spends a few hundred dollars on one medium or millions of dollars on a variety of media, the goal is still the same: to reach the right people at the right time with the right message.

Media strategy is the way media planners determine the most cost-effective way to reach the target audience and satisfy the media objectives. Specific media strategies are based on analyzing and comparing various ways to accomplish the media objectives, and then selecting the approach that is estimated to be the most effective alternative. The idea is that there are always multiple ways to reach an objective, but which way is the best?

Strategies That Deliver Reach and Frequency   In certain situations, for example, when the objectives call for high reach, the strategies used would involve creating broad exposure using many media vehicles. For example, high-reach strategies might be used in order to provide reminders for a well-known brand or to introduce a new product that has a broadly defined target market.

If the objectives specify high frequency, then the media strategies will probably be narrower in focus with a more limited list of media vehicles. That would be the case for niche products with tightly defined target markets (low reach) or for products that need a high level of information and explanation. High-frequency strategies are also used to counter competitive offers and to build the brand's share of voice in a highly cluttered category. Sometimes a low-frequency objective is specified when there is less need for repetition. If you are advertising a two-liter Coke for 89 cents, you don't need to repeat the message a lot, but if you are trying to explain how DVR systems work, then you may need more frequency.

Media Mix Selection   The reach and frequency objectives also lead to decisions about the media mix. We mentioned earlier that you can rarely generate an acceptable reach level with just one media vehicle. Most brands use a variety of targeted media vehicles, called a **media mix,** to reach current and potential customers. ESPN, for example, uses TV, magazines, radio, and the Internet, as well as original programming on its own ESPN channel, to promote its programs.

Media mixes are used for a number of reasons. The first is to reach people not reached by the first or most important medium. Using a variety of media vehicles distributes the message more widely because different media tend to have different audience profiles. Of course, these different audience groups should generally fit within the brand's target market.

Some people even reject certain media: television advertising, for example, is considered intrusive and Internet advertising is irritating to some people. Other reasons for spreading the plan across different media include adding exposure in less expensive media and using media that have some attractive characteristics that enhance the creative message. On the other hand, an *Ad Age* columnist believes media planners shouldn't give up traditional media just because digital media have become "sexy" and are seen as having lower costs.[4]

Still, the reason for choosing a particular medium or a set of media vehicles depends on the media objectives. What media will best deliver what effects—and can you reinforce and extend those effects with a mix of media? If audience reach is an objective, then television still reaches the largest audience; if frequency is important, then radio may be the best media vehicle to use. Print and television are considered more trustworthy, so they might be used by a media planner for a campaign that seeks to establish credibility for a brand or believability for a product claim. The *Practical Tips* box summarizes the reasons media planners choose various media.

An analysis of one industry's media mix choices presents an interesting argument about the logic of the media mix. The telecom industry (AT&T, Verizon, Sprint) was critiqued by BIGresearch and a team of media researchers from Northwestern University. Based on consumer research and a customized analytical model, the team was able to develop an idealized set of media allocations. In comparison to actual expenditures, the team concluded that the industry overspends on television at the expense of others, such as the Internet, radio, magazines, and outdoor. In particular, the consumer-based research determined an under-use of the Internet based on amount of time, its ability to influence purchase, and its lower costs.[5]

Media choices are sometimes designed to deliver the strategy of using one medium to deliver an audience to another medium or marketing communication tool. For example, mass media have frequently been used to promote special events and sales promotions. The emergence of the Internet has intensified what you might call a two-step media platform. Print and broadcast, which are basically informative and awareness building

This ad demonstrates the use of a creative print ad to drive traffic to a website.

media forms, are often used to drive traffic to a brand's website, which is more interactive and experiential. The Frontier "Web" ad is an example of this use.

Geographical Strategies   Another factor planners use in analyzing the target audience is geography. Are potential customers found all over the country, therefore calling for a national campaign, and does the client have the budget to afford such an extensive media plan? In most cases, the media plan will identify special regions or DMAs to be emphasized with a **heavy-up schedule,** which means proportionately more of the budget is spent in those areas. The company's sales coverage area (i.e., geography) is a major factor used to make this decision. There's no sense advertising in areas where the product isn't available. Most national or regional marketers divide their market geographically. The amount of sales produced in each geographic market will vary, and marketers try to match advertising investments with the amount of forecasted sales or the sales potential.

To determine which geographical areas have the highest (and lowest) rate of consumption for a particular product category, marketers compute a **category development index (CDI)** for each market in which they are interested. Then they calculate a **brand development index (BDI),** which estimates the strength of their brand in the various geographical areas. If General Mills were to bring out a new line of grits, for example, it wouldn't advertise nationally because most grits are consumed in the South.

PRACTICAL TIPS

When to Use Various Media

Use newspapers if . . .

- You are a local business and want extensive local market coverage.
- You sell a product that has a news element, such as new features or formulation.
- You are creating a news element through a sale or some other event.
- You want to reach an upscale, well-educated audience.
- You need to explain how something works, but it doesn't need to be demonstrated.
- The quality of the image is not a factor.

Use magazines if . . .

- You have a target audience defined by some special interest.
- You have a product that needs to be shown accurately and beautifully and a high-quality image is important.
- You need to explain how something works, but it doesn't need to be demonstrated.

Use out-of-home media if . . .

- You are a local business and want to sell to a local market.
- You want to remind or reinforce a brand image or message.
- You need a directional message.
- You need a situational, place-based message.
- Your product requires little information.

Use directories if . . .

- You are a local business or can serve local customers.
- You want to reach people who are searching for your type of business.
- You need to provide basic inquiry and purchase information.
- You need to provide directional information.
- You have a small to moderate budget.

Use radio if . . .

- You are a local business and want to reach a local market.
- You want to build frequency.
- You have a reminder message.
- You know the timing when your audience is considering the purchase.
- Your audience's interests align with certain types of music or talk shows.
- You have a message that works well in a musical form or one that is strong in mental imagery.

Use national television if . . .

- You need to reach a wide audience.
- You have a message that benefits from motion, sight, and sound.
- Your message calls for action or drama.
- You need product demonstration—how to use it, how it works.
- Your audience's interests align with a certain type of program (particularly on cable TV).
- You want to prove or demonstrate something so people in your audience can see it with their own eyes.
- You want the halo effect of a big TV ad to impress other stakeholders, such as dealers and franchisees.

Use local or spot television if . . .

- Your product is not distributed nationally.
- You want to "heavy up" in certain cities or regions where sales are higher.

Use movie ads if . . .

- Your brand can benefit from being associated with a movie's story and stars.
- The people in the audience match your brand's target audience.

Use product placement if . . .

- You want your brand to be associated with a movie or program's story and stars.
- The people in the audience match your brand's target audience.
- There is a natural fit between the product and the movie's storyline.
- There is an opportunity in the storyline for the brand to be a star.
- The placement will appeal to the brand's stakeholders.
- You have the budget for a campaign to support the placement.

Use the Internet if . . .

- Your target audience is difficult to reach with traditional media.
- You want to create buzz.
- You want your target audience to engage in dialogue with others.
- You want to provide information.
- You want to collect customer information.
- You want to engage your audience in an online activity, such as a game.
- You want to reach people on their own time.

Now taking reservations for October.

BERTUCCI'S
brick oven ristorante®

SHOWCASE

A billboard located at Kenmore Square above the Bertucci's restaurant is just two blocks from Fenway Park. Developed by the Boston University AdLab group, this billboard illustrates a message delivered at the right time and the right place.

A CDI is calculated for product categories. It is an index number showing the relative consumption rate of a product in a particular DMA or region as compared to the total universe (national or regional). A BDI is an index of the consumption rate of a brand in a particular market. The CDI tells you where the category is strong and weak, and the BDI tells you where your brand is strong and weak. CDI data can be found in industry and government sources, and BDI information is available through such services as Simmons and Scarborough, as well as company data.

Different strategies are used to deal with these levels, and they have implications for the media mix and schedule. Planners typically don't make heavy allocations in weak sales areas unless strong marketing signals indicate significant growth potential. Conversely, strong sales markets may not receive proportional increases in advertising unless clear evidence suggests that company sales can go much higher with greater advertising investment. When there is a lot of competitive activity, a heavy-up strategy may be used to defend the brand's market share.

Scheduling Strategies   When should a potential customer be exposed to a brand message? Scheduling strategies are designed to identify the best times for consumers to come in contact with a brand message.

For many product categories, prospective customers have one or more ideal times or places at which they are most receptive to receiving and paying attention to a brand message. This ideal time/place is called an **aperture,** and becomes an important factor in scheduling media placements. Movies and restaurants advertise on Thursdays and Fridays, knowing these are the days when potential customers are planning for the coming weekend. Ads for sporting goods, beer, and soft drinks pop up at athletic venues because sports fans are thinking about those products as they watch the game.

Regardless of whether a company spends a few hundred dollars on one medium or millions of dollars on a variety of media, the goal is still the same: to reach the right people at the right time with the right message. If advertising budgets were unlimited, most companies would advertise every day. Not even the largest advertisers are in this position, so media planners manipulate schedules in various ways to create the strongest possible impact given the budget. Three scheduling strategies involve timing, duration of exposure, and continuity of exposure.

- *Timing Strategies: When to Advertise?* Timing decisions relate to factors such as seasonality, holidays, days of the week, and time of day. These decisions are driven by how often the product is bought and whether it is used more in some months than in others. Timing also encompasses the consumers' best aperture and competitors' advertising schedules. Another consideration is **lead time,** or the amount of time allowed before the beginning of the sales period to reach people when they are just beginning to think about seasonal buying. Back-to-school advertising is an example. Advertising typically starts in July or early August for a

Principle
The CDI tells where the category is strong and weak, and the BDI tells where the brand is strong and weak.

Principle
Advertising is most effective when it reaches the right people at the right time and place with the right message.

school calendar that begins in late August or September. Lead time also refers to the production time needed to get the advertisement into the medium. There is a long lead time for magazines, but it is shorter for local media, such as newspapers and radio.

*   ***Duration: How Long?*** For how many weeks or months of the year should the advertising run? If there is a need to cover most of the weeks, advertising will be spread rather thin. If the amount of time to cover is limited, advertising can be concentrated more heavily. Message scheduling is driven by use cycles. For products that are consumed year-round, such as fast food and movies, advertising is spread throughout the year. In general, if you cannot cover the whole year, you should heavy up the schedule in higher purchase periods. For example, movie marketers do most of their newspaper advertising on the weekends, when most people go to movies.

    Another question is how much is enough. At what point does the message make its point? If the advertising period is too short or there are too few repetitions, then the message may have little or no impact. If the period is too long, then ads may suffer from **wearout**, which means the audience gets tired of them and stops paying attention.

*   ***Continuity: How Often?*** **Continuity** refers to the way the advertising is spread over the length of a campaign. A **continuous strategy** spreads the advertising evenly over the campaign period. Two other methods to consider, pulsing and flighting, are shown in Figure 14.4.

A **pulsing strategy** is used to intensify advertising before a buying aperture and then to reduce advertising to lower levels until the aperture reopens. The pulse pattern has peaks and valleys, also called *bursts.* Fast-food companies such as McDonald's and Burger King often use pulsing patterns as they increase media weight during special promotional periods. Although the competition for daily customers suggests continuous advertising, they will greatly intensify activity to accommodate special events such as new menu items, merchandise premiums, and contests. Pulsed schedules cover most of the year, but still provide periodic intensity.

After a media schedule has been worked out in terms of what media will run when and for how long, these decisions are plotted on a **media flow chart.** Across the top is the calendar for the period of the campaign and down the side is the list of media to be used in this campaign. Bars are then drawn across the calendar that identify the exact timing of the use of various media. When the chart is complete, strategies such as pulsing and flighting are easy to observe. You can also see where reminder advertising in less expensive media (in-store signs) may fill in between bursts and pulsing in more expensive media such as television. You can see a flow chart in the media plan example that follows later in the chapter.

A **flighting strategy** is the most severe type of continuity adjustment. It is characterized by alternating periods of intense advertising activity and periods of no advertising, called a *hiatus.* This on-and-off schedule allows for a longer campaign. The hope in using nonadvertising periods is that the consumers will remember the brand and its advertising for some time after the ads have stopped. Figure 14.5 illustrates this awareness change. The jagged line represents the rise and fall of consumer awareness of the brand. If the flighting strategy works, there will be a **carryover effect** of past advertising, which means consumers will remember the product across the gap until the next advertising period begins. The critical decision involves analyzing the *decay* level, the rate at which memory of the advertising is forgotten.

Size and Position Strategies   In addition to selecting the media mix, a media planner works with the creative team to determine the appropriate size and length of the message for each medium. This question of scope and scale applies to all media—even transit advertising, as the Yellow Cab ad illustrates.

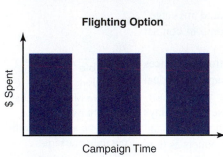

FIGURE 14.4

The Strategies of Pulsing and Flighting

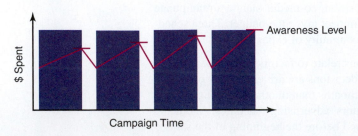

FIGURE 14.5

Consumer Awareness Levels in a Flighting Strategy

Media Weighting   Media planners often use decision criterion called **weighting** to help them decide how much to budget (we have referred to this as "heavy up") in each DMA or region and for each target audience when there is more than one. For example, if a media planner is advertising disposable contact lenses, there might be two target segments to consider: consumers who need help with their eyesight and the eye doctors who make the recommendations. You may recall the discussion of push and pull strategies in Chapter 2, which is also relevant here. If the strategy is to encourage the consumer to ask the doctor about the product, the planner might recommend putting more emphasis on consumer publications to execute a **pull strategy** rather than focusing on professional journals for eye doctors, which would represent a **push strategy.** A weighting strategy might be to put 60 percent of the budget on consumers and 40 percent on doctors.

In the case of DMAs, weak markets may be given more than their share of media weight in the hopes of strengthening the brands in these markets, a practice known as *investment spending*. On the other hand, if competition is extremely heavy in a brand's strong markets, the strategy may be to give them more than their proportional share of media dollars to defend against competitors. Weighting strategies are also used in terms of seasonality, geography, audience segments, and the level of brand development by DMA.

This photo illustrates the use of transit advertising—in this case a panel on the top of a taxi—to advertise the *Wall Street Journal*. The media plan would give direction to the decisions about the size of the sign and the duration of its appearance.

Step 4: Media Metrics and Analytics

Like every other aspect of marketing communication, media plans are driven by questions of accountability. And because media decisions are based on measurable factors, identifiable costs, and budget limitations, media planners are engrossed in calculating the impact and efficiency of their media recommendations. As a MediaBank executive said, "Media departments are no place for guessing. With millions—even tens or hundreds of millions—of dollars at stake, clients want hard data showing that their budgets are being well spent."[6]

Impact: GRPs and TRPs   Among the most important tools media planners use in designing a media mix is a calculation of a media schedule's gross rating points and targeted rating points. As we've suggested, reach and frequency are interrelated concepts that, when combined, generate an estimate called gross rating points. **Gross rating points, or GRPs,** indicate the weight, or efficiency, of a media plan. The more GRPs in a plan, the more "weight" the media buy is said to deliver.

To find a plan's GRPs, you multiply each media vehicle's rating by the number of ads inserted into each media vehicle during the designated time period and add up the total for the vehicles.

Once the media vehicles that produce the GRPs have been identified, computer programs can be used to break down the GRPs into reach and frequency (R&F) numbers. These R&F models are based on consumer media use research and produce data showing to what extent audiences, viewers, and readers overlap.

To illustrate how GRPs are determined and the difference in R&F from one media plan to another (using the same budget), look at the two media mixes that follow. Both are for a simple TV media plan for a pizza brand. As you will remember from Chapter 12, a *rating point* is 1 percent of a defined media universe (country, region, DMA, or some other target audience description) of households unless otherwise specified. *Insertions* are the number of ads placed in each media vehicle/program within a given period of time (generally four weeks). For example, in Table 14.1, if the plan delivered a household rating of 6 with eight insertions, the program *Survivor* would achieve an estimated 48 GRPs.

Using the same budget, the two different media mixes produce different GRP totals. A good media planner will look at several different mixes of programs that reach the target audience, figure the GRPs for each, and then break this calculation into R&F estimates for each plan. Because ratings are in percentages, the GRPs in both the plans in these tables indicate they reach more than 100 percent. Of course, this is impossible, just as it's impossible to eat 156 percent of a pie. This is why these numbers are called *gross* rating points; they include exposure duplication. Nevertheless, knowing the GRPs of different plans is helpful in choosing which plan delivers more for the money budgeted.

How would computer models calculate reach and frequency numbers based on achieving 208 GRPs in plan A? The media mix model would estimate something close to the following: R = 35, F = 6.9. (Even though reach is a percent, industry practice is to not use the percent sign for reach numbers.) For plan B where the number of GRPs is 176, the estimated R&F would be R = 55, F = 3.2.

Table 14.1A   Calculating GRPs for Plan A (R = 35; F = 6.9)

Program	HH Rating	Insertions	GRPs
Survivor	6	8	48
Lost	7	8	56
American Idol	9	8	72
24	4	8	32
		Total	208

Table 14.1B   Calculating GRPs for Plan B (R = 55; F = 3.2)

Survivor	6	8	48
Desperate Housewives	7	8	56
Boston Legal	5	8	40
Monday Night Football	4	8	32
		Total	176

How do you decide which is best? If a brand has a tightly targeted audience and wants to use repetition to create a strong brand presence, then plan A might be a wise choice because it has a higher frequency (6.9 vs. 3.2). If, however, a brand has a fairly simple message where frequency is less important, a planner would probably choose plan B because it has significantly higher reach. The reason for the higher reach (55 vs. 35) with plan B, even though it has fewer GRPs, is that plan B has a much more diverse set of programs that attract a more diverse audience than plan A. But because plan B has a higher reach, it also has a lower frequency.

It is important to remember that GRPs are a combination of R $\times$ F. When R increases, F decreases, and vice versa. Once experienced planners are given budgets, they generally have a good feel for how many GRPs those budgets will buy. The planning challenge is to decide whether to find a media mix with more reach or more frequency. This depends, of course, on media objectives.

Principle

Reach and frequency are interrelated: when reach increases, frequency decreases, and vice versa, within the constraints of the advertising budget.

The two media mixes shown previously are based on HH rating points. For products that have a mass-market appeal, HHs are often used in targeting. However, for more specialized products, such as tennis racquets, sports cars, and all-natural food products, target audiences can be more narrowly defined. For example, let's say that those consuming the most natural food products are females, ages 25 to 49, with a college degree; in addition, we know that they participate in at least one outdoor sport. This would be the target audience for most brands in this category. Therefore, when developing a media plan for a natural food brand, a media planner would be interested not so much in a media vehicle's total audience, but on the percentage of the audience that can be defined as being in the campaign's target audience. Those not in the target are called waste coverage.

Since the total audience obviously includes waste coverage, the estimate of **targeted rating points (TRPs)** adjusts the calculation to exclude the waste coverage so it more accurately reflects the percentage of the target audience watching a program. Because the waste coverage is eliminated, the TRPs are lower than the total audience GRPs. Targeted rating points are, like R&F, determined by media usage research data, which is available from syndicated research services like MRI and from the major media vehicles themselves.

To illustrate the difference between HH GRPs and TRPs, we'll use media plan A, shown previously. As shown in Table 14.2, the first column is HH rating points, while the new second column shows targeted rating points, or the percent of homes reached that include a female, age 25 to 49, with a college degree and an affinity for at least one outdoor sport. The insertions remain the same, but the TRPs are greatly reduced, as you can see when you multiply targeted ratings by insertions. When the 80 TRPs are compared to the 208 HH GRPs, you can see that 128 GRPs (208 – 80 = 128) were of little or no value to a natural food brand. The less waste, the more efficient the media plan.

Table 14.2 Calculating TRPs for Plan A

Program	HH Rating	Targeted Rating	Insertions TRPs	Total TRPs
Survivor	6	3	8	24
Lost	7	3	8	24
American Idol	9	1	8	8
24	4	3	8	24
			Total	80

Another reason to tightly describe a target audience, especially in terms of lifestyle, is to take advantage of the many media vehicles—magazines, TV programs and channels, and special events—that connect with various types of lifestyles. Examples of media that offer special interest topics are *Runners World,* which features topics of interest to runners; *This Old House,* the TV program that describes home improvement and remodeling; *Self* magazine, which focuses on health and fitness; and *Budget Travel* for those looking for interesting but economical trips and vacations.

We've been discussing the basic steps in media planning. Let's now consider the tools and techniques of media strategy.

Cost Efficiency

As mentioned earlier, one way to compare budgets with the competition is called *share of voice.* It sets the budget relative to your brand's and your competitors' market share. For example, if your client has a 40 percent share of the market, then you may decide to spend at a 40 percent share of voice in order to maintain your brand's competitive position. To calculate this budget level, you need to find the total ad spending in your category, as well as the share of market owned by your brand and your key competitors.[7] For example, if the category ad spending totals $10 million, and you want your share of voice to be 40 percent, then you would need to spend $4 million ($10 million × 0.40 = $4 million).

At the end of the planning process, after the media mix has been determined, the media planner will prepare a pie chart showing *media allocations,* a term that refers to allocating the budget among the various media chosen. The pie chart shows the amount being spent on each medium as a proportion of the total media budget. The pie chart visualizes the media mix and the relative importance of each vehicle in the mix.

Although much of the discussion in this book has been focused on measured advertising media and their objectives, it's useful to note that the other IMC disciplines are also concerned about proving their efficiency. Public relations, for example, has established metrics comparable to those used in evaluating advertising media. The *A Matter of Principle* box explains how important it is to integrate not only media planning, but also evaluations of efficiency comparing these other areas with advertising media planning. The author also explains the concept of *earned media,* in contrast to purchased (and measured) media.

CPMs, TCPMs, and CPPs   Advertisers don't make decisions about the media mix solely in terms of targeting, geography, and schedule considerations. Sometimes the decision comes down

Integrating Advertising and PR Media Planning

Clarke Caywood, *Professor and Director of the Graduate Program in Public Relations,*
Medill Graduate School, Northwestern University

Ask advertising directors in a company or agency what profitable target media they have chosen for message delivery for their new corporate or product/service brand strategy. They will probably give a list of traditional mass media advertising vehicles.

Then ask the PR director in the same company or company PR agency what the targeted media will be for the same program. It will often be a list of news and feature story outlets.

In an integrated approach to media planning, the communication leaders should be targeting the same media to reach similar readers, viewers, and listeners. If not, the C-Suite—chief executive officer, chief financial officer, and chief marketing officer—in the client company would want to know why not.

These newer models of media planning seem to be aligned with the growth of the large holding companies that contain advertising, direct database marketing, e-commerce, public relations, and, now, media buying agencies where coordination and cross-functional planning are essential.

In the IMC program at Medill, we define integrated media planning as "coordinated research, planning, securing, and evaluation of all purchased and earned media." **Earned media** is used by marketing and PR practitioners to differentiate paid media about a product, service, or company (advertising, promotions, direct mail, Web ads, etc.) from positive or negative broadcast, print, and Internet media articles and simple mentions

about the product, service, or company. The term *earned* is used to avoid the term *free*, which accurately suggests the company does not pay the media for the placement, but it does not address the fact that the publication of such stories requires hours of effort or years of experience by PR professionals to persuade journalists to cover the product, service, or company for the benefit of their readers or viewers.

Just as selecting media for advertising has become a science and management art, the field of selection and analysis of earned media (including print, broadcast, and blogs) for public relations is now more of a science. Today the existence of far richer database systems assists media managers who want to know which reporters, quoted experts, trade books, new publications, broadcasts, bloggers, and more are the most "profitable" targets for public relations messages. In other words, when we refer to *media planning*, we mean coordinating and jointly planning the earned media of public relations along with advertising and other purchased media.

Using the new built-in media metric systems, PR directors can calculate return on investment on advertising versus PR. With PR, they can read and judge a range of positive, neutral, or negative messages, as well as share-of-mind measures of media impact, advertising equivalency estimates, and other effectiveness indicators (see www.biz360.com).

Now, when the chief marketing officer and other C-Suite officers ask the integrated agency directors of advertising, public relations, or IMC if the media are fully planned to reach targeted audiences, they can answer affirmatively.

---

to cold, hard cash. The advertiser wants prospects, not just readers, viewers, or listeners; therefore, they compare the cost of each proposed media vehicle with the specific vehicle's ability to deliver the target audience. The cheapest vehicle may not deliver the highest percent of the target audience, and the highest priced vehicle may deliver exactly the right target audience, so the selection process is a balancing act between cost and reach.

The process of measuring a target audience's size against the cost of reaching that audience is based on calculations of efficiency as measured by two commonly used metrics: cost per thousand and cost per point.

The term **cost per thousand (CPM)** is industry shorthand for the cost of getting 1,000 impressions. CPM is best used when comparing the cost of vehicles within the same medium (comparing one magazine with another or one television program with another). This is because different media have different levels of impact. To be more precise and determine the efficiency of a potential media buy, planners often look at the **targeted cost per thousand (TCPM).**

To calculate a CPM for a broadcast commercial, you need only two figures: the cost of an ad and the estimated audience reached by the vehicle. Multiply the cost of the ad by 1,000 and divide that number by the size of the broadcast audience. You multiply the cost of the ad by 1,000 to calculate a "cost per thousand."

In the case of print, CPMs are based on circulation or number of readers. *Time* magazine has a circulation of 4 million but claims a readership of 19.5 million. The difference between circulation and readership is due to what is called **pass-along readership.** In the case of *Time,* this means each issue is read by about five people. As you would suspect, media vehicles prefer that agencies use readership rather than circulation for figuring CPM because this produces a much lower CPM.

- *Calculating CPM* In the following example, CPM is calculated based on *Time* readership and the price of a one-page, four-color ad, $240,000. Remember, you want to know what it costs to reach 1,000 readers.

$$CPM = \frac{Cost\ of\ ad \times 1,000}{Readership}$$

$$CPM = \frac{\$240,000 \times 1,000}{19,500,000} = \$12.31\ CPM$$

- *Calculating TCPM* To figure the TCPM, you first determine how many of *Time*'s readers are in your target audience. For the sake of discussion, we'll say that only 5 million of *Time*'s readers fall into our target audience profile. As you can see from the following calculation, the TCPM greatly increases. This is because you still have to pay to reach all the readers, even though only about one-fourth of them are of value to you.

$$TCPM = \frac{Cost\ of\ ad \times 1,000}{Readers\ in\ target\ audience}$$

$$TCPM = \frac{\$240,000 \times 1,000}{5,000,000} = \$48.00\ TCPM$$

- *Calculating CPP* Now we'll look at how to determine **cost per point (CPP),** which estimates the cost of reaching 1 million households based on a program's rating points. Divide the cost of running one commercial by the rating of the program in which the commercial will appear. If a 30-second spot on *Lost* costs $320,000, and it has a rating of 8, then the cost per rating point would be $40,000:

$$CPP = \frac{\$320,000}{8\ rating} = \$40,000\ CPP$$

- *Calculating TCPP* To figure the *targeted cost per point (TCPP),* the rating points based on the target audience you want to reach, determine what percentage of the audience is your target. In the case of *Lost,* we will estimate that half of the audience is our target. Thus, the overall rating of 8 is reduced to 4 (50% × 8 = 4 rating). Now we divide the one-time cost of $320,000 by 4 and find the TCPP is $80,000:

$$TCPP = \frac{\$320,000}{4\ target\ rating} = \$80,000\ TCPP$$

We can do this calculation to compare several different programs and identify those with lower costs.

CPMs have a wide range. A media planner may calculate a CPM of $56 to reach some 44 million viewers of the Super Bowl.[8] In contrast, in the real estate example given earlier, *iMapp.com* might charge a CPM of $125 to reach a small, but select group of realtors. iMapp is twice as expensive as the Super Bowl ad (not in real dollars, but in CPM), but the higher CPM is justified because of the tight targeting. Media planners are constantly balancing cost with audience characteristics to decide if the media vehicle makes sense given the target audience size and characteristics.

A MATTER OF PRINCIPLE

When Is Too Many Too Much?

Tom Duncan, *IMC Founder and Director Emeritus, University of Colorado and Daniels School of Business at the University of Denver*

The questions advertisers have to ask themselves when approving a plan that involves nontraditional media is whether they are using this tool effectively and with respect for consumers. Are advertisers trying to find every possible contact point they can identify or are they creating logical associations that consumers will appreciate?

The fact is that we are inundated with commercial messages from advertising of all sorts in all kinds of unexpected places that we routinely encounter. Message clutter is overwhelming every aspect of our daily lives.

Think about something as noncommercial as attending a symphony. You may find a new car in the lobby as well as promotional signs for any number of products—not to mention the symphony itself, which is promoting concerts and season subscriptions. Of course, there are ads in the program, but there may also be ads in the bathrooms and around the snack counter you visit at intermission. When you leave, you'll probably see more posters in windows adjoining the concert hall. You might even find a flyer tucked under the windshield wiper on your car.

There is a difference between "buying eyeballs" and delivering messages in a context that will intersect with a target audience's interests.

Wilson Sporting Goods, for example, sponsors Tennis Camps by furnishing practice balls and making racquets available that participants can try for free. Even though the camp may be surrounded by Wilson, the message is relevant and the brand experiences are positive.

The point is that the less relevant the messages, the more irritating they become.

Why is this a problem?

The tipping point in impact is when the percentage of irrelevant messages is so high that people respond by tuning out ALL commercial messages—the relevant along with the irrelevant.

One reason TiVo became popular is because viewers can time-shift programs and zip through commercials. In what ways will consumers create defense mechanisms to protect themselves from nontraditional media that assault them in unwanted ways in inappropriate times?

How many messages can we surround them with before they rebel?

Media Optimization   In our earlier discussion of media mix strategy, we looked at the efficiency of various media plans. Tools that help estimate the most optimum use of various media plans using computer models involve calculating the weight of a media schedule and optimizing the schedule for the greatest impact. These **optimization** techniques enable marketers to determine the relative impact of a media mix on product sales and optimize the efficiency of the media mix.

Generally the models can create an unlimited number of media combinations and then simulate the sales produced by each. Chrysler's digital agency, Organic, has designed a system to determine the best way to allocate the marketing communication budget. Here's how it works: "The system calculates how much ad spending is needed to meet certain sales targets and then analyzes how both online and offline ads affect Web activity and, ultimately, sales."[9] Using optimization models, the media planner can make intelligent decisions, given factors such as budget, timing, and so forth. Other optimization services are CPM Advisors (*www.cpmadvisors.com*), Aggregate Knowledge (*www.aggregateknowledge.com*), and Telmar (*www.telmar.com*).

The issue of media optimization, however, is bigger than just numbers and estimates of efficiency. It also involves questions of media overload and consumer irritation, as the *A Matter of Principle* feature argues.

A Sample Media Plan

Media plans do not have a universal form, but there is a common (and logical) pattern to the decision stages as we have outlined in this chapter. To illustrate one style of presentation in a real-life setting, we use an actual media plan for a Women's Health Services program based in hospitals. This media plan example was contributed by Amy Hume, who was media director

WOMEN'S HEALTH SERVICES MEDIA PLAN

Launched in winter 2009–10 in hospitals throughout the central United States, the Women's Health Services Program (WHSP) combines the health care services that women may be exposed to throughout their lives under one roof. It brings together services beyond just gynecology, like oncology, dermatology, cardiology, and more. It aids women by providing one central point of contact—a concierge—to coordinate their appointments.

Communication Objectives

- Establish awareness of a new Women's Health Services Program opening in select local hospitals throughout the Heartland of the U.S.
- Generate buzz and word of mouth
- Drive requests for information via Web and phone

Strategic Plan Development

While "all women" were the target, we knew that the best opportunity started with wealthy, more educated women who would act as influencers in the market. As a result, we focused, demographically, on,—Working Women Ages 30–54 with HHI $75M+, with or without kids.

It was important for us to gain further insight into their behaviors and attitudes relating to health care, communication and everyday routines. Via both syndicated research and primary research we uncovered many insights that helped direct the plan:

Activities/Behaviors

- They work out?—either at home, in a club, or outdoors.
  - They exercise to manage their weight, be more relaxed, reduce health problems.
  - While most women are not passionate about working out, many say it is an essential part of their lives.
- They travel to/from work an average of 7.5 miles—either in car or public transportation (depending on the market).
- They go to a coffee shop usually 1x/day—both independents and chains.
- They use the Internet for e-mail, social networking and to research just about anything.
  - But particularly health-related issues—2/3 of online health site users are female.
- Women make 75% of health care decisions, spend 2/3 of health care $, and account for 2/3 of hospital procedures.

Attitudes

- Women's most influential source of information or advice is their circle of friends:
  - Women rely on advice and opinions of those individuals around them who have proven themselves in the past.
  - They respond to anecdotes/storytelling—they will connect to an engaging narrative relating the lives and experiences of other women.
  - Through our primary research we found that many women have phone conversations with female relatives once/day.
    - Conversation serves many purposes in women's lives: recharging, validation, and learning.
- Women focus on the emotional—happiness, peace of mind, fulfillment, self-confidence—vs. more traditional, material, outward manifestations of success.
- When choosing health care they are looking for:
  - "Someone who knows me," "Ability to help with issues," "Treat me as an individual."
    - It's important for women to be communicated to on a personal level.
  - They believe it's stressful and hard to find a physician who's interested in their overall health.

(continued)

at the Denver-based Barnhart Communications when she prepared this plan. Let's briefly explore each major section in this plan:

- ***Objectives*** Media objectives are designed to deliver on the campaign's overall communication objectives. The primary communication objective for this Women's Health Services campaign was to build awareness. The media-related objectives that would deliver this awareness involved two tasks: generating buzz among the target audience and creating

A graduate of the University of Colorado, Amy Hume was nominated by Professor Tom Duncan.

With this background and research, we were able to establish our key strategies.

Strategies
- Overall, we determined that we would be most effective by using a combination of traditional and non-traditional vehicles that intersect women in relevant, yet respectful places—and in non-traditional ways.
- We knew that it was important to seek contacts that increase relevance—that tie into her perception of healthy living—nutrition, fitness, and relaxation—and into her passions—family and hobbies.
- Also, we needed to recommend contacts that would help provide impact, and thus increased receptivity of the message. Those that would signal "for me" (personal, part of my world), be trustworthy, and provide opportunity for narrative/storytelling.
- Finally, it was important to get out of the traditional health care mold and get her to react and engage.

Who (Target)
Active Female Health Managers
- Working women, married, ages 30–54, with or without kids
- More likely to ask their doctor to send them to a preferred specialist or hospital
- Indirectly, their knowledge, experience, and passion for updated health information makes them a valuable resource?—they have a large sphere of influence.

Where (Geography)
While the program itself was launching in 10 cities, we decided to focus on the more efficiently priced, mid-sized metro areas in the Central U.S. —Minneapolis, Denver, Kansas City, St. Louis, and Kansas City.

When (Timing/Seasonality)
Launch September 2009 to lead up to multi-city opening. Also coincides with time of "renewal" with the back-to-school mentality.
Provide additional support in January as people are making resolutions—mostly in the area of health.
Follow up with an effort in May tied into Women's Health month.

SAMPLE MEDIA PLAN FOR WOMEN'S HEALTH SERVICES

	2005						2006						BUDGET
	JULY	AUGUST	SEPTEMBER	OCTOBER	NOVEMBER	DECEMBER	JANUARY	FEBRUARY	MARCH	APRIL	MAY	JUNE	
Magazines			▬		▬						▬		$ 720,000
Radio			▬		▬		▬				▬		$ 600,000
Out of Home			▬										$ 300,000
Place-Based													
Health Clubs			▬				▬						$ 180,000
Coffee Sleeves			▬										$ 90,000
Produce Section			▬										$ 45,000
Mall boards			▬										$ 45,000
Online													
Media			▬				▬						$ 300,000
Website			▬										tbd
Events			▬									▬	$ 200,000
GRAND TOTAL													$ 2,480,000

How Much (Weight Levels/Budget)
We analyzed competitive advertising pressure of other hospitals and health centers in these markets as well as prominent women's programs like Brigham & Women's, Oregon Health & Science University Center for Women's Health, and the Iris Cantor Women's Health Center. We determined that there was little consistent mass media pressure in any market by these entities.

enough interest that the campaign would cause the target to search for information using the website and phone number provided in the campaign materials.
- ***Strategic Plan Development: Consumer Insights*** The key to this media plan is understanding the consumer market for the Women's Health Services Program (WHSP). Background research from the campaign's situation analysis is used to describe the women in this market in terms of their activities and behaviors, as well as their attitudes and feelings.

Due to the absence of substantive competitive reach and frequency benchmarks by competition or like programs, based weight level objectives on history and experience:
- During launch, generate 85% reach/4.0 frequency per month
  - For follow-up months, 65%/3.0 as budget allows

We were working with a Year One budget of $3.0MM to cover all markets.

What (Vehicle Selection)

Magazines: Be where they're searching for health care information—62% of women ranked magazines as their #1 source of information for healthy eating habits, fitness, health, and overall well-being. They will provide the opportunity for long-form messaging. Recommend use of local magazines as well as regional editions of national magazines to provide reach.

Radio: Close to 50% of active health managers listen to the radio everyday; and 50% always listen when they're in their car; they rely on radio to keep them informed. But, they tend to change the station when commercials come on. Thus, we need to use radio in a non-traditional manner. Recommended using 1–2 top-reaching stations per market and establish relationships with key DJs. Bring them to the Center's pre-opening to experience the staff, the atmosphere, and expose them to the services so that they will then talk about the Center during their shows. This will allow women to hear from a trusted source, yet via a good reaching medium, while not immediately turning the dial.

Out-of-Home: Use traditional billboards and transit advertising to intersect women during their daily routine. Helps create a surround-sound approach.

Place-Based: Based on their daily routines and behaviors, we recommended placements in Health Clubs, Coffee Shops, Grocery Stores, and Mall/Retail Centers. The messaging would need to be specially tailored to these environments and placements.

Internet:
- Other websites: Determine key sites within each city and talk with top-rated health sites nationally to gain a presence—particularly contextually via articles. Research blogs and chat rooms to determine other electronic avenues for contact.
- Social media: Use social networking technologies like Twitter to push out news about the doctors and other specialists working in the programs, information on events .
- WHSP website: Develop a website that will provide resources and links for women including the opportunity for community such as: blogging, chat rooms, message boards, as well as a feedback and research tool. Aggregate content that affects all women, but be specific when it comes to each community to ensure the local flavor and expertise. Also recognize that women will need to be pulled into the site via news, information—important to first go where they are first.
- Hospital websites: Tie into the partner hospital websites to create a special women's corner that links to the WHSP site.

Events/Seminars: Invite women in each community to a grand opening celebration with 2–3 key speakers. Follow up with quarterly seminars, which will encourage women to spread the word—"bring your sister or your mom." Develop a membership program that will provide an opportunity for Brand Ambassadors, creating a women's health care "community."

- ***Key Media Strategies*** Identifying the appropriate media involved locating those apertures where messages about the WHSP would be most welcome. That involves understanding the patterns in the target audiences' lives and the intersection of their activities with media opportunities. Another important aspect of media strategy is spelling out the media mix, which includes the various media to be used and strategies that drive how they support and reinforce one another. For the WHSP, the key decision was to use both traditional media and nontraditional vehicles that are specific to their lives and personal activities. The key strategic decisions in this media plan can be summarized as who, where, when, how much, and what.

WHAT IS THE BIG PICTURE OF MEDIA PLANNING?

As we have noted previously, when most people think about media, they think about traditional mass media and advertising. Media planning in an IMC context is complicated by the ways media interact in integrated programs. We'll discuss two of these practices that add complexity to the process: IMC planning and global media planning.

IMC and Contact Point Planning

When IMC planners think about media, they think about message delivery systems and that includes all of the media used in various types of marketing communication. Direct response, for example, which is the topic of Chapter 16, can appear in traditional media (print with fill-in-blanks to get more information about a brand or place an order; infomercials on TV), but also in letters mailed directly to the home or office, telemarketing (phone calls to the home or office), and in digital forms, such as e-mail and Twitter. Public relations places stories in all of the traditional media including trade media, but also uses publicity tours, speeches and interviews with executives, special events, corporate videos, blogs, and websites, to name a few.

As DePaul University marketing professor Steve Kelly says, "Because the Internet allows marketers to make their marketing dollars measurable and accountable, much like the direct marketers have done for years, the goal now is to make all marketing communications measurable. Thus, integrated marketing communications becomes the goal." He explains, "IMC tries to tie it all together. IMC is the goal of most marketers, but multichannel is what they actually do."[10]

An example of IMC multimedia planning comes from *The Today Show*, which launched a new recipe website and mobile application in sponsorship with Unilever. The "Cooking School" website contains previously aired segments of "Today's Kitchen" and streaming video *webisodes*, as well as recipes, cooking tips, and promotions for Unilever brands such as Bertolli, Country Crock, Hellmann's, and Ragu. The recipes can be downloaded at home or to a mobile device. A Smartphone app allows users to compile recipes and build shopping lists. The "Cooking School" partnership links mobile, online, and broadcast media.[11]

Another distinctive feature of IMC media plans is its emphasis on contact points. Media planning in an IMC campaign focuses on every important contact point. These can include a variety of experiential media, as well as conventional media. Think about all the ways you come in contact with a brand message when you fly on an airline—reservations, check in, baggage checking, the gate, the cabin attendants and officer's messages over the loudspeaker, the seats and food and other cabin features, departure and arrival times, deplaning, baggage again, not to mention customer service when you miss a plane or a bag gets lost. That's just a brief list and you can probably add to it. A list of contact points an IMC planner might consider would be endless, but a sample list is available online on this book's website (*www.pearsonhighered.com/moriarty*).

Dentsu's ContactPoint Management   Tokyo-based Dentsu, which is the world's largest individual agency, has a strong IMC orientation, which shows up in the way Dentsu planners create IMC media plans. Dentsu's ContactPoint Management offering is a section in its IMC 2.0 model that identifies a wide diversity of contact points, including but not limited to such separate communication functions as public relations, sponsorship, direct-response marketing, events, word of mouth (WOM), in-store (signage, POP, personnel), sales promotion, traditional advertising media (broadcast, print, out-of-home), sports, entertainment, interactive (Web, podcasting), mobile media, and new out-of-home (OOH) media. Let's take a closer look at Dentsu's approach to IMC media planning.[12]

The objective of Dentsu's ContactPoint Management planning is to select the most effective contact points required to achieve the desired communication goals and to implement optimum integrated communication programs that eliminate waste. ContactPoint Management focuses on two strategies that are critical in delivering effective integrated communication:

1. Identify the value contact points, that is, the emotion-driving points at which or during which consumers come in contact with a brand.
2. Move away from the traditional B2C model, in which business targets a consumer with a message, to a more interactive B2C2C model, in which a business talks to consumers who talk to other consumers. This approach uses mass media to stimulate interconsumer communications, or word of mouth, which delivers messages more persuasively.

Media selection recognizes that (1) contact points that work well must differ depending on the communication goal and (2) contact point effectiveness will differ from product category to product category and from target to target.

An example of how Dentsu manages a full set of brand contact points comes from an automotive campaign where two target audiences have been identified as Fathers (male, 50s) and Daughters (female, 20s). The communication objective is to position the new subcompact car model as "fun driving for grown men" and "a small cute model for young women."

The various contact points considered are evaluated and ranked using a proprietary contact point planning system called VALCON (Value ContactPoint Tracer). Dentsu planners also have access to hundreds of media-related databases with vast volumes of contact point information to consult in this process. The final decisions about media usage are based on the roles and effects of the various media.

For the new subcompact, contact points were evaluated based on three objectives: their ability to launch a new product (recognition, build awareness), arouse interest (evaluation), and make the target feel like buying (intention, attitude). Here are the results by points assigned to various options:

	Father		*Both*		*Daughter*
Awareness	1. Newspaper				1. Train poster
	2. OOH ads				2. TV ad
		3.	Direct mail	4.	3. Magazine ad
Interest	1. Car on display at event	3.	Car on streets	1.	
		4.	TV ad	2.	3. Automaker's website
		2.	Catalog	5.	
		5.	Newspaper insert	8.	4. Cars owned by friends
Intention	3. Car magazine story	2.	Catalog	1.	
		1.	Car on display	2.	
		6.	Test drive	3.	
					4. TV ad

As you can see, the plan calls for contact points that reach both audiences (TV ads, catalogs, street media, newspaper inserts, and direct mail). Newspaper ads, OOH ads, the car on display at the dealer's showroom, and car magazine stories were added or emphasized for the Father audience. For the Daughter audience, magazine ads, a website, transit ads, radio ads, family WOM, and TV ads were added. Here is how this complex media plan is diagrammed in terms of its effects.

	Recognition	*Evaluation*	*Attitude*
Father	Newspaper and OOH ads, car display at dealer		Car magazine stories
Both	TV ads, catalogs, street media, newspaper inserts, direct mail	TV ads, friends WOM	Catalog, car display at dealer, test drive
Daughter	Magazine and transit ads, website	Radio ads, family WOM	TV ads

Cross-Media Integration   Media selection also considers message needs. Here is where media planning and message planning intersect. Brand reminders, for example, are often found in television commercials and in OOH media. More complex information-laden messages are more likely to be found in magazines, direct mail, or publicity releases. If you want to stimulate immediate action, you might use daily newspapers, radio, or sales promotion.

With the increasing push into digital media, the chief marketing officer at a digital media company reminds planners that "Brand advertising is about telling a story, not just directing traffic."

The *Atlantic Monthly* magazine used a multiplatform campaign that integrated messages from neon signs to create an event that was filmed for videos that were seen on a website.

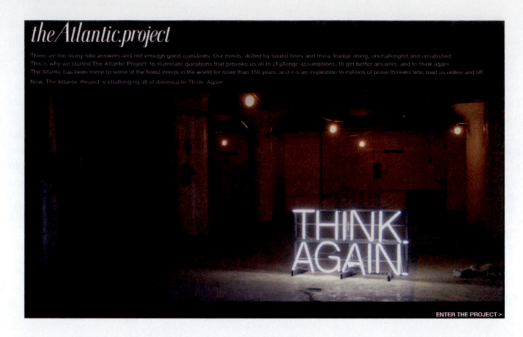

He calls for refocusing on media basics: "Interactivity has given us new options to tell a story, social media have given us tools to make it spread, and digital more broadly has forced advertisers to consider utility to the user." But he insists: "The basics persist—find paths to the consumers where you can get scale, buy attention, and repeat."[13]

The challenge is to create *cross-media integration*, which means the various media work together to create coherent brand communication. Planners seek to create a synergistic effect between the messages delivered in different media. In traditional media, this is sometimes called **image transfer** and refers to the way radio, in particular, reinforces and re-creates the message in a listener's mind that was originally delivered by other media, particularly TV.

An example of cross-media integration comes from the revitalization campaign for the *Atlantic Monthly* magazine. To reinforce its position as an intellectual leader, the campaign used the slogan: "Think. Again." To bring that idea to life, the campaign presented 14 of *Atlantic's* most thought-provoking questions as 14 huge neon signs placed around New York. At night the creative team taped interviews with viewers as they wondered about the brightly lit messages. These videos, which showcased the personal, profound, and sometimes hilarious responses, were housed on a website and used as a hub for a debate of these great issues. So it was OOH marketing that created an event that turned into videos that enlivened a website (see *http://thinkagain.theatlantic.com*). In this case, to quote media scholar Marshall McLuhan, media became the message. Was it successful? The magazine saw a double-digit increase in readership and the number of visitors to *TheAtlantic.com* increased by 27 percent over the previous year.

Global Media Planning

Advertising practitioners can debate global theories of advertising, but one fact is inescapable: a true global medium does not currently exist, which means global media plans have to piece together worldwide coverage using a variety of media tools. Television can transmit the Olympics around the globe, but no one network controls this global transmission. An advertiser seeking global exposure, therefore, must deal with different networks and different vehicles in different countries.

Satellite transmission now places advertising into many homes, but its availability is not universal because of the *footprint* (coverage area of the satellite), technical limitations, and regulations of transmission by various governments. Satellites beam signals to more than one country in Europe, the Asian subcontinent, North America, and the Pacific, but they are regional, not global, in coverage. Despite its regional limitation, satellite transmission is still an enormous factor in the changing face of international advertising. Star TV, with an audience spanning 38 countries, including Egypt, India, Japan, Indonesia, and Russia's Asian provinces, reaches a market of some 2.7 billion people. It is closely followed by CNN and ESPN. Sky Channel, a U.K.-based network, offers satellite service to most of Europe, giving advertisers the opportunity to deliver a unified message across the continent.

The North American, European, Asian, and Latin American markets are becoming saturated with cable TV companies offering an increasing number of international networks. Such broadcasters include the hugely successful Latin American networks of Univision and Televisa, whose broadcasts can be seen in nearly every Spanish-speaking market, including the United States. One of Univision's most popular programs, *Sabado Giganta*, is seen by tens of millions of viewers in 16 countries.

HOW DOES MEDIA BUYING WORK?

So far in this chapter, you've read about media plans and the key steps you would take to develop a media plan, and you looked at some important big picture issues related to media planning. As you recall, the media plan is a recommendation that the client must approve before any further steps are taken. In fact, planning is only the first stage in advertising media operations. Once the plan directions are set, media buyers convert objectives and strategies into tactical decisions. They select specific media vehicles and negotiate and contract for the time and space in media. In this section we explain how the media buyer makes the media plan come to life. A media buyer has distinct responsibilities as outlined in Figure 14.6.

Media Buying Complexities

Buying is a complicated process. The American Association of Advertising Agencies lists no fewer than 21 elements of a media buy. The most important one, however, is matching the media vehicle to the strategic needs of the message and the brand. In this section, we examine the most important buyer activities: providing information to media planners, selecting the media vehicles, negotiating costs, monitoring the media choices, evaluating the media choices after the campaign, and handling billing and payment.

- *Provide Inside Information* Media buyers are important information sources for media planners. They are close enough to day-to-day changes in media popularity and pricing to be an important source of inside current information. For example, a newspaper buyer discovers that a key newspaper's delivery staff is going on strike, or a magazine buyer's source reveals

Principle
Media buyers should be consulted early in planning as they are a good source of information on changes in media.

FIGURE 14.6
The Functions of a Media Buyer

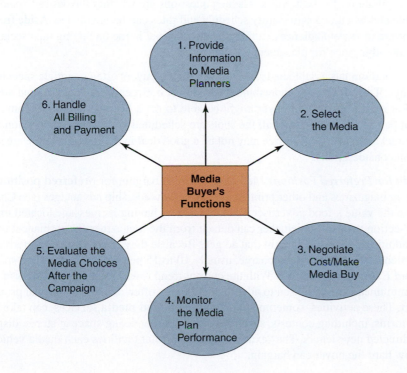

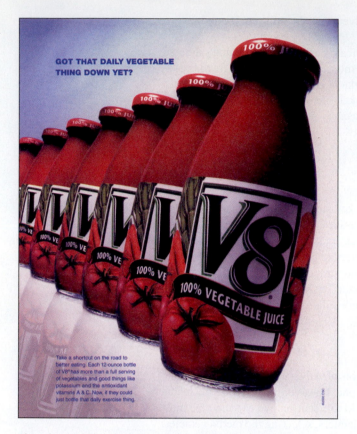

The physical characteristics of a magazine can affect its ability to deliver the desired message. For example, this V8 ad, which appeared in *Reader's Digest*, uses simple visuals and minimal copy to accommodate the smaller page size. *Reader's Digest* may not be the best choice for a complex ad.

that the new editor of a publication is going to change the editorial focus dramatically. All of these things can influence the strategy and tactics of current and future advertising plans.

- ***Select Media Vehicles*** The media planner determines the media mix, but the buyer is responsible for choosing the specific media vehicles. A *Mediaweek* article, for example, identifies patterns in media buyers' decision making. A study reported in 2010 found that ESPN was the top cable choice of media buyers, followed by Disney, TNT, TBS, the Food Network, USA, HGTV, Comedy Central, and Bravo. In terms of buys on network TV, the study found that ABC was best, followed by Fox, NBC, and CBS.[14] In terms of programs, *American Idol* has been the most-watched show on TV since 2007, even though its numbers started dropping in 2009. More than 25 million watched the show in 2009.[15] Online media buying is usually handled through ad networks and the big portals. AOL, Yahoo, Google, and Microsoft are four of the five biggest online ad networks; the Microsoft Media Network is the fastest growing service.[16]

Armed with the media plan directives, the buyer seeks answers to a number of difficult questions as various media vehicles are considered. Does the vehicle have the right audience profile? Will the program's current popularity increase, stabilize, or decline? How well does the magazine's editorial format fit the brand and the message strategy (see the V8 ad example)? The answers to those questions bear directly on the campaign's success.

- ***Negotiate*** Just as a person buying a car often negotiates for the best price, so does a media buyer negotiate for the best prices. The key questions are whether the desired vehicles are available and whether a satisfactory schedule and rates can be negotiated. Aside from finding the aperture of target audiences, nothing is more crucial in media buying than securing the lowest possible price for placements.

  Every medium has a published rate card, but media buyers often negotiate special prices for volume buys. The buyer must understand the trade-off between price received and audience objectives. For example, a media buyer might be able to get a lower price for 30 commercials on ESPN, but part of the deal is that half the spots are scheduled with programs that don't reach the primary target audience. So the price may not be a good deal in the long run. Here are some other negotiation considerations:

- ***Bargain for Preferred Positions*** Media buyers must bargain for **preferred positions,** the locations in magazines and other print media that offer readership advantages (see Chapter 12). Imagine the value a food advertiser would gain from having its message located in a special recipe section that the homemaker can detach from the magazines for permanent use. How many additional exposures might that ad get? Because they are so visible, preferred positions often carry a premium surcharge, usually 10 to 15 percent above standard space rates.
- ***Demand Extra Support Offers*** With the current trend toward using other forms of marketing communication in addition to advertising, buyers often demand additional promotional support. These activities, sometimes called **value-added media services,** can take any number of forms, including contests, special events, merchandising space at stores, displays, and trade-directed newsletters. The "extra" depends on what facilities each media vehicle has and how hard the buyer can bargain.

- *Monitor Performance* A media buyer's responsibility to a campaign does not end with the signing of space and time contracts. The media buyer is responsible for tracking the performance of the media plan as it is implemented and afterward as part of the campaign evaluation. Buys are made in advance, based on forecasted audience levels. What happens if unforeseen events affect scheduling? What if newspapers go on strike, magazines fold, or a television show is canceled? Buyers must fix these problems. Underperformance and schedule problems are facts of life. Poorly performing vehicles must be replaced, or costs must be modified. Buyers also check the publication issues to verify whether advertisements have been placed correctly. Buyers also make every attempt to get current audience research to ensure that schedules are performing according to forecast. Media buyers are even found out "riding the boards," which means they check the location of the outdoor boards to verify that the client is receiving the outdoor exposure specified in the plan.
- *Postcampaign Evaluation* Once a campaign is completed, the planner's duty is to compare the plan's expectations and forecasts with what actually happened. Did the plan actually achieve GRP, reach, frequency, and CPM objectives? Did the newspaper and magazine placements run in the positions expected? Such analysis is instrumental in providing guidance for future media plans.
- *Monitor Billing and Payment* Bills from the various media come in continuously. Ultimately, it is the responsibility of the advertiser to make these payments. However, the agency is contractually obligated to pay the invoice on behalf of the client. Keeping track of the invoices and paying the bills are the responsibility of the media buyer in conjunction with the accounting department.

In addition to negotiating, bargaining, buying, and monitoring the execution of a media plan, media buyers also have to deal with situations that crop up and complicate the planning. In effect, they are also troubleshooters. Buyers deal with the temporary snags in scheduling and in the reproduction of advertising messages that are sometimes unavoidable. Buyers must be alert for missed positions or errors in handling the message presentation and ensure that the advertiser is compensated appropriately when they occur. A policy of compensating for such errors is called "making good on the contract," known as **make goods.** Here are some of the common problems they may run into:

- *Program Preemptions* Special programs or news events sometimes interrupt regular programming and the scheduled commercials. In the case of long-term **program preemptions,** such as war coverage, buyers may have difficulty finding suitable replacements before the schedule ends.
- *Missed Closings* Magazines and newspapers have clearly set production deadlines, called **closings,** for each issue. Sometimes the advertising materials do not arrive in time. If the publication is responsible, it will make good. If the fault lies with the client or the agency, the publication makes no restitution.
- *Technical Problems* Technical difficulties are responsible for numerous goofs, glitches, and foul-ups that haunt the advertiser's schedule. **Bleed-throughs** (the printing on the back side of the page is visible and conflicts with the client's ad on the front side) and **out-of-register color** (full-color printing is made from four-color plates, which sometimes are not perfectly aligned) for newspapers, torn billboard posters, broken film, and tapes out of alignment are typical problems.

The media buyer's life got even more complicated in 2010 with the live broadcast of the Academy Awards where E! Entertainment and Google worked feverishly to make real-time placements that would match the drama playing out onstage. The E! online channel was able to alter its Oscar-related ads within minutes to reflect not just the winners, but also the content of the speeches, the onstage events, what the presenters were wearing, and other features of the coverage.[17]

Multichannel Buying (and Selling) It should be clear from this review of media buyers' responsibilities that this is a challenging job. A number of media services are available to help make buying for complicated media plans easier.

General Electric and its media arm, NBC Universal, for example, promoted its media opportunities using a multichannel plan that includes broadcast, cable, and the Internet, as well as original programming on its own channels. But the difference is that the media deals are packaged around a cause, such as the environment or wellness. Campbell Soup, for example, sponsored health segments on NBC's *The Today Show*, as well as Dr. Nancy Snyderman's MSNBC health program.[18] The idea is to match the media use of the target audience in all its complexity.

Newspapers have long offered simplified buys through such companies as Nationwide Newspapers, which can handle classified and display advertising in more than 21,000 newspapers. The Newspaper National Network is a trade association representing some 9,000 newspapers that also handles ad placement. In the digital world, DoubleClick's DART for Advertisers (DFA) service helps advertisers manage online display and search marketing campaigns across online channels. All of these services not only place ads, but also provide performance data to help optimize a buy, as well as report on the effectiveness of a marketer's specific plan.

On the other side of that coin is the *cross-media buy,* which is made easier by media companies that sell combinations of media vehicles in a single buy. This approach makes it easier to buy media across all of these platforms with a single deal rather than six phone calls. These **multichannel** deals are also a result of media convergence. As content moves across these various forms of new media, so also does advertising. Giant media groups, such as Viacom and Disney, are packaging "deals" based on the interests of the target audience. ESPN, for example, serves the sports market and can provide media integration that includes TV, magazines, radio, and the Internet. The media conglomerate Disney created a one-stop buying opportunity for advertisers targeting kids. To create this opportunity, Disney reorganized its ad sales staff to create one sales force for its various properties that reach children—two cable networks Disney Channel and Toon Disney, kids' programming on ABC, Radio Disney, *Disney.com,* and Disney Adventures magazine.

Global Media Buying   The definition of global media buying varies widely, but everyone agrees that few marketers are doing it yet. However, many are thinking about it, especially computer and other information technology companies that are being pursued by media such as CNN. Today, the growth area is media buys across a single region. As media become more global, however, some marketers are beginning to make the leap across regions. About 60 percent of ad buys on CNN International are regional, and 40 percent are global.

In Europe, the rise of buying "centrals" came about with the emergence of the European Union and the continuing globalization of trade and advertising. *Buying centrals* are media organizations that buy across several European countries. Their growth also began with the development of commercial broadcasting and the expansion of media choices. These firms have flourished in an environment of flexible and negotiated rates, low inflation, and a fragmented advertising market. The buying centrals have nearly three-fourths of the media market in France, nine-tenths in Spain, and about two-fifths in Britain, Holland, Italy, and Scandinavia.

The important thing, however, is to be able to consider cultural implications in media use. For that reason media planning and buying companies are also specializing or buying companies that know specific cultures, such as the Hispanic market in the United States and the Chinese market in Asia. Zenithoptimedia, for example, is a global media-buying company that has created ZO Multicultural, a multicultural unit that helps clients trying to reach ethnic markets.

Media Planning and Buying Trends

Advertising experts have been proclaiming the demise of mass media advertising for a number of years. It reached a high buzz level when Bob Garfield, an *Advertising Age* columnist, got industry-wide attention with his book, *The Chaos Scenario,* in which he speculated about the media landscape in coming years when over-the-air network TV is gone and everyone accesses their news, entertainment, and advertising any way they wish: TV, phone, camera, laptop, game console, or MP3 player. His concept of "listenomics" emphasizes the importance of consumer-in-charge media choices.[19]

The truth is that the media landscape is dynamic and changing so fast that it's hard to keep track of how the media business is practiced. All of these changes create new ways of operation and new opportunities for innovative media planners and buyers.

Unbundling Media Buying and Planning   We've mentioned before the growth of media-buying services, such as the media megashop Starcom MediaVest, as separate companies that specialize in media buying. This is a shift in the way the media industry is organized, a change referred to as **unbundling media services.** This happens when an agency transforms its media department into a separate profit center, apart from the agency. This then allows the media group to work for clients who may be competitors to some of those handled by the agency. Because these companies control the money, they have become a powerful force in the advertising industry, leading to a tug of war over control of planning. Faced with competition from these independent media companies, many large agencies have set up or bought their own buying services to compete with the independents and go after outside business.

Some of these media companies are now offering **consolidated services,** which means bringing the planning and buying functions back together. To take advantage of this consolidation argument, some media companies are also adding special planning teams for other related areas such as events, product placement, Internet, and guerilla marketing programs. WPP's MindShare created an agency-within-the-agency called the Wow Factory to develop ideas for nontraditional media.[20] For a major presentation to Coca-Cola, Starcom MediaVest pulled a team together that represented basic media planning and buying, research, consumer insights, programming, product placement, entertainment marketing, and integration solutions.[21] At this point, these big media companies begin to look more like traditional agencies.

Online Media Buying   A bigger threat to agencies than media-buying services comes from Google and Yahoo!, which, although not ad agencies, are making inroads into media buying and selling. Google is using its website to sell ads primarily to small advertisers and publishers who find its automated advertising network, Google Adworks, to be a cost-effective way to connect with one another. Agencies are trying to figure out if Google and Yahoo! are friends or enemies and what their move into online media buying will do to the revenue stream. Google, however, is betting that its expertise in search advertising, which matches ads to user interests, will give it an advantage over traditional ad media services.

New Forms of Media Research   As we mentioned earlier, one challenge media planners face is the lack of reliable audience research and measurement metrics for the new media. The traditional "measured" media with their CPMs were at least somewhat predictable in level of impact. But the metrics for online media—hits and clicks—don't really tell us much about impact. Comparing TRPs and clicks is like comparing apples and oranges.

We also know that exposure does not equal attention, which is a huge problem for evaluating the impact of television. In other words, just because the television is on does not mean anyone is watching; and just because a program is on does not mean anyone is watching the ads.

Search advertising on the Internet is also complicating things because, if it's successful, it steals viewers away from the original site. Does ESPN benefit when viewers leave its site to click on the banner ad for StubHub Ticket Center? As one critic observed, search advertising may make sense as a form of direct marketing, but it is a nightmare for content publishers who sell advertising on their pages. In such a situation, how do you evaluate efficiency of the publisher's site? Of the search advertising? If one is a winner, doesn't that automatically mean the other is a loser?

Viral marketing is equally difficult to measure, although YouTube is developing analytic data to help media planners assess the impact of the video-sharing site. Other companies such as Visible Measures, Unruly Media, and Millward Brown's Link provide viral monitoring services that assess the impact not only of YouTube, but also of multiple online platforms. As such services mature, marketers will become smarter about selecting marketing communication messages with the most viral video potential.[22]

Another problem is that media research is based on each medium as a silo—separate studies for separate media. Most of the research services are unable to tell you much about the effectiveness of combined media; the impact such as seeing the same message on television and then reading about it in a newspaper story or ad is difficult to evaluate.

Looking Ahead

That point leads to the next part of the book in which we review specific areas of marketing communication, such as public relations, direct response, sales promotion, and sponsorships—all of which are important aspects of multiplatform IMC programs. Then we'll apply this wider world of IMC to specific situations, such as retail, business-to-business, nonprofit, and international marketing. We'll end Part 5 with a discussion of evaluation and wrap up the effectiveness theme that is so important in today's brand communication.

Beauty of a Campaign

This chapter identified media strategies that are relevant to advertisers as they decide how to reach their audience effectively. The point is that the key to effective customer-focused advertising is staying sensitive to consumers and understanding how they think, act, and feel—and where they'll be able connect with the brand message.

The provocative copy in the Dove "Campaign for Real Beauty" challenges the audience to reconsider how they define beauty and to love their bodies, no matter what their age or shape. The campaign generated a huge buzz. But did it work to sell the product?

According to Unilever, the campaign resulted in a 24 percent sales increase during the advertising period across the entire Dove brand.

The brand also fared well globally. When it was launched in the United Kingdom, sales of Dove Firming Lotion reportedly increased by 700 percent in the first seven months after the posters appeared. It generated a substantial press interest, with about 170 editorial pieces written in the first four months after the launch in Great Britain.

The campaign radically changed the Dove brand image with its culturally relevant message. Initial publicity generated more than 650 million media impressions in the United States, estimated to be worth more than $21 million in free media exposure.

Moreover, the definition of beauty portrayed in advertising really seems to be changing. When asked about the images in Dove ads, 76 percent said women in the ad are beautiful, and 68 percent said, "It made you think differently about the brand."

Advertising Age named the Dove's "Evolution" Web film as one of its best non-TV campaigns of the decade. The viral film earned more than 6 million hits and lots of mentions in the national press on shows like *Good Morning America* and *The View*, which translates to about $150 million worth of media time. Although the video drew some criticism, overall the response was overwhelmingly positive. The play, *Finding Body and Soul*, won a Festival of Media award. Beautiful.

Key Points Summary

1. **What is a media plan and what is the role of media research in developing media plans?** A media plan identifies how a brand can connect with its customers and other stakeholders in effective ways that resonate with the target audience. Media researchers gather, sort, and analyze the data used by media planners in making their planning decisions.

2. **What are the four steps in media planning and why are they important?** Step one identifies the media use patterns of the target audience and the times and places where they would be more receptive to brand messages. Step two states the media objectives in terms of reach and frequency. This step includes selecting the most appropriate media and developing a media mix that reaches the target audience in various ways. The third step is to develop media strategies that fine-tune the plan in terms of the reach/frequency relationship, geography, scheduling and timing, size and position in a media vehicle, and the way media vehicles are

weighted in terms of their impact for this audience and brand situation. The final step is to use media metrics to analyze and predict the effectiveness (impact) and cost efficiency of the plan.

3. **How do IMC and global marketing affect media plans?** IMC focuses on contact points where brand experiences contribute to brand perceptions. IMC contact point planning is complex and uses multiplatform and multichannel programs. Global marketing programs need to be supported by media planning and buying across multiple countries and regions.

4. **What are the responsibilities of media buyers?** Media buyers have inside information about the media industries that they feed back into the planning. Their responsibilities as buyers include providing information to media planners, selecting media vehicles, negotiating rates, monitoring the media plan's performance, evaluating the effectiveness of the media buy, and handling billing and payments.

Words of Wisdom: Recommended Reading

Azzaro, Marian, *Strategic Media Decisions,* 2nd ed., Chicago: The Copy Workshop, 2008.

Katz, Helen, *The Media Handbook: A Complete Guide to Advertising Media Selection, Planning, Research, and Buying,* 2nd ed., Mahwah, NJ: Erlbaum, 2009.

Kelley, Larry, and Donald Jugenheimer, *Advertising Media Planning: A Brand Management Approach,* 2nd ed., Armonk, NY: M. E. Sharpe, 2008.

Sissors, Jack, and Roger Baron, *Advertising Media Planning,* 6th ed., New York: McGraw-Hill, 2002.

Key Terms

aperture, p. 433
average frequency, p. 428
bleed-throughs, p. 449
brand development index (BDI), p. 431
carryover effect, p. 434
category development index (CDI), p. 431
closings, p. 449
consolidated services, p. 451
continuity, p. 434
continuous strategy, p. 434
cost per point (CPP), p. 439
cost per thousand (CPM), p. 438

designated marketing area (DMA), p. 424
earned media, p. 438
effective frequency, p. 429
flighting strategy, p. 434
frequency, p. 428
frequency distribution, p. 429
frequency quintile distribution analysis, p. 429
gross rating points (GRPs), p. 435
heavy-up schedule, p. 431
image transfer, p. 446
lead time, p. 433
make goods, p. 449

measured media, p. 424
media flow chart, p. 434
media mix, p. 430
media objectives, p. 427
media plan, p. 424
media strategy, p. 430
multichannel, p. 450
optimization, p. 440
out-of-register color, p. 449
pass-along readership, p. 439
preferred positions, p. 448
program preemptions, p. 449
pull strategy, p. 435
pulsing strategy, p. 434
push strategy, p. 435

reach, p. 427
share of voice, p. 424
targeted cost per thousand (TCPM), p. 438
targeted rating points (TRPs), p. 436
targeted reach, p. 428
unbundling media services, p. 451
value-added media services, p. 448
wasted reach, p. 428
wearout, p. 434
weighting, p. 435

Review Questions

1. Explain the differences between media planning and media buying.
2. What is aperture, and how is it used in media planning?
3. How are gross impressions and gross rating points calculated?
4. What are some of the strategic considerations that determine the level of reach? Level of frequency?
5. Explain the differences among continuous, flighting, and pulsing schedules.
6. Explain the differences between GRPs and TRPs. How are they used to estimate the impact of a media plan?
7. Explain the differences among CPMs, TCPMs, and CPPs. How are they used to estimate the cost efficiency of a media plan?
8. In what ways do IMC and global marketing plans add complexity to media planning?
9. What do media buyers do?

Discussion Questions

1. You have just begun a new job as a media planner for a new automobile model from General Motors. The media planning sequence will begin in four months, and your media director asks you what data and information you need from the media research department. What sources should you request? How would you use each of these sources in the planning function?
2. The marketing management of McDonald's restaurants has asked you to analyze the aperture opportunity for its breakfast entrees. What kind of analysis would you present to management? What recommendations could you make that would expand the restaurant's nontraditional, as well as traditional, media opportunities.
3. In performing an aperture analysis, choose one of the following products: video games (Nintendo, for instance), men's cologne (such as Axe), computer software (such as PhotoShop), or athletic shoes for aerobics (Reebok, for ex-

ample). For the brand you selected, analyze the marketing situation and give your intuitive answers to the following questions:
   a. How does aperture work for this product?
   b. Which media vehicles should be used to maximize and leverage the prospect's media aperture?
   c. Explain how the timing and duration of the advertising can improve the aperture opportunity.
4. *Three-Minute Debate* You have been hired as a media consultant for the Women's Health Services Project campaign outlined in this chapter's sample media plan. You and another member of your team disagree on whether the plan should be focused more on reach or frequency. Working with a small team of your classmates, explain and justify your point of view to your class.

Take-Home Projects

1. *Portfolio Project* You have been asked to develop a media plan for a new reality show that you have created. Focus on the Internet as a primary medium for this launch. Go to both *www.google.com/adsense* and *http://searchmarketing.yahoo.com*. Indicate how you would use the information provided by these sites in developing your media plan for this new reality TV show. Write a one- to two-page report.

2. *Mini-Case Analysis* Outline the key decisions in the Dove "Real Beauty" campaign. What were the media strategies that contributed to the success of this campaign? Dove's Men+Care personal care product line was mentioned in this chapter. Using your "Real Beauty" analysis as a model, develop a proposal for a media plan for this men's line.

Team Project: The BrandRevive Campaign

In Chapters 11, 12, and 13, you developed ideas about various types of media that might be used in your BrandRevive project. Now let's pull everything together in a media plan for your brand.

- Use the four steps discussed in this chapter as an outline and develop your team's ideas for each section of the plan.

- Prepare a pie chart that shows the budget allocation percentages you recommend for each media vehicle; also prepare a flow chart that shows the scheduling you would recommend for your brand.

- Present and explain your media plan in a PowerPoint presentation that is no longer than three slides.

Hands-On Case

The Century Council

Read the Century Council case in the Appendix before coming to class.

1. What target market insights led to the development of The Stupid Drink media plan? Do you agree with The Stupid Drink campaign team that the closer they can get to the underage binge drinking on college campuses, the better chance they have of having a positive influence? Why or Why not?

2. Since binge drinking is a national problem, should the media plan use only national media instead of campus by campus plan? Why or why not?

5 PRINCIPLES: IMC AND TOTAL COMMUNICATION

Hundreds of different communication activities deliver brand messages both formally through planned communication programs and informally through other activities. This section provides a framework for you to understand how all of these programs and tools can work together to engage target audiences with consistent, persuasive messages that get people talking about a brand.

In this part we introduce a collection of key marketing communication tools whose activities need to be coordinated as part of an integrated communication program. To help you understand how this works to deliver effective brand communication, consider the summary of lessons learned by Professor Tom Duncan, one of the early leaders in IMC education.

Lessons We Have Learned about IMC

Originally IMC was about creating "one voice, one look" across all messages in a campaign. So the print ad "looked like" the television commercial and the billboard matched the website. We now know that a more effective approach to IMC has moved from this narrow "execution" focus to a much broader focus on branding and customer brand perceptions. Rather than just using advertising to sell products, companies now want to use everything that sends a message to create a coherent brand presence that leads to long-term brand relationships.

Tom Duncan
IMC Founder and Director
Emeritus, University
of Colorado and Daniels
School of Business at the
University of Denver

Although IMC has been around for 20 years, few understand the breadth—and depth—of this communication focus. It's not just advertising; it's not just marketing communication; it's everything a brand says and does. IMC involves the entire organization.

IMC is a common-sense ongoing process for managing brand perceptions and experiences, as well as customer expectations about the brand. IMC planning delivers the brand essence (position, personality, image) in all marketing communication, but also at all brand contact points. It engages all stakeholders in meaningful and often interactive brand experiences. When these best practices are applied, they lead to solid brand relationships and that leads to enhanced brand equity.

The chapters in this part introduce you to the various marketing communication tools and platforms, including public relations, direct response marketing, and promotions. We tie everything up with a chapter on the IMC umbrella which reviews basic IMC principles and practices, as well as the big picture of total communication. The last chapter focuses on how these various tools evaluate effectiveness.

Public Relations

It's a Winner

Campaign:	**Corporation:**	**Agency:**	**Award:**
"Save-A-Landmark"	Hampton Hotels	Cohn & Wolfe	PRSA Silver Anvil

CHAPTER KEY POINTS

1. What is public relations?
2. What are the different types of public relations programs?
3. What key decisions do public relations practitioners make when they create plans?
4. What are the most common types of public relations tools?
5. Why is measuring the results of public relations efforts important, and how should that be done?

The Ultimate Road Trip

The quest started with Hampton Hotels' challenge to the public relations firm Cohn & Wolfe to create awareness among customers of the 1,600 Hampton hotels across the United States and position the brand as a civic-minded industry leader. The destination was a campaign that helped save many landmarks of historical and cultural significance.

So why should a midpriced hotel brand, which includes Hampton Inn and Hampton Inn & Suites, care about preserving the nation's landmarks when its business is renting rooms?

A road map in the form of research guided the way. Results from a survey of about 1,000 people revealed that 9 out of 10 Americans believe it is important to preserve the country's roadside landmarks. Furthermore, 83 percent of respondents indicated that corporations ought to share responsibility for preserving the nation's landmarks.

The interest in preserving these sites is a natural fit for Hampton. Three-quarters of the people staying in Hampton's properties drive. Given the number of hotels crisscrossing the country, the travelers are likely to encounter these important places marking significant events in the country's history as they drive to their destinations.

Also Hampton stands for traditional American values, civic responsibility, and devout patriotism. Even its logo is red, white, and blue. So there seemed to be mutual interests between the goals of the corporation and its guests.

But the most important reason for undertaking this project is to build goodwill, the greatest asset any organization can have. A well-informed public with a positive attitude toward an organization is critical to the organization's survival— and that is why creating goodwill, this positive attitude, is the primary goal of most public relations programs.

Here's how Cohn & Wolfe, together with Hampton, created a campaign that generated great pride for the hotel and helped preserve culturally or historically important roadside landmarks. Some of the highlights of the program included:

- Building a "Save-A-Landmark" website offering vacation or weekend "drive-abouts" to landmarks across the country

- Making the website interactive by permitting visitors to suggest and vote for landmarks that needed saving
- Involving nearly 1,000 Hampton employees, who proudly participated in the restoration projects.

To date, this 10-year initiative has helped save more than 40 landmarks, from the world's largest Santa Claus in North Pole, Alaska; to 100-year-old mission bells in San Diego, California; to an antique wooden carousel in New Orleans; to the Eleutherian College in Madison, Indiana, the first college in pre-Civil War America to admit students regardless of race or gender. Most recently, Save-A-Landmark refurbished the National Civil Rights Museum (seen in opening photo), originally the Lorraine Motel and site of the assassination of Martin Luther King, Jr. Hampton has donated more than $2.5 million and hundreds of thousands of volunteer hours toward the project.

For more information about how these efforts have affected Hampton's reputation as a company that cares, turn to the end of the chapter and read the *It's a Wrap* feature.

Sources: Eric Litchfield, Cohn & Wolfe; www.hamptonlandmarks.com.

When you hear about Hampton taking responsibility to improve the communities where its hotels are located, doesn't that make you feel good about deciding to sleep there? You don't have to think hard to discover lots of other corporations and organizations trying to make their audiences feel good about their brand and gain the goodwill of the public, which is one objective of public relations. We focus our discussion in this chapter on the role of public relations in an organization, exploring how goodwill can be used effectively in a marketing communication program. You'll read about the types of PR programs, planning, and tools, and also about gauging their effectiveness.

WHAT IS PUBLIC RELATIONS?

Public relations is a fundamental communication discipline covering a wide range of functions that help an organization connect with the people it touches. Those functions include internal relations, publicity, advertising, press agentry, public affairs, lobbying, issues management, investor relations, and development.

Public relations is used to generate goodwill for an organization. That mission is as broad in scope as the definition suggests: "**Public relations** is the management function that establishes and maintains mutually beneficial relationships between an organization and the publics on whom its success or failure depends."[1] A field that is rapidly changing and growing, public relations is increasingly used to build and maintain reciprocal relationships through dialogue and two-way communication in our networked society.

Public relations focuses on all the relationships an organization has with its various publics. By **publics,** we mean all the groups of people with which a company or organization interacts: employees, members, customers, local communities, shareholders, other institutions, and society at large. Another term for this is **stakeholders,** which refers more specifically to people who have a stake, financial or otherwise, in a company or organization. In the Hampton case, the "Save-A-Landmark" campaign reaches multiple publics, including the residents of the areas where the hotels are located, travelers, and its employees.

Public relations is practiced by a wide range of organizations—companies, governments, trade and professional associations, nonprofit organizations, the travel and tourism industry, educational systems, labor unions, politicians, organized sports, and the media. Most organizations have in-house public relations departments that handle the organizations' public relations work, although many also hire outside public relations agencies. Public relations is a dynamic, global profession. One organization, The Global Alliance for Public Relations and Communications Management, represents 160,000 pros in about 70 countries. Find out more about this group at *www.globalalliancepr.org*.

On one level, public relations is a tactical function in that PR staff produce a variety of communication tools to achieve corporate image objectives. On a higher level, it is a management function that monitors public opinion and advises senior corporate managers on how to achieve positive relationships with various audiences (publics) to effectively manage the organization's image and reputation. Its publics may be external (customers, the news media, the investment community, the general public, government bodies) and internal (shareholders, employees). Sir Martin Sorrell, CEO of WPP Group, one of the largest advertising and marketing services groups in the world, believes that "public relations and public affairs are probably higher up on the CEO's agenda than advertising, market research, or other forms of specialist communication." As Sorrell notes, public relations practitioners have "access to the CEO's office," which can give them more influence on corporate policies.[2]

Public Opinion

Public relations programs are built on an understanding of public opinion on issues critical to the organization, such as the company's impact on the environment and its local community or workers' rights and how a company deals with its employees. **Public opinion,** the term describing what a group of people thinks, expresses beliefs based on their experiences with people, events, institutions, or products.

The public relations strategist researches the answers to two primary questions about public opinion to design effective public relations programs. First, which publics are most important to the organization, now and in the future? Second, what do these publics think? Public opinion is sometimes confused with mass opinion. Public opinion differs from mass opinion in that public opinion examines specific subgroups rather than a more general mass audience. Particular emphasis falls on understanding the role for each of the publics of **opinion leaders,** important people who influence the opinions of others

Reputation: Goodwill, Trust, and Integrity

Public **goodwill** is the greatest asset any organization can have. A well-informed public with a positive attitude toward an organization is critical to the organization's survival—and that is why creating goodwill is the primary goal of most public relations programs.

Sometimes a totally unexpected crisis can threaten an organization's respect and trust. For example, managers at Domino's Pizza had to deal with two employees in a North Carolina store who thought it would be funny to post a YouTube video of themselves messing with ingredients— think "mozzarella curl in the nostril" and "sneezing on a salami." It wasn't real funny to the company when it had to place ads nationwide apologizing for the antics of the two.[3]

Beyond responding to immediate issues, a public relations program that is tuned to creating goodwill operates as the conscience of the organization. Creating goodwill demands that both public relations professionals and the clients they represent act with integrity. Howard Rubenstein, an elder statesman in public relations, advises clients and colleagues that deliberately deceiving is "a career limiting move." He has a paperweight in his office at his agency to remind him, "If you tell the truth, you don't have to remember anything."[4]

To underscore the importance of acting ethically as a prerequisite for creating goodwill, public relations organizations have created codes of ethics, which encourage ethical behavior of industry members. The Public Relations Society of America's *Code of Professional Standards for the Practice of Public Relations* spells out core values of conduct, such as truth, accuracy, fairness, and responsibility to the public. It also includes specific provisions regarding the free flow of information, fair competition, disclosure of information, protection of confidential and private information, and avoidance of conflicts of interest.[5] Other industry organizations, such as the International Association of Business Communicators (IABC) and the Council of Public Relations Firms, offer similar codes.

It is critical for public relations professionals to act ethically. It is equally important for the clients and organizations they represent to act with integrity. The trust on which goodwill is based comes from corporate integrity. One communication expert who has experience with multinational

Principle
Public relations is the conscience of the company, with the objective of creating trust and maintaining the organization's integrity.

corporations and the U.S. State Department contends that corporate reputation and corporate responsibility are inseparable.[6]

Principle
Reputation is earned based on what you do, not on what you say about yourself.

A reputation for integrity involves more than image. Image is a perception based on messages delivered by advertising and other marketing communication tools. Reputation, however, is based on an organization's actual behavior. Image mirrors what a company says about itself, but reputation reflects what other people say about the company.[7]

The value of a good reputation is difficult to measure. Although considered a soft asset, one that is not usually included in a company's financial statement, it can be significant in determining company and brand value. The lack of a good reputation can be devastatingly costly, as British Petroleum discovered after weeks, even months, of trying to deal with an oil leak in the Gulf of Mexico and its decision to reimburse businesses harmed by the spill.

Comparing Public Relations and Advertising

Designing ads, preparing written messages, and buying time or space are the key concerns of advertisers. Their objective is to create the consumer awareness and motivation that deliver sales. The goal of public relations specialists is communicating with various stakeholders, managing the organization's image and reputation, creating positive public attitudes, and building strong relationships between the organization and its constituents.

Ultimately, the difference between advertising and public relations is that public relations takes a longer, broader view of the importance of image and reputation as a corporate competitive asset and addresses more target audiences. Public relations and advertising also differ in how they use the media, the level of control they have over message delivery, and their perceived credibility. Daniel Edelman, founder and chairman of Daniel J. Edelman, Inc., a major public relations firm, describes this as the "golden age of public relations," in part because of the many ways PR engages with its publics who are active participants in the communication process.[8] Here are some specific differences between public relations and advertising:

Pepsi invites customers to submit ideas about good causes that need support, which are listed on the campaign's website and then voted on by visitors to the site.

• *Media Use* In contrast to buying advertising time and space, public relations people seek to persuade media gatekeepers to carry stories about their company. **Gatekeepers** include writers, producers, editors, talk-show coordinators, and newscasters. Although public relations has a distinguished tradition, people often mistake it for **publicity,** which refers to getting news media coverage. Publicity, however, is focused on the news media and their audiences, which is just one aspect of public relations, and it carries no direct media costs. Even when public relations uses paid-for media like advertising, the message focuses on the organization, with little or no attempt to sell a brand or product line.

• *Control* In the case of news stories, the public relations strategist is at the mercy of the media gatekeeper. There is no guarantee that all or even part of a story will appear. PR writers write the story, send it to the media, and cross their fingers that this story will appear. In fact, there is the real risk that a story may be rewritten or reorganized by an editor so that it no longer means what the strategist intended. In contrast, advertising runs exactly as the client who paid for it has approved and it runs as scheduled.

• *Credibility* The public tends to trust the media more than they do advertisers. This consumer tendency to confer legitimacy on information simply because it appears in the news is called the **implied third-party endorsement** factor. Thomas Harris, in his book *Value-Added Public*

Relations, observes that today's sophisticated and skeptical consumers know when they are being informed and when they are being "sold to." He explains, "PR closes the marketing credibility gap because it is the one marketing communication tool devoted to providing information, not salesmanship."[9]

In a recent study researchers found that a media placement has about the same effectiveness as advertising. Contrary to the oft-repeated assumption that editorial coverage generates more value than equivalent advertising, they did not find that PR scored higher on most of the measures: brand recognition, message believability, overall interest, or consumer preference.[10]

Another way to build credibility is through **corporate social responsibility.** John Paluszek, senior counsel at Ketchum, an expert in the area of public relations corporate social responsibility, and a member of our advisory board, says, "One of the great growth areas for PR is corporate social responsibility/sustainable development/corporate citizenship."[11] Many examples confirm this trend of doing well by doing good. For example, Bill Gates' philanthropic efforts boosted public opinion of Microsoft and generated goodwill for his corporation in the process. General Electric's Ecomagination campaign helps raise awareness of sustainability issues (*http://ge.ecomagination.com*). The Pepsi Refresh Project aims to raise at least $20 million for donations to local organizations and causes proposed by the public in health, arts and culture, the environment, and education.[12] Often these efforts use advertising to accomplish their public relations goals.

WHAT ARE THE DIFFERENT TYPES OF PUBLIC RELATIONS PROGRAMS?

The word *relations* in *public relations* refers to relationships with various stakeholders. In fact, the main subspecialties in the field—public affairs, media relations, employee relations, and financial relations—call attention to important relationships with such groups as the general public, media, employees, and the financial community. Figure 15.1 outlines the various publics, or stakeholders, for a multinational company. The term **relationship marketing** introduces a point of view in marketing planning that evolved from public relations.[13]

The key publics addressed by relationship programs in public relations are the media, employees, members, shareholders and others in the financial community, government, and general public. Here are the specialty areas that focus on these relationship programs:

- *Media Relations* The area that focuses on developing media contacts—that is, knowing who in the media might be interested in the organization's story—is called **media relations.** When you say *public relations,* most people immediately think about publicity, which indicates the importance of this media function. The organization initiates publicity and provides pertinent information to the media. A successful relationship between a public relations person and editors and producers is built on a PR person's reputation for honesty, accuracy, and professionalism. Once this reputation is tarnished or lost, the public relations person cannot function effectively as a liaison between a company and the media.
- *Employee Relations* Programs that communicate information to employees are called **employee relations.** This function may belong to public relations, although it may also be the responsibility of human resources. A related program is called **internal marketing,** which deals with communication efforts aimed at informing employees about marketing programs and encouraging their support.
- *Financial Relations* All the communication efforts aimed at the financial community, such as press releases sent to business publications, meetings with investors and analysts, and the annual report, which the federal government requires of publicly held companies, are referred to as **financial relations.**
- *Public Affairs* Corporate communication programs with government and with the public on issues related to government and regulation are called **public affairs.** For example, a company building a new plant may need to gain the approval of government health and public safety regulators. Public affairs also includes lobbying. **Lobbying** occurs when a company provides information to legislators to get their support and vote on a particular bill. It also

FIGURE 15.1

Twenty Key Publics
Of the 20 key publics of a
typical multinational corporation, relationship management programs focus on the
media, employees, the financial community, government,
and the general public.

Source: Fraser P. Seitel, *The
Practice of Public Relations,* 11th
ed., Upper Saddle River, NJ:
Prentice Hall, 2011: 10. Printed
and electronically reproduced by
permission of Pearson Educaiton,
Inc., Upper Saddle River, N.J.

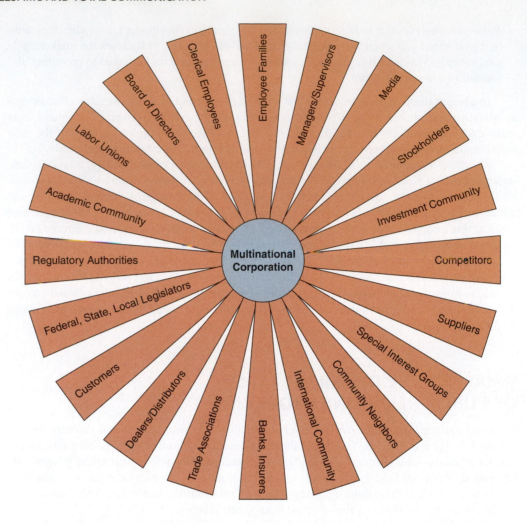

includes communication efforts with consumer or activist groups that seek to influence government policies. **Issue management** is another term for this function. In addition to government relations, public affairs programs also monitor public opinion about issues central
to the organization's interest and develop programs to communicate to and with the public
about these issues.

• *Recruitment* Public relations professionals are sometimes involved in employee recruitment,
working with human resources and also membership recruitment for organizations. This
may involve preparing ads, websites, and literature on the company or organization, as well
as arranging events.

• *Fund-Raising* The practice of raising money by collecting donations is called **fund-raising
(or development).** It is used by nonprofit organizations, such as museums, hospitals, and
emergency groups such as the Red Cross and directed to potential donors. Professional
fund-raisers know how to make the initial contacts that inspire other people to participate,
how to use other marketing communication tools such as advertising, and how to make the
best use of special events and public recognition. Sometimes fund-raising is called **strategic
philanthropy.**

• *Cause Marketing* When companies, such as Hampton Hotels, associate themselves with a
good cause by providing assistance and financial support, the practice is called **cause marketing.** This topic, along with the related areas of nonprofit marketing, public communication campaigns, social marketing, and mission marketing, will be discussed in more detail in
Chapter 18. Häagen-Dazs' association with the disappearance of honeybee colonies, which
was described in the opening case of Chapter 3, is an example of cause marketing.

Other areas of public relations, such as corporate reputation management, crisis management, marketing public relations, and public communication campaigns are distinctive because of

their focus rather than their target audience. The Showcase features student-produced work. If you're interested in working public relations, you can gain experience while you're in school, as these students did. See *The Inside Story* by Mark Thomson at *www.pearsonhighered.com/moriarty* for an example of an unusual career that relates to public relations.

Corporate Reputation Management   The area that focuses on an organization's image and reputation is called **corporate relations.** The overriding goal of **reputation management** in a corporate relations program is to strengthen the trust that stakeholders have in an organization. Public relations expert Fraser Seitel offers advice about the importance of managing corporate image in *The Practice of Public Relations:*

> Most organizations today understand that corporate image is a fragile commodity, and to improve that image they must operate with the "implicit trust" of the public. That means that for a corporation in the 21st century, winning favorable public opinion isn't an option—it's a necessity, essential for continued long-term success.[14]

Since corporate reputation is a perception, it is earned through deeds, not created by advertising. Starbucks and Walmart offer examples of corporations working hard to create positive perceptions. Cause marketing, which we just mentioned, is one way corporations demonstrate their social responsibility.

Starbucks is battling misperceptions that characterize it as a corporate giant with a media- and consumer-focused PR initiative called "Starbucks Shared Planet," which you can read about on its website (*www.starbucks.com*). The program shows Starbucks' efforts in the areas of ethical sourcing, environmental stewardship, and community involvement. Visitors to the interactive site are even offered the opportunity to customize their own global responsibility report.

Walmart, one of the world's biggest companies with more than $400 billion in annual sales, also faces the challenge of maintaining a positive image. Walmart's corporate website explains its efforts to be a good corporate citizen (go to *www.walmart.com,* then click on "Corporate Website"). You can read about its commitments to the disaster relief efforts for Haiti and Chile earthquake victims, to employing veterans, to building sustainability, and to improving health and wellness. One story describes Walmart's efforts to help educate American families about eating healthy foods. Reputation management is critically important to companies that want to earn goodwill from their constituencies.

Crisis Management   There is no greater test for an organization than how it deals with a crisis. The key to **crisis management** is to anticipate the possibility of a disaster and plan how to deal with the bad news and all the affected publics. Toyota's recall of defective cars in 2010, cyanide-laced Tylenol (a classic case from 1982), and the 2010 BP Deepwater Horizon oil disaster are all examples of crises that public relations professionals would handle, or at least consult with the corporations' top executives. Tiger Woods' admission of infidelity caused a crisis for the brands like Gatorade, Gillette, and Accenture who'd hired him as a spokesperson.

Preparing for a potential crisis helps organizations weather the storm. By analyzing the potential for emerging crises and identifying resources to cope with them, an organization can be ready to respond quickly and meaningfully.[15] Effective crisis plans can help to both avoid crises and ease the damage if one occurs. A plan outlines who contacts the various stakeholders who might be affected (employees, customers, suppliers, civic and community leaders, government agencies), who speaks to the news media, and who sets up and runs an on-site disaster-management

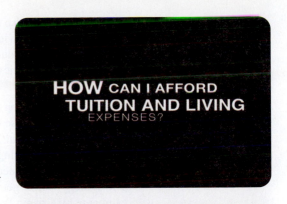

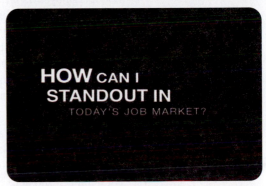

SHOWCASE

Students in Boston University's student-run agency, Adlab, created an online video aimed at recruiting students to BU's ROTC program. Professors John Verret and Tobe Berkovitz provided this work on behalf of their students, who created this promotion in three days.

center. Companies also should conduct unannounced crisis training during which staff must drop everything and deal with a simulated crisis as it unfolds. One example of crisis preparation is a contingency plan to educate consumers and reassure them that it's safe to eat pork should fears of the swine flu pandemic rise.

Public Communication Campaigns   Used as a way to change public opinion, **public communication campaigns** also discourage socially harmful behaviors, such as driving in areas with high levels of air pollution. Sometimes they are engaged in counter marketing as they try to argue against other advertising messages. For example, the Florida *truth*® campaign by the Porter Novelli agency was designed to counter big tobacco companies' advertising that appeals to teenagers. The strategy was to get young people to rebel against the tobacco industry. An extension of that campaign by Crispin Porter + Bogusky featured teens in one award-winning commercial piling body bags outside Phillip Morris's New York headquarters. The campaign produced the largest single-year decline in teen smoking in nearly 20 years.

Taken to the global level, public diplomacy is public relations writ large. President Obama and Secretary of State Hillary Clinton manifest efforts to promote the United States' interests internationally. You can read about a public communication campaign to change public opinion about the war in Iraq in the *A Matter of Principle* box.

Marketing Public Relations   One area where advertising and public relations overlap is **marketing public relations (MPR).** Tom Harris, author of *The Marketer's Guide to Public Relations,* says MPR is the fastest growing area of public relations. He defines MPR as the process of planning and delivering programs that encourage sales and contribute to customer satisfaction by providing communication that addresses the needs and wants of consumers.

MPR is different from a more general public relations approach in its consumer, brand, and sales focus. However, the need to establish a credibility platform is similar in both; that's what PR brings to marketing and is PR's greatest strength in an integrated marketing communication program. In other words, MPR supports marketing's product and sales focus by increasing the brand's credibility with consumers.

An example of MPR is a public relations push engaged in recently by some school districts to recruit students and the state funding that accompanies higher enrollments. Washington, D.C., and Denver Public School districts are two examples of public schools hoping to communicate a positive image, attract more students and convince voters to support school levies and bond issues.[16]

This has been a review of different types of public relations programs and should give you a sense of the breadth of the activities, as well as the career opportunities in this field. The short exercise below might help you decide if public relations is the career for you.

TEST YOURSELF: WOULD YOU LIKE TO WORK IN PUBLIC RELATIONS?

Here's a short list of required skills for public relations managers or public affairs specialists:

1. Knowledge of how public relations and public affairs support business goals
2. A knack for discerning which opponents to take seriously
3. The ability to integrate all communication functions
4. An understanding of how to control key messages
5. The ability to have influence without being too partisan
6. A talent for synthesizing, filtering, and validating information
7. An aptitude for information technology
8. A global perspective

Source: Doug Pinkham, "What It Takes to Work in Public Affairs and Public Relations," *Public Relations Quarterly,* Spring 2004: 15.

A MATTER OF PRINCIPLE

Can Advertising Help the U.S. Government Sell Ideas and Attract Tourists?

Alice Kendrick, *Professor, Southern Methodist University*, and
Jami Fullerton, *Professor, Oklahoma State University*

Twice in the past decade the U.S. government has forged new ground by using advertising to launch important post-9/11 strategic efforts—improving the faltering image of the United States and increasing failing tourism numbers.

In late 2002, at a time when America's image was declining abroad, the U.S. State Department launched its first integrated marketing campaign targeted to the Muslim world. Charlotte Beers, a former Madison Avenue advertising executive whom Secretary of State Colin Powell recommended for the post of Under Secretary of State for Public Diplomacy and Public Affairs after 9/11, spearheaded the effort. Roper organization surveys showed that the U.S. people and Muslims in various countries agreed about the importance of faith, family, and learning. The initial focus of the Shared Values Initiative (SVI) featured testimonial "mini-documentary" commercials about American Muslims living prosperous lives and practicing their faith in the United States. Other media were used as well.

The State Department reported that up to 288 million people saw the messages in Kuwait, Malaysia, Pakistan, and Indonesia and via the Pan-Arab satellite in other countries. A survey in Indonesia showed that commercial recall and main message registration were as high as 67 percent. Some believed it was inappropriate to use advertising in public diplomacy efforts, and many journalists and politicians labeled the campaign a failure.

More information about this controversial campaign is available at *www.svibook.com*.

In 2006 the U.S. Department of Commerce used a reported $24 million in congressional appropriations for a campaign to encourage travel to the United States. International travel had fallen from $103 billion in 2000 to only $80 billion in 2003. Even in 2010, projections were that U.S. tourism would dip 19 percent below 2000 levels.

Commercials were targeted to adults 26 to 60 years old and featured Hollywood movies old and new. Clips from movies related to U.S. destinations, such as *King Kong, Oklahoma!, Sweet Home Alabama*, and *Maid in Manhattan* were shown with the name of the movie (in the movie logotype) superimposed over the visual. Spots ended with the tagline "You've seen the film, now visit the set." Also displayed was the U.S. travel website address, *www.discoveramerica.org*.

M&C Saatchi–Los Angeles created the spots and Walker Media in London placed the media buy. The initial flight, which ran in the United Kingdom from December 10, 2004, through February 22, 2005, at a cost of $4.1 million, included 546 TV rating points, 677 aboveground posters, and another 125 Underground posters. A reported 12.8 million targeted consumers were aware of the campaign and 55 percent of those who saw the campaign mentioned the United States as a "Dream Destination" versus 45 percent who did not. A public relations effort, headed by Edelman PR, and cross-promotions with movie theatres and other retailers were also part of the campaign.

The Commerce Department cited survey research whose projections resulted in an increase of 362,500 *additional* visitors to the United States as a result of the campaign, which government officials said translated into more than $481 million in incremental spending including $79 million in state, local, and federal taxes.

Note: Alice Kendrick and Jami Fullerton coauthored Advertising's War on Terrorism: The Story of the U.S. State Department's Shared Values Initiative, Spokane, WA: Marquette Books, 2006.

WHAT KEY DECISIONS GUIDE PUBLIC RELATIONS PLANS?

Planning for a public relations campaign is similar to planning an advertising or IMC campaign. The plan should complement the marketing and marcom strategies so the organization communicates with one clear voice to its various publics. The plan also identifies the various key publics and the public relations activities that PR people use to address the interests of its various publics. In addition to identifying key targets, public relations plans also specify the objectives that give direction to the PR program or campaign. Assessing the effectiveness of the campaign in achieving its objectives is important, just as it is for advertising campaigns.

Research and SWOT Analysis

Research is used by an organization, as well as outside PR agencies, throughout the planning and implementation of a PR plan. It's also used afterward to determine if the effort was successful and if the organization is spending its money wisely on the public relations efforts.

The PR effort may also begin with a more formal type of background research, called a **communication audit** to assess the internal and external PR environment that affects the organization's audiences, objectives, competitors, and past results. An annual audit or a campaign-specific audit can be used to ensure that a program is on track and performing as intended. Often **benchmarking** is used to identify baselines from previous audits or audits of other related companies and industries so there is a point of comparison. A **gap analysis,** which measures the differences in perceptions and attitudes between groups or between the organization and its publics, may be part of the analysis.

Practitioners categorize publics so they can develop effective public relations plans to address issues. They consider **latent publics** as those who are unaware of their connection to an organization regarding some particular problem. **Aware publics** are those who recognize the connections between the problem and themselves and others but who do not communicate about it. **Active publics** are those who communicate and organize to do something about the issue or situation.[17] For the "Save-A-Landmark" campaign, Hampton Hotels wants to reach active publics and let them know about Hampton's efforts. It also wants to transform latent and aware publics into active publics who will connect Hampton's brand with saving historical and cultural landmarks.

Since public opinion is so central to public relations programs, companies often use ongoing research to monitor opinions and attitudes. The Porter Novelli agency annually tracks American institutions' credibility and consumers' concerns about such topics as health, nutrition, and their lifestyles. The agency suggests that such information is useful in identifying people's orientation to health messages. It's also helpful in targeting various types of publics based on their general attitudes toward key issues, such as antismoking. The survey has consistently found that the credibility of institutions such as government, the media, and corporations is declining.

As in marketing or advertising planning, a PR plan begins with background research leading to a situation analysis, or SWOT analysis, that evaluates a company's strengths, weaknesses, opportunities, and threats. This analysis reflects a general understanding of the difficulty of changing people's attitudes about issues such as corporations and their role in protecting the environment. Understanding the nature of the problem makes it easier to determine the appropriate communication objectives and the target stakeholder audiences, or publics, who will be addressed by the PR efforts. In public relations planning, the situation analysis can include such topics as changes in public opinion, industry and consumer trends, economic trends, governmental regulations and oversight programs, and corporate strategies that affect a company's relationships with stakeholders.

Targeting

As in other marketing communication areas, it is important to understand the target audience before designing the campaign. Research is conducted to identify the appropriate publics to which to address the public relations message. When Hampton Hotels asked Americans their opinions, they found that 9 out of 10 people believed that roadside landmarks should be saved and that most of those surveyed, 83 percent, thought that corporations should share the responsibility for doing so. Creating the "Save-A-Landmark" campaign was a natural connection between consumers and the innkeeper, and research provided a key insight.

Objectives and Strategies

A variety of objectives guides a PR plan, and the organization can use myriad strategies to carry out the plan. Public relations objectives are designed by PR planners to make changes in the public's knowledge, attitudes, and behaviors related to a company, brand, or organization. Usually, these objectives focus on creating credibility, delivering information, and building positive images, trust, and corporate goodwill.

A company may also seek to change behavior, but that is a difficult task. Before changing behavior, a communication effort may need to change people's beliefs, attitudes, and feelings. In many PR efforts, these communication effects are easier to accomplish and measure than behavior change. Typical public relations objectives include:

- Creating a corporate or organization brand
- Shaping or redefining a corporate reputation
- Positioning or repositioning a company or brand
- Moving a brand to a new market or a global market
- Launching a new product or brand
- Disseminating news about a brand, company, or organization
- Providing product or brand information
- Changing stakeholder attitudes, opinions, or behaviors about a brand or company
- Creating stronger brand relationships with key stakeholders, such as employees, shareholders and the financial community, government, members (for associations), and the media
- Creating high levels of customer (member) satisfaction
- Creating excitement in the marketplace
- Creating buzz (word of mouth)
- Involving people with the brand, company, or organization through events and other participatory activities
- Associating brands and companies with good causes.

Change Agent Strategies   Changing the attitudes that drive behavior is central to public relations programs. **Change agent** programs can be internal strategies focused on employees (sometimes called internal marketing) or external and focused on other publics, such as customers and other stakeholders. Regardless of the reason for change, "communication with principal stakeholders ranks high in the hierarchy of factors that predict success. Communication is second only to the main stakeholders' participation in the process."[18]

Involvement Strategies   Public relations uses participation to intensify stakeholder involvement with a company or brand. Involvement can create interest and a feeling of excitement, but more importantly it can drive loyalty. Getting people to participate in an action plan is one way to drive behavior change. For example, Pizza Hut's "Book It" effort is an incentive program used by schools to offer free pizzas to reward students for reading.

Principle
Before changing behavior, a communication program may need to change beliefs, attitudes, and feelings.

The Big Idea

Creative ideas are just as important in public relations as in advertising—and for the same reason: to get attention. The Clark County Desert Conservation Program in Nevada wanted to promote desert environments and threats to their ecology. Mojave Max, a desert tortoise that is at least 50 years old, became the group's mascot and announces the arrival of spring, just like Punxsutawney Phil does in the East. Who would have thought you could make a media star of a tortoise? The 15-pound Max has become the poster reptile for desert ecology and attracts the attention of children as well as adults.

Mojave Max is a desert tortoise used as a mascot for a desert conservation program in Nevada.

A publicity stunt aimed at generating attention for the cartoon series *Aqua Teen Hunger Force* resulted in a bomb scare in Boston.

PR stunts designed to get publicity are also part of the promotional arsenal. Janet Jackson's big exposure during the 2004 Super Bowl half-time show is an example of a stunt that got lots of visibility for the performer. Critics say the over-exposure was in poor taste, but other PR experts say it was an example of a stunt that will be talked about for years. Jackson also gathered twice the number of U.S. press mentions as the Super Bowl commercials did that year.[19] Denny's gave away 2 million free Grand Slam breakfasts after running a 30-second ad that aired during the Super Bowl in 2009 in an effort to reacquaint customers with its brand.[20]

Sometimes PR stunts generate negative publicity, such as the attempt by a guerrilla marketing campaign to promote *Aqua Teen Hunger Force* for Turner Broadcasting System's Cartoon Network and its *Adult Swim* block of programs. In an attempt to generate attention for the show, promoters placed electronic light boards under bridges that showed cartoon characters giving passing motorists the finger. It generated more than attention, causing a bomb scare that shut down bridges and terrified Bostonians. The two promoters were charged with using a hoax device to create panic and disorderly conduct.[21] TBS's chairman and CEO issued an apology immediately. TBS agreed to pay $2 million in compensation for the emergency response efforts, and the head of the Cartoon Network was forced to resign from a position he had held for 13 years.[22] Some argue that this stunt was a marketing campaign gone bad, while others thought it much ado about nothing. Was this effective public relations? Is any publicity good publicity?

PR's Role in IMC

In integrated programs, advertising and public relations aim at selected targets with different but complementary messages. Note that the term *strategic communication* is more often used than *IMC* in public relations programs. As one researcher observed, "In IMC, company assets and product assets are managed at the same time."[23] In many companies, advertising and public relations are separate, uncoordinated functions. People working in public relations are often trained as journalists, with little background in marketing, and they focus on corporate image rather than product sales. These different orientations can sometimes create inconsistencies in an organization's communication efforts.

Public relations uses a variety of marketing communication tools just as advertising does. Advertising is particularly useful in corporate image and reputation programs. Direct marketing is sometimes useful in sending out corporate books and DVDs. The Internet is important because the corporate website is one of the primary ways to disseminate information about an organization. PR activities, such as publicity and special mailings of DVDs, can help drive traffic to the corporate website. Sales promotion is used in support of PR activities, such as special events. In some cases, it's hard to know whether an event is a sales promotion or public relations effort. But it's not just the use of these tools that makes PR a viable IMC function, it's also the fact that PR can contribute valuable effects, such as credibility.

A study conducted by *Advertising Age* and the Council of Public Relations Firms asked marketers in what roles they considered public relations effective. They responded that raising awareness was most effective (83 percent), followed by providing credibility (67 percent), reaching influencers (63 percent), educating consumers (61 percent), prompting trial use of products (28 percent), persuading skeptics (22 percent), and driving sales (22 percent).[24] They also indicated that the most important contribution to marketing programs is in providing media contacts (67 percent).

The same study suggested that PR and advertising need to merge or at least find common ground as the media fragments and consumers gain more control of their time and media habits. Messages aimed at reaching mass audiences in the shifting media environment are less effective, and new opportunities are emerging for public relations, publicity, and product placements to be integral parts of integrated marketing communication programs One way that advertising and PR have worked together is in the Ad Council's work, such as the classic Smokey the Bear campaign.

WHAT ARE THE MOST COMMON TYPES OF PUBLIC RELATIONS TOOLS?

The public relations practitioner has many tools, which we can divide into two categories: controlled media and uncontrolled media. **Controlled media** include house ads, public service announcements, corporate (institutional) advertising, in-house publications, and visual presentations. The sponsoring organizations pay for these media. In turn, the sponsor maintains total control over how and when the message is delivered. **Uncontrolled media** include press releases, press conferences, and media tours. The most recent new media are electronic, which might be categorized as **semi-controlled media.** Corporations and businesses control their own websites, for example, but other websites (particularly those that are set up by critics and disgruntled ex-employees), blogs, and chat rooms about the company are not controlled.

Likewise, companies set special events and sponsorships in place, but participation by the press and other important publics is not under the control of the sponsoring company. Word of mouth, or buzz, is important to PR programs because of the persuasive power of personal conversation. PR programs, particularly employee communication programs, may be designed to influence what people say about the company, but ultimately the comments are outside the company's control. Table 15.1 summarizes these tools.

CLASSIC
An early animated television commercial for Smokey Bear can be seen at www.youtube.com/watch?v5mLdaj8n_zto. Smokey holds a poster with the famous slogan "Only You Can Prevent Forest Fires."

Table 15.1   Public Relations Tools

Controlled Media (company controls the use and placement)	**Uncontrolled Media** (media controls the use and placement)
• House ads	• News release (print, audio, video, e-mail, faxes)
• Public service ads	• Features (pitch letters)
• Corporate, institutional, advocacy advertising	• Fillers, historical pieces, profiles
• Publications: brochures, flyers, magazines, newsletters	• The press conference and media advisory (media kits, fact sheets, background info)
• Annual reports	• Media tours
• Speakers	• Bylined articles, op-ed pieces, letters to the editor
• Photographs	• Talk and interview shows
• Films, videos, CD-ROMs	• Public service announcements
• Displays, exhibits	
• Staged events	
• Books	

Semi-Controlled Media (some aspects are controlled or initiated by the company, but other aspects aren't)

• Electronic communication (websites, chat rooms)
• Special events and sponsorships
• Word of mouth (buzz)
• Weblogs (blogs)

Advertising

Public relations programs sometimes employ advertising as a way to create corporate visibility or strengthen relationships with its various stakeholder audiences. The primary uses of advertising are house ads, public service announcements, and corporate advertising.

House Ads   An organization (or a medium, such as a newspaper, magazine, or broadcast station) may prepare a **house ad,** which is an ad for use in its own publication or programming. Consequently, no money changes hands. For instance, a local television station may run a house ad announcing its new fall programming within its evening news program; likewise, a company may run an ad advocating a point of view or promoting a special employee benefit program within its corporate magazine. These house ads are often managed by the public relations department.

Public Service Announcements   The ads for charitable and civic organizations that run free of charge on television or radio or in print media are called **public service announcements (PSAs).** The United Way, the American Heart Association, the Greater Chicago Food Depository (see the accompanying ad), and local arts councils all rely on PSAs. These ads are prepared just like other print ads or commercials, and in most instances ad agencies donate their expertise and media donate time and space to run the ads.

The Advertising Council represents a PR effort for the entire advertising industry and has produced most of the PSAs you see on television and in print, such as the "Friends Don't Let Friends Drive Drunk" campaign, the United Negro College Fund ("A Mind Is a Terrible Thing to Waste"), the "Keep America Beautiful" anti-litter campaign, and the more recent "I Am an American" campaign that was developed following the tragic terrorist attacks of September 11, 2001. The classic Smokey Bear campaign ("Only You Can Prevent Forest Fires") is one of its longest and best-recognized efforts. Another classic is the "Pollution: Keep America Beautiful" campaign featured here.

Getting donated time and space is not easy. The PSA directors at various media receive a barrage of public service campaigns every week on different issues, and they must choose which ones to run. There is no guarantee which markets will see the campaign elements, and there is no guarantee that the same people will see the print and TV versions of a campaign. Some PSA campaigns do not get any airtime or print placements.

Studies of PSA effectiveness can help guide nonprofit organizations. For instance, a look at PSAs to combat drunk driving, particularly among the college population, found that the usual anti–drunk-driving messages are not as relevant to this audience as they might be. They do not address the students' greatest fear: being pulled over and charged with a DUI. The study also found that a localized PSA, one that mentions or uses a local community angle, is more meaningful to the college-age group.[25]

Professor Herb Rotfeld recognizes that many campaigns have produced effective PSAs to help address social ills in the *A Principled Practice* box. Yet he questions whether these campaigns alone can solve the social problems they seek to address, especially considering their dependency on the generosity of media outlets to offer free time and space. PSAs can help make people aware of social problems, but they may not eliminate them.

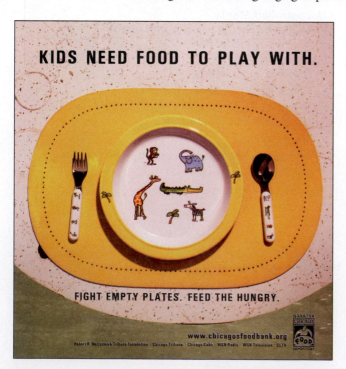

KIDS NEED FOOD TO PLAY WITH.

FIGHT EMPTY PLATES. FEED THE HUNGRY.

www.chicagosfoodbank.org

Robert R. McCormick Tribune Foundation · Chicago Tribune · Chicago Cubs · WGN Radio · WGN Television · CLTV

SHOWCASE

Matt Miller, art director at Goodby, Silverstein & Partners, explained the strategy behind this ad for the Greater Chicago Food Depository. "Even though it may be hard to hear, the truth is, people are skeptical of charities these days. The Greater Chicago Food Depository wanted to stand out among the rest. [It wanted] to reassure Chicagoans that the food and money they donate goes to other less fortunate Chicagoans. And that's why we created the "Fight Empty Plates" campaign."

Matt Miller is a graduate of the University of Colorado where he was a student of Professor Brett Robbs.

A PRINCIPLED PRACTICE

The Social Impact of Public Service Advertising

Herbert Jack Rotfeld, *Professor of Marketing, Auburn University*

Government and public agencies concerned about date rape, drunk driving, road rage, unsafe sexual practices, underage cigarette smoking, illegal drug use, and even littering all expect advertising to reduce the incidence of these not-infrequent socially undesirable activities. Yet no one asks whether mass media advertising *can* persuade anyone to change their "problem" behaviors. The power of advertising is presumed and people behind most public service advertising campaigns see advertising itself as the solution.

The Advertising Council, which is dedicated to using the great resources of the advertising industry to serve the public interest, is the largest producer of public service mass communication campaigns in the United States. Free public service work from anyone is admirable, and the Advertising Council's dedication to public service is a wonderful credit to business groups supporting it. But many Advertising Council campaigns finish their efforts with few people ever knowing they existed, running their entire span with few target consumers ever seeing the commercials. Since the Advertising Council and other groups depend on time or space donated by the media for public service announcements (PSAs), they take the placements they can get for free. No one is in a position to make certain the free media placements reach the intended audience.

There are examples of successful communication efforts that are locally targeted and carefully planned and that appeal to the values of a closely defined audience. Over the long term, some campaigns can change the public agenda, increasing public awareness and changing general perceptions of issues previously ignored. But in most cases, advertising can't do anything to help solve the problem. Instead, for a variety of reasons, the people involved with public health issues acquire a misplaced trust in the power of advertising to change the world.

Advertising is not magic.

Maybe, sometimes, in some ways, it can do some good with some people, but that weak collection of "maybes" is not a valid basis for all the faith it gets from people wanting to serve social goals. And for the deep-seated problems behind many social ills, mass media advertising is a very weak tool.

Yet despite these intrinsic limitations and inherent problems, many people feel that they are doing "something" by advertising. And generating conversation might be a step in helping the general public recognize the problem. But it would be misplaced trust in the power of mass communication to think that advertising alone is the solution.

Corporate Advertising   With **corporate advertising,** a company focuses on its **corporate image** or viewpoint. There is less emphasis on selling a particular product unless it is tied in to a good cause. For that reason, the ad or other campaign materials may originate in the public relations department rather than the advertising department.

An example of corporate advertising that is tied to a socially redeeming program is the Target Guest Card. To increase use of the credit card, the Martin/ Williams agency of Minneapolis had to find a compelling reason for people to shop at Target and use the card. Target's typical customer is female, ages 25 to 54, and her most important concern is her family. The agency team proposed a "Take Charge of Education" campaign, a simple fund-raising program for local schools tied to use of the Target Guest Card. One percent of the value of the purchases made with the card would go to a qualifying K–12 school of the cardholder's choice. The fund-raising program for schools showcases Target's commitment to education, an area of great importance to Target customers. So far Target has given more than $273 million to schools.[26] It gives 5 percent of its income—$3 million—to communities every week.

Corporate identity advertising is another type of advertising that firms use to enhance or maintain their reputation among specific audiences or to establish a level of awareness of the company's name and the nature of its business. "The Johnson & Johnson Campaign for Nursing's

The Advertising Council has sponsored a number of public communication campaigns in support of good causes. The participating agencies donate their time and talent, and media donate the time and space to run the PSAs. This one is for new dads and encourages them to learn more about parenting.

Future" celebrates the profession and helps recruit and retain nurses in one of its initiatives. Companies that have changed their names, such as Accenture (formerly Andersen Consulting), have also used corporate identity advertising.

Sometimes companies deliver point-of-view messages called **advocacy advertising.** General Electric's Ecomagination campaign that we mentioned before, for example, shows that the company wants to be a caretaker of the environment and is creating products in line with that philosophy. Another example comes from Procter & Gamble. Following the 1989 Exxon Valdez oil spill P&G recognized that many animals are injured or killed by the 24 million gallons of oil that typically pollute North American waters each year. In response it created a campaign for Dawn liquid dishwashing detergent . The soap, known to be tough on grease, yet gentle, connects naturally with the advocacy effort to rescue birds and marine mammals harmed by oil spills. Dawn's "Everyday Wildlife Champions" campaign aims to inspire people to get involved.[27] Dawn urges consumers to go to *www.dawnsaveswildlife.com* to enter numbers printed on the back of bottles, which triggers a $1 donation from Procter & Gamble to wildlife groups. Consumers can also volunteer to help wildlife causes via Facebook.

Dawn's environmental cause-related campaign proved particularly timely in light of the massive BP oil spill in the Gulf of Mexico in 2010. Donating more than 12,000 bottles of Dawn to animal rescuers on the Gulf coast, Procter & Gamble enhanced its reputation and built goodwill based on its long-standing marketing relationship between wildlife rescue organizations and the brand.[28]

Publicity

Moving away from controlled messages, consider the various tools and techniques used by media relations specialists to get publicity in the news media on behalf of a company or brand. Human footwear maker Teva created sandals for an Asian elephant with foot problems. The result was an article and photo that ran as a news items. PR expert Tom Harris calls this type of media coverage "an endorsement that money can't buy."[29]

Media relations is often seen as the most important core competency for PR professionals. Media relations specialists know media that would be interested in stories about their companies. They also develop personal contacts with reporters and editors who write regularly on topics related to their organization's industry. As Carole Howard, author of a media relations book, explains, "Good media contacts proliferate once they are established."[30] In addition to personal contact, the primary tool used in media relations is the news release, along with press conferences and media tours.

News Releases   The **news release** is the primary medium used to deliver public relations messages to the various external media. Although the company distributing the news release controls its original form and content, the media decide what to present and how to present it. What the public finally sees, then, is not necessarily what the originating company had in mind, and so this form of publicity offers less control to the originating company.

The decision to use any part of a news release is based on an editor's judgment of its news value. **News value** is based on such considerations as timeliness (something just happened or is about to happen), proximity (a local angle), impact (importance or significance), or human interest.

News releases must be written differently for each medium, accommodating space and time limitations. Traditional journalism form is followed, which means the 5W format is standard—in other words, the release should lead with answers to questions of who, what, why, when, where, and how. The more carefully the news release is planned and written, the better the chance it has of being accepted and published as written. Note the tight and simple writing style in the news release from global public relations and communication firm Weber Shandwick.

The news release can be delivered in a number of ways—in person, by local delivery service, by mail, by fax, or by e-mail. Sometimes a company is hired that specializes in distribution, such as the U.S. Newswire. Originally these companies sent news releases by mail or delivery services,

For immediate release
Contact:
Cassie Cataline | 703.852.5709
ccataline@kettler.com
OR
Erica Chlada | 410.558.2100
echlada@webershandwick.com

KETTLER PURCHASES PENTAGON CITY LAND FOR $220 MILLION
Ten-Phase, 3,200-unit Transit Oriented Development

McLean, VA. May 14, 2007— Kettler, one of the Washington area's leading diversified real estate development and property management companies, announced today that it has purchased 19.6 acres in Pentagon City from affiliates of Vornado Realty Trust for approximately $220.4 million. Kettler closed on the initial 11 acres today for $104.3 million, and plans to purchase the remaining acreage over the next year.

"This purchase gives us a long-term stake in one of Washington's most dynamic urban neighborhoods, and it deepens our established commitment to Arlington County and Pentagon City," said Robert C. Kettler, founder and chairman of Kettler.

For more than seven years, Kettler (formerly KSI) has been the ground lessee of the 19.6 acres for a ten-phase apartment development of 3,850 units. With today's purchase the firm takes title to the land under its existing and future buildings on the tract, which lies east and west of the Pentagon City Fashion Centre. To date, the firm has built 1,050 high rise apartments on the first three of the ten phases, including The Metropolitan at Pentagon Row, The Metropolitan at Pentagon City and The Gramercy at Metropolitan Park.

According to Kettler President, Richard W. Hausler, "The Pentagon tract is unique for its size and location on two major Metro lines with rail access to every part of the D.C. area." Over coming years, he said, "We look forward to working with Arlington County in completing this extraordinary transit oriented development."

Established Kettler developments on the Pentagon land include The Metropolitan at Pentagon City, which delivered 325 units in 2002 and The Metropolitan at Pentagon Row, which delivered 326 units in 2005. The latest Kettler undertaking in Pentagon City is The Gramercy at Metropolitan Park, a 399-unit apartment building which is nearing completion and set to open this summer. The Gramercy features architecture and interiors by renowned New York architect, Robert A.M. Stern. Future phases of Pentagon development include an additional 2,183 units -- and Stern also penned the master plan for these upcoming phases.

"Robert A.M. Stern brings a new dimension in urban design to this market," stated Kettler.

About Kettler

Based in Northern Virginia and celebrating its 30th anniversary in 2007, Kettler is a leading developer of award-winning, mixed-use residential and commercial properties across the Washington Metropolitan area. In 2007, Kettler was named one of the area's largest private companies by the Washington Business Journal and is one of the nation's top 15 multifamily developers. Kettler has developed more than five million square feet of commercial space and more than 50,000 homes. The company also owns and manages 9,000 apartments in 40 locations. Current projects include urban and transit-oriented developments, multifamily housing, commercial and mixed-use developments and resort communities.

###

The format of this piece from Weber Shandwick shows a typical news release format. It includes contact information at the top and a headline that summarizes the point of the news release.

but today news releases are more likely to be distributed electronically through satellite and Web-based networks. PR Newswire, U.S. Newswire, and BusinessWire are services that provide targeted distribution to special-interest media outlets or handle mass distribution of news releases, photos, graphics, video, audio, and other materials. If your organization decides to use e-mail, here is a set of guidelines for delivery:[31]

- Use one reporters name and address per "to" line.
- Keep subject line header simple.
- Boldface "FOR IMMMEDIATE RELEASE" on the first line above the date.
- Catch attention with a good headline.
- Limit length (shorter than print's 500-word limit).
- Use the 5W format.
- Do not include attachments.
- Link to a URL where other background information and photos are posted.
- Remember readability and use short paragraphs, bullets, numbers, and lists to keep it scannable.
- Put contact information below the text.
- Close with conventional end signs such as "30" or "######."

Video news releases (VNRs) contain video footage for a television newscast. They are effective because they show target audiences the message in two different video environments: first as part of a news report and then reused later in an advertisement. Of course, there is no guarantee that a VNR will be used. One study found that VNRs aired in the Miami market were used because they had high visual quality and simple stories.[32] The online video channel Skype also offers a new way to deliver VNRs.

Pitch Letters   Ideas for **feature stories,** which are human interest stories rather than hard news announcements, have to be "sold" to editors. This is done using a **pitch letter** that outlines the subject in an engaging way and sells a story idea. Companies use this form to feature interesting research breakthroughs, employees, or corporate causes. Not only is the distribution of press releases moving online, so are the letters pitching editors with story ideas. Ragan Communications, publisher of *Interactive Public Relations*, lists some tips for getting reporters and editors to read e-mail pitch letters in the *Practical Tips* box.

Press Conferences   A **press conference**—an event at which a company spokesperson makes a statement to media representatives—is one of the riskiest public relations activities because the media may not see the company's announcement as being real news. Companies often worry about whether the press will show up for a press conference. Will they ask the right questions, or will they ask questions the company cannot or does not want to answer?

To encourage reporters to cover press conferences, companies may issue a **media kit,** usually a folder that provides all important background information to members of the press, either before or when they arrive at the press conference. The risk in offering media kits (also called press kits) is that they give reporters all of the necessary information so that the press conference itself becomes unnecessary.

Media Tours   A **media tour** is a press conference on wheels. The traveling spokesperson makes announcements and speeches, holds press conferences to explain a promotional effort, and offers interviews.

Publications

Organizations may provide employees and other publics with pamphlets, booklets, annual reports, books, bulletins, newsletters, inserts and enclosures, and position papers.

PRACTICAL TIPS

How to Write E-Mail Pitch Letters

1. Never list all recipients in the "To" line. No one wants to see all the reporters who received the pitch, since these story ideas are supposed to be made available to the medium on an exclusive basis—in other words, no other medium will be offered that story.
2. Avoid attachments. They take time to open and read, and busy reporters often dismiss them. They can also carry viruses.
3. Keep your pitches less than a page in length. The first paragraph should capture the who, what, and why of the story.
4. Help reporters do their jobs. Some reporters won't rewrite a news release because they want to write the story their own way. For those reporters, provide them with a great story idea, including visuals and other resources, and with contacts, so they can round out the story.
5. Make it personal. Use their first names and mention the publication name.
6. Keep subject-line headers to fewer than four or five words. The header should be clear and to the point; don't waste the space running the term "press release" itself.
7. Never follow up an e-mail pitch by asking, "Did you get it?" Instead, call within an hour (things move quickly in the online world) to ask reporters if they need more information.

Source: "Seven Tips for Getting Your E-Mail Pitches Read," direct mailing from Ragan Communications, September 2000.

The Securities and Exchange Commission (SEC) requires that each publicly held company publish an **annual report.** A company's annual report is targeted to investors and may be the single most important document the company distributes. Millions of dollars are spent on the editing and design of annual reports. These reports are especially important to stockholders and potential investors.

Some companies publish material in print or online, often called **collateral material,** to support their marketing public relations efforts. Corporate publications, marketing, and sales promotion departments and their agencies also produce training materials and sales kits to support particular campaigns. Think about the high-quality brochures and booklets you can pick up at car dealerships when you go in to look at new cars. Another example, Owens Corning Fiberglass Insulation offers information on home insulation projects as an integral part of its promotion effort.

Zines provide another outlet for businesses. At the *eZineArticles.com* website, contributors write their own content and publish it online, making it available for others to publish on their own sites as well. The site doesn't like overtly promotional content, but a company can provide a service piece related to its business—any kind of "how-to" piece is welcome. For example, if you have a client that does faux painting, a general article on the art of faux painting and how to use it as a design element can also carry a short bio and link to your client's site.

SHOWCASE

Collateral material such as this Health Profile brochure for Global Health Services organizes and explains services the company provides.

Owner of his own design studio, Musion Creative, Michael Dattolico graduated from the University of Florida where he was a student of Professor Elaine Wagner.

Other Tools

In addition to advertising, publicity, and publications, public relations practitioners have various other types of materials and activities in their professional toolkits.

DVDs, CDs, Podcasts, Books, and Online Video   DVDs and podcasts have become major public relations tools for many companies. Corporate books have also become popular with the advent of simplified electronic publication. Costing $1,000 to $2,000 per minute to make, videos are not inexpensive. However, they are an ideal tool for distributing in-depth information about a company or program. Because they are easier to duplicate, DVDs are reducing this cost. Some companies have taken stock of the YouTube phenomenon and are using online video to reduce costs and draw attention to messages on corporate websites. Monsanto, for example, posted video clips of testimonials from farmers using Monsanto products on its site, hoping to attract customers, employees, and policy makers.

Speakers and Photos   Many companies have a **speakers' bureau** of articulate people who will talk about topics at the public's request. Organizations as varied as Apple Computer, Harvard University, and the Children's Hospital in Houston, Texas, all have speakers' bureaus that can arrange presentations to local groups and classes.

Some publics, particularly the news media, may want pictures of people, products, places, and events. That's why PR departments maintain files of photographs that are accurate, up to date, and well composed. The permissions for ads in this book were provided because they present the advertisers in a positive light. Companies seldom give permission to use ads that authors intend to criticize.

Displays and Exhibits   Displays and exhibits, along with special events and tours, may be important parts of both sales promotion and public relations programs. Displays include signage and booths, racks, and holders for promotional literature. A model of a new condominium complex, complete with a literature rack offering brochures about its development, is an example of a display. Exhibits tend to be larger than displays; they may have moving parts, sound, or video and usually are staffed by a company representative. Booth exhibits are important at trade shows, where some companies may take orders for much of their annual sales.

Special Events and Tours Some companies stage events to celebrate milestones, such as key anniversaries and introductions of new products. Toy company Mattel celebrated Barbie's 50th birthday by re-releasing a dozen retired models to celebrate different eras, such as Barbie in 1970s bell bottoms and as an 80s rocker with a spiky pink wig. Her birthday party included an appearance at New York's Fashion Week with outfits designed by top fashion designers.[33]

These are high-visibility activities designed to get maximum publicity. Special events can be the public relations manager's responsibility as well as a sales promotion activity. The use of fancy staged events has seen the most growth. Corporate sponsorship of various sporting events like golf tournaments and car races has evolved into a favorite public relations tactic.

Nonprofits also use events as promotional opportunities. For example, the American Museum of Natural History used a coordinated, branded media event to announce the unveiling of a 47-million-year-old fossil. The event was timed to coincide with an article in a scientific journal, as well as a History Channel film, a book release, an exclusive news arrangement with ABC, and a website.[34]

Thomas Harris, cofounder of Golin/Harris Communications, considers Steve Jobs to be one of the world's greatest public relations people. When Jobs took the stage to announce the Apple iPhone, the product launch generated an estimated $400 million in free publicity. According to Harris, by the time the iPhone went on sale six months later, it had already been the subject of 11,000 print articles and had generated 69 million hits on Google for what bloggers were calling the "Jesus phone." Jobs repeated the feat with the announcement of Apple's iPad, generating lots of buzz for its new tablet. Harris also had to do damage control with a large press conference when the new iPhone 4 was panned for its antenna problems.

Events can also be important for internal communication. Learning objectives and employee buy-in for a new campaign are often accomplished through meetings, seminars, and workshops sponsored by a company, typically in conjunction with training materials and other publications. To facilitate internal marketing, **town hall forums** are sometimes used. Forums provide management with an opportunity to make a presentation on some major project, initiative, or issue and invite employees to discuss it.

In addition to media tours, tours of all kinds are used in public relations programs, such as plant tours and trips by delegates and representatives. You are probably familiar with one form—the campus tour used by colleges in recruiting new students. Realizing the importance of these events, some colleges are hiring consulting companies to train the volunteer guides in appearance, presentation, and more relaxed "walks" designed to give a better sense of what makes a school distinctive.

The Spokane Regional Convention and Visitors Bureau and the International Trade Alliance in Spokane, Washington, teamed up to travel to Calgary, Alberta, to promote Spokane as an area for trade and tourism. Thirty-seven Spokane business leaders, travel suppliers, and trade professionals embarked on the four-day mission to Calgary. The group chartered a 50-passenger motor coach, which doubled as a

Steve Jobs unveils the iPad, generating lots of buzz for the new Apple tablet.

traveling billboard. "Team Spokane," as they were known, attended industry trade shows and a consumer travel show. John Brewer, former president and general manager of the Spokane Regional Convention and Visitors Bureau, deemed the effort a phenomenal success.

Another example is the *truth*® tours, the largest national youth smoking-prevention campaign for teens. These tours reach some 500,000 teens annually with information about cigarette smoking and its harmful effects.[35]

Online Communication

PR practitioner and author Fraser Seitel says, "While it is irrefutable that the Internet and social media have changed communication forever with newfound immediacy and pervasiveness, it isn't the case that the Internet has replaced human relationships as the essence of societal communications. Nor have the new techniques replace human relationships as the essence of the practice of public relations."[36] E-mail, **intranets** (which connect people within an organization), **extranets** (which connect people in one business with its business partners), Internet advertising and promotions, and websites and social media, such as blogs, Facebook, and Twitter, have opened up avenues for public relations activities.

Jason Cormier, co-founder of social media agency Room214, points out in the *A Matter of Practice* feature that social media can be a useful tool in public relations because it stimulates word of mouth. We know from Chapter 4 that word of mouth is one of the most powerful communication tools available to marketing communicators and particularly to public relations campaigns.

SHOWCASE

Named "The Spokane Stampede," the mission allowed Spokane County hospitality suppliers to network and conduct business with media, travel agents, meeting and tour group planners, and potential leisure travelers in Calgary, Alberta. This visit was a step toward developing stronger ties between Canada and the Spokane region for economic development and community relations.

A graduate of the University of West Florida, John Brewer was nominated by Professor Tom Groth.

External Communication   As a workshop conference on the Web's usefulness in public relations notes, "The World Wide Web can be considered the first public relations mass medium in that it allows managed communication directly between organizations and audiences without the gatekeeping function of other mass media."[37] Hampton Hotels involved the public by letting people learn about the landmark project and vote directly on which landmarks should be refurbished on its website (*www.hamptonlandmarks.com*).

Corporate websites have become an important part of corporate communication. These sites can present information about the company and open up avenues for stakeholders to contact the company. Website newsrooms distribute a company's press releases to the media and other interested stakeholders. One study noted that the Web's interactive dimension is particularly important: "If you build a highly interactive and informative website, then you can capitalize on building brand and corporate image through longer and more intense exposures than any other type of campaign." The study also found that interactivity—being able to contact the company—is more important than the actual information.[38]

In addition to websites, the Internet has become the favorite tool of media relations professionals as well as journalists. Furthermore, most press releases are now distributed online either by sending them directly to reporters or to such services as PR Newswire, which then handles mass distribution online to appropriate publications.

Internal Communication   E-mail is a great way for people at separate worksites to communicate. You can get a fast reply if people on the other end are checking their mail regularly. It is also an inexpensive form of internal communication. Internal company e-mail may have its public relations downside, however. It can be used in court. Some of the most damaging evidence the federal government presented against Microsoft in its antitrust suit in 1998 came from e-mail messages exchanged within the company.

A MATTER OF PRACTICE

Engaging Word of Mouth through Online Influencers

Jason Cormier, Co-Founder and Managing Partner, Room214.com

A key to understanding social media is found in one of the oldest yet most effective forms of marketing, word of mouth. We exercise word-of-mouth marketing every time we refer a friend, family member, or coworker to something we like (or dislike). This could be a restaurant, movie, product, service, or brand. For most of history, word-of-mouth marketing has been limited in terms of how it is seeded and spread. Social media enables marketers to guide and prioritize who gets the word first, providing a powerful channel by which to help others spread information about something or someone.

How? One way is through a host of self-publishing tools that have enabled a new wave of user-generated content. For marketers, that means more data that can be applied to research for online advertising, as well as to the emerging field of influencer marketing. Identifying and persuading influencers has been a long-time public relations objective.

Social media agencies, such as Room214, typically access a range of online monitoring and Web-based business intelligence tools for gaining new insights about online conversations. From blog and Twitter posts to online forums and mainstream media sites, marketers can gauge the volume of conversation around any given topic they choose. For example, language and semantic clustering tools are used to automate the identification of key themes and emerging topics within these online conversations.

Other features include the ability to identify authoritative sources (called **key influencers** or mavens),

and conduct sentiment analysis to determine if the tone within conversations is positive, negative, or neutral.

In addition to paid advertising within social networks, the realm of *online influencer*, or **maven marketing,** has quickly emerged. A popular form of this is blogger outreach, involving a process by which influential bloggers are contacted in the hope that they will write about the topic being pitched. For example, online savings program SmartyPig.com implemented a highly effective blogger outreach campaign, reaching out to influential bloggers in the financial community to solicit feedback about a product launch while also making them aware of something new and relevant to their audience. Unlike traditional public relations, the "pitch" to a blogger must take on an entirely different tone to be effective. If the communication is not relevant and authentic to the blogger's audience and to the blogger, respectively, the response will likely be nonexistent or negative.

In SmartyPig's case, a great deal of product loyalty and online visibility was earned from the very start of their business. Their success in this area has led to additional entry points into mainstream media, including coverage in the *Wall Street Journal* and other major industry trade publications. They have also been able to leverage online relationships to help build leadership and participation within social networks. (They were the first in the banking industry to use Facebook Connect technology.)

Bloggers are but one subset of online influencers. While the segmentation, outreach, and tracking of influencers support a broad range of social media and word-of-mouth tactics, the most important thing to stay grounded in is that social media is only a component (not a replacement) of an overall marketing mix—one that is most effective when public relations and advertising are smartly integrated.

Internal company networks have great benefits. Intranets and corporate portals (an extensive collection of databases and links that are important to people working in a company) encourage communication among employees in general and permit them to share data, such as customer records and client information. Some companies urge employees to set up personal home pages as part of the company portal, which allows them to customize the material they receive and set up their own links to crucial corporate information such as competitor news, product information, and case histories.

Web Challenges   The Internet presents at least as many challenges to public relations professionals as it does opportunities. Search engine optimization is a major issue for online experts who continually try to improve the process of key word searching that leads interested Web users to their sites.[39]

Although the Internet makes it possible to present the company's image and story without going through the editing of a gatekeeper, it is much harder to control what is said about the company on the Internet. According to Parry Aftab, a lawyer specializing in computer-related issues, "It used to be that you could control the information because you'd have one spokesman who represented the company. Now where you have thousands of employees who have access to an e-mail site, you have thousands of spokesmen."[40] All employees have "an inside view" of their company, whether sanctioned by the PR department or not.

Gossip and rumors can spread around the world within hours. Angry customers and disgruntled former employees know this and have used the Internet to voice their complaints. A number of these people have set up websites, such as the Official Internet AntiNike website, *alt.destroy.microsft,* I Hate McDonald's, Toys R Us Sucks, GTE Sucks, Why America Online Sucks, Packard Bell Is Evil, and BallySucks. As a defense against this negative press, some companies are registering domain names that might cause them trouble. For example, JP Morgan Chase bank owns *IHateChase.com, ChaseStinks.com,* and *ChaseSucks.com,* but not *chasebanksucks.com,* which is an active website critical of the company.

When Motrin posted an online ad on a Saturday about mothers who carried their babies in slings suggesting that this fashion caused back pain, outraged mommy-bloggers and Twitterers wasted no time calling for boycotts. Makers of Motrin responded by the end of the weekend with an apology and removed the ad.[41]

Some companies monitor the Internet to see what is being said about them so they can respond to protect their reputations. Thousands of companies have hired eWatch, a firm that provides Web monitoring services, to collect such information.

THE BOTTOM LINE

As you've seen throughout this chapter, businesses and organizations have many ways to reach their publics. It's critical to find a way to break through the media clutter for public relations as well as advertising messages. Some tips from an article[42] about how small businesses can communicate their messages effectively include:

- *Wrap Your Story Around a Bigger Idea* Find a broader context or news hook for your product or service and show how your company fits into it.
- *Keep It Short and Personal* When reaching out to journalists, a few quick sentences via e-mail, free from industry jargon, explaining who you are and what your business is usually will suffice. Try to keep the first e-mail readable without having to scroll down. Also, referring to past works by journalists shows you understand their area of coverage.
- *Pay Attention to Web Basics* Building a website and getting good rankings on search engines such as Yahoo! and Google can help customers find businesses, especially new ones. Consider blogging as a way to tell your story and interact with the public. Using sites such as *technorati.com* can help turn up other like-minded bloggers. Podcasting and online video-sharing sites such as *YouTube.com* can help tell your story, but do it creatively, avoiding purely commercial pitches.
- *Host Events* These don't have to be expensive, but small themed events with food and drink for customers can be a good draw, particularly on streets crowded with multiple merchants.
- *Seek Out Brand Ambassadors* Find customers willing to talk up your product to others, and encourage their word-of-mouth marketing with discounts or first looks at new products and sales.
- *Publish a Newsletter* It sounds old fashioned, but with so much information coming to people online these days, a mailed paper newsletter to customers can seem more personal than mass e-mails and help your business stand out.

Why Measure Public Relations Results?

As in all marketing communication areas, public relations evaluation is based on setting measurable objectives from the beginning of planning. Objectives that specify the impact the program seeks to have on the various publics can be evaluated by the PR manager if they contain benchmarks and target levels.

However, measuring the impact of public relations efforts has been difficult. It's hard to know what effect clips (or news stories about the company or organization) have on the bottom line, for example. Catalogs from retailers that feature over-the-top gifts have some value, even if the items are never sold, because publicity has its own value. The theory is that even consumers who don't purchase the swanky gifts like a $1.8 million Virgin Galactic Charter to Space, available through Neiman Marcus, still want to be associated with such luxury.[43] It is also difficult to separate the effects of public relations from advertising or direct mail. In an effort to solve this problem, Procter & Gamble has developed an analytic tool to quantify the sales impact of public relations. In the end, public relations activities need to be evaluated against specific objectives established in the public relations plan.

Rapid changes in the media environment further complicate measurement metrics. The Public Relations Society of America has convened a group of experts to collaborate and recommend standardized methods to measure program effectiveness.[44]

Figure 15.2 illustrates that various public relations tactics are controlled, semi-controlled, or uncontrolled messages. They all play a role in a communication campaign plan. The model identifies perception, emotion, cognition, persuasion, association, and behavior as categories of effects that might need to be measured in an evaluation program.

In the past, public relations practitioners have tracked the impact of a campaign in terms of output (how many news releases led to stories or mentions in news stories) and outcome (attitude or behavior change). PR firms and companies have hired companies such as BurellesLuce that specialize in monitoring media coverage. Such tracking and the evaluation of attitude and behavior change is done to prove the effectiveness of the PR program, so that they can learn from their efforts and fine-tune future campaigns. To get a comprehensive picture of PR's impact, practitioners evaluate process (what goes out) and outcome (media use, effect on the target audience).

Although some still argue that not all the value of public relations programs is measurable,[45] others claim that is it possible to increase the use of metrics to determine what impact the cam-

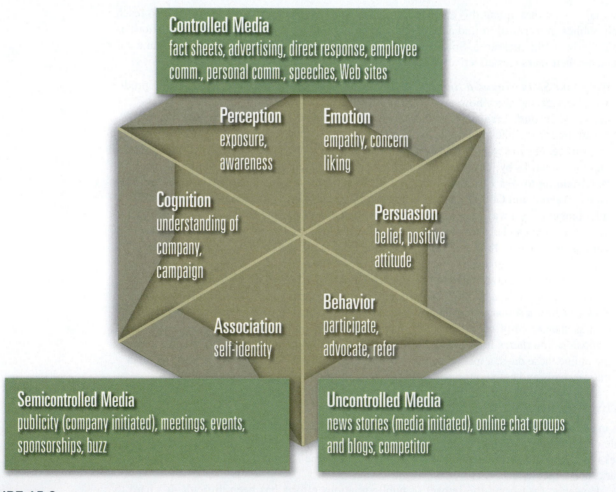

FIGURE 15.2

Communication Campaign Plan

This variation of the Facets of Effects model shows that even in public relations the media and messages must work together to deliver communications objectives.

paign is having on sales and business. The public relations community is rethinking the impact of digital and social media.[46] Some key concerns are integrating how results from traditional and new media affect the results of the whole campaign and moving from a mind-set that considers impressions to one that looks at engagement and conversion rates.

Looking Ahead

This is the first in a set of chapters that focuses on specific marketing communication areas. In this chapter we reviewed the practice of public relations, as well as its specialty areas, planning practices, and tools. The next chapter will look at direct-response practices.

IT'S A WRAP

Milestones for Hampton's Landmark Campaign

In this chapter you've read about the importance of earning a good reputation. Goodwill is invaluable. But companies can't thrive on goodwill alone. It is also essential for an organization to be profitable. The Hampton Hotels "Save-A-Landmark" campaign achieved its goal of creating awareness, which, in turn, increased hotel revenue and generated goodwill.

Hampton Hotels earned its good reputation, in part, by becoming a civic-minded industry leader and helping restore more than 40 landmarks, which are living symbols of American ingenuity, pride, and history. This campaign helped strengthen relationships with its publics: its guests, its communities, and its employees.

Media took notice of these good works, with major news organizations, magazines, and newspapers covering the Save-A-Landmark project. In 10 years, the program has generated an estimated nearly 5.3 billion in media impressions and resulted in close to $25 million in ad equivalency for the brand.

Two weeks after the campaign launched, the Save-A-Landmark website generated nearly $70,000 in online bookings and more than $700,000 in its first year. The site has since resulted in more than $3 million of incremental revenue for the brand.

For these outstanding efforts the "Save-A-Landmark" campaign received much recognition. President George W. Bush presented the *Preserve America* Presidential Award to Hampton Hotels. It also received the National Preservation Honor Award from the National Trust for Historic Preservation, a Silver Anvil, and more than 75 other industry awards.

Key Points Summary

1. **What is public relations?** Public relations is a management function that communicates to and with various publics to manage an organization's image and reputation. Public relations professionals perform a wide range of functions that help an organization connect with the people it touches. Those functions include internal relations, publicity, advertising, press agentry, public affairs, lobbying, issues management, investor relations, and development.

2. **What are the different types of public relations programs?** In addition to the key areas of government, media, employee, and investor relations, PR programs also include corporate relations and reputation management, crisis management, marketing public relations (MPR), and public communications campaigns.

3. **What key decisions do public relations practitioners make when they create plans?** Planning for a public relations campaign begins with a SWOT, or situation analysis, that is used as background to identify the target audience and develop objectives and strategies. Research is needed when planning a PR program and evaluating its effectiveness.

4. **What are the most common types of public relations tools?** Uncontrolled media tools include the news story that results from a news release or news conference. Controlled media are tools that the company uses to originate and control content. Some examples of these are house ads, corporate advertising, and public service ads. Semi-controlled tools are controlled in that the company is able to initiate

use of the tool, but uncontrolled in that content is contributed by others. A few examples include electronic communication (websites and chat rooms), word of mouth (buzz), and social media such as blogs, Facebook, and Twitter.

5. **Why is measuring the results of public relations efforts important, and how should that be done?** The evaluation effort is made to determine how well a PR program meets its objectives. Public relations evaluation usually focuses on outputs and outcomes and may include relationship management and excellence. The impact of a public relations program is difficult to measure and evaluation standards are evolving with the development and use of digital media.

Words of Wisdom: Recommended Reading

Borden, Kay, *Bulletproof News Releases: Help at Last for the Publicity Deficient,* 2nd ed., Marietta, GA: Franklin-Sarrett Publishing, 2002.

Broom, Glen M., *Cutlip and Center's Effective Public Relations,* 10th ed., Upper Saddle River, NJ: Pearson Prentice-Hall, 2009.

Caywood, Clarke L. (Ed.), *The Handbook of Strategic Public Relations & Integrated Communications,* New York: McGraw-Hill, 1997.

Harris, Thomas, and Patricia Whalen, *The Marketer's Guide to Public Relations in the 21st Century,* Florence, KY: Thomson (South-Western), 2006.

Scott, David Meerman, *The New Rules of Marketing and PR: How to Use Social Media, Blogs, News Releases, Online Video, and Viral Marketing to Reach Buyers Directly,* 2nd ed., Hoboken, NJ: Wiley, 2010.

Seitel, Fraser P., *The Practice of Public Relations,* 11th ed., Upper Saddle River, NJ: Pearson Prentice-Hall, 2011.

Yale, David R., and Anne Knudsen (Eds.), *Publicity and Media Relations Checklists,* Chicago: NTC Business Books, 1995.

Key Terms

active publics, p. 468
advocacy advertising, p. 474
annual report, p. 477
aware publics, p. 468
benchmarking, p. 468
cause marketing, p. 464
change agent, p. 469
collateral materials, p. 477
communication audit, p. 468
controlled media, p. 471
corporate advertising, p. 473
corporate identity
 advertising, p. 473
corporate image, p. 473
corporate relations, p. 465
corporate social
 responsibility, p. 463

crisis management, p. 465
employee relations, p. 463
extranets, p. 479
feature stories, p. 476
financial relations, p. 463
fund-raising
 (or development), p. 464
gap analysis, p. 468
gatekeepers, p. 462
goodwill, p. 461
house ad, p. 472
implied third-party
 endorsement, p. 462
internal marketing, p. 463
intranets, p. 479
issue management, p. 464
key influencers, p. 480

latent publics, p. 468
lobbying, p. 463
marketing public relations
 (MPR), p. 466
maven marketing, p. 480
media kit, p. 476
media relations, p. 463
media tour, p. 476
news release, p. 474
news value, p. 474
opinion leaders, p. 461
pitch letter, p. 476
press conference, p. 476
public affairs, p. 463
public communication
 campaigns, p. 466
public opinion, p. 461

public relations, p. 460
public service announcements
 (PSAs), p. 472
publicity, p. 462
publics, p. 460
relationship marketing, p. 463
reputation management,
 p. 465
semi-controlled media, p. 471
speakers' bureau, p. 477
stakeholders, p. 460
strategic philanthropy, p. 464
town hall forums, p. 478
uncontrolled media, p. 471
video news releases
 (VNRs), p. 476

Review Questions

1. Explain why public opinion is important to the success of public relations.
2. Compare and contrast the practice of advertising and the practice of public relations.
3. What is marketing public relations, and how does it differ from other forms of public relations, such as corporate relations?
4. In analyzing PR tools, compare the use of controlled and uncontrolled media. Explain the difference between the two categories.
5. What are the primary tools of publicity?
6. In evaluating the effectiveness of public relations, explain the difference between output and outcome evaluations.

Discussion Questions

1. Why is public opinion so important to the success of public relations? In how many different ways does it affect the success of a program like Hampton Hotels' "Save-A-Land-mark" campaign?
2. What is reputation management, and how does it intersect with advertising programs? Find a corporate reputation campaign and analyze its effectiveness.
3. *Three-Minute Debate* Think about a publicity stunt that backfired, such as the *Aqua Teen Hunger Force* bomb scare in Boston. Is all publicity good publicity? Or was this just a bad idea that hurt the client? Organize into a team, pick a point of view, and prepare to present it to your classmates.

Take-Home Projects

1. *Portfolio Project* Identify a local organization that might benefit from a public relations plan. Study the organization's situation, identify a problem that can be addressed with public relations, and outline a plan to help the organization. Prepare your proposal in a three-page (maximum) paper.
2. *Mini-Case Analysis* Study Häagen-Dazs's efforts to solve the problem of the disappearing honeybee colonies on its website. Look at the corporate social responsibility program on Ben & Jerry's website. Compare and contrast their efforts to be good corporate citizens.

Team Project: The BrandRevive Campaign

Determine objectives and describe how you would employ public relations tools to help you launch your revitalization campaign. First, reread your initial planning decisions for this campaign, then apply the strategies to your use of public relations:

- What are the key problems that might be addressed through public relations?
- What are your objectives for a PR effort?
- Compile a list of all stakeholders and key relationships. Decide who are your key target audiences for this PR effort.
- What is your Big Idea for this PR effort?
- Build your list of PR tools that would be appropriate to use in this situation.
- How would you measure the effectiveness of this effort?
- Present and explain your ideas in a PowerPoint presentation that is no longer than three slides.

Hands-On Case

The Century Council

Read the Century Council case in the Appendix before coming to class.

1. Which promotional and which public relations efforts in the case do you believe will be most successful? Develop at least two new promotional efforts and two new public relations opportunities to strengthen this campaign on your campus.
2. Reviewing the public relation tools in this chapter, find at least two tools you could use effectively on a national basis to increase the impact of The Stupid Drink campaign.

Direct Response

It's a Winner

Campaign:	Organization:	Agency:	Award:
"The Gecko"	GEICO	The Martin Agency, Richmond, Virginia	DMA Echo

CHAPTER KEY POINTS

1. How does direct-response marketing work?
2. What are the primary tools and media available to direct-response programs?
3. How are databases used in direct marketing?
4. What are the trends and challenges facing direct-response marketing?

He's Cute; He's Green; He Sells Insurance

Odds are that you know this little fellow. Maybe you were one of the half-million people who voted to make the GEICO Gecko one of two favorite advertising icons. The Gecko's biography will show you what a far-reaching impact he's had on the car insurance business and how direct marketing can successfully employ spokes-creatures to replace a sales force.

A subsidiary of Warren Buffett's Berkshire Hathaway corporation, GEICO is the leading direct-response auto insurer in a category dominated by major brands, such as Allstate and State Farm. Its biggest marketing challenge is to generate inquiries for rate quotes and to motivate people to call or go online to find out how they can save money, which is reflected in its long-standing brand promise, "15 minutes could save you 15 percent or more on car insurance."

The birth of The Gecko (that's his whole name) occurred in 1999 as ad honchos at The Martin Agency labored over what to do with an account they had for GEICO, an acronym for the not-so-catchy-sounding Government Employees Insurance Company. One member of the creative team noted that customers often mispronounced "GEICO" as "Gecko," and someone drew a doodle of the little guy.

The Gecko tells fundamental truths about the human condition in goofy ways. The oddball humor caught on with the audience, although Ted Ward, vice president for marketing for GEICO, admits he didn't immediately fall in love with the little guy. Ward said, "I quickly became much more fond of him as we sold more policies. I'm a big fan of anything that makes our phone ring or website click. He really has helped us brandwise."

Ted Ward described the business: "We have essentially a direct-to-consumer business model. We try to strip out costs to deliver the lowest price—which includes having very few agents in a process by having a superior technology model, which back in the '70s was direct mail; in the '80s and '90s, a telephone; and in the last 10 years, the online delivery of rates."

It's not just GEICO's endearing icon that makes the campaign work. GEICO uses The Gecko strategically to accomplish the work that its rival auto insurers do by hiring an army of sales middlemen.

You may have noticed that GEICO doesn't just stick with The Gecko in all of its commercials. The reason has much to do with the size of the market, which includes just about anyone who drives a car. Realizing that one creative approach will not appeal to everyone, GEICO uses a diverse approach to reach a wide audience.

That means The Gecko appeals to some, while the indignant Cavemen capture others' attention, and customer testimonials with celebrities like Little Richard reach even others. Another twist is a campaign dubbed "Rhetorical Questions" that doesn't feature any of the company's mascots. Instead commercials ask rhetorical questions, such as "Does Elmer Fudd have trouble with the letter R?" and "Did *The Waltons* take way too long to say goodnight?"

Lessons learned? The concept is simple: different strokes for different folks. The different creative approaches are GEICO-ized by using a common humorous tone.

If it's true that imitation is the sincerest form of flattery, you can see the effect GEICO's advertising has had on the industry. Watch competitors' like State Farm and Allstate, which have advertised for years with gentle, homespun messages promoting family and security. They are now including more humor, high action, and other attention-getting techniques to make you remember their brand when it comes time to buy auto insurance.

Just how successful are The Gecko and his pals' efforts to sell insurance? Turn to *It's a Wrap* at the end of the chapter to find out.

Sources: GEICO.com; Theresa Howard, "Gecko Scores Well in *USA Today* Ad Track," *USA Today*, July 16, 2006; Suzanne Vranica, "GEICO's Gecko Shook Up Insurance Ads," *The Wall Street Journal*, January 2, 2007: B1; Stuart Elliott, "GEICO's Lizard Offers a New Message of Reassurance," *The New York Times*, February 19, 2009; Mya Frazier, "GEICO Ad Chief Builds Insurer into Master Marketer," June 19, 2006, *http://adage.com*; Lavonne Kuykendall, "GEICO Advertising Spending Tops among Auto Insurers in '06," September 19, 2007, *www.insuranceheadlines.com*; Elena Malykhina, "GEICO Answers Its Own Questions," December 28, 2009, *www.adweek.com*.

Direct marketing is an exciting, dynamic field that is becoming more dominant in marketing communication because many, if not most, marketers are moving to more interactive forms of customer communication. Marketers use direct marketing in every consumer and business-to-business (B2B) category. IBM, Xerox, and other manufacturers selling office products use direct-response marketing communication, as do almost all banks and insurance companies. Airlines, hotels, and cruise lines use it. Packaged-goods marketers such as General Foods, Colgate, and Bristol Myers; household product marketers such as Black and Decker; and automotive companies use it. Direct marketing shows up in membership drives, fund-raising, and solicitation for donations by nonprofit organizations such as the Sierra Club and Audubon Society and by political associations, so it is also used by other marcom tools, such as public relations.

In this chapter we will discuss the practice and process of direct-response marketing communication (DMC), the key players, the tools of direct marketing, and the principles of integrating direct marketing into the total brand communication effort.

WHAT IS DIRECT-RESPONSE MARKETING COMMUNICATION?

Why do you suppose marketers continue to use "junk mail" that fills up mailboxes? Or e-mail spam? Or phone calls by telemarketers? Can these tools possibly be effective?

As you know from your own observations and from reading the previous chapters, most marketing communication messages have been carried by mass media as "one-way" messages that talk "at" customers and prospects. Although these messages are cost efficient (i.e., have a lower cost per thousand CPM), they are not as effective as DMC messages that are more interactive and have the potential to create higher levels of customer engagement.

As the Internet and mobile communication devices have become more pervasive and sophisticated, marketers are shifting more and more of their marcom budgets into direct-response

Principle
Marketers use new media forms to talk directly with, rather than at, customers and other stakeholders, creating higher levels of customer engagement.

marketing communication. Because this type of messaging is specifically designed to motivate an immediate response, it is sometimes also called direct-response marketing. And because DMC is designed to generate immediate responses, this means it is also easy to tell quickly if the messages are meeting their objectives. In other words, unlike mass media advertising and public relations, the effects of DMC are more immediate and more measurable.

The Direct Marketing Association is the professional association for this category of marketing communication. We'll define **direct-response marketing** as a multichannel system of marketing that uses a variety of media to connect sellers and customers who deal with each other directly rather than through an intermediary, such as a wholesaler or retailer. There are two pieces to the direct marketing business: first, direct marketing relies on communication that is sent in some form direct to the consumer and, second, the response (sales, sign-up, request for information) comes directly back to the source. In both cases there is no intermediary, such as a retailer.

As noted in Figure 16.1, direct marketing includes a strong focus on market research to guide strategy and database development to better target customers and prospects and invite them to interact with a company. Using an interactive communication model, the contact is designed to elicit an immediate response, usually a sale, as well as invite customers to contact a company. It also helps marcom planners listen to what their customers are saying as they respond.

The most important function of direct marketing is that it opens up the door for interactivity— and why is that important? In the Part 5 opener Duncan said that the best practices of IMC engage stakeholders in meaningful and often interactive brand experiences. Interactivity— two-way communication—is considered to be the heart of DMC and drives its ability to create engaging, relation-building contacts. If marketing is a conversation with consumers about a brand, then one of the most intimate marcom tools in the toolkit is **direct-response marketing communication.**

Some marketers see direct response as more limiting than brand or image advertising because it doesn't reach as many people or, if it does, the traditional cost of reaching each individual is higher per impression. Proponents justify the higher costs by noting that the objective is action rather than recall or attitude change and action is the most desired, if not the hardest, impact to achieve. Today the higher cost argument is weak. This is because the Internet and mobile

Principle
Direct marketing may have higher costs per impression than mass media, but it is less expensive in the long run because its messages are tightly targeted to reach prime prospects.

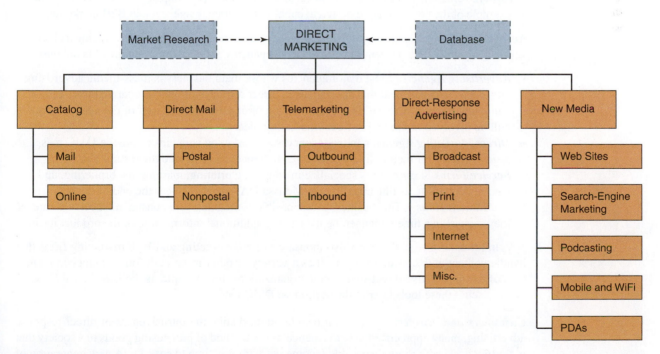

FIGURE 16.1

The Direct Marketing Industry
The direct marketing industry begins with research and database development. Its main tools are catalogs, direct mail, telemarketing, direct-response advertising, the Internet, and other new media.

media eliminate the cost of message delivery—the media cost (although there may still be a cost for producing these messages).

Direct marketers use a variety of traditional and nontraditional media, including catalogs, direct mail, telemarketing, mass-media advertising, the Internet, and new forms of media such as cell phones, smart phones (iPhones, Droids), BlackBerries (personal digital assistants, or PDAs), and social media such as Facebook and Twitter. Recently direct response has come to mean more than just advertising as it has expanded into new media that support entertainment platforms and social networks.

Who Are the Key Players?

The four main players in direct-response marketing communication are (1) marketers who use direct response to sell products or services; (2) agencies that specialize in direct-response advertising; (3) phone, mail, or Internet media that deliver messages; and (4) consumers who are the recipients of the information and sometimes initiators of the contact.

Marketers   Who do you suppose are the biggest users of direct marketing? Traditionally, the types of companies that have made the greatest use of direct marketing have been book and record clubs, publishers, insurance companies, sellers of collectibles, and gardening firms.

More recently, computer companies have used the direct-response model effectively. Dell, for example, has built its business platform on direct marketing of computers directly to consumers rather than through dealers, as its competitors do. This is also true for GEICO.

Why don't Compaq, Hewlett-Packard, and IBM copy the Dell model and sell computers directly? For one thing, their retail dealers, who deliver big sales to these companies, would retaliate if these companies started experimenting with direct sales. Furthermore, it takes a lot of effort and infrastructure to set up a direct-marketing business. Rather than an army of sales reps, Dell employs an army of people in fulfillment who take the order, match the product to customer specifications, handle the money, and arrange for shipping.

But direct marketing can contribute to the brand impression, as well as sales. In some cases, if the contacts are irritating, the message may be negative, but if the messages are well done and targeted to appropriate audiences, then they may be appreciated. Skilled direct marketers, supported by research findings, have discovered that the appearance of a direct-response message—the character and personality communicated by the graphics—can enhance or destroy, not only the brand image, but also the credibility of the product information. The Crane & Company "Banknote" brochure is an example of the power of good design to enhance corporate image, even in B2B marketing.

Agencies and Media Companies   The four types of firms in direct-response advertising include advertising agencies, independent direct-marketing agencies, service firms, and fulfillment houses:

- ***Advertising Agencies*** Most major agencies whose main business is mass-media advertising either have a department that specializes in direct response or own a separate direct-response company. Even if there isn't a special division or department, the staff of the agency may still be involved in producing direct marketing pieces.
- ***Direct Marketing Agencies*** Independent direct marketing agencies create the DMC messages, arrange for their delivery to a target audience, and evaluate the results.
- ***Service Firms*** Service firms specialize in supplying printing, mailing, list brokering, and data management, as illustrated by the Melissa DATA website near the end of the chapter.
- ***Fulfillment Houses*** This business is responsible for making sure consumers receive whatever they request in a timely manner, be it a catalog, additional information, or the product itself.

In terms of media, there are also thousands of telemarketing and Web marketing firms that handle contact with consumers, as well as a variety of other more traditional media companies. One of the most active direct-mail media organizations, for example, is the U.S. Postal Service. We'll discuss these tools later in the section on DMC media.

Customers and Prospects   Although people might dislike the intrusiveness of direct-response advertising, many appreciate the convenience. It is a method of purchasing goods in a society that is finding itself with more disposable income but with less time to spend it. A new generation of consumers armed with push-button phones and a billfold full of credit cards likes to shop from home. This push-button shopper is joined by an even larger group of mouse-clicking shoppers. Although it takes some daring to order a product you can't see, touch, feel, or try out, more and

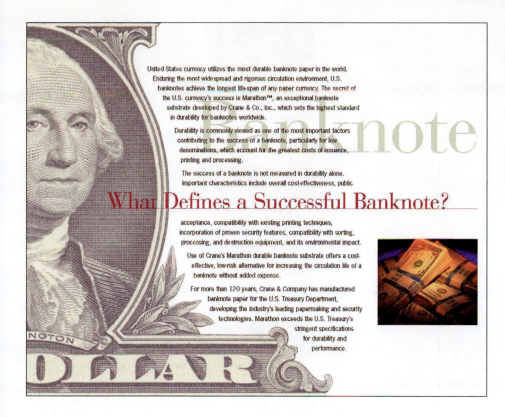

United States currency utilizes the most durable banknote paper in the world. Enduring the most widespread and rigorous circulation environment, U.S. banknotes achieve the longest life-span of any paper currency. The secret of the U.S. currency's success is Marathon™, an exceptional banknote substrate developed by Crane & Co., Inc., which sets the highest standard in durability for banknotes worldwide.

Durability is commonly viewed as one of the most important factors contributing to the success of a banknote, particularly for low denominations, which account for the greatest costs of issuance, printing and processing.

The success of a banknote is not measured in durability alone. Important characteristics include overall cost-effectiveness, public

What Defines a Successful Banknote?

acceptance, compatibility with existing printing techniques, incorporation of proven security features, compatibility with sorting, processing, and destruction equipment, and its environmental impact.

Use of Crane's Marathon durable banknote substrate offers a cost-effective, low-risk alternative for increasing the circulation life of a banknote without added expense.

For more than 120 years, Crane & Company has manufactured banknote paper for the U.S. Treasury Department, developing the industry's leading papermaking and security technologies. Marathon exceeds the U.S. Treasury's stringent specifications for durability and performance.

SHOWCASE

This beautifully designed B2B brochure was created by Peter Stasiowski when he was art director at Gargan Communications in Dalton, Massachusetts. It promotes the durability of Crane & Company's banknote paper. You're looking at the cover (which wraps front to back) and an inside page. Crane is the primary provider of banknote paper to the U.S. Mint. The impact of the piece comes from the unity of creative concept, the product itself, the selling premise, and the well-designed visual elements. What do you think? Is this an effective piece of B2B marketing communication?

Stasiowski is a graduate of the advertising program at the University of West Florida, and his work was nominated for inclusion in this book by Professor Tom Groth.

more consumers are confident and willing to take a chance buying online. To help reduce risk, many customers check out brands and goods in regular retail stores, then buy online. Also numerous websites have been created that publish consumer reviews of online companies.

What Is Included in the DMC Process?

As outlined in Figure 16.2, there are five basic steps in traditional direct marketing: (1) the establishment of objectives and strategic decisions (research helps marketers target, segment, prospect, and set objectives); (2) the communication of an offer (the message) by the seller through the appropriate medium; (3) response, or customer orders; (4) fulfillment, or filling orders and handling exchanges and returns; and (5) relationship building through maintenance of the company's database and customer service.

Objectives and Strategies   DMC planning begins by delineating the specific objectives. Direct marketing can be used to (1) provide in-depth product information, (2) drive traffic to a store or website, (3) develop leads for or follow-up sales contacts or other direct-response efforts (**lead generation,** also called **prospecting**), (4) drive a response, (5) retain or strengthen customer relationships, and (6) test offers to predict their effectiveness.

The most typical DMC objective is to create sales, or some other action, by convincing customers to order products, make payments, or take some other action, such as visiting a dealer, returning a response card, or visiting a website **Conversion rates** are the percentage of contacts who actually take action, and this is the most important metric used in evaluating DMC programs. Relationship building is also important because direct marketers seldom make a profit on the first sale to a new customer; profit comes from subsequent sales.

Nonprofits also are big users of direct-response marketing practices, using them to generate donations, memberships, and volunteers. UNICEF, for example, used a creative mailer for its child soldier campaign. The challenge was to communicate the idea that Africa has the world's highest number of child soldiers fighting in wars they don't believe in for causes they don't understand. UNICEF's goal is to save these kids from war and give them an opportunity to rejoin society. The Y&R Johannesburg agency in South Africa took on this challenge and developed a direct-response program that was sent to UNICEF supporter lists, as well as potential corporate sponsors.

Principle

Relationship building is critical because direct marketers seldom make a profit on the first sale to a new customer; profit comes from subsequent sales.

FIGURE 16.2

The Direct-Response Process

The direct marketer's challenge is to manage the five steps in the DMC process, not only so their messages generate purchases, but also so they build a long-term relationship with consumers.

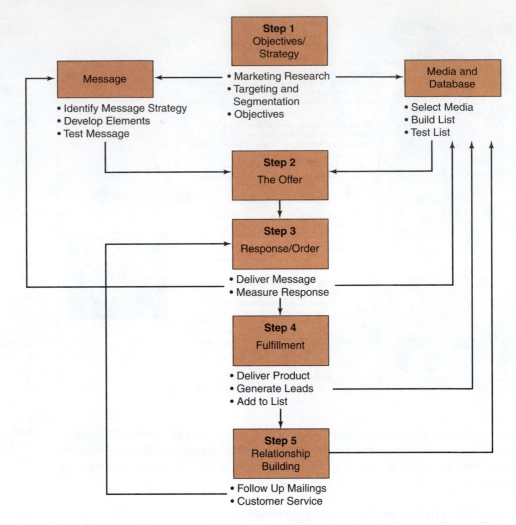

Direct marketers make these basic objectives more specific by spelling out such factors as timing, amount of increase, and the acquisition of information about consumers' specific behavior, such as where they see the product. For example, a local Ford dealership might expect its direct-marketing program to increase showroom traffic by 60 percent in the next 90 days, but one objective also might be to test the effectiveness of a booth at a local shopping center.

Targeting   One of the most important decisions made in direct marketing is selecting those who are to receive the offer. As we have said, for those DMC messages conveyed via catalog, phone calls, and mail, the CPM is high. Therefore, if the DMC effort is to have a positive return on investment (ROI), it is critical that the target prospects have a higher-than-average interest in the brand offer.

The best customer prospects of direct marketers are current customers. If someone has bought from a company several times before, they are much more likely to buy again from that company than someone who has never bought from that company. In other words, current customers have already been sold on the brand, so it is much easier (i.e., less costly) to motivate them to buy again.

Direct marketers have identified three criteria that help them predict who is most likely to repurchase: **recency, frequency, and monetary (RFM)**. The more recently customers bought from a company, the more likely they are to buy again. The more frequently customers have bought from a company, the more likely they are to buy again. Finally, the more money customers have spent buying from a company, the more likely they are to buy again. Computer models are used to do ongoing analyses of customers' buying behaviors and to produce lists, using these criteria, of who the company can best afford to send more catalogs, e-mails, and promotional letters. Similar to media planning, this modeling is also called **optimization**.

For acquiring new customers, a targeting strategy is to *profile current customers* and then look for potential customers who have similar profiles from databases of customer information. For example, if Wendy's finds that a high percentage of its customers in a college town are graduate stu-

Principle

The more recently customers have bought from a company, the more frequently they have bought, and the more they have spent all increase the odds that they will buy again.

This direct-mail piece from the UNICEF campaign appears to contain a packet of toy soldiers, but when opened, they turn out to be figures of children doing normal childhood activities, such as playing soccer and riding bikes. The message on the package, which is also the campaign theme, is "Turn Soldiers Back Into Children." Do you think this is an effective public service piece?

dents, then it should try to find mailing lists of graduate students to mail promotional coupons to because this target audience has a higher probability of responding than the average person.

The Offer   All direct marketing messages contain an **offer,** typically consisting of a description of the product, terms of sale, and payment, delivery, and warranty information. In its offer, a successful DMC campaign must communicate benefits to buyers by answering the enduring question, "What's in it for me?" Also, many DMC offers include an incentive for responding quickly, because marketers know that the longer people think about responding, the less likely they will respond.

All of the variables that are intended to satisfy the needs of the consumer are considered part of the offer. These variables include the price, the cost of shipping and handling, optional features, future obligations, availability of credit, extra incentives, time and quality limits, and guarantees or warranties. The offer is supported by a message strategy, a media strategy, and the database.

Message and Media Strategy   DMC messages are often longer and contain more explanation and detail because as stated before, if this message doesn't provide enough information and motivate the receiver to respond to it in some way, the message is wasted. To be persuasive, messages must contain clear comparisons or details about decision factors, such as price, style, and convenience.

Because DMC messages can be individually targeted, the more personalized the message the better. For example, when a customer orders a book from *Amazon.com*, the company's system immediately suggests similar books. When one of the airlines sends out promotional offers to its frequent flyers, these messages often show the number of miles traveled in the past year and the number of rewards earned year to date. This is obviously a personalized message and definitely attracts more attention.

A DMC message should reflect whether the offer is a one-step offer or two-step offer. Because a **one-step offer** asks for a direct sale response, it must include a mechanism for responding to the offer. A **two-step offer** is designed to gather leads, answer consumer questions, set up appointments, and drive customers to a website or retail store.

Finally the message needs to counter consumers' reluctance to buy. Buying something through direct marketing has elements of risk because there is no salesperson or store to rely on for assistance and information. Most direct-response messages will include copy intended to put the buyer's mind at rest. Guarantees and warranties are important, but another strategy was used in a GEICO flyer to newspaper subscribers, and also in similar looking ads in the business press, to reassure buyers about the company's reliability.

The Response/Order   Generating a response is the third step in the direct marketing process (see Figure 16.2). To maximize the response/order rate, the DMC message must make it as easy as possible for customers to respond. One way to do this is to offer a variety of ways in which to

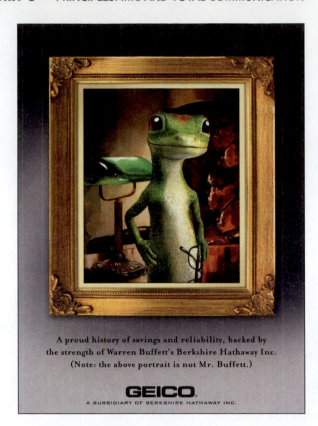

More than just a lighthearted lizard, The Gecko is smart enough to deliver a reassuring message to jittery consumers in an economic downturn that GEICO is financially stable, even mentioning investment giant and corporate owner Warren Buffett and his Berkshire Hathaway company in the flyer.

respond—online, mail, phone, and fax. Also, if phone is one channel, then the more hours the phone lines are open, the better. When customers respond online, it is important that the company immediately acknowledge the response, thanking the customer for the order and advising when the product will arrive. The types of customer service offered, such as toll-free telephone numbers for product support, free limited-time trials, and acceptance of several different credit cards, are important techniques for overcoming customer resistance to responding. To create urgency, the direct marketing message may also include a promotional device such as a gift or limited-time-only price deal.

Fulfillment and Customer Follow-Up   The next step in the direct marketing process is called **fulfillment,** which is responding to customers' responses by getting the product to those who order it. Fulfillment includes all of the back-end activities of processing the transaction, including delivering the product, receiving payment, and providing customers with tracking numbers so they can trace the delivery of their orders. The most critical aspect of successful direct marketing, however, is maintaining a customer relationship.

Relationship Building   Direct marketers use a database to track customer interactions and transactions, the final step in Figure 16.2. Measuring and evaluating consumer behavior helps the direct marketer understand not only how the customers have responded to direct marketing messages but predict their future behavior and build a relationship.

Direct marketing (DM) is not a "shot-in-the-dark" approach. DM professionals continually evaluate and accurately measure the effectiveness of various offers in a single campaign. By employing such measurement tools as tracking printed codes on mail-in responses that identify different offers and using different telephone numbers for each commercial (by time slot, station, or length), the DM professional can clearly identify those offers that yield the best results and modify the campaign to take advantage of them. Because of this constant evaluation,

Principle

Because direct marketing messages are constantly being measured, it is good practice to learn what works and to modify succeeding campaigns based on those results.

there is an emphasis in DM on learning what is most effective and employing that information in succeeding efforts. Such accurate measurements and adjustments are largely responsible for DMC's success.

WHAT ARE THE PRIMARY MEDIA OF DMC?

Personal sales is the original and most effective—and also most expensive—form of direct marketing. Sales persons are found in stores, they knock on the doors of homes, and they also make calls on business prospects. Personal sales are also a part of home parties, which are sponsored by such companies as Mary Kay and Weekenders.

Avon, which was named ninth on a list of "The Ten Most Successful Brands of 2010," is one of the biggest direct sales companies with its millions of sales representatives and some $11 million in revenue.[1] A new Avon little sister brand is Mark, a college program for direct sales on campus. The Mark college co-eds roam dormitories and sorority houses selling Mark beauty products and fashion accessories. In early 2010, there were more than 40,000 Mark Girls signed up in North America. The new organization combines personal sales with an e-boutique, iPhone app, and Facebook e-shop.[2]

Beyond personal sales, direct marketing employs five primary tools to achieve its objectives: (1) direct mail, (2) catalogs, (3) telemarketing, (4) direct-response advertising, and (5) online e-marketing. What is typical of all of these forms is that they offer an opportunity for in-depth information. Copywriter and professor, Karen Mallia, who wrote the Part III opener, observes that "direct marketers have known for years that people considering expensive or complex products want information, and people will be persuaded when that information is delivered in copy that sells while it tells. Much Internet advertising is simply direct marketing in electronic form: e-mails are just another kind of "letter," and search-engine advertising is direct copy at its tightest."

Direct Mail

Of those organizations that use direct marketing, **direct mail** is the most popular method. Anyone with a mailing address has received direct mail. Advertising mail represented more than 63 percent of all mail received by households, according to the U.S. Postal Service's *Household Diary Study*.[3]

A direct-mail piece is a print advertising message for a product or service that is delivered by mail. It may be as simple as a single-page letter or as complex as a three-dimensional package consisting of a letter, a brochure, a sample, a premium, and an order card with a return envelope. With the advances in digital printing, it is now possible to personalize not only the address and salutation on the letter but also other parts of the information as well as the offer. Called **variable data campaigns,** these marketing messages can be highly targeted, even unique to the recipient. Kodak's NexPress Digital Production Color Press is specifically designed for this application.

The following guidelines can be helpful for putting together direct-mail pieces:

* Get the attention of the targeted prospect as the envelope comes from the mailbox.
* Create a need for the product, show what it looks like, and demonstrate how it is used.
* Answer questions, as a good salesperson does, and reassure the buyer.
* Provide critical information about product use.
* Inspire confidence, minimize risk, and establish that the company is reputable.
* Make the sale by explaining how to buy, how to order, where to call, and how to pay for the purchase.
* Use an incentive to encourage a fast response.

Most direct mail is sent using a third-class bulk mail permit, which requires a minimum of 200 identical pieces. Third class is cheaper than first class, but it takes longer for delivery. Estimates of nondelivery of third-class mail run as high as 8 percent. The response rate for direct mail can vary from 0.1 to 50 percent, but it's typically in the 2 to 3 percent range. The primary variables are the offer and target audience. Offers mailed to current customers generally have a higher response rate than those sent to noncustomers.

Because of the high level of nonresponse, direct mail is also a fairly costly tool in terms of CPM. It can be cost efficient, however, because it can be designed to reach a highly targeted audience with an offer of interest. It also is much easier to calculate the actual payout rate—at what point do the returns of the investment begin to exceed the costs? That's why it is considered so much more accountable than other forms of marketing communication. As summarized here, direct mail has a number of advantages and limitations:

Advantages and Limitations of Direct Mail

Advantages	*Description*
Tells a story	The medium offers a variety of formats and provides enough space to tell a complete sales story.
Engages attention	Because direct mail has little competition when it is received, it can engage the reader's attention.
Personalizes the message	Because of the use of databases, it is now possible to personalize direct mail across a number of consumer characteristics, such as name, product usage, purchase history, and income.
Builds in feedback	Direct mail is particularly conducive to marketing research and can be modified until the message design matches the needs of the desired target audience.
Reaches the unreachable	Direct mail allows the marketer to reach audiences that are inaccessible via other media.

Limitations	*Description*
Negative perceptions	The main drawback of using direct mail is the widespread perception that it is junk mail. According to a Harris-Equifax Consumer Privacy Survey, about 46 percent of the public see direct-mail offers as a nuisance, and 90 percent consider them an invasion of privacy.
Cost	Direct mail has a higher cost per thousand than mass media. A great deal of this high cost is the cost of postage. (However, it reaches a more qualified prospect with less waste.) Another cost factor is the maintenance of the database.
Mailing list	To deliver an acceptable response rate, the quality of the mailing list is critical. It must be maintained and updated constantly.
Response rate	Because of the changing nature of mailing lists, as well as the difficulty of keeping relevant data in the database, the response rate can be as low as 2 or 3 percent. Even with that low response, however, database marketers can still make money.
Vulnerability	Direct-mail delivery is vulnerable to natural disasters as well as catastrophes such as the 9/11 terrorist attacks.

Direct-Mail Message Design   The functions of a direct-mail message are similar to the steps in the sales process. The message must move the reader through the entire process, from generating interest to creating conviction and inducing a sale. It's all done with a complex package of printed pieces. Most direct-mail pieces follow a fairly conventional format. They usually consist of an outer envelope, a letter, a brochure, supplemental flyers or folders, and a reply card with a return envelope. These can be one-page flyers, multipanel folders, multipage brochures, or spectacular **broadsheets** that fold out like maps big enough to cover the top of a table.

How the direct-mail piece looks is as important as what it says. The most critical decision made by the target is whether to read the mailing or throw it away, and that decision is based on the attractiveness and attention-getting power of the outer envelope. A mailing for Krispy Kreme got attention when it created a coupon mailer in the shape of a box of doughnuts. Attached to the mailer was an offer to buy a box of a dozen and get another dozen free. Instead of the usual 2 to 3 percent response rate, Krispy Kreme got an 11 percent response. The envelope should spark curiosity through a creative idea as the Billings mailer for its "Trailhead" campaign illustrates.

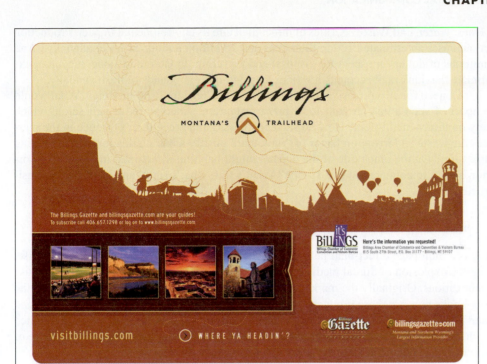

SHOWCASE
This envelope is used by the Billings Chamber of Commerce/ Convention & Visitors Bureau to send information about visitor, tourism, and relocation opportunities. It reinforces the new brand identity campaign, which we described in Chapter 7, and carries the campaign's "Trailhead" logo and slogan, as well as the "explore" graphics.

The Billings, Montana, "Trailhead" brand identity campaign was provided by John Brewer, president and CEO of the Billings Chamber of Commerce/ Convention & Visitors Bureau. A graduate of the University of West Florida, Brewer was nominated by Professor Tom Groth.

Historically, the letter has been the most difficult element in a direct-mail package to develop and therefore the focus of much research. Over the years many techniques have proven effective in getting consumers to read a direct-mail letter, flyer, or brochure. Here are some hints for writing an effective direct-response letter:

1. *Get Attention* To grab attention or generate curiosity, use pictures and headlines that tout the product's benefits.
2. *Be Relevant* Send the right message to the right person.
3. *Personalize* Use a personalized salutation. If the individual's name is not available, the salutation should at least be personalized to the topic, such as "Dear Cat Lover."
4. *Use a Strong Lead-In* Begin the letter with a brief yet compelling or surprising statement. For example, "Dear Friend: I could really kick myself!"
5. *The Offer* Make the offer as early in the body of the letter as possible and dramatize it.
6. *The Letter* Explain the details of the offer and use testimonials or evidence that clearly describes benefits to the customer to create conviction.
7. *Drive to Website* Use short pieces and drive interested prospects to the website for details.
8. *The Closing* End by repeating the offer and stating additional incentives or guarantees and a clear call to action.
9. *Test, Test, Test* Check every single element—small changes can boost conversion rates dramatically.

One advantage of direct mail is that it has a tactile quality that is missing in most other forms of marketing communication. An insurance company once sent out a mailing that contained one leather glove. A message accompanying the glove invited recipients to call the insurance agency if they would like to have the matching glove and hear a little more about the company's insurance policies. Other ideas about using direct mail creatively are offered in *The Inside Story* feature at *www.pearsonhighered.com/moriarty*.

How does "snail mail" compare to e-mail? One direct marketer, Per Annum, which sells planners, diaries, and albums for the corporate gift market, found that its orders dropped 25 percent when the company changed from direct mail to e-mail. The company had been spending $20,000 a year on personally signed letters that offered a discount on early orders. The company realized the change was a mistake even though the e-mail messages were cheaper. It depends on the offer, of course, but in this case the reduced cost wasn't worth the decrease in sales.[4]

Issues: Trees, Water, and Waste   Critics of direct mail cite its environmental impact. Production of direct mail uses an estimated 100 million trees and 28 billion gallons of water annually.[5] And untold millions of dollars are spent for disposal and recycling. In Colorado alone, recycling experts estimate that junk mail accounts for more than 340 million pounds of trash annually.

Is there a need for an aggressive ban on direct mail? Consider local mailings. What would be the impact of such a ban on your local pizza restaurant, video store, or hair salon, which might rely on direct-mail offers? How do such businesses announce their presence in the market? Does the waste and irritation factor of "junk mail" justify a ban on this form of marketing communication? On the other side of the debate, might banning direct mail infringe on an organization's right to commercial free speech? What's fair, what's right, and what's a responsible marketer to do?

Catalogs

A **catalog** is a multipage direct-mail publication (in print) that shows a variety of merchandise. Following the explosion of digital media, however, catalogs have also evolved into easy-to-use online publications. Originally the market of the big retailers Sears and Montgomery Ward, the glossy big books now are those produced by such retail giants as Lands' End, Eddie Bauer, and L.L.Bean. The industry estimates than more than 17 billion catalogs are mailed in the United States each year—that's about 50 for every person.[6] The industry also accounts for a big share of the paper consumed annually—more than either magazines or books.

The growth in the 21st century is in specialty catalogs, which are aimed at niche markets. Duluth Trading Company, for example, sells tough work clothes, and Soft Surroundings sells upscale women's clothing and home accessories. One of the most interesting catalogs is the Neiman Marcus Christmas Book, which features highly expensive fantasy gifts, such as a $250,000 two-seater plane complete with flying lessons, a $10 million Zeppelin, or a $10 million stable of racehorses.[7]

The traditional catalogs all have a variety of brands and products but there are also brand catalogs whose merchandise is all from the sponsoring brand. J. Crew, for example, features J. Crew-branded clothing. Marriott invites travelers to purchase its bed, bath, and room decor products from a catalog that is available in its rooms. The real growth in this field is in the area of specialty catalogs. There are catalogs for every hobby and for more general interests.

The reason paper catalogs continue to be such a force in direct marketing is that they pay. Glossy catalogs still move people to buy in ways that digital images don't, although catalogs can drive traffic to websites where the actual purchase is made.[8]

Online catalogs cross the line between e-commerce and direct marketing. *Amazon.com*'s website, for example, contains complete information about the product offerings, such as book reviews, as well as a way to place an order, pay for it, and contact customer service if there is a problem. The website operates like a direct-mail catalog, but interactivity makes it even more useful than a print version can be. Customers can make inquiries and the company can use its databases to personalize customer communication.

Principle
The reason the catalog industry is growing is because catalogs deliver a lasting impression.

Even though some issued warnings early on about how the Internet would kill off catalogs, in fact they are increasing in number. The reason—lasting impressions—is that most people hang onto catalogs for weeks, giving them a longevity that beats all other media except, perhaps, for magazines. As technology has improved, catalog marketers have refined their databases and culled consumers who receive catalogs but don't order from them.

Another factor in the effectiveness of catalogs is the nature of the interactions between customers and the company, whether over the phone or the Internet. Lands' End has been a model of customer care that leads not just to brand loyalty, but also brand love. Lands' End has been recognized for doing things like marshalling a corps of some 200 employee volunteers who respond to customer mail. The company has even been known to replace products before the customers discover they are faulty. Jeanne Bliss, chief customer officer at Lands' End, who helped create this culture of customer care explains that this high-touch approach has won Lands' End a lot of love, a point she writes about in her book, *I Love You More Than My Dog*.[9]

Some catalog retailers have their own stores, such as title nine, Williams-Sonoma and Tiffany's. Banana Republic, which began as a catalog marketer and then moved into retailing, is now launching its first catalog since 1988. Many large retailers are now multichannel, using catalogs, websites, and stores. Some marketers, such as L.L.Bean, have also seen their catalog mail-

Note how the catalog and web page work to build the brand for title nine through a consistent visual look and brand personality.

ings drive business to their websites. Bean expects that its online sales will soon overtake its catalog business, but it will still send out catalogs as a way to generate online sales. The advantages and limitations of marketing communication via catalogs are listed here:

Advantages and Limitations of Catalogs

Advantages	Description
Targeted	Can be directed at specific market segments.
Engages attention	Employs high-quality design and photography
Complete information	Extensive product information and comparisons are provided.
Convenience	Offer a variety of purchase options.

Limitations	Description
Negative perceptions	Catalogs are viewed as junk mail by many recipients.
Costs	The cost per thousand catalogs is higher than that for mass media.
Response rate	The response is relatively low at 3 to 4 percent.
Mailing list	Databases must be constantly maintained.

A number of marketers are using video or CD catalogs because these provide more information about their products. Car companies, for example, use online catalogs or CDs. The message can be interactive and feature animated illustrations. The catalog presents graphic descriptions and detailed text on the current models, including complete specifications. With some, you can even custom design your dream car.

Telemarketing

Before telemarketing calls were greatly limited by government-supported do-not-call lists, more direct marketing dollars were spent on **telemarketing** phone calls than on any other DMC

SHOWCASE

This is a CD cover designed by Michael Dattolico for his client Microflex, a B2B company in the automotive industry.

Owner of his own design studio, Musion Creative, LLC (*www.musioncreative.com*), Michael Dattolico graduated from the advertising program at the University of Florida where he was a student of Professor Elaine Wagner.

medium. That's because telemarketing is a form of personal sales, but a lot less expensive. An in-person sales call may cost anywhere from $50 to $1,000 after factoring in time and transportation. In comparison, a telephone call ranges from $2 to $15 per call. That is still expensive if you compare it to the CPM of an advertisement placed in any one of the mass media ($10 to $50 per thousand); however, the returns are much higher than those generated by mass advertising because they are intrusive, personalized, and interactive. The caller also can respond to buyers' objections and make a persuasive sales argument.

A typical telemarketing campaign usually involves hiring a telemarketing company to make a certain number of calls using a prepared script. These callers work in **call centers,** which are rooms with large banks of phones and computers. Most calls are made from databases of prospects who were previously qualified on some factor, such as an interest in a related product or a particular profile of demographics and psychographics. Occasionally a **cold call** is used, which means the call center staff are calling random numbers, but this practice has a much lower response rate.

There are two types of telemarketing: inbound and outbound. An **inbound telemarketing** or incoming telemarketing call is initiated by a customer. The consumer can be responding to an ad, catalog, e-mail, or fax. L.L.Bean's telephone representatives are trained to handle inbound calls in such a helpful manner that the company often features their friendly approach in its catalogs. Calls originating from the firm are outgoing or **outbound telemarketing.** These calls typically generate the most consumer resistance because they are uninvited, intrusive, and unexpected.

Telemarketing Message Design　　The key point to remember about telemarketing messages is that they need to be simple enough to be delivered over the telephone. If the product requires a visual demonstration or a complicated explanation, then the message might be better delivered by direct mail. The message also must be compelling. People resent intrusive telephone calls, so there must be a strong initial benefit or reason-why statement to convince prospects to continue listening. The message also must be short; most people won't stay on the telephone longer than two to three minutes for a sales call.

Issues: Intrusion, Fraud, and Privacy　　Telemarketing has its drawbacks. Perhaps the most universally despised telemarketing tool is **predictive dialing.** Predictive dialing technology makes it possible for telemarketing companies to call anyone—even those with unlisted numbers. Special computerized dialing programs use random dialing. This explains why, from time to time, when you answer your phone you simply hear an empty line; the predictive dialer has called your number before a call agent is free. Many people consider these calls a nuisance, and they can even be alarming, because burglars have been known to call a house to see if anyone's home before they attempt a break-in.

Telemarketing's reputation also has been tarnished by fraudulent behavior, such as promising a product or service in exchange for an advance payment, convincing consumers they need some kind of financial or credit protection that they don't really need, or enticing consumers to buy something by promising them prizes that are later discovered to be worthless. In response to these telemarketing abuses, the Federal Trade Commission enacted the Telemarketing Sales Rule (TSR) in 1995 to protect consumers. The TSR prohibits telemarketers from calling before 8 A.M. or after 9 P.M., imposes strict informational disclosure requirements, prohibits misrepresentative or misleading statements, and provides for specific payment collection procedures. More recently, FTC regulations have required telemarketing firms to identify themselves on Caller ID.

Call centers are large rooms with multiple stations for staff who make the calls (outbound) or answer calls from people placing orders (inbound).

The most serious restriction on telemarketing—a program that consumers love—is implemented by state and national "do-not-call" lists. The national Do Not Call Registry had 31.6 million sign-ups even before it took effect in 2003 and had grown to more than 149 million by 2007. Telemarketing companies responded by challenging the legality of these lists in court based on what they believe to be an illegal restriction on commercial free speech. In late 2004, however, the U.S. Supreme Court let stand a lower court ruling that the industry's free speech rights were not violated by the do-not-call list.

The do-not-call lists do not restrict companies from calling their own customers, and they allow nonprofits to continue calling and market research firms to continue conducting phone surveys. Telemarketers subscribe to the database and check the list at least monthly for numbers they need to delete. The subscription cost is $62 for each area code with a $17,000 maximum for a national list. The no-call list registration expires after five years, so consumers are finding that they may have to reregister.[10]

Some phone companies offer their customers a service called "Privacy Manager" that screens out sales calls. For customers who have Caller ID, numbers that register as "unavailable" or "unknown" are intercepted by a recorded message that asks callers to identify themselves. If the caller does so, the call rings through.

Direct-Response Advertising

The common thread that runs through all types of direct-response advertising is that of action. The move to action is what makes direct-response advertising effective. Syracuse University Professor John Philip Jones points to direct advertising as being more effective than general advertising and says advertisers have a lot to learn from direct marketers.[11]

Print Media   Ads in the mass media are less directly targeted than are direct mail and catalog, but they can still provide the opportunity for a direct response. Ads in newspapers and magazines can carry a coupon, an order form, an address, or a toll-free or 900 telephone number. The response may be either to purchase something or to ask for more information. In many cases the desired response is an inquiry that becomes a sales lead for field representatives.

CLASSIC

For most of its life, the Sears catalog was sent to homes via the Postal Service and shoppers could order directly from the "Wish book" with their merchandise also delivered to them by mail. Some surprising offerings included the Sears Motor buggy from 1909 to 1912 and from 1908 to 1940 Sears sold some 75,000 mail-order homes from its catalogs.

A classic example of the power of direct-response advertising is the "97-Pound Weakling" ads for the Charles Atlas body building mail-order courses that featured a cartoon telling the story of a scrawny guy who decides to bulk up after a well-built lifeguard kicks sand in his face and steals his girlfriend. The business was launched in 1928 when Atlas partnered with adman Charles Roman to promote the Charles Atlas exercise system and correspondence course. The campaign created a multimillion-dollar business and the "97-pound weakling" who turned into a "he man" became a pop culture icon.

Catalogs also have been effective direct-response marketers for as long as there has been mail. The famous Sears catalogs began in 1888 with a line of watches and jewelry. In 1894 the offerings were expanded to include sewing machines, bicycles, saddles, musical instruments and a host of new items. In 1896 the slogan "Cheapest Supply House on Earth" was added to the cover. For more on the history of this iconic direct-response vehicle, visit *http://www.searsarchives.com/*.

Broadcast Media   A direct-response commercial on radio or TV can provide the necessary information (usually a simple, easy-to-remember toll-free phone number or Web address) for the consumer to request information or even make a purchase. Radio's big advantage is its highly targeted audience. In contrast, television is a good medium for direct marketers who are advertising a broadly targeted product.

Direct-response advertising on television used to be the province of late-night TV with pitches for Vegematics and screwdrivers guaranteed to last a lifetime. As more national marketers, such as GEICO, move into the medium, the direct-response commercial is becoming more general in appeal, selling clothes and entertainment as well as insurance and financial services.

Direct-response TV also makes good use of the **infomercial** format. Infomercials blur the lines between retail and direct response. Infomercials have been around since the emergence of the cable industry and have become a multibillion-dollar industry. An infomercial is typically 30 or 60 minutes long and tends to be played during nonprime-time periods. The Salton-Maxim Juiceman infomercial took the company from $18 million to $52 million in sales overnight and made a marketing superstar of George Foreman. The Salton commercial made Juiceman the brand to buy, whether direct from television or from a local department store or mass merchant.

Today, the infomercial is viewed as a viable medium because (1) consumers now have confidence in infomercials and the products they sell; (2) with the involvement of upscale advertisers, the quality of infomercial production and supportive research has improved; (3) consumers can be better segmented and infomercials are coordinated with respect to these audiences; and (4) infomercials can easily be introduced into foreign markets. Marketers are more likely to use the infomercial format if their product needs to be demonstrated, is not readily available through retail outlets, and has a relatively high profit margin.

Telebrands, a direct-response TV (DRTV) marketer, for many years used pitchman Billy Mays until he died in 2009. Using a reality show format, the company offered tryouts for the Mays replacement. Even *AdAge* columnist Larry Dobrow tried out for the position. Mays was the undisputed king of TV pitching and sold as much as 70 percent of the gadgets offered on air.

A leading direct-response auto insurer, GEICO uses its Gecko character as a spokes-creature to sell its products on television, as well as in print.

The Telebrands president admitted that "you can double the response with the right pitch person vs. no pitch person."[12]

Cable television lends itself to direct response because the medium is more tightly targeted to particular interests. QVC and the Home Shopping Network reach more than 70 million households and service their calls with huge phone banks.

The Internet and New Forms of Direct Response

Direct marketers saw the Internet's potential early. Actually, direct marketing—particularly catalog marketing—is the model for e-commerce. *Amazon.com* is the leader of the pack, but other companies that sell merchandise direct include Columbia House Online (*www.columbiahouse.com*), eBags (*www.eBags.com*), and CDNow (*www.cdnow.com*). Because of its interactive dimension, the Web is moving direct marketers much closer to one-to-one marketing.

The technology of the Internet also has produced dramatic changes in the direct-mail industry. At a most basic level, the Internet has facilitated the ease in producing and distributing traditional direct mail by e-mail. E-mail marketing software and advertising assistance is available from such companies as Constant Contact (*www.constantcontact.com*), which even provides e-mail templates. Services such as Constant Contact and MailNow offers a streamlined process that allows users to point-and-click their way through a series of predesigned e-mailer templates priced and sorted by industry, as well as select mailing lists and various mail media (postcards, letters, flyers, or newsletters). Customers can customize the mailer with their logo and other proprietary images or copy.

Another feature of Internet direct marketing is greater sampling opportunities. Online music stores now have hundreds of thousands of music clips for shoppers to listen to before making a purchase. Eddie Bauer lets site visitors "try on" clothes in a virtual dressing room. It also sends them e-mail messages offering special prices on items based on their past purchasing patterns.

Today, the use of extensive database information and innovative e-mail technology, combined with creative marketing strategies, has brought the benefits of highly personalized, inexpensive messages to far-reaching mass campaigns. E-mail marketing is developing and becoming more strategic as new technologies are developed. Three basic types of e-mail campaigns are used in marketing communication:

* Addressable to current customers
* Addressable to prospects
* Unsolicited and often unwanted, or spam.

An option in the "addressable" category is one that is still evolving and that is the idea of sending automated direct marketing messages via GPS-enabled mobile devices, such as iPhones. Various

Television shopping networks handle sales orders by using hundreds of customer service agents.

innovations are being tested to make these geomarketing techniques useful without becoming a privacy issue.[13]

Well-known corporate brands such as BMW are using e-mail as a DMC tool. In one campaign, the company invited existing and prospective customers to view a collection of Web movies about new BMW models. Another campaign notified BMW owners of a new section at *BMW.com* reserved strictly for their use. Called the "Owner's Circle," the section allows owners to obtain special services and set up profiles that track maintenance items specific to their cars. Shortly after the mailing, enrollment in the Owner's Circle doubled, and participation in BMW's financial services program tripled.

Issue: Spam   Although e-mail marketing has enjoyed increased success, the practice has received intense criticism for generating too much unwanted e-mail, otherwise known as **spam.** The FTC has determined that 90 percent of all spam involving business and investment opportunities contains false or misleading information. The problem also exists with nearly half of the messages promoting health products and travel and leisure. This is why Congress passed the CAN-SPAM Act in 2003. The problem is so big that some industry experts estimate that more than half of all e-mail messages are spam.

Amazon has filed lawsuits in U.S. and Canadian courts to stop e-mail spammers it says have been fraudulently using its identity to send out spam, a practice known as **spoofing.** Facebook has been plagued with spam and began offering its users a complimentary six-month subscription to McAfee's Internet Security Suite, which railroads spam as well as viruses.[14] One of the largest e-mail marketers, OptInRealBig, has been sued by the state of New York for allegedly sending misleading and fraudulent e-mail solicitations. Microsoft also sued the company for bombarding its Explorer service with spam.

Critics would like to see the government close down the bulk e-mail operations. There are technological problems to controlling these practices, however, and spammers have proven creative in finding ways to get through filters. It's become a worldwide problem as spammers from outside the United States have helped to double the volume of unwanted e-mail. A register of spammers known as *Rokso,* or Register of Known Spam Operations, has been created. It's a kind of "most wanted" list maintained by Internet hosts and service providers like AOL, whose computers strain to handle the huge amounts of e-mail and are quick to kick off known spammers. An antispam website called *spamhaus.org* also tracks spam senders, and Congress has various proposals for regulating spam.

Is spam cost effective? Spammers solicit business from sources like AOL's profiles where people indicate their interests and activities. A spammer might send out 100,000 e-mails and get only two to five clients, which seems like a totally unacceptable number of responses. But a spammer who charges $300 to send out 100,000 messages or $900 for a million might make $14,000 to $15,000 on those few responses. That's not a bad return when you consider the cost of getting into the business—a computer and an Internet connection.

Here are some of the ways consumers can reduce the amount of unwanted direct mail or spam they receive:[15]

- If you enter a contest or order an item by mail, you may wind up on a mailing list. To protect your contact information, check the "opt-out" box and write "No mailing lists" beside your contact information.
- Use the "Contact Us" link on retailers' websites to ask to be taken off mailing lists.
- Check the "Privacy" link at the bottom of a company's home page for directions on removing your name from its mailing lists.
- The Mail Preference Service of DMA permits you to register for $5 to get off mailing lists (*www.dmaconsumers.org/cgi/offmailing*).

- To get off credit card solicitation lists, call 888-5-OPT-OUT. A recorded message will ask for your contact information, but that's just confirmation. This service already has your contact information; providing it by phone confirms your identity so your request can be processed.
- To register for the federal do-not-call list, go to *donotcall.gov* and sign up. That will cut down on unwanted phone calls from marketers.
- To reduce the amount of spam you receive, register at e-MPS, which is DMA's e-mail Preference Service (*http://dmaconsumers.org/consumers/optoutform_emps.shtml*).

You might note that in most cases, if you have a relationship with a company—which means you've ordered something within the past 12 months—you won't be deleted from those lists. Blanket requests to end unsolicited calls or mail may not apply to charities and politicians because of First Amendment issues. Nonprofit organizations do a lot of solicitations by mail.

Permission Marketing   Because spam is a huge problem for legitimate e-mail marketers, they are now using an approach called **permission marketing.** This approach attempts to address the spam problem by asking potential consumers for their permission to send them e-mail. Solutions to the problem usually incorporate one of two permission marketing strategies for consumers to control their inclusion on lists. **Opt in** means that all bulk mailers have to get your permission before sending a promotion. Legitimate direct marketers use this permission form, which is tougher for spammers to abuse and more sensitive to consumer rage when they do. **Opt out** means that e-mailers can send the first e-mail but must give recipients the means to refuse any further e-mails from that business. These options give customers control over the amount and type of e-mail messages they receive, and companies reduce wasted resources on marketing to uninterested individuals. The concept at the heart of permission marketing is that every customer who opts in to a campaign is a qualified lead.

Principle
Opt-in and opt-out strategies make e-mail campaigns more acceptable because customers give permission to marketers to contact them. At the heart of permission marketing is the idea that every customer who opts in to a campaign is a qualified lead.

WHY ARE DATABASES THE FOUNDATION OF DMC?

Looking back, you'll note that Figures 16.1 and 16.2 both begin with databases. Why is that so? Direct marketers use **databases** to keep track of current customers and identify prospective customers. They are also a segmentation tool to communicate relevant offers to customers and prospects. Another benefit for companies that keep track of their customers' online behavior is that they are better able to personalize their DMC messages. A database is at the heart of direct marketing.

For example, consider how Carnival Cruise Lines uses databases to manage its customer relationships. Information is gathered at check-in when customers get their Sail & Sign card, which serves as money on the cruise (it also allows Carnival to track its customers' purchases and activities). New customers receive a standard card but returning passengers get a gold card that triggers "Welcome back" messages from staff. Frequent cruisers get a platinum card and automatic membership in the Concierge Club with perks such as priority embarking and debarking, dining times, and spa reservations. These data are then used to target follow-up e-mail and direct-mail offers.

The authors of a set of books that focus on one-to-one marketing defined it as a strategy that delivers customer-focused objectives by treating different customers differently. Through the use of databases, they describe the *learning relationship* that results from customer dialogue. Here is how this data-driven relationship works:[16]

> If you're my customer and I get you to talk to me, I remember what you tell me, and I get smarter and smarter about you. I know something about you competitors don't know. So I can do things for you my competitors can't do, because they don't know you as well as I do. Before long, you can get something from me you can't get anywhere else, for any price. At the very least you'd have to start all over somewhere else, but starting over is more costly than staying with us.

An example of using a database to identify good customers and treat them differently comes from a direct-response campaign designed by Wisconsin-based Carlson Marketing that segmented customers by usage. By analyzing its database, a large multinational packaged goods company was able to send a premium quality direct-mail piece with a unique shape to the top 15 percent of the company's 200 million customers. The middle-tier customers—55 percent of the customer base—received a more modest flat mail piece and the bottom group received cost-effective e-mails.

How Do Databases Create a Circular Process?

Principle
DMC is a continuous process beginning and ending with a database of prospect and customer information.

A database is important at both the beginning of the direct-marketing process and at the end of the process where it captures and updates information for the next interaction. It's a circular process. If an important objective is to build relationship programs, then the information gathered through customer interaction feeds back into the process and becomes an input for the next round of communication efforts.

DMC is possible because of innovations in computer technology that have helped companies keep up with their customers. People move, have children, marry, divorce, remarry, change jobs, age, and retire and change their purchase behavior through all of these changes. The purpose of the database is to produce up-to-date information on customers and prospects as well as their interactions with the company. According to the DMA, a good marketing database has these primary objectives:[17]

• Record names of customers, expires (names no longer valid), and prospects.
• Store and analyze responses.
• Store and analyze purchasing performance.
• Continue direct communication with customers.

The database management process is illustrated in Figure 16.3. It begins with an initial information collection point. This could be the completion of a warranty card, entering a contest or sweepstakes, opting in on a website, or filling out a card at a trade show, to name a few. The second stage is to enter the data into the computer to merge it with other information already in the file or added at the same time. Stage 3 allows the marketer to assess the data and determine the relevant level of detail. In stage 4, the direct marketer can create clusters of characteristics and behaviors representing valuable consumer segments or target markets (audiences). Stage 5 applies the database to the specific marketing problems or strategies. An example might be sending coupons to a particular customer segment. In stage 6, the direct marketer makes decisions about data sharing and partnerships. A manufacturer may decide that his retail outlets could use the data. Finally, the database goes through a refinement process that includes corrections, updates, additions, and deletions.

Lists

Customer and prospect lists that contain contact information (addresses, phone numbers, and e-mail and other online addresses) are used by all areas of direct marketing. Direct-mail lists that match

FIGURE 16.3

The Database Marketing Process
Using database marketing, planners can continually improve the effectiveness of their marketing communication campaigns.

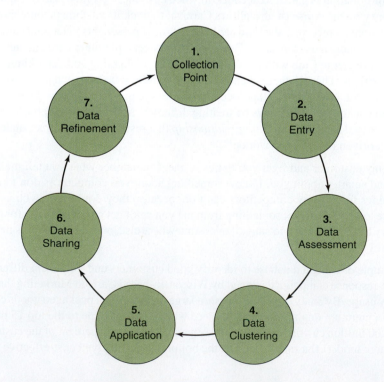

market segments identified in the marketing communication plan can be purchased or rented from list brokers who maintain and sell thousands of lists tied to demographic, psychographic, and geographic breakdowns. They have further classified their data on such characteristics as hobbies, affiliations, and personal influence, such as the Response Alliance database of decision makers. Geography is a common classification; American households can be broken down by their postal carrier routes. For instance, one company has identified 160 zip codes it calls "Black Enterprise" clusters, inhabited by "upscale, white-collar, black families" in major urban fringe areas.

Marketers own their own lists or rent lists based on customer characteristics, such as geography, age, gender, and personal interests (sailboat owners, college students). There are three types of lists:

- A **house list** is made up of the marketer's own customers or members in its most important target market. It is its most valuable list. These lists are compiled when stores offer credit plans, service plans, special sale announcements, and contests that require customers to sign up. Some stores, such as Radio Shack, fill in customers' names and addresses at the cash register.
- A **response list** is made up of people or households who have responded to some type of direct-response offer. The more similar the product to which they responded is to the marketer's product, the more valuable the list because these people should be similar to the company's current customers. For example, if you sell pet food, you might like a list of people who have responded to a magazine ad for a pet identification collar. Two important criteria are obvious from such a list: these people very likely have a pet, and they are open to buying from a catalog, mail offer, or website.
- A **compiled list** is a list of some specific category, such as sports car owners, new home buyers, graduating seniors, new mothers, association members, or subscribers to a magazine, book club, or record club. Luxury car manufacturers are always interested in lists of people who belong to country clubs, own a yacht, or own luxury cars, because these people obviously like and can afford such luxuries.

New lists can be created by merging and purging. If you want to target older women in New England who play tennis, for example, most list houses would be able to put together a database for you by combining lists, called **merging,** and then deleting the repeated names, called **purging.**

This is a postcard mailed to B2B direct marketers offering lists classified into 47 different types of buying characteristics. It separates prospects in terms of 47 "buying influence selectors" that include such factors as job function, industry, and decision-making patterns.

For example, you may want to develop a list of people who are in the market for fine furniture in your city. You could buy a list of new home buyers and combine that with a list of people who live in a desirable census tract. These two lists together—a compiled list—would let you find people who have bought new homes in upscale neighborhoods.

A company can hire database management firms whose sole purpose is to collect, analyze, categorize, and market an enormous variety of detail about customers. Companies such as National Decision Systems and Donnelly Marketing Information Systems are only a few of the firms that provide these **relational databases**—that is, databases that contain information useful in profiling and segmenting as well as contact information. Donnelly, for example, developed Hispanic Portraits, a database of households that segments the U.S. Hispanic population into 18 cluster groups.

Services such as Prodigy and Melissa DATA (see the website download) provide users with online buying services, remember purchases, and, over time, can build a purchase profile of each user. This kind of information is valuable to marketers, resellers, and their agencies. It's also of concern to consumer activists and consumers who worry about privacy.

Nintendo uses the 2 million names in its database when it introduces more powerful versions of its video game system. The names and addresses are gathered from a list of subscribers to its magazine, *Nintendo Power*. The company believes that many of its current customers will want to trade up systems, and this direct communication makes it possible for Nintendo to speak directly to its most important target market about new systems as they become available. Nintendo began its database in 1988 and credits database marketing with helping it maintain its huge share of the $6 billion to $7 billion video game market.

Data Mining   The practice of sifting through and sorting information captured in a company's database to target customers and maintain a relationship with them is called **data mining**.[18] Such information includes comprehensive profiles based on demographics, lifestyle, and behavior, as well as basic contact information.

The Melissa DATA website explains the services offered by this company in database collection and maintenance.

How is data mining used? Marketers collect information about their customers to better target customers who might really be interested in their offers. This is called *behavioral targeting,* to which we referred in Chapter 5. Instead of sending mass e-mails (spam) to everyone on a list, marketers can send information to people who are really interested in their product or service based on their past purchases and other product-related actions.

Data mining is also used to spot trends and patterns—frequent flyers may also be buyers of international phone cards, for example. Using the practice discussed earlier called *prospecting,* data mining also can be used to profile prospects based on key characteristics of current customers. If a grocery store that uses a loyalty card to track its customers' purchases notices that the young families in its customer pool live in certain neighborhoods, then it can target family-oriented promotions to those particular neighborhoods rather than spraying them across its entire geographical market.

Like the recycling symbol, this "i" will help people understand why they got the ad or online message. When they click on the symbol, the copy explains that the marketer used their Internet surfing behavior to identify their interests.

The Privacy Issue   Privacy is a huge concern for all direct marketers, not just those engaged in e-commerce. Companies are increasing the amount of data they collect on their customers in order to do better behavioral targeting—sometimes with their permission and knowledge, but often without customers even being aware of the practice. In an attempt to avert regulation, the direct-marketing industry has developed an icon—a little stylized "i"—to use on ads and other online messages that use behavioral targeting.[19]

Privacy is particularly an issue with data mining. D'Souza and Phelps call it the "privacy paradox,"[20] meaning that you can't do narrow targeting without collecting personal information. That may make direct-response targeting more efficient with consumers getting fewer unwanted contacts, but at what point is efficiency of targeting compromised by privacy concerns? What is the impact of privacy concerns on consumers' purchasing behavior? Research by D'Souza and Phelps found that privacy concerns do matter and that privacy policies and marketing strategies are interdependent. This issue is discussed in the *A Principled Practice* feature.

DMC TRENDS AND CHALLENGES

Direct marketing speaks in the voice of the brand and, as Duncan noted in his comments in the Part 5 opener, the brand voice needs to be true to the brand. In other words, direct marketing offers a great opportunity to convey the essence and personality of a brand in a one-on-one conversation with a customer or prospect. So what needs to be done to develop and protect this brand voice? Planning an integrated approach is critical, and keeping the message consistent across international borders is also important.

Principle
Direct marketing conveys the essence and personality of a brand in a one-on-one conversation with a customer or prospect.

Integrated Direct Marketing

Historically, direct marketing is the first area of marketing communication that adopted an integrated marketing approach. In fact, some people refer to DMC as **integrated direct marketing (IDM).** As technology has provided more and better ways to interact with customers, the challenge to direct marketers has been to integrate direct mail, catalogs, telemarketing, websites, e-mail, text messaging, and instant messaging with other marketing communication, such as advertising—and to do so with a consistent brand voice that reflects the brand strategy.

Two reasons integration plays so well in the direct-response market is because of its emphasis on the customer and its measurability. The coordination problem is a challenge due to the deluge of data bombarding customers from many different channels. The only way to manage the information is to focus it around customer needs and interests. By using databases, companies can become more sensitive to customer wants and needs and less likely to bother them with unwanted commercial messages.

Linking the Channels   Instead of treating each medium separately, as some advertising agencies tend to do, DMC companies seek to achieve precise, synchronized use of the right media at the right time, with a measurable return on dollars spent. Here's an example: Say you do a direct-mail

A PRINCIPLED PRACTICE

PRIVACY: *The Need to Use but Not Abuse Consumer Information*

Joseph E. Phelps, *University of Alabama*
Jimmy Peltier, *University of Wisconsin, Whitewater*
George R. Milne, *University of Massachusetts, Amherst*

In your advertising and marketing communication classes (including this one) you will be encouraged to collect and examine all of the information that is available in order to develop the consumer insights necessary to select the optimal audience and then develop and deliver messages that will move this audience to respond in the desired way.

To accomplish this task, marketing professionals are collecting and using more individual-level consumer information than ever before. Information such as names, addresses, demographic characteristics, lifestyle interests, shopping preferences, and purchase histories have been collected for many years. New information channels have emerged that provide marketers with the ability to capture more information and to capture that information in real time. For example, marketers can easily track online behaviors and use that information to deliver behavioral-based marketing communication.

Radio-frequency identification (RFID) and video surveillance allow for the tracking of product and customer in-store movements. GPS-based functions in mobile devices also provide location-tracking abilities. Marketers have the ability to capture, store, and analyze tremendous amounts of consumer information.

This information helps marketers to better understand and cater to the wants and needs of their customers and to more effectively identify and communicate with prospective customers. However, because marketers have the ability to piece together personally identifying information (PII) from multiple sources, consumers have a real concern regarding their "digital dossier" and how their information dossiers are generated, utilized, and shared, particularly if there is a potential for their information to be used with negative personal and financial consequences.

As you become a marketing communicator, these consumer concerns should be important to you for multiple reasons, each of which revolves around your responsibilities to practice in the best interests of your customers, society, and the ongoing success of the organization for which you work. You need to understand consumer privacy concerns and privacy regulations because you will have the ethical, and in many cases, legal responsibility to thoughtfully protect consumers' personal information while using this data effectively. Your responsibility to the long-term success of your company is critical, and consumer privacy concerns represent an important, yet too often ignored factor influencing the potential long-term success. Developing and maintaining long-term customer relationships require organizations to consider the negative impact that privacy concerns have on trust.

Thus, careful consideration of the amount and types of information collected and how that information will be used is critical. It is also essential to make sure that consumers are aware when information is being collected, what is being collected, and how that information will be used. This transparency is difficult to accomplish with emerging media that collect data in ways that are often invisible to the consumer. No one said the job would be easy.

Balancing the use of individual-level consumer information with consumer privacy is, however, a necessary task for which there are legal, ethical, and bottom-line business ramifications. You need consumer information to create great marketing communication, to direct it to the proper audience, and to build long-term relationships. Be sure to treat that information with the respect and protection it deserves.

campaign, which generates a 2 percent average response. If you include a toll-free 800 number in your mailing as an alternative to the standard mail-in reply—with well-trained, knowledgeable people handling those incoming calls with a carefully thought-out script—you can achieve a 3 to 4 percent response rate. If you follow up your mailing with a phone call within 24 to 72 hours after your prospect receives the mailing, you can generate a response two to eight times as high as the base rate of 2 percent. So, by adding your 800 number, you bring the response rate from 2 percent to 3 or 4 percent. By following up with phone calls, you bring your total response rate as high as 5 to 18 percent.

The principle behind integration is that not all people respond the same way to direct-response messages. One person may carefully fill out the order form. Someone else may immediately call the 800 number. Most people, if a DMC message grabs them, tend to put it in the pending pile. That pile grows and grows, and then goes into the garbage at the end of the month. But, if a phone call or e-mail follows the direct-mail piece, the marketer may get the wavering consumer off the fence. Hewlett-Packard, AT&T, Citibank, and IBM have all used integrated direct marketing as a multimedia effort to improve their direct marketing response rates.

Safeway Stores has become interested in integrated direct marketing. Essentially, Safeway has signed up manufacturers such as the Quaker Oats Company and Stouffer Food Corp. (owned by Nestlé) for a database marketing program that provides trade dollars in exchange for quality customer data. The program exemplifies the convergence of two trends: grocers looking for manufacturers to supplement their own shrunken marketing budgets and manufacturers eager to allocate new field marketing support dollars are working more closely as partners. A number of manufacturers whose products are carried in Safeway stores fund Safeway's quarterly mailings in exchange for in-store support and sales data.

A common problem with IDM is that direct marketing messages and advertising messages often do not reinforce each other as well as they should because the two functions—advertising and direct marketing, which often are handled by different agencies—don't talk to one another. This will change, however, as clients demand more coordination of their marketing communication programs. The point is that direct marketing can add impact to an IMC campaign and increase its efficiency.

Creating Loyalty One of the best practices noted by Duncan in the Part 5 opener is the development of solid customer-brand relationships. When effective, one-on-one communication leads to a customer retention strategy that ultimately increases brand loyalty. Direct response is a highly targeted form of marketing communication that lets planners focus on their best customers and inform, encourage, or reward them for their brand loyalty. Frequent flyer/buyer programs are examples of database-driven reward programs that help keep customers loyal.

Perhaps the most ambitious attempt to create consumer loyalty is through a concept called **lifetime customer value (LCV).** LCV is an estimate of how much purchase volume companies can expect to get over time from various target markets. To put it formally, LCV is the financial contribution through sales volume of an individual customer or customer segment over a length of time. The calculation is based on known consumption habits plus future consumption expectations. The estimate of the contribution is defined as return on investment, or revenue gains as a function of marketing costs. In simpler terms, by knowing your consumers' past behavior, you can decide how much you want to spend to get them to purchase and then repurchase your product, and you can track your investment by measuring the response.

Consumer resistance to direct marketing must be considered in efforts to build loyalty. Changing consumers' attitudes about direct marketing has not been easy because consumers resent companies that know too much about them. If the company can demonstrate that it is acting in the consumer's best interest rather than just trolling for dollars, it might gain and maintain consumers' loyalty. Saks Fifth Avenue, for example, identified the customers who account for half of all sales and offered the group exclusive benefits through a program called Saks First. The benefits include fashion newsletters and a first crack at all sales.

The most important goal, however, is supporting brand building, and some marketers have been concerned that DMC's emphasis on accountability and emphasis on driving sales has made it less focused on the brand presence. One back-end operation, GSI Interactive, which had been known for its handling of online sales, created a spin-off called True Action that is tasked with

Principle
One-on-one communication leads to a strengthened customer relationship and, ultimately, increased brand loyalty.

the mission of building brands. The point is that, as a True Action executive observed, if the agency doesn't understand the base business, "they can make dumb decisions."[21]

Global Considerations in DMC

The direct marketing industry is growing fast in many Far Eastern and European countries—in some places, even faster than in the United States. The global trend is fueled by the same technological forces driving the growth of direct marketing in this country: the increasing use of computer databases, credit cards, toll-free phone numbers, and the Internet, along with the search for more convenient ways to shop. The growth may be even greater in business-to-business marketing than in consumer marketing.

Direct marketing is particularly important in countries that have tight restrictions on advertising and other forms of marketing communication. However, these countries often have restrictions on direct marketing as well. Privacy issues are even more intense in some countries than in the United States. In some countries, lists are not available, or they may be of poor quality. Databases can be more freely transferred between European countries than they can between the United States and European countries.

Some countries have instituted outright bans on direct marketing, although these restrictions seem to be loosening up. China lifted its national ban on direct sales, such as Amway and Avon, in late 2005. The ban had been in place since 1998 because of a series of scandals and frauds.[22]

Governmental regulation of the postal service may also place limitations on the use of direct mail. For example, language and characters are a problem, particularly for American companies that may not understand that the letter *e* isn't the same as *é, è, ê,* or *ë* in an address. Computers and typesetting systems have to accommodate these differences. The format of the address has to be exactly correct in some countries, such as Germany, where the Deutsche Post has strict rules about correct address formats. In Hungary the street name is in the third line of the address, whereas it is on the second line along with the postal code in Germany. Presorted mail in a wrong format may result in charges to the end user that significantly raise the cost of the mailing.

What Are the Advantages and Limitations of DMC

In addition to interactivity, which is its greatest gift to marketing communicators, another big advantage of direct marketing over indirect marketing, such as advertising, can be summarized in one word: accountability. DMA describes this strength as the ability to track, measure, and optimize marketing communication.[23] Other advantages include the following:

- Direct marketing messages can be personalized, which makes them much more persuasive than nonpersonalized (mass-media) messages.
- Direct marketing results are measurable so the ROI is easily known.
- Direct marketing technology allows for the collection of relevant information about the customer, contributing to the development of a useful database and selective reach, which reduces waste.
- Products have added value, through the convenient purchase process and reliable/quick delivery mechanisms of direct marketing. Purchase is not restricted to a location.
- The marketer controls the product (rather than the wholesaler or retailer) until delivery.
- Advertising carrying direct marketing components is more effective than advertising not using direct marketing.
- Direct marketing affords flexibility both in form and timing.

Like all tools, direct marketing has some weaknesses. Most notably, consumers are still reluctant to purchase a product they cannot touch and feel. Another weakness is the annoyance associated with direct marketing, such as too many catalogs, junk mail, online pop-ups, ad clutter, spam e-mail, and unwelcome phone calls. There are serious problems with customer privacy and data sharing as well as concerns about identity theft. Finally, in the tension between creating a long-term brand image and driving immediate sales, direct marketing tends to be more attuned to the latter. But that doesn't mean brand building is impossible with direct marketing. In particular, direct marketers, such as L.L.Bean, *Amazon.com*, Nature Conservancy, and Dell Computer, have built strong brands primarily through direct marketing.

Looking Ahead

Direct-response marketing communication is an important tool in the IMC toolkits because it is uniquely designed to deliver interactivity. As we have said, dialogue-based communication is the foundation for brand relationships. DMC is also important because of its ability to track effectiveness. Now in the next chapter let's consider the various ways people are engaged in brand experiences through promotions.

IT'S A WRAP

The Gecko and Friends Drive Customer Response

In this chapter we identified many benefits of using direct-response marketing. It can reach a large, diverse audience efficiently to generate customers for auto insurance. GEICO's aggressive effort to blanket the nation with an array of campaigns, including The Gecko, the Cavemen, the customer/celebrity testimonials, and "Rhetorical Questions," teaches an important brand communication lesson about direct marketing. It demonstrates how effective direct-response advertising and a little bit of humor can sell a product to a wide-ranging and varied audience, even in a tough economy.

One report estimated 2007 auto-industry advertising expenditures at $1.7 billion, with GEICO, Allstate, Progressive Corp., and State Farm accounting for about 73 percent of the total. GEICO reportedly spent $561 million on advertising in 2008. In lieu of a sales force, direct advertising does the job.

The Gecko and Caveman have earned their way into the hearts of consumers, winning many awards including the Direct Marketing Association's Echo award. The Caveman joined The Gecko as a favorite brand icon, having been elected to the Madison Avenue Advertising Walk of Fame. According to the GEICO website, "The Caveman, still perturbed with GEICO for its 'So easy, a caveman could do it' slogan, did not attend the award ceremony."

Key Points Summary

1. **How does direct-response marketing work?** Direct marketing always involves a one-on-one relationship with the prospect. It is personal and interactive and uses various media to effect a measurable response. The four main players in direct marketing are the marketers, the agencies, the media that deliver the message, and the consumers. The process involves setting objectives and strategies, targeting, deciding on the offer, developing a message and media strategy, facilitating the response or order, filling the order, and evaluating the direct marketing effort.

2. **What are the primary tools and media available to direct-response programs?** Direct-response media include direct mail, catalogs, telemarketing, direct-response advertising in print and broadcast media, and the Internet and other new forms of media.

3. **How are databases used in direct marketing?** Direct marketing advertising has benefited from the development and maintenance of a database of customer names, addresses, telephone numbers, and demographic and psychographic characteristics. Advertisers use this information to target their campaigns to consumers who, based on demographics, are likely to buy their products.

4. **What are the trends and challenges facing direct-response marketing?** Direct marketing communication (DMC) has been an innovator in the use of integrated strategies, particularly those that link the various channels used in DMC campaigns. A challenge has been to create brand loyalty and long-term brand relationships using DMC tools. Another challenge is global marketing because of the different legal requirements in various countries.

Words of Wisdom: Recommended Reading

Bliss, Jeanne, *I Love You More Than My Dog,* New York: The Penguin Group, 2009.

Key Terms

broadsheets, p. 496

call centers, p. 500

catalog, p. 498

cold call, p. 500

compiled list, p. 507

conversion rates, p. 491

data mining, p. 508

databases, p. 505

direct mail, p. 495

direct-response
  marketing, p. 489

direct-response marketing
  communication, p. 489

fulfillment, p. 494

house list, p. 507

inbound telemarketing, p. 500

infomercial, p. 502

integrated direct marketing
  (IDM), p. 509

lead generation, p. 491

lifetime customer value
  (LCV), p. 511

merging, p. 507

offer, p. 493

one-step offer, p. 493

opt in, p. 505

opt out, p. 505

optimization, p. 492

outbound telemarketing, p. 500

permission marketing, p. 505

predictive dialing, p. 500

prospecting, p. 491

purging, p. 507

recency, frequency, and monetary (RFM), p. 492

relational databases, p. 508

response list, p. 507

spam, p. 504

spoofing, p. 504

telemarketing, p. 499

two-step offer, p. 493

variable data campaigns, p. 495

Review Questions

1. What are the advantages and disadvantages of direct-response marketing communication?

2. What are the six steps in the direct marketing process?

3. What are the five tools or media of direct marketing and how do they differ?

4. What is a database, and how do direct marketers use it?

5. If you are using data mining to develop a prospecting program for a client, what would you be trying to accomplish?

6. What is the objective of data-driven relationship programs?

7. Explain CRM and how it relates to database marketing.

8. What is permission marketing and what strategies can be used to overcome the problems of spam?

9. How is integrated direct marketing used in an IMC program?

10. What is a loyalty program, and how does LCV enter into the planning for such a program?

Discussion Questions

1. Most people hate telemarketing. Say you work for the local campus environmental organization. How could you conduct a campus and community telemarketing effort that would not generate resistance? Apply your ideas to developing a telemarketing program to promote campus fundraising for a good cause, such as a campus Habitat for Humanity project. Your primary targets are students, faculty, and staff.

2. Kali Johnson, a recent college graduate, is interviewing with a large garden product firm that relies on television for its direct-response advertising. "Your portfolio looks very good. I'm sure you can write," the interviewer says, "but let me ask you what is it about our copy that makes it more important than copy written for Ford, Pepsi, or Pampers?" What can she say that will help convince the interviewer she understands the special demands of direct-response writing?

3. One of the smaller, privately owned bookstores on campus is considering a direct-response service to cut down on its severe in-store traffic problems at the beginning of each semester. What ideas do you have for setting up

some type of direct-response program to take the pressure off store traffic?

4. The success of infomercials helps validate direct marketing as a revenue generator. What characteristics of a product must you consider when determining whether to use an infomercial to promote it?

5. *Three-Minute Debate* How does the recent fervor surrounding personal privacy affect direct marketing—

specifically, telemarketing and e-mail advertising? You are designing a direct-marketing campaign for a local record store that employs telemarketing and e-mail advertising, but your client is concerned because of privacy issues. Argue either for or against the use of these tools in this situation. Working with a small team of your classmates, develop a brief presentation to explain your recommendation to the client.

Take-Home Projects

1. *Portfolio Project* Check out a set of three catalogs and their companion websites in a particular category (such as *www.llbean.com, www.eddiebauer.com, www.landsend. com*). In what ways are they similar and different? Pick one of the brands:

   • Identify what direct marketing strategies the company employs. Which do you think are the most successful? Why? What are the least effective?
   • Analyze the brand image as presented in the catalog and online. Develop a proposal to make the brand image more distinctive and yet consistent across the two media formats.

2. *Mini-Case Analysis* Explain how GEICO operates as a direct-to-consumer insurer in the auto insurance market. Why would you think humor would be an effective creative strategy in this situation? You may also remember that we have suggested that being single-minded is a wise strategy. Why, then, does GEICO use different approaches? If you were on the GEICO team and had been asked to submit ideas for the next year's campaign, what would you recommend? Develop and explain an idea that you think would continue the unusual strategy GEICO is using.

Team Project: The BrandRevive Project

For this chapter, develop a proposal for a direct marketing communication component for your brand.

• Use the five-step process as an outline for your DMC plan (set the objectives/strategy, message and media, develop the offer, deliver the message and measure the response, provide

suggestions for fulfillment, and build relationships with customer follow-up).
• Explain how you would use databases in your DMC effort.
• Analyze the privacy issues created by your plan and explain how you would manage customer concerns about privacy.

Hands-On Case

The Century Council

Read the Century Council case in the Appendix before coming to class.

1. What is the chief advantage of direct marketing with this target audience?

2. The Stupid Drink campaign kicks off with a postcard being sent to the home of every new and returning college student announcing The Drinking Institute's discovery of The Stupid Drink. Is that a good idea to leak the discovery before students get to college? Is it a good idea to do this in front of their parents?

Promotions

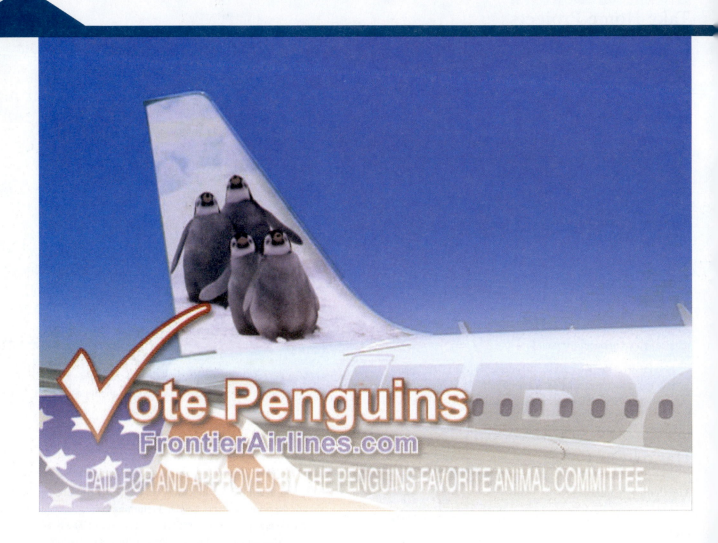

Vote Penguins
FrontierAirlines.com
PAID FOR AND APPROVED BY THE PENGUINS FAVORITE ANIMAL COMMITTEE.

It's a Winner

Promotion:	Company:	Agency:	Award:
"Denver's Favorite Animal"	Frontier Airlines	Grey Worldwide	Gold Effie for sustained success, regional Emmy

CHAPTER KEY POINTS

1. What are the current trends and practices in planning promotions?
2. How are various consumer promotions used?
3. What are the types and purposes of trade promotions?
4. How do multiplatform promotions—sponsorships and events, loyalty programs, and partnership programs—work?
5. How are promotions used strategically in terms of brand building, integration, and effectiveness?

Frontier Campaigns for Favorite Animal Votes and Web Hits

How do you follow up a successful campaign like Frontier Airline's "Flip to Mexico" campaign? (See Chapter 8's opening story.) Frontier handed Shawn Couzens and Gary Ennis, creative directors from Grey Worldwide in New York City, their next challenge: Drive consumers to the website. Airlines prefer passengers to book on the Web rather than via phone with agents because the company saves money, and capturing e-mails builds the airline's database.

Sometimes to reach the marketing and campaign objectives, advertisers need to be willing to take risks to be rewarded. How far could Couzens and Ennis push Frontier?

Couzens explained, "We would never do something 'out there' just to do it. It has to line up with the strategy and reflect who we are. A brand is a lot like a person. It has a distinct personality, a unique identity, and a belief system. And just like a person, if we misrepresent the brand, then people won't trust it. So, whenever we embark on an assignment, we ask, 'Is this consistent with our brand personality? Does this deliver on our brand promise?' And if the idea doesn't fit who Frontier is or what people expect from us, then we dump it."

The Grey team created an online contest that let citizens vote for their favorite animal. Seven of the animals campaigned via the Frontier website in a satire of real political campaigns. Would people pick Grizwald the Bear, Flip the Dolphin, Hector the Otter, Jack (who else?) the Rabbit, Larry the Lynx, the Penguins, or Sal the Cougar?

Couzens described how the contest fit the brand: "Fortunately, our brand personality is easygoing, friendly, and fun. We're 'a whole different animal,' so we can do things that demonstrate how different and unique we are—and that comes through not just in the ads but in the brand experience as a whole."

Fans could go to Frontier's home page to get to the contest, then click on a squeaky door to enter the virtual Campaign Headquarters. Once there, visitors could interact with various aspects of the campaign: They could listen to a debate between trash-talking contestants, order posters of their favorite animal, watch commercials on a TV set, order real press kits with T-shirts, listen to each contestant's platform, join a YouTube group, or participate in an online forum.

Here's a sample of the animals' political platforms: Griz the Bear wants to give voters free all-you-can-eat buffets, back massages, and free flights for every man, woman, and child, none of which, unsurprisingly, are endorsed by Frontier. Jack runs on an environmental platform. He promises lower health care costs, a statewide cap on fuel costs, and reductions in greenhouse emissions. Hector apparently chooses to run on his good looks: He is cute and cuddly and can make squishy sounds with his cheeks. The commercials even let the candidates engage in a bit of political backbiting.

Built-in fun on the site captured visitors' attention with a clock that actually told time, a spinning fan, and a coffee cup that spilled when you clicked on it.

The results? Turn to the *It's a Wrap* section at the end of the chapter to see who won the hearts of Frontier fans.

Sources: Shawn M. Couzens and Garry Ennis interview, February 21, 2007; Shawn Couzens interview, October 23, 2009; www.frontierairlines.portline.com/HQ_restore.html, February 25, 2007; www.thewhitehouseproject.org, February 25, 2007; "Denver's Favorite Animal," Effie Awards Brief of Effectiveness, www.nyama.org.

Frontier's "Denver's Favorite Animal" campaign is an example of an award-winning promotion that captivated viewers and involved them personally in building loyalty to the airline. Sales promotion is about the fun, creative, and exciting ideas that the promotion industry uses to spur action and build strong brand relationships. In this chapter, we will explain the difference between consumer and trade promotions, as well as other programs, such as loyalty programs, tie-ins, and sponsorships, that cross the line between advertising, PR, and promotion. First let's discuss the concept and basic principles of sales promotion.

WHY SALES PROMOTION?

When a marketer increases the value of its product or brand by offering an extra incentive to purchase it, the marketer is creating a **sales promotion,** which is the subject of this chapter. In most cases the objective of sales promotion is to encourage action. Promotions in a more general sense can also help build brand identity and awareness, as the Frontier Airlines case illustrates, but their primary contribution to most marketing communication programs is to drive behavior.

The Promotion Marketing Association (PMA) is the professional organization serving this $2 trillion industry. Founded in 1911, the organization promotes excellence in promotion marketing and showcases such practices in its Reggie Awards program. Although the breadth of the industry has exploded with the new opportunities provided by the Internet, a simple definition identifies the key elements of promotion marketing as follows: "The media and non-media marketing pressure applied for a predetermined, limited period of time at the level of consumer, retailer, or wholesaler in order to stimulate trial, increase consumer demand, or improve product availability."[1]

Let's examine this definition. First, it acknowledges that consumers are an important target for promotions, but so are other stakeholders, such as the company's sales representatives and members of the trade (wholesalers, retailers). Second, the definition recognizes that sales promotion is a set of techniques that prompts members of three target audiences—consumers, sales representatives, and the trade (distributors, retailers, dealers)—to take action, preferably immediate action.

Simply put, sales promotion affects demand by offering an incentive to act, usually in the form of a price reduction, but it also may offer additional amounts of the product, cash, prizes and gifts, premiums, special events, and so on. An example of a promotional incentive was a $1 million offer by Netflix to consumers who could offer ideas for improving its movie recommendation software. Promotions may also just contribute to a fun brand-relationship building experience, as Frontier Airlines' favorite animal contest illustrates.

Principle
Sales promotion is primarily designed to affect demand by motivating people to act.

Why Is Sales Promotion Growing?

Over the years, advertising and sales promotion have been battling for their share of the marketing communication budget, but sales promotion, including both consumer and trade promotions, now accounts for more than half of the budget. Until the 1980s, advertising was the dominant player in the marketing communication arena. But during the 1980s more marketers found themselves driving immediate bottom-line responses through the use of sales promotion.

Accountability   In terms of the need for accountability for marketing communication efforts, most U.S. companies focus on immediate profits, a drive that sales promotion satisfies. Because the benefits of advertising are often more apparent in the long term, companies invest more money in sales promotion when they want quick results. Product managers are under pressure to generate quarterly, or even monthly or weekly, sales increases. Arlene Gerwin, a marketing consultant who consults on promotional planning, explains, "Sales promotions deliver more immediate consumer response and a quicker payback than advertising."[2] Hence the pressure for short-term profits leads to bigger sales promotion budgets.

Another aspect of accountability is result driven. Sales promotions are relatively easy to evaluate in terms of their impact on sales and whether a sales promotion strategy has accomplished its objectives. Because promotions operate in a finite time frame and deliver action, in Gerwin's view, it is relatively easy and quick to evaluate their success because there is usually an immediate response of some kind.

It also is easier to compute a return on investment (ROI) for promotions than for advertising. This process is known as **payout planning** and means that the results derived from a promotion can be estimated and compared with the projected costs of the effort. If the promotion doesn't deliver more than it costs, then it is not a good idea, at least financially. Admittedly there may be other reasons for conducting a promotion, but usually the go/no-go decision is based on the effort's ROI.

For example, Moonfruit, a company that helps small businesses build do-it-yourself websites, gave away 10 MacBook Pros as part of a birthday celebration. To be eligible, participants had to send a creative Tweet, an idea that exploded on Twitter, brought lots of people to the company's website, and generated tons of publicity. If handled through a traditional advertising campaign, the exposure would have cost far more than the price of 10 MacBook Pros.[3] (Check out Moonfruit at *www.moonfruit.com*.)

Media Shifts   Advertisers also cite other economic reasons for the shift. Traditional media costs have escalated to the point where alternative types of media must be considered. As the networks have raised their advertising prices, their share of prime-time television viewers has dropped dramatically. The proliferation of media and competition for audiences' attention also factor in the need for accountability. Advertisers, therefore, are exploring marketing communication forms that cost less and produce immediate, tangible results. Sales promotion can deliver these results.

Global incentive programs are also experiencing explosive growth and much of that relates either to IMC or changes in global media. The international product manager for one promotional company indicates that the number of clients seeking global incentive programs has increased dramatically. Some of the reasons for this growth include the interest of multinational corporations in aligning all units with corporate goals, increasing bottom-line efficiency, and taking advantage of the rise of the Internet.[4]

Marketplace Changes   Other reasons for the move to sales promotion match changes in the marketplace, such as these:

- *Consumer Behavior* Shoppers today are better educated, more selective, and less loyal to brand names than in the past, which means they are more likely to switch brands.
- *Pricing* Consumers have come to expect constant short-term price reductions such as coupons, sales, and price promotions.
- *Market Share* In most industries, the battle is for market share rather than general product growth. Sales promotion encourages people to switch products, increasing market share.
- *Parity Products* Sales promotion is often the most effective strategy for increasing sales of a parity product when the products in the category are largely undifferentiated. When products are similar, promotions become the tie-breaker in the consumer's decision making.

- *The Power of the Retailer* Dominant retailers, such as Safeway, Walmart, Toys "R" Us, and Home Depot, demand a variety of promotional incentives before allowing products into their stores.

Principle
Sales promotion reduces the risk of trying a new product by giving something of added value to motivate action.

From the consumers' perspective, sales promotion reduces the risk associated with a purchase by giving them something of *added value* such as a coupon, rebate, or discounted price. Promotions typically offer the consumer added value, or "more for less," as a Southwest Airlines promotion illustrates. Developed in conjunction with Alamo, the promotion promised those who fly Southwest and rent vehicles from Alamo that they could earn double Rapid Rewards credit toward a free flight—for a limited time, of course.

Sales Promotion Planning

Similar to advertising and other marcom areas, promotions are developed with a plan, sometimes called a creative brief. This summarizes the usual planning decisions, such as SWOTs, brand positioning strategy, promotional objectives, targeting and consumer insights, budget, scheduling, and timing.

An example comes from the launch of Via, Starbucks' instant coffee. To demonstrate that the instant product tastes like its regular brew, the company promoted a "taste challenge" that took place at Starbucks stores on the launch weekend. Customers were able to sample a cup of brewed coffee and a cup of Via to see if they could tell the difference. The event was promoted with television commercials and on social marketing sites.

Promotional Big Ideas   From this document promotional planners develop their ideas—in fact, a Big Idea is just as important for sales promotion as it is for advertising. In many cases, the promotion is part of a bigger integrated marketing communication (IMC) plan, and one of the requirements is that the promotion's Big Idea should support the campaign's creative idea. For example, Frontier's long-running position as a different kind of animal is reflected in a short-term promotional campaign to choose a favorite animal from the spokes-animals on the planes' tails.

The challenge is to come up with exciting, interesting promotional ideas that are involving and capture the attention of the target market—and that includes consumers, as well as trade partners in the industry. One of the wackiest promotional ideas recently used was for the KitKat candy bar. It involves the use of religion, which is certainly novel but also raises some questions about the appropriateness of the idea. Professor Karen Mallia describes the promotion in the *A Principled Practice* feature and asks "Why religion? Why a candy bar?" Her answer: "Shock works—as a combination of norm violation and surprise. Religion is the last taboo. It's one area creatives haven't heavily mined for ideas, because few clients are willing to risk offending people."

As part of an integrated program, sales promotion has different functions than other marcom tools. For example, although advertising is designed to build long-term brand awareness, sales promotion is primarily focused on creating action. Marketing consultant Gerwin explains, "The objective of advertising is quite different from that of sales promotion. Advertising is usually viewed as a longer-term investment. Over time, advertising builds brand equity by establishing a consistent image or feeling for a brand." In contrast, she explains that "sales promotions are more immediate, involving a finite time period. Sales promotions offer the consumer something more tangible."[5]

What Are the Primary Categories of Sales Promotion?

The most common sales promotion strategies target the three audiences of promotions: consumer, trade, and sales force. The first two—customer sales and trade support—have direct implications for advertising and marketing communication and are the focus of this chapter.

The third category, sales force promotions, are also important in building trade support. These include two general sets of promotional activities directed at the firm's salespeople to motivate them to increase their sales levels. The first set of activities includes programs that better prepare salespeople to do their jobs, such as sales manuals, training programs, sales presentations, and supportive materials (training films, slides, videos, and visual aids). The second set of activities deals with promotional efforts or incentives for retails to use as in-store promotions and other programs that motivate salespeople to work harder, such as contests.

A PRINCIPLED PRACTICE

Finding Jesus. In a Candy Bar?

Karen L. Mallia, *Assistant Professor, University of South Carolina*

It was Good Friday, and a man in the Netherlands claimed to see the face of Jesus in his Kit Kat bar. Two of his coworkers even corroborated his sighting. He reported, "I was amazed. I just took a bite and then saw the face of Christ in it."

This wasn't just another Virgin Mary-in-the-grilled-cheese story, but a digital promotion created by Kit Kat's advertising agency, UbachsWisbrun/JWT, Amsterdam. To all the world, it appeared to be a "real" person responding to a website request for religious sightings.

When audiences increasingly avoid traditional media advertising, how do brands get their message across? Viral efforts. Promotions. Books. Candy bars. Anything but conventional "ads."

The Kit Kat social media promotion was involving and engaging—just as campaigns in the 21st century should be. It caused a groundswell in the blogosphere stretching from the Netherlands to Australia. Some saw the Shroud of Turin, while others said it looked more like a troll or Darth Vader. People chimed in for and against religion; several keen-eyed observers contended the image wasn't real, but a Photoshop job. (Quite right.) But practically no one suspected it was a marketing communication effort.

And FYI, the Kit Kat promotion has won several creative awards for its innovative use of media. (Do a Google search for Kit Kat Jesus) to see what the buzz was all about.)

To get people's attention in a life of media overload, advertisers keep pushing the limits farther and farther—in messages, as well as media choices. Cre-

ative people must dig deeper into their cultural knowledge bank for inspiration, and many are finding it in religious symbols, images, and stories.

Using religious symbolism also dovetails with another concurrent trend: the decreasing emphasis on words and increasing reliance on nonverbal communication in advertising. Religious concepts function as mnemonics. Our brains put together a larger "picture" from visual shorthand. In the same way logos and other devices trigger our association with a brand, religious concepts and symbols create a much bigger memory than what the content would at first glance imply. Contemporary media, such as the Internet, are great at delivering messages based on images.

My research suggests that not only is the use of religious imagery on the rise, but the way it's used is increasingly dramatic and controversial. The change in tenor is best illustrated with the use over the years of priests in advertising. In 1975, Xerox Corporation's "Brother Dominic" spot starred a sweet, earnest monk invoking a "miracle" in duplicating 500 illuminated manuscripts. Fast-forward to 1991, when Benetton shocked the world with a priest and nun kissing. In 2005, Stella Artois' "Skating Priests" spot swept award shows with a riveting homage to filmmaker Krzysztof Kieślowski, and surreal, almost sinister humor. It's over before you realize that a group of priests would rather see their fellow priest drown than lose a beer. In 2006, Pirelli tire launched a worldwide campaign with "The Call," a 10-minute Web film starring John Malkovich as a priest called on to exorcise a car, and Naomi Campbell as the devil. The dramatic tone brings a new level of darkness to advertising featuring priests.

Will the religious fervor in advertising continue or prove to be a passing fad? Will it be used in other more creative promotions? Should it be? Keep your eye on the Web—and your tea leaves.

In the rest of this chapter we examine the two primary categories of promotion—consumer promotions, then trade promotions. Another section covers other types of promotions that blur the lines between promotions, advertising, and public relations. Finally, we discuss overarching issues that relate to promotional strategy.

CONSUMER PROMOTIONS

Although trade promotion claims the greatest percent of the promotion budget, we'll start with consumer promotions because these are familiar to most people. Consumer sales promotions are directed at the ultimate user of the good or service. They are intended to provide an incentive so

Principle
Consumer promotions provide an incentive so consumers will look for a particular brand.

that when consumers go into a store they will look for a particular brand. The primary strengths of consumer sales promotions are their variety and flexibility, as well as their accountability.

WHERE YA HEADIN'?

You could be headin' ⊗ for the Winner's Circle

Celebrate the New Billings Brand with some cool new swag!

fill out the entry form below and return to the Gazette for your chanve to WIN!

Billings
MONTANA'S △ TRAILHEAD

Billings Gazette
COMMUNICATIONS
The Source

Dinner for 2 plus 2 night stay at the Crowne Plaza
CROWNE PLAZA BILLINGS
GRAND PRIZE

Name:	Name:
Billing Address:	Shipping Address:
Apt. / Ste. /Rm.	Apt. / Ste. /Rm.
City: State: Zip:	City: State: Zip:

SHOWCASE

The Billings "Trailhead" campaign used weekly drawings with the winners receiving caps, as well as dinner and two nights at the Crowne Plaza Hotel for the grand prize winner.

John Brewer, president and CEO of the Billings Chamber of Commerce/Convention & Visitors Bureau, graduated from the University of West Florida. He was nominated for inclusion in this book by Professor Tom Groth.

What Are the Tools of Consumer Promotions?

A product manager can use and combine many promotion techniques to meet almost any objective. Sales promotion works for all kinds of businesses, including movies as *The Inside Story* you'll read later in the chapter illustrates. Here's a summary of the most common types of consumer promotions.

- *Price Deals* A popular sales promotion technique is a **price deal,** a temporary price reduction or a sale price, or even freebies. *Giveaways* of some books, usually those that are in the public domain, such as Jane Austen's *Pride and Prejudice,* were used by *Amazon.com* to promote its Kindle e-reader.[6] Amazon also sometimes gives away limited numbers of certain new titles to spark interest in a new book. The Billings, Montana, "Trailhead" branding campaign that we discussed in Chapter 7 also used a giveaway to build excitement for the new brand identity.

  Freebies can be a killer if the company doesn't adequately predict the consumer response. That happened to KFC when it introduced its new grilled chicken. In what it thought was a great idea, the KFC promotion team got Oprah to announce a deal for freebie meals. Unfortunately, KFC wasn't prepared for the enormous response and its stores ran out of food, angering millions of customers. Next it tried to make good on its giveaway with downloadable coupons from its website, but because of problems online, many customers gave up on that offer as well. Even with all the bad press, the KFC president found a silver lining: "There's no one in America right now who doesn't know we're selling grilled chicken," he said.[7]

  The four common price deals include:

  1. A *cents-off deal* is a reduction in the normal price charged for a good or service (for example, "was $1,000, now $500," or "50 percent off") announced at the point of sale or through mass or direct advertising.
  2. *Prize-pack deals* provide the consumer with something extra through the package itself—a prize in a cereal box, for instance.
  3. *Bonus packs* contain additional amounts of the product free when consumers purchase the standard size at the regular price. For example, Purina Dog Food may offer 25 percent more dog food in the bag.
  4. *Banded packs* are more units of a product sold at a lower price than if they were bought at the regular single-unit price. Sometimes the products are physically packaged together, such as bar soap and six-packs of soft drinks.

  One result of price deals can be price wars such as when Walmart and *Amazon.com* took turns reducing hardback book prices in late 2009 as Walmart tried to steal Amazon's position as the number one bookseller. Sales of new releases that normally sell for $28 to $29 were offered by *Walmart.com* for $20. Amazon matched that price and Walmart responded with a $9 price. Authors were particularly concerned that the price war would reset the price point for new hardbacks.[8]

- *Refunds and Rebates* A **refund** or **rebate** is a marketer's offer to return a certain amount of money to the consumer who purchases the product. Sometimes the refund is a check for a certain amount of money; at other times it may be a coupon to encourage repeat use.

- *Sampling* Allowing the consumer to try the product or service is called **sampling.** Advertisers can distribute samples to consumers in numerous ways. Sampling tables, particularly for food products, can be set up in stores. Small samples of products can show up with newspapers and on house doorknobs, in doctors' and dentists' offices, and, most commonly, through the mail. An interesting offer by Millstone Coffee involved an empty bag delivered with a newspaper in the newspaper's plastic bag that could be taken to the store and filled with a half-pound Millstone sample of their choice. Advertisers can design ads with coupons for free samples, place samples in special packages, or distribute samples at special in-store displays. Product samples influence consumers more than other types of in-store promotions, according to one survey.

  Sampling is not just an in-store activity. Consider car rentals. A *Washington Post* columnist took automakers to task for selling low-budget, stripped down models to car rental companies. His point was that car rentals are an unrecognized sampling opportunity and if the experience is uncomfortable or the performance is underwhelming, then the car maker has suffered a possibly fatal hit to its brand experience. His point: it would make more sense for an automobile manufacturer to display the best samples of its cars in the rental market, even if that means selling them to rental car companies at a loss.[9]

  Sampling has also become a mainstay of interactive promotions on the Internet. Some companies sample their products on their Web page.[10] Recently, Dove enticed customers with free samples of its new Dove Body Nourishers and Dove Ultimate Clear deodorant; however, most farm out the efforts to online companies that specialize in handling sample offers and fulfillment. Some of these online sampling companies are *freesampleclub.com, startsampling.com, freesamples.com,* and *sampleville.com.* In addition, freebie portals such as *amazingfreebies.com, nojunkfree.com,* and the *freesite.com* have endless offers for gratis goodies.

- *Premiums* A **premium** is a tangible reward for a particular act, usually purchasing a product or visiting the point of purchase. Premiums are a type of incentive that works by adding value to the product. Examples of premiums are the toy in Cracker Jacks, glassware in a box of detergent, and a radio given for taking a real estate tour. Premiums are either free or low in price. The two general types of premiums are direct and mail. Direct premiums award the incentive immediately, at the time of purchase. The four variations of direct premiums are (1) store premiums, given to customers at the retail site; (2) in-pack premiums, inserted in the package at the factory; (3) on-pack premiums, placed on the outside of the package at the factory; and (4) container premiums, in which the package is the premium. Mail premiums require the customer to take some action before receiving the premium. A **self-liquidator** premium usually requires that a payment be mailed in along with some proof of purchase before the customer receives the premium. The payment is sufficient to cover the cost of the premium. Another type of mail premium requires the customer to save coupons or special labels attached to the product that can be redeemed for merchandise.

- *Coupons* The two general types of **coupons** that provide a discount on the price of a product are retailer and manufacturer coupons. Coupons have always been popular but with the recent Great Recession, research found that 40 percent of U.S consumers used coupons, a 10 percent increase from the previous year. The study estimated that shoppers save some $3 billion with coupons.[11]

  Retailer-sponsored coupons can be redeemed only at the specified retail outlet. Manufacturer-sponsored coupons can be redeemed at any outlet distributing the product, such as the McDonald McCafe brochure, which was filled with coupons for the new coffee offerings. They are distributed directly (direct mail, door-to-door), through media (newspaper and magazine ads, free-standing inserts), in or on the package itself, or through the retailer (co-op advertising). Manufacturers pay retailers a fee for handling their coupons. Coupons have moved online with social marketing sites like Groupon that

Cellfire is a company that sends digital coupons. Instead of using e-mail, the coupons are sent via text message and loyalty card. Check out this system at *www.cellfire.com*.

sends coupon e-mails to consumers who have signed up for special deals, such as group discounts for restaurants, car rentals, personal shoppers, and other services.[12]

• *Contests and Sweepstakes* Contest and sweepstakes promotions create excitement by promising "something for nothing" and offering impressive prizes. **Contests** require participants to compete for a prize or prizes based on some sort of skill or ability. **Sweepstakes** require only that participants submit their names to be included in a drawing or other chance selection. In keeping with a society that is in love with cell phones, sweepstakes are now offered via mobile marketing. Redbook and Procter & Gamble's Max Factor brand have both sponsored such promotions. A **game** is a type of sweepstakes. It differs from a one-shot drawing type of sweepstakes because the time frame is longer, so it establishes continuity by requiring customers to return several times to acquire additional pieces (such as bingo-type games) or to improve their chances of winning.

Sweepstakes and contests are effective promotional tools for driving people to marketers' Internet sites. As part of the Coke Zero campaign (see Chapter 7), Crispin Porter + Bogusky created the Department of Fannovation and invited NCAA fans to submit ways to improve the fan experience. Fans downloaded a brief to submit for a chance to win $10,000 and a trip to the basketball finals. The results from Internet sweepstakes, contests, and games can be huge because of the multiplier effect of interaction and social media.

• *Specialties* **Specialty advertising** presents the brand's name on something that is given away in an attempt to remind consumers about the brand. Items include calendars, pens and pencils, T-shirts, mouse pads, tote bags, and water bottles. The ideal specialty item is one that is kept out in the open where other people can see it, such as a coffee mug.

Promotional Media   The types of sales promotions we just listed can be delivered in various media, including print, broadcast, and online. Direct mail has dominated the delivery of special promotions but much of that has moved online. The Internet in particular is useful for distributing coupons, inviting participation in games and sweepstakes, and even in sampling.

Frontier Airlines' favorite animal contest used the Internet effectively to increase Web traffic with the goal of increasing the online purchase of flights. Advertisers can use the Internet for sales promotion programs in a number of ways, including sampling, sweepstakes and contests, price deals, and coupons. The "Bunny" promo for Frontier was delivered to Frontier's EarlyReturns members by e-mail.

Internet promotion is one of the hot areas of sales promotions. Many advertising campaigns include a campaign-dedicated website, such as the "microsite" designed as a tie-in. The Cheetos campaign described in Chapter 6, for example, was supported with an online website, *Orangeunderground.com,* that displayed the work of a social network of practical jokers committing Random Acts of Cheetos—in other words, using Cheetos to turn things orange.

Some sites offer price promotions only to online purchasers. The promotions might be discounted prices, rebates, or free offers such as

This is an example of an e-mail price promotion sent to Frontier's frequent flyers. Even though it's promoting a sale price, it's still faithful to the Frontier image and "different kind of animal" campaign theme.

frequent flyer miles. Incentive programs offered by online marketers FreeRide Media (*www.freeride.com*), MotivationNet (*www.mypoints.com*), and Netcentives (*www.clickrewards .com*) offer discounts to customers who enroll with them before buying from other merchants.

Coupons can be delivered via the Internet. Several sites have been designed for this. Catalina's ValuePage Web site (*www.valupage.com*) allows users to print coupons they can use at 7,000 supermarkets. The coupon is printed with a barcode and is used with the shopper's store card. If a product were to offer coupons this way, the site could link the shopper's Internet information with store card information, which the brand manager could use in determining the effectiveness of the coupon strategy.

Promotional Campaigns   Special promotions are usually approached as a campaign because they involve a variety of media and reach many stakeholders; they also have a limited time frame. Promotional planners are continually looking for new ways to engage consumers. In particular, the Internet has opened up new opportunities, with viral media driving a high level of social interaction that reinforces the involvement dimension of promotions. The KitKat promotion discussed earlier is an example of an innovative use of social media for a promotional idea.

An example of a full-blown promotional campaign is the effort that accompanies the opening of a big budget movie, as described in *The Inside Story* feature on the following page.

How Are Consumer Promotions Used?

Although an action response is the goal of most sales promotions, some programs such as the Frontier Airlines campaign are designed to build awareness first, but always with action as the ultimate goal. Consumers get to choose the animal they like best to represent Frontier, but in the long run the airline wants consumers to book flights online. What better way to get them to the site than generating Web traffic via an entertaining contest?

To demonstrate the strategy behind the use of these promotional tools in a new product launch, let's suppose we are introducing a new corn chip named King Corn. Promotion is particularly useful to launch the corn chip because it has a number of tools designed to encourage trial, but it can also be used later in the brand's life to maintain or increase its share of market and to remind and reward loyal customers. Promotions, in other words, deliver on a number of our Facets of Effects and drive a specific set of objectives.

Awareness   Our first challenge is to create awareness of this brand, which is the real strength of advertising and, you may remember from Chapter 5, the first step in consumer decision making. However, sometimes awareness can be increased when advertising is combined with an appropriate promotion to call attention to the brand name to get people to try the product. Awareness-building promotion ideas for this new corn chip might include colorful point-of-purchase displays, sponsorship of a King Corn team, or a special event that will attract people in the target market.

Trial   Creating awareness will only take the product so far, however. Consumers must also perceive King Corn as offering some clear benefit compared to the competition. Sales promotion does this by arranging for experiences, such as special events where people can try the product or see it demonstrated. Trial is one of the most important objectives of promotion, but it is essential to get the right people, the targeted audience, involved with the product. Sales promotion has other tools that lead to trial, such as sampling. An effective way to get people to try King Corn is to give away free samples at events, in stores, or through direct mail to the home. Sampling is an effective strategy for introducing a new or modified product or for dislodging an entrenched market leader by enticing potential users to try the product. As a general rule of thumb, retailers and manufacturers maintain that sampling can boost sales volume as much as 10 times when used with a product demonstration and 10 to 15 percent thereafter. Sampling is generally most effective when reinforced on the spot with product coupons. Most consumers like sampling because they do not lose money if they do not like the product. To be successful, the product sampled must virtually sell itself with a simple trial experience.

Another way sales promotion can motivate people to try a new product like King Corn is to offer a price deal—you try this product and we will give it to you cheaper than the usual price. These price deals are usually offered through coupons, refunds, rebates, or premiums. Refunds and

THE INSIDE STORY

The Intersection of the Movie and Promotion Industries

Heather Schulz, *University of Texas at Austin*

Today, movies "open wide" across thousands of theaters on the same day, and by Monday of that first weekend a movie is often decided to be a flop or a hit. Because of this relatively new reliance on opening weekend, movie companies spend more every year on their production and promotion budgets. To help pay for these big budget movies, many companies are teaming up with the advertising and promotion industries using cross-promotion, product placement, and licensing techniques.

Avatar is a good example. This science fiction film utilizing the latest 3D stereoscopic filmmaking technology was released in the United States on December 18, 2009. *Avatar* was written and directed by James Cameron, who has had previous blockbuster success with films such as *The Terminator*, *Terminator 2: Judgment Day*, and *Titanic*. The production budget was $237 million, with an additional $150 million spent on a global advertising campaign. It is arguably the most expensive film ever made.

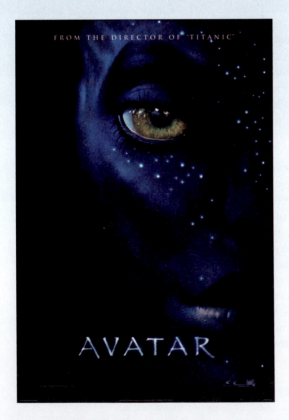

One strategy of the *Avatar* marketing plan was to cross-promote the movie on Coke Zero 12-packs and on McDonald's Happy Meals and Big Macs. Other franchising partners included LG, Panasonic, and Mattel. During the Fox TV network's World Series and NFL games, several 30-second spots were shown during a single commercial break. *Avatar* is already number one for both the all-time worldwide box office list ($2.056 billion) and the all time U.S. box office sales ($606 million).

An example of a movie that turned into a brand franchise is *Jurassic Park*. Released on June 11, 1993, it was directed by Stephen Spielberg who had previous success with films such as *Jaws* and *E.T.: The Extra-Terrestrial*. The budget for *Jurassic Park* was $63 million, and worldwide it eventually grossed more than $900 million.

One interesting aspect of *Jurassic Park*'s promotional strategy was to include the merchandise in the movie itself. All the products placed in John Hammond's gift shop from T-shirts to lunchboxes to stuffed animals were produced for sale in real life. The movie also included the integration of Ford Explorers into the movie's plot as the vehicles that carry the visitors on their tour.

One example of a movie that opened wide, but was a commercial flop is *Dr. Seuss' The Cat in the Hat*. Released on November 21, 2003, it was directed by Bo Welch who had previous success with films such as *Beetlejuice*, *Edward Scissorhands*, and *Men in Black*. The budget for the film was $109 million, and another $100 million was spent to cross-promote the movie with advertisers such as MasterCard, Procter & Gamble, Pepsi/Frito Lay, Burger King, Hershey's, Kellogg's, Kraft, Rayovac, Smucker's/Jif, and even the U.S. Postal Service. However, the film only grossed $139 million worldwide.

Movie	Opening Weekend Box Office
Avatar	$77 million
Jurassic Park	$50 million
Dr. Seuss' The Cat in the Hat	$38 million

As you can see, there is no recipe for success. Movie producers have to decide on a case-by-case basis what promotional tools they want to use far ahead of time and then suffer or reap the consequences when the movie finally comes out for that big opening weekend.

A doctoral student in advertising at the University of Texas, Heather Schulz got her M.S. from the University of Illinois and her B.J. from the University of Nebraska-Lincoln where she was a student of Professor Nancy Mitchell.

rebates are effective because they encourage consumers to purchase a product before a deadline. In addition, refunds stimulate sales without the high cost and waste associated with coupons.

Coupons mainly encourage trial, induce brand switching, and reward repeat business. The main advantage of the manufacturer's coupon, such as those that run in consumer magazines, is that it allows the advertiser to lower prices without relying on cooperation from the retailer to distribute them. Announcements for cents-off deals include the package itself and signs near the product or elsewhere in the store. Advertising for these deals include sales, flyers, newspaper ads, and broadcast ads.

Maintain or Increase Market Share In addition to encouraging trial of a new product, another purpose of price deals is to convince prospective users to switch from an established competing brand, such as Cheetos in the King Corn case. Later, after the King Corn brand is established, a price deal can be used to reward loyal users and encourage their repeat business. Price deals are particularly effective in those situations where price is an important factor in brand choice or if consumers are not brand loyal.

To maintain a brand's presence, increase its market share, or counter competitive actions, marketers use promotional tools such as coupons, premiums, special events, and contests and sweepstakes. The Blue Bunny brochure was used as a Sunday newspaper supplement. It features the entire Indulge line of low-carb and low-fat products, as well as coupons to encourage trial.

The Blue Bunny brochure uses strong appetite appeal in its visuals to emphasize the good taste of its low-carb and low-fat products and coupons to encourage consumers to try the product line.

In addition to serving as a reward for buying a product, premiums can enhance an advertising campaign or a brand's image. Characters like the Campbell's Soup Kids, Tony the Tiger, Cap'n Crunch, and Ronald McDonald are used on premiums, such as soup or cereal bowls, to reinforce the consumer's association of the brand with the character. Cereal manufacturers are among the biggest users of in-pack premiums as reminder devices.

Brand Reminder In addition to new product launches, promotions are also used in the reminder stage. This means that you change advertising copy to remind customers about the positive experience they had with the product and use sales promotion to reinforce their loyalty with coupons, rebates, and other rewards. After the initial purchase you want the customer to remember the brand and repeat the purchase, so specialty items, such as a King Corn snack bowl, can serve as a brand reminder. Specialty advertising serves as a reminder to the consumer to consider the product. Specialties also build relationships, such as items given away as New Year or thank-you gifts (the calendar hanging in the kitchen). Advertisers use specialty items to thank customers for patronage, to reinforce established products or services, and to generate sales leads.

TRADE PROMOTIONS

Consumer awareness and desire mean nothing unless King Corn is available where the consumer thinks it should be. Somehow the trade must be convinced that the product will move off the shelves. Marketers know they must engage the trade in the program if their consumer promotions

SHOWCASE

These kits were sent by Kuni Automotive to the smart car company to win dealerships in three cities. Karl Schroeder, a member of the agency team that came up with this idea, reported that the Kuni executives "loved the kits and even requested more."

Karl Schroeder is a copywriter at Coates Kokes in Portland, Oregon. A graduate of the University of Oregon, he was nominated by Professor Charles Frazer.

Principle

Consumer promotion is of little use if the product isn't available where the consumer can find it.

are to be effective. Consumer promotion has little impact if the product isn't available where the consumer can find it. In such programs, *trade* refers to all the people involved in the distribution channel, including buyers, brokers, distributors, wholesalers, dealers, franchisees, and retailers.

Trade promotions are usually directed at distribution channel members, a practice that is sometimes referred to as **channel marketing.** It can also be used in any kind of situation where one business is promoting its services to another, which also includes personal sales and materials used in sales presentations. An example comes from Kuni Automotive, a small group of auto dealerships that was pitching the smart car company to get dealerships in Portland, Seattle, and Denver. Karl Schroeder, copywriter at the Coates Kokes agency in Portland, explained the Big Idea behind the sales presentation kit his team designed to win the dealerships. Kuni "needed something that would stand out and give them instant name recognition with the people at smart." The idea was to send a set of kits before sending the official paperwork proposal. "They were all shrink wrapped. They came with scissors, glue, colors, points of interest for each city, smart cars, dealership buildings, and even customers ready to buy." Kuni was successful in winning two smart centers in Portland and Denver with this promotion.

Typically companies spend more than half of their total promotion budget on promotions directed at the trade, which is to say that although consumer promotion is highly visible, trade promotion is equally important as a marketing communication strategy. Let's look at the types of trade promotion.

What Are the Types of Trade Promotion?

Trade advertising directed at wholesalers and retailers provides trade members with information about the new product and its selling points. In addition, trade promotion techniques, especially price discounts, point-of-purchase displays, and advertising allowances, motivate retailers to provide shelf space for products and consumer promotions. Resellers, the intermediaries in the distribution channel, employ millions of people, including salespeople in retail and those in wholesaling, who help distribute the products manufacturers make. The King Corn manufacturer in our fictional example will be more encouraged that the product is acceptable if resellers are willing to carry and help promote it. Many promotional devices designed to motivate resellers to engage in certain sales activities are available to the manufacturer. Here are the most common types of trade promotion tools:

• *Retailer (Dealer) Kits* Materials that support retailers' selling efforts or that help representatives make sales calls on prospective retailing customers are often designed as sales kits.

The Kuni Automotive kits are good examples of this type of promotional sales materials. Sales kits contain supporting information, such as detailed product specifications, how-to display information, and ad slicks—print ads that are ready to be sent to the local print media as soon as the retailer or dealer adds identification, location, promotion price, or other information.

Nintendo launched its Wii game with demonstrations at entertainment and video game trade shows.

- *Trade Incentives and Deals* Similar to consumer price deals, a manufacturer may reward a reseller financially for purchase of a certain level of a product or support of a promotion. These promotional efforts can take the form of special displays, extra purchases, superior store locations, or greater local promotion. In return, retailers can receive special allowances, such as discounts, free goods, gifts, or cash from the manufacturer. The most common types of **trade deals** are buying allowances for increasing purchases and advertising allowances, which include deals on cooperative advertising and display allowances, or deals for agreeing to use promotional displays.

- *Contests* As in the case of consumer sales promotion, advertisers can develop contests and sweepstakes to motivate resellers. Contests are far more common than sweepstakes, mainly because resellers find it easy to tie contest prizes to the sale of the sponsor's product. A sales quota is set, for example, and the retailer or person who exceeds the quota by the largest percentage wins the contest.

- *Point-of-Purchase Promotions* According to the Point-of-Purchase Advertising International (POPAI) association, the marketing-at-retail industry includes three forms: manufacturer-designed displays distributed to retailers who their products and create a personality for their stores, and signs and displays used by retailers to cue their brand images and differentiate their stores from those of competitors.[13] These are referred to as **point-of-purchase (PoP) materials.** Although PoP forms vary by industry, they can include special racks, display cartons, banners, signs, price cards, and mechanical product dispensers, among other tools.

- *Trade Shows and Exhibits* The **trade show** is a place where companies within the same industries gather to present and sell their merchandise and to demonstrate their products. Exhibits are the spaces that are designed to showcase the product.

How Is Trade Promotion Used?

The ultimate gauge of a successful trade promotion is whether sales increase. Trade promotions are primarily designed to get the cooperation of people in the distribution channel and to encourage their promotion of the product to consumers. Sales promotion brings resellers to that point of conviction. There are two primary roles for a trade promotion:

1. *Trade Support* To stimulate in-store merchandising or other trade support (for example, feature pricing, superior store location, or shelf space)
2. *Excitement* To create a high level of excitement about the product among those responsible for its sale.

In addition, trade promotion is also used to accomplish other marketing objectives, such as manipulating levels of inventory held by wholesalers and retailers and expanding product distribution to new areas of the country or new classes of trade.

Demand: Push-and-Pull Strategies   As explained in Chapter 3, manufacturers hope to see their trade partners push a product. To understand the role of trade promotion, consider how sales promotion is used in push-and-pull strategies. Consumer and trade promotions interact through

Principle

Consumer and trade promotions interact through complementing push-and-pull strategies.

complementing push-and-pull strategies. If people really want to try King Corn based on what they have heard in advertising and publicity stories, they will ask their local retailers for it, which is called a *pull strategy;* that is, by asking for it, they will pull the product through the distribution channel. Sometimes the advertising and publicity are focused on a sales promotion, which can be used to intensify demand for the product. By conducting a contest in conjunction with sampling, for example, we can increase the pull of a promotion at the same time we get people to try the new product.

However, you might use a *push strategy* to push the product through the channel by convincing (motivating or rewarding) members of the distribution network to carry King Corn. For example, we want grocery stores not only to carry them, but also to allocate good shelf space in the crowded chip aisle. Here are the most common types of incentives and trade deals used with retailers as part of a push strategy:

- *Bonuses* A monetary bonus, also called *push money* or *spiffs,* is paid to a salesperson based on units the salesperson sells over a period of time. For example, an air conditioner manufacturer might give salespeople a $50 bonus for the sale of one model and $75 for a fancier model, within a certain time frame. At the end of the sales period, each salesperson sends in evidence of total sales to the manufacturer and receives a check for the bonus amount.
- *Dealer Loader* These are premiums, comparable to a consumer premium, that a manufacturer gives to a retailer for buying a certain amount of a product. A buying loader rewards retailers for buying the product. Budweiser offered store managers a free trip to the Super Bowl if they sold a certain amount of beer in a specified period of time. Display loaders reward retailers by giving them the display after the promotion ends. For example, Dr. Pepper built a store display for the July 4th holiday that included a gas grill, picnic table, basket, and other items. The store manager was awarded these items after the promotion ended.
- *Buying Allowances* A manufacturer pays a reseller a set amount of money or offers a discount for purchasing a certain amount of the product during a specified time period.
- *Advertising Allowances* The manufacturer pays the wholesaler or retailer a certain amount of money to advertise the manufacturer's product. This allowance can be a flat dollar amount, or it can be a percentage of gross purchases during a specified time period.
- *Co-op Advertising* In a contractual arrangement between the manufacturer and the resellers, the manufacturer agrees to pay a part or all of the retailers' advertising expenses.
- *Display Allowance* A direct payment of cash or goods is given to the retailer if the retailer agrees to set up the point-of-sale display.

Attention   Some trade promotions are designed to get the attention of both trade members and their customers. PoP displays, a promotional tool we mentioned earlier, are designed to get the attention of shoppers when they are in the store and to stimulate impulse purchases. They are used by retailers, but provided by manufacturers. As we have moved to a self-service retail environment in which fewer and fewer customers expect help from sales clerks, the importance of PoP materials continues to increase. POPAI has found that the PoP forms that have the greatest impact on sales are displays that tie in with entertainment, sports, or charities.

In the *Practical Tips* feature, marketing consultant Arlene Gerwin explains how best to plan effective PoP promotions.

In addition to getting attention in crowded aisles and promoting impulse purchases, marketers are designing PoP efforts to complement other promotional campaigns. As part of getting attention, retailers appreciate PoP ideas that build store ambience. Club Med designed a floor display for travel agents that featured a beach chair with a surfboard on one side and a pair of skis on the other to show that Club Med has both snow and sun destinations. Advertisers must design PoP displays that appeal to both end users and the trade. Retailers will use a PoP only if they are convinced that it will generate greater sales.

Motivation   Most trade promotions are designed to, in some way, motivate trade members to cooperate with the manufacturer's promotion. Incentives such as contests and trade deals are used. If conducted properly with a highly motivating incentive or prize, contests can spur short-term sales and improve the relationship between the manufacturer and the reseller. They encourage a higher quantity of purchases and create enthusiasm among trade members who are involved with

PRACTICAL TIPS

Planning Point-of-Purchase Promotions

Arlene Gerwin, *Marketing Consultant and President, Bolder Insights*

Ever since retail establishments came into existence, there has been some form of PoP promotion—carefully hand-painted signs announcing a sale can be seen in photos of 19th-century country general store windows. Inside the store, special displays of merchandise sometimes promoted seasonal prices or special deals.

Point-of-purchase promotions usually fall under the definition of marketing tactics, however objectives, strategies, and tactics are as important in planning PoP promotions as they are in the development of the overall marketing plan.

- *SMART Plans* Effective PoP promotions support the marketing plan and deliver on its strategies by being Strategic, Measurable, Actionable, Realistic, and Timely—that is, SMART.
- *Objectives* The most successful PoP promotions are developed against a clear set of objectives, such as countering competitive actions. A PoP campaign should be long range and strategic.
- *Big Idea* The best PoP promotions develop from campaignable, ownable "Big Ideas" that extend over a minimum of one year or more and should be in line with the overall marketing objectives.
- *Brand Fit* When the promotion becomes intricately intertwined with the brand or service, it enhances the brand image.

- *Bridge* PoP displays serve as a bridge linking trade and consumer promotions. The most powerful offers are delivered directly to consumers in the retail environment but they need retailer support to be strategically placed. Trade and consumer promotions should work in tandem often with a push–pull strategy—trade for push and consumer for pull.
- *Timing* PoP promotions should consider the consumer product-use cycle and not artificially inflate sales volume at the expense of short-term sales spikes.
- *Co-Promotions* Two brands that share PoP materials and link their products in a single promotion can make the shoppers' task easier if they have similar target audiences and consumer usage patterns.
- *Realistic Tactics* The specific tools in a PoP promotional plan should be affordable, on strategy, and produced on time.
- *Detailed Budgeting* Avoid Murphy's Promotions Law: designs that look great on paper often present unanticipated production complications, not to mention the unpredictable complications of natural disasters and ill-timed strikes. Whenever possible, test a prototype of the display in stores.
- *ROI* Because PoP promotions are planned across a finite time period and their costs can be predicted, planners can evaluate the promotion's ROI and estimate the payback.
- *Flexibility* Use contingency planning and have an arsenal of tactics waiting in the wings in case of unplanned complications.

---

the promotion. Trade incentive programs are used to stimulate frequency and quantity of purchase and encourage cooperation with a promotion.

Information   Trade shows display products and provide an opportunity to sample and demonstrate products, particularly for trade buyers, the people who buy for stores. The food industry has thousands of trade shows for various product categories, and the manufacturer of King Corn would want to sponsor an exhibit featuring the new corn chip at the appropriate food shows. Trade shows permit companies to gather information about their competition. In an environment where all the companies are attempting to give a clear picture of their products to potential customers, competitors can easily compare quality, features, prices, and technology.

MULTIPLATFORM PROMOTIONS

So far we have looked at consumer sales promotions and trade promotions. But marketers have more promotion techniques at their disposal. In this section, we focus on sponsorships, event marketing, loyalty programs, and co-marketing or partnership promotions. Many of these promotion techniques, such as sponsorships and event marketing, cross over to other areas of marketing and blur the lines between promotions, advertising, and public relations.

Sponsorships and Event Marketing

Sponsorships occur when companies support an event, say, a sporting event, concert, or charity, either financially or by donating supplies and services. **Event marketing** means building a product's marketing program around a sponsored event, such as the Olympics or a golf tournament. Both are used because of the excitement they generate for both the consumer and trade audiences.

Sponsorships and event marketing include sports sponsorships (events, athletes, teams); entertainment tours and attractions; festivals, fairs, and other annual events; cause marketing (associating with an event that supports a social cause); and support for the arts (orchestras, museums, etc.). Cause marketing sponsorship is a growth area with spending at around $1.6 billion in 2009 and it has been found by a Chicago research firm to be growing faster than sports and arts sponsorships.[14]

An innovative example of street-based promotional events comes from New York City, which has closed parts of Broadway to create pedestrian plazas. In addition to civic activities, companies can rent these spaces for commercial events such as when the Bravo Network's *Top Chef* cooking competition held a promotion there, or when Glidden Paint set up large paint can product literature displays and a team of young men and women in bright-colored T-shirts handed out paint chips and advice on colors and decorating.[15]

Sponsorships typically cost a lot of money. Sponsors for major golf tournaments, for example, are expected to invest between $6 million and $8 million. The *A Matter of Practice* box discusses the explosion of sports-related promotions.

Companies undertake sponsorships to build brand associations and increase the perceived value of the brand in the consumer's mind. The important thing is that the event must project the right image for the brand. That's particularly important in troubled economic times when companies with budget problems find it hard to justify spending money on glitzy events. Companies that use sponsorships focus their efforts on supporting causes and events that matter most to employees and customers. Unilever signed on as sponsor for the *Today Show's* food and recipe website, called Cooking School. The idea is to feature Unilever's brands, such as Bertolli, Country Crock, and Ragu. Although the most common sponsorships are around events, particularly sporting events, brands can also sponsor product-related websites that are particularly effective at creating sales or recruiting people. The *2BLIKEu.com* network is a consumer products social network that lets companies sponsor product pages.

Hundreds of companies sponsor NASCAR cars both to reach the sport's expanding fan base and to link their brand to a winning car and driver. Sponsors shell out in excess of $650 million to get NASCAR's top 35 cars in the Nextel Cup Series to put their logos on the car. The investment pays. Marketing analysts estimate that Dale Earnhardt, Jr., earns the equivalent of $150 million in televised exposure time for his sponsor Budweiser, quite a bargain considering Anheuser-Busch, and other sponsors, spend much less on the sponsorships.

Just think about sponsorships associated with football bowl games and other sporting events. The first bowl to have a sponsor, the Sunkist Fiesta Bowl, led the way in 1986, followed by the Tostitos Fiesta Bowl, the Outback Bowl, the Meinecke Car Care Bowl, and others. A twist on the sports sponsorship concept comes from convenience store chain 7-Eleven, which made a deal with the Chicago White Sox that their games would start at 7:11. Of course, when the club lost the 7-Eleven sponsorship, it also got a new start time—7:10.

The importance of sponsorships is growing worldwide. Mengniu Milk, a Mongolian milk company, raised its profile by backing the NBA in China. Beyond exposure, these events give corporations the opportunity to build their image and reputation by associating with an activity that audiences enjoy.[16]

Event Marketing   The term *event marketing* describes the practice of linking a brand to an event, such as the Jose Cuervo beach volleyball tournament. Marketers use related promotional events, such as a tour or the appearance of the product or its spokesperson at a mall or sporting event, to gain the attention and participation of people in the target audience who attend the event. The event showcases the brand, often with sampling, coupons, other incentives, and attention-getting stunts. To be successful, the event must match the brand to the target market's lifestyle.

Advertising through Sports

John Sweeney, *Professor, Head of Advertising and Director of Sports Communication Program, University of North Carolina*

There has been remarkable growth in the relationship between sports and advertising. The *Sports Business Journal* estimates that advertising in sports totaled more than $27 billion in 2001. The entire sports industry approaches $200 billion and includes advertising, tickets, licensing, equipment, media, sponsorships, and travel. The games we watch and play have become very big business.

The first reason for the enormous growth in sports advertising comes from the fracturing of media in general. We have gone from a nation of three national television networks to hundreds of cable channels, DVDs, VODs, Webcasts—and that's just one medium. There is so much clutter in the media marketplace that many advertisers choose to align themselves with leading sports leagues and events. This sponsorship locates a product in a place where millions of people feel deep loyalty and passion. And that location can be more powerful—in creating a relationship—than scattering messages across random programs.

The second reason for the rise of sports is the way both leagues and sponsors have organized to make sports an effective tool for marketing. Leagues now operate as singular brands in the marketplace. The NFL organizes itself to sell exclusive national media rights and sponsorships and distribute licensed merchandise. This seems simple enough until you realize that it requires 32 fiercely competitive teams to move in a disciplined manner for the good of marketing. It is politically demanding but the rewards are breathtaking. The National Football League makes $2 billion a year in media rights and sells more than $3 billion in licensed goods.

Sponsors have also organized to leverage their association with major leagues and events. In a fractured media world, companies present their sponsorship across dozens of media platforms. Visa uses its Olympic sponsorship throughout the world in television, print, interactive, outdoor, and numerous other ways involving the more than 19,000 banks that work under the card name. The Olympics is a perfect event for a global strategy.

Even seemingly small sports events can hold tremendous value for advertisers. Volvo sponsors the Volvo Ocean race, a grueling sailing competition where boats race for over nine months covering 37,000 miles. It is called by many the "Everest of Sailing." The race claims extraordinary coverage with more than 13,000 print articles and 30,000 online articles published in 101 countries. The event reaches over a billion listeners on radio and 1.3 billion television viewers from 46 countries. There were more than 89 million visitors to the website with a million fans visiting the site more than 100 times during the 2008–09 race. An estimated 500,000 people came to each port to see the boats. It is clear that there is a lot more to running a sponsorship than placing an ad.

The new world of sports marketing continues to grow in both popularity and cost. And—as our sports become a standard strategy for advertisers—they face the same demands for accountability as other marketing methods. The modern sports sponsorship must prove its effectiveness just like the traditional print campaign or television commercial. In that way, it has joined the big time of marketing with both enormous money and equal pressure to succeed.

Nintendo and Target paired up to set up Wii exercise kiosks that offered Target customers an opportunity to sample the new Wii Fit Plus Experience game. The kiosks were placed in front of stores and in parking lots for weekends during the last half of January 2010 creating a *sampling event* at a time when people are falling off their New Year's resolutions and looking for other fitness ideas.

Events can also be used to build goodwill as a holiday promotion by Yahoo! demonstrated. The online firm sent employees to airports to pay for airline customers' baggage fees. The stunt was described as "one small act of kindness," but it reinforced Yahoo's brand promise: "Yahoo makes your life easier."

Business-to-business promotions also use events to reach trade audiences, which can include the sales staff, distributors, retailers, and franchisees. These stakeholders are invited to participate in the event as a reward for their support.

The granddaddy of all events is the Super Bowl, which is also an Ad Bowl as there sometimes is as much interest in the advertising as in the game. The ads are the most expensive on television; prices can top $3 million for a 30-second commercial—and that's just the cost of the time. Don't forget there is a significant budget tied up in the production of the commercials because they have to be highly professional in order to justify the costs. The reason these costs make sense is because they also reach huge audience. The 2010 game, which featured the New Orleans Saints winning their first Super Bowl at the expense of the favored Indianapolis Colts, broke all audience records for viewership to become the most watched program in history.

It's not just the commercials, however, that get the attention of marketers. The TV spots are also the opportunity for wide-ranging promotional campaigns that involve publicity, PoP displays, video clips, websites and social media, search-engine ads, and relationship programs with important partners, such as retailers and shareholders. YouTube, for example, gets involved by sponsoring a Super Bowl Ad Blitz channel where viewers can vote for their favorite spots. Viewers are known to rewatch spots online on YouTube, AOL, Yahoo!, and other sites. They also pass along favorite commercials to friends and family.

Read about what research shows is a good Super Bowl commercial in the *A Matter of Principle* box. Check out Super Bowl commercials on *www.superbowl-ads.com* and *www.youtube.com/superbowl*. MSNBC has collected the 10 best of them at *www.msnbc.msn.com/id/16691199* and the 10 worst at *www.msnbc.msn.com/id/16790823*.

Ambush marketing is the term given to promotional stunts used at events, such as the Olympics and the soccer and rugby World Cups, by companies that are not official sponsors. Ambush marketing typically occurs when one brand is trying to undermine the presence of a competitor that is sponsoring an event. If it can create enough confusion, it can reduce the return on the official sponsor's investment at the same time it can pick up additional visibility through pub-

A MATTER OF PRINCIPLE

Who'll Win the Next Super Bowl Ad Championship? It Might Be You.

Bonnie Drewniany, *Associate Professor, University of South Carolina*

Doritos has been scoring touchdowns with consumer-generated Super Bowl ads since 2007. A commercial created by a 22-year-old for less than $13 was the fourth most popular spot in the 2007 *USA Today* Ad Meter. The commercial, which shows a dorky guy trying to impress a woman while he's driving and munching on Doritos, beat out ads that cost upwards of $1 million to produce.

In 2008, the chipmaker invited amateur musicians to submit original songs for a video that aired during the big game. While that spot fumbled in the Ad Meter, a consumer-generated commercial that was created for the previous year scored much better. The fourth most popular spot of 2008 featured a man dressed as a giant mouse with an obsession for Doritos Nacho Cheese chips.

Doritos upped the ante in 2009, with a $1 million prize if the consumer-generated spot won the Ad Meter. It seemed like an impossible challenge, since Anheuser-Busch had won the advertising championship every year since 1999. But two "nobodies from nowhere" did just that. Two unemployed brothers from Indiana won the

million-dollar prize for creating the top-rated commercial. The ad, which cost less than $2,000 to produce, features a man trying to predict if he will get free Doritos chips. He gets the answer he wants by throwing a snow globe at the vending machine.

To make the 2010 competition even more enticing, Doritos offered a total prize giveaway of $5 million if the consumer-generated ads swept all top-three rankings. As it turns out, only one spot made it to the top three. "Underdog," which shows a dog training his master with an anti-bark collar, took the number two spot and earned its creator $600,000.

Doritos scored numerous other touchdowns in 2010. "House Rules," which features a little boy telling his mom's boyfriend to "keep your hands off my mama, and keep your hands off my Doritos," generated the most Tweets, was the most popular ad on the Web, and the most replayed ad on TiVo. And the Nielsen Company reports that the Doritos-clad Samurai spot was seen by an estimated 116.2 million viewers, making it the most watched commercial of all time.

So what's the lesson in all this for advertising agencies and aspiring creatives? Engage consumers with your brand. Listen to what they like. And make your brand central to your message.

licity. At the 2010 World Cup, 36 Dutch women were kicked out of their country's soccer game against Denmark. Why? They were accused of wearing orange mini-dresses to promote an unlicensed beer by Dutch brewery Bavaria at the World Cup event. American firm Anheuser-Busch, maker of Budweiser beer, was one of the official sponsors of the World Cup; Bavaria was not. FIFA, organizer of the event, said ambush marketing was not permitted. This was not the first time Bavaria was accused of being involved in Ambush marketing. In a 2006 World Cup match, Dutch fans were forced to take off the orange lederhosen given to them by Bavaria. The idea of fans removing their pants in itself was potentially amusing, and the ambush tactic detracted from the official sponsor Anheuser-Busch.

To help promote the opening of the movie *Spider-Man*, inflatables like this one were placed along buildings in major cities throughout the world.

Other Promotional Support Advertisers use blimps, balloons, and inflatables—even skywriting planes—to capture attention and create an aura of excitement at events. Everybody has probably heard of the Goodyear blimp, but other companies sponsor dirigibles as well. MetLife, which uses characters from the popular Peanuts comic strip in its advertising, has two blimps, Snoopy I and Snoopy II, that connect with the corporate campaign to provide brand reminder messages. Inflatables, giant models of products, characters, and packages, are used at all kinds of events, including grand openings, sporting events, parades, trade shows, beaches, malls, and other places where they can make an impression for a new product rollout. A giant inflatable, such as Spider-Man on a building, demands attention and provides an entertaining and highly memorable product presentation. Its effectiveness comes from its huge size and three-dimensional shape.

Loyalty Programs

Another type of program that crosses the line between advertising and promotion is frequency, or loyalty, programs. A **loyalty program,** also called a **continuity** or **frequency** program (such as airline frequent flyer programs), is a promotion to increase customer retention. Marketers typically design loyalty programs to keep and reward customers for their continued patronage, which is why they are called *continuity programs*. Typically, the higher the purchase level, the greater the benefits.

Today loyalty programs are synonymous with the word *frequent*. The frequent flyer club, first created by United and American Airlines in 1981, is the model for a modern continuity program. These programs offer a variety of rewards, including seat upgrades, free tickets, and premiums based on the number of frequent flyer miles accumulated. Although the frequent flyer programs were originally established to create customer loyalty, they have turned into a rewards program. For example, people can earn miles through credit card purchases. Continuity programs work in competitive markets in which the consumer has difficulty perceiving real differences between brands. TGI Friday's, for example, has used a "Frequent Fridays" program with several million members. The key to creating a successful loyalty program is offering memorable incentives that consumers want.

Marketers like membership programs because they also generate information for customer databases. The enrollment application at TGI Friday's, for example, captures name, address, telephone number, birth date, and average visit frequency. The database can also record the restaurant locations, date, time, purchase amount, and items ordered on each visit. Marketers can then use this information to more specifically target customers with promotions and advertising materials.

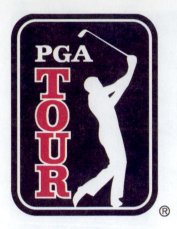

The PGA licenses the use of its logo to other advertisers who want to associate themselves with the PGA Tour event and pros.

Partnership Programs

Another promotion tool that crosses the lines is the partnership program. **Co-marketing** involves manufacturers developing marketing communication programs with their main retail accounts, instead of for them. If done right, these partnerships strengthen relationships between manufacturers and retailers. Co-marketing programs are usually based on the lifestyles and purchasing habits of consumers who live in the area of a particular retailer. The partnership means that the advertising and sales promotions build equity for both the manufacturer and the retailer. For example, Procter & Gamble and Walmart might develop a spring cleaning promotion directed at Walmart shoppers that features P&G cleaning products sold at reduced prices or with premium incentives.

An interesting experience with an electronic-coupon partnership between Kroger and P&G ended after a tug-of-war about the click-through of customers to each others' website. P&G got a lot of clicks, more so than did Kroger. Kroger, of course, was unhappy when its viewers would move to the *P&eSaver.com* site rather than staying with *Kroger.com*.[17] So who is the dominant player in this distribution channel—the manufacturer or the retailer? Kroger finally decided it didn't need to compete with P&G via a coupon website.

Co-Branding   When two companies come together to offer a product, the effort is called **co-branding.** An example of co-branding is when American Airlines puts its logo on a Citibank Visa card and awards AAdvantage points to Citibank Visa card users. Both companies are equally present in the product's design and promotion, and both get to build on the other company's brand equity.

Licensing   With **licensing,** legally protected brand identity items, such as logos, symbols, and brand characters, must be licensed—that is, a legal contract gives another company the right to use the brand identity element. In brand licensing, a company with an established brand "rents" that brand to other companies, allowing them to use its logo on their products and in their advertising and promotional events. Fashion marketers such as Gucci, Yves St. Laurent, and Pierre Cardin have licensed their brand names and logos for use on everything from fashion accessories to sunglasses, ties, linens, and luggage, and they do this because it makes them money and extends their brand visibility. The PGA Tour is a golf brand that has become recognizable through an elaborate, integrated marketing campaign. Charles Schwab, the financial investment house, has used the PGA Tour logo as a part of its advertising. This lets the company associate its brand with a golf event that has a lot of interest and positive associations for the target audiences.

Tie-Ins and Cross Promotions   Another type of cooperative marketing program is a **tie-in** or **cross promotion,** which is an effective strategy for marketers using associations between complementary brands to make one plus one equal three. For example, Doritos may develop a tie-in promotion with Pace salsa in which bottles of salsa are displayed next to the Doritos section in the chip aisle (and vice versa). The intent is to spur impulse sales. Ads are also designed to tie the two products together, and the sponsoring companies share the cost of the advertising.

But cross promotions are not only used by packaged goods. Billings, Montana, for example used a promotion in its "Trailhead" rebranding campaign with Pepsi-Cola. A half a million special Pepsi cans with the campaign logo and slogan offered $5.00 off a the "Trailhead" cap when visitors

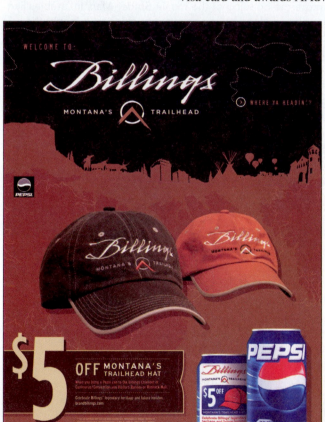

SHOWCASE

As another element in the Billings, Montana, rebranding campaign that we discussed earlier, a cross-promotion enlisted Pepsi-Cola to sponsor special cans with a premium offer on a "Trailhead" cap.

These promotional materials were provided by John Brewer, a graduate of the University of West Florida who was nominated by Professor Tom Groth.

brought the can to the Chamber of Commerce. The promotion also was supported with a PoP poster in stores where Pepsi was sold.

The biggest cross promotions are arranged around movies and other entertainment events. The Aflac duck became a passenger in a commercial for the Pixar movie *Up* who is shown hitching a ride on the balloon-borne house. The voice-over on the Pixar-created commercial explained that Aflac "can help keep your dreams afloat," which reflected Aflac's position as a friend who provides support in a time of need.[18]

Some products tie in with worthy causes. A number of companies support breast cancer awareness and research, including KitchenAid, Yoplait, and Sun Chips. Pink products total a big percentage of the Komen Foundation's $200 million in annual revenue for breast cancer education and research. In the long run, sponsors and their charities mutually benefit.

Tie-ins and cross promotions succeed because brands can leverage similar strengths to achieve a bigger impact in the marketplace. Typically, marketers align themselves with partners that provide numerous complementary elements, including common target audiences, purchase cycle patterns, distribution channels, retailer penetration, and demographics to drive their products and promotions through retail channels and into the minds of consumers.

Should beer manufacturers be allowed to "borrow" school colors in local marketing of their products? That was the question when Bud Light's "fan cans" hit the stores in limited markets during college football season. What do you think? If you were brand manager for Bud Light and your promotion manager presented this idea, how would you decide what to do?

An interesting, although questionable, promotion was Bud Light's use of "Fan Cans" in college colors. It raised questions about licensing and rogue "tie-in" strategies that aren't sanctioned by the schools. In the fall of 2009, Anheuser-Busch had a great idea to tie in with the start of college football season by issuing Bud Light in cans with collegiate colors, some 27 different color combinations to be exact. "Show your true colors with Bud Light" the promotional materials announced. Retailers reported that Bud Light's "Fan Can" promotion seemed to be a hit among football fans in those cities where wholesalers choose to participate.[19]

Several problems surfaced with this promotion. Some universities complained that the colored cans infringed on the schools' trademark licensing. Anheuser-Busch agreed not to offer the promotion in areas where the schools protested. Others complained that it promoted drinking among students, many of whom were underage. A Federal Trade Commission senior attorney, Janet Evans, followed up on that complaint expressing "grave concern" about its impact on underage drinking.

The company responded that it takes the problem of underage drinking very seriously. Anheuser-Busch's vice president of corporate social responsibility explained that these cans were only being made available in communities where purchasers must be age 21 or older to drink. Anheuser-Busch stood by its rights to sell Bud Light using colors associated with universities—and to sell these cans to college fans. Furthermore, there are lots of fans who are not underage and think the game-day promotion is cool.

PROMOTION STRATEGY

As we explained in Chapter 2, promotions are just one element of the marketing communication mix available to marketers. Here we discuss the strategy behind the use of promotions, as well as how advertising and promotions complement each other, particularly in building brands.

Promotion Objectives

Our earlier discussion of the use of promotion identified a number of reasons for using promotions, and these can easily be translated into objectives. Many of the reasons focused on the use of promotions in a new product launch and how that can deliver trial. Promotions can offer consumers an immediate inducement to try or buy a product, often simply by making the product more valuable. Sales promotions can make consumers who know nothing about the brand develop awareness and trial and persuade them to buy the product again once they've tried it. It can push the product through the distribution channel by generating positive brand experiences among resellers and buyers in many places along the channel and purchase continuum.

In addition to helping to introduce a new product and create brand awareness, promotions can build a brand over time by reinforcing advertising images and messages. Promotions can create an affinity between brands and buyers and provide new channels for reaching audience segments. They can create brand involvement and positive experiences that people associate with the brands.

Promotions are not effective in achieving all marketing objectives. For example, promotions alone cannot create an image for a brand. They cannot do much to change negative attitudes toward a product, overcome product problems, or reposition a brand. Brand building, however, is an interesting challenge to promotion, so let's look at it in more depth.

The Issue of Brand Building   For years a heated debate has focused on sales promotion and brand building. Advertisers claim the strength of advertising is creating and maintaining brand image, and sales promotion's price deals actually negate all their hard work by diverting the emphasis from the brand to the price. The result, sales promotion critics complain, is a brand-insensitive consumer. Consider McDonald's, which has long based its image on everyday value, one of the four pillars of McDonald's marketing mantra: quality, service, cleanliness, and value (QSC&V). Advertisers contend that price promotions like a 99-cent Big Mac damage more than the company's bottom line because the price promotion undercuts the value pillar. In other words, if value is central to McDonald's pricing, then it wouldn't need to offer special sale prices. On the other hand, in difficult economic times, the special-price strategy may also convey the message that companies are sensitive to customers' needs and adjusting its prices in order to be supportive.

Procter & Gamble's division manager of advertising and sales promotion explains it this way: "Too many marketers no longer adhere to the fundamental premise of brand building, which is that [brand] franchises aren't built by cutting price but rather by offering superior quality at a reasonable price and clearly communicating that value to consumers." The price-cutting promotions began in the 1970s fostering a buy-only-on-sale orientation that some branding experts believe has caused long-term brand building to suffer. Critics point to a general decline in consumer brand loyalty as just one negative result of price-based promotions.

The problem is that brand building is a long and time-consuming process of establishing the brand's core values. Promotion, whether a sale price, premium, coupon, or some other incentive, is inherently short term, so the promotion can undermine the brand's established values if not handled carefully. Analyst Doug Brookes says that even in economic downturns promotion strategies can be designed to balance both long-term brand building and short-term price promotion with the help of predictive analytic techniques that optimize ROI.[20]

Sales promotion experts argue that their practices can help to build brand image. They refer to many cereal brands, rental car companies, airlines, and hotels that have used a variety of well-planned sales promotion strategies (like loyalty programs, for example) to enhance their brand images. An example comes from a classic promotional ad for Eagle Shirtmakers. Second, they acknowledge that continuous promotion—particularly continuous price promotion—does not work well with brand building, except for discount marketers, whose image is built on the notion of sale prices, although even Walmart is rethinking its "always low prices" positioning strategy.

According to one industry expert, the solution is to make advertising more accountable and promotion more brand focused. In other words, the advertising and promotion need to work more closely together and, in particular, short-term campaigns shouldn't be at odds with one another. More integration is needed when planning marketing communication programs.

Promotion Integration

Advertising and promotion both contribute to the effectiveness of a marketing communication plan, primarily because they do different things and have different objectives. In an effective plan,

[ADVERTISEMENT]®

[OVER]

[cont. from preceding page]

SEND FOR YOUR FREE EAGLE SHIRTKERCHIEF (SHIRTKIN?) (NAPCHIEF?)

AS far as we know this is a brand new invention. Perhaps you will be able to figure out how to realize its full potential. ★ It all started when we tried to devise something to send you—short of an actual shirt—to illustrate a few of the fine points of fine shirt making. A sample to take with you when you go shirt shopping. ★ So first we hemmed a piece of fine shirting; *20 stitches to the inch*, just like in our shirts. At this point you could still call it a handkerchief. ★ But it did seem a shame not to show one of our threadchecked buttonholes, so we did. It makes a pretty good shirt protector: just whip it out of your breast pocket and button it on the second from the top to avoid gravy spots. Good. And tuck your tie in behind it. ★ But then somebody in Pockets said, "Look, if you let us sew a pocket on it, it will show how we make the pattern match right across, no matter what." ★ So if anyone knows what you can use a pocket in a handkerchief/napkin for we will be glad to hear. We will give a half-dozen shirts for the best answer. Make it a dozen.

Eagle Shirtmakers, Quakertown, Pa.
Gentlemen :
Please send me whatever it is. (Signed)_____
Address_____City_____State_____

CLASSIC

San Francisco ad man Howard Gossage was known for his sense of humor and tongue-in-the-cheek promotional ideas. This ad for Eagle Shirtmakers featured what you might call a premium—a handkerchief made from the shirt fabric, which also made it a sample. The wry copy is in classic Gossage ad writing style.

---

the two work together, along with other marketing communication tools, to accomplish the overall marketing communication objectives.

The major differences between advertising and sales promotion concern their methods of appeal and the value they add to the sale of the product or service. Advertising is primarily used to create a brand image and high levels of brand awareness over time; promotions are primarily used to create immediate action. To accomplish this immediate goal, sales promotion may rely heavily on rational appeals, such as price deals. In contrast, advertising often relies on emotional appeals to promote the product's image. In other words, advertising tends to add intangible value—brand personality and image—to the good or service. Promotions add tangible value to the good or service and contribute greatly to the profitability of the brand.

Here is a summary of the differences between these two marketing tools in terms of their primary orientations:

Advertising	Sales Promotion
• Creates a brand image over time.	• Creates immediate action.
• Relies on emotional appeals.	• Added value strategies rely on rational appeals; impulse appeals use emotion.
• Adds intangible value to a product or service through image.	• Adds tangible value to product or service.
• Contributes moderately to short-term profitability.	• Contributes greatly to short-term profitability.

Some objectives that advertising and promotion share include increasing the number of customers and increasing the use of the product by current customers. Both objectives attempt to change audience perceptions about the product or service, and both attempt to make people do something. Of course, advertisers accomplish these tasks in different ways. In most cases, advertising is needed to support promotions. Price deals, for example, are advertised as a way to build traffic in a store. Contests, sweepstakes, and special events won't work if no one knows about them.

Similar to direct-response and other marcom tools that we discuss in this book, promotions are strategically designed to work within a mix of brand messages and experiences to build brand strength and presence. Marketing consultant Gerwin explains, "When all the marketing tasks are driven by a common strategy and shared objectives, the company communicates with the consumer in a single voice with the consistent creative approach. For publicly held companies, this ultimately translates into building shareholder value and increasing the stock price."[21]

An example of a multiplatform promotion that demonstrates how a variety of media and tools can work together was the Voyeur Project for HBO that won a Grand Prix at the Cannes Film Festival. The idea for the promotional campaign was to project a massive film on the wall of a building in New York showing the illusion of looking inside eight fictional apartments. Each apartment and its inhabitants depicted a different story, which reinforced HBO's position as "the greatest storyteller in the world."

It was also an event—street teams passed out invitations to the showings, which were held at different times on a street in New York. Street viewers could hold up their invitations and see clues about the storylines and they also could interact through mobile messaging. Viewers at home could go online and zoom in on the various stories, or they could go to HBO On Demand and see the film *The Watcher* that tied in with one of the storylines about an assassin murdering an FBI agent.

Created by BBDO and a team of partner agencies, other content about the storylines was found online on Web mini-sites, as well as in photo and video clips on social media platforms, such as Flickr and YouTube. It was an event, an outdoor advertising experience, an online experience, and it involved many bloggers who followed the stories and commented to their digital communities. See the film at *www.youtube.com/watch?v=QCr853VVo9c*

Promotion Effectiveness

Because promotions are so focused on action, it makes sense that sales volume is the primary measure of their effectiveness. After all, they are called *sales promotions*. Response rate—consumers calling the company, sending back a card—is also important to sales promotion. So are redemption rates, which are the rates at which people redeem coupons, refunds, and rebates. These rates are used to evaluate the effectiveness of promotional programs. All of these will be discussed in more detail in Chapter 19.

An important dimension of sales promotion effectiveness is payout planning. The goal of creating a payout plan is to produce promotions that increase sales and profits. Needless to say, a promotion should not cost the company more money than it brings in.

An example of poor payout planning comes from Maytag and an ill-fated U.K. promotion. It was a simple offer: Customers in Great Britain and Ireland were offered two free airline tickets to the United States or Continental Europe when they purchased at least $150 worth of Hoover products. Hoover planned to use the commissions it made from land arrangements, such as hotel reservations and car rentals, to help pay for the airline tickets. How did the promotion turn into a catastrophe? Unfortunately, the commissions were less than anticipated, and the ticket demand was far greater. Maytag's travel agents began attaching unreasonable demands to the free tickets, expensive extras, inconvenient airports, and undesirable departure dates to discourage acceptance of the offer. All these strategies turned happy winners into complaining customers. In the aftermath, Hoover fired three top executives and set up a $30 million fund to pay for the airline tickets.

The trade press is full of stories about poorly designed or performing promotions. Such failures hurt companies' reputations, waste money, and sometimes even hurt consumers. For example, Burger King once had to recall 400,000 toy boats given away with kids' meals after reports that children had been stuck with metal pins that came off the boats too easily. That recall came a week after McDonald's recalled a Happy Meal "Scooter Bug" toy. In 1999 the fast-food industry reeled from the deaths of two infants who suffocated from containers used in a Pokémon promotion. About 25 million of those toys were recalled.

Looking Ahead

As you've read in this chapter, promotions can successfully deliver sales to a company, but they must be well planned and executed if they are to enhance the brand's reputation. The next chapter, which will wrap up our discussion of IMC, as well as introduce various specialized areas of marketing communication, will also reinforce the idea that all the tools we have presented in this book must work together to create a consistent and coherent brand image.

IT'S A WRAP

Consumers Vote Frontier the Winner

Similar to the "Flip to Mexico" campaign (described in the opening case in Chapter 8), Frontier's "Denver's Favorite Animal" campaign proved to be a winner. Fans engaged in the democratic process in a mock election, posting more than 4,000 entries on the forum and logging more than a million votes.

Recognizing that all the candidates were male, more than 1,000 fans signed a petition to draft the only female animal, Foxy the Fox, into the race. Even the White House Project, an organization that supports women in politics, got into the act, creating its own "Draft Foxy" commercial and posting a story online urging people to vote for Foxy as Denver's favorite animal.

In case you were wondering, the Penguins were announced the winners of the favorite animal contest in a 60-second commercial that ran during the last half hour of the Academy Awards. Maybe they had a little bump in popularity from *Happy Feet*, a movie about penguins that won an Academy Award for Best Animated Feature Film that same night.

Frontier won big, too. Web traffic was up more than 50 percent over the same period in the previous year. Online bookings increased 18 percent. Another benefit—online enrollments in Frontier's frequent flyer program increased by about a third. Throughout the campaign, the much-talked about campaign garnered an estimated value in ad equivalency dollars from exposure on TV news, newspaper stories, PR releases and events, and social networking, proving that the characters were more popular than ever.

Frontier's advertising has been recognized with more than 80 awards. Frontier won a Gold Effie for sustained success. The advertising was nominated for Best of Show at the International Mobius Awards for two years in a row. It was awarded a Silver Clio for the prestigious Content & Contact category and won a Silver Effie as well. A 2010 ad for a 43-hour super sale that ran during Super Bowl XLIII (43) also received top honors in the sustained success campaign category of the North American Effie Awards. "Denver's Favorite Animal" campaign received a nomination for a National Emmy for Outstanding Achievement in Advanced Media Technology. It won further recognition, along with creators Couzens and Ennis when it was selected as one of the "Amazing Animal Ads" aired on *Animal Planet*.

Key Points Summary

1. **What are the current trends and practices in planning promotions?** Sales promotion offers an "extra incentive" to take action. It gives the product or service additional value and motivates people to respond. Sales promotion is growing rapidly for many reasons. It offers the manager short-term bottom-line results; it's accountable; sales promotion is less expensive than advertising; it speaks to the current needs of the consumer who wants to receive more value from products; and it responds to marketplace changes. Effective promotional plans are based on Big Ideas.

2. **How are various consumer promotions used?** Sales promotions directed at consumers include price deals, coupons, contests and sweepstakes, refunds, premiums, specialty advertising, continuity programs, and sampling. Their purpose is to pull the product through the distribution channel.

3. **What are the types and purposes of trade promotions?** Sales promotions directed at the trade include point-of-purchase displays, retailer merchandising kits, trade shows, and price deals such as discounts, bonuses, and advertising allowances. These are used to push the product through the channel.

4. **How do multiplatform promotions—sponsorships and events, loyalty programs, and partnership programs—work?** Sponsorship is used to increase the perceived value of a brand by associating it with a cause or celebrity. Internet promotions can be used to drive people to a sponsor's Web page. Licensing "rents" an established brand to other companies to use on their products. Loyalty programs are designed to increase customer retention. Partnership programs, such as co-branding and co-marketing programs, are designed to build stronger relationships between manufacturers and retailers and between two brands that market related products to a similar target audience.

5. **How are promotions used strategically in terms of brand building, integration, and effectiveness?** Promotions offer an incentive to action and stimulate trial, which is important in launching a new product. In brand building promotions can reinforce advertising images and messages and encourage or remind consumers to buy the brand again. They can be used to push or pull a product through the distribution channel by creating positive brand experiences. Interactive promotions are more involved. Sales promotions are used with advertising to provide immediate behavioral action. They are effective when the return on the investment more than covers the cost of the promotion.

Words of Wisdom: Recommended Reading

Liljenwall, Robert, *The Power of Marketing at Retail,* Alexandria, VA: Point-of-Purchase Advertising International, 2008.

Martin, Patricia, *Made Possible By: Succeeding with Sponsorships,* Chicago: LitLamp Communications, 2008.

Mullin, Roddy, *Sales Promotion: How to Create, Implement and Integrate Campaigns That Really Work,* 4th ed., Philadelphia, PA: Kogan Page, 2008.

Saget, Allison, *The Event Marketing Handbook: Beyond Logistics and Planning,* Chicago: Dearborn Publishing, 2006.

Key Terms

ambush marketing, p. 534

channel marketing, p. 528

co-branding, p. 536

co-marketing, p. 536

contests, p. 524

coupons, p. 523

cross promotion, p. 536

event marketing, p. 532

game, p. 524

licensing, p. 536

loyalty (continuity, frequency) program, p. 535

payout planning, p. 519

point-of-purchase (PoP) materials, p. 529

premium, p. 523

price deal, p. 522

rebate, p. 523

refund, p. 523

sales promotion, p. 518

sampling, p. 523

self-liquidator, p. 523

specialty advertising, 524

sponsorship, p. 532

sweepstakes, p. 524

tie-ins, p. 536

trade deal, p. 529

trade show, p. 529

Review Questions

1. Define sales promotion and explain how it differs from other marcom areas.

2. Why is sales promotion growing?

3. Explain the three audiences for sales promotion and the two primary categories used to reach those audiences.

4. What are the primary objectives that consumer promotions can deliver?

5. What are the key objectives of trade promotions?

6. List the primary tools of consumer and trade promotions.

7. What media are used to communicate about sales promotions?

8. How do push and pull marketing strategies relate to sales promotion to consumers? To trade audiences?

9. Why are sponsorships and events used by marketers?

10. Define loyalty programs and explain why they are useful.

11. How and when are partnership promotions used?

Discussion Questions

1. This chapter has covered a number of promotion methods and tools. Some techniques tend to increase product use, and others are used to get new consumers to try the product. Which methods belong with which objective and why?

2. You have been named promotion manager for Maybelline, a well-known brand of cosmetics. You know the brand has been successful in using sales promotion plans lately, but you are concerned about how to use promotions successfully without harming the brand. How is sales promotion weak in building and maintaining a brand and how can it be used to strengthen a well-known brand? What kind of promotions would you suggest for maintaining and strengthening this brand franchise?

3. *Three-Minute Debate* You have just been named product manager for a new FDA-approved pharmaceutical, a diet pill that helps reduce hunger. Should you use a push or pull strategy to introduce this new product? Organize into small teams with each team taking one side or the other. Prepare a presentation that explains your point of view and present it to your classmates.

Take-Home Projects

1. *Portfolio Project* Select a print ad for a national marketer. Redesign the ad, including the use of a consumer sales promotion. Now design a second version orienting the ad to a trade audience. Write a one-paragraph explanation for each ad that summarizes the objectives and strategy you are proposing.

2. *Mini-Case Analysis* Why do you think the "Denver's Favorite Animal" campaign was so successful? What lessons might you learn about promotional planning from this case? If you were on the Grey team, what would you do next to continue the momentum? Come up with a big idea for a new promotion for the next year and explain how it would work and what it would accomplish.

Team Project: The BrandRevive Campaign

For your BrandRevive client, develop a promotion plan for the next year. It should fit into the overall marketing communication strategy that you have developed in past chapters.

- What was the Big Idea you decided on for this brand? How can that Big Idea come to life as a promotional idea?
- What consumer promotions would you recommend and why?
- What trade promotions would you recommend and why?
- How could sponsorships or event marketing contribute to your marketing communication plan?

- Is there a place for a loyalty program? What would you propose and how would it work?
- What about partnership programs? What opportunities are there for co-branding or co-marketing programs? Is licensing a possibility? What tie-ins and cross promotions would you suggest using.
- Summarize your best ideas and explain how you would track their effectiveness.
- Present and explain your promotional plan in a PowerPoint presentation that is no longer than three slides.

Hands-On Case

The Century Council

Read the Century Council case in the Appendix before coming to class.

1. When students first arrive on campus, The Stupid Drink mock beer pong game will be set up in the middle of campus giving away prizes. Chances are most freshmen will be with their parents at this point. Do you think this will be effective at inciting discussion?

2. Create at least five additional promotional materials that you feel will make this campaign more effective on your campus.

The IMC Umbrella

HONDA
The Power of Dreams

MATCH **CR-V**
WITH YOUR MOBILITY

H:N markaðssamskipti / SÍA

It's a Winner

Campaign:	Company:	Agency:	Award:
"Match"	*Honda*	*H:N Marketing Communication, Reykjavík*	Effie Iceland

1. What do we mean by *total brand communication* in IMC programs?
2. What is retail marketing communication all about, and what makes it distinctive?
3. How does business-to-business marketing communication work?
4. What are the basic goals and operations of nonprofit and social marketing?
5. Which strategic decisions underlie effective international marketing communication?

Match CR-V to Your Lifestyle*

After winning a gold Effie for an advertising campaign leading to outstanding sales results, what do you do for an encore?

The advertising business is a "what-have-you-done-for-me-lately" kind of business. A lot of clients are only as happy as their latest advertising campaign results.

Having taken the Honda CR-V from being a distant fourth as the most sold small SUV in Iceland to a close second with a successful marketing campaign, what can you do to top the results? You make it the number one selling small SUV in the country.

The Honda dealership in Iceland challenged us to make the new-from-the-ground-up CR-V the best selling small SUV in Iceland. Like most new car models, the new CR-V was more luxurious and more expensive than its predecessor. To meet the challenge of becoming number one, the new CR-V was completely changed visually to cast a less rugged and more urban image.

The Icelandic climate, road conditions, and mentality have always inflated the need for four-wheel-drive vehicles. Much like in the United States, the better performance of four-wheel-drive vehicles has increased the demand for such vehicles in the last decade and a half. Close to half the vehicles sold in Iceland were four-wheel drive, but the majority of those were full-size SUVs or pickups.

Most ads for the SUV segment focused on off-road capabilities and mountain activities. Our earlier research showed that the people buying those types of vehicles were not necessarily involved in those activities. Rather, we found that what people wanted from those cars was mostly space, both for people and stuff (groceries, luggage, kids, and sporting equipment), and minimum off-road capabilities. They wanted the ability to drive on dirt and gravel roads and the benefit of not being stuck in town (or at home) on heavy snow days.

Having successfully analyzed the market to maximize sales of the older version of the CR-V by carving out a unique identity in the Icelandic market and stressing the extra urban connection with the target group, we now had to expand on our market research to find a new niche to match the newer version.

---

*This chapter opening story was contributed by Ingvi Logason, Principal, H:N Advertising, Reykjavík, Iceland.

Our research also showed that the Honda brand was seen as high quality, well built, and reliable. Furthermore, the last campaign had managed to change the image from a car that was expensive and dull to one that was a great value (although not inexpensive) and safe.

We needed a strategy that could build on the previous campaigns.

We set very ambitious objectives. In year 1 we intended to lower the average age of the new CR-V buyer from 47 years old to 45 years old. We aimed to increase strong purchase intent for the Honda SUV for those under 40 years old to 30 percent (an increase of 20 percent), while maintaining the status quo among older buyers. We also aimed to move the top-of-mind scores to fourth place among all car brands (up two spots). This goal helped support the sales objective of increasing sales to a 12 percent market share in the small SUV segment. Historically, reaching this goal would be enough to be make the CR-V the highest seller in the market.

We had good insight from our previous campaigns for the older generation CR-Vs. So we decided to simplify the message and exploit it further by taking the campaign all urban. We would go all in on the prospect's lifestyle and the car's urban connection with the key phrase "Match CR-V . . . [to your lifestyle]."

We built a campaign positioning the CR-V as "an ultra inner-city SUV with space and maneuverability for your daily activities." At the same time, competitors were promoting their small SUVs as sport SUVs or off-roaders.

Our Big Idea was to challenge the target group to compare the new CR-V to their lifestyle. Their real usage was mostly for daily chores: grocery shopping, driving children to school, and so on, with a light mixture of rural activities.

All our headlines challenged the target group to match the car to specific tasks, chores, and situations. All headlines started with the challenge "Match CR-V . . ." and were the building blocks for universal themes in all promotional materials for the CR-V, making good use of digital media and promotional activities along with more traditional media. When tested these headlines were shown to engage the target group and their imaginations. Different target groups identified with different headlines.

The result was beyond our dreams. You can find out more about what we achieved by turning to the end of the chapter and reading *It's a Wrap*.

The Honda CR-V case is about an award-winning integrated campaign that illustrates how international marketers make decisions about their local advertising. It combines two of the subjects we cover in this chapter, integration and international advertising. Other topics in this chapter are retail, business-to-business (B2B), and nonprofit marketing communication. All these specialized areas use many of the basic marketing communication IMC principles and generally strive to coordinate their messages; however, there are some distinct differences that we will call to your attention in this chapter.

IMC MANAGEMENT

We're near the end of this book. If you have any interest in working in marketing or marketing communication, what have you learned about integrated marketing communication that might help you in your career? The industry is definitely moving in that direction. A study by the Association of National Advertisers (ANA) in 2008, for example, found that 74 percent of ANA members said they were using IMC for most or all of their brands. The association's CEO sees that as a call for "Renaissance Marketers" who understand the essentials of IMC. He describes them as "a new breed of holistic professionals who are system thinkers, customer-centric believers, innovators, and dreamers."[1] So there's definitely a job opportunity here—does that sound like you?

Maybe you're even thinking about starting a business or going to graduate school and becoming a consultant. If so, it's important to understand the concept of advertising has broadened to include almost everything that sends a brand message, a practice we have been calling IMC. If you go to work in marketing or marketing communication, you may be asked to help plan an IMC campaign. So let's wrap up our chapters on the various types of marketing communication and see how what you've learned in this book fits together from a manager's perspective.

One lesson you may have learned is that in marketing communication campaigns, the objective is to create consistency among all the marcom tools. That's essentially a tactical approach, one that's focused on orchestrating consistent brand messages. In the Part 5 opener, Duncan referred to this as a "one-voice, one-look" strategy, which is a critical goal for campaigns. So let's look at the type of IMC planning that delivers marketing communication consistency. Then we'll turn to the big picture of managing a *total brand communication* program.

Managing IMC Campaigns

An IMC campaign is a complex set of interlocking, coordinated activities that has a beginning and end. An IMC campaign plan outlines the objectives and strategies for a series of different but related marketing communication efforts that appear in different media, use different marketing communication tools, and convey different but complementary brand-consistent messages to a variety of stakeholders using strategic consistency. Strategic consistency comes from the creative theme and the consistent presentation of the brand position and personality, even when different stakeholders groups receive different types of messages and interact with the brand in different ways.

Consistency is a product of a carefully designed multiplatform and multimedia plan. For example, consider the CR-V campaign. The agency's owner, Ingvi Logason, explained:

> The media emphasis had been on print with support from TV and the Internet. We shifted the emphasis to a 360-degree integrated approach where we focused, among other things, on media with large reach at the expense of high frequency. TV and interactive Web banners were at the forefront of the campaign with support from newspaper, radio, and event marketing. We also extended the traditional media with sponsorship of some big sports and cultural events that tied in with the car owners' lifestyles.

Stan Richards, founder of the Dallas-based Richards Group explains the process his agency goes through in planning an integrated campaign. It's also the creative brief for what he calls *spherical branding*, which means no matter what your angle of vision, the brand always looks the same:[2]

- *Three-Part Positioning* Target audience? Competitors? Most meaningful brand benefit?
- *Brand Personality* Five to six words that define the brand's personality
- *Affiliation* What club do you join when you adopt a brand?
- *Brand vision* A statement of the brand's "highest calling."

The IMC Mix The decision about which marcom tools to use in a campaign is based on an analysis of their strengths and weaknesses and how they can best be employed to meet the campaign's objectives. As we explained in Chapter 7, certain tools are better at delivering specific objectives. Table 18.1 provides a more extensive outline of the tools and their objectives. As you look over the list, think about what's required to launch a new product. In that situation, which tools would you select as the most appropriate?

Managing 360-Degree Communication

Another lesson you may have learned from our previous discussions is that IMC is a philosophy, a way of managing a brand with a singular vision of what the brand stands for. Unlike the short-term IMC campaign approach, this is a philosophy that delivers total communication over the life of a brand. We are calling this *360-degree communication* because a unifying brand vision

Table 18.1   Typical Objectives for Various IMC Tools

Advertising Reach wide audience through mass media; acquire new customers; establish brand image and personality; define brand position; identify points of differentiation and competitive advantage; counter competition; deliver reminders.

PR Announce news; affect attitudes and opinions; maximize credibility and believability; generate likability; create and improve stakeholder relationships; stimulate buzz.

Consumer Sales Promotion Stimulate behavior; generate immediate response; intensify needs, wants, and motivations; reward behavior; stimulate improvement and relevance; create pull through the channel; encourage repeat purchase.

Trade Sales Promotion Build industry acceptance; push through the channel; motivate cooperation; energize sales force, dealers, and distributors.

Point of Purchase Increase immediate sales; attract attention at decision point; create interest; stimulate urgency; encourage trial and impulse purchasing.

Direct Marketing Stimulate sales; create personal interest and relevance; provide information; create acceptance and conviction; encourage repeat purchase; maintain relationship.

Sponsorship and Events Build awareness; create brand experience; create opportunity for participation, interaction, and involvement; create excitement; stimulate buzz.

Packaging Increase sales; attract attention at selection point; deliver product information; create brand reminder at point of purchase.

Specialties Reinforce brand identity; provide continuous brand reminder; reinforce satisfaction; encourage repeat purchase.

Guerilla Marketing Intercept prospects where they work, live, and visit; create curiosity and excitement; provide opportunity for involvement; stimulate buzz.

Customer Service Answer questions; solve customer problems; record complaints and compliments; turn bad customer experiences into positive experiences; listen to consumer perceptions and record feedback; notify appropriate departments of complaints and compliments; test market communication strategies and copy points.

surrounds all the brand's interactions with all its stakeholders—and this vision must be shared by everyone involved with the brand.

At this "total communication" level, a manager's goal is to monitor all brand experiences to ensure they are working together to support the brand vision. As we have said, messages are delivered by every element of the marketing mix, as well as every marcom message and every brand experience at every brand contact point.

The problem is departmental *silos* with each marcom function going its own way. The solution according to the ANA report cited earlier is "a team of colleagues who have the responsibility vision, understanding, and commitment to engage in a media-agnostic planning process."[3] The only way to monitor and plan for a diversity of brand communication is through **cross-functional management.** Departmental silos that generate inconsistent messages is an organizational problem and every department involved in delivering the brand message should be part of the team that monitors and plans the brand communication. The point is that you can't be integrated externally if you are not integrated internally.

Ninth Principle of IMC
A brand can't be integrated externally if it is not integrated internally.

Ninth Principle of IMC

A brand can't be integrated externally if it is not integrated internally.

The importance of the need for a shared vision from a manager's viewpoint was in evidence when the new chief executive at Ford realized that what the troubled car company needed after the auto meltdown of the late 2000s was a unifying vision. To rally the troops, he had a motivating vision printed on laminated, wallet-size cards and given to the thousands of Ford employees. It proclaimed: "One Ford . . . One Team . . . One Plan. . . . One Goal." The statement conveyed a strategy for returning Ford to its leadership position and undergirded the launch of the Ford Focus, the firm's first truly global car.[4]

A Management Case Study   On the big picture level, IMC is both a philosophy of management and a tool for creating and monitoring total brand communication. The best example comes from the Tokyo-based Dentsu agency, which has aimed at providing *total communication service* to its clients for decades.[5] But until the 2000s, the agency was only able to do multimedia coordination at a one-voice, one-look level. New technology and a new management philosophy, however, created a new way of doing business.

To truly operate with an IMC orientation, Dentsu underwent a total reorganization and designed a comprehensive new IMC toolkit. Now the giant agency's employees have sophisticated tools to actually deliver on that total communication promise with a more advanced approach that Dentsu calls IMC 2.0. It defines IMC 2.0 as "an ongoing systematic process for creatively planning, production, and evaluating brand communication that creates customer relationships, builds strong brands, and increases sales and profits."[6]

To engineer this turnaround, it first held an IMC audit, conducted by IMC leader Professor Tom Duncan, to determine its IMC strengths and weakness internally, as well as in the eyes of key clients. Then it created an IMC Development Division with the mission of undertaking the IMC R&D arm. That division has some 90 to 100 staff members dedicated to basic research into IMC processes. The agency also created an IMC online site with more than 250 planning tools, models, and processes that can be used in IMC 2.0 projects. This portal also provides access to case studies, training modules, articles, and research on IMC. It registers more than 2,000 unique visits a day from Dentsu employees.

An IMC Planning Center with 350 people from a variety of media and marcom areas was established. The staff members assigned to this department are given intensive IMC training so they have the skills to work in cross-functional IMC teams on client projects brought to them by various account groups. The agency's Brand Creation Center, an existing brand consulting group, was also integrated into the IMC Planning Center. Finally, each of Dentsu's 22 account groups has 5 to 10 embedded account planners who are trained in IMC practices. These planners help educate clients on the goals of IMC and establish a common language for planning.

It's a work in progress—and one complicated by the worldwide recession—but Dentsu's IMC executives and managers believed that the investment in reorganization was justified. The effort didn't come cheap: Dentsu initially dedicated some 600 of its 4,500 employees to IMC development and client services.

The Management of Synergy   We have mentioned elsewhere in the book that one goal of integration is message synergy. Because everything a brand does sends a message, IMC planners strive to manage a total communication program to deliver a consistent brand presence. As Duncan said in the Part 5 opener, "It's not just advertising . . . it's everything a brand says and does." The end result is brand message **synergy**, a foundational truth that means when all the pieces work together, the whole is greater than the sum of its parts.

Another way to understand this synergy in the IMC context is the say–do–confirm *integration triangle*. This triangle identifies three key aspects that must work together to create integration: (1) what the company or brand says about itself (*say*), (2) how the company or brand performs (*do*), (3) and what other people say about it (*confirm*). Figure 18.1 shows these relationships. The important principle here is that, since a brand is an integrated perception, a brand is what people say about it—and that defines your brand's reputation. Furthermore integration fails if there are gaps between what the marketing communication says, what the brand does (performance, social responsibility), and what others say (reputation). Those gaps are the ultimate test of integration. Because a brand is an integrated perception, a brand is what people say about it—it fails as an integrated perception if there are gaps between say, do, and confirm.

In most cases the drive for brand consistency is a strategic need, but at other times it reflects cost efficiency. IMC programs can be more effective because of their repetition, and this reinforcement, along with synergy, creates more cost-efficient campaigns. Managers have learned that using multiple tools and channels in a consistent way

Tenth Principle of IMC
Integration happens when what your brand says matches what it does and what others say about it.

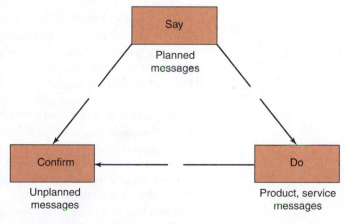

FIGURE 18.1

The Integration Triangle
The say–do–confirm model explains how planned marketing communication messages (say) are either reinforced or undercut by messages delivered by the product or service marketing mix (how well the brand and company perform its business) and unplanned messages (what others say). Why do you think we say that a brand is integrated when there are no gaps between the say, do, and confirm messages?

Source: Adapted from Tom Duncan and Sandra Moriarty, *Driving Brand Value,* New York: McGraw-Hill, 1997: 91.

is more profitable and builds longer lasting customer relationships than just relying on one tool, such as advertising.

Ten Principles of IMC

An *Adweek* article on new marketing principles, urges managers to use what we are calling big picture thinking: "shifting from campaign thinking to conversation thinking," what the author called "Think 365—not 360."[7] The point is to become an indispensable part of people's daily lives whenever or wherever a customer needs what a brand offers. That ongoing, multichannel, multi-platform, multistakeholder approach to the practice of IMC is what we have been referring to in previous chapters when we have described the principles and practices of IMC. We also added two more in the previous discussion, so we now have a set of ten principles of IMC.

Let's summarize this total brand communication philosophy by compiling the complete set of IMC principles that we have developed in this book. The 10 basic principles that we believe guide IMC practices are shown in Table 18.2. These are a manager's toolkit to guide the design of a 360-degree brand communication program.

As we said at the beginning of this chapter, a number of different marketing communication situations can benefit from an IMC approach. Let's now consider the practice of our first specialty area—retail marketing.

Table 18.2   Ten Principles of IMC

First Principle of IMC *Everything communicates.*

Everything in the marketing mix sends a message. Everything a brand does, and sometimes what it doesn't do, can send a message. One cannot NOT communicate. Receiving messages is as important as sending messages. Integrating the marketing communication is futile if contrary and more powerful messages are being sent by other brand actions.

Second Principle *A brand is a unified vision (the art) and a complex system (the science).*

Third Principle *Brand relationships drive brand value.*

Interactivity leads to brand involvement. When two parties interact, both learn about the other. Customer retention is just as important as customer acquisition.

Fourth Principle *Integration equals integrity.*

Mission marketing adds trust to brand relationships.

Fifth Principle *People automatically integrate brand messages and experiences.*

Synergy occurs when all the messages work together to create a coherent brand perception.

Sixth Principle *Stakeholders overlap.*

Seventh Principle *All contact points deliver brand messages.*

Everything that delivers a message to a stakeholder about a brand is a contact point. Both good and bad. Maximize and leverage the good ones and minimize the bad ones.

Eighth Principle *Strategic consistency drives synergy.*

At every point of contact with every stakeholder, the essence of the brand should be the same. Strategic consistency, rather than one-look, one-voice executions, drives synergy.

Ninth Principle *You can't be integrated externally if you are not integrated internally.*

A core brand strategy—a shared vision—drives the entire organization. Cross-functional organization delivers unity of vision, and unity of vision drives an integrated brand perception.

Tenth Principle *Integration happens when what your brand says matches what it does and what others say about it.*

A brand fails as an integrated perception if there are gaps between say, do, and confirm brand communication.

RETAIL MARKETING COMMUNICATION

The face of retailing is changing as malls convert to open-air markets, eBay operates an international flea market, and the Internet becomes a primary information source for buyers. *Clicks and bricks* are changing places as store-based retailers (*bricks*) set up websites and e-marketers (*clicks*) set up stores. NikeTown stores sell sports as entertainment and ESPN takes the X Games to malls. The more the retail world changes, the more need there is for information and promotion.

A significant part of the U.S. economy, big stores such as Walmart, Target, Kohl's, Sears, and JCPenney, accounts for more than 10 percent of all U.S. consumer goods spending. According to branding consulting firm Interbrand, the three most valuable retail brands in the United States are Walmart with a brand value estimated at $154 billion. Target is second at $25.5 billion, and Best Buy is third at $17.8 billion. Others in the top 10 were Home Depot, Walgreens, CVS, Sam's Club, Dell, Coach, and *Amazon.com.*[8]

In some estimates, retail accounts for nearly half of all the money spent on advertising. Retail marketing communication has two missions: (1) selling the brand of the retail store, as the Saks ad demonstrates, and (2) selling individual branded items the store carries. Best Buy, for example, uses marketing communication to promote itself as these ads demonstrate, but it also sells a variety of electronics brands—everything from Adobe to Yamaha with hundreds of brands in between. Increasingly, retail food and drug chains are giving more space and promotional support to their own **store brands,** also called **private-label brands** or **house brands.**

A positive, distinctive image is a valuable asset and especially important for upscale retailers like Saks Fifth Avenue. This visual shows both a thumbnail and the produced ad. What do you think this ad says about the image of Saks?

The three basic types of retail stores are those that are *independently owned* such as a barber shop, those that are part of a *franchise* such as KFC and Hertz, and those that are owned by a major *corporation* such as Starbucks and Macy's. Retailers such as Sears, Staples, Home Depot, and Best Buy advertise nationally and locally. Local advertising is targeted at consumers who live within a geographical market, what we called a Designated Market Area (DMA) in Chapter 14.

For franchises, local owners may pay a percent of sales to headquarters to help pay for national advertising. These stores also are generally required to use a certain percent of their sales to do local advertising. When there are several different franchises in a local market (auto dealers, for example), they may form a co-op advertising committee, pool their money, and run local advertising.

Of course, another popular form is online retailing. More than just retail websites for existing stores, the iTunes and iApp electronic storefronts have created a new face for retail selling—not just to people sitting at their computers, but also to those using mobile media wherever they may be. Technology is changing shopping. A boutique in Manhattan, for example, offers a new way to shop using a cell phone—shoppers standing outside a store window, even if the store is closed, can point the phone at merchandise and buy it.[9]

Retail Communication Planning

As mentioned previously, retailers sell not only a range of product brands, they also sell themselves as destinations for buying a selection of products. A positive, distinctive image is a valuable asset and especially important for upscale retailers like Saks Fifth Avenue. Retailers who want to build a brand image, particularly an upscale one, must clearly and consistently communicate that image to consumers through advertising, other forms of marketing communication, pricing strategies, location, and the physical appearance of the store.

Retail Objectives   Customers base their decisions about where to shop on the quality of the shopping experience, as well as on such retail decision factors as choice, selection, and service. These, in turn, affect retail marcom objectives.

The primary objective is to build **store traffic,** which marketing communication does by featuring reduced prices on popular items and promoting an appealing store image and shopping experience. In addition to traffic, most retailers use advertising to help attract new customers, build store loyalty, increase the amount of the average sale, maintain inventory balance by moving out

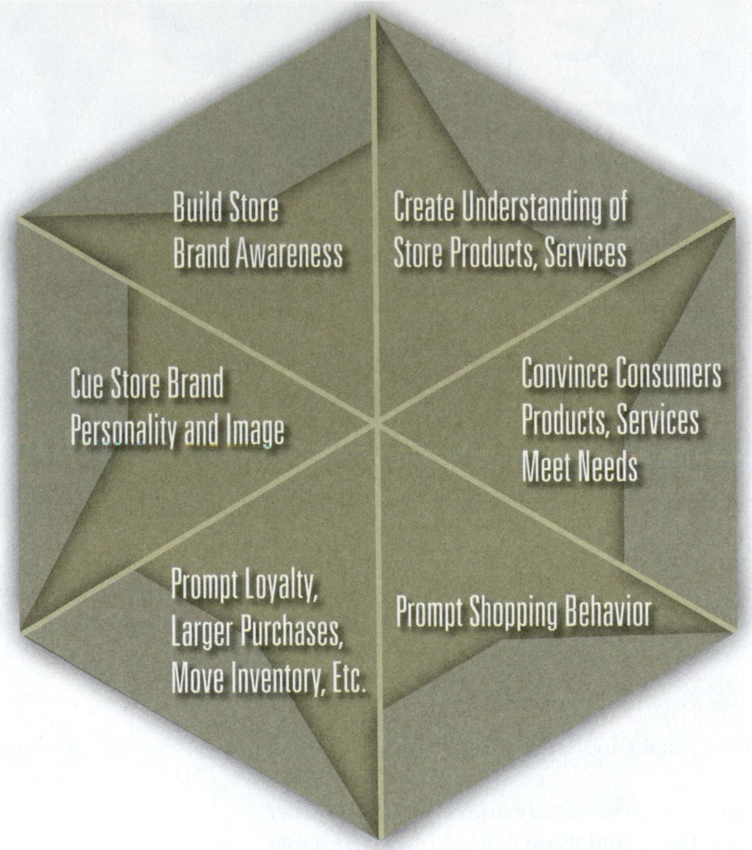

FIGURE 18.2

Retail Advertising Objectives
The objectives for retail marketing communication can be organized around the six basic elements in the Facets of Effects mode (from upper left clockwise): Perception, Cognition, Persuasion, Behavior, Association, Emotion.

overstocks and outdated merchandise, and counter seasonal lows (see Figure 18.2). Another characteristic of retail advertising is an inherent sense of urgency—"weekend special," "prices good this Saturday only," or "while supplies last." To build loyalty or to motivate consumers to switch from a competitor, retail stores also use frequent buyer programs and special services such as banking, pharmacies, and even coffee shops.

Retail promotional strategies focus on retail benefits, such as an unusual or varied selection of merchandise, friendly and knowledgeable clerks, or prestige brands. Many retailers use any reason they can find to have a sale (President's Day, back-to-school, tax time, overstocks). Stores also search for themes to use in their advertising, such as an exotic place (Madras, India, was the theme of a special JCPenney sale). Revisit Table 18.1 and decide what you think would be the most appropriate marketing communication tools for a retail business to use.

Retailers suffered from the recession of the late 2000s and generally used sales and discounts to attract customers; however, that is a risky strategy for luxury stores that sell high-end goods because it may "re-train" customers to expect price deals. Such a strategy undercuts the luxury position. One solution used by some high-end stores was to severely limit their inventory, in effect, intensifying demand. The exclusivity strategy fit better with the stores' luxury positioning.[10]

Principle

The first strategic consideration in retail advertising is geography.

Retail Targeting   In targeting consumers, a retailer's first strategic concern is geography: Where do my customers live? How far will they drive to come to my store? In large DMAs individual retailers who only have one or two stores try to find media that just reaches those within their stores' shopping area (generally a two- to five-mile radius).

The next concern is consumer taste, which may also reflect geography. National retailers try to develop offers that appeal to consumers in different parts of the country, as well as in different neighborhoods. H.E.B. Supermarkets operates its stores in both central and south Texas. In San Antonio, the stores located in Mexican-American neighborhoods have a very different merchandise assortment, as well as different advertising than do its stores in other locations. Sometimes special sales are used to reach special target audiences as the Virgin "Forever 70s" sale demonstrates, which has some fun with the type of person who might be interested in 70s music.

Cooperative Advertising

One way local retailers can compensate for their smaller advertising budgets and limited expertise is to take advantage of **cooperative (co-op) advertising** (Chapters 2, 8, 12, and 17), in which the national brand reimburses the retailer for part or all of the advertising expenses. Also called **ad allowances** or **promotional allowances,** these co-op funds have become so common that most retailers won't even consider taking on a new brand, especially one in a heavily advertised category, without receiving some support. Large drug and discount chains periodically produce special advertising supplements. Their suppliers are offered an opportunity to buy space in these supplements. The result is that much or all of retail advertising is paid for by the brands carried in the advertising.

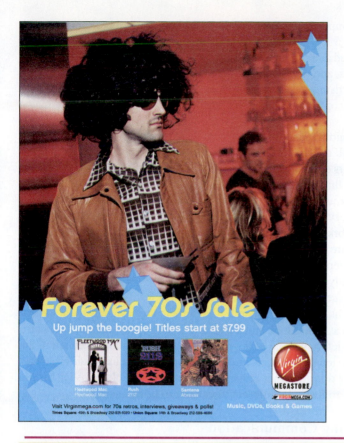

SHOWCASE

For Virgin Megastore's "Forever 70s" sale, Chris Hutchinson came up with the idea of a character who was stuck in the 70s—his music, his style, his lingo, his attitude. Where to find this cool cat? The perfect person turned out to be the art director himself who worked out a great outfit—a huge Afro, tight bellbottoms, and an orange leather jacket that his father wore in the real 1970s. The photographer shot on the run to get a semi-documentary look. The client loved the print so the art director directed himself in a set of TV spots, as well. The sale was a huge success nationwide.

A graduate of the University of Oregon's advertising program, Chris Hutchinson was nominated for inclusion in this book by Professor Charles Frazer.

Creating the Retail Ad

Prior to actually writing copy or drawing a layout, creative advertising experts Jeweler and Drewniany suggest that advertisers answer this question: Why would you shop in your store? Possible answers to this question can provide direction for the creative process. They suggest these typical reasons:[11]

- Store's personnel
- Store's location
- Store's pricing policy
- Store's products
- Store's history
- Store's stand on social responsibility issues.

Price, for example, can be a factor in establishing a store's image and a reason for shopping. Most discount stores signal their type of merchandise with large, bold prices. Other retailers emphasize price by offering coupons in their print advertising. Featuring prices doesn't necessarily apply only to ads that give the store a bargain or a discount image, however. Price can help the consumer comparison shop without visiting the store. Discounters like Target and Walmart also use a **price-value strategy** that suggests they offer the best quality you can get for that price level.

Because the main object of retail ads is to attract customers, store location (or telephone number, if advertising is a service) is essential. For merchandise that is infrequently purchased, such as cars, furniture, wallpaper, and hearing aids, the ad should include a map or mention a geographic reference point (for example, three blocks north of the state capitol building) in addition to the regular street address.

Most retail advertising is created and produced by one or a combination of the following: in-house staff, local media, ad agencies, and/or freelancers. The larger the retail operation, the more likely it is to have an in-house advertising staff because few outside agencies are prepared to handle the large number of day-to-day copy changes and the fast deadlines that are typical of major retail advertising.

In the case of national chains and franchises, the national headquarters provides ad formats, TV commercials, and radio spots, all of which can be localized. All local media also are willing to create and produce ads for retailers as a way to get them to use their media. With the exception of television stations, most provide this service free.

Local retailers will sometimes use local agencies to create a campaign they can run over time. If successful, as the Virgin story illustrates, the creative idea may become a national campaign. Generally outside agency work is the most costly way to produce retail ads on a regular and frequent schedule so agencies are used instead to create image ads or campaigns.

Small- and medium-sized retailers often save money by using stock artwork in their ads and other promotional materials. All daily newspapers subscribe to click art services that provide a wide range of photographs and line art drawings (some for free, others for a fee). Larger retailers or upscale specialty retailers, such as Tiffany's, generally have their art designed by a staff or agency designer to give all their ads a similar look and a distinct image. Some manufacturers also provide a **dealer tag,** which is time left at the end of a radio or television spot or space left at the bottom of print materials, where the local store is mentioned. Retail chains make their broadcast production more efficient by using a **donut** format in which the opening and closing sections are the same, while the middle changes to focus on different merchandise or local stores.

The Media of Retail Marketing Communication

At the national level, retail chains use a variety of traditional and nontraditional media—newspapers, magazines, television, outdoor, the Internet, guerilla marketing. Manufacturers also provide window banners, free-standing displays, and special direct-mail pieces, such as four-color supplements for the local paper that carry the store's name and address. Other media used by retailers include banners, posters, **shelf talkers** (signs attached to a shelf that let the consumer take away some piece of information or a coupon), and other merchandising materials, such as end-of-aisle displays and shopping cart ads. New interactive electronic kiosks with touch-screen computers, CD-ROM databases, full graphics, and product photos are moving into the aisles in many stores, where they provide more information about more products than the store can ever stock on its shelves.

Unlike national advertisers, local retailers generally prefer reach over frequency since the majority of their advertising is for special promotions. Because retailers can choose from many local media, they are careful to use media that minimize waste. That's why direct mail is now the second-largest advertising medium used by retailers (newspapers are first).

Newspapers have always made up the bulk of retailer advertising because the local newspaper fits the retailer's desire for geographic coverage and immediacy (although local businesses are moving some, if not most, of their advertising online and sites like Craig's List are seriously cutting in to the classified advertising revenues). Retailers can gain some measure of audience selectivity by advertising in specific sections of the paper, such as sports (for sporting goods stores) and financial pages (for banks and loan companies), and in **zone editions** (certain versions of the paper that go to certain counties and suburbs). Free-distribution newspapers called **shoppers** are also popular advertising vehicles for retailers, as are **preprints,** also called **free-standing inserts (FSIs),** which are placed inside newspapers.

Many of the top 50 markets in the United States have at least one local magazine offering retailers high-quality, four-color ads to reach upscale consumers. Some national magazines have regional or metropolitan editions that also enable local retailers to buy exposure within their trading area only.

Nearly all major markets now have at least one local independent station and a public television station. The *A Matter of Practice* feature explains how television advertising can be used for revitalizing a retail brand image. Radio is used by local retailers because it has a relatively low cost, a high degree of geographic and audience selectivity, and flexibility in scheduling.

A MATTER OF PRACTICE

"Life Is Great" at SPAR

Daryl Bennewith, *Strategic Director TBWA Group, Durban, South Africa*

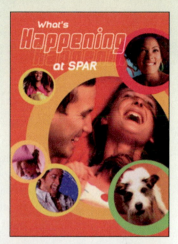

"All will benefit from united co-operation" was the original philosophy Adrian van Well, the founder of SPAR, introduced in 1932.

Today the SPAR Group Ltd. in South Africa operates six modern distribution centers that service just over 900 SPAR grocery stores across the nation as well as stores in neighboring countries.

The success of any business, as we know, is dependent on the brand's ability to occupy a position in the mind of the consumer, which will motivate them to shop at SPAR stores.

In 2006 we began taking the brand in a new direction by building a position on a young, modern, and energetic platform and gearing the marketing communication campaigns to communicate this message.

The first phase of the campaign was vibrant and attention grabbing to match the "happening" concept, which set out to communicate that there is always something exciting and new going on at SPAR. This campaign was communicated through television, leaflets, news, and radio. Three main themes, "Jumpin'," "Shakin'," and "Bubblin'," were used to convey the spirit and image of the brand.

The next phase was an exciting effort to reinforce and evolve the up-tempo positioning of the SPAR brand, while still retaining its youth and energy. This campaign approach was born out of SPAR's realization that the brand needed to remain "Forever Young." This taps into the global focus on preserving youth through attitude, products, diet, and exercise and has emotional appeal to the consumer of the future, through the celebration of what life has to offer.

This campaign, known as "Life's Great," required an element of innovative, creative execution to inspire and motivate consumers to build a relationship with SPAR. That element was using one of the country's hottest bands, Prime Circle, to write and perform the song for the TV campaign.

Our campaign song was released on the latest Prime Circle album, received air time on radio, and was played in clubs around the country. Since the song was prereleased in the SPAR ad, all future airplay that the song receives prompted recognition and recall of the campaign, entrenching the message that "Life Is Great" at SPAR.

As SPAR continues to prosper and attain new heights, the communication strategy will lead the way, ensuring that the brand stays relevant, exciting, and forever young.

In 2009 SPAR achieved excellent results and continued to create a lasting solid brand position—and that truly makes life great!

The Internet is making a huge difference in business operations. Some retailers are selling as much online as they do from their stores—a successful clicks-and-bricks strategy. In addition to online business, retailers have found interesting ways to use the Web for marketing communication. Some fashion retailers, for example, employ their own bloggers who review the store's lines.[12]

Staying on top of fashion is challenging for trendy retailers such as Abercrombie & Fitch, which really suffered during the recent recession. Even with a high level of sale prices, the retailer's woes seemed to suggest a more basic problem with its "once unerring sense of style." Analysts said that A&F's look was stale and the company was no longer in touch with hot trends.[13] Retail, particularly in fashion, can be a tricky business.

BUSINESS-TO-BUSINESS MARKETING COMMUNICATION

As we explained early in the book, advertising directed at people in business who buy or specify products for business use is called **business-to-business (B2B) advertising.** Business marketing is the marketing of goods and services to other businesses. Although personal selling is the most common method of communicating with business buyers, business advertising is used to create corporate brand awareness, enhance the company's reputation, support salespeople and other channel members, and generate new business leads. It also reinforces the brand position as the Interprint ad illustrates.

B2B Buying Behavior

Principle

B2B buyers are driven by rational, pragmatic considerations, and those concerns must be addressed by B2B advertising.

Businesses buy goods and services for two basic reasons: (1) they need ingredients for the products they manufacture, and (2) they need goods (such as computers, desks, and chairs) and services (legal, accounting, maintenance) for their business operations. Business marketing differs from consumer marketing in terms of who buys a product, what the buying motive is, and how the buying decision is made. Buying decisions are often made by committees on behalf of the people who use the products, and the actual purchase is negotiated by a specialist in that category called a **buyer.** Department stores, for example, have a team of buyers who select the merchandise for their different departments.

Purchasing objectives in B2B marketing center on rational, pragmatic considerations such as price, service, quality of the good or service, and assurance of supply. For that reason, B2B communication tends to use rational strategies and focus on reasons and benefits.

Types of B2B Marketing Communication

Businesses are grouped according to the **North American Industry Classification System (NAICS),** which was formerly known as the *Standard Industrial Classification (SIC) system* (see *www.census.gov/epcd/www/naics.html*). This system allows a marketer to determine its customers' business category and then obtain media lists that include the publications this group uses. The primary B2B industries are classified as industrial, government, trade, professional, and agricultural:

"At some point, my QC audit became their QC clinic."

INTERPRINT
IP

SHOWCASE

Peter Stasiowski, a former advertising agency creative director, now works as marketing and communication manager for a printing company. His B2B ads are beautifully designed and written, as these ads for the company's quality control standards and environmental stewardship illustrate.

A graduate of the University of West Florida, Peter Stasiowski was nominated by Professor Tom Groth.

• **Industrial** Original equipment manufacturers (OEMs), such as International Harvester and General Motors, purchase industrial goods or services that either become a part of the final product or aid business operations. **Industrial advertising** is directed at OEMs. For example, when General Motors purchases tires from Goodyear, information needs focus on whether the purchase will contribute positively to the final vehicle. When Goodyear purchases the packaging materials used to ship the tires it manufactures, information needs focus on prompt, predictable delivery.

- *Government* The largest purchasers of industrial goods in the United States are federal, state, and local governments. These government units purchase virtually every kind of good, from $15 hammers to multimillion-dollar missiles. Such goods may be advertised in *Commerce Business Daily* or *Defense News*. These purchases are usually made by bids and contracts, and the decision is made on price and specifications.
- *Trade/Channel Marketing* **Trade advertising** is used to persuade distribution channel members, such as distributors, wholesalers, dealers, and retailers, to stock the manufacturer's products. *Chain Store Age, Florist's Review*, and *Pizza and Pasta* are examples of trade publications, and there are thousands more covering every possible product category. Resellers want information on the profit margins they can expect to receive, the product's major selling points, and the producer's plans for consumer advertising and other promotional support.
- *Professional* Advertising directed at a group of mostly white-collar workers such as lawyers, accountants, technology consultants, doctors, teachers, funeral directors, and advertising and marketing specialists is known as **profession advertising.** Advertisers interested in attracting professionals advertise in publications such as the *Music Educators' Journal* and *Advertising Age*.
- *Agricultural* Agricultural advertising promotes a variety of products and services, such as animal health products, seeds, farm machinery and equipment, crop dusting, and fertilizer. Large and small farmers alike want to know how industrial products can assist them in the production of agricultural commodities. They turn to such publications as *California Farmer* and *Trees and Turf* for such assistance.

Creating B2B Communication

In terms of objectives, B2B advertising is used to create and maintain brand awareness and to support the personal selling function. As a result, B2B objectives center on creating company awareness, increasing overall selling efficiency, and generating leads (see Figure 18.3). When buyers are aware of a company's reputation, products, and record in the industry, salespeople are more effective. Also advertising in trade magazines and general business publications is a much less expensive way to reach influencers than personal sales calls. In other words, advertising is used to presell, and personal sales are used to close sales.

As in consumer advertising, the best B2B ads are relevant and understandable and strike an emotional chord in the prospective client. Business-to-business marketers follow these guidelines to create effective ads:

- Make sure the ad selects the strongest benefit and presents it prominently and persuasively.
- Dramatize the most important benefit, either by showing the product in action or by visualizing a problem and offering your product or service as a solution.

FIGURE 18.3
Business-to-Business Objectives
Similar to retail, the B2B objectives can be organized according to the Facets of Effects Model.

- Make sure the visual is relevant to the key message. It should help readers understand how your product or service works or instantly show that you understand the problem.
- Make the offer as clear as possible. What exactly do you want the reader to do as a result of seeing your ad?
- Provide contact information. It should be easy for the potential customer to follow through with a response.

B2B Media

Although some business marketers use traditional consumer media, most rely on general business or trade publications, industrial directories, consumer media, websites, direct marketing, or some combination of these media.

- *General Business and Trade Publications* As we saw in Chapter 12, business and trade publications are classified as either horizontal or vertical. **Horizontal publications** are directed to people who hold similar jobs in different companies across different industries. For example, *Purchasing* is a specialized business publication targeted to people across industries who are purchasing agents. In contrast, **vertical publications,** such as *Iron Age and Steel* or *Advertising Age*, are targeted toward people who hold different positions in a particular industry.
- *Directory Advertising* Every state has an industrial directory, and there are also a number of private ones. One of the most popular industrial directories is the New York–based *Thomas Register*. The 19-volume *Register* contains 50,000 product headings and listings from 123,000 industrial companies selling everything from heavy machine tools to copper tubing to orchestra pits.
- *Consumer Media* Sometimes businesses advertise in consumer magazines, such as *Golf, Time,* or *Newsweek,* in the hope of building widespread brand recognition, such as the "Intel Inside" campaign. There also has been some growth in business television programming, which provides a good message vehicle for certain B2B companies. For example, Financial Network News (FNN) produces its own business shows and carries the syndicated business shows *This Morning's Business* and *First Business*.
- *The Internet and B2B* The Internet is a key medium for B2B advertisers. Company websites allow business clients to view product lists, place orders, check prices and availability, and replace inventories automatically. The Internet is also a primary research tool used by B2B marketers to check out competitors and to find areas of new business and suppliers. One of the most popular B2B sites on the Internet is the FedEx site, which allows clients to track packages, obtain price information, and learn about FedEx software and services. It receives 1.7 million tracking requests a month, 40 percent of which probably would have been called in to the company's 800 number if the website were not available. Because handling each call costs approximately $1, its website saves FedEx more than $8 million a year.
- *B2B Direct Marketing* Direct mail has the capacity to sell a B2B brand, provide sales leads, and lay the groundwork for subsequent sales calls. Business advertisers use print and online catalogs and product literature to reach their target markets, which support the selling function by providing technical data about the product and supplementary information concerning price, availability, delivery, and warranties. Direct marketing is widely used because most target audiences are smaller than the audiences for many consumer brands; therefore, B2B marketers can target their messages (because they know names and addresses) and greatly minimize media waste.

Customer service and technical support departments are important in many different business categories, but particularly in B2B. Calling a customer help line frequently gets you a message about wait time, a robotic recording, an impenetrable non-U.S. accent, or a cheerfully inept live person. The message: "Your call is (not that) important to us," which is also the title of a book critical of customer service industry practices.[14] One solution to the customer service problem in computer technical support is to enlist volunteers who are "super-users." So you think no one would work for a company for free, right? That's exactly how a corps of Web-savvy people created the open-source Linux operating system. Verizon and other companies have found that there are groups of experts who find social (and intellectual) rewards in solving problems and, in some cases, contributing to product development and improvement.[15]

Social media have become important to B2B marketers because they offer personal contact, which is ideal for tightly targeted programs. An IBM social media manager has some ideas for B2B marketers on how to use Twitter for segmenting prospects in terms of the desired response. Her point is that within businesses, you may want to contact people in different parts of the organization with specific messages. Here is a summary of this strategy in terms of public relations and promotion activities looking at who to follow and the appropriate objectives for reaching that group. If you were assigned to develop a Twitter strategy for your student center on campus, what ideas would you adopt and adapt from this table?

Twitter Strategy for B2B Marketing			
Strategy	Who to Follow ...	Create What ...	Engage How ...
Customer Relations	Customers/prospects	Relevant content, tips, company info	Answer questions, respond to comments
Crisis Management	Your brand, category, issues	Resources, updated info, explanations	Answer questions, respond to comments, raise issues, provide info
Reputation Management	Industry leaders, interest groups, news	Insight, expertise, thought leaders	Join conversation, add value/info, transparency
Event Coverage	Those interested in attending, media	Updates/schedules, interviews, behind the scenes	Set up Tweet-ups, talk to attendees, ask/answer questions
Product Promo	Customers/prospects	Links to promos, insider info on sales, discount codes	Check replies, answer questions, provide info
Issue Advocacy	Those interested in your cause, industry	Health tips, disaster alerts, fund-raising	Know followers, thank them for support, get followers involved

Adapted from Ogilvy PR 360 Degree Digital Influence, "A Strategic Approach to Using Twitter." Used with permission. www.OgilvyPR.com.

NONPROFIT OR SOCIAL MARKETING

Effective marketing and advertising techniques are not only important for businesses, but also for nonprofit organizations involved in community issues, public policy, and good causes. Nonprofit marketing is used by organizations such as hospitals, government agencies, zoos, museums, orchestras, religious organizations, charities, and universities and schools to "sell" their services, programs, and ideas.

Many people make the mistake of thinking that competition only exists between for-profit companies. Nothing could be farther from the truth. Nonprofits often have to compete as hard, if not more so, than for-profit companies because they know individuals and businesses have just so much money and time to donate to nonprofit organizations. It is also a myth to think that nonprofits are not businesses. The Red Cross and the Salvation Army, for example, have hundreds of full-time paid staff and multimillion-dollar annual budgets.

Nonprofit organizations have a number of goals, such as *membership* (AARP, chambers of commerce), *donations* (Red Cross, United Way, American Cancer Society), *participation* (Habitat for Humanity), *sales* (museum gift shops), *recruitment* (the military, universities), *attitude change* (political parties), *advocacy* (Weyerhauser for forest management), and *visits* or *attendance* (state tourism programs, art museums).

Another goal is action, as the SORPA recycling ads from Iceland demonstrate. Agency founder Ingvi Logason explains that "SORPA was founded to encourage people to reduce waste and increase recycling. Seen at first as a troublesome addition to daily life, SORPA quickly managed with clever marketing to earn an 80 percent positive rating by the Icelandic public."

SHOWCASE

Contributed by Ingvi Logason, this work by his agency H:N Marketing Communication, in Reykjavík, Iceland, for the local SORPA recycling center urged people to participate in recycling. He explained, "From day one the marketing strategy, concept and platform, has been very consistent—always positive, encouraging, and built around light colors. These two print ad examples were part of an overall image/reminder campaign that has the company aiming for even higher positive ratings. SORPA is now maintaining over a 90 percent positive rating."

A graduate of the University of West Florida, Ingvi Logason was nominated by Professor Tom Groth.

Fund-Raising

One activity that almost all nonprofits do is **fund-raising,** sometimes called **development,** often under the guidance of a *development officer* who is a professional specializing in fund-raising. Groups such as Save the Children and the Nature Conservancy use sophisticated segmentation and message strategies to target audiences and raise funds.

Universities and other organizations such as museums and hospitals use **capital campaigns** designed to raise a specified amount of money in a set time frame to finance new buildings, equipment purchases, and other programs. These campaigns operate with a carefully designed strategy that involves sophisticated motivation strategies based on segmentation, targeting, goal setting, and leadership identification. Events, direct marketing, and campaign literature are important tactical tools.

Social Marketing and Public Communication

The use of marketing programs and marketing communication tools to create awareness of a social need is called **social marketing.** It is also used to motivate consumers and businesses to act in certain ways, such as give money, volunteer time, or adopt certain policies. The anti-smoking and antidrug campaigns are examples of social marketing.

Social marketing is also called public communication. **Public communication campaigns** are undertaken by nonprofit organizations as a conscious effort to influence the thoughts or actions of the public. The biggest and longest running program is the Advertising Council, which is a network of advertising agencies, media, and suppliers that donate their services to create ads and campaigns on behalf of socially important causes: crime prevention, child abuse, mental illness, and the environment. The "Smoky Bear" fire prevention effort is one of the longest running and best-known Ad Council campaigns.

Another example comes from Jeremy Boland, art director at Borders Perrin Norrander in Portland, Oregon, who contributed a campaign that he directed from the 2008 presidential campaign. It's an example of integrated planning for a public communication effort. You can see the "Things Are Fine" campaign at *www.thingsarefine.org.* Boland describes the effort as "a hugely impactful campaign to get the youth demographic out and vote in this last presidential election." Boland said it was "overwhelming how well received on a global level it was" and it has been described as "one of the most memorable campaigns from the election."

Cause and Mission Marketing

An annual study, the Edelman Consumer Study, found that almost 60 percent of the world's consumers do business with a company because it supports good causes.

Concern for social issues is increasingly important for for-profit companies because they want to be seen as socially responsible. Pepsi, for example, launched the Pepsi "refresh project" dedicating at least $20 million in 2010 to nonprofits and causes consumers propose on the campaign's website (*www.refresheverything.com*). Visitors can vote on the ideas suggested during the previous month. A media blitz to announce the effort included appearances by Kevin Bacon and Demi Moore on NBC's *Today Show*, ads on other broadcast networks, and messages on AOL, Facebook, Hulu, MTV, *Parade*, and Yahoo!.[16]

Adopting a good cause and helping in its fund-raising and other community-oriented efforts is called **cause marketing.** For example, Walmart was an early responder to the Hurricane Katrina disaster with truckloads of water as well as special placement help for its employees who were affected. Target has donated a huge amount of money to its local communities as part of its community caring effort. Carol Cone, founder of the Cone agency, which specializes in cause marketing, calls these efforts *passion branding* because they link brands to causes for which people feel passion. (Check out this agency at *www.coneinc.com*.) For example, Celestial Seasonings supports the "Red Dress" campaign for women's heart health, which is part of the bigger American Heart Association's Go Red for Women campaign. The Cone agency was behind the "Red" campaign, as well as Yoplait's Save Lids to Save Lives, and Avon's Breast Cancer Crusade. Being a good corporate citizen, as we discussed in Chapter 3, is good for the bottom line. An article in *Advertising Age* explained the bottom-line importance of such strategies as: "Companies do well by doing good."[17]

Professor Scott Hamula explains that "in addition to operating with a sense of social responsibility, marketers engage in philanthropy through cause marketing." The primary goals, he says, are "to help communities and nonprofit organizations while generating goodwill, positive word-of-mouth, and the hope that people will look more favorably on these brands when making their next purchase decision." He explains how this works in the *A Principled Practice* feature.

A **societal marketing** philosophy describes the operations of companies whose corporate mission reflects their desire to do good—the business philosophies of Ben & Jerry's, Tom's of Maine, and the Body Shop, for example. Their commitment is expressed in the way they design, source their ingredients, produce, and market their products. We mentioned in Chapter 3 that embedding social responsibility deep in the brand essence and operations is the idea behind our **Fourth Principle of IMC** that *integration equals integrity*.

If a commitment reflects a company's core business strategy, as in Dove's "real women" campaign and Avon's support of breast cancer research, it is called **mission marketing.**[18] See also Interprint's "environmental stewardship" ad, which

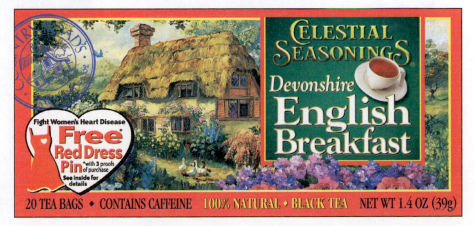

Celestial Seasonings links its brand to the "Red Dress" campaign using the symbol of the dress on its tea packages.

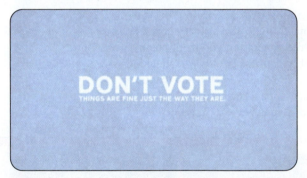

SHOWCASE

The award-winning "Things Are Fine" campaign to mobilize youth voters in the 2008 presidential campaign was featured in *Communication Arts, Adweek, Ad Critic,* and the *One Show.*

The "Things are Fine" campaign includes:

Web site: animated flag opening

Posters: oil noose, Made in China, price of war, battered george

Spread the Word: bookmarks, personal blogs, social network links, email and IM formats

TV: "polar bear," "crayon–orange" key frames (also "church and state" "flag disintegrating," "Freedumb,")

A graduate of the advertising program at the University of Colorado, Jeremy Boland was a student of Professor Brett Robbs.

A PRINCIPLED PRACTICE

Pause for the Cause: Boosting Brands and Building Goodwill with Cause Marketing

Scott Hamula, *Associate Professor, Ithaca College*

Things are really tough out there for brands: lots of competition, savvier consumers, media messages that just don't break through the clutter like they used to, and occasional pieces of bad publicity. Today, though, some brands are turning to corporate social responsibility, not only because it is the right thing to do, but also as a way for brands to more clearly differentiate themselves in this dynamic marketplace.

An increasingly popular form of customer engagement is called cause-related marketing. From a local pizzeria donating money to pay for a neighborhood Little League team's baseball shirts to Ford Motor Company donating vehicles to an earthquake-ravaged disaster area in China, brands act as good corporate citizens.

This socially responsible promotional strategy occurs when a brand or company aligns itself with a nonprofit organization to generate both sales and charitable donations at the same time. Simply put, it's "buy my product and I'll donate to your cause." This approach tends to make a lot of sense. Surveys continue to show that, given two very similar products, consumers are more likely to purchase the brand that is associated with a cause they care about.

American Express Company is often credited with starting cause-related marketing in the early 80s when it pledged to donate 5 cents to the arts in San Francisco whenever a member used their American Express card to make a purchase and $2 for each new card member.

To launch and sustain a successful cause-related marketing program, a brand must first know what issues are important to its customers so as to align itself with a cause that's a good match. An example of this would be Yoplait yogurt's "Save Lids to Save Lives" campaign. Since this brand's primary target market is women, Yoplait linked itself with the Susan G. Komen Fight for the Cure organization, which is dedicated to fighting against breast cancer worldwide and is often recognized by its pink ribbon symbol. During Yoplait's annual drive, for every pink lid sent in, the brand donated 10 cents, up to $1.5 million. Some brands like Pier 1 Imports go as far as creating specific products for its annual partnership with Komen including a candle whose design is remodeled every August, a pink jewelry box, and a pink shawl. For more information on these and other cause-related marketing programs, visit the Cause Marketing Forum at *www.causemarketingforum.com*.

What do you think? Is cause marketing limited to certain types of industries or is this a strategy with more universal appeal for brands in a variety of categories?

---

appeared earlier in the B2B section. Mission marketing links a company's mission and core values to a cause that connects with the company's and its customers' interests. It is more of a commitment than cause marketing because it reflects a long-term brand building perspective and the mission becomes the focal point for integrating all the company's marketing communication.

In addition to a societal marketing business philosophy, corporate public relations activities are sometimes designed to create a positive company image by emphasizing a company's concern for social issues and the steps it takes to make a positive contribution to society. Societal marketing also engages the entire brand organization and its stakeholders, particularly its employees, through their commitment to the effort.

Principle
Cause marketing and mission marketing are driven by the passion employees and other stakeholders, as well as customers, feel for a good cause.

INTERNATIONAL MARKETING COMMUNICATION

The globalization of marketing communication is driven by the development of international media, globalization of brands, and the spread of market-based economies in countries and regions such as China, South America, India, and Eastern Europe. Also, the expanded use of English as an international language is helping spread Western marketing ideas to the rest of the world. The

Dedicated to World Peace Through World Trade

The title "World Headquarters" has been given to this building because it is the center from which are directed the far-flung activities of International Business Machines Corporation in seventy-nine different countries of the world.

This building was dedicated to the cause of world peace through world trade. Every International Business Machine representative in every country is an unofficial ambassador for better international understanding, working toward the day when the people of all nations, through a greater exchange of goods and services, ideas and ideals, shall live and work together for the advancement of civilization.

CLASSIC

IBM used this "World Peace" ad to demonstrate its commitment to world trade and the international marketing of its products.

Internet has also had a huge impact on bringing the ability to market internationally to even the smallest of companies.

Stages of Marketing Development

Virtually every product category can be divided into local, national, regional (trading bloc), and international markets and brands. Typically this involves a process that begins when a national company expands to a few foreign markets by **exporting** its products. Then at the second stage it begins to internationalize its operations by selling to a group of markets in a region (Europe or Asia, for example) and eventually moves to a global perspective, the third stage, with brands sold throughout the world. An example of a company adopting an international perspective comes from the "World Peace" ad used by IBM in 1938.

A characteristic of globalized companies is that the **country of origin** label often doesn't apply. Nokia and Motorola, even though they are not U.S. companies, are both familiar brands to U.S. consumers. Country of origin, however, can be a problem as McDonald's found out when its restaurants were targeted because it represented America at a time when the country's political actions were being criticized worldwide. McDonald's has been boycotted in the Philippines and Argentina, as well as in many Arab countries—not for anything it does but simply because of its image as an iconic American brand. Efforts by McDonald's local franchisees have included trying to present a local face by using its employees in traditional dress standing outside the store and by making contributions to local charities.

The SPAR grocery store chain that we described earlier in the *A Matter of Practice* feature originated in the Netherlands in 1932 and is now present in 33 countries on four continents. The SPAR model is for each store to have its own personality and range of products, which are adapted to its individual market.

The Global versus Local Debate

There is an old axiom, "All business is local." An extension of this saying is "Think globally, act locally." Although advertising campaigns can be created for a global market, they must be relevant to a transaction that is completed at or near home or in the office.

A classic article by Harvard Business School professor Theodore Levitt as long ago as 1983 ignited a debate over how to conduct global marketing. Levitt argued that companies should operate as if there were only one global market. He suggested that differences among nations and cultures were not diminishing and people throughout the world are motivated by the same desires and wants.[19] Other scholars argued that Levitt misinterpreted the importance of cultural differences and cited the success of such brands as Coca-Cola, PepsiCo, and McDonald's in developing products and marketing for the various cultures they serve.[20]

In support of Levitt's thinking, some researchers propose sets of what they call *universal values* that cross cultures. They include such values as these:

1. Protecting the family
2. Honesty
3. Health and fitness
4. Self-esteem
5. Self-reliance
6. Justice
7. Freedom
8. Friendship
9. Knowledge
10. Learning

Dutch scholar Geert Hofstede, an expert on cultural differences, insists that the impact of national culture on business and consumption patterns is huge and should be accommodated in marketing and advertising strategies. The universals, in other words, are not as common as Levitt said. Based on a study of 116,000 IBM employees around the world, Hofstede found their cultural differences to be stronger than the legendary IBM corporate culture that he assumed would be a standardizing influence. Hofstede also found that the American values of taking initiative, personal competency, and rugged individualism are not universal values and that some cultures prize collective thinking and group norms rather than independence. A *Practical Tips* box at *www.pearsonhighered.com/moriarty* explains what one researcher has learned about the application of Hofstede's principles to advertising.

The outgrowth of the local-versus-global debate has been three schools of thought on advertising across national borders:

- *Standardization* The **standardization** school of thought contends that differences between countries are a matter of degree, so advertisers must instead focus on the similarities of consumers and a consistent brand presentation.
- *Localization (Adaptation)* The **localization** or **adaptation** school of thought argues that advertisers must consider differences among countries, including local culture, stage of economic and industrial development, stage of life cycle, media availability, research availability, and legal restrictions.
- *Combination* This approach reasons that a combination of standardization and localization may produce the most effective advertising. Some elements of brand identity and strategy, for example, may be standardized, but advertising executions may need to be adapted to the local culture.

The reality of global advertising suggests that a combination approach is often best. The challenge for advertisers is to balance variations nationally or regionally with a basic global brand plan that maintains brand consistency. The adaptability continuum shown in Figure 18.4 elaborates on these three perspectives.

As we have said, most companies use the combination approach or lean toward localization. Honda, for example, uses a decentralized strategy for its CR-V. The auto manufacturer has a global brand guideline that all agencies must follow; however, these guidelines apply mostly to use of the logo. There is a global website with a standard look and format. The marketing communication strategy varies with the market. In Iceland, as Ingvi Logason explained, "We created a completely unique strategy based on our local research and knowledge." The following list summarizes the benefits of standardization and local strategies:

When to Use a Standardization Strategy

- Standardization will lead to savings through economies of scale (production, planning, control).
- Standardization ensures that the brand messages of a product are complementary and reinforcing.
- The company maintains control over the image projected by all brand communication for the brand.
- Global media create opportunities for global marketing.
- Converging buyer wants and needs mean that buyers everywhere will increasingly want the same products.

Principle
International marketers strive for a consistent brand strategy that still allows them to honor cultural differences when those differences are relevant to the brand's marketing strategy.

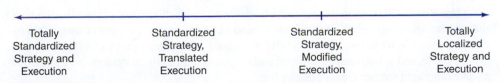

| Totally Standardized Strategy and Execution | Standardized Strategy, Translated Execution | Standardized Strategy, Modified Execution | Totally Localized Strategy and Execution |

FIGURE 18.4

The Adaptability Continuum
Most global companies fall in the middle and right side of the continuum in their global strategies.

High-Context

- Japanese
- Chinese
- Arabic
- Greek
- Spanish
- Italian
- English
- French
- North American
- Scandinavian
- German

Low-Context

FIGURE 18.5

High- to Low-Context Cultures
The language of advertising messages is not as easy to craft in high-context cultures as in low-context cultures, where the meaning of a sentence is not so dependent on surrounding sentences.

- There is little or no competition in many foreign markets.
- Graphic and visual approaches can be used to overcome cultural differences.

When to Use a Localized Strategy

- A better fit with local markets means the marketer is less likely to overlook local variations that affect buyer behavior.
- As a general rule, the fewer number of people who have to approve decisions, the faster they can be made.
- Getting local managers and employees involved and motivated is much easier if those people have a say in the strategic decisions.
- Creating localized messages can be a more effective use of the budget because cost reductions resulting from globalization often are offset by mistargeted ads.
- Strategically sound messages are more likely to be successful and communicate effectively with the local audience. The chance of cultural blunders decreases with localized strategies.

Cultural Meanings The major distinction in cross-cultural communication is between **high-context cultures**, in which the meaning of a message can be best understood when contained within contextual cues, and **low-context cultures** in which the message can be understood as it stands.[21] In other words, in Japanese a word can have multiple meanings. Listeners or readers will not understand the exact meaning of a word unless they clearly understand the context in which the word is used. In contrast, English is a low-context language—most of its words have clearly defined meanings that are not highly dependent on the words surrounding them. Figure 18.5 lists cultures from the highest to lowest context, with Japanese being the highest context culture. This model helps explain the difficulties of advertising in other languages.

Advertising messages constructed by writers from high-context cultures might be difficult to understand in low-context cultures because they may offer too much detail to make the point clearly. In contrast, messages authored by writers from low-context cultures may be difficult to understand in high-context cultures because they omit essential contextual detail.

Central Control versus Local Adaptation As noted previously, some marketers develop tightly controlled global campaigns with minimum adaptation for local markets. Others develop local campaigns in every major market. Most companies are somewhere in the middle. How are global campaigns created? International advertising campaigns have two basic starting points: (1) success in one country and (2) a centrally conceived strategy. Planning approaches also include variations on the central campaign and bottom-up creativity:

- *Local Initiative* A successful campaign, conceived for national application, is modified for use in other countries. Wrigley, Marlboro, IBM, Waterman, Seiko, Philips, Ford, and many other companies have taken successful campaigns from one country and transplanted them around the world, a practice called *search and reapply*. When a local campaign is found to be successful, that campaign is taken to one or two countries that are similar to see how well the campaign works in these areas. If it is successful, use of the campaign is expanded and can eventually become the brand's primary international campaign. What is interesting about this strategy is that it provides additional motivation for local agencies. While all local agencies want to do a good job to keep their local business, it is a major ego boost—not to mention the additional financial awards—when a local campaign is taken beyond its original country's borders.

  The Honda CR-V is an example. As Logason explains, "Because of the effectiveness of the original campaign—both the insights behind the strategy and the idea of ownership of the 4×4 concept, which was so successful in Iceland—the campaign caught the eye of the global office, and it has been distributed and showcased globally to dealers in other markets as an example of strong, clever positioning."

- *Centrally Conceived Campaigns* The second approach, a centrally conceived campaign, was pioneered by Coca-Cola and is now used increasingly in global strategies. Microsoft uses a centralized strategy for its Xbox video game system; since it was a new brand, a consistent marketing strategy was deemed to be essential. Although the centralization concept is simple, its application can be difficult. A work team, task force, or action group (the names vary) assembles from around the world to present, debate, modify, if necessary, and agree on a basic strategy as the foundation for the campaign. Cost is a huge factor. If the same photography and artwork can be used universally, this can save thousands of dollars over each local variation.

- *Variations on Central Campaigns* Variations on the centrally conceived campaign also exist. For example, BBDO's many local agencies were used to adapt the creative ideas for all the markets served by DaimlerChrysler (now Chrysler after the company split). The office that develops the approved campaign would be designated the **lead agency** and would develop all the necessary elements of the campaign and prepare a standards manual for use in other countries. Because photography, artwork, television production, and color printing are costly, developing these items in one location and then overlaying new copy or rerecording the voice track in the local language saves money. However, because some countries, such as Malaysia, require that all campaign materials be locally produced, this approach gives direction to the message but still allows for local requirements to be met.
- *Bottom-Up Creativity* Sometimes a competition may be used to find the best new idea. For example, to extend McDonald's "I'm Lovin' It" campaign, McDonald's global chief marketing officer held a contest among McDonald's ad agencies all over the world. One winner, which became part of the international pool of ads, came from China, which is developing a lively creative advertising industry that produces edgy, breakthrough ads for young people. McDonald's strategy was not just to do the creative work in the United States but rather to "Let the best ideas win."

Planning International Strategies

Assuming that the campaign has been approved centrally, with a local application approach, its execution must be adapted to suit the local market, and that may involve modifying basic strategy decisions, such as objectives, targeting, and perhaps even positioning.

International Objectives The problem of managing brand consistency is largely responsible for limiting most international or global marketing objectives to awareness and recall, two effective yet easily attainable marketing communication measures, although more specific objectives may be needed in individual markets. For example, a brand may be well known in one market, so its primary objective, then, is reminder. At the same time it may be newly launched in another country, so the objectives there are awareness building and trial.

Targeting Issues International marketers need to answer three basic targeting questions: (1) What countries? (2) What level of market development? (3) Which cultural cohort groups?

- *What Countries?* This is generally the easiest to answer because it is driven by where the brand is distributed.
- *Market Development Level* Countries, especially developing countries, vary greatly in market infrastructure, literacy levels, economic level, and level of media development. Some countries' standard of living is such that luxury brands, for example, would not find a large enough segment of the population to cover the cost of setting up distribution and supporting the brand with marketing communication and a sales force.
- *Cultural Cohorts* A cultural cohort is a segment of customers from multiple countries sharing common characteristics that translate into common wants and needs. New mothers are an example. Regardless of their nationality, new mothers want their babies to be happy and healthy. Teenagers are another cohort—teens in Tokyo and New York City may have more in common than a teen and his father.

Positioning the Brand Positioning is one of the key strategic elements that brands usually try to keep consistent from country to country. An example comes from a Vodafone campaign created by an Argentinian agency, Santo, which was identified as *Ad Age*'s International Agency of the Year

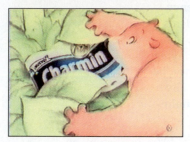

Charmin continues to emphasize softness through the device of a cuddly bear, even in Mexico where this commercial ran. Note that it is largely a nonverbal execution, which is easier to use for global campaigns than those with a lot of words.

in 2010. For Vodafone, the mobile telecommunication brand, Santos came up with the line: "Power to You." *Ad Age* heralded it as a simple, direct global idea that's easy to adapt to local campaigns.[22]

Research is often conducted to identify the problems and opportunities facing the product in each of the international markets to be entered, as the Charmin commercial illustrates. Particularly important is a good understanding of consumer buying motives in each market. This is almost impossible to develop without locally based consumer research. If analysis reveals that consumers' buying behavior and the competitive environment are the same across international markets, it may be possible to use standardized positioning throughout.

The international consulting firm Accenture faced a strategic problem when Tiger Woods, the brand's long-time celebrity spokesperson, faced allegations of extramarital affairs. Because he was so well known internationally and represented the firm's high-performance position around the world, Accenture felt it needed to replace his long-running campaign. Much of Accenture's brand communication appears as images in airports, so the problem was to find universal imagery that continued to reflect the Accenture brand position. After conducting research and testing a number of ideas, the decision was to use animals—an elephant, chameleon, frogs, and fish—in unexpected and challenging situations. For example, one of the electronic posters shows an elephant balancing on a surfboard with text that reads "Who says you can't be big and nimble?"[23]

Setting the Budget   All the budgeting techniques discussed in Chapter 7 apply in foreign markets. When preparing a single plan for multiple markets, many companies use an objective-task budgeting approach that entails a separate budget for each foreign market. (Remember that this approach looks at the objectives for each activity and determines the cost of accomplishing each objective.) This technique adds some flexibility to localize campaigns as needed. However, local practices also may affect the budget decision. Most notably, the exchange rate from country to country may affect not only the amount of money spent in a particular market, but also the timing of the expenditures. The cost of television time in Tokyo is approximately twice what it is on U.S. networks, and, rather than being sold during an up-front market every spring, Japanese TV time is wholesaled several times during the year.

Executing an International Campaign   The execution of a global campaign is usually more complex than a national plan. The creative may need to be reshot with local models and settings as well as language translation. Language is always a problem for a campaign that is dependent on words rather than visuals as the primary meaning carrier. A team of language experts may be needed to adjust the terms and carry over the meanings in the different languages. The Pepsi slogan "Come Alive," for example, was translated in Taiwan as "Pepsi will bring your ancestors back from the dead." KFC's "Finger Lickin' Good" slogan translated into Chinese as "Eat Your Fingers Off."

Product names can even be a problem. In Canada, Mercedes-Benz found that its GST model name is also the familiar initials of a tax commonly referred to in English as the "gouge and screw tax."

Regulations, censorship, and favoritism toward local companies create barriers to entry for foreign companies trying to enter some markets, particularly China. U.S.-based technology giants, such as Google, Yahoo!, and eBay have been outmaneuvered by their Chinese competitors. Twitter and Facebook are regularly blocked by the Chinese government.[24]

Government approval of television commercials can be difficult to secure in some countries. As advertisers move into international and global advertising, they also face many of the same ethical issues that advertisers deal with in the United States, such as the representation of women and advertising to children, but they may also have to deal with questions about the Americanization or Westernization of local cultures.[25] An example comes from a Nike ad used in China that showed LeBron James teaching moves to martial arts masters. Chinese officials banned it because they consider it insulting to national dignity.

But it's not just government bans that can trouble ad strategies. Social responsibility is taken seriously in some countries and, with the Internet and e-mail, consumer concerns can create a huge issue. For example, an ad by fashion house Dolce & Gabbana showed a bare-chested man pinning a glamorous woman to the ground while his buddies looked on. Consumers in Spain, Italy, and the United States complained that it trivialized violence against women, and the many e-mail complaints led the company to drop the ad.

International Media Buying In terms of the media buy, media are different in every country—not only different, but also developing and evolving. As a result, it is absolutely essential that a local agency be used to handle the media buy. In the early 1990s in China, for example, there was hardly an advertising industry or advertising media opportunities. China is widely recognized as the world's most fragmented market. Television, for example, has 95 percent penetration with more than 2,200 channels. Internet use in China reached 384 million registered users in 2009. That's only 29 percent of China's population, so you can see the incredible growth opportunities for this medium.[26]

Adjustments may need to be made for seasonality. For example, a campaign in the Southern Hemisphere, especially for consumer goods, requires major changes from a Northern Hemisphere campaign. In the Southern Hemisphere, summer, Christmas, and back-to-school campaigns are all compressed from November through January. Holidays also differ based on

Accenture's replacement campaign for its well-known celebrity, Tiger Woods, used different types of animals—who are less likely to make unfortunate headlines. Accenture's slogan "High Performance. Delivered." continued to be used in the new campaign with its animals in challenging, but semi-humorous, situations.

local history and religion and often affect retail and government activities. Christmas, for example, is celebrated in Christian lands, Ramadan in countries with Muslim populations, and Hanukkah everywhere there are Jewish population centers.

Everything takes longer internationally—count on it. The New York business day overlaps for only three hours with the business day in London, for two hours with most of Europe, and for one hour with Greece and not at all with Japan, Hong Kong, the Middle East, or Australia. For these reasons e-mail that permits electronic transfer and telecopy transmission is a popular mode for international communication. E-mail and fax numbers have become as universal as telephone numbers on stationery and business cards in international companies. The calendar is an enemy of business in other ways. France and Spain virtually close down in August for vacation.

Organizing for International Marketing Communication

Agencies must develop an organizational structure to manage global brand messages. The organizational structure depends heavily on whether the client company is following a standardization or localization strategy. Some agencies exercise tight control, while others allow more local autonomy. All these approaches fall into three groups: tight central international control, centralized resources with moderate control, or a match of the client's organization—if the client is highly centralized, then the agency account structure will be highly centralized.

The IMC Factor in International Campaign Planning

Integrated marketing communication means that all the messages a consumer receives about a brand work together to create a coherent brand impression. To do that on a global level requires both horizontal and vertical coordination. The vertical effort represents the coordination of the key planning decisions, such as targeting, positioning, objectives, strategies, and tactics across all the various tools used in the communication program. The horizontal level requires coordination across all countries and regions involved in the plan.

Because of this complexity, it takes a dedicated manager to ensure that all the various marketing communication activities stay consistent to the brand and campaign strategy. *The Inside Story* explains how an account director at Dentsu, the world's largest single agency, approaches integration on behalf of his clients.

Because of the complexity, IMC planners use planning grids to plot strategic coordination of messages across countries and across marcom programs. The table below illustrates how such a grid might be constructed. The messages are plotted indicating how they may vary locally for different cultures, as well as what brand elements are used, such as position or personality, to maintain consistency. Some companies sell not just one brand but a portfolio of subbrands or brand extensions, and the challenge is to maintain brand consistency across these different product lines in different countries. There may also be differences in the message strategy for different stakeholder groups. For each country the planner describes the following brand message variations:

- Country specific changes
- Audience specific changes
- Brand consistency elements (the unchangeables)

Marcom Tool	Country A	Country B	Country C	Country D
Advertising				
Direct Response				
Public Relations				
Etc.				

Looking Ahead

This chapter started with IMC and then reviewed a number of specialized marketing areas: retail, B2B, nonprofit, and international. In most of these specialized areas an important strategy for marketing communicators is to drive consistency through all their messages and brand experiences. It's cost effective as well as more effective communication. The next chapter will wrap up this marketing communication journey with a discussion of evaluation—the last and most important step in proving the effectiveness of IMC programs and campaigns.

Chasing the Same Dream

Masaru Ariga, *Group Account Director, Dentsu Inc., Tokyo, Japan*

Without doubt, markets are getting similar to one another. But I feel that fundamental differences exist in the business of communication.

The societal implications of advertising itself are significantly different between Japan and the United States. The meaning of advertising generally goes beyond just a means of selling in Japan. People "enjoy" advertising. Good advertising becomes the talk of the town and often invigorates corporate reputations, providing a ripple effect on employee satisfaction and recruitment of talented people. Bad advertising does exactly the opposite.

It is understandable, therefore, that Japanese advertisers tend to think of advertising more holistically than their American counterparts. Consumers and society do remember the messages a company sends. Successful companies, therefore, need to have a long-term and holistic view of communication activities.

In Japan, the client–agency relationship also tends to be considered longer term. In fact, a food company I handle has been Dentsu's client for more than a century—since the agency was founded in 1901. While short-term accountability should not be undermined, the fact that agency and advertiser are solidly intertwined, sharing common values and history, is definitely a plus for building a strong, cohesive brand. After all, a brand develops in consumers' minds over a long period of time.

Advertisers rely on agencies for a wider range of communication issues in Japan than in the United States—advertising agencies are called in for much of what an American company would have called in consulting firms or specialized agencies. In the case of a hotel/transportation conglomerate I am responsible for, Dentsu's work includes creating the mission statement, internal marketing, hotel naming and logo or mark design, and even industrial design of a new commuter train and signage for the stations. Those tasks are in addition to conventional marketing communication such as mass media advertising, PR, sales promotion, events, and the Internet. I make sure that my team provides holistic solutions to the business issues of clients in a cohesive way.

I believe that the power of integrated communication is still undervalued. When communication activities are truly integrated based on a solid mission and direction, a company can obtain a strong, durable competitive edge.

After all, true IMC requires organizational integration by which people in a variety of fields creatively chase the same dream. But it is extremely difficult for different people to have the same dream. Hand in hand with top management, I feel an agency can play a critical role to "coordinate" disoriented messages and guide the organization to move forward in the same direction.

Masaru Ariga was in the first graduating class in 1992 from the IMC Master's program at Northwestern University; his undergraduate degree was from Waseda University in Tokyo.

IT'S A WRAP

Driving Honda's CR-V to Number One

According to Ingvi Logason, owner of the H:N agency in Iceland, the results of his agency's campaigns over several years for the Honda CR-V campaign were phenomenal. You may remember that the goal was to increase the sales of an international auto brand, the Honda CR-V, in Iceland. It also was designed as an integrated campaign. Here is how Logason explains the encore campaign's success: "In a market where competitive SUVs were being heavily subsidized, we sold all cars with close to no discounts (3 to 5 percent off list price is standard in Iceland), which demonstrated the brand's strength."

His proof: Interest among intended new buyers measured 33 percent (3 percentage points above our aim of 20 percent increase), top-of-mind scores placed the brand at 3 (1 higher than our goal). The average age of the new CR-V buyer was 43 years of age (exceeding our target by 2 years) and this led to a 15 percent market share in the small SUV section, 25 percent over the target, and the largest in the car market by far. Furthermore the campaign made the new CR-V the fourth most sold car in the country—the best-selling Honda ever in Iceland.

Not only was the CR-V the best-selling Honda, the campaign drove the CR-V to become the best-selling small SUV to achieve the position of category leader—outselling the closest competitor 4 to 3. Today Honda in Iceland has by far the highest market share of all Honda dealerships in Europe.

Logason concludes, "All in all it was a textbook campaign of strategic planning where creative insight derived from research yielded great results. We challenged the target group and created a visual image in their mind of them owning the car. It was done in a simple, yet meaningful way that built a bridge between a brand and buyer."

Key Points Summary

1. **What do we mean by *total brand communication* in IMC programs?** Integration is both a way to develop campaigns that maximize consistency among all the marcom tools and a philosophy that monitors and manages all brand messages with all stakeholders at all contact points—not just the traditional marketing communication. The latter delivers total brand communication with a consistent vision for the life of the brand. Total communication means everything communicates—messages are delivered by every element of the marketing mix, as well as every marcom message and brand experience.

2. **What is retail marketing communication all about, and what makes it distinctive?** Retailers are merchants who sell directly to consumers. Most retail businesses are locally owned and advertise at the local level. However, retail advertising at the national and international levels is becoming more common. Co-op advertising with manufacturers and service providers is common. Retail advertising directed at a local audience typically focuses on attracting customers through price and promotion information. It may also focus on store image, product quality, and style. The main

medium used for retail advertising is newspapers. However, retailers also use shoppers, preprinted inserts, magazines, television, radio, and the Web. Apart from traditional store retailing, some businesses engage in nonstore retailing, including use of the Web.

3. **How does business-to-business marketing communication work?** Business-to-business advertising is used to influence demand and is directed at people in the business arena who buy or specify products for business use. Its objectives include creating company awareness, increasing selling efficiency, and supporting channel members. Compared to the consumer market, the market for business goods is limited. Decision making tends to be shared by a group of people, and purchasing decisions center on price, services, product quality, and assurance of supply. B2B media consist of general business and trade publications, directories, direct mail, catalogs, the Web, and consumer media.

4. **What are the basic goals and operations of nonprofit and social marketing?** Nonprofits use all the tools of mar-

keting communication to achieve their goals, which tend to focus on fund-raising and recruitment. Social marketing uses marketing programs and marketing communication tools for the good of society. It can be a corporate strategy or a strategy used by a nonprofit organization. Cause marketing and mission marketing are tools used to align companies with socially responsible business practices.

5. **Which strategic decisions are behind international marketing communication?** Marketing begins with a local brand, expands to a regional brand, and, finally, goes global. Advertising and marketing communication follow the same path. The biggest strategic decision involves how much of the marketing communication strategy is globalized or localized. Ultimately, such campaigns should be centrally controlled and centrally conceived. There should also be local applications and approval. In international as in all IMC campaigns, the challenge is to create brand consistency in all messages and customer experiences with the brand.

Words of Wisdom: Recommended Reading

IMC

Kitchen, Philip, and Patrick De Pelsmacker, *Integrated Marketing Communications: A Primer,* New York: Routledge, 2004.

Percy, Larry, *Strategic Integrated Marketing Communications,* Oxford, UK: Butterworth-Heinemann, 2008.

Schultz, Don, Stanley Tannenbaum, and Robert Lauterborn, *The New Marketing Paradigm: Integrated Marketing Communications,* Lincolnwood, IL: NTC, 1996.

Schultz, Don, and Heidi Schultz, *IMC, The Next Generation: Five Steps for Delivering Value and Measuring Financial Returns,* New York: McGraw-Hill, 2004.

Retail

Levinson, Jay, Elly Valas, and Orvel Wilson, *Guerilla Retailing,* Boulder, CO: The Guerilla Group, 2004.

Liljenwall, Robert, *The Power of Marketing at Retail,* Washington, DC: Point-of-Purchase Advertising International, 2008.

Negen, Bob, and Susan Negen, *Marketing Your Retail Store in the Internet Age,* Hoboken NJ: John Wiley, 2007.

Schultz, Don, Martin Block, and BIGResearch, *Retail Communities: Customer-Driven Retailing,* Worthington, OH: Prosper Publishing, 2010.

B2B

Brennan, Ross, Louise Canning, and Raymond McDowell, *Business-to-Business Marketing,* Thousand Oaks, CA: Sage, 2007.

Hutt, Michael, and Thomas Speh, *Business Marketing Management: B2B,* Mason, OH: South-Western Cengage, 2009.

Yellin, Emily, *Your Call Is (Not That) Important to Us,* New York: Free Press, 2009.

International

de Mooij, Marieke, *Global Marketing and Advertising,* Thousand Oaks: Sage, 2010.

Frith, Katherine, and Barbara Mueller, *Advertising Societies: Global Issues,* New York: Peter Lang, 2003.

Mueller, Barbara, *Dynamics of International Advertising,* New York: Peter Lang, 2004.

Key Terms

ad allowances, p. 552
adaptation, p. 565
business-to-business (B2B)
   advertising, p. 556
buyer, p. 556
capital campaigns, p. 560
cause marketing, p. 561
cooperative (co-op)
   advertising, p. 552
country of origin, p. 564
cross-functional
   management, p. 548
dealer tag, p. 554

development, p. 560
donut, p. 554
exporting, p. 564
free-standing inserts
   (FSIs), p. 554
fund-raising, p. 560
high-context culture, p. 566
horizontal publications, p. 558
house brands, p. 551
industrial advertising, p. 557
lead agency, p. 567
localization, p. 565
low-context culture, p. 566

mission marketing, p. 561
North American Industry
   Classification System
   (NAICS), p. 556
preprints, p. 554
price-value strategy, p. 553
private-label brands, p. 551
profession advertising, p. 557
promotional allowance, p. 552
public communication
   campaigns, p. 560

shelf talkers, p. 554
shoppers, p. 554
social marketing, p. 560
societal marketing, p. 561
standardization, p. 565
store brands, p. 551
store traffic, p. 551
synergy, p. 549
trade advertising, p. 557
vertical publications, p. 558
zone editions, p. 554

Review Questions

1. Explain the difference between planning an IMC campaign and planning a 360-degree total communication program.

2. How do retail advertising objectives differ from B2B objectives?

3. What are the types of B2B advertising, and how do these differ from more general consumer advertising?

4. Explain how both for-profit companies and nonprofit organizations can use social marketing.

5. What is a public communication campaign, and how does it differ from product advertising? Give an example.

6. Explain cause marketing and mission marketing. How do they differ?

7. How does culture relate to the decision to globalize or localize a campaign?

8. Explain how a global IMC program is more complex than an IMC program operated nationally.

Discussion Questions

1. Choose a restaurant in your community. What types of people does it target? Would you recommend that its advertising focus on price or image? What is (or should be) its image? Which media or marcom area should it use?

2. You work for a large sporting goods chain that would like to focus all of its local philanthropic activities in one area. You believe the company could benefit from a mission marketing program. What should be in a proposal for the marketing VP that explains mission marketing? Why do you think a mission marketing project might work for the company?

3. You have gotten a new assignment to be on a launch team for an upscale pen made in Switzerland under the brand name of Pinnacle. Its primary advantage is that it has an extremely long-lasting cartridge, one that is guaranteed to last for at least five years. The pen is available in a variety of forms, including roller ball and felt tip, and a variety of widths, from fine to wide stroke. Use the adaptability continuum to analyze the globalization or localization options for launching this pen first in Europe and then globally. What would your recommendation be on standardizing the advertising?

4. Define the difference between a high-context and a low-context culture. If you are an international student, analyze your own culture and compare it with the United States. If you are from the United States, try to see your country through the eyes of someone from another country. In class illustrate the difference by finding two ads in this textbook that you think effectively demonstrate these two message strategies. Explain how they work and which viewpoint you think they present.

5. *Three-Minute Debate* Two of your friends have just purchased a sandwich shop and intend to turn it into a gourmet sandwich shop that features different types of sandwiches from different countries. They found a good lease in a neighborhood shopping center, but the costs of franchising, leasing, and other charges have left them very little for advertising. With limited funds, Tom and Wendy are arguing about how to best get the word out about their new business. Should they use advertising, social media, guerilla media, events, or sales promotion? Pick a form and develop an argument why your team thinks this approach should be the lead medium or platform. Prepare a three-minute presentation with no more than three PowerPoint slides.

Take-Home Projects

1. *Portfolio Project* Compare the brand positioning and customer-focused content of three of the following B2B sites: *www.accenture.com, www.ibm.com, www.nielsen.com, www.forrester.com, www.strategicbusinessinsights.com*, and *www.newpig.com*. Write a one- to two-page report on your analysis of the three sites you selected. What would you recommend to improve their usefulness to B2B customers?

2. *Mini-Case Analysis* The CR-V campaign in Iceland has been receiving effectiveness awards for years. Why do you think that is so? What are the strengths of its marketing communication approach? What might you suggest to continue to improve the impact of this series of campaigns?

Team Project: The BrandRevive Campaign

It's time to begin the wrap up of the campaign you have been building for your BrandRevive client.

- Analyze the needs of your BrandRevive client in terms of retail, B2B, nonprofit, and international marketing. For those areas that are relevant, write proposals that explain how your campaign would be extended into those special types of marketing situations.

- Analyze your BrandRevive campaign that you have been developing in terms of its 360-degree or total brand communication orientation. Make whatever adjustments are needed and then prepare a discussion of how your campaign delivers an integrated program. Use the Richards Group creative brief to summarize your planning.
- Present and explain these dimensions of your plan in no more than three PowerPoint slides.

Hands-On Case

The Century Council

Read the Century Council case in the Appendix before coming to class.

1. How could you increase the consistency of "The Stupid Drink" campaign so that the overall impact was greater?

2. If you wanted to go global with this campaign, what would you need to learn about each new market before you ran the campaign?

CHAPTER 10

Evaluation
of Effectiveness

It's a Winner

Title:
"Colorado Pass Club: It's Why We Live Here"

Client:
Vail Resorts

Agency:
In-house

CHAPTER KEY POINTS

1. Why and how is marketing communication evaluation conducted?
2. Can you list and explain the stages of message evaluation?
3. What are the key areas of media evaluation?
4. How are IMC tools, campaigns, and programs evaluated?

The Colorado Pass—The Coolest Club on the Slopes!*

Here's the problem: How do you not only maintain share of market but increase business for a ski resort in a competitive landscape? I work for Vail Resorts and that's one of our biggest challenges.

Although the business from the destination market is important to the financial health of the company, so are season passes. Season-pass sales are a significant contributor to the bottom line and provide revenue stability by locking in revenue early in the ski season. Lift ticket revenue is 35 percent of all company revenue; season passes represent approximately 33 percent of that lift ticket revenue. In fact, most season passes are purchased before the season even begins. However, season-pass purchases are conducted in a very competitive environment because our resorts go up against other Colorado resorts to secure the largest share of the 5 million skiers in the local market.

Our company is in a unique position to attract skiers and snowboarders because of its five mountains—Vail, Beaver Creek, Breckenridge, Keystone, Heavenly-Lake Tahoe—and Arapahoe Basin (a partner resort). Our largest competitors in Colorado, where competition is the fiercest, include Copper Mountain, Winter Park, Aspen, and Steamboat Springs. The company offers a few different types of season passes, but we'll focus on the Colorado Pass™, our marquee pass.

One of our strengths is our robust customer databases, which contain transactional information (a history of products purchased) and traditional marketing information. The combination of the two permits very strong database segmentation for e-mail and direct-mail efforts. We also track revenue generated from those efforts so that we can assess their ROIs and strengthen the next campaign. We can also tell if a guest has booked a trip or purchased a product through our e-mails or direct mail and can ensure that they aren't served up the same message again—keeping our communication effective and meaningful.

Vail Resorts has more than 500,000 total e-mail subscribers for various programs; more than 70,000 of these are Colorado Pass holders. In accordance with

---

*This chapter opening story was contributed by Jennifer Wolfe-Kimbell, Senior Marketing Manager at Vail Resorts, Broomfield, Colorado.

the "canned spam" laws, everyone on the list has opted in and asked for e-mail promotions and information. This is a perfectly qualified database of customers—they own our product and raised their hands for more information.

As we headed into the selling season for 2009–2010 season passes, the marketing department was charged with ensuring that (1) our loyal pass holders stayed loyal and renewed—locking them in for the season, (2) previous pass holders returned, and (3) individuals with competitor passes converted to the Colorado Pass.

Once we had secured a healthy base of season-pass holders we had to focus on generating revenue for the various lines of business within the company (lodging, ski school, rentals, dining). The challenge for us was that it had been a particularly difficult landscape. The recession was in full swing and we had to contend with cautious consumers, elevated gas prices (something the drive market was sensitive to), and a relatively low snow season (this group lives for snow days).

Beyond encouraging our pass holders to renew their passes, what could we do to take advantage of that pass holder database?

The concept of the Colorado Pass Club (CPC) was introduced as the 2006–2007 ski season wound down. The objectives for the CPC were to distance the Colorado Pass from competitive passes by offering elevated benefits. In particular, we wanted to create a sense of community among Colorado Pass holders. Moving forward, we wanted to continue to drive awareness of the inclusive and exclusive aspects of the pass program.

To further the sense of community and ownership within our pass holder group we developed the tagline "It's Why I Live Here." This tagline strategically positions our resorts and having a pass with other iconic Colorado experiences. Skiing, and being outdoors, is an integral part of living in Colorado. We felt that this statement spoke to a broad market, tapped into sense of pride and exclusivity about living in Colorado, and complemented the CPC efforts well.

Our CPC program included biweekly e-mails full of promotions, offers, and discounts exclusively for pass holders. Promotions ranged from dining and event tickets to deeply discounted lodging, ski tune-ups, and discounts on gear. We also gave away tickets to sporting events, free mountain lunches, gas cards, and tickets to music events. Called "Random Acts of Pass Holder Kindness," these offers were diverse enough to create a strong response and a lot of interest and to elevate the perceived value of the season pass.

Many of our efforts were also supported by radio spots and a special CPC website that recapped the contents of our biweekly e-mails. Slowly these e-mails started creating buzz in the pass holder community, and soon they were being forwarded to friends and family.

Not only did the CPC e-mails generate interest and excitement with Colorado Pass holders, they generated trackable revenue—everything from lodging purchases to ski school lessons, to equipment rentals and, of course, season pass renewals. In fact, our e-mail programs were one of the strongest performing channels for our promotions!

We decided to leverage the passion around our season passes and launched a referral program, rewarding skiers for referring their friends to buy a pass—furthering our intent of building a community. We were able to test various versions of e-mails—we learned that simpler was better and started to reframe offers by coming up with a few high-impact offers rather than several small gestures.

As the program continues to evolve, we have learned quite a bit about our pass holders and have begun to not only offer them great benefits and expressions of appreciation, we engage them in a dialogue and use this group for surveys about product attributes and program improvements.

We also designed unique ways to engage them with content by running contests asking why they haven't skied more. When our pass holders responded with stories about job loss, bad equipment, the need for improved ski technique, we responded by finding one pass holder a job, giving gift certificates to replace equipment, and signing them up for free ski school! The pass holder community loved it.

The result cemented the Colorado Pass Club as the most important club for Colorado skiers. You can find out more about what we achieved by turning to the end of the chapter and reading *It's a Wrap*.

Throughout this book you've read about the effectiveness of advertising. We've emphasized that effective campaigns do more than win awards for creativity. They work hard to achieve the campaign's communication and marketing goals, as does the Colorado Pass Club campaign for Vail. As you will see in this chapter, there are many ways to evaluate the effectiveness of various aspects of an advertising and marketing communication program. Specifically, four categories of work get evaluated in advertising and marketing communication programs: the message execution, the media, the campaign, and the other marketing communication areas and their synergistic effect as part of an IMC program. This chapter discusses the basic concept of the evaluation of effectiveness and then examines those four areas.

IMPACT: DOES IT WORK?

What makes a marcom message effective? The fact that people like it—or the fact that it moves people to some kind of action? The classic campaign for Avis is an example of one that works on both levels—people like it and it drove the company to record sales levels. When advertising works—when marketing communication is effective—it has impact and generates a response of some kind from its target audience. The critical phrase—"as intended"—means there are multiple objectives and, therefore, multiple ways to evaluate the effectiveness of marketing communication campaigns and programs.

Let's just consider advertising to begin with. Many executives feel advertising works only if it produces sales. Syracuse University Professor John Philip Jones, who has written many books and articles on the topic, estimates that of the $500 billion spent annually on advertising globally, only 41 percent—less than half—produces sales.[1] Jones contends that "advertising must generate an immediate jolt to sales before it can be expected to produce any further effect."[2] Simon Broadbent, another leading figure in effectiveness research, disagreed with Jones's short-term sales focus and suggested instead that advertising should emphasize long-term brand building.[3]

Determining advertising effectiveness based on sales can be difficult because of the impact of other marketing mix factors. For example, an article in *Business 2.0* reported that an ad for the Six Flags amusement park was a smash success in viewer surveys. However, because attendance at the company's 31 theme parks

Avis is only No.2 in rent a cars. So why go with us?

We try harder.
(When you're not the biggest, you have to.)
We just can't afford dirty ashtrays. Or half-empty gas tanks. Or worn wipers. Or unwashed cars. Or low tires. Or anything less than seat-adjusters that adjust. Heaters that heat. Defrosters that defrost.

Obviously, the thing we try hardest for is just to be nice. To start you out right with a new car, like a lively, super-torque Ford, and a pleasant smile. To know, say, where you get a good pastrami sandwich in Duluth. Why?

Because we can't afford to take you for granted.
Go with us next time.
The line at our counter is shorter.

CLASSIC

According to *Advertising Age*, the Avis "We Try Harder" campaign was one of the top 10 in advertising history. It was the ultimate simple idea that conveyed a great idea that was truthful and believable. The strategy—to state strongly a self-effacing underdog position—also tapped into people's sympathy for underdogs. The copy defined what it means to try harder (and what a leader in the car rental business should be providing)—clean ashtrays, full gas tanks, wipers that work, washed cars, heaters and defrosters that work—and the lines at the counter are shorter. It also subtly suggested the problems you might find with #1—Hertz. Created by the legendary Doyle Dane Bernbach agency in 1962 when Avis's market share was only 11 percent, the campaign drove a turnaround for the company. Four years later, Avis's market share was 35 percent and the campaign got credit for a 300 percent increase in business.

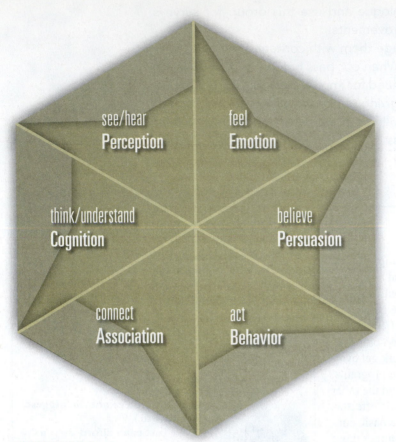

see/hear
Perception

feel
Emotion

think/understand
Cognition

believe
Persuasion

connect
Association

act
Behavior

FIGURE 19.1

The Facets of Effects Model

Principle

If you can't measure it,
you can't manage it.

fell after the campaign instead of increasing, it must be deemed ineffective. But sales are not the only reason brands advertise: one of the major objectives of advertising is to create higher levels of brand awareness. Perhaps the Six Flags awareness level increased, but the reason people didn't come to the parks has to do more with the lack of new attractions or maybe an external factor such as an increase in the price of gas. Does that mean the advertising is ineffective?

It's our view that marketers intend for their messages to accomplish a variety of goals, such as build a brand relationship, recruit volunteers or donations, or entice people to visit a website, which is why the other 60 percent of ads studied by Jones may be effective in their own way. That's why this book uses the Facets Model of Effects to broaden the way we evaluate message effectiveness.

Evaluating Effectiveness

The most important principle in this chapter—possibly in this book—is a well-known maxim: "If you can't measure it, you can't manage it."

Some evaluation is informal and based on the judgment of an experienced manager. There is always a need for the intuitive analysis of experienced professionals. The important thing, however, is to recognize early in the planning stage the need for a formal evaluation mechanism, as Professor Mark Stuhlfaut explains. Evaluation should be "planned in" to any campaign. Evaluation determines the success of a marketing communication, but it also feeds back into the ongoing brand communication plan. Figure 19.2 illustrates that process, and Professor Stuhlfaut's *A Matter of Principle* features builds on the idea of a cycle beginning and ending with research.

In addition to intuition and judgment, measurement that tracks consumer response is also needed and can be built into a campaign plan as structured feedback, such as response cards and calls. Often, however, the evaluation effort involves a more formal research project, which also needs to be part of the campaign planning.

Personal insights into what makes an ad great are important, but why do we also need formal evaluation? The first reason is that the stakes in making an advertising misstep are high. By the time an average 30-second commercial is ready for national television, it has cost about $200,000 in production costs. If it is run nationally, its sponsor can invest several million dollars in airtime. The second reason is advertising optimization, or reducing risk by testing, analyzing, tracking brand performance, and making changes where possible to increase the effectiveness of the advertising. The third reason is to learn what works and what doesn't—in other words, to identify best practices so a brand's advertising continues to improve.

Types and Stages of Evaluation

Evaluation is done through testing, monitoring, and measurement. Testing is used to predict results, monitoring tracks performance, and measurement evaluates results. In other words, for major campaigns a sample of the ads is typically tested before they run as a way to predict effectiveness. Ideally, the results of preliminary evaluative research should be available before large sums of money are invested in finished work or in media buys.

As a campaign unfolds, the performance is tracked to see whether any elements need to be changed. Sales may fall, or they may not increase as rapidly as expected. Is the advertising at fault? The results, the actual effects, are measured after the ad or campaign runs. Diagnostic research also is used in all three stages to deconstruct an ad to spot message problems. Four types of research are used in evaluation:

1. **Developmental research** through pretesting estimates the likelihood that an ad idea will work or that one idea is better than another.
2. **Concurrent research** using tracking studies and test marketing monitors the way the campaign is unfolding and how the messages and media are working.
3. **Post-testing research** evaluates impact after the campaign is over or after the ad ran. Postcampaign research encompasses benchmark or baseline studies to gauge movement. These can be research company norms, or they can be based on previous campaigns by this brand.
4. **Diagnostic research** deconstructs an ad to see what elements are working or not working. Researchers who evaluate commercials use frame-by-frame or moment-by-moment analysis to identify strengths and weaknesses in an ad.

Facets: Measuring Responses

Most advertisers would be happy if evaluation could simply tell them how much the advertising contributed to their sales effort. That's difficult for a number of reasons. Factors other than advertising affect sales (e.g., pricing, distribution, product performance, competition), and that makes it hard to isolate advertising to determine its impact. Furthermore, advertising effects tend to be delayed, so it's difficult to link the advertising seen at one time to a purchase made days or weeks later. Exceptions are direct-response advertising and ads carrying promotional offers good for only a limited time.

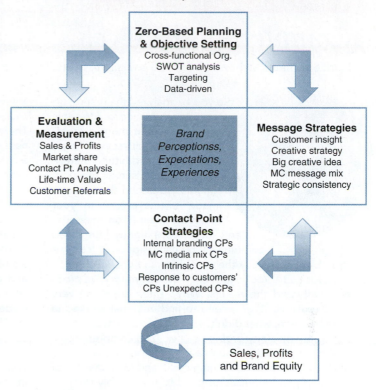

IMC Brand Optimizer Model

FIGURE 19.2
IMC Brand Optimizer Model
This IMC model created by Professor Tom Duncan illustrates that evaluation is a circular process—IMC plans start by gathering information and move through the various steps in the planning process to come back to the last step in the process, which is again gathering information. This time, however, information is gathered to determine what works and what doesn't. That information feeds back into the process and the organization learns from the results.

Usually advertising is measured in terms of its communication effects—the mental responses to a message, which become *surrogate measures* for sales impact. Such factors as awareness of the advertising, purchase intention, preference, and liking all suggest that the advertising message can make a positive contribution to an eventual purchase decision. According to research professionals at Ipsos ASI, one of the largest U.S. providers of advertising pretesting, "Ads work best when they engage viewers' interest, when consumers enjoy watching them, when they are relevant, and when they tell their story in a unique and interesting way."[4] Those are some of the dimensions of effectiveness, but others also are important, as we know from our discussion of how advertising works in Chapter 4.

On the other hand, some ads don't work, and it is just as important to understand why that happens. Some confuse the audience or fail to get attention or connect with consumers. In many cases, people can't remember the brand. In some cases, the ad can even boomerang, an effect mentioned in a feature on antidrug ads in Chapter 4. The same problem was noted with anti-smoking ads when the American Legacy Foundation announced that a study of smoking prevention ads by the tobacco industry actually increased the likelihood that teens would try smoking.[5]

Good evaluation objectives are based on a model of human response to an advertisement that identifies key effects. We developed the Facets Model of Effects in Chapter 4 as a guide for both setting objectives and evaluating effectiveness. Table 19.1 groups the key factors of effectiveness and then matches them to the types of research questions advertisers can use to determine effectiveness.

Principle
Good evaluation plans, as well as effective professional work, are guided by a model of how people respond to advertising.

A MATTER OF PRINCIPLE

Completing the Cycle

Mark Stuhlfaut, *Assistant Professor, University of Kentucky*

So you've analyzed the market up and down, honed a strategic position, spent months creating the most attractive image, produced hard-hitting materials, placed ads in all the right media, stretched the budget, made sure everyone in your marketing chain is on message, and launched a tightly integrated communication campaign. . . . It's time to sit back and enjoy the afterglow . . . right?

Not quite. You're job isn't finished until you've properly evaluated the results. Why? There are three very good reasons: (1) you need to find out what worked in the campaign, what didn't, and what could have worked better to solve any problems now; (2) a comprehensive evaluation provides valuable information that will serve as input for the next planning cycle; and (3) managers of marketing communication need to responsibly demonstrate the effectiveness of their efforts to clients and corporate management—you owe it to them to prove that their investment of resources in your programs and their trust in you were worth it.

Where do you start? A good beginning is to go back to the campaign's goals to see if they were met, which brings back the importance of having clear, measurable, and attainable objective statements.

What standards should you employ to know if you've succeeded? Sales data? They're one indicator, but too many intervening factors make tying marketing communication to sales figures difficult and not very meaningful. Therefore, other measures, such as the levels of awareness, comprehension, importance, and brand preference, are more useful for communication managers to determine whether the campaign was effective.

A thorough review takes more than a few quick surveys. Sure, you'll want to conduct quantitative and qualitative research to get feedback from consumers or customers. But you should also contact all the key stakeholders in the market—such as company sales personnel, distributors, dealers, editors, broadcasters, consultants, and other friendly third parties (FTPs)—to see if their communication needs were satisfied by the campaign. Include these important people in your evaluation, and you'll not only gain helpful information, you'll build strong relationships for the future.

The best evaluation techniques aren't something you add on to a campaign; they're something you build in to every phase of the process. Assess alternative positions early in the campaign's development. Compare different concepts in the rough layout stage. The earlier you test, the cheaper it is, and the better chance you have to get it right.

It's easy to say you don't have the time or the money to evaluate the campaign's elements. But consider the cost of not getting it right. The effort made to evaluate the effectiveness of the campaign before and after launch will pay off in the long run.

The Vail Resorts' Colorado Pass Club launch is an example of how a model of effects can be developed for a specific campaign and used to drive not only the planning of the effort, but also the evaluation of its effectiveness. One of the goals to a successful ski season, according to Vail's Jennifer Wolfe-Kimbell, is to lock in revenue as early as possible. This can happen in multiple ways. For Colorado ski resorts, two groups of skiers bring in the bucks: in-state season pass holders and out-of-state visitors or "destination skiers." In-state skiers purchase season passes prior to the ski season and provide a surge of revenue going into the season. Destination skiers provide incremental revenue throughout the season by booking vacations and purchasing the lion's share of daily lift tickets, lodging and dining sales, ski school lessons, and rentals.

WHAT IS MESSAGE EVALUATION?

Copytesting is a general term that describes various kinds of research used at different stages in the advertising development process—before, during, and after an ad or campaign has run. Before we talk about specific types of studies, consider first the various copytesting services and the factors they feel are important to evaluate.

Table 19.1   Effectiveness Research Questions

Effect	Research Questions
Perception	
Awareness/noticed	Which ads do you remember seeing?
	Which ads were noted?
Attention	What caught your attention?
	Did the ad stand out among the other ads and content around it?
	What stood out in the ad?
Recognition (aided)	Have you seen this ad/this campaign?
	Sort elements into piles of remember/don't remember.
Relevance	How important is the product message to you? Does it speak to your interests and aspirations?
Emotional/affective	What emotions did the ad stimulate?
	How did it make you feel?
Liking/disliking	Do you like this brand? This story? The characters (and other ad elements)?
	What did you like or dislike about the brand? The ad?
Desire	Do you want this product or brand?
Cognition	
Interest	Did you read/watch most of it? How much?
	Did it engage your interest or curiosity?
	Where did your interest shift away from the ad?
Comprehension/ confusion	What thoughts came to you? Do you understand how it works? Is there anything in the ad you don't understand? Do the claims/product attributes/benefits make sense?
	Do you have a need for this brand or can it fulfill a need for you?
Recall (unaided)	What happened in the commercial? What is the main message? What is the point of the ad?
Brand recall/linkage	What brand is being advertised in this ad?
	[In open-ended responses, was the brand named?]
Differentiation	What's the difference between Brand X and Y?
Association	When you think of this brand, what (products, qualities, attributes, people, lifestyles, etc.) do you connect with it?
	Do you link this brand to positive experiences?
Personality/image	What is the personality of the brand? Of whom does it remind you? Do you like this person/brand personality?
	What is the brand image? What does it symbolize or stand for?
Self-identification	Can you see yourself or your friends using this brand?
	Do you connect personally with the brand image?
Persuasion	
Intention	Do you want to try or buy this product/brand?
	Would you put it on your shopping list?
Argument/ counterargument	What are your reasons for buying it? Or for not buying it—or its competing brand(s)? How does it compare to competitors' brand(s)?
	Did you argue back to the ad?
Believability/ conviction	Do you believe the reasons, claims, or proof statements?
	Are you convinced the message is true? The brand is best?
Trust	Do you have confidence in the brand?
Behavior	How many people buy, try, call, send, click, visit, attend, inquire, volunteer, donate, advocate, or whatever the desired action?
	What is the rate of change?

Copytesting

Copytesting companies have different specialties that focus on different effectiveness dimensions. The most successful of these companies have conducted enough tests that they have developed **norms** for common product categories. In other words, after they pretest an ad, they can compare its score with scores from comparable ads. Norms allow the advertiser to tell whether a particular advertisement is above or below the average for the brand or its product category. Without norms the advertiser would not know whether a score of 23, for example, is good or bad.

Most of these companies have also developed diagnostic methods that identify strong and weak points of the ad. Here is a list of some of the more prominent companies and the types of tests they provide:

- *Ameritest:* brand linkage, attention, motivation, communication, flow of attention and emotion through the commercial
- *COMSCORE ARSgroup:* persuasion, brand/ad recall, communication
- *Ipsos ASI:* recall, attention, brand linkage, persuasion (brand switch, purchase probability), communication
- *Mapes & Ross:* brand preference change, ad/brand recall, idea communication, key message delivery, like/dislike, believability, comprehension, desire to take action, attribute communication
- *Millward Brown:* branding, enjoyment, involvement, understanding, ad flow, brand integration, feelings about ad, main stand-out idea, likes/dislikes, impressions, persuasion, new news, believability, relevance
- *RoperASW:* overall reaction, strengths and weaknesses, understanding, clutter busting, attention, main message, relevance, appeal, persuasiveness, motivate trial, purchase intent.

Now let's consider how the services of such companies and the research they conduct can be used at various points in the development and evaluation of a marketing communication effort. This outline is based on the Facets Model of Effects that we first introduced in Chapter 4.

Message Development Research

Deciding what facts to convey in marketing communication is never easy. Research is needed to develop and test alternative message strategies. Planners conduct research with members of the target audience to develop the message strategy and test the relative effectiveness of various selling premises—hard sell or soft sell, informational or emotional, and so forth. Insights into consumer motivations and purchasing decisions help solve the often-difficult puzzle of selecting the most relevant information and motivating promise as well as the emotional appeal that best engages the audience.

Concept Testing   Advertising and other marketing communication messages usually incorporate a Big Idea, a creative concept that is attention getting and memorable. Research in **concept testing** compares the effectiveness of various message strategies and their creative ideas. This testing often relies on a *key concept card*, which is an artist's drawing of the visual idea with a sentence underneath that captures the essence of the idea. A researcher may use a pack of three, five, or more idea cards or rough layouts to elicit consumer responses in a mall or through discussions in a focus group.

An example of effective concept testing that was used in a campaign's development is Volvo's GLBT campaign, which was the first campaign of its kind to receive an Advertising Research Foundation (ARF) David Ogilvy award. Witeck-Combs Communications in collaboration with Prime Access, Inc., developed a set of concepts and rough ad executions representing a range of GLBT-specific imagery and copy. Ford and Volvo managers selected their top three choices from the group of proposed ad ideas. The messages were tested to assess the constructs of branding, communication, and persuasion, including the concept of consumer connection, or whether the ad makes consumers feel closer to the brand. These constructs were measured in four ways—cognitive, behavior, emotional, and aspirational dimensions.

Pretesting   Another type of evaluative research, called **pretesting,** helps marketers make final go/no-go decisions about finished or nearly finished ads. Pretesting differs from concept testing or message strategy research, which reveals the strengths and weaknesses of different versions of a concept or approach as marketers develop them. Pretesting assesses the strength of the finished message and predicts how well it will perform.

In terms of print advertisements, the ideas to be tested are often full mockups of the ad. In television, advertisers can test the commercials as storyboard ideas or **photoboards** (still photos arranged as a storyboard), but more often commercials are in the form of **animatics** (drawings or still photos shot on videotape synchronized with a rough version of the audio track). Advertisers can show these versions of the commercial to individuals, to focus groups, or in a theater testing situation. They follow the viewing of the advertisement with a survey, a more open-ended interview, or a set of questions for a group discussion.

Diagnostics   Many advertisers and agencies are moving away from copytesting methods that rely on single scores to evaluate an ad and turning to methods that are more focused on diagnosing strengths and weaknesses. The reason is that they believe an advertisement is too complex to be reduced to one factor and one simple score. Instead they are using research methods designed to diagnose the strengths and weaknesses of their advertising ideas to improve the work while it is still in development or to learn more from the ad to improve subsequent advertisements.

> **Principle**
> Advertising effects are too complicated to be reduced to a single score.

In theater tests for TV commercials, for example, respondents may have a black-box device and can press a button to record different types of responses—indicating what they liked or didn't like or how long they paid attention by letting up on the button when their attention shifts.

Moment-by-moment tests of commercials provide an analysis of the impact of the internal logic of the commercial. The Ameritest company, whose work is described in the *A Matter of Practice*, looks at two dimensions of moment-by-moment tests: a *Flow of Attention* measure and a *Flow of Emotion* measure. The procedure involves showing a **clutter reel,** a group of commercials that includes the test commercial, competitors' commercials, and other ads, and conducting interviews afterward. The Ameritest method uses a **picture sort** to diagnose the viewer's attention to and emotional engagement with different elements in the commercial. The viewers receive a deck of key frames from the commercial and sort them into images they remember seeing and ones they don't remember. Then they sort them into five categories from strong positive to strong negative. The researchers tabulate the sets to depict the flow of impact for both attention and emotion. In particular, they want to identify and analyze key moments in the commercial such as the solution to a problem or the introduction of the brand and analyze them in terms of viewers' attention and emotion.[6] The *A Matter of Practice* box takes you through this analysis.

During Execution: Concurrent Testing

Concurrent testing takes place while the advertising is running. There are three primary techniques: coincidental surveys, attitude tests, and tracking studies. The first two assess communication responses; tracking studies evaluate actual behavior.

The **coincidental survey** technique is most often used with broadcast media. Random calls are made to individuals in the target market. By discovering what stations or shows people are tuned to, the researcher can determine whether the target audience has seen/heard the ad and, if so, what information or meaning the audience members now have of the brand. This technique can be useful in identifying basic problems. For example, several years ago Pepsi discovered that the use of Madonna as a spokesperson was a terrible mistake.

In Chapter 4 we discussed the relationship between an attitude—a favorable or unfavorable disposition toward a person, brand, idea, or situation—and consumer behavior. This relationship is the basis of *attitude tests*. Researchers survey individuals who were exposed to the ad, asking questions about the spokesperson, the tone of the ad, its wording, and so forth. Results that show strong negative attitude scores may prompt the advertiser to pull an ad immediately. A favorable attitude indicates that people are more likely to purchase a brand than if they have an unfavorable attitude.

Tracking Studies   Studies that periodically (generally every three or six months) measure top-of-mind brand awareness (first brand mentioned) are called **tracking studies.** These studies can

A MATTER OF PRACTICE

Finding Moments of Truth

Charles E. Young, *President, Ameritest*

The most powerful search engine of all is the human eye, which scans advertising film, television commercials, and Web videos, continuously deciding on an unconscious level whether the visual information streaming toward it is important enough to let into consciousness. Because our conscious minds have limited bandwidth or workspace, much of the imagery that advertisers are trying to communicate to consumers is ignored or deleted by our preconscious eye-brain filters as so much visual spam.

Ameritest's Picture Sorts® is a set of nonverbal research tools that have been developed for the Internet to survey the right-brained scanning and sorting processes involved in visual communication. These tools make use of the power of still photographs to capture an instant of time and store our fleeting emotions.

By sorting a randomized deck of pictures taken from the ad itself—which is like the visual vocabulary of the film—the ad researcher can reconstruct consumers' moment-by-moment attention and emotional response to an ad they just saw. Three different sorting exercises enable the advertiser to perform the equivalent of putting on 3-D glasses to see advertising through the eyes of its target audience.

The Flow of Attention® graph, the first of three measurement dimensions, is like a visual spell-checker that the researcher can use to analyze whether or not a piece of advertising film or Web video has been put together well according to principles of proper film syntax or good visual grammar. The Flow of Attention graph reveals the hidden structure of audience attention to moving pictures, which, like music, follows a rhythmic beat of cognitive processing. The beat, or focal points of attention, is where the most important information in an ad, like the brand identity, is conveyed.

From the emotional hook at the beginning, to the turning points in a story, to the surprise ending of a funny commercial, engaging the emotions of consumers is essential to motivating them. The Flow of Emotion® graph measures not only the volume of emotions pumping through ad film but also reveals which of four archetypal dramatic structures is being used in the creative design. Knowing this structure tells the advertiser when the timing is exactly right to first introduce the brand in the ad, which might be at the beginning, or somewhere in the middle, or not until the end of a commercial.

The Flow of Meaning® tool shows the researcher where key communication points or brand values are being cued visually. Meaning is created when thought and emotion come together, in a few memorable and emotionally charged moments in a commercial when memories are being created. Because there are three distinct memory systems in the mind, branding moments come in three flavors: (1) images that convey concepts or rational ideas go into our knowledge, or semantic, memory system; (2) images that evoke emotions go into our emotion, or episodic, memory system; and (3) images that rehearse or mirror the behavior the advertiser is trying to influence go into our action, or procedural, memory system (where memories of how you ride a bike or play a violin are stored). Taken together, this learn–feel–do imaging process is how the long-term work of advertising is performed, building a brand's image.

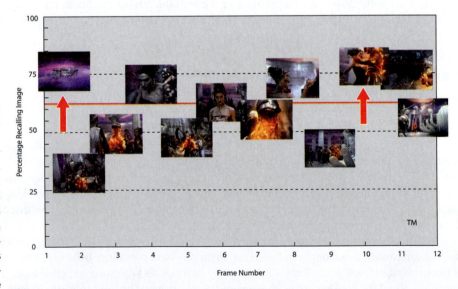

This diagram demonstrates the flow of attention across a commercial for Unilever's Thermasilk. The selected still frames represent those places in the commercial where the attention is high (above the red line) or low (below the red line). Note the highest attention points, which are indicated with the red arrows. In this commercial, that tight shot of the face is the "moment of truth," the most highly attended to frame in this execution.

also measure unaided and aided awareness of an ad and trial and repeat purchases. They sometimes ask the same questions of competing brands.

Tracking studies show how a marketer's brand is performing over time, especially after changes are made in the marketing communication. Because several different measures are taken, findings can indicate if there is an attention-getting problem, a recall problem (saw message but can't remember what it said), a trial problem (remembered the advertising but not moved to try the brand), or a repeat problem (tried the brand but have not repurchased for some reason).

Brand tracking is an approach that tracks the performance of the brand rather than or in addition to the advertising. The assumption is that with fragmented media and an abundance of high-quality but similar products, it is more important to track the brand because it reflects the quality of the customer's brand relationship. That's at the heart of the Colorado Pass Club campaign. Instead of focusing on attributes and claims about a product, this research identifies how customers are involved with the brand and whether they are more favorably disposed toward it than toward other brands. As Peppers and Rogers point out, you also need a centralized customer database that allows you to track customer activity across channels.[7]

This analysis as depicted in Figure 19.3 is also based on the factors identified in the Facets Model of Effects.

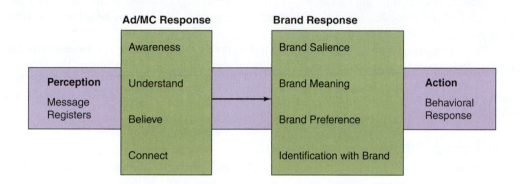

FIGURE 19.3
Tracking Brand Response

Brand tracking studies generally use sets of brand-related questions, but Bain & Company, a highly respected consulting firm, is promoting the use of a single-question test to track attitudes to a brand. Called *net promoter*, it tracks the response to a simple question: "How likely is it that you would recommend us to a friend or colleague?"[8] Another single measure is **brand penetration,** which is the number of customers who purchase the brand relative to the total population in the market.[9]

Although these single measures are useful as a broad indication of brand effectiveness, the other questions found in brand tracking studies, such as those about awareness and credibility, for example, are particularly important in an IMC program because they provide diagnostic information about areas of marketing communication that might need to be changed or refined.

Because spending information enters the analysis, much of the focus of tracking studies is on the target market, the selection of media vehicles, the schedule, the marketing communication mix, and the media mix. Account planners use several methods to collect tracking data, such as the attitude tests discussed earlier and wave analysis, consumer diaries, and pantry checks:

- *Wave Analysis* **Wave analysis** looks at a series of interviews during a campaign. The tracking begins with a set of questions asked of a random sample of consumers on a predetermined date. After the person is qualified as hearing or seeing the ad, the researcher asks a series of follow-up questions. The answers serve as a benchmark and allow adjustments in the message content, media choice, and timing. Perhaps two months later, the researcher makes another series of random calls and asks the same questions. The second wave is compared with the first until management is satisfied with the ad's market penetration and impact.
- *Consumer Diaries* Sometimes advertisers ask a group of representative consumers to keep a diary during a campaign. The consumers record activities such as brands purchased, brands used for various activities, brand switches, media usage, exposure to competitive promotions,

and use of coupons. The advertiser can then review these **consumer diaries** and determine factors such as whether the message is reaching the right target audience and whether the audience is responding to the message as intended. One common unfavorable finding from consumer diaries is that no attitude or behavioral change occurred because of exposure to the campaign.

- *Pantry Checks* The **pantry check** provides much of the same information as the diary method but requires little from the consumer. A researcher goes to homes in the target market and asks what brands or products they have purchased or used recently. In one variation of this procedure, the researcher counts the products or brands currently stocked by the consumer. The consumer may also be asked to keep empty packages, which the researcher then collects and tallies.

Test Markets   A **test market** might serve to evaluate product variations, as well as elements of a campaign or a media mix. These are generally conducted in two or more markets with the same number of similar markets chosen to act as controls. In the control markets the researcher can either (1) run no advertising or (2) continue to run the old ad. The new advertising (or product variation) is used in the test cities. Before, during, and after running the advertising, marketers compare sales results in the test cities. Some cities, such as Buffalo, Indianapolis, and San Antonio, are considered excellent test markets because their demographic and socioeconomic profiles are representative of either the United States or a particular target market. Furthermore, they are relatively isolated as media markets so the advertising impact is less likely to be affected by what is happening in other markets.

The possibilities for isolating variables in test markets are almost limitless. Researchers can increase the frequency of advertising or try a different media schedule, for example. They can see whether an ad emphasizing brand convenience will stimulate sales to two-career families. They can try an ad that plays up the brand's fiber or vitamin content or compare the effectiveness of a two-for-one promotion versus a cents-off coupon.

Post-Testing: After-Execution Research

Another evaluation method is post-testing, which occurs after the marketing communication has been used to determine if it met its objectives. The most common evaluative research techniques account planners and advertising researchers use include memory tests, persuasion tests, direct-response counts, frame-by-frame tests, in-market tests such as test markets, and brand tracking.

Some of these more traditional post-testing methodologies were discussed in Chapter 6, however, there is another type called **heuristics** that is relevant for certain types of post-testing evaluation. Harley Manning, vice president for customer experience at Forrester Research, describes heuristics as a type of expert review that Forrester uses to evaluate the performance of websites in terms of brand attributes (information provided) and user descriptions and goals as measured against "a valid set of rules (heuristics) that identify known types of user experience flaws." Manning explains that Forrester uses that type of expert-review research to gauge how well the sites served consumers (keep the brand promise).

The idea is that advertising—and other types of marketing communication messages—vary in the way they affect people, so the measurements also must be different.

Breakthrough: Attention   Most advertising is evaluated in terms of its ability to get and keep attention. This is a simple concept but difficult to measure. Similar to pretesting, some researchers use instantaneous tracking in a theater setting where viewers with a keypad indicate what they watch and don't watch—or rather what interests them and doesn't interest them. The Ameritest methodology asks respondents who have just watched a collection of ads to indicate which ones interested them.[10] Another firm's method asks viewers to rate how enjoyable the ad is, which confounds the attention score with a liking response. Other methodologies use noted scores for print ads or ask viewers to recognize the concept of a commercial and attach it to a brand.

Engagement Tests   Interest in a commercial is determined by concentration and excitement. **Eye-tracking** research is a mechanical technique that traces **saccadic eye movement**, the path the eye takes in scanning an ad. Because scanning involves a lot of stops and starts and revisits, this complex map of how a visual is scanned identifies what first caught the viewer's attention—the visual point of entry—and where it moved to next. It also records those elements the eye kept revisiting either to focus on because they were appealing visuals or because they needed more study. It also shows what elements didn't get noticed at all. The e-Motion system from the New Jersey–based firm PreTesting Group identifies eye fixations but also the amount of vibrations in the retina. The vibration is very minute, but it does indicate a level of excitement—the more the retina vibrates, the more interested the viewer.[11]

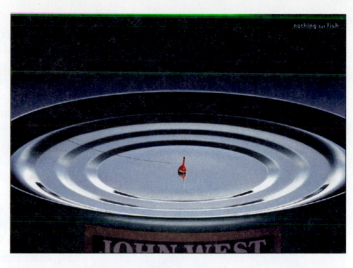

A beautifully done image for John West, a British beer, uses a simple photograph of the top of a can. It takes on new meaning when the can's rings are associated with the rings in water from a fishing bobber. The question is do people get the association and understand the larger meaning of "Relax with a Can of John West."

Understanding and Comprehension Tests   These tests are used as part of the diagnostic effort, but it is particularly important in post-testing to determine if consumers understood the message. Another comprehension problem can emerge from creative strategies that are engaging, but ask consumers to puzzle out the meaning. Ambiguity is sometimes used particularly because it is engaging, but it can also be a risky strategy, one that benefits from testing. An example is a billboard for a British beer brand John West, which is given a dramatic touch by making the rings on top of the can look like rings of rippling water cast from a fishing bobber.

Memory Tests   Memory tests are based on the assumption that an advertisement leaves a mental residue with the person who has been exposed to it; in other words, the audience has learned something. One way to measure an advertisement's effectiveness, then, is to contact consumers who saw the ad and find out what they remember. Memory tests fall into two major groups: recognition tests and recall tests.

One way to measure memory is to show the advertisement to people and ask them whether they remember having seen it before. This kind of test is called a **recognition test**. In a **recall test**, respondents who have read the magazine are asked to report what they remember from the ad about the brand. In aided recall tests, the interviewer may go through a deck of cards containing brand names. If the respondent says, "Yes, I remember seeing an advertisement for that brand," the interviewer asks the interviewees to describe everything they can remember about the ad. Obviously recall is a more rigorous test than a recognition test.

Similarly, a TV commercial is run on network television within a regular prime-time program. The next evening, interviewers make thousands of random phone calls until they have contacted about 200 people who were watching the program at the exact time the commercial appeared. The interviewer then asks a series of questions, such as the following:

• Do you remember seeing a commercial for any charcoal briquettes?
• *If No* Do you remember seeing a commercial for Kingsford Charcoal briquettes? (memory prompt)
• *If Yes to Either of the Above* What did the commercial say about the product? What did the commercial show? What did the commercial look like? What ideas were brought out?

The first type of question is called an **unaided recall** question because the particular brand is not mentioned. The second question is an example of **aided recall**, in which the specific brand name is mentioned. The answers to the third set of questions are written down verbatim. The test requires that the respondent link a specific brand name, or at least a specific product category, to a specific commercial.

Brand Linkage Tests   Testing for brand linkage is basically a test of memorability, however, the important aspect of this measure is not whether the message is remembered, but whether it

Pacific Life uses an image of a leaping whale to reflect its image of a confident insurance company that excels in its market.

associates the brand with the memory. If the commercial fails to establish a tight connection between the brand name and the selling message, the commercial will not get a high recall score. This is also called a test of "brand linkage." The long-running Pacific Life campaign with its image of a leaping humpback whale is a good example of a visual that serves as a strong brand reminder and associates the brand with strength and performance.

Emotion Tests   Advertising is just beginning to move into this area of research. There are several ways to get at the emotional response. Ameritest uses photo sorts with still frames from commercials to identify the positive and negative moments that touch people's emotions.[12] Other researchers are wiring up viewers of television ads to monitor brain activity using a functional magnetic resonance imaging (fMRI) machine. The fMRI images identified ads from the 2007 Super Bowl that produced anxiety, fear, anger, and insecurity, as well as positive feelings.[13]

Likability Tests   A study by the Advertising Research Foundation (ARF) compared a variety of different copytesting methods to see if any of them were better able to predict sales impact. Surprisingly, it wasn't awareness, recall, communication, or persuasion measures that won out but rather **likability tests.** Likability, however, is not easy to measure because it's difficult to know if the consumer likes the ad, the brand, or some other factor, such as the person giving the test. A number of the copytesting companies offer a likability score, but they suggest it needs to be interpreted relative to other consumer responses. Questions that try to evaluate likability investigate factors such as these: personally relevant, important to me, stimulates interest or curiosity, creates warm feelings, enjoyable, entertaining, and fun.

Persuasion Tests   Another evaluative research technique is a **persuasion test,** or attitude change test. The basic format is to ask consumers how likely they are to buy a specific brand. Next they are exposed to an advertisement for that brand, usually as part of a collection of brands. After exposure, researchers again ask them what they intend to purchase. The researcher analyzes the results to determine whether *intention to buy* has increased as a result of exposure to the advertisement. This test is sometimes referred to as an **intend-to-buy** or **motivation test.** The validity of a persuasion test depends in part on whether participants in the experiment represent a good sample of the prospects the advertiser is trying to reach. A dog food advertiser, for example, would not be interested in responses from people who do not own dogs.

Inquiry Tests   A form of action response, **inquiry tests** measure the number of responses to an advertisement. The response can be a call to a toll-free number, an e-mail or website visit, a coupon return, a visit to a dealer, an entry in a contest, or a call to a salesperson. Inquiry tests are the primary measurement tool for direct-response communication, but they also are used to evaluate advertisements and sales promotions when the inquiry is built into the message design. Inquiry tests also are used to evaluate the effectiveness of alternative advertisements using a split-run technique in magazines, where there are two versions of the magazine printed, one with ad A and the other with ad B. The ad (or direct-mail piece) that pulls the most responses is deemed to be the most effective.

Scanner Research

Many retail outlets, especially drug, discount, and food stores, use electronic scanners to tally up purchases and collect consumer buying information. When you shop at your local Safeway, for example, each product you buy has an electronic bar code that conveys the brand name, the product code, and its price. If you are a member of Safeway's frequent buyer program and have a membership card that entitles you to special promotional offers, the store can track your purchases.

Scanner research is also used to see what type of sales spikes are created when certain ads and promotions are used in a given market. Both the chain and the manufacturers of the brands are interested in this data. The regional Safeway system may decide to establish a consumer panel so it can track sales among various consumer groups. In **scanner research,** you would be asked to join a panel, which might contain hundreds of other customers. You would complete a fairly extensive questionnaire and be assigned an ID number. You might receive a premium or a discount on purchases for your participation. Each time you make a purchase, you also submit your ID number. Therefore, if Safeway runs a two-page newspaper ad, it can track actual sales to determine to what extent the ad worked. Various manufacturers who sell products to Safeway can do the same kind of testing. The panel questionnaire also contains a list of media that each member reported using, so media performance can also be evaluated.

Scanner research reads the information from a shopper's identification card and records that along with product information. Many retail outlets use electronic scanners to track sales among various consumer groups.

Using scanner data and the cooperation of local cable networks, researchers are closer to showing a causal relationship between advertising/promotion and sales because of **single-source research.** Single-source research companies, such as A. C. Nielsen, arrange to have test commercials (and sometimes test newspaper ads) delivered to a select group of households (HHs) within a market, comparing it to a control group of HHs. The purchasing behavior of each group of HHs is collected by scanners in local stores. Because advertising is the only manipulated variable, the method permits a fairly clear reading of cause and effect. Data collected in this way are known as *single-source data* because advertising and brand purchasing data come from the same HH source.

Syracuse University Professor John Philip Jones, who spent many years at J. Walter Thompson (JWT), has used single-source data from JWT combined with Nielsen TV viewing data to prove that advertising can cause an immediate impact on sales. His research has found that the strongest campaigns can triple sales, while the weakest campaigns can actually cause sales to fall by more than 50 percent.[14]

Although fairly expensive, single-source research can produce dependable results. Advertisements are received under natural conditions in the home, and the resulting purchases are actual purchases made by consumers. One drawback, besides cost, is the three to six months required to set up and run this test. Critics also say that single-source research is better for short-term immediate sales effects and doesn't capture very well other brand-building effects.

MEDIA EVALUATION

Advertising has little chance to be effective if no one sees it. Analyzing the effectiveness of the media plan is another important part of evaluation. Did the plan actually achieve reach and frequency objectives? Did the newspaper and magazine placements run in the positions expected and produce the intended GRP and CPM levels? In other words, did the advertisers get what they paid for?

A classic case of the power of media, particularly the repetition of commercials, is the "Please Don't Squeeze the Charmin" campaign that began in 1964. Because it dominated the airwaves for 20 years, it was hugely visible and built incredible brand awareness—awareness that led Charmin to dominate its category. It and its brand character, the comical grocer Mr. Whipple, was not only one of the best remembered campaigns, but also one of the most parodied campaigns ever made because the Whipple character was so goofy. Yet, it made Charmin one of the most successful brands in the history of Procter & Gamble. So what do you think: Does it make sense to use an irritating campaign with a lot of repetition in order to build brand awareness and memory? Could this strategy work in our time? What would an IMC planner say about this strategy?

Evaluating Audience Exposure

For major campaigns, agencies do post-buy analyses, which involve checking the media plan against the performance of each media vehicle. The critical question is whether the reach and frequency objectives were obtained.

Verifying the audience measurement estimates is a challenge. Media planners are working sometimes with millions of dollars, and they can't afford to get it wrong. We discussed how various media channels measure their audiences. For print, services such as the Audit Bureau of Circulations (ABC), Experian Simmons (formerly known as SMRB), and Mediamark (MRI+) provide data. Likewise for broadcast, Arbitron, RADAR, and A. C. Nielsen provide audience monitoring. Initially media planners use these estimates to develop a media plan, and media buyers use them later to verify the accumulated impact of the media buy after the campaign has run.

Media planning oversight is usually handled in-house by the media buyer, but it can also be contracted by the advertiser to independent companies who specialize in conducting media audits of the agency's media planning and buying operations. Nissan and Procter & Gamble are examples of companies that have hired outside media-auditing firms to confirm the execution of their media plans.

As the job gets more complex, media planners are being asked to prove the wisdom of their recommendations in an area where the data they use are sometimes suspect or unreliable, particularly if there are problems with the media measurement companies' formulas and reporting systems. Nielsen, for example, has been subject to much criticism for its television ratings.

Another issue is the impact of video recorders and DVRs. What do viewers see and remember as they skip or fast forward through commercials? Tests have shown that viewers do remember some of the spots, or at least the brands. The easiest to recall were ones that had been seen before. Other characteristics of successful ads have the brand's logo in the middle of the screen and leave it on the screen for more seconds than in a normal TV commercial. It also helps if the action isn't too fast with many screen changes. Simple commercials are easier to see and remember when zipping.[15]

To better understand the problems in media evaluation, let's look at two areas where media performance is hard to estimate: out-of-home media and new media, including the Internet.

Out-of-Home Media   As you would expect, accurately measuring the mobile audience for outdoor advertising is challenging. Traffic counts can be gathered, but the problem is that traffic does not equal exposure. Just because a car drives by a board doesn't mean that the driver and/or passengers see it, particularly since some outdoor boards are more attention getting than others, as the "road rage" board illustrates.

New Media   Similarly, the measures of effectiveness used to evaluate offline campaigns don't seem to transfer well to the online world. Is the website visitor or banner ad viewer similar to a member of the print or broadcast audience? The online industry hasn't been able to establish online equivalencies for GRPs and CPMs and is still trying to define what makes an effective Internet ad and to develop a system that accurately measures online effectiveness. At the heart of the problem is the question of what exactly is to be measured and how that equates to other media: readers, viewers, visitors, hits, click-throughs, or minutes spent with a site? Web-analytic firms are developing more sophisticated tracking programs to measure user activity in terms of Web pages visited, time spent, and click-throughs.

Alternative media, such as word of mouth, social media, and guerilla marketing campaigns, are even harder to measure and media planners search for reliable indicators of exposure numbers and buzz from these new sources that equate to the performance of traditional mea-

DO YOU GO INTO REVERSE EVERY TIME YOU DRIVE?

Don't drive like a dipstick.

This outdoor board from the United Kingdom attracted attention because of its interesting visual but also because of its challenging idea. Research based on traffic counts find it difficult to account for the emotional impact of messages like these.

sured media. Research company Millward Brown has designed a metric for online word of mouth (WoM) to track and analyze sentiments expressed on social networks, blogs, and chat rooms.[16] Procter & Gamble has created TREMOR, which develops buzz campaigns, but is also used to design analysis techniques to track measurable business results for WoM campaigns.

An example of using new media analytical tools to assess performance comes from the Taco Bell "Drive-Thru Diet" campaign, which promoted the fast-food chain's "Fresco" menu. Although the campaign wasn't presented as a weight-loss program, it generated a significant amount of buzz questioning the strategy. According to Zeta Buzz, a firm that tracks postings on blogs, message boards, and social media, Taco Bell's buzz rating dropped six points—the volume of postings increased but the tone was much more negative, which indicated the strategy was backfiring.[17]

Another interesting experiment was conducted by Boston University college students and the Mullen ad agency using Twitter to get near-instantaneous feedback on how viewers were reacting to Super Bowl ads. The project was designed "to use a new medium to comment on an old medium," according to Mullen's chief creative officer.[18]

ROI and Media Efficiency

Advertisers continue to improve how they measure *advertising ROI* (return on investment, which means the costs of creating and running the advertisement versus the revenue it generates). Another way to look at it is the cost-to-sales ratio.

Since the dollar impact for advertising—and public relations, especially—is difficult to measure, ROI is hard to calculate. The campaigns must be carefully designed not only to increase sales, but also to ensure that advertisers can isolate the impact of the message and verify that the advertising caused the increase in sales. ROI is easier to calculate for direct marketing (because there are fewer variables between the message and the sales) and for sales promotion (because there is an immediate response, which is easier to link to the message).

One question related to ROI is this: How much spending is too much? That is, how do you determine whether you are overadvertising or underadvertising? That's one of the key reasons to use test marketing. If a campaign is launched in several different, but matched, cities at different levels of media activity, a comparison of the campaign results (sales or other kinds of trackable responses) can determine the appropriate level and type of media spending.

Wearout   The point where the advertising, because it has been seen multiple times, no longer stimulates much of a response is called **wearout**. This is also the point where recall stabilizes or declines and irritation levels increase because people are tired of hearing or seeing the same ad.

Wearout is a combination of creative impact and media buying. The more intrusive or the less interesting the creative technique, the higher the level of irritation. It's like a joke: you may pay attention the first couple of times you hear it, but then it gets "old." Other types of advertising are less prone to wearout. Good jingles, for example, can be repeated almost endlessly. The more people like to hum along, the less likely there will be a wearout problem.

The issue is how long and how much is needed to create the necessary impact. John Philip Jones, who has done extensive research into effectiveness issues, argues that research supports higher continuity. He recommends spreading the budget out and adding weeks to the media schedule as much as possible.[19] Another way to evaluate such decisions is through media optimization models.

Media Optimization   One of the biggest challenges in media planning is media efficiency—getting the most for the money invested. You may remember from Chapter 14 that media planners operate with computer models of **media optimization**—or the optimum media performance—that are used in making decisions about media selection, scheduling, and weights (amount of budget). Models are always theoretical, so one result of postevaluation is that the actual performance of a plan can be compared with the results projected by the media planner's model. The goal of media optimization is to optimize the budget—to get the most impact possible with the least expenditure of money. That is the critical finding derived from the comparison of performance with projections. In addition to meeting the reach and frequency objectives, was the media plan efficient?

A new dimension to the efficiency question comes from a program by media company Starcom to measure the effectiveness of various media used by client Applebee's. The objective was to develop a model that compares the value of video ads, both on-air and online, across a number of NBC properties. The model will establish the relative value of the ads and also interaction across channels.[20]

EVALUATING IMC TOOLS, CAMPAIGNS, AND PROGRAMS

Evaluation is the final and, in some respects, most important step in an advertising campaign because it determines whether the campaign effort was effective. A campaign evaluation will assess the campaign's performance in terms of its message and media objectives. It employs either internal performance data or results from an outside research organization that monitors brand performance, such as Gallup-Robinson, Decision Analyst Inc., and Millward Brown. The important thing to remember in planning an evaluation program is that evaluation has to be built into the marketing communication plan from the very beginning.

An IMC campaign employs various marcom tools, such as sales promotion, public relations, direct marketing, events and sponsorships, personal sales, packaging, point of purchase (PoP), and specialties. You'll find that most of these areas have their own metrics by which performance is measured.

Even though an IMC campaign is evaluated in terms of its overall impact on a brand, the pieces of the mix may also be evaluated to determine the effectiveness of their performance. Advertising may be the most visible; however, other marketing communication tools, such as sales promotion, are better at getting people to respond with an immediate purchase, and public relations is particularly strong at building credibility. Let's look briefly at these other marketing communication areas in terms of their evaluation.

Marcom Tools

Principle
Advertising is particularly effective in accomplishing such objectives as creating exposure, awareness, and brand image and delivering brand reminders.

As Table 19.2 illustrates, marketers can use the Facets Model of Effects to identify the objectives commonly associated with the various marketing communication areas as well as the types of measures used to evaluate performance. The idea is that certain marketing communication functions, such as public relations and sales promotion, do some things better than other areas. Therefore, in an integrated plan, we would use the best tool to accomplish the desired effect. In Table 19.2, the main effects are located in the first column, with a collection of surrogate measures identified in the second column (this list is not inclusive, it's just a sample). The last column lists the communication tool or tools that may be most appropriate for achieving the objective.

Advertising   How do you describe effective advertising? You've been watching it for most of your life. One brand manager's answer to that question is presented in the *Practical Tips* at *www.pearsonhighered.com/moriarty*. An examination of Table 19.2 shows that advertising is particularly effective in accomplishing a number of objectives, such as creating exposure, awareness, and a brand's image. It is also good at providing brand reminders to the customer and encouraging repurchases. The preceding discussions about copytesting, message development research, concurrent testing, post-testing, and the evaluation of media cover the most common advertising methodologies. Many of these research methods are used by other marcom areas, but they all are derived initially from advertising.

Evaluation doesn't just happen at the end of a campaign or after the ad is run. It has to be planned into the campaign from the very beginning as this planning meeting illustrates.

Direct Response   The objective of direct-response communication is to drive a transaction or generate

Table 19.2   Message Effectiveness Factors

Key Message Effects	Surrogate Measures	Communication Tools
Perception	Exposure	Adv media; PR, PoP
	Attention	Adv; sales promo (SP), packaging; PoP
	Interest	Adv; SP; PR, direct; PoP
	Relevance	Adv; PR; direct; PoP
	Recognition	Adv; PR, packaging; PoP, specialties
Emotional/Affective	Emotions and liking	Adv; SP, Packaging; PoP
	Appeals	Adv; PR; sales; events/spnsrshps
	Resonate	Adv; PR; events/spnsrshps
Cognition	Understanding	Adv; PR; sales; direct
	Recall	Adv; SP; PR, PoP, specialties
		Adv; PR; packaging
Association	Brand image	Adv; PR; events/spnsrshps
Persuasion	Attitudes	Adv; PR; direct
	Preference/intention	Adv; PR; sales; SP
	Credibility	PR
	Conviction	PR; sales; direct
	Motivation	Adv; PR; sales; SP
Behavior	Trial	SP; sales; direct, PoP
	Purchase	SP; sales; direct
	Repeat purchase	Adv; SP; sales; direct, specialties

some other type of immediate behavioral response, such as a donation or visit to a dealer. What makes this marketing communication tool so attractive to marketers is that response is so easily measurable. Some advertisements request direct response via a toll-free number, a mail-in coupon, a website or e-mail address, or an offer embedded in the body copy. Instead of depending on consumers' memories, measures of a message's persuasive abilities, or some other indirect indication of effectiveness, the advertiser simply counts the number of viewers or readers who request more information or buy the product.

Principle
Direct-response communication drives action and that makes it highly measurable.

In some ways, direct response mechanisms are the easiest marketing communication tool to evaluate both in terms of message effectiveness and in terms of ROI efficiency—the sales-to-cost ratio. The efficiency of a direct-response offer is measured in terms of responses per thousand (RPM). To calculate the RPM, use the following formula:

$$\frac{\text{Total responses}}{\text{Total mailed}} \times 1,000 = \text{RPM}$$

This calculation lets you compare the response rate of alternative mailings. For example if one mailing of 15,000 pulled 750 responses, then the RPM was 50 per 1,000. If a different mailing of 12,000 pulled 800 responses, then the RPM was 66 per 1,000, making it a more effective offer.

Sales Promotion   Sales promotion programs for packaged goods and other products that use distribution channels need to evaluate both the impact of consumer (or end-user) direct promotions and promotions targeted at retailers and other channel members. You will recall the discussions of promotional allowances offered to retailers who agree to feature a brand in their ads or provide special in-store display and price discounts. These are measured by proof of performance such as copies of store ads and pictures of in-store displays. One responsibility of the sales force is to do store checks to verify that stores are doing what they promised. Promotions that contain a response device, such as coupons, have a built-in evaluation measure.

As for consumer promotions, the following evaluation measures are the most popular:

Principle

Proof of performance, various types of responses to promotional tactics, and payout planning provide built-in evaluation measures for promotions.

Measure	% Used
Sales	46
Response rates	20
Awareness	10
Other mix	9
Redemption rates	4

The efficiency of a sales promotion offer can be evaluated in terms of its financial returns more easily than advertising. We compare the costs of a promotion, called a **payout analysis,** to the forecasted sales generated by the promotion. A **break-even analysis** seeks to determine the point at which the total cost of a promotion exceeds the total revenues generated, identifying the point where the promotion is not wise to do. Figure 19.4 depicts this analysis.

Principle

Ultimately, public relations efforts are evaluated in terms of opinion change and relationship tracking.

Public Relations   The evaluation of public relations examines the success of getting a message out to a target audience in terms of *output* (materials produced and distributed) and *outcomes* (acceptance and impact of the materials). Outcomes can be measured in terms of changes in public opinion and relationship tracking. The output evaluation is conducted by asking questions such as these: How many placements (news releases that ran in the media) did we get? How many times did our spokesperson appear on talk shows? How much airplay did our public service announcements receive or how much and what kind of buzz are Twitters generating? The results are presented in terms of counts of minutes, mentions, or inches.

Content analysis also helps determine the favorability of the coverage, share of voice, and issue and competitor coverage. Ongoing public opinion tracking studies ask these questions: Has there been a change in audience knowledge, attitudes, or behavior (e.g., pretesting versus post-testing)? Can we associate behavior change (e.g., product trial, repeat purchase, voting, or joining) with the public relations effort? The most common measures of output and outcomes in public relations are summarized here:

Output Objectives Achieved

- *Production* Number of PR messages, such as news releases or brochures, generated.
- *Distribution* Number of media outlets (TV stations, newspapers) receiving PR products.
- *Coverage* Number and size of clips, column inches, or minutes of time or space.
- *Impressions* Media placements multiplied by circulation or broadcast reach.
- *Advertising Value* Equivalent ad costs for time or space.
- *Content Analysis* Positive or valence (whether the story or mention seems to be more positive or negative), key messages (the idea in the story), sources, and prominence.

Outcome Objectives Achieved

- *Awareness* Aided and unaided recall.
- *Attitudes* Perceptions, preferences, and intent to buy.
- *Behavior* Did target do what you wanted them to do?

The search for methods to tie public relations activities to bottom-line business measures, such as ROI (return on investment), is like the quest for the Holy Grail. PR practitioners would like to demonstrate ROI because it would provide even more support for the importance of PR effects. A surrogate ROI measure can be based on shareholder value, which can be seen as a company or brand's reputation capital. For example, research conducted on companies with the most effective employee communication programs has determined that they provide a much higher total return to shareholders. Recently Web-based analytical tools are making it possible to connect earned media results to online business goals, such as generating website traffic, sales leads, revenue, and donations for nonprofit organizations.[21]

Website Evaluation Evaluating the communication effects of website advertising is still a new game. Some performance indicators are traffic volume, such as **page views** or the simple number of visitors to a site. Banner advertising and other online ads are evaluated using **click-through rates,** and the one thing the industry has learned is that this form of advertising is decreasing in effectiveness. One problem is that people who have little or no interest in the product may click on the banner by accident or curiosity. Because this type of advertising is sold by **pay-per-click (PPC),** the advertiser has to pay regardless of the reason for the click. Pop-up banners can get more attention, but they are also seen as more irritating.

Instead of click-through rates, some advertising uses a **cost-per-lead** metric that records how well the click-through generates prospects, an attempt to get at ROI. The most important metric for Internet advertising, however, is **conversion rate,** which is the percentage of visitors to a site who complete a desired action, such as playing a game, signing up for a newsletter, or buying something. Of course, online sales are an important measure of a website's effectiveness.

The more sophisticated conversion rate services not only measure how well the site generates action but also how customers navigated the site. This information is obtained by tracking where they come from, what search terms they used, how they move around within the website, and where they go when they leave. It gives a more comprehensive picture of the path visitors and customers use in navigating a site.

Forrester Research has been developing methods for evaluating websites for years. The company tracks effectiveness of website performance in terms not only of making a brand promise, but in terms of also delivering easy-to-find and use information. Harley Manning, a Forrester vice president, reported that his company's research has found that "on average sites did a better job of making the brand promise than they did of meeting customer needs." Manning explains how this research is used to evaluate good and bad performing websites in *The Inside Story.* (Check Forrester's website at *www.forrester.com.*)

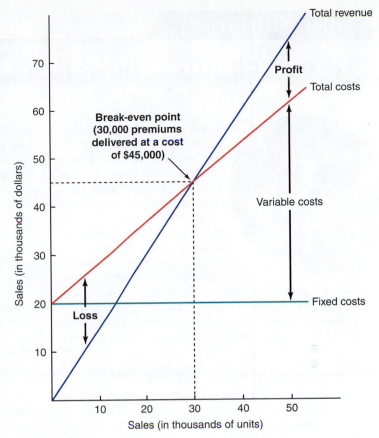

FIGURE 19.4

A Sales Promotion Break-Even Analysis

At the break-even point, where 30,000 premiums are delivered at a cost of $45,000, the sales revenues exactly cover, but do not exceed, total costs. Below and to the left of the break-even point (in the portion of the diagram marked off by dashed lines), the promotion operates at a loss. Above and to the right of the break-even point, as more premiums are sold and sales revenues climb, the promotion makes a profit.

Special Advertising Situations

The various types of advertising identified in Chapter 18 are evaluated using many of the tools discussed previously; however, they each have their own particular objectives that affect how they are evaluated.

The primary objective of *retail advertising* is to generate store traffic. The results of traffic-building promotions and advertising are simple counts of transactions as well as the change in sales volume of brands receiving promotional support. Participation counts can be used to estimate the pull of special events. Loyalty is evidenced through participation in frequent buyer programs and measured in terms of registration, store visits, and average purchases per visit.

In *B2B marketing*, a common form of evaluation is a count of sales leads based on response devices such as calls, e-mails, and cards returned to the advertiser. Another common B2B objective is *conversion*, similar to the conversion rate in the online discussion; this refers to the number of leads that turn into customers who make a purchase. Conversion rates, which are percentages of the leads, are also calculated for most marketing communication tools used in support of B2B programs.

THE INSIDE STORY

How Web Sites Build Brands (Or Don't)

Harley Manning, *Vice President and Research Director, Customer Experience, Forrester Research, Inc.*

Brand is at or near the top of the priority list for companies doing business on the Web. In one Forrester survey, decision makers at 148 companies rated building the brand as the second most important goal for their business-to-consumer sites. The same group said that when considering new content and features for their sites, building the brand was as important as supporting customer goals.

So if online brand building is so important, how can companies make sure that their websites build their brands? To answer that question, we started by interviewing brand strategists at seven of the largest interactive agencies, including Razorfish and Tribal DDB Worldwide. We also talked to marketers at two companies that we respect for their brand management expertise: Johnson & Johnson and Procter & Gamble.

We found broad agreement that websites serve two equally critical functions: *They are both a communication medium and a delivery channel. In other words, consumers expect sites to not just make the brand promise but also to keep that promise by providing value in the form of detailed product information that's easy to find and use.*

As a result of our initial research, we created a methodology that grades how well sites make the brand promise and keep the brand promise. Our approach is a type of heuristic evaluation, sometimes referred to as an expert review. Standard heuristic evaluations date from the late 1990s and depend on three factors: detailed user descriptions, relevant user goals, and a valid set of rules (or heuristics) that identify known types of user experience flaws. We stuck with that approach to gauge how well the sites served consumers (i.e., kept the brand promise).

To measure how well sites make the brand promise, we created a variation on the standard expert review methodology. Instead of starting with user descriptions and goals, we begin by identifying the *brand attributes of the site* we intend to grade. We do this by looking at their annual reports and the public statements made by their executives. Then we collect above-the-line collateral ranging from annual reports to magazine ads to TV commercials. This preparation lets us check sites for cross-channel consistency of logos, colors, typography, and layout as well as consistency with intended brand attributes such as "reliable" or "innovative" (two of the most common).

We've been using this methodology now for about four years. During that time we've spotted a number of interesting trends. For one, websites on average do a poor job of building either major aspect of brands online: in an analysis of more than 150 reviews we found that only 8% of sites passed both halves of our test.

We also found that, *on average, sites did a better job of making the brand promise than they did of meeting customer needs.* Sixty sites passed our tests for making the brand promise but only 17 did an adequate job of serving customers' goals. For example, sites from companies as diverse as Nike, Edward Jones, BP, and Coca-Cola excel at online copy and imagery, but fall flat on user experience basics like providing the right content or making that content easy to read via easily legible text.

Like other types of advertising, *nonprofit organizations* need to communicate efficiently and effectively, particularly as they are stewards who must ensure that limited funding is used effectively and efficiently. Evaluation of communication for foundations and nonprofit organizations is an emerging field, and challenges to assessing effectiveness are many. Activities and behaviors being measured are complex and campaigns are often a multi-phase effort. There are no standard and widely accepted guidelines for communication evaluation for the nonprofit sector. Nonetheless, measuring success of a campaign begins with setting objectives and evaluating the progress toward achieving the objectives.[22]

International marcom is difficult to evaluate because of market differences (e.g., language, laws, cultural norms) and the acceptability of various research tools. There may also be incompatibilities among various measurement systems and data analysis techniques that make it difficult to compare the data from one market with similar data from another market. An international evaluation program for advertising should focus, at least initially, on pretesting because unfamiliarity with different cultures, languages, and consumer behaviors can result in major miscalculations. Pretesting helps the advertiser correct major problems before miscommunication occurs. To evaluate the global/local question, the best approach is to test two ads that are both based on the global advertising strategy: a locally produced version of the advertising and an original ad produced locally.

Campaign and Program Evaluation

While it is ideal to know how each marketing communication function has performed, the reality in most campaigns is that a variety of functions and media are used to reach and motivate customers to respond. Time is a factor as well. We mentioned in the beginning of this chapter that there is a debate about advertising's ability to impact short-term sales results as well as long-term branding.

University of Southern California Professor Gerard Tellis reminds us that advertising not only has *instantaneous* effects (consumer responds immediately) but also *carryover* effects (delayed impact).[23] Any evaluation of campaign effectiveness needs to also be able to track both types of effects over time. Differential effects also complicate the ongoing evaluation of IMC programs that operate with a 360-degree total communication philosophy, although tracking may be easier in some ways because the evaluation is continuous.

The Synergy Problem   The problem with evaluating campaigns—particularly IMC campaigns—is estimating the impact of synergy. Intuitively we know that multichannel communication with messages that reinforce and build on one another will have more impact than single messages from single sources; however, that can be difficult to prove. As Bob Liodice, CEO of the Association of National Advertisers, observes, "there is no single, consistent set of metrics that transcends discipline-centric measurements."[24]

If the campaign planning is well integrated, which means each specialty area cooperates with all others in message design, delivery, and timing, then there should be a synergistic effect. This means that the overall results are greater than the sum of the individual functional areas if used separately.

A number of studies have attempted to evaluate IMC impact by comparing campaigns that use two or three tools to see what is gained when more message sources are added to the mix. For example, a study by the Radio Ad Effectiveness Lab reported that recall of advertising is enhanced when a mix of radio and Internet ads are used rather than just website advertising alone.[25] A study published in the *Journal of Advertising Research* developed a multidimensional approach based on evaluation of four factors including unified and consistent communication, strategic consistency in targeting (different messages for different audiences), database communication, and relationship programs.[26] Such studies of both the platforms and components of IMC are beginning to tease out the effects of synergy, but they are a long way from evaluating the effects of a total communication program.

The most common way of measuring a campaign's total impact is the brand tracking approach mentioned previously. As various ingredients in the campaign are added and taken away, changes in tracking study results can show the effects and help identify what combinations of marketing communication functions and media work best for a brand. In other words, has the brand become stronger on critical dimensions of the image, such as personality and positioning cues, because of the campaign?

A complication in evaluating programs is the need to consider other messages and contact points beyond traditional marketing communication. As we have said, in a 360-degree total communication program, brand experiences, such as those involved with customer service and WoM, may be even more important than traditional marketing communication. *A Principled Practice* feature by Professor Keith Murray demonstrates how these unconventional message effects can be measured.

Connecting the Dots   The challenge in campaign and program evaluation is to pull everything together and look at the big picture of campaign performance rather than the individual pieces and parts. One of the first places to start is defining the objectives—all the various effects—and then adequately and realistically measure the campaign's performance against those objectives. Here's an example that demonstrates how evaluation methods can be matched to the original campaign objectives.

Effie award winner UPS wanted to reposition itself by broadening its package delivery image.[27] Although UPS owned ground delivery, it lost out to Federal Express in the overnight and international package market. UPS knew from its customer research that to break out of the "brown and ground" perception, the company had to overcome the inertia of shipping managers who use UPS for ground packages and FedEx for overnight and international. The company also had to shift the perception of senior executives from a company that handles packages to a strategic partner in systems planning. From these insights came three sets of objectives that focused on

A PRINCIPLED PRACTICE

Can a Broken Guitar Really Hurt United?

Keith Murray, *Associate Dean, College of Business, Bryant University*

It's been a YouTube hit and made the e-mail rounds for a long time—the "United Breaks Guitars" video. It's the story of a musician who made a trip on United Airlines (UA) and was compelled to "check" his Taylor guitar as baggage— which is how UA came to be vulnerable to the charge that, in the handling of it, they damaged the instrument.

When asked to make it right—to pay for fixing the Taylor guitar—UA declined.

The musician, Dave Carroll, responded by writing a ballad about the experience and posting it on YouTube and the Internet. (See it at *www.youtube .com/watch?v=5YGc4zOqozo*.)

A lot of people viewed the clip; it's catchy and tells the story in an amusing way. People have sent it to their friends . . . and friends have sent it to their friends, which has led now to literally millions of people seeing it! You can also see a CBS report about the incident at *www.youtube.com/watch?v= PGNtQF3n6VY&feature=related*.

So was UA smart to ignore this incident? In other words, did UA really "save" the $1,200 it would have taken to fix the guitar in the first place?

It seems clear that UA might have been short sighted. If you "do the numbers," you come to the conclusion that UA may have paid a much higher price than it realized!

The table following shows how much money might have been—and is still being?!!—lost by UA from 8 million people (in 2010) seeing the YouTube clip and deciding *against* using UA. It gives various levels of impact from 1 to 10 percent. It also compares the percent of this lost revenue against UA's sales revenue in 2008.

# of $500 Trips NOT Taken in a Year	Percent of Viewers Influenced by YouTube Videos to NOT Patronize UA in a 12-Month Period			
	1%	2%	5%	10%
One trip	$30M	$60M	$150M	$300M
% '08 revenue	0.15	0.31	0.78	1.56
Two trips	$60M	$120M	$300M	$600M
% '08 revenue	0.31	0.63	1.56	3.13

What the calculations show is compelling. If only 1 percent of those who learned of the broken Taylor guitar were affected by the story, then UA only lost somewhere between $30 million and $60 million. However, if the negative influence is higher, then UA could arguably have forgone as much as half a *billion* dollars, or about 3 percent of its annual sales! In any case, all of these figures stand in stark contrast to the $1,200 asked for by Mr. Carroll in the first place!

This gets to the real point of the story: If UA (or any company) has a flawed system to handle and remedy customer complaints—in other words, if UA has customer service "issues" that produce unsatisfactory results for customers—then it can pay a very high price for its poor service. And the damage is exponential, because the average person tells about 10 people about a bad brand experience—all of which has a chilling effect on patronage by those who hear such tales of woe!

These numbers show the huge impact of failure to pay attention to customer complaints and service system problems. Can one little broken Taylor guitar—and all the other little failures each day—affect a mammoth company like United Airlines? You bet.

---

breaking through awareness, breaking the inertia trance, and breaking the relevance trance. Here's how the campaign performed on those objectives. Notice the mix of perception, image, and behavioral measures.

Objective 1: Breaking through Awareness

- Awareness of the Brown campaign outpaced *all* past UPS advertising measured in the 10-plus-year history of its brand tracking study.
- Among those aware of the campaign, correct brand linkage to UPS was 95 to 98 percent across all audiences (compared to a historical average of 20 to 40 percent for past UPS advertising).

- "What Can BROWN Do for You?" has taken hold in popular culture. For instance, the tagline was mentioned in both *Saturday Night Live* and *Trading Spaces* shows.

Objective 2: Breaking the Inertia Trance

- With shipping decision makers, the brand showed steady and significant gains in key measures like "Helps my operation run more smoothly," "Dynamic and energetic," and "Offers a broad range of services."
- International shipping profitability increased 150 percent, and overnight volume spiked by 9.1 percent after the campaign ran. The targeted companies' total package volume increased by 4.39 percent.
- From the start of the campaign in March to the year-end, annual ground shipping revenue grew by $300 million.
- The campaign was a hit in terms of response with a 10.5 percent response rate and an ROI of 1:3.5. In other words, every dollar spent on the campaign generated $3.5 dollars in revenue.

Objective 3: Breaking the Relevance Trance

- For the first time in the 10-plus-year history of the brand tracking study, UPS leads FedEx in all image measures among senior-level decision makers. All significant brand image measures continued upward.
- Among senior decision makers, the biggest gains were in key measures like "For people like me," "Acts as a strategic partner to my company," "Helps in distribution and supply chain operations," and "Provides global competitive advantage."
- At the start of the campaign, annual nonpackage (supply chain) revenue was approximately $1.4 billion. By the end of the year, nonpackage revenue had almost doubled to $2.7 billion.

Bringing It All Together   Beyond connecting the objectives to the measurements, advertisers continue to search for methods that will bring all the metrics together and efficiently and effectively evaluate—and predict—brand communication effectiveness. A small Florida agency, Zimmerman Advertising, positions itself specifically on that issue. It promises to deliver long-term brand building as well as short-term sales. The president explains, "The biggest problem marketers face today is connecting advertising to retail sales." To help determine the impact of its ads on sales, Zimmerman measures ad response immediately using a toll-free number and proprietary software that tracks sales to specific ads.[28]

The giant media research company, Nielsen, has undertaken a project to find the links in its various marketing metrics. In particular, the company wants to connect its Nielsen Media Research TV ratings with its A.C. Nielsen retail scanner and consumer panel data. Then it wants to mix in data from its Nielsen/NetRatings for online advertising and Nielsen Buzzmetrics online-buzz measurement system.[29] This is just one example of how important it is to connect the dots to draw an accurate picture of consumer response to marketing communication.

Ultimately, the goal is to arrive at holistic, cross-functional metrics that are relevant for integrated communication, a task undertaken by Dell Computers and its agency DDB. Given Dell's direct-marketing business model, the company had extensive call and order data in its database. DDB helped organize the collection of detailed marcom information, which made it possible to begin linking orders to specific marcom activities. This new marcom ROI tracking system made it possible for Dell to recognize a 3 percent gain in the efficiency of its marketing communication. As the metrics system became more sophisticated, it also began to move from a reporting and metrics evaluation engine to a strategic tool providing deeper insights into consumer behavior.[30]

Many pieces are still missing in the evaluation of advertising, not to mention more complex IMC programs. Research think tanks are struggling to find better ways to measure consumers' emotional connections to brands and brands' relationships with their customers[31] and how those connections and relationships are affected by various types of marketing communication messages. But let's end with an inspirational video called "Life Lessons from an Ad Man." It's a little old, but Rory Sutherland makes a good point about having fun even as you contemplate how marketing communication creates intangible value for brands. See it at: *www.ted.com/talks/ rory_sutherland_life_lessons_from_an_ad_man.html*.

COLORADOPASS™

IT'S A WRAP

The Colorado Pass Club Comes to Pass

In this final chapter we have reviewed various methods of evaluating the effectiveness of a campaign. No campaign uses all of them, but all successful campaigns have to do some kind of evaluation in order to determine success. The Colorado Pass is an example of an IMC program that carefully monitors its marketing communication messages to evaluate the effectiveness of its brand-relationship building objectives. Jennifer Wolfe-Kimbell, senior marketing manager at Vail Resorts, explains how this program has been evaluated.

Our marketing mix for season-pass sales includes e-mail campaigns, direct-mail campaigns, online banner advertising, newspaper print in local and regional papers, local radio spots, and local TV spots. The passes are sold online and onsite at retail locations, resort ticket offices, and special events throughout Colorado and the region.

Fiscal Year 2009 Results (Based on Third Quarter Results) The number of total season passes sold for the 2008/2009 ski season was a 12.2 percent increase, which is greater than the increase in the number of passes sold for the 2007/2008 ski season. Combined with an 8.3 percent increase in the pass price, these results drove a 21.8 percent increase in season-pass revenue.

Season-pass holders skied more on average in the 2008/2009 ski season than the previous year. They used the season pass an average of 10.6 times in 2008/2009 compared to 9.7 times per season pass in the prior season.

Fiscal Year 2010 Results (Based on Second Quarter Results) Vail Resorts experienced a $3.1 million or 6.2 percent increase in total season-pass revenue including the Colorado Pass. The increase in season-pass revenue was generated in spite of overall flat visitation from all skiers, as well as season-pass holders, and fewer visits per pass. This demonstrated the value of the program, even in periods of challenging snow conditions. Despite adverse factors such as historically low snowfall and a struggling economy, we were pleased with the outcome of our brand-relationship building efforts. This positive report on the company was attributed to the following:

- The strength of the pass programs. In fact, decline in out-of-state visitation was mitigated by growth in visits from local season-pass holders, which was up 17 percent.
- Higher guest expenditures on ski school and retail sales and rentals.
- A 9 percent increase in the number of season passes sold. In fact, record season-pass sales locked in higher revenue prior to the start of the season (despite fewer pass visits) further illustrating the strength and importance of our pass programs.

Our pass holders loved the CPC Club—and Vail Resorts loved the results, as well.

Key Points Summary

1. **Why and how is marketing communication evaluation conducted?** Marketing communication evaluation is used to test, monitor, measure, and diagnose the effectiveness of marcom messages. The factors tested are the key effects outlined in a model of advertising effectiveness.

2. **Can you list and explain the stages of message evaluation?** Message evaluation is conducted before (pretesting), during (tracking), and after (post-testing) an ad or campaign has run. Diagnostic evaluation can be conducted at all three stages.

3. **What are the key areas of media evaluation?** Media evaluation begins by verifying the media exposure in terms of

the achievement of the reach and frequency objectives, as well as the audience measurement reports of the media used. Media ROI evaluations consider questions such as how much is enough, particularly in terms of advertising wearout.

4. **How are IMC tools, campaigns, and programs evaluated?** A campaign's performance is assessed in terms of how well it meets its message and media objectives. IMC plans also assess the performance of the various marketing communication tools, as well as the synergistic effect of the elements working together.

Words of Wisdom: Recommended Reading

Davis, John, *Measuring Marketing: 103 Key Metrics Every Marketer Needs,* Hoboken, NJ: John Wiley, 2007.

Jones, John Philip, *When Ads Work: New Proof That Advertising Triggers Sales,* 2nd ed., Armonk, NY: M. E. Sharpe, 2007.

Noble, Paul, and Tom Watson, *Evaluating Public Relations: A Best Practice Guide to Public Relations Planning, Research, and Evaluation,* Philadelphia: Kogan Page, 2007.

Tellis, Gerard, *Effective Advertising,* Thousand Oaks CA: Sage, 2004.

Young, Antony, and Lucy Aitken, *Profitable Marketing Communications: A Guide to Marketing Return on Investment,* Philadelphia: Kogan Page, 2007.

Young, Charles, *The Advertising Research Handbook,* Seattle, WA: Ideas in Flight, 2005.

Key Terms

aided recall, p. 589
animatics, p. 585
brand penetration, p. 587
break-even analysis, p. 596
click-through rates, p. 597
clutter reel, p. 585
coincidental survey, p. 585
concept testing, p. 584
concurrent research, p. 581
consumer diaries, p. 588
conversion rate, p. 597

cost-per-lead, p. 597
developmental research, p. 581
diagnostic research, p. 581
eye-tracking, p. 588
heuristics, p. 588
inquiry tests, p. 590
intend-to-buy test, p. 590
likability tests, p. 590
media optimization, p. 593
moment-by-moment tests, p. 585

motivation test, p. 590
norms, p. 584
page views, p. 597
pantry checks, p. 588
payout analysis, p. 596
pay-per-click (PPC), p. 597
persuasion test, p. 590
photoboards, p. 585
picture sort, p. 585
post-testing research, p. 581
pretesting, p. 584

recall test, p. 589
recognition test, p. 589
saccadic eye movement, p. 588
scanner research, p. 591
single-source research, p. 591
test market, p. 588
tracking studies, p. 585
unaided recall, p. 589
wave analysis, p. 587
wearout, p. 593

Review Questions

1. Why do marketers evaluate their advertising and marketing communication programs?

2. This chapter suggests that evaluation is most useful when based on a model of advertising response. Why is that so?

3. Why are diagnostic research methods becoming more important?

4. What is a tracking study and how is it used? A test market?

5. What is single-source research, and how does scanner data relate to it?

6. What is media efficiency, and how does that relate to ROI?

7. Why is an IMC campaign difficult to evaluate?

Discussion Questions

1. Many creative people feel that formal copytesting research doesn't do justice to their ideas. In particular, they feel that research results are designed to reward cognitive approaches and don't do a good job of evaluating brand image ads and emotional ads. From what you have read in this chapter about copytesting, why do they feel that way? Do you believe that is a legitimate criticism of copytesting?

2. Most clients want a quick and easy answer to the question of whether the ad works. Advertising professionals, however, tend to believe that a one-score approach to copytesting is not appropriate. Why do they feel that way? If you were helping an agency prepare for a presentation on its copytesting results, what would you suggest the agency say to explain away the idea that you can evaluate an ad with a single test?

3. *Three-Minute Debate* You are hiring a research consulting company to help a client evaluate the effectiveness of its advertisements. One of the consultants recommends using focus groups to evaluate their effectiveness. Another consultant suggests that focus groups aren't very effective for post-testing and recommends other measures. Which viewpoint do you believe is most insightful?

4. Explore the websites of two copytesting companies, such as Ameritest (*www.Ameritest.net*), Ipsos ASI (*www.ipsos.com*), Millward Brown (*www.millwardbrown.com*) or the ARS Group (*www.ars-group.com*), and compare the services they offer. If you were looking for a company to pretest a campaign for a cosmetic product, which one would you prefer? Why?

Take-Home Projects

1. *Portfolio Project* Put together a portfolio of 10 ads for a set of product categories targeted to a college audience. Set up a focus group with participants recruited from among your friends and ask them to look at the ads. In a test of unaided awareness, ask them to list the ads they remember. Identify the top performing ad and the bottom ad in this awareness test. Now ask the focus group participants to analyze the headline, the visual, and the brand identification of each ad. How do the two ads compare in terms of their ability to get attention and lock the brand in memory?

2. *Mini-Case Analysis* Reread the chapter opening story about the Colorado Pass Club. Explain what is meant when we say the point of this campaign is to build a brand relationship. How did this campaign succeed in that objective? How was effectiveness determined for the Colorado Pass? If you were on the marketing team and were asked to develop a broader set of evaluation tools, what would you recommend and why?

Team Project: The BrandRevive Campaign

This is it. You're now at the last steps in the development of a campaign for your BrandRevive client.

- First, develop an evaluation proposal for your campaign. How would you measure the effectiveness of your campaign ideas?
- Finally, bring all your ideas together as a complete campaign. From everything you've done in the preceding chap-

ters, as well as the evaluation proposal you just drafted after reading this final chapter, synthesize and consolidate your best ideas. Compose a campaign presentation of no more than 30 PowerPoint slides. This is a showcase presentation, so give your team a title and create a title for your campaign. Practice and present it to your class. Good luck and good work.

Hands-On Case

The Century Council

Read the Century Council case in the Appendix before coming to class.

1. If you worked for the Century Council, how would you pretest this campaign prior to using it across the country and spending a full $10 million on it?

2. How did "The Stupid Drink" team evaluate their progress step by step through the campaign development process?

3. If you worked for the Century Council, how would you evaluate the market success of "The Stupid Drink" campaign from year to year?

The Century Council 2009 American Advertising Federation Case Study

THE STUPID DRINK: THE DRINK BETWEEN DRINKING . . . AND DRINKING TOO MUCH

The following case was written by Edward Russell, associate professor of advertising at the S. I. Newhouse School of Public Communications at Syracuse University in Syracuse, New York. Professor Russell is the faculty adviser to The NewHouse, a student-run advertising agency on the campus of Syracuse University and winner of the 2009 American Advertising Federation National Student Advertising Competition. The competition is the oldest and largest advertising competition in the United States.

How Do You Curb Binge Drinking on College Campuses?

Drinking on college campuses is absolutely frightening! Every year there are countless DUI's, arrests, unwanted sexual advances and worst of all . . . nearly 2,000 students a year die of alcohol poisoning. We must do something and we must do something right now!

This isn't a problem. Drinking is fun. College is all about meeting new people, becoming independent from your parents and having the time of your life.

The problem? Both completely opposite points of view are legitimate. Drinking can be dangerous *and* drinking can be a fun social event. So how do you get people to stop doing something they enjoy?

TRENDS IN COLLEGE BINGE DRINKING

The National Institute on Alcohol Abuse and Alcoholism's National Advisory Council defines binge drinking as such:

A binge is a pattern of drinking alcohol that brings blood alcohol concentration (BAC) to .08 or above. For a typical adult, this pattern corresponds to consuming five or more drinks in a two-hour span for men or four or more drinks in a two-hour span for women.

According to a U.S.-based "Monitoring the Future" study, 45% of male college students reported binge drinking and 37% of female students binge drink. But this isn't a U.S. problem; the same trends show up in Europe, Australia, Asia, and South America. College students drink heavily; they always have.

You might assume that with all of the emphasis on healthy living in our culture today that binge drinking, like smoking, would be on the decline. You would be wrong. Binge drinking on college campuses has remained pretty steady since 1993.

What happens to binge drinkers? According to the CORE Institute at Southern Illinois University at Carbondale, 63% of college students reported having a hangover, 54% were nauseous, 38% did something they regretted later, 34% experienced memory loss, 31% missed a class, etc., etc., etc. While no one would ever rationally choose to feel badly the next morning, these problems aren't such a big deal to a college student. Let's just say, the risk-to-fun ratio generally falls in favor of the fun part.

Although the legal drinking age in the United States is 21, it isn't that difficult for a college student to get alcohol on most campuses. It's nearly impossible for the authorities to enforce the law as drinking gets pushed deeper and deeper underground. According to a 2006 National Survey on Drug Use and Health, approximately 1% of 12-year-olds report drinking enough to qualify as binge drinking. This percentage of the population who are binge drinkers increases every year until it peaks with 50% of 21-year-olds being binge drinkers.

It almost seems silly to ask in a college textbook why college students drink. You know the answer. It can be fun. The CORE study showed that 74% say it gives them something to do, 62% say it allows you to have more fun, and 58% of males and 48% of females say consuming alcohol facilitates bonding.

THE PROBLEM

How do we curb an activity (binge drinking) that is associated with more positive experiences than negative experiences for students? We had to start with obvious solutions.

Tougher enforcement! But how? Police can't be everywhere all the time. Bar raids and checking IDs in liquor stores can only go so far toward curbing accessibility to alcohol. It's simply not practical to think we can stop underage binge drinking this way. The laws are already in place and enforced, and the problem is still with us. We can't solve the problem legally.

Just say no. Students hate authorities telling them what to do and not do. At the very time they are experiencing their first taste of independence, well-meaning groups that try to tell them not to drink, smoke, eat *trans* fats, or whatever are unwelcome voices and aren't effective. If that type of message worked, the problem would have been solved decades ago. The authoritarian approach to stopping binge drinking simply does not work.

Inform them of the consequences. Everyone reading this knows there are serious potential consequences associated with the overconsumption of alcohol. However, we also all believe we are invincible. Bad things happen to other people. Telling people what they already know but don't believe doesn't work.

Turn off the culture. Movies, TV, YouTube videos, thousands of websites, fraternities, sororities, beer and liquor companies with multimillion-dollar advertising budgets all tell us constantly that drinking with friends is fun; in fact, it is often portrayed as hilarious. You can't turn off the culture, and you can't be dishonest.

We knew what wasn't working; we didn't know what would work. So we started looking around the world of public service advertising at case studies and award-winning work and interviewed experts from other industries. Well-meaning failed communications campaigns outnumber successful case studies in this area by at least ten to one. However, no other attempt rang as true and had the business results to prove its success as much as the *truth*® campaign for the American Legacy Foundation created by Arnold Worldwide and Crispin Porter + Bogusky. Clearly, there is a difference between stopping cigarette smoking among teens and curbing binge drinking on college campuses, but there was a lot we could learn here. Our biggest lesson was we had to identify a "bad guy." One of the brilliant ideas behind the *truth* campaign is that it didn't attempt to blame you, the user. It blamed the tobacco company instead. We had a similar situation. Drinking isn't bad; out-of-control binge drinking is.

Research: What We Learned about Drinking—Yours and Our Own

So how do we curb binge drinking on college campuses? It took the AAF NSAC team from Syracuse University 1,556 in-depth surveys, 75 expert interviews, 15 observational ethnographies, a deprivation study, and a review of journal articles to discover one very simple observation:

Freshmen drink very differently than seniors.

Freshmen tend to get together, drink a lot fast to get as drunk as possible, and be social around people they don't yet know. Seniors get together with friends they value and share a few drinks to enjoy those times more. That's a huge piece of information.

Think about this: When you were a freshmen, chances are you "learned" to drink with other freshmen who also didn't really know how to drink. No wonder we drink too much too fast. Over four years of college we actually "learn" to drink.

Then it occurred to us . . . *what if we could shorten the learning process?* What if we could take the four years of "learning to drink" and shorten that into three to six months? Would that curb binge drinking? We weren't sure. So, we went to bars and frat houses to observe binge drinkers in their environment. We observed them before they drank, while they drank, and even the morning after they drank. We talked to students about binge drinking and found out that nearly no one thinks of himself or herself as a "binge drinker." To the students, the term "binge" implies people that aren't *capable* of limiting their consumption of alcohol. These students aren't alcoholics; they're just partying and having a great time. Sure it gets out of control once in a while, but they definitely don't see that as a "problem."

So we changed the words we used. Instead of talking about "binge" drinking, we talked about "drinking too much." Just changing the terminology we used caused a radical change in the responses we received. Students know what drinking too much is. Most had experienced it firsthand; all had seen it for themselves.

There is a line between "drinking" (which can be a lot of fun) and "drinking too much" (which can lead to unwelcome consequences). The more we discussed the idea of this line, the more we realized we had all crossed the line at one time or another, and none of us really wanted to cross it again.

Strategy: What We Want to Do and What We Want to Communicate

We want to "curb underage binge drinking." We aren't trying to stop drinking. As communicators, it is crucial that we accept what we can change and what we can't change. College students are going to drink. However, if we can speed up this learning process of "how to drink" we have the potential of avoiding unwelcome consequences and maybe even saving lives.

We headed back to the bars and fraternity houses to try and figure out *where* that line is. But, it's not a line. It's a drink. The line between drinking and drinking too much is actually one drink. There is one drink between "in control" and "out of control." There is one drink between a fun night with friends and a night of regrettable consequences. There is one drink where your judgment decreases and consumption increases.

We decided to name our "bad guy." We didn't have to look very far to hear how students refer to drinking too much. A college student in one of our focus groups referred to his weekend as "getting stupid" and the name "The Stupid Drink" stuck.

Strategy Our strategy was to teach students how to drink responsibly by identifying and stigmatizing the one drink (The Stupid Drink) that separates enjoyable drinking from negative consequences that occur from drinking too much. In doing this, we hypothesized we could greatly reduce the prevalence of binge drinking on college campuses.

Target audience Naive drinkers on college campuses who haven't yet learned how to drink responsibly. They tend to be freshmen and sophomores away from home for the first time, but can also be juniors and seniors caught up in out-of-control social drinking situations.

The "Big Idea" The Stupid Drink is the drink between drinking and drinking too much. For some, The Stupid Drink might be indicated by a feeling; for some, a number of drinks; and for others, it might even be one type of alcohol such as tequila.

Tonality We know authoritarian messages don't work with this newly independent young adult. And although students respond well to humor, we have to be extremely careful we don't allow the seriousness of the message to get lost.

Confirming Our Strategy

Before we began creating communications, we tested the idea. We explained the concept to a group of serious college drinkers and checked back with them after a weekend of partying. It worked. Our test group reported back that they figured out where their Stupid Drink was and to a person really didn't *want* to drink beyond that. They reported having a lot more fun and feeling a lot better the day after. They were sold. And, they were safe.

We realized we had come upon a universal insight. We all have a stupid drink—professors, students, parents, etc. There is one drink between being in control and out of control for all of us.

Students also talked about how easy it was to talk about their "stupid drink" around friends as well as tell others when they were beyond their stupid drink. We knew for our concept to be effective, the term had to be very natural in any setting. This was all becoming very exciting.

CREATIVE EXECUTIONS

The plan for our messaging is to begin several weeks before freshmen get to campus with a postcard sent home announcing the discovery of The Stupid Drink and encouraging students to check out The Drinking Institute online. Because we wanted to "teach" our fellow students safe and responsible drinking habits, we created a fictitious "Drinking Institute" headed by friendly scientists such as Bill Ney, the Science Guy. In a television commercial and viral video, The Drinking Institute announces its revolutionary discovery after years of research. It discovered The Stupid Drink—the drink between drinking and drinking too much.

The Drinking Institute website allows students to visit this fictitious institute, roam the halls, do experiments on subjects, and come to their own conclusion about drinking too much. A Facebook application allows students to tag their friends with "symptoms of stupid" after they have gone too far such as "handsy friend." Is your best friend slurring her speech? Our mobile messaging application allows you to text another with her "symptom of stupid" during a party. Drinking at a sporting event? The Stupid Drink billboard will prove an effective reminder at just the right time.

Bars love people who drink and have a good time. They don't like patrons who get sick in the bar or go out and get hurt afterward. Our bar coasters with cute definitions of The Stupid Drink such as "the line between 'I'm good' and 'my bad'" and The Stupid Drink ID stamp will allow bars to remind patrons to have a great time, but not to go beyond their stupid drink. If you are drinking beer in a bar, sooner or later you will visit the restroom where our Symptoms of Stupid bathroom posters will remind you that you don't want to make a fool of yourself by exhibiting one of these symptoms (e.g., dancing like a "pro" or "personal space invasion").

We want to not only build a general awareness of The Stupid Drink idea, we want to get as close to the actual drinking situation as possible. We want The Stupid Drink message to be in the bars, in the fraternity parties, in the dorms—wherever college students go to drink.

Promotions and Public Relations

Curbing binge drinking among college students is a huge task. We want to enlist the help of those who care the most about this. That's why we created a website for college administrators to share their best practices with each other, and for parents to learn about what to expect and how they can help their child become a responsible, safe independent adult.

Press releases will celebrate the discovery of The Stupid Drink and campus events will help bring the message as close to the actual drinking event as possible. We developed a "Shoot Till You Miss" beer pong game but instead of beer, participants win prizes. But, hit the middle glass, The Stupid Drink, and it's game over. Urban Dictionary and Wikipedia entries for The Stupid Drink give it credibility and legitimacy.

Media

There is never enough money in advertising to accomplish all you want to, but by investing the money smartly you can maximize the impact of your plan. Our $10 million plan will go a long way toward helping us curb binge drinking.

To stretch our budget, we divided the colleges into Tier 1 and Tier 2 schools based on alcohol consumption and size of campus (per *The Princeton Review* list of "Party Schools" and *Playboy*'s list of party schools). The Tier 1 schools would receive the full program with all advertising executions. Tier 2 schools would receive a reduced level in part because the drinking problem isn't as severe at these schools.

At Syracuse University, we no longer talk about "traditional vs. nontraditional" media. With this generation, the world is their medium and anything is possible. Viral videos, websites, Facebook applications, mobile messaging, Twitter, bar coasters, search engine optimization, campus newspapers, postcards, stadium billboards, cable television (e.g., MTV, ESPN, VH-1, and Comedy Central), dorm room stickers and posters, sidewalk clings, decks of cards, and bar stamps all worked together to deliver our message from August through May to 967 colleges and universities, 7,500,000 college students or 74% of the entire student population.

But will The Stupid Drink campaign curb binge drinking on college campuses? Our postevaluation research clearly demonstrated that 95% of college students understood our message and 89% reported that they actually thought about the idea while out drinking. If we are right, almost no one reading this now will look at drinking too much in the same way again.

Syracuse University's "The NewHouse Advertising Agency" student members include Maria Sinopoli, Paul Savaiano, Peter Ceran, Gregory Rozmus, and Erica Bruno on the presenting team with strong support from Christina DiPhillips, Amanda Dwyer, Danielle Eck, Laurin Garbarino, Blair Gontowicz, Erica Gorlick, Ronald Hughes, Andrea Serra, Stephen Shoemaker, Jonathan Smolin, Allison Yoest, Kate Overholt, David Ma, Alison Leung, Pam Sidran, and Agatha Lutoborski. Faculty Adviser Ed Russell with incredible support from Newhouse professors Dr. James Tsao, Kevin O'Neill, and Amy Falkner.

GLOSSARY

3-D Television *(p. 377)* Television programs that have been filmed using technology that creates the illusion of depth, which is the third dimension—the other two being width and height.

A

Account executive *(p. 24)* A person who acts as a liaison between the client and the agency.

Account management *(p. 23)* People and processes at an ad agency that facilitate the relationship between the agency and the client.

Account planner *(p. 210)* The person responsible for the strategy and its implementation in the creative work.

Account planning *(pp. 25, 210)* A process of using research to gain information about the brand in its marketplace, the consumer's perspective, or both, and to use that research to contribute directly to advertising development.

Account services *(p. 23)* The account management function of an agency, which acts as a liaison between the client and the agency.

Acquired needs *(p. 135)* A driving force learned from culture, society, and the environment.

Active publics *(p. 468)* Those people who communicate and organize to do something about an issue or situation.

Ad allowances *(p. 552)* In cooperative advertising, funds are provided by manufacturers to retailers who feature the manufacturers' products in the retailers' local advertising.

Adaptation *(p. 565)* See Localization.

Added value *(p. 41)* A marketing activity, such as advertising, makes a product more appealing or useful.

Addressable media *(p. 327)* Media, such as mail, the Internet, and the telephone, that carry messages to identifiable customers or prospects.

Addressable television *(p. 377)* Television technology that permits the signal to be personalized to a home.

Adese *(p. 265)* Formula writing that uses clichés, generalities, stock phrases, and superlatives.

Adoption *(p. 149)* The willingness to try new products.

Adoption process *(p. 149)* Buying behavior that reflects the speed with which people are willing to try something new.

Advertainment *(p. 344)* A form of persuasive advertising in which the commercials look like TV shows or short films, and provide entertainment as opposed to high levels of information.

Advertisement *(p. 6)* A notice about a product (good, service, or idea) that is designed to get the attention of a target audience.

Advertiser *(p. 18)* A person or organization that initiates the advertising process.

Advertising *(p. 7)* Paid nonpersonal communication from an identified sponsor using mass media to persuade or influence an audience.

Advertising agency *(p. 20)* An organization that provides a variety of professional services to its client who is the advertiser of a product.

Advertising department *(p. 20)* A department within the company that acts as a facilitator between outside vendors and internal advertising management.

Advertising plan *(p. 53)* A plan that proposes strategies for targeting the audience, presenting the advertising message, and implementing media.

Advertising research *(p. 163)* The process of gathering information about consumers and the marketplace in order to make sound strategic planning decisions.

Advocacy *(p. 121)* A type of advertising that communicates a viewpoint.

Advocacy advertising *(p. 474)* A type of corporate advertising that involves creating advertisements and purchasing space to deliver a specific, targeted message.

Affective response *(p. 109)* A response caused by or expressing feelings and emotions.

Affiliates *(p. 370)* A station that contracts with a national network to carry network-originated programming during part of its schedule.

Agency networks *(p. 23)* Large conglomerations of agencies under a central ownership.

Agency-of-record (AOR) *(p. 20)* An advertising agency that manages the business between a company and the agencies it has contracts with.

AIDA *(p. 103)* A hierarchy of effects identified as Attention, Interest, Desire, and Action.

Aided recognition (recall) *(pp. 174, 589)* When one can remember an idea after seeing a cue.

Ambush marketing *(p. 534)* In event marketing, a competitor advertises in such a way that it steals visibility from the designated sponsor.

Analogies *(p. 251)* A statement that finds some point of similarity between two things that are otherwise dissimilar.

Animatics *(p. 585)* Drawings or still photos shot on videotape synchronized with a rough version of an audio track.

Animation *(pp. 282, 312)* A film or video technique in which objects or drawings are filmed one frame at a time.

Annual report *(p. 477)* A financial document legally required of all publicly held companies.

Answer print *(p. 314)* The finished version of the commercial, with the audio and video recorded together.

Aperture *(pp. 373, 433)* The ideal moment for exposing consumers to an advertising message.

Appeal *(p. 237)* An advertising approach that connects with some need, want, or emotion that makes the product message attractive, attention getting, or interesting.

Argument *(p. 119)* A cognitive strategy that uses logic, reasons, and proof to build convictions.

Art director *(p. 14)* The person who is primarily responsible for the visual image of the advertisement.

Association *(p. 115)* The process used to link a product with a positive experience, personality, or lifestyle.

Association tests *(p. 172)* A way to check consumer perceptions by asking people what comes to mind when a word or brand is mentioned.

Attention *(p. 13)* Concentrating the mind on a thought or idea.

Attitude *(pp. 116, 145)* A learned predisposition that we hold toward an object, person, or idea.

Attributes *(p. 239)* A distinctive feature of a product.

Avatars *(p. 409)* A representation, character, or personality constructed by a computer user to serve or represent that person.

Average frequency *(p. 428)* The average number of times an audience has an opportunity to be exposed to a media vehicle or vehicles in a specified time span.

Aware publics *(p. 468)* Those people who recognize the connection between a problem and themselves or others but do not communicate about it.

Awareness *(p. 109)* The degree to which a message has made an impression on the viewer or reader.

B

Back translation *(p. 284)* The practice of translating ad copy into a second language and then translating that version back into the original language to check the accuracy of the translation.

Bandwagon appeals *(p. 117)* The idea that people respond to popular causes and ideas and want to join up or adopt a trendy viewpoint.

Bandwidth *(p. 393)* In electronic communication, this is what governs the amount of digital information or data that can be sent from one place to another in a given time.

Banner ad *(p. 402)* Small, often rectangular-shaped graphic that appears at the top of a Web page.

Banners *(p. 282)* See "banner ad."

Behavioral targeting *(p. 154)* The practice of identifying groups of people who might be in the market for a product based on their actions—particularly the patterns of their online behavior.

Beliefs *(p. 116)* A term related to a person's cognitive processing—how they arrive at a position, viewpoint, or decision based on their knowledge, attitudes, and opinions.

Believability *(p. 119)* The extent to which a marketing communication message is accepted as true.

Benchmarking *(pp. 199, 468)* Comparing a result against some other known result from a comparable effort.

Benefit *(p. 239)* Statement about what the product can do for the user.

Big Idea *(p. 244)* A creative idea that expresses an original advertising thought.

Bleed *(p. 360)* A full-page ad with no outside margins—the printed area extends to the edge of the page.

Bleed throughs *(p. 449)* In printed communication, the image on one side of a sheet of paper can be seen on the other usually because the ink has thoroughly saturated the paper.

Blind headline *(p. 269)* An indirect headline that gives little information.

Blog *(p. 405)* A personal diary-like Web page.

Blogola *(p. 73)* Company representatives who pose as consumers or paid bloggers who post endorsements as customer reviews online without the sponsorship being made known to readers, also known as flogging.

Body copy *(p. 265)* The text of the message.

Brag-and-boast copy *(p. 265)* Self-important copy that focuses on the company rather than the consumer.

Brainfag *(p. 249)* In creative thinking, this is the point where concentration ceases to produce ideas because of mental fatigue and the mind closes down.

Brainstorming *(p. 250)* A creative thinking technique using free association in a group environment to stimulate inspiration.

Brand *(p. 44)* A name, term, design, or symbol that identifies the goods, services, institution, or idea sold by a marketer.

Brand advertising *(p. 11)* An advertising strategy that focuses on creating an image or perception of a brand.

Brand communities *(p. 134)* Groups of people devoted to a particular brand, such as the Harley Owners Group (HOG) for Harley-Davidson.

Brand development index (BDI) *(p. 431)* A numerical technique used to indicate a brand's sales within a particular market relative to all other markets where the brand is sold.

Brand equity *(p. 51)* The value associated with a brand; the reputation that the brand name or symbol connotes.

Brand extension *(p. 52)* Use of an established brand name with a related line of products.

Brand icon *(p. 240)* A character used to represent the brand.

Brand identity *(p. 48)* Unique characteristics of a product within a product category.

Brand image *(pp. 50, 207)* A special meaning or mental representation created for a product by giving it a distinctive name and identity.

Brand licensing *(p. 52)* A partner company rents the brand name and transfers some of its brand equity to another product.

Brand linkage *(pp. 115, 207)* The extent to which an advertising message is connected to the brand and locked into the memory of people who see the message.

Brand loyalty *(pp. 51, 119)* The degree of attachment that a customer has to a particular brand as expressed by repeat sales.

Brand management *(p. 44)* An organizational structure that places a manager or management team in charge of a brand's total marketing efforts.

Brand meaning *(p. 44)* Perceptions of ideas and images of products or services often based on product attributes and performance.

Brand name *(p. 15)* The part of the brand that can be spoken, such as words, letters, or numbers.

Brand penetration *(p. 587)* The number of customers who purchase a certain brand compared against the total market population.

Brand personality *(p. 50)* The image projected by a brand that often resembles characteristics of people.

Brand position *(p. 50)* The location a brand occupies in consumers' minds relative to its competitors.

Brand promise *(p. 50)* Communication that sets expectations for what a customer believes will happen when the product is used.

Brand relationship *(p. 51)* Communication aimed at delivering reminders about familiar brands and building trust.

Brand transformation *(p. 46)* A brand's meaning is more valuable than the products, goods, or services it represents.

Brand value *(p. 51)* Enhanced meaning of a brand that adds worth to products and services.

Branded apps *(p. 347)* A software program mounted on a cell phone, computer, or social networking page that contains information sponsored by or related to a brand.

Branded entertainment *(p. 344)* Programs, such as the Hallmark Hall of Fame, that are sponsored by a particular brand.

Branding *(p. 44)* The process of creating a unique identity for a product.

Break-even analysis *(p. 596)* A type of payout plan that seeks to determine the point at which the total cost of the promotion exceeds the total revenues, identifying the point where the effort cannot break even.

Broadband *(p. 393)* A bandwidth that has more capacity to send data and images into a home or business through a cable television wire than the much smaller capacity of a traditional telephone wire or television antenna system.

Broadcasting media *(pp. 327, 369)* Media, such as radio, television, and interactive media, which transmit sounds or images electronically.

Broadcast network *(p. 374)* A national group of affiliated stations through which programming and advertising are distributed.

Broadsheets *(p. 496)* A newspaper with a page size eight columns wide and 22 inches deep.

Brokers *(p. 332)* People or companies who sell space (in print) or time (in broadcast) for a variety of media.

Business-to-business (B2B) advertising *(pp. 11, 556)* Targets other businesses.

Business-to-business (B2B) market *(p. 37)* Organizations that have products for use in conducting their business.

Buyer *(p. 556)* A specialist who negotiates an actual purchase in a certain category.

Buzz *(p. 9)* Gossip created by people over a popular interest in something.

C

Cable radio *(p. 370)* A technology that uses cable television receivers to deliver static-free music via wires plugged into cable subscribers' audio systems.

Cable television *(p. 376)* A form of subscription television in which the signals are carried to households by a cable.

Call centers *(p. 500)* Facilities with banks of phones and representatives who call prospects (outbound) or answer customer calls (inbound).

Call to action *(pp. 120, 243, 272)* A concluding line that tells people how to buy the product.

Call-out *(p. 267)* A block of text separate from the main display copy and headline where the idea is presented.

Campaign *(p. 12)* A comprehensive advertising plan for a series of different but related ads that appear in different media across a specified time period.

Campaign plan *(p. 194)* A comprehensive outline of all activities for a series of related advertisements and other marketing communication efforts.

Capital campaigns *(p. 560)* Fund-raising method used to raise a certain amount of money in a set period of time to finance new buildings, equipment, and so on.

Captions *(p. 270)* Text that explains what is happening in a corresponding photo or illustration.

Carrot mob *(p. 116)* A technique used by environmentalists to reward companies that support green marketing.

Carryover effect *(p. 434)* A measure of residual effect (awareness or recall) of the advertising message some time after the advertising period has ended.

Casting *(p. 280)* Finding the right person for the role.

Catalog *(p. 498)* A multipage direct-mail publication that shows a variety of merchandise.

Category development index (CDI) *(p. 431)* A numerical technique that indicates the relative consumption rate in a particular market for a particular product category.

Cause marketing *(pp. 76, 464, 561)* Sponsoring a good cause in the hope that the association will result in positive public opinion about the company.

Cease-and-desist order *(p. 87)* An FTC remedy for false or deceptive advertising that requires an advertiser to stop its unlawful practices.

Change agent *(p. 469)* Programs and individuals whose goal it is to change the attitudes that drive behavior.

Channel market *(p. 37)* The members of a distribution chain, including resellers or intermediaries.

Channel marketing *(pp. 37, 528)* Advertising and promotion efforts directed at members of the distribution channel.

Channel of communication *(p. 100)* The media through which an advertisement is presented.

Channel of distribution *(p. 36)* People and organizations involved in moving products from producers to consumers.

Channels (media) *(p. 20)* Media or companies such as local newspaper or radio stations that transmit communication messages from the advertiser to the audience and from consumers back to companies.

Chat room *(p. 407)* A website that allows users to share information.

Circulation *(p. 335)* The number of copies sold.

Claim *(p. 239)* A statement about the product's performance.

Claim substantiation *(p. 86)* The reasonable basis for making an assertion about product performance.

Classified advertising *(pp. 13, 357)* Commercial messages arranged in the newspaper according to the interests of readers.

Claymation *(p. 312)* A stop-motion animation technique in which figures sculpted from clay are filmed one frame at a time.

Clichés *(p. 244)* Generic, nonoriginal, non-novel ideas.

Click art *(p. 296)* See Clip art.

Click fraud *(p. 413)* Clicking on a website or online advertisement to mislead the count either to increase the volume for the sponsor or to damage a competitor.

Click-through *(pp. 283, 402)* The act of clicking on a button on a website that takes the viewer to a different website.

Click-through rates *(p. 597)* A method of measuring the effectiveness of online advertising by dividing the number of times the ad was presented on a website by the number of times it was clicked on by viewers.

Clip art *(p. 296)* Generic, copyright-free art that can be used by anyone who buys the book or service.

Closing *(p. 449)* Represents the last date to send an ad to production.

Closing paragraph *(p. 272)* The last paragraph of body copy in an ad that sums up the selling message, usually ending with a call to action.

Cloud computing *(p. 411)* The practice of managing an organization's files online rather than on a server or hard drive.

Clutter *(p. 101)* The excessive number of messages delivered to a target audience.

Clutter reel *(p. 585)* A reel of commercials used in ad testing on which one ad is the one being tested and the others are included to simulate the clutter of a typical advertising break in a program.

Co-branding *(pp. 52, 536)* A product offered by two companies with both companies' brands present.

Co-marketing *(p. 536)* Programs through which manufacturers partner with retailers in joint promotions.

Code-of-ethics *(p. 79)* The rules and standards for a system of socially responsible professional practice.

Cognition *(p. 113)* How consumers respond to information, learn, and understand.

Cognitive dissonance *(p. 136)* A tendency to justify the discrepancy between what you receive and what you expected to receive.

Cognitive learning *(p. 114)* When advertisers want people to know something new after watching or hearing a message.

Coincidental survey *(p. 585)* Random phone calls made to viewers to determine what shows they are watching at that time.

Cold call *(p. 500)* Contacts that are made to leads that have not been qualified as interested; also includes cold calls made by telemarketers to random phone numbers.

Collateral materials *(pp. 274, 477)* Brochures and other forms of product literature used in support of an advertising, public relations, or sales promotion effort.

Color separation *(p. 307)* The process of splitting a color image into four images recorded on negatives; each negative represents one of the four process colors.

Commercial speech *(p. 82)* Our legal right to say what we want to promote commercial activity, as defined by the First Amendment.

Commission *(p. 25)* The amount an ad agency charges to the client, often a percentage of media cost.

Communication audit *(p. 468)* A type of background research that assesses the internal and external PR environment that affects the organization's audience, objectives, competitors, and past results.

Communication brief *(p. 214)* A strategy document that explains the consumer in-

sight and summarizes the message and media strategy.

Comparative advertising *(p. 71)* A message strategy that explicitly or implicitly compares the features of two or more brands.

Comparison *(p. 240)* An advertising strategy that compares two or more brands.

Competitive advantage *(pp. 40, 204)* Features or benefits of a product that let it outperform its competitors.

Compiled list *(p. 507)* In database marketing, a list that is created by merging several lists and purging duplicate entries.

Composition *(p. 304)* The art of arranging the way the elements in a photograph are positioned.

Comprehension *(p. 114)* The process by which people understand, make sense of things, and acquire knowledge.

Comprehensives *(p. 304)* A layout that looks as much like the final printed ad as possible.

Concept testing *(pp. 173, 584)* When a simple statement of an idea is tried out on people who are representative of the target audience in order to get their reactions to the Big Idea.

Concepting *(p. 244)* Creating a big idea.

Concurrent research *(p. 581)* Research that occurs as a campaign is underway to monitor how the message and media strategies are working in order to make adjustments if needed to improve the effectiveness of the effort.

Conditioned learning *(p. 115)* Learning through association by connecting a stimulus to a reward through repeated exposure to a stimulus that eventually leads to the reward.

Consent decree *(p. 87)* A formal FTC agreement with an advertiser that obligates the advertiser to stop its deceptive practices.

Considered purchase *(p. 118)* Buying something after gathering and evaluating information.

Consolidated services *(p. 451)* Company action of bringing planning and buying functions together.

Consumer *(p. 40)* The buyer or user of goods, services, and ideas.

Consumer behavior *(p. 130)* The process of an individual or group selecting, purchasing, using, or disposing of products, services, ideas, or experiences to satisfy needs and desires.

Consumer diaries *(p. 588)* A record kept of brands purchased, what they are used for, if consumers switched from one brand to another, and consumer response to coupons and other offers.

Consumer insight research *(p. 172)* Research that seeks to determines the underlying motivations that drive consumer attitudes and behaviors.

Consumer magazine *(p. 359)* A publication oriented to a general (non-business) audience.

Consumer market *(p. 37)* Selling products to a general (non-business) audience.

Consumer research *(p. 163)* A type of market research that identifies people who are in the market for a product.

Consumer research panel *(p. 179)* Information provided by an ongoing group of carefully selected people interested in a particular topic or product category.

Contact points *(pp. 35, 218, 337)* The media, as well as other places and ways, where a consumer engages in a brand experience.

Content analysis *(p. 171)* Research that analyzes articles, news stories, and other printed materials for themes and positive or negative mentions of a brand or company.

Contest *(p. 524)* A form of promotion that requires participants to compete for a prize or prizes based on some sort of skill or ability.

Continuity *(pp. 434, 535)* Even, continuous advertising over the time span of the advertising campaign.

Continuous strategy *(p. 434)* A media strategy that spreads the advertising evenly over a period.

Continuous tone *(p. 306)* Photographs are images that have a range of tones from white to black and all the shades of gray in between.

Controlled circulation *(p. 360)* Publications that are distributed, usually free, to selected individuals.

Controlled media *(p. 471)* Media that the direct marketer either owns or has delivered through carefully controlled criteria by a contracted company.

Convergence *(p. 328)* Because of the digitization of media forms, specialized media, such as newspapers and television, are becoming more alike in their content and how they are delivered online.

Conversion rates (*pp. 491, 597*) In sales, changing a prospect into a customer.

Conviction (*p. 119*) A particularly strong belief that has been anchored firmly in one's attitudes.

Cookies (*p. 413*) Web "bugs" that can be placed on your computer by a Web server to track your online movements.

Cool hunters (*p. 150*) People who specialize in spotting trends.

Co-op advertising (*p. 356*) Also called cooperative advertising; an arrangement between a retailer and manufacturer in which the manufacturer reimburses the retailer for all or part of the retailer's advertising costs.

Cooperative advertising (*pp. 356, 552*) See Co-op advertising.

Copycat advertising (*p. 247*) Using some other brand's creative idea.

Copytesting (*pp. 174, 253*) Evaluating the effectiveness of an ad, either in a draft form or after it has been used.

Copyright (*p. 82*) The owner or creator of certain types of original works have the sole right to reproduce and distribute the work.

Copywriter (*p. 261*) The person who writes the text for an ad.

Core values (*p. 132*) Underlying values that govern a person's (or a brand's) attitudes and behavior.

Corporate advertising (*pp. 11, 473*) A type of advertising used by firms to build awareness of a company, its products, and the nature of its business.

Corporate culture (*p. 134*) The values and attitudes that shape the behavior of an organization and its employees.

Corporate identity advertising (*p. 473*) Promotional method aimed at enhancing or maintaining a company's reputation in the marketplace.

Corporate image (*p. 473*) A perception of a company that its stakeholders create in their minds from messages and experiences with the company.

Corporate relations (*p. 465*) Relations between a corporation and the public involving an organization's image and reputation.

Corporate social responsibility (*p. 463*) Programs designed to create a platform of good citizenship for corporations and other organizations.

Corrective advertising (*p. 87*) An FTC directive that requires an advertiser to run truthful ads to counter deceptive ads.

Cost per lead (*p. 597*) Record of how well a click-through generates prospects.

Cost per point (CPP) (*p. 439*) A method of comparing alternative media vehicles on the basis of what it costs to deliver 1,000 readers, viewers, or listeners; the cost of an advertising unit (30-second TV or radio spot, for example) per 1,000 impressions.

Cost per thousand (CPM) (*p. 438*) The cost of exposing each 1,000 members of the target audience to the advertising message.

Country of origin (*p. 564*) Indication of the country that globalized companies consider their base of operation.

Coupons (*p. 523*) Legal certificates offered by manufacturers and retailers that grant specified savings on selected products when presented for redemption at the point-of-purchase.

Coverage (*p. 371*) The degree to which a particular advertising medium delivers audiences within a specific geographical area.

Crawl (*p. 310*) Computer-generated letters that move across the bottom of the screen.

Creative boutique (*p. 23*) An advertising agency that specializes in the creative side of advertising.

Creative brief (*pp. 214, 231*) The document that outlines the key strategy decisions and details the key execution elements.

Creative concept (*p. 244*) A Big Idea that is original, supports the ad strategy, and dramatizes the selling point.

Creative director (*p. 228*) The person responsible for managing the work of the creative team.

Creative platform (*p. 231*) A document that outlines the message strategy decisions for an individual ad.

Creative strategy (*p. 231*) The determination of the right message for a particular target audience, a message approach that delivers the advertising objectives.

Credibility (*p. 119*) The believability or reliability of a source of information.

Crisis management (*p. 465*) Management of people and events during times of great danger or trouble.

Critical touchpoint (CTP) (*p. 338*) A touch-point experience that connects the brand and customer on an emotional level and leads to a yes or no decision about a brand purchase or relationship.

Cross-functional management (*p. 548*) A practice that uses teams to coordinate ac-

tivities that involve different areas in and outside a company.

Cross-functional organization (*p. 54*) a team involving members from all of the relevant parts of a company that interact with customers, other stakeholders, and with outside agencies.

Cross-functional planning (*p. 218*) A type of planning that involves people from different parts of an organization, particularly all those departments whose work in some way has impact on the customer.

Cross-media (*p. 332*) See Multichannel.

Cross promotion (*p. 536*) A type of cooperative marketing program in which marketers use associations between complementary brands to create a joint promotional program.

Crowdsourcing (*p. 178*) Aggregating the wisdom of Internet users in a type of digital brainstorming that collects opinions and ideas from a digital community.

Cultural and social influences (*p. 135*) The forces other people exert on your behavior.

Cultural imperialism (*p. 70*) Imposing a foreign culture on a local culture; usually referred to as the impact of Western culture, products, and lifestyles on a more traditional culture.

Culture (*p. 132*) The complex whole of tangible items, intangible concepts, and social behaviors that define a group of people or a way of life.

Customer (*p. 40*) Current or prospective purchaser of a product.

Customer satisfaction (*p. 119*) The degree to which there is a match between the customer's expectations about a product and the product's actual performance.

Customer service (*pp. 38, 340*) The process of managing customers' interactive experiences with a brand, particularly those experiences based on complaints or requests for information or service.

Cut (*p. 314*) An abrupt transition from one shot to another.

Cutouts (*p. 365*) Irregularly shaped extensions added to the top, bottom, or sides of standard outdoor boards.

D

Dailies (*p. 313*) Processed scenes on film that a director reviews to determine what needs correcting.

Data mining (*pp. 154, 508*) Shifting through and sorting a company's computer database records to target customers and maintain relationships with them.

Database marketing *(p. 414)* A tool and industry that utilizes databases to predict trends and monitor consumers in order to more effectively implement direct-marketing strategies.

Databases *(p. 505)* Lists of consumers with information that helps target and segment those who are highly likely to be in the market for a certain product.

Daypart *(p. 371)* The way the broadcast schedule is divided into time segments during a day.

Dealer tag *(p. 554)* Time left at the end of a manufacturer's TV or radio commercial to insert local retail store information.

Debossing *(p. 308)* A depressed image created on paper by applying heat and pressure.

Deceptive advertising *(p. 86)* Advertising that misleads consumers by making claims that are false or by failure to fully disclose important information.

Delayed effects *(p. 124)* An advertisement's impact occurs at a later time (than its time of delivery).

Demand creation *(p. 65)* An external message creates a want or need.

Demographics *(p. 139)* Human traits such as age, income, race, and gender.

Demonstration *(p. 239)* An advertising strategy that shows how the product works.

Designated marketing area (DMA) *(pp. 145, 424)* Households in each major U.S. metropolitan area, or TV or radio broadcast coverage area.

Development *(p. 560)* Department of a company focused on fund-raising.

Developmental research *(p. 581)* A type of research that tests alternative ideas to determine which has the best likelihood of being successful and delivering on the strategy.

Diagnostic research *(p. 581)* A type of research that deconstructs a message to determine what elements are working or not working in order to make corrections or strengthen the execution of the strategy.

Diaries *(p. 181)* In advertising research, consumers record their consumption activities, including media use.

Die-cutting *(p. 307)* Using a sharp-edged stamp to cut irregular shapes in printed materials.

Differentiation *(pp. 40, 114)* An advertising strategy that calls to the consumer's attention the features that make a product unique or better than the competition.

Diffusion *(p. 149)* Adoption of new ideas based on Everett Rogers' Diffusion of Innovations theory.

Digital displays *(p. 365)* Outdoor advertising that uses digital technology to create an image.

Digital marketing *(p. 55)* Using new media and electronic media, particularly the Internet, to reach customers and make a sale.

Digital video recorder (DVR) *(p. 378)* Technology that allows people to record TV programs and play them back when they want.

Digitization *(p. 307)* Converting art into computer-readable images.

Direct action *(p. 120)* Immediate response to advertising, such as completing an order form and sending it back by return mail.

Direct mail *(p. 495)* A type of direct marketing that sends the offer to a prospective customer by mail.

Direct marketing (DM) *(p. 42)* A type of marketing that uses media to contact a prospect directly and elicit a response without the intervention of a retailer or personal sales.

Direct-action headline *(p. 268)* A headline that is straightforward and informative and leads to some kind of action.

Direct-response advertising *(p. 11)* A type of marketing communication that achieves an action-oriented objective as a result of the advertising message.

Direct-response marketing *(p. 489)* A multi-channel form of marketing that connects sellers and customers directly rather than through an intermediary, such as a retailer.

Direct-response marketing communication *(p. 489)* A type of marketing communication that achieves an action-oriented objective as a result of a message delivered directly to a prospective customer.

Directional advertising *(p. 362)* Tells people where to go to find goods and services.

Discretionary income *(p. 143)* The money available for spending after taxes and necessities are covered.

Display advertising *(p. 356)* Sponsored messages that can be of any size and location within the newspaper, except the editorial page.

Display copy *(p. 265)* Type set in larger sizes that is used to attract the reader's attention.

Distribution *(p. 42)* In marketing, the channel of distribution describes the route a product takes moving from its manufacturer to the customer.

Distribution chain *(p. 36)* The companies involved in moving a product from the manufacturer to the customer.

Divergent thinking *(p. 247)* In creative thinking, people trying to come up with a creative idea are advised to move away from logical thinking (inductive, deductive) and look for unexpected ideas by making mental jumps and creative leaps.

Domain name *(p. 392)* Sometimes referred to as a Web address, the domain name is the part of the address that identifies the host server on which a website resides.

Donut *(p. 554)* A form of broadcast commercials in which the opening and closing sections are the same, while the middle changes to focus on different merchandise or local stores.

Double-page spread *(p. 360)* An advertisement that crosses two facing pages in a magazine.

Dubbing *(p. 316)* The process of making duplicate copies of a videotape.

E

E-business *(p. 395)* The practice of conducting business online.

E-commerce *(p. 395)* Selling goods and services through electronic means, usually over the Internet.

Earned media, *(p. 438)* A term used in public relations, it refers to the media impressions delivered through publicity rather than through advertising media buys.

Effective *(p. 16)* Marketing communication is deemed to be effective when it accomplishes its objectives.

Effective frequency *(p. 429)* A planning concept that determines a range (minimum and maximum) of repeat exposures for a message.

Effectiveness *(p. 27)* Assessment about the extent to which objectives are met.

Effects *(p. 27)* The type of impact delivered by an advertisement or other marketing communication.

Embedded research *(p. 184)* Research that is measured through real purchase and use situations which benefits the consumer, manufacturer, and retailer.

Embossing *(p. 308)* The application of pressure to create a raised surface image on paper.

Emotional appeals *(p. 112)* Message strategies that seek to arouse our feelings.

Employee relations *(p. 463)* Relations between the company and its workers.

Endorsement *(p. 72)* Any advertising message that consumers reasonably believe reflects the opinions, beliefs, or experiences of an individual, group, or institution.

Endorser *(p. 240)* A person who testifies on behalf of the product (goods, service, or idea).

Engagement *(pp. 119, 328)* Advertisement that gets and holds the attention of its audience.

Ethics *(p. 76)* A set of moral principles that guide our actions.

Ethnographic research *(p. 181)* A form of anthropological research that studies the way people live their lives.

Evaluative research *(p. 174)* Research that determines how well the ad or campaign achieved its goals.

Event marketing *(p. 532)* Creating a promotion program around a sponsored event.

Evoked set *(p. 151)* A set of brands that come to mind when a product category is mentioned.

Exchange *(p. 35)* The process whereby two or more parties transfer something of value to one another.

Execution *(p. 231)* The different variations used to represent the message of a campaign.

Experiential marketing *(p. 338)* Marketing strategies and events that connect a brand and a prospective customer in a personal and involving way.

Experimental research *(p. 168)* Scientific research in which an investigator controls most of the key variables in order to study the impact of manipulating one or more—changing the product's price or the type of appeal in an ad, for example.

Expert panel *(p. 179)* A type of research that involves obtaining the opinions from a group of people who are recognized as experts in the area being studied.

Exporting *(p. 564)* Selling items to a foreign country.

Exposure *(pp. 107, 335, 378)* The opportunity for a reader, viewer, or listener to see or hear an advertisement.

Extensions *(p. 365)* Embellishments to painted billboards that expand the scale and break away from the standard rectangle limitations.

Exterior transit advertising *(p. 367)* Advertising posters that are mounted on the sides, rear, and tops of vehicles.

Extranets *(pp. 392, 479)* Networked systems of electronic communication that allow employees to be in contact with each other in one business with its business partners.

Eye-tracking *(p. 588)* A mechanical technique that tracks the eye's response while reading an advertisement to determine interest.

F

False advertising *(p. 71)* Advertising that is misleading or simply untrue.

Family *(p. 135)* Two or more people who are related by blood, marriage, or adoption and live in the same household.

Fast-moving consumer goods (fmcg) *(p. 37)* European term for package goods.

Feature analysis *(p. 204)* A comparison of your product's features against those of competing products.

Feature story *(p. 476)* In the media, these are human-interest stories, in contrast to hard news.

Features *(pp. 202, 239)* A product attribute or characteristic.

Federal Communications Commission (FCC) *(p. 84)* A U.S. government agency that regulates broadcast media and can eliminate ads that are deceptive or offensive.

Federal Trade Commission (FTC) *(p. 17)* A U.S. government agency responsible for regulating several advertising issues including banning deceptive or misleading advertising.

Fee *(p. 25)* An hourly amount charged to the client by the agency.

Fee system *(p. 25)* A compensation tool for advertisers requiring that client and agency agree on an hourly fee or rate or negotiate a charge for a specific project.

Feedback *(p. 100)* Response to a message by a receiver that is conveyed back to the source.

Film-to-tape transfer *(p. 311)* A procedure by which film is shot, processed, and then transferred to videotape.

Financial relations *(p. 463)* Communications with the financial community.

Flash mob *(p. 120)* A sudden and conspicuous gathering of people in public places generated by viral e-mail messages, telecommunications or social media.

Flighting strategy *(p. 434)* An advertising scheduling pattern characterized by a period of intensified activity called a flight, followed by a period of no advertising called a hiatus.

Focus groups *(p. 177)* A group interview led by a moderator.

Foil stamping *(p. 308)* The application of a thin metallic coating (silver, gold) molded to the surface of the image with heat and pressure.

Font *(p. 300)* The basic set of letters in a particular typeface.

Four Ps *(p. 35)* The marketing mix, which includes the product (design and performance), price (value), place (distribution), and promotion (marketing communication).

Four-color printing *(p. 307)* A printing process that replicates the full color of a photograph although it only uses four colors of ink.

Free association *(p. 250)* Getting a new idea by creating a juxtaposition between two seemingly unrelated thoughts—usually done by describing everything that comes into your mind when you are given a word to think about.

Free-standing insert (FSI) *(pp. 357, 554)* Preprinted advertisement placed loosely in the newspaper.

Frequency *(pp. 335, 428, 535)* The number of times an audience has an opportunity to be exposed to a media vehicle or vehicles in a specified time span.

Frequency distribution *(p. 429)* A media planning term describing exactly how many times each person is exposed to a message by percentage of the population (reach).

Frequency quintile distribution analysis *(p. 429)* A media planning analysis technique that divides a target audience into five equal-sized groups, each containing 20 percent of the audience, and establishes an average frequency of exposure for each of these segments (also called quintile analysis).

Friendship focus groups *(p. 178)* Group interviews with people who know one another and have been recruited by the person who hosts the session, which is usually held in that *person*'s home.

Fulfillment *(p. 494)* The back-end operations of direct marketing, which include receiving the order, assembling the merchandise, shipping, and handling returns and exchanges.

Full-service agency *(p. 22)* An agency that provides clients with the primary planning and advertising services.

Fund-raising (or development) *(pp. 464, 560)* The practice of raising money by collecting donations, sometimes called development or strategic philanthropy.

G

Gaffer *(p. 314)* Chief electrician on a film shoot.

Game *(p. 524)* A type of promotional sweepstakes that encourages customers to return to a business several times in order to increase the chances of winning.

Gap analysis *(p. 468)* A research technique that measures the differences in perceptions and attitudes between groups or between them and the organization.

Gatefold *(p. 360)* Four or more connected pages that fold in on themselves.

Gatekeepers *(p. 462)* Individuals who have direct relations with the public such as writers, producers, editors, talk-show coordinators, and newscasters.

Generic brands *(p. 46)* Products with no brand identification often appearing in black and white packages and projecting the image of a low-cost brand.

Global brand *(p. 56)* One that is marketed with the same name, design, and creative strategy in most or all of the major regional market blocs.

Globalization *(p. 184)* The deepening relationships and broadening interdependence among people from different countries.

Goodwill *(pp. 52, 461)* A positive attitude about a company among the general public.

Green marketing *(p. 76)* Companies whose promotional efforts help preserve the environment.

Grip *(p. 314)* Individual who moves the props and sets on a film shoot.

Gross impressions *(pp. 335, 379)* The sum of the audiences of all the media vehicles used within a designated time span.

Gross rating points (GRPs) *(p. 435)* The sum of the total exposure potential of a series of media vehicles expressed as a percentage of the audience population.

Guaranteed circulation *(p. 361)* Publications such as magazines guarantee to their advertisers that a certain number of copies will be sold or distributed to subscribers.

Guerrilla marketing *(p. 342)* A form of unconventional marketing, such as chalk messages on a sidewalk, that is often associated with staged events.

Gutter *(p. 360)* The white space, or inside margins, where two facing magazine pages join.

H

Halftones *(p. 306)* (Continuous tone): Image with a continuous range of shades from light to dark.

Hard sell *(p. 235)* A rational, informational message that emphasizes a strong argument and calls for action.

Hard-sell approach *(p. 206)* Method of selling that uses reasons to persuade consumers.

Hashtags *(pp. 102, 411)* Mashed-together phrases marked with a hash symbol (the pound sign) that indicates what topic the Twitter tweet addresses.

Headline *(p. 266)* The title of an ad; it is display copy set in large type to get the reader's attention.

Heavy-up schedule *(p. 431)* In media planning, a schedule can be designed that spends proportionately more of the budget in certain key ways, such as season or geography.

Heuristics *(p. 588)* A programmed approach to the analysis of some type of performance that uses expert opinion as a technique of evaluation.

Hierarchy of effects *(p. 103)* A set of consumer responses that moves from the least serious, involved, or complex up through the most serious, involved, or complex.

High involvement *(p. 118)* Perceiving a product or information as important and personally relevant.

High-context culture *(p. 566)* The meaning of a message is dependent on context cues.

High-definition TV (HDTV) *(p. 377)* A type of television set that delivers movie quality, high-resolution images.

Hits *(p. 413)* The number of times a website is visited.

Holding companies *(p. 23)* One or more advertising agency networks, as well as other types of marketing communication agencies and marketing services consulting firms.

Home page *(p. 399)* The opening page on a website.

Horizontal publication *(pp. 359, 558)* Publications directed at people who hold similar jobs.

House ad *(p. 472)* An ad by an organization that is used in its own publication or programming.

House brand *(pp. 46, 551)* See Store brands.

House list *(p. 507)* A compilation of a company's past customers or members.

Household *(p. 135)* All those people who occupy one living unit, whether they are related or not.

Households using television (HUT) *(p. 378)* A measure of households using TV.

Humor *(p. 240)* An advertising message strategy that tries to be funny to attract an audience, build a positive brand connection, and lock the product in memory.

I

Idea *(p. 244)* A thought or product of thinking.

Ideation *(p. 249)* The process of creating an idea.

Illumination *(p. 249)* The point when a new idea strikes.

Image *(p. 9)* The use of intangible attributes to create a specific perception.

Image advertising *(p. 242)* A type of advertising that creates a unique brand meaning.

Image transfer *(pp. 277, 446)* When the presentation in one medium stimulates the listener or viewer to think about the presentation of the product in another medium.

IMC research *(p. 163)* Research used to plan and evaluate the performance and synergy of all marketing communication tools.

Immersion *(p. 249)* Gathering information and concentrating your focus on a problem.

Impact *(pp. 103, 247)* The effect of the message on the audience.

Implied third-party endorsement *(p. 462)* When the media endorse a product and the public finds it credible.

Impression *(pp. 335, 378)* In media planning, one person's opportunity to be exposed to an advertising message.

In-depth interview *(p. 176)* One-on-one interview using open-ended questions.

In-house agency *(p. 22)* An agency within an advertiser's organization that performs all the tasks an outside agency would provide for the advertiser.

Inbound telemarketing *(p. 500)* Incoming calls initiated by the customer.

Incubation (*p. 249*) A step in the ideation process, when you turn your attention elsewhere and let your subconscious play with a problem.

Independent stations (*p. 376*) Local stations unaffiliated with a national network.

Indirect action (*p. 120*) Delayed response to advertising such as recalling the message and later in the store selecting the brand.

Indirect advertising (*p. 83*) Advertising that features a related product or idea instead of the primary (controversial) product.

Indirect-action headlines (*p. 268*) Headlines that aim to capture attention although they might not provide much information.

Industrial advertising (*p. 557*) Advertising directed at suppliers or original equipment manufacturers (OEMs).

Infomercial (*p. 502*) Infomercials are extended TV commercials that use the techniques of direct response communication to make an offer to viewers who are prospects for the brand.

Ingredient branding (*p. 52*) Acknowledging a supplier's brand as an important product feature.

Inquiry tests (*p. 590*) Evaluation that measures the number of responses to a message.

Insight mining (*p. 213*) Finding some nugget of truth in a stack of research findings that lead to a key understanding of how consumers feel, think, or behave.

Instant messaging (IM) (*p. 346*) Exchanging text-based messages in real time via an Internet communications service.

Institutional advertising (*p. 11*) A type of corporate advertising that focus on establishing a corporate identity or viewpoint.

Institutional markets (*p. 37*) Usually a nonprofit organization, such as hospitals, government agencies, or schools, that buy products to use in delivering their services.

Integrated direct marketing (IDM) (*p. 509*) A method of achieving precise, synchronized use of a tightly targeted medium at the right time, with a measurable return on dollars spent. Also known as integrated relationship marketing.

Integrated marketing communication (IMC) (*pp. 17, 53*) The practice of unifying all marketing communication efforts so they send a consistent brand message to target audiences.

Intend-to-buy test (*p. 590*) An evaluation determining if people are more likely to buy a product once they are exposed to an advertisement for it.

Intention (*p. 119*) A preference that motivates consumers to want to try or buy a brand.

Interactive communication (*p. 101*) Personal conversations between two people.

Interactive television (*p. 377*) A television with computer capabilities.

Interactivity (*p. 328*) Communication strategies that make it possible for consumers to send messages back and forth to the brand and to each other.

Interest (*p. 108*) Activities that engage the consumer.

Interior transit advertising (*p. 367*) Advertising posters that are mounted inside vehicles such as buses, subway cars, and taxis.

Interlock (*p. 314*) A version of the commercial with the audio and video timed together, although the two are recorded separately.

Intermediaries (*p. 37*) Companies that buy finished or semi-finished items and resell them for a profit.

Internal marketing (*pp. 217, 463*) Providing information about marketing activity and promoting it internally to employees.

International advertising (*p. 70*) Advertising designed to promote the same product in a number of countries.

International brand (*p. 56*) A brand or product that is available in most parts of the world.

International marketing (*p. 56*) Marketing programs that manage and promote the same brand in several countries or globally.

Internet (*p. 391*) A linked system of international computer networks.

Intranets (*pp. 392, 479*) Networked systems of electronic communication that allow employees to be in touch with one another from various locations.

Intrusive (*p. 108*) Marketing communication messages that intrude on people's perception in order to grab attention.

Intrusiveness (*p. 336*) Techniques used by messages and media to grab attention by being disruptive or unexpected.

Involvement (*p. 118*) The intensity of the consumer's interest in a product.

Issue management (*p. 464*) The practice of advising companies and senior management on how public opinion is coalescing around certain issues.

J

Jingles (*pp. 276, 371*) Commercials set to music.

K

Key frame (*p. 281*) An image from a commercial that sticks in the mind and becomes the visual that viewers remember when they think about the commercial.

Key influencers (*p. 480*) Persons of knowledge or authority who serve as opinion leaders within a social network.

Key visual (*p. 281*) Image that conveys the heart of the concept.

Key words (*pp. 282, 392*) A word or phrase typed into a search engine to finds websites relevant to a certain topic.

Kiosks (*p. 367*) Multisided bulletin board structures designed for public posting of messages.

Knowledge structure (*p. 116*) See Network of associations.

L

Latent publics (*p. 468*) Those people who are unaware of their connection to an organization regarding a problem.

Layout (*p. 303*) A drawing that shows where all the elements in the ad are to be positioned.

Lead agency (*p. 567*) In international marketing, the agency that develops the campaign.

Lead generation (*pp. 43, 491*) The identification of prospective customers.

Lead paragraph (*p. 272*) The first line or paragraph of the body copy that is used to stimulate the reader's interest.

Lead time (*pp. 355, 433*) Production time; also time preceding a seasonal event.

Leads (*p. 43*) The identification of potential customers, or prospects.

Left-brain thinking (*p. 247*) Logical, linear, and orderly thought; inductive or deductive.

Legibility (*p. 302*) How easy or difficult a type is to read.

Licensing (*p. 536*) The practice whereby a company with an established brand "rents" it to another company.

Lifestyle (*p. 135*) The pattern of living that reflects how people allocate their time, energy, and money.

Lifetime customer value (LCV) (*p. 511*) An estimate of the revenue coming from a particular customer (or type of customer) over the lifetime of the relationship.

Likability tests (*p. 590*) Evaluation of positive responses to an ad.

Liking (*p. 113*) Positive feelings about the brand that are aroused by a brand message.

Line art *(p. 306)* Art in which all elements are solid, with no intermediate shades or tones.

Link *(p. 392)* A path used to connect to a website.

Lobbying *(p. 463)* A form of public affairs involving corporations, activist groups, and consumer groups who provide information to legislators in order to get their support and to get them to vote a certain way on a particular bill.

Local advertising *(p. 11)* Advertising targeted to consumers who live within the local shopping area of a store.

Local brand *(p. 56)* A brand that is marketed in one specific country.

Localization *(p. 565)* A strategy in international advertising that adapts the message to local cultures.

Logo *(pp. 49, 295)* A distinctive brand mark that is legally protected.

Low-context cultures *(p. 566)* The meaning of a message is obvious without needing a sense of the cultural context.

Low involvement *(p. 118)* Perceiving a product or information as unimportant.

Low-power FM (LPFM) *(p. 370)* Nonprofit, noncommercial stations that serve a small area market, such as a college campus.

Loyalty (continuity, frequency) program *(p. 535)* A program designed to increase customer retention by rewarding customers for their patronage.

M

Make goods *(p. 449)* Compensation that media give to advertisers in the form of additional message units. These are commonly used in situations involving production errors by the medium and preemption of the advertiser's programming.

Market *(p. 37)* An area of the country or a group of buyers.

Market research *(p. 163)* A type of marketing research that investigates the product and category, as well as consumers who are or might be customers for the product.

Market segmentation *(p. 137)* The process of dividing a market into distinct groups of buyers who might require separate products or marketing mixes.

Market selectivity *(p. 355)* When the medium targets specific consumer groups.

Marketer *(p. 35)* The company or organization behind the product.

Marketing *(p. 34)* Business activities that direct the exchange of goods and services between producers and consumers.

Marketing communications *(pp. 9, 43)* The element in the marketing mix that communicates the key marketing messages to target audiences.

Marketing concept *(p. 39)* An idea that suggests that marketing should focus first on the needs and wants of the customer, rather than finding ways to sell products that may or may not meet customers' needs.

Marketing imperialism *(p. 70)* Marketing practices that result in imposing foreign cultural values on a local culture with different values and traditions.

Marketing mix *(p. 35)* A blend of four main activities: designing, pricing, distributing, and communicating about the product.

Marketing plan *(pp. 39, 192)* A written document that proposes strategies for using the elements of the marketing mix to achieve objectives.

Marketing public relations (MPR) *(p. 466)* A type of public relations that supports marketing's product and sales focus by increasing the brand's and company's credibility with consumers.

Marketing research *(p. 169)* Research that investigates all elements of the marketing mix.

Marketing services *(p. 20)* This includes a variety of suppliers hired by marketers, such as researchers and various types of marketing communication agencies.

Mass media *(pp. 21, 327)* Communication channels, such as newspapers or television, used to send messages to large, diverse audiences.

Maven marketing *(p. 480)* People who are considered expert or knowledgeable about some topic.

Measured media *(pp. 327, 424)* Media used in advertising that are evaluated by auditing companies that track performance data, such as circulation, readership, and viewership.

Mechanicals *(p. 304)* A finished pasteup with every element perfectly positioned that is photographed to make printing plates for offset printing.

Media *(pp. 20, 326)* The channels of communication that carry the ad message to target audiences.

Media buyer *(p. 332)* Specialists who implement the media plan by contracting with various media for placement of an advertisement.

Media flow chart *(p. 434)* A planning document that shows how the media plan will run in terms of the scheduling of the various media used.

Media kit *(p. 476)* Also called a press kit, a packet or folder that contains all the important information for members of the press.

Media mix *(pp. 334, 430)* Selecting the best combination of media vehicles, nontraditional media, and marketing communication tools to reach the targeted stakeholder audiences.

Media objective *(p. 427)* Goals or tasks a media plan should accomplish.

Media optimization *(p. 593)* The best use of various communication methods to promote the company.

Media plan *(pp. 332, 424)* A decision process leading to the use of advertising time and space to assist in the achievement of marketing objectives.

Media planners *(p. 332)* Media specialists who develop the strategic decisions outlined in the media plan.

Media planning *(p. 332)* The way advertisers identify and select media options based on research into the audience profiles of various media.

Media relations *(p. 463)* Relationships with media contacts.

Media reps *(p. 332)* Media salespeople who sell media time and space for a variety of media outlets.

Media research *(p. 173)* The process of gathering information about all the possible media and marketing communication tools available to be used in a marketing communication plan.

Media researchers *(p. 332)* The specialists who gather information about media audiences and performance.

Media salespersons *(p. 331)* People who work for a specific medium and call on media planners and buyers in agencies to sell space or time in that medium.

Media strategy *(p. 430)* The decisions media planners make to deliver the most effective media mix that will reach the target audience and satisfy the media objectives.

Media tour *(p. 476)* A traveling press conference in which the company's spokesperson travels to different cities and meets with the local media.

Media vehicle *(pp. 20, 327)* A single program, magazine, or radio station.

Media-buying services *(p. 23)* Specialized businesses that purchase media for clients.

Media/medium *(p. 326)* **media** is plural when it refers to various channels, but singular—**medium**—when it refers to only one form, such as newspapers.

Medium *(p. 20)* A single form of communication (television, billboards, online media).

Mental rehearsal *(p. 120)* Visualization of imagined actions that is the predecessor to the behaviors with which the advertiser hopes the consumer will feel comfortable and familiar.

Merging *(p. 507)* The process of combining two or more lists of data.

Message *(p. 100)* The words, pictures, and ideas that create meaning in an advertisement.

Message development research *(p. 173)* Research findings gathered by planners to help decide message strategy.

Message strategy *(p. 231)* The determination of the right message for a particular target audience that delivers the advertising objectives.

Metaphors *(p. 183)* A figure of speech in which a term or phrase from one object is associated with something entirely different to create an implicit comparison.

Micro-blog *(p. 407)* A small blog—Twitter, for example.

Micro-sites *(p. 402)* Small websites that are offspring of a parent website.

Microtargeting *(p. 154)* The practice of using vast databases of personal information to predict attitudes and behavior of selected groups.

Minisites *(p. 402)* Smaller websites that exist on a marketing partner's site permitting viewers to click on the minisite for additional information without leaving the original website.

Mission marketing *(pp. 76, 561)* Linking the mission of the company to a good cause and committing support to it for the long term.

Mission statement *(p. 192)* A business platform that articulates the organization's philosophy, as well as its goals and values.

Mixer *(p. 314)* The individual who operates the recording equipment during a film shoot.

Mobile marketing *(p. 346)* The use of wireless communication to reach people on the move with a location-based message.

Moment-by-moment tests *(p. 585)* A research method that evaluates viewers' response to a commercial frame by frame.

Morals *(p. 76)* The framework for separating right from wrong and identifying good behavior.

Morning drive time *(p. 371)* On radio the day part that reaches people when they are commuting to work.

Morphing *(p. 310)* A video technique in which one object gradually changes into another.

Motivation *(p. 116)* An unobservable inner force that stimulates and compels a behavioral response.

Motivation test *(p. 590)* Research that evaluates consumers' intention to act.

Motive *(p. 136)* An internal force—like the desire to look good—that stimulates you to behave in a particular manner.

Multichannel *(pp. 332, 450)* An advertising plan that uses several different forms of media, such as TV, print, radio, and online.

Multiplatform *(p. 334)* In IMC planning, multiple functional areas and tools, such as public relations and sales promotion, are used to deliver messages and create brand interactions, a practice referred to as multiplatform communication.

N

Navigation *(pp. 318, 400)* The action of a user moving through a website.

Needs *(p. 114)* Basic forces that motivate you to do or to want something.

Netcasting *(p. 392)* Using video on personal sites (vlogs) or corporate sites particularly broadcasting TV or radio online.

Network of associations *(pp. 116, 172)* The linked set of brand perceptions that represent a person's unique way of creating meaning.

Neuromarketing *(p. 137)* The brain-science approach investigating how consumers think.

News release *(p. 474)* Primary medium used to deliver public relations messages to the media.

News value *(p. 474)* The quality of information that makes it of interest to news editors based on such considerations as timeliness, proximity, impact, or human interest.

Newsprint *(p. 305)* An inexpensive paper with a rough surface, used for printing newspapers.

Niche market *(p. 138)* Subsegments of the general market which have distinctive traits that may provide a special combination of benefits.

Niche media *(p. 327)* Communication channels used to reach audience segments defined by a specialized interest, such as ethnicity or profession.

Noise *(p. 100)* Anything that interferes with or distorts the advertising message's delivery to the target audience.

Nonprofit advertising *(p. 11)* Advertising programs used by nonprofit organizations, such as charities, associations, and hospitals.

Nontraditional delivery *(p. 360)* Delivery of magazines to readers through such methods as door hangers or newspapers.

Norms *(pp. 132, 584)* Simple rules that each culture establishes to guide behavior.

North American Industry Classification System (NAICS) *(p. 556)* The federal system of grouping businesses based on the major product or service provided.

O

Objective *(pp. 27, 190)* The goal or task an individual or business wants to accomplish.

Objective-task method *(p. 209)* Budgeting approach based on costs of reaching an objective.

Observation research *(p. 180)* Qualitative research method that takes researchers into natural settings where they record people's behavior.

Off camera *(p. 278)* In television, a voice that is coming from an unseen speaker.

Offer *(p. 493)* A direct marketing tool that provides potential customers with an item's information, description, terms of sale, and often an incentive for quick action in buying.

Offline advertising *(p. 411)* Advertising in traditional media that is designed to drive consumers to an advertiser's website.

Offset printing *(p. 307)* A printing process that prints an image from a smooth-surface chemically treated printing plate.

On location *(p. 280)* Commercials shot outside the studio.

One-order, one-bill *(p. 356)* When media companies buy newspaper advertising space for national advertisers and handle the rate negotiation and billing.

One-step offer *(p. 493)* A message that asks for a direct sales response and has a mechanism for responding to the offer.

Online video *(p. 378)* Television programming delivered via a computer.

Open-ended questions *(p. 176)* A qualitative research method that asks respondents to generate their own answers.

Opinion leaders *(pp. 117, 461)* Important people who influence others.

Opt in (Opt out) *(p. 505)* In e-mail advertising (and direct mail) consumers agree to be included or not included in the list.

Optimization *(pp. 440, 492)* Computer modeling that helps media planners determine the relative impact and efficiency of various media mixes.

Original *(p. 247)* Unique and the first of it's kind.

Out-of-home advertising *(p. 364)* All advertising that is displayed outside the home, from billboards, to blimps, to in-store aisle displays.

Out-of-register color *(p. 449)* When the four colors used in full-color printing are not perfectly aligned with the image.

Outbound telemarketing *(p. 500)* Telemarketing sales calls initiated by the company.

Outdoor advertising *(p. 364)* Advertising on billboards along streets and highways.

Overlines *(p. 267)* Text used to set the stage and lead into the headline of copy.

P

Pace *(p. 281)* How fast or slowly the action progresses in a commercial.

Package goods *(p. 37)* Products sold for personal or household use.

Packaging *(p. 338)* Both a container and a communication vehicle, a package delivers a brand message in the store, as well as a reminder message when used at home or in the office.

Page views *(p. 597)* The number of times a website is visited.

Painted outdoor bulletins *(p. 365)* A type of advertisement that is normally created on-site and is not restricted to billboards as the attachment.

Pantry checks *(p. 588)* A researcher checks home-owners' pantries to determine their purchases.

Parity products *(pp. 46, 202)* Products that really are the same, such as milk, unleaded gas and over-the-counter drugs; also known as undifferentiated products.

Participant observation *(p. 181)* A research method in which the observer is a member of the group being studied.

Participations *(p. 380)* An arrangement in which a television advertiser buys commercial time from a network.

Pass-along readership *(p. 439)* The view that a magazine, although only bought by one consumer, may actually be read by several; difference between circulation and readership.

Payout analysis *(p. 596)* A comparison of the cost of a promotion against the forecasted sales generated by the promotion.

Pay-per-click (PPC) *(p. 597)* Online advertising where a company is charged every time a potential customer visits (clicks) on their website.

Payout planning *(p. 519)* A way to evaluate the effectiveness of a sales promotion in terms of its financial returns by comparing the costs of the promotion to the forecasted sales of the promotion.

People meters *(p. 379)* Boxes on a TV set that record viewing behaviors.

Perceived risk *(p. 149)* The relationship between what you gain by making a certain decision and what you have to lose.

Percentage-of-sales method *(p. 209)* A budgeting technique based in the relationship between the cost of advertising and total sales.

Perception *(p. 107)* The process by which we receive information through our five senses and acknowledge and assign meaning to this information.

Perceptual map *(p. 205)* An analytical technique that plots the mental positions held by consumers of a set of competitors on a matrix.

Permission marketing *(p. 505)* A method of direct marketing in which the consumer controls the process, agrees to receive communication from the company, and consciously signs up.

Permission to believe *(p. 242)* Credibility building techniques that increase consumers' conviction in making decisions.

Personal sales *(p. 43)* Face-to-face contact between the marketer and a prospective customer.

Personal selling *(p. 43)* Face-to-face contact between the marketer and a prospective customer that intends to create and repeat sales.

Personalization *(p. 328)* In the shift away from mass communication strategies, media are being used to deliver information related to an individual's personal information, behavior, and interests.

Persuasion *(p. 116)* Trying to establish, reinforce, or change an attitude, touch an emotion, or anchor a conviction firmly in the potential customer's belief structure.

Persuasion test *(p. 590)* A test that evaluates the effectiveness of an advertisement by measuring whether the ad affects consumers' intentions to buy a brand.

Photoboards *(pp. 282, 585)* A mockup of a television commercial that uses still photos for the frames.

Picture sort *(p. 585)* Viewers receive a deck of photos and sort them into categories as requested by the researcher.

Pitch letter *(p. 476)* A letter to a media outlet that outlines a possible story idea that the PR person would like to provide.

Podcasting *(p. 101)* The practice of using audio shows broadcast from the Web to be downloaded to an MP3 player.

Podcasts *(p. 411)* Audio shows broadcast from the Web that an be downloaded to an MP3 player.

Point of differentiation *(p. 41)* The way a product is unique from its competitors.

Point-of-purchase (PoP) display *(p. 151)* A display designed by the manufacturer and distributed to retailers to promote a particular brand or line of products.

Point-of-purchase (PoP) materials *(p. 529)* In-store merchandising materials that use such promotional materials as aisle displays, shelf signs, and window posters to feature a brand and its promotional offer.

Pop-ups and pop-behind *(p. 402)* Types of ads that burst open on the computer screen either in front of or behind the opening page of a website.

Population *(p. 139)* An entire group of people from which a sample is drawn.

Portal *(p. 392)* A website that provides doors or links to other websites.

Position *(p. 202)* A brand location in the consumer's mind relative to competing brands based on the relative strengths of the brand and its competitors.

Positioning *(p. 40)* The way in which consumers perceive a product in the marketplace.

Post-testing research *(p. 581)* A type of research that uses a number of methods to evaluate the effectiveness of a program after it has been implemented.

Postproduction *(p. 314)* In TV production, assembling and editing the film after the film has been shot.

Predictive dialing *(p. 500)* Technology that allows telemarketing companies to call anyone by using a trial and error dialing program.

Preference *(p. 119)* Favorable positive impression of a product that leads to an intention to try or buy it.

Preferred positions *(p. 448)* Sections or pages of print media that are in high demand by advertisers because they have a special appeal to the target audience.

Preferred-position rate *(p. 357)* Charges by media for space or time that are in high demand because they have a special appeal to the target audience.

Premium *(p. 523)* A tangible reward received for performing a particular act, such as purchasing a product or visiting the point-of-purchase.

Preprints *(p. 554)* Advertising circulars furnished by a retailer for distribution as a free-standing insert in newspapers.

Proproduction *(p. 313)* The process of outlining every step and decision to be made in the production process in a set of production notes that are compiled from a preproduction meeting with the creative team, producer and other key participants.

Press conference *(p. 476)* A public gathering of media people for the purpose of establishing a company's position or making a statement.

Pretesting *(pp. 174, 584)* Evaluative research of finished or nearly finished ads that leads to a go/no-go decision.

Price *(p. 42)* An amount a seller sets for a product that is based not only on the cost of making and marketing the product, but also on the seller's expected profit level.

Price copy *(p. 42)* A term used to designate advertising copy devoted to information about the price and the associated conditions of a particular product.

Price deal *(p. 522)* A temporary reduction in the price of a product.

Price-value strategy *(p. 553)* Promotional method suggesting customers buying a certain product will get the best quality possible at a particular price.

Primary research *(p. 165)* Information that is collected from original sources.

Prime time *(p. 373)* Programming on TV that runs between the hours of 8 p.m. and 11 p.m.

Print production *(p. 22)* A department that takes a layout, type, and artwork and turns it into a reproducible format.

Printed poster *(p. 365)* A type of billboard that uses printed formats in standardized sizes that are pasted to the board's surface.

Privacy policy *(p. 414)* A statement on a company's website that explains what user data it collects and how it uses the data.

Private label brands *(p. 551)* See Store brands.

Private labels *(p. 46)* Also called store brands, house brands, or private labels; products manufactured to the store's requirements and labeled with a brand distinctive to that store.

Pro bono *(p. 11)* Situation in which all services, time, and space are donated.

Problem avoidance message *(p. 240)* A message strategy that positions the brand as a way to avoid a problem.

Problem solution message *(p. 240)* A message strategy that sets up a problem that the use of the product can solve.

Process colors *(p. 307)* Four basic inks—magenta, cyan, yellow, and black—that are mixed to produce a full range of colors found in four-color printing.

Product category *(p. 35)* Classification to which a product belongs.

Product development *(p. 40)* Improvement of goods and services to meet customer needs more efficiently and effectively.

Product differentiation *(pp. 40, 202)* A competitive marketing strategy that tries to create a competitive difference through real or perceived product attributes.

Product placement *(p. 342)* The use of a brand name product in a television show, movie, or event.

Product reviews *(p. 391)* A record of opinions by people who have purchased a particular item.

Product-as-hero *(p. 240)* A form of the problem-solution message strategy.

Product-driven philosophy *(p. 39)* A marketing approach that starts with the development of a product, rather than with consumer needs.

Production notes *(p. 313)* A document that describes in detail of every aspect of a commercial's production.

Professional advertising *(p. 557)* Advertising that is targeted at professionals.

Profiles *(p. 153)* A composite description of a target audience using personality and lifestyle characteristics.

Program preemptions *(p. 449)* Interruptions in local or network programming caused by special events.

Projective techniques *(p. 182)* A psychoanalytic research technique that asks respondents to generate impressions to gather insights about consumers and brands.

Promise *(p. 239)* Found in a benefit statement, it is something that will happen if you use the product.

Promotional allowances *(p. 552)* Retail advertising that is focused on price or a special sale.

Prospecting *(p. 491)* In database marketing, this is the process of identifying prospects based on how well they match certain user characteristics.

Prospects *(p. 43)* Potential customers who are likely to buy the product or brand.

Psychographics *(p. 145)* All psychological variables that combine to share our inner selves and help explain consumer behavior.

Psychological pricing *(p. 42)* A strategy that tries to manipulate the customer's purchasing judgment.

Public affairs *(p. 463)* Relations between a corporation, the public, and government involving public issues relating to government and regulation.

Public communication campaigns *(pp. 466, 560)* Social issue campaigns undertaken by nonprofit organizations as a conscious effort to influence the thoughts or actions of the public.

Public opinion *(p. 461)* People's beliefs, based on their conceptions or evaluations of something, rather than on fact.

Public radio *(p. 370)* A network of radio stations that use public broadcasting material usually provided by National Public Radio (NPR).

Public relations *(p. 460)* A management function enabling organizations to achieve effective relationships with various publics in order to manage the image and reputation of the organization.

Public Service Announcements (PSAs) *(pp. 11, 371, 472)* A type of public relations advertising that deals with public welfare issues and typically is run free of charge.

Public television *(p. 377)* Broadcast TV stations that generally function based on donations rather than commercial advertising.

Publicity *(p. 462)* Information that catches public interest and is relayed through the news media.

Publics *(p. 460)* All groups of people with which a company or organization interacts.

Puffery (p. 71) Advertising or other sales representation that praises a product or service using subjective opinions, superlatives, and similar techniques that are not based on objective fact.

Pull strategy (pp. 43, 435) A strategy that directs marketing efforts at the consumer and attempts to pull the product through the channel.

Pulsing strategy (p. 434) An advertising scheduling pattern in which time and space are scheduled on a continuous but uneven basis; lower levels are followed by bursts or peak periods of intensified activity.

Purging (p. 507) The process of deleting duplicative information after lists of data are combined.

Push strategy (pp. 43, 435) A strategy that directs marketing efforts at resellers, where success depends on the ability of these intermediaries to market the product, which they often do with advertising.

Q

Qualitative research (p. 167) Research that seeks to understand how people think and behave and why.

Quantitative research (p. 167) Research that uses statistics to describe consumers.

R

Radio Network (p. 372) A group of local affiliates providing simultaneous programming via connection to one or more of the national networks through AT&T telephone wires.

Radio script (p. 277) A written version of a radio commercial used to produce the commercial.

Random sample (p. 175) The type of research sample requiring that each person in the population being studied has an equal chance of being selected to be in the sample.

Rate card (p. 356) A list of the charges for advertising space.

Ratings, Rating Points (pp. 335, 379) Percentage of population or households tuned to a program.

Reach (pp. 335, 427) The percentage of different homes or people exposed to a media vehicle or vehicles at least once during a specific period of time. It is the percentage of unduplicated audience.

Reason to believe (p. 119) Supporting or proving an advertising claim intensifies believability.

Reason why (p. 239) A statement that explains why the feature will benefit the user.

Rebate (p. 523) A sales promotion that allows the customer to recover part of the product's cost from the manufacturer in the form of cash.

Recall (p. 109) People remember seeing an ad and what the ad said.

Recall test (p. 589) A test that evaluates the memorability of an advertisement by contacting members of the advertisement's audience and asking them what they remember about it.

Receiver (p. 100) The audience for an advertisement.

Recency, frequency, and monetary (RFM) (p. 492) The three criteria that help direct marketers predict who among the customer base is likely to be repeat buyers.

Recognition (p. 109) An ability to remember having seen something before.

Recognition test (p. 589) A test that evaluates the memorability of an advertisement by contacting members of the audience, showing them the ad, and asking whether they remember having seen it before.

Reference group (p. 134) A group of people that a person uses as a guide for behavior in specific situations.

Referrals (p. 121) When a satisfied customer recommends a favorite brand.

Refund (p. 523) An offer by the marketer to return a certain amount of money to the consumer who purchases the product.

Regional brand (p. 56) A brand that is available throughout a regional trading block.

Registered (p. 305) When the four colors used in full-color printing are perfectly aligned with the image.

Relational database (p. 508) Databases used for profiling and segmenting potential customers as well as providing contact information.

Relationship marketing (pp. 337, 463) The ongoing process of identifying and maintaining contact with high-value customers.

Release prints (p. 316) Duplicate copies of a commercial that are ready for distribution.

Relevance (p. 108) The message connects with the audience on a personal level.

Relevant (p. 247) Ideas that mean something to the target audience.

Reliability (p. 183) In research, reliability means you can run the same test over again and get the same results.

Reminder advertising (p. 243) An advertising strategy that keeps the brand name in front of consumers.

Repositioning (p. 205) Developing a new position for the product as the marketing environment changes.

Reputation (p. 17) A general estimation in which a company is held by the public, based on its practices, policies, and performance.

Reputation management (p. 465) The trust stakeholders have in an organization.

Reseller (p. 37) Intermediaries in the distribution channel, typical wholesalers, retailers, and distributors who buy products from manufacturers and then resell them to the ultimate user.

Resonance (p. 113) A message that rings true because the consumer connects with it on a personal level.

Response list (p. 507) In direct marketing, a list that is compiled of people who respond to a direct-mail offer.

Retail advertising (p. 11) A type of advertising used by local merchants who sell directly to consumers.

Retainer (p. 25) Agency monthly compensation based on an estimate of the projected work and its costs.

Return on investment (ROI) (pp. 55, 191) Return on investment means that the costs of conducting the business should be more than matched by the revenue produced in return.

Right brain thinking (p. 247) A type of divergent thinking that is intuitive, holistic, artistic, and emotionally expressive.

ROI of creativity (p. 246) Ideas that are relevant, original, and have impact.

Rough cut (p. 314) A preliminary edited version of the commercial.

Rough layouts (p. 304) A layout drawn to size but without attention to artistic and copy details.

Run-of-paper (ROP) rate (p. 357) In newspaper advertising, a rate based on a locaton that is at the discretion of the publisher.

Rushes (p. 313) Rough versions of the commercial assembled from unedited footage.

S

Saccadic eye movement (p. 588) The path the eye takes in scanning an ad.

Sales kits (p. 331) Packets of information used by media representatives and other types of sales personnel.

Sales levels (p. 167) The amount of a particular product customers buy.

Sales promotion (p. 518) Marketing activities that add value to the product for a limited period of time to stimulate consumer purchasing and dealer effectiveness.

Sample *(p. 174)* In research, a subset of the population that is representative of the key characteristics of the larger group.

Sampling *(p. 523)* Allowing the consumer to experience the product at no cost.

Satellite radio *(p. 370)* Subscription radio programming delivered by satellite to receivers anywhere in the continental United States.

Satellite television *(p. 376)* Subscription television programming delivered by satellite to locations with satellite dishes.

Scanner research *(p. 591)* Research that tracks consumer purchases and compares the marketing communication received by the consumer's household.

Scenes *(p. 281)* Commercials are planned with segments of action that occur in a single location.

Screen *(p. 307)* Used to convert continuous tone art to halftone by shooting the image through a fine screen that breaks the image into a dot pattern.

Script clerk *(p. 314)* The person who checks the dialogue, other script details, and times the scenes.

Search engine *(p. 392)* Internet services that locate information based on key words.

Search marketing *(p. 403)* Marketing communication strategies designed to aid consumers in their search for information.

Search optimization *(p. 404)* The practice of maximizing the link between topics that consumers search for and a brand-related website.

Secondary research *(p. 164)* Information that already has been compiled and published.

Segmenting *(p. 137)* Dividing the market into groups of people who have similar characteristics in certain key product-related areas.

Selective attention *(p. 108)* The process by which a receiver of a message chooses to attend to the message.

Selective perception *(p. 107)* The process of screening out information that doesn't interest us and retaining information that does.

Self-liquidator *(p. 523)* A type of mail premium that requires a payment sufficient to cover the cost of the item.

Selling premise *(p. 239)* The sales logic behind an advertising message.

Semicomps *(p. 304)* A layout drawn to size that depicts the art and display type; body copy is simply ruled in.

Semi-controlled media *(p. 471)* Media, such as the Internet, whose messages can be controlled by an organization in some ways, but that also contains totally uncontrolled messages.

Semiotic analysis *(p. 173)* A qualitative research method designed to uncover layers and types of meaning.

Set *(p. 280)* A constructed setting in which the action of a commercial takes place.

Share of audience *(pp. 335, 379)* The percent of viewers based on number of sets turned on.

Share of market *(pp. 37, 193)* The percentage of the total market in a product category that buys a particular brand.

Share of mind *(p. 209)* The extent to which a brand is well known in its category.

Share of voice *(p. 424)* One brand's percentage of advertising messages in a medium compared to all messages for that product or service.

Share of wallet *(p. 208)* The amount customers spend on the brand.

Shelf talkers *(p. 554)* Signs or coupons attached to a shelf that customers can take away for information or discounts.

Shoppers *(p. 554)* Free-distribution newspapers retailers use to attract customers.

Showing *(p. 366)* The percentage of the market population exposed to an outdoor board during a specific time.

Single-source research *(p. 591)* A test that is run after an ad campaign is introduced that shows a causal relationship between marketing communication and sales.

Situation analysis *(pp. 39, 196)* The first section in a campaign plan that summarizes all the relevant background information and research and analyzes its significance.

Skyscrapers *(p. 402)* Extra-long narrow ads that run down the right or left side of a website.

Slice-of-life message *(p. 240)* A type of problem-solution ad in which "typical people" talk about a common problem.

Slogans *(p. 241)* Frequently repeated phrases that provide continuity to an advertising campaign.

Smart phones *(p. 345)* High-end cell phones, such as the BlackBerry or iPhone, with computing and photographic capabilities that can access the Internet, as well as perform traditional telephone functions.

SMCR model *(p. 100)* A communication model that identifies the Source, Message, Channel, and Receiver.

Social class *(p. 134)* A way to categorize people on the basis of their values, attitudes, lifestyles, and behavior.

Social games *(p. 409)* Like a computer game except it's played with friends—an example is FarmVille and Second Life.

Social learning *(p. 115)* People learn by watching others.

Social marketing *(p. 560)* Marketing with the good of society in mind.

Social media marketing *(p. 405)* Marketing strategies that take advantage of the interactivity found on social media, such as Facebook and My Life.

Social networking *(p. 397)* Social media, such as Facebook, which represents a network, or community, of friends—marketing strategies use this network of personal contacts as communication opportunities.

Social responsibility *(p. 65)* A corporate philosophy based on ethical values.

Societal marketing *(p. 561)* A business philosophy that describes companies whose operations are based on the idea of socially responsible business.

Soft sell *(p. 235)* An emotional message that uses mood, ambiguity, and suspense to create a response based on feelings and attitudes.

Soft-sell approach *(p. 206)* Method of selling that tries to persuade consumers by building an image for a brand and touching consumers' emotions.

Sound effects *(p. 276)* Lifelike imitations of sounds.

Source *(p. 100)* The sender of a message, the advertiser.

Source credibility *(p. 119)* Belief in a message one hears from a source one finds most reliable.

Spam *(p. 504)* Blasting millions of unsolicited e-mail ads.

Speaker's bureau *(p. 477)* A public relations tool that identifies a group of articulate people who can talk about an organization.

Specialty advertising *(p. 524)* Free gifts or rewards requiring no purchase and carrying a reminder advertising message.

Spokes-character *(p. 240)* A created or imaginary character who acts as a spokesperson.

Spokesperson *(p. 240)* A message strategy that uses an endorser, usually someone the target audience likes or respects, to deliver a message on behalf of the brand.

Sponsorship (cause or event) *(pp. 380, 532)* An arrangement in which a company contributes to the expenses of a cause or event to increase the perceived value of the sponsor's brand in the mind of the consumer.

Spoofing *(p. 504)* A practice used by e-mail spammers who assume the identity of a company or organization to send fraudulent spam e-mails.

Spot announcements *(p. 381)* Ads shown during the breaks between programs.

Spot buy *(p. 376)* Broadcast advertising bought on a city-by-city basis rather than through a national buy.

Spot color *(p. 300)* The use of an accent color to call attention to an element in an ad layout.

Spot radio advertising *(p. 372)* A form of advertising in which an ad is placed with an individual station rather than through a network.

Stakeholders *(pp. 35, 216, 460)* Groups of people with a common interest who have a stake in a company and who can have an impact on its success.

Standard Advertising Unit (SAU) *(p. 356)* A standardized system of advertising sizes in newspapers.

Standardization *(p. 565)* In international advertising, the use of campaigns that vary little across different cultures.

Stereotype *(p. 68)* The process of positioning a group of people in an unvarying pattern that lacks individuality and often reflects popular misconceptions.

Stickiness *(pp. 108, 400)* Ad messages that hold the audience's interest long enough for the audience to register the point of the ad; also refers to the amount of time a viewer spends on a website.

Stock footage *(p. 309)* Previously recorded film, video, or still slides that are incorporated into a commercial.

Stop motion *(p. 312)* An animation technique in which inanimate objects are filmed one frame at a time, creating the illusion of movement.

Store brands *(pp. 46, 551)* A variety of products branded with a particular store's name.

Store traffic *(p. 551)* The number of people who come to a store to shop.

Storyboard *(pp. 282, 305)* A series of frames sketched to illustrate how the story line will develop.

Straightforward message *(p. 239)* A factual message that focuses on delivering information.

Strategic business unit (SBU) *(p. 191)* A division of a company focused on a line of products or all the offerings under a single brand name.

Strategic consistency *(p. 218)* Messages vary with the interest of the stakeholder but the brand strategy remains the same, projecting a coherent image and position.

Strategic philanthropy *(p. 464)* Philanthropy involves contributions of time, resources, or money to a good cause—it's strategic when it is aligned with an organization or brand's mission.

Strategic planning *(p. 190)* The process of determining objectives, deciding on strategies, and implementing the tactics.

Strategic research *(p. 163)* All research that leads to the creation of an ad.

Strategy *(p. 190)* The design or plan by which objectives are accomplished.

Streaming video *(pp. 347, 393)* Moving images transmitted online.

Structural analysis *(p. 253)* Developed by the Leo Burnett agency, this method evaluates the power of the narrative or story line, evaluates the strength of the product or claim, and considers how well the two aspects are integrated.

Subheads *(p. 270)* Sectional headlines that are used to break up a mass of "gray" type in a large block of copy.

Subliminal *(p. 109)* Refers to messages transmitted below the threshold of normal perception so that the receiver is not consciously aware of having seen it.

Subscription television *(p. 376)* Television service provided to people who sign up for it and pay a monthly fee.

Substantiation *(p. 239)* Providing support for a claim, usually through research.

Superstations *(p. 376)* Independent but high-power television stations.

Superstitials *(p. 402)* Short Internet commercials that appear when you go from one page on a website to another.

Supplements *(p. 357)* Syndicated or local full-color advertising inserts that appear in newspapers throughout the week.

Suppliers *(p. 18)* Organizations, professionals, and specialized businesses that provide goods and services.

Supply chain *(p. 36)* The network of suppliers who produce components and ingredients used by a manufacturer to make its products.

Support *(p. 239)* The proof, or substantiation needed to make a claim believable.

Survey research *(p. 174)* Research using structured interview forms that ask large numbers of people exactly the same questions.

Sweeps *(p. 379)* In television programming, these are quarterly periods when more extensive audience data are gathered.

Sweepstakes *(p. 524)* Contests that require only that the participant supply his or her name to participate in a random drawing.

Switchers *(p. 149)* Television viewers who change channels.

SWOT analysis *(pp. 39, 196)* An analysis of a company or brand's strengths, weaknesses, opportunities, and threats.

Symbolic meaning *(p. 115)* Communication conveyed through association.

Syndication *(p. 372)* This is where local stations purchase television or radio shows that are reruns or original programs to fill open hours.

Synergy *(pp. 109, 549)* The principle that when all the pieces work together, the whole is greater than the sum of its parts.

T

Tabloid *(p. 142)* A newspaper with a page size five to six columns wide and 14 inches deep.

Tactic *(p. 190)* The specific techniques selected to reflect the strategy.

Tag clouds *(p. 412)* A visual representation of the relative importance of key-words associated with an organization or concept.

Tagging *(p. 411)* In Twitter, a technique of marking a keyword by inserting a hash symbol (#).

Taglines *(p. 241)* Clever phrases used at the end of an advertisement to summarize the ad's message.

Tags *(p. 411)* In Twitter, a method of marking and categorizing comments and keywords.

Take *(p. 313)* Each scene shot for a commercial, sometimes done repeatedly for the same scene.

Talent *(p. 280)* People who appear in television commercials.

Target market *(p. 139)* The market segment(s) to which the marketer wants to sell a product.

Targeted cost per thousand (TCPM) *(p. 438)* The cost to expose 1,000 likely consumers of a product to an ad message.

Targeted rating point (TRP) *(p. 436)* The practice of adjusting a television program's rating points to more accurately reflect the percentage of the target audience watching the program.

Targeted reach *(p. 428)* The practice of identifying key characteristics of the target population to better match media audience profiles.

Targeting, Target audience *(pp. 15, 152)* People who can be reached with a certain advertising medium and a particular message.

Teaser *(p. 240)* A message strategy that creates curiosity as the message unfolds in small pieces over time.

Telemarketing *(p. 499)* A type of marketing that uses the telephone to make a personal sales contact.

Television script *(p. 281)* The written version of a television commercial specifying all the video and audio information.

Test market *(p. 588)* A group used to test some elements of an ad or a media mix in two or more potential markets.

Testimonial *(p. 72)* See "endorsement."

Text messaging (TM) *(p. 346)* Communicating using brief messages keyboarded into a cell phone.

Theater of the mind *(p. 275)* In radio advertising, the story is visualized in the listener's imagintion.

Think/Feel/Do model *(p. 103)* A model of advertising effects that focuses on the cognitive, emotional, and behavioral responses to a message.

Thumbnail sketches *(p. 304)* Small preliminary sketches of various layout ideas.

Tie-ins *(p. 536)* Preprinted ads that are provided by the advertiser to be glued into the binding of a magazine.

Time-shifting *(p. 378)* Using digital video recorders (DVRs) to record television programming for playback at some other time.

Tint blocks *(p. 307)* A screen process that creates shades of gray or colors in blocks.

Tip-ins *(p. 308)* Preprinted ads that are provided by the advertiser to be glued into the binding of a magazine.

Tone of voice *(pp. 231, 263)* Ad copy is written as a conversation or an announcement and the voices carry emotional cues.

Touch points *(pp. 54, 218, 338)* The contact points where customers interact with the brand and receive brand messages.

Town hall forums *(p. 478)* Meetings within an organization as part of an inter-nal marketing program to inform employees and encourage their support.

Tracking studies *(p. 585)* Studies that follow the purchase of a brand or the purchases of a specific consumer group over time.

Trade advertising *(p. 557)* A type of business-to-business advertising that targets members of the distribution channel.

Trade deal *(p. 529)* An arrangement in which the retailer agrees to give the manufacturer's product a special promotional effort in return for product discounts, goods, or cash.

Trade show *(p. 529)* A gathering of companies within a specific industry to display their products.

Trademark *(pp. 49, 82)* When a brand name or brand mark is legally protected through registration with the Patent and Trademark Office of the Department of Commerce.

Traditional delivery *(p. 360)* Delivery of magazines to readers through newsstands or home delivery.

Traffic department *(p. 22)* People within an agency who are responsible for keeping track of project elements and keeping the work on deadline.

Trailers *(p. 382)* Advertisements shown in movie theaters before the feature.

Transformation *(p. 115)* Creating meaning for a brand that makes it a special product, one that is differentiated within its category by its image.

Trend spotters *(p. 150)* Researchers who specialize in identifying trends and fads that may affect consumer attitudes and behavior.

Trial *(p. 120)* Trying a product is usually the first step in making a purchase.

Tweets *(p. 407)* A short comment of 140 characters made by Twitter users.

Two-step offer *(p. 493)* A message that is designed to gather leads, answer consumer questions, or set up appointments.

Typography *(p. 300)* The use of type both to convey words and to contribute aesthetically to the message.

U

Unaided recall or recognition *(pp. 174, 589)* When one can remember an idea all by oneself.

Unbundling media services *(p. 451)* Media departments that separate themselves from agencies becoming separate companies.

Uncontrolled circulation *(p. 360)* Publications that are distributed free usually in racks in high-traffic areas.

Uncontrolled media *(p. 471)* Media that include the press release, the press conference, and media tours.

Underlines *(p. 267)* Text used to elaborate on the idea in the headline and serve as a transition into the body copy.

Underwriting *(p. 377)* In public broadcasting, a sponsor contributes funds to pay for the cost of the programming.

Undifferentiated strategy *(p. 137)* A view of the market that assumes all consumers are basically the same.

Uniform resource locators (URLs) *(p. 82)* Internet domain names that are registered and protected.

Unique selling proposition (USP) *(p. 239)* A benefit statement about a feature that is both unique to the product and important to the user.

URL *(pp. 82, 392)* A website address.

Usage *(p. 148)* Categorizing consumers in terms of how much of the product they buy.

User-generated ads *(p. 398)* Promotional copy on personal websites developed by the site's owner to promote a product, service, viewpoint, or cause.

V

Validity *(p. 183)* The research results actually measure what they say they measure.

Value added, value added media services *(p. 448)* A marketing or advertising activity that makes a product—or a media buy—more valuable.

Value billing *(p. 25)* A practice by marketers of paying agencies for creative and strategic ideas, rather than for executions and media placement.

Values *(p. 132)* The source of norms; values are not tied to specific objects or behavior, are internal, and guide behavior.

Values and Lifestyle System (VALS) *(p. 132)* A research method that categorizes people into lifestyle groups.

Vampire creativity *(p. 253)* Big ideas that are so powerful that they are remembered but not the brand.

Variable data campaigns *(p. 495)* A direct-mail piece featuring messages that are personalized through the use of digital technology.

Vertical publications *(pp. 359, 558)* Publications targeted at people working in the same industry.

Video editing *(p. 314)* Processing of recorded videotape to improve its final presentation; may include time manipulation and sound additions.

Video news releases (VNRs) *(p. 476)* Contain video footage that can be used during a television newscast.

Videographer *(p. 305)* Person who shoots images with a video camera.

Viral marketing *(pp. 340, 401)* A strategy used primarily in Web marketing that relies on consumers to pass on messages about a product.

Viral video *(pp. 347, 409)* The practice of sending interesting videos digitally from a variety of sources, such as ads or YouTube, to friends and colleagues in a vast network of personal connections.

Virtual communities *(p. 397)* An online group of people interested in a particular topic or brand.

Visualization *(p. 296)* Imagining what the finished copy will look like.

Vlogs *(p. 179)* Video blogs used for online distribution of personal video essays.

Voice-over *(p. 278)* A technique used in commercials in which an off-camera announcer talks about the on-camera scene.

W

Wants *(p. 111)* Motivations based on desires and feelings.

Wasted reach *(pp. 381, 428)* Advertising directed at a disinterested audience that is not in the targeted audience.

Wave analysis *(p. 587)* In research, a series of interviews conducted at different points in a campaign.

Wearout *(pp. 434, 593)* The point where the advertising gets tired and there is no response or a lower level of response than at the advertising's launch.

Website *(p. 399)* Sometimes called a "home page," this is the online presence of a person or organization.

Webcasting *(p. 370)* Radio transmitted through audio streaming over the Internet.

Webisode *(p. 344)* Web advertisements that are similar to TV programs with a developing storyline.

Weighting *(p. 435)* In media planning decision criteria are used to determine the relative amount of budget allocated to each medium.

White space *(p. 307)* Areas in a layout that aren't used for type or art.

Widgets *(p. 402)* Tiny computer programs that allow people to create and insert professional-looking content into their personal websites, as well as their computers, and other electronic media screens.

Word-of-mouth *(pp. 117, 329)* Free advertising that comes from people talking about a product.

World Wide Web *(p. 391)* The structure of the information interface that operates behind the Internet.

Y

Yellow Pages *(p. 362)* A form of directory advertising that lists the names of people or companies, their phone numbers, and addresses.

Your-name-here copy *(p. 265)* Pompous writing used in corporate communication that contains generic claims that do not differentiate the company.

Z

Zap *(p. 382)* Changing channels when a television commercial comes on.

Zines *(pp. 359, 395)* Magazines or newsletters that are only available online.

Zip *(p. 382)* Fast forwarding past commercials in a previously recorded program.

Zone editions *(p. 554)* Special versions of a newspaper that go to certain counties or suburbs.

CREDITS

CHAPTER 1

2 Courtesy of William Weintraub; **3** Courtesy of Regina Lewis; **4** Courtesy of Burger King Corporation, Anthony Martinez, and Tim Smith/Atreyu. The BURGER KING® trademarks and advertisements are used with permission from Burger King Corporation; **10** Copyright © 2004 Apple Computer, Inc. All rights reserved. Courtesy of Anya Major, FM Agency; and David Graham, Acting Associates. Used with permission; **12** © TJX Companies, Inc. All rights reserved; **12** © 2004 The Pharmaceutical Research and Manufacturers of America (PhRMA). All rights reserved; **12** Courtesy of Aflac Incorporated; **13** © 2010 The Procter & Gamble Company. All rights reserved; **15** Alphonse Marie Mucha/Mucha Trust/ADAGP, Parts/Swim Ink 2, LLC/ CORBIS All Rights Reserved; **16** Courtesy The Procter & Gamble Company; **16** Trademarks are used with permission of Volkswagen Group of America, Inc.; **16** © PepsiCo, Inc. All rights reserved; **16** © 2004 Computer Associates International, Inc. All rights reserved. PHOTO: © Peter Steiner/CORBIS; **16** Courtesy of H.J. Heinz Company; **17** Courtesy of HutchProjects; **17** Courtesy of Chris Hutchinson; **19** Courtesy of Wende Zomnir; **19** Courtesy of Urban Decay; **21** Bruce Ayres\Getty Images Inc. - Stone Allstock; **21** DOUG MARTIN\Photo Researchers, Inc.; **21** David Hanover\Getty Images, Inc. – Reportage; **21** Getty Images - Stockbyte, Royalty Free; **21** Getty Images - Stockbyte, Royalty Free; **24** Courtesy of Jennifer Cunningham; **28** The BURGER KING® trademarks and advertisements are used with permission from Burger King Corporation.

CHAPTER 2

32 Robert Galbraith\Reuters Limited; **33** PRNewsFoto\Nintendo; **35** Courtesy of Urban Decay; **35** Courtesy of Wende Zomnir; **36** Courtesy of Peter Stasiowski; **36** Courtesy of INTERPRINT, Inc.; **36** Courtesy of INTERPRINT, Inc.; **38** © The Stride Rite Corporation. All rights reserved; **38** © GE Aircraft Engines, a division of General Electric Company. All rights reserved. Courtesy of HSR Business to Business, Inc.; **38** Reprinted with permission of Sunkist Growers, Inc. Sunkist and design are trademarks of Sunkist Growers, Inc. © 2004 Sherman Oaks, California, U.S.A. All rights reserved; **40** © 2004 United Air Lines, Inc. Courtesy of Fallon Worldwide.

PHOTO © Images.com/CORBIS; **40** Charles Platiau\Reuters Limited; **41** Courtesy of The Idaho Potato Commission; **42** Jeff Greenberg\ Alamy Images; **43** Getty Images, Inc.; **45** Courtesy of Giep Franzen; **47** Courtesy of Procter & Gamble Company. All rights reserved; **47** © 2007 The Procter & Gamble Company. All rights reserved; **48** Lisa Poole\ AP Wide World Photos; **48** Molly Riley\ Reuters Limited; **48** Reproduced with permission of Schering-Plough HealthCare Products, Inc., a subsidiary of Merck & Co., Inc. All rights reserved. DR. SCHOLL'S is a registered trademark of Schering-Plough Healthcare Products, Inc.; **48** Paul Sakuma\AP Wide World Photos; **48** Getty Images, Inc./Tim Boyle; **48** Stan Honda/AFP/GETTY IMAGES; **48** Christof Stache \AP Wide World Photos; **48** John Keatley\Redux Pictures; **49** borkur.net/ Flickr; **49** Courtesy of Xerox Corporation. Used with permission; **50** Courtesy of The Hain Celestial Group, Inc.; **51** Courtesy of BU AdLab; **52** Intel and the Intel logo are trademarks or registered trademarks of Intel Corporation or its subsidiaries in the United States and other countries; **52** Copyright © The McGraw-Hill Companies, Inc. Reproduced with permission of The McGraw-Hill Companies, Inc. No redistribution or reproduction without the permission of The McGraw-Hill Companies, Inc.; **54** Courtesy of Ed Chambliss; **56** Andy Kropa\Redux Pictures; **56** Jim Wileman\Alamy Images; **56** Getty Images, Inc./Bloomberg/Ian Waldie; **57** PRNewsFoto\Nintendo.

CHAPTER 3

62 © 2010 HDIP, Inc. All rights reserved. Used with permission. The Häagen-Dazs® brand is a registered trademark; **66** Craig Frazier/Craig Frazier Studio; **66** Getty Images, Inc.; **68** Courtesy of Herbert Jack Rotfeld; **71** Courtesy of Dunkin' Brands, Inc.; **72** Courtesy of Ivan Preston; **73** Fred R. Conrad/The New York Times/Redux; **74** © Shell International Limited. All rights reserved. Courtesy of HÉR & NÚ; **74** Courtesy of Ingvi Logason; **77** Courtesy of Fred Beard, PhD; **77** © Copyright 1991 Benetton Group S.p.A. - Photo: Oliviero Toscani; **78** Courtesy of Steve Edwards; **87** General Motors LLC. Used with permission, GM Media Archives; **90** © 2010 HDIP, Inc. All rights reserved. Used with permission. The Häagen-Dazs® brand is a registered trademark.

CHAPTER 4

94 Courtesy of Regina Lewis; **96** Courtesy of Ford Motor Company; **104** © 2010 Port of Vancouver USA. Used with permission; **104** © 2010 Port of Vancouver USA. Used with permission; **104** © 2010 Port of Vancouver USA. Used with permission; **104** Courtesy of Karl Schroeder; **105** Courtesy of Citizenship and Immigration Canada; **108** Courtesy of the Peace Corps; **110** Courtesy of Sheri Broyles; **110** © 2004 American Association of Advertising Agencies. Reprinted with permission; **111** Courtesy of Nightlife Navigators, University of Florida; **112** Courtesy of Ann Marie Barry; **113** © 2004 American Airlines, Inc. All rights reserved. Courtesy of TM Advertising. Used with permission; **115** Sandra Moriarty; **117** Courtesy of Marilyn Roberts; **118** © Central Florida YMCA. All rights reserved. Courtesy of Fry Hammond Barr; **118** Used with permission of Lara Mann; **120** Courtesy of the Rare Book and Special Collections Division of the Library of Congress; **121** Courtesy of T-Mobile Limited; **122** Courtesy of American Association of Advertising Agencies; **123** Courtesy of Trent Walters; **123** Courtesy of the Department of Transportation; **125** Courtesy of Ford Motor Company.

CHAPTER 5

128 Abby Dings; **132** © ConocoPhillips Company. All rights reserved. Courtesy of Bulldog Drummond; **132** Courtesy of Chris Hutchinson; **133** Courtesy of Sunny Tsai; **134** Courtesy of Virginia Commonwealth University. Used with permission; **137** © 2004 KM Labs. All rights reserved; **141** Courtesy of Trent Walters; **143** © The Procter Gamble Company. Used by permission; **144** Courtesy of Jason Chambers; **153** Courtesy of The Procter & Gamble Company and Clairol Inc.; **155** Courtesy of Dave Rittenhouse; **156** Frances M. Roberts\Newscom.

CHAPTER 6

160 Courtesy of Frito-Lay, Inc.; **161** Courtesy of Frito-Lay, Inc.; **163** David Young-Wolff\ PhotoEdit Inc.; **164** www.census.gov; **165** Courtesy of Perdue Farms Incorporated; **168** Courtesy of Connie Pechmann; **170** Courtesy of Ingvi Logason; **170** Courtesy of Icelandic Lamb and Hér & NÚ Advertising Agency; **172** © American Dairy Association managed by Dairy Management, Inc. All rights reserved; **175** Michael Newman\PhotoEdit Inc.; **175** RON CHAPPLE\Getty Images, Inc. – Taxi; **176** Courtesy of the Billings Chamber of Commerce; **177** Courtesy of Karl Weiss; **178** Michael Newman\PhotoEdit Inc.; **178** Courtesy of Nottingham-Spirk; **180** Courtesy of Kate Stein; **183** © 2004 Great Brands of Europe, Inc. All rights reserved. Reprinted with permission; **185** Courtesy of Frito-Lay, Inc.

CHAPTER 7

188 Nadine Laubacher; **191** Courtesy of Pat Fallon; **191** Courtesy of Fred Senn; **193** Courtesy Toms of Maine; **195** Courtesy John Brewer; **195** Courtesy Billings Chamber of Commerce; **197** Courtesy of Kellogg Company and the Leo Burnett Company. Special K® is a registered trademark of Kellogg Company. All rights reserved; **197** Courtesy of Kellogg Company and the Leo Burnett Company. Special K® is a registered trademark of Kellogg Company. All rights reserved; **197** Courtesy of Amy Hume; **200** Courtesy of Nightlife Navigators, University of Florida; **201** Courtesy of Peggy Kreshel; **203** Army materials courtesy of the U.S. Government; **203** U.S. Navy materials courtesy of the U.S. Government; **203** Courtesy of the U.S. Marines Corps; **203** Courtesy of the United States Air Force and GSD&M; **206** Courtesy of Bill Barre; **207** Courtesy Billings Chamber of Commerce; **208** Copyright © Dow Jones & Company, Inc. All rights reserved worldwide; **209** Copyright 1999-2004 American Express Company. All rights reserved. Courtesy of Jerry Seinfeld and Ogilvy & Mather; **212** Courtesy of Joyce M. Wolburg; **215** Courtesy of SeaPort Airlines; **215** Courtesy of SeaPort Airlines; **215** Courtesy of Karl Schroeder; **217** Courtesy of Susan Mendelsohn; **219** Getty Images, Inc./Susana Gonzalez/Bloomberg.

CHAPTER 8

222 Courtesy of Karen Malia; **224** Courtesy of Frontier Airlines and Grey Worldwide; **228** Courtesy of Sheila Sasser; **229** Courtesy of Michael Dattolico; **230** CORBIS- NY; **230** ALBERT EINSTEIN and related rights TM/© of The Hebrew University of Jerusalem, used under license. Represented exclusively by Corbis Corporation.; **230** Doris Bry\AP Wide World Photos; **233** Trademarks are used with permission of Volkswagen Group of America, Inc.; **234** Courtesy of Frontier Airlines and Grey Worldwide; **237** Elf Sternberg /Flickr; **237** © 2004 Quaker Oats Company. All rights reserved; **238** Courtesy of Ronald E. Taylor; **239** Courtesy of Kellogg Company and the Leo Burnett Company. Special K® is a registered trademark of Kellogg Company. All rights reserved; **240** Courtesy of BU AdLab; **242** © 2004 Wm Wrigley Jr. Company. All rights reserved. Courtesy of Leo Burnett;

242 Courtesy of Sonia Montes Scappaticci; **243** Reprinted with permission of Sunkist Growers, Inc. Sunkist and design are trademarks of Sunkist Growers, Inc. ©2004 Sherman Oaks, California, U.S.A. All rights reserved; **243** Courtesy of Harley-Davidson and Carmichael Lynch. All rights reserved; **245** Courtesy of Tom Groth; **246** Courtesy of Road Crew. Used with permission; **246** Courtesy of Harley-Davidson and Carmichael Lynch. All rights reserved; **247** Courtesy of the California Milk Advisory Board and Goodby, Silverstein & Partners; **248** © 2004 Michelin North America, Inc. All rights reserved; **249** Courtesy of Linda Conway Correll; **250** Courtesy of Carlsberg A/S; **252** Courtesy of Shawn Couzens; **252** Courtesy of Gary Ennis; **252** Courtesy of Frontier Airlines and Grey Worldwide; **254** Courtesy of Frontier Airlines and Grey Worldwide.

CHAPTER 9

258 © 2005 Chick-fil-A, Inc. All rights reserved; **261** Courtesy of NYNEX; **262** © Central Florida YMCA. All rights reserved. Courtesy of Fry Hammond Barr; **262** Used with permission of Lara Mann; **264** Courtesy of Fred Beard; **267** Courtesy of the Corporate Angel Network; **267** © 2007 E. I. du Pont de Nemours and Company. All rights reserved. Used with permission; **269** Courtesy of Johnson & Johnson; **269** Courtesy of Johnson & Johnson; **269** Courtesy of Michael Dattolico; **272** Courtesy of Jean Grow; **273** © 2007 Nike Inc. All rights reserved. Used with permission; **274** © 2004 Register-Guard. All rights reserved. Courtesy of Coates Kokes; **274** Courtesy of Karl Schroeder; **277** Courtesy of Trent Walters; **279** Courtesy of Chuck Young; **279** Young, Charles, *The Birthplace of a Brand,* White Paper, exhibit 1. Reprinted with permission of Charles Young; **284** © 2005 Chick-fil-A, Inc. All rights reserved.

CHAPTER 10

288 © 2007 Wm. Wrigley Jr. Company. All rights reserved. Used with permission.; **290** © 2007 Wm. Wrigley Jr. Company. All rights reserved. Used with permission; **291** © 2007 Wm. Wrigley Jr. Company. All rights reserved. Used with permission; **291** Courtesy of Andy Dao; **291** Courtesy of Matt Miller; **292** AP Wide World Photos; **293** Courtesy of Edoardo Teodoro Brioschi; **293** DAMIEN MEYER/AFP/GETTY IMAGES; **294** © 2007 Columbia Sportswear Company. All rights reserved. Used with permission. Courtesy of Borders Perrin Norrander; **294** Courtesy of Jeremy Boland; **294** Courtesy of Central Florida YMCA and Lara Mann. Used with permission; **294** Used with permission of Lara Mann; **295** Courtesy of LCP Machines; **295** Courtesy of MicroFlex; **295** Courtesy of Galtronics Corporation Ltd.; **295** Courtesy of Michael Dattolico; **296** Courtesy of SeaPort Airlines; **296** Courtesy

of Karl Schroeder; **297** Courtesy of Amy Niswonger; **297** Courtesy of Amy Niswonger; **297** Courtesy of Amy Niswonger; **297** Archimage\Alamy Images; **298** Used by permission of Sony Electronics, Inc.; **298** Courtesy of Maxell Corporation of America; **299** Shepard Falrey/Mannie Garcia/ AP Photo; **300** Courtesy of New Balance Athletic Shoe, Inc.; **300** Courtesy of Nike; **302** © 2007 Frontier Airlines. Used with permission. Courtesy of Grey Worldwide; **303** Schwinn is a division of Pacific Cycle, LCC. © 2004 Pacific Cycle, LCC. All Rights Reserved; **305** © 2004 Greater Oklahoma City Chamber of Commerce. All rights reserved. Used with permission; **309** © 2007 Specialized Bicycle Components. All rights reserved. Used with permission. Courtesy of Aaron Stern; **309** Courtesy of Aaron Stern; **310** Used with permission of Lara Mann; **311** © 2004 Electronic Data Systems. All rights reserved. Used with permission. Courtesy of Fallon Worldwide; **312** © 2007 Metro. All rights reserved. Used with permission. Courtesy of Karl Schroeder; **312** Courtesy of Karl Schroeder; **315** Courtesy of Tom Fauls; **315** Courtesy of Tom Fauls; **316** Courtesy of Borders Perrin Norrander; **316** Courtesy of Jeremy Boland; **317** Courtesy of Harley Manning; **318** © 2007 Wm. Wrigley Jr. Company. All rights reserved. Used with permission.

CHAPTER 11

322 Courtesy of Larry Kelly; **324** Courtesy of Unilever; **327** Copyright © The Miami Herald. All rights reserved; **328** Courtesy of Donald Jugenheimer; **329** © STAN HONDA/Agence France Presse/Getty Images; **330** Courtesy of Michael McNiven; **330** Courtesy of Dean Krugman; **331** Courtesy of Digital Offsite; **331** Courtesy of Michael Dattolico; **337** Courtesy of Bruce Bendinger; **339** Tom Carter\PhotoEdit Inc.; **339** Courtesy of the SAS Institute, Inc.; **340** Courtesy of Burger King Corporation, Anthony Martinez, and Tim Smith/Atreyu. The BURGER KING® trademarks and advertisements are used with permission from Burger King Corporation; **341** © 2008 Zappos.com Inc.; **342** Courtesy of Melissa Lerner; **343** Courtesy of Nationwide, TM Advertising, and Diesel FX. Photographer: Rey Nungaray/TM Advertising; **344** Courtesy ACTIVISION PUBLISHING, INC.; **344** Courtesy of Diego Conteras; **345** Courtesy of Sonia Montes Scappaticci; **346** © Darren Robb/Photographer's Choice/Getty Images; **347** Courtesy of Eichborn AG and Jung von Matt/Neckar GmbH; **349** Courtesy of Unilever.

CHAPTER 12

352 Courtesy of Aflac Incorporated; **355** Courtesy of AT&T Intellectual Property and HTC America. Used with permission. Photography – Andric. Painting – Guido Daniele; **357** Courtesy of Aflac Incorporated;

358 Courtesy of The Condé Nast Publications, The Hearst Corporation, Meredith Corporation, Time Inc., and Wenner Media LLC.; 359 Michael Newman\PhotoEdit Inc.; 362 Courtesy of Terminex; 362 Courtesy of Steven Tran; 363 Courtesy of Joel Davis; 364 Courtesy of the Department of Transportation; 364 Courtesy of Trent Walters; 365 Courtesy of Elisa Guerrero. Product image courtesy of Olympus Corporation of the Americas; 365 Courtesy of Elisa Guerrero; 366 Courtesy of James Maskulka; 367 LouLouPhotos\Shutterstock; 368 Courtesy of Texins Activity Centers; 368 Courtesy of Michael Dattolico; 370 Courtesy of the Department of Transportation; 370 Courtesy of Trent Walters; 372 ©2007 Arbitron Inc. All rights reserved. Used with permission; 375 Courtesy of Bruce Vanden Bergh; 375 NEWSCOM/AMERICAN MOVIE CLASSICS (AMC)/RADICAL MEDIA; 378 © 2004 TiVo, Inc. All rights reserved; 380 Courtesy of Keep America Beautiful, Inc. All rights reserved; 382 Courtesy of Avista Corporation; 382 Courtesy of Karl Schroeder; 383 © Cinema Advertising Council. All rights reserved; 384 Courtesy of Aflac Incorporated.

CHAPTER 13

388 Courtesy of the U.S. Army. and Ignited LLC.; 394 Courtesy of Brian Sheehan; 394 Courtesy of HowStuffWorks.com and Toyota Motor Sales; 396 Courtesy of Diego Contreras; 396 Courtesy of Microsoft; 397 AP Wide World Photos; 398 Courtesy of Daimler and smart USA; 400 Courtesy ACTIVISION PUBLISHING, INC.; 400 Courtesy of Diego Contreras; 402 © Zippo Manufacturing Company. All rights reserved. Courtesy of Blattner Brunner, Inc.; 404 Courtesy of Google; 405 Trademarks are use with permission of Volkswagen Group of America, Inc.; 406 Courtesy of David Rittenhouse; 407 Courtesy of Irene Hoofs and www. Bloesem.com; 409 Courtesy of GEICO; 412 Courtesy of The Phelps Group; 413 Courtesy of the Interactive Advertising Bureau; 414 Courtesy of TRUSTe; 415 Courtesy of the U.S. Army and Ignited LLC.

CHAPTER 14

418 Dove/PA Wire \AP Wide World Photos; 421 Courtesy of Holly Duncan Rockwood; 421 AP Photo/Electronic Arts, Inc. via Obama Campaign; 426 Courtesy of Heather Beck; 428 © 2007 Courtroom Television Network LLC. All rights reserved. Used with permission. Courtesy of Aaron Stern; 428 Courtesy of Aaron Stern; 431 © 2007 Frontier Airlines. Used with permission. Courtesy of Grey Worldwide; 433 Courtesy of BU AdLab; 435 Christina Heeb/laif\Redux

Pictures; 438 Courtesy of Clarke Caywood; 440 Courtesy of Tom Duncan; 441 Courtesy of Amy Hume; 446 Courtesy of the Atlantic Media Company; 448 © 2004 Campbell Soup Company. All Rights Reserved; 452 Courtesy of the Dove brand.

CHAPTER 15

456 Courtesy of Tom Duncan; 458 Courtesy of Hilton Worldwide, Inc.; 462 Courtesy of Pepsi-Cola North America, Inc.; 465 Courtesy of BU AdLab; 467 Courtesy of Alice Kendrick; 467 Courtesy of Jami Fullerton; 469 AP Wide World Photos; 470 Todd Vanderlin\AP Wide World Photos; 471 Smokey Bear image used with the permission of the USDA Forest Service; 472 Courtesy of Greater Chicago Food Depository; 472 Courtesy of Matt Miller; 473 Courtesy of Herbert Jack Rotfeld; 474 Courtesy of the National Fatherhood Initiative and the Ad Council; 475 Courtesy of Weber Shandwick. Used with permission; 477 Courtesy of Johnson & Johnson; 477 Courtesy of Michael Dattolico; 478 Paul Sakuma\AP Wide World Photos; 479 Courtesy of the Billings Chamber of Commerce; 479 Courtesy of John Brewer; 480 Courtesy of Jason Cormier; 483 Courtesy of Hilton Worldwide, Inc.

CHAPTER 16

486 © 2007 GEICO. All rights reserved. Used with permission. Courtesy of The Martin Agency; 491 © 2004 Crane & Co., Inc. All Rights Reserved. Courtesy of Gargan Communication; 491 Courtesy of Peter Stasiowski; 493 Courtesy of UNICEF; 494 © 2009 GEICO. Reprinted with permission from GEICO. All rights reserved; 497 Courtesy of the Billings Chamber of Commerce; 497 Courtesy of John Brewer; 499 Courtesy of Title Nine; 500 Courtesy of Michael Dattolico; 500 Courtesy of MicroFlex; 501 James Schnepf\James Schnepf Photography, Inc.; 502 © Bettmann / CORBIS All Rights Reserved; 503 © 2004 GEICO. All rights reserved. Used with permission. Courtesy of The Martin Agency; 504 Courtesy Home Shopping Network; 507 © 2004 Edith Roman Associates. All rights reserved; 508 Courtesy of Melissa DATA Corp; 509 Courtesy of the Future of Privacy Forum; 510 Courtesy of Joseph E. Phelps; 510 Courtesy of Jimmy Peltier; 510 Courtesy of George R. Milne; 513 © 2007 GEICO. All rights reserved. Used with permission. Courtesy of The Martin Agency.

CHAPTER 17

516 Courtesy of Frontier Airlines and Grey Worldwide; 521 Courtesy of Karen Mallia; 522 Courtesy of the Billings Chamber of Commerce; 522 Courtesy of John Brewer;

524 Courtesy of Cellfire Inc. and Hollywood Entertainment Corporation; 524 Courtesy of Frontier Airlines and Grey Worldwide; 526 Courtesy of Heather Schultz; 526 Archives du 7eme Art/Photos 12/Alamy; 527 © 2004 Wells' Dairy, Inc. All rights reserved; 528 Courtesy smart center Portland; 528 Courtesy of Karl Schroeder; 529 PRNewsFoto\Nintendo; 531 Courtesy of Arlene Gerwin; 533 Courtesy of John Sweeney; 534 Courtesy of Bonnie Drewniany; 535 Eric Risberg\AP Wide World Photos; 536 © 1995-2004, PGA TOUR, Inc. All rights reserved; 536 Courtesy of the Billings Chamber of Commerce; 536 Courtesy of John Brewer; 537 Andrew Hoxey/Andrew Hoxey Photography; 539 Courtesy of Phillips-Van Heusen Corporation; 541 Courtesy of Frontier Airlines and Grey Worldwide.

CHAPTER 18

544 Courtesy of Honda Motor Co., Ltd. and Hér & NÚ Advertising Agency; 551 © 2007 Saks Fifth Avenue. All rights reserved. Used with permission; 553 Used with permission of Virgin Entertainment Group. All rights reserved. Courtesy of Bulldog Drummond; 553 Courtesy of Chris Hutchinson; 555 Courtesy of Daryl Bennewith; 555 Courtesy of the the SPAR Group Ltd.; 556 Courtesy of INTERPRINT, Inc.; 556 Courtesy of Peter Stasiowski; 560 Courtesy of SORPA bs and Ingvi Logason. Used with permission; 560 Courtesy of Ingvi Logason; 561 Courtesy of The Hain Celestial Group, Inc.; 562 Courtesy of Borders Perrin Norrander; Courtesy of Jeremy Boland; 563 Courtesy of Scott Hamula; 564 Courtesy of IBM Corporation; 568 Courtesy of Procter & Gamble Company. All rights reserved; 569 Courtesy of Accenture Ltd.; 571 Courtesy of Masura Ariga; 572 Courtesy of Honda Motor Co., Ltd. and Hér & NÚ Advertising Agency.

CHAPTER 19

576 Courtesy of Vail Resorts Management Company; 579 Courtesy of Avis Rent A Car System, LLC.; 582 Courtesy of Mark Stuhlfaut; 586 Courtesy of Chuck Young; 586 Courtesy of Unilever PLC and Ameritest/CYResearch Inc. Used with permission; 589 © 2004 John West Foods Ltd. All rights reserved. Used with permission; 590 © 2004 Pacific Life Insurance Company. PHOTO: © Brandon D./CORBIS. All rights reserved. Used with permission; 591 David Young-Wolff\PhotoEdit Inc.; 592 Courtesy of J. Walter Thompson, London. "Anti-Aggressive Driving Campaign," 1996; 594 Stone/Loren Santow; 598 Courtesy of Harley Manning; 600 Courtesy of Keith Murray; 602 Courtesy of Vail Resorts Management Company.

ENDNOTES

CHAPTER 1

1 Ad Age Staff, "More Bigwigs Weigh In on What to Do in a Downturn," *Advertising Age*, April 13, 2008, http://adage.com/print?article_id=135947.

2 TNS Media Intelligence, Marketing Charts, June 10, 2009, www.marketingcharts.com.

3 Stephen Fox, *The Mirror Makers: A History of American Advertising and Its Creators* (New York: Vintage Books, 1985); "Advertising History Timeline," *Advertising Age*, 2005.

4 Bill Bernbach Interview, *Printer's Ink*, January 2, 1953: 21.

5 Parekh Rupal, "Agency of the Year: Crispin Porter & Bogusky," *Advertising Age*, January 19, 2009, http://adage.com.

6 Jeremy Mullman and Natalie Zmuda, "Coke Pushes Pay-for-Performance Model, *Advertising Age*, April 27, 2009, http://adage.com.

7 John Galvin, "The World on a String," *Point*, February 2005: 13–18.

8 Suzanne Vranica, "CareerBuilder Offers Ad Bounty," *The Wall Street Journal*, May 13, 2009: B5.

9 Mike Carlton, "The Future Isn't What It Used to Be," Carlton Associates Inc. Agency White Paper, May 12, 2009.

CHAPTER 2

1 http://www.marketingpower.com/Community/ARC/Pages/Additional/Definition/default.aspx

2 Mark Stewart, quoted in Michael Bush, "What's the Next Marketing Platform?" *Advertising Age*, December 9, 2009, http://adage.com.

3 James B. Twitchell, "Lydia E. Pinkham's Vegetable Compound," Chapter 2, in *Twenty Ads That Shook the World*, New York: Three Rivers Press, 2000: 26–37.

4 Raymund Flandez, "Entrepreneurs Strive to Turn Buzz into Loyalty," *The Wall Street Journal*, July 21, 2009: B4.

5 Frank Striefler, "Five Marketing Principles Brands Should Embrace in 2010," *Adweek*, January 13, 2010, www.adweek.com.

6 Randall Stross, "When the Price Is Right, the Future Can Wait," *The New York Times*, June 22, 2009: B1.

7 Theresa Howard, "Food Marketers Turn to Value with Dollar-per-Meal Strategy," *USA Today*, May 19, 2009: 21.

8 Tom Duncan and Sandra Moriarty, *Driving Brand Value: Using Integrated Marketing to Manage Profitable Stakeholder Relationships*, New York: McGraw-Hill, 1998.

9 Giep Fanzen and Sandra Moriarty, *The Science and Art of Branding,* Armonk, NY: M.E. Sharpe, 2009.

10 Sandra Predicuini, "Store Brands Are in Demand," *Orlando Sentinel,* May 26, 2009: 1.

11 Kathie Canning, "The Power of Private Label," *The Costco Connection,* October 2009: 24–25.

12 Ben Moger-Williams, "Adventures in Translation," November 21, 2008, http://benmojo.blogspot.com/2008/11/chinese-coke-tasty-happy.html; "Branding in Chinese, the Coca-Cola Story," Csymbolf (Shan Associates), http://csymbol.com.

13 Sandra Moriarty and Giep Franzen, "The I in IMC: How Science and Art Are Integrated in Branding," *International Journal of Integrated Marketing Communication,* 1, No. 1, Spring 2009: 29.

14 John Burnett and Sandra Moriarty, *Marketing Communications: An Integrated Approach*, Upper Saddle River, NJ: Prentice Hall, 1998: 14.

15 Andrew Lingwall, "IMC and Its Integration into Programs of Journalism and Mass Communication," *Journal of Advertising Education,* Fall 2009: 25.

16 Tom Duncan and Frank Mulhern, eds., A *White Paper on the Status, Scope and Future of IMC,* University of Denver, March 2004: 10.

17 Tom Duncan, "The Evolution of IMC," *International Journal of Integrated Marketing Communication,* 1, No. 1, Spring 2009: 17.

18 Aaron Patrick, "Publicis Chief Seeks Unity Within," *The Wall Street Journal*, July 12, 2006: B3.

19 Emily Bryson York, "General Mills Sees Profits Climb 49%; Marketing Outlay Increased 37% in Most Recent Quarter," *Advertising Age*, December 17, 2009, http://adage.com.

20 John Galvin, "The World on a String," *Point*, February 2005: 13-18.

21 Brian Steinberg, "Putting a Value on Marketing Dollars," *The Wall Street Journal*, July 27, 2005: 25.

22 York, "General Mills Sees Profits Climb 49%."

CHAPTER 3

1 CSR (Corporate Social Responsibility) Wire, www.csrwire.com.

2 Harris Poll, "Majorities of Americans Lay at Least Some Blame for Economic Crisis on Media and Advertising Agencies for Causing People to Buy What They Couldn't Afford," Harris Interactive, April 15, 2009, www.harrisinteractive.com.

3 Charles Goodrum and Helen Dalrymple, *Advertising in America: The First 200 Years,* New York: Harry N. Abrams, 1990.

4 Randee Dawn and Alex Ben Block, "Brands Take 'American Idol' Stage," *Brandweek,* May 12, 2009, www.brandweek.com.; Kenneth Hein, "Do Top Shows Prime Kids for Obesity-Inducing Fare?" *Brandweek*, December 12, 2005: 12.

5 James Rucker, "10 More Advertisers Drop Glenn Beck," August 27, 2009, www.alternet.org.

6 Anna Mehler Paperny, "Virgin Ads Too Sexy for Calgary, Mississauga Transit," *The Globe and Mail*, January 8, 2010, www.theglobeandmail.com.

7 Interview with Jean Kilbourne by Renee Montagne, *NPR Morning Edition* transcript, June 22, 2004.

8 Dennis J. Ganahl, Thomas J. Prinsen, and Sarah Netzley, "A Content Analysis of Prime Time Commercials: A Contextual Framework of Gender Representation," Broadcast Education Association, Las Vegas, NV, 2001; Mark R. Barner, "Sex-Role Stereotyping in FCC-Mandated Children's Educational Television," *Journal of Broadcasting & Electronic Media*, 43, 1999: 551–564; Scott Coltrane and Michele Adams, "Work-Family Imagery and Gender Stereotypes: Television and the Reproduction of Difference," *Journal of Vocational Behavior*, 50, 1997: 323–347.

9 Dennis J. Ganahl, Thomas. J. Prinsen, and Sarah B. Netzley, "A Content Analysis of Prime Time Commercials: A Contextual Framework of Gender Representation," Broadcast Education Association, Las Vegas, NV, 2001.

10 Fara Warner, "Imperfect Picture: Advertisers Have Long Struggled to Adjust to Women's Changing Roles at Work and Home," in *Facing Difference: Race, Gender, and Mass Media,* ed. S. Biagi and M. Kern-Foxworth, Thousand Oaks, CA: Pine Forge Press, 1997: 223–224.

11 Ken Wheaton, "Verizon Wireless Proves Bigotry Is Alive and Well," January 27, 2009, http://adage.com.

12 Joan Voight, "Realistic or Offensive?" *Adweek,* September 2, 2003: 16–17.

13 Michelle Wirth Fellman, "Preventing Viagra's Fall," *Marketing News*, August 31, 1998: 1, 8.

[14] Herbert Rotfeld, "Desires Versus the Reality of Self-Regulation," *Journal of Consumer Affairs*, 37, Winter 2003: 424–427; Nanci Hellmich, "Weight-Loss Deception Found Ads for Many of Those Pills, Patches, Creams, and Wraps Are Grossly Exaggerated," *USA Today*, 2002.

[15] Joe Morgan, "Barclays Forced to Withdraw 0% Campaign by OFT," *The London Times*, November 19, 2003: 4M.

[16] Herbert J. Rotfeld and Kim B. Rotzoll, "Is Advertising Puffery Believed?" *Journal of Advertising*, 9, No. 3, 1980: 16–20, 45.

[17] Noreen O'Leary, "Weight Watchers Wins 1st Round vs. Jenny Craig, *Adweek*, January 21, 2010, www.adweek.com.

[18] Stephanie Clifford, "Coat Maker Transforms Obama Photo into Ad," January 6, 2010, www.nytimes.com.

[19] Word of Mouth Marketing Association, "Ethics Code," September 21, 2009, www.womma.org/ethics/code.

[20] Eric Tegler, "Ford Is Counting on Army of 100 Bloggers to Launch New Fiesta," *Advertising Age*, April 20, 2009, http://adage.com.

[21] Josh Bernoff, "When and How to Pay a Blogger," *Advertising Age*, May 26, 2009, http://adage.com.

[22] Bruce Horovitz, "Wendy's Will Be 1st Fast Foodie with Healthier Oil," *USA Today*, June 8, 2006.

[23] Stuart Elliott, "More Liquor Ads Pour onto Broadcast TV," *The New York Times*, February 9, 2009, www.nytimes.com.

[24] Bill McInturff, "While Critics May Fret, Public Likes DTC Ads," *Advertising Age*, March 26, 2001: 24; David Goetzi, "Take a Heaping Spoonful," *Advertising Age*, November 6, 2000: 32; Angetta McQueen, "Watchdog Blames Ad Spending for High Drug Costs," *The Denver Post*, July 22, 2001: 4C.

[25] Theresa Howard, "Push Is on to End Prescription Drug Ads Targeting Consumers," *USA Today*, August 10, 2009, www.usatoday.com.

[26] Minetter E. Drumwright and Patrick E. Murphy, "The Current State of Advertising Ethics," *Journal of Advertising*, 38, No. 1, Spring 2009: 83–107.

[27] Ana Campoy, "Hot Job: Calculating Products' Pollution," *The Wall Street Journal*, September 1, 2009: B1.

[28] Philip Patterson and Lee Wilkins, *Media Ethics: Issues and Cases*, 6th ed., Boston: McGraw-Hill, 2008.

[29] Lydia Saad, "Honesty and Ethics Poll Finds Congress' Image Tarnished," December 9, 2009, www.gallup.com.

[30] Sherry Baker and David L. Martinson, The TARES Test: Five Principles for Ethical Persuasion, *Journal of Mass Media Ethics*, 16, Nos. 2 & 3, 2001: 148–175.

[31] Tom Spalding, "Peeps Maker Sues Greeting Card Firm," *USA Today*, October 7, 2009, www.usatoday.com.

[32] Chris Adams, "Looser Lip for Food and Drug Companies?" The *Wall Street Journal*, September 17, 2002: A4.

[33] Database and Internet Solutions, January 31, 2010, www.dbt.co.uk.

[34] Federal Trade Commission, "FTC Publishes Final Guides Governing Endorsements, Testimonials," October 5, 2010, www.ftc.gov/opa/2009/10/endortest.shtm.

[35] Michael Bush, "Direct-Mail Spending Down in 2008 and Still Falling," *Advertising Age*, March 3, 2009, http://adage.com.

[36] Jack Neff, "Duracell Agrees to Modify Robo-War Duck Ad," *Advertising Age*, February 6, 2002, http://www.adage.com; Daniel Golden and Suzanne Vranica, "Duracell's Duck Ad Will Carry Disclaimer," The *Wall Street Journal*, February 7, 2002: B7.

[37] John J. Burnett, "Gays: Feelings about Advertising and Media Used," *Journal of Advertising Research*, January–February 2000: 75–86.

[38] Roy F. Fox, "Hucksters Hook Captive Youngsters," *Mizzou*, Summer 2002: 22–27.

CHAPTER 4

[1] Peter Holloway, "Maximizing Communicational Effectiveness," in *Conference Proceedings of Seminar on How Advertising Works and How Promotions Work*, April 1991, The Netherlands: European Society for Opinion and Marketing Research: 149–153.

[2] Louise Marsland, "How Much Advertising Actually Works?" SAMRA Convention 2006 News, www.bizcommunity.com.

[3] First Research Industry Profiles, July 20, 2009, www.firstresearch.com.

[4] Ennis Higgins, "Conversations with David Ogilvy," in *The Art of Writing Advertising*, Chicago: Advertising Publications, 1965.

[5] David Carr, "24-Hour Newspaper People," *The New York Times*, January 15, 2007, www.nytimes.com.

[6] Kelly Spors, "The Customer Knows Best," *The Wall Street Journal*, July 13, 2009: R5.

[7] Virginia Heffernan, "Hashing Things Out," *New York Times Magazine*, August 9, 2008: 13.

[8] Demetrios Vakratsas and Tim Ambler, "Advertising Effects: A Taxonomy and Review of Concepts, Methods, and Results from the Academic Literature," Marketing Science Institute Working Paper, Cambridge, MA: MSI, 1996: 96–120; Thomas Barry and Daniel Howard, "A Review and Critique of the Hierarchy of Effects in Advertising," *International Journal of Advertising*, 9, No. 2, 1990: 429–435; Michael Ray, "Communication and the Hierarchy of Effects," in *New Models for Mass Communication Research*, ed. P. Clarke, Beverly Hills, CA: Sage Publications, 1973: 147–175; Thomas Barry, "The Development of the Hierarchy of Effects: An Historical Perspective," *Current Research and Issues in Advertising*, 10, Nos. 1 & 2, 1987: 251–295.

[9] Michael Applebaum, "Caring Enough about Loyalty," *Brandweek*, August 9, 2004: 16–17.

[10] Ray, "Communication and the Hierarchy of Effects," 1973; Richard Vaughn, "How Advertising Works: A Planning Model," *Journal of Advertising Research*, 20, No. 5, 1980: 27–33; and "How Advertising Works: A Planning Model Revisited," *Journal of Advertising Research*, 26, No. 1, 1986: 57–66.

[11] Gergely Nyilasy and Leonard Reid, "Agency Practitioner Theories of How Advertising Works," *Journal of Advertising*, 38, No. 3, Fall 2009: 86.

[12] Sandra Moriarty, "Beyond the Hierarchy of Effects: A Conceptual Model," *Current Issues and Research in Advertising*, 1, 1983: 45–56.

[13] Nyilasy and Reid, "Agency Practitioner Theories," 86.

[14] David Ogilvy, *Confessions of an Advertising Man*, New York: Dell, 1963, 119; American Advertising Federation Advertising Hall of Fame, www.advertisinghalloffame.org/members.

[15] Phred Dvorak, "Canada Issues a Wake-Up Call, You May Be a Citizen," *The Wall Street Journal*, April 17, 2009: A8.

[16] Nyilasy and Reid, "Agency Practitioner Theories," 87.

[17] Charles E. Young, *The Advertising Research Handbook*, Seattle, WA: Ad Essentials, 2005: 37.

[18] Charles E. Young, "Co-Creativity," Ameritest Reports, 2007, www.ameritest.net: 1.

[19] Ogilvy & Mather website, retrieved August 2009 from www.ogilvy.com.

[20] Ivan Preston, "The Association Model of the Advertising Communication Process," *Journal of Advertising*, 11, No. 2, 1982: 3–14; Ivan Preston and Esther Thorson, "The Expanded Association Model: Keeping the Hierarchy Concept Alive," *Journal of Advertising Research*, 24, No. 1, 1984: 59–65.

[21] Preston, "The Association Model," 6.

[22] Tom Duncan and Sandra Moriarty, *Driving Brand Value: Using Integrated Marketing to Manage Profitable Stakeholder Relationships*, New York: McGraw-Hill, 1997.

[23] Erik du Plessis, *The Advertised Mind*, London: Kogan Page, 2005: 4.

[24] Ann Marie Barry, "Perception Theory," Chap. 3 in *The Handbook of Visual Communication*, ed. Ken Smith, Sandra Moriarty, Gretchen Barbatsis, and Keith Kenney, Mahwah, NJ: Lawrence Erlbaum, 2005: 23–62.

[25] Jon D. Morris, Chongmoo Woo, James Geason, and Jooyoung Kim, "The Power of Affect: Predicting Intention," *Journal of Advertising Research*, May/June 2002: 7–17.

[26] Russell I. Haley and Allan L. Baldinger, "The ARF Copy Research Validity Project," *Journal of Advertising Research*, April/May 1991: 11–32.

[27] Kevin Helliker, "The End of the Affair," *The Wall Street Journal*, April 4–5, 2009: W3.

[28] David Stewart and David Furse, *Television Advertising: A Study of 1000 Commercials*, Lexington, MA: Lexington Books, 1986.

[29] Thomas J. Page, Jr., Esther Thorson, and Maria Papas Heide, "The Memory Impact of Commercials Varying in Emotional Appeal and Product Involvement," Chap. 15 in *Emotion in Advertising*, ed. Stuart J. Agrees, Julie A. Edell, and Tony M. Dubitsky, New York: Quorum Books. 1990: 255–281.

[30] Preston, "The Association Model"; Ivan Preston and Esther Thorson, "Challenges to the

Use of Hierarchy Models in Predicting Advertising Effectiveness," in *Proceedings of the 1983 American Academy of Advertising Conference*, ed. Donald Jugenheimer, Lawrence, KS: University of Kansas: 27–33.

[31] Michael Solomon, *Consumer Behavior*, 8th ed., Upper Saddle River, NJ: Prentice Hall, 2004: 109.

[32] Jeremy Caplan, "Boycotts Are So 20th Century," *Time*, June 8, 2009: 54.

[33] Todd Cunningham, Any Shea, and Charles Young, "The Advertising Magnifier Effect: An MTV Study," September 2006, www.ameritest.net.

[34] Neal Conan, "Bob Garfield's 'Chaos Scenario'," *NPR Talk of the Nation* transcript, August 6, 2009: 4, www.npr.org.

[35] David Robinson, "It All Happens So Suddenly," Book review of Bill Waski's *And Then There's This*, *The Wall Street Journal*, June 12, 2009: A13; Simon Dumenco, "And Then There's This Article: 7 Truths About Viral Culture," *Advertising Age*, August 12, 2009, www.adage.com.

[36] Charles Young, "Imaging the Four Types of Brand Memory Tags in Restaurant Advertising, 2007," Ameritest/CY Research, 2008: 15, www.ameritest.net.

[37] Richard Cross and Janet Smith, *Customer Bonding: Pathway to Lasting Customer Loyalty*, Lincolnwood, IL: NTC, 1995: 54–55.

[38] Erik du Plessis, *The Advertised Mind: Ground-Breaking Insights into How Our Brains Respond to Advertising*, London: Millward Brown, 2005: 4.

[39] Jesse Shapiro, "A 'Memory-Jamming' Theory of Advertising," *Capital Ideas*, April 2006: 12–15.

[40] John Philip Jones, "Over-Promise and Under-Deliver," in *Conference Proceedings of Seminar on How Advertising Works and How Promotions Work*, April 1991, The Netherlands: European Society for Opinion and Marketing Research: 13–28.

[41] John Philip Jones, *When Ads Work: New Proof That Advertising Triggers Sales*, 2nd ed., New York: Lexington Books, 2007.

[42] Alex Williams, "Back by Popular Demand," *The New York Times*, May 24, 2009: 8.

CHAPTER 5

[1] Sarah MacDonnell, "2–9-Innovator Series: Apple's Ad-Man," *ByLines* (CU SJMC alumni publication), Spring 2009: 19.

[2] "Consumers Are Saving More and Spending and Borrowing Less," The Harris Poll News Release, June 26, 2009, www.harrisinteractive.com.

[3] Dave Taylor, "The Odd World of the Cult of Apple," *Boulder Daily Camera*, January 7, 2009: 9.

[4] Susan Mendelsohn, private e-mail, September 20, 2009.

[5] Brian Martin, "Remember to Give Them What They Want (It's Really Very Simple)," *Advertising Age*, February 3, 2010, http://adage.com.

[6] Eugene Schwartz, *Breakthrough Advertising*, Stamford, CT: Bottom Line Books, 2004: 4.

[7] Ann Marie Barry, "Perception Theory," Chap. 3 in *The Handbook of Visual Communication*, ed. Ken Smith, Sandra Moriarty, Gretchen Barbatsis, and Keith Kenney (Mahwah NJ: Lawrence Erlbaum, 2005): 23–62.

[8] Thomas Hargrove and Guido H. Stempel III, "Judging Generations," *Daily Camera*, March 3, 2007: D3.

[9] Michael Winrip, "They Warned You about Us," *The New York Times*, January 25, 2009, Styles: 1.

[10] Brad Stone, "The Children of Cyberspace: Old Fogies by Their 20s," *The New York Times*, January 9, 2010, www.nytimes.com.

[11] "Head-Turners," *Incentive*, March 2006: 10.

[12] "'Trophy Kids' Shake Up Workplace," *Indianapolis Star*, October 26, 2009: D1.

[13] "Seven in 10 U.S. Adults Say They Watch Broadcast News at Least Several Times a Week," 2006 Harris Poll #20, February 24, 2006, www.harrisinteractive.com/harris_poll.

[14] Tamar Lewin, "If Your Kids Are Awake, They're Probably Online," *The New York Times*, January 20, 2010, www.nytimes.com.

[15] "Growing Old in America: Expectations vs. Reality," Pew Research Center, June 29, 2009, http://pewsocialtrends.org.

[16] MCorp Consulting, "Insights and Influence in 140 Characters of Less. . . ." *Touchpoint Insights*, October 2009, http://blog.mcorpconsulting.com.

[17] Mickey Meeco, "What Do Women Want? Just Ask," *The New York Times*, October 29, 2006: 29.

[18] "Graduate Degree Attainment of the U.S. Population," U. S. Census Bureau, July 2009, www.cgsnet.org; Aimeee Heckel, "Layoffs Hit Men Hardest," *Boulder Daily Camera*, October 25, 2009: D1; Richard Stengel, "The American Woman," *Time*, October 26, 2009.

[19] Alan Kirkpatrick, "Creating Equity," *Bylines* (CU SJMC alumni publication), Spring 2009: 15.

[20] Bob Witeck, personal communication, September 2, 2009; Bob Witeck and Wesley Combs, "Gay Buying Power," Chap. 6 in *Business Inside Out*, New York: Kaplan Publishing, 2006.

[21] Peter Francese, "Trend Analysis: U.S. Consumers—Like No Other on the Planet," *Advertising Age*, January 2, 2006: 4.

[22] Thomas T. Semon, "Income Is Not Always Predictor of Spending," *Marketing News*, March 31, 2003: 6.

[23] R. Thomas Umstead, "BET: African-Americans Grow in Numbers, Buying Power," *Multichannel News*, January 26, 2010, www.multichannel.com.

[24] Carl Izzi, "A Primer on the New America for CMOs," *Advertising Age*, January 15, 2010, http://adage.com.

[25] Sam Roberts, "Census Data Show Recession-Driven Changes," *The New York Times*, September 22, 2009, www.nytimes.com.

[26] Hope Yen, "Census: Recession Had Sweeping Impact on U.S. Life," Associated Press, September 22, 2009, http://hosted.ap.org; Conor Daugherty and Miriam Jordan, "Recession Hits Immigrants Hard," *The Wall Street Journal*, September 22,, 2009: A3.

[27] "Country of Birth, Hispanic Fact Pack," supplement to *Advertising Age*, 2009 edition, July 27, 2009: 39.

[28] Gary Silverman, "Hispanics in Tune with TV Advertising," *Financial Times*, March 4, 2004: 18.

[29] Jack Neff and Emily York, "ANA Urges Marketers: We Must Be the Ones to Lead the Country Out of Recession," *Advertising Age*, November 9, 2009, www.adage.com.

[30] "Mohammad Now Top Male Name in England, World," *NPR Morning Edition*, September 17, 2009, www.npr.org.

[31] Richard Stengel, "The Responsibility Revolution," *Time*, September 21, 2009: 38–40.

[32] Joseph White, "Dude, Where's My Car?," *The Wall Street Journal*, October 28, 2009: D1.

[33] MindBase website, retrieved December 2006 from www.yankelovich.com.

[34] Laura Lorber, "Older Entrepreneurs Target Peers," *The Wall Street Journal*, February 16, 2010: B6.

[35] Michael Sanserino, "Peer Pressure and Other Pitches," *The Wall Street Journal*, September 14, 2009: B6.

[36] Kate Stein, "Shop Faster," *The New York Times*, April 16, 2009, www.nytimes.com.

[37] Everett Rogers, *Diffusion of Innovations*, 3rd ed., New York: The Free Press, 1983.

[38] Kelly Crow, "The Girl-Scout Cookie Makeover," *The Wall Street Journal*, January 26, 2007: W2.

[39] Jim Edwards, "Why Buy?" *Brandweek*, October 3, 2005: 21–24.

[40] Bryan Walsh, "America's Food Crisis and How to Fix It," *Time*, August 31, 2009: 31–37; Paul Kaihla, "Sexing Up a Piece of Meat," *Business 2.0*, April 2006: 72–74. at http://www.time.com/time/health/article/0,8599,1917458,00.html.

[41] Steve Smith, "The Next Frontier: Behavior," *MediaPost Publications*, January 16, 2007, www.mediapost.com.

[42] Becky Ebenkamp. "The Big Problem with Micro Trends," *Brandweek*, January 21, 2008: 12–15.

CHAPTER 6

[1] Christopher Noxon, *Rejuvenile*, NY, NY: Crown Publishing Group, 2006.

[2] Gina Chon, "To Woo Wealthy, Lexus Attempts Image Makeover," *The Wall Street Journal*, March 24–25, 2007: A1.

[3] Karl Weiss, IMC Marketing Research course handout, University of Colorado, January 2001.

[4] Julia Chang, "More Than Words," *Sales & Marketing Management*, September 2006: 14.

[5] "Research for R.O.I.," Communications Workshop, Chicago: DDB, April 10, 1987.

[6] Ilan Brat, "The Emotional Quotient of Soup Shopping," *The Wall Street Journal*, February 17, 2010: B6.

[7] Jackie Boulter, "Creative Development Research," Chap. 6 in *How to Plan Advertising*, 2nd ed., ed. Alan Cooper, London: Thomson Learning and Continuum, 2004: 81.

[8] "Analysis of a Commercial: OnStar and Batman," http://student.claytonstate.net/ ∼csu11197/3901/project1.

[9] Roger Wimmer and Joseph Dominick, *Mass Media Research*, 8th ed., Belmont, CA: Wadsworth/Thomson Learning, 2007.

[10] Peverill Squire, "Why the 1936 Literary Digest Poll Failed," *Public Opinion Quarterly*, 1988, 52:125–133.

[11] Susan Mendelsohn, personal communication, December 20, 2003.

[12] Leigh Ann Steere, "Culture Club," *Print*, March/April 1999: 4–5.

[13] Jeff Howe, "The Rise of Crowdsourcing," *Wired*, June 2006, www.wired.com.

[14] Emily Steel, "Marketers Find Web Chat Can Be Inspiring," *The Wall Street Journal*, November 23, 2009: B8.

[15] Shay Sayre, *Qualitative Methods for Marketplace Research*, Thousand Oaks: CA: Sage Publications, 2001: 31.

[16] Russell W. Belk, ed., *Highways and Buyways: Naturalistic Research from the Consumer Behavior Odyssey*, Provo, UT: Association for Consumer Research, 1991.

[17] Sayre, *Qualitative Methods*: 20.

[18] Ellen Byron, "Seeing Store Shelves Through Senior Eyes," *The Wall Street Journal*, September 14, 2009: B1.

[19] Thomas Davenport, Jeanne Harris, and Ajay Kohli, "How Do They Know Their Customers So Well?" *MIT Sloan Management Review*, Winter 2001: 63–72.

[20] Joe Ruff, "Research Goes Beyond Focus Groups," *The Denver Post*, December 6, 2004: 2E.

[21] Antonio Regalado, "McCann Offers Peek at Lives of Low-Income Latins," *The Wall Street Journal*, December 8, 2008; B6.

[22] Regina Lewis, personal communication, November 21, 2006.

[23] Larry Soley, "Projective Techniques for Advertising and Consumer Research, *AAA Newsletter*, June 2010, 6:2, 1, 3–5.

[24] Emily Eakin, "Penetrating the Mind by Metaphor," *The New York Times*, February 23, 2002, www.nytimes.com.

[25] Sandra Yin, "New or Me Too," *American Demographics*, September 2002: 28.

[26] Mendelsohn, personal communication.

[27] Jim Edwards, "Victory Dance for the Vain: A Reporter Goes 'Under,'" *Brandweek*, October 3, 2005: 23.

[28] Robin Couler, Gerald Zaltman, and Keith Coulter, "Interpreting Consumer Perceptions of Advertising: An Application of the Zaltman Metaphor Elicitation Technique," *Journal of Advertising*, 30, No. 4, Winter 2001: 1–14; Eakin, "Penetrating the Mind"; Daniel Pink, "Metaphor Marketing," *Fast Company*, 14, March 31, 1998: 214, http://www.fastcompany .com; HBS Division of Research, The Mind of the Market Laboratory, "ZMET," www.hbs.edu.

CHAPTER 7

[1] Pat Fallon and Fred Senn, *Juicing the Orange: How to Turn Creativity into a Powerful Business Advantage*, Boston: Harvard Business School Press, 2006.

[2] Julie Jargon, "Hardee's, Carl's Hope to Steer Angus Eaters," *The Wall Street Journal*, August 19, 2009: B5.

[3] Jeff Howe, "The Rise of Crowdsourcing," *Wired*, June 2006, www.wired.com; Brian Sheehan, "Unilever's So-Called Crowd-sourcing," September 28, 2009, http://adage .com.

[4] Tom Duncan and Sandra Moriarty, *Driving Brand Value: Using Integrated Marketing to Manage Profitable Stakeholder Relationships*, New York: McGraw-Hill, 1997.

[5] Emily York, "General Mills Sees Profits Climb 49%; Marketing Outlay Increased 47% in Most Recent Quarter," *Advertising Age*, December 7, 2009, http://adage.com.

[6] New York City Commission on Human Rights, *Minority Employment and the Advertising Industry in New York City*, June 1978.

[7] Nancy Hill and Bob Liodice, "Why We're Building an Army to Advance Industry Diversity," *Advertising Age*, October 5, 2009, http://adage.com.

[8] Al Ries and Jack Trout, *Positioning: The Battle for Your Mind*, New York: McGraw-Hill, 1981.

[9] Carl Bialik, "New Vehicles Leave MPG Standard Behind," *The Wall Street Journal*, August 26, 2009: A12.

[10] Nick Bunkley, "With Low Prices, Hyundai Builds Market Share," *The New York Times*, September 22, 2009, www.nytimes.com.

[11] Suzanne Vranica, "Veteran Marketer Promotes a New Kind of Selling," *The Wall Street Journal*, October 31, 2008: B4.

[12] Al and Laura Ries, "Q&A: Launch a New Brand," *Next Space*, No. 1, 2006, www.oclc.org.

[13] Larry Kelley and Donald Jugenheimer, *Advertising Account Planning*, Armonk, NY: M.E. Sharpe, 2006: 68.

[14] Jack Trout, "Branding Can't Exist without Positioning," *Advertising Age*, March 14, 2005: 28.

[15] Giep Franzen and Sandra Moriarty, *The Science and Art of Branding*, Armonk, NY: M.E Sharpe, 2009: 5.

[16] John Williams, "Emotional Branding: What's Love Got to Do with It? Plenty!" April 16, 2008, www.entrepreneur.com.

[17] Julie Ruth, "Implementing Strategy for Success," *AAA Newsletter*, June, 2010: 5–6.

[18] Suzanne Vranica, "Ads to Go Leaner, Meaner in '09," *The Wall Street Journal*, January 5, 2009: B8.

[19] Bill Lindelof, "Tiger's Fall Cost Sponsors $12 Billion," *Boulder Daily Camera*, December 29, 2009: 3C.

[20] "AmEx Plans Jerry Seinfeld-Meets-Superman Internet Show," *Advertising Age*, February 4, 2004, http://adage.com.

[21] Joe Ruff, "Research Goes beyond Focus Groups," *The Denver Post*, December 6, 2004: 2E.

[22] Regina Lewis, personal communication, November 21, 2006.

[23] "What Is Account Planning? (and What Do Account Planners Do Exactly?)" Account Planning Group (APG), www.apg.org.uk.

[24] Susan Mendelsohn, personal communication, January 8, 2004.

[25] Suzanne Varanica, "J&J Joins Critics of Agency Structure," *The Wall Street Journal*, May 11, 2007: B4.

[26] Laurie Freeman, "Planner Puts Clients in Touch with Soul of Brands," *Advertising Age*, February 8, 1999, www.adage.com.

[27] Charlie Robertson, "Creative Briefs and Briefings," Chap. 4 in *How to Plan Advertising*, 2nd ed., ed. Alan Cooper, London: Thomson Learning and the Account Planning Group, 2004: 62.

[28] Jon Steel, *Truth, Lies and Advertising: The Art of Account Planning*, New York: Wiley, 1998; "Tests Ahead for Account Planning," *Advertising Age*, September 20, 1999: 36.

[29] "More Bigwigs Weigh In on What to Do in a Downturn," *Advertising Age*, April 13, 2008, http://adage.com.

CHAPTER 8

[1] Mark Stuhlfaut and Margo Berman, "Pedagogic Challenges: The Teaching of Creative Strategy in Advertising Courses," *Journal of Advertising Education*, Fall 2009: 37.

[2] Bonnie L. Drewniany and A. Jerome Jewler, *Creative Strategy in Advertising*, 10th ed., Boston: Wadsworth, Cengage Learning, 2011: 1.

[3] Try Montague, Keynote Speech, Effie Awards Gala, June 7, 2006, www.effie.org/gala/ montague.html.

[4] Lee Earle, "Creative Message Strategy as a Framework for Course Planning, Preparation, and Pedagogy Or: Everything I Know about Teaching I Learned from Advertising," *Journal of Advertising Education*, Fall 2005: 22–28.

[5] William Weir, "Character Counts: Brand Icons Get Story Lines, Emotions," *The Seattle Times*, November 2, 2006, http://seattletimes .nwsource.com.

[6] Kevin Keller, *Strategic Brand Management*, 3rd ed., Upper Saddle River, NJ: Prentice Hall, 2008: 76–81.

[7] Eric Pfanner, "Hewlett-Packard Takes a New Tack: Being Cool," *The New York Times*, July 25, 2006, www.nytimes.com/2006/07/25/ business/media/25adco.html.

[8] Bob Garfield, "Anti-Texting PSA Converts at Least One Viewer, "*Advertising Age*, September 2, 2009, www.adage.com; "Hard-Hitting Video Shows Dangers of Texting while Driving," MSNBCcom, August 25, 2009, www.msnbc.com.

[9] Charles Frazer, "Creative Strategy: A Management Perspective," *Journal of Advertising*, 12:4 (1983): 36–41.

[10] Ron Taylor, "A Six Segment Message Strategy Wheel," *Journal of Advertising Research*, November-December 1997, 7–17.

[11] William Wells, "How Advertising Works," speech to the St. Louis AMA, September 17, 1986.

[12] Edd Applegate, *Strategic Copywriting*, Lanham, MD: Rowman & Littlefield, 2005.

[13] Darren Rovell, Friday June 18, 2010, CNBC.com.

[14] Reported in Thomas Page Jr., Esther Thorson, and Maria Heide, "The Memory Impact of Commercials Varying in Emotional Appeal and Product Involvement," *Emotion in Advertising*, New York: Quorum Books, 1990: 255–268.

[15] Stuart Elliott, "Home Depot Taps the Weepy Part of Reality TV," *The New York Times,* February 12, 2007, www.nytimes.com.

[16] Mark Stuhlfaut, "How Creative Are We? The Teaching of Creativity Theory and Training," *Journal of Advertising Education*, 11, No. 2, Fall 2007: 49–59.

[17] Jan Rijkenberg, *Concepting*, Henley-on-Thames, UK: World Advertising Research Center, 2001.

[18] Andrew Newman, "No Actors, Just Patients in Unvarnished Spots for Hospitals," *The New York Times,* May 4, 2009, www.nytimes.com.

[19] Bob Garfield, "The Top 100 Advertising Campaigns of the Century," *Advertising Age,* March 29, 1999, www.adage.com.

[20] Rupal Parekh, "Domination Wanted: VW Dumps Crispin in Bid to Triple U.S. Sales," *Advertising Age,* August 24, 2009, www.adage.com.

[21] James Webb Young, *A Technique for Producing Ideas*, 3rd ed., Chicago: Crain Books, 1975.

[22] Jerri Moore and William D. Wells, *R.O.I. Guidebook: Planning for Relevance, Originality and Impact in Advertising and Other Marketing Communications*, New York: DDB Needham, 1991.

[23] John Eighmy, *The Creative Work Book*, Iowa City: University of Iowa, 1998: 1.

[24] Thomas Russell and Glenn Verrill, *Kleppner's Advertising Procedure*, 14th ed., Upper Saddle River, NJ: Prentice Hall, 2002: 457.

[25] Janet Forgrieve, "Ad Agency's Colo., Fla. Offices on Same Team," *Rocky Mountain News Rocky Business*, March 8, 2007: 6.

[26] Sheri J. Broyles, "The Creative Personality: Exploring Relations of Creativity and Openness to Experience," unpublished doctoral dissertation, Southern Methodist University, Dallas, 1995.

[27] Ibid.

[28] A. Kendrick, D. Slayden, and S. J. Broyles, "Real Worlds and Ivory Towers: A Survey of Top Creative Directors," *Journalism and Mass Communication Educator*, 51, No. 2, 1996: 63–74; A. Kendrick, D. Slayden, and S. J. Broyles, "The Role of Universities in Preparing Creatives: A Survey of Top U.S. Agency Creative Directors," in *Proceedings of the 1996 Conference of the American Academy of Advertising*, ed. G. B. Wilcox, Austin: University of Texas, 1996: 100–106.

[29] Linda Conway Correll, "Creative Aerobics: A Technique to Jump-Start Creativity," in *Proceedings of the American Academy of Advertising Annual Conference*, ed. Carole M. Macklin, Richmond, VA: American Academy of Advertising, 1997: 263–264.

[30] Graham Wallas, *The Art of Thought*, New York: Harcourt, Brace, 1926; Alex F. Osborn, *Applied Imagination*, 3rd ed., New York: Scribner's, 1963.

[31] Goeffrey Fowler, Brian Steinberg, and Aaron Patrick, "Mac and PC's Overseas Adventures," *The Wall Street Journal*, March 1, 2007: B1.

[32] Doris Willens, *Nobody's Perfect: Bill Bernbach and the Golden Age of Advertising*, Self published using Amazon's CreateSpace, 2009.

[33] Al Ries, "Advertising Could Do with More of Bernbach's Genius," *Advertising Age*, July 6, 2009, www.adage.com.

CHAPTER 9

[1] Tom Murphy, "Drug Brand Search Extends from A to Z," *Boulder Daily Camera*, January 18, 2008: 9A.

[2] Ennis Higgins, "Conversations with David Ogilvy," in *The Art of Writing Advertising*, Chicago: Advertising Publications, 1965.

[3] Yumiko Ono, "Sometimes Ad Agencies Mangle English Deliberately," *The Wall Street Journal*, November 4, 1997: B1.

[4] Susan Gunelius, "10 Advertising Words to Avoid in 2009," MSNBC.com, December 15, 2008, www.msnbc.com.

[5] Susan Gunelius, *Kick-Ass Copywriting in 10 Easy Steps*, Irvine, CA: Entrepreneur Press, 2008.

[6] David Ogilvy, *Ogilvy on Advertising*, New York: Vintage, 1985.

[7] Gail Collins, "Come Visit. Live Life. Eat Cheese." *The New York Times*, April 25, 2009, www.nytimes.com.

[8] Sandra Dallas, "Road to Pave? Remember Burma-Shave!" *BusinessWeek*, December 30, 1996: 8; Frank Rowsome Jr., *The Verse by the Side of the Road*, New York: Dutton, 1965.

[9] Paul D. Bolls and Robert F. Potter, "I Saw It on the Radio: The Effects of Imagery Evoking Radio Commercials on Listeners' Allocation of Attention and Attitude toward the Ad," in *Proceedings of the Conference of the American Academy of Advertising,* ed. Darrel D. Muehling, Lexington, KY: American Academy of Advertising, 1998: 123–130.

[10] Peter Hochstein, "Ten Rules for Making Better Radio Commercials," Ogilvy & Mather's *Viewpoint*, 1981.

[11] Adapted from Bonnie L. Drewniany and A. Jerome Jewler and, *Creative Strategy in Advertising*, 10th ed., Wadsworth, Cengage Learning, 2011.

[12] Adapted from John Burnett and Sandra Moriarty, *Marketing Communications: An Integrated Approach*, Upper Saddle River, NJ: Prentice Hall, 1998: 296–297.

[13] Blessie Miranda and Kuen-Hee Ju-Pak, "A Content Analysis of Banner Advertisements: Potential Motivating Features," Annual Conference Baltimore, Association for Education in Journalism and Mass Communication, August 1998.

CHAPTER 10

[1] Sandra Dolbow, "Brand Builders," *Brandweek*, July 24, 2000: 19.

[2] Theresa Howard, "Ads Try Grins to Appeal to Users' Smarter Sides," *USA Today*, September 31, 2005: 4B.

[3] Kunur Patel, "Lessons from the Microsoft Photoshop Fiasco," *Advertising Age,* August 31, 2009, www.adage.com.

[4] Loretta Chao and Betsy McKay, "Pepsi Steps into Coke Realm: Red, China," *The Wall Street Journal,* September 12, 2007, www.wsj.com.

[5] Bill Marsh, "Warmer, Fuzzier: The Refreshed Logo," *The New York Times*, April 31, 2009: 2.

[6] Noreen O'Leary, "Legibility Lost," *Adweek*, October 5, 1987: D7.

[7] Kathy Lohr, "Ads Add a Certain Glow to Atlanta's City Buses," National Public Radio, March 23, 2007, www.npr.org.

[8] Charles Goldsmith, "Adding Special to Effects," *The Wall Street Journal*, February 26, 2003: B1.

[9] Stuart Elliott, "JanSport Sings 'Do-Re-Mi' to Teens," *New York Times Direct*, April 29, 2003, www.nytimes.com.

[10] Stuart Elliott, "Is That Honda Commercial Real?" *The New York Times Direct*, June 10, 2003, NYTDirect@nytimes.com; "Honda's Cog Does It Again, Taking the Grand Clio," *AdForum Alert*, May 19, 2004, adforum.com.

[11] Laura Ruel and Nora Paul, "Eyetracking Points the Way to Effective News Article Design," *Online Journalism Review*, March 13, 2007, www.ojr.org.

[12] Heather McWilliams, "Zooming in to Web Video," *Business Plus*, March 5, 2007: 3.

CHAPTER 11

[1] Larry Kelley and Donald Jugenheimer, *Advertising Media Planning*, Armonk, NY: M. E. Sharpe, 2004: 11.

[2] "About AARP, The Magazine," AARP Press Center, November 15, 2009, www.aarpmagazine.org.

[3] TNS Media Intelligence, January 14, 2010, www.tns-mi.com/prodMediaMarketCoverage .htm.

[4] Erwin Ephron, "Engagement Is Many Different Things," *Admap*, April 2006: 41–42; Joe Mandese, "Medialink," *Admap*, April 2006: 10.

[5] "TNS Media Intelligence Reports U.S Advertising Expenditures Declined 14.7 Percent in First Nine Months of 2009," TNS Media Intelligence News Release, December 8, 2009, www.tns-mi.com.

[6] "2009 Set to Show First Revenue Decline for Nation's Top 100 Media Cos.," *Advertising Age*, December 28, 2009, www.adage.com.

[7] Wayne Friedman, "Covering All Bases: CBS RIOT Sells Cross-Platform," *MediaPost*, February 13, 2007, http://publications .mediapost.com; Brian Steinberg, "Disney Combines Ad Staff for Selling Kids' Media," *The Wall Street Journal,* February 6, 2007: B2.

[8] "TNS Media Intelligence Reports U.S. Advertising Expenditures Declined 14.3 Percent in First Half 2009," TNS Media Intelligence News Release, September 16, 2009, www.tns-mi.com.

[9] Newspaper Association of America, *The Source: Newspapers by the Numbers 2006,* January 2007: 3–4, www.naa.org.

[10] Wayne Friedman, "Blockbuster: Best Super Bowl Ratings in 7 Years," *MediaPost,* February 6, 2007, http://publications.mediapost.com.

[11] Tom Duncan and Sandra Moriarty, "How Integrated Marketing Communication's 'Touch Points' Can Operationalize the Service-Dominant Logic," Chap. 18 in *The Service-Dominant Logic of Marketing,* ed. Robert Lusch and Stephen Vargo, Armonk, NY: M. E. Sharpe, 2006: 240.

[12] Chris Herring, "Coke Bottle Is Part Plant," *The Wall Street Journal,* January 25, 2010: B7.

[13] Philip Gray, "Using Milk-Carton Ads to Build Strong Brands," *The New York Times,* August 27, 2009, www.nytimes.com.

[14] David Kesmodel, Lauren Etter, and Alica Mundy, "Tobacco Giants Challenge Law," *The Wall Street Journal,* September 1, 2009: R3; Leslie Wayne, "Fight Grows over Labels on Household Cleaners," *The New York Times,* September 16, 2009, www.nytimes.com.

[15] Michael Bush, "What's the Next Marketing Platform? How to Measure Success? Ad Age's Media Mavens Answer the Big Questions," *Advertising Age,* December 9, 2009, www.adage.com.

[16] Joe Mandese, "Simultaneous Research Study Reveals Consumers Buzz Most over Word-of-Mouth, Not Ads," *MediaPost Publications,* January 19, 2007, http://publications.mediapost.com.

[17] Steve Knox, "Why Effective Word-of-Mouth Disrupts Schemas," *Advertising Age,* January 25, 2010, www.adage.com.

[18] Theresa Howard, "McDonald's Filet-O-Fish Ad Makes a Big Splash," *USA Today,* April 5, 2009, www.usatoday.com.

[19] Jack Neff, "Unilever's CMO Throws Down the Social-Media Gauntlet," *Advertising Age,* April 13, 2009, www.adage.com.

[20] Marc Ransford, "Average Person Spends More Time Using Media Than Anything Else," Ball State University News Center Press Release, September 23, 2005, www.bsu.edu. Janet Kornblum, "Americans Will Devote Half Their Lives to Forms of Media Next Year," *USA Today,* December 15, 2006: 6A; Bob Dart, "Americans to Spend 9 1?2; Hours a Day with the Media," *Tampa Tribune:* 2, 13.

[21] Wayne Friedman, "TV Product Placement Delivers for '24,'" *Media Post,* January 19, 2010, www.mediapost.com.

[22] N. E. Marsden, "What TV Is Really Selling," *Washington Post,* October 30, 2009, www.washingtonpost.com.

[23] Mei Fong, "In China, Brands Come with Plots," *The Wall Street Journal,* June 12, 2009: B6.

[24] Jessica Vascellaro and Emily Steel, "Giving Mobile Ads a Makeover," *The Wall Street Journal,* January 28, 2010: B7.

[25] Ken Mallon and Duncan Southgate, "Where Digital Marketing Is Heading in 2010 (Part I), *Advertising Age,* December 29, 2009, www.adage.com.

[26] Julie Jargon, "Domino's IT Staff Delivers Slick Site, Ordering System," *The Wall Street Journal,* November 24, 2009: B5.

[27] Michael Bush, "Texting Trumps Talking in U.S., Just Not as Ad Platform," *Advertising Age,* February 18, 2010, http://www.adage.com.

[28] Matt Kapko, "Secrets Behind Three eBranded iPhone App Successes," February 23, 2009, www.imediaconnection.com.

[29] Brad Stone, "Nintendo Wii to Add Netflix Service for Streaming Video," *The New York Times,* January 13, 2010, www.nytimes.com.

[30] Abbey Klaaseen, "Viral Video: Now That's How You Sell a Mobile Home," *Advertising Age,* November 5, 2009, www.adage.com.

[31] Katy Bachman, "Visa to Advertise on Super Bowl Trays," *Media Week,* January 26, 2010, www.mediaweek.com.

CHAPTER 12

[1] Nat Ives, "Out of 25 Biggest Newspapers, Only Wall Street Journal Gains Circ," *Advertising Age,* October 26, 2009, http://adage.com.

[2] Robert Wilonsky, "At *The Dallas News,* a New 'Bold Strategy': Section Editors Reporting to Sales Managers," *Dallas Observer New Blog,* December 3, 2009, http://blogs.dallasobserver.com.

[3] "The Full Story on Magazine Circulation Vitality," Magazine Publishers Association, September 2009, www.magazine.org.

[4] Russell Adams and Shira Ovide, "Magazines Team Up to Tout 'Power of Print,'" *The Wall Street Journal,* March 1, 2010: B4.

[5] Stephanie Clifford, "For Wired, a Revival Lacks Ads," *The New York Times,* May 18, 2009, www.nytimes.com.

[6] Emily Steel, "Meredith Builds Up a Sideline in Marketing," *The Wall Street Journal,* February 25, 2010: B6.

[7] *Magazine Handbook,* New York: Magazine Publishers Association: 17.

[8] "Time Magazine," downloaded July 10, 2010, Mahalo.com.

[9] *Magazine Reader Experience Study,* Chicago: Northwestern University Media Management Center, www.mediamanagementcenter.org; *Magazine Handbook:* 5.

[10] Cathie Gandel, "White Pages Phone Books Fading Away," *AARP Magazine,* October 2009: 8.

[11] Eric Pfanner, "Old Medium Dusted Off," *International Herald Tribune,* July 9, 2007: 11.

[12] Andrew Vanacore, "Apple's iPad: Publishers See Signs Tablet Can Restore Ad Money," *Silicon Valley Mercury News,* June 3, 2010, MercuryNews.com.

[13] Shira Ovide, "Out-of-Home Advertising Pulls in a Banner Year," Outdoor Advertising Association of America Press Release, January 10, 2007; Outdoor Advertising Association of America, "Frequently Asked Questions," www.oaaa.org/faq.

[14] Kunur Patel, "Windvertising!" *Creativity,* April 7, 2009, http://creativity-online.com.

[15] *The Signage Sourcebook,* South Bend, IN: The Signage Foundation, 2003.

[16] Stuart Elliott, "People and Accounts of Note," *The New York Times,* November 23, 2009, www.nytimes.com.

[17] Stephanie Clifford, "As Storefronts Become Vacant, Ads Arrive," *The New York Times,* May 12, 2009, www.nytimes.com.

[18] Sarah McBride, "Mixed Signals in Web Radio," *The Wall Street Journal,* December 1, 2009: B10.

[19] Paul Farhi, "Limbaugh's Audience Size? It's Largely Up in the Air," *Washington Post,* March 7, 2009, www.washingtonpost.com.

[20] Andrew Hampp, "Radio Listeners Don't Change Dial during Ads," *Advertising Age,* February 12, 2007, http://adage.com; Bill Rose, Phillipe Generali, and Jon Coleman, "What Happens When the Spots Come On?" 2007 Study by Arbitron, Media Monitors, and Coleman, www.arbitron.com.

[21] Ron Winslow, "Watching TV Linked to Higher Risk of Death," *The Wall Street Journal,* January 12, 2010: D1.

[22] Amy Chozick, "What Your TV Is Telling You to Do," *The Wall Street Journal,* April 7, 2010: D1.

[23] Sam Schechner and Shira Ovide, "Record Draw for Super Bowl," *The Wall Street Journal,* February 9, 2010: B6.

[24] Holman Jenkins, Jr., "The Economics of Jay Leno," *The Wall Street Journal,* November 18, 2009: A17; Joe Flint, "Jay Leno's New Time Slot Wreaks Havoc for NBC Affiliates," *Los Angeles Times,* October 19, 2009, www.latimes.com; Lynn Elber, "NBC to Pull the Plug on Leno's Prime-Time Show," Fox News, January 11, 2010, www.foxnews.com.

[25] David Carr and Tim Arango, "A Fox Chief at the Pinnacle of Media and Politics," *The New York Times,* January 20, 2010, www.nytimes.com.

[26] "Primetime Scorecard," Cabletelevision Advertising Bureau Press Release, July 17, 2006, www.onetvworld.org.

[27] David Goetzi, "Interactive Ads Pay Off for Cablevision," *Media Daily News,* January 12, 2010, www.mediapost.com.

[28] Daisuke Wakabayashi, "Sony Pins Future on a 3-Revival," *The Wall Street Journal,* January 7, 2010: A1; Suzanne Vranica, "Marketers Face Zooming Costs as ESPN Launches 3-D Channel, *The Wall Street Journal,* June 10, 2010: B1.

[29] Sam Schechner and Nat Worden, "NBC in Hand, Comcast Now Faces New Hurdles," *The Wall Street Journal,* December 4, 2009: B1.

[30] Stephanie Clifford, "TiVo Promotes Ads It Hopes You'll Talk to, Not Zap," *The New York Times,* April 23, 2009, www.nytimes.com.

[31] Paul Bond, "The Growing Use of DVRs," *The Hollywood Reporter,* April 28, 2009, http://hollywoodreporter.com.

[32] Steve McClellan, "Average Super Bowl Commercial Drew 93 Million Viewers," *Mediaweek.com,* February 8, 2007, http://mediaweek.com.

[33] Mandalit del Barco, "Ethnic Outlets Thriving in Sinking Media Market," *NPR*, April 7, 2009, www.npr.org.

[34] Emily Bryson York, "Subway Caught Up in Fan Effort to Save NBC Series 'Chuck'," *Advertising Age*, April 27, 2009, http://adage.com.

[35] Bob Lodice, "10 Events That Transformed Marketing," *Advertising Age*, January 18, 2010, http://adage.com.

[36] John Consoli, "MillerCoors and Asics Bring Action to Ads on ESPN," *The New York Times*, April 14, 2009, www.nytimes.com.

[37] Katherine Rosman, "As Seen on TV . . . and in Aisle 5," *The Wall Street Journal*, January 28, 2010: D1.

[38] Jon Lafayette, "Study Shows TV's Impact on Consumer Purchasing Behavior," *TV Week*, April 16, 2009, www.tvweek.com.

[39] Joe Mandese, "Medialink," *Admap*, April 2006: 10.

[40] Sarah McBride, "In Theaters: Commercials Aplenty," *The Wall Street Journal*, February 8, 2007, www.wsj.com.

[41] Martha Woodroof, "In a 24/7 World, What Is a Magazine?" *NPR*, August 30, 2009, www.npr.org; Suzanne Vranica, "WPP Chief Tempers Hope for Ad Upturn," *The Wall Street Journal*, September 21, 2009: B1.

[42] Theresa Howard, "CBS, Pepsi Max Put Video in Some Magazine Ads," *USA Today*, August 19, 2009, http://usatoday.com.

CHAPTER 13

[1] Ben McConnell and Jackie Huba, *Citizen Marketers: When People Are the Message*, Chicago: Kaplan Publishing, 2007.

[2] Emily Steel, "AOL, Yahoo Face Off to Impress Madison Avenue," *The Wall Street Journal*, September 24, 2009; Abbey Klaassen, "The State of Search Marketing: 2009, *Advertising Age*, November 2, 2009; Internet World Stats, "Top Ten Companies in Internet, Top Ten Brands in Internet," downloaded July 12, 2010, http://www.internetworldstats.com/top10.htm.

[3] Randall Stross, "Broadband Now! So Why Don't Some Use It?" *The New York Times*, October 18, 2009: 4.

[4] Christina Binkley, "The Forgotten Market Online: Older Women," *The Wall Street Journal*, May 21, 2009: D8.

[5] Thomas Friedman, "Is China the Next Enron?" *The New York Times*, January 12, 2010, www.nytimes.com.

[6] Aaron Back, "China's Big Brands Tackle Web Sales," *The Wall Street Journal*, December 21, 2009: B2.

[7] Geoffrey Fowler and John Stoll, "GM Program with eBay Creates Buzz But Few Sales, *The Wall Street Journal*, August 21, 2009: B1; Geoffrey Fowler, Scott Morrison, and Sharon Terlep, "GM's Vaunted Effort to Sell Cars on eBay Stalls," *The Wall Street Journal*, September 30, 2009: B1.

[8] "Realtor Awarded for Online Marketing," *Daytona Beach News Journal*, May 20, 2009: 10A; Ed Burd, personal communication, May 29, 2009.

[9] John Williams, "The New Rules of E-Branding," Entrepreneur.com, February 25, 2008, www.entrepreneur.com.

[10] Utpal Dholakia and Silvia Vianello, "The Fans Know Best," *The Wall Street Journal*, August 17, 2009: R7.

[11] Joe Mandese, "Simultaneous Research Study Reveals Consumers Buzz Most over Word-of-Mouth, Not Ads," *MediaPost Publications*, January 19, 2007, http://publications.mediapost.com.

[12] Ty Montague, Keynote Speech. Effie Awards Gala, June 7, 2006, http://www.effie.org/gala/montague.html.

[13] Michael Bush, "What's the Next Marketing Platform? How to Measure Success? Ad Age's Media Mavens Answer the Big Questions," *Advertising Age*, December 9, 2009, http://adage.com.

[14] Evan Hessel and Taylor Buley, "How to Know Your Web Ad Is Working," Forbes.com, April 29, 2009, www.forbes.com.

[15] Eleftheria Parpis, "VW Plays 'Truth & Dare' Online," Adweek.com, May 5, 2009, http://adweek.com.

[16] Jessica Vascellaro, "Why Email No Longer Rules," *The Wall Street Journal*, October 12, 2009: R1.

[17] Kit Eaton, "Online Ads Turn a Corner: More Spent on Internet Ads Than TV in U.K.," Fast Company.com, September 30, 2009, www.fastcompany.com.

[18] Erik Sass, "Tipping Point: Digital Ad Revs to Top Print in 2010," *Media Daily News*, March 8, 2010, www.mediapost.com.

[19] Jessica Vascellaro, "Google Says Internet Advertising Picked Up Steam in Third Quarter," *The Wall Street Journal*, October 16, 2009: B1.

[20] ZenithOptimedia, "Global Advertising Downturn Slows Despite Disappointing Q1," Press Release, July 6, 2009, www.zenithoptimedia.com.

[21] Emily Steel, "AOL to Produce News, Video by the Numbers," *The Wall Street Journal*, November 30, 2009: B8.

[22] Emily Steel, "Drug Makers to Press for Guidance on Web Marketing," *The Wall Street Journal*, November 12, 2009: B4.

[23] Jessica Vascellaro, "Google Decides to Find Its Creative Side," *The Wall Street Journal*, October 6, 2009: B8.

[24] Ashlee Vance, "Times Web Ad Show Security Breach," *The New York Times*, September 15, 2009, www.nytimes.com.

[25] Suzanne Vranica, "Element of Choice Draws in Online Viewers," *The Wall Street Journal*, February 4, 2010: B11.

[26] Esther Thorson, personal communication, April 20, 2009; Abbey Klaasen, "The State of Search Marketing: 2009," *Advertising Age*, November 2, 2009, http://adage.com; ZenithOptimedia, Global Advertising Downturn Slows.

[27] Brad Stone, "Google Adds Live Updates to Results," *The New York Times*, December 8, 2009, www.nytimes.com.

[28] Brad Stone, "Craigslist Expands Legal Battle Against Spammers," October 8, 2009, http://bits.blogs.nytimes.com.

[29] Emily Steel, "AOL, Yahoo Face Off to Impress Madison Avenue," *The Wall Street Journal*, September 24, 2009: B8.

[30] Emily Steel, "Pricing Tensions Shake Up Web Display-Ad Market," *The Wall Street Journal*, September 21, 2009, p. B6.

[31] Emily Steel, "Target-Marketing Becomes More Communal," *The Wall Street Journal*, November 5, 2009: B10.

[32] Emily Steel, "Web Sites Debate Best Values for Advertising Dollars," *The Wall Street Journal*, August 13, 2009: B7.

[33] Bush, "What's the Next Marketing Platform?"

[34] Douglas Quenqua, "Blogs Falling in an Empty Forest," *The New York Times*, June 7, 2009, www.nytimes.com.

[35] Martha Irvine, "Bloggers Getting Older," *Boulder Daily Camera*, February 4, 2010: 7A.

[36] Douglas MacMilan, "Blogaola: The FTC Takes on Paid Posts," *Business Week*, May 19, 2009, www.businessweek.com; N. E. Marsden, "What TV Is Really Selling," *Washington Post*, October 30, 2009, www.washingtonpost.com.

[37] Brandon Griggs and John Sutter, "Oprah, Ashton Kutcher Mark Twitter 'Turning Point'," CNN, April 18, 2009, www.cnn.com.

[38] Tom Mueller, "Advertising, Media, and the Convergence Model," *AEJMC News*, January 2010: 18–19.

[39] Mark Zuckerberg, "An Open Letter," December 1, 2009, http://blog.facebook.com/blog.php?post=190423927130.

[40] Laura Sydell, "Facebook, MySpace Divide Along Social Lines," National Public Radio, October 21, 2009, www.npr.org.

[41] "BIGresearch Profiles Social Media Users; Not All Created Equal," News Release, August 13, 2009, www.bigresearch.com.

[42] Ibid.

[43] Sean Corcoran, "The Broad Reach of Social Technologies," August 25, 2009, www.forrester.com.

[44] Jack Neff, "P&G Embraces Facebook as Big Part of Its Marketing Plan," *Advertising Age*, January 25, 2010, http://adage.com.

[45] Beth Bulik, "Army of Tweeting Tax Pros Leads H&R Block Social Push," *Advertising Age*, January 4, 2010, http://adage.com.

[46] Simon Dumenco, "Everything I Know about Marketing I Learned from Susan Boyle," *Advertising Age*, April 20, 2009, http://adage.com.

[47] Laure Hansen, "What Happened to Second Life?" BBC News, November 20, 2009, http://newsvote.bbc.co.uk.

[48] Natalie Zmuda, "Behind Coca-Cola's Biggest Social-Media Push Yet," *Advertising Age*, November 17, 2009, http//adage.com.

[49] Emily Steel, "Shift in Search-Ad Tactics Seeks More for Less," *The Wall Street Journal*, October 22, 2009: B7.

[50] Ken Mallon and Duncan Southgate, "Where Digital Marketing Is Heading in 2010 (Part Two)," *Advertising Age*, December 30, 2009, http://adage.com.

[51] Brian Stelter, "Web-TV Divide Is Back in Focus with NBC Sales," *The New York Times*, December 4, 2009, www.nytimes.com.

52 Brian Stelter, "Xbox Takes on Cable, Streaming TV Shows and Movies," *The New York Times*, January 19, 2010, www.nytimes.com.

53 Walter Mossberg, "No File! No Icon! Litl Is a Big Idea, But Still Cloudy," *The Wall Street Journal,* December 31, 2009: D1.

54 James Hookway, "Web Censoring Widens across Southeast Asia," *The Wall Street Journal*, September 14, 2009: A10.

55 Susanna Hamner, "Pay-Per-Click Web Advertisers Combat Costly Fraud," *The New York Times*, May 13 2009, wwwnytimes.com.

56 Emily Steel, "Web Privacy Efforts Targeted," *The Wall Street Journal*, June 25, 2009: B10.

57 Emma Hall, "U.K. Falls Behind on Online Privacy," *Advertising Age*, November 5, 2009, http://adage.com.

CHAPTER 14

1 Jack Neff and Rupal Parekh, "Dove Takes Its New Men's Line to the Super Bowl," *Advertising Age*, January 5, 2010, http://adagecom.

2 "TV Ads Most Helpful; Web Banners Most Ignored," *MC Marketing Charts*, July 1, 2009, www.marketingcharts.com.

3 Tom Van Riper, "Super Bowl Ads: A Whole New Ballgame," *Forbes*, January 13, 2010, www.forbes.com.

4 Judy Shapiro, "9 Digital Marketing Mistakes I Won't Make Next Year," *Advertising Age,* December 29, 2009, http://adage.com.

5 Chrissy Wissinger, "Prosper MediaPlanIQ: Telecom Companies Need to Reallocate Ad Expenditures," BIGresearch Press Release, www.bigresearch.com.

6 John Bauschard, "New Cross-Media Analytics Can Alleviate Guesswork," AdAgeDaily, December 16, 2009, http://adagedaily.com.

7 Carla Lloyd, "Modern Media Planning," Chap. 5 in *Strategic Media Decisions,* 2nd ed., ed. Marian Azzaro, Chicago: The Copy Workshop, 2008: 183–184.

8 Carla Lloyd, "Creative Media Analysis," Chap. 4 in *Strategic Media Decisions,* 2nd ed., ed. Marian Azzaro, Chicago: The Copy Workshop, 2008: 149.

9 Emily Steel, "Modeling Tools Stretch Ad Dollars," *The Wall Street Journal,* May 18, 2009: B7.

10 Steve Kelly, personal communication, January 11–13, 2010.

11 Elaine Wong, "Unilever Signs On as Sponsor of *Today Show*'s 'Cooking School,'" *Brandweek*, January 12, 2010, www.brandweek.com.

12 "Dentsu Launches Next-Generation Communication Planning System IMC ver.2.0™," Dentsu Press Release, April 13, 2006; "Integrated Communication by Use of ContactPoint Management®," PowerPoint Presentation, Tokyo, November 2006.

13 Troy Young, "It's Not the Impression That Counts. It's What You Do with It." *Advertising Age*, January 19, 2010, http://adage.com.

14 Anthony Crupi, "ESPN Tops Beta Research Survey," *MediaWeek,* January 12, 2010, www.mediaweek.com.

15 Ethan Smith and Shira Ovide, "Blunt But Popular Simon Cowell Will Bow Out of 'American Idol'," *The Wall Street Journal*, January 12, 2010: B1; Amy Chozick, "The Queen of Unmean," *The Wall Street Journal,* January 8, 2010: W9.

16 Mike Shields, "Ad Network Business Dominated by Big Players," *Media Week*, January 14, 2010, www.mediaweek.com.

17 Emily Steel, "Web Sites Target Oscars Fans; Ads Will Reflect Show Events," *The Wall Street Journal*, March 4, 2010: B7.

18 Suzanne Vranica, "NBC Universal Tees Up Cause-Related Shows," *The Wall Street Journal,* October 19, 2009: B4.

19 Bob Garfield, *The Chaos Scenario*, Nashville, TN: Stielstra Publishing, 2009.

20 Kate Fitzgerald, "Trolling for Media Plan's Role," *Advertising Age* Special Report, March 3, 2003: S10–S12.

21 Claire Atkinson, "Coke Catapults Starcom MediaVest," *Advertising Age*, February 9, 2004: S6, S10.

22 Ken Mallon and Duncan Southgate, "Where Digital Marketing Is Heading in 2010 (Part I), *Advertising Age,* December 29, 2009, http://adage.com.

CHAPTER 15

1 Glen M. Broom, *Cutlip and Center's Effective Public Relations,* 10th ed., Upper Saddle River, NJ: Pearson Prentice-Hall, 2009: 1, 308.

2 Martin Sorrell, "Assessing the State of Public Relations," *The Strategist,* 3, No. 4, Winter 1998: 48.

3 Bob Garfield, "Domino's Does Itself a Disservice by Coming Clean about Its Pizza," *Advertising Age*, January 2010, http://adage.com; "Pizza Workers Fired after YouTube Joke," UPI, April 15, 2009, www.upi.com.

4 Claire Atkinson, "Rubenstein: PR Maestro," *Advertising Age*, October 11, 2004: 46.

5 Public Relations Society of America, www.prsa.org.

6 Bennett Freeman, "Substance Sells: Aligning Corporate Reputation and Corporate Responsibility," *Public Relations Quarterly*, Spring 2006: 12–19.

7 Tom Duncan and Sandra Moriarty, *Driving Brand Value: Using Integrated Marketing to Manage Profitable Stakeholder Relationships*, New York: McGraw-Hill, 1997.

8 Daniel J. Edelman, "The Golden Age of Public Relations," *Public Relations Quarterly*, Spring 2006: 20–21.

9 Thomas L. Harris, *Value-Added Public Relations: The Secret Weapon of Integrated Marketing*, Lincolnwood, IL: NTC Business Books, 1998.

10 David Michaelson and Don W. Stacks, "What Research Says—Advertising vs. PR Effectiveness," Institute for Public Relations, February 28, 2007, www.instituteforpr.org.

11 John Paluszek, personal communication, August 3, 2009.

12 Stuart Elliott, "Pepsi Invites the Public to Do Good," *The New York Times*, February 1, 2010, nytimes.com.

13 Sandra Moriarty, "IMC Needs PR's Stakeholder Focus," *AMA Marketing News,* May 26, 1997: 7.

14 Fraser P. Seitel, *The Practice of Public Relations*, 11th ed., Upper Saddle River, NJ: Pearson Prentice-Hall, 2011: 72–73.

15 Jonathan Salem Baskin, "CMOs, Go Beyond a PR Plan to Prepare for an Inevitable Product Crisis," AdAge.com, March 8, 2010, http://adage.com.

16 Stephanie Simon, "Hard-Hit Schools Try Public-Relations Push," *The Wall Street Journal*, August 17, 2009: A3.

17 Broom, *Cutlip and Center's Effective Public Relations*.

18 Tamara Gillis, "In Times of Change, Employee Communication Is Vital to Successful Organizations," *Communication World,* March–April 2004: 8.

19 Claire Atkinson, "PR Firms Praise Janet Jackson Breast Stunt," AdAge.com, February 9, 2004, http://www.adage.com.

20 Michelle Chapman, "Denny's Promotion Hits Grand Slam," *The Tampa Tribune*, February 4, 2009, http://www2.tbo.com.

21 Dan Lothian, Fran Fifis, and Deborah Feyerick, "Two Plead Not Guilty to Boston Hoax Charges," February 1, 2007, www.cnn.com.

22 Harry R. Weber, "Cartoon Network Head Resigns after Scare," ABC News, February 10, 2007, http://abcnews.go.com.

23 Harris, *Value-Added Public Relations*.

24 Paul Holmes, "Senior Marketers Are Sharply Divided about the Role of PR in the Overall Mix," *Advertising Age*, January 24, 2005: C1, C2.

25 Alyse R. Gotthoffer, "Exploring the Relevance of Localization in Anti-Drinking and Driving PSAs," in *Proceedings of the American Academy of Advertising Conference*, ed. Darrel D. Muehling, Lexington, KY, 1998: 214.

26 Target, http://www.target.com/tcoe.

27 Andrew Adam Newman, "Tough on Crude Oil, Soft on Ducklings," *The New York Times*, September 25, 2009, www.nytimes.com.

28 Jack Neff, "Dawn's Wildlife Rescue Efforts Shine in Gulf Coast Oil Spill," May 4, 2010, adage.com; Leslie Kaufman, "Ad for a Dish Detergent Becomes Part of a Story," *The New York Times,* June 15, 2010, nytimes.com.

29 Thomas Harris, "iPod, Therefore iAm," *ViewsLetter,* September 2004: 3.

30 Carole Howard, "Working with Reporters: Mastering the Fundamentals to Build Long-Term Relationships," *Public Relations Quarterly,* Spring 2004: 36.

31 Fraser P. Seitel, "E-Mail News Releases," *O'Dwyer's PR Services Report,* March 2004: 37.

32 Anne R. Owen, "Avant-Garde or Passé: Using Video News Releases Internationally," in *Proceedings of the American Academy of Advertising Conference*, ed. Carole M. Macklin, St. Louis, 1997: 290.

33 Tom Harris, "Barbie Joins AARP," *ViewsLetter,* April 2009: 3–4.

34 Tim Arango, "Seeking a Missing Link, and a Mass Audience," *The New York Times,* May 19, 2009, www.nytimes.com.

35 "Truth Kicks Off Its 10th Annual Summer Tour," June 26, 2009, www.legacyforhealth .org.

36 Seitel, *The Practice of Public Relations:* 360.

37 Candace White and Niranjan Raman, "The World Wide Web as a Public Relations Medium," Association for Education in Journalism and Mass Communication Annual Conference, Baltimore, MD, August 1998.

38 Michelle O'Malley and Tracy Irani, "Public Relations and the Web: Measuring the Effect of Interactivity, Information, and Access to Information in Websites," Association for Education in Journalism and Mass Communication Conference, Baltimore, MD, August 1998.

39 Jill Whalen, "Online Public Relations," *High Rankings Advisor,* 109, August 18, 2004, www.highrankings.com.

40 Michael Markowitz, "Fighting Cyber Sabotage," *Bergen Record,* October 4, 1998, www.bergen.com.

41 Lisa Belkin, "Moms and Motrin," *The New York Times,* November 17, 2008, www.nytimes.com.

42 "Blogging and Beyond," *The Wall Street Journal,* September 25, 2006: R3.

43 Vanessa O'Connell, "It's the Publicity That Counts," *The Wall Street Journal,* November 17, 2006: B1, B4.

44 "PRSA Seeks Industry Agreement on Measurement Standards," September 15, 2009 http://media.prsa.org.

45 Eric Webber, "You Can't Quantify Everything," AdAge.com, September 9, 2008, http://adage.com.

46 Michael Bush, "PR Metrics Evolve to Show How Discipline Drives Sales," AdAge.com, October 5, 2009, http://adage.com.

CHAPTER 16

1 "Direct Sales Giant Avon Ranked 9th 'Most Successful Brand of 2010,'" MLM The Whole Truth, December 21, 2009, www.mlm-thewholetruth.com.

2 Camille Sweeney, "Avon's Little Sister Is Calling," *The New York Times,* January 13, 2010, www.nytimes.com.

3 John Mazzone and John Pickett, The Household Diary Study: Mail Use & Attitudes in FY 2008, U.S. Postal Service, March 2009: 40.

4 Tom Evans, "Firms Hold Fast to Snail Mail Marketing," *The Wall Street Journal,* January 12, 2009: B5.

5 "Junk Mail Impact," January 28, 2010, www.41pounds.org.

6 Jeffrey Ball, "In Digital Era, Marketers Still Prefer a Paper Trail," *The Wall Street Journal,* October 16, 2009: A13.

7 Vanessa O'Connell, "The Shrinking of the Fantasy Gift," *The Wall Street Journal,* October 7, 2009, www.wsj.com.

8 Ball, "In Digital Era, Marketers Still Prefer a Paper Trail."

9 James Arndorfer, "A Loyalty Even Man's Best Friend Can't Beat," *Advertising Age,* January 21, 2010, http://adage.com.

10 Jennifer Kerr, "Warning: No-Call List Expires," *Boulder Daily Camera,* September 22, 2007: 13A.

11 Louise Marsland, "SAMRA Convention 2006 News," Bizcommunity.com, March 15, 2006, www.bizcommunity.com.

12 Jack Neff, "Behind the Search for the Next Great DRTV Pitchman," *Advertising Age,* January 25, 2010, http://adage.com.

13 Ken Mallon and Duncan Southgate, "Where Digital Marketing Is Heading in 2010," *Advertising Age,* December 29, 2010, http://adage.com.

14 Brad Stone, "Facebook Joins with McAfee to Clean Spam from Site," *The New York Times,* January 13, 2010, www.nytimes.com

15 Suzanne Barlyn, "Block That Catalog!" *The Wall Street Journal,* February 8, 2007: D3; Jenny Stamos, "Say No to Junk Mail," *Woman's Day,* November 1, 2006: 16.

16 Don Peppers and Martha Rogers, "The Principles of Data-Driven Relationships," in *Advertising Principles & Practices,* 8th ed., Upper Saddle River, NJ: Prentice Hall, 2009: 458.

17 Pradeep K. Korgaonkar, Eric J. Karson, and Ishael Akaah, "Direct Marketing Advertising: The Assents, the Dissents, and the Ambivalents," *Journal of Advertising Research,* September/October 1997: 41–45.

18 Tom Duncan, Advertising & IMC, 2nd ed., Boston: McGraw-Hill Irwin, 2005: 262–263.

19 Stephanie Clifford, "A Little 'I' to Teach about Online Privacy," *The New York Times,* January 27, 2010, wswww.nytimes.com.

20 Giles D'Souza and Joseph Phelps, "The Privacy Paradox: The Case of Secondary Disclosure," *Review of Marketing Science,* 7, No. 4, 2009: http://www.bepress.com/romsjournal/vol7/iss1/art4.

21 Kunar Patel, "How a Back-End E-Tail Operation Looks to Grow into a Digital Shop," *Advertising Age,* November 9, 2009, http://adage.com.

22 Mei Fong, "Avon's Calling, But China Opens Door Only a Crack," *The Wall Street Journal,* February 26, 2007: B1.

23 Direct Marketing Association 2006 Annual Report, 10.

CHAPTER 17

1 American Marketing Association website, www.marketingpower.com/mg-dictionary.php.

2 Arlene Gerwin, "Sales Promotion Planning," Chap. 4 in *The Power of Point-of-Purchase Advertising: Marketing at Retail,* ed. Robert Liljenwall, 3rd ed., Washington, DC: Point-of-Purchase Advertising International, 2008: 63.

3 Bob Garfield and Neal Conan "Bob Garfield's 'Chaos Scenario,'" NPR, August 6, 2009, www.npr.org.

4 Leo Jakobson, "Incentives without Borders," *Incentive,* March 2006: 12–17.

5 Gerwin, "Sales Promotion Planning"; 63.

6 Motoko Rich, "With Kindle, the Best Sellers don't Need to Sell," *The New York Times,* January 23, 2010, www.nytimes.com.

7 Bruce Horovitz, "Match the Food to the Logo," *USA Today,* May 27, 2009: B1.

8 Miguel Bustillo and Jeffrey Trachtenberg, "Wal-Mart Strafes Amazon in Book War," *The Wall Street Journal,* October 16, 2009: A1.

9 Warren Brown, "Chrysler's PT Cruiser: Time for Fad to Fade," *Daytona Beach News Journal,* May 15, 2009: 6A.

10 "Stores Are Media: BIGresearch's Simultaneous Media Survey Ranks the Influence of In-Store Media on Purchase Decisions," www.bigresearch.com, September 20, 2006.

11 Jill Stravolernos, "78 Percent of Americans Get Coupons from Newspapers," *Boulder Daily Camera Business Plus,* January 11, 2010, p. 8; John Waggoner, "Consumers Open Wallets, But Not for New Stuff," *USA Today,* May 19, 2009: B1, http://usatoday.com.

12 Kanur Patel, "Groupon Takes Coupons into the Social-Media Age," *Advertising Age,* December 21, 2009, http://adage.com.

13 Dick Blatt, "Foreword," in *The Power of Marketing at-Retail,* ed. Robert Liljenwall, Alexandria, VA: Point-of-Purchase Advertising International, 2008: 9.

14 Suzanne Vranica, "NBC Universal Tees Up Cause-Related Shows," *The Wall Street Journal,* October 19, 2009: B4.

15 Michael Grynbaum, "New York Traffic Experiment Gets Permanent Run," *The New York Times,* February 11, 2010, www.nytimes .com; Libby Nelson, "Broadway's Car-Free Zones: This Space for Rent," *The New York Times,* July 9, 2009, www.nytimes.com.

16 Adam Thompson and Shai Oster, "NBA in China Gets Milk to Sell Hoops," *The Wall Street Journal,* January 22, 2007: B1.

17 Jack Neff, "P&G and Kroger Call It Quits on Coupon Partnership," *Advertising Age,* December 22, 2009, http://adage.com.

18 Eleftheria Parpis, "Disney-Pixar, Aflac Duck 'Up' to New Tricks," *Adweek.com,* May 7, 2009, http://adweek.com.

19 Dashiell Bennet, "'Fan Cans' Let You Chug for Alma Mater," *Deadspin,* August 31, 2009, http://deadspin.com/5342510/fan-cans-let-you-chug-for-alma-mater; John Hechinger, "FTC Criticizes College-Themed Cans in Anheuser-Busch Marketing Efforts," The Wall Street Journal, August 25, 2009: B1; Emily Fredrix, "Anheuser-Busch Pulls Promotions at Some Colleges," AP and boston.com, August 25, 2009, www.boston .com; "A-B Ends Some Bud Light 'Fan Cans' Promotions Amid Complaints," Street & Smith's Sports Business Journal, August 26, 2009, www.sportsbusinessjournal.com.

20 Doug Brooks, "How to Balance Brand Building and Price Promotion," Advertising Age, December 29, 2009, http://adage.com.

21 Gerwin, "Sales Promotion Planning": 63.

CHAPTER 18

1 Bob Liodice, "Essentials for Integrated Marketing: As More Power Shifts to Consumers, Need Grows for Common Metric and 'Renaissance Marketers,'" *Advertising Age,* June 9, 2008, http://adage.com.

2 Stan Richards, "It's Been a Rocket Ride," *The Dallas Business Journal,* April 7, 2006, dallas .bizjournals.com.

3 Liodice, "Essentials for Integrated Marketing."

4 Bill Vlasic, "Ford's Bet: It's a Small World After All," *The New York Times,* January 10, 2010, www.nytimes.com.

5 Tom Duncan and Sandra Moriarty, "How One Agency Re-Organized to Walk the New IMC Talk," *Admap,* September 2007: 35–38; Thomas Duncan, "IMC and Branding: Research Propositions," *International Journal of Integrated Marketing Communications,* 1, No. 1 (Spring 2009): 17–23.

6 IMC Consulting Visit by Tom Duncan and Sandra Moriarty with Dentsu, Tokyo, Japan, January 2006.

7 Frank Strifler, "5 Marketing Principles Brands Should Embrace in 2010," *Adweek,* January 13, 2010, www.adweek.com.

8 Elaine Wong, "Walmart, Target, Best Buy Named Most Valuable Brands," *Brandweek,* March 11, 2010, www.brandweek.com.

9 Stephanie Rosenbloom, "Cellphones Let Shoppers Point, Click, and Purchase," *The New York Times,* February 27, 2010, www.nytimes .com.

10 Stephanie Rosenbloom, "Luxury Stores Trim Inventory and Discounts," *The New York Times,* November 19, 2009, www.nytimes.com.

11 Jerome Jeweler and Bonnie Drewniany, *Creative Strategy in Advertising,* 9th ed., Belmont, CA: Wadsworth, 2007: 240–244.

12 Vanessa O'Connell, "The New Fashion Bloggers," *The Wall Street Journal,* February 7, 2007: B1.

13 Elizabeth Holmes, "Abercrombie & Fitch's Style Sense Wears Thin with Some Shoppers," *The Wall Street Journal,* February 3, 2010: B1.

14 Barbara Phillips, "Please, Stay On the Line," *The Wall Street Journal,* March 24, 2009: A15.

15 Steve Lohr, "Customer Service? Ask a Volunteer." *The New York Times,* April 26, 2009, www.nytimes.com.

16 Stuart Elliott, "Pepsi Invites the Public to Do Good," *The New York Times,* February 1, 2010, www.nytimes.com.

17 Nick Bartle, "Finding the Real Bottom Line," *Advertising Age,* January 27, 2010, http://adage.com.

18 Tom Duncan and Sandra Moriarty, *Driving Brand Value: Using Integrated Marketing to Manage Profitable Stakeholder Relationships,* New York: McGraw-Hill, 1997.

19 Theodore Levitt, "The Globalization of Markets," *Harvard Business Review,* May–June 1983: S8–S9.

20 Philip Kotler (with Kevin Keller), *Marketing Management,* 12th ed., Upper Saddle River, NJ: Prentice-Hall, 2006.

21 Edward Hall, *Beyond Culture,* Garden City, NY: Anchor Press/Doubleday, 1976.

22 Aixa Rocca and Valentina Vescovi, "Santo Is *Ad Age*'s International Agency of the Year," *Advertising Age,* January 25, 2010, http://adage.com.

23 Emily Steel, "After Ditching Tiger, Accenture Tries New Game," *The Wall Street Journal,* January 14, 2010: B1.

24 David Barboza and Brad Stone, "China, Where U.S. Internet Companies Often Fail," *The New York Times,* January 16, 2010, www.nytimes.com.

25 Katherine Frith and Barbara Mueller, *Advertising and Societies: Global Issues,* New York: Peter Lang, 2002.

26 "China Internet Population Hits 384 Million," Reuters, January 15, 2010, http://www.reuters.com/article/idUSTOE60E06S20100115.

CHAPTER 19

1 Louise Marsland, "How Much Advertising Actually Works?" *SAMRA Convention 2006 News,* March 15, 2006, www.bizcommunity .com/Archive/196/119/9593.html.

2 John Philip Jones, *When Ads Work: New Proof That Advertising Triggers Sales,* 2nd ed., Armonk, NY: M. E. Sharpe, 2007: xvii.

3 Simon Broadbent, *When to Advertise,* Henley-on-Thames, UK: Admap Publications, 1999.

4 David Brandt and Dave Walker, "Copy Testing under the Gun?" *Ipsos Ideas,* August/September 2003: 3.

5 "Trick or Treat? Tobacco Industry Prevention Ads Don't Help Curb Youth Smoking and Should Be Taken Off the Air," American Legacy Foundation Press Release, October 31, 2006, www.americanlegacy.org.

6 Charles E. Young, "Capturing the Flow of Emotion in Television Commercials: A New Approach," *Journal of Advertising Research,* June 2004: 202–209; Chuck Young and John Kastenholz, "Emotion in TV Ads," *Admap,* January 2004: 40–42.

7 Don Peppers and Martha Rogers, "Delivering a Smarter Multichannel Experience," *Sales & Marketing Management,* April 2007: 11.

8 Scott Thurm, "One Question, and Plenty of Debate," *The Wall Street Journal,* December 4, 2006: B3.

9 Vikram Mahidhar and Christine Cutten, "Navigating the Marketing Measurement Maze," *Journal of Integrated Marketing Communications,* 2007: 41–46.

10 Charles Young, *Advertising Research Handbook,* Seattle, WA: Ideas in Flight, 2005: 53–58.

11 Lee Weinblatt "Q&A: Testing Firm Keeps Eye on TV Ad Effectiveness," *Brandweek,* January 22, 2007: 8.

12 Young, *Advertising Research Handbook:* 95–102.

13 Debra Sherman, "Super Bowl Ads Fumble, Brain Scans Show," *Washington Post,* February 5, 2007, www.washingtonpost.com.

14 Jones, *When Ads Work.*

15 Stephanie Kang, "Why DVR Viewers Recall Some TV Spots," *The Wall Street Journal,* February 26, 2008: B5.

16 Brian Morrissey, "New Campaign Metric: Social Chatter," *Adweek,* January 27, 2010, www.adweek.com.

17 Emily York, "Taco Bell Takes Heat Over 'Drive-Thru Diet' Menu," *Advertising Age,* January 4, 2010, http://adage.com.

18 Chris Reidy, "Locals Plan Twitter Experiment on Super Bowl Ads," *Boston Globe,* January 30, 2009, www.boston.com.

19 Louise Marsland, "How Much Advertising Actually Works?" *SAMRA Convention 2006 News,* March 15, 2006, www.bizcommunity .com/Archive/196/119.html.

20 Anthony Crupi, "Starcom, NBCU, Applebee's to Gauge Value of Video Ads," *Media Week,* May 17, 2009, http://mediaweek.com.

21 Institute for Public Relations, "Using Web Analytics to Measure Impact," E-Mail Release, February 15, 2010.

22 Communications Consortium Media Center, "Guidelines for Evaluating Nonprofit Communications Efforts," April 2004, www.mediaevaluationproject.org/Paper5.pdf.

23 Gerard Tellis, *Effective Advertising,* Thousand Oaks CA: Sage, 2004: 6.

24 Bob Liodice, "Essentials for Integrated Marketing: As More Power Shifts to Consumers, Need Grows for Common Metric and 'Renaissance Marketers,'" *Advertising Age,* June 9, 2008, http://adage.com.

25 "Unaided Advertising Recall Significantly Higher with Mix of Radio and Internet," *Research Brief,* February 23, 2007, www.centerformediaresearch.com.

26 Dong Lee and Chan Park, "Conceptualization and Measurement of Multidimensionality of Integrated Marketing Communication," *Journal of Advertising Research,* 47:3 (September 2007), 222–236.

27 2004 Effie Brief provided by UPS and the Martin Agency.

28 Ellen Neuborne, "Ads That Actually Sell Stuff," *Business 2.0,* June 2004: 78.

29 Jack Neff, "Nielsen Tasks Mandel with Proving Ads Work," *Advertising Age,* December 4, 2006: 1.

30 Marlene Bender and Art Zambianchi, "The Reality of ROI: Dell's Approach to Measurement," *Journal of Integrated Marketing Communications,* 2006: 16–21.

31 Jack Myers, "Jack Myers' Weekend Think Tank: Can the Rules of Research Change?" *MediaPost Publications,* January 5, 2007, http://publications.mediapost.com.

INDEX